Watching **TV**

Television and Popular Culture

Robert J. Thompson, *Series Editor*

Other titles in Television and Popular Culture

Critiquing the Sitcom: A Reader
Edited by Joanne Morreale

Gen X TV: The Brady Bunch to Melrose Place
Rob Owen

Inside the TV Writer's Room: Practical Advice for Succeeding in Television
Edited by Lawrence Meyers

Prime-Time Authorship: Works About and by Three TV Dramatists
Douglas Heil

Prime Time, Prime Movers: From I Love Lucy to L.A. Law America's Greatest TV Shows and the People Who Created Them
David Marc and Robert J. Thompson

Screwball Television: Critical Perspectives on Gilmore Girls
Edited by David Scott Diffrient with David Lavery

Starting Your Television Writing Career: The Warner Bros. Writers Workshop Guide
Abby Finer and Deborah Pearlman

The Story of Viewers for Quality Television: From Grassroots to Prime Time
Dorothy Collins Swanson

Teleliteracy: Taking Television Seriously
David Bianculli

Television's Second Golden Age: From Hill Street Blues to ER
Robert J. Thompson

Watching TV

Six Decades of American Television

EXPANDED SECOND EDITION

Harry Castleman *and* Walter J. Podrazik

Syracuse University Press

The paper used in this publication meets the minimum requirements of American National Standard for Information Sciences—Permanence of Paper for Printed Library Materials, ANSI Z39.48-1992.

ISBN: 978-0-8156-3220-7

Library of Congress Cataloging-in-Publication Data

The Library of Congress has catalogued the second edition as follows:

Castleman, Harry
  Watching TV: six decades of American television / Harry Castleman and Walter J. Podrazik – 2nd ed.
    p. cm. – (Television series)
  ISBN 0-8156-2988-5 (alk. paper)
  1. Television broadcasting—United States—History. I. Title: Watching television. II. Podrazik, Walter J. III. Title. IV. Series.

  PN1992.5.U5C37 2003
  791.43'0973—dc22   2003061750

Manufactured in the United States of America

Book design, McGraw-Hill edition: Nancy Dale Muldoon.
Second edition book design: Walter J. Podrazik.
Second edition book half-title page, title page, and paperback cover design: Syracuse University Press.

Contents

ACKNOWLEDGMENTS   vi

INTRODUCTION: Three Stars in the East   ix

1. The World Is Waiting for the Sunrise   1
2. Shadows in the Cave   5
3. The Dawn   9
4. 1944–45 Season: We Want to Find Out First Where TV's Goin'   15
5. 1945–46 Season: After the Storm   20
6. 1946–47 Season: TV Gets the Green Light   24
7. 1947–48 Season: Vaudeville Is Back   30
8. 1948–49 Season: The Freeze   37
9. 1949–50 Season: Behind the Ion Curtain   45
10. 1950–51 Season: What's My Crime?   53
11. 1951–52 Season: The Thaw   63
12. 1952–53 Season: Grade-B TV   73
13. 1953–54 Season: Point of Order   81
14. 1954–55 Season: Showbiz in a Hurry   90
15. 1955–56 Season: The Road to Reruns   99
16. 1956–57 Season: It's Been a Tremendous Strain   108
17. 1957–58 Season: Oh, Dem Oaters   115
18. 1958–59 Season: *Dotto* Goes Blotto   122
19. 1959–60 Season: Adventures in Syndication   128
20. 1960–61 Season: The Vast Wasteland   136
21. 1961–62 Season: I Still Have the Stench in My Nose   143
22. 1962–63 Season: CBS + RFD = $$$ 150
23. 1963–64 Season: Hands Across the Ocean   158
24. 1964–65 Season: The Unloved Messenger   166
25. 1965–66 Season: The Second Season   175
26. 1966–67 Season: Same Is the Name of the Game   184
27. 1967–68 Season: The Whole World Is Watching   192
28. 1968–69 Season: The One Punch Season   200
29. 1969–70 Season: Effete and Impudent Snobs   207
30. 1970–71 Season: Totally Committed and Completely Involved   215
31. 1971–72 Season: Not Just Another Pretty Face   223
32. 1972–73 Season: Ideological Plugola   231
33. 1973–74 Season: The New Centurions   239
34. 1974–75 Season: Affirmative Access   246
35. 1975–76 Season: Freddie or Not?   253
36. 1976–77 Season: The Big Event   260
37. 1977–78 Season: T & A TV   267
38. 1978–79 Season: Born Again Broadcasting   274
39. 1979–80 Season: Gleam in the Eye   282
40. 1980–81 Season: The Strike   289
41. TRANSITION 1927–81: Stop and Start It All Again   294
42. 1981–82 Season: Freddie's Blues   299
43. 1982–83 Season: Send in the "A" Team   305
44. 1983–84 Season: After *M*A*S*H*   313
45. 1984–85 Season: We Are the World   317
46. 1985–86 Season: Isn't That Amazing?   323
47. 1986–87 Season: Finally a Fourth   329
48. 1987–88 Season: The Boomer Years   335
49. 1988–89 Season: The Goddess   341
50. 1989–90 Season: Mmmm … Doughnuts   346
51. 1990–91 Season: The Live Storm   351
52. 1991–92 Season: The Sax Man   356
53. 1992–93 Season: Nothing Much   361
54. 1993–94 Season: The Truth That's Out There   366
55. 1994–95 Season: In the Blink of an Eye   372
56. 1995–96 Season: Ready for Reform   377
57. 1996–97 Season: All Around the Dial   383
58. 1997–98 Season: Devil with the Blue Dress On   390
59. 1998–99 Season: Sex and Violence   396
60. 1999–2000 Season: Not the Final Answer   402
61. 2000–01 Season: Reality Is Bad Enough   408
62. 2001–02 Season: Ground Zero   414
63. 2002–03 Season: Go Pound Sand   420
64. 2003–04 Season: Game Change   426
65. 2004–05 Season: ZigZag and JibJab   431
66. 2005–06 Season: Here's the Deal   438
67. 2006–07 Season: What *Else* Is On?   444
68. 2007–08 Season: Called Third Strike   452
69. 2008–09 Season: Change Is Now   459
70. 2009–10 Season: The End of the World as We Know It   464

CONCLUSION: On Beyond Zebra   470

INDEX   477

Acknowledgments

We would like to thank the following for their help, both in this edition and in the original publication.

Businesses and Institutions (from A to Z):

ABC News (special thanks to Tony Brackett, Trevor Julien, and Mike Duffy); AT&T Co. (special thanks to Sheldon Hochheiser and Ray O'Connell)

Bing Crosby Productions, Inc. (special thanks to J.R. Rodgers); Bret Adams Limited; George Burns

C-SPAN (special thanks to Brian Lamb, Steve Scully, Shelly Siders, Robin Scullin, Mike Michaelson, Lee Ann Long, Howard Mortman, and Deb Lamb); Carsey Werner Mandabach (special thanks to Suzanne Habbershaw); Capitol Radio (UK) (special thanks to Howard Hughes); CBS Photo Archives (special thanks to David Lombard); CBS (special thanks to Martin Silverstein, James Sirmans, and Anne Nelson); CBS News (special thanks to David Buksbaum, Geraldine Newton-Sharpe, and Robert Levithan); Chicago Public Radio (special thanks to Tish Valva, Justin Kaufmann, and Steve Edwards); Chicago Scenic Studio (special thanks to Ken Zommer); Classic Media, Inc. (special thanks to Jeremy Drosin); CNN (special thanks to Jane Maxwell); Crew Neck Productions (special thanks to John Scheinfeld)

Danny Thomas Productions; David Shapira and Associates, Inc.; Digital Focus–Photography

Edie Adams Foundation (special thanks to Edie Adams)

Federici Video (special thanks to Joe Federici); Irving Fein; Filmways, Inc. (special thanks to Robert Mirisch); Bill Fitz-Patrick (White House photographer); 498 Productions, LLC (special thanks to Bruce Spizer); Fox News (special thanks to Stephen Hirsh in Washington)

International Creative Management (special thanks to Toni Howard); ITC Entertainment, Inc. (special thanks to Edward Gilbert, Murray Horowitz)

Jack Barry-Dan Enright Productions (special thanks to Dan Driscoll); Rick Jasculca at Jascula/Terman; Jonathan Lehrer Communications; Judy Thomas Management

Knights of Good Productions, Inc. (special thanks to Kim Evey)

Lakeview Photo and Portrait Studio (Lake Zurich, Illinois); Library of Congress; Lucille Ball Productions, Inc. (special thanks to Gary Morton)

MacNeil Lehrer Productions (special thanks to David Sit, Mike Fritz, Dave Gustafson); MTM Enterprises (special thanks to Patricia Ahmann); Miss America Organization (special thanks to Liz Puro); Museum of Broadcast Communications (special thanks to staff members Madeline Mancini, Raissa Jose, Steve Jajkowski, Daniel Berger, and Gina Loizzo)

NASA; National Archives; NBC News (special thanks to Bob Asman); NBC Studios (special thanks to LeeAnn Platner); NBC 5 Chicago (special thanks to Diana Borri and Edward S. Mann)

The George Foster Peabody Awards, administered by the Grady College of Journalism and Mass Communication at the University of Georgia (special thanks to Horace Newcomb and Eric Holder); Peekskill Enterprises, Inc. (special thanks to Jack Philbin)

Second City Toronto (special thanks to Carlie Baxter); SFM Entertainment (special thanks to John Firestone); Smithsonian Institution (special thanks to Hal Wallace, David Allison, and John McDonough); Sonny Fox Productions (special thanks to David Eagle); Sony Pictures Television (special thanks to Edward Zimmerman and to Marc Rashba); Stock Montage (special thanks to Shirley Neiman)

Tandem Productions (special thanks to Lynne Naylor, Barbara Brogliatti, Virginia Carter); Studs Terkel; *The Tonight Show* with Jay Leno (special thanks to Walter Lewis and Carrie Simons); The Tribune Company (special thanks to Mitch Locin); Twentieth Century Fox (special thanks to Andy Bandit and Shanna Wegrocki)

United Talent Agency (special thanks to Allison Band); U.S. House of Representatives Radio TV Press Gallery (special thanks to Tina Tate); U.S. Senate Press Photographers' Gallery (special thanks to Jeff Kent and Mark Abraham); Universal Studios Licensing LLLP (special thanks to Roni Lubliner)

Viacom Inc. (special thanks to Mallory Levitt, Debbie Artim, Rebecca Borden, and, especially, Tad Jankowski)

WCIU in Chicago (special thanks to Neal Sabin); WGN Radio (special thanks to Steve King and Johnnie Putman); White Cherry Entertainment (special thanks to Ricky Kirshner); William Morris Agency; *Who Wants to be a Millionaire* in Great Britain (special thanks to David Briggs and Chris Tarrant); WTBS (special thanks to Edwin Jay); WTTW Channel 11 in Chicago (special thanks to Randy King and Rich Samuels)

For the front cover photography, special thanks to:

Peter Sills at Digital Focus for the cover shot and finishing work; Barbara Brown for the photograph used as the TV screen image; and, for the period room setting, thanks to Bud and Marge Podrazik, Mark Podrazik, Paula Schipiour, Irene Zima, Jake and Dorothy Dumelle, Steve Bulwan, and young viewers Liam Sills, Zachary Sills, and David Podrazik.

For unique TV references and resources, special thanks to:

Bruce DuMont, president and founder of the Museum of Broadcast Communications in Chicago (www.museum.tv)

Ron Simon, curator of television and radio at the Paley Center for Media in New York and Los Angeles (www.paleycenter.org)

Colleagues and Friends: Eileen Berman, Lana Brown, Tom Campbell, Bob Chapman, Chris Dumelle, Robert Ellisberg, Michael Epstein, Nadine Epstein, Steve Jones, Jack Kelly, Justin Kulovsek, Tom LaPorte, Howard Leib, Tekki Lomnicki, Cindy Myers, Bob Petersen, John Powell, Maria Rafa, Martin Rich, Sharon Ross, R. Craig Sautter, Danette Sills, Chuck Stepner, Marjorie Tsang, Paula Uscian, Bev Weintraub, Don Wilkie, Flawn Williams, and Dean Yannias.

At Syracuse: Robert Thompson and the staff of Syracuse University Press.

VERY SPECIAL THANKS TO:
- Peter Sills for taking us along the digital pathway.
- Mark Abraham for sharing photos from his news portfolio.
- Mark Lewisohn, for sharing our passion for accuracy.
- Edward S. Mann, our man in master control.
- Dick Fiddy, for a UK data base tour.
- Jonathan Lehrer for guest hosting.
- John O'Leary for his liberal good humor.
- Rev. Michael Class, S.J., for his conservative good humor.
- Al Sussman for his critical comments, line by line.

And to PJ Dempsey, Michael Mills, Mike Tiefenbacher, Tom Schultheiss, and Tony Sauber for helping to make the original 1982 edition happen.

Family thanks from Harry to:

Lloyd and Fay, who never thought that watching TV would pay off for their son in the end.

Claire for appreciating much of what her father wanted to pass on to her, and for getting him to appreciate what is good now.

Laura for caring.

Family thanks from Wally to:

Walter and Julia, who were always willing to adjust the family schedule to accommodate their son's fascination with the tube.

Grace Dumelle for patient support and a sense of perspective in dealing with the siren call of the television world.

And as usual:

Harry would like to thank Wally.
Wally would like to thank Harry.

NOTES ON THE PRIME TIME FALL SCHEDULE GRIDS

The fall schedule grids display the prime time programming of the major commercial broadcast networks, arranged according to Eastern time. They reflect the initial offering in each slot at the start of each fall season and do not show changes that may have occurred later that season.

The schedule grids reflect 100% clearance. That is:

1) They present every series in the time period they were first generally available from the networks for airing by individual network affiliates. However, these affiliates often altered the network schedules a bit to fit their own needs. Sometimes this meant presenting shows on a delayed basis in a different time period; other times it meant not airing particular shows at all.

2) Thus, the fall schedule grid lineup may not reflect exactly what an individual affiliate in a specific market chose to air in those timeslots that fall.

A title set entirely in UPPER CASE indicates a new program making its first appearance on television that fall.

In three cases, program titles appearing for the first time in one of the fall schedule grids are not considered new programs.

1) Programs that premiered during a prior winter, spring, or summer season and are merely returning for their first fall season;

2) Programs that previously premiered outside of prime time, or somewhere other than on the major broadcast networks, and were then moved to a fall prime time slot.

3) Programs that previously appeared on a fall schedule but under a different name.

A network time period split by a horizontal line between program titles indicates that the shows alternate each week in the same slot.

If a title is preceded by the # symbol, that program appears only once each month.

A title followed by other titles in parentheses is an "umbrella" series. The other titles identify specific programs aired under the umbrella title. These usually alternated on a week-to-week basis.

The ^ symbol indicates a program carried only on the network's Midwestern stations.

The shape and layout of the schedule grids alters over the course of the book to reflect the changing number of major commercial broadcast networks as well as the changing time periods considered to constitute evening prime time.

The *Watching TV* website can be found at www.watchingtv.org

Email Harry Castleman at hc@watchingtv.org

Email Walter J. Podrazik at wp@watchingtv.org

President Dwight D. Eisenhower took the oath of office on January 20, 1953. *(National Archives)*

Jackie Gleason, Audrey Meadows, Art Carney, and Joyce Randolph: *The Honeymooners.* *(CBS Photo Archive © 2003 CBS Worldwide, Inc. All Rights Reserved.)*

Three Stars in the East

JANUARY 19, 1953, WAS A MONDAY. It was the day of a subtle but significant shift in twentieth century America. Though it had been almost thirty years since John Logie Baird had demonstrated the world's first experimental television, fifteen years since the first American TV sets had gone on sale, and nearly five years since Milton Berle had become the first television superstar, it was not until January 19, 1953, that three separate events marked the point at which television became synonymous with American popular culture.

As they did every Monday night, millions of Americans turned to CBS at 9:00 P.M. to watch the top-rated show in the country, *I Love Lucy*. That night the audience for the program was greater than usual because Lucy Ricardo was to become a mother. This development was set in the fictional world of situation comedy, but, at the same time, it was also very real. On *I Love Lucy* that evening, Lucy Ricardo gave birth to a healthy baby boy, nicknamed "Little Ricky" after his father, Ricky Ricardo. Earlier that same day, Lucille Ball, who played Lucy Ricardo, gave birth herself to a real life healthy baby boy, named Desi Arnaz, Jr. after *his* father, Desi Arnaz. Interest in the two births had steadily grown over the previous three months through baby-related plots on the weekly series and in publicity photos and feature articles in popular magazines. The widespread attention paid to the double drama of celluloid TV pregnancy and real life pregnancy practically overshadowed the other big news story of the day: the inauguration of Dwight D. Eisenhower as president and Richard M. Nixon as vice president.

January 19, 1953, was the last day in office for President Harry Truman and it ended twenty years of uninterrupted leadership by Democratic presidents, who had taken the country through a major depression and a world war. The new Republican administration marked not only a significant shift in political style and priorities, but also a dramatic change in the election process itself. The Eisenhower-Nixon ticket was the first to reach national office by the deliberate and successful use of television. Eisenhower owed his nomination to the dominant presence of television at the 1952 Republican convention and to the skillful use of the new medium by his campaign managers. Richard Nixon, Eisenhower's running mate, had saved himself from an almost certain dumping from the Republican slate by responding to charges of maintaining a "secret slush fund" with an unprecedented personal appeal to the country, via television, in his famous "Checkers" speech. Appropriately, the Eisenhower inauguration on January 20, 1953, was the first to be televised live, coast-to-coast, giving millions of Americans their first glimpse at the pageantry and ceremony in the American style of transferring power.

The fact that all three births (Desi Arnaz, Jr., Little Ricky, and the Eisenhower administration) came within twenty-four hours of each other was coincidental, but it serves as a convenient landmark in the history of television. The ascension of Eisenhower and Nixon ended the medium's long struggle to be taken seriously by government officials and important newsmakers. The nationwide attention lavished on the *I Love Lucy* birth episode was solid evidence that the American viewing public had totally accepted television's Hollywood-flavored sitcom characters as part of its daily life. By January 19, 1953, television had become the most powerful mass medium in the land.

The appearance of Little Ricky and Desi Arnaz, Jr. (the first by-products of television's premiere couple) also ushered in a brand new generation of Americans, the first to spend their entire lives growing up in the world of video images. Under the influence of the nation's new electronic babysitter, these children acquired a video vision of life which increasingly intertwined the shape and makeup of the fantasy world they observed on the tube and the hopes and dreams they nurtured for the real world they lived in. While watching TV, the new video generation grew up with perfect parents such as Ozzie and Harriet, Donna Reed, and Fred MacMurray; perfect heroes such as the Lone Ranger and Superman; perfect buddies such as Howdy Doody and the Mouseketeers; and the generation's own personification—the perfect kid—Jerry Mathers as the Beaver. In the immediacy and intimacy of television, these fantasy characters became as real, if not more real, than the world itself. Unlike any previous form of entertainment, television brought lifelike images directly into homes throughout the country by the mere flick of a switch, allowing people thousands of miles apart to see, share, and learn the same things together. This simple fact made television the ultimate miracle of twentieth century technology.

Since the first major experiments in television during the 1920s, ecstatic visionaries had been struck by the near miraculous technical nature of the new medium and they had painted rosy pictures of it as the "savior of our culture." Once TV arrived, nearly everyone marveled at the amazing process itself and watched almost anything that aired, from roller derby to serious drama, yet it quickly became clear that the high expectations had ignored the hard realities of the business interests that had worked to develop television.

Lucille Ball and Desi Arnaz *(center)* as Lucy and Ricky Ricardo, America's #1 sitcom couple, along with Vivian Vance as neighbor Ethel Mertz and Richard Keith as Little Ricky. *(CBS Photo Archive © 2003 CBS Worldwide, Inc. All Rights Reserved.)*

Television was conceived by the same people responsible for commercial radio. Like radio, television was structured around just a few programming networks, paid for by commercial advertisers, and dedicated to attracting the largest possible audience. At heart, TV was just a very fancy new way to present mainstream entertainment and sell some soap at the same time. This came as a rude shock to the visionaries and, within a few years, they were calling television a mental wastebasket for the dregs of American creativity. Like their original great expectations, this later letdown was far removed from the reality of the medium.

To be understood, American television must be viewed as the embodiment of contradiction: a miracle of spectacular technical achievement imprisoned by the demands of its mundane day-to-day operations. So-called "high class" programming almost always competes with mass appeal presentations because, with 365 days a year to fill, programmers cannot possibly stock each moment of each day with uplifting culture. In spite of all its limitations, this mundane miracle still produces great moments of popular culture and, to varying degrees, special moments of brilliance that rekindle the awe felt by the first TV owners. Yet, in the game of American television, the bottom line has always been the bottom line and, to this day, it still is.

Watching TV in Mayberry, North Carolina. (*From left*) Gomer (Jim Nabors), Andy (Andy Griffith), Aunt Bee (Frances Bavier), and Opie (Ron Howard). *(CBS Photo Archive © 2003 CBS Worldwide, Inc. All Rights Reserved.)*

1. The World Is Waiting for the Sunrise

FOR A LONG TIME people were, and felt, apart from each other. Communication between cities and countries took time and, as late as the nineteenth century, people's lives and global events moved at a very slow pace. Then, almost within one lifetime, in one amazing century (1840–1940), the whole concept of communication was turned inside out.

The upheaval began on the afternoon of May 24, 1844, when Samuel Morse, sitting in the United States Supreme Court building in Washington, tapped out a series of electric dots and dashes on his new telegraph machine. Forty miles away, assistants in Baltimore received and decoded the message sent through the telegraph wires stretched between the two cities. Morse's first message was "What hath God wrought?" It was an appropriate comment on the entire revolution in communication that was just beginning.

Implications of the Morse message were staggering. For the first time in human history, people in two separate cities could converse with each other instantaneously. The new invention spawned a network of telegraph cable that covered the country within a few years and soon thereafter spanned the oceans. News became a same day medium. Using dots and dashes sent over wires, people could learn of events within twenty-four hours of their occurrence anywhere in the Western world. Yet this was only the beginning. Thirty-two years after Morse's breakthrough, Alexander Graham Bell provided the next communication link, the telephone. With this, the human voice itself could be sent over the wires.

The new-found ability to bridge great distances and bring people together tickled the imaginations of nineteenth century romantic visionaries. Ignoring the more pragmatic side of human nature, they naively predicted that the new technology would be developed and expanded for great humanitarian and social reasons. Soon, it was said, leaders of the world would be linked by cable and, with such channels of instant communication open, permanent world peace would naturally result. Instead, the new inventions were used to make money. Through such major companies as Western Union and American Telephone and Telegraph (AT&T), both the telegraph and telephone became a means for private communication in which, for a fee, customers could send personal and business messages. Though this was a much less exalted

purpose than the overnight end to all war, it provided an equally important change in the social pattern of society. With an ever expanding flow of information, world events grew increasingly complex and, consequently, individuals, businesses, and governments wanted to communicate even faster and farther.

In 1896, Guglielmo Marconi, a young Italian who had relocated to London, demonstrated the next step in communication technology, the wireless telegraph. This device could flash dot and dash messages limited distances through the air without any connecting cable. Wireless communication was perfect for situations which could not be handled by regular telegraph and telephone wires, such as ship-to-shore contact. In July 1897, the Marconi Wireless Telegraph Company was formed in Britain and, two years later, a branch office was established in America.

As the new century began, the Marconi company led the way in commercial message wireless service and, by the outbreak of World War I in 1914, wireless telegraphy was a thriving business in the United States. Other companies such as General Electric and Westinghouse became involved in wireless research and development as well, though they all assumed that the most lucrative aspect of wireless communication would be transmitting personal messages for customers, like the telegraph and telephone.

At the same time, there were also thousands of amateur "ham" operators who took the basic wireless design and built home machines, tapping out their own messages into the dark. A few intrepid souls such as Reginald Fessenden and Lee de Forest began crude wireless voice broadcasts, a process dubbed "radio." Within a few years, voices filled the air as well as dots and dashes. Wireless fanatics sat for hours at their equipment, listening for distant messages and sending their own. Some young executives such as American Marconi's David Sarnoff saw great potential in the dedicated listenership and proposed that the communication giants expand beyond private messages into the area of free informational and entertainment voice broadcasting. Such suggestions were ignored because there did not seem to be any great profit in this.

When the United States entered World War I, the military took over all important wireless transmitters for use in the war effort. Following the armistice of November 1918, the administration of President Woodrow Wilson toyed with the idea of retaining gov-

June 2, 1896

Guglielmo Marconi is awarded a British patent for his wireless telegraphy system. In December in London's Toynbee Hall, Marconi publicly demonstrates his invention for the first time.

July 20, 1897

The Marconi Wireless Telegraph Company is established in London. This is the great-grandfather of NBC.

November 22, 1899

Marconi sets up a U.S. branch office, the American Marconi Wireless Telegraph Company, in Trenton, New Jersey.

August 25, 1900

First appearance of the word "television." A report from the International Congress of Electricians, meeting in Paris, uses the term in a caption.

May 14, 1901

The United States Navy officially retires its fleet of homing pigeons in favor of wireless telegraphy.

September 30, 1906

American Marconi hires fifteen-year-old Russian immigrant David Sarnoff as a $5.50-a-week office boy.

December 24, 1906

Reginald Fessenden becomes the first to broadcast an entertainment program via radio. From his transmitter in Marshfield, Massachusetts, Fessenden performs "O Holy Night" on the violin, plays a few records, and reads from the Bible.

February 5, 1907

Lee de Forest begins irregularly scheduled programming from a broadcasting station on the roof of the Parker Building in New York City.

---

ernmental control of all broadcast facilities, but the private enterprise spirit won out and commercial wireless service was restored. An important part of the plan to end governmental control of broadcasting was the promise by American Marconi to separate itself from its "foreign" (British) roots. In the fall of 1919, General Electric set up the Radio Corporation of America (RCA), which absorbed American Marconi that November. When commercial wireless service resumed in March 1920, RCA was the largest broadcasting company in America.

Looking for a competitive edge in the postwar marketplace, the Westinghouse company hatched a scheme to expand the market for its wireless equipment by producing ready-made wireless receivers. Instead of restricting itself to the limited world of dedicated amateurs, Westinghouse aimed for the general public. In late 1920, Westinghouse set up a rooftop broadcasting station (KDKA) in Pittsburgh to provide free entertainment and information programs that could be picked up by home radio receivers. For its inaugural broadcast, KDKA carried up-to-the-minute results of the presidential race between Warren Harding and James Cox, using information telephoned in by reporters from a Pittsburgh newspaper office. Leo Rosenberg, a Westinghouse public relations man, read the reports on the air. In the weeks preceding the broadcast, Westinghouse launched an intense publicity campaign for both the election night coverage and its "easy to operate" radio sets. The enthusias-

tic response to both was much stronger than anticipated, so Westinghouse went ahead with a followup. It began nightly radio broadcasts running at least an hour and featuring talk, music, speeches, and sports. The success of KDKA convinced the major industrial firms that free radio broadcasting could be used to increase sales of radio equipment dramatically. Over the next few years, Westinghouse, General Electric, AT&T, and RCA set up radio broadcasting stations in major cities across the nation.

The phenomenal growth in equipment sales that resulted from the free broadcasts turned radio into a spectacular moneymaker. Yet almost immediately the costs of providing enough entertainment to fill the stations' expanding program schedules began to escalate as well. Searching for a way to meet rising costs and further increase profits, broadcasters soon realized that a veritable gold mine of a different sort lay at their feet. Instead of merely selling tubes and radio sets, the companies operating radio stations could sell the air itself. They could charge other companies for the privilege of inserting commercial messages into their entertainment programs. With the acceptance of radio advertising by the general public, radio as a profitable commercial medium became economically feasible, with no apparent limit to its possible growth.

With the potential for so much money and power at stake, hundreds of individuals and corporations quickly set up their own radio stations throughout the country, with very little governmental oversight. By the mid-1920s, broadcasting had deteriorated into a series of vicious battles as station owners jockeyed for choice frequency allocations and arbitrarily increased their transmitting signal strength. They wanted to round up as large an audience as possible in order to attract and satisfy advertisers. For more than a year there was near chaos in the radio spectrum. At last, in desperation, the industry itself asked the government to step in and, in early 1927, Congress passed legislation establishing the Federal Radio Commission (FRC) to sort out the broadcasting mess. In doing so, the government set up a basic conflict in American broadcasting that would remain present throughout its further development: the battle between "crass" commercial interests and "class" programming.

Rather than assigning individual station owners permanent control of particular frequencies as expected, the Radio Act of 1927 took a dramatically different approach and defined the airwaves as belonging to the public. It authorized the FRC to issue only limited

The earliest radio listeners needed headphones to hear the few stations on the air. *(National Archives)*

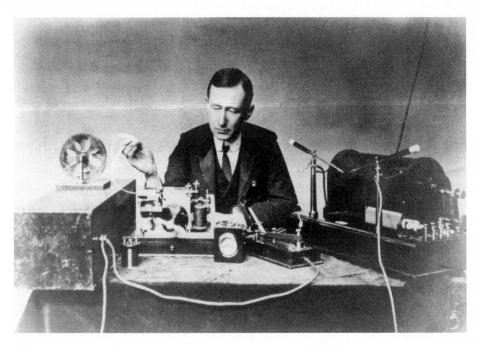

Young Guglielmo Marconi and one early version of his wireless telegraph apparatus. *(Smithsonian Institution; Marconi's Wireless Telegraph Co., Ltd.)*

licenses which permitted the temporary use of, but not the actual ownership of, the airwaves. Station owners were required to apply for renewal of their licenses every few years. In granting a renewal, the FRC was to judge whether, overall, the station owner had used the frequency assigned to serve the "public interest, convenience, and necessity." Though the commission was also forbidden by law to act as censor on specific programs or in day-to-day operations, this licensing procedure gave it a powerful tool of influence. Previously, profit had been the sole motivation behind broadcasting. With the FRC sitting in judgment, station owners were forced to also make concessions to the public good that they could point to at renewal time, even though some of these concessions might not be profitable at all.

Just before the FRC was established to bring order to the airways, the major communication companies were busy themselves developing a system to meet the growing demand for radio programming nationwide. AT&T, GE, RCA, and Westinghouse had been fighting each other throughout the decade for control over the various lucrative aspects of radio broadcasting and its hardware. In July 1926, they hammered out their differences and set up the mechanism for a national source of radio programming, a "network." RCA, GE, and Westinghouse, the major producers of radio equipment, formed the National Broadcasting Company (NBC), based in New York City, to offer commercial entertainment and information programs to stations throughout the country. AT&T, which completely withdrew from actual station operation, provided the vital cross-country telephone cable link that made a national network possible. Programming was "fed" over AT&T lines for simultaneous broadcast by the individual stations subscribing to the NBC service. As a result, the opportunity for profit was established at each stage: equipment, commercial time, and cable use. In turn, listeners throughout the country were treated to highly professional New York-based entertainment.

NBC actually consisted of two separate networks, called NBC Red and NBC Blue. Though governed by the same company, they featured different programs and could be sold to different radio stations in the same reception area, or "market." Less than a year after NBC's first broadcast in November 1926, a rival network service was organized, the Columbia Broadcasting System (CBS). The new network began operating in September 1927, on shaky economic footing and was virtually bankrupt the night of its debut.

Less than two months later, Columbia Records, its chief financial backer, pulled out of the venture. The network floundered for nearly a year before William S. Paley, the twenty-six-year-old son of a Philadelphia cigar manufacturer that was one of CBS's few regular sponsors, bought a controlling interest in the network and

April 15, 1912

News of the sinking of the SS *Titanic* reaches America via wireless. One of the main sources of information from the disaster is the Marconi wireless station atop New York's Wanamaker department store, with twenty-one-year-old David Sarnoff as the station manager. Wireless receives an important publicity boost with its role in the crisis.

October 17, 1919

General Electric sets up the Radio Corporation of America, which on November 20 takes control of American Marconi. David Sarnoff is RCA's commercial manager.

November 2, 1920

Westinghouse's KDKA in Pittsburgh reports on the Warren Harding-James Cox presidential race, ushering in a new approach to radio.

August 28, 1922

WEAF, AT&T's New York City radio station, broadcasts the first radio commercial: a pitch for a suburban housing development.

November 14, 1922

Just as America is beginning commercial radio, England goes noncommercial as the British Broadcasting Corporation (BBC) begins programming. A government-chartered monopoly, the BBC is funded by a license fee paid by consumers on the purchase of radio (and later, TV) sets.

December 1, 1922

Edward Belin gives a public demonstration of "television" in Paris. His system transmits flashes of light a few feet.

became its president. Within a few years, Paley's careful budgeting and emphasis on popular entertainers put CBS on stable financial footing. By 1938, CBS was strong enough to purchase Columbia Records as a wholly owned subsidiary.

Though CBS consistently took second place to NBC in both number of hit shows and the number of listeners, the two systems were set up in essentially the same way. NBC and CBS used both "owned and operated" stations (so-called O&Os) and independent "affiliates" in their respective networks. The O&O stations, located in the major metropolitan areas, were the most valuable. The networks themselves owned these and operated them as a major source of network revenue and an important outlet for network programming. Affiliates were independent stations throughout the country which contracted to broadcast as much of the networks' programming as they felt like, or could be pressured into accepting. Through the affiliates and O&Os, NBC and CBS maintained a virtual hammerlock over radio station programming from coast to coast. By 1930, just ten years after the KDKA breakthrough, the pattern of American network broadcasting had taken shape. The networks had become the country's primary source of radio programming, presenting top stars singing, telling stories, acting out dramas, and reporting the latest headline news. The networks, however, ceded control over many of their program slots to the sponsors. These blocks of time (usually fifteen minutes, thirty minutes, or an hour in length) would be purchased by the sponsors, who would then fill them with programs that they created and produced.

Almost as soon as NBC and CBS began network operations, industry insiders felt a need to measure how one network was faring against the competition. Unlike newspapers and magazines, radio networks could not count the number of copies sold to determine how many people were steady customers, so an unofficial system of measuring audience size was instituted at the end of the 1920s. Archibald Crossley's research organization began to compile program "ratings" by calling homes and asking what radio station, if any, the folks there were listening to. It was impossible to call everyone in the country, so instead Crossley contacted people in carefully targeted small sample areas, usually consisting of several hundred or sometimes a few thousand households. Their answers were extrapolated into an estimate of how many listeners a show probably had nationwide. There was a margin of statistical error inherent in such a procedure but, for want of anything better, everyone in radio accepted "the Crossleys" as literally true. The early ratings confirmed the obvious—NBC was far ahead of CBS. Because a network's advertising rates depended on its popularity as determined by the Crossleys, ratings soon became crucial in decisions on what shows stayed and what shows were axed.

The most important finding of the first ratings was that radio listenership had enlarged tremendously in the late 1920s, confirming radio's status as a national mass medium. It joined two other entertainment forms that had also experienced dramatic growth in the 1920s, phonograph recordings and motion pictures. Phonographs, pioneered by Thomas Edison about the time of the birth of the telephone, began appearing in the homes of millions of Americans in the 1920s along with easy to operate and relatively cheap playback machines called "victrolas." Motion pictures, which had attained tremendous popularity without the benefit of sound since the turn of the century, made a dramatic leap forward in 1927 with the development of sound-on-film movies, called "talkies."

All three young media, to varying degrees, sought to remove the barriers between average people and popular entertainment. Yet, all three were flawed. Phonographs were severely limited in length, radio was entertainment for the sightless, and movies could only be seen at a neighborhood theater. By the mid-1920s, enterprising scientists had developed a working model of a greater wonder, a device which could bring both sight and sound to the home virtually free of charge.

It was called television.

2. Shadows in the Cave

AT THE START OF THE TWENTIETH CENTURY, the inventors who had sent first dots and dashes, then spoken words, into the air proclaimed that they were on the verge of doing the same for moving images. Over the years, the arrival of this tantalizing process, called "television," was constantly postponed. By the early 1920s, scientists had only developed methods of transmitting shadows, not detailed pictures. Nevertheless, on April 5, 1923, David Sarnoff, then RCA vice president and general manager, confidently declared to a meeting of the RCA board of directors that soon "television will make it possible for those at home to see, as well as hear, what is going on at the broadcast station." He urged the company to enter the potentially lucrative new field, predicting that eventually television would be in the home of every American. In the previous decade, company executives had fumbled the lead in radio broadcasting by ignoring a Sarnoff memo proposing entry into that field, and RCA did not intend to repeat the mistake for television. Along with General Electric and Westinghouse, the company began to invest more and more money in television development and research.

Ironically, an outside independent Scottish inventor, John Logie Baird, beat these powerful companies and produced the world's first working television on his own. On March 25, 1925, Baird gave his first public demonstration, at Selfridge's department store on Oxford Street in London. On a four by two inch screen, observers saw the image of a doll, but it was little more than a silhouette. Just over six months later, Baird, working at his home laboratory at 22 Frith Street in the Soho section of London, was at last able to successfully transmit a full image, of a ventriloquist's dummy called "Stooky Bill." Baird publicly unveiled his breakthrough on January 26, 1926, to a group of about fifty members of the Royal Institute who were gathered at his Soho lab. The crude image flickered quite a bit, but the details of a moving human face could clearly be seen. Television had been born.

The first television systems were based on a mechanical process that used rapidly spinning disks containing spiral perforations to transmit the action. The spinning disks in the camera and receiving unit would "see" a rapid succession of tiny flashes of reflected light through the perforations. If the disks were spinning fast enough, the tiny flashes would be perceived by the human eye as forming a coherent, moving image. The process was akin to the techniques used to create the illusion of movement in film, where a series of still photos flashed by so quickly that the subjects appeared to move. Though very awkward and bulky, mechanical television was only slightly more complicated than the radios of the day and, as late as 1930, amateur mechanics magazines included instructions on how to build television sets at home from scratch. It was generally felt that if television progressed at the same rapid rate as radio, within five years the system could easily be in homes throughout the country. Such predictions appeared to be more than idle speculation in the late 1920s, when it seemed that science fiction could barely stay ahead of science fact.

In March 1927, Fritz Lang's German film "Metropolis," concerning life in the future, opened in New York City. Among the film's many special effects was an elaborate television-telephone system used by the industrial wizard who ruled the fictional city. A mere thirty days later, such a system was used in real life, tying together New York, New Jersey, and Washington. This first American intercity TV transmission was viewed at AT&T's Bell Telephone labs in New York City. Secretary of Commerce Herbert Hoover delivered an opening congratulatory message from Washington via telephone cable and then a comedy skit was sent over the air from nearby New Jersey. In this, a vaudevillian named A. Dolan, portraying an Irishman (with side whiskers and a broken pipe), told a few jokes in brogue, then quickly donned blackface and told more jokes, this time in what was called a "Negro dialect." Sent out as a moving image made up of eighteen horizontal "lines of resolution," the entire show appeared as a bluish-green hazy picture on a two-by-three-inch screen. Nonetheless, on April 8, 1927, the *New York Times* proudly proclaimed in a front page headline: "Far Off Speakers Seen As Well As Heard Here." A subheadline added: "Like a Photo Come to Life."

The excitement expressed by the *New York Times* infected the electronics industry as a whole. David Sarnoff called the event inspiring and said that it proved television had "passed the point of conjecture ... the possibilities of the new art are as boundless as the imagination." The Federal Radio Commission optimistically declared that "visual radio is just around the corner" and set aside frequencies for the new medium, just above the AM radio band.

At first, it seemed as if all the enthusiasm was justified. In January 1928, GE and RCA held the first public demonstration of home television sets, in Schenectady, New York. David Sarnoff appeared on the promotional show, calling it "an epoch-making development." Though at that point GE had produced only three of the bulky spinning disk sets for home use, a larger number did go on sale later that year for $75 each. In May 1928, General Electric's Schenectady station, W2XCW (later WRGB), became the world's

June 13, 1925

Charles Francis Jenkins holds the first public demonstration in America of an early form of television at his Connecticut Avenue laboratory in Washington. Moving silhouette images of a small windmill are seen on a ten-by-eight-inch screen five miles from the transmitter.

January 26, 1926

Television is born. In his London laboratory, John Logie Baird demonstrates the world's first working television system.

November 15, 1926

The National Broadcasting Company (NBC) goes on the air. Heard on twenty-six radio stations located as far west as Kansas City, the NBC network is the first national source of radio programming.

September 7, 1927

Philo T. Farnsworth constructs the first all-electronic television system.

September 18, 1927

Though nearly bankrupt, the struggling new Columbia Broadcasting System (CBS) takes to the air on sixteen radio stations, challenging NBC.

July 2, 1928

The first advertisement for a ready-made television set appears in the brand new magazine called *Television*. Manufactured by the Daven Corporation of Newark, New Jersey, the set costs $75.

July 20, 1928

The FRC grants RCA a license for a New York television station, W2XBS, which goes on the air in September.

September 28, 1928

William Paley acquires control, and becomes president, of CBS.

August 19, 1929

The Amos 'n Andy Show. (NBC-Blue Radio). Freeman Gosden (Amos) and Charles Correll (Andy), radio's first situation comedy superstars, make it to a network after four years of local broadcasts. Their fifteen-minute show runs weekdays, beginning at 7:00 P.M.

November 20, 1929

The Rise of the Goldbergs. (NBC-Blue Radio). Gertrude Berg (as Molly Goldberg) heads one of radio's first funny ethnic families, struggling for financial security in a new land.

fully sent out the first color television images: a red and blue scarf and a man sticking out his tongue. The Federal Radio Commission began issuing noncommercial television station licenses so that an expanded schedule of experimental broadcasts could be conducted. RCA received one of the first licenses and, in the fall of 1928, W2XBS (later WNBC) went on the air in New York City. Because no human could stand extended stretches under the intense light needed for the experimental broadcasts, W2XBS used a statue of Felix the Cat, which slowly revolved on a platter, as its moving test pattern.

By the fall of 1929, Baird had begun regular television service in London and twenty-six stations were operating in America, including five in the New York area. Programming was spotty and set sales were slow, but broadcasters felt the possibility for real economic growth in television was almost at hand. They urged the FRC to lift the ban on commercial television broadcasting, but the commission disagreed. Though continuing to encourage experimentation and expansion in television, it felt that approval of commercial broadcasting on a par with radio would have to wait for further technical improvements as well as a significant increase in station operation and set sales. Broadcasters felt that such developments hinged on commercial backing, but the argument soon became irrelevant as two factors combined to stop the television boom cold: the introduction of a new television system and the beginning of the Great Depression.

Since 1919, Vladimir Zworykin, a Russian immigrant, had been hard at work for Westinghouse and, later, RCA in pursuit of an alternative method of transmitting TV pictures, the all-electronic television system. In the 1920s Zworykin devised an early model iconoscope, the "eye" of an electronic TV camera, and, later, the

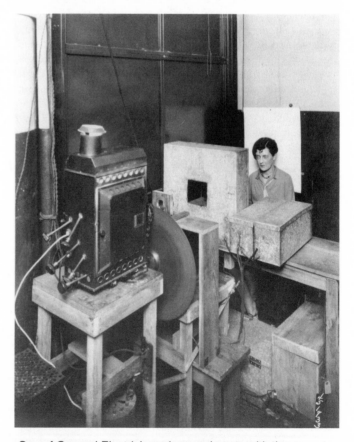

One of General Electric's early experiments with the cumbersome "spinning disk" mechanical television system. *(Smithsonian Institution)*

first regularly operating television station, simulcasting programs with General Electric's Schenectady radio station, WGY, for half an hour three days a week. At this point, television was primarily viewed as an adjunct to radio, not a competitor. In the experimental simulcasts by RCA and GE, television was literally visual radio, merely adding pictures to the audio then being broadcast on radio.

Throughout 1928 and most of 1929, enthusiasm for the new medium continued to grow. W2XCW broadcast the first outdoor scene, the first television play, and even covered the acceptance speech by Democratic presidential candidate Alfred E. Smith from Albany, New York. In July, John Logie Baird, in London, success-

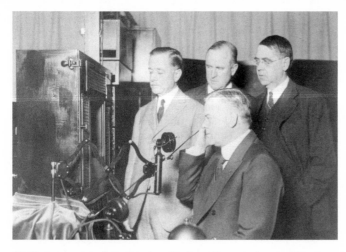

U.S. Secretary of Commerce Herbert Hoover *(seated)* took part in the country's first public inter-city television broadcast. *(Property of AT&T. Reprinted with permission of AT&T)*

receiving end of the process, the kinescope picture tube. Once again, though, it was a feisty independent that beat the established companies and put all the elements together. In 1927, twenty-one-year-old inventor Philo T. Farnsworth developed the first practical all-electronic television system, and filed key patents for its components. Even mighty RCA eventually ended up licensing some of Farnsworth's work, though only after years of trying to buy him out or to supersede him through its own patent claims. In the end, both Farnsworth's and Zworykin's work were needed for television to move forward.

In essence, the all-electronic television system used an electron gun to "spray" tiny flashes of light into very thin horizontal lines of resolution, from the top to the bottom of a TV screen. This accomplished the same task as the spinning disk, but with a much smaller device that provided greater clarity. Because the electronic system operated at a faster rate than the mechanical one, less light was needed to illuminate the subjects in the studio and the resulting picture appeared better defined and more lifelike. As television technology improved, the number of lines used to form the picture increased, and the images became even sharper.

From the start, mechanical television had been awkward, bulky, and incapable of a very sharp picture. The new electronic system solved all these problems but imposed one new one: the two systems were incompatible. A mechanical TV set could not pick up the images sent out by an electronic system, and vice versa. Because the electronic system provided a more saleable product in the long run, it was only a matter of time before the industry would adopt it. As a short term result, all the mechanical spinning disk sets were doomed to obsolescence and this meant at least a five-year hiatus in the expansion of television into American homes. Consumers and station operators might have been able to absorb such an expensive television adjustment without too much trouble, if not for the Great Depression.

The Wall Street "crash" of October 1929 sounded the death knell for early television. Much of the financing for experimentation and set construction evaporated. Most American station owners could not afford the changeover from the mechanical to the electronic system, so they went off the air. No new sets were being produced and there was little chance that very many people outside New York City would be watching anyway. Only the two giants of American radio broadcasting, NBC and CBS, could afford to keep television alive.

With personal income plummeting, radio became the average

citizen's cheapest source of entertainment. Situation comedies such as *Amos 'n Andy* and *The Rise of the Goldbergs,* soap operas such as *One Man's Family,* and entertainers such as Rudy Vallee kept people glued to their radios and kept the networks in the black. NBC and CBS used the income from their successful network radio operations to subsidize flashy moves in television. In 1931, NBC received permission to build a large, powerful TV antenna atop the Empire State building. CBS opened its own New York TV station, W2XAB (later WCBS) with New York Mayor Jimmy Walker presiding at the ceremony, and Kate Smith and George Gershwin providing the music. W2XAB then seized the initiative from NBC's W2XBS and commenced a fairly regular schedule of

January 3, 1930
David Sarnoff becomes president of RCA.

July 21, 1931
CBS begins its television operations with the birth of W2XAB in New York.

February 15, 1932
The George Burns and Gracie Allen Show. (CBS Radio). After some well-received guest appearances on NBC in 1931, George and Gracie are snapped up by CBS for a radio show of their own.

May 2, 1932
The Jack Benny Program. (CBS Radio). The master of comic timing takes to the air. Benny popularizes the concept of a "family" of supporting players for a comedy-variety program, adding Don Wilson in 1934 and both Eddie "Rochester" Anderson and Dennis Day in 1937.

July 2, 1932
Live radio coverage of Franklin Roosevelt's speech at the Democratic National Convention in Chicago marks the first time a candidate officially accepts a party's presidential nomination in person at the proceedings, instantly redefining the future dynamic of political conventions.

November 21, 1932
An out-of-court settlement of a government antitrust suit forces General Electric and Westinghouse to dispose of their interests in NBC, leaving the network as a wholly owned RCA subsidiary.

January 30, 1933
The Lone Ranger. Tales of the Western masked man establish a new radio network. The program starts out on just one station, WXYZ in Detroit, but is soon picked up by other major independents, including WGN in Chicago and WOR in New York. In 1934, they form the Mutual Broadcasting System (MBS).

February 23, 1933
CBS's W2XAB suspends television broadcasts.

June 19, 1934
The Communications Act of 1934 becomes law, supplanting the Radio Act of 1927. The Federal Radio Commission is revamped into the Federal Communications Commission.

March 22, 1935
The Nazi TV network goes public.

A mid-1930s German prototype of home television sets. *(National Archives)*

entertainment and discussion programming in the evening for those few in New York who had receivers. CBS television even covered the 1932 presidential election.

On October 11, 1932, the "stage and screen division" of the Democratic National Committee held a thirty-minute political rally on W2XAB. Master of ceremonies Wayne Pierson introduced celebrities who, in turn, explained why they were supporting Franklin Roosevelt. On election day, November 8, the *New York Times* exalted that "television set owners, believed to be a few hundred, will catch a glimpse of the future when they see the way Americans will get the election returns in the '40s. W2XAB will televise pictures of the candidates and bulletins, beginning at 8:00 P.M."

Two weeks before Roosevelt's inauguration, though, W2XAB suspended broadcasts when it became impossible to overcome the effects of the worsening depression. Though CBS was in solid financial shape overall, television was proving to be a dead-end investment for the time being. The problem was the lack of sets. Almost everyone already had a radio, but only a handful of people possessed TV sets. Even though RCA probably could have begun mass production of commercial electronic televisions by 1935, very few people would have been able to afford one.

The healthiest Western economy in the mid-1930s was that of Germany under Adolf Hitler. There, the National Socialist (Nazi) Party was strongly committed to propaganda efforts in the popular arts and mass media, and it set up the first relatively public electronic television system in the world. On March 22, 1935, after six months of extensive testing, the Reichs Rundfunk in Berlin began

three-day-a-week broadcasts, at 180 lines, using the world's first mobile TV units. The Reich, like RCA, was capable of producing TV sets for home use in 1935, but wanted to wait until the price could be reduced enough to put television in the reach of the average German consumer. In place of home sets, the Nazis temporarily compromised by setting up eleven viewing rooms in Berlin, where members of the public, after obtaining a free ticket, could view one of the ninety-minute film programs broadcast via television. By January 1936, transmissions consisting of live and filmed segments were increased to one hour each day (with repeats). In August, the Berlin Olympics were televised to twenty-eight public viewing rooms, using three cameras and two mobile vans for the coverage. These viewers, like Hitler himself, saw close-up the record-breaking performance of black American Jesse Owens as he triumphed over the best of Germany's "Aryan" athletes.

German home TV sets went on sale in July 1939, but the outbreak of war two months later prevented many sales. However, telecasting in Berlin was soon increased to six hours a day in order to boost war morale and entertain the soldiers in hospitals. The Berlin broadcasts did not cease until November 23, 1943, when Allied bombing destroyed the German transmitter, though Nazi-controlled telecasts continued from the Eiffel Tower in Paris until August 16, 1944.

Right behind the Germans in bringing electronic television to the public were the British. The government-run British Broadcasting Corporation (BBC) had taken over Baird's fuzzy thirty-line mechanical television operations in August 1932. Three years later, the BBC signed off to retool for "high definition" all-electronic television. The necessary new receivers went on sale in London in August, 1936, as the BBC resumed test broadcasts. On November 2, 1936, the BBC officially inaugurated its electronic television service, operating each weekday for an hour in the afternoon and an hour in the evening. It acquired its first mobile vans in May, 1937, in time to cover the coronation parade of King George VI. Three cameras sent the scene to an estimated 50,000 people watching on 3,000 sets. Before World War II intervened, France, Russia, Italy, and Japan also commenced electronic television service, with Japan broadcasting the first televised baseball game eight years before America.

As a result of the length and severity of the depression in the United States, the country lost the lead in television development to Europe. In the mid-1930s, television in the U.S. was largely moribund, having almost shut down completely after the "false start" of mechanical TV. It took a very powerful company and a very persistent man to pump some life back into the industry in the middle of the Great Depression. That company was RCA and that man was David Sarnoff.

3. The Dawn

JUST AS NAZI GERMANY BEGAN its regular television broadcasting service in 1935, David Sarnoff, by then president of RCA, acted to revive television in the United States. Though the lingering economic depression made mass market set sales impractical, he was determined to keep the idea of television before the public while firmly establishing RCA and NBC as the unquestioned leaders in the medium. At a meeting of RCA stockholders on May 7, 1935, Sarnoff announced a $1 million program to take television "out of the lab" and "around the corner," saying that, "in the sense that the laboratory has supplied us with the basic means of lifting the curtain of space from scenes and activities at a distance, it may be said that television is here. But as a system of sight transmission and reception, comparable in coverage and service to the present nationwide system of sound broadcasting, television is *not* here, nor around the corner."

Sarnoff's plan called for experimental broadcasts that would showcase the dramatic technical and artistic breakthroughs in the quality of television and, at the same time, generate public curiosity and excitement. Television was to put aside the 1920s concept of radio simulcasting and present its own programming instead. Picture quality was set at the much sharper transmitting signal of 343 lines and new receivers were to be placed in highly visible locations for easy public viewing. RCA was practically the only company in America capable of mounting such an expansive campaign then, due largely to the continued success of its network radio operations and equipment sales. Even though the end of simulcasting was, in effect, the quiet declaration that television and radio were to go their separate ways, radio would continue to pay for the very expensive experiments in television for nearly two decades.

After fourteen months of construction and testing, NBC's W2XBS began the all-electronic, phase of American television on July 7, 1936. David Sarnoff presided over a special telecast, which featured comedian Ed Wynn. There was no effort to rush electronic TV sets onto the market because both the technical engineers and program producers wanted to use the experimental phase to discover what would and would not work on television. Besides, the government's ban on commercial TV was still in effect, though this "limitation" actually helped NBC's program producers. They could run any film and stage any play they wished without having to worry about paying for commercial authorization. As a result, over the next three years, W2XBS aired a wide range of material.

Even though RCA did not push set sales during this experimen-

tal phase, executives kept news about television constantly before the public, so every few months reporters were brought to NBC's New York studios in Rockefeller Center to witness another test broadcast. During 1937 and 1938 they saw Gertrude Lawrence's play "Susan and God" (with the original Broadway cast), humorist George Ade's vaudeville act "The Mayor and the Manicure," Claudette Colbert in the film version of "I Met Him in Paris," and an adaptation of a Sherlock Holmes short story, "The Adventure of the Three Garridebs." Just before Christmas 1937, W2XBS obtained America's first two mobile TV vans and they began to roam within twenty-five miles of New York City, sending signals back to the transmitter via microwave. At the time, these telecasts were quite newsworthy and the press came away suitably impressed (reviewers called the mobile broadcast of a fire "very graphic"). Often, though, the excitement of the moment went unchecked and easily fed the public relations vision of the medium as a force that would revolutionize entertainment, if not the world. In the early 1950s, even the *New York Times* would look back ruefully at its early enthusiasm for the promise of television as "a vital new form of electronic theater that augured an exciting and challenging new cultural era … the imperishable wonders of a vibrant and articulate stage would be spread to the far corners of the land."

They had fallen into the same trap as their predecessors. Telephones were going to bring world peace, but instead brought pay phones. Radio was going to bring grand opera and learned discussion into the home, but instead delivered cigarette and soap commercials. Television's cultural visionaries saw the amazing tube as nothing less than the savior of the nation's artistic soul, even as television's business planners saw it as a moneymaker potentially more lucrative than network radio.

Even though W2XBS was the only New York City station operating in 1937, technicians were already hard at work on a system that would make possible a national television network similar to the existing radio network. Due to technical limitations, electronic television could not use regular AT&T phone lines for long distance hookups as radio did, so it was necessary to devise a thicker, more complex cable, called a "coaxial cable," and construct an alternate cable system throughout the country. In November 1937, the first AT&T coaxial cable link was established, connecting New York with Philadelphia, which also had one television station in operation. The Philco company's W3XE (later KYW) began to occasionally share programs with W2XBS via the cable, though it was usually a New York-to-Philadelphia sharing.

November 2, 1936

The BBC officially inaugurates its all-electronic television service. England is the first country in which home sets capable of receiving the improved signal are actually put on sale.

January 25, 1937

The Guiding Light. (NBC-Red Radio). The start of one of the few top radio soap operas to survive the challenge of television. In the early 1950s, it makes a smooth transition to video.

May 6, 1937

Chicago radio reporter Herbert Morrison provides a defining moment in on-the-spot news coverage at the "*Hindenburg* disaster." Recording an account of a much publicized landing in New Jersey by a trans-Atlantic German passenger air zeppelin, Morrison instantly switches his narrative when the ship suddenly bursts into flame. His horrified, powerfully moving description ("Oh, the humanity!") airs the next day on WLS, in Chicago, and the disc recording is also carried by the NBC network.

November 9, 1937

The first link in the chain. The New York to Philadelphia television coaxial cable opens.

March 13, 1938

CBS World News Roundup. (CBS Radio). Edward R. Murrow makes his first on-the-air broadcast for CBS's new daily news show, which emphasizes on-the-spot reporting.

July 20, 1938

The Department of Justice sues the eight major Hollywood studios for anti-trust violations in the so-called Paramount Case, claiming they unfairly control both the production and the projection of movies.

August 8, 1938

Paramount Pictures, one of the eight major Hollywood studios, buys an interest in DuMont Labs.

October 30, 1938

Orson Welles achieves overnight national notoriety with his staging of "The War of the Worlds" on CBS Radio's *Mercury Theater* anthology. He presents the 1898 H. G. Wells tale of a Martian invasion as a contemporary breaking news story, even "interrupting regular programming" for its grim fictional updates. With real-life tensions high over a possible war in Europe, this blurring of news and fiction about invaders "landing in New Jersey" is unexpectedly accepted as real by many listeners, especially on the East Coast.

NBC's W2XBS practically monopolized domestic television progress through the late 1930s. In August 1937, CBS served notice that, after letting its New York City license lie dormant for more than four years, it would reinject network competition into the television market by soon resuming its telecasts. It announced plans for constructing television studios in Grand Central Station, though CBS's W2XAB did not return to the air until October 1939. During that time, David Sarnoff moved NBC and RCA into the next phase of their expansion initiative.

By early 1939, the American economy had picked up and RCA felt it was time to launch a full-scale drive to promote home television set sales. W2XBS was technically capable of presenting reasonably high quality signals and programming from both in the studio and on remote, so Sarnoff decided to put the station on a regular daily broadcast schedule which could be effectively publicized. As a dramatic kick-off event, NBC covered the opening of the 1939 New York World's Fair.

At 12:30 P.M. Sunday, April 30, 1939, the 200 television sets already in use in New York City, and the twelve special receivers at the RCA Pavilion at the fair, carried a milestone in American broadcasting. Producer Burke Crotty directed the one-camera program, opening with a graceful view of the Trylon and Perisphere (the symbols of the fair), sweeping over to the Court of Peace, and resting on the opening day crowd and assembled VIPs. President Franklin Roosevelt (the first president to appear on television) delivered an opening address, as did many other dignitaries, but once again it was David Sarnoff of RCA who captured the moment, "Now we add sight to sound. It is with a feeling of humbleness that I come to this moment of announcing the birth, in this country, of a new art so important in its implication that it is bound to affect all society. It is an art which shines like a torch in the troubled world."

It was such prose that, four years later, prompted the Television Broadcasters Association to bestow Sarnoff with the title Father of American Television.

On Monday, May 1, the day after the fair opened, the first American electronic television sets went on sale. There were twenty-five models, ranging from $200 to $1,000. Throughout the run of the fair, an NBC mobile van remained stationed at the RCA exhibit, attracting large crowds of curious viewers who delighted in seeing themselves on television. However, there was no immediate rush to buy home sets. Though not as awkward as the old mechanical models, the new sets were still rather large and bulky. Many included a complicated tilted-mirror viewing device because it was feared that looking directly at the screen itself could cause damage to the eyes. NBC confidently pressed on with its expanded broadcasting schedule anyway and, during the next few months, W2XBS racked up numerous television firsts: first baseball game on American TV; first TV professional baseball game; first TV prize boxing bout; first TV football game; first TV professional football game; first TV college basketball game; first TV professional hockey game; and the first televised circus.

These events were usually covered by one NBC mobile van which was severely restricted by the limitations of the equipment. There was only one television camera in the van and no means for the announcer to monitor the on-air signal. As a result, it became very difficult to coordinate the descriptions and pictures in complicated wide-open team sports such as baseball and hockey. Boxing and wrestling, on the other hand, were much easier to follow because both involved only two contestants and took place in small, well-lit arenas. Announcers such as Bill Stern, Dennis James, and Ben Grauer could sit ringside, reasonably certain that their descriptions would match the actions on the screen. Consequently, early television favored the one-on-one boxing and wrestling contests over major team sports, and sports announcers became some of the first familiar television personalities, turning up throughout the broadcast day—even on non-sports events. In addition to his play-by-play duties, Dennis James hosted two weekly shows, *Dennis James Sports Parade* and *Television Roof* (scenery and interviews from atop the Rockefeller Center). Ben Grauer did the special "play-by-play" report on the festivities surrounding the New York premiere of "Gone With the Wind" on December 19, 1939.

In spite of NBC's many well-publicized events and the return to the air of CBS's W2XAB in October, fewer than 1,000 TV sets were sold in New York by November 1939. The Federal Communications Commission (FCC), the successor to the FRC, analyzed the lack of public support for television and concluded that people would not buy sets until there were more stations and better programs available. NBC felt the best chance for such growth in the industry rested in commercial television, but the FCC felt that there were a number of vexing technical problems still to be worked out before opening up TV for sponsors. CBS, having just returned to active television broadcasting, was inclined to support the FCC's more cautious approach. Executives at both NBC and CBS did agree that one of the major stumbling blocks to popular acceptance of television was its monochrome nature. Television pictures appeared only in black and white. Most agreed that television in color would be more appealing and saleable, but just how and when to add color to the system posed a perplexing problem.

The television industry's uncertainty over color was similar to problems the movie industry faced thirty years before in adding sound and color to film. When movies were developed at the turn of the century, some argued that commercial motion pictures should be withheld until the entire system was perfected and color, sound, and depth could be incorporated into the projection process. Others felt that the public would be willing to accept silent black and white two-dimensional films until something better came along, and this view prevailed. It proved to be an astute business decision and, as a result, the film industry made a great deal of money on silent pictures while color and sound techniques were worked out.

In television, successful but crude color broadcasting had been demonstrated in 1928, only three years after the first black and white transmissions, but the development of a system for acceptable high quality color images proved to be a very difficult next step. With initial black and white set sales very slow in 1939, the industry faced the question: Should it delay the promotion and mass production of black and white sets until a color system could be developed? Tackling the problem head on, RCA unveiled a prototype color system to the FCC in February 1940. Seven months later, CBS proposed its own system. The two differed in various technical aspects but were identical in one vital respect: they were incompatible with black and white television sets. Both proposed color systems were based on the spinning disk method used for television in its mechanical era. The black and white sets then in use would merely pick up static when trying to tune in a color broadcast. This meant that unless a compatible system could be devised, one day home owners would have to buy new sets specifically designed for color. In early 1941, when NBC and CBS began test color broadcasts, the prospect of junking all the TV sets then in use did not appear to be a distasteful solution. There were only 3,000 black and white TV sets in New York City and far fewer in other major cities. Throughout the country, there were fewer than ten TV stations on the air.

The debate over the proposed color TV systems was just the latest battle in the decade-long rivalry between the two major radio networks, NBC and CBS. All through the 1930s virtually all the important progress in American television had come from either one network or the other. Though some other major industrial firms were involved in local television operations (Zenith in Chicago, Philco in Philadelphia, and General Electric in Schenectady), it was generally assumed that the two big radio chains would monopolize any future system of network television. One company, however, dared to challenge NBC and CBS on their own turf, DuMont Laboratories.

Allen B. DuMont, who had worked with Charles Francis Jenkins in the earliest days of television, had set up his own research corporation in New Jersey in 1931 and, during the decade, DuMont

became an important electronics manufacturer. When NBC and CBS appeared ready to resume full-scale TV operations in the late 1930s, DuMont Labs announced that it would join them—as a full-fledged television broadcasting power mass producing TV sets, applying for its own stations across the country, and setting up its own national network. Such a grandiose plan required more financial backing than the healthy, but limited, electronics base of DuMont, so in August 1938, DuMont sold about 40% of its stock to Paramount Pictures. With this influx of capital, DuMont's TV sets were right beside RCA's in the department store showrooms when TV sets went on sale in May 1939. That same year, DuMont applied for a TV station in New York City to serve as headquarters for its network operations.

DuMont faced two critical problems, aside from financial resources, as it tried to start its own television network. The company had no established stars and no experience in running any broadcast stations. NBC and CBS had a ready-made pool of radio

October 29, 1939
CBS's New York TV station, W2XAB, returns to the air.

January 12, 1940
General Electric's television station in Schenectady is linked to New York City, via microwave.

March 23, 1940
Truth or Consequences. (NBC-Red Radio). Ralph Edwards becomes radio's number one gamesman as the host of a slick stunt show. Contestants who fail to answer simple quiz questions must "suffer the consequences" and participate in some outlandish, usually slapstick, "punishment."

April 13, 1940
The FCC grants DuMont its first television station license: W2XWV in New York.

June 24, 1940
The Republican National Convention opens in Philadelphia and becomes the first convention to be televised.

February 20, 1941
NBC begins on-the-air tests of its color television system.

July 1, 1941
Commercial television begins in the United States with Lowell Thomas, *Truth or Consequences,* and *Charades.*

October 14, 1943
NBC sells its Blue radio network to Edward Noble, owner of the Life Savers candy company.

October 18, 1943
Perry Mason. (CBS Radio). Erle Stanley Gardner's literary sleuth turns up as a foppish playboy in a sudsy daytime serial starring Bartlett Robinson.

April 27, 1944
CBS asks the FCC to kick television "upstairs" to UHF in order to facilitate the shift to color broadcasting.

May 21, 1944
DuMont's New York TV station, W2XWV, at last goes commercial as WABD.

By 1937, television had won a spot in London's home entertainment showrooms alongside radio. *(National Archives)*

talent (performers, producers, technicians) that could be shifted to television when the time came. DuMont had a ready-made pool of technicians, but had to start from scratch in finding creative programming talent. In the crucial area of signing up affiliates for a television network, NBC and CBS also held a tremendous advantage because they had been in radio since the 1920s. Most of the firms beginning local TV operations were companies that owned radio stations. They were accustomed to dealing with NBC and CBS, and they expected to do so again as soon as network television became feasible. DuMont had to first become a broadcaster itself, and then develop a working relationship with the other broadcasters in order to win a large number of TV affiliates in the future.

Essential to the DuMont strategy was a healthy string of owned and operated stations located in key cities. These formed the nucleus of any network because they allowed it to showcase programs and stars for potential affiliates. Once commercial television began turning a profit, the O&Os would also serve as an important source of income for the network. Though DuMont lacked the program experience and radio network income of NBC and CBS, at this early stage of television its entry into the field was a realistic business gamble. It was already a feisty competitor to RCA in the manufacture and sale of sets and, once it obtained its O&Os, DuMont could develop its own stars and be ready to flourish when television really caught on.

Into all this, a monkey wrench was thrown to jam DuMont's expected growth. On May 8, 1940, RCA claimed to the FCC that DuMont was trying to get inferior technical standards adopted for television to protect the film industry because DuMont was really controlled by Paramount Pictures, its major stockholder. The

immediate charge went nowhere, but the underlying claim stuck. Paramount Pictures, though not owning a majority of DuMont stock, was strong enough to elect half of the eight-member board of directors and the FCC ruled that, under its definition, Paramount controlled DuMont. Therefore, the FCC would treat the two companies as one entity. This distinction had important ramifications because the commission had set an ownership limit of five O&Os for any television broadcaster. In 1940, DuMont had already obtained a license for New York and was applying for one in Washington. Paramount had applied for licenses in Los Angeles and Chicago. These three applications were granted in June 1940, but, according to the FCC, if either company received another television license, the DuMont-Paramount "combine" would reach its limit of five O&Os. After that, neither would be granted licenses for any more stations. Paramount and DuMont contended that they were not the same organization and so deserved more stations. DuMont pointed out that if it was to become a creditable national television network, it had to have a full slate of O&Os operational in the major cities as soon as possible. As long as the FCC stuck to its interpretation of DuMont's ties with Paramount, those hopes were mortally wounded.

Despite the complications facing experimental television at the beginning of the 1940s, spurts of technical and program expansion continued. DuMont's first station, W2XWV in New York, signed on in October 1940. In June, NBC used a "network" of three stations to cover a major news event, the Republican National Convention in Philadelphia. Four NBC cameras sent twenty-five hours of political shenanigans live over Philco's station in Philadelphia, via coaxial cable to NBC's W2XBS in New York, and then over the new microwave link to the General Electric station in Schenectady. As the general public watched (if the elite few who then owned TV sets could be called general), the convention delegates selected a dark horse candidate, Wendell Willkie, as their presidential nominee. The Democratic convention was held in Chicago, far from any coaxial cable connection, so television was limited to newsreel reports of the renomination of President Franklin Roosevelt. Election night television coverage in November, though, was the first to go beyond merely posting vote totals. NBC even brought in as announcers radio news star Lowell Thomas and veteran broadcaster Leo Rosenberg (who had performed in the vanguard radio election night coverage on KDKA in 1920).

Through 1941, NBC continued to urge the FCC to approve commercial television, feeling that it was the only way enough money would ever be available to develop entertaining programs to attract a larger audience. In May 1941, the commission at last agreed and announced that commercial television could begin in America on July 1, 1941. To qualify for commercial status, stations were required by the FCC to be on the air for at least fifteen hours a week and to broadcast at an improved transmitting signal of 525 lines. The FCC also authorized new call letters to take effect when the stations began commercial telecasts. In New York, the only city in which all three fledgling networks were already in direct competition, NBC's W2XBS would become WNBT (later WNBC), CBS's W2XAB would become WCBW (later WCBS), and DuMont's W2XWV would become WABD (later WNEW).

Appropriately, W2XBS, the main pioneering force in American television, was the first to make the changeover, transforming itself into WNBT at 1:30 P.M. on July 1, 1941. WNBT's first commercial rates were $120 for an hour-long sponsored program during the evening and $60 for an hour program during the day. The first day's broadcast schedule contained nothing momentous—the station did not have the money for it yet—and the first commercial was very simple. During a time, temperature, and weather report, a watch bearing the name Bulova was shown ticking for sixty seconds. That was it. No catchy jingle. No pretty girls. Just a ticking watch.

The programming itself was equally primitive. Lowell Thomas read the news, but, without accompanying visuals, his newscast was essentially just a radio program. In contrast, quiz and game shows offered very cheap and easy visual action (slapstick, stunts, excited contestants), so the day's schedule was overflowing with them. Ralph Edwards hosted a test video episode of *Truth or Consequences,* sponsored by Ivory Soap. *Uncle Jim's Question Bee,* another quiz show, followed. Soon thereafter came *Charades,* the animated parlor game which quickly became one of television's first format clichés. It was what every run-of-the-mill programmer instinctively thought of when ordered to come up with something "new and visual" for television.

NBC soon applied for permission to upgrade to commercial status its stations in Washington, Philadelphia, and Chicago. Throughout the country, twenty-three television stations were either on or in the process of construction, including Paramount's Chicago station, WBKB (later WLS). Television seemed ready to take off at last. Once again, though, outside forces intervened to put the medium back into the freezer.

On May 27, 1941, just after the FCC authorized commercial television broadcasts, President Roosevelt declared an "unlimited national emergency" as America found itself being drawn into World War II. War came to the United States on December 7, 1941, when the Japanese bombed Pearl Harbor in Hawaii. CBS's WCBW broadcast an unprecedented nine-hour news special on the attack, anchored by Dick Hubbel, but then television practically shut down. American industry was ordered to cut down on unnecessary production and devote itself to the huge war effort. Station construction was halted. All but nine stations went off the air, and those that remained drastically cut their schedules. Each of the three network stations in New York went from broadcasting on four nights a week to just one. By the end of 1942, NBC and CBS had locked their studios, falling back on filmed shorts, a few live sports remotes, and civil defense instruction films. Hospitals requisitioned as many TV sets as they could find for the entertainment of wounded servicemen. Police stations acquired sets so that the squad could take notes on the generally dull civil defense flicks. All production of home TV sets ceased. The few thousand who owned sets had to treat them with love and care because anybody with enough technical skill to fix a TV set had been absorbed by the military. If a set stopped working, it had to sit idle "for the duration." Even the top brass at the networks got involved in the war effort. William Paley of CBS was in the military's Psychological Warfare branch, while NBC's David Sarnoff was in uniform in the Signal Corps, where, by the end of the war, he had achieved the rank of Brigadier General (allowing him, for the rest of his life, to be called "General Sarnoff").

During the war years, the most important development in American broadcasting was the government-induced divestiture by NBC of its Blue radio network. The process began one day after the FCC approved the beginning of commercial television in 1941,

"Now we add sight to sound." The symbols of the 1939 New York World's Fair: *(center)* The Trylon and Perisphere. *(Property of AT&T. Reprinted with permission of AT&T.)*

when the commission issued a proposed new set of rules to govern the relations between radio networks and their affiliates. The FCC felt that NBC and CBS enjoyed a near monopoly of the airwaves, so most of the new rules were aimed at loosening the hold the networks had on the operation of local stations.

Under the FCC's new rules, the radio networks could no longer prevent their affiliates from airing a few shows offered by other networks, and the maximum duration of contracts tying a station to a particular network was reduced from five to two years. In giving affiliates a stronger voice in their own affairs, the FCC hoped to encourage the growth of new networks.

Another new rule went a step further and, in effect, ordered the creation of a new network by stating that no network could operate two competing chains at the same time. This section really applied solely to NBC which, for years, had run both its Red and Blue networks, maintaining itself as number one in the radio ratings. NBC fought this ruling in the courts for two years, but lost. In October 1943, NBC sold the Blue network to Edward J. Noble for $8 million. In June 1945, it was renamed the American Broadcasting Company (ABC). Although Blue-ABC was a new network in a legal sense, it retained most of its old identity, hit programs, and top personalities in the transfer of owners. It even came equipped with three radio O&Os. For television, the arrival of ABC meant that there was a new competitor applying for stations, though ABC had to play catch-up for years. It was even behind DuMont.

The tide of World War II turned in favor of the United States and its allies in 1943 and, under the glow of this optimism, the networks began to awaken television from its nearly comatose state. The three New York TV stations had each been operating only one night of the week (NBC's WNBT on Monday; CBS's WCBW on Thursday; and DuMont's W2XWV on Sunday), but by New Year's 1944, all three had expanded their broadcast hours to fill each night of the week (DuMont on Sunday, Tuesday, and Wednesday; NBC on Monday and Saturday; and CBS on Thursday and Friday).

NBC and DuMont were especially optimistic about launching full-scale network television operations as soon as the war ended. DuMont was anxiously awaiting the FCC's go-ahead to change W2XWV from experimental to commercial status and, in preparation, it was trying hard to gather performing and production talent. The network brought in Broadway producer Irwin Shane to organize a regular live dramatic series, *Television Workshop,* which won critical praise for its version of "Romeo and Juliet." Doug Allen acted as host of another studio program, *Thrills and Chills.* The title was slightly misleading, though, because Allen merely conducted interviews with studio guests who narrated their own travel films.

Through the war years, DuMont had been the only network doing any live-in-studio productions but, on April 10, 1944, NBC at last reopened its TV studios after two and one-half years of old films and remote broadcasts. Network and FCC dignitaries were on hand to introduce what was boldly billed as the first world premiere movie on television, "Patrolling the Ether." It turned out to be a turgid two-reel MGM short which dramatized the FCC's work in tracking down illegal radio transmitters. Still, a brand-new film short for television was something to brag about in 1944. Since television's earliest days, and especially during the slow war years, programmers had plugged in virtually any film, regardless of subject matter or age, just to fill dead spots in the schedule.

On May 25, little more than a month after resuming studio programming, NBC was involved in one of the first instances on record of television censorship. Eddie Cantor, one of the first big radio stars to appear on television, was in the middle of a duet with Nora Martin on "We're Having a Baby, My Baby and Me," when the sound was cut off. The song was considered "suggestive." As Cantor commenced a hula-type dance, the cameraman was ordered to change the focus of the picture to a soft blur.

CBS reopened its studios on May 5, 1944, with the premiere of the *CBS Television News* (hosted by Ned Calmer), a fifteen-minute wrap-up of news headlines using newsreel film. Under the direction of a recently hired producer, Worthington "Tony" Miner, CBS also began to develop entertainment shows. Miner's strategy was simple: He took successful CBS radio shows (usually game shows) and brought them to TV to see if they worked with video added. Lacking NBC's years of television program experience, CBS would have preferred a few more years of experimentation while the technicians, bureaucrats, and producers sorted out television's teething pain problems: program development, frequency allocation, and color. CBS urged that color be added to television before any postwar expansion took place, feeling that it would be best to abandon the few thousand TV sets then in service and move television to a new set of frequencies which would be more adaptable to color broadcasting. Though it developed some new shows, CBS maintained that television was still in the "experimental" stage. Consequently, it did not join in the early bidding for new television station licenses in other cities and limited television operations to its sole outlet in New York City.

A milestone in reverse took place in the summer of 1944 as the two major political parties staged their presidential nominating conventions and, for the last time, essentially disregarded television. Both conventions took place in Chicago, even though the city was not yet connected to the minuscule coaxial cable system. Just as in the 1940 Democratic convention, East Coast viewers had to be satisfied with same-day newsreel coverage. The established newsreel firms (RKO-Pathé and 20th Century-Movietone), which were more concerned with producing reports for the nation's movie theaters, flew the footage to New York for the special broadcasts. Only one concession was made to television at the 1944 conventions: Republican Governor Earl Warren of California pre-filmed his keynote address so that it could be carried on the three-station NBC network as he was delivering it in Chicago.

While the politicians practically ignored television that summer, major advertisers were beginning to seriously consider the commercial possibilities of the medium. There had not been much chance to dabble in commercial television before the war but, once peacetime began and things returned to normal, Madison Avenue felt that video advertising might be worth trying. The first major ad man to publicly display his faith in the future of commercial television was J. Walter Thompson, head of one of radio's largest advertising and program production firms. In the summer of 1944, he personally took charge of his company's premiere foray into television, "The Peanut Is a Serious Guy." This light hearted fifteen-minute opus on DuMont was nothing more than an entertaining plug for peanuts. Nonetheless, Thompson felt that such basic TV experience would prove invaluable in a few years because, he stated flatly, television was going to be "the biggest ad medium yet."

4. We Want to Find Out First Where TV's Goin'

ON FRIDAY, SEPTEMBER 29, 1944, THE FIRST successful long-lasting commercial network television program premiered, *The Gillette Cavalcade of Sports.* That evening, Steve Ellis, the announcer for the Gillette Razor Company's radio sportscasts, did the blow-by-blow description as world featherweight champion Willie Pep easily defeated Chalky Wright in fifteen rounds. The entire NBC television network – New York, Philadelphia, and Schenectady – carried that first program and the series became a Friday night fixture on NBC, lasting sixteen years.

The Gillette Cavalcade of Sports was an outgrowth from radio. Gillette had joined with Mike Jacobs's 20th Century Sporting Club in the late 1930s to present weekly boxing matches over the NBC radio network, which met with considerable success. In October 1943, NBC television began occasional sports broadcasts from Madison Square Garden for servicemen in hospitals, carrying such events as the rodeo and boxing. By mid-1944, it was clear that television boxing and wrestling were quite popular. Telecasts from Madison Square Garden, local semi-professional matches, and a few professional prize fights drew a strong response. With hordes of servicemen expected back soon from the war, Gillette felt it might be wise to expand its sports coverage and get in on the ground floor of television by adding a TV version to its regular radio broadcasts. It scheduled telecasts for three nights of the week: boxing from St. Nicholas Arena on Monday, wrestling from the same spot on Tuesday, and, the main draw, boxing from Madison Square Garden on Friday.

Gillette's commitment to weekly television sponsorship, coming so soon after J. Walter Thompson's initial entry into television over the summer, gave the video industry a much-needed shot of respectability among the hard-to-impress skeptics on Madison Avenue. It proved that advertising on television was no longer a farfetched fantasy for the future, but could be a daily commercial reality.

The success of Gillette's sports show (with its roots in radio) also showed that, while radio and television had ostensibly gone their separate ways a decade before when NBC ended its reliance on simulcasts, the two media were still inexorably tied. Not only did radio provide the funds to pay for television expansion, it also supplied ideas for shows. Programmers would look at established radio hits and restage them for television, hoping to attract a similar loyal following of fans to the new medium. Besides sports,

radio stunt and game shows in the style of *People Are Funny* and *Truth or Consequences* had the most obvious visual appeal. The format consisted of handsome interchangeable male hosts using the lure of cash or gifts to lead unsuspecting, eager, basically naive average Americans through demeaning yet undeniably funny shenanigans. In these audience participation programs, the antics were much more entertaining when seen rather than merely described.

The first network radio game show to be made into a weekly television series was *Missus Goes A' Shopping.* CBS had brought it to the air two months before the premiere of NBC's Gillette boxing, but because it was unsponsored the program was not considered as important to television's progress. Host John Reed King, a veteran of the same sort of thing from radio's *Double or Nothing* game, presented such stunts as a woman trying to slide a quarter off her nose without moving her head and a 250-pound truck driver trying to squeeze into a girdle. CBS producer Worthington Miner added some clever visual production bits to this generally undistinguished show and perhaps it was his touch that won *Missus Goes A' Shopping* rave reviews. One critic wrote: "This removes all doubts as to television's future. This is television."

Simple stunt and game shows were the easiest choice among radio programs being considered for television and were especially appealing to CBS (which still treated TV as chiefly experimental) and the newly established Blue (ABC) network. In fact, the first television program by ABC-Blue was a TV version of a mediocre radio game show, *Ladies Be Seated* (hosted by Johnny Olson), which began on February 25, 1945. Five months later, Blue was officially renamed the American Broadcasting Company, though it still did not have a home base for its television operations. It had applied for stations in New York, Chicago, and Los Angeles, but the FCC had put a halt to processing applications for the duration of the war. As a result, ABC was forced to bicycle along the East Coast, producing television shows in the studios of General Electric's WRGB in Schenectady and DuMont's WABD in New York. Among the productions in this jerry-rigged television operation were a video version of radio's *Quiz Kids* and a ten-week variety series, *Letter to Your Serviceman,* with Joey Faye, Burt Bacharach, and Helen Twelvetrees as headliners.

DuMont did not have a stable of radio shows to draw from, so it put more emphasis on formats specifically designed with video in mind. Instead of radio game shows, the network dabbled in trave-

	7:00	7:30	8:00	8:30	9:00	9:30	10:00	10:30	
M O N									ABC
									CBS
									DUM
			The War As It Happens	Televiews	GILLETTE CAVALCADE OF SPORTS				NBC
T U E									ABC
									CBS
									DUM
					GILLETTE CAVALCADE OF SPORTS				NBC
W E D									ABC
									CBS
									DUM
									NBC
T H R									ABC
			CBS News	local		MISSUS GOES A' SHOPPING			CBS
									DUM
									NBC
F R I									ABC
			CBS News	AT HOME SHOW	local	Opinions On Trial	Will You Remember		CBS
									DUM
					GILLETTE CAVALCADE OF SPORTS				NBC
S A T									ABC
									CBS
									DUM
									NBC
S U N									ABC
									CBS
				Thrills And Chills	Irwin Shane's Television Workshop				DUM
									NBC

logue presentations such as *Magic Carpet* and breezy cooking instruction such as *Shopping with Martha Manning*. Like game shows, these were cheap, visual, and easy to produce, though the subject matter of travel and cooking ultimately proved just as dull and trivial. However, because they were so simple, such programs proliferated for years on all the networks, serving as inexpensive filler with such appropriate titles as *The World in Your Home* and *I Love to Eat.*

When striving for class and recognition, however, DuMont continued to concentrate on drama and achieved mixed success. In the fall, DuMont presented the first televised version of "A Christmas Carol" by Charles Dickens as well as the first full-length musical comedy specifically written for television, "The Boys from Boise." "A Christmas Carol" was well received but "The Boys from Boise" (staged by the Charles M. Storm Theatrical Company) suffered from the technical shortcomings of mid-1940s television. The cameras could focus clearly on only a limited area of action and so, on the small TV screen, movement seemed very cramped.

As a result, the life and bounce of a wide-open stage show was absent and the meager plotline typical of such musical-comedy efforts wore through very quickly.

All of the TV networks were anxious to develop a successful TV format for music because music and musicians were the essential ingredients of radio. Programmers assumed that, to a degree, the same would hold true for television. CBS launched its own modest efforts at television music with a special fifteen-minute solo program featuring Victor Borge, a recent Danish émigré, and a weekly variety show hosted by Paquita Anderson, *At Home,* which featured regular appearances by singer-guitarist Yul Brynner. Developing musicians with TV experience seemed vital because, in network radio, most of the big stars had begun as singers or instrumentalists, and even the comedy giants included musical bits or singing sidekicks in their comedy-variety shows for a change of pace. In fact, that fall CBS Radio promoted to top billing just such a pair of second bananas: Ozzie and Harriet Nelson.

Ozzie and Harriet had become man and wife in the mid-1930s,

three years after Harriet Hilliard joined Ozzie Nelson's band. While later becoming the symbols of middle-aged parenthood at its best, at that time Harriet was quite a beautiful young singer and Ozzie was a very popular dance band leader. The two gained national recognition during their 1941–44 supporting stint on Red Skelton's radio comedy show. Their relaxed ribbing of each other concerning marital spats and their young children made them well-liked radio personalities who showed they could handle comedy as well as music. When Skelton was drafted into the army, the Nelsons received their own show.

Billed as "America's favorite young couple," Ozzie and Harriet began their radio series on October 8, 1944, their ninth wedding anniversary. Over the years, their personal and professional lives had become intertwined in the public's mind, so their program was structured to continue that impression. On *The Adventures of Ozzie and Harriet,* Ozzie Nelson, band leader, portrayed a fictitious Ozzie Nelson, band leader. In both worlds, he and Harriet had two young sons, eight-year-old David and four-and-one-half-year-old Eric (known later as Ricky). At first, child actors (Tom Bernard and Henry Blair) played David and Ricky, but by 1948 the real Ozzie Nelson allowed his real sons on air to portray their fictional counterparts.

The Nelsons thus became another successful example of the "mirror of reality" sitcom approach, in which celebrities were placed into a setting in which their fictional characters were almost identical with real life. Top radio comedian Jack Benny had developed this style in the 1930s by playing a comedian surrounded by a talented supporting cast, who was trying to stage a radio comedy show aided by a talented supporting cast. In Benny's program, though, showbiz life usually remained the focus and what emerged was a very funny comedy-variety show about putting on a comedy-variety show. Ozzie and Harriet shifted the emphasis almost completely to family home life in California, with occasional nods to the professional work that made the comfortable lifestyle possible. Their program was really a domestic situation comedy about a very likable family and their friends and neighbors. *The Adventures of Ozzie and Harriet* was a pioneering innovation and a tremendous success. The format carried them through both long radio and, later, television runs. It served as the model for other television performers in the mid-1950s, such as Danny Thomas in *Make Room for Daddy,* who wanted to place their show business characters into warm family settings.

Whatever plans the networks may have had for increasing the amount of music on TV were dealt a severe setback at the start of 1945 by James C. Petrillo, president of the American Federation of Musicians (AFM), the largest of the musicians' unions. Petrillo had become one of the most powerful men in American broadcasting by using radio's reliance on music as an effective bargaining tool. He had won fat pay raises for "his boys" in the radio orchestras by calling crippling musician walkouts during protracted contract negotiations throughout the late 1930s and early 1940s. Petrillo claimed that large raises were necessary to rectify the inordinately low-paying labor contracts that had been signed by his predecessors when radio was not yet a lucrative mass medium. He had no intention of falling into the same trap himself with television, so in February 1945, before any bad video contract precedents could be set, he decided to put a total ban on all television appearances by any AFM musicians. There were no specific negotiating points on the table, just the desire to avoid premature agreements. Before making any deals, Petrillo said, "We want to find out first where TV's goin'!"

The Petrillo ban, which lasted three years, was a crippling blow to television at this stage because it eliminated some of the most

WTOP's Arthur Godfrey covered the Independence Day ceremonies at Arlington National Cemetery in July 1945. *(National Archives)*

popular radio talent, techniques, and formats, such as musical-variety shows and shows with famous singers. Without live music, television would never get off the ground. The few musical-variety shows tested on television after the Petrillo ban went into effect demonstrated the futility of such ventures without live musicians. Performers on a test TV version of ABC radio's popular *Breakfast Club* with Don McNeill tried to mime (or "lip synch") records, but the results were disastrous. Until the networks and Petrillo came to an understanding, television had to restrict itself to boxing, drama anthologies, cheap film shorts, cooking instruction, game shows, and, to a very limited extent, news.

The television networks had made little effort to establish any news service by 1944 because television as a whole was not yet profitable and there seemed no reason to spend money in such a low return area. Instead, the networks used theatrical newsreel companies as the cheapest source of news film, even though most of these reports barely qualified as news. The newsreels were generally light, upbeat, and oriented toward highly visual events such as far-off natural disasters, the christening of a new ship, or the finals of a beauty pageant. There was very little on-the-spot sound and no in-depth reporting. Instead, an announcer delivered breezy narration in stentorian tones while hokey "appropriate" music matched the action (a news clip of an earthquake in Japan would be accompanied by Japanese-style music).

In the 1930s, there had also been a similar scarcity of news on the radio, with most reports consisting of a few headlines supplied by the major newspaper wire services, or leisurely observations by commentators such as Lowell Thomas (NBC) and H.V. Kaltenborn (CBS). The outbreak of World War II changed all that as CBS made a concerted drive to become the top radio news service. Emphasizing on-the-spot coverage, the network built a solid corps of battle-trained correspondents (led by Edward R. Murrow) who brought their sharpened reporting skills back to the States when the war ended.

The same sort of style was impossible in the early 1940s for television, which lacked the technology, personnel, and finances for on-the-spot coverage. In the first half of 1945, as the war in Europe ended and the leadership of many major powers changed

---

September 29, 1944
Gillette Cavalcade of Sports. (NBC). The first successful, long-lasting commercial network television series.

October 8, 1944
The Adventures of Ozzie and Harriet. (CBS Radio). "America's favorite young couple" begin twenty-two years of weekly shenanigans.

December 11, 1944
Chesterfield Supper Club. (NBC Radio). Perry Como's first musical-variety series, in which he follows Bing Crosby's formula of easy, natural singing.

January 15, 1945
House Party. (CBS Radio). After a year as sole host of *People Are Funny*, Art Linkletter adds a second show, one with less slapstick and more interviews.

February 25, 1945
Though it has no "home base" station of its own, the Blue network gamely begins television operations with a video version of its radio game show *Ladies Be Seated.*

April 15, 1945
NBC Television Theater. (NBC). Producer Edward Sobol begins Sunday night television drama on NBC, with Robert Sherwood's "Abe Lincoln in Illinois." Twenty-nine-year-old production assistant Fred Coe takes over as producer in 1946.

April 30, 1945
Arthur Godfrey Time. (CBS Radio). Slotted as an unsponsored summer filler, the "old redhead" stays on for twenty-seven years.

April 30, 1945
Queen for a Day. (MBS). Distraught women vie for fabulous prizes by describing their personal crises (on cue). Jack Bailey becomes emcee of this tearfest in January 1946.

May 13, 1945
NBC sets up its own television news film department.

June 7, 1945
The Adventures of Topper. (NBC Radio). Roland Young recreates his movie role as host to a pair of ghosts.

June 15, 1945
The Blue network officially is renamed the ABC network.

July 2, 1945
Beulah. (NBC Radio). After a stint on the *Fibber McGee and Molly* show, the popular character of Beulah, a black maid dubbed "queen of the kitchen," begins "her" own program. Beulah is actually played by a small white man, Marlin Hurt.

---

hands, world events moved too quickly for newsreel orientation, yet the networks continued to rely on them. Television could only pretend that it was covering the news. On V-E Day, May 7, 1945, not one television network had its own news-gathering operation.

That day, all three networks managed to assemble specials on the end of the war in Europe, but most of the coverage consisted of live pickups of the celebrating crowds in New York City's Times Square. A week after V-E Day, NBC decided to get the jump on its television competition and established the NBC Television News Film Department. It was a lovely title, but all the department consisted of was a few cameramen who made extensive use of a 35mm camera "borrowed" from the government. For news anywhere outside New York, NBC continued to purchase newsreels.

On August 8, 1945, NBC did present the first network-produced television news show, *The NBC Television Newsreel,* but it was virtually indistinguishable from the coverage provided by the theatrical newsreel companies. For example, as the country celebrated the end of the war against Japan one week later, the program merely featured more live pickups of cheering crowds at Times Square. Since mid-1944, CBS had been presenting fifteen minutes of news on the nights that the network was on the air, but *The CBS Television News* relied solely on material purchased from the newsreel firms. Anchor chores on the CBS newscast fluctuated for over two years until late 1946 when twenty-nine-year-old Douglas Edwards became the regular anchorman (a post he held for more than fifteen years). Edwards resisted the assignment at first because he feared that television news was a dead-end occupation. In the mid-1940s, the only road to broadcast news stardom was on radio, which had made a celebrity out of Ed Murrow and, more recently, Arthur Godfrey.

Godfrey began his radio career as "Red Godfrey, the warbling banjoist" on Baltimore's WFBR in 1929. During the 1930s, he served a long stint as a disk jockey on CBS affiliate WTOP in Washington, where he pioneered a "natural" style of announcing. Godfrey tried to sound like a "regular Joe" rather than an officious announcer mechanically hustling some sponsor's products. He presented himself as an honest fellow who ad-libbed and talked directly to each individual listener, sharing just what was on his mind. The stuffy commercial scripts that shamelessly plugged sponsor products frequently served as a springboard for his comments, and Godfrey became infamous within the radio industry for his on-the-air ribbing of advertising. ("Boy, the stuff they ask me to read!"). The audience grew to love Godfrey and, because he directed his comments at the commercial presentation rather than at the product itself, their support kept nervous sponsors and programmers at bay.

National newspaper columnist Walter Winchell ran some complimentary reviews and this gave Godfrey a national reputation. Godfrey served a brief stint on the small Mutual radio network in the late 1930s and, in 1941, he secured a morning slot on CBS radio's local New York station. He handled this new assignment while still remaining in Washington by pre-recording the New York show. After finishing his early morning chores at WTOP, Godfrey would start all over again and record onto disc (or "transcribe") another music and gab show which would be shipped up the East Coast for airing the following morning. By early April, 1945, Godfrey was a radio workaholic, on the air ten hours a week from WTOP and sending another seven and one-half hours to New York. Though Godfrey was popular locally, the CBS radio network was not sure whether he could be sold nationally. It decided to give him a test run in the spring and summer of 1945, when the network's *American School of the Air* (a highly acclaimed educa-

The funeral procession for President Franklin Roosevelt. *(National Archives)*

tional show) took a summer vacation. CBS ran the educational program on a "sustaining" (unsponsored) basis anyway, so Godfrey was given the weekday morning network show unsponsored. If he caught on, it might be possible to snare a brave national sponsor and keep the show going on its own in the fall. Just two weeks before Godfrey's scheduled network debut, President Roosevelt died.

Franklin D. Roosevelt had been in the White House for twelve years and he was the only president many Americans had ever known. "FDR" engendered very deep emotions in almost everyone; he had helped the country out of the Great Depression and had led it to the brink of victory in World War II. Though his death was not totally unexpected—he had been quite ill for a while—it was still a jolt.

On April 14, 1945, the whole country turned to radio for coverage of Roosevelt's funeral in Washington. Arthur Godfrey, as top man at CBS's WTOP, had the assignment of narrating the network's radio coverage of the slow caisson parade down Pennsylvania Avenue. Like everybody else, Godfrey was overcome with emotion that day, but, unlike his broadcasting brethren, he let those emotions show. As the parade moved slowly by, Godfrey talked of the millions of people listening who were "getting ready for suppertime." When the car carrying the new president passed, Godfrey choked as he spoke of the man who "just had such burdens fall upon him, God bless him, Harry Truman!" As Roosevelt's coffin came into sight, Godfrey broke down and sobbed into the microphone, "Oh God, give me strength!" It was a natural reaction for a man whose radio style was based on naturalness. Nobody else on the air that day better captured the way the country felt. When Godfrey began *Arthur Godfrey Time* on April 30, he already seemed like a close friend to many listeners.

Arthur Godfrey remained a daily fixture in broadcasting for the next thirty years, though he had no exceptional performing talent (his banjo and ukulele playing were only average and his jokes only mildly humorous), and his program (standard musical-variety with comedy) was different only in that it was ad-libbed. Years before the heyday of television, though, Godfrey had discovered the secret of longevity that would prove so important in the decades to come: personality. Because he was not tied to an act or theatrical style, Godfrey could remain on the radio day after day, year after year, and still not use up his material or overstay his welcome. People did not tire of him because he was an interesting person to listen to. He was himself.

Advertisers noted that, despite Godfrey's reputation for ribbing sponsor scripts, his approach to commercials was very effective. He was not just selling something, he was recommending it to his radio friends. Listeners enjoyed visiting with Godfrey, trusted him, and bought what he asked them to. He was the ideal pitchman.

5.   After the Storm

WHEN WORLD WAR II OFFICIALLY ENDED on September 2, 1945, there were fewer than 7,000 working television sets in the United States. There were only nine television stations on the air: three in New York City, two each in Chicago and Los Angeles, and one each in Philadelphia and Schenectady. Programming on all of them was spotty. Yet within sixty days, three events occurred which signaled the approaching expansion of television and the end of this torpid era of American broadcasting.

On October 8, the government lifted its wartime ban on the construction of new television stations and television sets. Over the previous four years, the FCC had received several applications for television station licenses, but had taken no action because most of the country's industry was occupied with War Department contracts. With the wartime restrictions at an end, manufacturers could start to gear up for the production of TV station equipment and home sets on a mass market scale. People once again began to take an active interest in acquiring commercial television stations and the FCC received a steady stream of applications, chiefly from major cities in the East and Midwest. Though the commission's own bureaucratic procedures kept it from moving very fast processing the requests, within a year television managed to expand in areas outside New York, Chicago, and Los Angeles.

Near the end of October, Gimbel's Department Store in Philadelphia held the first large-scale television demonstration in years. Aside from the RCA Pavilion display at the 1939 New York World's Fair, most Americans had never seen a working television system close up. More than 25,000 people came to Gimbel's over three weeks for a chance to watch NBC programs from New York and local shows sent out by Philco's Philadelphia station. Because the major set producers had not yet retooled for domestic work, it would be another eleven months before large numbers of postwar sets reached the stores, so most of the sets on sale in 1945 were actually RCA and DuMont prewar models. Nonetheless, the public's response to even these old sets demonstrated great potential for television sales and it brought TVs back into store showrooms for the first time in years.

In October, RCA held its first public demonstration of a brand new type of television camera, the image orthicon, the first major improvement in TV cameras since Vladimir Zworykin's iconoscope of the late 1920s. The image orthicon was 100 times as sensitive as the other cameras then in use. This not only produced a sharper picture overall but also extended television's "depth of field." Previously, television cameras could show clearly only a relatively small area of stage or playing field. With the image orthicon, much more remained sharply in focus, so television producers could present indoor productions that occupied an entire stage, and outdoor events that were spread over large playing fields.

The first tangible benefits from the new camera turned up in the field of sports. The networks stepped up their interest in wide-open team sports. NBC began regular Saturday afternoon telecasts of college football games in the fall of 1945 and, the next summer, it made professional baseball an important part of its local New York programming. NBC also realized that the image orthicon camera allowed the already very popular one-on-one boxing matches to be presented with "crystal clarity." With a sharp new product to display, NBC and Gillette staged what was billed as the first "television sports extravaganza," the Joe Louis-Billy Conn heavyweight fight at Yankee Stadium in June 1946.

The Louis-Conn fight was heavily promoted in the East Coast television cities as both an important sports event and a special television program. By the time it aired, Washington had been connected to the East Coast coaxial cable network, so NBC added DuMont's experimental Washington station, W3XWT (later WTTG), to its four-city ad hoc fight network. Even though the program was an NBC exclusive, there was no reluctance to include a DuMont O&O in the hook-up because it was the only way the event could be seen in Washington. In the immediate postwar years, competing network affiliates in a market were rare, so any station on the coaxial cable would be offered a show if it was the only outlet in a new TV city.

The fight was a tremendous success, with an estimated audience of 150,000 watching on more than 5,000 TV sets, as Louis defeated Conn in eight rounds. Announcer Ben Grauer compared the event to the 1921 Jack Dempsey-Georges Carpentier bout which, as the first heavyweight championship fight on radio, generated similar excitement in its time. Tube veterans and television novices raved about the new clarity provided by the image orthicon camera. One reviewer said, "This is the sort of event that'll make people buy televisions, not the endless boring cooking shows that seem to turn up on every channel."

Gillette had proved its point. There was a huge potential audience for TV sports. For every TV set tuned to the fight, there were, on average, thirty people watching, many of whom were seeing an event on television for the first time. NBC inserted frequent refer-

RCA's new image-orthicon cameras allowed better coverage of sporting events. *(National Archives)*

ences to Gillette's weekly *Cavalcade of Sports* show, hoping that the excitement over the Louis-Conn fight might translate into a greater number of regular TV viewers. The chief stumbling block to this strategy was that, aside from sports, no other program format had shown itself to be a sure-fire video hit, worthy of a sponsor's support or a viewer's investment in a home set.

Network programmers turned again and again to radio for precedents and ideas, but not all radio translated well into video. Game shows continued to appear all over television, both as clones of radio hits and as original video productions, but none could capture a sponsor. In the 1945–46 season, television presented such short-lived experiments as *Cash and Carry* (with Dennis James), *Play the Game* (more charades), and *See What You Know* (with Bennett Cerf). NBC's suspense radio thriller, *Lights Out*, failed in its attempt to cross over to TV in 1946. On radio, the program used spooky sound effects and the power of suggestion to create masterpieces of audio horror. During a few test television episodes, equivalent video tricks were either impossible or too expensive. As a result, the stories in the television version emerged as much too tame to match the reputation of the original.

NBC was more successful with *The NBC Television Theater*, a weekly drama series launched in April 1945. Following DuMont's lead, NBC turned to the stage for inspiration, presenting drama productions with firm roots in the legitimate theater rather than radio. By 1946, Fred Coe had taken over production chores for the series, and he displayed a tremendous understanding of drama as both a serious and entertaining form. In its first year, *NBC Televi-*

September 29, 1945

NBC begins regular Saturday afternoon telecasts of college football games, featuring the few East Coast schools that will allow television coverage. In the first game, Columbia defeats Lafayette, 40 to 14.

October 5, 1945

Meet the Press. (MBS). Martha Rountree and Lawrence Spivak lead weekly, unrehearsed radio interviews with newsmakers. The first guest is U.S. Chamber of Commerce president Eric Johnson.

October 8, 1945

The war-induced freeze on handling new station applications ends. ABC officially files for three television O&Os, including one in New York.

October 25, 1945

NBC unveils its new image orthicon camera.

October 27, 1945

Harry Truman makes his first live television appearance as president: a Navy Day speech in New York's Central Park.

December 1, 1945

Army beats Navy (on NBC) in their annual football contest, the first event to be televised with the new image orthicon camera.

January 9, 1946

William Paley, president of CBS since 1928, moves up to chairman of the board. Frank Stanton is the new president.

February 12, 1946

Washington is linked to the East Coast television network. General Dwight Eisenhower is shown laying a wreath at the Lincoln Memorial.

March 1, 1946

New York City begins a final six weeks without television as NBC joins CBS and DuMont in signing off temporarily for frequency alignment. On April 15, DuMont's WABD is the first to return to the air.

April 15, 1946

The DuMont television network is officially inaugurated and becomes the first TV network to have two O&Os on the air, connected by coaxial cable.

May 9, 1946

Hour Glass. (NBC). Vaudeville comes to television and it seems to work.

June 6, 1946

Here's Morgan. (ABC). Taking advantage of television's visual nature, Henry Morgan, radio's reigning bad boy, illustrates his monologue about the intense light necessary in a TV studio by stripping to the waist—on camera.

June 19, 1946

Joe Louis overcomes Billy Conn in television's first "sports extravaganza."

July 2, 1946

Arthur Godfrey's Talent Scouts. (CBS Radio). Godfrey enters prime time, as host of an amateur talent show.

Day	Net	7:00	7:30	8:00	8:30	9:00	9:30	10:00	10:30
MON	ABC								
MON	CBS								
MON	DUM								
MON	NBC			Wings Of Democr.	local	Televiews	Gillette Cavalcade Of Sports		
TUE	ABC								
TUE	CBS			CBS News	local	Missus Goes A' Shopping			
TUE	DUM								
TUE	NBC								
WED	ABC			KING'S RECORD SHOP					
WED	CBS			CBS News	local	A.A.U. Boxing Bouts			
WED	DUM								
WED	NBC								
THR	ABC								
THR	CBS								
THR	DUM								
THR	NBC		The Children's Program						
FRI	ABC								
FRI	CBS			CBS News	local	PHOTOCRIME / There Ought To Be Law			
FRI	DUM								
FRI	NBC			FRIDAY NT. Q'BACK	World In Your Home	Gillette Cavalcade Of Sports			
SAT	ABC								
SAT	CBS								
SAT	DUM								
SAT	NBC								
SUN	ABC								
SUN	CBS								
SUN	DUM								
SUN	NBC			NBC NEWS	local	NBC Television Theater			

sion *Theater* presented: Noel Coward's "Blithe Spirit"; "Angel Street," a ninety-minute thriller using the entire Broadway cast of four people (an ideal size for television staging); and "Mr. and Mrs. North," adapted from a Broadway show taken from a radio series based on magazine articles, with Efrem Zimbalist, Jr. in a bit part. Critics who had barely heard of television just months before began to praise NBC's television drama productions as being as good as or better than anything running on Broadway. Under Fred Coe, the performers, scripts, and direction were top notch and, almost single-handedly, Coe made NBC the leader in serious TV drama for a decade. He was NBC's equivalent to Worthington Miner at CBS, a producer with superb television instincts.

The NBC Television Theater ran Sunday night, usually starting about 9:00 P.M. (NBC devoted the time slot to drama for the next twelve years). From the beginning, the network had high hopes for the series. Though it remained unsponsored for more than three years, the critical acclaim given to *The NBC Television Theater* served as a reminder to viewers that television could expand be-

yond theretofore typical fare such as newsreels, games, cooking, film shorts, and sports. Just like Broadway, television could present high quality entertaining stories.

While pleased at the artistic success of its unsponsored Sunday night drama, NBC was still searching for a formula that could generate a commercial television hit. Comedy-variety and musical-variety programs were among the network's most successful radio shows then on the air, so in May 1946, despite the continued ban on live music by James Petrillo's musicians union, NBC and Standard Brands, one of the major advertisers on radio, gambled with the first big budget TV variety show, *Hour Glass.*

In adapting the variety format to television, *Hour Glass* took a simple approach: On each program a host introduced four or five performers (nonmusical) who stood in front of the curtain backdrop or a simple set, did their individual acts, and departed. The show was really nothing more than a series of vaudeville routines staged before a camera, yet *Hour Glass* served as an important experiment in TV programming. Though this pioneer television

Members of Congress gathered at the Statler Hotel in Washington to view the first "television sports extravaganza": the Joe Louis–Billy Conn heavyweight fight. *(Harris & Ewing Photo / Stock Montage)*

vehicle rarely could afford a "name" act, its weekly talent budget of $4,000 was far higher than any previous video series. There was also money for better lighting, sets, props, and writers.

Because *Hour Glass* was the first program of its type on television, it started out ragged and uncertain. Singer Evelyn Eaton, the program's first host, had to lip-synch her records because of the Petrillo ban. During the show's first weeks, the pretty young women showing off the sponsor's products frequently forgot their lines and the ads often dragged on for five minutes. By the fall, the show had tightened up and such fluffs were rare. Actress Helen Parrish took over the hosting chores and she proved more adept at projecting her personality through television and catching the imagination of viewers. Parrish became one of the first performers to be stopped in the streets of New York City and recognized as a television personality. *Hour Glass* attracted a loyal following and soon Edgar Bergen, one of radio's biggest stars, did a guest spot.

Hour Glass was the only commercial success of the TV season, yet it lasted less than a year. The program was the most expensive television production at the time and there were still not enough stations, sets, or viewers to justify such a costly experiment. Standard Brands could not point to any dramatic increase in sales as a result of its television advertising and there seemed to be no end in sight to the stagnant situation in live television music. Just as important, the FCC's continuing indecision on whether to adopt new technical standards to allow color broadcasting was serving as a deterrent to new station applications. In early 1947, the program was canceled. *Hour Glass* had been just slightly ahead of its time.

Yet *Hour Glass* set very important programming precedents in its brief run and became the model for future television variety shows. It demonstrated the surprising fact that the simple vaudeville format—long judged passé on stage—seemed tailor-made for the home screen.

6. TV Gets the Green Light

NETWORK RADIO WAS AT THE HEIGHT of its golden age in the fall of 1946. The nation was resuming peacetime activities. More people had radios than ever before, and they spent more time than ever listening. There seemed to be an almost perfect mixture of news, familiar entertainment programming, and promising new series available. Network news operations, staffed with battle-trained correspondents, were given a larger share of the weekly schedule. Nationally known commentators such as Walter Winchell, Ed Murrow, and H.V. Kaltenborn had very popular regular slots in the early evening. In the ratings for evening entertainment shows, Jack Benny was number one, closely followed by Bob Hope, *Fibber McGee and Molly,* and Edgar Bergen. The strength of relative newcomers such as Red Skelton and Arthur Godfrey augured well for the future.

The NBC network was the unquestioned champion of radio. Through the early 1930s, the Crossley ratings showed NBC far ahead of CBS. In 1935, the Hooper organization supplanted Crossley as the most respected radio ratings source, and NBC continued its healthy lead in "the Hoopers." Even the 1943 government-induced sale by NBC of its Blue network (which became ABC) had not shaken NBC's financial stability and dominance in the ratings. Though stars such as Jack Benny and Fred Allen might hopscotch between NBC and CBS in constant search of a better contract deal, NBC always maintained the strongest roster of programs. As the fall of 1946 approached, NBC had claims on Jack Benny, Bob Hope, Edgar Bergen, Bing Crosby, Fred Allen, Perry Como, Red Skelton, Kay Kyser, Dennis Day, George Burns and Gracie Allen, Bud Abbott and Lou Costello, Eddie Cantor, Alan Young, and Art Linkletter, plus such popular continuing programs as *Amos 'n Andy, Fibber McGee and Molly, Life of Riley, Du-Pont's Cavalcade of America, The Voice of Firestone, The Bell Telephone Hour, Dr. I. Q., Mr. and Mrs. North, The Great Gildersleeve, Duffy's Tavern, Mr. District Attorney, The Aldrich Family, The Kraft Music Hall, Truth or Consequences,* and *The Grand Ole Opry.*

NBC's schedule included several popular sitcoms as well as a few high caliber drama and music shows (usually financed by large industrial corporations in order to promote a positive company image), but the network based its ratings strategy on the strength of its line-up of established singers and comedians. NBC favored the variety format to showcase its stars and used them as hosts of comedy-variety and musical-variety vehicles. CBS's radio schedule was structured essentially the same way, but without as many big names. At CBS, there were such celebrities as Kate Smith, Frank Sinatra, Dinah Shore, Jimmy Durante, and Arthur Godfrey, plus a smattering of musical and dramatic programs such as *Texaco Star Theater, Lux Radio Theater, Suspense, The Thin Man,* and *Your Hit Parade.*

In January 1946, William Paley, president of CBS since 1928, was promoted to the position of chairman of the board. During the war, Paley was away from broadcasting, serving as head of the government's Department of Psychological Warfare, and, upon his return to civilian life, he was eager to begin a concerted drive to move CBS ahead of NBC and into the role as America's number one network. Paley chose Frank Stanton, a man who had worked his way up the CBS corporate ladder over nine years, to succeed him in the post of president, and the two began their task by analyzing CBS's strengths. CBS had earned the reputation for superiority in radio news during the war by pioneering the on-the-spot style of reporting. In an equivalent move in the entertainment field, the Paley-Stanton team decided that, instead of merely trying to imitate NBC's approach to programming, they would give CBS a distinctively different "feel" from the competition. At NBC, sitcoms were generally passed over in favor of variety formats, so CBS began to encourage ideas for popular sitcoms, adding to the handful—led by *The Adventures of Ozzie and Harriet*—it already had on the air. The network also attempted to break from the accepted practice of program control by advertisers and their production companies to produce some shows completely on its own instead.

In the early days of radio, the networks had willingly turned over artistic and production control of their radio programs to the sponsors. At the time, the networks needed the advertising revenue to fund their fledgling but rapidly expanding operations, and felt relieved that some of the production burden had been removed. The sponsors, in turn, did not usually hire the talent and organize the shows themselves, but instead contracted with advertising agencies such as J. Walter Thompson and Young & Rubicam, which actually put the shows together. Soon it became clear that the networks had lost control of what they were broadcasting. For all practical purposes, popular shows on competing networks often sounded the same because the same agencies had created them. With those additional parties in the production process also laying claim to a share in each program's profits, the networks found their portions noticeably reduced. Because this policy was very lucrative to the "outside" producers, the networks found it next to impossi-

In the 1930s and 1940s, network radio was the prime source of home entertainment, with high quality productions such as Bell Telephone's prestigious concert series *The Telephone Hour*. Here, conductor Donald Voohees *(center)* welcomes guest artist Lily Pons *(left)* in 1942. *(Property of AT&T. Reprinted with permission of AT&T.)*

ble to eliminate on established shows. The only way around the status quo was to retain control on new programs and hope that they became big hits as well.

The sponsor-agency combination turned out very slick packages that worked well in popular comedy, adventure, music, and variety formats. These were light entertainment vehicles perfect for showcasing sponsor products and big name stars. Applying the same standards to drama, however, tended to eliminate any serious or controversial productions. Shows such as *The Lux Radio Theater* usually settled for fluffy star-laden melodrama. Appropriately, one of the first series in CBS's postwar independence drive was an ambitious radio drama anthology, *Studio One*, under the direction of Fletcher Markle. The program began in April 1947 with a poignant and exciting adaptation of Malcolm Lowrey's "Under the Volcano," a masterpiece on the alcoholic mind. Subsequent *Studio One* productions continued to emphasize high quality writing rather than glamorous stars. The network hoped that such distinctive network-controlled programs, combined with its established shows and stars, would eventually push it to the top. As long as NBC had so many big name stars under its banner, this was about the best strategy CBS could pursue.

The battle for supremacy in network radio was between NBC and CBS. Far behind, but still turning profits in this golden age of radio, were the two other networks, ABC and the Mutual Broadcasting System (MBS). Mutual was the third oldest independent radio network, formed in 1934 by owners of a few powerful radio stations not affiliated with either NBC or CBS. As a self-proclaimed "voluntary association of independent broadcasters" (thus the name "Mutual"), the network allowed its affiliates much more local control over network programming decisions and did not even have any owned and operated stations. While the individual stations did quite well, as a network Mutual was always on very shaky financial grounds and could rarely afford high budget series.

Since the mid-1930s, Mutual had been playing an unsuccessful game of catch-up with the other networks and, in 1946, found itself last in the network radio ratings race, suffering the inherent frustrations of that position. Any hit shows developed by Mutual were inevitably snatched by the competition, so the network lost such programs as *Dick Tracy, The Lone Ranger, It Pays to Be Ignorant, Kay Kyser's Kollege of Musical Knowledge, Juvenile Jury, The Green Hornet,* and *Roy Rogers.* In the other direction, Mutual served as the dumping ground for network shows on their last legs such as *Lights Out, Sergeant Preston of the Yukon,* and *Sky King.* Nonetheless, even Mutual found gold during this era of broadcasting prosperity, chiefly with flashy but inexpensive game and quiz shows such as *Queen for a Day* and *Twenty Questions.*

The prestige program of the Mutual network was *Meet the Press,* a simple panel show with an important innovation. Previously, most radio interview programs consisted of tame reporters lobbing softball questions at that week's guest. Items of substance were rarely covered. In 1945, thirty-year-old Martha Rountree, a freelance writer, and Lawrence Spivak, editor of the magazine *American Mercury,* convinced Mutual to try a different interview approach, an unrehearsed interrogation with bite. Each week on *Meet the Press* an important, often controversial, public figure was grilled by some of the nation's top reporters. During the give and take between the guests and the questioners, important revelations and admissions sometimes slipped out and soon the national news services were covering *Meet the Press* as a legitimate news event itself. On one program, for instance, labor leader John L. Lewis unveiled a threat of a national coal strike. For a while, Mutual had toyed with the idea of entering television, but its loose organization and meager financial resources eventually forced it to ignore video altogether. *Meet the Press,* however, was brought to television in late 1947 by NBC.

The ABC radio network ran ahead of Mutual in the ratings, coming in a distant but still respectable third. Even though it was

Day	Net	7:00	7:30	8:00	8:30	9:00	9:30	10:00	10:30
MON	ABC								
MON	CBS								
MON	DUM				BOXING FROM JAMAICA ARENA				
MON	NBC		Your Esso Reporter	Televiews		Gillette Cavalcade Of Sports			
TUE	ABC			Play The Game					
TUE	CBS								
TUE	DUM				Serving Through Science				
TUE	NBC								
WED	ABC					^ Wrestling From Chicago			
WED	CBS								
WED	DUM			Magic Carpet	local	FARAWAY HILL	BOXING FROM JAMAICA ARENA		
WED	NBC								
THR	ABC			CHARM SCHOOL	local	Ladies Be Seated			
THR	CBS			CBS News	Judge for Yourself / There Ought To Be Law	SPORTS FROM MADISON SQAURE GARDEN			
THR	DUM					Cash And Carry			
THR	NBC		In Town Today / Your Esso Reporter	Hour Glass					
FRI	ABC								
FRI	CBS								
FRI	DUM					WRESTLING FROM JAMAICA ARENA			
FRI	NBC		Friday Nt. Q'back	YOU ARE AN ARTIST	I LOVE TO EAT / World In Your Home		Gillette Cavalcade Of Sports		
SAT	ABC								
SAT	CBS			Week In Review	SATURDAY REVUE	King's Party Line			
SAT	DUM								
SAT	NBC								
SUN	ABC								
SUN	CBS			CBS News	Shorty / SPORTS ALMANAC	SPORTS FROM MADISON SQAURE GARDEN			
SUN	DUM								
SUN	NBC			Face To Face / Geograph. Speaking	BROADWAY PREVIEWS				

technically the newest independent radio network, ABC's network roots (as NBC Blue) stretched back twenty years. As a result, ABC had a much stronger and more formal network organization than Mutual. Though it could not possibly match the depth of programming by NBC and CBS, ABC carried as varied a selection as possible, including comedy and adventure staples such as *Lum and Abner, Gangbusters,* and *The Lone Ranger,* as well as prestige programs such as *The Theater Guild of the Air* (later *The U.S. Steel Hour), The American Town Meeting of the Air,* and commentary by political gadfly Drew Pearson. Like Mutual, however, ABC turned increasingly to quiz shows for its most successful popular programming. In 1947, ABC had the most popular quiz show on the air, *Break the Bank,* which handed out the largest prizes (up to a then hefty $9,000) and offered one of the most enthusiastic quiz hosts, Bert Parks. He displayed an amazing knack for getting caught up in the quiz itself, urging contestants through their paces, and sounding as if he truly cared whether or not they won.

Television did not enter into the overall broadcast picture very much going into the fall of 1946, and seemed as distant a threat to radio's supremacy as ever. Few television stations were on the air, very few TV sets were in people's homes, broadcast schedules were brief and irregular, and there were next to no hits or stars to attract an audience. The debate over the adoption of a color TV system seemed to go on forever and there were moves afoot to discard all the TV sets then in use and shift television to a different set of broadcast frequencies.

Beneath this apparent weakness, there was a dramatic expansion building. Special events such as the Louis-Conn boxing match in June 1946 and regular series such as *Hour Glass* had demonstrated the public's interest in television. In September 1946, the first large batch of postwar television sets rolled off the assembly lines and into department stores. For the first time ever, interest in TV began to translate into sales. People began to buy television sets in great numbers.

The rise in television set production that fall was nothing short of phenomenal. In the first eight months of 1946, only 225 TV sets were produced in the United States. In September, 3,242 were turned out. On November 4, RCA put its first postwar models on sale and, to pump up interest, NBC-TV aired a star-studded special edition of *In Town Today,* with Bob Hope, Edgar Bergen, and Ben Grauer. By January 1947, the monthly TV set production figure had jumped to 5,437 and, by May, it reached 8,690.

This sudden surge of TV set production added a sense of urgency to resolving the important technical questions that still faced the industry. The central problem was color. Because both RCA and CBS's proposed color systems used the spinning disk concept, they were incompatible with the black and white sets then being manufactured and sold. Since 1940, the FCC had been cautiously considering the wisdom of ordering the few TV sets then in use to be junked in favor of new ones designed for color reception. At mid-decade, however, the color question became entangled in yet another problem: frequency allotment.

In the late 1930s, the FCC had assigned television stations space on the VHF (Very High Frequency) band (channels 1 to 13), even though, practically speaking, this could accommodate only about 400 TV stations throughout the country without cross-signal interference. This was barely enough to support two national networks with affiliates in all major American cities and certainly could not provide outlets for three or four networks.

In April 1944, CBS executive vice president Paul W. Kesten suggested that both the color and frequency problems could be solved in one fell swoop by "kicking TV upstairs" into the UHF (Ultra High Frequency) band (channels 14 to 83). In UHF, there would be room for four times as many TV channels, and broadcasts in spinning disk color could commence at once. In 1944, with the war still on and no new television sets in production, the transition could be relatively easy. The few people who owned TV sets would have to buy new ones but, Kesten said, in the long run it would be worth it.

Most of the other important television powers disagreed and CBS was virtually alone in supporting this plan. RCA-NBC, DuMont, Philco, and General Electric were already heavily committed to TV stations in VHF and to the promotion of black and white TV sets. They saw such a radical proposal as harmful to their own best interests and an unnecessary delay to the progress of commercial television in the United States. Once the war ended, they observed, network operations would begin in earnest as TV station construction and set production resumed. CBS countered that color was essential to television's success and that the move to UHF offered the best solution to the problem. The network insisted that television was still only "experimental" in its monochrome stage and, to show that it was serious, CBS restricted itself to broadcasts on its sole outlet, WCBW in New York City.

During 1945 and 1946, the FCC held lengthy hearings on CBS's suggestion. RCA insisted that the CBS color system would not be ready for five to ten years, while CBS countered with a string of "surprise" demonstrations of progress in its color system, which it claimed would be ready by mid-1947, at the latest.

The psychological turning point of the struggle came at the end of October 1946, when RCA held its own "surprise" demonstration of a brand new color system that would make the CBS spinning disk version obsolete. The big news was that the new RCA color system was partially compatible with black and white sets. When a converter was attached to an existing set, RCA's system would allow reception of shows sent out both in black and white and in color. This meant that the TV sets already in operation could be kept and, with a flick of a switch, could be used no matter what sort of program was sent. RCA promised the FCC that, within five years, further improvements would make the RCA color system

totally compatible with black and white sets, and the bulky converters would be unnecessary. Without any new equipment at all, owners of old TV sets would then see color shows in black and white, and those who bought RCA's color sets could see black and white shows without any problem.

RCA's promised compatible system involved far fewer headaches for the TV industry and for TV set owners, but CBS's noncompatible system seemed the closest to being ready for mass use. When sales of black and white VHF sets began multiplying in the fall of 1946, it became clear that the time for some sort of decision was at hand. If the CBS plan was to succeed, it had to be approved as soon as possible, before sales of monochrome sets increased further. In March 1947, the FCC issued a ruling, stating that, despite the promises, CBS's color system was not yet ready for commercial use. The commission added that, in the meantime, there was no reason to prevent Americans from buying and using black and white television sets. This fateful statement relieved manufacturers and potential station applicants, who were worried over the possibility that the entire television system could be pulled out from under them in a sudden move to color. Though the FCC had simply put aside the pesky color question for the foreseeable future, this decision, in effect, made black and white VHF the ap-

September 14, 1946
Professional football comes to prime time (on an experimental basis) as DuMont airs one Saturday night contest between the New York Yankees and Buffalo Bisons of the All-American Football Conference. Dennis James helps on the play-by-play.

September 22, 1946
Broadway Preview. (NBC). Fred Coe, with help from the Dramatists Guild, presents television "sneak previews" of plays under consideration for Broadway runs.

October 2, 1946
Faraway Hill. (DuMont). Television's first regular soap opera series stars Flora Campbell as Karen St. John, a young city widow who moves to the country and finds a new love. This vanguard effort fades by Christmas.

October 17, 1946
CBS begins televising sports (other than boxing) from Madison Square Garden, opening with a rodeo contest. John Henry Faulk, a new CBS acquisition from Texas, handles the announcing chores.

November 1, 1946
WCBW, CBS's New York TV station, becomes WCBS.

January 3, 1947
Television covers Congress for the first time, carrying its opening day ceremonies live. Three days later, President Truman's state of the union address before the House and the Senate is also broadcast.

January 9, 1947
ABC temporarily ceases television programming in order to sink its money into station construction.

May 7, 1947
Kraft Television Theater. (NBC). New York says "cheese" and Kraft smiles.

By late 1946, the postwar television production lines rolled at a record pace. *(National Archives)*

proved television system for the country. The path seemed clear at last for a rapid expansion in TV growth because, intended or not, the FCC had given commercial TV the green light.

Almost immediately following the FCC decision, applications for stations began pouring in. Within a few months, the number of stations on the air more than doubled. Most of the new licenses were for cities that previously had no TV stations at all, such as St. Louis, Detroit, Baltimore, Milwaukee, and Cleveland.

As more TV stations signed on across the country, local non-network programs began to reach a fair level of quality and talented local personalities began to emerge from cities other than New York. By mid-1947, WBKB, in still far-off Chicago, had developed several performers who would later become network stars. Young Dave Garroway, a former NBC page, added a touch of humor to *Remember the Days,* a weekly thirty-minute sustaining series that consisted of old silent films. As host, Garroway not only read the subtitles but also gently poked fun at the stylized flicks. One reviewer thought that the show was too cute, asking, "Won't we be doing the same thing to 1947 television one day?" A few months later, Fran Allison, who played the gossipy Aunt Fannie on radio's *Breakfast Club,* and Burr Tillstrom, a puppeteer, began a daily kiddie show on WBKB, *Junior Jamboree* (sponsored by RCA). The program focused on Fran's interaction with a group of puppet characters, especially Kukla, a well meaning little bald man, and Ollie, a scatterbrained dragon. Allison's gentle good humor and Tillstrom's imaginative puppet characterizations made the team regional celebrities and soon won *Kukla, Fran and Ollie* a network slot on NBC.

By the end of 1947, Washington, Philadelphia, and Baltimore had joined New York City, Chicago, and Los Angeles in having more than one TV station on the air. Stations connected to the East Coast coaxial cable began establishing regular network affiliations, though most stations continued to accept programs from two, three, or even four networks-for the time being. With its long head start in video programming, NBC was the most successful in signing up TV affiliates.

CBS was the apparent loser in the color TV shuffle. Expecting its color system to be approved and television "kicked upstairs" to UHF, the network had been lax in developing regular programming, seeking out sponsors, signing up TV affiliates, and applying for other owned and operated TV stations outside New York City.

Grudgingly accepting the fact that black and white VHF TV was here to stay—at least for a few years—CBS applied for a Chicago O&O.

Two months after the FCC's "no go" to color, CBS began an ill-fated drive to make up for lost time in TV programming and to leapfrog into the TV lead by adopting a distinctively different "feel" from the competition. The network closed its TV studios at Grand Central Station in favor of all on-location ("remote") and filmed broadcasts. CBS announced plans to sharply increase, in the fall of 1947, telecasts of live sports events such as college football, basketball, hockey, track and field, and the rodeo. In addition, cooking shows would originate from famous restaurants, drama shows would come from theaters, and children's shows would be staged in parks throughout New York City. The Douglas Edwards news broadcasts would continue, but with Edwards relegated to the role of off-screen newsreel narrator.

CBS touted its outside-the-studio broadcasts as a great leap forward in television. The other networks merely televised the inside of a studio, which, it was said, was too much like radio with pictures. CBS promised to bring the world (or at least New York City) directly into viewers' living rooms. CBS's move was, at best, ill-timed and highly unrealistic. Television's bulky technology was not yet ready for extensive out-of-the-studio broadcasting and, with little preparation, CBS had nothing special to offer potential sponsors and potential viewers with its new format.

DuMont adopted a much more reasonable middle ground. The network also could not match NBC's in-studio expertise, but, unlike CBS, DuMont launched a more limited series of remote telecasts. The network copied NBC's already successful prime time sporting schedule and began an extensive series of on-location sports telecasts in the fall of 1946, with a series of Monday-Wednesday-Friday boxing and wrestling matches from New York's Jamaica Arena. NBC had aired a number of wrestling matches, but it had always concentrated on boxing, so DuMont emphasized wrestling, and eventually turned it into a national fad. Like boxing, wrestling was confined to a small space and limited to just a few contestants at a time, which made it ideal for television coverage. Unlike boxing, wrestling had been a sport of only marginal interest until the arrival of television. Very quickly, the promoters of wrestling began to emphasize the theatrical values of the contests above the sport itself, which TV insiders soon nick-named "flying beef." Before and after matches, the wrestlers threatened each other in pre-planned interviews and confrontations. Once in the ring, such colorful characters as Haystack Calhoun, Gorilla Monsoon, and Gorgeous George played up every stomp, scream, and painful grimace to the audience for maximum effect. DuMont's ringside wrestling announcers patterned their actions to fit this style. Dennis James added such touches as snapping chicken bones next to his microphone when a wrestler was put in a particularly painful-looking hold. As wrestling grew increasingly popular, James became known for his trademark phrase, "OK, Mother" which he used to begin explanations of the sport directed toward housewives in the audience.

DuMont's on-location sports programming was a rousing success and wrestling remained a part of the network's schedule through the next decade. Unlike CBS, DuMont continued to try in-studio program formats as well, achieving mixed results. *Faraway Hill,* network television's first soap opera series, was short-lived, but *Small Fry Club,* starring "Big Brother" Bob Emery, became television's first hit children's show. By April 1947, *Small Fry Club* aired Monday through Friday, 7:00–7:30 P.M., beginning the television day with kiddie games and clowns for the small fry lucky enough to have a TV set at home. (After a successful five-

May 11, 1947
CBS closes its Grand Central Station studios and begins a schedule of all-remote and film telecasts.

June 1, 1947
The Jack Paar Show. (NBC Radio). One of the "postwar" generation of comics, Paar begins a summer substitute series for Jack Benny and then, in the fall, moves over to ABC Radio for his own regular weekly program.

June 8, 1947
Lassie. (ABC Radio). The perspicacious canine travels from the movies to radio.

June 16, 1947
News from Washington. (DuMont). The first nightly network television news show. Walter Compton is anchor, but the program lasts only eleven months.

June 29, 1947
Strike It Rich. (CBS Radio). Warren Hull is emcee of "the quiz show with a heart." Poor unfortunates plead for help and the studio audience decides which ones get the loot.

July 6, 1947
Candid Microphone. (ABC Radio). Allen Funt starts sticking his nose into other people's business.

year network run, Emery relocated to a local Boston station where he remained a comforting uncle figure to yet another generation of children.)

NBC continued to televise college football on Saturday afternoons and boxing matches in the evening two nights a week, but its primary focus remained on attracting advertisers for in-studio programming. The Borden Milk company sponsored a series of variety programs that served as try-outs (or "pilots") for formats that might work on TV, all without live music (the Petrillo ban was still in effect). Fred Coe beefed up the Sunday night drama show with assistance from the Dramatist's Guild. For a while, the lead-in to the drama slot was *Geographically Speaking,* starring world traveler Mrs. Carveth Wells, who narrated films of her world trips. The show ended abruptly after twenty-six weeks when she ran out of films.

The radio talk show duo of Tex and Jinx made a more conscious effort to adapt to television, experimenting with three different program forms that season on NBC. John Reagan "Tex" McCrary (newspaperman-turned-commentator) and his wife, Eugenia Lincoln "Jinx" Falkenburg (tennis player-swimmer-glamour girl), had been on NBC's local New York radio outlet since early 1946, leading a low-key, intelligent celebrity talk show program. On April 27, 1947, they brought their successful format to television in *At Home with Tex and Jinx.* From a studio set resembling a fancy apartment, Tex and Jinx entertained their famous friends and showed home movies. (Apparently they took trips, too.)

During the summer of 1947, Tex and Jinx took a brief vacation, but NBC wanted to continue their Sunday evening broadcasts, so, in spite of the network's preference for live programming, a filmed

series was shown in its place. The new format, *Ringside with Tex and Jinx,* moved the show's locale from the couple's "apartment" to their favorite club haunts, where they continued to hobnob with their celebrity chums.

The success of the duo's Sunday evening program earned them an additional assignment, the first commercial network daytime television program. On May 16, *The Swift Home Service Club* began a one-year residency on NBC, Friday from 1:00 to 1:30 P.M. Geared toward the housewife audience, the show featured Tex and Jinx (especially Jinx) giving tips on interior decorating and home economics, while their ever-present celebrity friends tossed *bons mots.* Apparently Tex's chief responsibility was to sample, with relish, Swift's taste-tempting meat products specially prepared for the show. Because television broadcasting still required enormous amounts of light, the resulting heat could wreak havoc on the food. The mayonnaise went bad often enough that an off screen bucket was kept close at hand so that Tex could immediately vomit, if necessary.

The longest-running and most important program that NBC brought out in the 1946–47 season was *The Kraft Television Theater,* which began in May. NBC and Fred Coe had been staging weekly unsponsored dramas for some time, but the Kraft dramas were different. Not only were they sponsored by a major national concern, they were also produced by an outside firm, the J. Walter Thompson agency. All the early NBC and CBS video productions were "in-house," so it came as quite a surprise to the industry that NBC would allow its first major sponsored TV drama series to be run by outsiders.

Kraft and J. Walter Thompson had been long-time partners in staging *The Kraft Music Hall* on radio, so the television arrangement made good business sense. It also offered NBC a ready-made sponsored vehicle to plug into its slowly expanding schedule. If the Kraft series caught on, the network might have an easier time finding support for its own drama series. In spite of network fears that the agency would turn out a slick and shallow *Lux Radio Theater* style drama series, *The Kraft Television Theater* maintained a remarkably consistent, high quality approach over the years (rarely stupendous but generally quite good). Though the first presentation of the series, the slightly dull melodrama "Double Door," did not receive rave notices, another part of the program did.

Kraft's new McLaren's Imperial Cheese had been introduced to the market in early 1947 but, at one dollar a pound, was doing quite poorly in sales. Kraft subscribed to the notion that television might be an excellent advertising medium on a par with radio and decided to use Imperial Cheese as the acid test. For the first two weeks, all of the ads run on Kraft's drama show were for McLaren's Imperial Cheese. For two weeks, pretty model Dana Wyatt demonstrated the tastability of the cheese. For two weeks, the ever-convincing voice of Ed Herlihy expounded on the wonders of this new cheese marvel. By the third week, every package of McLaren's Imperial Cheese available in New York City had been sold.

Now this was news! Mrs. Carveth Wells could show all the travelogues she wanted, but this was something to make Madison Avenue sit up and take notice. Everyone had always suspected that television, with its combined visual and aural appeal, would probably be the "biggest ad medium yet," but until Kraft, nobody had proved it.

7. Vaudeville Is Back

IN SEPTEMBER 1926, RCA PLACED A FULL PAGE AD in the nation's major newspapers announcing the birth of NBC and the beginning of network radio broadcasting, saying, "The day has gone by when the radio receiving set is a plaything. It must now be an instrument of service … The purpose of [NBC] will be to provide the best program[ing] available for broadcasting in the United States."

Only two years later, NBC began operating an experimental television station. However, it was not until January 5, 1948, that the followup ad appeared, announcing network TV under the headline "1948–TELEVISION'S YEAR." The ad touted, "an exciting promise is now an actual service to the American home. After twenty years of preparation, the NBC television network is open for business."

NBC proudly spoke of the four TV stations already programming its network material, with stations in Boston and Baltimore to open soon. In 1947, it was pointed out, the number of TV sets operating in America had increased by more than 2,000 percent, from 8,000 to 170,000.

The ad further noted, "Nineteen forty-seven marked the end of television's interim period. Nineteen forty-eight marks TV's appearance as a major force."

In almost awe-struck tones the ad concluded with the declaration, "The greatest means of mass communications in the world is with us."

The excitement that followed Kraft's successful entry into TV in the summer of 1947 had continued into the fall as more and more sponsors invested money in television entertainment. Throughout the fall, the networks launched new television vehicles and the quality of their programming began to rise noticeably. In October, DuMont presented gossip columnist Jack Eigen in a nightclub setting, surrounded by glamour girls. For fifteen minutes, Eigen talked about the latest showbiz rumors and chatted with whatever celebrity he could corral. (Both Frank Sinatra and Fred Allen were on the show, but only via a telephone hookup.) In November, NBC brought Mutual radio's popular *Meet the Press* interview program to TV, after convincing a sponsor, General Mills, that the show was not too controversial for television. Fred Coe enlisted help for his NBC Sunday night drama presentations from two respected Broadway organizations, the Theater Guild and the American National Theater Academy (ANTA). In December, DuMont restaged "A Christmas Carol," using twelve sets and a cast of twenty-two.

Still, it was another sports remote that produced the most exciting television in the fall of 1947: baseball's annual World Series contest, the first to be televised. All eight TV stations on the East Coast coaxial cable broadcast the seven game "subway" series between the New York Yankees and the Brooklyn Dodgers, two bitter cross-town rivals. With Gillette and the Ford Motor Company as sponsors, CBS, NBC, and DuMont organized a "pool" coverage system in which the three networks each carried all of the games but took turns on the play-by-play and camera chores. Bob Stanton of NBC was the broadcast voice for games one and seven, Bill Slater took games two, five, and six for DuMont, and Bob Edge handled games three and four for CBS. Close-up cameras presented viewers at home and in bars with sharp, clear pictures of every phase of the game: the antics of baseline coaches giving complicated signals, the challenging stance by a batter waiting for a pitch, and the dejection on the face of a pitcher taken out of the game. Television, in effect, provided the best seats in the house and gave the dramatic championship match a greater sense of theater than ever before as the Yankees won the series, four games to three.

Viewer response to the World Series was even greater than the reaction to the Louis-Conn fight of the year before. The TV audience was estimated to be at least 3.8 million, and retailers reported a sharp increase in TV set sales during early October. Welcome as this news was, the World Series was merely another short-term special event. The TV networks were still searching for regular weekly hit series to solidify their position as the primary source of video programming. They were a bit anxious to find such material because the very concept of national live TV networks was under attack from the West Coast.

In June 1947, Jerry Fairbanks, a former producer of film shorts at the Paramount studios in Hollywood, announced that he was setting up a TV film unit. He promised to supply programs directly to individual stations (bypassing the networks), a process called "syndication," dispatching filmed episodes through the mail for airing at each station's pleasure. Not only did this represent a considerable saving when compared to the potential cost of using AT&T's coaxial cable, but, with coast-to-coast network TV hookups still years away, Fairbanks offered a ready supply of programs to new TV stations not yet connected to the cable. He filmed seventeen episodes of a crime drama series, *Public Prosecutor* (at the unconventional length of twenty minutes per episode), but the networks were able to pressure the local TV station managers into ignoring the service. The networks feared that if local stations began to obtain filmed shows directly from a syndicator, they might eventually decide not to use network programming at all. Stressing that television should be *live,* not filmed, the networks assured the locals that once the cable connections were made, stations would receive much better material if aligned with a national network. In the meantime, for those in the hinterlands, DuMont supplied the stopgap solution when it announced development of a method of preserving live TV shows by filming them directly from a television monitor. These kinescope recordings, popularly known as "kines," meant that while a local station waited for the arrival of live network TV in its area, it could still obtain network programs, albeit delayed a week or two. Though the kines were often grainy and hard to hear, they allowed the TV networks to beat Fairbanks at his own game. Finding no buyers, Fairbanks dropped the idea and, as a result, his *Public Prosecutor* series stayed on the shelf until the early 1950s.

The success of the networks in scuttling the Fairbanks film proposal had as much to do with the standoffish attitude of Hollywood to television, and vice versa, as their own influence on the locals. All the major film studios considered TV to be a prime competitor for the future, and they refused to allow any of their feature films, producers, directors, or stars to appear on television in any form. Consequently, they also gave Fairbanks no support in his scheme. Their strategy was to treat the upstart television with disdain and not give it any help or support, hoping that it would just fade away.

While Hollywood viewed television as a possible economic threat in the future, the movie industry had to concentrate on handling a more immediate crisis in the fall of 1947: the growing fear that Hollywood films might be used to spread Communist propaganda. Only two years after World War II had ended, the new "Cold War" between the United States and the Soviet Union dominated the nation's thinking. Many Americans truly felt that the country was in danger of being infiltrated by sinister forces. They looked with suspicion at the many pro-Soviet organizations in the United States, which had been formed during the Great Depression of the 1930s and the war camaraderie of the 1940s, and regarded them as a subversive fifth column that could not be counted on in the seemingly inevitable struggle with Communism.

Newsletters and magazines, such as *Counterattack* (founded in May 1947, by two former FBI agents), sprang up to publicize the names of Americans suspected of having ties to Communism. Congressional committees such as the House Un-American Activities Committee (HUAC) held public hearings designed to document "Red" collusion wherever it could be found. One of the first targets of HUAC was the film community of Hollywood, which possessed the most popular system for capturing the nation's attention in an effective, entertaining manner. The committee feared that Communists seeking to subvert the national will would logically try to take over various parts of the film industry as a quick way to reach the American public.

In October 1947, HUAC opened public hearings to prove that Communists had been writing, producing, and starring in "suspicious" Hollywood films for years. The hearings, which featured some of Hollywood's leading producers and stars, were broadcast live by many stations along the East Coast television coaxial cable. These were the first important congressional hearings ever to allow television coverage and they provided the first national television exposure for a young first term congressman from California, Richard M. Nixon, a HUAC member. At first, Hollywood's bigwigs treated the hearings as a joke, but they soon realized that, in

the national climate of fear and suspicion, the committee was looking for a scapegoat. Fearing that a lack of cooperation might lay the industry open to a governmental takeover, the movie moguls offered up for sacrifice the "ten unfriendlies," ten writers with alleged leftist and Communist connections who had refused to cooperate with HUAC. The writers' refusal to answer questions on their political backgrounds had infuriated the members of HUAC, who loudly observed that they "must be hiding something." The ten unfriendlies were suspended from their jobs and "blacklisted," that is, nobody in Hollywood would hire them any more because they had been linked to communism. Soon, blacklisting spread from these ten to others who worked in movies. In each case, the mere accusation of leftist ties was tantamount to being pronounced guilty, and the blacklisted artists were rarely given a chance to try and "clear" themselves. Writers, producers, directors, and actors suddenly found themselves out of work because of unsubstantiated charges made by unseen accusers. At first, television was mostly untouched by blacklisting because it was felt that TV in 1947 was not even worthy of infiltration.

As television continued to expand through the fall and winter, though, that situation was rapidly changing. Applications for stations, which had been crawling in at one or two per month the year before, averaged three a week by the end of 1947. Set sales were climbing and the January 1948 declaration by NBC that network television had arrived served as a signal that the time had come for serious efforts at regular weekly programming.

Less than two weeks after the NBC ad, DuMont revived the long-successful radio variety standard, *The Original Amateur Hour.* Major Edward Bowes had run the series on radio from the early 1930s until it ended in 1945, just before he died. Bowes had assumed a wholesome, fatherly, yet realistically critical role introducing new talent to the nation. The possibility of rags-to-riches stardom had made the show very successful on radio and DuMont had high hopes for the TV version. Ted Mack, who had worked under the tutelage of Bowes, took charge, adopting the same approach in welcoming the aspiring performers. Though DuMont took a chance and slotted the program earlier than practically anything else then on (Sunday night, 7:00-8:00 P.M.), it became a very popular video hit. But how popular?

Television was being run by people familiar with radio formats and strategies and, as they began to develop more expensive new video series, they felt the need for program ratings just as in radio. Less than one month after *The Original Amateur Hour* premiered, the Hooper organization, radio's most respected ratings service, conducted the first television rating sweep, in New York City. Ted Mack's show walked away with the number one slot, registering a 46.8% rating (that is, of the televisions in the homes contacted, 46.8 percent were on and tuned to *The Original Amateur Hour).* The J. Walter Thompson agency, an early believer in TV advertising, was the first ad agency to subscribe to Hooper's rating service.

In early 1948, NBC also found itself with a hit show, though it took a while longer to catch on. *Puppet Television Theater* had begun at Christmastime 1947 as a one-hour children's show running Saturday afternoons at 5:00 P.M. By April 1948, two weekday episodes were added and the series was renamed *Howdy Doody* after the main puppet character. The idea behind the show was simple: a few kids, a few puppets, a clown, and some music. What made it click was the personality and verve of the program's ringmaster, "Buffalo" Bob Smith, a former New York disc jockey who had previously been the host of a relaxed Arthur Godfrey-type morning radio show for adults. Smith seemed to enjoy the children present in the "peanut gallery" and his efforts to entertain them

	7:00	7:30	8:00	8:30	9:00	9:30	10:00	10:30	
MON									ABC
									CBS
	Samll Fry Club	Doorway To Fame	SHOWCASE	Swing Into Sports	Boxing From Jamaica Arena				DUM
		NBC News	local	Gillette Cavalcade Of Sports					NBC
TUE									ABC
									CBS
	Small Fry Club	PHOTOGRAPHIC HORIZONS	LOOK UPON A STAR	local	MARY KAY & JOHNNY	Boxing From Park Arena			DUM
									NBC
WED									ABC
					Sports From Madison Sqaure Garden				CBS
	Small Fry Club	local	CAFÉ DE PARIS	local	JACK EIGEN				DUM
		Kraft Television Theater		In The Kitchen	local	CURRENT OPINION			NBC
THR									ABC
			CBS News	TO THE QUEEN'S TASTE	Sports From Madison Sqaure Garden				CBS
	Small Fry Club	Birthday Party	local	CHARADE QUIZ	local	WRESTLING FROM JEROME STADIUM			DUM
		NBC News	MEET THE PRESS	MUSICAL MERRY-GO ROUND	You Are An Artist	EYE-WITNESS			NBC
FRI									ABC
									CBS
	Small Fry Club	THE GAY COED	local	Magic Carpet	local	Wrestling From Jamaica Arena			DUM
		Campus Hoopla	World In Your Home	Gillette Cavalcade Of Sports					NBC
SAT									ABC
			CBS News	THE SCRAPBOOK	Sports From Madison Sqaure Garden				CBS
									DUM
									NBC
SUN									ABC
	SCRAPBOOK, JUNIOR EDITION	local	Week In Review	Sports From Madison Sqaure Garden					CBS
									DUM
		Author Meets The Critics	THEATER GUILD TELEVISION THEATER A.N.T.A. PLAYHOUSE		REVIEW OF THE NEWS				NBC

came out in an ingratiating but not condescending form. He supplied the voices to most of the puppets (such as Howdy Doody, Phineas T. Bluster, and Captain Scuttlebutt), giving each an individual personality. The live characters such as Princess Summer-Fall-Winter-Spring and the mute clown Clarabell (played by Bob Keeshan, later renowned as Captain Kangaroo) shared his enthusiasm and helped to make the humans as warm and friendly as the puppets. By the fall of 1948, the program aired Monday through Friday.

Howdy Doody was one of television's first superstars. Small fry seized control of the family TV set in the late afternoon and demonstrated that they could become quite devoted to a television character. Mothers were not upset because, when the kids were occupied with *Howdy Doody,* they could relax. In the postwar "baby boom" era, television had a practical function. It was an excellent babysitter. As a result, the late afternoon and very early evening "after school" timeslots were recognized as prime "kidvid" hours perfect for programming geared toward children,

whose parents were still too busy with everyday household tasks to settle down and watch.

Television was becoming an item of interest to more and more households. Newspapers began accepting the medium as a fact of life and grudgingly agreed to print daily broadcast schedules for no charge, just as they did with radio. CBS, which had been airing only remote telecasts for almost a year, realized that NBC and DuMont had seized the initiative in television programming. Having attracted only a few sponsors for its outdoor broadcasts, the network conceded defeat in February 1948 by announcing that it would soon reopen and greatly enlarge its studios at Grand Central Station. ABC, which had abstained from TV production for a year while awaiting construction of its home base in New York, decided not to wait until the August completion date but geared up instead for a mid-April kick-off, using its affiliates on the East Coast.

All the networks realized that if their new program drive was to go anywhere, they would need live music. They at last came to terms with James C. Petrillo's American Federation of Musicians and the total ban on live television music ended. Within hours, CBS and NBC staged a nip-and-tuck race to be the first network to present live music on television. CBS won by ninety minutes. Eugene Ormandy and the Philadelphia Orchestra hit the air at five in the afternoon on March 20, while Arturo Toscanini and the NBC Orchestra weighed in at 6:30 P.M. These orchestral presentations, however, were not really representative of the future of live television music. Soon, pop-oriented musical programs appeared, modeled after the popular radio music shows, showcasing singers in either an all music format (usually a fifteen-minute slot) or more elaborate musical-variety shows (a half-hour or an hour long).

Though CBS was far behind NBC in developing studio entertainment programming and signing up new TV stations as affiliates, once it decided to reenter in-studio commercial television in earnest, the network quickly became the chief competitor to NBC, leapfrogging the competition. This was a reflection of CBS's radio strength. It was a very strong number two in radio behind NBC and the two were generally regarded as the powerhouses of broadcasting. As television stations decided to align themselves with a network, it made sense to go with one of the two biggest in radio.

CBS's only holdover from its all-remote concept was the network's first effort in theatrical drama, *Tonight on Broadway.* Producer Worthington Miner took TV cameras to New York theaters in order to present hit Broadway plays, beginning with "Mr. Roberts," starring Henry Fonda. Miner treated the series like any other remote event and positioned the cameras from the perspective of an audience member sitting in the theater so that the entire stage was visible at all times on the TV screen. While dead center, twenty rows from the front, might have been perfect for a patron at the theater, it was deadly for viewers at home who tried to follow the action on their eight-inch screens. (Opera glasses were not much help.) The tiny figures were lost in the open expanse of stage, but it was felt that this was the only way to correctly convey the feel of theater. The cameras were there to present the event

exactly as a member of the audience would see it. Home viewers were, in effect, sneaking in for free.

The resurrected ABC also dabbled in drama with its first new series in April, *Hollywood Screen Test.* Originating at first from Philadelphia, the program was a combination drama-anthology and talent show in which two performers who had Broadway experience, but who were not yet stars, appeared in a scene with a celebrity veteran. Just as in *The Original Amateur Hour,* there was the lure of seeing stars-in-the-making, but the overall quality of production was much higher. The show was set up as if it were an actual West Coast "screen test," which not only served as an innovative format but also covered up the lack of expensive scenery. The series lasted five years for ABC, with veteran Neil Hamilton acting as host for all but the first few months.

Through the spring of 1948, the networks' TV schedules expanded tremendously to include elementary versions of basic entertainment formats that were popular on radio. NBC presented *Barney Blake, Police Reporter,* starring Gene O'Donnell as a reporter-as-cop. On DuMont, real-life husband and wife Johnny and Mary Kay Sterns faced the humorous trials and tribulations of married life in the appropriately titled situation comedy, *Mary Kay and Johnny.* Kyle MacDonnell, one of the first singing stars to make a name on television, hosted a series of pleasant fifteen-minute musical vehicles for NBC: *For Your Pleasure, Kyle Mac-Donnell Sings,* and *Girl About Town.* All the networks had quizzes such as *Americana Quiz* and *Charade Quiz.* DuMont offered the imaginative *Court of Current Issues,* in which actors would argue a case in a courtroom setting and the studio audience acted as jury. This seemed the perfect setting for a television discussion show.

While television developed its selection of entertainment vehicles in an effort to duplicate some of the draw of network radio, a dramatic and symbolic change took place in radio programming. On March 21, the day after the Petrillo ban ended for television music, *Stop the Music* premiered on ABC Radio. It was a musical

Milton Berle, the first host of *Texaco Star Theater,* soon became known as Mr. Television. *(Smithsonian Institution; Allen B. DuMont Collection)*

October 27, 1947

You Bet Your Life. (ABC Radio). After several misfired flops, Groucho Marx, the great ad-libber, finds a successful radio format under producer John Guedel. The setup is simple: Groucho acts as host of a quiz show that devotes most of its time to his jokes.

November 13, 1947

Boston is connected to the East Coast network, though it does not yet have any television stations on the air.

November 18, 1947

Mary Kay and Johnny. (DuMont). Television's first weekly situation comedy.

February 9, 1948

The Frederick W. Ziv Company, radio's largest program syndicator, sets up a television film branch to help fill the many programming gaps on the local TV stations.

February 16, 1948

Camel Newsreel Theater. (NBC). Fox-Movietone produces NBC's first nightly television news show.

April 15, 1948

ABC resumes television broadcasting, using as its temporary headquarters WMAL in Washington and WFIL in Philadelphia.

April 28, 1948

CBS resumes in-studio television broadcasts as the Douglas Edwards news show becomes a Monday through Friday production. By fall, twenty-five-year-old Don Hewitt becomes the program's first regular producer.

May 3, 1948

The Supreme Court upholds the antitrust decision in the ten-year-old "Paramount Case." The eight major movie studios must begin to divest themselves of their theater chains.

---

quiz show conceived by Louis G. Cowan, directed by Mark Goodson, and slotted in one of the toughest time periods of the radio week: Sunday night against Edgar Bergen and Fred Allen. Surprisingly, within months, Fred Allen, a member of radio's top ten for a decade, had dropped to thirty-eighth place. By the end of the year, Edgar Bergen took his Sunday night show off the air for a season. *Stop the Music* had beaten them both.

Quiz and game shows had been a part of radio for years, but *Stop the Music* was different. It was a quiz that directly connected entertainment with the personal greed of listeners at home, offering prizes for merely tuning in. The contest was simple: Phone numbers from across the nation were selected at random. While host Bert Parks dialed a number, the show's musical regulars began performing a popular song. As soon as the home contestant picked up the phone, Parks would say "Stop the music!" and ask the listener to identify the song that had just stopped playing. If correct, the listener would win a prize and a chance to identify a much more difficult "mystery melody" worth as much as $30,000. Though the odds against being called were astronomical, enough listeners felt it was wise to tune in and be prepared. Just in case. Besides, the music was good, Parks was energetic as ever, and the show was entertaining in its own right.

In the fall of 1948, Allen offered insurance (up to $5,000) to any listeners who lost out on winning on *Stop the Music* because they were tuned to him. "In other words," Allen said, "my listeners can only lose thirty minutes." That was not quite true. With a top prize of up to $30,000 on *Stop the Music* they could lose up to $25,000. But in any case, the offer came too late. Large numbers of similar giveaway shows appeared, at the expense of both established comedians such as Allen and youngsters such as Danny Thomas and Jack Paar. By June 1949, Allen quit radio in disgust.

At the time radio was about to meet television in a head-to-head battle for advertising dollars, *Stop the Music* demonstrated that a game show could topple a highly paid star. This offered radio sponsors an attractive way to cut costs yet still have a top rated show. Even with all that fancy prize money, quiz show budgets were much less than the salaries of top radio stars who at the time made as much as $30,000 a week. A subtle shift in priorities began to take place. Though radio was still regarded as important to sponsors, the high-class high-budget formats had become expendable if necessary. Lower-budget quizzes could pull in high radio ratings while advertisers directed more of their money to television.

The giveaway quiz show fad did spill over into TV in mid-1948, but none of the programs became big hits. Video production budgets were still relatively small so the TV quiz programs looked cheap rather than magical and glamorous. The shows simply did not appear as visually exciting as the equivalent radio programs sounded. They remained just one more experimental format for television programmers in search of hit shows and prestige events.

The 1948 presidential race provided the networks with an excellent opportunity to boost television's stature. President Harry Truman, who had assumed office when Franklin Roosevelt died, was running for his first elected term and the Republicans felt certain they could beat him. As the race heated up through the spring and summer, the networks devoted as much air time as possible to the various campaigns. Most of the stories appeared on the fifteen-minute nightly newsreel shows that the networks had established over the previous year in an effort to upgrade the image of their news departments. DuMont had been first in the summer of 1947 with Walter Compton's *News from Washington*. NBC soon followed with *Camel Newsreel Theater,* a ten-minute collection of newsreels completely produced by Fox-Movietone (which even took responsibility for hiring the show's off-screen announcing trio of Ed Thorgensen, George Putnam, and Helen Claire). In April 1948, as part of its return to in-studio broadcasts, CBS brought Douglas Edwards back on camera and retitled the daily program *Douglas Edwards and the News.* ABC joined the others in the summer with *News and Views,* which used a rotating anchor crew, including TV's first anchorwoman, Pauline Frederick.

In addition to coverage on the newsreel shows, that summer CBS gave thirty-minutes of time to a different presidential candidate each week on *Presidential Timber.* Republican Harold Stassen was the first to appear. At the time, the radio networks banned the "dramatization of political issues," so most political forays into radio were generally dull discussions and speeches by either the candidate or a chosen representative. Television had no such ban, so Stassen hired an ad agency to produce a thirty-minute film to run in his segment of *Presidential Timber.* The film did not spend much time on "the issues" at all, but instead served as a warm pictorial biography meant to promote Stassen as a "nice guy" rather than just a speechmaker.

The planners of both party nominating conventions had noted the staggering growth of television set sales in 1947 and realized that a city connected to the Eastern coaxial cable network offered the opportunity for a tremendous publicity boost at convention

Paul White *(left)*, who helped create the CBS news organization in the early 1930s, and Douglas Edwards. *(CBS News/CBS Photo Archive © 2003 CBS Worldwide, Inc. All Rights Reserved.)*

time. Both parties chose Philadelphia and, by the time the first gavel fell, there were eighteen stations from Boston to Richmond sending out the proceedings to ten million viewers watching on 300,000 sets.

There was little to distinguish one network's convention coverage from another's because all four of them used the same pictures, provided by a common pool camera set up to focus on the main podium. There were no additional pickups from roving floor reporters, though NBC set up a small studio off the convention floor ("Room 22") in which Ben Grauer conducted on-the-spot, off-the-cuff interviews with political bigwigs. To anchor coverage of the proceedings, the networks rotated among their top reporters. CBS featured Ed Murrow, Quincy Howe, and Douglas Edwards, while NBC had H.V. Kaltenborn and Richard Harkness. ABC made extensive use of Walter Winchell, while DuMont, which had no formal news staff, hired Drew Pearson as its main commentator.

The Republican convention was generally uneventful and dull as Governor Thomas Dewey from New York easily beat Harold Stassen, but the Democrats staged a drawn-out free-for-all. Minnesota's Hubert H. Humphrey, a candidate for the U.S. Senate, led a floor fight over inclusion of a civil rights plank in the party platform and, in response, Southern Democrats walked out and formed their own splinter party, popularly known as the Dixiecrats, which chose Strom Thurmond as their candidate for president. The Democratic nominee, President Harry Truman, fell victim to the floor wrangling along the way and his acceptance speech was delayed until 2:00 A.M. By then most viewer-voters were asleep and consequently missed a truly electrifying presentation. Though Truman was a horrible reader of prewritten speeches, when he started

speaking ad-lib from the heart, his oratory was close to perfection. This was the style he used for his acceptance address and it resulted in one of the best speeches of his life.

It was also a very good television speech. By not reading from a script, Truman could look the camera (and the voter) in the eye, without the distracting pauses and downward glances of most speech readers. He came across on TV as a sincere natural man who was not so much the President of the United States as "one of the guys." Truman's speech vividly demonstrated the personal intimacy possible through television. Sharp politicians sensed that television might be even more important than first suspected, but they were not yet ready to incorporate the medium into a full-scale presidential campaign. That fall, Governor Dewey turned down an advertising agency's suggestion to concentrate on short "spot announcements" for television. Instead, he and President Truman both restricted their use of TV to a few live pickups of large political rallies. It was generally agreed that television played very little part in Truman's come-from-behind victory.

While politicians were just beginning to experiment with television, the era of testing had passed for entertainment programming. The networks and sponsors were ready for a dramatic breakthrough to tie it all together. Kraft's McLaren Cheese promotion demonstrated how effective television advertising could be. The top-rated Ted Mack show proved that viewers liked variety. The vaudeville styled *Hour Glass* had attracted a devoted following in 1946 without any live music, and now the Petrillo ban was lifted. The total number of TV sets in the country was doubling every four months. It was time to move!

On pages 26 and 27 of the May 19, 1948, issue of the entertainment trade weekly *Variety,* the William Morris talent agency placed a two-page ad with a large headline:

May 6, 1948
The FCC takes away channel one from television, giving the military use of the frequency instead.

July 5, 1948
My Favorite Husband. (CBS Radio). Lucille Ball plays a wacky wife whose zany escapades make life difficult for her banker husband and his short-tempered boss (played by Gale Gordon). Jess Oppenheimer produces this "in-house" CBS radio sitcom.

July 19, 1948
Our Miss Brooks. (CBS Radio). In another successful home-grown CBS radio sitcom, Eve Arden plays Connie Brooks, a level-headed, believable teacher at mythical Madison High School. She is backed by the omni-present Gale Gordon as the blustery principal, Osgood Conklin.

July 26, 1948
The Bob Howard Show. (CBS). Piano-playing Bob Howard becomes the first black to host a network television series, appearing in a fifteen-minute weekday evening musical show.

August 10, 1948
ABC at last gets its own home-base television station as WJZ (later WABC) goes on the air in New York.

August 11, 1948
News and Views. (ABC). Six different anchors handle ABC's first television news show.

VAUDEVILLE IS BACK

The Golden Age of variety begins with the premiere of *The Texaco Star Theater* on television, Tuesday, 8:00–9:00 P.M. E.D.T., starting June 8 on NBC and its affiliated stations in New York, Washington, Boston, Philadelphia, Baltimore, Richmond, and Schenectady.

WANTED – Variety artists from all corners of the globe. Send particulars to the William Morris Agency.

A radio version of *The Texaco Star Theater* had played since the fall of 1938, but that mixed variety and drama under a succession of celebrity hosts (including Ken Murray, Fred Allen, James Melton, Alan Young, and Gordon MacRae). The new television version was conceived as a throwback to the vaudeville houses (such as New York City's famed Palace Theater), which had thrived from the turn of the century until the advent of radio and talkies.

In vaudeville, a few acts would appear on stage, perform, and step off, beginning with the unknowns and working up to the headliners. An emcee would introduce the performers and attempt to give the show some continuity. NBC felt that a big budget television version of the vaudeville form might catch on, just as *Hour Glass* had done in its brief run. With imaginative production, a good selection of talent, and a strong host, *Texaco Star Theater* could be a big hit. Finding the right host was the most difficult part of the formula, so the network decided to spend the summer giving a few candidates trial runs. It quickly settled on Milton Berle to open the series. Berle was a successful nightclub comedian who had been a flop in numerous attempts to make it on network radio, but he had brought down the house on a heart fund auction program televised by DuMont on April 7. It seemed that the added visual nature of television was just the extra plus Berle needed and, on June 8, he stepped out for the first *Texaco Star Theater*. It was as if television had been reinvented.

Reviewers were ecstatic: "Television's first real smash!" "Let the hucksters make way for the show folk!" As emcee, Berle delivered a cleaned-up version of his nightclub routine, with visual mannerisms impossible to convey over radio, then introduced a succession of acts (including Pearl Bailey). Yet that was just the beginning. Berle also had an amazing sense of timing and pacing. When he saw the show was lagging, he would dash on stage and ham it up, holding the program together with the force of his personality. Unlike old-time vaudeville and every other variety show previously on television, Berle's *Texaco Star Theater* opened fast, stayed fast and tight, and finished fast. Even the one commercial—known as the middle ad—was integrated into the act as a funny plug by pitchman Sid Stone, whose "tell ya' what I'm gonna do" come-on soon became a national catch phrase.

Instead of staging the show for the studio audience, the producers were more interested in giving the viewers at home a sharp, clear picture. Cameras were placed on stage instead of presenting the view seen by the audience sitting in the theater. The resulting closeups produced an immediacy and intimacy unmatched by radio and theater. This marriage of vaudeville and video techniques produced a new form, vaudeo. There had never been anything else like it on television.

NBC had hoped for success, but had not expected a hit of such proportions. After Berle's three appearances in June and July, a rotating group of emcees took over (including Henny Youngman, Morey Amsterdam, and George Price), but none could generate anything near the excitement of Berle. The format and his personality had meshed perfectly. After frantic importuning by NBC, Berle signed to become permanent host of *Texaco Star Theater* beginning in September.

Twelve days after Berle's June premiere, CBS unveiled its own television vaudeville show, *Toast of the Town,* with Ed Sullivan as host. Sullivan had been a Broadway newspaper columnist for almost twenty years and his Broadway contacts made him the perfect choice to head a variety show drawing on new talent. CBS producer Worthington Miner first spotted the somewhat dour, low-key Sullivan as a potential for television, and chose him to emcee the 1947 Harvest Moon Ball, staged and televised in Madison Square Garden by CBS and the *New York Daily News.* He used him again in a 1948 Easter Sunday variety benefit, and *Toast of the Town* soon followed.

Coming so soon after Berle's spectacular, Sullivan's June 20 debut suffered in comparison. He was judged by the same standards even though Berle had been chosen for his abilities as a performer and Sullivan for his skills as an off-stage producer who could unearth new talent. *Toast of the Town* itself was much closer to a traditional vaudeville set up than *Texaco Star Theater*, as Sullivan merely introduced a succession of acts and stepped aside. At first, even the cameras were placed back out with the audience in the theater rather than moving them right up front to benefit the home viewers.

Jack Gould of the *New York Times* called the selection of Sullivan as emcee "ill advised," saying: "his extreme matter-of-factness and his tendency to introduce friends in the audience add up to little sparkling entertainment."

In a medium centered on performing talent and warm intimacy, Sullivan was the permanent exception to prove the rule. He had neither, but his knack for finding talent on the verge of making it big was uncanny. Two of the seven performers on the opening show were the then unknown "zany comic" team of Dean Martin and Jerry Lewis (paid $200 for their appearance). Nonetheless, jokes about Sullivan's stage mannerisms never ceased, even after the show became a big success. Budding impressionists cut their teeth on mimicking his scrunched stance and his frequently repeated phrases such as "And now, right here on our stage" and "really big shew." For years, husbands would turn to their wives in the glowing dark and opine, "He's got no talent. He'll never last." It was Sullivan who had the last laugh as his program ran for twenty-three years. Fred Allen explained the incongruity: "Ed Sullivan will stay on television as long as other people have talent."

8.   The Freeze

THE EXPANSION OF TELEVISION during the first nine months of 1948 was nothing short of miraculous. Set manufacturers could hardly keep up with the demand for new product. The FCC could hardly keep up with the paperwork of applications for new stations. All four television networks planned major program premieres in the fall, treating the new TV season with the same respect as a new radio season. To the television industry, the era of "the greatest means of mass communications in the world"—also known as "the biggest ad medium yet"—had arrived at last. There seemed to be no limit to the coming boom. At the end of September, though, a long festering technical problem cast a chill over this euphoria.

In the 1930s, when the FCC had first set technical standards for television broadcasting, it frankly had no idea how far apart stations assigned to the same channel should be. If they were too close to each other, signals would clash and many home viewers would receive a jumble of images. In 1945, the commission set 150 miles as the minimum distance between stations on the same channel but, during 1948, when the number of TV stations on the air almost tripled, there were more and more reports of cross-station interference. The FCC felt impelled to do something quickly because unlike the question of color, which could be postponed indefinitely, signal interference was an obvious, irritating, and immediate problem which would only get worse as more stations signed on. Yet the FCC really needed time to study the situation and to work out new standards, so on September 30, 1948, the commission put a freeze on processing applications for new television stations.

When the freeze was announced, there were thirty-seven stations on the air in twenty-two cities, with eighty-six other stations already approved and in the process of preparing to sign on. These new stations would be allowed to go on the air, but the 303 station applications sent in but not yet acted on were filed away until the FCC could work out the frequency problem. The commission said that the freeze would be in effect for only a short time (approximately six months), so the networks took no immediate notice of it. At worst, they felt, there would be a slight pause in the rapid rise of television. Instead, the freeze extended three-and-one-half years and placed television in a peculiar state of suspended animation, just on the verge of expanding into a national mass medium. From 1948 to 1952, advertisers and programmers were given the opportunity to refine their formats and techniques while serving a large, but limited, audience. While part of the nation continued to wait breathlessly for the long-postponed arrival of television, people in the rest of the country became caught up in the new focus of popular entertainment.

The most exciting event of the new season was the return of Milton Berle, the uncrowned king of television, to the *Texaco Star Theater*. Milton was back and NBC had him. What's more, he was still "boffo!" The magic chemistry that had powered Berle's few summer appearances continued to charge his fall shows. When the first ratings came in, Berle and *Texaco* were so far out in front that the number one slot was virtually conceded to them, and the other networks lowered their sights and aimed for number two. By November, *Texaco Star Theater* had an 86.7% rating (meaning that of all sets, including those not turned on, 86.7 percent were tuned to Berle on Tuesday) and a 94.7% share (meaning that of all sets then being used, 94.7 percent were tuned to Berle). Milton Berle had a hammerlock on the Tuesday-at-8:00 P.M. time slot that he would keep for almost eight years.

It soon became clear that any program slotted against Berle's show was going to lose big, and sponsors knew it. So the other networks began to fill early Tuesday evening with extremely weak programming (usually unsponsored) that had little hope of attracting a large audience anyway. One of the first to do so was DuMont, which moved out its promising *Court of Current Issues* and moved in *Operation: Success,* a program of self-help tips for disabled veterans.

Milton Berle's program seemed irresistible with its fast-paced tempo aimed directly at the home audience. Gradually, the program evolved from basically a vaudeville format into an even stronger vehicle for Berle's dominating personality: a "sketch" show. This formalized Berle's habit of butting into routines by adding as a regular feature scenes with Berle and his guests performing together. This provided better continuity as well as the assurance that Berle would appear throughout the show as often as possible. Although sometimes he seemed to be staging a one man production, Berle also introduced some very talented performers as *Texaco Star Theater* became one of the prime television showcases for new talent. Sid Caesar, a rising young comic, appeared on one of the early shows to recreate an airplane skit he had performed in the feature film "Tars and Spars." In March, band leader Desi Arnaz soloed with his hot bongo drumming.

Number two in the ratings behind Berle was Ed Sullivan's *Toast of the Town,* which also served as a television springboard for new talent. In February, Jackie Gleason, who was then starring

Day	Net	7:00	7:30	8:00	8:30	9:00	9:30	10:00	10:30
MON	ABC	News And Views · local	Kiernan's Corner	ON TRIAL	^ VAUDEO VARIETIES		^ SKIP FARRELL SHOW	local	
	CBS	local · Places, Please	CBS News · Face The Music	local		Sports From Madison Sqaure Garden			
	DUM	Doorway To Fame	Camera Headlines · local	Champaign & Orchids · local	Swing Into Sports	local	Court Of Current Issues		local
	NBC	^ KUKLA, FRAN AND OLLIE	American Song · Camel Newsreel	CHEVROLET ON BROADWAY	Americana Quiz	Gillette Cavalcade Of Sports			
TUE	ABC	News And Views · local	CHILD'S WORLD	local	AMERICA'S TOWN MEETING		^ TOMORROW'S CHAMPIONS (to 12 Midnight)		
	CBS	ROAR OF THE RAILS · local	CBS News · Face The Music	local		We, The People	Straws in the Wind / People's Platform	local	
	DUM	OFF THE RECORD	Camera Hedlines · INS Telenews	OPERATION: SUCCESS	local	Boxing From Park Arena			
	NBC	^ KUKLA, FRAN AND OLLIE	MUSICAL MINIATUR. · Camel Newsreel	Texaco Star Theater		MARY MARGARET McBRIDE SHOW		Gillette Cavalcade Of Sports	
WED	ABC	News And Views · local	BUZZY WUZZY · local	Club Seven	Quizzing The News	Wrestling From Washington			
	CBS	local · Places, Please	CBS News · Face The Music	KOBB'S KORNER	Winner Take All	local	TOURAMENT OF CHAMPIONS		
	DUM	Birthday Party	Camera Headlines · local	Photographic Horizons	THE GROWING PAYNES	Boxing From Jamaica Arena			
	NBC	^KUKLA, FRAN OLL. · Story Of The Week	You Are An Artist · Camel Newsreel	Girl About Town · PICTURE THIS	PHIL SILVERS ARROW SHOW	Kraft Television Theater		NBC News · The Village Barn	
THR	ABC	News And Views	local	FASHION STORY	Critic-At-Large	ABC FEATURE FILM		local	
	CBS	local	CBS News · Face The Music	To The Queen's Taste	Sports From Madison Square Garden				
	DUM	ADVENTURES OF OKY-DOKY	Camera Headlines · Jack Eigen	local	Charade Quiz	Wrestling From Park Arena			
	NBC	^ KUKLA, FRAN OLL. · Paris Fashions	MUSICAL MINIATUR. · Camel Newsreel	PRINCESS SAGAPHI · Nature Of Things	Lanny Ross Swift Show	BOB SMITH'S GULF ROAD SHOW	DUNNINGER & WINCHELL BIGELOW SHOW	local	
FRI	ABC	News And Views · local	RED CABOOSE · local	Candid Michrophone	Gay 90s Revue	BREAK THE BANK	^ MUSIC IN VELVET	local	
	CBS	YOUR SP. SPECIAL · Places, Please	CBS News · Face The Music	What's It Worth	Capt. Billy's Music Hall	local			
	DUM	Key To The Missing	Camera Headlines · local	Television Fashions On Parade	local	Wrestling From Jamaica Arena			
	NBC	^ KUKLA, FRAN AND OLLIE	Musical M.-G.-Round · Camel Newsreel	NBC Presents	Stop Me If You've Heard This One	I'D LIKE TO SEE	Gillette Cavalcade Of Sports		GREATEST FIGHTS
SAT	ABC	News And Views · local	Joe Hasel Sports · Three Abo. Town	local		^ STAND BY FOR CRIME	^ SUPER CIRCUS	local	
	CBS	local				Sports From Madison Square Garden			
	DUM	local							
	NBC	local		THE EYES HAVE IT	Television Screen Magazine	SEMI-PRO BASKETBALL FROM JAMAICA ARENA			
SUN	ABC	local	THE SOUTHERNAIRES	Hollywood Screen Test	ACTOR'S STUDIO	^ ABC TELEVISION PLAYERS	local		
	CBS	Week In Review · local	STUDIO ONE / FORD TELEVISION THEATER HOUR		DENNIS JAMES CARNIVAL	Toast Of The Town		AMERICA SPEAKS	local
	DUM	Original Amateur Hour		local					
	NBC	Mary Kay & Johnny · Review Of The News	WELCOME ABOARD	Author Meets The Critics	Meet The Press	PHILCO TELEVISION PLAYHOUSE		local	

on Broadway in "Along Fifth Avenue," delivered a comedy monologue about a man in love with a jukebox. Later that month, young nightclub comic Larry Storch offered some hilarious impersonations and, in June, Sam Levenson, a former schoolteacher, presented his view of life in New York City in a monologue that drew strong critical praise. Sullivan also arranged for the first television appearances by established stars such as Faye Emerson, Rosemary Clooney, Vaughn Monroe, Peter Lind Hayes, Skitch Henderson, Bil and Cora Baird's puppets, Frankie Laine, and Frank Fontaine. Unlike Berle, Sullivan continued to present his guests in a pure vaudeville format, always stepping aside once the introductions were finished. He also included a greater variation in types of guests than Berle, placing concert singers, circus animal acts, acrobats, and ballet troupes alongside more traditional comedy and popular music performers. Sullivan boasted that he put on a show with something for everybody in the family.

Even though Berle and Sullivan had only been on the air since June, their shows had become the standards other television series tried to copy. The makeup of the program schedule for the fall of 1948 made it quite clear that television had adopted yet another radio trait: mass imitation. Nervous radio sponsors, desiring the largest possible audience for their programs, tended to choose carbon copies of already successful formats rather than risk audience rejection with an untested concept. The same was holding true for television. Berle and Sullivan had vividly demonstrated the popularity of vaudeo shows, so the airwaves were filled with similar programs trying to cash in on this proven path to video success. Combined with the expected deluge of new musical-variety shows launched after the Petrillo ban was lifted, these gave viewers their first overdose of a hit formula.

Russ Morgan hosted *Welcome Aboard,* which was ostensibly set aboard a ship, and featured numerous guest appearances by Sullivan's first finds, Dean Martin and Jerry Lewis. Frank Fontaine and later Jan Murray hosted *Front Row Center,* while Morey Amsterdam's show brought forward the talents of second banana Art Carney. NBC slotted Phil Silvers to host *The Arrow Show* but, because he was also starring in "High Button Shoes" on Broadway at the time, Silvers had to rush from the studio immediately after his live TV program in order to appear live on stage. After a few months of this madness, Silvers gave up *The Arrow Show*. NBC placed Perry Como's casual fifteen-minute *Supper Club* after the fights on Friday, marking the first attempt at late night network programming.

Band leader Fred Waring conducted the classiest musical-variety show of the season, and the most expensive at the time ($20,000 each week). Waring rarely used guests, relying instead on his sixty-five-member family of dancers, singers, and musicians. In contrast, some of the season's weaker vehicles included ABC's *American Minstrels of 1949*, which placed twenty-six-year-old Jack Carter and the blackface duo of Pick and Pat into a cumbersome mix of the vaudeville era and the minstrel age; *Paul Whiteman's TV Teen Club,* which presented only mildly uptempo big band dance music; Bob Smith's attempt at a weekly half-hour of song and chat, similar to his pre-*Howdy Doody* Godfrey-esque radio show; and the unwieldy team of ventriloquist Paul Winchell and Dunninger, the mind-reading mentalist.

The prime exponent of pure and simple variety was "the old redhead," Arthur Godfrey, who quickly became as much of a workaholic on television as he was on radio. Godfrey's first television series was a simulcast of his Monday night radio hit, *Talent Scouts,* in which he played the genial Ted Mack role. A month later he added *Arthur Godfrey and His Friends,* a Wednesday night television version of his popular morning radio show in which he headed a close knit "family" of musical performers. Like Godfrey, the show was extremely low-key. Guests came on, engaged in chit-chat, and sang a song or two. One of the program's regulars performed a number. Godfrey recommended some products he truly believed in, played his ukulele, told a few slightly ribald jokes, and said goodnight. His warm, sincere personality carried over to television perfectly as he transformed such potentially boring routines into entertaining visits with an old friend. Both shows immediately became top ten hits and remained so for years.

One vaudeville format that failed miserably in the transition to television was the hellzapoppin' humor of Ole Olsen and Chic Johnson, the hosts of *Fireball Fun-For-All*, Milton Berle's summer replacement. For three decades, Olsen and Johnson had specialized in cornball punchlines and comic anarchy, including exploding scenery, stooges in gorilla suits, pop-up midgets, seltzer bottles, and gobs of custard pie. Their very busy productions worked well with a live audience in a large theater, but they were stopped cold by television. Even though the writers worked out detailed scripts and camera shots in advance, the very nature of their act (which Olsen and Johnson brought unaltered to television) made it impossible for the camera crews to follow close up, so the action was generally shown in long shots. As a result, the complicated bits were completely lost to the home audience watching on eight-inch screens. Without the impact of the visuals, Olsen and Johnson's cornball humor bombed.

In the summer of 1949, one year after Berle and Sullivan had first appeared, DuMont launched its big effort in vaudeo, *Cavalcade of Stars,* with Jack Carter as host. By then, there had been so many others like it already that *Cavalcade of Stars* was almost lost in the crowd. The only unique feature of the program was its unorthodox time slot: Saturday night at 9:00 P.M. The other networks did not place any of their stronger programs on Saturday because it was assumed that on "date night" the home audience would put television aside (as it had done with radio) and go out. Instead, more people stayed at home with the TV set than the networks had expected, so *Cavalcade of Stars* built a moderate (but not overwhelming) following and served as a training ground not only for

Carter, but also for his successors as the show's host: Jerry Lester, Jackie Gleason, and Larry Storch. Each, like Carter, went on to success with other networks after a stint with the program.

The less-than-spectacular performance by *Cavalcade of Stars* even against weak competition was a grim disappointment to DuMont, which badly needed a smash hit show. Though all the networks had ignored the FCC-imposed freeze at first, after the flurry of fall premieres it became apparent that, as a result of the freeze on new stations, the competition for affiliates would be tighter than ever before. During the freeze, there were many cities with only one television station, and, consequently, these stations found themselves besought by all four networks to air programs. Broadcasters in one-station markets regularly took programs from all the networks, depending on which shows were doing the best. DuMont and ABC were especially hurt by this situation because NBC and CBS, the leaders in network radio, had the biggest names and already occupied the top of the TV ratings. By the middle of 1949, the two major networks dominated the airtime on most stations, at the expense of the two smaller networks. *Cavalcade of Stars* demonstrated how difficult it was to break this cycle, even with a reasonably good show. ABC and DuMont needed smash hits just to catch the attention of local programmers and have them consider airing their material. This became a circular "Catch-22" situation because if local stations regularly chose the most popular programs, how could any new show build an audience and become a hit? Soon, however, DuMont realized that the tight market limitations of the freeze had also provided it with one important weapon it could use to fight back: the city of Pittsburgh.

Before the freeze took effect, DuMont had won FCC approval for its third O&O station, WDTV (later KDKA-TV), the first television station in Pittsburgh. During the freeze years, this gave the network the only television outlet in one of the nation's largest markets, so sponsors that wanted to be seen in Pittsburgh had to "play ball" with DuMont. This monopoly over the Pittsburgh airwaves soon became one of the network's most important assets and it won sponsors for a number of DuMont shows that would have been otherwise ignored. One of the most peculiar program deals took place in early 1949 when Admiral agreed to run its *Admiral Broadway Revue* on DuMont as well as NBC (which had more affiliates than any other TV network) in order to get into Pittsburgh. The simultaneous placement allowed DuMont to tout the program to local stations as a DuMont show and to try to interest them in its other network offerings. This short cut to credibility failed because broadcasters considered *The Admiral Broadway Revue* an NBC program anyway, so it never became the "DuMont hit" the network so desperately needed.

NBC had its own problems with *The Admiral Broadway Revue,* chief among them the fact that its Broadway-based producer, Max Liebman, concentrated on the theatrical nature of the presentation itself and did not take the vital next step of directing the stage action toward the audience at home. He brought together a talented group of young performers—comics Sid Caesar, Imogene Coca, and Mary McCarthy as well as dancers Marge and Gower Champion—and each week staged a very funny Broadway-style revue that worked well in the theater but came across as choppy and distant on the TV screen. Instead of demanding intimate camera placement, Liebman was content to let the crews shoot the stage from a distance out in the audience. *The Admiral Broadway Revue* ended after a thirteen-week run when Admiral pulled out as sponsor, though Liebman learned from his mistakes and had considerably more success the following season when he returned with a restructured version of the program, retitled *Your Show of Shows.*

When the FCC approved DuMont's request for a TV station in

Washingtonians watched the 1949 World Series on a set displayed in a store window. *(National Archives)*

Pittsburgh, the commission reiterated its belief that DuMont was controlled by its major stockholder, Paramount Pictures, and said that it would not grant any more TV licenses to either Paramount or DuMont. The FCC had set an ownership limit of five TV stations for any one group and because it classified Paramount and DuMont as one organization, it counted the two Paramount stations (WBKB in Chicago and KTLA in Los Angeles) and three DuMont stations (WABD in New York, WTTG in Washington, and WDTV in Pittsburgh) as reaching that limit. Both companies refused to accept the FCC's decision as final and planned to continue the fight once the freeze was lifted. Paramount wished to establish TV stations in Boston, Detroit, and Dallas, while DuMont intended to push for O&Os in Cincinnati and Cleveland. With the battle over network TV affiliates already so intense, DuMont felt that it needed five O&Os as a solid base for expanding its network. Paramount also felt that it badly needed the income from some extra television stations because the end of a decade-long legal case had jeopardized the financial structure of the big Hollywood studios.

In 1938, the Department of Justice had filed an anti-trust suit against eight major film studios (including Paramount), claiming that they were monopolizing the movie business by controlling both the production and projection of films. The "big eight" not only created most of the movies in Hollywood, but also owned and ran large national chains of movie theaters, which routinely obtained exclusive screening rights to the latest films. By 1948, the Supreme Court ended the marathon suit (popularly called the "Paramount Case") by siding with the government and ordering the eight studios to end their production-exhibition arrangement. Along with the others, Paramount had to divest itself of its chain of theaters, a major source of the company's revenue.

In 1949, Paramount Pictures, Inc., split in two. The Paramount Pictures Corporation was set up to continue making movies. It also kept control of KTLA and about 30% of DuMont. A separate company, United Paramount Theaters, was created to manage the movie theaters and run WBKB. The Justice Department was satisfied that Paramount had complied with the Supreme Court's ruling, but the FCC was not so sure. Preoccupied with the freeze, the commission refused to say whether it accepted the Paramount/United Paramount split as total. Until it did decide, it would continue to assume that DuMont and the two Paramounts were one organization that owned five TV stations and was not entitled to any more.

The FCC's slow pace in sorting out technicalities placed broadcasters in a squeeze between their day-to-day business reality and the commission's decision process. Without the expansion of television into new markets, the smaller networks found themselves consistently lagging behind as NBC and CBS solidified their hold in TV. Potential station applicants and investors across the country were forced to scuttle their television plans because they had no idea when the freeze would end. Yet during the freeze period, important growth did take place within the areas already served by television. Set sales continued to climb and the size of the home audience expanded. Both advertising and production budgets increased. Producers worked out some of the rough spots in such formats as variety and drama. The networks tried out programs in other time periods such as the morning and early afternoon. Through all this, work on the cross-country coaxial cable continued, bringing the industry closer to live, nationwide TV.

In September 1948, a Midwest coaxial cable network began operations, connecting Chicago, St. Louis, Detroit, Milwaukee, Toledo, Buffalo, and Cleveland. On January 11, 1949, the Philadelphia-Pittsburgh-Cleveland link connected the Midwest cable with the East Coast network (Boston to Richmond) so that, for the first time, one quarter of the nation's population was within reach of live network programming. One of the first shows on the East-

Midwest hookup was the inauguration of President Truman. Ninety-one-year-old Luther Parsons, who had seen the March 4, 1889, inauguration of Benjamin Harrison, watched the Truman ceremony on television and declared that seeing it from his home in Philadelphia was "the much more comfortable way."

One month after the inauguration broadcast, NBC took over control of its nightly news show, bringing in a live on-camera announcer, John Cameron Swayze, a comparatively fancy set, and a new title, *Camel News Caravan*. The new program soon passed Douglas Edwards and became the number one network news show, remaining so for seven years. At heart, though, both Edwards and Swayze were doing essentially the same thing and neither program could match the depth of network radio news coverage. Television still relied on the newsreel organizations for films of news events that were more visual than newsworthy. There was very little on-the-spot reporting. Important but more complex stories were usually left for sketchy summaries by the news anchors. In his reports, Swayze would chirp, "Let's hop-scotch the world for headlines!" and then read a few bulletins taken from the wire services.

While news was still regarded as the domain of radio, much was expected of live television drama. New York based critics—surrounded by theater—viewed drama as one of the best forms television could present. Yet in 1948 and 1949, television drama was still far from their expectations. Original stories were rare and producers still needed to develop their production techniques. The biggest problem, however, was the sheer bulk of material required. Each week there were eight or nine programs, with no reruns.

Television writers turned to previously written plays, books, and short stories for scripts, but even these required a great deal of work. Everything had to be adjusted to television's limitations and cut down to fit a sixty- or thirty-minute format. In addition, the Hollywood studios applied as much pressure as possible to try and keep television away from hot Broadway property that was under consideration for film. Hollywood lawyers even argued that the studios' exclusive rights to film adaptations of some shows meant that the television kinescope recordings could not be allowed because they were really *films* of the productions. Just to be safe, TV producers usually concentrated on material that the Hollywood studios either had no legal claim to or did not care about.

CBS had assigned its top producer, Worthington Miner, the task of developing a major dramatic program for the fall of 1948 and he responded with a TV version of *Studio One*. The program consisted of the usual book and theater adaptations, but Miner's production skills transformed the material into high quality television drama. He adapted most of the first season's stories himself and used both theater veterans and fresh talent (including young Charlton Heston) in the casts. In his adaptation of William Shakespeare's "Julius Caesar," Miner demonstrated just how effective television drama could be. Using *Studio One*'s tight budget to his advantage, Miner staged the story in modern dress, an approach successfully used on stage by Orson Welles and the Mercury Theater Company in 1937. As a result, the television production had an immediate, eye-catching punch that made the story instantly accessible. The Roman legions, dressed in pseudo-Nazi attire, clearly suggested the recent battle against fascism in World War II and brought the themes of totalitarian oppression and political conspiracy from ancient Rome to contemporary society. In one very effective sequence, Miner moved the camera into a tight closeup on the eyes of one of the Roman conspirators and played the actor's prerecorded voice to reveal his inner thoughts. Viewers experienced the unnerving but exciting sensation that they had jumped inside the man's mind as he thought about the assassination of Caesar. That was something even Broadway could not do!

Viewers who had considered Shakespeare too highbrow and inscrutable found the program comprehensible and exciting. Critics praised the production as an example of the high quality television drama they had been hoping for.

At NBC, the Philco corporation signed on in the fall of 1948 as the first sponsor for the network's three-year-old Sunday night drama showcase, which became *The Philco Television Playhouse*. Producer Fred Coe's first efforts for Philco were adaptations of Broadway productions and classic plays. In the second season he shifted to adapting books and presented the program as a novel-a-week. Gradually, as Coe turned more and more to original scripts rather than adaptations, the program improved and eventually became known as the most innovative drama series on television.

The obvious solution to the adaptation problem was original material. In 1948, however, TV writers felt it was tough enough just turning out the adaptations on a weekly basis. Soon, out of

---

September 19, 1948
Stained Glass Windows. (ABC). Catholic, Protestant, and Jewish faiths alternate in this Sunday afternoon religious show. It is joined two months later by *Lamp Unto My Feet* on CBS, as the networks quickly settle on obscure weekend slots as the place for less profitable "cultural" fare. Soon Sunday afternoons become known as "egghead" time.

September 20, 1948
The Midwestern television coaxial cable network begins operation connecting Chicago, St. Louis, Detroit, Milwaukee, Toledo, Buffalo, and Cleveland.

October 3, 1948
The National Football League becomes the first professional sports organization to allow regular weekly network television coverage. As with radio, the Sunday afternoon NFL contests are on ABC, because both NBC and CBS do not consider professional football worth covering. On this first Sunday telecast, Joe Hasel does the play-by-play as the Washington Redskins defeat the New York Giants, 41 to 10.

October 22, 1948
Break the Bank (ABC). Radio's big money quiz show fad is transplanted to television by ABC, the network that started the trend on radio. Bert Parks is emcee of what becomes ABC's first top ten television show.

November 22, 1948
Columbia Records releases the first *I Can Hear It Now* album, an audio montage of news events between 1933 and 1945. CBS's Ed Murrow narrates and NBC Radio's Fred Friendly produces.

December 17, 1948
The Morey Amsterdam Show. (CBS). Amsterdam brings his comedy-variety format to television from CBS Radio, playing the smart-mouthed emcee of the "Golden Goose" nightclub. He is aided and abetted by his bumbling doorman (played by Art Carney) and a dumb cigarette girl (played by Jacqueline Susann).

December 24, 1948
Supper Club. (NBC). Perry Como pioneers late night television as host to a fifteen-minute music show aired Friday nights at 11:00 P.M.

practical necessity, the thirty-minute anthology programs were forced to come up with original scripts. Adaptations used on the thirty-minute anthologies such as *Chevrolet on Broadway, Colgate Theater,* and *Actor's Studio* required extensive, time-consuming editing anyway and usually the finished product barely resembled the original work. The producers realized it could be cheaper and faster to use original scripts. Most of these vanguard efforts were horrible, but it really did not matter. Critics, who could barely keep up with all the television drama, had quickly dismissed the thirty-minute form and devoted most of their attention to the sixty-minute anthologies. There were fewer hour shows, they had bigger budgets, and they seemed more worthwhile and important. Though the thirty-minute showcases sometimes featured high quality productions, they remained practically unnoticed by critics and instead served as unheralded television training for aspiring writers such as young Paddy Chayefsky.

The thirty-minute dramas were also in the vanguard of the use of film. A few anthology series such as *Your Show Time* and *Fireside Theater* either began as all-film operations or turned to film after a brief live stint. The networks were still a bit leery about putting filmed shows on the air, and the hour dramas were restricted to just a few film clips for transitions and for some outdoor action shots that could not be staged in the studio. Producers learned that combining live action and film always held a danger of an embarrassing technical flub. For example, one script called for a quick cut from an actor jumping through a studio prop window live to a film of a figure falling to the ground. Instead, the film clip came in two seconds too late and viewers saw the actor hit the safety of the studio floor and scamper away.

The networks generally favored live action over cheap-looking film formats because, from a practical viewpoint, live television emphasized the networks as a source of original programming. The programs themselves seemed more intimate and immediate, pre-senting the home viewers the opportunity to follow the action as it happened. For instance, in the Chicago-based *Stand By for Crime* on ABC, a fictional police homicide chief would narrate a story in flashback, list the suspects, and then ask home viewers to call in with their guesses as to who was guilty.

In spite of television's progress, with the freeze in effect network radio remained the only means for advertisers to reach consumers throughout the country at once, and it was still the main entertainment force in television cities as well. The major comedy and variety performers shied away from any serious commitments to television, and radio was still regarded as the main stage for the continuing battle for network primacy between NBC and CBS.

Since World War II, CBS Radio had been engaged in a concerted drive to break from its perennial number two status. The network chipped away at NBC's radio lead with a string of lightweight situation comedies such as *My Friend Irma* (with Marie Wilson as the archetypical dumb blonde) and *My Favorite Husband* (with Lucille Ball as the archetypical scatterbrained housewife), but NBC still had the top comics. With its virtual monopoly on popular big name humor, NBC seemed well insulated from even the most imaginative CBS program strategy. Determined to move his network into the top spot, CBS chairman William Paley came up with an ingenious ploy to lure NBC's comedy talent to CBS.

In September 1948, Paley convinced *Amos 'n Andy*'s creators Freeman Gosden and Charles Correll that by selling CBS the rights to the characters of Amos and Andy (for $2 million), they could substantially reduce their taxes. By treating the program as a business package, which they happened to perform in, Gosden and Correll declared much of the income from the show's sale as a capital gain on an investment, and their tax rate dropped from 77% to 25%. NBC doubted the legality of Paley's maneuver and failed to make equivalent offers to its other stars. Soon Jack Benny, Ed-

The popular ethnic humor of *The Goldbergs* came to television with *(from left)* Eli Mintz as Uncle David, Gertrude Berg as Molly Goldberg, and Philip Loeb as her husband Jake. *(CBS Photo Archive © 2003 CBS Worldwide, Inc. All Rights Reserved.)*

gar Bergen, Groucho Marx, Bums and Allen, and Red Skelton rode "Paley's Comet" to the opposition.

It was the biggest programming coup in radio history. CBS had captured the core of NBC's big name star roster and seemed ready to take over as number one after two decades of effort. CBS radio was the immediate beneficiary of the shift but, as Paley later recalled in an interview with the industry magazine, *Broadcasting*, "I was not only thinking of radio, where I wanted to bolster our standing and please our audience ... I wanted people who I thought would be able to transfer from radio to television."

Development of television vehicles for the new CBS stars would take a few years, especially with situation comedy formats such as *Amos and Andy*. In the meantime, CBS brought its reliance on situation comedy over to television with a strong video version of another popular radio show, *The Goldbergs*. CBS's ace producer, Worthington Miner, developed the program for television and it became the network's first major TV situation comedy.

Since 1929, *The Goldbergs* had run as a popular radio show presenting the members of a Jewish immigrant family as they grew up and adjusted to life in their new home, the East Side of New York City. Gertrude Berg, who played Molly Goldberg, wrote, produced, and directed the radio program, which was one of several very successful "ethnic" comedies that thrived during the 1930s and 1940s, including *Lum and Abner* (Arkansas hillbillies), *Amos and Andy* (blacks in Harlem), and *Life with Luigi* (Italians in Chicago). The characters in these shows obviously reflected ethnic stereotypes, usually in their dialect and misspoken English ("It's time to expire" for "Let's go to sleep"), but within their settings, they were natural and homey.

In its transition to television in January 1949, *The Goldbergs* retained its rich ethnic flavor and concern for everyday family problems. Unlike the brash, snappy vaudeo shows of the time, the program drew its humor from the complications that evolved as the characters faced generally realistic working class situations. Molly managed the household while her husband, Jake (Philip Loeb), ran a small clothing business. Though they worried about keeping the family solvent, their chief concerns were domestic. Jake was a strong father who loved his children yet did not hesitate to punish them when they deserved it. Molly served as both peacemaker and family gossip, always on the lookout for a "perfect match" for either their teenage son, Sammy (Larry Robinson), or daughter, Rosalie (Arlene McQuade). Molly's Uncle David (Eli Mintz) also lived with the family, tossing in homey aphorisms. For the latest in neighborhood news, Molly leaned out the window and summoned her upstairs neighbor by yelling, "Yoo-hoo, Mrs. Bloom!"

While drama programs at the time followed the anthology-adaptation format, the situation comedy of *The Goldbergs* presented viewers with slices of life involving familiar characters they could return to week after week, like old friends. Within six months, CBS added another warm family comedy to its schedule, *Mama*, which caught on and ran for eight years.

Mama presented the growing pains and light humor in the lives of a Norwegian immigrant family in San Francisco during the first years of the twentieth century. The series was based on the book by Kathryn Forbes, *Mama's Bank Account,* which had been turned into a play and theatrical film earlier in the decade (both called "I Remember Mama"). Each episode of the series opened with the family's oldest child, Katrin, looking at the family photo album, thinking back to her childhood and the people and places she had known so well. She remembered many things: "I remember the big white house ... and my little sister Dagmar, and my big brother Nels, and, of course, Papa. But most of all, I remember Mama."

Like *The Goldbergs, Mama* focused on down-to-earth problems

January 12, 1949
Kukla, Fran and Ollie. (NBC). After two months on the midwestern network, Chicago's first major contribution to network television arrives on the East Coast.

January 21, 1949
Your Show Time. (NBC). The first all-film series on network television dramatizes one-act plays, with Arthur Shields as narrator. Naturally, this venture comes from Los Angeles.

January 25, 1949
The first Emmy awards are handed out by Walter O'Keefe at the Hollywood Athletic Club. *Pantomime Quiz,* a local Los Angeles show, is named "Most Popular TV Program."

January 31, 1949
These Are My Children. (NBC). Television's first daytime soap opera airs weekday afternoons from Chicago, radio's soap capital.

April 9, 1949
The telethon is born. Milton Berle stays on the air for fourteen hours to raise $1.1 million for cancer research.

May 5, 1949
Blind Date. (ABC). Arlene Francis transfers her successful radio game show to television. Anxious bachelors, hoping to be picked for a night out, take turns trying to woo a beautiful female hidden from their sight by a studio wall.

May 5, 1949
Crusade in Europe. (ABC). Time-Life produces the first television documentary series, studying World War II.

July 7, 1949
Dragnet. (NBC Radio). Jack Webb dramatizes real life police cases, presenting policemen not as glamour boys or boobs, but as dedicated professionals.

faced by an immigrant family, and both series extolled the family as the most important force in a decent society. "Mama" Hansen (Peggy Wood), like Molly Goldberg, kept a watchful eye on the household while "Papa" Hansen (Judson Laire) worked to support his family. Neither the parents nor their children were always right and members of the family occasionally grew frustrated, angry, and confused with each other. Though the turn-of-the-century pacing was sometimes extremely slow, *Mama* lasted longer on television than any of the other ethnic series of the 1940s and 1950s, as viewers followed it almost like a soap opera. Its Broadway-based cast performed each episode live until the series was canceled in 1956.

Television grew a great deal during the first year of the freeze, establishing important foundations in comedy, drama, and variety. Nonetheless, there was still very primitive programming through most of the broadcast day and, as the networks expanded into new time periods, they ran anything they could.

Two fifteen-minute programs designed to showcase model railroads premiered in the fall of 1948. *Roar of the Rails,* on CBS, used a model railroad train going around and around the same track to illustrate stories told by a narrator about the railroads.

ABC's *Tales of the Red Caboose* ran *films* of a model railroad train going around and around the same track while a narrator told stories about the railroads. They were sponsored by the makers of American Flyer and Lionel model trains, respectively.

In November, DuMont tried expanding its schedule to run from 10:00 A.M. until 11:00 P.M., with a daytime line-up aimed primarily at housewives (chiefly cooking and fashion shows). This caused Jack Gould, television critic for the *New York Times,* to quip, "the idea of a nation of housewives sitting mute before the video machine when they should be tidying up the premises or preparing the formula is not something to be grasped hurriedly. Obviously it is a matter fraught with peril of the darkest sort."

The nation was saved for a while because DuMont's daytime schedule was an utter failure and served to give daytime television a bad name for years.

In January 1949, NBC unveiled television's first daytime soap opera, *These Are My Children,* which used blackboards as cue cards, giving the performers a far-away look in their eyes as they strained to read their lines.

In March, ABC brought the violent cheesecake of Roller Derby contests to the air. This gimmick sport consisted of teams of women on roller skates going around and around a roller rink shoving and punching each other trying to score game points. It had been around (and around) since 1935, but attracted very little popular attention until the summer of 1946, when WNBT in New York City used some live telecasts to fill out its local schedule. ABC looked at DuMont's success with theatrical-style wrestling matches and decided to try the same stunt with Roller Derby. The sport was the same sort of constant mindless theatrical action. Even though there were complicated rules, everyone essentially ignored them. ABC's Ken Nydell did the skate-by-skate description and Joe Hasel did the color, as such healthy young women as Midge "Toughy" Brashun and Ann "Red" Jensen threw football- and wrestling-style blocks and punches against their opponents. ABC's strategy succeeded and Roller Derby became a national fad.

When summer arrived, the networks were further pressed. Summer was traditionally the time when the top performers took vacations, along with much of the home audience. With very few filmed series and no reruns available, the networks used the period to experiment. Hollywood's boycott of television prevented most American movies from reaching the air, so CBS dug up somewhat dated British product for *The CBS Film Theater of the Air.* This was the first of many early network movie series that relied on obscure foreign or cheap domestic films to fill out holes in the broadcast day. DuMont used *Program Playhouse* to test pilots for possible series. ("Hands of Murder" earned a spot in the fall 1949 lineup.) NBC's *Theater of the Mind* anthology featured psychological drama, while ABC's *Stop the Music* game show (with Bert Parks) tried to duplicate its radio success.

Yet summer proved to be a rich viewing time for those who stayed indoors and sorted through the filler. In addition to *Mama* and *Cavalcade of Stars,* there were offbeat new programs for both children and adults.

Worthington Miner was the producer of *Mr. I Magination* on CBS, which starred Paul Tripp as a magical engineer who took ideas from children's letters and staged them as skits in which the suggestions came true. DuMont's *Captain Video* series, featuring the "guardian of the safety of the world," brought to life Flash Gordon and Buck Rogers style adventures on an absurdly minuscule budget. Despite the constraints, the series worked and became a hit as children realized that Saturday afternoon movie adventure serials were available five nights a week at home. Young viewers also eagerly tuned to NBC to see decade-old Hopalong Cassidy movies starring William Boyd as the virtuous Western cowboy.

Perhaps the most unusual and innovative show of the summer was NBC's unsponsored *Garroway at Large,* placed in a bleak Saturday slot (10:00 P.M.), then still considered television's Siberia. Dave Garroway ran the program as a variety show, only it did not look like one. He had no studio audience or elaborate backdrops. Instead, he calmly meandered about the studio, working with his guests and talented family of regulars, including Jack Haskell, Cliff Norton, and Connie Russell. They sang, told stories, and performed in short skits, always at a very casual pace and usually with the cameras, mikes, and cables in sight. In one sequence, Garroway and Jack Haskell walked onto a simple outdoor set consisting of a few fake trees, some tools, a shovel, and a bucket. As they discussed the song Haskell was about to sing, the studio crew walked on camera and took the props away, one by one, leaving the set bare as he began his song. Another time, the show went for two minutes without any words or music. First, the camera panned the studio, following Cliff Norton as he hid behind boxes and trunks, occasionally mugging to the camera. Connie Russell joined him and silently the two sneaked into a room with a printing press that was turning out counterfeit money. All this served as the lead-in to the duo's rendition of a popular hit tune, "Counterfeit Love."

More than any other variety host then on TV, Garroway understood how important visual imagery was to the new video art. Even with a bare-bones budget, he realized that a few simple actions in the intimate medium of television could produce a program that was visually entertaining to the home viewer. Reviewers were not quite sure exactly what Garroway had in mind, but they liked it, seeing him as NBC's equivalent to the casual Arthur Godfrey.

The key to Garroway's program was its location, Chicago. Television shows from Chicago always had much less money than those in New York and therefore the people working there had to innovate. They were also generally outside the rigid traditions of network radio and Broadway, the two cultures that dominated New York TV, and so were more inclined to take a fresh approach to production. For instance, instead of staging a big finale, Garroway would smile and say "Peace," adding some unusual description of Chicago as his closing line, such as: "This program came to you from Chicago, where even pigs can whistle."

In spite of all the progress in television, it was still losing money. In 1948, the entire TV industry lost $15 million. None of the networks, and none of their O&Os, made money. The profits in network radio kept television afloat. Yet, sponsors could barely contain their attraction to the glowing tube. By the summer of 1949, they had begun to shift their attention toward television and, wherever possible, they began cutting back the radio budgets to more "cost effective" programs. Even with the freeze in effect, television was demonstrating its ability to produce popular entertainment in the best radio tradition. Besides, the cheaply produced quiz shows on radio offered a perfect alternative to the high-budget, high-class radio series. No matter how good the ratings were for prestige comedy, variety, and drama programs, those shows could not match the commercial value of radio quizzes, which attracted a large audience at only a fraction of the price.

As radio and television approached a fateful head-to-head battle for audience support, radio was losing its best weapon—a high level of program quality. And that just drove more people into the arms of the waiting television set salesman.

9. Behind the Ion Curtain

WHILE GIVEAWAY QUIZ SHOWS DOMINATED network radio in 1949, it was generally assumed that the bulk of these programs would fade away just like any other format craze, with a few of the better ones hanging on to become stable hits as the next gimmick appeared. During the summer of 1949, however, the FCC decided that it did not want to wait.

On August 19, 1949, the FCC ruled that giveaway quiz shows such as *Stop the Music* violated the federal law prohibiting lotteries and that stations which carried the programs after October 1 would not have their licenses renewed. The commission claimed that the shows met the legal definition of a lottery because they required radio listeners to expend something of value (the time it took to listen to a program) in order to be able to win if called at home. Technically, the FCC's rule applied only to shows that telephoned people (such as *Break the Bank, Winner Take All,* and *Stop the Music),* but the point was clear: The FCC wanted to rid the airwaves of quiz shows.

The networks took the issue to court, saying that the FCC had no business sticking its nose into programming decisions. They might not like the quiz shows themselves, but the sponsors wanted them and so did the audience, according to the ratings. In court, the networks managed to block the FCC's new rule from going into effect while the case dragged on. During the court presentations, it became increasingly clear that the FCC was on very shaky legal footing because its charter specifically prohibited program censorship. Even if the giveaways were illegal, the issue was probably outside the commission's jurisdiction. Eventually, in 1954, the Supreme Court knocked down the FCC ruling, but by then most of the giveaway shows had been taken off the air. The FCC's charge had given the giveaway shows a taint of illegality which drove away listeners and scared off sponsors. By November 1949, ABC's *Stop the Music* had lost one-half of its radio audience and CBS Radio had taken four quiz shows off the air. Nonetheless, producers still felt games and quizzes were viable, so they temporarily turned away from the brash come-ons of the big money giveaways and focused on more restrained formats such as celebrity panels.

Most of the new television quiz shows in the 1949–50 season followed a similar strategy, emphasizing guest celebrities *(What's My Line?),* funny antics *(Beat the Clock* and *Pantomime Quiz),* and revamped parlor games *(Twenty Questions).* Still, giveaway shows did not completely disappear. *Stop the Music* continued to run on both television and radio until 1952 and, just weeks after the

FCC's August 1949 quiz ruling, ABC came out with one of the most blatantly exploitative television giveaways yet, *Auction-Aire.* Libby Foods sponsored this weekly live auction in which contestants both at home and in the studio bid on merchandise, not with cash but with labels from Libby products. On the second week's show, bidding had reached the astounding level of 20,000 labels when an anonymous viewer called and said, "I'll give you 30,000 labels if you take this show off the air." This generous offer was refused but it raised an obvious question: What sort of person would have 30,000 Libby labels lying about the house? Whatever the explanation, it was clear that the something-for-nothing illusion of the giveaway shows struck a responsive nerve and a campaign by the FCC would not kill this interest.

In some ways, the FCC's heavy-handed attempt to purge the airwaves of giveaway shows merely reflected its frustration over the proliferation of what it viewed as a particularly "crass" format. Since the 1920s, culture-minded citizens and profit-oriented businesses had fought over the content and effects of the new forms of popular entertainment: movies and radio. Businesses produced what sold, explaining that they were giving the public what it wanted. At the same time, special interest groups worked to remove what they viewed as dangerous and offensive material (no matter how popular) and tried to promote uplifting high quality culture instead. However, not everybody agreed on what was uplifting, proper, or offensive, so the battle never ended and the self-appointed guardians of the public morality remained ever alert for new dangers.

Just as the FCC's crusade against giveaway shows was driving most of the big radio quizzes off the air, television began to supplant radio as the focus for popular entertainment trends. During 1950, television viewing matched radio listening in New York and other major cities and, in this first year of real head-to-head competition, radio ratings plummeted. Though network radio continued to make money (in 1949 radio made $56 million while television lost $25 million), it was clear that, once the FCC lifted its freeze on television's growth, thereby putting an end to radio's monopoly in many markets, the older medium would not be able to match the allure of television. The radio networks joined advertisers in adapting radio to a new marketplace. Instead of high program ratings (which, relative to television, were increasingly irrelevant) they began to emphasize sales effectiveness (the cost-per-listener). To this end, the networks turned to less expensive musical disc jockey shows (using prerecorded music). By the

Day	Net	7:00	7:30	8:00	8:30	9:00	9:30	10:00	10:30
MON	ABC	local	Author Meets The Critics	local	Science Circus	ABC Barn Dance	MR. BLACK	Roller Derby	
	CBS	Roar Of The Rails / PAUL ARNOLD	CBS News / Sonny Kendis	SILVER THEATER	Arthur Godfrey's Talent Scouts	Candid Camera	The Goldbergs	Studio One	
	DUM	Captain Video	Manhattan Spotlight / Vincent Lopez	Newsweek Views The News	AL MORGAN SHOW	And Everything Nice	Wrestling From Sunnyside Arena With Dennis James		
	NBC	Kukla, Fran And Ollie	Morton Downey / Cam. News Caravan	Chevrolet Tele-Theater	VOICE OF FIRESTONE	Lights Out	BAND OF AMERICA	Quiz Kids	local
TUE	ABC	local	On Trial	local				Tomorrow's Champions (to 12 Midnight)	
	CBS	PRIZE PARTY	CBS News / Sonny Kendis	SUGAR HILL TIMES		Actor's Studio	Suspense	THIS WEEK IN SPORTS / Blues By Bargy	PANTOMIME QUIZ
	DUM	Captain Video	Manhattan Spotlight / Vincent Lopez	Court Of Current Issues		THE O'NEILLS	FEATURE THEATER		local
	NBC	Kukla, Fran And Ollie	Roberta Quinlan / Cam. News Caravan	Texaco Star Theater		Fireside Theater	THE LIFE OF RILEY	Original Amateur Hour	
WED	ABC	local		Wendy Barrie Show	PHOTO CRIME	YOUR WITNESS	Wrestling From The Rainbo In Chicago		
	CBS	STRICTLY LAUGHS / PAUL ARNOLD	CBS News / At Home Show	Arthur Godfrey And His Friends		Dunninger & Winchell Bigelow Show	Tournament Of Champions		
	DUM	Captain Video	Manhattan Spotlight / Vincent Lopez	Flight To Rhythm	local	THE PLAINCLOTHESMAN	Famous Jury Trials	local	
	NBC	Kukla, Fran And Ollie	Morton Downey / Cam. News Caravan	CRISIS	The Clock	Kraft Television Theater		Break The Bank	local
THUR	ABC	local	THE LONE RANGER	Stop The Music		STARRING BORIS KARLOFF	THE RUGGLES	Roller Derby (to 11:15)	
	CBS	Dione Lucas On Cooking	CBS News / Sonny Kendis	FRONT PAGE	INSIDE U.S.A. / THEATER OF ROMANCE	ED WYNN SHOW	local	Blues By Bargy	local
	DUM	Captain Video	Manhattan Spotlight / Vincent Lopez	MYSTERY THEATER		Morey Amsterdam Show	Boxing From Sunnyside Arena With Dennis James		
	NBC	Kukla, Fran And Ollie	Roberta Quinlan / Cam. News Caravan	HOLLYWOOD PREMIERE	Mary Kay And Johnny	Fireball Fun-For-All		MARTIN KANE, PRIVATE EYE	local
FRI	ABC	local	TOUCHDOWN	MAJORITY RULES	Blind Date	AUCTION-AIRE	Fun For The Money	Roller Derby	
	CBS	STRICTLY LAUGHS / PAUL ARNOLD	CBS News / AMAZING POLGAR	Mama	MAN AGAINST CRIME	54th Street Revue / # Ford Television Theater Hour	People's Platform	CAPITOL CLOAKROOM	
	DUM	Captain Video	Manhattan Spotlight / Vincent Lopez	HANDS OF MURDER	THE FAMILY GENIUS	FISHING AND HUNTING CLUB OF THE AIR	Program Playhouse	AMATEUR BOXING FROM CHICAGO	
	NBC	Kukla, Fran And Ollie	Morton Downey / Cam. News Caravan	ONE MAN'S FAMILY	We, The People	VERSATILE VARIETIES	THE BIG STORY / Believe It Or Not	Gillette Cavalcade Of Sports	Greatest Fights
SAT	ABC	local	Hollywood Screen Test	Paul Whiteman's TV Teen Club		Roller Derby			
	CBS	Lucky Pup (from 6:45) / local	Quincy Howe / Blues By Bargy	Winner Take All	local	Premiere Playhouse		local	
	DUM	local		Spin The Picture		Cavalcade Of Stars		WRESTLING FROM THE MARIGOLD IN CHICAGO	
	NBC	local	Nature Of Things / Leon Pearson	TWENTY QUESTIONS	SESSIONS / STUDS' PLACE	Who Said That?	Meet The Press	The Black Robe	local
SUN	ABC	PAUL WHITEMAN'S GOODYEAR REVUE	COMEDY THEATER	Think Fast	THE LITTLE REVUE	LET THERE BE STARS		Celebrity Game	YOUTH ON THE MARCH
	CBS	Tonight On Broadway	This Is Show Business	Toast Of The Town		Fred Waring Show		Week In Review	local
	DUM	Front Row Center		CHICAGOLAND MYSTERY PLAYERS	CINEMA VARIETIES	Cross Question		local	
	NBC	Leave It To The Girls	THE ALDRICH FAMILY	Supper Club	Colgate Theater	Philco Television Playhouse		Garroway-At-Large	HANK McCUNE SHOW

summer of 1950, almost all of radio's superstars decided it was time to jump ship and they made plans to switch to television by the fall. Advertising agencies, which had been easing out of the more expensive radio programs whenever possible for more than a year, eyed the expansive postwar baby boom and marked their calendars for 1955—when these offspring would become new TV consumers. Television was the marketplace for the future.

During the 1949–50 season, television also became the new scapegoat for the ills of society. With seventy new TV stations on the air (approved before the FCC freeze went into effect), there were sixty-five cities in the country with at least one television station. More and more people had sets, making television an established part of society. Some saw the tube as the ultimate way to reach out and touch people, while others considered it a disruptive force which was already getting out of control.

Throughout the country, ad-hoc commissions sprang up to study the problem of television, focusing on what they saw as instances of excessive and unnecessary sex and violence. Some blamed television for an increase in juvenile delinquency, pointing to the violence on TV cop shows as a bad influence on children. Dr. Daniel L. Marsh, president of Boston University, told his 1950 graduating class: "If the television craze continues with the present level of programs, we are destined to have a nation of morons."

Others warned of the potential danger to unstable adults lured by the urge to "make a big splash" on television. One such offbeat act of television violence took place in Texas where, on June 11, 1950, Sanford B. Twente boasted to a waitress, "just watch me at the end of the fifth inning." Later that day, he barged into the announcing booth during KLEE-TV's telecast of a Houston versus Dallas minor league baseball game, at the end of the fifth inning. Viewers heard Twente exclaim, "I've got something to tell you!" Announcer Dick Gottlieb replied, "Not now, this mike is live." Seconds later, there was the sound of a gunshot. The camera focused on the players and fans turning to stare at the announcing booth; then the cameraman swung around to show the inside of the booth and Twente, slumped dead, in the arms of an engineer.

Coroner Tom Mays, who happened to be watching the game at home, turned in his preliminary verdict of suicide without ever going to the hospital. The game continued after a short break.

Protests over sex settled on more symbolic connections and issues because there was not any sex, per se, on television in 1950. Instead, people focused on actions that seemed to suggest an erosion in moral attitudes and the encouragement of irresponsible behavior. Two of the first symbols were women's necklines and Arthur Godfrey's tongue.

Arthur Godfrey's natural broadcasting style occasionally resulted in a few bawdy stories and suggestive "blue" jokes, which went over the air uncensored. What upset some people even more than the jokes themselves, however, was the fact that Godfrey was never reprimanded by CBS. It appeared that nobody at the network felt capable of telling him to "clean up his act" because he was too important and powerful. Godfrey was practically a one-man network on CBS, doing eight hours and forty-five minutes of radio and TV broadcasting per week. His two TV programs never left the top ten that season and he was directly responsible for thousands of dollars in advertising. Wayne Coy, chairman of the FCC, drew attention to this turnaround in authority, noting, "when a comedian gets so big that his network can no longer handle him, then I think we have a case of the tail wagging the dog … it seems to me, that the question of just how bad poor taste can get before it merges over into downright obscenity or indecency may be settled one of these days."

Performers such as Faye Emerson and Ilka Chase upset some people in a different way. They were attractive women who frequently wore lowcut gowns as part of their image as television "glamour girls." For years, such beautiful women had appeared on TV wearing mildly suggestive costumes, usually in background roles on "sophisticated" nightclub formats. Emerson and Chase merely stepped to the forefront as individual stars who dressed in slightly more daring outfits as part of their overall promotion strategy, and they were quite successful at it. Emerson was a regular on three different panel shows and in April 1950 won her own prime time variety program on NBC. Chase appeared in her own interview show for CBS in February, *Glamour-Go-Round* (with Durward Kirby). Both Emerson and Chase capitalized on creating the impression of introducing viewers to the ultimate in witty, sophisticated society.

As women such as Ilka Chase and Faye Emerson became popular stars, they attracted both approving stares and outraged criticism. In doing so, they sparked animated discussions on the proper attire for women in public and the issue soon became a national *cause celebre.* Most viewers did not care one way or the other about such supposedly scandalous behavior, though, and merely used the controversy as an excuse to look at beautiful women and to talk about looking at beautiful women. The issue served as a perfect springboard for routines and one-liners by television comedians and punsters. On the humorous panel show *This Is Show Business,* which featured Clifton Fadiman, George S. Kaufman, and Abe Burrows as "problem consultants" to famous celebrity guests, French actress Denise Darcel asked if her sisters should come and work in the United States amid the lowcut controversy. Abe Burrows quickly said "Yes!" suggesting that "LS/MFT," the slogan of the show's sponsor, Lucky Strike cigarettes, did not stand for "Lucky Strike Means Fine Tobacco" but really meant: "Let's See More French Tomatoes."

The most important aspect of the interest in sex and violence on television in 1950 was that it vividly demonstrated the medium's tremendous growth. All of the networks were expanding, but NBC, as the number one network, expanded the most. NBC was reaping the rewards of being the first to begin network television broadcasting. It had the longest association with the older, established TV stations, giving it the best collection of network affiliates and the best showcases for its network programming. By early 1950, NBC had sold out almost all of its available commercial slots in the popular evening hours, or "prime time" (approximately 8:00–11:00 P.M.), so it began looking for new periods to sell. In studying viewer habits, the network noticed a shift from the patterns of radio. Previously, people had listened to their favorite radio shows between 7:00 P.M. and 10:00 P.M., then turned off the set and read the paper or cleaned the dishes. With television, families finished the housework first, tuned in about 8:00 P.M., and watched until it was time for bed. NBC concluded that they might be induced to stick around another hour (11:00 P.M. until midnight) with just the right program. After a very careful search, the network selected twenty-six-year-old Los Angeles comic Don "Creesh" Hornsby to host *Broadway Open House,* a casual mixture of comedy-variety and talk. The day of the scheduled May 22, 1950, premiere, Hornsby died of a sudden attack of polio.

NBC delayed the show for a week, then filled in with guest hosts, including Tex and Jinx, Pat Harrington, and Dean Martin and Jerry Lewis. By June, a new format was ready. The *Broadway Open House* slot was split between two performers: Morey Amsterdam handled Monday and Wednesday, while Jerry Lester took Tuesday, Thursday, and Friday. Amsterdam was a borscht-belt vaudeville comic who was already a TV veteran from his own

The Lone Ranger was one of the first important filmed TV series, with Clayton Moore *(right)* as the Lone Ranger and Jay Silverheels *(left)* as his companion, Tonto. (*The Lone Ranger and Tonto are trademarks of and copyrighted by Classic Media, Inc.*)

September 5, 1949
Pat Weaver becomes NBC's programming chief.

October 10, 1949
RCA at last unveils a totally compatible color television system.

October 24, 1949
"Battleship Bismarck" plays on *Studio One* and provides young Charlton Heston his first starring role. He portrays a conscience-troubled Jewish gunnery officer on a large Nazi ship.

November 11, 1949
John Daly leaves CBS News for ABC.

November 26, 1949
Studs' Place. (NBC). Another off beat high-quality (rarely sponsored) television series from Chicago. Writer-philosopher Studs Terkel acts as barkeep, sharing stories and songs with his "regulars," including a folk singer and a jazz pianist. The show is relaxed and loose, with a blue and lonesome tone.

January 1, 1950
Mark Woods, ABC's first president, becomes vice-chairman of the board. Forty-year-old Robert Kinter moves up to become the youngest network president in television.

January 30, 1950
Robert Montgomery Presents. (NBC). The first major defection from Hollywood's closed ranks. Montgomery directs and occasionally stars in this fancy, top-class drama showcase.

April 9, 1950
"Star Spangled Revue." (NBC). Max Liebman produces a vanguard big-budget television special. Host Bob Hope makes his first major television appearance and is the first important radio comic to take the plunge into video.

prime time series and a string of guest spots on panel shows. Lester had spent a few months hosting DuMont's *Cavalcade of Stars,* replacing Jack Carter. In the new form, the late night program quickly became a hit. The number of television sets in use after 11:00 P.M. increased dramatically and the show registered ratings as high as many prime time shows.

Broadway Open House was loose and had no formal script. There was light chat, strains of comedy and variety, a family of regulars, and some guests. Above all, the program ran on the personality of its hosts. Though Amsterdam did a good show, Lester quickly attracted the more devoted following. He was described as "a middle-aged Mickey Rooney, a walking seltzer bottle who never runs out of fizz." Lester cultivated the image of *Broadway Open House* as a late night private party and viewers picked up the spirit, latching onto his catch phrases and in-jokes. A detractor once labeled him a bean bag, so Lester immediately formed the fictitious Bean Bag Club of America, naming himself as president. Seventy thousand people wrote in to join.

In addition to his own offbeat humor, Lester used a family of regulars including dancer Ray Malone, the Milton Delugg Orchestra, and Dagmar. Jennie Lewis, who used the stage name Dagmar, was a tall, buxom blonde who delivered dry spicy one-liners, somewhat in the style of Mae West. Her deft, often suggestive,

comments frequently stole the show, though some sensitive viewers described Dagmar as "nothing more than a walking pin-up picture," apparently even more dangerous than Faye Emerson and Ilka Chase. Nonetheless, Dagmar's wit and figure made her the most popular member of Lester's supporting crew.

Broadway Open House lasted only one year as first Amsterdam, then Lester, left the program. Lester tried to bring his style of late night zaniness to prime time but there his offbeat personality worked against him as the much larger and more diverse evening audience found his oddities harder to accept. Dagmar hosted a brief late night show of her own, *Dagmar's Canteen,* but it folded after only four months. NBC used a few other hosts for *Broadway Open House,* but none seemed to have a similar rapport with the home viewers. Reluctantly, the network turned the time slot back to the local affiliates. NBC had demonstrated the viability of late night TV, but had also discovered the importance of finding just the right personality for the slot.

Broadway Open House was only one of NBC's television innovations in 1950. Though the network had lost some of its top radio comedy talent to CBS in the Paley's Comet raids of 1948, NBC was determined to maintain its momentum in television. It pressed to develop not only new time periods but new programs and formats uniquely suited to TV. In August 1949, NBC hired Sylvester "Pat" Weaver, who had been vice president for radio and television at the powerful Young & Rubicam ad agency. Weaver became chief of programming and almost immediately began testing creative new ideas.

Weaver's first project was a two-and-one-half-hour concept he called *Saturday Night Revue.* The previous season, DuMont's *Cavalcade of Stars* had demonstrated that viewers were willing to stay home on Saturday night to watch television, so Weaver planned a full night of special entertainment that could realistically compete with feature films and live theater. As first conceived, *Saturday Night Revue* consisted of an hour-long film or play done especially for television, followed by an hour of Broadway revue material, and ending with a thirty-minute nightclub variety segment. Weaver's grandiose plan faced staggering financial and casting problems, as well as strong opposition by the other networks.

In early 1950, AT&T still had only a few coaxial cable links connecting TV stations in the East and Midwest, and the networks fought with each other for use of these cables on a show-by-show basis. NBC, with the largest number of popular shows and the most affiliates, consistently grabbed the choice slots on the cable. ABC, CBS, and DuMont quickly realized that the proposed *Saturday Night Revue* would tie up the East-to-West cable all night and, in effect, prevent any of their Saturday night programming from being aired in the Midwest. DuMont was particularly incensed because the NBC show would directly affect its *Cavalcade of Stars,* which had broken the ground for Saturday night broadcasting. DuMont complained to the FCC, which, after complicated legal maneuvering, forced NBC to make two concessions: The first hour of the *Saturday Night Revue* would originate in Chicago (thereby freeing one of the East-to-West cable lines), and NBC was forbidden to insist that stations take the entire two-and-one-half hours as a package. Instead, the show was to be offered in thirty-minute blocks so that local programmers—especially in those crucial one-station markets—could run fare from other networks as well.

Ironically, the forced partitioning of *Saturday Night Revue* made the entire project economically feasible by allowing NBC to institute a revolution in sponsorship. Previously, there had been three ways to sponsor a show: sustained (paid for by the network), co-op (no national advertising, but local stations inserted commercials from local sponsors), or, the most common form, direct sponsorship (one sponsor paid for an entire program). Weaver conceived a new form, participating sponsorship, which allowed a number of national sponsors to carve a program into separate blocks of time, each considered its own segment. With the costs of television rising rapidly, such a move was inevitable because there were few sponsors that could continue to bankroll an entire program alone. *Saturday Night Revue,* for example, cost $50,000 a week to produce. Multiple sponsorship eventually became the norm for television, and sponsors never attained the overall level of control in video that they had enjoyed on radio.

Besides devising a method to encourage sponsorship for NBC's expensive new show, Weaver also revised its structure. He dropped the costly idea of an original film or play every week and broke *Saturday Night Revue* into just two programs: *The Jack Carter Show* (one hour of standard vaudeo from Chicago) and *Your Show of Shows* (ninety minutes of comedy-variety from New York). Nonetheless, Madison Avenue agencies played it cozy, waiting to see if NBC could make the two and one-half hour format work. Consequently, when the two shows premiered at the end of February 1950, not one of their fifteen commercial slots was sold.

The Jack Carter Show was fairly funny, but nothing special. Carter had recently departed from DuMont's *Cavalcade of Stars* and did not change his act much for the new program. In contrast, *Your Show of Shows* marked a major improvement by producer Max Liebman and headliners Sid Caesar and Imogene Coca over their previous series, *Admiral Broadway Revue.* This time, their television comedy-variety act worked perfectly. Part of the improvement was a reflection of more polished writing. At the same time, the Broadway-based Liebman adjusted his techniques to meet television's demand for intimacy, bringing the camera "up on stage," which managed to convey to the viewers at home the humor and excitement of the wide-open production. Above all, Caesar blossomed. His frequent coughing and throat-clearing, which had marred his *Admiral Broadway Revue* performances, were gone. He was cooler, more controlled, and better suited to carry a wide range of skits with Coca. Though *Your Show of Shows* included fine supporting crews of singers and dancers, as well as a weekly guest star host (Burgess Meredith the first two weeks), the comedy sketches featuring Caesar and Coca transformed the show into truly exceptional entertainment.

The most obvious vehicles for the two were man and woman settings, and these ranged from starry-eyed lovers on a first date to an unhappy couple trying to put some romance back into their tired marriage. In these sketches, Caesar and Coca conveyed the humor and drama of everyday life, yet they functioned just as well in more abstract settings such as a pair of lions looking out at the visitors to the zoo. Both could also handle solo spots. Coca excelled in comic dance and singing while Caesar demonstrated remarkable versatility in monologues, pantomime, and crazy dialects. They were soon joined by sidemen Carl Reiner and Howard Morris, and the ensemble of four was able to tackle virtually any comedy routine concocted by the writers (including then-unknowns Neil Simon and Mel Brooks). They reached heights of gleeful frenzy in parodies of movie and television titles including *This Is Your Life,* "Shane," "The Mark of Zorro," and "From Here to Eternity." With such a strong basic cast, *Your Show of Shows* became a long-lasting hit and it quickly sold all of its ad slots.

Your Show of Shows was better than almost anything else then on TV, so Jack Carter's merely adequate program suffered in comparison. Yet Carter's presence infuriated the Chicago television community, which felt that the town's reputation for innovation was being hurt. Instead of drawing on the still unsponsored home-grown talents such as Dave Garroway and Studs Terkel, NBC had used a New York flavored, New York run program for its required telecast from Chicago. The network seemed to consider Chicago's own creative talent irrelevant, while national sponsors treated the city like a cowtown that did not warrant a business trip.

Chicago received such cavalier treatment because ultimately the city was not important to the networks' future expansion plans. It was merely an O&O city that, by circumstance (the route of the coaxial cable construction), became a convenient location for some stopgap TV production. Once the coast-to-coast cable was completed, Chicago programs would become largely expendable. Television, like radio and the movies, would operate from the two coasts.

New York and California had been battling for control of American popular culture since the early 1900s, when Hollywood replaced Long Island as the nation's movie capital. In the late 1930s, Los Angeles had supplanted New York as the main locale of network radio programming. New York TV people prepared for another conflict as the theater-oriented East Coast and the Hollywood-based West Coast faced off over television production. Network television was oriented toward live performances, so the technical limitations facing Los Angeles in 1950 gave New York City the upper hand for the moment. The West Coast was not connected to the coaxial cable and, going into the 1949–50 season, the networks carried very few filmed series. Some Hollywood production was inevitable, though. New York studio space was already tight and the network schedules were still expanding. CBS bought land out in Los Angeles for a future television city and also launched the first important use of Los Angeles-made kines, *The Ed Wynn Show.*

Kinescope recordings were films of live shows shot directly off a picture tube monitor as they played. They were grainy, lacked

---

June 4, 1950
The Steve Allen Show. (CBS Radio). While *Our Miss Brooks* is gone for the summer, twenty-eight-year-old Steve Allen gets his first network comedy series.

June 26, 1950
The Garry Moore Show. (CBS). After a few years as junior partner to Jimmy Durante on radio, Garry Moore gets his own weekday evening comedy-variety series on television, with Durward Kirby as his sidekick.

July 10, 1950
Your Hit Parade. (NBC). A video version is added to a fifteen year radio smash. Dorothy Collins and Snooky Lanson sing the top seven songs of the week, plus three up-and-coming "extras." On this first program, "My Foolish Heart" is number one.

July 20, 1950
Arthur Murray Party. (ABC). Part variety, part dance instruction, this is *the* perennial summer replacement show. By the fall of 1953, it will have been on all four television networks, the first show to achieve such a distinction.

August 19, 1950
ABC becomes the first television network to begin Saturday morning programming for children, offering the informational *Animal Clinic* and the Western circus setting of *Acrobat Ranch.*

definition, and were generally a poor substitute for live television. Viewers in cities not connected to the East Coast coaxial cable watched them because there was no other way to receive the New York-based network shows. *The Ed Wynn Show* reversed the process and originated live in Los Angeles, sending kines to the East Coast. Wynn staged a revue show, mixing variety, comedy, and his own low-key mimicry and whimsy. He drew on the talent based in Hollywood for guest spots. In December, he sang a duet with Buster Keaton and, in January, did a great pantomime bit with Lucille Ball, who was making her television debut. Viewers out East liked the program, but they hated the kines. Accustomed to high-definition live telecasts, they were appalled by the gray grainy quality of the picture and the poor sound reproduction. Although other series such as *The Alan Young Show* (another comedy revue) and *The Ruggles* (a sitcom) were staged lived in Los Angeles and shipped out as kines, negative viewer reaction made it obvious that live West Coast productions would have to wait for the cable connection.

Film was an obvious way around the cable problem and, in the 1949–50 season, the concept of filming shows for television received important boosts. At the time, the networks generally regarded film as inferior to live presentations and most filmed efforts seemed designed to prove the point. The *Fireside Theater* drama anthology, produced by the Hal Roach studios, consisted of low budget episodes churned out in just a few days each. Both *The Life of Riley* (starring Jackie Gleason) and *The Hank McCune Show,* two filmed sitcoms, were stilted and cheaply produced. Ed Wynn quipped, "In the beginning, a television set cost hundreds of dollars and you could see a few bad shows. In a couple of years, you'll be able to buy a television set for a few dollars and see hundreds of bad shows."

Apart from these, there was a dramatic exception in the fall of 1949, the wide open Western adventures of *The Lone Ranger.*

In looking at the TV success of Hopalong Cassidy, the struggling ABC saw that Saturday matinee-style heroics on television were very popular with children. The network was searching for any sort of hit, so it decided to take a chance on brand new filmed-for-television adventures of a popular radio cowboy hero, the Lone Ranger. The TV series was pure pulp adventure, following the radio legend of a daring masked lawman (played by Clayton Moore) and his faithful Indian companion, Tonto (Jay Silverheels), who fought for law and order in the amorphous old West of the 1870s. The Lone Ranger helped anyone in need, never accepted payment for his services, and always defeated the bad guys. Unlike previous filmed series, *The Lone Ranger* was treated like a medium-budget adventure movie and the first season's fifty-two episodes (there were no reruns) cost $1 million to produce. The money was well spent. Kids found the outdoor action and scenery a thrilling release from the "cooped up" New York studio productions and they made *The Lone Ranger* one of ABC's first TV hits.

Several months after the masked man appeared, TV film pioneer Jerry Fairbanks unveiled a cheaper but more efficient way to produce filmed TV series, the multi-cam system. In February 1950, the previously live New York based *Silver Theater* moved out West and became the first to use the multi-cam process, which was designed to combine the feel of live TV with the perfectibility and permanence of film, without a large increase in budget. Three film cameras with thirty minutes of film in each were positioned in the studio and used like regular TV cameras. All three operated continuously and the director could monitor what they were shooting. Like live shows, a program could be done in one smooth take, from start to finish. Like filmed shows, the action could be stopped to correct mistakes or to change lighting, and then resumed. When editing time was added, an average half-hour show took three days to complete, while its live equivalent took five, including rehearsals. The multi-cam made West Coast filmed series a viable alternative to live shows from New York City, and the focus of East Coast objections shifted from technical limitations to the programs themselves.

The New York branch of the TV industry had seen Hollywood assume control of movies and radio, and some executives feared that if the same happened with television the medium would soon be reduced to mindless fluff. They criticized California productions in general as flashy, light, and empty, pointing to the first wave of West Coast filmed TV sitcoms as confirming their worst apprehensions. *The Hank McCune Show,* for instance, was just like Hollywood's theatrical "screwball" comedies that featured empty-headed adventures of lovable, inoffensive bumblers. The series even "faked" its laughter by dubbing the sound of an audience onto the audio track of the film (creating a "laugh track"), though no audience had been present at the filming. Another program, *The Life of Riley,* was an all-around loser with terrible scripts, cheap sets, and a weak supporting cast. However, the show did have one saving grace: Jackie Gleason in the lead role of Chester A. Riley.

For six years on radio, William Bendix had played Chester Riley as yet another simple-minded, lovable middle class bumbler who could turn the most innocent task into a silly crisis. Though Riley would frequently sputter and moan ("What a revoltin' development this is!"), it was all show. He was really a pushover and the problems, which were inevitably just simple misunderstandings, melted away every week. Under Bendix, Riley never really got angry and his chief appeal was a predictable soft heart and forgiving nature.

In 1949, William Bendix was under an exclusive film contract which prevented him from continuing the role on TV, and Jackie Gleason got the job instead. Gleason played Riley a bit differently from the image Bendix had cultivated on the radio. Though Gleason's Riley was also a simple man with a soft heart, his anger was more threatening and he seemed capable of really popping off in a situation. This made the moments of forgiveness and resolution more believable. However, Gleason's expressive interpretation went against the public's image of Riley and there was some resistance to it. Gleason was good, but he was not Chester A. Riley! More important, the writing and overall production on the show was exceptionally weak, so Gleason did not have the support to build a following for his version of Riley. After six months, the program was off the air.

Though a failure itself, *The Life of Riley* provided Gleason with important television exposure as he demonstrated his ability to shine in a show despite weak writing and production. When Jerry Lester left DuMont's *Cavalcade of Stars* to do *Broadway Open House,* the network signed Gleason as the new host, beginning in July 1950. Under Gleason, *Cavalcade of Stars* came closest to DuMont's dream of a hit comedy-variety show and, in September, the network helped it along by moving the program to Friday night, against NBC's boxing matches and away from *Your Show of Shows.*

On *Cavalcade of Stars,* Gleason was surrounded by the usual variety trappings of music (the Sammy Spear Orchestra) and dancing (the June Taylor Dancers), but the revamped program worked because of his energy and versatility. His characters ranged from a down-and-out bum to an arrogant playboy, and his facial expressions could carry a scene without a word of dialogue (only Sid Caesar could top Gleason's contortions of pain). For his sidekick Gleason chose Art Carney and the two developed into smooth comic foils. Carney served as an especially effective balance to Gleason's more boisterous characters, playing a stern father to haughty Reginald Van Gleason III or the prim but caustic Clem Finch to loudmouth Charlie Bratten. In 1951, they introduced what soon became their most popular character sketch, "The Honeymooners," featuring Gleason as a blustery Brooklyn bus driver, Ralph Kramden; series regular Pert Kelton as Kramden's wife, Alice; and Carney as Ed Norton, an obliging sewer worker who was Kramden's best friend. By 1952, Gleason had blossomed into a first rate television star and, in the fall, he jumped to CBS – taking Carney and the June Taylor Dancers with him. As always, DuMont's *Cavalcade of Stars* had been merely a stepping stone to a better salary and a bigger budget.

At the same time that Jackie Gleason was toiling on the ill-fated *Life of Riley,* other stars-to-be were working in the hinterlands of broadcasting, also in search of their lucky break. Future talk show host Mike Douglas was a singer on *Kay Kyser's Kollege of Musical Knowledge* (a musical quiz show); Jim McKay, later a renowned sportscaster, arrived in New York to host *The Real McKay* (a local chit-chat variety show set on his patio); and actor Jack Lemmon played "a brash young lad from Kalamazoo" who was trying to break into show business by serving as houseboy to a famous drama critic (played by Neil Hamilton) on ABC's *That*

Wonderful Guy. At the New Jersey state fair, Trenton disc jockey Ernie Kovacs failed in his effort to break the marathon radio broadcasting record of one week, while in nearby Camden, Ed McMahon played a red-nosed circus clown on CBS's *Big Top.*

Despite the many successful new programs and emerging stars, television was still losing money at a disturbing rate. ABC's president Mark Woods explained that his network had expanded too fast to meet expenses and announced major cost-cutting moves: ABC cut 20% from its TV budget in the winter of 1950 and canceled all of its Monday and Tuesday programming. These actions saved the network from total collapse. By the fall of 1950, ABC's five O&Os were nearing the black, but in the tight freeze market the network still had serious problems attracting viewers and selling its shows to sponsors. Even number one NBC was beginning to feel the squeeze. Though it was actually selling more commercial time than ever, costs for programs had shot up. More important, the networks could not yet charge advertisers premium rates because the FCC freeze limited television coverage across the country. Established markets might reach a higher saturation of TV sets, but there were still millions of people who had never seen a television program. The nation had settled into a peculiar social division: One half of the country was going TV crazy while the

On June 25, 1950, Communist forces invaded South Korea, and the U.S. was drawn into war. *(U.S. Army)*

other half, "behind the ion curtain," had to imagine what everybody else was talking about. Though the FCC had instigated the freeze in 1948 merely to investigate signal interference and channel separation, the commission soon found the issue mired in the more complicated questions of UHF frequencies and color. The promised six month halt in processing new station applications had already extended for one and one-half years, and there was no sign that the freeze would be ended in the foreseeable future.

Apart from the stagnation of the freeze, darker shadows tainted American television that season. Since World War II, Americans had become increasingly concerned about the safety of the United States as Communist forces seized control of governments in both Europe and Asia. Congressional committees such as HUAC and private organizations such as *Counterattack* had assumed the task of identifying Communists, Communist sympathizers, and so-called fellow-travelers throughout American society. In response, the Hollywood film industry had begun blacklisting writers and actors charged with having suspicious ties to leftist organizations, usually without ever corroborating the accusations. By 1948, blacklisting had become an established but rarely discussed practice in network radio as well. After examining the programming and the personnel files of the four radio networks, *Counterattack* evaluated each one, concluding that, "NBC and Mutual are the least satisfactory to the Communists … ABC is about halfway between most satisfactory and least satisfactory, and CBS is the most satisfying network to the Communists."

At first, television had been dismissed as unimportant, but, as the medium grew, so did concern over its potential for misuse by Communist subversives. Through 1949, television sponsors and network executives also quietly adopted the practice of blacklisting as protection against charges of helping the Communist cause.

Blacklisting was a vague process. There were no lists as such, only individual campaigns and reports published by self-proclaimed Communist investigators who would tout every rumor and innuendo as fact. A brave network or sponsor could decide to ignore such accusations and hire the "suspicious" talent anyway. Ed Sullivan chose to do just that by scheduling dancer Paul Draper for an appearance on *Toast of the Town* in January 1950. Reluctantly, the network and sponsor went along, even though Draper had been blacklisted from network television for more than a year.

On Sullivan's show Draper danced to, of all things, "Yankee Doodle Dandy." Benson Ford, of the Detroit Ford family (who owned Sullivan's sponsor, Lincoln Mercury) happened to be in the audience that night and was shown clapping when Draper finished. In spite of this apparent corporate approval, a concerted letter writing and phone campaign produced hundreds of complaints about Draper's appearance. At first Sullivan defended his decision to have Draper on the show, but after intense pressure from the American Legion, the Catholic War Veterans, and banner headlines in the *New York Journal American,* Sullivan backed down, agreed to clip Draper from the kine being sent to the nonconnected stations, and issued a public apology, saying he was opposed to "having the program being used as a political forum, directly or indirectly." Draper's dismissal was the first public acknowledgement that television had begun blacklisting writers and performers. A network talent chief candidly complained, "Now we spend our time trying to satisfy our top brass that the actors have never been on the left side of the fence. If one of them has even had his picture taken with a known Communist, even if it was several years ago, he's a dead duck as far as we're concerned."

Two weeks after the Draper incident, an obscure senator from Wisconsin, Joseph McCarthy, gave a speech in Wheeling, West Virginia, in which he stated, "I have here in my hand a list of 205 [State Department employees] that were known to the Secretary of State as being members of the Communist Party and are still working and shaping the policy of the State Department."

McCarthy, in fact, did not have any such list, but his bold accusations brought him national attention. Within weeks, McCarthy had been embraced by crusaders against Communism as the popular new leader of the movement. Others had said much the same thing, but McCarthy, a dramatic and crafty individual who did not bother with corroboration or offer the opportunity for rebuttal, went further with his charges. He knew how to appeal to people's gut feelings and fears. Adopting the theory that nobody was too high to accuse, McCarthy offered the public reasons for the rise of Communism: American traitors. Russia had the atomic bomb and some American scientists confessed to passing secrets to the Russians. If the scientific world was rife with traitors, why not the world of government, the military, or, for that matter, the world of broadcasting?

On June 22, the publishers of *Counterattack* issued a special pamphlet, *Red Channels* ("The Report of Communist Influence in Radio and Television"), which was designed as a handy reference source for blacklist-minded networks and sponsors. It contained the names of 151 entertainment personalities said to have ties with the Communist Party. Among those listed were Leonard Bernstein, Lee J. Cobb, Ben Grauer, Pert Kelton, Gypsy Rose Lee, Philip Loeb, Burgess Meredith, Arthur Miller, Zero Mostel, Pete Seeger, Howard K. Smith, and Orson Welles. Like previous efforts by *Counterattack*, many of the listings were based on rumor and hearsay information. In less paranoid times, the audacity of such sweeping accusations without substantiation might have been dismissed outright.

Instead, three days later, the eternal vigilance called for by *Red Channels* seemed completely vindicated as Communist forces invaded South Korea.

10. What's My Crime?

THE KOREAN WAR WAS NOT a television war. Film cameras were too bulky to allow the extensive on-the-spot battlefield reporting that would mark coverage of the war in Vietnam more than a decade later. In 1950, TV news crews barely covered events at home, so there was no reason to expect them to turn up in Korea. More important, the networks saw no need to supplant the official information supplied by the government. A month after the invasion of South Korea by Communist forces from the north, NBC was the only TV network there with a technical crew, and that consisted of merely three cameramen and one reporter. Instead, most television coverage of the Korean War consisted of live pick ups of debates at the United Nations and frequent one-minute battle summaries. The little film footage shown at home came largely from the U.S. Signal Corps.

The idea that television news could be an independent force, like newspapers, had not occurred to most people. Both the government and the networks regarded television as an entertainment medium which, in special cases, could be used by officials to communicate directly with the voters. In this spirit, NBC created a weekly series, *Battle Report Washington,* which was designed for administration spokesmen who wished to address the nation on war-related questions. The government controlled the show and said whatever it wished, without any second-guessing or cross-examination from NBC reporters. To debunk propaganda emanating from Moscow and Beijing, DuMont contributed *Our Secret Weapon—The Truth,* a weekly panel show produced by Freedom House. CBS, in its part to promote civil defense, aired a timely forty-five minute documentary in September, "What To Do During an A-Bomb Attack," hosted by a thirty-three-year-old reporter the network had just picked up from United Press International, Walter Cronkite.

The news from the battlefront was rather grim during the summer of 1950. By the end of August, the North Koreans controlled most of the peninsula; the U.N., American, and South Korean forces held only a small enclave in the south near Pusan. At home, the question of Communist influence in the United States was no longer restricted to the theoretical level. The nation was at war. With American boys "being felled by Red bullets," no sponsor wanted to be charged with "satisfying the Communists" by putting one of their fellow-travelers on national television. Publications such as *Red Channels* became unofficial Madison Avenue bibles on performers with alleged Communist connections and soon the practice of blacklisting again broke out into the open.

At noon on August 27, 1950, the cast of *The Aldrich Family* (a frothy TV situation comedy that had been transferred from radio a year earlier) assembled in NBC's New York studios for a final rehearsal for that night's season premiere. The only news expected to come from that day's broadcast was the response to the performances of two new members of the cast: Richard Tyler who replaced Bob Casey as Henry, and Jean Muir who replaced Lois Wilson as Henry's mother, Alice. The rehearsal never took place. A spokesman from the Young & Rubicam ad agency announced that Jean Muir was being temporarily suspended from the program because of protests the agency had received about her background. Muir, it was learned, had been listed in *Red Channels.* She was cited as one of twenty actors named in grand jury testimony in August 1940 as a member of the Communist Party (an association she denied and an association never proved). She was also said to have been a member of such leftist groups as the Artists' Front to Win the War and the Congress of American Women, and was a subscriber to *Negro Quarterly.* Muir denied knowing about many of the groups and publications, but it did her no good.

On August 29, the show's sponsor, General Foods, dropped Muir permanently from *The Aldrich Family* cast, saying that it made no difference whether she was guilty or not: Muir had become too controversial and her presence on the program could hurt sales. This reasoning became a model for other blacklisting cases. It did not matter how truthful the charges of Red tainting were. The very fact that somebody had been accused at all made them guilty of being too controversial. Muir, like most blacklisted people, spent her energies trying to disprove the charges without realizing that it was already too late.

The extensive news coverage given to Muir's firing combined with the bad battle news from Korea to produce a sharp upswing in the number of sponsors who agreed to let publications such as *Red Channels* be the final arbiter of TV employment. Before the Muir case, a few well-known broadcasting figures had withstood the pressure from the blacklist lobby and defended the rights of their associates. Robert Kinter, the new president of ABC, had rejected demands that he fire Gypsy Rose Lee (a *Red Channels* target), who hosted an ABC radio show, *What Makes You Tick.* Gertrude Berg had persuaded General Foods to allow Philip Loeb (who was also listed in *Red Channels)* to continue to appear as Molly Goldberg's husband, Jake, on *The Goldbergs.* After the Muir firing, even having a friend "upstairs" meant nothing for all but the most popular celebrities.

	7:00	7:30	8:00	8:30	9:00	9:30	10:00	10:30	
M O N	Club Seven	Hollywood Screen Test	TREASURY MEN IN ACTION	DICK TRACY	COLLEGE BOWL	On Trial	ABC Feature Film		ABC
	Stork Club	CBS News	PERRY COMO	LUX VIDEO THEATER	Arthur Godfrey's Talent Scouts	HORACE HEIDT SHOW	The Goldbergs	Studio One		CBS
	Captain Video	local	Susan Raye	Visit With The Armed Forces	Al Morgan Show	Wrestling From Columbia Park With Dennis James			DUM
	Kukla, Fran And Ollie	Roberta Quinlan	Cam. News Caravan	THE SPEIDEL SHOW WITH PAUL WINCHELL	Voice Of Firestone	Lights Out	Robert Montgomery Presents MUSICAL COMEDY TIME	Who Said That?		NBC
T U E	Club Seven	BEULAH	ALL-AMERICAN FOOTBALL GAME	Buck Rogers	BILLY ROSE'S PLAYBILL	CAN YOU TOP THIS?	Life Begins At 80	Roller Derby	ABC
	Stork Club	CBS News	Faye Emerson	PRUDENTIAL FAMILY THEATER Sure As Fate	VAUGHN MONROE CAMEL CARAVAN	Suspense	DANGER	We Take Your Word		CBS
	Captain Video	local	Joan Edwards	Court Of Current Issues	Johns Hopkins Science Review	Cavalcade Of Bands	STAR TIME		DUM
	Kukla, Fran And Ollie	Little Show	Cam. News Caravan	Texaco Star Theater	Fireside Theater	Armstrong Circle Theater	Original Amateur Hour		NBC
W E D	Club Seven	CHANCE OF A LIFETIME	FIRST NIGHTER	DON McNEILL'S TV CLUB	Wrestling From The Rainbo In Chicago (to 12 Midnight)			ABC
	Stork Club	CBS News	PERRY COMO	Arthur Godfrey And His Friends	TELLER OF TALES	The Web	Blue Ribbon Bouts	SPORTS SPOT		CBS
	Captain Video	Manhattan Spotlight	Susan Raye	local	Famous Jury Trials	The Plainclothesman	Broadway To Hollywood Headline Clues	local		DUM
	Kukla, Fran And Ollie	Roberta Quinlan	Cam. News Caravan	FOUR STAR REVUE	Kraft Television Theater	Break The Bank	STARS OVER HOLLYWOOD		NBC
T H U R	Club Seven	The Lone Ranger	Stop The Music	Holiday Hotel	Blind Date	I COVER TIMES SQUARE	Roller Derby (to 11:15)		ABC
	Stork Club	CBS News	Faye Emerson	BURNS & ALLEN SHOW / The Show Goes On	The Show Goes On	Alan Young Show	BIG TOWN	TRUTH OR CONSEQUENCES	NASH AIRFLYTE THEATER		CBS
	Captain Video	Manhattan Spotlight	Joan Edwards	local	ADVENTURES OF ELLERY QUEEN	Boxing From Eastern Parkway With Dennis James			DUM
	Kukla, Fran And Ollie	Little Show	Cam. News Caravan	YOU BET YOUR LIFE	Hawkins Falls	Kay Kyser's Kollege of Musical Knowledge	Martin Kane, Private Eye	WAYNE KING SHOW		NBC
F R I	Club Seven	LIFE WITH LINKLETTER	Twenty Questions	NEW YORK GIANTS FOOTBALL HUDDLE	PULITZER PRIZE PLAYHOUSE	PENTHOUSE PARTY	Studs' Place		ABC
	Stork Club	CBS News	PERRY COMO	Mama	Man Against Crime	Ford Television Theater Hour MAGNAVOX THEATER	STAR OF THE FAMILY	Beat The Clock		CBS
	Captain Video	Manhattan Spotlight	Susan Raye	local	HOLD THAT CAMERA	Hands Of Mystery	Roscoe Karns, Inside Detective	Cavalcade Of Stars		DUM
	Kukla, Fran And Ollie	Roberta Quinlan	Cam. News Caravan	Quiz Kids	We, The People	Versatile Varieties	The Big Story / The Clock	Gillette Cavalcade Of Sports	Greatest Fights	NBC
S A T	SANDY DREAMS	LIFE WITH THE ERWINS	Paul Whiteman's TV Teen Club	Roller Derby			ABC
	Big Top (from 6:30)	Week In Review	Faye Emerson	Ken Murray Show	FRANK SINATRA SHOW	SING IT AGAIN		CBS
	Captain Video	Country Style	SATURDAY NIGHT AT MADISON SQUARE GARDEN			DUM
	Hank McCune	One Man's Family	Jack Carter Show	Your Show Of Shows	Your Hit Parade		NBC
S U N	Paul Whiteman's Goodyear Revue	SHOWTIME U.S.A.	HOLLYWOOD PREMIERE THEATER	SIT OR MISS	Marshall Plan In Action	Faith For Today	OLD FASHIONED REVIVAL HOUR	Youth On The March		ABC
	Gene Autry Show	This Is Show Business	Toast Of The Town	Fred Waring Show	Celebrity Time	What's My Line		CBS
	Starlit Time	RHYTHM RODEO	local	Arthur Murray Show	They Stand Accused		DUM
	Leave It To The Girls	The Aldrich Family	COLGATE COMEDY HOUR	Philco Television Playhouse	Garroway-At-Large	TAKE A CHANCE		NBC

In the wartime atmosphere of Communist expansion into Korea, sponsors and networks were determined to avoid controversial performers at any cost. In December 1950, CBS, still stinging from the charge of being "the most satisfying network to the Communists," went so far as to announce that it would require all 2,500 of its employees to take a loyalty oath. In May 1951, General Foods dropped *The Goldbergs* because of the continued presence of Philip Loeb, even though the program had increased the sales of Sanka coffee an amazing 57% among TV viewers and had occasionally been a top ten TV show. No other sponsor stepped forward and CBS soon took the popular series off the air. NBC picked up options to the program, but also could not find a sponsor willing to accept the show with Loeb. In January 1952, Gertrude Berg gave in and agreed to dismiss Loeb (who was unable to find work elsewhere and later committed suicide). Within a month the show was back on (with Harold J. Stone as Jake) but it never recaptured the following or feeling of its CBS run. The united front put up by sponsors in forcing Loeb off *The Goldbergs* was dramatic proof that blacklisting had become firmly established as an unofficial but iron-clad rule that advertisers, networks, and performers had to accept as part of the broadcasting business.

Networks and ad agencies established elaborate procedures for checking the acceptability of individuals under consideration as writers, directors, and performers. They funneled the names of all prospective talent through a company executive in charge of personnel "security," who would, in turn, consult self-appointed authorities on Communist subversion such as Vincent Hartnett, who had helped write *Red Channels*.

Using as a base the single issue of *Red Channels* (published in June 1950), such consultants provided up-to-date information on further charges of Communist infiltration. The clearance procedure on talent was usually conducted by phone and consisted of little more than the agency or network security chief ticking off a list of names and being told "Yes" or "No" by the consultant after each one. Just as in *Red Channels,* the consultants often relied on hearsay evidence as well as words and actions twisted out of context.

The blacklisting process was well insulated from criticism and rebuttal because the people identified as suspicious were never confronted with the charges. Instead, they were merely told that they were "not right" for the job (too tall, too short, and so forth). It was only after being consistently turned down that individuals realized they had probably been blacklisted, but they faced a nearly impossible situation. There were no formal charges to dispute and no accusers to face. As a result, dozens of people were added to blacklists and effectively denied employment without a word of explanation or formal accusation. The networks viewed this system as a distasteful, but necessary, procedure forced upon them by the sponsors and by the paranoid state of the country. Blacklisting was seen as the networks' way of policing themselves in a wartime situation, when it was wise to be extra cautious anyway.

Though the practice of blacklisting proved to be a traumatic experience for those affected, the viewing public found it only vaguely disturbing. Only a few incidents, such as the Philip Loeb firing, ever received general press coverage. Most Americans simply assumed that people would not be accused of Communist connections unless there was some truth to the charges. Because blacklisting usually only affected second-level TV personalities (the superstars were generally left alone), the general public found the situation easy to ignore. Viewers turned to television for entertainment, not disturbing news, and blacklisting remained a behind-the-scenes internal problem that would have to be resolved by the people within the industry. Even the news of the Jean Muir firing in August 1950 was soon superseded in the public's mind by the glittering events of the new season premieres.

In September, viewers were treated to the most exciting fall season since Milton Berle's first appearance, as the nation's most popular radio stars made the plunge into video. With a great deal of advance publicity, NBC unveiled *The Colgate Comedy Hour* and *Four Star Revue,* two lavishly furnished comedy-variety hours staged live, in huge New York theaters, with flashy sets, music, dancing, and skits. The two shows were the network's vehicles for bringing to TV nine of its top comedy acts: Eddie Cantor, Dean Martin and Jerry Lewis, Fred Allen, Bob Hope, and Bobby Clark on *The Colgate Comedy Hour,* and Jimmy Durante, Ed Wynn, Danny Thomas, and Jack Carson on *Four Star Revue.* In order to avoid the wear and tear of a week-in, week-out routine, each of the nine had a separate production staff and was scheduled to appear as host only about once a month, rotating the chores with the other headliners. This was thought to be the perfect solution to the pressures that frequently faced such performers as Sid Caesar and Milton Berle, whose writers had to come up with material for an entire program every week. Even though the rotating procedure was very expensive ($50,000 a week), NBC felt this was the best way to produce comedy blockbusters and the network confidently slotted the programs against the two most popular shows on CBS: *The Colgate Comedy Hour* aired on Sunday versus the number three rated *Toast of the Town,* while *Four Star Revue* took on the number two ranked *Arthur Godfrey and Friends* on Wednesday.

In September and October, as the stars each made their first appearances, ratings were high and reviewers were ecstatic in their praise of the two shows. It looked as if NBC had pulled off a minor miracle. Though the network had lost a slew of big comedy names to CBS Radio in 1948, NBC appeared to be on the verge of locking up the field of TV comedy. Week after week, viewers saw top-notch material that had taken the stars years to polish and perfect.

Eddie Cantor's first program showcased a "Cavalcade of Cantor," reprising his many hits and ending with Cantor in blackface singing "Ain't She Sweet" and "Ma, He's Making Eyes at Me." Cantor made it a point to give exposure to new talent and during the season he featured the TV debuts of Eddie Fisher and sixteen-year-old Joel Grey, son of veteran borscht-belt comedian Mickey Katz. Dean Martin and Jerry Lewis, who had become big radio and film stars by 1950, brought back to television their highly polished combination of Martin's romantic crooning and Lewis's zany

Studs' Place embodied the "Chicago School" of television with improvisational innovation on a tight budget: *(from left)* front: Studs Terkel, Beverly Younger, and guest John Barclay; back: Chet Roble and Win Stracke. *(Courtesy NBC, Chicago)*

"swell nonsense." Comedy newcomer Norman Lear usually wrote many of their segments. Ed Wynn came in from the West Coast and used the cavernous Center Theater in New York as a TV playground, staging such show-stopping routines as bicycling French singer Edith Piaf around on top of a movable piano. Bob Hope added hilarious visual double takes to his radio style of sharp one-liners and clever skits, while Jimmy Durante drew on his electric personality and unbeatable charm with lady guests.

There were some problems. Danny Thomas, one of the youngest of the nine, did not click at first. His opening monologues were good (Thomas assumed the pose of belligerent underdog), but the rest of the show emerged as static and bland. Instead of projecting his personality to the folks at home, Thomas began to play to the studio audience. He frequently lapsed into wartime flag-waving that came over only as bad corn. By March, though, Thomas gained more confidence and the show improved tremendously. He was helped by better writing and the adoption of the more cohesive "book show" style. In this process, an hour-long comedy-variety show tied together its sketches and music with a thin continuing thread, such as Thomas and his crew taking a train ride to Miami.

The three other stars had more serious problems. Los Angeles comic Jack Carson's shows were replete with bad timing and insufficient planning. Bobby Clark, whose appearances were produced by famed showman Mike Todd, was lost amid a bevy of beautiful legs (a Todd trademark), sloppy slapstick routines, and erratic production work. The big failure, though, was Fred Allen. After being away from audiences for a year (following his radio banishment by *Stop the Music),* Allen seemed rusty, spiteful, and uncomfortable in the role of emcee. He had not performed on the open stage for eighteen years, yet NBC placed him, like the others, in a huge Manhattan theater that often swallowed up guests and hosts that did not come on brash and brassy. Allen was a humorist used to the close, relaxed atmosphere of a radio studio and he never hid his disdain for television, which added an unwanted Scrooge-like element to his already acerbic character. For Allen's long-time radio fans, one of the big letdowns in the television show was the treatment of Allen's Alley. Instead of using talented character actors to flesh out the residents of the famed fictional street, the program presented Ajax Cassidy, Titus Moody, Mrs. Nussbaum, and Senator Claghorn as puppet characters, turning the program into some bizarre sort of Kukla, Fred, and Ollie show.

Of the September array of NBC comedy celebrities, Allen was the first to fall. He left the show in December, citing high blood pressure and issuing a parting blast at the network, which he said had forced the revue format on him. "I'm through with this kind of television," Allen said, adding that if he returned it would be in a low-key thirty-minute format closer to the style used by Chicago's Dave Garroway.

CBS also brought a number of radio stars to TV in the 1950–51 season, including some that had been lured to the network in the Paley's Comet talent raids of 1948. Edgar Bergen, Jack Benny, and Bing Crosby did occasional specials, while Frank Sinatra had a weekly series running against *Your Show of Shows.* Despite the big budget variety shows in its schedule, though, CBS felt that situation comedy was a more stable television form that would be easier to exploit in the long run. The network felt such programs could overcome some of the weaknesses of the variety format by presenting viewers with continuing characters, settings, and stories, rather than week after week of unrelated skits, which often looked like sixty minutes of random activity. Consequently, CBS, as it had previously done in radio, concentrated on sitcoms, trying to give its programming a different "feel" from NBC and hoping to develop a blockbuster hit that could push it ahead of NBC in the TV

ratings race. In the fall of 1950, however, the network had only one new sitcom ready, *The George Burns and Gracie Allen Show.* Even that aired only on alternate Thursdays, live from New York.

George Burns and Gracie Allen performed an effortless transition into television, bringing to the new medium the characters they had developed through twenty-five years in vaudeville and on radio. They were a real life husband and wife comedy team and they played themselves in a domestic setting. George was the long-suffering straightman and Gracie was the mistress of malapropism who seemingly was on a different plane of reality from the rest of the world. The structure of the series was simple: Using a very thin plot line to hold each episode together, George and Gracie interacted with each other and various members of the supporting cast, in effect staging their familiar comedy routines throughout the program. George described the show as having "more plot than a variety show and not as much as a wrestling match."

The Burns and Allen Show drew elements from both Jack Benny and Ozzie and Harriet. Like Benny, George and Gracie portrayed performers who put on a weekly comedy show, but while they often talked about their fictional television program, they never got near the studio. Instead, like Ozzie and Harriet, they used their showbiz identities as a springboard for behind-the-scenes homelife escapades. In these, George and Gracie were joined by their announcer, Harry Von Zell, and their next door neighbors, Blanche Morton (Bea Benaderet) and her straight-laced C.P.A. husband, Harry (played by a succession of actors: Hal March, John Brown, Fred Clark, and Larry Keating). Each week's complications were very simple, inevitably the result of some household or showbiz misunderstanding by Gracie. Though in some ways the program's plots were very much like Hollywood's "screwball" theatrical comedies and the first wave of West Coast filmed TV sitcoms, the excellent writing and emphasis on the comic characters and routines raised the show far above such routine fare. Even when the program became a weekly series in 1952, moving out West and onto film, it retained its high quality production and unique point of view. Gracie Allen was not a dumb blonde or a two-faced schemer. She merely followed her own illogical logic to its nonsense conclusions, leaving everyone who crossed her path totally confused. "If she made sense," George quipped, "I'd still be selling ties."

While Gracie was the comic center of the program, George's special outlook added extra flavor. Going beyond the simple role of straightman to Gracie, George took mischievous delight in confusing people himself because, of all the characters in the show, George alone acknowledged that they were all doing a comedy program and that ultimately none of the complications were meant to be taken seriously. Looking directly into the camera, he made frequent witty asides to the audience, delivering both comic monologues and comments on the story to that point. George usually knew what everybody else in the show was doing, occasionally getting this information just as the home viewer did, by watching the program on TV while it was still in progress. He became a special confidant to the audience at home, acting as both a character and an omniscient observer. As a result, *The Burns and Allen Show* emerged as a relaxed, leisurely visit with some very funny people.

Though the show did well in its time slot against tough competition, the program was not a runaway hit in its early years. CBS's sitcom strategy had yet to be proved for television. In fact, by January 1951, there was not one sitcom listed among TV's top ten rated shows. According to the A.C. Nielsen Company (which had taken over the Hooper ratings service in early 1950), NBC dominated the television ratings chart with comedy-variety hours,

George Burns and Gracie Allen, successful radio stars since 1932, made an effortless transition to CBS television in 1950. *(Courtesy George Burns)*

drama anthologies, and Friday night boxing. CBS was represented at the top of "the Nielsens" with a few of its own variety, drama, and sports shows, but the network continued to bank on sitcoms for the future. In the summer of 1951, when most of the comedy-variety stars were on vacation, CBS presented a new show that it felt would usher in the age of presented a new show that it felt would usher in the age of sitcom supremacy on television: *The Amos 'n Andy Show.*

Since May 1949, CBS had been scouring the country in search of an all-black cast for the TV version of radio's *Amos 'n Andy,* building as much interest and anticipation as possible. With its proven success and viewer loyalty from radio, the series seemed a good choice by CBS for a possible breakthrough in television situation comedy. Created by Freeman Gosden and Charles Correll, two white men, *Amos 'n Andy* had been one of radio's first nationwide sensations, becoming a national obsession soon after arriving on the NBC network in 1929. People planned their lives around the 7:00–7:15 P.M. weekday radio broadcasts. Movie theaters altered show times and some piped in the program for patrons.

Amos 'n Andy had begun as the humorous adventures of two black men, focusing on their home lives, friends, and the funny situations they got into. Amos Jones (portrayed by Gosden) was the respectable straightman, a hard-working, church-going solid citizen, happily married with two children. Andy Brown (Correll) was the good natured comic foil, a pudgy addlebrained bachelor. They lived in the Harlem area of New York City and operated the "Fresh Air Taxi Cab Company, Incorpulated," which consisted of one rundown old car that did not even have a windshield. Amos did most of the work while Andy loafed or chased women. They

both socialized with George Stevens, nicknamed the Kingfish, who was the head of the Mystic Knights of the Sea Lodge and a fast talking conniver. The Kingfish (also played by Gosden) was always ready to fleece Andy with some new get-rich-quick scheme and, as the series evolved in the 1930s, he began to supplant Amos, whose character was a bit too straight for many comic situations and misunderstandings. Governor Huey Long of Louisiana, a great fan of the show, even adopted the nickname Kingfish for himself.

Though the Kingfish put on a boastful front as a big-time operator, his schemes were generally penny ante manipulations and he was caught as the fall guy almost as often as Andy. Over the years, the Kingfish became the main character of the series, with more and more attention given to his home life. There the Kingfish was just a hen-pecked husband, dominated by his wife, Sapphire (Ernestine Wade), and hounded by his sour mother-in-law (Amanda Randolph). As a result, the Kingfish emerged as an earthy, uneducated, but lovable conniver rather than as a cruel and malicious schemer. The only chance he ever had to show off was down at the lodge where he could always talk Andy into another hair-brained venture or berate Lightnin', the lodge's shuffling dim-witted janitor.

Like most hit radio comedies of the era, *Amos 'n Andy* had its share of stock phrases. During the program's heyday in the 1930s, many of these became part of the nation's vocabulary, including "I'se regusted!" "Ow-wah, ow-wah, ow-wah!" "Now ain't that sumpin'!" and "Holy mackerel, Andy!" Even into the 1940s when it became a half-hour weekly series, *Amos 'n Andy* was still a top ten radio show with a strong following. The program was a logical first choice for CBS's famed Paley's Comet talent raids of 1948 and the network had high hopes that a TV version of *Amos 'n Andy* would be just as successful and long-lasting as the radio show. Freeman Gosden and Charles Correll, who did their radio show from Los Angeles, personally supervised the long casting process and they produced the TV pilot film for the series, on the West Coast, at the then expansive cost of $40,000.

Amos 'n Andy was the first important television situation comedy filmed in Los Angeles, and it used a program formula that was identical to the vanguard West Coast filmed sitcoms of the previous season, only with a bigger budget and better overall production. These filmed series, like Hollywood's theatrical "screwball" comedy films, relied on simple cardboard characters placed in silly situations that could be easily repeated and endlessly exploited. In this form of comedy, the situation became all important. The stereotyped characters ran through the paces of the plot as if it were an obstacle course, serving as mouth-pieces for one-liners as they reacted to the absurd events. This formula had worked well for movie and radio comedies and CBS thought that *Amos 'n Andy* could produce television's first smash hit sitcom with this style.

Like the formula screwball comedies, the TV series relied on misunderstood situations and misfired schemes, ploys that allowed even the most trivial actions to become the basis for an outlandish story. In one episode, the Kingfish (Tim Moore) discovered that Andy (Spencer Williams) was in possession of a rare coin (a nickel worth $250) and tricked him into giving it up. However, the Kingfish then mistakenly used that nickel at a public pay phone to call a rare coin dealer, so he talked Andy into helping him to break open the coin box with a crowbar to retrieve it. The two were caught and taken to court, but were soon rescued by their level-headed friend, Amos (Alvin Childress), who helped convince the judge to release them. Another week, the overage Kingfish received a draft notice intended for another, much younger, George Stevens. He felt honored to serve his country at middle age and proudly reported for the Army physical. When the Army turned him down, the Kingfish

September 7, 1950

Truth or Consequences. (CBS). After ten years on radio, Ralph Edwards brings his popular audience participation show to television, intact. "Consequences" on the first video episode include a wife throwing trick knives at her husband, and the sentimental reunion of a wounded G.I. and his mother (after a thirty-one-month separation).

September 18, 1950

NBC Comics. (NBC). Animated cartoons come to network television in a fifteen-minute late afternoon weekday program made up of four three-minute cartoon series: "Danny Match" (a young private eye), "Space Barton" (interplanetary adventures), "Johnny and Mr. Do-Right" (a school boy and his dog), and "Kid Champion" (a young boxer).

September 25, 1950

The Kate Smith Show. (NBC). NBC succeeds with the first major venture in afternoon network television: an hour of music and variety.

October 6, 1950

Pulitzer Prize Playhouse. (ABC). Alex Segal directs ABC's first major dramatic series. The acting and writing are top-notch, with scripts from a number of Pulitzer Prize winning authors such as Maxwell Anderson, Thornton Wilder, and James Michener.

October 16, 1950

Following the lead of NBC and Kate Smith, CBS jumps into afternoon television with two hour-long variety shows. Garry Moore (moving from evenings) and Robert Q. Lewis are the hosts.

December 15, 1950

Hear It Now. (CBS Radio). Ed Murrow is reunited with Fred Friendly (recently signed to CBS) and together they create "a document for the ear."

felt ashamed and had Andy hide him at the lodge, where he wrote postcards "from training camp" and sent them to Sapphire.

Inevitably, a few words of explanation cleared up such situations, and the characters were ready to do it all again the following week. These simple stories were silly but funny, and the actors were good in their comic roles. (Ernestine Wade as Sapphire and Amanda Randolph as Sapphire's Mama came directly from the radio version.) However, instead of giving CBS its first important sitcom success, *Amos 'n Andy* created nothing but problems once it hit the air.

Because *Amos 'n Andy* was the first major television sitcom series from Los Angeles, the inherent weaknesses of the screwball style were painfully evident. Characters in West Coast comedies were exaggerated comic caricatures living in a fantasy world of formula humor. Even though *Amos 'n Andy* was much better than such dismal TV vehicles as *The Hank McCune Show,* East Coast critics still had serious reservations about the form. However, *Amos 'n Andy* faced an additional problem. Because the series was also the first television program to deal exclusively with blacks, the underlying silliness of the characters was interpreted by some as a putdown directed specifically against blacks. Protests began almost immediately after the program premiered. The National Association for the Advancement of Colored People (NAACP) blasted the series, complaining that it "depicts the Negro in a

stereotyped and derogatory manner … it strengthens the conclusion among uninformed or prejudiced people that Negroes and other minorities are inferior, lazy, dumb, and dishonest."

Though there had been a great deal of ballyhoo over the search for an all-black cast for *Amos 'n Andy,* the fact that the performers were black was almost secondary to the types of plots and characters in the series. Both were, in fact, totally interchangeable with scores of "white" sitcoms that both preceded and postdated *Amos 'n Andy.* Gosden and Correll had never used the incongruity of white men playing black roles as a source of laughs, and the approach in the television version also avoided situations that might have been staged as cheap racial putdowns. *Amos 'n Andy* was set up in an essentially all-black world, where whites were rarely seen. If the Kingfish was outsmarted, it was by a black con artist, not a white one. There were black lawyers and black doctors to balance off black stooges. As in any screwball comedy, the stories depended on misunderstandings and crazy antics by such tried and true stereotypes as a money-hungry bumbler, a slow-witted second banana, a shrewish wife, and a battleaxe mother-in-law. In *Amos 'n Andy,* these familiar comic caricatures just happened to be black. Nonetheless, the NAACP was outraged that the first major television program to feature blacks prominently was a screwball situation comedy, a form which included as a matter of course comic caricatures that the organization was particularly sensitive to seeing identified with blacks. For example, the minor supporting character of Lightnin' (Horace Stewart), the janitor at the lodge, was shiftless, lazy, and dumb. Worse yet, he spoke with a high-pitched drawl ("Yazzah") and walked with a lazy shuffle.

Reacting to the characters and the stories, the NAACP urged a boycott of the show's sponsor, Blatz beer. The boycott never caught on, but then again neither did the show. Television's *Amos 'n Andy* never attracted anywhere near the loyalty and support of the radio version, and for CBS it was an expensive disappointment. Instead of dethroning Milton Berle and comedy-variety, *Amos 'n Andy* secured only marginal ratings and, after two years, the show was taken off the air. Fifteen years later, in response to continued sensitivity over the program's perceived racial tone, CBS even withdrew *Amos 'n Andy* from circulation as an off-network rerun.

In a way, *Amos 'n Andy* was kicked off the air for the wrong reason. Though its black stereotyped characters were gone, the underlying assumptions for West Coast screwball sitcoms remained. In that light, *Amos 'n Andy* was merely the harbinger of a successful trend, with its black characters no more nor less demeaning than their white equivalents. Throughout the decade that followed, similar screwball series flourished featuring white performers, while a generation of black talent was rarely offered another opportunity to helm a broad comedy.

Instead, if cast at all, black performers often found themselves in domestic roles, such as in the setting for another new West Coast filmed sitcom with a black character in the title role, ABC's *Beulah.* Arriving in October 1950, six months earlier than *Amos 'n Andy,* the series received far less attention, even though it, too, dealt in old-fashioned stereotypes. While *Amos 'n Andy* presented an essentially all black world that included business professionals as well as sitcom schemers, *Beulah* cast blacks almost exclusively as servants in a suburban setting that was barely removed from the antebellum world of "Gone With the Wind."

Beulah's taint of racial deprecation had begun on radio. The character of Beulah was created by a white man, Marlin Hurt, and had first appeared in 1944 as part of *The Fibber McGee and Molly Show.* In 1945, ABC Radio gave Beulah "her" own show, with Hurt continuing the character in the new series. Each week, he got his first big laugh by exploiting the incongruity between his radio character and his physical appearance. After an introduction by the studio announcer leading up to Beulah's first appearance, Hurt, previously unseen by the studio audience, jumped into place and yelled, in character, "Somebody bawl for Beulah?" The sight of a small white man with the voice of a large black woman never failed to touch off a roar of laughter from the studio audience. When Beulah shifted to CBS Radio in 1947, a real black woman (Hattie McDaniel) took the title role, but the program never lost its condescending attitude, even in the transfer to television.

In the television version, McDaniel played Beulah for only a few episodes in the middle of the run, with Ethel Waters (followed by Louise Beavers) taking the lead. No matter the performer, Beulah remained the much put-upon "Mammy" for a bland suburban white middle-class family, running their day-to-day domestic lives as "queen of the kitchen." Beulah was presented as a reassuringly warm and non-threatening woman who often rescued the "masters of the household" from their own simple misunderstandings and complications. Still, Beulah was ultimately just hired help, whose path came through the back door. In the program's supporting cast, there were no noticeable black professionals; instead, Beulah had a nondescript shiftless boyfriend, Bill (Percy Harris), and a scatter-brained girlfriend, Oriole (Butterfly McQueen). Unlike *Amos 'n Andy*, *Beulah*'s bland stories and setting saved it from being an obvious target for harsh racial criticism at the time. Yet, the program did little to advance the range of television roles for black comic performers as it reinforced safe but still stereotypical images, relegating even the title character to a subservient position.

The Los Angeles-produced filmed sitcoms introduced in the 1950–51 season were, at best, only marginally successful. Yet there would be more. As the coast-to-coast coaxial cable neared completion, television executives prepared to link the operations of the two centers of popular entertainment in America, New York and Los Angeles. Increased Hollywood production was inevitable as the East and West branches of television moved into a new phase of their battle for dominance in the medium.

With the final hookup of the East-West cable targeted for the fall of 1951, the networks eliminated practically all of their remaining Chicago-based productions. Executives found that it made more sense to draw on the resources of the two coasts instead. New York-based producers had tremendous expertise with complicated in-studio productions, especially live drama, plus a rich stock of Broadway performers to draw from. Los Angeles had talent proficient in filmed productions and was also the home of the top stars in radio comedy and variety (many of whom had temporarily relocated out East for the move to television). Chicago programming was totally expendable. Throughout the season, most of the Chicago-based variety programs (usually unsponsored anyway) were replaced by more easily sold programs live from New York or on film from Los Angeles. Even *Garroway at Large,* the most popular of the Chicago television stable, found itself without a sponsor at the end of the season.

One of the last successful network programs to come out of Chicago was a low-key new game show, DuMont's *Down You Go,* hosted by a professor of English from Northwestern University, Bergen Evans. Even though it was created by Louis G. Cowan, who had conceived such flashy vehicles as *Stop the Music, Down You Go* had a distinctively different flavor from other network programs, chiefly because of its Chicago-based production. Using fresh, unknown talent rather than a panel of familiar big name celebrities, *Down You Go* emerged as one of the wittiest, most relaxed game shows on television. The mechanics of the game were simple: Using clues provided by Evans, the four panelists had

to guess a slogan, sentence, word, or phrase, filling in each word, letter by letter. For "I don't want to set the world on fire," Evans suggested that this was "the usual excuse for those who have no burning ambition." Evans and the panel members obviously enjoyed working with each other and their personal charm and effortless good humor consistently came through to the home audience. The program stood out favorably against the competition and ran on DuMont for four years, subsequently appearing briefly on each of the other three networks as well.

Though the top rated programs in the 1950–51 season were variety shows, drama anthologies, and sports contests, the networks usually selected a game, panel, or quiz show format to fill holes in their schedules. Such programs were easy to stage, inexpensive, and practically interchangeable. Only a few ever stood out. Besides *Down You Go*, there were two other distinctive game shows that season, *You Bet Your Life* and *Strike It Rich.*

Strike It Rich began on television as a CBS daytime offering and was soon added to the network's nighttime schedule as well. Hosted by Warren Hull and occasionally by Monty Hall, *Strike It Rich* described itself as "the quiz show with a heart," though critics claimed it merely exploited the weaknesses of contestants in order to garner high ratings. The program featured people in need, including such unfortunates as someone who needed money for an expensive operation, a childless couple looking for an orphan to adopt, and a widow needing funds to start a new life. After answering a few simple qualifying questions, the contestants had to stand in front of the audience, tell their stories, and plead for assistance.

December 25, 1950
The Steve Allen Show. (CBS). "Steverino" shifts to television (weekday evenings) with a simple format that will serve him well for years: He plays the piano, interviews guests, and talks to the audience. The following May, Allen is moved to noontime and his show expands to an hour.

December 25, 1950
"One Hour In Disneyland." (NBC). Walt Disney's first television special. He quickly displays a great blend of television showmanship and commercialism, incorporating plugs for upcoming Disney films in a "best of Disney" retrospective.

January 20, 1951
The Cisco Kid. Duncan Renaldo plays a Mexican equivalent to the Lone Ranger in a syndicated adventure series distributed to the local stations by Ziv. Just to be prepared, the episodes are filmed in color.

April 23, 1951
Ed Thorgensen and the News. (DuMont). The second of DuMont's three attempts at its own nightly news show. This version uses a top newsreel announcer, but settles for a very cheap set (even by DuMont's standards). One month later, the program is gone.

May 14, 1951
Time for Ernie. (NBC). Ernie Kovacs makes it to network television in a brief afternoon series. In July, he is moved into the *Kukla, Fran and Ollie* time period.

August 24, 1951
After two months under the leadership of Jack E. Leonard, *Broadway Open House* is closed, ending (for the moment) NBC's experiment in late night television.

Senator Estes Kefauver *(seated, left)* campaigning in the 1952 New Hampshire presidential primary. He used the notoriety gained from televised crime hearings in 1951 to mount a serious bid for the Democratic nomination. *(National Archives)*

The loudness of the applause by the audience in response to their presentations determined who received the most money. Afterward, home viewers were invited to phone in pledges for those who still needed additional help.

Strike It Rich regularly crossed the line between entertainment and exploitation. Reacting to the absurd mechanics of the program, humorist Al Capp proposed that the show use a Misery Meter which would measure the strength of each tale of woe. The scale began with "sad," and worked its way through "depressing," "heartbreaking," "sickening," and "sickeningly heartbreaking" before reaching the ultimate: "unbearably tragic." The program was regularly criticized for its maudlin tone, but the most dramatic expression of outrage took place in the studio control room one day when the show's director was ordered to broadcast a tight closeup of the legs of a crippled person attempting to walk. Instead, the director silently stood up, walked out of the control room, and never returned.

You Bet Your Life, the season's most successful new game show, was far removed from such tactics. The program had begun on radio as a vehicle for the ad-lib wit of Groucho Marx, and continued unchanged in the move to television. Prior to *You Bet Your Life,* Groucho had been a flop on radio in four short-lived scripted programs. In 1947, John Guedel, the creator of Art Linkletter's audience participation shows *People Are Funny* and *House Party,* talked Groucho into trying the quiz show format. At first Groucho resisted, feeling that the role of quizmaster was beneath his professional dignity. Once the program started rolling, it quickly became apparent that Guedel had found the perfect setting for Groucho's wit. The quiz portion of *You Bet Your Life* was unimportant; it served as the excuse to have pairs of contestants brought out to be interviewed by Groucho before "playing the game." Groucho did not see the contestants before they were introduced by announcer George Fenneman, so Groucho's comments once they met were spontaneous.

In order to assume control over such a potentially volatile for-

mat, the show's producers carefully selected the contestants, looking for people that could play well against Groucho. For further control, one hour of material was recorded live before a studio audience, then edited down to a thirty minute program. This allowed the producers to assemble a tight package and to discard unsuccessful exchanges and exceptionally risqué comments. The format clicked and *You Bet Your Life* became a top ten radio show for NBC. When the program came to television, the producers merely added a camera. Television viewers could then see Groucho's leering eyes whenever a beautiful woman appeared, and the flustered attempts at composure by any contestant whom fate had saddled with a funny-sounding name—a favorite target of Groucho's quips. *You Bet Your Life* continued on television virtually unchanged until the early 1960s, a monument to Groucho's creativity and Guedel's insight.

While *You Bet Your Life* shot into the top ten for NBC, Groucho's brother, Chico Marx, bombed in *The College Bowl,* an odd musical comedy on ABC. Cast as the owner of a campus malt shop, Chico played essentially the same type of character as he did in the successful Marx Brothers feature films, singing nonsense songs at the piano and cracking horrible puns in Italian dialect. He was surrounded by a crew of young singers and dancers (including eighteen-year-old Andy Williams) who played the local "campus types" that hung around the malt shop. There was constant singing, dancing, and light humor, but the scripts were terrible, the staging lackluster, and the program never caught fire.

Another major disappointment for ABC was the performance of a TV film version of Chester Gould's comic strip crimefighter, Dick Tracy. The show was unable to duplicate the success of ABC's only big hit, *The Lone Ranger,* even though it possessed many of the same pulp adventure elements in an urban crime setting. From its beginning in 1931, the Dick Tracy comic strip presented a violent world of clearcut good guys, bad guys, crime, and punishment. Tracy joined the police force as a plainclothes detective following the murder of his fiancée's father, and his pursuit of bizarre criminals such as Flattop, Prune Face, and Pouch inevitably included a graphic, fatal shoot-out. Through the 1930s and 1940s, the comic strip inspired a successful radio show and a series of theatrical films starring Ralph Byrd. Yet the television series, which even had Byrd repeating the title role, never took off.

One unexpected problem the producers faced was that when the series began filming in early 1950, Congress was going through one of its first seizures against television violence. Word was flashed to Los Angeles to tone down Tracy's escapades. Consequently, the first two episodes of *Dick Tracy* shown in September were very mild. The third and fourth episodes, filmed after the congressional heat had cooled, brought Tracy back to his more familiar tough guy stature. The fifth show featured two murders, a gun fight, and a fist fight. The sixth show opened with a hanging. Even so, the program failed to make a dent in Arthur Godfrey's Monday night audience.

ABC's poor showing in the fall served to compound the network's shaky financial position. While NBC and CBS battled for ratings points at the top, ABC was fighting for its life. The network had saved some money the previous season by substantially cutting back its schedule, but when ABC resumed seven-day-a-week programming, it found the money and ratings problems worse than ever. Though ABC had a few hits such as *The Lone Ranger* and *Stop the Music,* the rest of its programs were regularly trounced by the other networks. Worse yet, all through 1950, TV production costs multiplied at a staggering rate and, for the first time, the networks' television budgets surpassed their radio budgets. All the other networks pumped money into TV broadcasting from other, more profitable, parts of their corporate setup. NBC was part of RCA, CBS owned Columbia Records, and DuMont made TV sets. ABC had to sink or swim with its radio and TV operations alone.

ABC saw no hope for a quick upswing in either the number of viewers or the number of affiliates. The outbreak of the Korean War had forced a sharp reduction in TV set production, and the FCC's unending freeze on new TV station construction had halted such expansion. ABC decided that if a new source of income was not found, the network would not be able to continue. In May 1951, after flirting with a merger offer from CBS, ABC announced plans to merge with United Paramount Theaters. United Paramount had been formed when Paramount Pictures was ordered by the Supreme Court to divest itself of the ownership of movie theaters while the studio continued to produce films. Besides offering ABC much-needed cash, United Paramount had a number of officials steeped in Hollywood techniques and tradition. It was felt that such an influx of West Coast showmanship could give the young and struggling ABC a distinctive flair, contrasting with the New York orientation of the other three networks.

The parties asked the FCC to approve the merger before September to allow ABC to begin the next season on a new footing. Perhaps they should have specified which September they intended, because two seasons slipped by while the FCC sat on the merger request. The FCC was still struggling with the comparatively simple decision of whether or not to accept the Paramount Pictures-United Paramount split. Because the FCC repeatedly had contended that Paramount Pictures controlled DuMont, the ABC request would go nowhere until the FCC decided whether to accept United Paramount as a separate entity. Only then would the commission get into the question of whether a theater chain should own a television network. As the bureaucrats at the FCC chewed on these questions, ABC watched its financial reserve sink lower and lower.

Though the FCC postponed a decision on ABC's merger request, during the 1950–51 season the commission ended, for the moment, ten years of deliberation on another topic: color. In October 1950, the FCC voted to approve CBS's noncompatible process as the country's official color television system. The Korean War and the freeze on station construction had temporarily halted the growth in TV set sales but, even so, when the decision was announced there were nine million black and white sets in use that would have to be scrapped and replaced by new color models. Even though RCA had, in the fall of 1949, produced a working, totally compatible color system, the FCC justified its decision by pointing out that CBS's was better in quality and ready at the moment. The RCA system appeared to be a few more years from commercial viability.

RCA appealed the FCC decision, taking the battle all the way to the Supreme Court. The legal wrangling delayed CBS's commercial color debut for more than seven months and, during that time, RCA decided to carry the fight into the public sector. In December 1950, RCA called in television critics from the major newspapers for a demonstration of its compatible color system. The improvement from the previous RCA public exhibitions was substantial and the critics noted that there was only a slight difference in quality between the CBS and RCA systems. This effectively changed the nature of the color debate. Some people observed that the FCC had chosen noncompatible color just as a compatible color system was nearing completion. They questioned the wisdom of asking the nation's viewers either to invest in expensive new color sets or to miss out on important chunks of color TV programming that could not be picked up by black and white models. In May of 1951, however, the Supreme Court turned down RCA's legal appeal and it appeared that CBS had won. Most TV set manufacturers said they would go along with the decision and produce the new color sets when there was an evident public demand for them.

At 4:30 P.M. Monday, June 25, 1951, Arthur Godfrey walked onto the stage of CBS's Grand Central Station studios and was seen in lovely, spinning disk, noncompatible color by the 400 guests watching on eight color sets at CBS, and by other viewers gathered around the thirty color receivers then available in the New York City area. The program was broadcast in color to Boston, Philadelphia, Baltimore, and Washington, though it is doubtful that anyone outside the control rooms of those CBS affiliates saw anything but jumbled static. Sixteen sponsors (such as the makers of multitinted automobiles and vibrantly colored lipsticks) paid $10,000 for the privilege of being seen by a handful of people. CBS felt color would follow the progression of black and white television the previous decade: Early test programs would be seen by next to nobody, a few brave sponsors would stake out some turf in this goldmine of the future, and eventually a few hit shows would lure the reluctant public into the color TV showrooms.

Following the opening day special, no hit shows turned up. No brave sponsors presented themselves. The war-conscious public refused to give up its old black and white sets and showed complete apathy toward color television. CBS soon realized that the FCC approval had come too late. The network had a multi-million dollar lemon on its hands. In October 1951, National Production Authority chairman Charles Wilson (whose top aide was CBS chairman William Paley) politely asked CBS to cease all color television operations for the duration of the national emergency resulting from the war in Korea. Before the print was dry on Wilson's request, CBS graciously agreed to this virtual death sentence for the government-ordered monopoly it had fought so long for. Everybody said publicly that the halt in color operations was just temporary and the FCC continued to limit tests of compatible color to outside regular broadcast hours. Within the television industry, however, it was felt that noncompatible color was dead.

The public's indifference to color television had nothing to do with its feelings toward TV in general. Viewing levels were greater than ever. In fact, three months before color's inauspicious debut, interest in a new television programming event swept the country. Alternately labeled "What's My Crime" and "Underworld Talent Scouts," this program had everything a hit TV show needed: a cast Hollywood could not beat, an ad-libbed script better than any drama, and free publicity from the morning papers. There was suspense, personality conflict, suspicious motivation, and real life human drama. The program was the traveling road show staged by the Senate Crime Committee, Senator Estes Kefauver, chairman.

The committee's investigation into organized crime began to attract attention in early February 1951, when local Detroit TV coverage of the proceedings pulled in top ratings. The story broke into the headlines later that month in St. Louis when nationally known betting expert James J. Carroll refused to testify if television cameras were present. Carroll's lawyer called such television coverage "an invasion of privacy," and observed that his client, "may be ridiculed and embarrassed as a result." When the hearings moved to New York City in mid-March, all the TV networks decided to run them live, during their nearly empty daytime hours. Over the course of the broadcasts, daytime viewing reached twenty times its usual level. TV viewing parties sprang up and people suddenly became aware of the previously untapped power that television had for conveying and even creating events.

Committee Counsel Rudolph Halley and Senator Kefauver became instant celebrities as they probed into the shady activities of such underworld bigwigs as Frank Erickson, Frank Costello, and Joe Adonis before millions of television viewers. One of the most dramatic and damaging of the sessions took place when Frank Costello, like James Carroll, said that he would not testify with television cameras present. Unlike Carroll, Costello then modified his stance and agreed to a compromise: the network cameras could show only his hands during the testimony. In a strange way, this arrangement backfired for Costello because it attracted much more attention than if his face had been routinely shown like the others. Instead, viewers were given an eerie contrast between a calm voice seeking exoneration and the fidgeting hands of a clearly nervous

man. After hours of intense questioning under the hot TV lights, Costello said, "I am not going to answer another question!" and walked out of the committee room. Thirty million viewers saw him leave and the committee cited Costello for contempt.

In spite of the publicity and increased daytime viewing from the hearings, the networks were happy when they came to an end. Extended broadcasting without commercial sponsors meant losing money. In fact, when a night session was held, NBC and CBS stuck with their regular programming and only ABC and DuMont, both with few sponsored shows, continued the broadcasts.

Television's coverage of the Kefauver hearings was called the advent of electronic journalism. Had the hearings been reported only in the newspapers and on the brief nightly TV news shows, they would not have received such wide public attention. Instead, the issues and personalities involved became household topics simply because they had been on live TV. One reviewer marveled that "[Television] has shown that it can arouse public interest to a degree which virtually beggars immediate description." With the next presidential election little more than a year away, politicians with foresight realized that television could be something more than a mute conveyor of convention hoopla.

The Kefauver hearings had other peculiar forms of fallout. The networks saw that there was a tremendous audience waiting for daytime broadcasting and they prepared to exploit it. They also increased the number of crime dramas about the mob throughout the prime time schedule. Senator Kefauver decided to use his newly acquired national celebrity status to run for the Democratic presidential nomination the following year. Though he lost that bid, Kefauver was a serious contender right up to the party's nominating convention.

Perhaps the man who made the best use of his association with the televised hearings was Halley, the committee counsel. In September he became host of the network show *Crime Syndicated*. Even though he appeared only at the beginning and end of the program, laboriously reading cue cards, the exposure was enough to help secure his election in November as president of the New York City Council. Now, *this* was a facet of television that politicians could really understand.

11. The Thaw

AT 10:30 P.M. (EASTERN TIME), September 4, 1951, coast-to-coast network television became a reality. In the fifty-two cities joined by the coaxial cable, 94 of the 107 television stations then on the air in the United States broadcast the same event: President Harry Truman's address to the opening session of the Japanese Peace Treaty Conference at San Francisco's Opera House.

Before the completion of the Western cable hookup, only 45% of the American homes with a television could be reached by live network TV. Afterward, 95% of the TV homes, from Atlanta north to Boston, west to San Francisco, and south to San Diego, could all watch the same thing at the same time. By the opening of the political conventions in the summer of 1952, only one TV station (KOB in Albuquerque, New Mexico) was not hooked in with the national networks.

All four television networks carried President Truman's speech from the West Coast and, at the end of September, regular commercial coast-to-coast programming began with a string of star-studded variety hours from Hollywood. Still, the most effective demonstration of the electronic magic of transcontinental sight did not take place until Sunday afternoon, November 18, on the premiere broadcast of CBS's *See It Now* (a television version of Edward R. Murrow's respected *Hear It Now* radio news documentary series). On that first show, Murrow sat before two television monitors in CBS's New York City Studio 41 and asked director Don Hewitt to punch up a live signal from the West Coast on one monitor, while showing a scene from New York City on the other. Instantly, a panorama of the Golden Gate Bridge, Alcatraz, and the San Francisco skyline appeared alongside the view of the Brooklyn Bridge, Manhattan, and New York Bay. For the first time, Americans could see both coasts of their vast continent at once, live and instantaneously. Murrow, a man not easily moved, said he was "very impressed" with this technical miracle, and that he expected a lot from TV.

The biggest change in programming caused by the coast-to-coast link was the immediate availability of Los Angeles as a live origination point. Performers who had moved East to host the top variety shows on NBC and CBS immediately transferred back to the West Coast, where their film and radio careers had long been centered. Television was at last ready for coast-to-coast operation. More big money sponsors began to buy television commercial time because there were, via cable, enough markets capable of receiving the networks' signals to justify the investment. With more people tuning in and more sponsors interested in purchasing spots, the cost of advertising on a prime time show shot up. On NBC and CBS, the two most successful networks, prime time was soon filled with sponsors and, by the end of 1951, their network TV profits exceeded those of their network radio operations for the first time. Television also registered an overall profit in 1951, with 93 of the 108 TV stations on the air finishing in the black.

Yet even amid this expansion there was disappointment. Though DuMont and ABC also saw their network television incomes increase, they were far behind CBS and NBC. The continuing FCC freeze on new stations still kept many cities without television at all, or limited to just a few stations. Pacific residents, who for years had endured the low quality kines of live East Coast fare, found themselves inconvenienced even with the live cable connection. Due to the difference in the time zones, the top live prime time hits began at 5:00 P.M. out West so that the East Coast viewers could see the shows at 8:00 P.M.

The biggest disappointment voiced by many viewers was that, aside from the technical magic of bridging the cross-country chasm, there was very little excitement over the approach of the 1951–52 season. For the first time since the arrival of Milton Berle more than three years before, the networks' fall line-ups consisted primarily of familiar shows returning for another season. Compared to the avalanche of superstar talent that had descended upon TV for the first time during the 1950–51 season, the upcoming season seemed very dull. With most of radio's top talent on television, the period of continuous innovation and expansion appeared to have come to an end.

Television reviewers, bemoaning the absence of any exciting new headliners on the horizon, pointed out that prime time had become too valuable for experimentation, especially at NBC and CBS. The problem was that television had automatically adopted radio's rigid approach to the time period. Programmers assumed that the best way to keep an audience was with the same format, week-in and week-out. With ad slots in the evening sold out, they saw no reason to risk upsetting this rhythm with out-of-the-ordinary fare. As a result, newcomers went through try-outs as second bananas, in fringe hours, and, ironically, on network radio. In these settings, new and different personalities could attempt to carve out a niche for themselves and spring into prime time as headliners.

In 1951, there were many such stars-to-be still toiling in relative obscurity, waiting for their lucky break. Steve Allen was host of a ninety-minute daytime TV variety talk show on CBS, and also

FALL 1951 SCHEDULE

	Net	7:00	7:30	8:00	8:30	9:00	9:30	10:00	10:30
MON	ABC	local	Hollywood Screen Test	MR. D.A. / AMAZING MR. MALONE	Life Begins At 80	CURTAIN UP!		Bill Gwinn Show	Studs' Place
	CBS	local	CBS News / Perry Como	Lux Video Theater	Arthur Godfrey's Talent Scouts	I LOVE LUCY	It's News To Me	Studio One	
	DUM	Captain Video	local	Stage Entrance	Johns Hopkins Science Review	Wrestling From Columbia Park With Dennis James			
	NBC	Kukla, Fran And Ollie	Roberta Quinlan / Cam. News Caravan	Paul Winchell And Jerry Mahoney Show	Voice Of Firestone	Lights Out	Robert Montgomery Presents / Somerset Maugham Theater		Who Said That?
TUE	ABC	local	Beulah	Charlie Wild, Private Detective	How Did They Get That Way?	United Or Not	On Trial	ACTOR'S HOTEL	CHICAGO SYMPHONY CHAMBER ORCH.
	CBS	local	CBS News / Stork Club	Frank Sinatra Show		CRIME SYNDICATED	Suspense	Danger	local
	DUM	Captain Video	local	What's The Story	KEEP POSTED	COSMOPOLITAN THEATER		Hands Of Destiny	local
	NBC	Kukla, Fran And Ollie	Little Show / Cam. News Caravan	Texaco Star Theater		Fireside Theater	Armstrong Circle Theater	Original Amateur Hour	
WED	ABC	local	Chance Of A Lifetime	FROSTY FROLICS		Don McNeill's TV Club / Arthur Murray Party	The Clock	CELANESE THEATER / KING'S CROSSROADS	
	CBS	local	CBS News / Perry Como	Arthur Godfrey And His Friends		Strike It Rich	The Web	Blue Ribbon Bouts	Sports Spot
	DUM	Captain Video	local	Adventure Playhouse		GALLERY OF MADAME LIU-TSONG	Shadow Of The Cloak	International Playhouse	
	NBC	Kukla, Fran And Ollie	Roberta Quinlan / Cam. News Caravan	KATE SMITH EVENING SHOW		Kraft Television Theater		Break The Bank	Freddy Martin Show
THR	ABC	local	The Lone Ranger	Stop The Music		HERB SHRINER TIME	GRUEN GUILD THEATER	Paul Dixon Show	At Home Show / Red Grange
	CBS	local	CBS News / Stork Club	Burns And Allen Show / Garry Moore Show	Amos And Andy	Alan Young Show	Big Town	Racket Squad	Crime Photographer
	DUM	Captain Video	local	Georgetown University Forum	Broadway To Hollywood Headline Clues	Adventures Of Ellery Queen	local	Bigelow Theater	local / FOOTBALL THIS WEEK
	NBC	Kukla, Fran And Ollie	Little Show / Cam. News Caravan	You Bet Your Life	Treasury Men In Action	Ford Festival		Martin Kane, Private Eye	Wayne King Show
FRI	ABC	local	Life With Linkletter / Say It With Acting	MARK SABER MYSTERY THEATER	Stu Erwin Show	CRIME WITH FATHER	Tales Of Tomorrow / Versatile Varieties	DELL O'DELL SHOW	Industries For America
	CBS	local	CBS News / Perry Como	Mama	Man Against Crime	SCHLITZ PLAYHOUSE OF STARS		Live Like A Millionaire	Hollywood Opening Night
	DUM	Captain Video	local	Twenty Questions	You Asked For It	Down You Go	Front Page Detective	Cavalcade Of Stars	
	NBC	Kukla, Fran And Ollie	Roberta Quinlan / Cam. News Caravan	Quiz Kids	We, The People	The Big Story	The Aldrich Family	Gillette Cavalcade Of Sports	Greatest Fights
SAT	ABC	The Ruggles	Jerry Colona Show	Paul Whiteman's TV Teen Club		LESSON IN SAFETY	HARNESS RACING		
	CBS	Sammy Kaye Show	Beat The Clock	Ken Murray Show		Faye Emerson's Wonderful Town	The Show Goes On	Songs For Sale	
	DUM	local	THE PET SHOP	local		Wrestling From The Marigold In Chicago With Jack Brickhouse			
	NBC	ASSEMBLY VI	One Man's Family	All Star Revue		Your Show Of Shows		Your Hit Parade	
SUN	ABC	Paul Whiteman's Goodyear Revue	BY-LINE	Admission Free		In Our Time	Marshall Plan In Action	BILLY GRAHAM'S HOUR OF DECISION	Youth On The March
	CBS	Gene Autry Show	This Is Show Business / # Jack Benny Program	Toast Of The Town		Fred Waring Show		Celebrity Time	What's My Line
	DUM	local		Pentagon: Washington	Rocky King, Inside Detective	The Plainclothesman	They Stand Accused		
	NBC	SOUND-OFF TIME	YOUNG MR. BOBBIN	Colgate Comedy Hour		Goodyear/Philco Television Playhouse		RED SKELTON SHOW	Leave It To The Girls

served as one of the network's favorite panel show substitutes. Jack Paar, who had starred in a few unsuccessful comedy series on network radio, was host of the NBC radio quiz, *The $64 Question.* Even in this simple setting, his fiery personality proved unnerving to network executives. When the quiz show's sponsor pulled out and NBC asked all involved to accept a pay cut, Paar promptly walked off the show (a dramatic action that became a Paar trademark). Buff Cobb and her husband, Myron (Mike) Wallace, were brought by CBS from Chicago to New York, where they became hosts of an endless series of afternoon TV chit-chat shows, some of which aired during CBS's brief and unreceivable color run. Merv Griffin was a lead vocalist on *The Freddy Martin Show,* one of the numerous unsuccessful attempts to bring the big band sound to TV. Soon thereafter Griffin had a solo hit record, "I've Got a Lovely Bunch of Coconuts," and he began to appear as a TV guest on his own.

Going into the 1951–52 season, the few new prime time series that evoked any anticipation featured as headliners performers who had served similar warm-up stints in previous late night or afternoon programs. Industry insiders watched to see whether stars such as Kate Smith, Jerry Lester, and Garry Moore would be able to transfer their magic to prime time competition. Yet, what would prove to be the most popular and important new show of the season was barely considered in the preseason projections. Critics did not expect anything more than run-of-the-mill Hollywood TV production from a new filmed series, *I Love Lucy.*

Through the 1940s, Lucille Ball had pursued a career as a Hollywood film star, but never had any big hits. In 1948, she began a more successful venture, playing the part of a scatter-brained suburban housewife on the CBS Radio sitcom, *My Favorite Husband.* That series ended in 1951 just as her real favorite husband, Cuban band leader Desi Arnaz, was involved in his own radio show for CBS, *Your Tropical Trip.* Each week, Arnaz mixed his bouncy, infectious Latin "babaloo" rhythms with a hokey giveaway segment-for instance, a contestant who could guess how many bags of coffee Brazil produced the previous year would win a trip to South America. The program was a disaster and vanished in April 1951, after only a three-month run.

The two were then able to try their hands at a television comedy vehicle and CBS, still eager to develop the TV sitcom form, encouraged them. Lucy and Desi had made several competent guest appearances together on TV variety shows and, with Lucy's radio mentor, Jess Oppenheimer, serving as producer and writer, they developed a domestic sitcom premise and submitted it to the network. Immediately, several points of disagreement arose. CBS wanted them to do the show live from New York, like George Burns and Gracie Allen. Lucy wanted it on film from Los Angeles, so she could be at home with her husband. CBS also balked at the suggestion that Desi Arnaz play her husband in the series. Network brass doubted that he could carry the acting for the comic role. Though a competent band leader and talented song and dance man, Desi was also a foreigner with a heavy accent, and the network feared that audiences would not accept him. Lucy held firm on both points, which CBS agreed to only after some horse trading. CBS demanded that Lucy and Desi take a pay cut, to help make up for the added expense of film production. The couple went along with the cut, as long as CBS allowed them to retain ownership and total production control over the series. After both sides approved the arrangement, Lucy and Desi formed their own TV film production company, Desilu, which would produce the show, and they set about assembling a cast and turning out the first filmed episodes.

At the time, Los Angeles TV films were usually produced by small independent filmmakers because the big studios still refused to become involved with television production. Most of these filmed series adhered to a predictable formula and suffered from inadequate scripts, cheap sets, and weak acting. Though there were a few good Los Angeles productions under way, most were considered inferior to live East Coast shows. In their series, Lucy and Desi stuck with the basic screwball comedy formula, but unlike the others they carefully fashioned it into a delicate balance of exaggerated domestic farce and believable comic characters.

The setup for *I Love Lucy* was an intriguing variation of the "mirror of reality" formula successfully used by Jack Benny, Burns and Allen, and Ozzie and Harriet for years on radio, focusing on both professional and domestic situations. Desi Arnaz played Ricky Ricardo, a Cuban band leader who worked in a Manhattan nightclub, the Tropicana. Lucille Ball played his showbiz-starved wife, Lucy. This combination allowed Arnaz to, in effect, play himself while Ball took off as the comic center for the show, using her talents for slapstick and comic timing that were matched only by Sid Caesar and Jack Benny.

Though the series was filmed in Hollywood, the action was set in New York City, and—in an important break from many previous filmed comedies and radio sitcoms—the two stars were not presented as an already successful suburban couple. Instead, Ricky Ricardo was an up-and-coming, but still struggling, nightclub performer who lived in a middle class Manhattan brownstone within a comfortable but not extravagant family budget. The characters of Lucy and Ricky were especially believable because they resembled the real life Lucy and Desi in a setting that viewers found easy to relate to and accept. The apartment building itself was owned by a down-to-earth middle-aged couple, Fred and Ethel Mertz (William Frawley and Vivian Vance), who were the landlords, upstairs neighbors, and best friends to Lucy and Ricky.

I Love Lucy was set in this essentially real world with three normal characters and one zany but lovable madcap: Lucy. This effectively combined the best of two strains of comedy. From the warm and natural style championed by *The Goldbergs* came a concentration on character interaction. From the Hollywood screwball comedy style exemplified by *Amos 'n Andy* came absurd coincidences and misunderstandings as the basis for the plots. Ball played the Lucy character as a sharp but scatterbrained housewife who inevitably misunderstood conversations and events, turning everyday complications into comic disasters. The other three reacted as basically normal people caught up in a screwball situation. Together they formed a strong performing ensemble that could

With the completion of the AT&T coaxial cable, coast-to-coast network television became a reality. Using this link, President Truman's address at the opening session of the Japanese Peace Treaty Conference was seen throughout the country. *(Property of AT&T. Reprinted with permission of AT&T.)*

September 3, 1951

Search for Tomorrow and, three weeks later, *Love of Life* lather up the soap opera suds for television, giving CBS the lead in developing this daytime radio staple for TV.

September 10, 1951

The CBS "eye," designed by William Golden, becomes the CBS logo.

September 29, 1951

Television coverage of NCAA collegiate football is reduced to a single national "game of the week" carried by one network (NBC) on Saturday afternoons.

September 30, 1951

The "fourth" television network, DuMont, steals the Sunday afternoon NFL professional football games from the "third" network, ABC.

October 3, 1951

Celanese Theater. (ABC). Alex Segal directs ABC's second major drama series, showcasing material by the "Playwrights Company" (including Maxwell Anderson, Robert Sherwood, Elmer Rice, and Eugene O'Neill).

October 4, 1951

After four years of "pooled" coverage, baseball's World Series begins twenty-six years as the exclusive property of NBC.

November 27, 1951

The Dinah Shore Show. (NBC). NBC's female equivalent to Perry Como eases into a relaxed fifteen-minute weekday show.

December 24, 1951

"Amahl and the Night Visitors." (NBC). Gian-Carlo Menotti presents the first written-for-television opera, a gentle Christmas fantasy of a twelve-year-old boy who befriends the three kings searching for Jesus. The opera becomes a Yuletide tradition on NBC for sixteen years.

---

handle practically any comedy situation, no matter how silly it might appear on the surface.

In one of the first episodes of the series, Lucy, engrossed in a lurid murder novel, overheard Ricky talking on the telephone and became convinced that he was trying to kill her. She asked Ethel to help her avoid Ricky's clutches while a confused Ricky turned to Fred for suggestions on what could possibly be wrong with Lucy. Like any misunderstood situation, the mix-up took only a few words of explanation to clear up at the end, but the sharp script and strong performances by each character turned such silly fluff into engaging comedy.

Other stories focused on deliberate schemes by Lucy, especially as she tried to follow Ricky into the glamorous world of show business. Ricky always insisted that Lucy stay home as a loving wife, but she used any outlandish disguise and complicated lie to end up on stage or to just meet famous stars and directors. Ethel inevitably acted as Lucy's accomplice, slightly scared of Lucy's schemes but eager underneath to give them a try. Usually, Lucy's hard-fought-for tryouts turned into hilarious failures.

Often, the program avoided show business completely and focused on domestic complications. Sometimes the Ricardos argued with the Mertzes. Other times, the wives and husbands teamed up

against each other. In other situations, all four neighbors took on a common problem. Through all the settings, the energy between the Ricardos and the Mertzes served as the driving force behind the show. They faced situations together as believable, humorous people. Even with Lucy's zany schemes, the farce never completely overshadowed the characters and the characters never got in the way of the humorous situations. As a result, *I Love Lucy* emerged as a perfect combination of sharp comic writing and acting.

The production style used in filming *I Love Lucy* also represented a careful mix of techniques, combining the best traits of both Hollywood films and live TV staging. As in a theatrical film, there was full screen action, effective editing, and well-planned direction. As in live sitcoms, character movement was generally continuous and compact, staying within a few basic sets: the Ricardo apartment, Ricky's nightclub, and one or two special "location" scenes. There was also a studio audience present for the filming, so the comedy was staged for real people responding to the energy of the players.

I Love Lucy premiered on CBS on October 15, 1951, in a choice time slot: Monday night, following the number two rated *Arthur Godfrey's Talent Scouts*. Reviewers marveled at how well the Ricardos and Mertzes walked the tightrope between character and caricature, and how well producer-writer Jess Oppenheimer had made use of the standard screwball elements. Within four months, *I Love Lucy* deposed Milton Berle's *Texaco Star Theater* as television's top-rated show, and *Lucy* stayed there for the next four years. In the process, the Ricardos became the first TV family to be taken to heart by the entire nation, becoming just as real and alive as the characters of radio's *Amos 'n Andy* had been to a previous generation.

For CBS, *I Love Lucy* accomplished what the network had hoped television's *Amos 'n Andy* would do. It proved the strength and acceptability of TV sitcoms, giving the network a strong weapon against NBC's flashy comedy-variety hours. Sitcoms presented viewers with continuing characters, settings, and stories, rather than a mixed bag of skits, and CBS planned to bring others to the schedule as soon as possible.

It quickly became evident that many of the new sitcoms would be quite a letdown from the careful craftsmanship of *I Love Lucy*. Radio's *My Friend Irma* began a live TV version in January 1952, featuring Marie Wilson as a female even more scatterbrained than Lucy Ricardo. (Irma was once convinced that her cat was a missing friend, reincarnated.) Though adequate, the series had nowhere near the energy of *I Love Lucy. My Little Margie,* the summer replacement for *I Love Lucy,* had terrible scripts and a cast of characters that seemed designed to embody as many offensive Hollywood stereotypes as possible. Produced by the Hal Roach studios, *My Little Margie* featured Gale Storm in the title role of a bratty, know-it-all young girl; Charles Farrell as her dad, Vernon Albright, an emasculated, mushy widower; Clarence Kolb as George Honeywell, Albright's boss, a stuffed-shirt, blustery capitalist; Gertrude Hoffman as the eighty-three-year-old Mrs. Odettes, who gave senility a bad name; and Willie Best as Charlie, the black elevator operator, who made *Amos 'n Andy*'s Lightnin' look like a Rhodes scholar. Yet even this series became a big enough summer hit to be picked up as a winter replacement the following season. It was clear that while there might be many successful *I Love Lucy*-inspired sitcoms, few would match the quality of the original.

A summer sitcom that achieved success with a radically different style was *Mr. Peepers,* a low-key live NBC series produced by Fred Coe. Wally Cox portrayed Robinson J. Peepers, a quiet slow-

The first TV sitcom superstars: *(from left)* Lucille Ball, Vivian Vance, Desi Arnaz, and William Frawley. *(CBS Photo Archive © 2003 CBS Worldwide, Inc. All Rights Reserved.)*

tempered high school biology teacher in the small Midwestern town of Jefferson City. Unlike the screwball sitcoms, the humor in *Mr. Peepers* developed from just slightly exaggerated situations that the soft spoken Peepers encountered. His friends Harvey Weskit (Tony Randall), a brash history teacher, and Mrs. Gurney (Marion Lorne), a befuddled English teacher, served as excellent comic foils to his mild manner, and the stories emerged as whimsical visits with friendly, good-natured people. The show was originally scheduled for just a summer run, but viewer response was so strong that NBC used it early in the 1952–53 season as a replacement series. The program ran until 1955 and, at the end of the second full season, the mild mannered Peepers summoned the courage to ask Nancy Remington (Patricia Benoit), the school nurse, to marry him.

One of NBC's first major experiments in filmed TV series was not a sitcom but a crime show, *Dragnet,* which the network brought in as a winter replacement in early 1952. Under the direction of producer-narrator-star Jack Webb, *Dragnet* had begun in the summer of 1949 on radio, featuring Webb as Sergeant Joe Friday of the Los Angeles police department and Barton Yarborough as his partner, Sergeant Ben Romero. The series broke from radio's romanticized image of crime fighting and emphasized instead the mundane legwork necessary for success by real policemen. Stories were based on "actual cases" from the Los Angeles police department and each week, following the opening theme ("Dum-De-Dum-Dum"), the announcer reminded the audience, "The story you are about to hear is true. Only the names have been changed to protect the innocent." Webb's clipped narration described each case step by step, introducing to the general public the jargon and methodology of police work as well as his own catch phrases such as "Just the facts, ma'am." Listeners, who did not know any more about the cases than Friday and Romero did, followed the painstaking investigations clue by clue and became caught up in the excitement of piecing together the solutions to real life urban crimes. Each show tied everything together at the con-

January 6, 1952
Hallmark Hall of Fame. (NBC). Actress Sarah Churchill (daughter of Winston) serves as host of a Sunday afternoon drama anthology. Later, as a series of floating specials, the *Hall of Fame* productions serve as one of television's classiest series.

January 7, 1952
Arthur Godfrey Time. (CBS). A television simulcast of Godfrey's morning radio variety show pushes CBS-TV up to a 10:00 A.M. starting time.

April 26, 1952
Gunsmoke. (CBS Radio). William Conrad plays marshal Matt Dillon in a Western that takes dead aim at adults.

June 19, 1952
I've Got a Secret. (CBS). Garry Moore hosts another of Mark Goodson and Bill Todman's celebrity panel quiz shows, emphasizing the sharp banter of its regulars. The format is simple: Each contestant has a secret which the panel attempts to guess.

June 30, 1952
The Guiding Light. (CBS). CBS adds this veteran fifteen-year-old radio soap opera to its afternoon television lineup.

July 7, 1952
The Republican National Convention opens in Chicago. CBS has a new anchor, Walter Cronkite.

July 21, 1952
The Democratic National Convention program book ominously warns delegates "Television will be watching YOU!" citing the *eight* cameras that might catch them unawares in closeup while "covering every inch" of the hall.

clusion with a crisp report on the trial and punishment given to the apprehended criminal. Without resorting to the sounds of excessive violence, *Dragnet* turned investigative police work into exciting and popular radio entertainment.

The television version of *Dragnet* continued the methodical style of the radio show and its dedicated support for the average cop on the beat. *Dragnet* first appeared at Christmastime in a special "preview" episode featuring Webb, Yarborough, and guest Raymond Burr as a deputy police chief. Yarborough died on December 19, so when the show came to the regular NBC television schedule in January 1952, Webb tried out a few new assistants, eventually choosing Ben Alexander as his new partner, officer Frank Smith. Like the radio version three years before, TV's *Dragnet* marked a major change from the standard crime shows proliferating on television. In series such as *Martin Kane, Private Eye,* the hero was a loner detective so the police were presented as fumbling fools who would probably trip over a dead body before they realized that a crime had been committed. Series such as *Dick Tracy, Mr. District Attorney,* and *Racket Squad* consisted entirely of character stereotypes. The bad guys wore slouch hats and needed a shave while the smooth know-it-all heroes relied on third-degree grillings and coincidence to break a case. *Dragnet,* on the other hand, pictured police neither as boobs nor glamour boys, but as dedicated human beings who solved crimes by careful deduction, using brains rather than brawn.

Dragnet was a tremendous success and, like *I Love Lucy,* set a program style that would be imitated for years. Both shows also made filmed television series respectable. While most of the programs emanating from Los Angeles were still live, the television networks ceased considering filmed series as simply filler. The major Hollywood studios continued to treat television as a leper, but smaller, independent studios were more than happy to fill the new demand for filmed product.

The *I Love Lucy*-inspired boom in sitcom development served as a direct challenge to NBC's emphasis on comedy-variety giants. Even Milton Berle, the network's biggest star, felt the pressure. Though he began the season by knocking off his first serious Tuesday night competition in years (CBS's *Frank Sinatra Show),* Berle dropped as *I Love Lucy* climbed. After being dethroned by *Lucy,* Berle began changing his program's tone, aiming the show more and more toward the kids, adopting a new cognomen, Uncle Miltie. In mid-season, large numbers of adults began to turn from the *Texaco Star Theater* to a new, unexpected source of competition: God. DuMont, which prided itself (out of financial necessity) on producing "sensibly priced" entertainment, threw up against Berle a concept considered too ridiculously simple for the other networks to take seriously: a sermon. For thirty minutes each week on *Life Is Worth Living,* Roman Catholic Bishop Fulton J. Sheen delivered a strong but sensitive religious presentation. He was not plugging a particular doctrine, but rather was discussing everyday problems and the help a faith in God could bring. He even had a sense of humor, often joking about his competition with Berle. One quip had it that both worked for the same boss, Sky Chief.

Even with the challenges to Berle, NBC stuck with its big name variety shows – highlighted by *The Colgate Comedy Hour* and *All Star Revue* (the renamed *Four Star Revue*) – because overall they were still producing top ratings. Throughout the 1950–51 season, *The Colgate Comedy Hour* had regularly defeated its Sunday night competition, Ed Sullivan's *Toast of the Town.* For the new season NBC came up with another TV winner, Red Skelton.

Red Skelton's television act centered on little hats, big grins, his rubber face, and a ready-made roster of already familiar characters from radio including Clem Kadiddlehopper, Willie LumpLump,

Bolivar Shagnasty, and the infamous Mean Widdle Kid. Each week, Skelton merely stepped on stage in front of a curtain and performed, vaudeville style. His decade-long success on radio carried over to television and he shot straight into TV's top ten.

NBC also tried to expand comedy-variety into a new, earlier time period that season, in an attempt to duplicate the early-evening radio success of Jack Benny. For years, Benny had led off CBS's Sunday night radio line-up with his top-rated 7:00 to 7:30 P.M. program, so NBC slotted *Chesterfield Sound Off Time* for the same period, which was unusually early for TV variety. Once again, there was a rotating format, with Bob Hope, Fred Allen, and Jerry Lester taking turns as the show's host. Hope was just as good as always; Lester, who had quit the late night *Broadway Open House* in May, failed with a mix of bland scripts and racy ad-libbed humor; and Allen was once again saddled with hosting a vaudeville show, a task unsuited to his nature. *Sound Off Time* vanished by Christmas, only to be replaced by another variety show, *Royal Showcase.* This was also unable to snare a large audience, though it did feature Fred Allen's best TV performances ever. Appearing as a guest two times in the spring, Allen at last brought to life the characters of his famed Allen's Alley. If this had been done eighteen months earlier, Allen might have become the TV star everyone expected him to be, using his familiar stock of characters in much the same way as Red Skelton.

NBC's experiment with early evening variety achieved only occasional success. However, there was a much more serious problem beginning to show in the network's comedy-variety showpieces, *The Colgate Comedy Hour* and *All Star Revue.* Nightclub and film commitments of the original regulars disrupted the smoothly balanced rotating schedule that had been set up for the two shows and, as the major headliners decreased the number of their appearances, NBC was forced to rely increasingly on less popular substitute hosts. These included Donald O'Connor, Martha Raye, Ezio Pinza, Ben Blue, Tony Martin, the Ritz Brothers, Jack Paar, Spike Jones, Abbott and Costello, and Jerry Lester. Colgate was sinking $100,000 per week into its show (which totaled $3 million per year, then the highest budget in television) and desperately wanted only the familiar big names as headliners. But the top stars were getting tired of the routine. They found their backlog of material used up very quickly and were forced to fall back on writers who could turn out only so much greatness on a week-to-week basis. At the end of the season, Danny Thomas quit the grind, exploding, "TV is for idiots! I don't like it … it has lowered the standards of the entertainment industry considerably. You … work years building routines, do them once on TV, and they're finished. Next thing you know, you are, too … When and if I ever do my own TV show, I'd like it to be a half-hour on film."

Eventually most of the other major headliners echoed the criticisms of both Danny Thomas and the previously departed Fred Allen. Television comedy-variety used up routines at an incredible rate and performers quickly had to settle for presentations that were just average, frustrating themselves and disappointing viewers. Their shows began to look the same, with the same guests, the same format, and the same material.

As *The Colgate Comedy Hour* turned more frequently to lesser light substitute hosts, Ed Sullivan's show began to nibble away at NBC's hold over the Sunday at 8:00 P.M. slot. After being consistently beaten in the 1950–51 season, Sullivan had decided to give his show a new wrinkle in the hope of drawing even with the celebrity-studded variety hour on NBC. In September 1951, the budget for *Toast of the Town* was increased and Sullivan began doing elaborate special tribute shows. Throughout the season, entire programs were turned over to salutes to Oscar Hammerstein,

Television coverage of the 1952 Democratic convention gave home viewers the best seats in the house. *(National Archives)*

Helen Hayes, Bea Lillie, Cole Porter, and Richard Rodgers, with the featured artist as headliner and well-known friends as the supporting cast. These tribute shows were, in effect, floating specials that aired within the *Toast of the Town* framework. When stars such as Dean Martin and Jerry Lewis were on *The Colgate Comedy Hour,* NBC still came out on top. However, when viewers were faced with headliners such as Spike Jones or Abbott and Costello, Sullivan's specials provided an attractive alternative on CBS.

NBC's programming chief, Pat Weaver, learned a lesson from Ed Sullivan's success against *The Colgate Comedy Hour* and, late in the fall of 1951, he proposed that NBC adopt the idea of regularly scheduled specials as part of its network strategy. Weaver felt such programs, which he dubbed "spectaculars," could be used to keep NBC's TV schedule vibrant by breaking the weekly routine that too many shows had fallen into. He suggested that a two-hour spectacular could be scheduled to appear about once a month, financed by the regular sponsor of the time slot. Television's big advertisers, as well as NBC itself, were not receptive to this idea. They believed that week-in, week-out regularity in programming was the best way to keep an audience, with Christmas specials such as "Amahl and the Night Visitors" the only exception. Their resistance meant that Weaver had to hold off implementing his "spectaculars" idea for a little while, but he was able to get another

of his pet projects on the air more quickly: *Today,* a two-hour news and information series broadcast in the early morning.

At the start of 1952, daytime TV programming was still sparse. A few stations signed on at about 10:00 A.M., but nothing of any importance took place until about 4:00 P.M. One exception was in Philadelphia where, each weekday morning from 7:00 A.M. to 9:00 A.M., WPTZ ran *Three to Get Ready,* a loose show led by former radio disc jockey Ernie Kovacs. The program had begun in late November 1950 and featured some live music, records, time-and-weather checks, and great doses of Kovacs's own peculiar television humor. He read fan letters on the air, performed skits he had written himself, shot off toy guns after puns, picked his teeth, and even held an audition for goats. *Three to Get Ready* did unexpectedly well in the local ratings and the success of Kovacs apparently convinced NBC that Weaver's idea for an early morning show might attract network viewers as well.

Chicago's Dave Garroway, who had been without a show for a few months, was chosen as the low-key host for the new program, originally dubbed *Rise and Shine* but retitled *Today* before its premiere. NBC budgeted the concept at $40,000 per week and took out full page ads in trade magazines, declaring the show to be "a revolution in television," and that, via *Today,* "the studio becomes the nerve center of the planet." When the program began in January 1952, though, such proclamations could only be regarded as promises for the future. Skeptical advertisers withheld support and there was only one sponsor for the premiere.

On the home screens the first *Today* broadcast appeared as an almost meaningless hodge-podge. The cast and crew were squeezed into a tiny street-front New York City studio that had originally been a public display showroom for RCA TV sets. There, viewers could see three teletype machines, weather maps, wire photo displays, clocks set to the times of various world cities, record players, newspapers, the crowd outside the studio, and, oh yes, the show's regular cast of Dave Garroway, Jim Fleming, and Jack Lescoulie. Throughout the program there were frequent cuts to live reports from the Pentagon, Grand Central Station, and the comer of Michigan Avenue and Randolph Street in Chicago, as well as live phone reports describing the weather in London, England and Frankfurt, Germany. Viewers were bombarded with data and they reacted to *Today* with confused indifference. *Today* did not seem to have any point other than to show off fancy gadgets. Before long, NBC toned down the video tricks and adopted a news, reviews, features, and interviews format more suited to Garroway's relaxed nature. By May, the show was in the black.

Today was so successful that WPTZ, in order to carry it, was forced to shift the Ernie Kovacs *Three to Get Ready* program to noon, a move soon followed by his departure to New York City. There, Kovacs did a few daytime network shows for NBC, but soon found himself on the CBS local New York affiliate doing a morning show against his old nemesis, *Today.* His new show continued the loose and off-beat style of *Three to Get Ready,* with such features as visits from Tondelayo, an "invisible" cat that was visible to everybody, and Yoo-Hoo Time. Kovacs noticed that most members of a studio audience began waving as soon as a camera was pointed in their direction, so he generously set aside Yoo-Hoo Time for just such activity. A display card showed the name of a person in the audience who was invited to stand up and wave to his heart's content, egged on by Kovacs. Actor Peter Boyle also made guest appearances, often appearing as either a rotund Irish cop on the beat or a rotund uncle-figure who urged the kiddies to "Eat up like Uncle Pete!" When the makers of Serutan ("Natures spelled backwards") took over five minutes of his morning slot, Kovacs insisted for weeks on referring to himself as Ernie Scavok. Above all, Kovacs constantly ribbed the effusive wall gadgets and world-wide air of the competing *Today* show. He hung up signs on his set with such helpful descriptions as: "London," "Cloudy," "Frown," and "Trenton."

On the other side of the broadcast day, the networks were experimenting with new late night telecasts, but these were far less successful than the early morning *Today.* One of the worst shows was CBS's gauche attempt at sophistication, *The Continental,* which aired Tuesday and Thursday nights, 11:15 to 11:30 P.M. Renzo Cesana played a TV gigolo who sat in an apartment setting, trying to look like a swank European mélange of Charles Boyer and Ezio Pinza. Cesana sipped fancy drinks, puffed expensive cigarettes, sang, and pitched woo to the presumably palpitating housewives at home. The camera was supposed to be their eyes and ears, so Cesana acted as if the viewers were really in the room with him. He handed cigarettes and drinks to the camera, gushing sweet nothings such as "Don't be afraid, darling, you're in a *man's* apartment!" Trying to tickle romantic fantasies, Cesana went on and on that he loved the marvels of a woman's smile, that he valued champagne that did not tickle your nose, and that his ladies looked great in Cameo stockings. Inevitably this led to a plug for women's stockings, revealing the great lover as a pitchman in a rented tuxedo. One critic labeled this extended commercial "the most needless program on television."

The expansion by the television networks into the fringe operating hours reflected the increasing growth in the country's economy, despite the fighting in Korea. The war had settled into a peculiar state in July 1951 as cease-fire and armistice talks began. Though these dragged on for two more years while thousands of American soldiers remained in Korea, the level of fighting toned down sufficiently for domestic production facilities to be returned to civilian use. Manufacturing and consumer buying picked up and it was against this background that television programming and sponsor support took off with the coast-to-coast cable connection and the success of shows such as *I Love Lucy.* Though the FCC freeze still prevented television from touching many areas, viewer interest in television cities was greater than ever. Competing magazines listing the week's TV fare hit the stands, giving the home viewer a choice of *TV Preview, TV Review, TV News, TV Views, TV Forecast, TV Digest, TV Today,* and an early version of *TV Guide.* Besides the program listings, these magazines usually featured short puff piece articles on individual shows, star biographies, and ads. The program listings sometimes served as plugs themselves with the sponsor's name as part of the title in such shows as *Texaco Star Theater, Pabst Blue Ribbon Bouts,* and *Chesterfield Sound Off Time.* Most TV magazines and newspapers drew the line, though, at an ABC Sunday night adventure show whose official title was *Your Kaiser-Frazer Dealer Presents "Kaiser-Frazer Adventures in Mystery" Starring Betty Furness in "By-Line."* Despite the sponsor's determined effort to squeeze in an extra plug while taking as much column space as possible, the title in print was inevitably shortened to *By-Line.*

As television's popularity grew, those concerned about the medium's persuasive effects on others became increasingly vocal. Aspiring politicians discovered that they could catapult themselves into the headlines by claiming that sex and violence on television was corrupting the nation and that such programming should be halted by federal fiat. Those who wanted to clamp down on television pointed to seemingly ominous incidents such as one that took place in Detroit on January 22, 1952. There, John R. Sikron, a forty-six-year-old deputy sheriff in Macomb County, had been arguing with his wife over whether the family should watch CBS's thriller series, *Suspense,* claiming that the show was too violent for her and their six children to see. During the argument, Sikron's fifteen-year-old son, Jerry—who later explained that he could not stand to see his father push his mother around—picked up his father's shotgun and shot his dad through the back, killing him.

In the early days of motion pictures, there had been similar charges that violence on the silver screen translated into violence in real life. When governmental intervention appeared imminent in the 1920s, the major studios called in a respected former postmaster general, Will Hays, to help draw up a morality code which would govern the content of all Hollywood films. With a self-regulating code in effect, the demand for federal censorship abated. In 1951, the self-appointed guardians of the public morality began looking askance at examples of television sex and violence, such as Dagmar's cleavage and Dick Tracy's mayhem, and TV moguls decided to adopt a Hollywood-style code of ethics. The networks hoped that their declaration of support for industry self-regulation would assuage the vocal critics, prevent federal intervention, and prove that television was doing its part to keep the country square with God. There were four basic rules laid down to guide all producers of television programs:

1. Shows will not sympathize with evil.
2. Shows will not degrade honesty, goodness, and innocence.
3. Figures exercising lawful authority should not be ridiculed.
4. Law breakers must not go unpunished.

In October, the proposed television code was adopted by the National Association of Broadcasters (NAB), which asked its members to voluntarily agree to abide by it. On the day the code went into effect, March 1, 1952, television industry publications proudly proclaimed that 77 of the 108 American television stations had taken the pledge. The airwaves had been cleansed and the nation could sleep in peace.

That may have been enough for the television industry, but it was not enough for U.S. Representative Ezekiel C. Gothings, a Democrat from Arkansas. He induced the House Interstate Commerce Committee to hold public hearings on the morality of TV programs. One witness, conservative radio commentator Paul Harvey, complained that television had become an outlet for comics schooled in the "bawdy night life" of New York City, who were disseminating their "purple" jokes to the nation, thereby imposing "their distorted views on the rest of the forty-seven states." Representative Gothings himself presented the committee with a more specific bill of particulars. One night, he announced, he had viewed a network variety show in which ". . . a grass-skirted young lady and a thinly-clad young gentleman were dancing the hootchie-kootchie to a lively tune and shaking the shimmy!"

In spite of such shocking observations, the committee at large accepted the explanations and assurances of the network presidents who testified at the hearings. The TV executives admitted that much of what was on television was bad, but quickly pointed out that many books and many plays were also bad. Television was just another mass medium which was trying to appeal to a mass audience. Some banality had to be expected with so many hours to fill. Besides, they concluded, the public was not forced to watch everything on television and, in fact, if a viewer chose carefully, there were many good shows throughout the schedule. In its final report, the committee stated that there was too much crime and suggestiveness on television, but government control would be worse than the moments of poor taste. The committee also commended intra-industry self-regulatory measures, such as the NAB code, which, it pointed out, was already having a beneficial effect. Dagmar's neckline had gone up.

Interest in the effects of television on the public became more intense during 1952 because, in April, the FCC at last ended its freeze on processing station applications and cleared the way for television to eventually reach nearly every home in America. The commission had first ordered the freeze in 1948 to study and revise frequency allocations in order to solve problems of cross-station interference. After three and one-half years of deliberation, the FCC announced a comprehensive new set of rules. First, the commission squeezed 220 additional stations into the VHF band, raising that system from its previous maximum of 400 to a new level of 620. It also opened seventy channels (14 to 83) on the UHF spectrum for television broadcasting, making 1,400 new UHF stations available nationwide. Both systems combined permitted more than 2,000 TV stations in 1,291 cities. This meant that, theoretically, television at last had enough channels to allow operations by four (or more) national TV networks. In a bold step, the FCC also reserved 242 channels (mostly in the UHF spectrum) for independent noncommercial educational stations. By July, less than three months after "the thaw" took place, almost 600 station applications had been received by the FCC, many for the new UHF band.

The chief flaws in the new television status quo were in the setups for both the UHF system and the noncommercial stations. None of the eighteen million TV sets in use in 1952 were able to receive the UHF frequencies, and set manufacturers saw no reason to spend extra money to include the feature unless their customers

demanded it. With plenty of entertainment available on VHF, the public ignored the new system. Few people purchased UHF converters for existing sets or asked for UHF capabilities on new sets. Almost immediately, fierce battles began over the more accessible VHF frequencies as applicants realized their competitive value. In launching the new system, the FCC might have unofficially declared certain cities as all-UHF, giving manufacturers a captive audience for UHF sets, but this did not occur. Instead, the commission decided to let the subtle pressures of supply and demand solve the UHF problem.

Most of the newly created noncommercial channels were on the UHF band, so their future hinged on the success of the new system. Yet, they also faced an additional, fundamental problem of their own: funding. The FCC had left this important aspect of noncommercial television unsettled. It was not clear where the money was to come from if the stations were to be both noncommercial and independent of the government. San Francisco's KQED (one of the few educational stations located on the VHF band) soon hit upon the concept of a yearly on-air auction to raise operating funds, but the UHF stations, with far fewer potential viewers, could not do even that. The only major source of revenue for noncommercial TV came from the Ford Foundation, which donated $11 million to establish the Educational Television and Radio Center (forerunner of the National Educational Television Network) to produce and distribute educational programs. However, through poor organization and faulty funding, both of the major TV cities, New York and Los Angeles, did not have an educational station at all. Without them, noncommercial television remained, for all practical purposes, a very expensive television laboratory.

The failure of UHF and the lack of major market outlets for educational TV prevented the noncommercial system from having any influence on American TV programming for more than a decade. Commercial television experienced no such delay. At the time of the thaw, there were only 108 stations (all VHF) on the air in sixty-three cities, and thirty-seven of those cities—places such as St. Louis, Pittsburgh, Buffalo, New Orleans, Houston, and Indianapolis—still had only one TV station each. Within a year, the number of TV stations on the air increased from 108 to 200, and another 200 were in the process of construction.

The birth of live coast-to-coast television and the surge in TV station growth assured by the thaw made television a much more important factor in the 1952 presidential campaign. The politicians remembered the amazing effects of television during the 1951 Kefauver hearings and prepared to exploit it. At the same time, CBS and NBC decided to build some much-needed television news respectability with early and extensive coverage of the 1952 electoral process.

In March, for the first time, CBS and NBC film crews descended upon New Hampshire, turning the state's previously unimportant presidential primary into a vital national bellwether. Among the Republicans, General Dwight Eisenhower scored a surprise write-in victory and the wide play this received on TV made "Ike" a credible candidate. The quality and depth of the two networks' coverage of New Hampshire showed that television could cover news on its own, independent of radio and newsreels. Candidates soon discovered that they had to augment their speech writing staffs to have new catchy phrases ready for the ever-present TV cameras. As with the comedy-variety shows, television quickly used up political material. Without new lines, candidates ran the risk of turning off the public with "the same old stuff."

The most important breakthrough in television's news stature came in June when Eisenhower held his first big campaign press conference. Though the event marked the beginning of his active run for the Republican nomination (after leaving military service), Eisenhower's press aides—in collusion with the newspaper and newsreel reporters—announced that television crews would be barred from covering the press conference. This practice was not at all unusual in those days, but CBS's William Paley decided to take a stand. He boldly announced that CBS was sending a camera crew anyway and Eisenhower would have to throw it out. Fearing bad publicity, Eisenhower's people let CBS (and the late-coming NBC) into the conference. This marked milestone in TV journalism. For the first time, TV news had stood up for itself, and won.

At the Republican National Convention in July, the Eisenhower aides showed that they had learned their lessons well. When the forces of Eisenhower's chief rival, Ohio Senator Robert Taft (who controlled the convention machinery), tried to sneak through an important delegation challenge out of sight of the cameras, Eisenhower's people suddenly appeared all over television talking about "convention rigging," "the big steal," "smoke-filled rooms," and "steam-rollered conventions." Incensed viewers sent telegrams to the convention and the public outcry that resulted from the charges on television swayed enough delegates to put Eisenhower over the top, landing him the presidential nomination. Television news coverage had been proved even more powerful than many people had imagined. TV had not only come of age, it was also affecting who was chosen to lead the country.

12. Grade-B TV

IN SPITE OF THE GREAT STRIDES made in television coverage of politics in the spring and summer of 1952, the real beginning of political television took place at 9:30 P.M. (Eastern time), September 23, 1952, when, live from NBC's El Capitan studio in Hollywood, California Senator Richard M. Nixon faced the nation, and won. Nixon had made a name for himself as a congressman a few years before by "getting" Alger Hiss, an accused Soviet spy in the State Department, and, in 1952, Republican presidential nominee Dwight Eisenhower chose Nixon as his running mate. Soon thereafter, stories began circulating that a group of California businessmen were supplying Nixon with a secret slush fund. Republican leaders, primarily concerned with ensuring Eisenhower's election, urged him to drop the young senator from the ticket, but Eisenhower gave Nixon a few days to clear himself. Nixon talked the Republican National Committee into buying a half-hour of radio and television time so that he could explain his side of the story. With pressure mounting for Nixon's ouster, tension on the day of the broadcast was quite high, because nobody knew what Nixon was going to say.

Nixon's presentation that night demonstrated that he was one of the first major politicians to grasp fully the impact and nature of television as a political tool. His performance was a playwright's dream. The young star (with his devoted wife, Pat, at his side) faced the allegations on his own, trying to save his honor in a world turned cruel and hard. The charges concerning the $18,235 in a supplementary expenditures fund were quickly dismissed. Yes, Nixon admitted, he received the money, but he denied any sinister or illegal motives. It was not an under-the-table gift, Nixon said, but merely a fund to help him better serve his constituents. Then almost immediately, Nixon left the original topic behind and launched into a brilliant "Just Plain Bill" portrait of himself as simple, down-home folk. He told a tear-jerker story of his impoverished background and minimal current financial holdings. He described his war record, the two-year-old car he drove, the mortgage on his home, and his repayments of loans, with interest, to his parents.

The Horatio Nixon story culminated in the ultimate heart-tug, a little dog. He had used such sure-fire gambits as mom, the family hearth, the poor-boy-makes-good, and the story of a struggling young couple, so all that remained were cute little puppies and young children. Near the end of the speech, Nixon disclosed that, yes, he had received a gift from a supporter after all:

One other thing I probably should tell you, because if I don't, they'll probably be saying this about me too. We did get something—a gift … A man down in Texas heard Pat on the radio mention the fact that our two youngsters would like to have a dog and, believe it or not, the day before we left on this campaign trip, we got a message from Union Station, saying they had a package for us. We went down to get it, and you know what it was? It was a little cocker spaniel dog in a crate that he sent all the way from Texas. [It was] black and white and spotted, and our little girl—Trisha, the six-year-old—named it Checkers, and you know, the kids love the dog, and I just want to say this right now, that regardless of what they say about it, we're gonna keep it.

What a scenario! All it needed was some organ music underneath and the nation would have been awash in bathos. Who could resist such a presentation? Nixon correctly assumed that television (which everyone had said was an intimate medium) was the perfect way to get to people's hearts for an emotional response. The "little people" came to Nixon's defense and flooded the Eisenhower campaign headquarters with telegrams urging Nixon's retention on the ticket. Television industry people, while admiring the showmanship in Nixon's presentation, were vaguely disturbed by its implications. It was an implied declaration that a clever politician could, via television's immediacy, reduce politics to personalities, issues to emotions, and complexities to simplifications. Certainly this was not a new trend in politics. President Franklin Roosevelt's references to "my little dog Fala" on radio back in the 1940s were close to Checkers in such intent. However, television had elevated this to a much higher level of effectiveness.

The rest of the campaign was dull by comparison. Eisenhower, always uncomfortable in front of television cameras, relied chiefly on ad agency-produced short spots, many of which featured cartoon marching bands endlessly repeating "I Like Ike! You Like Ike! Everybody Likes Ike!" Adlai Stevenson, the Democratic nominee, stuck to the more traditional half-hour speech format.

Election night itself was not all that dramatic, either. It was evident early on that Eisenhower and Nixon would win, and NBC and CBS's much-touted Univac computers made little difference in the speed of calling the races. The only news about the news coverage was the surge in popularity of CBS, which decided to stick with its successful new convention anchor man, Walter Cronkite. The CBS sponsor, Westinghouse, also stuck with its anchor, commercial spokeswoman Betty Furness.

FALL 1952 SCHEDULE

Day		7:00	7:30	8:00	8:30	9:00	9:30	10:00	10:30	Net
M O N		local	Hollywood Screen Test	Mark Saber - Homicide Squad	United Or Not	ABC ALL STAR NEWS		local		ABC
		local	CBS News / Perry Como	Lux Video Theater	Arthur Godfrey's Talent Scouts	I Love Lucy	LIFE WITH LUIGI	Studio One		CBS
		Captain Video	local	Pentagon: Washington	Johns Hopkins Science Review	Guide Right	FOOTBALL SIDELINES / FAMOUS FIGHTS	Boxing From Eastern Parkway With Ted Husing	Ringside Interview	DUM
		local	Those Two / Cam. News Caravan	Paul Winchell - Jerry Mahoney Show	Voice Of Firestone	Hollywood Opening Night	Robert Montgomery Presents		Who Said That?	NBC
T U E		local	Beulah	local						ABC
		local	CBS News / HEAVEN FOR BETSY	LEAVE IT TO LARRY	RED BUTTONS SHOW	Crime Syndicated / City Hospital	Suspense	Danger	local	CBS
		Captain Video	local	Life Is Worth Living	Keep Posted	WHERE WAS I?	Quick On The Draw	Meet The Boss	local	DUM
		local / SHORT ST. DRAMA	Dinah Shore / Cam. News Caravan	Texaco Star Theater / # BUICK CIRCUS HOUR		Fireside Theater	Armstrong Circle Theater	TWO FOR THE MONEY	CLUB TIME / Bob Considine	NBC
W E D		local	The Name's The Same	ABC ALL STAR NEWS		Adventures Of Ellery Queen	Wrestling From The Rainbo In Chicago (to 12 Midnight)			ABC
		local	CBS News / Perry Como	Arthur Godfrey And His Friends		Strike It Rich	Man Against Crime	Blue Ribbon Bouts	Sports Spot	CBS
		Captain Video	New York Giants Quarterback Huddle	local		STAGE A NUMBER		local		DUM
		local	Those Two / Cam. News Caravan	I MARRIED JOAN	Scott Music Hall / CAVALCADE OF AMER.	Kraft Television Theater		THIS IS YOUR LIFE	local	NBC
T H R		local	The Lone Ranger	ABC ALL STAR NEWS	Chance Of A Lifetime	PERSPECTIVE	POLITICS ON TRIAL	NFL FOOTBALL HIGHLIGHTS	local	ABC
		local	CBS News / HEAVEN FOR BETSY	Burns And Allen Show	Amos And Andy / FOUR STAR PLAYHOU.	BIFF BAKER, U.S.A.	Big Town	Racket Squad	I've Got A Secret	CBS
		Captain Video	local		Broadway To Hollywood Headline Clues	TRASH OR TREASURE	What's The Story	Author Meets The Critics	local	DUM
		local / SHORT ST. DRAMA	Dinah Shore / Cam. News Caravan	You Bet Your Life	Treasury Men In Action	Dragnet / Gangbusters	FORD THEATER	Martin Kane, Private Eye	Ask Me Another	NBC
F R I		local	Stu Erwin Show	ADVENTURES OF OZZIE AND HARRIET	ABC ALL STAR NEWS	Tales Of Tomorrow	local			ABC
		local	CBS News / Perry Como	Mama	My Friend Irma	Schlitz Playhouse Of Stars	OUR MISS BROOKS	MR. AND MRS. NORTH	local	CBS
		Captain Video	local	HOLLYWOOD OFF-BEAT	Rebound / DARK OF THE NIGHT	Life Begins At 80	local	Twenty Questions	Down You Go	DUM
		HERMAN HICKMAN / local	Those Two / Cam. News Caravan	RCA Victor Show	GULF PLAYHOUSE	The Big Story	The Aldrich Family	Gillette Cavalcade Of Sports	Greatest Fights	NBC
S A T		Paul Whiteman's TV Teen Club	Live Like A Millionaire	Feature Playhouse					local	ABC
		Stork Club	Beat The Clock	JACKIE GLEASON SHOW		JANE FROMAN'S U.S.A. CANTEEN	MEET MILLIE	BALANCE YOUR BUDGET	Battle Of The Ages	CBS
		local	The Pet Shop	local		Wrestling From The Marigold In Chicago With Jack Brickhouse				DUM
		Mr. Wizard	My Little Margie	All Star Revue		Your Show Of Shows			Your Hit Parade	NBC
S U N		You Asked For It	The Hot Seat	ABC ALL STAR NEWS		PLAYHOUSE ONE	THIS IS THE LIFE	Billy Graham's Hour Of Decision	ANYWHERE U.S.A.	ABC
		Gene Autry Show	This Is Show Business / # Jack Benny Program	Toast Of The Town		Fred Waring Show	Break The Bank	The Web	What's My Line	CBS
		Georgetown University Forum	local			Rocky King, Inside Detective	The Plainclothesman	Arthur Murray Party	Youth On The March	DUM
		Red Skelton Show	DOC CORKLE	Colgate Comedy Hour		Goodyear/Philco Television Playhouse		THE DOCTOR	local	NBC

In December, fulfilling a campaign promise, Eisenhower flew to Korea. TV news, still flexing its muscles, was able to force the Eisenhower staff into allowing a TV camera crew to join the print, radio, and newsreel members of the press pool. The heavily advertised Korean trip turned out to be something of a "news snooze." Even as President-elect, Eisenhower was unable to produce any significant progress in the stalled peace talks, and there was little exciting footage relayed to the folks back home. It remained for CBS and Ed Murrow, just a few days after Eisenhower's return, to bring the Korean War into the living room.

For two and one-half years, most of the day-to-day television coverage of the Korean War had consisted of Washington-based battle reports, or mild combat footage, often supplied by the government itself. Just before Christmas, Murrow's *See It Now* crew filmed soldiers at the front. The film was hastily returned to New York where it was quickly edited for presentation on December 28, an amazing turnaround time for a one-hour documentary. The program ignored the usual topics of why the war was being fought, how the fighting was going, and what political games of one-upmanship were transpiring at the truce talks. Murrow focused instead on average people and how they reacted under the intense pressure of a stalemated war. One reviewer called the program "a visual poem" because some of the show's best moments contained very little dialogue. These included a native girl in a South Korean military uniform singing "Silent Night" in a plane flying over enemy territory, a French officer who kept shrugging his shoulders as he noted that nobody really knew how to end the war, and a weary patrol being given its orders and then trudging off to face the enemy. Such scenes gave the show a feel for detail unrivaled at the time. Seeing the war portrayed in such human terms came as almost a shock to viewers at home, and they were deeply moved by the show. Seven months later, an armistice was signed, officially ending the three years of fighting in Korea. For many, Ed Murrow's Christmas documentary served as their only real glimpse of the confusion, frustration, and personal dedication of the forces stationed halfway around the world.

Television news was becoming increasingly important to American life. Network coverage of the 1952 presidential campaign, as well as the use of television by the Eisenhower-Nixon ticket, had proved to be decisive factors in the outcome of the race. Prominent newsmakers were beginning to treat television with more respect. Yet television remained, above all, a popular entertainment medium. Although millions viewed the broadcast of Eisenhower's presidential inauguration—the first to be shown live, coast-to-coast—far more watched *I Love Lucy* as a matter of course every week. In fact, on January 19, 1953, the night before the inauguration, a record number of viewers tuned in the program to see a special event: the birth of Lucy and Ricky Ricardo's first child.

At the time, pregnancy was considered a fairly taboo topic for broadcast, especially in a comedy format. Desi Arnaz and Lucille Ball were sticking their necks out a bit by devoting so much attention in that season's episodes to Lucy's pregnancy, but because Lucy was pregnant in real life, it would have been harder to avoid it. Production of the 1952–53 *I Love Lucy* episodes began a few months earlier than usual. In June 1952, five post-birth shows were filmed while Lucy showed no growth. In August, as she grew larger, the pre-baby shows were filmed. To ensure the acceptability of the treatment of so delicate a subject, a priest, a rabbi, and a minister were present during production to lend divine approval. The nation, which had already come to accept the Ricardos as real, became caught up in this latest development. What could make more sense in this natural show than for the couple to have a baby, certainly a common enough occurrence? As the new year approached, the big event drew closer. Lucy began having cravings for papaya milk shakes, and Ricky experienced sympathetic morning sickness. In an event that was a press agent's utopia, the real baby and the celluloid baby arrived within hours of each other, almost overshadowing the Eisenhower inauguration the next day.

About 70% of the nation's TV sets were tuned to *I Love Lucy* that night, and this tremendous ratings performance boosted CBS past NBC in that week's Nielsen ratings. Occasionally, CBS had topped NBC before, but this was the first of a string of weekly CBS victories that, by spring, put the network slightly ahead of NBC in the season's average. For two years after that, NBC insisted (by relying on alternate measuring methods) that it was still number one, but by 1955 CBS's lead was clear no matter how you looked at it and NBC had to concede that it had become number two. CBS's sitcom strategy had paid off. After more than twenty-five years, CBS had displaced NBC as America's number one network.

Besides boosting CBS to the top, *I Love Lucy* also touched off a stampede toward West Coast films, the first wave of which arrived for the 1952–53 season. Between 1951 and 1952, the number of filmed TV series almost doubled, going from twenty-five to forty-six. There were new crime, adventure, and drama anthology series, though sitcoms were regarded as the most important ventures as everyone hoped to duplicate the instant success of *I Love Lucy*. A large number of new shows began on film while some series that had been previously done live such as *The George Burns and Gracie Allen Show* transferred to celluloid.

One of the important advantages of a filmed series was that it could be rerun. This lowered the overall cost of a season's shows by allowing a thirteen-week summer rerun cycle consisting of selected episodes from the previous thirty-nine weeks. Reruns also helped the networks to fill the summer programming gaps that opened when many top stars were on vacation. The rerun value of filmed series, however, went beyond summer filler and opened a whole new market not possible with live network shows. Once a popular network filmed series completed its prime time network run, the films could be sold to individual stations for local broadcast and, conceivably, even to other countries.

Interest in film, and its rerun value, was inevitable as television continued to grow. The need to fill so many hours of broadcasting each day put both the networks and local programmers into the same position that Hollywood had been in years before with its theatrical features. In order to keep the public occupied in between big name features and large budget spectaculars, the studios regularly churned out screwball comedies, soap opera-ish romances, kiddie Westerns, and pulp adventure sagas all labeled "grade-B" movies. As television expanded, the appearance of TV equivalents to grade-B films was almost unavoidable.

Through the late 1940s, West Coast filmmakers such as Jerry Fairbanks worked to develop such filmed television series, but most of these vanguard efforts were terrible. They were also not considered very important to the networks' schedules, which were oriented toward live productions from New York, especially variety and drama vehicles. However, local stations desperately needed material to use when there was no network program, especially before completion of the coast-to-coast coaxial cable. In 1948, Frederick Ziv, radio's top program syndicator, set up a television branch to produce and distribute TV films to local stations. By the 1950s, Ziv was the most important independent syndicator in television, with material aimed chiefly at the 7:00 P.M. and 10:30 P.M. periods, when the networks often did not offer any shows to their affiliates. Besides Ziv, the Hal Roach studios, Screen Gems, and Revue also produced such TV films. In aiming programs at the syndication market, the Hollywood-based producers devised virtual carbon copies of Hollywood's grade-B theatrical films because their interchangeable plots and characters made them practically timeless.

The success of *I Love Lucy* prompted NBC to attempt a few filmed sitcoms in the fall of 1952. This strategy got off to a disastrous start, though, with what was generally regarded as the worst new sitcom of the new season, *Doc Corkle,* a highly-touted series starring Eddie Mayehoff as a screwball neighborhood dentist. The show was panned by critics, shunned by viewers, and abandoned by its sponsor. After three weeks, NBC replaced the program with its surprise success of the previous summer, *Mr. Peepers.* NBC's other new filmed sitcom entries for the fall were *I Married Joan* and *My Hero. I Married Joan,* starring Joan Davis and Jim Backus, was a competent copy of *I Love Lucy*. Backus played a believable judge who handled other people's domestic problems in court while facing complications at home from his own scatterbrained wife, Joan. *My Hero,* on the other hand, was a weak slapstick vehicle for Bob Cummings, who not only starred in the show but was its co-writer, co-executive producer, and part owner. He played a dopey California real estate salesman and, said one critic, brought a "magnificent terribleness" to his role.

Another unsuccessful NBC filmed comedy was the previously live *Red Skelton Show.* For the fall of 1952, Skelton changed to film production while NBC moved him to the Sunday at 7:00 P.M. period, hoping that his established success could turn the early evening slot into a strong lead-in for the entire evening. Instead, the filmed series fell badly in the ratings. Skelton continued to rely almost entirely on the bare-bones vaudeville setting of acts performing on a simple stage, and these appeared stale and cheap compared to even simple filmed sitcom stories. In March, when Skelton was ill, it was decided to take advantage of having the shows on film, and instead of using a substitute host, reruns of very recent shows were inserted to fill the time. This strategy backfired and Skelton's ratings fell further. At this point, NBC let

The inauguration of Dwight Eisenhower was covered live on all networks. *(National Archives)*

Skelton escape to CBS, where he returned, live, in the fall of 1953 with a much more rounded variety format (and a larger budget) that lasted seventeen years.

Even with the failure of Red Skelton on film and the proliferation of weak sitcoms, the continued high quality and success of *I Love Lucy* and the transplanted *Burns and Allen Show* demonstrated that filmed comedy series could be both well done and popular. While rejecting terrible shows such as *Doc Corkle,* viewers continued to show their willingness to accept and support the TV film format. For the fall of 1952, CBS and ABC each presented a successful new filmed sitcom with, respectively, *Our Miss Brooks* and *The Adventures of Ozzie and Harriet.*

Our Miss Brooks, on CBS, was a Desilu production that featured Eve Arden as Connie Brooks, an English teacher at Madison High School. The show had begun on CBS Radio in July, 1948 just two weeks after Lucille Ball's *My Favorite Husband* premiered, and was still a hit when the TV filmed version began. Arden played Brooks as a wise-cracking tough gal with a heart of gold who was both human and humorous in facing the daily grind of a high school teacher. She was constantly at odds with the school's blustery, authoritarian principal, Osgood Conklin (Gale Gordon), while trying to control her pupils, especially her main classroom problem, the squeaky-voiced Walter Denton (Richard Crenna). Perhaps her biggest problem was Philip Boynton (Robert Rockwell), a handsome biology teacher, who was too shy to respond to her advances and suggestions of marriage. At home, her elderly landlady, Mrs. Davis (Jane Morgan), constantly offered words of advice on every situation: how to handle the principal, how to control the students, and how to snare Philip Boynton.

Our Miss Brooks reflected the same care and craftsmanship that went into *I Love Lucy,* with an effective reversal of that show's setup: Connie Brooks was presented as the level-headed person surrounded by exaggerated, though generally realistic, characters.

The cast was especially effective together (Gordon, Crenna, and Morgan all came over with Arden from the radio version) and the stories evolved from their comic misunderstandings and interaction. The strong, independent personality of Connie Brooks set her apart from other female sitcom characters in the 1950s. Yet, in keeping with the prevailing social philosophy of the era, she was also presented as just waiting for her wedding day so she could retire from teaching and become a good wife. Until that day, Miss Brooks led a Victorian social life, never going beyond a discussion of the reproduction of horned toads with Mr. Boynton. There was, however, a happy ending. Though shyly avoiding romance with Miss Brooks for eight years on radio and television, in a movie adaptation of the series, Mr. Boynton finally popped the question.

ABC's *Adventures of Ozzie and Harriet,* like *Our Miss Brooks,* had begun on radio in the 1940s. There, Ozzie and Harriet Nelson had pioneered a style of domestic comedy in which they essentially played themselves: a happily married showbiz couple with two sons, David and Ricky. The only change made for television was that Ozzie and Harriet dropped all references to their show business careers and instead played solid middle-aged parents raising their family full time in a classy Los Angeles suburb. When the program came to television, David was fifteen and Ricky was twelve, and, over the next fourteen years, the main focus of the series was on their lives, from the teen years to young adulthood.

The Adventures of Ozzie and Harriet was not a screwball sitcom, but rather a continuing story about growing up in suburban America. The Nelsons were relaxed and natural people and the humor on the show developed from everyday problems and simple misunderstandings that the family and their friends and neighbors faced. Though the setting was an idealized household and the complications were as simple and noncontroversial as needing money for a date, the program was very much in the spirit of radio's epic family series, *One Man's Family,* and was very effective in presenting the growing pains and daily lives of a very likable TV family. Even Ricky's moment as a heart-throb rock'n'roller was incorporated. As Ozzie and Harriet proudly looked on, Ricky played his songs to screaming teenage fans on the show, and then he did the same in real-life concerts. From 1957 to 1964, he had more than a dozen top ten hits, including "Teenager's Romance," "Travelin' Man," "Poor Little Fool," and "Hello Mary Lou." In time, first David, then Ricky, got married. Even then, they never lost touch with the folks back home and, by the early 1960s, all three couples—Ozzie and Harriet, David and June, Rick and Kris—were introduced at the beginning of each episode as part of "America's favorite family."

On radio, the Nelsons had been one of many families that listeners followed with affection and interest, including the strong ethnic characters on programs such as *Life with Luigi* (Italians in Chicago) and *The Goldbergs* (Jews in New York). While Ozzie and Harriet thrived on television, however, the ethnic TV shows were in retreat. During the 1952–53 season a television version of *Life with Luigi* ran only three months, NBC's revival of *The Goldbergs* flopped, and CBS canceled *Amos 'n Andy.* Unlike their radio counterparts, ethnic TV shows touched off embarrassing criticism and controversy for the networks. Even though *Life with Luigi* came to television virtually unchanged from radio (including many performers from the radio cast) it was criticized for ethnic stereotyping. Despite the all-black cast for TV's *Amos 'n Andy,* black groups such as the NAACP urged a boycott of the program's sponsor. At the same time, the ethnic shows were not runaway big hits in the TV ratings. The networks decided that they were just not worth the trouble. As a result, programmers turned increasingly to comedies that avoided obvious ethnic slants while focusing on nondescript white middle class life, usually in safe, homogeneous suburbs. This dovetailed perfectly with the settings of many Los Angeles filmed sitcoms which were generally set in faceless California suburbs. *The Goldbergs* even tried to adapt to this new style in its final revival attempt in 1955. After twenty-six years of city living, the family moved to the suburbs, but this approach was an even worse failure. Not only were the Goldbergs visibly ethnic, they were *right next door!*

The increasing interest in noncontroversial settings and characters removed an important edge from the television sitcom form. Through the remainder of the decade, only a handful of new shows would have the touch of reality found in *I Love Lucy* or the expressive ethnic characters found in *Amos 'n Andy.* Even with well written, funny scripts, most of the new series would be trapped in a bland Neverland beneath the ever-present California sun. A perfect example of this approach was NBC's revival of *The Life of Riley,* a winter replacement series that began in January 1953.

Chester A. Riley (William Bendix) was a lovable bumbler who lived in a quiet nondescript Los Angeles suburb that was never disturbed by anything more than a harmless misunderstanding. It never even got cold there. His wife, Peg (Marjorie Reynolds), faithfully stood by him in any situation and was interested only in housework and raising their two children. Babs (Lugene Sanders) and "Junior" (Wesley Morgan), were an adult's view of perfect kids, always in some lovable mixup but at heart never selfish or malicious. Occasionally, the Rileys had friendly spats with their next-door neighbors, Jim and Honeybee Gillis (Tom D'Andrea and Gloria Blondell), but afterward they always remained good friends. Riley was presented as the comic focus of the series, and his simpleminded bumbling and misunderstandings touched off the weekly complications with his family and neighbors.

This setup had already failed in the 1949–50 season with a completely different cast, including Jackie Gleason as Riley. *The*

Life of Riley had been one of the first network radio sitcoms to transfer to television as a filmed series, but that version had a weak supporting cast for Gleason, terrible scripts, and cheap sets. Though the revival with Bendix (who had played Riley in the radio show and was now free of his movie contract) reflected better overall production and writing, several problems remained. The supporting characters were still lifeless stereotypes, overshadowed by the silly situations and reduced to mouthpieces for one-liners. More important, Bendix's Riley was too predictably powerless to carry the series. Jackie Gleason's Riley had at least seemed capable of blowing his stack, bringing a stronger comic tension to the character. With Bendix, it was a foregone conclusion that Riley would forgive and forget because he was as bland as everyone else. Yet despite all its shortcomings, the revived *Life of Riley* caught on and ran until 1958, a sure sign of the growing popularity of such noncontroversial sitcoms.

The failure of the ethnic comedies along with the success of *The Life of Riley* also reflected a subtle change in social attitudes across the country. In the expanding postwar economy of the early 1950s, more and more blue-collar Americans (like Chester A. Riley) were achieving their personal dream of joining the middle class and

---

September 20, 1952
The Jackie Gleason Show. (CBS). The "Great One" comes to CBS from DuMont, bringing along Art Carney, the June Taylor dancers, Joe the Bartender, the Poor Soul, and The Honeymooners. Pert Kelton is left behind, though, as Audrey Meadows becomes Alice Kramden number two.

October 3, 1952
Death Valley Days. Stanley Andrews is "the old Ranger," host and narrator to this popular syndicated Western anthology. Already a twenty-two-year radio veteran, this show runs another twenty years on television without ever receiving a network slot.

October 9, 1952
ABC All Star News. (ABC). ABC reenters television news with a five-night-a-week prime time combination of straight news, man-on-the-street interviews, and filmed reports. Against the standard entertainment fare of the competition, the program dies by Christmas.

October 26, 1952
Victory at Sea. (NBC). A twenty-six-week Sunday afternoon documentary series on the naval battles of World War II, using film from ten countries and an original musical score by Richard Rodgers.

December 30, 1952
The Ernie Kovacs Show. (CBS). CBS gives Ernie Kovacs a four-week tryout opposite NBC's Milton Berle.

January 15, 1953
Rod Serling's "Ward Eight" wins the $1,000 first prize in a TV script contest held by WTVN in Cincinnati.

February 1, 1953
You Are There. (CBS). Up-and-coming CBS newsman Walter Cronkite gets his own Sunday evening show on which he serves as anchor for a simulated news report covering an important event from history. Actors portray the historical figures while actual CBS reporters tell the story "from the scene."

February 2, 1953

Action in the Afternoon. (CBS). A true oddity. Though this Western is ostensibly set in Montana during the 1890s, the program is actually done live weekday afternoons from a backlot in Philadelphia.

March 1, 1953

WJZ becomes WABC in New York City.

March 19, 1953

NBC presents the first national telecast of Hollywood's Academy Awards ceremony. Bob Hope is emcee and Gary Cooper wins the "Best Actor" Oscar for his role in "High Noon."

April 1, 1953

The Adventures of Superman. One of the great syndicated television series of the 1950s brings Krypton's man of steel to life in the person of George Reeves. The program adheres faithfully to the straight-laced spirit of the Superman comic books, promoting "truth, justice, and the American way." And, of course, no one ever seems to notice the obvious resemblance between mild-mannered reporter Clark Kent and his famous alter ego.

April 3, 1953

TV Guide, previously a regional publication, becomes a national weekly, combining different editions containing local program listings with national feature articles. On the first cover: Lucille Ball and her new baby.

April 18, 1953

Rod Brown of the Rocket Rangers. (CBS). Future *Batman* major domo William Dozier produces a Saturday morning kiddie space opera. Cliff Robertson stars as the clean cut Rod Brown and Jack Weston plays his bumbling sidekick, "Wormsey."

May 30, 1953

ABC brings major league baseball to network television with Saturday afternoon "game of the week" broadcasts. For the first contest, Dizzy Dean and Buddy Blattner report the play-by-play as the Cleveland Indians beat the home team Chicago White Sox, 7 to 2.

moving to the clean, homogeneous suburbs. They wanted to leave behind the distinctive problems of urban life, and television programs with obvious ethnic or racial settings were disturbing, especially as comedies. Such stories served as reminders to people of both where their family had probably been some twenty years earlier and where other families still lived. It was much more reassuring to follow bland American families such as the Nelsons and the Rileys.

The move toward a lighter approach to entertainment on TV also reflected the growing influence of the Hollywood branch of the industry, as the medium shifted its operations westward. West Coast TV production received tremendous boosts from the opening of the coast-to-coast coaxial cable and the ratings success of filmed series such as *I Love Lucy* and *Dragnet.* In late 1952, both CBS and NBC opened new "television city" studio production facilities in California (CBS near Hollywood; NBC in Burbank), so that, for the first time, New York and Los Angeles were competing on an equal footing. The preference for one or the other location more and more reflected a choice in program philosophy. As with radio,

the West Coast TV producers worked well in light comedy, adventure, and variety formats done Hollywood style. Applying their approach to drama, however, tended to eliminate serious or controversial productions, especially in the filmed drama anthology series.

Radio producers had faced a similar philosophical choice during the 1930s. In 1936, when the producers of the New York-based *Lux Radio Theater* needed to boost sagging ratings, they moved out West. Once in California, they quickly adopted the West Coast emphasis on flashy stars over the weekly stories as the main attraction for listeners. In 1953, *The Lux Video Theater* made the complementary change for television, becoming one of the first TV drama series to originate from CBS's new television city.

Much of the difference in the approach to drama between the two coasts came from the dissimilar philosophies behind New York and Los Angeles entertainment productions. The East Coast, Broadway-based live TV plays were, by their very nature, imperfect. Like any individual performance on Broadway, mistakes were bound to occur and often did. Even the best performances were usually gone after one broadcast because few were kept on kines. Yet these limitations were a source of strength. Producers were more willing to experiment with new ideas and challenging themes because the plays were one-shot affairs. If they did not work, there was always next week.

The fluffy West Coast Hollywood-influenced filmed dramas, on the other hand, were designed, like filmed sitcoms, to play for years, especially in post-network syndication runs. As a result, they took fewer chances. One of the first West Coast TV producers explained, "Most of us are from the motion picture business, where we worked under a code for a long time, so we automatically observe good taste in programs. We must also consider the rerun value of a film, which would be impaired if we injected controversial material. You don't have this on live television."

As the Hollywood branch of TV asserted more influence on television production, this more restrictive attitude sometimes spilled over into the networks' overall approach to drama so that, given a choice, some executives would opt for the more cautious route in programming. The most obvious instances of this took place in the TV drama scripts that were adaptations from other sources, some of which were changed to seem "nicer" for television. Sometimes the changes were humorous and trivial, as when General Electric discovered that the episode it was sponsoring on *Studio One Summer Theater* was Rudyard Kipling's "The Light That Failed." GE forced CBS to change the title to "The Gathering Night." Other revisions went further, completely changing the thrust of a story.

Though *Schlitz Playhouse* proudly proclaimed that it was presenting the first Ernest Hemingway play to appear on television, "Fifty Grand," it did not point out the major alterations made to the story. In Hemingway's original plot, the central character, a boxer, bet against himself and deliberately threw a fight in order to win some money. The modified story had the boxer bet on himself to win, and then be beaten. By losing the fight, he learned the evils of gambling, gave up the habit, and went back home to his wife. In much the same vein, *The Lux Video Theater* performed a frontal lobotomy on "The Brooch," the first work by William Faulkner to be presented on television. The original story featured a mama's boy who permitted his mother to rule over his wife (described as "the trampy type"). When his wife left him, the boy realized his unending dependence on his mother, and killed himself. The television version presented him as a nice young kid who married the sweet young thing from next door. The mother tried to interfere in their lives, but the husband stood up to her, the mother gave in, and they all lived happily ever after. The producers said that the new self-regulating TV code forbade presenting suicide as a possible solution for someone's problems, but clearly the people at *Lux* could have eliminated the suicide while keeping the point and tenor of the play. The reasoning behind such alterations was best described by Frank Wizbar, director of the Hollywood-based filmed drama series, *Fireside Theater:* "We sell little pieces of soap, so our approach must be the broadest possible … we never take a depressing story."

There were people, chiefly on the East Coast, who were fighting this attitude toward television drama. They took their productions in the opposite direction, venturing into areas theretofore thought too topical for television. In early 1952, Fred Coe made an important change in his NBC drama showcase. He decided to stop relying so much on adaptations and start cultivating writers who could turn out original works. Previously, some thirty-minute drama anthology series had turned to original scripts, but most of them were slapdash, hackneyed, and meant just to fill time. With his original stories, Coe hoped to substantially upgrade *The Philco/Goodyear Television Playhouse* (the program had taken on Goodyear as an alternate sponsor in 1951). Throughout 1952, Coe tried out plays by young unknown writers who were not shackled by years of experience on Broadway or in Hollywood and seemed better able to create works that were specifically tailored for the small screen. Most of the new plays tended to be extended character sketches, taking one or two people and placing them in engrossing lifelike situations. One of Coe's first finds was a Texan, Horton Foote, who came up with "The Travelers," a mildly amusing look at two Texas women who were husband hunting in New York City.

By 1953, other hour-long drama shows began seeking new writers, and original television dramas began attracting critical acclaim. *Kraft Television Theater* presented two compelling originals by Robert Howard Lindsay, "The Chess Game" and "One Left Over." The first depicted an atheist alcoholic who, after discussing the idea with a priest, confessed to a murder he did not commit in order to save a young man he knew was being framed. The second portrayed the struggles of a young husband who lost his wife and two of his children in a car crash. The man had to overcome his grief and carry on life with his remaining daughter. Both plays were out of the ordinary for that era: alcoholics were seldom acknowledged much less portrayed with dignity; and death and its consequences were rarely discussed at all. Though dealing with these highly emotional subjects, both plays avoided easy, maudlin cliches.

Fred Coe's year-long search for good, original material at last paid off on May 24, 1953, when he presented Paddy Chayefsky's "Marty," starring Rod Steiger. "Marty" was well-suited for television in that it concerned the close, cramped life of simple people. Unlike most of its contemporaries (theater and tube), "Marty" did not concern itself with prominent people doing momentous things or beautiful people doing remarkable things. Instead, it focused on common people doing common things. Marty, as played by Steiger, was a not-so-young local butcher who still lived with his mother. She wished he would get married (to almost anybody) because she felt it was not right for anyone not to be married. Marty, who knew his looks were, at best, average, had tried and failed at meeting girls and had no desire to endure the pain of rejection again. After persistent nudging from his mother and his friends, Marty attended a weekly neighborhood ballroom dance where he met and fell in love with an equally lonely young woman (played by Nancy Marchand) who was no beauty herself. It was a simple story, told well, that used television's close quarters to its advantage.

The importance of "Marty" to the TV industry was that, for the first time, serious filmakers in Hollywood showed some interest in a production done for television. "Marty" received next to no publicity from NBC before its airing, and afterward the play was not even reviewed by many leading television critics. It was Hollywood that declared "Marty" worthy of merit by making a movie version (starring Ernest Borgnine). The word was out that television drama could be a source of high quality, commercial material. Established playwrights began taking television more seriously, while unknown writers and actors saw the opportunity for exposure they had been looking for. Viewers, too, began to notice the increased respect being paid to television drama. Previously, important theatrical films had been based on novels, short stories, and Broadway plays, but never on television scripts. Hollywood was, in effect, saying that original television drama could be just as good as live theater and popular literature. If there was such a thing as television's golden age, this marked the beginning of it.

Yet just as television drama was coming of age, Worthington Miner, one of TV drama's founding fathers, found himself without a job. After four years with *Studio One,* Miner had switched to NBC in the spring of 1952. He produced a brief summer series, *Curtain Call,* as a warm-up for a projected hour-long program in the fall (labeled "Studio Miner" because it had no real title). However, NBC was unable to sell this show and instead of "Studio Miner" the network presented *I Married Joan* and *The Scott Music Hall* with Patti Page. Throughout 1952 and 1953, Miner sat idle while NBC searched for a time slot. A new hour-long series (this one had a title, *Gallery*) was scheduled to start alternating with the new *Hallmark Hall of Fame* on Sunday afternoons, but the Hallmark company had no desire to cut back. It was enjoying great success featuring Sarah Churchill and Maurice Evans in Shakespeare classics. As a result, Miner found himself out in the cold.

The difficulty that even a veteran of Miner's stature faced in securing a new slot demonstrated the increasing competition for advertising dollars. With prime time filling up with filmed series, the non-prime time hours were becoming increasingly important to the networks as a repository for experimental "class" programming. Such material might be brought to prime time as a special prestige hit, but only after it had proved itself in the less critical time period. NBC placed *The Hallmark Hall of Fame* on Sunday afternoons and CBS did the same with Edward R. Murrow's *See It Now* news program. In November 1952, CBS added to its Sunday afternoon schedule *Omnibus,* a ninety-minute production by the Ford Foundation's Radio and TV Workshop, directed by Alex Segal and hosted by Alistair Cooke. Cooke described the series as a "vaudeville show of the arts and skills of man," though some reviewers saw it as being closer to a long-haired *Toast of the Town* with some *Studio One* on the side. The first episode featured excerpts from "The Mikado," "Tales of Anne Boleyn," and a William Saroyan original (with Sidney Poitier in a bit part). One of the highlights of the new series was a patient explanation of the great works of Beethoven by young conductor Leonard Bernstein. With its "mixed bag" approach, *Omnibus* constantly experimented in a generally unexplored field: adapting different forms of classical culture to popular tastes. Occasionally the program fell into the habit of repetition and condescension, but, as Cooke observed, "If you aim at the stars you sometimes land on the roof."

It was this willingness to try new ideas that might even fail that gave the so-called golden age of TV its life. Vehicles such as *Omnibus* as well as the top-of-the-line prime time drama showcases treated television drama as an exciting challenge. But this uninhibited spirit was soon doomed by technological progress. In 1953, technicians were already demonstrating early versions of video tape recorders, which would eventually sound the death knell for live television by providing an easy way to prerecord and preserve any show. What's more, the move to film and Los Angeles-style production continued to pick up steam.

The network that was leading the way in the marriage of television and Hollywood was granted salvation in 1953. On February 9, the FCC approved the merger of ABC and United Paramount Theaters, having decided that United Paramount was not connected to the Paramount Pictures-DuMont "cartel." ABC, which lost $141,000 in 1952 and owed $12 million, received an influx of $30 million with its marriage to United Paramount. The network felt that it could at last compete with NBC and CBS as an equal. Within one month, ABC's radio and TV O&Os signed up $4 million of new advertising business. By the summer, George Jessel, Ray Bolger, Paul Hartman, Cesar Romero, Danny Thomas, Sammy Davis, Jr., and Joel Grey were signed to headline shows (though the last two never made it to the air). U.S. Steel, which had sponsored *Theater Guild of the Air* on radio since 1945, agreed to come to television on ABC, rather than NBC, which had the radio show. ABC even finally moved out of its old headquarters in the RCA building (a remnant of the network's earlier days as NBC Blue).

ABC was not the only innovative force busy in television. Steve Allen reactivated the concept of a late night variety-talk show (on New York's WNBT), while KNXT in Los Angeles featured *Carson's Cellar,* a Friday night comedy-variety show starring Johnny Carson, who listed as his co-writer a fellow named Joe Twerp. Canada's top TV news commentator, Lorne Greene, came to New York to plug his stopwatch invention. Paul Newman portrayed Nathan Hale on CBS's historical dramatization series, *You Are There,* while newcomer James Dean "stole the show" from Walter

Hampton in "Death Is My Neighbor" on the *Danger* drama anthology. Dean played a young psychotic who nearly killed someone, a role he soon mastered on the movie screen. While all this was going on, young Philadelphians were watching WFIL-TV where, five days a week, radio disc jockeys Bob Horn and Lee Stewart presented *Bandstand,* a program taken over four years later by Dick Clark. In 1952, the kids were "gone" over Johnny Ray.

ABC did manage one humorous triumph over its competition to start the summer of 1953. With NBC and CBS neck and neck in the ratings, practically any event became an opportunity for one-upmanship. As a result, the two turned the June 2nd coronation of Great Britain's Queen Elizabeth into a childish race to be the first on the air with film from England of the ceremony, pompously dubbed "the birth of world TV." Both CBS and NBC hired speed pilots to fly in the films when they arrived in Canada. Appropriately, the two speed demons were late and NBC had to ask for footage from number three ABC, which calmly beat them both simply by arranging to pick up a Canadian television feed from Montreal.

Earlier in the day, NBC had faced other embarrassing technical problems when wire photo and live phone reports from London during *Today* were interrupted by ads from General Motors brazenly touting cars described as "queen of the road" and "royal carriages." British egos were also offended by J. Fred Muggs, a baby chimp that had become *Today*'s on-air mascot in February. He was shown bouncing about the studio making chimp noises in between reports on the coronation. People felt that his antics degraded a solemn occasion by injecting a circus atmosphere. Though NBC eventually issued a semi-apology, at the so-called "birth of world TV" American television had put its worst foot forward, pairing the queen of England with a monkey.

13. Point of Order

ON MARCH 25, 1953, THE SEEMINGLY ENDLESS battle over the development of color television technology reached a dramatic climax with the collapse of the CBS forces. The erosion of CBS's strength had begun in 1951, despite the government-ordered monopoly status granted to the CBS noncompatible color system in June of that year. Within months, CBS had discovered that few television set owners had any desire to discard black and white sets in favor of expensive color models, and by October the network had "temporarily" suspended its color broadcasts under the guise of complying with wartime production cutbacks. For longer than a year, CBS allowed the losing venture of noncompatible color television to lie dormant, while RCA's ever-improving compatible color process was limited to off-hour experimental broadcasts. Eighteen months after the much ballyhooed inauguration of CBS color, the viewing public found itself effectively denied any color broadcasts at all. In March 1953, the House Committee on Interstate and Foreign Commerce began hearings on the color question, trying to determine whether color TV was ready for the public or not.

RCA sensed the mood of the committee and saw the opportunity for victory. The company carefully modified its approach by presenting the RCA color process under the umbrella of the National Television Systems Committee (NTSC), an industry-wide group of twenty top television set manufacturers. As the NTSC color process, the proposal offered CBS a face-saving opportunity to terminate its noncompatible system officially. Rather than surrender to RCA, its hated rival, CBS could adopt a conciliatory stance and step aside in favor of a "new" color system with broad-based industry support. Following an RCA-NTSC demonstration that was almost identical to many previous RCA presentations, CBS president Frank Stanton announced, on March 25, that CBS had "reluctantly but realistically" recognized that it would be "economically foolish" to attempt to persuade the public to discard twenty-three million black and white television sets to institute CBS color. Without specifically endorsing RCA, Stanton ended the decade-old battle with the almost weary admission, "perhaps this time it is different, perhaps this time they have found the answer."

Others were more enthusiastic. Committee chairman Charles A. Wolverton said he was "astounded" by the quality of RCA-NTSC color, and his committee urged the FCC to approve the system forthwith. Wolverton said, "Color TV is ready for the public; there is no reason for more delay." RCA submitted its petition to the FCC in June, and the commission took a few months to ruminate.

On December 17, 1953, in one of the few instances in which the FCC publicly admitted a change of heart, the commission reversed its October 1950 decision favoring CBS color and approved the RCA-NTSC system. Immediately, NBC scheduled several color holiday specials, including the perennial "Amahl and the Night Visitors" (which reached the air first, only three days after the FCC ruling), the traditional *Dragnet* Christmas story, and the New Year's Tournament of Roses parade. By this time, the Korean armistice had been signed and the remaining limits on domestic production had been lifted, so NBC expected color TV set sales to skyrocket over the next twelve months.

NBC pursued color broadcasting with more vigor than the other networks in 1954. Realizing that its technicians still needed a good deal of practical experience, the network set up a rotating color broadcast schedule in the first part of the year. NBC broadcast, on the average, ten color programs each week, selecting different shows each week for treatment in color. By March virtually every NBC program had been telecast in color at least once.

The addition of color to some programs such as quiz, discussion, and children's shows did not seem to add much. The same held true for news. The only new information conveyed in the February 16 color telecast of the *Camel News Caravan* was the color of the bathing suits in the cheesecake feature footage (shot in Florida) and the color of John Cameron Swayze's ever-present carnation (red that day). However, women's programs—with those colorful fashions and taste-tempting food tips—were enhanced by color. The process was also an enormous aid to musical productions in programs such as "Amahl and the Night Visitors" and *Your Hit Parade*, so NBC began staging lavish musical-variety specials as sure-fire promotions for color. Advertisers, too, found color a welcome bonanza. Kraft was nearly apoplectic over the vibrant yellow luster of products like Velveeta, which provided a rich complement to the sincere voice of Ed Herlihy ("then smother it with thick Velveeta cream sauce"). Car manufacturers emphasized their two-tone auto-behemoths while cigarette companies presented their brands in bright, decorative packs. CBS went a little more slowly, restricting its color tryouts to a Friday afternoon variety show called *The New Revue,* with Mike Wallace and his wife, Buff, as hosts. ABC decided to postpone color broadcasting until the public demanded it.

There was no public demand for color TV. Only 8,000 of the expensive color sets were produced in the first six months of 1954 and manufacturers discovered that they were very hard to sell.

	7:00	7:30	8:00	8:30	9:00	9:30	10:00	10:30	
MON	local	J. DALY & THE NEWS	JAMIE	Sky King	OF MANY THINGS	Junior Press Conference	THE BIG PICTURE	This Is The Life	local	**ABC**
	local	CBS News	Perry Como	Burns And Allen Show	Arthur Godfrey's Talent Scouts	I Love Lucy	Red Buttons Show	Studio One		**CBS**
	Captain Video	MARGE AND JEFF	local	Twenty Questions	The Big Issue	Boxing From Eastern Parkway With Chris Schenkel			Ringside Interview	**DUM**
	local	Arthur Murray	Cam. News Caravan	Name That Tune	Voice Of Firestone	RCA Victor Show	Robert Montgomery Presents		Who Said That?	**NBC**
TUE	local	J. DALY & THE NEWS	Cavalcade Of America	local		MAKE ROOM FOR DADDY	U.S. STEEL HOUR / THE TV HOUR		The Name's The Same	**ABC**
	local	CBS News	Jane Froman	Gene Autry Show	Red Skelton Show	This Is Show Business	Suspense	Danger	See It Now	**CBS**
	Captain Video	MARGE AND JEFF	local	Life Is Worth Living	Pantomime Quiz	local				**DUM**
	local	Dinah Shore	Cam. News Caravan	Buick Berle Show / # BOB HOPE SHOW		Fireside Theater	Armstrong Circle Theater	JUDGE FOR YOURSELF	Bob Considine	It Happen. In Sports	**NBC**
WED	local	J. DALY & THE NEWS	Mark Saber Homicide Squad	At Issue	THROUGH CURTAIN	ANSWERS FOR AMERICANS	TAKE IT FROM ME	DR. I.Q.	Wrestling From The Rainbo In Chicago (to 12 Midnight)	**ABC**
	local	CBS News	Perry Como	Arthur Godfrey And His Friends		Strike It Rich	I've Got A Secret	Blue Ribbon Bouts	Sports Spot	**CBS**
	Captain Video	MARGE AND JEFF	local	Johns Hopkins Science Review	JOS. SCHILDKRAUT PRESENTS	COL. HUMPHREY FLACK	ON YOUR WAY	STARS ON PARADE	The Music Show	**DUM**
	local	Eddie Fisher	Cam. News Caravan	I Married Joan	My Little Margie	Kraft Television Theater		This Is Your Life	local	**NBC**
THR	local	J. DALY & THE NEWS	The Lone Ranger	Quick As A Flash	WHERE'S RAYMOND	BACK THAT FACT	Kraft Television Theater		local	**ABC**
	local	CBS News	Jane Froman	MEET MR. McNUTLY	Four Star Playhouse	Lux Video Theater	Big Town	PHILIP MORRIS PLAYHOUSE	City Hospital / Place The Face	**CBS**
	Captain Video	MARGE AND JEFF	local	New York Giants Quarterback Huddle	Broadway To Hollywood Headline Clues	What's The Story	Author Meets The Critics	The Big Idea	local	**DUM**
	local	Dinah Shore	Cam. News Caravan	You Bet Your Life	Treasury Men In Action	Dragnet	Ford Theater	New Adventures Of Martin Kane	local	**NBC**
FRI	local	J. DALY & THE NEWS	Stu Erwin Show	Adventures Of Ozzie And Harriet	PEPSI COLA PLAYHOUSE	PRIDE OF THE FAMILY	THE COMEBACK STORY	SHOWCASE THEATER	local	**ABC**
	local	CBS News	Perry Como	Mama	TOPPER	Schlitz Playhouse Of Stars	Our Miss Brooks	My Friend Irma	PERSON TO PERSON	**CBS**
	Captain Video	MARGE AND JEFF	local	Front Page Detective	MELODY STREET	Life Begins At 80	NINE THIRTY CURTAIN	Chance Of A Lifetime	Down You Go	**DUM**
	local	Eddie Fisher	Cam. News Caravan	DAVE GARROWAY SHOW	The Life Of Riley	The Big Story	Campbell TV Soundstage	Gillette Cavalcade Of Sports	Greatest Fights	**NBC**
SAT	Paul Whiteman's TV Teen Club	Leave It To The Girls	Talent Patrol	Music From Meadowbrook	Saturday Night Fights	Fight Talk	Madison Square Garden Highlights	local		**ABC**
	Meet Millie	Beat The Clock	Jackie Gleason Show		Two For The Money	MY FAVORITE HUSBAND	Medallion Theater	Revlon Mirror Theater		**CBS**
	local		National Football League Pro Football							**DUM**
	Mr. Wizard	Ethel And Albert	BONINO	Original Amateur Hour	Your Show Of Shows / # All Star Revue			Your Hit Parade		**NBC**
SUN	You Asked For It	FRANK LEAHY	NOTRE DAME FOOTBALL		Walter Winchell	Orchid Award	JUKE BOX JURY		Billy Graham's Hour Of Decision	**ABC**
	LIFE WITH FATHER	Private Secretary / # Jack Benny Program	Toast Of The Town		Fred Waring Show / Gen. Electric Theater	MAN BEHIND THE BADGE	The Web	What's My Line		**CBS**
	local	OPERA CAMEOS	local		Rocky King, Inside Detective	The Plainclothesman	DOLLAR A SECOND	Man Against Crime		**DUM**
	Paul Winchell Show	Mr. Peepers	Colgate Comedy Hour		Goodyear/Philco Television Theater		LETTER TO LORETTA	Man Against Crime		**NBC**

Westinghouse staged a big color push and found after one month that it had sold only thirty sets, nationwide. On one of the variety specials NBC held to promote color, emcee Bob Hope quipped that there was a "tremendous" audience watching in color, "General Sarnoff and his wife."

ABC was more than willing to let NBC occupy itself with color. Entering its first full season with the financial backing of United Paramount, ABC stuck to the more basic goal of winning over the television audience with fancy new black and white programming in order to catapult itself into direct competition with CBS and NBC. Such a leap would have been astounding, because when the merger with United Paramount was approved, ABC's ratings were only about 50% of CBS's and its status was much closer to that of the ailing DuMont system.

As the new season commenced, ABC presented a seemingly impressive line-up of new shows, highlighted by drama and situation comedy. The two showcases for drama represented a tentative vote of confidence in the struggling network by two major spon-

sors, United States Steel and Kraft Foods. Kraft had decided to launch a second weekly hour-long drama series, not on NBC (home of its Wednesday night series) but on ABC. U.S. Steel, too, had passed over NBC (home of its radio series) and scheduled *The U.S. Steel Hour* for ABC. While such support was gratifying and impressive, the network was banking on comedy as its chief ratings weapon.

ABC expected quick success with its new roster of veteran comics (George Jessel, Paul Hartman, Ray Bolger, and Danny Thomas) while holding high hopes for a new sitcom, *Jamie*. The list of newly acquired talent was formidable, but none of the shows became hits and ABC was unable to place a series in the top ten. The network was doing better in the ratings overall, winning some time slots and coming in number two in a few more, but the hoped-for leap to respectability did not take place. The chief stumbling block was one that would plague ABC for the rest of the decade: affiliates. Because station investment and construction was just gearing up after the freeze and Korean War, many large and medium-size cities still had only one or two channels operating. As a result, ABC had fewer affiliates than either NBC or CBS. In addition, many of ABC's affiliates were UHF stations and, because most home sets lacked UHF converter attachments, the network's programs, no matter how good, could not be picked up by large numbers of viewers. Until its affiliate situation improved, ABC would remain far behind the two television leaders.

Though its potential success was severely limited, ABC approached the season aggressively, out to score substantial gains despite the affiliate handicap. The network's emphasis on comedy vehicles was a sound strategy, building on a proven formula that had taken CBS to the top. ABC won warm critical praise for two of its new shows, though there were some disappointments.

The much-touted *Jamie* series proved to be the biggest letdown. Eleven-year-old Brandon De Wilde played Jamie, a young orphan living with his aunt. There, he became best friends with Grandpa (played by sixty-three-year-old Ernest Truex), who understood Jamie's loneliness and frustration at being an extra burden to an unwilling relative. Despite the age difference, the two constantly shared adventures and experiences together, often just sitting and gazing thoughtfully at the sky, perhaps searching for a brighter tomorrow. Though the pilot for the program had won rave reviews the previous season on the network's anthology series, *ABC Album,* the sentimentality dished out on the weekly series frequently overshadowed both the plots and the characters.

Veteran George Jessel was also lost in a great gush of tears and sentiment. He began the season as host of two programs, *The Comeback Story* and *George Jessel's Show Business.* The *Show Business* variety program included music and monologues and featured Jessel in his favorite, familiar role of toastmaster general of the United States, leading combination toast-roasts of celebrities. This show was squirreled away Sunday at 6:30 P.M., just before *You Asked For It,* while *The Comeback Story* received a Friday night prime time slot. As host to this maudlin copy of *This Is Your Life,* Jessel presented each week the tear-filled life story of a once famous celebrity who had fallen from grace but was battling back. Doing both shows proved too much for Jessel and in December Arlene Francis took over *The Comeback Story* while Jessel continued the Sunday variety series. In its terrible time slot, though, this barely lasted the season.

Pride of the Family, Paul Hartman's vehicle, turned out to be just an average Los Angeles filmed sitcom. Though Hartman was a talented dancer and satirist, he appeared as a bumbling father who, like Chester A. Riley, had a loving, faithful wife (played by King Kong's former flame, Fay Wray) and two bland teenage children, Junior (Bobby Hyatt) and Ann (Natalie Wood). Apart from these drab disappointments, ABC's new sitcom schedule contained two jewels, *Where's Raymond?* and *Make Room for Daddy,* which both featured stars essentially playing themselves.

Where's Raymond? cast Ray Bolger as Ray Wallace, a professional song and dance man who had a habit of arriving at the theater only minutes before he was to step on stage, causing the supporting crew to wonder constantly: "Where's Raymond?" Once he began performing, everyone forgot the frustrations and watched the charming, whimsical star. The show was less a sitcom and more a loose musical comedy tied together by a slim thread of situation. Bolger's stage act was the true focus of the series. Each week's musical numbers often incorporated his character bits from Broadway and feature films (such as the Scarecrow in "The Wizard of Oz"), and the show was greatly admired by critics as one of the more imaginative filmed series to come from Los Angeles. With ABC's affiliate problem, though, *Where's Raymond?* never developed a large following and ran only two seasons.

In *Make Room for Daddy,* Danny Thomas (who apparently had concluded that television was no longer "just for idiots") portrayed a show business father and, in effect, himself. The character of nightclub comedian Danny Williams was almost identical to the character Danny Thomas had been projecting for years in his own nightclub act and on television comedy-variety shows. In the sitcom setting, Thomas was given a strong TV family for support, consisting of Jean Hagen as his wife, Margaret; eleven-year-old Sherry Jackson as his daughter, Terry; and six-year-old Rusty Hamer as his son, Rusty. The concept was perfect for Thomas, resolving the many objections that had driven him from television variety the previous year. Unlike the random skits of a comedy-variety show, *Make Room for Daddy* provided a workable setting that allowed stories to be built around both domestic and show business complications.

Make Room for Daddy was filmed at Desilu and, like *I Love Lucy* and *Our Miss Brooks,* reflected important touches of real life. The Williams family lived in a New York City apartment, rather than a Los Angeles suburb. Danny was not a bumbler or a dummy, but an intelligent, principled, often stubborn, father and husband. Margaret was a loving but creditable wife, and the children were cute, though pushy and conniving often enough to seem real. More important, Danny Williams actually worked. His nightclub act was sometimes incorporated into the show and he even had to "go on the road" to perform. This served as an important basis of the humor at home because his absences caused family problems,

Make Room for Daddy did not become a hit until it moved from ABC to CBS in 1957. After the switch, the cast included: *(from left)* Marjorie Lord, Sherry Jackson, Angela Cartwright, Danny Thomas, and Rusty Hamer. *(Danny Thomas Productions and SFM Entertainment LLC)*

September 27, 1953

I Led Three Lives. From Ziv, America's leading television syndicator, comes Richard Carlson, a man renowned for subduing aliens in grade B science fiction film adventures. Playing an undercover agent for the FBI, he battles a more clear and present danger, the Communist Party, U.S.A.

October 2, 1953

Person to Person. (CBS). In addition to his Tuesday night *See It Now* chores, Ed Murrow hosts a Friday night celebrity interview show, originating directly from the stars' homes. One of the first guests is Massachusetts senator John F. Kennedy and his new bride, Jacqueline.

October 3, 1953

DuMont brings professional football to prime time for the first time. A national "game of the week" airs Saturday nights, while regional games are televised on Sunday afternoons. In the first NFL prime time contest, the Pittsburgh Steelers overcome the New York Giants, 24 to 14.

October 9, 1953

Topper. (CBS). A delightfully wacky sitcom about two married ghosts who can be seen only by Leo G. Carroll ("host to said ghosts") as the befuddled Cosmo Topper.

October 12, 1953

John Daly and the News. (ABC). After four years, ABC resumes early evening nightly news.

October 20, 1953

The Bob Hope Show. (NBC). Leaving the *Comedy Hour* rotation, Hope secures his own regular monthly comedy-variety series.

---

especially when he tried to compensate upon returning. The kids shamelessly exploited him to cover their mischief, until Danny caught on. Then, he exploded. When Thomas bellowed, the show crackled with energy. The moments of forgiveness and reconciliation that followed were especially effective because they showed that, underneath, he had a heart of gold and really loved his family.

Make Room for Daddy demonstrated that a believable father could serve as an effective comic focus for a series. Critics were effusive in praising the program, but the ratings were disappointing. Sixty stations carried the premiere episode (a good figure for ABC) and by November the show was on 112 stations, the largest number of any ABC program. Yet this could not match coverage by NBC and CBS, so *Make Room for Daddy* remained rather a cult program for three years. It became a big hit only when it moved to CBS in 1957.

Even with ABC's strong new line-up, NBC and CBS again dominated television, with their combined ratings more than four times ABC's meager numbers. Like ABC, they also included a healthy dose of comedy, though NBC continued to emphasize both filmed sitcoms and live comedy-variety hours. In fact, the network introduced only one new sitcom in the fall, *Bonino,* while bringing *My Little Margie* over from CBS.

Bonino was NBC's own "daddy" TV show, a live production by Fred Coe featuring one of the network's favorite variety guest stars, singer Ezio Pinza, as a concert singer whose career conflicted with his family life. Though the premise of *Bonino* resem-

bled that of *Make Room for Daddy,* Coe took it the opposite direction. Unlike Danny Williams, Babbo Bonino was established as a widower who gave up his far-flung touring schedule in order to return home and raise his six children (one of whom was played by Van Dyke Parks, who later became a rock musician and wrote music for TV commercials). The series was strongly ethnic and the children were considerably more independent than Terry and Rusty Williams, but the stories lacked the driving force of a personality like Danny Thomas. The program never took off, even though making Bonino a widower opened up a wide range of possibilities. Such a character offered the best of two comedy worlds: children to add a family touch, and girlfriends for sex appeal. Though not much happened in this series (which ended after just three months), many TV widowers followed Bonino and they exploited both angles extensively.

Prior to his stint on *Bonino,* Ezio Pinza had alternated with singer Dennis Day on *The RCA Victor Show* during the 1951–52 season. In the fall of 1952, Day became the sole star of the program and in the 1953–54 season the show went to film and its title was officially changed to *The Dennis Day Show.* Through each permutation, Dennis Day played himself, Dennis Day, an often naive but determined young bachelor-vocalist living in Hollywood and trying to get ahead in show business. His character had been developed on Jack Benny's radio show during the 1940s and came virtually unchanged to television. (He also continued on Benny's program.) Cliff Arquette, who had appeared occasionally on Benny's radio series himself (playing Jack Benny's father) brought his Charlie Weaver character to television as the janitor for Day's apartment building. NBC seemed to consider the filmed series to be either a sleeper hit or doomed from the start because the network threw it to the wolves by placing it against *I Love Lucy* on Monday night.

Jack Benny, who had perfected the "mirror of reality" style of a comedian playing himself two decades earlier on radio, continued his own steady expansion into television that season. Beginning in the fall of 1950, Benny had done occasional floating specials on CBS television, while maintaining his successful Sunday night CBS radio show. By 1951, he settled on 7:30–8:00 P.M. Sunday as a good television slot, appearing there about once a month. By slowly increasing his television work, he developed an excellent feel for the medium before attempting more frequent exposure. He had seen too many comedians burn themselves out trying to do too much on a weekly basis. In the fall of 1953, Benny's TV show appeared every third week and the following season he agreed to an every-other-week schedule.

The Jack Benny radio show combined the variety and situation comedy formats by presenting Benny as the low-key star of a comedy-variety show about trying to put on a comedy-variety show. The show-within-a-show setup allowed Benny to act in a very relaxed, natural manner and gave him the option of shifting back and forth from variety to sitcom. Sometimes the comedy-variety show was presented intact, with guests, songs, and sketches. Other times, the show would never start at all as the action focused on backstage complications and Benny's home life. For television, he continued this winning format intact.

What separated Jack Benny's show from others that used a similar formula was Benny's uncanny sense of comic timing and delivery, combined with his strong supporting cast. The familiar characters that had surrounded him for years on radio made the transition to television almost as easily as he did, drawing on their own well-established personalities. Portly Don Wilson the announcer portrayed Don Wilson the announcer; Eddie Anderson continued as Benny's valet, Rochester; and Dennis Day the vocalist played Dennis Day the vocalist (a role he obviously relished). Mel Blanc (the voice of Bugs Bunny, Daffy Duck, and other Warner Bros. cartoon zanies) appeared as an assortment of crazy characters including Professor Le Blanc, Benny's frustrated violin teacher; Sy, a very concise Mexican who spoke in one word sentences; and the sputtering personality of Benny's limousine, a misfiring old Maxwell.

At the center of the show was the easily identifiable character of Jack Benny, the vain miser. Benny employed an excellent crew of writers who came up with continuing routines that fit the character: he had a pay phone in his house, kept his money in a subterranean bank vault, and filled his Maxwell with gasoline one gallon at a time. As a master of delivery and timing, Benny used such material for years. Though Fred Allen once said that Jack Benny couldn't ad-lib a belch after a Hungarian dinner, it was obvious that he did not have to. Benny's elongated double-takes and phrases such as "Well!" "Now cut that out!" and "Wait a minute!" became legendary. He could milk a bit better than anyone. Once, when confronted by an armed robber who demanded, "Your money or your life," Benny took an extended, deliberate pause (building audience anticipation and laughter) before delivering his anguished reply, "I'm thinking it over!"

Jack Benny's television show, like his radio program, became a top ten hit. Even with this success, Benny did not drop his weekly radio show until 1955 (he was one of the last of the big name comics to do so) and he did not begin doing his television show on a weekly basis until the fall of 1960.

With the strong showing by Jack Benny and the continued top ratings by veteran filmed sitcoms such as *I Love Lucy* and *Our Miss Brooks,* CBS held on to a very slim lead as the number one television network (though NBC still challenged that claim, touting its own numbers that still showed it as number one). The strength of CBS's sitcoms in the 1953–54 season contrasted sharply with the downturn in NBC's comedy-variety vehicles. Both of the network's top-of-the-line showcases, *All Star Revue* and *The Colgate Comedy Hour,* were in serious trouble, in artistic quality as well as in ratings strength.

In the fall, NBC reduced *All Star Revue* to a once-a-month offering placed in the *Your Show of Shows* time slot and, by December, after Martha Raye had often been called upon to act as host, the title was changed to *The Martha Raye Show.* The remaining headliners from *All Star Revue* were merged into *The Colgate Comedy Hour* rotation so that the Sunday night show was divided almost evenly (but erratically) among Dean Martin and Jerry Lewis, Jimmy Durante, Eddie Cantor, Donald O'Connor, and Bud Abbott and Lou Costello. Ed Sullivan's show regularly topped this line-up in the ratings and, at a yearly budget of $6 million, the Colgate program was turning into a growing disappointment. Colgate's producers seemed unable to find fresh new talent to act as hosts, and the old timers, who often repeated their old routines over and over again, began to irritate many home viewers. During one of the frequent appearances by Abbott and Costello, a frustrated viewer, Frank Walsh of West Hampstead, Long Island, took out his gun and shot his television set. He later told police he thought the show was too loud. Naturally, such a cult figure could not be ignored by the medium he wished to destroy. Less than a week later, Frank Walsh of West Hampstead, Long Island, appeared on *Strike It Rich* ("the program with a heart") and won—what else—a new television set.

The erosion of the comedy-variety format during the 1953–54 season was not limited to NBC's *Colgate Comedy Hour.* Stars throughout the networks' schedules were suffering from escalating costs and format fatigue. The grueling weekly TV schedule that Jack Benny so carefully avoided was taking its toll. Even Godfrey stumbled.

As a virtual one-man network for CBS radio and television, Arthur Godfrey appeared invulnerable. With his consistently high ratings, Godfrey was responsible for millions in advertising revenue and stood practically beyond network criticism. If he decided to tell a slightly risqué story or to change around the format of one of his programs, sponsors and network executives accepted it. Over the years, he had built his own strong organization to handle the multi-million-dollar enterprise, taking care of booking and paying guests, as well as managing his own cast of regulars. Godfrey treated his shows as both a business and family affair, acting like a benevolent father who was determined to take care of his performing family.

Since 1951, Godfrey's "family" had included young singer Julius La Rosa. La Rosa soon became the most popular member of the supporting cast, with his fresh, modest personality generating a tremendous following, second only to Godfrey himself. In the fall of 1953, as his career continued to expand, La Rosa violated an unwritten rule of Godfrey's organization: He arranged his own business deals, hiring an agent and signing an independent recording contract. Godfrey's response came a short time later.

On Monday, October 19, as Godfrey was nearing the conclusion of his morning radio-television simulcast program, he brought La Rosa to the microphone and began a fatherly reminiscence of how he had brought the young singer so far so fast. La Rosa, he noted, seemed to be on the verge of stardom on his own. He had signed

---

November 13, 1953
The Jack Paar Show. (CBS). Paar hosts an easy-paced daytime variety show, assisted by a family of regulars that includes Edie Adams and Jose Melis.

December 4, 1953
Sylvester "Pat" Weaver becomes president of NBC-TV.

December 30, 1953
The first compatible color TV sets, built by the Admiral corporation, go on sale. Price: $1,175.

January 3, 1954
"The Bing Crosby Show." (CBS). Even more hesitant toward television than Jack Benny, "Der Bingle" headlines his first television show. He will continue to do a few specials each season, resisting a weekly series for nearly a decade.

February 22, 1954
Breakfast Club. (ABC). ABC returns to the daytime television battles with a video version of Don McNeill's veteran radio variety hour. Though the program is sold out on radio, the network cannot give away ads for the television series, which is carried by only a few stations.

May 23, 1954
Earn Your Vacation. (CBS). Johnny Carson debuts on network television as host of a short-lived game show.

July 9, 1954
It's News To Me returns to the air on CBS with a new quizmaster, the ubiquitous Walter Cronkite. John Henry Faulk remains a regular panelist.

an independent recording deal and was going to become "a great big name." Godfrey asked La Rosa to sing "I'll Take Manhattan" (which he sang). Then, as the show was ending, Godfrey said: "Thanks ever so much, Julie. That was Julie's swan song with us; he goes now out on his own, as his own star."

What this meant was that Julius La Rosa had been fired.

At a press conference the next day, Godfrey was pressed to explain why he so suddenly dismissed one of his protégés. Godfrey responded that La Rosa did not understand that on his show "we have no stars ... we're all one family." By trying to venture into independent recording as a star outside that family, La Rosa had, Godfrey said, lacked "humility." To the general public, however, it appeared just the opposite. It was Godfrey who seemed to lack humility, firing an aide who had become very popular on the show.

Immediately after the firing, La Rosa became an instant *cause celebre.* He was signed to appear on a number of Ed Sullivan's programs where he acted very humble, but was lost in some silly production numbers. Later, La Rosa was host of a few TV summer replacement musical series, but he never really made it big on his own. But something did happen to Godfrey. He began losing his audience. For a decade, the Old Redhead had been Mr. Nice Guy, Mr. Natural. After his firing of La Rosa, he appeared instead to be an evil taskmaster, jealous of every scrap of publicity. This was clearly a wild over-reaction to the La Rosa incident, but the public's view of Godfrey had become jaundiced. By March 1954, neither of his two television shows was in the top ten, an unprecedented situation at that time. Though he remained on the tube for another five years, and on radio into the 1970s, Godfrey was never able to regain the stature he had before the October day he gave young La Rosa the kiss of death.

Another television institution, *Your Show of Shows,* ended its successful run in 1954. The program had been one of NBC's first comedy-variety blockbusters, but unlike many others that followed it, *Your Show of Shows* quit while it was still in top form. Performers Sid Caesar, Imogene Coca, Carl Reiner, and Howard Morris were still sharp and the writers, including Neil Simon and Mel Brooks, were often brilliant. Nonetheless, the program's ratings had dipped a bit in the 1952–53 season, so producer Max Liebman instituted a few changes for the fall of 1953. He dropped the Billy Williams Quartet and the dance team of Bambi Lynn and Rod Alexander, invited more guests, and worked with an increased budget. It soon became apparent that there was a more fundamental problem that could not be solved by such minor tinkering.

Viewers who followed the program show after show, season after season, had come to know the cast and writers inside out and there was little either could do that seemed fresh and new. Even very funny skits were somehow familiar and repetitious. The escalating costs of the program applied further pressure. With a budget of $100,000 to $125,000 per week ($4 million per year), the loss of even one sponsor pushed the program into the red. In February 1954, Caesar, Coca, and Liebman decided that they had done all they could in *Your Show of Shows* and made plans to split up and start fresh as headliners of their own shows in the fall. The last three *Your Show of Shows* programs recapitulated the most popular skits of the series, which had become a TV legend while it was still on the air. The tear-filled final program on June 5 featured a guest appearance by Pat Weaver, the man responsible for selling the show's original concept in 1949. All the central figures from *Your Show of Shows* had varying degrees of success in their subsequent series, but none of them was able to assemble such a pool of consistently successful writing, producing, and acting talent again. Fortunately, there were kines saved of a number of their hilarious performances and, in 1973, some of them were stitched together

and released as a feature film "Ten from *Your Show of Shows.*" In this way, these landmarks of TV comedy, still as sharp and fresh as ever, went on to influence a new generation of TV comedians.

The appearance of Pat Weaver on the final edition of *Your Show of Shows* reflected his increased public stature at NBC. Just before New Year's 1954, Weaver was promoted to the post of president of NBC, in hopes of meeting the challenge of CBS's continued strong ratings. At once, he reactivated his concept of regularly scheduled special programs (dubbed "spectaculars") which had run into network and sponsor opposition when first proposed in 1951. This time, Weaver presented the spectaculars as the means to catapult NBC back into a clear lead in the TV ratings, and he was able to convince the sponsors to try it. Weaver signed Max Liebman to coordinate the project, which was slated to begin in the fall of 1954.

One reason that skeptical sponsors were more receptive to the concept of spectaculars was that another Weaver innovation, *Today,* had turned into the biggest money-making show on television. Even J. Fred Muggs, the program's mascot chimp, had become a celebrity and turned up as a guest on a number of NBC variety shows. Unfortunately, Muggs lacked the sense of camaraderie that usually existed among showbiz folk and he began biting people. After he bit Martha Raye on the elbow in April, Muggs was sent on a worldwide promotional tour. There, he attracted the attention of the Soviet newspaper, *Izvestia,* which described J. Fred Muggs as, "A symbol of the American way of life ... Muggs is necessary in order that the average American should not look into reports on rising taxes and decreasing pay, but rather laugh at the funny mug of a chimpanzee."

In March 1954, CBS launched *The Morning Show* in an attempt to duplicate NBC's success with *Today.* The new show included a similar mixture of news, interviews, and features, with Charles Collingwood as the news anchor and Walter Cronkite as the genial host. Like *Today, The Morning Show* had its own flashy wall gadgets and animal mascots, though Humphrey the hound dog and Charlamane the lion were puppet characters (from Bil and Cora Baird) and much easier to control than J. Fred Muggs. However, the wall gimmicks were just as confusing and silly as *Today*'s. At appropriate moments in the program, Cronkite pointed to an electric weather map that was covered with special effects meant to resemble falling rain, snow, and clouds. On the home screen, it seemed more like a giant pinball machine than a helpful guide to the nation's weather. Cronkite soon tired of his role as entertainer-bon vivant and left *The Morning Show* in August, though the program continued under a cavalcade of successors including Jack Paar, John Henry Faulk, Will Rogers, Jr., and Dick Van Dyke. None of them could boost the program anywhere near *Today's* ratings and, after three years, CBS gave up and canceled the show.

Pat Weaver had more success with NBC's new one-hour features and interview program, the late-morning *Home* show, also begun in March 1954. Like many other daytime shows, *Home* was aimed at housewives, but Weaver treated them with considerably more respect, assuming that they were intelligent, perceptive viewers. With Arlene Francis and Hugh Downs as hosts, *Home* avoided the glamour chit-chat formula in favor of a more down-to-earth style of dealing with fashion, food, home decorating, leisure activities, home gardening, and children. It was an immediate hit and dominated late morning programming for three and one-half years, before succumbing to the competitive pressures from a line-up of popular soap operas on CBS.

By the summer of 1954, Pat Weaver's amazing programming abilities and willingness to innovate had generated new excitement at NBC. With Weaver back, three of the four television networks

In the fall of 1953, after two years of Sunday afternoon broadcasts, *See It Now* with Ed Murrow *(foreground)* moved into prime time. *(CBS News/CBS Photo Archive © 2003 CBS Worldwide, Inc. All Rights Reserved.)*

were once again in the position of tremendous growth and expansion, after the slowdown caused by the FCC freeze and the Korean War. CBS was solidifying its newly-won ratings lead, NBC was banking on Weaver's leadership skills, and ABC was drawing on the money and Hollywood experience of United Paramount.

The only network that was slipping was DuMont, which was in both financial and programming distress in early 1954. The FCC continued to prevent DuMont from acquiring any new owned and operated stations, and the failure of UHF meant that there still were not enough TV stations in most major cities to provide strong affiliates for all four networks. DuMont inevitably came up last in the competition. Actually, DuMont did have a brand new project that it hoped would provide a boost in its network prestige and income, a giant new television production facility located in New York. However, instead of serving as DuMont's successful equivalent to the expansion by the other three networks, the five-studio $4 million "telecenter" proved to be a very expensive failure.

Over the years, while the DuMont network had been losing money, the parent DuMont Labs had made enough to keep the overall DuMont operations solvent. In building the New York telecenter (the biggest on the East Coast), DuMont funneled what little company profits there were away from program development and into the future facility. This strategy, while logical, proved to be a mistake. By the time the telecenter was completed and dedicated on June 14, 1954, television producers interested in using expanded facilities were heading west. As a result, while the telecenter remained largely unused, DuMont's programs reflected the painful absence of money.

The network's new offerings for the 1953–54 season were practically doomed from the start by low budgets resulting in mediocre scripts and productions. *Love Story* was a simpering romance anthology, *The Stranger* was a stale pulp adventure featuring a mysterious Shadow-like character, and *Melody Street* required the performers to lip synch to other people's records. Even a series such as *Colonel Humphrey Flack,* with a moderately good character actor (Alan Mowbray) as lead, could not compensate for DuMont's inadequate budgets. Compared to the flashy variety shows, big name sitcoms, and classy drama programs on the other networks, DuMont's series looked cut rate. Fewer and fewer viewers and local stations bothered to even consider DuMont's offerings. The only large audience DuMont attracted in 1954 tuned in for a show that the network itself did not stage: the Army-McCarthy hearings broadcast in April, May, and June.

Senator Joseph McCarthy had been awarded his own committee and staff when the Republicans took control of Congress after the 1952 elections. As a member of the president's party, the majority party in Congress, McCarthy acted as if he had been given a blank check to pursue his far-flung investigations of Communist infiltration into any area of public life he wished. He often used the mass media to rally support and to blunt criticism, bending broadcast rules to suit his needs.

In 1949, the FCC had formally articulated a Fairness Doctrine applying to broadcasters in reporting important public issues. Previously, stations had been obliged to cover issues fairly, but also to refrain from expressing their own editorial views. The commission said in the Fairness Doctrine that stations could editorialize on the air, as long as their overall coverage provided "reasonably balanced presentations" of current issues. McCarthy interpreted this to mean that anytime anyone on television took a stand on a controversial issue, an equal and opposing opinion had to be presented. He sold the public on this view and cajoled the individual stations and networks into accepting it, giving him free access to television for the flimsiest of reasons. In November 1953, after much huffing and puffing, McCarthy even received "equal time" to reply to a TV speech by former President Harry Truman.

In his speech, Truman had merely used the word "McCarthyism"—as the senator's process of guilt-by-inference had been labeled—while defending himself against charges from the new Republican attorney general, Herbert Brownell. That did not matter to McCarthy, who ignored everything Truman said and used the television time to launch a thinly veiled assault on his brother Republicans in the Eisenhower administration for not doing a good enough job weeding out Communists. McCarthy also promised to intensify his latest investigation, which was aimed at finding Red subversives in the U.S. Army. For once, it seemed as if McCarthy had aimed his sights too high. President Eisenhower and the Republican leaders felt McCarthy needed to learn who was boss, and they waited for an appropriate opportunity to discipline him.

On March 7, 1954, CBS broadcast a speech from Miami by former Democratic presidential candidate Adlai Stevenson, who blasted the Republican Party in general and Senator McCarthy in particular. Though this program was part of the network's policy of regularly offering air time to major political figures, McCarthy immediately demanded equal time to reply. On March 8, the Republican National Committee pulled an end-run around McCarthy by announcing that Vice President Richard Nixon, not McCarthy, would respond to Stevenson. This was the break the networks had been waiting for, and CBS rejected McCarthy's request. McCarthy fumed: "They will grant me the time, or they will learn what the law is. I will guarantee that."

This threat could not be lightly dismissed, and CBS was quick to point to the Republican Party action as the reason for its refusal. Though the networks had always resented McCarthy's heavy-handed demands, he had successfully intimidated them because they knew he generally had strong support from the public and powerful allies in the government. Executives went along to avoid embarrassing public controversies and, more important, threats of trouble from the FCC. McCarthy had effectively handpicked two of Eisenhower's nominees for the FCC and the commission almost routinely followed McCarthy's suggestions to investigate "suspicious" broadcasters. In one case, Edward Lamb (an Ohio station owner who had failed to carry McCarthy's speeches) found himself enmeshed in FCC actions meant to deprive him of his stations' licenses because of alleged Communist connections. Lamb aggressively defended himself and placed full-page ads in the *New York Times* and other papers offering $10,000 to anyone who could prove he was a Communist. Three years of expensive, drawn-out hearings ensued, and only the depth of Lamb's financial resources and the eventual fading of McCarthy's influence prevented him from being beaten. The message of the Lamb case had not been lost on other broadcasters: Don't mess with McCarthy.

However, McCarthy's seemingly invulnerable stature was shaken when the Republicans circumvented his request for equal time after Stevenson's Miami speech. The next day, March 9, Senator Ralph Flanders of Vermont became the first Republican to attack McCarthy on the Senate floor. Later that night, CBS's Ed Murrow attacked McCarthy in a much larger forum.

Murrow's *See It Now* had moved into prime time on Tuesday evenings in the fall of 1953, after two years of Sunday afternoon broadcasts. In October, the program carried a report on a victim of McCarthy-style guilt by association, Lieutenant Milo Radulovich. In March, Murrow and producer Fred Friendly pieced together film clips and information on McCarthy that their crew had assembled and, on March 9, *See It Now* presented "A Report on Senator Joseph McCarthy."

In the program, Murrow deliberately let the film clips speak for themselves because they vividly illustrated McCarthy's style of using half-truths and vague associations to inflame audiences, badger witnesses before his committee, and embarrass people he had under suspicion. After each film sequence, Murrow came on camera, simply noted the inaccurate statements made by the senator, point by point, and then moved on to the next piece. At the conclusion of the report, Murrow underscored the presentation, taking a very strong editorial position:

> It is necessary to investigate before legislating, but the line between investigation and persecuting is a fine one, and the junior senator from Wisconsin has stepped over it repeatedly ... We must remember always that accusation is not proof, and that conviction depends upon evidence and due process of law ... This is no time for men who oppose Senator McCarthy's methods to keep silent, or for those who approve ... The actions of the junior senator from Wisconsin have caused alarm and dismay amongst our allies abroad and given considerable comfort to our enemies, and whose fault is that? Not really his. He didn't create this situation of fear; he merely exploited it, and rather successfully.

Murrow took this step with great trepidation. To spell out his judgment of McCarthy so clearly and firmly violated a cardinal rule in his style of journalism: Don't tell the viewer what the story is supposed to mean; instead present the facts and let the viewer decide. Murrow felt, however, that the issue of McCarthyism was too important and that, in this case, there should be a temporary suspension of the rules.

This suspension was both good and bad for television news. For one thing, it marked a shining moment in broadcast journalism in which Ed Murrow drew the American people's attention to a grave situation many were not aware of. Other reporters in the early 1950s had tried to expose McCarthy as a tricky operator, but none had Murrow's stature and vast television pulpit. Murrow's *See It Now* show on McCarthy set a standard for bravery and decisiveness that television journalists would measure themselves by for years.

The day after the Murrow broadcast, CBS was flooded with telegrams supporting the show, and Eisenhower praised Senator Flanders for his Senate speech criticizing McCarthy. The tide had turned. CBS turned down McCarthy's request that William F. Buckley appear in his place to respond to Murrow's program. McCarthy had to appear himself. Though McCarthy had often used television to air charges against other people, he was on foreign turf trying to respond to a well-produced documentary with his blustery style. Because Murrow had used McCarthy's own words throughout the report, McCarthy was put in the position of trying to respond to himself. William F. Buckley might have been able to sidestep this problem with the force of his cultivated, smooth manner, but McCarthy would not. Yet he also could not turn down the air time without losing face.

In his filmed reply, McCarthy assumed his usual approach to television: Take the offensive and use the air time to generate other news. He treated Murrow's broadcast as unimportant and not worthy of a detailed reply, turning instead to the juicier topic of a possibly sinister eighteen-month gap in the development of America's first hydrogen bomb. Six days later, while denying any connection with McCarthy's charges, the Atomic Energy Commission suspended the security clearance of J. Robert Oppenheimer, a top nuclear scientist who had urged delay in constructing the H-bomb. Though McCarthy's response to Murrow's program did stir up another controversy, it failed to blunt the impact of the original presentation. More than ever, McCarthy was open for attack.

Murrow's *See It Now* show on McCarthy demonstrated that the medium of television could serve as a powerful independent force with the ability to affect national politics even beyond a national election. Yet the broadcast also opened a Pandora's box of troubles. For the first time, a television newsman had taken a definite stand on a controversial topic and, naturally, there were many viewers who disagreed with his conclusions. They also questioned Murrow's decision to use *See It Now* to present his personal viewpoint over the air. "Who elected him?" the cry went. A suspicion began to grow that television could be used as a propaganda mouthpiece to champion unpopular causes.

Some of this suspicion was well founded and even some anti-McCarthy forces, who applauded Murrow's show, expressed reservations about the precedent that the *See It Now* episode had set. What would have happened if the tables were turned? If Murrow could awaken the nation with his thoughtful analysis, what could a clever rabble rouser do? What if McCarthy had known television techniques better than he did, and had responded with a slicker program wounding Murrow? Or what if McCarthy had been a broadcaster in the first place? If the networks allowed news anchors to take stands in their newscasts, what could prevent a sharper, better-looking version of Joseph McCarthy from putting everyone in his pocket? The fear of just such an event spread through CBS and, in later years, Murrow found the opportunity to express such a strong conviction on TV much harder to come by. For some people, Murrow's McCarthy broadcast marked the day the device they had so eagerly brought into their homes turned against them, challenging their pre-established views. Television and, more specifically, television news, would never be seen as the same benign servant it had appeared to be before March 9, 1954.

The attacks against McCarthy continued. On March 11, the Army put McCarthy on the defensive by charging that he and his assistant, Roy Cohn, had threatened to "wreck" the Army and Army Secretary Robert T. Stevens if a recently drafted McCarthy staff member, G. David Schine, was not given preferential treatment. Public hearings were scheduled for April to delve into the complicated Army and McCarthy charges and counter-charges.

The thirty-six days of public testimony at the Army-McCarthy hearings were broadcast live by DuMont and ABC, both of which had little or no daytime programming. NBC and CBS, which did, stuck to late night wrap-ups of each day's proceedings. At first, with the hearings entangled in procedural wrangling, the size of the viewing audience was less than expected. As the personalities and the issues involved sunk in, the public began to tune in. In May, a Cincinnati housewife wrote to a Democratic member of McCarthy's committee, "Just when do you think you can stop these hearings? My husband has given up his job, just sits and watches those hearings all day, and doesn't work anymore. Being a Democrat, he has laughed so much that he has become ill, and I don't think he'll be able to go back to work even if it was over."

It was soon apparent that all the parties involved knew that the hearings were being staged chiefly for the public. No decision on either side's contentions would be reached in the hearing room in Washington. Instead, throughout the country, the viewing public would decide which side "came over better." On this level, McCarthy lost. His image as a fearsome warrior who was never defeated collapsed and instead he appeared as a venal, cantankerous, pushy man who displayed no sensitivity for the feelings of other people. His frequent interjections of "Mr. Chairman, Mr. Chairman!" and "Point of order!" became national running gags. Panelists on game shows started using them for sure-fire laughs. There was even a song called "Point of Order, Baby, I Love You." McCarthy the person had been separated in the public's mind from the larger issue of anti-Communism. Once he became the butt of humor, McCarthy could never again make the nation cower.

In June the hearings ended. ABC and DuMont absorbed their financial losses and the Senate went on to condemn McCarthy in private. Joseph McCarthy was gone, but many of the other transgressions of the "McCarthy era," such as blacklisting, continued unabated for years.

14. Showbiz in a Hurry

ONCE THE ARMY-MCCARTHY HEARINGS ENDED and TV programming returned to normal, the prime topic of discussion in television circles was NBC's upcoming series of spectaculars. These were seen as the biggest strategic gamble of the new season because network chief Pat Weaver was risking his reputation on the belief that the American public was willing to disrupt its normal viewing patterns in favor of one-shot programming.

There had already been successful examples of Weaver's basic concept in the previous two seasons. To celebrate its fiftieth year in business, the Ford Motor Company, in 1953, had purchased the same prime time slot on all the networks and replaced the regularly scheduled programming with a lavish variety special, "The Ford Fiftieth Anniversary Show." Produced by Leland Hayward at a cost of $500,000, the program featured big name stars such as Mary Martin, Ethel Merman, and Helen Hayes, and won both critical praise and high ratings. General Foods did a similar show in early 1954 on its corporate anniversary. Both programs had a tremendous built-in advantage, however. Because they were on all the networks at once, there was no competition. Their ratings had to be high. Pat Weaver felt that such programming could succeed on a regular basis even carried by only one network, and he presented the spectaculars as the method to pump new life into the schedule and help NBC to regain its position as the number one network.

Sponsors found the concept of frequently scheduled specials disturbing because it disrupted the usual audience flow from one familiar series to another. After extended negotiations during the winter and spring of 1954, the spectaculars received advertising support, primarily based on Weaver's track record with such hit concepts as *Today* and *Your Show of Shows*. NBC's publicity department then went to work cranking out a mountain of promotional material to help create the impression that the entire television world was about to undergo a massive alteration and that NBC would crush its competition with the spectaculars. Once a month, ninety minutes of the network's normal entertainment schedule on Saturday, Sunday, and Monday would be replaced by Weaver's spectaculars: special programs of either variety, drama, comedy, or music.

Max Liebman, the former producer of *Your Show of Shows*, was put in charge of the Saturday and Sunday slots. The Monday night program, called *Producers' Showcase*, was to be a cooperative, supervised by Fred Coe, who had recently left *The Philco/Goodyear Television Playhouse*. Individual guest producers were

scheduled to handle the details of each Monday broadcast, while Coe assumed overall responsibility. Though the exact format of both Liebman and Coe's programs was unclear, sponsors knew that whatever form they took, the shows would be big, expensive, and in color (an added incentive to boost color set sales). The television industry anxiously awaited the night of the first spectacular, Sunday, September 12. It was a disaster.

For ninety minutes live from New York, Max Liebman presented "Satins and Spurs" in four acts, thirteen scenes, in color, at a cost of $300,000. Star Betty Hutton jumped, twirled, sang, and yelled the part of a rodeo performer in New York City who fell for a photographer from *Life* magazine. Critics described the production as loud and annoying, somewhat sophomoric, and certainly not spectacular. Though "Satins and Spurs" had been labeled an original musical comedy, they also noticed a strong resemblance to "Annie Get Your Gun," a Broadway musical comedy that had also starred Betty Hutton.

Worst of all, the ten-city Trendex ratings service (which emphasized speed by focusing on fewer cities than the national Nielsen ratings) indicated that Ed Sullivan's *Toast of the Town* had easily bested the first spectacular, registering twice the audience. From the start, the spectaculars were given a bad name. Betty Hutton said she was quitting television. Nervous sponsors began muttering that they felt as if they were throwing away their money and they sent their lawyers searching for ways to break their contracts. Liebman's second show, "Lady in the Dark," a Broadway adaptation starring Ann Sothern, barely beat its CBS competition, at a price of $500,000.

In spite of all the advance publicity, the nation's viewers had not joyfully risen to embrace the spectaculars, the competition had not been destroyed, and sales of color television sets were as abysmal as ever. Pat Weaver held firm, saying, "Take my word for it, this is it!" He knew that his spectaculars required a major change in audience habits. It would take time for the public to adjust to the idea of setting aside a familiar program routine for a one-time special. In October, a major psychological break occurred. The season's first national Nielsen ratings (which took almost a month to compile) gave the spectaculars generally higher ratings than the Trendex service had. Sensing that maybe the programs were not the disasters they first appeared to be, the skeptics decided to withhold final judgment for a while.

Despite the reprieve, the spectaculars still faced a tremendous uphill battle. Some of the difficulties were inherent in the format of a one-shot show. Unlike a weekly series, which could draw on its familiar structure, continuing characters, or running gags, the spectaculars had to present something entirely new for every outing. Each program required new scenery, a new story line, and a new line-up of stars. Even one month was not enough time to properly plan, write, and rehearse the productions.

The spectaculars faced an additional problem. Because of the tremendous ballyhoo that preceded them, public expectations were far higher than for any individual segment of a continuing series. Even with the live drama anthologies, which faced many of the same time and rehearsal pressures, there was always next week's production. With a once-a-month big budget spectacular, every presentation was expected to be special. Any Broadway producer could point out the problems of trying to throw together a successful show from scratch every few weeks. Even with adequate preparation and rehearsal, many plays and revues on Broadway flopped. Television compounded the difficulties and underscored failure. Unlike Broadway productions which could open, play awhile, and build an audience (or quietly close after unfavorable reviews), a TV spectacular had one chance. One night, no previews. Worse yet, there were only two or three other stations to choose from so that a failure, or even a mediocre effort, stood out much more on TV than it would on Broadway.

Trying to solve some of these problems, Max Liebman very quickly began to adopt some familiar trappings from regular series, especially on his Sunday spectaculars against Ed Sullivan. In late October he teamed Judy Holliday, Steve Allen, and Dick Shawn to form the central cast for a musical-comedy revue, "Sunday in Town." The team clicked and throughout the remainder of the season they reappeared on a number of Sunday evenings, with different guests but in the same sort of revue. Liebman saved his more unusual shows for Saturday night, when the competition was not as formidable. One of his best productions was a musical version of "Babes in Toyland" starring Jack E. Leonard as the inventor of castor oil, Wally Cox as a toymaker, and Dave Garroway as Santa Claus. By Christmas, spectaculars, while still viewed with deep suspicion, were pulling in decent ratings and were no longer a dirty word. It was Fred Coe, however, who wiped out any remaining doubts about the ratings potential of the spectaculars with his March 7 presentation of the Sir James Barrie fantasy classic, "Peter Pan."

Coe, like Max Liebman, had experienced difficulties at the beginning of the season with his spectacular slot. As a result, *Producers' Showcase* generally downplayed original productions and stuck to less risky adaptations of Broadway chestnuts. Though well done, these did not generate much excitement. They seemed to belie the spectacular buildup by focusing on well-worn material that could have just as easily fit into an average drama anthology program. With "Peter Pan," though, Coe brought a successful Broadway production to television almost intact only nine days after it had finished its theatrical run. Not only was interest in the show high, but the cast and crew were exceptionally sharp. In effect, they had been practicing for months for their TV appearance and the program reflected their confidence and energy.

"Peter Pan" was the story of a magical trip by several turn-of-the-century London children to another world. Working with a $700,000 budget and an excellent cast, Coe and producer Richard Halliday skillfully adapted the elaborate stage choreography for television, retaining both the sense of wonder and the spirit of youthful adventure from the original. Mary Martin as Peter Pan, an impish pixie, flew about the studio aided by nearly invisible wires, guiding the children under the care of the oldest child, Wendy Darling (Kathy Nolan), to Neverland. There they had a series of

adventures, culminating in a fearful battle with the villainous scalawag and pirate, Captain Hook (Cyril Ritchard). In the spirit of the fanciful evening, the Ford automobile commercials were staged as humorous productions, presented by Ernie Kovacs and Edie Adams.

The public response to "Peter Pan" was extraordinary. One-third to one-half of all Americans saw the program. Twenty-one million TV homes, containing sixty-five million to seventy-five million viewers, tuned in. "Peter Pan" became the highest rated show of television's brief history and served to convince sponsors that spectaculars could live up to Pat Weaver's promises. By the end of the season, all but one of the sponsors for NBC's spectaculars renewed.

Even CBS offered its own "minor spectacular" color programs for the 1954–55 season, though the network's two monthly shows (*Best of Broadway* and *Shower of Stars*) rarely reached the level of NBC's productions. CBS had decided to try such special programming late into the planning for the fall, and the lack of preparation and whole-hearted commitment showed through. *Shower of Stars,* which replaced the Thursday night drama anthology *Climax* once a month, wasted big name stars such as Betty Grable, Harry James, and Mario Lanza in splashy but slapdash variety programs. *Best of Broadway,* the monthly stand-in for CBS's Wednesday night boxing matches, usually stuck to merely adequate one-hour cutdowns of old Broadway classics. Yet even this show scored well when, like "Peter Pan," it used an experienced crew that had worked out the production kinks long before the play was brought to television. In January 1955, for example, members of the original Broadway cast of "Arsenic and Old Lace" (including Boris Karloff) reunited for a successful new television production of the macabre murder story.

Despite the recovery by the spectaculars after their unimpressive start, programmers, sponsors, and viewers soon came to realize that only a handful of the shows could possibly live up to the tremendous advance hype. This in itself represented an important shift in attitude because it broke the dependence on an unchanging weekly routine that the networks had automatically carried over from radio. Spectaculars proved that, with the right mix, a special program could succeed and provide a temporary, but dramatic, ratings boost for a network.

Pat Weaver's once-a-month spectacular schedule survived on NBC for three seasons, though to meet production deadlines the shows often settled for traditional variety showcases and safe Broadway adaptations in between truly "spectacular" events. By the late 1950s, the monthly frequency of such programming was reduced to a more realistic and manageable level and the term "spectacular" was replaced by the less bombastic description of "special." Nonetheless, even as irregularly scheduled specials, Weaver's concept provided an important opportunity to try something different on television, and they often served as a showcase for the best programming television had to offer.

In the prime time ratings race for the 1954–55 season the spectaculars proved too erratic to deliver consistent blockbuster ratings against CBS's strong weekly series, and CBS remained slightly ahead of NBC over the entire season. With full sponsor support after the success of "Peter Pan," though, Pat Weaver looked optimistically toward the following season for the flowering of the spectaculars and the promised return of NBC's supremacy.

Besides the spectaculars, the most important addition to the network's schedule that fall was the late night *Tonight* show. Pat Weaver had been tremendously successful with the early morning *Today* show and the mid-morning *Home* program, so in preparing for the 1954–55 season he turned his attention to the period im-

	Net	7:00	7:30	8:00	8:30	9:00	9:30	10:00	10:30
MON	ABC	Kukla, Fran & Ollie / John Daly & The News	The Name's The Same	COME CLOSER	Voice Of Firestone	College Press Conference	Boxing From Eastern Parkway		Neutral Corner
	CBS	local	CBS News / Perry Como	Burns And Allen Show	Arthur Godfrey's Talent Scouts	I Love Lucy	DECEMBER BRIDE	Studio One	
	DUM	Captain Video / M. BEATTY NEWS	local	ILONA MASSEY SHOW	local	Monday Night Fights From St. Nicholas Arena With Chris Schenkel			At Ringside
	NBC	local	Tony Martin / Cam. News Caravan	CAESAR'S HOUR # PRODUCER'S SHOWCASE		MEDIC	Robert Montgomery Presents		local
TUE	ABC	Kukla, Fran & Ollie / John Daly & The News	Cavalcade Of America	local	Twenty Questions	Make Room For Daddy	U.S. Steel Hour / Elgin Hour		Stop The Music
	CBS	local	CBS News / Jo Stafford	Red Skelton Show	HALLS OF IVY	Meet Millie	Danger	Life With Father	See It Now
	DUM	Captain Video / M. BEATTY NEWS	local	Life Is Worth Living	STUDIO 57	local			
	NBC	local	Dinah Shore / Cam. News Caravan	Milton Berle Show / Martha Raye Show # Bob Hope Show		Fireside Theater	Armstrong Circle Theater	Truth Or Consequences	IT'S A GREAT LIFE
WED	ABC	Kukla, Fran & Ollie / John Daly & The News	DISNEYLAND		New Stu Erwin Show	Masquerade Party	Enterprise U.S.A.	local	
	CBS	local	CBS News / Perry Como	Arthur Godfrey And His Friends		Strike It Rich	I've Got A Secret	Blue Ribbon Bouts # BEST OF BROADWAY	Sports Sp.
	DUM	Captain Video / M. BEATTY NEWS	local			Chicago Symphony Orchestra	Down You Go	GREATEST PRO FOOTBALL PLAYS	
	NBC	local	Eddie Fisher / Cam. News Caravan	I Married Joan	My Little Margie	Kraft Television Theater	This Is Your Life	Big Town	
THUR	ABC	Kukla, Fran & Ollie / John Daly & The News	The Lone Ranger	THE MAIL STORY	Treasury Men In Action	So You Want To Lead A Band	Kraft Television Theater		local
	CBS	local	CBS News / Jane Froman	Ray Milland Show	CLIMAX # SHOWER OF STARS		Four Star Playhouse	Public Defender	Name That Tune
	DUM	Captain Video / M. BEATTY NEWS	local	They Stand Accused		What's The Story	local		
	NBC	local	Dinah Shore / Cam. News Caravan	You Bet Your Life	Justice	Dragnet	Ford Theater	Lux Video Theater	
FRI	ABC	Kukla, Fran & Ollie / John Daly & The News	ADVENTURES OF RIN TIN TIN	Adventures Of Ozzie And Harriet	Ray Bolger Show	Dollar A Second	THE VISE	local	
	CBS	local	CBS News / Perry Como	Mama	Topper	Schlitz Playhouse Of Stars	Our Miss Brooks	THE LINEUP	Person To Person
	DUM	Captain Video / M. BEATTY NEWS	local			The Stranger	One Minute Please	Chance Of A Lifetime	TIME WILL TELL
	NBC	local	Eddie Fisher / Cam. News Caravan	Red Buttons Show #JACK CARSON SHOW	The Life Of Riley	The Big Story	DEAR PHOEBE	Gillette Cavalcade Of Sports	Gr. Momen. In Sports
SAT	ABC	local	COMPASS	LET'S DANCE		Saturday Night Fights	Fight Talk	Stork Club	local
	CBS	Gene Autry Show	Beat The Clock	Jackie Gleason Show		Two For The Money	My Favorite Husband	That's My Boy	WILLY
	DUM	local		National Football League Pro Football					
	NBC	Mr. Wizard	Ethel And Albert	HEY MULLIGAN	Place The Face	IMOGENE COCA SHOW # MAX LIEBMAN PRESENTS	Texaco Star Theater	GEORGE GOBEL SHOW	Your Hit Parade
SUN	ABC	You Asked For It	Pepsi Cola Playhouse	Flight #7	The Big Picture	Walter Winchell / Martha Wright	Soldier Parade	Break The Bank	local
	CBS	LASSIE	Private Secretary / Jack Benny Program	Toast Of The Town		Gen. Electric Theater # Fred Waring Show	HONESTLY CELESTE	FATHER KNOWS BEST	What's My Line
	DUM	local	Opera Cameos	local	Author Meets The Critics	Rocky King, Inside Detective	Life Begins At 80	The Music Show	local
	NBC	PEOPLE ARE FUNNY	Mr. Peepers	Colgate Comedy Hour # Max Liebman Presents		Goodyear/Philco Television Playhouse		Loretta Young Show	The Hunter

mediately following prime time. In 1950 and 1951, NBC had ventured into the post-prime time slot with a one-hour variety-talk program at 11:00 P.M., *Broadway Open House,* and had discovered that there was a surprisingly large reservoir of late night viewers. When host Jerry Lester left the program, the network was unable to come up with a personality that the affiliates would accept as a replacement, so, reluctantly, NBC turned back the time to the locals. They, in turn, were more than happy to run old movies and sell the lucrative commercial time themselves. Though not ruling out the resumption of network control, the affiliates made it clear that any new late night program would have to be worth more to them than their films.

Eager to reclaim the time, the network floated alternative plans such as a midnight mystery show and live extravaganzas from the streets of New York City, but these were dismissed as unproven and too risky. NBC soon revived the notion of the talk-variety format and began to search for an appropriate host. It was generally agreed that Jerry Lester's distinctive personality had made

Broadway Open House click and that if the network could find someone with similar strengths the locals would probably buy the show. The major stumbling block to launching such a program from scratch was that any new host, no matter how talented, needed time to build a following.

The solution to the late night problem began to emerge when Steve Allen joined NBC. Allen had previously served as a variety-talk host on a number of programs broadcast at odd hours on CBS and, in July 1953, he was given a forty-minute show (just before midnight) weeknights on NBC's local New York City station. In effect, this slot provided him with a major market showcase for his approach to late night television. He quickly demonstrated that his many years of experience as a television performer on five days a week had taught him the basics for survival in the daily grind. Above all, Allen realized that funny routines were not as important as a positive, identifiable personality. He observed, "If the audience likes you, they'll laugh at anything you say … The reason people don't tire of Arthur Godfrey is that he doesn't do anything.

The first live television coverage of the Miss America Pageant on September 11, 1954 (on ABC, hosted by John Daly and Bess Myerson), gave home viewers the opportunity to share the emotional excitement as Lee Ann Meriwether (of California) was awarded the crown as Miss America for 1955. *(Courtesy of Miss America Organization)*

Martin and Lewis put on a much better show, but the audience gets tired of them quicker. I have found that people get tired of you on TV nine times faster than they do on radio."

Allen drew on his dry, humorous appreciation for the irrelevant and often overlooked aspects of life to project a casual, distinctive TV personality. He also surrounded himself with a talented family of supporting players, beginning with singers Steve Lawrence and Helen Dixon (who was soon replaced by Eydie Gorme). By the fall of 1954, he had gained enough support from NBC affiliates to move his show (now titled *Tonight*) onto the network schedule, beginning September 27, 1954. For ninety minutes each week-night, the program was broadcast live across the country, and it slowly began to catch on with the national audience.

By the time *Tonight* began its network run, Allen's supporting family had grown to include former disc jockey Gene Rayburn as his announcer, band leader Skitch Henderson, and singer Andy Williams. Over the years other performers joined the troupe, but Steve Allen always remained the focus of the entertainment. Dubbed "the midnight Godfrey," Allen would stroll through the studio, play the piano, conduct humorous interviews with members of the audience, and ad-lib routines with the regulars. His most popular reoccurring bits were "man-on-the-street" interviews and his "reports to the nation." Though Allen was willing to try virtually any comic stunt (he once took a swim in a huge vat of gelatin), he also occasionally delved into serious non-showbiz topics with his guests. Under Allen, *Tonight* developed into a consistent ratings hit for NBC, reestablishing the network's hold on the slot and providing the model for late night entertainment that would survive for decades.

Just as *Tonight* reached the network schedule, twenty-nine-year-old Los Angeles-based comic Johnny Carson, a self-effacing, quiet charmer who had hosted a mundane prime time quiz show during the summer of 1954, received his big break on CBS. Red Skelton hurt himself one night in rehearsal for his live comedy-variety show and Carson, who wrote for Skelton, was picked as a last minute stand-in. Carson's on-the-spot cool won him his own prime

September 7, 1954
After a favorable Supreme Court ruling on giveaway quiz shows, *Stop the Music* returns to television, on ABC.

September 27, 1954
Morgan Beatty and the News. (DuMont). The third and final try by DuMont at a nightly news show.

October 3, 1954
Father Knows Best. (CBS). Robert Young plays an all-knowing, patient father. Low ratings nearly kill the series in its first season.

October 21, 1954
Ian Fleming's James Bond comes to the screen for the first time in "Casino Royale" on CBS's *Climax* anthology, though he is presented as an American agent (played by Barry Nelson). Peter Lorre steals the show as the villain playing with Soviet-supplied cash who Bond must beat at the gambling table.

November 7, 1954
Face the Nation. (CBS). A Sunday afternoon answer to NBC's *Meet the Press.* CBS's Ted Koop is moderator and Senator Joseph McCarthy is the first guest.

January 2, 1955
The Bob Cummings Show. (NBC). A product of the mind of Paul Henning. Bob Cummings plays an oversexed, swinging bachelor photographer. The series (later retitled *Love That Bob*) also has a great line-up of sidekicks: Rosemary DeCamp as Bob's widowed sister, Margaret; Dwayne Hickman as her son, Chuck; and Ann B. Davis as Bob's assistant, Schultzy.

time summer series on CBS in 1955. In *The Johnny Carson Show,* Carson appeared as emcee to a traditional comedy-variety mix of singers, dancers, guests, skits, and monologues, but it just did not work. After years of developing his "boy down the block" appeal into a strong ad-lib personality, he seemed to be miscast in a heavily scripted prime time format. Though the summer series continued into the fall, by the spring of 1956 Carson was taken out of the evening schedule and slotted into the daytime, where he flourished. He later compared the freedom allowed in daytime television (and, he might have added, late night) with the restrictions imposed in the closely watched prime time shows, especially as it related to comics. "I think that any comic who appears as a personality, week after week [in prime time] has got to lose ground in two or three years … in daytime, you can be relaxed and informal, but an easy informal show won't go [in prime time] because people aren't conditioned to it."

While the late night *Tonight* show and the spectaculars eventually caught on, the performance of NBC's comedy-variety showcases, the mainstay of the network's prime time schedule, proved to be disappointing. *Your Show of Shows* star Sid Caesar brought along sidekicks Carl Reiner and Howard Morris to his new vehicle, *Caesar's Hour,* but the program had a shaky takeoff with weak sketches and a lack of direction. Though the show stabilized by mid-season with the writing and production returning to Caesar's previous levels of quality, *Caesar's Hour* could not overcome CBS's powerful Monday night sitcom line-up. NBC also had Red Buttons, who had come over from CBS, but he was unable to find a format or writers that clicked. Every few months he reworked his show, but it died at the end of the season.

On Sunday, the sagging *Colgate Comedy Hour* lost the services of most of the few strong headliners it had left. Dean Martin and Jerry Lewis appeared infrequently; Jimmy Durante and Donald O'Connor moved to a reactivated *Texaco Star Theater* (Texaco had bailed out of Milton Berle's show in 1953, when production costs seemed to be soaring out of sight); and Eddie Cantor jumped ship entirely. Cantor signed with the independent film syndicator, Ziv, to do two years of half-hour variety shows, but the syndicated product seemed cheap in comparison to his previous network offerings. After a half-year of tepid local ratings, Cantor, citing ill health, parted ways with Ziv and retired from regular TV work.

After the many defections, *The Colgate Comedy Hour* focused more and more on flashy sets and production numbers rather than the comedy headliners. Singer Gordon MacRae became a semi-regular host and, during the summer of 1955, the Paramount studios supplied guest stars and clips from upcoming films. The studio treated the TV shows as little more than a chance to plug its new films for free, so programs such as a "behind the scenes peak" at "Pete Kelly's Blues" were really just sixty-minute ads. Yet even with these excesses, Paramount's involvement with a network television show reflected the fact that the long-standing Hollywood-television feud was beginning to cool.

In the early years of television, the major Hollywood studios chose to meet the TV challenge by treating the new medium with disdain. They refused to give it any help or support, pretending that television might fade away if they just ignored it. Network executives, who had seen radio profits in the 1930s diluted by the involvement of West Coast production agencies, were similarly wary of the major West Coast studios. As a result, when the networks began looking for sources of filmed programs, they had turned to small independent filmmakers. CBS and NBC, which early on recognized the many practical advantages of West Coast TV production, were able to keep almost complete control over any live and filmed work done for them in Hollywood. By 1954, both had built huge live studios in California and had established working agreements with the smaller filmmakers. As independents such as Desilu prospered, the possibility of the networks and the major studios working together seemed increasingly remote.

If the major studios had not been so determined to ignore the challenge of television in the 1940s, they might have realized from the beginning that the new competitor could also open a new field of production to them, films for television. They, not the small independents, should have led the way in producing TV sitcoms, spy chillers, and adventure yarns. Even following the ruling in the Paramount case of 1948 which forced the major studios to surrender control of their lucrative theater chains, they seriously questioned the viability of TV films and made no moves to court the networks.

There were a few exceptions to Hollywood's "hands off TV" policy, chiefly in efforts by individual film actors and producers. In February 1950, movie star Robert Montgomery began producing and often starring in an NBC drama anthology series sponsored by Lucky Strike. The fall of 1952 brought the first major defections to the television market: David Niven, Dick Powell, Charles Boyer, and Ida Lupino (four Hollywood veterans), who alternated as the stars of CBS's *Four Star Playhouse,* a thirty-minute filmed anthology. In 1953, long-time film leading lady Loretta Young began the sudsy *Letters to Loretta,* which staged heartthrob soapy situations described in Young's fan mail and cast her as a Dear Abby-style counselor who offered possible solutions after each story. That same year, matinee idol Ray Milland played the part of an addlebrained drama professor at a women's college in *Meet Mr. McNutley.* While bringing some big name Hollywood stars to television, these efforts in no way reflected a change of heart by any of the major studios or the networks. Instead, the Hollywood-network feud ended gradually as both sides discovered that they could use each other.

ABC, which was far behind CBS and NBC in the ratings, had made the first serious moves toward Hollywood at the beginning of the decade. More than the others, ABC needed help in producing and developing enough programs to fill its schedule, and the network was one of the first to rely on vanguard filmed series such as *The Lone Ranger.* ABC had also turned to Hollywood for financial help when, in 1953, it merged with United Paramount Theaters for a much-needed influx of cash. As Hollywood became an increasingly important television production center following such successes as *I Love Lucy* and *Dragnet,* ABC decided to take a chance with an established film studio in the hope of finding a blockbuster hit. On April 2, 1954, the network announced an agreement with the Walt Disney studios for a one-hour weekly series beginning in the fall of 1954, *Disneyland.*

ABC's agreement with Disney represented several important changes in television programming philosophy. Though Disney was not one of the eight major Hollywood studios, it was the largest to venture into full scale television production at the time. More important, by turning to Disney, ABC was tacitly admitting that unlike CBS and NBC it was willing to rely on outside sources (even established film studios) for major programs, thereby conceding some loss of network control. ABC paid a premium price for the Disney series, including funds toward the construction of a "Disneyland" amusement park planned for Anaheim, California. In return, the network received twenty one-hour programs, which were to be rerun to fill out the entire season.

ABC considered *Disneyland* its biggest hope for the 1954–55 season and very quickly sold out the available ad time on the show. The network also decided to use the program for a calculated assault against the programming strategies of the competition and scheduled it to run Wednesdays, from 7:30 P.M. to 8:30 P.M. At the time, CBS and NBC did not really begin prime time broadcasting until 8:00 P.M., filling the 7:30–8:00 P.M. period with fifteen minutes of news and fifteen minutes of musical entertainment. (Perry Como, Jo Stafford, and Jane Froman appeared on CBS while Tony Martin, Dinah Shore, and Eddie Fisher sang on NBC.) Only ABC had regularly scheduled half-hour programs in the 7:30 P.M. slot but, aside from *The Lone Ranger,* these had never made a significant difference in the ratings. As a one-hour program, however, *Disneyland* would be in progress when the other networks began their prime time shows, giving ABC a critical edge. Just as important, *Disneyland* would begin early enough to catch the attention of the nation's children by providing an attractive alternative to news and music. ABC was counting on them to raise a ruckus and control the channel selection as family viewing began for the evening. The kids came through.

Disneyland premiered on October 27, 1954, to rave reviews. One critic declared: "It's happened and it's wonderful!" Drawing on more than twenty years of theatrical material, as well as new features shot specifically for the television show, *Disneyland* presented a delightful combination of kiddie adventure yarns, travelogues, real-life nature stories, mildly educational documentaries, and classic Disney animation. It was the perfect family show and a resounding ratings success, providing ABC with its first top ten hit in five years.

Until his death in 1966, Walt Disney himself hosted the series, demonstrating how to mix promotion, education, and homespun humor into an enchanting visit to the "magic kingdom." Though in effect many of the shows were actually plugs for one of Disney's new theatrical features or for the new Disneyland amusement park, they were always entertaining. Disney the showman never forgot that people, especially children, watched television for pleasure and that they would accept a commercial pitch as well as some basic history and science if it was well done and fun to follow. One episode, meant to coincide with the release of Disney's "20,000 Leagues Under the Sea" (based on the Jules Verne novel), focused on the complex underwater photography techniques used in the production. The program was a perfect promotion for the film (which was a box office smash) yet also a worthwhile documentary (it received an Emmy). Viewers actually were interested in how the special effects had been staged for that adventure film.

The frequent glimpses of Disney's California amusement park put Anaheim, California, at the top of every child's list of dream vacation spots, but the most dramatic instance of fan support began in December when *Disneyland* touched off a nationwide fad with the first of five episodes fantasizing the life of Western hero Davy Crockett. In response to the stories (which starred Fess Parker in the title role and Buddy Ebsen as Crockett's sidekick, George Russel), a Davy Crockett mania swept the nation. It seemed as if every child (along with many adults) owned a "genuine imitation" Davy Crockett coonskin cap. Senator Estes Kefauver wore one through most of his 1956 campaign for the presidency. There were even seventeen recordings of "The Ballad of Davy Crockett."

By the spring of 1955, the competition on the other networks was reeling. NBC's *I Married Joan* was knocked off the air and Arthur Godfrey saw a huge chunk of his audience carved away. Due to a short production year, *Disneyland* operated on a 20–20–12 schedule its first season, meaning that twenty episodes were presented, then all twenty were repeated (beginning on March 26), and then twelve selected episodes were run a third time during the summer. This procedure was almost unheard of at the time (when a single rerun cycle of series episodes was still fairly unusual), yet the ratings for the Davy Crockett episodes actually increased for

the reruns, and the drop off in viewers for the third runs was nowhere near what had been feared. *Disneyland* proved once and for all the viability of reruns as well as the strength of kiddie-related programming. The series kept right on rolling on ABC through the mid- and late 1950s, serving as a display window for such Disney classics as "Alice in Wonderland," "Treasure Island," and "The Legend of Sleepy Hollow," as well as endless reels of cartoons featuring such familiar Disney characters as Donald Duck, Mickey Mouse, Goofy, and Pluto. The program moved to NBC in 1961 where it went to color and eventually became one of the longest running prime time series in television history.

The success of *Disneyland* in the 1954–55 season provided a tremendous boost to ABC and convinced executives both at the Hollywood studios and at the networks that a potential ratings bonanza lay at their feet. In planning for the fall of 1955, NBC and CBS joined ABC in scheduling programs produced by other major Hollywood studios as the first tentative follow-ups to *Disneyland.* At the same time, number one CBS also made a hasty decision to eliminate its 7:30–8:00 P.M. news and music block in the fall and to fill it instead with kidvid programming, determined not to cede the advantage in that market to ABC. (NBC resisted that temptation for two more years.) The performance of two other early evening kiddie-related series, *Lassie* and *Rin Tin Tin,* underscored the fact that children were increasingly important in program selection.

The Adventures of Rin Tin Tin, which led off ABC's Friday night schedule, became the network's second top ten program for the 1954–55 season. The show starred a perspicacious German shepherd, Rin Tin Tin, that barked out orders in a post-Civil War frontier camp, Fort Apache. Surrounding the canine was a set of characters that soon set the standard for kiddie TV action shows: a young child (Lee Aaker as Corporal Rusty, who owned Rin Tin Tin), his strong clean-cut male guidance figure (James Brown as Lieutenant Rip Masters), and the bumbling comic friend-of-the-hero (Joe Sawyer as Sergeant Biff O'Hara). The venerable quartet of animal, kid, man, and comic fool followed the grade B adventure formula of fights, frantic gunplay, and dramatic chases in a program that was, like *The Lone Ranger,* an effective television equivalent to the Saturday kiddie matinees and radio adventure shows of the 1930s and 1940s. Rin Tin Tin, in fact, had first appeared on the silver screen in 1923 and subsequently starred in a successful four-year radio adventure series before turning up at Fort Apache.

The other dog star of the season was CBS's Lassie, a cerebral collie that had also appeared in films and on the radio in the 1940s. In contrast to *Rin Tin Tin's* rugged Western adventures, television's *Lassie* adhered to the spirit of the heart-tugging MGM film "Lassie Come Home" and focused on "the world of love and adventure shared by a boy and his dog." Though the program included dramatic animal heroics to keep the children interested, the series was a gentle family show featuring tales of kindly people who were in trouble and received help from Lassie. A pair of young boys, Jeff Miller (Tommy Rettig) and Timmy (Jon Provost), along with a trio of mothers (played by Jan Clayton, Cloris Leachman, and June Lockhart) appeared successively as Lassie's sidekicks until the 1960s. Then the dog began wandering from the care of such families taking up first with a park ranger and later striking off on her own, sleeping under the stars with itinerant raccoons and squirrels. During her final season on CBS at the beginning of the 1970s, Lassie fell in love and gave birth to a litter of puppies.

Kidvid was yet another hit formula that was done best on film in Hollywood, rather than live from New York, and a line of imitations was inevitable. *I Love Lucy* had spawned dozens of screwball

Lassie easily stepped into the human world (just like on the weekly adventure series) and personally accepted a 1955 award from the Peabody's John E. Drewry *(right). (Courtesy Peabody Awards Collection)*

sitcoms, and copies of NBC's first important filmed series, *Dragnet,* were already on the air.

By early 1954, *Dragnet* was regularly coming in number two in the ratings, right behind *I Love Lucy,* and each of the networks had planned similar "docudrama" shows for the 1954–55 season. CBS presented the most blatant duplicate, *The Lineup,* a cop show produced in cooperation with the San Francisco police department. Warner Anderson played Lieutenant Ben Guthrie, a slightly more talkative version of *Dragnet's* Sergeant Joe Friday. Like Friday, he fought everyday crime in a generally realistic setting, with stories based on actual cases from the police department's files.

The next step in cashing in on the success of *Dragnet* was to take the docudrama format into another profession. NBC's Worthington Miner produced one of the best of such series, the "authentic medical dramatizations" of *Medic,* starring Richard Boone as Doctor Konrad Styner. Overall, *Medic* did a good job duplicating the manner in which real doctors handled life-or-death cases, as Miner combined in-house jargon (as on *Dragnet)* with such innovative touches as intercutting film footage of real-life surgery with closeups of a white-masked, profusely sweating Richard Boone. Along with doctors there were also lawyers, with Gary Merrill starring in NBC's live *Justice* series. Producer David Susskind drew from the files of the National Legal Aid Society and usually focused on poor people needing legal advice.

ABC also jumped on the docudrama form in the fall of 1954 and came up with an out-of-the-ordinary profession to portray. *The Mail Story* (subtitled "Handle With Care") dramatized cases from the files of the United States Post Office Department, stretching from stagecoach robbers in the 1800s to twentieth century instances of mail fraud. Postmaster General Arthur Summerfield even introduced the story on the first episode.

Although the networks continued to expand their reliance on Hollywood filmed series, they also maintained their New York-based drama anthologies. These East Coast programs were now particularly powerful because, after years of developing plays for television, the producers and writers had come of age. They had learned what worked best within the limitations imposed by live television and consequently turned out an amazing number of high quality original plays.

Aspiring new writers had flocked to the drama anthology programs because they knew that a successful TV production could be picked up by Hollywood and turned into a theatrical feature. This had happened in 1953 with Paddy Chayefsky's "Marty" and since then many of the most popular TV plays were selected for film treatment. The writers also came to realize that with so many anthology programs to fill, they had a constant opportunity to experiment and grow. Neither Broadway nor Hollywood offered so many script outlets, and many of the best TV writers used the shows to develop simple mood pieces and slices of life. They sharpened their sense of character interaction and dialogue, developing dramas that were often insightful examinations of human relationships. Their stories frequently focused on the difficult personal decisions faced by realistic people and the consequences of their actions. In the process of turning out these intimate, human stories, both the veterans and the newcomers produced a string of outstanding dramatic productions that matched and sometimes even surpassed the best works on stage and in the movies.

ABC's often retitled *Elgin Hour*, produced by Herb Brodkin, presented "Crime in the Streets" by Reginald Rose. John Cassavetes starred as the leader of a teenage gang in this perceptive portrayal of the bitterness, loneliness, and violence of slum life that turned natural born leaders into outlaws. *The Elgin Hour* alternated weekly with *The U.S. Steel Hour* (directed by Alex Segal), which had premiered in November 1953 with a David Davidson original, "P.O.W." In that story, Richard Kiley and Brian Keith played former Korean War captives who attempted to defend the ways they handled the pressures while in a prisoner-of-war camp. Gary Merrill was the American psychiatrist who listened intently to their stories.

In subsequent productions, *The U.S. Steel Hour* presented Frank Gilroy's "Last Notch," a serious Western featuring Jeff Morrow as George Temple, a mild mannered man who happened to be the fastest gun in town. Because people were constantly coming to town to challenge him, he found himself repeatedly facing total strangers and killing them. The story was in the spirit of two adult Westerns that had been successful theatrical films, "High Noon" (in 1952) and "Shane" (in 1953). In March 1955, *The U.S. Steel Hour* offered a much lighter tale, "No Time for Sergeants," based on the hit book by Mac Hyman. Andy Griffith (who had made a name for himself the year before with a left field hit record, "What It Was, Was Football") played Will Stockdale, a Georgia farm boy drafted into the Air Force. In uniform, he constantly bedeviled his sergeant (played by Harry Clark) with his unorthodox plowboy logic. The success of the TV play inspired a film, which was a virtual copy of the television production except that Don Knotts was cast as the goggle-eyed camp psychologist. In the 1960s, Andy Griffith again used that resilient set-up for *Gomer Pyle, U.S.M.C.*, a spinoff from his own successful TV series.

CBS's drama showcase, *Studio One*, produced by Felix Jackson, presented three works by the prolific Reginald Rose that season. "Thunder on Sycamore Street" touched on the sensitive issue of racial prejudice by depicting an analogous situation in which an ugly gathering of suburban neighbors wanted to get rid of an ex-convict that had moved into their town. As the mob grew increasingly hostile, a previously weak and silent neighbor stood up, horrified at his neighbors' actions, and defended the ex-con, causing the crowd to disperse. "The Incredible World of Horace Ford" cast Art Carney as a thirty-five-year-old toymaker on the edge of a nervous breakdown, longing to return to his childhood. In a delightful fantasy ending, his wish came true and he somehow returned to his old home street, set as it was when he was a boy.

The most powerful of Rose's works was "Twelve Angry Men," the story of a jury debating a life and death decision: whether to convict a young man of murder. The entire play was set inside the cramped jury room as each of the jurors struggled with his conscience. At the beginning all but one of the jurors voted guilty. The lone holdout (played by Bob Cummings) explained why he felt there was "a reasonable doubt" in the case and he then pressed the others to reexamine the evidence and reconsider their votes. In the heated arguments that followed, personal one-upmanship, peer pressure, and the desire to simply end the long deliberation became just as important as analyzing the case itself. One by one, the jurors changed their votes, shifting the total to eleven not guilty, one guilty. At the dramatic conclusion, the last man, frightened at the prospect of standing alone to defend his guilty decision to the others, agreed to the not guilty verdict.

NBC's top drama producer, Fred Coe, had left the Sunday night *Philco/Goodyear Television Playhouse* at the end of the 1953–54 season to supervise *Producers' Showcase*, but he left his old program in able hands. Under replacement Gordon Duff, Coe's stable of writers, including Paddy Chayefsky and Horton Foote, continued to turn out sensitive original works dealing with such situations as the disintegrating marriage of a man out of work, a woman who refused to be shut away in an old age home, and the inhabitants of a boarding house in a small Texas town. One story was particularly striking, Robert Alan Aurthur's "A Man Is Ten Feet Tall," which cast Sidney Poitier as a black dock worker who encouraged a white GI deserter (played by Don Murray) to straighten out his life and pull himself together. Because blacks then rarely had leading roles in TV drama, Poitier's appearance brought a special edge to the production. In May, Gore Vidal's satirical fantasy, "A Visit to a Small Planet," used a light, humorous touch to poke fun at the foibles of modern society, including its elaborate war-game strategies. Cyril Ritchard portrayed Mr. Kreton, an eccentric but superpowered visitor to planet Earth who arrived dressed in Civil War-era fashions, thinking it was 1860, not 1960. Realizing that he could not participate in the War Between the States, Kreton decided to direct a modern world war instead because, he observed, that's what mankind seemed to want anyway.

One of the most important dramas of the 1954–55 season was "Patterns," written by Rod Serling. The story appeared on NBC's *Kraft Television Theater* in January 1955 and received so much acclaim that it was restaged less than a month later. It provided the big break for Serling, who soon became one of television's top dramatic writers.

"Patterns" was set in the high pressure world of big business. An up-and-coming young executive, Frank Staples (Richard Kiley), joined a large New York organization and was assigned to work with one of the experienced old timers, Andy Sloane (Ed Begley). The two became good friends and worked well together, as Staples quickly demonstrated his sharp business acumen. He was shocked to discover, however, that Jim Ramsie (Everett

---

January 19, 1955
President Eisenhower allows television crews to film his press conferences for the first time. ABC gives the delayed films a weekly prime time slot.

January 19, 1955
The Millionaire. (CBS). Fabulously wealthy J. Beresford Tipton starts handing out million-dollar checks, through his executive secretary, Michael Anthony (Marvin Miller). Oddly, on the first episode, a woman *refuses* the loot because she does not want to be richer than her fiancé.

March 7, 1955
Steve Allen is emcee for the first nationwide telecast of the Emmy awards show, presented by NBC.

March 15, 1955
"No Time for Sergeants" plays on ABC's *U.S. Steel Hour*. What it was, was Gomer.

April 16, 1955
CBS captures the Saturday afternoon baseball game of the week from ABC. In 1957, NBC gets in on the action by signing away a few teams as a basis for a separate Saturday baseball series.

May 16, 1955
NBC announces an agreement to trade its Cleveland O&O to Westinghouse for WPTZ in Philadelphia. The Justice Department soon begins a lengthy investigation into the deal.

June 6, 1955
Chet Huntley defects from ABC to NBC.

July 21, 1955
CBS removes *See It Now* from the weekly prime time schedule, slotting it as an hour-long monthly floating special instead.

Sloan), the head of the company, was grooming him as a replacement for Sloane.

There was no obvious solution to the situation. Each man had to determine what was important to him, how hard to fight for it, and the consequences of his decision. Staples realized that he wanted and deserved the job, yet was determined to defend and protect his friend. Ramsie felt that Sloane was no longer effective and that, for the good of the company, Staples should replace him. Because Sloane had seniority and a good track record, though, Ramsie could not fire him outright, so he planned to pressure and humiliate him into retiring. Sloane himself had allowed his job to become the most important part of his life and could not conceive of quitting.

Building on these decisions, Serling developed "Patterns" into a highly charged, intensely exciting human debate. The confrontations between Ramsie and Staples were the most powerful because Staples was the only person in the entire company brave enough and strong enough to stand up to the boss, and both knew it. In fact, it was for that very reason that Ramsie was determined to promote Staples, at any cost. Following a public dressing down of Sloane by Ramsie at a board meeting, the humiliated executive collapsed of a heart attack. At first the enraged Staples threatened to resign, but then reconsidered and proposed a more lasting revenge. He agreed to stay with the company as one of its top executives and pledged to constantly criticize and attack Ramsie's every move, until he was toppled. Ramsie agreed. It was an acceptable price to pay for the good of the company.

Such standout works of original television drama provided spectacular moments of entertainment. New York-based TV critics, steeped in Broadway tradition, regarded the television anthology programs featuring original drama as the best possible use of the medium and called for more. In doing so, however, they ignored many obvious signs that the form was doomed to a short life cycle.

The nature of television drama in the 1950s made demands on writers and producers that were suicidal, even compared to the rigorous grind of the theater. On Broadway, there might be fifty major openings in a year, plus a dozen revivals and a number of continuing productions. All of these plays would be presented (or rerun) hundreds of times. At the start of 1955, there were ten regular hour-long drama anthologies on the four TV networks, accounting for thirty-five hours of programming a month. Adding the fourteen thirty-minute drama anthologies, the monthly total rose to sixty-three hours. To expect television to turn out even two good hour-long plays per week, over an entire season, was to expect it to almost double Broadway's normal yearly output. For television to consistently stock all of its anthology programs with good material bordered on the impossible. Yet the most amazing aspect about the "golden age of TV drama" was that the writers and producers managed to come up with as many good productions for as long as they did.

One reason the medium performed so well was that fresh talent emerged and eagerly turned out new stories for television. When the initial infusion passed, though, the high percentage of truly exceptional work had to pass as well. With so many anthology programs on the air, the demand for new TV plays began to outdistance the supply of good material, and the overall quality of original TV drama began to drop. Even returning to adaptations of books, films, and old plays (which had been the basis of most TV drama in the 1940s) did not offer much help because it was very hard to squeeze a wide open story line into sixty minutes, especially within the confines of a live television studio.

Writers found it harder and harder to create so many new settings and new characters week after week. Viewers found it harder and harder to get involved in the constantly changing worlds tossed out before them in the anthology programs. Television producers began to consider seriously alternatives to the highly praised anthology format. Successful series such as *Dragnet* and *Medic* suggested one answer; they provided viewers with a familiar cast and setting, yet still showcased well written stories. Perhaps it would be easier on everyone to work some dramatic themes into weekly drama series with continuing central characters, while saving more ambitious original stories for one-shot specials (such as Pat Weaver's spectaculars) or for a select number of special anthology shows. Such a strategy could reduce the production pressure while allowing the best writers opportunities to flourish.

There was another very practical reason for considering such changes in television drama. The anthology showcases were becoming less and less popular with the large corporations that had been acting as sponsors since the late 1940s. They recognized that, with almost 40 million TV sets in use in the United States in 1955, the average television viewer was no longer part of the elite upper middle class. Instead, there was an increasingly large audience (of both post-World War II baby boom youngsters and working class adults) that considered television to be primarily a source of light entertainment. These viewers preferred following the adventures of their favorite sitcom characters rather than searching out dramas which often posed disquieting questions on the basics of American life.

In August 1955, Philco pulled out of its alternating sponsorship of NBC's Sunday *Television Playhouse*. Dealers had complained that customers told them they wanted more "boy meets girl" shows rather than the often complicated realism dispensed by the *Playhouse* writers. Critical acclaim and respectable ratings were no longer enough to guarantee support even for a top flight show.

The networks were also beginning to cast a critical eye overall at the more limited-interest "class" programming in their prime time schedules. With the ratings race more heated than ever, programs that could not beat the competition by attracting the largest possible audience were becoming harder to justify. Original drama anthology programs were expensive to produce, increasingly difficult to sell to sponsors, and often disturbing to viewers.

It was not just drama that was squeezed. News, too, felt the crunch. *See It Now*, carried for years by Alcoa, found itself without a sponsor when Alcoa announced that it would replace Philco as the sponsor for NBC's Sunday night drama (with the assurance that the *Television Playhouse* would "lighten up"). Even without Alcoa, though, CBS was going to carry *See It Now* in its regular 10:30 P.M. Tuesday night slot into the fall of 1955, unsponsored if necessary. During the summer, however, a more compelling element entered the equation: *See It Now*'s time slot became too valuable. By September 1955, every advertiser in the business wanted to place a show on CBS at 10:30 Tuesday night, so it could follow *The $64,000 Question*.

15. The Road to Reruns

IN APRIL 1954, AFTER FIVE YEARS of legal debate, the Supreme Court ruled that the FCC's 1949 proposal to ban giveaway quiz shows was illegal. The commission had claimed that giveaway shows violated federal law concerning lotteries and should be barred from the airwaves. By definition, participants in a lottery had to expend "something of value" to win, and the FCC had stretched that to include programs such as *Stop the Music,* which required viewers to "spend" time watching the show in order to learn information necessary to win. Even though the Supreme Court agreed that giveaway shows were a complete waste of time, it rejected the commission's attempt to kick them off the air by defining them as lotteries.

During the five-year court battle, giveaway quiz shows had virtually disappeared anyway, with most new quizzers following the more cautious celebrity panel format that emphasized repartee over financial largess. Once the Supreme Court had cleared the good name of the giveaway format, the big money programs were primed for a comeback. In the fall of 1954, *Stop the Music,* which had started the giveaway trend on radio in 1947, returned on ABC-TV after an almost two-year hiatus. Despite network ballyhoo, the revived program managed to bring in only marginal ratings and could not generate anything near the excitement of its top ten TV run in the late 1940s. Some television programmers pointed to this as proof that the era of the big money quiz shows had passed. Louis G. Cowan, creator of *Stop the Music,* disagreed. He felt the idea was still good, it just needed a new package.

The FCC's actions in 1949 had effectively scuttled the giveaway quiz shows before television developed many strong vehicles that could convey visually the excitement of the contests. In early 1955, Louis Cowan's production company put together a big money quiz package that was specifically tailored to meet the demands of television. The show was based on a simple radio quizzer from the 1940s, *Take It Or Leave It,* which had run for ten years without any fancy frills or expensive gimmicks. On the radio show, contestants were asked to answer a series of increasingly difficult questions in order to earn an increasingly valuable cash prize. Each contestant selected a category of questions from a prepared list and, at any point along the way, could stop—keeping the money already won—or choose to move on to the next question and risk losing it all. The value of the questions doubled at each step: $1, $2, $4, $8, $16, $32, and finally, $64. *Take It or Leave It* eventually changed its name to *The $64 Question* because that was what most people came to call the show.

For the transfer to television, Cowan took the basic idea of *The $64 Question* and added mounds of show business hype. Instead of the sixty-four-dollar question, the goal became the sixty-four-*thousand*-dollar question. Upon reaching the $8,000 level, the contestant was placed inside an isolation booth. Ostensibly this was to prevent hearing clues yelled by members of the audience, but it was really done to increase the visual suspense for the home viewers. The contestant stood alone in the isolation booth, ready to face the challenge of the four big money questions: $8,000, $16,000, $32,000, and $64,000. To prolong the suspense, only the $8,000 and $16,000 questions were posed the first week. If these were answered correctly, the contestant was given a week to decide whether to keep the money or go on. If the $32,000 question was answered correctly the next week, the contestant was given another week to decide whether to keep the winnings or to try for the ultimate jackpot. As an added incentive to go for the $64,000 question, the contestant was permitted to bring into the isolation booth an expert in the chosen category for advice. To demonstrate the program's unimpeachable standards of honesty, a grand show was made of having armed guards surround the safety deposit box in which the questions were stored. A bank official regularly appeared on the show to testify that nobody who had any connection with the program had access to the safety deposit box, "except the editors" (an exception mentioned very quickly and, at the time, no one seemed to notice it).

The super-charged big money package, with veteran sitcom sidekick Hal March as emcee, premiered on CBS live from New York on June 7, 1955, as a summer replacement for the *Danger* drama anthology. Within one month, *The $64,000 Question* was the most popular television show on the air. People found it irresistible and became caught up in the hokey, but nonetheless real, human drama unfolding live before them. Unlike most previous big money quiz shows, *The $64,000 Question* asked tough, but not tricky, questions, written by Professor Bergen Evans, host of another Louis G. Cowan program, *Down You Go.* Contestants on *The $64,000 Question* were allowed to choose their own category of questions and this encouraged participation by smart but basically average people who happened to have a great deal of specialized knowledge in one particular topic. This helped the show's popularity enormously because members of the audience could see themselves in the ordinary, run-of-the-mill people competing, and they shared vicariously in the decision to "go for the big dough."

The producers had hoped for an enthusiastic public response to

FALL 1955 SCHEDULE

Day	Net	7:00	7:30	8:00	8:30	9:00	9:30	10:00	10:30
MON	ABC	Kukla, Fran & Ollie / John Daly & The News	Topper	TV Reader's Digest	Voice Of Firestone	Dotty Mack Show	Medical Horizons	The Big Picture	local
MON	CBS	local	ADVENTURES OF ROBIN HOOD	Burns And Allen Show	Arthur Godfrey's Talent Scouts	I Love Lucy	December Bride	Studio One	
MON	DUM	local				Monday Night Fights From St. Nicholas Arena With Chris Schenkel			At Ringside
MON	NBC	local	Tony Martin / Cam. News Caravan	Caesar's Hour / # Producer's Showcase		Medic	Robert Montgomery Presents		local
TUE	ABC	Kukla, Fran & Ollie / John Daly & The News	WARNER BROTHERS PRESENTS (KING'S ROW; CHEYENNE; CASABLANCA)		LIFE AND LEGEND OF WYATT EARP	Make Room For Daddy	Du Pont Cavalcade Theater	Talent Varieties	local
TUE	CBS	local	Name That Tune	NAVY LOG	YOU'LL NEVER GET RICH	Meet Millie	Red Skelton Show	$64,000 Question	My Favorite Husband
TUE	DUM	local							
TUE	NBC	local	Dinah Shore / Cam. News Caravan	Milton Berle Show / Martha Raye Show — CHEVY SHOW		Jane Wyman's Fireside Theater	Armstrong Circle Theater — PLAYWRIGHTS '56		Big Town
WED	ABC	Kukla, Fran & Ollie / John Daly & The News	Disneyland		MGM PARADE	Masquerade Party	Break The Bank	Wednesday Night Fights	
WED	CBS	local	BRAVE EAGLE	Arthur Godfrey And His Friends		The Millionaire	I've Got A Secret	U.S. Steel Hour / 20th CENTURY-FOX HOUR	
WED	DUM	local				What's The Story		local	
WED	NBC	local	Eddie Fisher / Plym. News Caravan	SCREEN DIRECTOR'S PLAYHOUSE	Father Knows Best	Kraft Television Theater		This Is Your Life	Midwestern Hayride
THR	ABC	Kukla, Fran & Ollie / John Daly & The News	The Lone Ranger	Life Is Worth Living	Stop The Music	Star Tonight	Down You Go	OUTSIDE U.S.A.	local
THR	CBS	local	SGT. PRESTON OF THE YUKON	Bob Cummings Show	Climax / # Shower Of Stars		Four Star Plyhouse	Johnny Carson Show	WANTED
THR	DUM	local							
THR	NBC	local	Dinah Shore / Cam. News Caravan	You Bet Your Life	THE PEOPLE'S CHOICE	Dragnet	Ford Theater	Lux Video Theater	
FRI	ABC	Kukla, Fran & Ollie / John Daly & The News	Adventures Of Rin Tin Tin	Adventures Of Ozzie And Harriet	CROSSROADS	Dollar A Second	The Vise	Ethel And Albert	local
FRI	CBS	local	ADVENTURES OF CHAMPION	Mama	Our Miss Brooks	THE CRUSADER	Schlitz Playhouse Of Stars	The Lineup	Person To Person
FRI	DUM	local							
FRI	NBC	local	Eddie Fisher / Plym. News Caravan	Truth Or Consequences	The Life Of Riley	The Big Story	STAR STAGE	Gillette Cavalcade Of Sports	Red Barber
SAT	ABC	local	Ozark Jubilee / # GRAND OLE OPRY			Lawrence Welk Show		Tomorrow's Careers	local
SAT	CBS	Gene Autry Show	Beat The Clock	Stage Show	THE HONEYMOONERS	Two For The Money	IT'S ALWAYS JAN	GUNSMOKE / # FORD STAR JUBILEE	Damon Runyan Theater
SAT	DUM	local							
SAT	NBC	local	BIG SURPRISE	Perry Como Show		People Are Funny	Texaco Star Theater / # Max Liebman Presents	George Gobel Show	Your Hit Parade
SUN	ABC	You Asked For It	FAMOUS FILM FESTIVAL			Chance Of A Lifetime	Original Amateur Hour	Life Begins At 80	local
SUN	CBS	Lassie	Private Secretary / Jack Benny Program	Ed Sullivan Show		General Electric Theater	ALFRED HITCHCOCK PRESENTS	Appointment With Adventure	What's My Line
SUN	DUM	local							
SUN	NBC	It's A Great Life	FRONTIER	Colgate Variety Hour / # Color Spread		Goodyear Television Playhouse / Alcoa Hour		Loretta Young Show	Justice

the program, but they were pleasantly surprised to receive an unexpected bonus from the nation's major newspapers, which devoted a great deal of space to the trials and tribulations of *The $64,000 Question*'s contestants. The weekly progress of the suddenly famous people was treated as a news item and reported in articles outside the TV page. The day after the first show, large write-ups described the performance of a housewife from Trenton who answered seven questions on the movies, but lost on the eighth. (She received a Cadillac as a consolation prize.) Then, a Staten Island policeman, Redmond O'Hanlon, worked his way through questions on Shakespeare and found himself facing what was soon to become a familiar, agonizing decision: keep the $8,000 or go for more. He went on, but stopped at $16,000, so public attention shifted to Mrs. Catherine E. Kreitzer, a Bible expert who eventually stopped at $32,000. (She did, however, "go on" to read a chapter from the Bible on Ed Sullivan's *Toast of the Town*.) Mrs. Kreitzer was followed by Gino Prato, a Bronx cab driver-opera buff, who reached the $32,000 plateau. All week,

New York was abuzz: Would Gino go on? A local radio station broadcast a recording of a phone call to Gino from his ninety-two-year-old father, who lived in Italy. Papa Prato urged caution and Gino, ever the dutiful son, took the money and ran. The tension became unbearable. Was there no American strong enough to stand up and challenge the fates on the $64,000 question? Just as the 1955–56 season began, such a man appeared. Appropriately, he was a soldier, twenty-eight-year-old Marine Corps Captain Richard S. McCutchen, who decided to try for the $64,000 question and chose his father as the expert to accompany him into the isolation booth. For the final question in the category of food and cooking (his hobby), McCutchen was asked to explain an exotic menu served to the king and queen of England in 1939. He answered correctly. McCutchen's boldness had paid off and his success at winning $64,000 (which, after taxes, came to about $32,000) was reported on page one of the staid gray *New York Times*.

On December 6, a twenty-eight-year-old psychologist, Dr. Joyce Brothers, became the second contestant to go all the way. In her chosen topic, boxing, she identified the caestus as the special gloves worn by gladiators in ancient Rome, and won $64,000. Dr. Brothers received so much publicity from her victory that she went into broadcasting full time, and became a well-known TV and radio personality. Around the time of Dr. Brothers's triumph, some major newspapers reached an unofficial agreement with each other to downplay their treatment of *The $64,000 Question.* There was a feeling that the free publicity generated by reporting the contestants' progress with such gusto had helped foster the program's sudden popularity. Whatever the cause, *The $64,000 Question* had become a television phenomenon by the fall of 1955, and it handily defeated all the returning series, staying the number one rated TV show throughout the 1955–56 season.

Many other programs used the distinctive game show as a hook. Almost every variety show did a take-off, and one of the best was by Dean Martin and Jerry Lewis on *The Colgate Variety Hour.* Martin played Hal April, emcee of *The $64,000,000 Question.* At the $16,000,000 plateau, Lewis, an unwilling contestant, was shoved into taking the next question. Instead of entering an isolation booth, he was pushed under water. Jackie Gleason wrote and starred in a serious play on the topic, "Uncle Ed and Circumstance," which aired on *Studio One.* Using the actual *$64,000 Question* set, Gleason played the family goat who suddenly came into favor by winning $64,000. The triumph on the quiz show provided him with a victory his relations could admire and gave him the inner strength to cut his home ties and go off on his own. He actually did not care about the prize money itself and gave it to his family. Gleason aired another quiz story that season on his regular weekly series. In a humorous Honeymooners tale, Gleason (as Ralph Kramden) went through the agony of mastering music, his chosen topic, only to get stagefright and blank out on the opening question of identifying "Swanee River."

Within the television industry, the sudden success of *The $64,000 Question* over the summer prompted a frantic race by all the networks to come up with copies. One of the first to appear was another Louis G. Cowan product, *The Big Surprise* (hosted by Mike Wallace), which premiered on NBC in October. Though the program increased the winning ante to $100,000, it lacked the raw edge of human emotion symbolized by the isolation booths of CBS's *$64,000 Question.* The first quiz clone that proved a ratings success was *The $64,000 Challenge* created by (who else?) Louis G. Cowan as a virtual carbon copy of his established hit. On *The $64,000 Challenge,* winning contestants from *The $64,000 Question* returned to the isolation booths to face new challengers and to try for a top prize of $128,000. Soon after its spring debut on CBS in 1956, *The $64,000 Challenge* joined *The $64,000 Question* in television's top ten list.

The spectacular success of *The $64,000 Question* came as a major surprise to the networks. In just a few months, the rank upstart quizzer had deposed *I Love Lucy* as the country's number one show. The preferences of the television audience were obviously changing and the network executives faced the difficult and sometimes puzzling task of trying to analyze them.

One reason that tastes were changing was that the audience was changing. As TV set sales continued to grow, the size and makeup of the audience had turned television into a more broadbased mass medium. Between 1952 and 1955, TV set ownership had almost doubled, growing from 34% of the country to 65%. In addition, the first wave of post-World War II baby boom children were almost ten years old and increasingly influential in setting family viewing patterns. With these important new factors affecting program selection, even previously successful stars, shows, and formats were on uncertain ground. Throughout the season there were

surprise failures and unexpected hits, some of which, like the big money quizzes, had been previously unsuccessful or dismissed as past their prime.

During the summer of 1955, just as *The $64,000 Question* was topping the ratings charts, a less meteoric but equally unexpected hit appeared on ABC: *The Lawrence Welk Show.* Over the previous seven years, band leaders such as Eddie Condon, Vincent Lopez, Sammy Kaye, Wayne King, and Freddy Martin had come and gone on TV with no success. They seemed to violate the cardinal rule of television by presenting a format that emphasized sound rather than visuals. When Lawrence Welk, who had been on TV locally in Los Angeles since 1951, brought his pleasant, unpretentious schmaltz to ABC's summer schedule, he was expected to follow the other band leaders to oblivion. Instead, Welk's Saturday night dance party, featuring his patented champagne music, turned into the sleeper hit of the season.

Welk led a relaxed hour of dance music, featuring a talented crew of supporting players including accordionist Myron Floren, singer-dancer Alice Lon, clarinetist Pete Fountain, and the singing Lennon Sisters. The key to the success of his simple, direct musical format proved to be an elusive enigma. Trying to duplicate the chemistry, a rash of musical hopefuls soon appeared: Guy Lombardo's *Diamond Jubilee* (part music, part giveaway, part *This Is Your Life), The Ina Ray Hutton Show* (featuring an all-female orchestra), *The Russ Morgan Show* (like Welk's, presented straight), and *It's Polka Time* (with lively emcee Bruno "Junior" Zielinski, who shouted loud, enthusiastic introductions to each song). None of these attracted a following like Welk, whose natural but cultivated accent and manner made him a popular national figure. (Even his trademark phrase "a vun and a two and a t'ree" became a popular gag line.) Unlike the failed competition, Welk not only continued to thrive on Saturday night, he also launched a successful spinoff series, *Lawrence Welk's Top Tunes and New Talent* in the fall of 1956, which ran three seasons.

One of the most important changes for the 1955–56 season was the expanded role of Hollywood in network programming. Following the success of *Disneyland* the previous season, ABC, CBS, and NBC had made agreements with several major studios for programs produced specifically for television. The networks hoped for another ratings bonanza and the studios hoped to duplicate Disney's ploy of using a profitable TV show to plug the latest theatrical features. Almost every one of the highly touted film industry productions was a disappointment.

Number one CBS showed the most restraint and selectivity in approaching the major studios, and secured the closest thing to an all-around Hollywood success that season, *The 20th Century Fox Hour.* Joseph Cotten hosted the bi-weekly series, which presented high quality sixty-minute adaptations of old movies such as "The Ox-Bow Incident" and "Miracle on 34th Street," and occasionally featured a few big name stars not usually seen on television.

NBC talked the Screen Directors Guild into producing a half-hour weekly drama anthology, *Screen Director's Playhouse.* Despite the participation by such distinguished feature film directors as John Ford and Fred Zinnemann, the series was bland and indistinguishable from every other thirty-minute drama anthology. NBC was also let down by the first world premiere on American television of a major feature length film, the British-made "The Constant Husband." The story was a light farce starring Rex Harrison as an amnesia victim who married several different women, and its November telecast drew universally tepid reviews. This created the impression that NBC had been taken for a ride by the British film studio, paying a great deal of money to show a film that would not have been a hit if released to the theaters.

September 17, 1955

The Perry Como Show. (NBC). Perry defects to NBC after CBS axes his early evening music show. For his new network, Perry hosts a lavishly-financed hour-long musical-variety program with Goodman Ace as a writer and the Ray Charles singers as back up.

September 22, 1955

Commercial television comes to Britain via the regionally based ITV network, at last providing competition to the government-sponsored BBC.

September 25, 1955

Toast of the Town becomes *The Ed Sullivan Show.*

September 28, 1955

NBC telecasts the first color World Series game: The New York Yankees beat the Brooklyn Dodgers 6 to 5 at Yankee Stadium.

October 16, 1955

Wide Wide World. (NBC). Another Pat Weaver programming innovation. Dave Garroway hosts a live ninety-minute potpourri every other Sunday afternoon. This first week, the roving cameras bring the Grand Canyon, Rockefeller Center, the Texas State Fair, and Florida's Weeki Wachee to the living rooms of America. In March, the series presents the U.S. premiere of the new British feature film of "Richard III," starring Sir Laurence Olivier.

October 26, 1955

Highway Patrol. Ziv, master of off-network syndication, scores with Broderick Crawford as the grumpy, rumpled highway patrol chief, Dan Matthews, who barks "ten-four" into his radio while chasing criminals over the nation's motorways.

October 31, 1955

NBC Matinee Theater. (NBC). At a daily cost of roughly $20,000, NBC sends out an hour-long live television drama show from Los Angeles each weekday afternoon. This Pat Weaver-inspired series is one of the first to be regularly broadcast in color.

ABC also turned to Britain for filmed material and purchased fifty features from the J. Arthur Rank studios to launch one of the first network schedulings of feature films in prime time, the Sunday evening *Famous Film Festival* (soon expanded to include *The Afternoon Film Festival*). Most Americans at the time found British drama too stiff and British accents too confusing to follow, so the network's experiment was unable to beat the tough competition of Ed Sullivan's *Toast of the Town.* Acceptance of prime time movies did not come about until NBC acquired the television rights to more recent Hollywood films six years later. Though disappointed by the failure of the prime time British films, ABC was much more concerned by the weak performances of its major new Hollywood-produced series, *MGM Parade* and *Warner Bros. Presents.*

The network ran the hour-long *Warner Bros.* adventure series Tuesday from 7:30 P.M. to 8:30 P.M., repeating the early starting time strategy that had worked so well with *Disneyland.* In order to fill the program each week, the studio set up *Warner Bros. Presents* as a showcase for three continuing series that rotated in the slot. Each was a television adaptation of a past Warner Bros. film.

The first in the series, *King's Row,* came from a competent but unexciting grade-B film about a small-town psychiatrist. Appropriately, the film inspired a competent but unexciting grade-B adaptation. Second in the series was *Casablanca,* a silly grade-Z yarn based on the grade-A film thriller. The original film had been set in Morocco during World War II and starred Humphrey Bogart as Rick, an American expatriate who operated a cafe in Casablanca, and Ingrid Bergman as Ilsa, his long-lost love from Paris, who was working underground against the Nazis. For the television adaptation, the setting remained Rick's cafe in Casablanca, but everything else was updated to the 1950s. The town was no longer overrun by Nazis, but by Russian spies on the lookout for nuclear secrets. Charles McGraw and Anita Ekberg took Bogart and Bergman's roles, though in keeping with the updated setting, Ekberg's character was transformed into Trina, a Swedish scientist. The magic of the original premise was smothered in 1950s relevancy. It was a close race, but *King's Row* was judged to be worse than *Casablanca,* and it was the first to be axed, replaced in January by *Conflict,* an undistinguished drama anthology.

The only member of the original Warner Bros. triumvirate to succeed was *Cheyenne,* a better-than-average stock Western starring Clint Walker as Cheyenne Bodie, a half-Indian government scout in the classic "strong silent type" mold. *Cheyenne* attracted a sizeable audience, composed largely of youngsters, that became caught up in the Western setting and adventures. When *King's Row* faded around New Year's, *Cheyenne* was increased to an alternate week frequency, with *Casablanca* and *Conflict* filling out the month.

The real reason for *Warner Bros. Presents* was not left to the imagination. Every week the last fifteen minutes was turned over to Gig Young who hosted "Behind the Camera at Warner Bros. Studios." Plug. Plug. Plug. More fascinating interviews with fascinating stars about their fascinating movies soon to open at a local fascinating movie theater.

The behind-the-scenes features on *Disneyland* were subtle and entertaining. It was possible for viewers to watch and enjoy that program without ever seeing the theatrical films involved, though it was likely they would attend after being teased by the well done background reports. The Warner Bros. features were little more than cheaply produced promotional trailers. The fifteen minutes of plugs, added to the normal commercial allotment, brought the one-hour program dangerously close to a fifty-fifty mix of entertainment and commercials. ABC's other new Hollywood showcase was even worse. *The MGM Parade* was set up as a weekly behind-the-scenes peek at the MGM studios in a half-hour mélange of old film clips, new film clips, shots of productions in progress, and a few interviews. The program was poorly paced, lacked cohesion, and played as a blatant plug for the studio.

The public reaction to both programs (with the exception of the *Cheyenne* segment) was largely negative and the ratings were nowhere near the blockbuster success of *Disneyland.* The major Hollywood studios soon realized that television had to be treated as more than a garbage dump for promotional messages. In the spring, MGM upgraded its program and presented several high quality episodes, such as a well researched review of the career of Greta Garbo. By then, however, the show had already been canceled. Warner Bros. scuttled the *Warner Bros. Presents* format at the end of the season, but carried over *Cheyenne* as a series on its own. The success of *Disneyland* and *Cheyenne* pointed to a simple, but effective, strategy. Leave the obvious plugs behind and produce programs that would stand on their own as profitable hits.

Though the major studios fared poorly in the initial attempts to package feature programs for the networks, their failure did little to slow the steady shift in the balance of power in television from New York to Hollywood. Later that season, in fact, the major studios successfully released nearly 2,000 pre-1948 theatrical films to television and in the process almost single-handedly killed off live local programming. Stations quickly snapped up the features because running the old films was much cheaper than anything else they could do. Like the networks, the locals were increasingly willing to cede control in return for reliable, popular product.

Throughout the years, Hollywood had consistently displayed a better grasp than New York of how to produce pop culture material that appealed to the average American. In the 1910s, the center of the U.S. film industry had shifted from the East Coast to the West Coast and, in the 1930s, the same thing had taken place in radio. By the 1950s, the ascendancy of Hollywood-based filmed sitcoms, crime shows, and adventure series gave the West Coast the upper hand in the battle for control over television. Even many live variety programs originated from Hollywood because that's where the stars lived. ABC was largely committed to California production and CBS was not far behind. With so much of its new programming originating from Los Angeles, CBS created the position of Manager of West Coast Network Programming. James Aubrey, general manager since 1952 of CBS's Los Angeles station, KNXT, became the first to fill the new post.

The success of programs such as *Disneyland* and *The Adventures of Rin Tin Tin* in the previous season had added to prime time another popular format that was easily done on the West Coast, kidvid adventure films. For the fall of 1955, CBS dumped its 7:30 to 8:00 P.M. news and music programs in favor of kiddie-oriented sagas such as *Sergeant Preston of the Yukon, Brave Eagle, The Adventures of Champion,* and the British-made *Adventures of Robin Hood.* These standard pulp adventure yarns focused on animals, young boys, and stalwart adults in rugged settings ranging from the frozen tundra to the forests of Sherwood. Though none of them produced outstanding ratings, they served their purpose and attracted a large pre-teen audience for advertisers.

CBS also made a bid for children in the early morning, taking one hour from the foundering *Morning Show* news program and installing Bob Keeshan (formerly Clarabell the clown on *Howdy Doody)* as the gentle Captain Kangaroo. ABC took its kidvid strategy to the late afternoon and challenged NBC's *Howdy Doody* with another Disney series, *The Mickey Mouse Club.* For one hour on film each afternoon, host Jimmie Dodd and a dozen young "Mouseketeers" performed in skits, sang songs, and introduced special features such as the Mickey Mouse Newsreel, safety lectures by Jiminy Cricket, nature films, Disney cartoons, and guest performers ranging from circus aerialists to veteran comedian Morey Amsterdam. There were also adventure serials such as "Corky and White Shadow," "Annette," "The Hardy Boys," and "Spin and Marty," usually featuring members of the Mouseketeers in the lead roles. (Annette Funicello was the most popular performer.) Local California children sometimes participated in the show as well, often taking part in studio contests. (In 1957, a youngster named Jerry Brown was a contestant. Seventeen years later, when the series was still being seen in reruns, Brown was elected governor of California and later became a candidate for president.) *The Mickey Mouse Club* proved so successful for ABC that *Howdy Doody* was soon banished to Saturday morning.

One format that had kept preadolescents enthralled long before television emerged was the Western, a popular setting for American adventure tales throughout the twentieth century. During the 1930s, near-mythic hero types such as Wild Bill Hickok, Hopalong Cassidy, Gene Autry, and Roy Rogers had filled countless Saturday movie matinees with hard-riding action interrupted by only a few "boring" love scenes. The stories were simple morality plays, with good and bad clearly defined and justice always triumphant over evil. When television arrived in the late 1940s, the kiddie Western made an easy transfer to the home screen where a new generation of children eagerly snapped them up in both reruns of the old films and new exploits made for television.

In the early 1950s, the assumption that Westerns were "just kid stuff" began to change as theatrical films such as "High Noon" and "Shane" placed more serious plots in Western settings. These stories became known as adult Westerns and did well at the box office. ABC staged a successful adult Western ("Last Notch") on its *U.S. Steel Hour* anthology in 1954 and, in the 1955–56 season, all three networks made tentative tests of the popularity of the format in a weekly series.

NBC handed Worthington Miner the task of developing a continuing adult Western, and Miner responded with *Frontier,* an anthology based on Western folklore. *Frontier* was an abysmal failure, partly because of its often pretentious plots (liberally sprinkled with heavy-handed psychology), but largely due to the absence of a continuing identifiable Western hero that viewers could latch onto.

ABC's *The Life and Legend of Wyatt Earp* was a half step removed from *Frontier* and considerably more successful. Most of

December 10, 1955
Mighty Mouse Playhouse. (CBS). The first animated cartoon on Saturday morning network television.

January 3, 1956
Do You Trust Your Wife? (CBS). Edgar Bergen, like Groucho Marx, hosts a quiz show that emphasizes humorous patter over the actual game.

January 3, 1956
Queen for a Day. (NBC). "Would you like to be queen for a day?" Jack Bailey asks. America's housewives respond in the affirmative, as NBC regains control of the weekday afternoon hours with this successful, heart-tugging audience participation show.

February 20, 1956
Good Morning. (CBS). A last gasp move to salvage CBS's version of *Today.* Will Rogers, Jr. takes over as host. Ratings rise at first, but *Today* appears to be unbeatable.

April 2, 1956
CBS presents the first daily thirty-minute television soap operas, *As the World Turns* and *The Edge of Night.*

May 28, 1956
After a year in prime time, *The Johnny Carson Show* is demoted to a daytime slot on CBS, replacing Robert Q. Lewis. Carson "loosens up" in his new slot, adopting a style similar to Steve Allen's. Nonetheless, CBS cans Carson in September.

August 13, 1956
The Democratic National Convention opens in Chicago. Along with Bill Henry, NBC adds as co-anchors two new faces: Chet Huntley and David Brinkley.

September 7, 1956
Pat Weaver quits as chairman of NBC.

On their simple kitchen set, the stars of *The Honeymooners*: *(from left)* Art Carney, Jackie Gleason, and Audrey Meadows. *(CBS Photo Archive © 2003 CBS Worldwide, Inc. All Rights Reserved.)*

the early episodes were based on allegedly historical events from a biography of frontier lawman Wyatt Earp (who had died in Los Angeles in 1929 at the age of eighty-two). To this base, ABC added a more traditional handsome leading man, Hugh O'Brian, as Sheriff Earp. As portrayed by O'Brian, Wyatt Earp was a genuinely interesting character and far beyond the one-dimensional heroic figures such as Hopalong Cassidy. Earp took his job seriously, but compassionately, first in Kansas (Ellsworth and Dodge City) and then in Tombstone, Arizona. The conflict between a previously lawless town and an effective, dedicated sheriff provided a strong basis for the weekly plots. The program was well executed and avoided obvious Western film clichés even within the obligatory fights, chases, and shoot-outs. (During a fist fight near the town water reservoir, *nobody* fell in!)

CBS based its adult Western series on its successful radio hit, *Gunsmoke*. The innovative radio Western had premiered in early 1952 (predating the breakthrough film "High Noon") as a finely crafted portrait of the old West as seen through the eyes of a tough but compassionate U.S. marshal, Matt Dillon (played by William Conrad). Dillon lived in a tough, violent West that cheated honest men and sometimes left the heroes frustrated and confused, even after winning a showdown. At the start, CBS Radio did not quite know what to make of the show and relegated it to an obscure time slot, where it stayed for one and one-half years before securing a sponsor. By that time, "High Noon" had won an Oscar and *Gunsmoke* was moved to a better time period, where it flourished.

In 1955, when CBS began to search for an adult Western television vehicle, all it had to do was look to its radio branch. For the video version, an entirely new cast was chosen, with the rotund, slightly grumpy William Conrad replaced by the tall, lean figure of James Arness. America's number one traditional Western film star, John Wayne, who had suggested Arness for the lead, introduced the first episode of the half-hour series, assuring old-time sagebrush fans by his presence that TV's *Gunsmoke* was worthy of their patronage. The program successfully maintained the tight combination of effective, inevitable violence and compelling slices of human drama that had worked so well on radio. In one story, Dillon spent most of the program in relentless pursuit of a killer, only to discover on confronting him that the man was not so much an evil murderer as a slightly psychotic individual who only wanted to be left alone. Dillon understood the man's desire for solitude, felt compassion, and cursed the circumstances that turned him into a killer, but nonetheless brought him in. It was his painful, necessary duty as marshal.

While NBC's *Frontier* was a flop, CBS's *Gunsmoke* and ABC's *Wyatt Earp* proved quite successful. Neither was a ratings smash in its first season, but both were solid performers, with a slowly but steadily growing legion of regular viewers. The two-out-of-three scorecard for adult Westerns, while not overwhelming, combined with the success of *Cheyenne* to underscore the surprising strength of the Western format. Once again, a durable Hollywood film staple provided yet another successful network television format. The growing feeling that Hollywood production represented the best chance for reaching the expanding TV audience pushed program activity westward, and it dealt the crippling blow to one of television's pioneers, the DuMont network.

For some time, DuMont had conceded the fact that it was not in the same league as CBS and NBC, preferring instead to bill itself as the reasonably priced network that allowed not-so-large sponsors a crack at television. This proved to be a workable, if limited, strategy that did attract a number of new sponsors to television for the network's few successful low-budget programs: *Cavalcade of Stars, Captain Video, Down You Go, Life Is Worth Living, Rocky King, The Plainclothesman, They Stand Accused, Life Begins at Eighty,* wrestling, and prime time NFL football. In time, however, even these inexpensive programs became impossible to maintain as television costs continued to escalate.

The turning point for DuMont came in January 1955 when the network sold its Pittsburgh O&O, WDTV, to Westinghouse for $9.7 million. (The station was promptly renamed KDKA-TV.) WDTV's position as the only television station in Pittsburgh had been the main reason DuMont stayed alive as long as it had, but by the end of 1954, DuMont Labs was in desperate need of cash. The network operation had never been very profitable, but TV set sales had always been great enough for an overall company profit. When the labs began sliding into the red, DuMont was forced to sell the only valuable property it owned, even though WDTV would remain the only commercial VHF station in Pittsburgh for three more years.

The sale of WDTV was an admission that the DuMont television network was a failure. In early 1955, DuMont began cutting its use of the costly coaxial cable connections, effectively reducing network output to almost nothing. The long-running Monday through Friday *Captain Video* serial ended April 1. *Down You Go, Chance of a Lifetime, Life Begins at Eighty,* and Bishop Sheen's *Life Is Worth Living* moved to ABC. By October 1955, DuMont maintained only one or two live sporting events.

While effectively out of the television network business, DuMont hoped to stay alive as a source of television programming. With more and more prime time programs on film, DuMont decided to offer its newly built five-studio New York telecenter as a convenient location for East Coast film production. It tried to convince New York producers to stay put and transfer to film without the expense of a cross-country shift, using a new DuMont TV film process, the electronicam. The lure of Hollywood was too hard to buck and, by the fall of 1955, only Jackie Gleason had signed on as a customer.

In the face of such an all-around failure, the Paramount side of the DuMont ownership staged a coup d'etat in August 1955 and at last took complete control of the company. By teaming with the investment firm of Loeb & Rhodes (another major DuMont stockholder) Paramount obtained a working majority of stockholders and instituted immediate changes. Dr. Allen DuMont was kicked upstairs to the figurehead position of chairman of the board, and Bernard Goodwin (a Paramount man) was installed as president. Soon thereafter, DuMont announced that it no longer considered itself a national television network.

Paramount's dramatic victory turned out to be a Pyrrhic one. In July 1957, Paramount was voted out of control when the Loeb & Rhodes faction teamed up with the owners of WNEW, a newly acquired New York City radio station. A year later, the DuMont network was officially put to rest when Paramount sold its remaining shares of stock and Dr. DuMont retired. DuMont Broadcasting, which had failed so miserably as a television network, was renamed Metromedia and, ironically, it ultimately became a very healthy string of independent radio and TV stations, similar to the Westinghouse ("Group W") organization.

DuMont's brief venture in 1955 as an East Coast production outfit did result in one major contribution to American television: the preservation of thirty-nine half-hour episodes of Jackie Gleason's *Honeymooners* series. By early 1955, three years after leaving DuMont for CBS, Gleason's Saturday night comedy-variety hour had replaced *Dragnet* as the number two television program. Despite the success of his proven format, Gleason decided to gamble and discard the variety part of his show in favor of a thirty-minute filmed situation comedy devoted exclusively to the long-running Honeymooners characters. CBS was very nervous over Gleason's plan because it practically invited rival NBC to counter with a strong hour-long program in a time slot previously conceded to CBS. After extended negotiations, Gleason got his way, but with some limitations. Though he signed a very generous contract which granted him a hefty percentage of the rerun profits for the filmed series, the deal was limited to one year, to see if it would work.

Despite network misgivings, Gleason's venture seemed to have every reason to succeed. The Honeymooners had been a part of his repertoire for years, originating during Gleason's tenure as host of DuMont's *Cavalcade of Stars*. When he transferred to CBS in the fall of 1952, Gleason brought the Honeymooners along, though at first it remained just another element in his stock of character skits. Soon it became evident that the Honeymooners was the most popular of all and sometimes the entire hour was devoted to a Honeymooners story. A Honeymooners series was the logical next step, lifting the familiar cast and concept, intact, from the variety show. Using the DuMont electronicam process, the episodes were filmed before a live audience which retained the spontaneous energy of the live sketches and helped the program to appear as just a continuation of Gleason's variety show.

The Honeymooners was a working class character piece, built around the chemistry between Jackie Gleason and Art Carney. Over the years the duo had developed superb physical and verbal comic timing together, carrying even weak sketches by the sheer force of their personalities. *The Honeymooners* was a showcase for two of their best characters and some of their most effective

interaction. Gleason played Ralph Kramden, a fat, loud-mouthed, but basically warm-hearted Brooklyn bus driver, while Carney was Ed Norton, an uneducated, clumsy, but cheerful and innately perceptive sewer worker. The two were best friends and constantly played off each other. When Ralph was blustery, Norton was befuddled. When Ralph was scheming, Norton was gullible. When Ralph was hurt, Norton was consoling. When Ralph was pompous, Norton was there to prick the balloon. Through it all they remained inveterate dreamers, convinced that just one lucky break could make them wealthy.

Equally important to *The Honeymooners*, however, was the relationship between Ralph and his wife, Alice (played by Audrey Meadows, who replaced Pert Kelton in the role when Gleason moved from DuMont to CBS). Ralph and Alice stood apart from the typical television sitcom couples of the time, which often contained a bland, lovable husband and a flighty, lovable housewife. Ralph Kramden was not a particularly lovable man. He had no patience, was often self-centered, quick tempered, and had an overblown estimate of his own importance. Alice was a bedrock of stability who knew Ralph's faults and still loved him in spite of (perhaps even because of) his occasional bursts of irrationality. Unlike Ralph and Norton, she had long ago accepted their lowly position in life and her realistic, almost fatalistic, personality provided a strong counterbalance to the flights of fancy the "boys" engaged in.

The emphasis on reality distinguished *The Honeymooners* from the mainstream of 1950s television sitcoms. The sets suggested a simple working class urban neighborhood. There were no split level suburban houses or expensive apartments. The Kramdens did not even own a telephone. In fact, there was very little scenery at all, just the all-too-familiar Kramden kitchen and a few occasional secondary locations. The entire world of *The Honeymooners*—the domestic squabbles, money shortages, the get-rich-quick schemes—took place on the basic set containing a door, a chest of drawers, a table, some chairs, a window, a stove, and an ice box.

I Love Lucy also had trappings of reality, but it used the setting as a launching pad for zany situations with a showbiz flavor. (In 1955, the *Lucy* plots revolved chiefly around Ricky's new movie career in Hollywood.) *The Honeymooners* accomplished something much more difficult, restricting the focus to average Americans facing everyday problems. In the process, the show brought out the humorous twists in the often mundane workaday world and demonstrated how funny reality could be.

Oddly, *The Honeymooners* did not do all that well. As part of the deal with Jackie Gleason, CBS was forced to accept *Stage Show*, a half-hour program from Gleason's production company. This gambit ("Buy me, buy my show") had been used by other stars in previous years to affect the selection of their summer replacement series. *Those Whiting Girls*, a Desilu production, became *I Love Lucy's* summer sub; *Caesar's Hour* was spelled by the Sid Caesar-produced *Caesar Presents;* and pinch-hitting for George Gobel was *And Here's the Show*, a product of Gobel's Gomalco Enterprises. However, unlike these short lived summer series, *Stage Show* (which had already *failed* as Gleason's summer replacement in 1954) was included in CBS's 1955 fall line-up, leading off the vital 8:00–9:00 P.M. Saturday night slot (preceding *The Honeymooners).* As feared, the program was a ratings disaster, sending viewers to a new Perry Como variety hour on NBC and away from *The Honeymooners.*

Stage Show was a straight vaudeville style vehicle, hosted by the musical Dorsey Brothers (Tommy on trombone, Jimmy on sax). Just like the "good old days," one performer after another appeared on stage, while the Dorsey Brothers and their orchestra filled the moments in between acts with a few musical numbers. The only exception to this predictable routine was the network television debut of "young hillbilly singer" Elvis Presley on January 28, 1956 (with his hip-churning renditions of "Blue Suede Shoes" and "Heartbreak Hotel"). At the start of 1956, CBS convinced Gleason to, at least, swap times with *Stage Show* so that the much stronger *Honeymooners* would lead off the 8:00 hour. Even after this move, though, Gleason could not regain the control of Saturday night he had previously enjoyed. In the spring of 1956, he decided to suspend the filmed *Honeymooners* series and in the fall return to his live hour-long variety format, which would occasionally contain some Honeymooners sketches. This was not only a mortal blow to DuMont's electronicam system (Gleason was its only customer) but also a loss to viewers of the future because there would be only thirty-nine half-hour episodes of *The Honeymooners* preserved in this format. Strangely enough, the series (which went into syndication one year later) garnered much better ratings as an off-network rerun than as part of the CBS schedule. The far-sighted Gleason raked in year after year of rerun profits as repeats of the show aired for decades, while he had only varying success with his reestablished variety format.

Another classic sitcom made its debut on CBS during the 1955–56 season, *You'll Never Get Rich* (later retitled *The Phil Silvers Show,* but popularly known as *Sgt. Bilko*). Phil Silvers had worked briefly as a TV variety show host during the late 1940s, and subsequently proved more popular as a variety show guest star. He usually played an underhanded type of fellow and the networks said he was not "warm" enough for a regular series. Nat Hiken, a former writer for Martha Raye, disagreed. He analyzed Silvers's acerbic characters and devised what he saw as the perfect setting: the United States Army.

With Hiken as director, Silvers portrayed Master Sergeant Ernest Bilko, a sly conman who served in the peacetime Army on a base filled with men who had nothing to do but eat, sleep, and gamble. This very workable situation gave Silvers a setting for a double-dealing character that could launch numerous money-making schemes and deceptions without really hurting anyone. In civilian life his actions would have appeared cruel and selfish. As a soldier, he was helping the GIs to pass away the time at an otherwise boring military base in Kansas, while lining his own pockets in the process. Best of all, Bilko did not have to worry about going to jail. He was already in the Army.

There was little chance of Bilko ever being caught because Hiken surrounded him with the most inept, disheveled Army outfit ever conceived. No commanding officer would ever be as blind and addlebrained as Colonel Hall (Paul Ford). No tub-of-flesh like Private Doberman (Maurice Gosfield) would be allowed in this or any other Army. The other borscht-belt confederates (played by Herbie Faye, Harvey Lembeck, Allan Melvin, and Joe E. Ross) seemed more appropriate in Broadway's Palace Theater than on Fort Baxter's parade ground. In effect it was vaudeville burlesque, complete with ridiculous outfits, breezy plots, and cardboard characters. But when had vaudeville ever been done so well on television? The scripts and supporting cast were excellent and the weekly schemes sheer magic. A setup took place in the first few minutes and, once again, Bilko would be off.

The entertaining joy of a Bilko con was its execution. He had an ear-to-ear grin that told everyone except the unknowing target that the master was at work. Bilko manipulated his boys and other military personnel like a Chicago ward heeler, buttering up bigwigs, choosing the perfect flunkies, and twisting every Army regulation to suit his needs. Though he was never allowed to get away with any really big sting, Bilko won most of the little battles

with the Army bureaucracy, earning the undying gratitude of an entire generation of former GIs.

Like *The Honeymooners, You'll Never Get Rich* began in a bad time slot. When it debuted, the program ran during the second half of NBC's Tuesday night comedy-variety rotation and it followed a weak CBS adventure saga, *Navy Log.* At mid-season, *Bilko* swapped slots with its lead-in, the ratings went up, and a pattern developed. When *Cheyenne* appeared on ABC's *Warner Bros. Presents,* the Western was the top show of the evening; when Bob Hope was on NBC, he was number one; and when neither of these two was present, Bilko, the old standby, came out ahead. The Bilko saga lasted for four years and, like *The Honeymooners,* stepped immediately from prime time to a lengthy and successful run in syndication.

As CBS almost routinely developed its sitcom hits, NBC's "old guard" comedy-variety showcases continued to fade. Bob Hope was the only consistent winner, but he appeared infrequently, alternating with Dinah Shore as host to *The Chevy Show.* That program shared the Tuesday-at-eight slot, on a rotating basis, with Martha Raye and Milton Berle. For the first time in eight years, Berle did not win his time slot. In fact, he lost big to Phil Silvers, who sometimes doubled Berle's ratings. Berle tried getting more serious and arty, expanded the scope of his guest list (one show opened with Elvis Presley singing "Hound Dog"), but it did no good. At the end of the season, NBC canceled the Tuesday night comedy hour and Milton Berle found himself without a show. With its stable of successful sitcoms and new quiz show hits, CBS was now clearly the top-rated network. Even NBC had to concede that fact by now.

Another veteran NBC comedy show axed during the 1955–56 season was Colgate's Sunday comedy-variety hour. At the start of 1956, NBC took control of the show and renamed it *The NBC Comedy Hour,* inaugurating a new format with Leo Durocher as emcee for the first three programs. The ratings for *The NBC Comedy Hour* were so bad that, by the spring, the old British films running on ABC outscored it. A final, frantic fix-up provided the show with a decent burial that summer. Satirist Stan Freberg was signed on (he conducted humorous dialogues with his handpuppet, Grover) and one-half of the writing staff was replaced by new writers shipped to the West Coast from New York (including nineteen-year-old Woody Allen, whose mother had to sign his contract because he was underage). In late June, the *Comedy Hour* expired and NBC brought in Steve Allen from the successful *Tonight* show in an attempt to salvage Sunday night.

The Pat Weaver-inspired big-budget spectaculars, which NBC was counting on to provide the winning edge in the ratings competition, also lost ground by the end of the season. Going into the fall, they began strong, still in the glow of "Peter Pan's" phenomenal success. Even CBS jumped whole hog into the field with *Ford Star Jubilee,* which presented an excellent adaptation of the Broadway hit, "Caine Mutiny Court Martial," as well as the television debuts of Judy Garland and Noel Coward. NBC's *Producers' Showcase* restaged "Peter Pan," presented some excellent "long hair" variety from impresario Sol Hurok, and revived and musicalized Thornton Wilder's "Our Town" (with Eva Marie Saint, Paul Newman, and Frank Sinatra, who introduced the hit tune, "Love and Marriage").

In spite of these successes, the ultra-high-budgeted, regularly scheduled spectaculars were in serious trouble by the end of the season. Ratings dropped to a generally disappointing level for such an expensive operation. Highly touted productions, such as CBS's filmed musical fantasy "High Tor" (with Bing Crosby and Julie Andrews) and Max Liebman's Maurice Chevalier variety special on NBC, bombed in the ratings. When such simple productions as

"Inside Beverly Hills" (puff interviews with film stars in their homes, hosted by Art Linkletter) registered the season's top ratings for spectaculars, the need to produce anything very elaborate and complicated was increasingly difficult to justify. When an economic recession hit, it became almost impossible.

Spectaculars had always been extremely expensive to stage and wildly unpredictable in the ratings. Only the largest sponsors had been able to cover the costs, and the 1956 recession forced even these bankrollers, chiefly auto companies such as Ford, to withdraw from the market. They preferred safer and cheaper programs. Increasingly, that meant West Coast filmed series. The other major programming type still emanating from New York, live drama, also felt the squeeze.

Though the prestigious New York-based drama series attracted all the critical attention, popular Los Angeles drama productions attracted more viewers. CBS had three of the top shows: *Alfred Hitchcock Presents* (with the master of suspense supplying pithy remarks before and after short plays of suspense); *Climax* (which successfully mixed New York style production with Los Angeles style stories and stars); and *General Electric Theater* (which became the top-rated drama show on television by showcasing its host, Ronald Reagan, as well as other top Hollywood names). In addition, Westerns such as *Gunsmoke* and ABC's *Wyatt Earp* presented well written drama with a familiar cast of characters and plenty of action.

The networks did not abandon live New York drama. They were just being more careful with it, limiting the number of showcases and trying to avoid upsetting sponsors and viewers. As a result, while there were still outstanding plays staged, the behind the scenes efforts required to turn them out added a further strain to the already high pressure production schedules. CBS, which had spirited *The U.S. Steel Hour* from ABC, managed to present several striking and memorable plays that season, including a strident Rod Serling original, "Incident in an Alley," which portrayed a policeman's guilt after killing a young boy. Another Serling play,

"Noon on Doomsday," faced strong sponsor and network pressure and had to be rewritten before airing. Originally it was to be about the highly publicized murder of a Southern black, Emmett Till; as it eventually aired, the locale was shifted to New England (where everyone *knew* there was no racial prejudice) and the victim became a white foreigner.

At NBC, Fred Coe at last won a program slot specifically devoted to producing plays written by his troupe of writers from the Sunday night *Television Playhouse. Playwrights '56,* sponsored by Pontiac, began with a David Davidson original, "The Answer," but the long-fought-for series was overshadowed by its strong competition on CBS, *The Red Skelton Show* and *The $64,000 Question.* In an almost eerie juxtaposition of events in the spring of 1956, NBC loudly celebrated Fred Coe's tenth anniversary with the network, then axed his show.

The biggest loser in the shifting fortunes of television in the 1955–56 season was Pat Weaver. The driving force behind *Your Show of Shows, Today, Home, Tonight,* and the spectacular quickly became the scapegoat for NBC's sinking fortunes. Throughout his career at NBC, Weaver had served as a seemingly bottomless well of innovative programming concepts, most of which were highly praised by the nation's television critics and popular with viewers. The fact remained, however, that NBC had fallen from first place and he had failed to bring it back to the top.

In December 1955, Pat Weaver was kicked upstairs to the position of chairman of the NBC Board of Directors. Robert Sarnoff, son and heir apparent to "the General," succeeded Weaver as network president. Weaver remained at his figurehead post for a few months and then quietly and politely retired from NBC. Many of Weaver's programming concepts, in fact many of his specific programs, continued successfully long after he was out of power. At the start of 1956, though, the feeling at NBC, and throughout the television industry, was that a new era in television was at hand and that the old generation of executives had to make way for the new.

16. It's Been a Tremendous Strain

CONFUSION AND UNEASINESS GRIPPED the television industry in the fall of 1956. Prime time programming was in flux, the economy was sluggish, and big advertisers were reducing their television budgets. There was pressure from Washington in the form of a new congressional proposal to sharply reduce the networks' control over program production. NBC faced a Department of Justice lawsuit charging that the network had used "undue force" in pressuring Westinghouse to sell its Philadelphia station to NBC. On top of all this, the long smoldering issue of blacklisting had erupted once again, focusing embarrassing national attention and public debate on what was still a common network practice.

The networks themselves had not been directly involved at first in the new blacklisting tempest. It developed in 1955 from an internecine power struggle within television's largest actors' union, the American Federation of Television and Radio Artists (AFTRA). One faction of AFTRA allied itself with Aware, Inc., an anti-Communist *Red Channels* inspired organization. The New York local of AFTRA took the opposite position and issued well-publicized condemnations of Aware's smear tactics and blacklist procedures.

Aware had been founded in December 1953 by Laurence Johnson, a Syracuse supermarket owner, and Vincent W. Hartnett, a self-appointed authority on Communist subversion who had helped write *Red Channels.* The organization continued, on a day-to-day basis, the crusade begun in the one issue of *Red Channels* published in 1950. Aware informed networks, sponsors, and agencies of supposed "leftist tendencies" of prospective actors, writers, and directors. It was a clearing house of blacklist information.

The New York local of AFTRA not only blasted Aware's tactics, it also singled out and criticized specific AFTRA members who belonged to Aware and who were cooperating with the Red-baiting House Un-American Activities Committee. The committee used their inside information to subpoena anti-Aware AFTRA members and to pressure them into revealing the names of other entertainers who might have suspicious backgrounds.

In November 1955, an independent anti-Aware slate, headed by CBS news correspondent Charles Collingwood, campaigned on an anti-Aware, anti-blacklisting platform and was elected to head the New York branch of AFTRA. Almost immediately, Aware launched an extensive smear campaign against these newly elected AFTRA leaders, focusing its attack on comic-personality Orson Bean and local WCBS radio raconteur-humorist John Henry Faulk. Collingwood was too well known and respected by viewers as a credible newsman for a smear campaign to work against him. Bean and Faulk, on the other hand, were second-level performers that people vaguely knew but not well enough to assume innocence. Though the two had never been previously linked with left-wing causes, stories suddenly began to spread calling into doubt their patriotic fervor. Some of Bean's personal appearances were canceled with little or no warning, and Faulk lost some of his sponsors. Collingwood held press conferences to denounce Aware's actions, but these had almost no effect. Even the courts seemed to offer no redress.

Lawyers for blacklisted entertainers had repeatedly found themselves trying to grapple with an elusive enemy. In filing personal damage suits, they had to prove that being blacklisted had caused their clients to suffer a personal injury. This was far from easy because no one ever admitted that the blacklisting process even existed, despite its pervasive influence. The publishers of *Red Channels,* the people usually cited in anti-blacklisting cases, stood on solid legal ground and said that *they* had nothing to do with an actor losing a job. They were simply pointing out, to whomever was interested, alleged connections between performers and certain subversive groups. It was the networks and sponsors, they said, that may have made improper use of their publications. The networks, sponsors, and agencies always insisted that they failed to hire particular defendants either because they were "just not right for the part" or because they were "too controversial."

This stance put the blacklisted actors on the defensive, trying to prove a non-event: that they were not hired because of the influence of a list they could not produce. The fact that everyone in the entertainment industry knew an informal blacklist existed did not matter; until someone could present an actual list of names to a court, and document how it was used to damage a career, judges would not accept as proven the very cornerstone of an anti-blacklisting case. Thus, there seemed to be no way to blame anyone, legally, for blacklisting. As a result, anti-blacklisting suits over the years were consistently turned aside.

In spite of the previous failures, John Henry Faulk decided to try again and hired nationally known lawyer Louis Nizer. In June

1956 he filed a $500,000 libel suit against Aware, Inc., Laurence Johnson, and Vincent Hartnett. Faulk contended that they had conspired to destroy his income, livelihood, and reputation by the publication of false accusations linking him with Communist infiltration and Communist front organizations. The suit also said that these actions were a patently "sour grapes" response to the defeat of Aware-backed candidates in the 1955 local AFTRA elections. Faulk contended that the Aware attacks had effectively kept him off television and had caused him to lose nineteen sponsors for his Monday through Friday WCBS radio show. The case immediately became bogged down in tedious legal wrangling that prevented the trial from commencing for years. Faulk managed to retain his WCBS program longer than a year, but the station at last gave in to pressure and fired him. In the process, Faulk's yearly salary dropped from $35,000 to $2,000. Lawyer Nizer said that Aware's actions had cut off Faulk's career "like a knife."

Faulk did not get his day in court until April 1962. It was only then, with cold war hysteria abated, that the very existence of a blacklist was corroborated by witnesses of considerable stature within the industry. Drama producer David Susskind and quiz show whiz Mark Goodson testified that groups such as Aware were used religiously by networks and sponsors to determine who was hired and who was fired. Susskind and Goodson explained that, as producers, they had to regularly submit names to agencies for "clearance." After a nine-week trial, the jury found Aware guilty in June 1962 and ordered it to pay Faulk $3.5 million in damages, even more than Nizer had asked for. Further appeals (and the death of defendant Johnson) brought the amount of the settlement down, but money was never the central issue in the case. The important point was that, after fifteen years, an American jury at last declared blacklisting to be illegal. Until then, even through the long legal process, blacklisting continued.

The start of the Faulk case in the summer of 1956 was merely the topping on a mound of upsetting problems for the television industry. Though the legal and governmental headaches were disturbing, they had to take a back seat to the more immediate issue of trying to make sense out of the era's vast changes in programming, ushered in by the rise of *The $64,000 Question.* There was no doubt that change was in progress, but what made the networks very nervous was that nobody could be sure just what the emerging new TV status quo would be. Throughout the season, superstar performers who had been top ten material just a few years before found their drawing power fading. Some of the veterans voluntarily decided to leave the television grind for a while; many more were canceled.

Of the three networks, NBC seemed the most willing to tear up old patterns and start from scratch because, despite its best efforts over the previous few years, the network's programming philosophy had left it still playing number two to CBS. As upstart ABC showed signs of a concerted drive toward equality with NBC and CBS, even NBC's number two position seemed in jeopardy. NBC's programming was in decline throughout the day. The Pat Weaver-inspired staples of prime time (spectaculars, hour-long dramas, and rotating big name comedy-variety shows) had failed to deliver consistently. NBC news veteran John Cameron Swayze was losing the nightly news race. In daytime, CBS's soap operas had a firm lock on the audience.

All through 1956 there was a complete shakeup in NBC executive personnel, reshaping the network's programming philosophy. Flashy, easy to produce quiz and game shows such as *Tic Tac Dough, The Price Is Right,* and *Queen For a Day* began to dominate NBC's daytime line-up. On the nightly news, Chet Huntley and David Brinkley (the two surprise stars of NBC's coverage of

the summer's political conventions) deposed anchor John Cameron Swayze.

With Pat Weaver gone, Robert Sarnoff, the new president of the network, named Robert Kinter as NBC's new programming boss. Previously, Kinter had been the president of ABC and he brought with him the policy of filling prime time with programming produced almost exclusively by outsiders. Such a policy had made sense at ABC, which from the beginning of its network operations had neither the background nor the finances to establish a comprehensive, in-house production unit. It seemed an unusual strategy for financially stable NBC because from the very early days of television both NBC and CBS had fought to retain control of programming either by producing most of their prime time shows themselves or by buying into the programs they purchased from independent producers. This policy had obvious economic benefits and gave the two networks a major role in deciding the direction and tone of programs being aired. Even though Kinter's policy surrendered such control to outsiders, he hoped to shake some life into his new network's ratings by adopting the policy that had provided ABC with its few major hits.

There was a sound political reason for Kinter's strategy as well. With NBC fighting a Department of Justice lawsuit in the Westinghouse-Philadelphia case, and Congress thinking of breaking up the networks' control of programming, Kinter's "outsiders" policy helped deflate public criticism of the networks. In doing so, it helped to hold off any governmental action that might radically alter the fundamental rules of television and cause the networks far greater losses in profits and control.

NBC had begun its major overhaul in prime time programming a few months before Kinter came on board. One of the most important changes took place on Sunday night during the summer of 1956 when late night personality Steve Allen came in to compete with Ed Sullivan. CBS used Sullivan, whose show was number two in the overall ratings, as the pivot in its successful Sunday night strategy. Sullivan's show was popular enough to boost the ratings of the programs both before and after his; as a result, CBS had a chain of hits to begin the evening. In order to improve its own ratings on the most popular night for TV viewing, NBC had to break up the solid CBS line-up. That meant beating Ed Sullivan.

Steve Allen took to the air in the summer to get a jump on the fall competition. He took the straight vaudeville style Sullivan used and added to it the popular sketches and the family of supporting characters he had built on the *Tonight* show. Transplanted virtually intact from Allen's late night format were his "man-on-the-street" feature and mock "report to the nation," as well as his increasingly popular band of regulars, including Don Knotts, Louis Nye, Tom Poston, Pat Harrington, Jr., and Bill (Jose Jimenez) Dana.

The Steve Allen-Ed Sullivan face-off became the biggest ratings battle of the 1956–57 season, and the pattern of combat soon emerged: it was a war of guest stars. Allen's June premiere featured Jerry Lewis, Bob Hope, and Sammy Davis, Jr., while Sullivan countered with an eighth anniversary show featuring Lucille Ball, Phil Silvers, and Marlon Brando. On his second show, Allen retaliated with the current teenage phenomenon in music, Elvis Presley. In contrast to his hip-swinging Dorsey Brothers and Milton Berle appearances, Elvis presented a "new Presley," more subdued and in more formal attire. His presence boosted Allen's ratings far above Sullivan's. Undaunted, Sullivan imperiously stated that despite the ratings, he would *never* have Mr. Presley on because he hosted *a family* show. Within two weeks, Sullivan signed Presley to do three shows for $50,000, the most he had ever paid a performer.

	7:00	7:30	8:00	8:30	9:00	9:30	10:00	10:30	
M O N	Kukla, Fran & Ollie / John Daly & The News	Bold Journey	Danny Thomas Show	Voice Of Firestone	Life Is Worth Living	LAWRENCE WELK'S TOP TUNES AND NEW TALENT		local	**ABC**
	local	Adventures Of Robin Hood	Burns And Allen Show	Arthur Godfrey's Talent Scouts	I Love Lucy	December Bride	Studio One		**CBS**
	local	NAT KING COLE / NBC News	ADV. OF SIR LANCELOT	STANLEY	CAN DO	Robert Montgomery Presents		local	**NBC**
			# Producer's Showcase						
T U E	Kukla, Fran & Ollie / John Daly & The News	Cheyenne / Conflict		Life And Legend Of Wyatt Earp	BROKEN ARROW	DuPont Theater	It's Polka Time	local	**ABC**
	local	Name That Tune	Phil Silvers Show	THE BROTHERS	HERB SHRINER SHOW	Red Skelton Show	$64,000 Question	Do You Trust Your Wife	**CBS**
	local	JONATH. WINTERS / NBC News	Big Surprise	NOAH'S ARK	Jane Wyman Show	Kaiser Aluminium Hour / Armstrong Circle Theater		Break The $250,000 Bank	**NBC**
W E D	Kukla, Fran & Ollie / John Daly & The News	Disneyland		Navy Log	Adventures Of Ozzie And Harriet	Ford Theater	Wednesday Night Fights		**ABC**
	local	GIANT STEP	Arthur Godfrey Show		The Millionaire	I've Got A Secret	U.S. Steel Hour / 20th Century-Fox Hour		**CBS**
	local	Eddie Fisher / NBC News	ADVENTURES OF HIRAM HOLIDAY	Father Knows Best	Kraft Television Theater		This Is Your Life	TWENTY-ONE	**NBC**
T H R	Kukla, Fran & Ollie / John Daly & The News	The Lone Ranger	CIRCUS TIME		WIRE SERVICE		Ozark Jubilee		**ABC**
	local	Sgt. Preston Of The Yukon	Bob Cummings Show	Climax / # Shower Of Stars		PLAYHOUSE 90			**CBS**
	local	Dinah Shore / NBC News	You Bet Your Life	Dragnet	The People's Choice	Tennessee Ernie Ford Show	Lux Video Theater		**NBC**
F R I	Kukla, Fran & Ollie / John Daly & The News	Adventures Of Rin Tin Tin	ADVENTURES OF JIM BOWIE	Crossroads	TREASURE HUNT	The Vise	RAY ANTHONY SHOW		**ABC**
	local	My Friend Flicka	WEST POINT	DICK POWELL'S ZANE GREY THEATER	The Crusader	Schlitz Playhouse Of Stars	The Lineup	Person To Person	**CBS**
	local	Eddie Fisher / NBC News	The Life Of Riley	WALTER WINCHELL SHOW	ON TRIAL	The Big Story	Gillette Cavalcade Of Sports	Red Barber	**NBC**
					# Chevy Show				
S A T	local	Famous Film Festival			Lawrence Welk's Dodge Dancing Party		Masquerade Party	local	**ABC**
	Beat The Clock	THE BUCCANEERS	Jackie Gleason Show		OH, SUSANNA	HEY, JEANNIE	Gunsmoke	High Finance	**CBS**
							# Ford Star Jubilee		
	local	People Are Funny	Perry Como Show		Caesar's Hour		George Gobel Show	Your Hit Parade	**NBC**
					# Saturday Color Carnival				
S U N	You Asked For It	Original Amateur Hour		Press Conference	Omnibus			local	**ABC**
	Lassie	Private Secretary / Jack Benny Program	Ed Sullivan Show		General Electric Theater	Alfred Hitchcock Presents	$64,00 Challenge	What's My Line	**CBS**
	TALES OF THE 77th BENGAL LANCERS	CIRCUS BOY	Steve Allen Show		Alcoa Hour / Goodyear Television Playhouse		Loretta Young Show	National Bowling Champions	**NBC**
		# Hallmark Hall Of Fame			# Chevy Show				

On September 9, at the start of the new season, Elvis Presley appeared live, from Los Angeles, on the Sullivan show, performing four songs ("Don't Be Cruel," "Love Me Tender," "Ready Teddy," and "Hound Dog") in the more familiar "Elvis the Pelvis" style, to the delight of screaming fans in the studio. Once again, Presley meant instant ratings success, as Sullivan's show grabbed more than 80% of the audience that night. Presley's second appearance (in October) did just as well. After this success, CBS grew nervous over the then-current wave of Presley detractors and when the singer returned in January for his third and final Sullivan show, the cameramen were instructed to show Elvis only from the waist up. This truncating of Presley inflamed proponents of the new rock'n'roll craze who felt their hero was being unfairly treated. After a particularly bouncy appearance by actress Jayne Mansfield on *Shower of Stars,* one Presley fan wrote to CBS, "If you can't show Elvis Presley from the waist down, don't show Jayne Mansfield from the waist up."

The wild competition for stars sometimes seemed humorous, but the stakes were high. At the start of the 1956–57 season, Sullivan maintained a healthy lead over Allen, but as the year wore on Allen whittled down the advantage until the race was a virtual tie. This was a tremendous improvement for NBC which had been decimated on Sunday night for several seasons running its moribund comedy-variety hour.

Steve Allen was also still in charge of the *Tonight* show. In the fall of 1956, his only concession to his added Sunday night duties was handing over the Monday and Tuesday night *Tonight* slots to perennial fill-in Ernie Kovacs, who brought his increasingly abstract and inventive style of television humor to perhaps his largest audience. By January, however, Allen felt that he was working himself too hard and left the late night slot altogether to devote his full attention to the prime time series. NBC found itself in the same position it had been in when Jerry Lester quit *Broadway Open House* in 1951. The network had to carry on a program based on a familiar character who had departed. NBC had failed miserably in its search for a successor to Lester and it very nearly did the same in 1957 with the poorly planned *Tonight! America After Dark.*

Instead of finding one successor to Allen, NBC set up *America After Dark* as a show with multiple hosts performing in four cities (New York, Chicago, Los Angeles, and a wild card city such as Miami or Las Vegas), turning it into an unwieldy sort of late night wide, wide world of entertainment. The format called for live remote broadcasts of top performing talent at nightclubs, cafés, and restaurants, as well as light features, hard news, and a few sports figures. The network chose newspaper columnists Hy Gardner, Earl Wilson, Bob Considine, and Irv Kupcinet as emcees, with *Today* show regular Jack Lescoulie as the only television veteran in sight. The columnists may have known their stars but they did not know how to act relaxed before the camera, appearing uncomfortable and spiritless.

Reviewers watching the first week's shows concluded that NBC was committing hara-kiri and seemed determined to kill off its late night programming. The live nightclub remotes and on-the-spot features were awkward and unimaginative. There was a good deal of name dropping and very little entertainment. Though the loose format *of America After Dark* had been set up to create a feeling of spontaneity (the strength of Allen's show), the program emerged instead as a jumble of unconnected, erratic, poorly timed ad-libs. Ratings took a nose dive and affiliates in major cities defected to the more stable format of airing old movies. It appeared as if NBC had once again botched its fragile hold on late night television. In June 1957, the network decided to make a last ditch attempt to save the slot by scrapping *America After Dark* and reverting to the more familiar desk and sofa talk show style. The new host, Jack Paar, was given an ultimatum: Register good ratings by Christmas or face extinction.

Premiering at the end of July, Paar's show faced a difficult challenge. Viewers in cities such as Houston, Cleveland, St. Louis, Nashville, Pittsburgh, and Boston were unable to see the program because the local NBC affiliates there kept showing old films, having decided that the new format was doomed. Additionally, Paar seemed to lack "warmth," an attribute felt necessary for late night hosts. In spite of these shortcomings, Paar not only managed to keep the show afloat, he made it a hit again. To support his own personality, Paar favored frequent appearances by guest performers over a family of regulars (only announcer Hugh Downs joined Paar each night). Among the many performers that often dropped by were Dody Goodman, a daffy blonde with a sharp tongue for intentional malapropisms; Cliff Arquette as Charlie Weaver, the country philosopher who read humorous and fictitious letters from his mother; and controversial social gadfly Elsa Maxwell, who constantly got Paar into trouble with her outrageous charges about well-known celebrities (such as calling Walter Winchell a "phony patriot" who never voted). Maxwell's slightly ribald and risqué style rubbed off on Paar, whose double-entendre jokes soon captured a national audience, thereby saving the show while bedeviling NBC's censors.

The *Tonight* show weathered a difficult transition but eventually became a success again under Jack Paar. In prime time, other formats and performers did not fare as well, with spectaculars, comedy-variety, and hour-long drama anthologies suffering major casualties. NBC's monthly Monday and Saturday spectaculars limped along until the end of the season, while CBS's *Ford Star Jubilee* did not even last until Christmas. The Ford show went out on a high note, though, presenting the television premiere of "The Wizard of Oz," the first major Hollywood film to appear on TV.

In comedy-variety, several titans were laid low. Even before the season began, NBC had divided Milton Berle's traditional Tuesday night slot between two half-hour shows, a Jack Webb medical drama (*Noah's Ark*) and a Louis G. Cowan quiz program (*The Big Surprise*). As a result, for the first time in eight years, Berle did not have a show. On CBS, Jackie Gleason made a well-publicized return to a live comedy-variety hour after his experiment with a weekly filmed *Honeymooners* series the previous season, but found his reception less than triumphant. His familiar format of glamour girls, dancers, and character skits had become a fond memory in its year-long absence, yet seemed repetitiously familiar when it reappeared. Worse yet, the Honeymooners segment was rarely presented, leaving the show almost devoid of its strongest element. NBC's slow and steady *Perry Como Show* soon garnered double Gleason's ratings. At the end of the season, Gleason temporarily retired from television after seven years of weekly shows.

Veteran Sid Caesar, whose program had been moved to Saturday in the fall to follow the successful *Perry Como Show*, could not carry over the audience from the strong lead-in show. Instead,

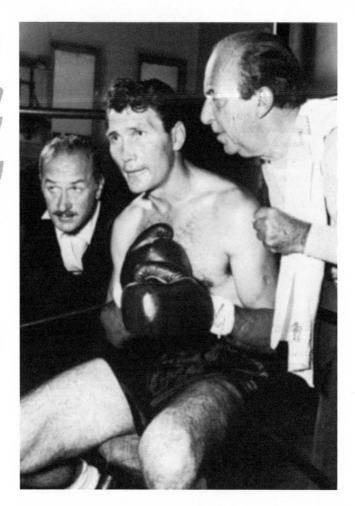

The second production of CBS's live drama series, *Playhouse 90*, was Rod Serling's "Requiem for a Heavyweight," starring *(from left)* Keenan Wynn, Jack Palance, and Ed Wynn. *(CBS Photo Archive © 2003 CBS Worldwide, Inc. All Rights Reserved.)*

Caesar's Hour was regularly defeated by ABC's *Lawrence Welk*. Viewing Caesar's enormous budget and low ratings, NBC tried to convince him to leave weekly television and to concentrate on occasional specials. Caesar balked at the idea and, after a brief fight, NBC canceled his show. Sid Caesar was generally considered one of the best comics on television, so his forced departure came as an especially upsetting blow to other TV comedians.

Even the king and queen of television sitcoms, Desi Arnaz and Lucille Ball, ended their weekly series at the end of the season, though they chose to quit while on top. *I Love Lucy*, in fact, had regained the number one spot for a time during the season and was still a Monday night blockbuster for CBS. The staff felt, however, that after six years they had done all they could with the half-hour program. The Ricardos and the Mertzes had gone through dozens of domestic plots, traveled to Hollywood, toured Europe, and, in the 1956–57 season, set up housekeeping in a Connecticut suburb. After some wrangling with CBS, which did not want to lose a winner, it was agreed that, after 180 episodes, *I Love Lucy* would cease weekly production at the end of the season. Beginning in the fall of 1957, though, the *Lucy* format would be continued in occasional one-hour specials for the network. At the same time, CBS would move the successful reruns of the older *I Love Lucy* episodes from early Saturday evening to prime time on Wednesday night.

September 30, 1956

Following the demise of DuMont, CBS picks up the Sunday afternoon National Football League contests. With this new larger forum, NFL professional football begins a sharp growth in popularity among America's gridiron fans.

October 23, 1956

The final nail in the coffin for live TV, as video tape is used on a network TV show for the first time. A two-and-one-half minute segment of singer Dorothy Collins, taped the day before, airs on NBC's *Jonathan Winters Show*.

October 29, 1956

NBC News. (NBC). The two stars of NBC's convention coverage, Chet Huntley and David Brinkley, take over NBC's nightly news. Brinkley reports from Washington, Huntley from New York. By 1958, the show is known as *The Huntley-Brinkley Report*, and their sign-off exchange of "Goodnight, Chet" and "Goodnight, David" becomes a familiar program trademark.

November 3, 1956

Hollywood's 1939 feature film classic, "The Wizard of Oz," appears for the first time on television (as the final presentation of CBS's *Ford Star Jubilee*). The annual airing of the movie becomes a TV family ritual for decades.

November 26, 1956

The Price Is Right. (NBC). Bill Cullen hosts a daytime quizzer in which contestants try to win shiny new merchandise by guessing the actual retail price (without going over).

December 17, 1956

CBS's James Aubrey temporarily defects, becoming ABC's chief programmer.

December 18, 1956

To Tell the Truth. (CBS). Bud Collyer, the radio voice of Superman, hosts another Mark Goodson-Bill Todman television quiz hit. Three contestants each claim to be the same person and a panel of celebrities tries to separate the bona-fide oddball from the two charlatans.

The hour-long drama anthologies, once a pillar of network television programming, also lost considerable ground during the 1956–57 season. *The Lux Video Theater, The Alcoa/Goodyear Television Playhouse*, and *Robert Montgomery Presents*, three old-time stalwarts, were canceled. A more important setback, though, was the treatment of a promising new NBC anthology series, *The Kaiser Aluminum Hour*, Worthington Miner's equivalent to Fred Coe's *Playwrights '56*.

Miner, who had been mostly inactive following his defection to NBC in 1952, formed a production arm called Unit 4 to produce the Kaiser show. He held the post of executive producer, while three others, Franklin Schaffner (a former director at *Studio One*), and Fielder Cook and George Roy Hill (both former directors of *The Kraft Television Theater*), rotated the weekly production and direction chores. From the start, Unit 4 turned out exciting, unique television drama for Kaiser, reminiscent of Miner's glory days at *Studio One*. Early successes included a bold and exciting adaptation of the Sophocles classic "Antigone" with Claude Rains, and "The Army Game," with Paul Newman (who had become a movie star with "Somebody Up There Likes Me") as a wise-guy draftee

with psychological problems. Like Coe's *Playwrights '56, The Kaiser Aluminum Hour* was placed in one of the toughest slots possible (against *The $64,000 Question* and the ever-resilient *Red Skelton Show)*, yet the program maintained respectable ratings. The problems facing the show came from the Young & Rubicam production agency, which controlled the program, and Henry Kaiser himself.

In November, Miner quit, after two projects were vetoed as being too controversial (an old John Galsworthy play on anti-Semitism in Britain and a new play on the Polish Poznan trials that followed the 1956 anti-Soviet riots). With Miner gone, the sponsor and agency began exerting their veto power more frequently and within three months they rejected: Robert Alan Aurthur's "Memphis by Morning" (on a tense racial situation), Loring Mandel's "The Healer" (on a faith healer who lost, then regained, his faith), and Reginald Rose's "The Gathering" (a sensitive portrait of a family under stress during an air raid, revealed at the end to be Russians living in Moscow). Repeated crisis sessions were held between the agency and the three remaining Unit 4 members. In February, Henry Kaiser personally appeared to inform the members of Unit 4 that they were fired. He said that they refused to produce the plays Kaiser wanted, those that were noncontroversial and more "Americana-oriented." There were too many people, Kaiser said, who tuned out their more realistic but more depressing plays. Franklin Schaffner of the Unit 4 group responded, "To offend no one is to stimulate no one."

As the era of original television drama anthologies approached its almost inevitable conclusion, CBS presented one last gasp of greatness, *Playhouse 90*, the last major attempt by a network to produce weekly high class drama. Produced by Martin Manulis, the new show represented a double risk for CBS: It marked the first attempt to produce live ninety-minute drama on a weekly basis (to ease the production schedule, however, a filmed play produced by Screen Gems filled the slot once a month) and it was scheduled on Thursday night, following *Climax*. This resulted in two and one-half hours of continuous drama on CBS, a line-up many assumed put too much faith in the attention span of the American public. CBS pressed on and, after faltering a bit with a weak first show, produced in *Playhouse 90* some of the best drama seen on television.

In October, on only its second episode, *Playhouse 90* presented one of its best plays, Rod Serling's "Requiem for a Heavyweight." It was a complex and dynamic character study starring Jack Palance as a washed-up, confused, dumb but honest boxer; Ed Wynn (in his dramatic debut) as the honest and faithful trainer; and his son Keenan Wynn as Palance's manager, who was torn between a desire to help his fighter and an urge to misuse him in order to make money. The masterful production seemed to defy the inherent time and space limitations of live television by using ingenious and complicated camera work. "It was so good," one critic noted, "it was hard to believe it was live."

In February, *Playhouse 90* presented another powerful original, "The Miracle Worker," the story of blind and deaf Helen Keller, starring Patty McCormack as Keller at age seven, Burl Ives as her father, and Teresa Wright as Helen's teacher, Anne Sullivan. The final dramatic scene, in which Sullivan broke through and communicated with Helen, combined the best in dramatic tension and honest sentimentality (a major factor in Hollywood's decision to turn it into a movie, starring Patty Duke).

In spite of CBS's valiant efforts with *Playhouse 90*, television's commitment to drama continued to move away from live New York anthologies and toward Hollywood filmed adventures. During the summer of 1956, when some of television's big stars were

Jack Barry, co-producer of *Tic-Tac-Dough*, hosted the daytime version of the show, which premiered in July 1956. *(Courtesy Barry-Enright Productions)*

Alda (father of Alan Alda) presented guest celebrities who attempted inane stunts while contestants from the audience tried to guess whether the stars "can do" or "no can do." The show itself was a "no can do" and became one of the first of many quiz shows to bite the dust that season.

In place of *Can Do*, NBC moved in *Twenty-One*. Hosted by Jack Barry, *Twenty-One* featured contestants who tried to accumulate twenty-one points by answering increasingly difficult questions. Like *The $64,000 Question*, *Twenty-One* made use of that deliciously symbolic tool, the isolation booth. In shifting from late Wednesday (where it had debuted in September) to Monday night (in *Can Do*'s old slot), though, *Twenty-One* seemed destined to meet the bleak fate of most of the other new quiz shows because it was placed opposite *I Love Lucy*. Instead, *Twenty-One* became *the* show that clicked. It came up with what every quiz show producer dreamed of: a contestant who caught the public's fancy. The contestant was thirty-year-old Charles Van Doren, a Columbia University English instructor and son of the well-known poet, Mark Van Doren.

Charles Van Doren had first appeared on *Twenty-One* on November 28 and overtook the reigning champion, Herbert Stempel, one week later. By January, Van Doren had reached a new high in quiz earnings ($122,000) while leading *Twenty-One* to a new high against *I Love Lucy* (only four rating points behind). As he increased his winnings, Van Doren became a widely discussed national figure. He was treated as a shining example of American intellect and youth, someone parents wanted their children to look

on vacation, *Gunsmoke* had surprisingly popped into the top ten, further encouraging the expansion of Westerns. For the 1956–57 season, the network schedules were stocked with such sagebrush sagas as *Broken Arrow, Tales of Wells Fargo*, and *Dick Powell's Zane Grey Theater*. These joined such grade-B adventure yarns as *Tales of the 77th Bengal Lancers, Wire Service*, and *Circus Boy* (which starred twelve-year-old Mickey Braddock who, a decade later as Micky Dolenz, appeared in another kiddie adventure show, *The Monkees*). CBS even ran *The West Point Story*, a filmed series from Ziv, a TV film syndicator that had been locked out of prime time by the networks for years. Though none of these new programs were runaway hits, they provided clear evidence of the drift in television drama. The most exciting and successful drama of the season, however, did not appear on any of the networks' anthologies, Westerns, or adventure series. It took place on a new quiz show.

After the initial spurt in popularity by *The $64,000 Question*, viewer interest in quiz shows had leveled off. The programs were easy to produce, though, and anxious sponsors (eager for cheap television time) insisted that the shows continue. In a time of economic slowdown, the sponsor's word carried added weight with the networks so they continued to slot new quiz programs, despite the rapid turnover of the shows throughout the season. Nobody seemed able to single out exactly what elements were needed to ensure success; consequently, endless variations of the same thing developed, with one aspect exaggerated. Many programs, such as *Break the $250,000 Bank* (with Bert Parks), inflated the potential jackpot well beyond a paltry $64,000. Others featured face-offs by celebrity contestants. *Can Do*, hosted by actor Robert

April 7, 1957
Hollywood Film Theater. (ABC). ABC presents old RKO feature films, beginning with "Rachel and the Stranger," in another unsuccessful attempt to bring movies to prime time.

April 8, 1957
The Jimmy Dean Show. (CBS). CBS gives up trying to beat *Today* at its own game and opts to fill the early morning slot with a country-style variety show.

April 28, 1957
Mike Wallace Interviews. (ABC). After five months as host of a "no holds barred" late night interview show in New York City, Wallace goes network. His technique of pressing for candid, controversial statements is dubbed "hot interviewing."

June 3, 1957
Sports Focus. (ABC). Up-and-coming sports commentator Howard Cosell gets his first regular network television show, a daily wrapup of the sporting world.

August 30, 1957
More vets fade from view. *Kukla, Fran and Ollie* is laid to rest by ABC.

September 13, 1957
WCBS radio gives in to blacklist pressure and fires John Henry Faulk.

September 29, 1957
After twelve years of Sunday night drama, NBC retires the *Television Playhouse* to make room for musical-variety with Dinah Shore.

up to. Unlike contestants on *The $64,000 Question,* those on *Twenty-One* were not able to choose the topic they wished to be queried on. Instead, they were subjected to an all-around interrogation, something that called for not just a sports fanatic or a drama enthusiast, but an all-around educated American. Van Doren certainly seemed to fit that bill. Without blushing, he quickly identified the Polish volunteer who became Washington's aide in the Revolutionary War (Kosciuszko); with a mere furrow of the brow he identified "caries" as another name for dental cavities; after nervously chewing his lip he correctly identified the "patellar reflex" as the reaction that occurs when a knee is tapped; and after a worried mop of his forehead, he identified which church in which city contained Leonardo da Vinci's fresco "The Last Supper" (Santa Maria delle Grazie, in Milan).

The nation was entranced. Charles Van Doren was said to have "gained the affection and esteem of millions throughout the nation." Viewers found Van Doren the one new television personality that they could become involved with. Millions tuned in *Twenty-One* just to follow the newly-anointed symbol of the state in his weekly battle of wits. His success was their success. His failure would be their failure.

Early in February, a few days after he staged a dramatic come-from-behind victory, Van Doren was on the cover of *Time.* After his February 11 performance, he offered a $50,000 movie contract. By the February 18 show, the tension was unbearable. Van Doren reached the level of $143,000 in earnings but, at the end of the program, was tied with Mrs. Vivienne Nearing, a New York lawyer. When the ratings for the February 18 program came in, they showed that *Twenty-One* had become the first regular series to beat *I Love Lucy* in its time slot. On February 25, newspaper ads posed the question: "Will the Lady Lawyer beat him?" Amazingly, they tied again. (Think of it; two ties in a row.) That night, *Twenty-One* was six points *ahead* of *Lucy,* and the producers were ecstatic. They were immediately frustrated, however, to discover that round two of their sudden-death contest would be delayed a week. As part of NBC's remaining regularly scheduled specials, *Producers' Showcase* was slated for its monthly appearance on March 4, preempting *Twenty-One* to present "Romeo and Juliet." A howl went up, demanding that the Bard be postponed so that the nation could see the latest act in a real-life drama. Despite the pressure, "Romeo

and Juliet" performed instead as scheduled, and the nation had to wait until March 11 to learn the answer to the question posed by that week's *Twenty-One* newspaper ad, which showed large photos of both Van Doren and Nearing with the simple caption: "Which one?"

After all the buildup, Van Doren was eliminated on the first question, being unable to give the name of the king of Belgium (Baudouin). The boy genius had been deposed in a bloodless joust and *Twenty-One* had to face its real test: Could it survive without Charles Van Doren, America's favorite egghead?

For a loser, Van Doren left *Twenty-One* in pretty good shape. He received $129,000 and accepted a job as a regular panelist on NBC Radio's *Conversation,* discussing such questions as "What is an educated man?" Nonetheless, on leaving he confided to anxious reporters, "It's been a tremendous strain." Soon thereafter, Van Doren signed an exclusive pact with NBC for five years at $50,000 per year.

Following Van Doren's departure, *Twenty-One* immediately dropped seventeen points in the ratings (from eight and one-half ahead of *I Love Lucy* on Van Doren's last week to nine behind only seven days later). While no longer in television's top ten list, *Twenty-One* had become a consistently top-rated show and quiz show producers were again given proof that quiz shows could lead to instant success, if only the right gimmick or the right character could be found. Perhaps the two elements were really one and the same thing.

Just a few months after Van Doren's triumph, the television industry, which had been sniffing all season to unearth the prophesied new trend in programming, was surprised to discover that *Gunsmoke* had slowly climbed into the number one position with practically no advance ballyhoo. It had quietly and unobtrusively advanced up the popularity lists while its other Western brethren held to steady, if not standout, ratings.

This meant that, in a season of flux, the only two formats to show a marked improvement were Westerns and quizzes. After two full seasons of vainly searching for what would attract the support of the expanding television audience, the networks concluded that the viewers had cast their votes for the old sage and the isolation booths. If that was what the public wanted, then Westerns and quizzes would be what it would get. In abundance.

17. Oh, Dem Oaters

THOUGH THE NETWORKS HAILED WESTERNS as a "sure thing" for the new season, there was a sense of caution among advertisers. The cowboy programs (nicknamed "oaters") needed to prove themselves in head-to-head competition with television's superstars. Kaiser Aluminum, sponsor of one half of a new ABC Western, *Maverick*, delivered an ultimatum to the network: Kaiser would guarantee sponsorship only until Christmas; if *Maverick* failed to deliver good ratings by then, Kaiser would pull out.

Maverick (produced by the Warner Bros. studios) was placed in a difficult time slot, Sunday night against the variety blockbusters of Ed Sullivan and Steve Allen. To gain some advantage over the competition, ABC duplicated a strategy that had worked well for *Disneyland,* and started *Maverick* one half hour before the two giants began, hoping to hook the audience before it fell into its usual viewing habits. The first ratings report, released in October, showed *Maverick* surprisingly strong in the tough slot, and ABC easily found a sponsor for the other half of the show. By Thanksgiving, the program had topped Steve Allen and in the spring it even beat Ed Sullivan. Only then were the sponsors, including Kaiser, convinced that Westerns could perform very well and might indeed be the "safest bet" in programming.

Though *Maverick* contained many facets of the traditional adult Western, it was actually the leader of a revisionist new wave that introduced a different brand of hero to television, the maverick, also known as the anti-hero. Television's first wave of cowboys such as the Lone Ranger and Hopalong Cassidy had merely carried on the standard stalwart stances of classic movie heroes. The second wave had focused on grimly realistic characters such as Matt Dillon, who found no joy in violent shoot-outs, but who accepted their necessity. The new breed of hero emerging in Westerns such as *Maverick* not only accepted violence but frankly sought it out for enjoyment (albeit on the side of justice). The maverick devoted his energies to aiding people in need, just as his familiar Western colleagues did, but was guided by self-interest and a good-hearted nature, rather than by a mythical "code of the West." Additionally, *Maverick* refused to take itself too seriously, injecting into the series elements of humor, a quality notably absent in most Westerns.

The Maverick brothers, (James Garner as Bret and Jack Kelly as Bart) roamed the West not as determined law enforcement agents, but as drifting playboys. They supported their gambling habits and expensive tastes with clever schemes and con games, though they usually saved their most outlandish exploits for overblown figures of authority, especially in defense of hopeless causes and mistreated underdogs. Bret and Bart occasionally worked as a team, but usually went their separate ways in search of high stakes and beautiful women (with Garner and Kelly alternating each week in the lead role). Garner was especially effective as the good-hearted slightly dishonest hero, and his roles in subsequent theatrical features and television series (such as "Support Your Local Sheriff" and *The Rockford Files*) often seemed to be Maverick in a different setting. *Maverick*'s writers also made a determined effort to avoid the usual Western plots, sometimes even adapting stories from classic literature. In fact, *Maverick* departed so often from the usual Western types that, in many ways, it really was not a Western at all. "We've done three shows in a row without so much as a gun or a horse," *Maverick* producer Roy Huggins proudly told *Variety* during the program's second season, further explaining, "What we set out to do was create a character that deliberately broke all the rules of the traditional Western hero. He's a little bit of a coward, he's not solemn, he's greedy, and not above cheating a little. He's indifferent to the problems of other people. He's something of a gentle grafter."

Another new wave Warner Bros. cowboy series on ABC that departed from the traditional image of the Western hero was *Sugarfoot,* which featured an anti-hero of a different sort. Tom Brewster (played by Will Hutchins) was a young wanderer who could not shoot (he abhorred guns), was shy, and was studying to become a lawyer (through a correspondence course). Though he became entangled in other people's problems week after week, he tried to solve them with as little violence as possible, relying on his boyish charm instead of his biceps to overcome evil. His lack of experience in traditional Western ways earned him the title of Sugarfoot (even more inexperienced than a "tenderfoot"). His emphasis on talk proved so unnerving that in the first episode the frustrated bad guy (played by Dennis Hopper) asked Sugarfoot, "Whaddya tryin' to do, talk me to death?"

CBS broke from the standard Western mold that fall with *Have Gun Will Travel,* presenting Richard Boone as a hired gun (Paladin) who operated on the blasphemous premise that he should be paid for protecting people in trouble. Of course, Matt Dillon was paid for being marshal of Dodge City, but the stories left the impression that he would have done it all for free anyway, motivated by principle and a sense of justice. Paladin, however, was little better than a mob hit man who spent his off hours lounging at his San Francisco hotel playing cards and entertaining women (of

Day	Net	7:00	7:30	8:00	8:30	9:00	9:30	10:00	10:30
MON	ABC	Sports Focus / John Daly & The News	American Bandstand	GUY MITCHELL SHOW	Bold Journey	Voice Of Firestone	Lawrence Welk's Top Tunes And New Talent		local
MON	CBS	local	Adventures Of Robin Hood	Burns And Allen Show	Arthur Godfrey's Talent Scouts	Danny Thomas Show	December Bride	Studio One	
MON	NBC	local	The Price Is Right	RESTLESS GUN	Tales Of Wells Fargo	Twenty-One	ALCOA/GOODYEAR THEA.: TURN OF FATE	SUSPICION	
TUE	ABC	Sports Focus / John Daly & The News	Cheyenne / SUGARFOOT		Life And Legend Of Wyatt Earp	Broken Arrow	Telephone Time	West Point	local
TUE	CBS	local	Name That Tune	Phil Silvers Show	EVE ARDEN SHOW	To Tell The Truth	Red Skelton Show	$64,000 Question	ASSIGNMENT: FOREIGN LEGION
TUE	NBC	local	Nat King Cole Show	George Gobel Show / Eddie Fisher Show		Meet McGraw	Bob Cummings Show	THE CALIFORNIANS	local
WED	ABC	Sports Focus / John Daly & The News	Disneyland		TOMBSTONE TERRITORY	Adventures Of Ozzie And Harriet	WALTER WINCHELL FILE	Wednesday Night Fights	
WED	CBS	local	I Love Lucy	BIG RECORD		The Millionaire	I've Got A Secret	U.S. Steel Hour / Armstrong Circle Theater	
WED	NBC	local	WAGON TRAIN		Father Knows Best	Kraft Television Theater		This Is Your Life	local
THU	ABC	Sports Focus / John Daly & The News	Circus Boy	ZORRO	THE REAL McCOYS	PAT BOONE CHEVY SHOWROOM	O.S.S.	Navy Log	local
THU	CBS	local	Sgt. Preston Of The Yukon	HABOURMASTER	Climax / # Shower Of Stars		Playhouse 90		
THU	NBC	local	Tic Tac Dough	You Bet Your Life	Dragnet	The People's Choice	Tennessee Ernie Ford Show	THE LUX SHOW WITH ROSEMARY CLOONEY	Jane Wyman Show
FRI	ABC	Sports Focus / John Daly & The News	Adventures Of Rin Tin Tin	Adventures Of Jim Bowie	PATRICE MUNSEL SHOW	FRANK SINATRA SHOW	Date With The Angels	COLT .45	local
FRI	CBS	local	LEAVE IT TO BEAVER	TRACKDOWN	Dick Powell's Zane Grey Theater	Mr. Adams And Eve	Schlitz Playhouse Of Stars	The Lineup	Person To Person
FRI	NBC	local	Saber Of London	COURT OF LAST RESORT	The Life Of Riley	M SQUAD	THE THIN MAN	Gillette Cavalcade Of Sports	Red Barber
SAT	ABC	local	KEEP IT IN THE FAMILY	Country Music Jubilee		Lawrence Welk's Dodge Dancing Party		Mike Wallace Interviews	local
SAT	CBS	local	PERRY MASON		DICK AND THE DUCHESS	Oh, Susanna	HAVE GUN, WILL TRAVEL	Gunsmoke	local
SAT	NBC	local	People Are Funny	Perry Como Show		CLUB OASIS / POLLY BERGEN SHOW	GISELE MacKENZIE SHOW	WHAT'S IT FOR	Your Hit Parade
SUN	ABC	You Asked For It	MAVERICK		BOWLING STARS	Open Hearing	COLLEGE FOOTBALL GAME OF THE WEEK	SCOTLAND YARD	local
SUN	CBS	Lassie	BACHELOR FATHER / Jack Benny Program	Ed Sullivan Show		General Electric Theater	Alfred Hitchcock Presents	$64,000 Challenge	What's My Line
SUN	NBC	Original Amateur Hour	SALLY	Steve Allen Show		Dinah Shore Chevy Show		Loretta Young Show	local

questionable virtue), while being attended to by two servants he addressed as "Hey Boy" and "Hey Girl." He was motivated entirely by his own self-interest, and cared little for the code of the West or for aiding people for the fun of it. Occasionally, when he detected that someone was trying to manipulate him, Paladin sacrificed payment and confronted his own employer, but only to protect his professional reputation. Usually, though, he was commissioned by "good" people who were simply unable to defend themselves.

Have Gun Will Travel incorporated many of the standard routines of the classic Western heroes, but gave them a diabolic twist in the character of Paladin. Though he was the hero of the series, Paladin always wore black (even in the desert heat), giving him an image as the Angel of Death. Appropriately, the death sequences in the show were the dramatic high point of each episode and choreographed as carefully as a ballet. At the inevitable final confrontation, Paladin and his foe respectfully squared off for what both knew would be a fatal shoot-out. Like Death itself, the dark-robed Paladin seemed to offer a chance to beat the fates with the draw of guns, but he always won. Afterward, though pleased at another victory, out of professional respect Paladin often leaned over to offer his dying adversary a final word of consolation. In many ways Paladin had more in common with his foes than with those who hired him, and this was one of the great strengths of this stand-out adult Western and anti-hero series. The characters in these stories turned a simple, traditional television morality play into a far more complex conflict.

Generally, all Western adventures took place after the divisive national politics of the Civil War yet before the American frontier ended, in a West largely untouched by Eastern civilization. Within the twenty-year period between 1870 and 1890 (the date American historian Frederick Jackson Turner declared as marking the closing of the frontier), virtually the entire American West lost its free-wheeling spirit, as town after town was cleaned up and readied for civilization and business expansion. Setting the stories in this very short period emphasized the theme of inevitable, necessary, but uncertain progress and gave an air of dramatic fatality to all the Westerns.

With civilization always just around the corner, Western heroes faced the same inescapable fate as the villains because both the good guys and bad guys were part of a vanishing breed. By 1890, when the outlaws were gone, the gun-toting marshals also became unnecessary. Traditional kiddie Westerns generally ignored this important conflict with change, but the new breed of Westerns used it to increase dramatic tension and develop the cowboy heroes into characters very similar to a classic private eye type, the inside-outsider.

For years, crime buffs had followed such inside-outsiders, usually coarse and surly private eyes typified by Humphrey Bogart's interpretation of Sam Spade in "The Maltese Falcon." These characters were strong-willed independents who refused to abide by the rules of behavior for normal society and often broke the letter of the law themselves in the pursuit of a personal code of justice. The best anti-hero and adult Westerns featured strong characters that embodied the traits of these reluctant heroes, from barely legal gunmen such as the Maverick brothers and Paladin to sensitive souls such as Matt Dillon and Sugarfoot. They all were, in effect, outlaws yet, through the vagaries of fate, they worked with the system if not always actually within it.

Of course, all television Westerns did not feature inside-outsiders and, despite the dramatic strength of the Western setting, there was no denying that many Western series used an inordinate number of cliché characters and weak scripts. NBC, the last network to commit itself to developing a new slew of cowboy dramas for the fall, had two of the season's more conventional programs. *Restless Gun* featured tight-lipped determination by strong silent type cowboys, while *The Californians* presented lawless San Francisco at the height of the Gold Rush. (Nonetheless, one NBC flak insisted, *"[The Californians] is not a Western; it's about California in the 1850s!"*) However, the network also came up with an hour-long epic oater, *Wagon Train,* an adult Western that successfully combined elements of a drama anthology series with a stable cast of regulars. Each week, a new group of pioneers (the guest stars) joined the wagon train on another regular run from St. Joseph, Missouri, across a treacherous expanse of Western territory to California. Ward Bond played the wagon master, Terry Wilson was his assistant, and Robert Horton served as the frontier scout. Though they acted as both protectors and counselors to the traveling party (fighting outlaws and hostile Indians), they often stepped aside in the stories and let the traumas and complications of the passengers carry the episodes. This scripting strategy not only saved wear and tear on the central cast, it also allowed a wide range of character study plots. *Wagon Train* managed to keep rolling with this workable format for eight seasons, setting the pattern later followed by *Bonanza* and *The Virginian*.

The general swing toward Westerns also meshed perfectly with the networks' increasing emphasis on youth-oriented adventure tales for early prime time. To satisfy children's desire for less complicated Western adventure, ABC and Walt Disney offered *Zorro,* a direct descendant of the old-fashioned Saturday matinee serials. Zorro, the alias of wealthy Spanish playboy Don Diego (Guy Williams), acted as a latter-day Robin Hood in nineteenth-century Spanish California, defending the town of Monterey from its evil ruler, Captain Monastario (Britt Lomond). Diego's transparent disguise (a simple Lone Ranger-ish mask around the eyes) should have fooled no one but, as in the adventures of Superman, the characters in the series were perpetually dumbfounded, particularly the portly Sergeant Garcia (Henry Calvin). *Zorro* provided two years of swashbuckling comic book-style exploits and became a minor fad, as thousands of urchins donned cheap plastic Zorro robes and brandished rubber-tipped swords.

The upsurge in Westerns of every type on the fall schedule (there were ten new oaters in September) was viewed with alarm by TV's comics, who rightly saw this trend as a direct challenge to them. Though comedy had been a staple of television for years, over the previous few seasons some of television's most successful comics, including Milton Berle, Jackie Gleason, and Sid Caesar, had faded from the screen. Those that remained (such as Red Skelton, Jack Benny, George Burns, and Bob Hope) vowed to "laugh the Westerns off the air" by mercilessly satirizing them at the start of the new season. For example, George Burns poked fun at the sometimes absurd distinctions made among the dozens of cowboy stories by insisting that his skit be classified as an adult Western because "every Indian in that scene is over twenty-one." By January, however, it was clear that the cowboys were having the last laugh, as Westerns occupied seven of the top ten positions in the ratings. Sid Caesar and Imogene Coca tried a reunion on ABC in late January, but their new show bombed. The only comedy successes that season were in the field of sitcoms, which produced one belated hit and three successful sleepers.

For three seasons, *Make Room For Daddy* had suffered from ABC's most vexing problem, a lack of reliable affiliates. In 1956, only eighty-three stations carried the program, and fifty of these aired it on delay. Though Danny Thomas had a viable format and a strong cast, the technical limitations of the ABC network had, in effect, reduced his program to a cult show, seen at odd times by a small corps of followers. Thomas shifted the series (renamed *The Danny Thomas Show*) to CBS beginning in the fall of 1957, and the network placed it in the prestigious Monday night slot vacated by *I Love Lucy* (which was now seen only in reruns on Wednesday night). At the start of the season, Thomas talked hopefully of attracting at least half of *Lucy's* old audience, and he brought in new characters and situations to help relaunch his show on its new network. During his final season at ABC, Danny had become a widower (Jean Hagen, who played his wife Margaret, had left the series, so her character was quietly killed), and had met a beautiful nurse (Kathy Daly, played by Marjorie Lord) who was, conveniently, a widow with a young daughter (played by Angela Cartwright). Danny began his residency at CBS by marrying Kathy and bringing the daughter into his own family, making *The Danny Thomas Show* seem almost brand-new, at a time when most situation comedies were running short of situations. With a fresh cast, new situations, and a better network (CBS carried the program on 195 stations), the show quickly passed its competition (NBC's quizzer, *Twenty-One*) and became a consistent member of television's top ten.

The only new situation comedies to survive the season were all slow starters: *Bachelor Father, The Real McCoys,* and *Leave It To Beaver*. *Bachelor Father* was simply another in a long line of television dads trying to raise a family without a wife. John Forsythe played a supposedly swinging Beverly Hills bachelor who found himself saddled with the responsibility of raising his thirteen-year-old niece, Kelly (Noreen Corcoran), after her parents were killed in a car crash. The series was slotted against *Maverick* and alternated with Jack Benny, so it did not have the opportunity to strike out on its own and become a hit until it defected to NBC in the summer of 1958. While *Bachelor Father* was a passable but generally uninspired show, the other two sitcom sleepers were exceptional comedies of the decade, with strong characters and genuinely funny situations.

The Real McCoys blazed a trail from the mountains of "West Virginny" to the farms of California's San Fernando Valley, turning rural humor into top-rated TV for ABC. Presiding head of this hillbilly clan was veteran sidekick Walter Brennan who, even though growing up fifteen miles north of Boston, was completely believable as the crusty, cantankerous, dyed-in-the-cornpone Grandpa Amos. Grandpa provided most of the humor in the series, usually outwitting everyone else (especially the city slickers) in spite of (or often because of) his backwoods naiveté and adherence to proven down-home aphorisms. Richard Crenna and Kathleen Nolan (as grandson Luke and his wife, Kate) played their characters straight, though inevitably everyone in the McCoy clan had to face the sputtering wrath of Grandpa. The family's Mexican-American hired hand, Pepino (Tony Martinez) served as the most frequent and convenient target for Grandpa's volatile temper.

The Real McCoys was pure comic fluff and seemed ABC's

perfect answer to CBS's reliance on sitcom superstars such as Lucille Ball, Jack Benny, Phil Silvers, and Danny Thomas. Though the program was practically ignored at the start of the season, by New Year's it had begun a slow and continuous rise in popularity. By early 1959, *The Real McCoys* became the first ABC sitcom to reach the top ten, winning both urban and rural support. Urban viewers laughed at the out-of-place hillbilly ways of the McCoys while rural viewers were amused by the clan's constant triumphs over the absurd, overly sophisticated city folk. (One of the program's writers, Paul Henning, used the same premise five years later and produced the even more successful *Beverly Hillbillies*.)

ABC also became the launching pad for another sleeper sitcom success, *Leave It To Beaver*. The program began in 1957 with an undistinguished season on CBS, losing against *Rin Tin Tin* and *Disneyland*. In the fall of 1958, *Leave It To Beaver* moved to ABC as a lead-in to *Zorro* and its fortunes began to rise immediately.

Leave It To Beaver was the most effective of the decade's "warm family" strain of sitcom, even outshining the Anderson family of the already popular *Father Knows Best* (which had debuted in 1954 on CBS and moved to NBC a year later). Both series presented small, close-knit families living in the vast expanse of television's interchangeable suburbs, but there were important differences between them. Though the Andersons rarely faced the ridiculous misunderstandings that usually occupied TV sitcom families (such as in *The Life of Riley*), the blandness of their characters ultimately undercut the attempts to introduce moderately realistic situations into the story lines. The Anderson children were especially disconcerting. Betty (Elinor Donahue), Bud (Billy Gray), and Kathy (Lauren Chapin) experienced the usual adolescent crises (allowance, school grades, dates), but everything seemed to happen *to* them. They were too nice and aseptically clean to ever get into trouble themselves. The Anderson kids were an adult's view of perfect children: They were never greedy, stupid, or mischievous, just unlucky or unwise. With the vital core of a warm family situation (the children) lacking credibility even for television reality, the frequent heart-to-heart talks in the den with their patient and understanding father (played by Robert Young) and their nervous reactions to minor crises (such as a misfired blind date) seemed hollow and phony.

Leave It To Beaver also contained its share of bland 1950s sitcom stereotypes. The Cleaver family lived in a typical television suburban home in a quiet neighborhood with shady trees and a nice front yard. Like nearly every TV father at the time, Ward (Hugh Beaumont) disappeared between 9:00 A.M. and 5:00 P.M. five days a week to an unknown job, though his real life's work seemed to be mowing the lawn and having weekly heart-to-heart talks with his sons (an annual event, at best, in real families). His wife, June (Barbara Billingsley), was a perfect TV mom who wanted nothing more out of life than a clean carpet, whiter-than-white laundry, and a well-done roast. She was a professional mother who always wore a semi-formal dress, even while doing the housework or baking cookies. (Billingsley received her basic training for this task by serving as the mother in the short-lived 1955 sitcom *Professional Father*.) Ward and June both stuck to the standard Hollywood image of adults, as did the other grownups in the series, such as stuffed-shirt Fred Rutherford (Richard Deacon), over-protective Mrs. Mondello (Madge Blake), and Miss Landers (Sue Randall), the pure and patient schoolteacher. The children in *Leave It To Beaver*, though, provided the crucial difference. More than any other kids then on TV, they were real.

The star ("Jerry Mathers as the Beaver") was a young boy, nearly ten years old, with an all-trusting Alfred E. Neuman-ish grin and an appropriate set of dimples. Despite his adorable appearance, the Beaver had very little of the "goodie two-shoes" qualities given to most of television's kids, and he actually engaged in normal, healthy preteen mischief. At the same time, he was honestly trying to decipher the way the world worked, and trying to understand whether people could be trusted or not. He often turned to his older brother Wally (Tony Dow) for help, and his brother responded with genuine concern tempered by total exasperation at the Beaver's frequent ineptitude (summed up in his often repeated phrase, "Aww, Beav'!"). Wally faced his own awkward problem: He was old enough to be interested in girls but too young to do anything about it. He tried to assert himself and create a good impression, even adopting a touch of 1950s teenage cool but Wally often ran into just as many problems as the Beaver. Even their friends were touched, to a lesser degree, by this more realistic portrayal of a kid's world. Straight-talking Whitey (Stanley Fafara), fat and selfish Larry Mondello (Rusty Stevens), perpetually flunking Lumpy (Frank Bank), and the brazenly two-faced Eddie Haskell (Ken Osmond) were a fair cross-section of suburban youth.

Leave It To Beaver managed to bridge the chasm between television's caricatures and the real world by keeping one part of the family equation close to reality. Though the adults were cardboard characters, the children in *Leave It To Beaver* were just like real kids: flawed and confused, usually good, but not above some exciting petty larceny. As a result, *Leave It To Beaver* emerged as a warm family show that offered real-life kids the opportunity to actually identify with children portrayed in a television series. More than any other sitcom at the time, it captured the essence of a child's everyday life in the late 1950s, building a strong and loyal following that watched the Beaver and Wally mature from mischievous kids to spirited teens.

ABC's early evening kidvid strategy had led both CBS and NBC to place similar fare in the 7:30–8:00 P.M. slot, pushing out both the fifteen-minute news and fifteen-minute music shows that had previously filled this period. NBC's success the previous few seasons with laid-back hour-long series featuring Perry Como and Dinah Shore suggested a new avenue of exposure for the displaced singers: a revival of the thirty- and sixty-minute musical-variety form, which had flourished in the early 1950s. For the fall of 1957 there were new musical-variety showcases for TV veterans Dean Martin, Nat King Cole, Patti Page, Eddie Fisher, and Frank Sinatra, as well as for new headliners Polly Bergen (from Pepsi-Cola ads and panel shows), Rosemary Clooney (from local television syndication), Pat Boone (from *The Arthur Godfrey Show*), Guy Mitchell (from the hit "Singin' the Blues"), Gisele MacKenzie (from *Your Hit Parade*), and Patrice Munsel (from the world of classical music). Only Pat Boone and Eddie Fisher survived to join Dinah Shore and Perry Como in returning the following fall.

Most of the new shows failed for lack of a very important element in a musical-variety program: variety. The new programs seemed almost the same, sharing the same guests and staging the same sort of production numbers over and over. Though a popular singer could easily carry a fifteen-minute show with a few lively numbers, much more was needed to fill the longer programs. The hosts were unable to tie together the individual segments of their new shows, frequently falling into stilted, artificial chit-chat as transition. Often, the same writers that had worked on the recently flopped comedy-variety hours supplied the transitional patter, repeating well-worn routines that had eventually strangled the big name comics. Against these odds, the battle for respectable ratings proved frustrating to both the musical stars and the networks.

Frank Sinatra, in his second attempt at a weekly television series, proved a major disappointment for ABC. His much-touted new program never found a consistent voice or rhythm, alternating between live and film presentations and frequently changing producers. CBS was frustrated at the failure of Patti Page's *The Big Record,* which the network had hoped to use to dominate Wednesday nights. Modeled after NBC's familiar *Your Hit Parade,* which used a cast of regulars to sing "cover" versions of the top tunes, *The Big Record* brought in the hit artists themselves to sing their own songs, live. From the opening show, though, everything seemed to go wrong. A trick piano for Hoagy Carmichael did not work properly. Eddie Cantor, who was miming a song, had to begin singing when somebody stopped the record. As Billy Ward's Dominoes were performing, stagehands had to restrain two policemen that barged into the New York studio with an arrest warrant for a member of the band. Most important, the program failed in its attempt to appeal to both teenagers and adults by including sharply conflicting styles of music: rock'n'roll and mainstream pop. Instead of attracting both audiences, it alienated them.

Nat King Cole, the first black to host a full-length network television variety show, faced a more serious problem. Cole had been a success with both black and white audiences as host of one of NBC's fifteen-minute musical spots during the 1956–57 season, so when these were eliminated in the summer of 1957, he received a thirty-minute summer slot that the network hoped would catch on and carry over into the fall. Throughout the summer, some of the top names in show business (such as Harry Belafonte, Peggy Lee, Tony Martin, and Ella Fitzgerald) appeared on his show for next to nothing, and Cole started to register very good ratings, coming within a few points of overtaking CBS's *$64,000 Question.* Despite such a strong performance, no sponsor offered to pick up the show, fearing the antipathy of Southern viewers toward seeing blacks on television. Defying the traditional handling of unsponsored programs, NBC bravely invested $17,500 each week (still just a fraction of the budget for most sponsored variety shows) to keep Cole on the air, hoping a sponsor would eventually come forward. In September, the network increased the weekly budget to $20,000 and kept the program on in prime time, but no commercial support emerged. When the show ended its run in December, Cole issued a devastating attack on advertisers, saying it was Madison Avenue, not the South, that was keeping blacks off television. He said the ad agencies deliberately refused to sponsor him, fearing that, as a black, he would be bad for "product identification."

Strangely enough, while many middle-of-the-road pop singers failed on television in 1957, raucous rock'n'roll music managed to make important inroads into the network schedule, and the genre even registered its first television hit. Alan Freed, one of the men responsible for popularizing rock'n'roll in the 1950s (with his radio programs and traveling stage shows) presented the first network television show devoted to the new sound, *Rock 'n' Roll Revue* (soon renamed *The Big Beat*), which premiered in the spring of 1957 on ABC. Each week Freed presented rockers such as the Clovers, the Del-Vikings, and Screaming Jay Hawkins, though as a concession to those in the TV audience not yet sold on the new sound, he also included less frenetic artists such as Guy Mitchell, June Valli, and Connie Francis. Despite his mixture of performers, Freed's program did not catch on. Rock'n'roll was still somewhat limited in appeal and Freed's own rough, unpolished manner, while perfect for his live stage shows, was unsuited to the demands of network television. *The Big Beat* faded at the end of the summer of 1957. What did succeed, though, was the unpretentious *American Bandstand,* which came to the ABC network weekday afternoon line-up on August 5, 1957, after playing five years as a local Philadelphia program.

For ninety minutes each day on *American Bandstand,* young disc jockey Dick Clark played the latest hit records while some

A heart-to-heart father and son talk between Ward Cleaver (Hugh Beaumont) and the Beaver (Jerry Mathers) on *Leave It To Beaver. (Courtesy of Universal Studios Licensing LLLP)*

high schoolers in the studio danced to the music. Occasionally, there were appearances by guest performers, but they usually only lip-synched their own records instead of singing live. Many reviewers predicted that *American Bandstand* would be a flop as a network show and they scoffed at the format, pointing out that local stations could easily produce a similar program on their own (at the time, many did). When the ratings arrived, however, they showed *American Bandstand* clobbering the competition from CBS and NBC. Though the concept was simple to stage, local stations found it much easier to take the network feed rather than to turn out their own versions.

Once *American Bandstand* was an established hit, plenty of sponsors turned up and the program was even given a brief run in prime time. In February 1958, Clark received a more suitable evening show, sponsored by Beech-Nut gum. The nighttime program closely resembled Freed's *The Big Beat,* only with more polish, as, live from a New York theater, Clark presented the big names of rock'n'roll in a mix of live singing and lip-synched numbers. Though there was no dancing staged in the theater, the exuberant teenage audience gave the show an exciting energy as it cheered such performers as Jerry Lee Lewis, Chuck Berry, Fats Domino, Fabian, Bobby Darin, and Annette Funicello.

Clark succeeded with rock on television while Freed did not for one important reason: Clark was a sharper businessman and packager. Alan Freed often seemed to be too caught up in keeping the frenzied movement of a live rock show intact to consider toning it down for the television cameras to follow. He also favored the raunchy, less familiar black rhythm and blues performers over more mainstream rockers. As a result, to the uninitiated, *The Big Beat* appeared visually confusing and Freed's own supercharged demeanor somewhat threatening.

September 29, 1957
DuPont Show of the Month. (CBS). CBS and David Susskind begin a series of irregularly slotted monthly dramas that pop up all over the schedule.

September 30, 1957
Do You Trust Your Wife? switches to weekday afternoons on ABC and features a new host: CBS reject Johnny Carson (assisted by sidekick Ed McMahon). In July 1958, the title of the show is changed to *Who Do You Trust?*

October 17, 1957
ABC's *Navy Log* dramatizes John F. Kennedy's wartime naval exploits aboard the *PT-109.* At the end of the episode, the junior senator from Massachusetts appears to chat about the events.

November 6, 1957
The Lucille Ball and Desi Arnaz Show. (CBS). Television's #1 sitcom couple begin a series of irregularly scheduled monthly specials. First up: a "flashback" on how Lucy and Ricky first met in Havana in 1940.

December 13, 1957
CBS axes *The Jimmy Dean Show* because of continued sponsor indifference—even though it is *ahead* of *Today* in the ratings.

January 6, 1958
Dotto. (CBS). Colgate drops sponsorship of *Strike It Rich* in the CBS daytime schedule and picks up a new game show for the slot.

January 11, 1958
Sea Hunt. Ziv brings local stations a diver-as-cop adventure series, produced by Ivan Tors and starring Lloyd Bridges.

Though a true rock'n'roll fan, Dick Clark treated the music first and foremost as a special business enterprise that had to be adjusted to meet the unique demands of television. He realized that the nature of a live rock performance did not transfer easily to the small, confining TV screen. While masters at their music, most rock performers were novices at projecting any visual, physical stage presence (beyond shaking) for television. Clark provided the necessary stabilizing control and guidance. He also recognized the need to place rock'n'roll in safer, more accessible surroundings for general consumption. On his programs, Clark was always neatly dressed, clean-cut, warm, and articulate. He usually emphasized less threatening personalities such as Fabian, who did toned-down versions of black rhythm and blues hits. With this approach, Clark ran away with the television teen market and soon his *American Bandstand* show was the most important outlet for new rock'n'roll music. (He could make or break a new disc just by deciding to play it on his show.) His Saturday night *Dick Clark Beech-Nut Show* lasted until 1960, while *American Bandstand* kept right on going, weathering the British invasion, acid rock, the rise of disco, and punk music, surviving to the end of the 1980s.

Live television drama continued to lose strength during the 1957–58 season as the networks and sponsors nitpicked the form to death while drastically increasing their commitment to filmed productions. Besides providing a boon for Westerns, this trend resulted in a new batch of police and private eye shows, including several new loner cop series and the revival of an old crime format.

Like the Westerns, they offered the public a mixture of familiar characters and dramatic action.

In *M Squad,* Lee Marvin played Chicago police lieutenant Frank Ballinger, a tight-lipped cop on a violent beat. As in Jack Webb's *Dragnet,* there was a deadpan voice-over narration to explain the story, but unlike that show *M Squad* emphasized physical beatings, frequent car chases, and constant gunplay. David Janssen, as *Richard Diamond, Private Detective,* and Frank Lovejoy in *Meet McGraw,* were both tight-lipped, long-suffering, know-it-all private eyes who disliked cops and turned to the police force only when necessary. Peter Lawford (*The Thin Man*) and Donald Gray (as a new one-armed British permutation of *Mark Saber*) both played dilettante detectives who exuded sophistication and occasionally even cooperated with the police. The best new crime series of the season, however, took an old, discarded television format and used it as the basis for a well-executed presentation of the systematic pursuit of justice, *Perry Mason.*

Courtroom drama (with its simple, inexpensive sets) had been a programming staple in the early days of television on such shows as DuMont's *They Stand Accused,* but had gone out of style with the move to filmed series that allowed action to take place outside the cramped confines of the studio. *Perry Mason* brought the courtroom saga back into the limelight. The character of Perry Mason had begun life in a series of murder mystery novels by Erle Stanley Gardner and, in the early 1940s, Mason moved from print to a radio soap opera series on CBS, which presented him as the playboy type. As portrayed by Raymond Burr for television, Perry Mason was a no-nonsense legal wizard who never lost a case.

Perry Mason was a triumph of technique over format, because every episode was virtually identical: Somebody in trouble came to Mason, who spent the first half of the story investigating the case. Inevitably, a murder would take place, and Mason would shift his attention to defending his client from this charge, farming out the tedious detective work to his flunky, Paul Drake (William Hopper). In court, Mason carefully questioned each witness, undercutting alibis, exposing contradictions, and shifting suspicion from one character to another, while playing a cat and mouse game with the long-suffering state prosecutor, Hamilton Burger (William Talman). At the dramatic showdown, Mason would reveal a vital piece of evidence (often brought in at the last minute by Drake), causing the guilty party to stand up and publicly confess.

The series was a straight whodunit, complete with a full range of suspects and clues that allowed the viewer to become an armchair detective. Because it was clear that Mason would win (he lost only one case in the nine year history of the series), the object was to keep one step ahead of him and spot the damaging evidence or false alibi, and zero in on the killer; or at least understand how Perry did. Afterward, he covered any remaining points of the case talking with Drake and secretary Della Street (Barbara Hale) back at the office.

Even though the series followed the same formula each week, it demanded that viewers think and alertly scan the suspicious characters in the episode. Though it seemed that every hack character actor in Hollywood eventually turned up as a suspect in *Perry Mason,* their character types contrasted well with the strong central cast to provide, for most people, a positive and generally believable portrait of the legal profession. Many practicing attorneys were not happy over such an image, however, finding it impossible to live up to the infallible standard Mason set. Salt Lake County attorney Frank Moss (later a United States senator from Utah) complained at a convention of prosecutors that, "A good number of jurors have become convinced, through watching television, that the prosecutor is some sort of trick artist, who pulls a rabbit out of his hat in the last reel … if he doesn't resort to theatrics, as the TV prosecutors do, they are inclined to bring in an innocent verdict."

As *Perry Mason* began its long run as a top-notch formula drama show, the long battle between New York and Los Angeles for control of America's television culture passed a symbolic turning point. New York lost. *Studio One*, for years one of the premiere showcases for live New York drama, moved to Hollywood and began accentuating big name stars, fancy scenery, and deep-voiced announcers over dramatic content. The trend was irreversible. In addition, video tape came into general use in 1957, dooming live television, and one of the last remaining reasons for the stars and networks to avoid the West Coast evaporated. It was all just so much easier out West: there was more room, a greater number of actors, and less red tape. All of the major film studios were now heavily committed to television production, and all three networks had virtually conceded control of program production to the filmmakers. Though the amount of prime time programming originating on the West Coast had been increasing slowly for years, in 1957 it jumped from 40% to 71%.

As the first generation of important network programmers passed from the scene, they left behind bitter comments. Former NBC president Pat Weaver, who failed that year in an abortive attempt to start a fourth network, labeled television "a jukebox to put in the corner to keep kids quiet." Fred Coe quit NBC stating, "I just wasn't happy doing nothing." Max Liebman and NBC parted

ways. All season, stories about great drama shows being emasculated by fearful sponsors and networks circulated in the press. Rod Serling said he was "giving up" writing television dramas after *Playhouse 90* tampered with two of his plays: "Aftermath" and "Panic Button."

"Aftermath," a story of a black lynching in the modern South (a topic that Serling had run into trouble with a few years earlier), had been scheduled to open the season for *Playhouse 90,* but sponsor protests forced a delay. Even after Serling changed the story to the lynching of Mexicans in the Southwest in the 1880s, it was not put on the air until June, when most people began their vacations and the number of viewers dropped. Retitled "A Town Has Turned to Dust," the play featured Rod Steiger as a cowardly sheriff torn between the law and the mob (led by William Shatner). Serling's "Panic Button" began as the story of a commercial airliner crash and the investigation that followed. Airline pressure forced Serling to change it to a charter plane, but then the charter companies complained. "We'll wind up with a Yellow Cab," an associate producer moaned. "TV has more sacred cows than India."

Playhouse 90 even permitted showman Mike Todd to take over one episode and turn it into a first anniversary party for his film "Around the World in 80 Days" (in which CBS had purchased a 10% interest the previous year). For "Around the World in 90 Minutes," Todd filled Madison Square Garden with 18,000 of his closest friends, and CBS carried the celebration live. Elizabeth Taylor (Todd's wife) passed out slices from an enormous birthday cake as luminaries paraded aimlessly beneath a giant balloon. Two hundred forty dancers stood by but never danced. Anchormen Walter Cronkite and Jim McKay tried to make sense of the proceedings and the speeches that ranged from tiresome testimonials to an unexpected call for world peace by Senator Hubert Humphrey. The camera work was generally shoddy and the interviews were constantly interrupted by ads. The *New York Times* television critic Jack Gould succinctly described the affair as "an elaborate bore."

The prostitution of a distinguished series like *Playhouse 90* with the airing of Todd's party was a symbol of the declining status of television drama. *Studio One, Climax,* and NBC's daytime *Matinee Theater* were canceled by the end of the season. Even the eleven-year-old *Kraft Television Theater,* the granddaddy of all TV drama anthologies, bit the dust in 1958. Though long a refuge of sensible dramatic entertainment, it was sacrificed in the spring of 1958 to effectuate Milton Berle's return to television the following fall. Even though Berle had been considered "dead" as a television personality only a few years before, he had stolen the show at the April 15 Emmy awards telecast, so Kraft decided to gamble and sign him for the next season. Though it was generally conceded that comedy-variety was in a bad slump, Kraft felt that the chance of success with Berle was better than continuing to support hour-long drama, which it saw as an increasingly moribund form.

In a last-ditch attempt to salvage the Kraft drama program, the J. Walter Thompson production agency withdrew from the show, and turned it over to David Susskind's Talent Associates (which had done a great deal of television drama work for CBS, especially on *Armstrong Circle Theater).* Susskind turned out a fabulous two-part live presentation of Robert Penn Warren's "All the King's Men," but it was too late. Kraft had settled on Berle and slated the oldest show on television for cancellation. Susskind, who was still very active on CBS, took the defeat personally, calling 1958 "the year of the miserable drivel."

Then there were the quiz shows.

February 17, 1958
Ollie Treyz becomes president of ABC-TV.

March 12, 1958
Game showman Louis G. Cowan becomes president of CBS-TV.

April 28, 1958.
James Aubrey returns to CBS as vice-president of creative services.

May 13, 1958
Dr. Allen DuMont resigns as chairman of the board of the DuMont Broadcasting Corporation, which is renamed the Metropolitan Broadcasting Corporation. Under new owner John Kluge, it becomes Metromedia Inc. in 1961.

July 1, 1958
Colgate brings *Dotto* to prime time on NBC.

July 7, 1958
Death of *See It Now.* Age: 7 years. Cause: CBS's new leaders feel the floating documentary series is expendable.

July 11, 1958
Robert Kinter becomes the president of NBC-TV as Robert Sarnoff assumes the position of NBC's chairman of the board.

August 4, 1958
Monday Night Fights, the final show of the old DuMont network, dies. At the end, it is carried on only five stations, nationwide.

October 1, 1958
Death of *Kraft Television Theater,* the oldest show on television. Final production: H. Julian Fink's "Presumption of Innocence."

18. *Dotto* Goes Blotto

REGULAR VIEWERS OF CBS WHO TUNED IN the network at 11:30 A.M. on Monday, August 18, 1958, expecting that day's edition of the quiz show *Dotto* instead heard studio announcer Ralph Paul stampede through a quick disclaimer, *"Dotto,* the program formerly presented at this hour, will no longer be seen. In its place, we bring you *Top Dollar."* Though the disappearance of this morning quizzer was quite sudden, the fact that one quiz show was being replaced with another was not that unusual. All through 1958, various quiz programs had appeared and disappeared with increasing regularity. Since the ratings triumph of *The $64,000 Question* in the summer of 1955, quiz shows had become a network programming staple, turning up throughout the schedule. They were the easiest format to use in quickly filling holes left by flopped programs or to serve as headliners in launching the new season.

Even though another runaway smash hit had not emerged since the spectacular performance by Charles Van Doren on *Twenty-One* in 1957, sponsors were happy to continue to bankroll the quiz programs. The television economy had been in a very weak state since 1956, and expensive, complicated filmed series often were a more risky and less attractive investment. Besides, sponsor identification was judged to be much higher on the quizzes than on sitcoms or Westerns, and without many of the problems. There were no temperamental stars demanding salary increases, and the possibility of sparking any controversy seemed remote. Best of all, quiz shows were very cheap to produce. All that fancy prize money was nothing compared to the usual price tag of a filmed series. It did not matter that most of the quiz programs were nearly identical and often disappeared after a short run. Another show with a slightly different gimmick would be brought in and there was always the possibility that ratings lightning would strike with the new program. It soon became clear, however, that *Dotto* was not just another quiz show that bit the dust. Instead, it marked the first step in the collapse of the house of cards that was the TV quiz show.

In the time between Charles Van Doren's final appearance on *Twenty-One* (March 1957) and the fall of *Dotto* (August 1958), quiz show producers had become increasingly fixated over the performance of each show and they tried every possible gimmick and format variation in the hope of attracting ratings equal to Van Doren's. Some offered very large amounts of cash or highly unusual prizes. In one extreme case, *Bid'n'Buy* (hosted by Bert Parks) planned to auction as one of its prizes the sparsely settled

Scottish island of Stroma, which producer Robert Stivers had purchased for $23,000, but canceled the proposed stunt at the last minute in response to the plaintive pleas of the British government. Others adopted off-beat formats such as ABC's *ESP* (hosted by Vincent Price), which tested the extra sensory perception of contestants who had to identify unseen playing cards from isolation booths. Christmas 1957 brought the home participation craze, which gave viewers at home the opportunity to win prizes at the same time as the studio contestants. By Easter 1958, a local New York program, *Bingo at Home* (hosted by Monty Hall), combined the home participation angle with a new wrinkle, bingo. The first network to pursue the bingo fad was CBS's thinly disguised *Wingo* (hosted by Bob Kennedy) which offered prizes of up to $250,000, though the rules were so complicated no one ever got close. NBC soon followed with *Music Bingo* and even old timers such as *The $64,000 Question* added a special bingo-type feature.

Through all these gimmicks, most quizzes earned adequate, if not spectacular, ratings while waiting for the next public hero to appear. No matter how many variations were devised, audience identification with contestants was the most important element for success. *The $64,000 Question* had featured Gino Prato and Dr. Joyce Brothers. *Twenty-One* found gold with Charles Van Doren. *Name That Tune* once featured Marine Major (and future astronaut) John Glenn, who won $15,000 by correctly identifying twenty-five songs, including "Far Away Places." Still, every show had to eventually face the same problem: The most popular contestants did not automatically win and could be knocked out at anytime by a less attractive challenger. Thus, the most important aspect of a quiz show seemed left to blind chance.

In the spring of 1958, however, quiz shows were still accepted by most people as a solid part of the TV culture and one that would continue to grow. CBS had its Louis G. Cowan-inspired *The $64,000 Question* and *The $64,000 Challenge* as well as the independently produced *Top Dollar, Dotto,* and *Name That Tune.* NBC concentrated on programs devised by Jack Barry and Dan Enright *(Twenty-One, Tic Tac Dough, Dough Re Mi,* and *Concentration)* and added other shows such as *The Price Is Right, Haggis Baggis,* and *Win with a Winner.* As the number of quiz shows on the air increased, the number of more serious news and drama shows decreased. Quiz show impresario Louis Cowan became president of the CBS television network in March 1958 and soon thereafter it was decided that CBS could do without controversial, expensive loss leaders such as *See It Now*—not even as an occasional floating special. At the same time, some producers went even further and brazenly claimed that quiz shows were really a true renaissance in live TV and the successors to the live drama productions from New York, which were rapidly fading from prime time. Television executives responded to anguished cries among critics over the apparent passing of the already mythical golden age of television by insisting that they were performing a public service, giving the people what they demanded: quiz shows and Westerns. TV had become a truly mass medium, they pointed out, and could no longer afford to cater to the elitist tastes of a small, over-educated minority.

Even so, there was uneasiness and exceptional pressure in quiz show circles during the spring of 1958. Sponsors were paying increasing attention to the performance of the quiz programs, and the generally acceptable ratings most quizzes had been coasting along on were beginning to be viewed as inadequate. During the summer, no fewer than ten new quiz shows appeared, but the genre's overall performance declined. Loretta Young's anthology series defeated *The $64,000 Challenge*. A mediocre Western, *The Californians*, nosed out *The $64,000 Question*. Ancient reruns of *I Love Lucy* beat new episodes of *Twenty-One*. *Dotto*, a smash hit on CBS in the daytime, flopped in a nighttime version on NBC. Halfway through the summer, even the off-beat *ESP* abandoned the quiz format and became a drama anthology, focusing on real life incidents of extrasensory perception. (At the end of each dramatization, Vincent Price interviewed the real people involved.)

One reason for the ratings decline was overexposure. The public was beginning to tire of the interchangeable formats used in each quiz program. More important, the programs were running out of new heroes. Without a consistent stream of heroes, viewer attention focused on the all-too-similar formats of each individual show, and the obvious weaknesses were exposed. By the middle of 1958, it became increasingly clear within the TV industry that quizzes were not a solid commodity, but a very unstable structure that needed just a slight push to collapse.

On May 20, 1958, Ed Hilgemeier, a twenty-four-year-old part-time butler and bit actor, was a standby contestant on the daytime version of *Dotto*. Backstage, Hilgemeier found a notebook belonging to a woman who had been the winning contestant on that day's show. The notebook contained answers to the questions she had been asked. Suspecting foul play, Hilgemeier showed the notebook to the woman's opponent and also protested to the show's producers. After receiving a $1,500 payoff, Hilgemeier was ready to forget the whole matter until he discovered that the disgruntled losing contestant had been given $4,000, just what the winning contestant had received. Feeling double-crossed, Hilgemeier filed a complaint on August 7 with the show's sponsor, Colgate. These maneuvers went on behind the scenes and out of the public eye, so the sponsor's public reaction came as a complete surprise. On August 16, Colgate abruptly announced it was terminating both the weekday morning (CBS) and Tuesday evening (NBC) versions of *Dotto*. No reason for the unexpected cancellations was given by either of the networks involved or the sponsor. Yet rumors quickly spread that a disgruntled contestant had charged the show with rigging and was taking his story to the D.A. Appropriately, on the morning of August 25, only hours after Teddy Nadler set a new quiz show prize record (he won $252,000 on *The $64,000 Challenge*), New York District Attorney Frank Hogan announced that his office was beginning an investigation into the possibly illegal activities of the producers of *Dotto*. What's more, added Hogan (who happened to be the Democratic nominee for the U.S. Senate that year), "If it leads to other shows, we will have to follow them up."

Even though *Dotto* was the only show publicly under suspicion, questions about other quiz shows began surfacing. On August 28, Herbert Stempel charged that the producers of *Twenty-One* had supplied him with answers during his reign as champion and that after he had been on top for four weeks (winning $49,000), they told him to "take a dive" in his match with Charles Van Doren in December 1956. This dramatic accusation changed the focus of the quiz show investigation from a relatively obscure program to one of America's new folk heroes, who was still a public celebrity. Van Doren happened to be guest-hosting the *Today* show that week and on August 29 he took the opportunity to issue an on-the-air denial, saying, "I'm sad and shocked ... it's enough to shake your faith in human nature ... I myself was never given any answers or told any questions beforehand, and, as far as I know, none of the contestants received any coaching of this sort ... the television quiz show in this country has become an institution. A quiz show is fundamentally a matching of wits, and it is an American tradition to do this. I, for one, think it's a good tradition."

Twenty-One producers Barry and Enright, as well as NBC itself, also issued categorical denials of Stempel's charges, with the network calling them "utterly baseless and untrue."

In September, quiz show contestants and producers began pilgrimages to Hogan's office, both voluntarily and involuntarily. Barry and Enright produced a dramatic audio tape of Stempel in which he seemed to be trying to blackmail them by demanding $50,000 or he'd talk. Stempel replied that the tape had been doctored. Barry, who was also host of *Twenty-One*, issued an on-the-air defense of the program on October 8, assuring home viewers that the *Twenty-One* producers had not abused the audience's trust and would not in the future, adding, "The truth will out." Jack

---

September 15, 1958
 ABC experiments with prime time news, moving John Daly's fifteen-minute report to 10:30 P.M., while also maintaining an early evening news show. Sponsor reaction is strong at first, but viewer reaction is cool. In May, 1959, Daly moves back to the early evening.

September 22, 1958
 Peter Gunn. (NBC). Both the networks and sponsors appear to be loosening up: After years of being blacklisted, actor Herschel Bernardi lands the role of Lieutenant Jacoby in this jazzy detective series.

September 24, 1958
 The Donna Reed Show. (ABC). A wholesome family sitcom with a pleasant, if idealized, cast of characters: Donna Reed plays the loving mother; Carl Betz is the respectable physician, husband, and father; and Shelly Fabares and Paul Petersen are the sweet, occasionally boisterous, children.

October 2, 1958
 "Days of Wine and Roses" on *Playhouse 90.* J. P. Miller's original story (later turned into a film) focuses on the destructive effects of alcoholism, with Cliff Robertson and Piper Laurie.

October 13, 1958
 ABC resumes daytime programming with *Day in Court, Liberace, Beat the Clock* and Dick Van Dyke as a quiz emcee in *Mother's Day.*

Day	Net	7:00	7:30	8:00	8:30	9:00	9:30	10:00	10:30
MON	ABC	local / ABC News	Polka-Go-Round		Bold Journey	Voice Of Firestone	Anybody Can Play	Traffic Court	John Daly & The News / local
MON	CBS	local	Name That Tune	THE TEXAN	Father Knows Best	Danny Thomas Show	ANN SOTHERN SHOW	WESTINGHOUSE DESILU PLAYHOUSE # Lucille Ball & Desi Arnaz Show	
MON	NBC	local	Tic Tac Dough	Restless Gun	Tales Of Wells Fargo	PETER GUNN	Alcoa-Goodyear Theater	Arthur Murray Party	local
TUE	ABC	local / ABC News	The Cheyenne Show (BRONCO) Sugarfoot		Life And Legend Of Wyatt Earp	THE RIFLEMAN	NAKED CITY	Confession	John Daly & The News / local
TUE	CBS	local	STARS IN ACTION	Keep Talking	To Tell The Truth	Arthur Godfrey Show	Red Skelton Show	GARRY MOORE SHOW	
TUE	NBC	local	Dragnet	George Gobel Show / Eddie Fisher Show		GEORGE BURNS SHOW	Bob Cummings Show	The Californians	local
WED	ABC	local / ABC News	Lawrence Welk's Plymouth Show		Adventures Of Ozzie And Harriet	DONNA REED SHOW	OLDSMOBILE SHOW WITH PATTI PAGE	Wednesday Night Fights	
WED	CBS	local	Twilight Theater	PURSUIT		The Millionaire	I've Got A Secret	U.S. Steel Hour / Armstrong Circle Theater	
WED	NBC	local	Wagon Train		The Price Is Right	KRAFT MUSIC HALL WITH MILTON BERLE	BAT MASTERSON	This Is Your Life	local
THR	ABC	local / ABC News	Leave It To Beaver	Zorro	The Real McCoys	Pat Boone Chevy Showroom	ROUGH RIDERS	This Is Music	John Daly & The News / local
THR	CBS	local	I Love Lucy	December Bride	YANCY DERRINGER	Dick Powell's Zane Grey Theater	Playhouse 90		
THR	NBC	local	Jefferson Drum	ED WYNN SHOW	Twenty-One	BEHIND CLOSED DOORS	Tennessee Ernie Ford Show	You Bet Your Life	Masquerade Party
FRI	ABC	local / ABC News	Adventures Of Rin Tin Tin	Walt Disney Presents		MAN WITH A CAMERA	77 SUNSET STRIP		John Daly & The News / local
FRI	CBS	local	Your Hit Parade	Trackdown	Jackie Gleason Show	Phil Silvers Show	Lux-Schlitz Playhouse	The Lineup	Person To Person
FRI	NBC	local	Buckskin	FURTHER ADVENTURES OF ELLERY QUEEN		M Squad	The Thin Man	Gillette Cavalcade Of Sports	Post-Fight Beat
SAT	ABC	local	The Dick Clark Beech-Nut Show	Jubilee U.S.A.		Lawrence Welk's Dodge Dancing Party		MUSIC FROM MANHATTAN	local
SAT	CBS	local	Perry Mason		WANTED: DEAD OR ALIVE	Gale Storm Show	Have Gun, Will Travel	Gunsmoke	local
SAT	NBC	local	People Are Funny	Perry Como Show		STEVE CANYON	CIMARRON CITY		BRAINS AND BRAWN
SUN	ABC	You Asked For It	Maverick		LAWMAN	Colt .45	ENCOUNTER		local
SUN	CBS	Lassie	Bachelor Father / Jack Benny Program	Ed Sullivan Show		General Electric Theater	Alfred Hitchcock Presents	$64,000 Question	What's My Line
SUN	NBC	Saber Of London	NORTHWEST PASSAGE	Steve Allen Show		Dinah Shore Chevy Show		Loretta Young Show	local

Narz, emcee *of Dotto,* said he knew nothing about any rigging, but one *Dotto* contestant who had won $900, Mrs. Regan Leydenfrost, said she had received "indirect help anyone but an idiot could follow." The Reverend Charles E. Jackson said that during the pregame runthrough before his appearance on *The $64,000 Challenge* he had been supplied with the correct answers. Another contestant, James E. Snodgrass, announced that he had received the answers in advance during his five appearances on *Twenty-One* but, unlike the others, he had proof. Before his appearances, he had mailed the answers to himself and he presented the district attorney sealed registered letters containing the evidence.

These charges surfaced just as the 1958–59 season began, and soon every quiz show on the air came under suspicion, throwing the networks' schedules into chaos. By mid-September, *Dotto, ESP, Haggis Baggis,* and *The $64,000 Challenge* were axed. In mid-October, *Twenty-One,* which had fallen from sixth to thirty-fifth in a matter of months, was kicked off NBC. In early November, *The $64,000 Question* departed, after giving away $2,106,800 and twenty-nine Cadillacs. At Christmas, even the local *Bingo at Home* was removed from the air, even though it was completely free of taint. The networks steadfastly claimed they were canceling the shows because of their bad ratings, and not in response to the many charges being leveled.

In late September a grand jury was impaneled to hear the mounting charges against the quiz shows, but it handed down only one indictment that year, charging Albert Freedman, producer of *Twenty-One,* with lying to the grand jury in October when he said that he had never supplied answers to contestants. The grand jury continued to conduct its business in 1959, but behind closed doors, so the issue of the quiz scandal faded from view for almost a year. Most of the quiz shows were off the air and, while there appeared to have been some cheating, nobody familiar to the public seemed to be at fault. Charles Van Doren, with his steadfast denials, seemed to escape the crisis unscathed and was signed on as a regular for *Today.* Van Doren delivered daily five-minute lectures on science, poetry, history, and famous people in what he felt was a marvelous opportunity to interest the nation in "the intellectual life."

NBC and CBS were adamant in their own statements of innocence, pointing out that almost every one of the quiz shows had been, like most programs on television, produced by outsiders over whom they had no direct control. ABC, which, by coincidence, had few quiz shows, eagerly pointed out that it was cleaner-than-clean. "You can't say anything bad about Westerns. That's our format and we're sticking with it."

With quiz shows knocked out of the picture just as the new season began, the networks rushed to replace the format and build a positive image for their other programming. At first, they attempted to portray the season as marking the reappearance of television's classic comics. Such an approach made sense because one sponsor, Kraft, had already abandoned its long-running dramatic showcase in favor of the much-heralded return of Mr. Television as host of *The Kraft Music Hall* (an umbrella title for comedy and variety shows borrowed from the network radio program Kraft had sponsored over the years). Unfortunately, it was the same old Milton Berle in the same old skits. His only new feature was a spotlight on up-and-coming talent, but even this was canned after a few months, not long before Berle himself was dropped. Jackie Gleason, also attempting yet another comeback, offered his old formula of familiar stock characters, the June Taylor dancers, and a parade of glamour girls, but without the assistance of sidekick Art Carney, who had been replaced by Buddy Hackett. The program was banished by New Year's. George Burns tried to make it without his long-time partner, Gracie Allen (who had retired from show business), using the remaining characters and the show-within-a-show premise from the *Burns and Allen Show*. He played a former comedian trying to make it as a theatrical producer and variety show host, but found himself outdistanced by syndicated reruns of his old show. By the end of the season, Burns also disappeared. Veteran Ed Wynn, who had achieved some success as an NBC variety host in the early 1950s, attempted to make the transition to situation comedy as a folksy, sentimental figure in the embarrassingly hokey setting of a lonely old widower trying to raise two orphaned granddaughters in a college town. *The Ed Wynn Show*, too was gone by New Year's. Despite the network's efforts to breathe new life into television comedy, the format that dominated programming and ratings again this season was the Western.

The networks exploited nearly every possible aspect of the old West and at one point in the season seven of the top ten shows were oaters (*Wagon Train, Gunsmoke, Maverick, Sugarfoot, The Rifleman, Cheyenne,* and *Have Gun Will Travel*), with only Danny Thomas, Perry Como, and Perry Mason breaking the near-monopoly. In order to stand out amidst this multitude of frontier heroes, some of the new shows emphasized unusual gimmicks that were either a part of the setting or used by the main character. Bat Masterson carried a cane, wore a derby hat, and used a custom built gun. Gene Barry, as Masterson, projected an air of suave sophistication in his portrayal of the dandified yet adept lawman who was usually looking out for himself, in the style of Maverick and Paladin. In *Yancy Derringer*, the producers went to a ridiculous extreme and tried combining at least eight saleable gimmicks into one program: The action took place in bawdy post-Civil War New Orleans and focused on the exploits of a former Confederate captain, Yancy Derringer (Jock Mahoney), a roguish riverboat gambler who used tiny pistols and knives instead of guns, and was good at judo besides. Derringer's compatriot and bodyguard was a stonefaced rifle-toting Indian (played by X Brands) who used sign language to communicate.

In opposition to the gimmick school were the Westerns that emphasized strong silent heroes such as Steve McQueen in *Wanted: Dead or Alive*, Eric Fleming and Clint Eastwood in *Rawhide*, John Russell in *Lawman*, George Montgomery in *Cimarron City*, Rory Calhoun in *The Texan*, and Kent Taylor in *The Rough Riders*. These characters spoke so infrequently that one critic (in a review of *The Rough Riders*) said the best acting was by the Rocky Mountains. Westerns were doing so well that even the loss of the leading man could be overcome by an enterprising producer. When production for the fourth season of *Cheyenne* began, star Clint Walker was out "panning for gold in contract land" (holding out for more money) so a new character, Bronco Lane (played by former Texas A&M football star Ty Hardin) was brought in. The series ran as scheduled, without even changing its name. When Walker returned the next season, *Bronco* was given its own slot.

The season's most successful new Western was ABC's *The Rifleman*, starring Chuck Connors as Lucas McCain. On the surface this appeared to be another gimmick Western, emphasizing the hero's use of a rifle in place of the traditional six-shooter, but the program's real attraction was the warm relationship between Lucas and his young son, Mark (Johnny Crawford). Every episode of *The Rifleman* centered on the son's learning something about life, either on his own or from his father. Once the audience ac-

Dotto's announcer Ralph Paul prepares to pick the name of a lucky home viewer who would be called by emcee Jack Narz and asked to identify the dotted celebrity caricature on the wall. *(CBS Photo Archive © 2003 CBS Worldwide, Inc. All Rights Reserved.)*

November 23, 1958

Ronald Reagan and his wife Nancy appear in *General Electric Theater*'s Thanksgiving production of "A Turkey for the President."

January 12, 1959

The Bell Telephone Hour. (NBC). After eighteen years as a radio showcase for musical diversity, the *Telephone Hour* comes to television as an occasional special. In the fall it receives a weekly slot.

February 6, 1959

On *Person to Person,* Ed Murrow conducts a live interview with Fidel Castro, who appears clad in pajamas.

March 8, 1959

The three Marx Brothers make their final appearance together in "The Incredible Jewel Robbery," a half-hour pantomime-style comedy on CBS's *General Electric Theater.* Harpo and Chico star, but Groucho makes a cameo appearance, delivering the only line of dialogue.

April 1, 1959

Under the vigorous leadership of a new president, John White, the National Educational Television network (NET) moves its headquarters from Ann Arbor, Michigan, to New York City. His long range goal: turn NET into a respectable alternative to the three commercial networks. The immediate goal: find a home base educational channel to serve New York City.

June 16, 1959

Death of George Reeves a.k.a. Clark Kent a.k.a. Superman. Age: 45. Suspected Cause: Typecasting.

July 16, 1959

Oh Boy. (ABC). Bad quality kines of Britain's premiere rock'n'roll television show (produced by Jack Good) receive a short summer run in the U.S.

September 25, 1959

Death of *The Mickey Mouse Club.* Age: 4 years. Cause: Growing up.

---

cepted Connors as both a tough guy and a gentle father, and Crawford as a believable son, the plots lost their significance, the showdowns became just window dressing, and the show became a hit.

Crime shows, though not as prominent as Westerns, also continued their steady growth. Like Westerns, they occasionally provided high quality stories even as they attempted to snare audiences with off-beat gimmicks. CBS's *Markham* presented Ray Milland as still another rich dilettante detective in the *Thin Man* mold who was in the business just for kicks, though the network insisted that the series was different: Markham was an investigator, not a private eye. *Naked City* touted realism, both in its story line (the day-to-day routine of a police detective, played by James Franciscus) and setting (the series was filmed entirely on location in New York City). *Man with a Camera* featured Charles Bronson as a freelance photo-journalist and virtual Superman who personally took on tough guys and tackled fleeing criminals, just for the opportunity to "get a good picture." The fights were the high point of each episode because the series was pure, predictable formula. The first episode wasted the team of Bronson and Billy Jack-to-be Tom Laughlin in an uninspired story of a fighter asked to take a dive.

Traffic Court came to ABC after years on local Los Angeles television. The series took the concept of "dramatizing actual cases from the files of …" and brought it to the trivial world of moving violations. Edgar Allan Jones, an assistant law school dean at the University of California, portrayed the austere traffic court judge while amateur actors played the repentant souls who had double parked or let their licenses expire. Such intense legal drama was apparently very popular in Los Angeles for, at the time, L.A. viewers could watch, within the same week: *Traffic Court, Court Martial, Divorce Court, Juvenile Court, Youth Court, Night Court, Municipal Court,* and *Day in Court.*

Confession was another ABC find from the hustings (this time, Dallas). It also focused on the criminal element, though it followed a format that seemed designed to overstep the boundaries of good taste. Convicted criminals who were trying to reform were brought before a panel and subjected to intense public questioning designed to reveal the depth of their commitment to a new way of life. Host Jack Wyatt led the process that often originated from the county jail with some criminals appearing under guard as they faced the panel. Clergymen, lawyers, psychologists, psychiatrists, penologists, and sociologists conducted the questioning, which one critic described as a "public dissection."

One series that broke from these formulas, though, was dropped by its sponsor for being too controversial. Herb Brodkin's *Brenner* marked a drastic shift from 1950s TV tradition and presented policemen who were not always right and who sometimes found their actions indistinguishable from the criminals they pursued. Edward Binns (as Lieutenant Roy Brenner) and James Broderick (as his son) portrayed honest but fallible policemen attempting to sort out the differences between justice and the law. Brenner was responsible for keeping the other policemen in line, and his son helped him by working as an undercover agent in the police vice squad. The series, based on a 1958 *Playhouse 90* story, "Blue Men," was both fifteen years ahead of its time (anticipating the 1970s "Serpico") and also a return to the inside-outsider type in the crime genre. Though Lever Brothers withdrew as sponsor after *Brenner*'s brief run in the summer of 1959, CBS felt strongly enough about the series to bring it back the next few summers with well-written new episodes. Despite the quality at every level, *Brenner* never caught the public's fancy.

The season's most successful new private eye show was *Peter Gunn* (starring Craig Stevens), a triumph of style over substance. A jazzy theme by Henry Mancini provided a rich backdrop for the series as it trod the traditional turf of blackmail, business intrigue, and murder, but peppered the all-too-predictable adventures with fascinating characters. Gunn himself hung out at Mother's, a jazz nightclub run by a tough but understanding woman (played by Hope Emerson). His girlfriend Edie (Lola Albright) sang there, and his contacts, including police Lieutenant Jacoby (Herschel Bernardi), often met him there. Gunn appeared as a grown-up, cynical boy scout who understood human nature but somehow kept hoping for the best anyway, and his character mixed well with his surroundings. The show became a hit for NBC in its first season and lasted for three years, shifting to ABC for its final season after the ratings slipped a bit.

ABC, which for years had been looking for a new hit show or hit format to make it appear respectable, found the answer in 1959 by unlocking the secret of the Westerns. All three networks had frantically tried to determine what made Westerns so appealing to the American public throughout the decade. At first, executives and producers assumed the Western setting itself was the attraction, because it provided a conveniently noncontroversial stage for modern morality plays. Next, they used gimmicks in setting and paraphernalia to try to make a new show stand out from the others. They consistently overlooked an obvious but nevertheless vital element that lay at the heart of the most popular Westerns: the characters.

In the best Westerns, the heroes were not wooden demi-gods but well rounded and interesting people. Looking at its success in series such as *Maverick, Cheyenne,* and *Sugarfoot,* Warner Bros. made the connection. Stars of its Westerns had not been well-known figures with an already established audience. Many were studio contract players who were well matched with the right role. As a result, the characters portrayed by actors such as James Garner, Clint Walker, and Will Hutchins were themselves appealing and consequently they *became* stars in the intimate medium of television. If viewers liked the central characters and cared about what happened to them, they would keep returning to the series to find out. That same type of appeal had kept viewers interested in such television heroes as Lucy and Ricky and Charles Van Doren and, in that light, Paladin, Matt Dillon, Lucas McCain, and the Maverick brothers were merely the latest entries in a continuing cycle. If that was the appeal of the Westerns, then there was no reason to keep such a winning formula stuck out West in the 1880s. By retaining the appealing characteristics of such heroes as Bret Maverick, along with the frequent incidents of "action" (a television euphemism for fights and violence), the producers at Warner Bros. concluded that a hit show could be set in almost any time and any place. The theory was put to the test in October 1958 when Warner Bros. combined the nucleus of its hit Westerns with the setting from a not-so-different format, private eyes. The result was *77 Sunset Strip* and the birth of a new program form: action-adventure series.

77 Sunset Strip took action, humor, sex appeal, and a set of characters that gelled, presenting, in effect, a modern day Western. The first episode of the series was actually a ninety-minute movie reject, "Girl on the Run," in which private detective Stuart Bailey (Efrem Zimbalist, Jr.) tracked down and captured a murderer (played by Edward Byrnes) before marrying the pretty girl at the end. Some elements were changed for the television series itself which began the following week. Zimbalist was still private detective Stuart Bailey who operated an investigation business on the swank Sunset Strip, but he was no longer married and no longer alone at work. His business was a partnership with Jeff Spencer (Roger Smith) and they were assisted occasionally by Byrnes, who was no longer a murderer but rather their parking lot attendant, Gerald Lloyd Kookson III (better known as Kookie). Roscoe (Louis Quinn), the firm's junior partner (a former horse player who retained his unmistakable Brooklyn charm even in the aseptic world of Los Angeles), and Suzanne Fabray (Jacqueline Beer), their switchboard operator, provided additional color. The cast had all the necessary elements to make the show a hit. Smith and Zimbalist were the epitome of suave sophistication, both intelligent and quick-witted. Their office repartee was light and breezy, with the putdowns usually directed at Kookie and Roscoe. Naturally they could solve any case without help from the police, and they displayed a fierce independence riding the streets of Los Angeles. Suzanne added the necessary sex appeal for the men while Kookie connected with young women as a dreamboat hipster who struck a calculating cool pose simply by chewing gum and combing his hair. Byrnes even released a hit record-paean, "Kookie, Kookie, Lend Me Your Comb." The show started out very slowly but turned into a solid ratings winner by the spring.

The success of *77 Sunset Strip*, along with that of *Maverick, The Rifleman, The Real McCoys,* and *Walt Disney Presents* (the re-named *Disneyland*) gave ABC its best ratings in its history. The network had more shows in the top ten (four) than either CBS or NBC, and by the end of the season ABC found itself not that far behind NBC in a battle for second place. This was unparalleled success for the network that was usually buried deep in the cellar. By unlocking the secret of the action-adventure series, Warner Bros. won the undying friendship of the ABC network and its new president, Ollie Treyz. Singing "Kookie, Kookie, lend me your format," ABC turned over to the studio 30% of its prime time schedule to fill for the fall of 1959.

19. Adventures in Syndication

AT THE BEGINNING OF THE 1950s, the television networks and the Hollywood studios viewed each other as mortal enemies and consequently kept their operations separate. The studios saw television as an unwelcome intruder while the two major networks, CBS and NBC, insisted that they would not give up their direct control over TV programming as they had done with radio. As the decade drew to a close, though, a totally altered relationship existed: Warner Bros., Screen Gems (Columbia Pictures), Twentieth Century Fox, and not-so-minor independents such as Desilu, Four Star Productions, Ziv, Talent Associates, and Goodson-Todman produced almost everything on television while all three networks acted as mere conduits, retaining complete control over only sports and news. This shift in power took place as network chieftains who favored in-house production (such as NBC's Pat Weaver) were replaced by people who supported abdication of network control, primarily out of economic self-interest. It was cheaper to let outside agencies take the financial risks necessary in developing programs; network executives could then sit back and pick and choose from the finished products. At the same time, direct and sustained governmental pressure was also at work, and over the years the networks were forced to "voluntarily" relinquish more and more controls.

Though the federal government, through the FCC, was expressly forbidden by law from dealing with program content (unless it was obscene or libelous), there were many ways to get around the rule. The FCC had made the first major attempt to control programming with its unsuccessful ban on big money quiz shows in 1949, but throughout the 1950s it was Congress, rather than the commission, that sought to influence what went over the air. Beginning in 1951, a seemingly endless stream of hearings dealing with the possible detrimental effect of sex and violence on television occupied congressional attention. Despite numerous impassioned outcries at these hearings over the deteriorating morals of the nation, none of the investigators ever uncovered a dramatic outrage that could be pinned on the networks as an example of a blatant abuse of the public's trust. Even in criticizing programming, no one could explain what level of sex and violence was harmful, if any. So in the mid-1950s Congress turned instead to the field of anti-trust action and here the potential for success seemed higher.

In the 1940s, such governmental pressure had forced NBC to give up its Blue radio network (which then became ABC) and had broken the grip that the eight major film studios held over Hollywood. Testing the waters again, the government suggested that television might be helped immeasurably by breaking the control the three networks held over programming and cited some possible benefits. Broadcasters would no longer all have to appeal to the lowest common denominator. Instead, by allowing a greater number of program producers access to the market, the government would encourage specialization similar to what was then occurring in AM radio (stations catered to specific but differing tastes such as rock'n'roll, classical, and middle of the road music) and perhaps even develop additional competing networks. In reaction to the congressional trust-busters breathing down their necks, the networks, in the late 1950s, acted to forestall any such legislation by relinquishing some programming control on their own. However, as Hollywood took more control of television production through the 1950s, the level of quality and innovation did not increase; it dropped noticeably. Hollywood firms were even more cautious than the networks and they tended toward safe imitations and duplications of the film industry's classic grade-B staples.

The Hollywood studios could not really be blamed for failing to initiate any bold innovations because even the supplier of the greatest amount of network programming for the 1959–60 season, Warner Bros., produced only seven hours each week. Each program was one-seventh of its total television commitment, and there was little room for shows that were likely to meet viewer resistance by being different. Warner Bros. felt it was taking a big enough risk in the new season by making a major commitment to the one-hour action-adventure format for ABC. Until the previous few seasons, the only successful sixty-minute shows had been variety and drama presentations, and it was not until *Maverick* and *Cheyenne* that regular filmed adventure series dared to go this extra length. After the success of *77 Sunset Strip* in 1958–59, ABC was willing to gamble with more of the same, and Warners, with some trepidation, delivered the new product. At first, it appeared as if the network's gamble had failed. Each of the new action-adventure programs opened to blistering critical reviews and low ratings, but ABC held firm. *77 Sunset Strip* had also opened in a weak position, then slowly built its ratings, becoming a hit by spring. The network had learned that a sixty-minute program needed a slightly longer time to prove itself; besides, the public was still getting used to the action-adventure format. ABC's patience paid off, the numerous echoes of *77 Sunset Strip* caught on, and by spring ABC found itself in second place in the network ratings race for the first time.

Each of the three new Warner Bros. action-adventure programs followed the previous season's winning formula to a tee ("two parts private eye, one part cutie pie"), just as ABC wanted. *Bourbon Street Beat* ("77 Gumbo Strip") presented blackmail, murder, drug smuggling, dames, fights, and wisecracks in the French Quarter of New Orleans through the eyes of suave and sophisticated Cal Calhoun (Andrew Duggan) and Rex Randolph (Richard Long). The two were assisted by Ricky Nelson-cum-Kookie protégé Ken Madison (Van Williams) and their shapely secretary Melody Mercer (Arlene Howell). There was the prerequisite jazz theme that ran through each episode, but it did little to punch up the predictable action sequences. *Hawaiian Eye* ("77 Surfboard Strip") presented blackmail, murder, pineapple smuggling, fights, and dames with the palm trees, beaches, and tropical sun of the country's newest state as a backdrop. The crew of detectives (played by Anthony Eisley, Grant Williams, and Robert "Kookie" Conrad) went through the paces of solving crimes and admiring the scenery, with assistance from a beautiful nightspot singer (Connie Stevens) and a local-color taxicab driver (Poncie Ponce). It would have been undiplomatic to ignore the country's other new state, so *The Alaskans* ("77 Tundra Strip") presented blackmail, murder, gold prospecting, dames, fights, and wisecracks in the "beautiful but dangerous Ice Palace of the Northland" in the 1890s. A pair of prospectors, Reno McKee (Jeff York), a rugged cowpoke with gold on his mind, and the aptly-named Silky Harris (Roger Moore), teamed up with a beautiful saloon entertainer, Rocky Shaw (Dorothy Provine), in search of gold and adventure, but they never seemed quite right in the lusty Klondike setting. Moore was too much the epitome of British *sang-froid* and Provine appeared far too Victorian for the part of cafe thrush to the earthy miners. Though these new entries pulled in respectable ratings by the end of the season, for the most part they failed to provide any solid foundation to sustain audience interest. In many ways, they were formula television at its worst.

Just because a program followed a predictable, repetitious formula did not automatically mean it was bad. On the contrary, some excellent television entertainment had emerged from such unchanging stalwarts as *Perry Mason, Peter Gunn,* and *Maverick,* but each of those added something special to the formula. *Perry Mason* drew the viewer into an elaborate murder puzzle with a wide range of clues and suspects. *Peter Gunn* filled its routine detective adventures with off-beat characters and a rich musical undercurrent. *Maverick,* probably the best of the Warner Bros. productions, showcased very appealing characters, clever plots, and humor that was neither forced nor overbearing. *77 Sunset Strip* was near the quality of *Maverick,* supporting the action with appealing, witty characters and usually adequate scripts. The new action-adventure series, in contrast, failed at almost every level. The main characters were handsome but weak, the supporting casts wooden and lifeless, and the stories offered nothing to supplement the action. There were no clever puzzles, baffling mysteries, or intriguing situations: just interchangeable tales of murder, blackmail, smuggling, fights, and dames. Despite all the action, the programs were also generally bland and inoffensive, offering adventures that were so noncontroversial and timeless that they could have come from any of the hundreds of grade-B Hollywood adventure films produced since the 1920s. Perhaps all these weaknesses could have been overlooked if they turned up in only one or two programs, but with ABC devoting so much of its attention in the new season to action-adventure (from Warner Bros. and other studios) and developing more of the same for the future, the genre was being diluted and overextended while it was just beginning. There were too many series, too soon. The only thing that distinguished one from another was the so-called exotic setting (Alaska, Hawaii, New Orleans). Though they were first-run network series, the programs seemed designed more for future syndication than current network programming.

Devising the perfect show for syndication was a minor artform and Ziv had perfected it over the years. When the networks had maintained more control over programs, Ziv, as an independent production company, had been practically locked out of the network schedules, so it began producing shows that could be sold individually to local stations. Such a strategy required programs that could be repeated indefinitely without appearing dated. Because local stations were even more reticent than the networks to take on a series that smacked of controversy, stories had to be safe and inoffensive as well. Though Ziv and other independent film producers eventually won a toe-hold in the network schedules by the mid-1950s, a program's potential for syndication remained their paramount concern. Filmed series cost a great deal to produce and, though a prudent producer could usually break even after a few years on the network, the real profit rested in years of local reruns in which the only new cost was duplicating the episodes. When the major studios ventured into network television, the potential profit in this rerun market did not go unnoticed, and in the late 1950s many network-filmed series (especially the sitcoms, Westerns, and action-adventure shows) began to take on the unmistakable look of syndication. The season's quintessential example of this trend was *Adventures in Paradise* from Twentieth Century Fox. The series was set in the alluring South Pacific, following the adventures of Adam Troy (Gardner McKay), the handsome, pipe-smoking skipper of the schooner *Tiki,* who cruised the ocean and visited countless island ports. The stories were negligible, Troy's character was emotionless and nondescript, and the supporting cast irrelevant. Nonetheless, the series was perfect for syndication since it was really nothing more than a travelogue through a swank tropical paradise. Though it remained on ABC for only three seasons, *Adventures in Paradise* was still being rerun in syndication through the 1970s. Of course, there were also high quality series worthy of continued off network reruns. One such program was ABC's most successful new action series for 1959–60, *The Untouchables.*

An amazing wave of nostalgia for the prohibition era surfaced in 1959 on television, beginning with the *Playhouse 90* presentation of "Seven Against the Wall" (produced by John Houseman). It was a realistic recreation of the Al Capone gang's St. Valentine's Day Massacre in Chicago. The realism was accentuated by using a well-known newscaster, Eric Sevareid, as narrator. A few months later, NBC began a short-lived series called *The Lawless Years,* which was based on the real-life exploits of Barney Ruditsky, a New York City plainclothes detective in the 1920s who worked to infiltrate and expose racketeers and bootleggers. The most successful exploitation of the era came in the spring with a two-part story on CBS's *Desilu Playhouse,* "The Untouchables," which was based on a book written by Eliot Ness, the federal agent who nailed Al Capone. Robert Stack portrayed the no-nonsense lawman, Neville Brand played Capone, and Bruce Gordon was Frank Nitti, Capone's assistant. Borrowing *Playhouse 90's* realistic touch of using a well-known newscaster to tell the story, Walter Winchell supplied the dramatic narration. The two episodes were favorably received and the concept was developed into a weekly series. In the fall of 1959, *The Untouchables* premiered, surprisingly, on ABC—a concrete example of the network's growing strength and credibility.

The Untouchables, produced by Quinn Martin, took real events and real characters and incorporated them into interesting and

	7:00	7:30	8:00	8:30	9:00	9:30	10:00	10:30	
M	local	Cheyenne / #Shirley Temple's Storybook		BOURBON STREET BEAT		ADVENTURES IN PARADISE		Man With A Camera		**ABC**
O	local	Masquerade Party	The Texan	Father Knows Best	Danny Thomas Show	Ann Sothern Show	HENNESEY	DuPONT SHOW WITH JUNE ALLYSON	**CBS**
N	local	Richard Diamond, Private Detective	LOVE AND MARRIAGE	Tales Of Wells Fargo	Peter Gunn	Alcoa-Goodyear Theater	Steve Allen Plymouth Show		**NBC**
T	local	Sugarfoot / Bronco		Life And Legend Of Wyatt Earp	The Rifleman	PHILIP MARLOWE	Alcoa Presents: One Step Beyond	Keep Talking	**ABC**
U	local		DENNIS O'KEEFE SHOW	THE MANY LOVES OF DOBIE GILLIS	TIGHTROPE	Red Skelton Show	Garry Moore Show		**CBS**
E	local	LARAMIE		FIBBER McGEE AND MOLLY	Arthur Murray Party	FORD STAR TIME		local	**NBC**
W	local	Court Of Last Resort	CHARLIE WEAVER'S HOBBY LOBBY	Adventures Of Ozzie And Harriet	HAWAIIAN EYE		Wednesday Night Fights		**ABC**
E	local	The Lineup		MEN INTO SPACE	The Millionaire	I've Got A Secret	U.S. Steel Hour / Armstrong Circle Theater		**CBS**
D	local	Wagon Train		The Price Is Right	Perry Como's Kraft Music Hall		This Is Your Life	WICHITA TOWN	**NBC**
T	local	Gale Storm Show	Donna Reed Show	The Real McCoys	Pat Boone Chevy Showroom	THE UNTOUCHABLES		TAKE A GOOD LOOK	**ABC**
H	local	To Tell The Truth	BETTY HUTTON SHOW	JOHNNY RINGO	Dick Powell's Zane Grey Theater	Playhouse 90			**CBS**
R	local	LAW OF THE PLAINSMAN	Bat Masterson	JOHNNY STACCATO	Bachelor Father	Tennessee Ernie Ford Show	You Bet Your Life	Lawless Years	**NBC**
F	local	Walt Disney Presents		MAN FROM BLACKHAWK	77 Sunset Strip		ROBERT TAYLOR IN THE DETECTIVES	Black Saddle	**ABC**
R	local	Rawhide		HOTEL DePAREE	Westinghouse Desilu Playhouse / #Lucille Ball & Desi Arnaz Show		THE TWILIGHT ZONE	Person To Person	**CBS**
I	local	People Are Funny	THE TROUBLESHOOTERS	Bell Telephone Hour / NBC SPECIALS		M Squad	Gillette Cavalcade Of Sports	Jackpot Bowling	**NBC**
S	local	The Dick Clark Beech-Nut Show	JOHN GUNTHER'S HIGH ROAD	Leave It To Beaver	Lawrence Welk's Dodge Dancing Party		Jubilee U.S.A.		**ABC**
A	local	Perry Mason		Wanted: Dead Or Alive	MR. LUCKY	Have Gun, Will Travel	Gunsmoke	Markham	**CBS**
T	local	BONANZA		THE MAN AND THE CHALLENGE	THE DEPUTY	FIVE FINGERS		It Could Be You	**NBC**
S	Colt .45	Maverick		Lawman	THE REBEL	THE ALASKANS		DICK CLARK'S WORLD OF TALENT	**ABC**
U	Lassie	DENNIS THE MENACE	Ed Sullivan Show		General Electric Theater	Alfred Hitchcock Presents	George Gobel Show / Jack Benny Program	What's My Line	**CBS**
N	RIVERBOAT		SUNDAY SHOWCASE		Dinah Shore Chevy Show		Loretta Young Show	local	**NBC**

entering stories. It was a good gangster show, depicting a violent era populated by cruel men who often could be overcome only by violence. Occasionally the writers were not completely faithful to history, but the effective presentation of the struggle between the "untouchable" lawmen (led by Eliot Ness) and the Capone mob (led by Frank Nitti) usually rendered the minor inaccuracies unimportant. The program was merely a re-creation of events in a bygone era, not a strict history lecture, and it was necessary to have clearly defined good guys and bad guys as well as innocent and not-so-innocent bystanders.

Nonetheless, *The Untouchables* upset many Italian-Americans because it appeared at a time when revelations about the Mafia were making front page news. They felt the program merely served to confirm a feeling among Americans that all gangsters were Italians and all Italians were gangsters. In reality, the Capone mob was almost completely Italian, so Quinn Martin had given the characters Italian names and used actors who could "look Italian" in these roles. In doing so, he had violated TV's unspoken ban on presenting identifiable ethnic personalities, a volatile topic in American broadcasting since World War II. Industry reluctance to showcase ethnicity had all but eliminated the ethnic school of humor in the early 1950s and ABC was sensitive to criticism of its new show. In response, the network downplayed the Italianness of the gangsters in the show's second season and had Martin add Italian agents to Ness's crew and non-Italian thugs to the Nitti mob (in a prohibition era equivalent of affirmative action). Even with

these modifications, the series still retained a strong flavor of the era.

The Untouchables was also criticized for being too violent with its abundance of gang war shoot-outs and ambushes by federal agents. Though frequent and intense, the violence was never gratuitous, rarely gruesome or morbid, and usually necessary to the story. After all, the program was dealing with gangsters in an era when such dramatic confrontations frequently took place. If Martin had sanitized the subject matter, he would have seriously undercut the very premise of the show and left it virtually indistinguishable from every other TV crime series. Instead, *The Untouchables* stood apart with its strong characters, good scripts, and very realistic setting. Though by no means perfect (over time, the nearly hysterical Walter Winchell narration became rather humorous), the series managed to deliver nearly everything an action-adventure show was supposed to.

The criticism of the violent tendencies and historical inaccuracies in *The Untouchables* was, in many cases, just fresh ammunition for people convinced that television was somehow responsible for most of the country's ills. In the fall of 1959, such nit-picking became unnecessary as the long percolating quiz show scandal provided them with the long sought "smoking gun" to clinch the argument against television.

The special grand jury investigating the charges against the quiz shows had met in secret throughout the winter and spring of 1959, so the entire matter had slipped out of sight for a while. On June

10, after hearing 150 hours of testimony from 200 witnesses concerning six quiz shows (many of which were, by that time, no longer on the air), the grand jury finished its work and handed over a 12,000 word report to Judge Mitchell D. Schweitzer. The grand jury's findings did not constitute an indictment, but rather a "presentment," that is, a report calling attention to illegal acts without holding specific people responsible. Because no trial would result from the presentment, Judge Schweitzer felt that the document would damage those named in it by not providing an opportunity for them to publicly clear their names, so he promptly sealed and impounded the report. Members of the grand jury pointed out that they had specifically avoided naming individuals and that no harm would occur. Most of the summer was spent arguing whether the report should be made public or not, and in August a compromise was reached. Judge Schweitzer agreed to show the minutes of the grand jury proceedings to Representative Oren D. Harris, the chairman of the House Committee on Interstate and Foreign Commerce, who had announced that his committee would hold public hearings on the quiz show question beginning October 6. Releasing the minutes was almost as good as showing the committee the actual report, so the matter was put to rest (the report never was made public) and attention shifted to Harris's committee.

Harris had bedeviled the broadcast industry for years with antitrust allegations and inconclusive hearings on sex and violence. With the quiz show investigation, he felt he had a clear-cut issue to use against television, even though there was doubt that concrete criminal charges could be leveled against anyone. After months of research, lawyers on both sides had been unable to uncover any law that quiz show riggers might have broken, so the committee hearings were merely a maneuver to put the matter before the public. It was felt that outraged viewers would demand changes in the laws regulating broadcasting after learning the depth of the quiz show rigging first hand.

The first witnesses before the committee were former *Twenty-One* contestants James Snodgrass and Herbert Stempel. Snodgrass offered his proof that he had been supplied answers in advance (the sealed registered letters that he had mailed to himself with the information) and Stempel claimed he had been told when to lose to Charles Van Doren (though he offered no hard evidence). A breakthrough occurred on October 9 when Dan Enright (one-half of the team that created *Twenty-One* and other top NBC quizzes) publicly acknowledged that "controls" (his euphemism for rigging) had been "a practice for many many years" on both his quiz shows and those of many others. The nighttime version of *Tic Tac Dough,* he revealed, was rigged 75% of the time. The daytime version was not fixed because it was not as vital to attract a large audience at that hour. "Deception is not necessarily bad," he explained. "It's practiced in everyday life ... it should be measured in terms of the hurt it inflicted on people." He said that the whole point of rigging was to ensure a dramatic flow of events while making certain that characters who appealed to the public became the returning champions. After Enright's confession, other people involved with other shows came forward to echo the same line. They had coached contestants merely to ensure good ratings. Hal March, emcee of *The $64,000 Question,* said: It got to the point where there were just too many quiz programs. Ratings began to drop and some producers turned to rigging to make sure the shows kept their audience. They just couldn't afford to lose their sponsors.

Despite the attempts to couch quiz show controls as just a necessary business practice, the admissions of rigging suggested that the situation was much worse and more widespread than had been previously suspected. More important, many of the contestants, including Charles Van Doren, had testified under oath that such rigging had not taken place. That exposed them to charges of perjury. Van Doren, then a regular *Today* show staff member, had even issued another complete denial at the start of the committee's hearings, then vanished. Harris issued a subpoena for Van Doren, but for days the former quiz kid could not be found. On October 13, he reappeared in New York City, saying that he had been in New England on vacation and had known nothing of the subpoena, but was ready to testify. By then, the quiz show question seemed to be turning itself into a national self-examination in which the country's self-esteem was at stake. Even President Eisenhower announced that he was worried over the disclosures and was instructing Attorney General William Rogers to look into the matter.

On November 2, 1959, Charles Van Doren, thirty-three-year-old symbol of American ingenuity, confessed he had been living a lie since 1956, saying "I would give almost anything I have to reverse the course of my life in the last three years." From the very beginning, he said, *Twenty-One* producer Albert Freedman had coached him in both answers and demeanor. Freedman had said that the then-current champion, Herbert Stempel, was hurting the show by being too successful and unpopular with the audience. Van Doren's job was to depose him. Van Doren said he asked to compete honestly, but Freedman replied that was impossible. Such things had to be prearranged. Besides, the methods didn't matter. The important thing was that Van Doren would be promoting the image of the intellectual before the nation. Van Doren said that Freedman then "instructed me how to answer the questions, to pause before certain of the answers, to skip certain parts and return to them, to hesitate to build up suspense, and so forth ... He gave me a script to memorize and before the program he took back the script and rehearsed me in my part."

Van Doren explained that soon after he became champ, and an unexpectedly popular contestant with the public, he asked Freedman many times to let him go; in January 1957 the producer agreed, but said it would take some time to arrange. In February, Van Doren faced Vivienne Nearing who he, was told, would be his final opponent. So that every possible twist could be milked for the maximum effect, the final contest was arranged to end in a succession of dramatic ties. On February 18, Van Doren and Nearing were tied. On February 25, they were locked in two more ties, and then the program took a one-week break while the nation held its breath. On March 11, Van Doren was told he would lose that night and was not given any of the answers. In a perverse twist of fate, he was honestly stumped by the first question directed to him and could not identify the current king of Belgium (a relatively simple question).

Van Doren confessed that he had been surprised by the public's warm and enthusiastic response to him, but took advantage of it with the feeling that he was "promoting the intellectual life." When the grand jury called him in on January 14, 1959, he, like the other contestants, lied to protect himself, his new-found friends, and his own professional image. They had even been coached again, this time in their testimony. When he saw the stonewall strategy coming apart, he ran to New England for some serious soul searching, and decided to tell the truth when he returned.

As a measure of the high regard Van Doren was held in, Representative Harris and other members of the committee responded to the lengthy testimony with effusive praise for the newly repentant sinner. He was commended for his fortitude and forthrightness in his soul-searching statement. Only Representative Steven Derounian of New York disagreed, observing: "I don't think an adult of your intelligence should be commended for telling the truth." It was this view that took hold. Columbia University fired Van Doren

October 12, 1959

Play of the Week. David Susskind brings the endangered species of drama anthologies to syndication. This weekly two-hour videotaped program is quickly hailed by critics as being as good as, if not better than, the few drama showcases remaining on the networks.

October 26, 1959

CBS Reports. (CBS). To counter the embarrassing quiz scandal, CBS basks in the desperately needed praise and prestige from "Biography of a Missile," the first presentation of its new documentary series from Ed Murrow and Fred Friendly.

November 17, 1959

Radio's payola scandal rolls in right behind the quizzes. ABC's Dick Clark is given an ultimatum by congressional investigators: Get rid of outside music interests, or else. Clark divests.

November 19, 1959

Rocky and His Friends. (ABC). Jay Ward and Bill Scott put together a classy package of tongue-in-cheek original cartoons, including: the adventures in history of a genius dog and his pet boy (Peabody and Sherman); twists on familiar fairy tales (narrated by Edward Everett Horton); and the cliffhanger escapades of Rocky the flying squirrel, Bullwinkle the moose, and their arch-enemies Boris Badenov and Natasha Fatale. First up: Bullwinkle discovers a super rocket fuel while baking.

November 20, 1959

Alan Freed is fired from WABC radio, due to his payola problems. Eight days later, he is fired from WNEW-TV.

December 8, 1959

Quiz show casualties reach the top: Louis G. Cowan is out, James Aubrey is in, at CBS.

---

from his assistant professorship, and NBC fired him from its staff. *New York Times* TV critic Jack Gould observed that "apparently many witnesses felt that going before a grand jury was just another little quiz game to which the answers could be rigged in advance." The anxious public, intensely interested in hearing Van Doren's side of the story, found the details of the preprogram coaching particularly galling. If Van Doren had really wanted to stop the charade, he could have deliberately answered incorrectly at any time. What's more, not only had Van Doren cheated, but all those nervous tics that viewers had identified with as he struggled to victory had been nothing more than acting craft.

Following the Van Doren testimony, a parade of other contestants, many from the Louis G. Cowan-inspired CBS quizzers, came forward and bared their souls. Each one added to the disillusioning revelations about some of America's television heroes. Staff assistants from *The $64,000 Question* revealed that they had ready access (as "editors") to the safe deposit box containing each week's questions, and that they had regularly used the privilege in order to prep contestants. Band leader Xavier Cugat confessed that he had received help in his appearance on *The $64,000 Challenge.* Thirteen-year-old actress Patty Duke, who had gone from successful appearances on *The $64,000 Challenge* to a Broadway role as Helen Keller in "The Miracle Worker," admitted that she had been merely acting on the quiz show as well. To many this seemed the lowest blow of all. Quiz show producers had even exploited an impressionable child. President Eisenhower said he was bewildered and dismayed by the extent of the quiz rigging, but preferred to view it as a latter day equivalent to the 1919 Black Sox World Series scandal, stating, "It doesn't reflect a general debasement of moral standards."

Though the extensive public hearings and revelations disappointed and outraged many, the only crime committed in the entire matter turned out to be lying to the grand jury. Most of the producers cooperated with the district attorney and copped pleas. In October 1960, twenty contestants from *Twenty-One* and *Tic Tac Dough,* including Charles Van Doren and Vivienne Nearing, were indicted for second degree perjury. For more than a year their cases were dragged through the courts, and nearly half decided to plead guilty. On January 17, 1962, Van Doren and the nine other remaining contestants pleaded guilty before Judge Edward Breslin, who suspended their sentences because "the humiliation was evident in their faces."

To the television industry, however, the revelations came as a major body blow to its prestige. After years of very vocal but disorganized carping, critics, both in and out of government, were handed more than enough ammunition to use in their efforts to alter the laws governing broadcasting. Viewers felt betrayed by the medium they had placed so much trust in. Television programmers had willingly manipulated their emotions and exploited their loyalties in order to pump up ratings and satisfy the sponsors, so there was very little public sympathy for the broadcasters. CBS president Frank Stanton, realizing the need for bold action to forestall any potentially devastating legislation, saved the situation by immediately canceling the only three big money quiz shows left on CBS (*The Big Payoff, Top Dollar,* and *Name that Tune*) while the quiz hearings were still in progress. In the process, he wrote off $15 million per year in ad revenue. Going beyond that, Stanton told a convention of news directors in New Orleans that, in the future, "we and we alone will decide not only *what* is to appear on CBS, but *how* it is to appear. We accept the responsibility for content and quality and for assuring the American people that what they see and hear on CBS is exactly what it purports to be."

Stanton's statement and quick action drew praise from the public, but Albert Freedman, the producer of *Twenty-One,* felt otherwise and argued that there was no reason to treat quiz shows differently from other entertainment programs, saying, "In the field of TV programming, saturated with murder and violence, it is my opinion that the quiz shows, as entertainment, were a breath of fresh air ... it is about time the television industry stopped apologizing for its existence and began to fight back. It should insist that programming be recognized and judged as entertainment and entertainment only."

It was only show business, he said, the same as magicians, Hollywood sets, radio sound effects, Western shoot-outs, movie stuntmen, TV lawyers' perfect records, and ghost writers for politicians. All of these did not present reality, but rather an approximation and re-creation of reality. The real crime perpetrated was the attempt to convince the public that the quiz shows were not approximations of reality, but living breathing reality itself. "Our only error was that we were too successful," he said. "The stakes were too high, and the quiz winners fused themselves into the home life and the hopes and aspirations of the viewers."

Stanton's firm action and brave announcements contrasted favorably with the self-serving statements of innocence that came from NBC and the "you can't blame us" attitude at ABC. By accepting both blame and responsibility, Stanton diffused much of the antipathy felt toward the networks. Legislation was eventually passed in reaction to the quiz scandal, but it was limited to the very narrow area of making it a crime to fix a quiz show. At the same time, CBS began a drive to upgrade the overall image of network television with positive reforms and programs that emphasized the passing of the quiz show era. The network reestablished at least partial control over programming; the old Edward R. Murrow *See It Now* series was reactivated under a new name, *CBS Reports;* and the ailing Louis Cowan, father of the big money quiz shows, was eased out of his position as head of the television network and replaced by James T. Aubrey.

Just as TV executives began the task of restoring their tarnished credibility, charges of industry misconduct in another area surfaced. Radio disc jockeys and music entrepreneurs were accused of accepting payola (bribes) in return for the exposure and promotion of individual recording artists. Once again, the illusion of popular entertainment was tainted by vested interests and personal gain. Investigations into the radio payola charges touched many people but quickly focused on the two titans of rock'n'roll, Dick Clark and Alan Freed, both of whom had far-reaching business interests ranging from radio and television programs to connections with record companies and song promoters. The two were acknowledged to be very influential in directing teen tastes throughout the country and this raised suspicions about their motives. Both were called before congressional committees to face heavy questioning, and the grilling left Clark shaken but Freed severely wounded. Though he insisted he had done nothing wrong, Freed was fired from his local New York radio and TV slots. (He died a few years later on the West Coast.) Clark quickly divorced himself from his outside business interests in order to remove even the possible impression of conflicts and he managed to keep his two ABC television shows. The careers of both men, however, illustrated the chief by-product of both the payola and quiz scandals: a tremendous increase in the level of fear in the broadcasting world. Even the slightest hint of controversy had to be avoided at all costs.

With TV blackened by the quizzes and radio damaged by payola, both tried desperately to win back the public's trust. Safe, reassuring programming became vital. Experimentation was out. Even a television program that was a critical and ratings winner, *Mr. Lucky,* found itself in trouble over its moral tone. The series, which had premiered in the fall, followed the adventures of a suave gambler, Mr. Lucky (John Vivyan), who operated his own casino aboard his yacht, the *Fortuna.* Lucky and his Latin sidekick Andamo (Ross Martin) cruised along the Pacific coast facing an assortment of odd-ball gamblers, corrupt Latin American dictators, and enticing females, while accompanied by rich Henry Mancini mood music. When the quiz scandals erupted, the sponsor demanded that Lucky stop gambling. He was corrupting the public morals (that is, he was providing bad product identification for the sponsor). It was not enough that the series stressed the personal integrity of Lucky and Andamo while emphasizing their efforts to keep the operation honest. The idea of a leading man running a floating crap game was too much to bear. So Lucky and Andamo transformed the *Fortuna* from a casino to a restaurant. How the sponsor expected dramatic tension to develop in a floating deli was never revealed because *Mr. Lucky* was soon canceled anyway. In this atmosphere of fear, *Mr. Lucky* earned the dubious distinction of being one of the highest rated shows to be axed in years. More and more, even sizable minorities or mildly esoteric tastes were being ignored in favor of safe, inoffensive formats.

Though tranquility was the new cornerstone of prime time entertainment, the networks did sharply increase the number of news and public affairs shows. They turned to them and hoped that the public would be impressed and forgive the lapses in taste of the quiz show era. This revival of informational programming marked a clear-cut shift of priorities because those same shows had been deliberately cut back by all the networks in favor of cheaper, flashier commercial fare since the middle of the 1950s.

CBS was the first to act, bringing *CBS Reports* to prime time even before the quiz scandal reached its peak. The floating hour-long documentary series, produced by Ed Murrow and Fred Friendly, presented high quality programs and managed to attract the support of sponsors, who were also interested in projecting a more positive image. Among the reports in the program's first season were: "Biography of a Missile" (the development of a new missile, the *Juno 2*, from design to launch); "Who Speaks for the South?" (both sides of the integration issue told by the people directly involved); "Trujillo, Portrait of a Dictator" (a look at the controversial Dominican leader who seemed headed for trouble; he was, in fact, assassinated the next year); and "Lippmann on Leadership" (the first television appearance by noted columnist Walter Lippmann).

January 3, 1960
  Sunday Sports Spectacular. (CBS). A Sunday afternoon experiment: The first attempt to offer a variety of less familiar sporting events, such as rodeo and stock car racing, on a weekly basis.

January 21, 1960
  CBS cuts *Playhouse 90* loose, lets it float. The series is quietly killed in 1961.

February 11, 1960
  Jack Paar walks out on his late night NBC show after a network censor nixes a somewhat randy bathroom joke. After fuming awhile, Paar returns March 7 and levels a searing blast at the newspaper columnists that criticized him about the incident.

April 1, 1960
  Television's foremost couple, Lucille Ball and Desi Arnaz, make their final appearance together in "Lucy Meets the Moustache" (with guest Ernie Kovacs). One month later, their divorce becomes final.

April 5, 1960
  Worthington Miner, last of NBC, replaces David Susskind as executive producer of *Play of the Week.*

May 12, 1960
  Frank Sinatra, in his fourth and final ABC special for the season, presents the return to television of Elvis Presley, who has just completed a stint in the Army. The Voice and the Pelvis duet on "Love Me Tender" and "Witchcraft."

June 24, 1960
  Death of *Gillette Cavalcade of Sports.* Age: 16 years. Cause: Bad punches.

July 31, 1960
  On the NBC *Chevy Mystery Show* anthology episode "Enough Rope," writers Richard Levinson and William Link introduce their detective character of Lieutenant Columbo (played by Bert Freed).

September 24, 1960
  Death of *Howdy Doody.* Age: 13 years. The decade is over. "Goodbye kids."

Shortly after the quiz scandal revelations, NBC also moved to boost its corporate image and offered *World Wide 60* as its public affairs showcase. Hosted by Frank McGee, the program occasionally turned out hard-hitting material such as "The Winds of Change" (an analysis of the changing situation in black Africa) and a look at Cuba, one year after Castro assumed power. Usually, though, it tended toward either well-produced travelogue type features (such as visiting scientists at the South Pole) or soft mood pieces such as "The Living End" (on old age). The network's main cultural drive, however, had actually begun in the fall with two of NBC's traditional strengths, class variety and live drama. *Sunday Showcase,* headed by Robert Alan Aurthur, featured dramas such as "What Makes Sammy Run" and "The American" (the story of Ira Hayes, played by Lee Marvin), as well as high class variety presentations such as "Give My Regards to Broadway" with Jimmy Durante and Ray Bolger. Another series, *Ford Star Time,* also mixed drama with its main strength, variety, and produced "Turn of the Screw," "The Jazz Singer" (Jerry Lewis re-creating the 1927 film classic), and a unique television sing-along, led by popular recording artist Mitch Miller. Despite these noble efforts to upgrade the quality of American television (and the networks' own public image), the 1959–60 season marked a significant, symbolic loss for serious television drama.

In the fall, CBS's *Playhouse 90* was reduced to an every-other-week feature alternating with *The Big Party,* a free swinging (actually scripted) gathering "live from New York City" that was filled with inveterate scene stealers and glittery showbiz folks (such as Rock Hudson, Eva Gabor, Sammy Davis, Jr., Carol Channing) ready to plug their latest song or film. This insipid plugfest was quietly put to sleep in January and, at the same time, *Playhouse 90* lost its regular Thursday night slot and became a floating special.

The era of regularly scheduled, large scale drama anthologies had passed. Even the once heated confrontations over controversial scripts had settled into a well-worn and hollow routine. CBS postponed the production of a Rod Serling play about Warsaw's Jewish ghetto, "In the Presence of Mine Enemies," (originally scheduled for presentation at the beginning of the season) when three sponsors objected, saying simply that the network had promised to get away from such depressing themes. There was not much of a fight and the story eventually aired on May 18 as one of *Playhouse 90*'s irregularly scheduled special broadcasts. Fittingly, the play was superficial, pretentious, and not worth squabbling over. (Its only memorable feature was a performance by Robert Redford as a young, sensitive Nazi.) Serling himself seemed to have written off TV drama showcases as a lost cause anyway, devoting his efforts instead to a new half-hour filmed series that premiered on CBS that fall, *The Twilight Zone.* He explained his transition to *Variety,* saying, "I'm tired of fighting the frustrated fights, copping pleas, fighting for points … in any case, the half-hour form is a fact of life, and as long as we have to live with it, we might as well try and do something meaningful in it. Even if they fail, I think my shows will be better than *My Little Margie.*"

Serling acted as executive producer, host, and frequent writer for *The Twilight Zone,* a suspense anthology similar to *Alfred Hitchcock Presents.* Both series presented "stories with a twist," but while Hitchcock's usually followed an O. Henry-ish style of trick ending, Serling's focused on events that often could not be explained at all. Many of the tales drew on science fiction themes, a number were genuinely amusing, and a few were actually scary. Though it never became a runaway hit, the series won a few Emmys and continued for five seasons (expanding to a full hour for one), maintaining Serling's high standards for the entire run.

Without a doubt, the provocative and engrossing tales were very much better than *My Little Margie.*

Serling's move to a weekly half-hour series was his acknowledgment that, for the most part, the public preferred that form. Occasionally a special might stir viewer interest, but inevitably the audience would return to familiar weekly series. In the 1959–60 season, Westerns continued to dominate this form, though as the season progressed their popularity seemed to be leveling off. At the start of the season, six of television's top ten program were Westerns but, by spring, the number had dropped to four of the top fifteen. Though there were more new Westerns in September than any other program format, most seemed content to rely on one obvious hook to snare viewers and so broke no new ground. *Tate* was about a one-armed sheriff. *Law of the Plainsman* featured a U.S. marshal who was a Harvard-educated Apache Indian. *The Rebel* was Johnny Yuma (Nick Adams), a troubled wanderer and former Confederate soldier. *Riverboat* was a floating *Wagon Train,* starring Darren McGavin and TV newcomer Burt Reynolds. *The Deputy* featured occasional appearances by Henry Fonda. Only two of the new series lasted more than a few years and they used the most unusual gimmick of all. The heroes in both *Laramie* and *Bonanza* worked on a ranch—something cowboys really did!

Laramie was competent but unexciting, while *Bonanza* was an epic family drama that relied on its four male leads, joined by frequent guest stars, to carry the program's workload. Former Canadian newscaster Lorne Greene played Ben Cartwright, father of three sons by three different wives. This was the reason, apparently, that Adam (Pernell Roberts), Hoss (Dan Blocker), and Little Joe (Michael Landon) had such different personalities. They constantly engaged in excessive fraternal scraps, but when the chips were down, father and sons clung together to protect the family name and family spread, the Ponderosa, from corrupt and thieving outsiders. As owners of a huge ranch in Nevada, the members of the Cartwright clan were required to make frequent business trips to neighboring towns, and to take an intense interest in any local scheme or development that might affect them. Such a wide open format allowed a great range of plots and the opportunity for individual guest stars to shine. It also permitted great expanses of gorgeous full color outdoor scenery, and this had a surprising effect on color TV set sales. NBC (the only network still pushing color) had assumed all along that variety spectaculars (live or on tape) would provide the motivation for the purchase of the expensive color sets, but dealers reported that *Bonanza,* one of the few color filmed series, had brought more people into the stores than years of such live fare. This was the first good news color manufacturers had heard in years, though even with this special attraction *Bonanza* was not a smash hit in its first season. Only after a few years and several time shifts did it build up a loyal audience that followed it for nearly fourteen years.

The most successful new show of the 1959–60 season was not a Western, but rather an unpretentious sitcom, *Dennis the Menace.* As in the popular comic strip the series was based on, Dennis perpetually bedeviled both his parents and his neighbor, Mr. Wilson, as he displayed his natural curiosity and affinity for mischief. Six-year-old Jay North played Dennis as a normal, believable kid in the *Leave It to Beaver* tradition, facing a world filled with incomprehensible adults.

One of the few 1950s sitcoms to deal with teenagers facing a bedeviling world also premiered in the fall, though unlike *Dennis* the show made no pretense at dealing with real characters. *The Many Loves of Dobie Gillis* was based on caricature and exaggerated situations that were handled with the comic timing and wit of such TV classics as *I Love Lucy.* The characters were funny, the scripts believable (in the context of their own world), and the series emerged as an effective but affectionate lampoon of middle class teenage life in the 1950s, displaying remarkable insight into an era that was still in progress.

Dwayne Hickman played the perpetually heartstruck Dobie Gillis, straight and clean-cut outside, but slightly wacko inside. Dobie had no gripes with society; all he wanted was women and money. He was constantly frustrated in the pursuit of both and, in George Burns-style asides to the audience, he tried to figure out just what had gone wrong with his latest scheme. His best friend and "good buddy," Maynard (Bob Denver), was a sharp contrast to Dobie's own image as a classic straight middle class teen. Maynard was a beatnik. He talked in jive, had a beard, wore old clothes, and did not seem to want anything out of life, especially a job (the very mention of work made Maynard jump). Besides fulfilling the age-old requirements for a comical leading man's best friend, Maynard G. Krebs (the *G*, he explained, stood for "William") marked the first regular TV appearance of a beatnik as an unconventional but normal and sensitive person beneath his garb and gab. (Before this, beatniks were usually presented as sadistically insane criminals that were subdued by colorless, methodical policemen.) Dobie and Maynard balanced each other perfectly and provided a strong base for their comic world.

The show's supporting cast was equally colorful. Herbert T. Gillis (Frank Faylen), Dobie's father, was a self-made man, the owner of the Gillis Grocery Store. He was an acceptably adult businessman who was obviously just off-beat enough to have fathered a boy such as Dobie. Zelda Gilroy (Sheila James) was the short, plain girl in love with Dobie, to no avail, since he was always pining for classic beauties such as Thalia Menninger (Tuesday Weld). Both Zelda and Thalia were much more intelligent than most TV females of the time; both knew what they wanted and what they did not want. Zelda wanted Dobie and Thalia wanted lots of money. In Dobie's world, there was also someone who had "lots of money," the spoiled Chatsworth Osborne, Jr. (Stephen Franken), whose family fortune represented opulent excess at its best. Neither Chatsworth nor his widowed mother was ashamed of the Osborne fortune (they rather enjoyed it) and though the series ridiculed their elitist manner and ideals (both matriarch and scion spoke in hilariously exaggerated Harvard accents), it never portrayed them as ogres. Rounding out the supporting cast were two minor characters that made occasional, but effective, appearances: Duncan Krebs (Michael J. Pollard) was Maynard's spacey cousin, and Milton Armitage (Warren Beatty) was a stuffy but talented rival for Thalia's attention. In his own way, though, Armitage could be as unconventional as the rest. In a school play, he once performed a hilarious take-off of Marlon Brando's interpretation of Stanley Kowalski in "A Streetcar Named Desire." All of these characters served to illustrate the pleasures and the frustrations Dobie faced in trying to grow up as a typical teenager of the 1950s.

This decade, which later gained such an identifiable (if not always accurate) character in retrospect, did not really end in December 1959. The moods, trends, and attitudes of the 1950s petered out over the next four years, during the administration of President John F. Kennedy. Nevertheless, three events took place in the 1959–60 season that seemed to symbolically mark a turning point in television culture and its passage into a new era.

In 1959, George Reeves, who had appeared as the man of steel in all 104 episodes of the six-year-old syndicated series, *The Adventures of Superman,* killed himself. In writing his obituary, many suggested that Reeves had chosen suicide out of frustration at being unable to escape his Superman image and that his epitaph might be that he died of typecasting. To millions of youngsters who heard the news, it brought a sobering realization that television was not reality and that even Superman could die.

In March 1960, Lucille Ball filed for divorce from Desi Arnaz. Lucy and Desi had been seen together only in monthly specials for the past few seasons, but their breakup officially ended, in reality and forever, a marriage whose fictionalized portrayal had been the cornerstone of television culture throughout the decade.

Finally, on September 24, 1960, NBC presented the 2,343rd-and-final episode of *Howdy Doody.* Howdy had been there when TV began and kids who watched the earliest episodes had children of their own who watched the last. It was a graceful farewell that rang down the curtain on one of the last remnants of television's infancy. For that first TV generation, there was perhaps never a more poignant moment on television than the last moment of that last show when Clarabell the clown, silent through all thirteen years of the program, looked into the camera and quietly spoke, "Goodbye kids."

20. The Vast Wasteland

SEVEN YEARS AFTER MERGING WITH United Paramount Theaters, the ABC television network had reached apparent respectability. The network's commitment to the action-adventure format had paid off and, though it was still far behind CBS, ABC had successfully nosed out NBC for the number two slot in the 1959–60 season. Just as the new decade began, ABC was often placing as many programs in the top ten as the other networks, sometimes even more. Ollie Treyz, president of ABC-TV since 1958, noted this improvement with considerable pride. He went even further, though, and asserted that ABC was actually number one, citing a special Nielsen ratings survey that measured markets in which all three networks had full time affiliates to back his claim. Despite these pronouncements, ABC was not yet generally considered at parity with its rivals and was still unmistakably the "third network." Though the number and strength of its affiliates had increased, ABC was far weaker than CBS and NBC. Its news, public affairs, sports, and daytime programming were virtually nonexistent. Even its success in prime time had come almost entirely from one program type, action-adventure, with only occasional hits in other genres. If the action-adventure format faded before a viable followup was found, ABC could slip back into oblivion in a very short time.

While it searched for potential new prime time hits, ABC began to expand both its news and sports coverage in an attempt to increase prestige and build on its momentum. Its first important move in these areas was the surprise acquisition of exclusive television rights to the 1960 Winter Olympics in Squaw Valley, California. For the privilege of carrying the first Olympics held in the United States since the advent of television, the network paid $167,000. ABC viewed this investment in the Winter Games as essentially a losing venture that was valuable only as a bargaining tool in an attempt to acquire the more profitable Summer Games scheduled for Rome. When it failed to win the rights to the Roman Games, ABC canceled plans for coverage of the winter contests, feeling that they would cost too much and not attract sufficient viewer interest. CBS picked up both the winter and summer TV rights and found itself producing all eighteen hours of winter coverage on an unsponsored basis, just as ABC had expected. When the Winter Games brought in unexpectedly high ratings, both the networks and sponsors were appropriately stunned. Events such as a dramatic down-to-the-wire hockey win by the U.S. over the Soviet Union captured the public's attention and revealed a substantial audience for types of sports previously considered of only marginal interest. In August, CBS followed up the success in Squaw Valley with twenty hours of sponsored, well-produced coverage of the events in Rome, featuring sportscaster Jim McKay. The extensive use of video tape made it possible to present events in the United States on the same day they occurred in Italy, giving the games an immediacy and tension that had been noticeably absent in the long-delayed film reports of previous years. For CBS, the Winter and Summer Olympic Games were both an artistic and ratings success. For ABC, they were a valuable lesson.

Though it had lost this contest to CBS, ABC saw that sports events were a natural area for it to pursue. CBS and NBC had not come up with many dramatic sports innovations in the previous half decade and ABC could compete on an equal footing, meet them head-on, and attempt to outbid them for established events. Or, it could pick up contests they had dropped or had not considered at all. ABC had already become the sole network outlet for one of the first TV sports, boxing, by attrition. CBS abandoned its *Blue Ribbon Bouts* in 1955 as a worn-out remnant of TV's early days, even though the show had maintained a relatively stable audience for seven years. ABC picked it up on the rebound and joined NBC and DuMont in carrying TV pugilistics through the 1950s. By the end of the decade, DuMont had folded and stories of corruption in the boxing profession and well-publicized deaths of boxers shortly after being pummeled in the ring had given the sport a sinister and subversive tinge that was reflected in lower ratings. In June 1960, NBC ended its association with boxing, dropping Gillette's *Cavalcade of Sports* matches after sixteen years. That left ABC alone in the field, and it continued to present weekly bouts until 1964.

As boxing declined during the late 1950s, other sports supplanted it as the chief focus of television athletics, and ABC scanned these for areas of possible expansion. Major league baseball was firmly in the grip of CBS and NBC, which both presented a weekend "game of the week." Beyond that, NBC had exclusive rights to the popular World Series contest. Television coverage of professional football, however, was especially attractive to ABC because it seemed to have elevated a game of rather limited appeal for thirty years into serious contention with baseball as the national pastime. Though NBC controlled college football telecasts and CBS presented the National Football League (which it had inherited from DuMont), the sport seemed ripe for plunder. Interest in the game was growing and there was serious talk about the formation of a new professional football league.

Television helped to develop this interest and appreciation for football by making the complicated game more comprehensible to the home audience. Video taped "instant replays" (which at first took nearly half an hour to air) provided viewers with the opportunity to see important plays repeated. This transformed the sport into a contest that was actually better seen on television than at the stadium. As the fans became more sophisticated, football became a frequent topic of discussion on television. Serious programs in the Sunday afternoon "egghead" slots began to examine the personalities and psychology of football in such well-produced entries as "The Violent World of Sam Huff" on CBS's *Twentieth Century* (hosted by Walter Cronkite). More important, plans for a new professional league to compete with the NFL for fan attention came through in late 1959. For the fall of 1960, ABC filched the Saturday afternoon NCAA college games from NBC and signed a TV pact for Sunday afternoon games with the brand new American Football League in a two-pronged drive for prominence in football. The NCAA games were a safe, established draw and the upstart AFL was a perfect mate to the upstart ABC. Although the AFL was clearly no match for the NFL in either talent or prestige, like ABC it had nowhere to go but up, and if either partner proved to be a success, the other would benefit.

ABC made its most daring move in the field of TV sports in April 1961 with the premiere of its Saturday afternoon *Wide World of Sports*. Hosted by former CBS sportscaster Jim McKay, *Wide World of Sports* was the brainchild of Roone Arledge, a sports producer ABC had picked up from NBC along with the NCAA football games. The show turned from the then accepted practice of slotting specific events one at a time in regular time periods to the revolutionary concept of presenting as many different sports as possible, often within the same program. Using both live and pretaped segments, the program resembled coverage of the Olympics as it brought together a diverse selection of contests from different venues. It exposed sports enthusiasts to events previously considered too limited in appeal for network television including track and field, auto racing, bowling, and tennis. The rapid pacing of the program as it shifted locales helped *Wide World of Sports* to lure viewers into accepting unfamiliar settings and events as part of an exciting afternoon of sports. The program was an unqualified success for ABC and over the years it established the network's reputation as an effective and innovative source for sports. In this area, ABC's expansion plans worked perfectly.

The network faced a more difficult challenge in upgrading its news and public affairs programming to compete with NBC and CBS because in this area it was unquestionably far behind in both experience and prestige. At the birth of network television in the late 1940s, ABC had started near the pace of its competition, offering *News and Views* in August 1948, just as the other networks were beginning nightly news shows. The Monday through Saturday show was structured exactly like a radio news and commentary program: one of the anchors would present the day's headlines and then offer a few minutes of interpretation. The anchor chores were rotated among a number of analysts such as George Hicks, Walter Kiernan, and the first female network news anchor, Pauline Frederick, but *News and Views* disappeared within one year. Although the format worked very well on radio, it was particularly ill-suited to television's voracious demand for visuals. For four years, ABC had no nightly news show and, for all practical purposes, no news department whatsoever. During this interregnum NBC and CBS significantly developed their television news resources and styles, while ABC settled for once-a-week commentary programs by individual radio analysts such as Paul Harvey and Walter Winchell.

As a sign of the growing strength and independence in the NBC and CBS news departments, neither allowed outside sources to produce news or news-related programs, keeping the nightly news shows and occasional news specials under direct network control. ABC, on the other hand, was forced to rely totally on outside sources for both film footage and program production, and it aired documentary series such as *Crusade in Europe, Crusade in the Pacific,* and *March of Time through the Years* from Time-Life in lieu of its own news and public affairs programming. Once the ABC-United Paramount Theaters merger of 1953 brought much-needed cash to the network coffers, ABC reactivated its news organization and resumed Monday through Friday newscasts in October 1953, with veteran newscaster-quiz master John Daly, formerly of CBS. Under Daly's leadership, ABC news improved substantially, even adopting the CBS-NBC dogma of "no outside documentaries." Unfortunately, due to the comparatively small budget for the ABC news department, this rule translated into no ABC documentaries at all. Most of ABC's affiliates refused to take the network's improved news posture seriously anyway and did not bother to carry Daly's fifteen-minute news show. In an attempt to remedy this situation, ABC moved the program into prime time (10:30–10:45 P.M.) during the 1958–59 season, but this shift placed it in a hopeless battle with the popular entertainment programs on the opposing networks. Even though ABC had upgraded its treatment of the news by 1960, it still had the weakest of the

September 11, 1960
Danger Man. (ATV). Patrick McGoohan portrays secret agent John Drake in this British series, which CBS brings to the States for a brief summer run beginning in April 1961.

September 26, 1960
The largest television audience yet—seventy-five million Americans—tunes in the first of four debates between presidential candidates John F. Kennedy and Richard M. Nixon. Howard K. Smith of CBS is moderator of the first (held in Chicago), which focuses on domestic affairs. Though the two are rated about even by radio listeners, television viewers give Nixon poor marks for personal appearance. He appears tired and haggard while Kennedy looks sharp and bright.

November 27, 1960
Issues and Answers. (ABC). The third network at last gets its own Sunday afternoon interview show. First guest: Senator Paul Douglas of Illinois.

December 16, 1960
Bill Shadel takes over ABC's nightly news show following the resignation of John Daly.

January 5, 1961
Mr. Ed. An off-beat syndicated series featuring Alan Young as Wilbur Post, a young architect who one day discovers that his horse, Mr. Ed, can talk. Allan "Rocky" Lane provides the voice for the good-natured palomino. The program is so successful that CBS puts it on network television in October, 1961, where it becomes a national hit.

January 7, 1961
The Avengers. Britain's ITV network presents the spy duo of Dr. David Keel (Ian Hendry) and a mysterious character referred to simply as Steed (Patrick Macnee).

FALL 1960 SCHEDULE

		7:00	7:30	8:00	8:30	9:00	9:30	10:00	10:30	
M O N		local	The Cheyenne Show (Cheyenne; Bronco; Sugarfoot)		SURFSIDE SIX		Adventures In Paradise		Peter Gunn		ABC
		local	To Tell The Truth	PETE AND GLADYS	BRINGING UP BUDDY	Danny Thomas Show	ANDY GRIFFITH SHOW	Hennesey	PRESIDENTIAL COUNTDOWN		CBS
		local	Riverboat		Tales Of Wells Fargo	KLONDIKE	DANTE	BARBARA STANWYCK SHOW	Jackpot Bowling With Milton Berle		NBC
T U E		EXPEDITION	BUGS BUNNY SHOW	The Rifleman	Life And Legend Of Wyatt Earp	STAGECOACH WEST		Alcoa Presents: One Step Beyond	local		ABC
		local		Father Knows Best	The Many Loves Of Dobie Gillis	TOM EWELL SHOW	Red Skelton Show	Garry Moore Show			CBS
		local	Laramie		Alfred Hitchcock Presents	THRILLER		NBC Specials			NBC
W E D		local	HONG KONG		Adventures Of Ozzie And Harriet	Hawaiian Eye		Naked City			ABC
		local	THE AQUANAUTS		Wanted: Dead Or Alive	MY SISTER EILEEN	I've Got A Secret	U.S. Steel Hour / Armstrong Circle Theater			CBS
		local	Wagon Train		The Price Is Right	Perry Como's Kraft Music Hall		PETER LOVES MARY	local		NBC
T H R		local	GUESTWARD HO	Donna Reed Show	The Real McCoys	MY THREE SONS	The Untouchables		Take A Good Look		ABC
		local	THE WITNESS		Dick Powell's Zane Grey Theater	ANGEL	Ann Sothern Show	Person To Person	DuPont Show With June Allyson		CBS
		local	THE OUTLAWS		Bat Masterson	Bachelor Father	Tennessee Ernie Ford Show	The Groucho Show	local		NBC
F R I		local	Matty's Funday Funnies	HARRIGAN AND SON	THE FLINTSTONES	77 Sunset Strip		Robert Taylor In The Detectives	THE LAW AND MR. JONES		ABC
		local	Rawhide		ROUTE 66		MR. GARLUND	The Twilight Zone	Eyewitness To History		CBS
		local	DAN RAVEN		THE WESTERNER	Bell Telephone Hour / NBC Specials		MICHAEL SHAYNE			NBC
S A T		local	THE ROARING TWENTIES		Leave It To Beaver	Lawrence Welk Show		Fight Of The Week	MAKE TH. SPARE		ABC
		local	Perry Mason		CHECKMATE		Have Gun, Will Travel	Gunsmoke	local		CBS
		local	Bonanza		THE TALL MAN	The Deputy	THE CAMPAIGN AND THE CANDIDATES		local		NBC
S U N		Walt Disney Presents (from 6:30)	Maverick		Lawman	The Rebel	THE ISLANDERS		WALTER WINCHELL SHOW		ABC
		Lassie	Dennis The Menace	Ed Sullivan Show		General Electric Theater	Jack Benny Program	Candid Camera	What's My Line		CBS
		Shirley Temple Show		NATIONAL VELVET	TAB HUNTER SHOW	Dinah Shore Chevy Show		Loretta Young Show	This Is Your Life		NBC

three network news organizations by far and found itself consistently losing in direct competition with CBS and NBC.

In the months following Charles Van Doren's revelations to Congress, the news departments at all three networks became very important to network prestige as the industry displayed a sudden deep concern for the value of news and public affairs, hoping that such programs could erase the black mark the quiz show scandal had given television. Some television executives saw such a public commitment as a perfect PR device to counter criticism of the industry and possibly even rekindle the notion of television as cultural savior. Because it lacked the resources and manpower, the ABC news department found itself hard pressed to instantly deliver some new documentary series similar to those announced by NBC and CBS, even on an irregular basis. However, ABC did successfully participate in a fortuitously timed event that allowed television to display its best side, the "great debates" staged in the fall of 1960 between the two major-party candidates for president. An act of Congress suspended the equal time law to allow the networks to broadcast four debates between Democrat John Kennedy and Republican Richard Nixon without being obligated to offer an equal amount of network time to each of the other legitimate, but minor, candidates for the presidency. For the first time in years, people again began talking about the fabulous nature of television and its ability to allow millions of people across the entire country to share an important and historic series of events. The debates

provided a windfall of good publicity for the networks, sparked strong voter interest in the election, and probably provided the thin margin of victory for Kennedy, who came across more effectively than Nixon in the vital first debate. For this special event, ABC News held its own, producing two of the four contests.

In the field of in-house documentaries, though, ABC just could not compete with CBS and NBC. The network was anxious to display its own documentary series and it convinced Charles Percy's Bell and Howell company to finance *Bell and Howell Closeup*, a series of floating specials produced by ABC News and similar to *CBS Reports*. The first few productions of the new series (which premiered in September 1960) were roundly panned so ABC turned again to Time-Life, relinquishing control of the series to the Time-Life film crew headed by Robert Drew. Daly viewed this production deal as a direct violation of his no outsiders policy and quit ABC at the end of 1960. Ironically, the new *Closeup* series was far removed from the industry-controlled public relations fluff Daly had feared and it presented some of the most imaginative television documentary work in years, satisfying ABC's desire for material that could match the work at NBC and CBS. Drew's first program in the series, "Yanki No!" took its cue from Ed Murrow's *See It Now* "Christmas in Korea" show, downplaying the role of the narrator and avoiding the artificial setting of formal interviews. It attempted to capture people and events "as they were" in a *cinema verite* style comparison between Cuba under Fidel Castro, who was on the verge of publicly announcing that he was a Communist, and South American countries run by right wing dictators. Drew's crew portrayed Latin Americans as generally restive and fearful under the military rulers supported by the United States government, and showed Castro's supporters happy and enthusiastic. Subsequent shows in the series tackled such diverse subject matter as the effect of automation on the U.S. labor force ("Awesome Servant") and the defiant attitude emerging among American blacks ("Walk in My Shoes"). In each of these, the *cinema verite* style seductively underplayed a far stronger editorial stance than most network documentaries of the time chose to assume. Though purporting to present things as they were, Drew's crew carefully selected the film clips they used in order to present a very specific viewpoint, without an easily identifiable narrator cast as an advocate of the position. This style was aimed at conveying a strong point about a controversial issue without confronting the viewers with dramatic accusations that might alienate them before the problem could be fully explored. Someone of the stature of Ed Murrow might be able to use the force of his personality and reputation to argue a specific point of view (as he had done in his broadcasts about Senator Joseph McCarthy) but such figures were the exception. Murrow, in fact, had sometimes found that the instances in which he had taken a strong stand made it that much harder to present other unrelated issues to people who had concluded he was biased and not to be trusted. Because heightened awareness of an issue was all that could ever be expected to result from even the best documentary, it was vital that the audience be willing to give the program a fair hearing. The *cinema verite* style in ABC's *Closeup* series allowed the audience such opportunities and gave the network the class documentaries it wanted, though the use of an outside crew merely postponed the necessary development and expansion of ABC's own news department for several more years.

The news department at NBC occasionally followed the *verite* style in its floating *NBC White Paper* series. The technique was used in such reports as "Sit In" (a personal study of the individuals involved in the sit-in tactics being used to integrate stores in Nashville), but the producers usually stuck to well-made but traditional in-depth overviews of controversial topics, being careful to avoid taking any stand, explicit or implied. The subject matter of these programs ranged from an analysis of the U-2 spy plane affair to an examination of both sides of a rebellion going on almost unnoticed in Portugal's African colony of Angola. Another NBC floating documentary series, *Project 20,* usually avoided such controversy entirely and focused instead on more cultural topics. One typical program, "The Real West," attempted to present a view of the old West more realistic and accurate than the fictional TV Westerns. Narrated by Gary Cooper, the program used old photographs and personal memoirs to portray the events leading to the closing of the frontier and the conquest of the nation's Indian tribes.

Of all the networks, CBS provided the most dramatic documentary of the season, "Harvest of Shame," one of the strongest pieces by Ed Murrow since the Army-McCarthy days. On November 25, 1960, in the middle of the Thanksgiving holidays, Murrow brought the living and working conditions of America's migrant farm laborers to the attention of the general public, which knew next to nothing about the topic. As a sort of updated *Grapes of Wrath,* the program depicted the squalid conditions of the migrant workers in sharp contrast to the wealth of their employers, the food growers. The growers' side of the issue was also presented, but Murrow took a firm stand and left no doubt in viewers' minds that he felt something had to be done, such as federal protection for the workers and industry-wide standards to guide the owners. The timing of the program combined with its firm and effective presentation of a strong point of view touched off a bitter national controversy over the issue of migrant farm labor. Growers complained that they were unfairly portrayed, while average citizens expressed their outrage at the situation and echoed Murrow's appeal for some corrective action. Though sixty minutes of film could never change a situation by itself, "Harvest of Shame" made a deep impression on the American public, and it emerged as one of the most incisive documentaries of Murrow's career. It was also his last major production at CBS because a few months later he accepted newly elected President John Kennedy's offer to become the director of the United States Information Agency. Murrow left behind a well-trained group of correspondents and colleagues at CBS who respected him and worked to maintain his journalistic principles. The door to his office retained his name plate for three years after he was gone. When CBS moved its offices into a new building, the "Murrow door" was taken off its hinges and moved as well.

Of course, even with the extra emphasis on public affairs by the networks during the 1960–61 season, such programming accounted for only a tiny fraction of prime time and was usually tucked away in some unprofitable time slot or presented as a floating, irregularly scheduled special. The networks' real concern rested, as usual, with the performance of their regular prime time shows and the possible emergence of any new program fad. For the most part, 1960–61 marked a discernible pause in the industry, with regular prime time programming continuing almost unchanged from the previous season. NBC and CBS presented their usual selection of Westerns and sitcoms while ABC continued to emphasize action-adventure. Both NBC and CBS also launched a few vehicles in the action-adventure format, but they regarded these as part of a still unproven fad and were ready to drop them at the end of the season if they did poorly.

As the viewing habits for the 1960–61 season developed, it became clear that the bread-and-butter staples were holding steady, but the action-adventure format was in serious trouble, especially for ABC. Though *77 Sunset Strip* and *The Untouchables* remained in the top ten, the new crop of third generation action-adventure clones proved to be the worst of all, registering generally poor ratings with only two shows surviving for the 1961–62 season. The new programs contained no original twist, only the same lifeless characters, tired plots, mindless murders, and so-called exotic settings. *The Aquanauts,* produced by Ivan Tors, presented the adventures of a team of free lance skindivers in Honolulu. *The Islanders* featured the adventures of a pair of handsome pilots and two beautiful women who operated a tiny airline service in the Spice Islands. *Hong Kong* cast Rod Taylor in warmed-over Charlie Chan-type adventures set in the mysterious Orient. One show managed to incorporate two clichéd settings in one season. Premiering in the fall as *Klondike,* it featured Ralph Taeger and James Coburn in a premise that was *The Alaskans* sideways, mixing cutthroat adventures and pure-as-the-snow innocence in the Northland's beautiful but dangerous palace of ice. By mid-season, the producers wrote off *Klondike* and put Taeger and Coburn in the new, but somehow familiar, *Acapulco.* This mixture of cut-throat adventures and pure-as-the-sand innocence in Mexico's beautiful but dangerous seaside paradise did not last three months.

As failure in the action-adventure format became more frequent, Warner Bros. began transplanting actors from the unsuccessful series to some of its remaining slots. *Cheyenne* became a rotating series, taking the *Sugarfoot* and *Bronco* shows under its banner. Roger Moore moved from the Alaskan frontier of the 1890s to the old West of the 1880s in the improbable role of Beau Maverick, the long-lost British cousin of Bret and Bart. James Garner

January 27, 1961

Sing Along with Mitch. (NBC). Goateed maestro Mitch Miller invites everyone to "sing along—loud and strong."

March 2, 1961

Newton Minow is sworn in as chairman of the FCC.

April 16, 1961

Death of *Omnibus.* Age: 9 years. In its final season, the show was relegated to a Sunday afternoon slot once a month on NBC.

April 17, 1961

ABC Final Report. (ABC). The first network attempt at late night news each weeknight (11:00–11:15 P.M.). At first, the program is carried only by ABC's O&O stations, but in October it expands to the entire network.

June 9, 1961

Worthington Miner's syndicated *Play of the Week* is canceled.

June 12, 1961

PM East/PM West. Westinghouse gets into late night television, syndicating ninety minutes of talk and variety five days a week. One-half of the program comes from New York (with Mike Wallace) the other half from San Francisco (with Terry O'Flaherty). In February 1962, the West portion is dumped.

July 17, 1961

John Chancellor takes over NBC's *Today* from Dave Garroway.

(brother Bret) had departed the series in a contract dispute and was seen only in *Maverick* reruns. Another refugee from *The Alaskans,* Dorothy Provine, brought her nightclub singer character to the studio's weak imitation of *The Untouchables, The Roaring Twenties.* Rex Reason and Donald May joined her as a pair of investigative reporters in search of hot scoops on the latest activities of bootleggers and mobsters. The series relied on a few artifacts of the period (raccoon coats, cars, the Charleston), acceptable 1920s-style music, and a sprinkling of "timely" phrases (such as "hotcha" and "Twenty-three skidoo") to cover the predictable plots. *The Roaring Twenties* was a mere shadow of the sharply produced *Untouchables,* and it faded after two seasons. One other new Warner Bros. action-adventure series, *Surfside Six,* also managed to hang on for two seasons while serving as yet another haven for members of the studio's action-adventure acting company. Van Williams moved in from *Bourbon Street Beat* while his partner, Troy Donahue, eventually moved on to *Hawaiian Eye.* Apparently the studio had run out of exotic foreign spots so it set the usual flip talk and detective pretty boys aboard a houseboat in Miami Beach (address: Surfside Six).

It was too much. After three years of variations on the "two parts private eye, one part cutie pie" formula, the public had had enough. As the 1960–61 season progressed, the Warner Bros./ABC action-adventure structure began sliding into the ocean. The other networks quickly shifted their energies back to other formats, but ABC had nowhere else to go. It had stumbled upon this formula almost by accident and the network was on the verge of returning to its pre-action-adventure number three status. Though ABC might still produce an occasional, isolated hit, it could no longer

automatically count on this formula as a continuing source of new programs. As the network began drawing up plans for the next season (a process which, at the time, was usually completed by March), it frantically searched for any formula that might provide a steady stream of shows, hoping that blind chance might strike again. ABC even tried expanding the dubious concept of bringing so-called "adult cartoons" to prime time, a format that had had a disappointing debut in 1960 with *The Flintstones.*

Through the summer and early fall of 1960, ABC's advance publicity touted *The Flintstones* as the "first adult cartoon show" and promised that it would be a satire on suburban life that would appeal to grownups as well as children. Rarely had a show been so erroneously hyped. When the program hit the airwaves in late September, it was immediately apparent that *The Flintstones* was actually just another kiddie cartoon series from the TV animation mill of Bill Hanna and Joseph Barbera, a team responsible for such characters as Tom and Jerry and Yogi Bear. Nonetheless, ABC's placement of the show at 8:30 P.M. (past the traditional kiddie hour), its choice of sponsor (Winston cigarettes), and its continuing ballyhoo indicated that the network was seriously aiming *The Flintstones* at adults. Unfortunately, while the program's faults might have been quietly passed over in a Saturday morning children's slot, they could not withstand the direct comparisons with other prime time fare.

Ironically, at the same time ABC was plugging *The Flintstones* as a cartoon series capable of entertaining all age groups, it was almost ignoring another prime time cartoon show on its schedule that really could, *The Bugs Bunny Show.* The series had been developed after Ollie Treyz discovered that an independent station in Chicago (WGN) had been running old Bugs Bunny cartoons in prime time (6:30 P.M. in the Midwest) with considerable success. Hoping to duplicate that success on the network, ABC bought the last of the Warner Bros. theatrical cartoons not yet released to television and presented them in a format that featured brand new introductions and transitions by Bugs and other popular Warner characters such as Daffy Duck, Elmer Fudd, Foghorn Leghorn, and Porky Pig. Because these cartoons were originally intended for release with Warner Bros. movies, the cartoonists had specifically aimed at entertaining the adults as well as the children with playful lampoons of Hollywood stars, popular movies, and then-current events. The animation, scripts, and characters reflected more than thirty years of sophisticated development by some of the best animators in Hollywood and they hopelessly outclassed anything produced specifically for television.

Hanna-Barbera could not possibly match the high standards of the best Warner Bros. cartoons, but in attempting to develop its own cartoon series for adults, the company did begin with a sensible strategy. It took the successful characters from a live-action adult sitcom (in this case, *The Honeymooners*) and created animated caricatures. To increase the potential for gags and satire, the cartoon characters were placed in a fully developed suburban community that happened to be set in the Stone Age. Veteran character actors Mel Blanc and Bea Benaderet were cast to do some of the voices. The series held great promise that was never realized. All the appealing elements of *The Honeymooners'* characters were lost in the transition to animation, and *The Flintstones* emerged as a dimwitted interpolation in a Stone Age setting. Fred Flintstone was noisy, boastful, and stupid. His neighbor, Barney Rubble, was a dolt. The interaction and scheming of the two lacked the wit, energy, humor, and deep affection of the Jackie Gleason-Art Carney original. Fred's wife, Wilma, possessed none of the intelligence, personality, and understanding of Alice Kramden. All of the cartoon characters came off merely as ... cartoon characters.

Perhaps the weak characters might have been tolerable if the promised satire on American life had come through. It did not. All Hanna-Barbera did was effect a one-to-one transplant of modern mechanical devices to Stone Age animal equivalents. Fred and Barney operated enormous dinosaurs instead of mechanical bulldozers. Fred drove a car powered by his own two feet. Pterodactyls with seats strapped to their backs served as airplanes. That was it. No witty satire. Just formula animation. Nonetheless, the series lasted six seasons on ABC, though the characters of Fred, Wilma, Pebbles (their daughter), Barney, Betty Rubble, and Bamm Bamm (their son) reached their most effective penetration of the market when the show ended its prime time run and moved to its natural home, the Saturday morning kiddie circuit, and then into syndication, spawning several spinoff series along the way.

For ABC's immediate future, *The Flintstones* provided a quick program fad for the network to exploit, and by the 1962–63 season, it had launched three additional "adult" cartoon series that followed *The Flintstones* style: *Top Cat* (a *Sergeant Bilko* imitation), *Calvin and the Colonel* (*Amos 'n Andy* of the animal world), and *The Jetsons* (*The Flintstones* backwards). Of course, the cartoon format was much too limited in appeal to serve as a substitute for the fading action-adventure series, but it underscored the return to ABC's patchwork style of filling its prime time schedule with virtually anything, in the hope that a flash hit would take hold.

For a change, ABC was not alone in feeling the absence of high quality new shows. All three networks had reached the bottom of a programming slump in 1960–61. Only two new series made it into the top ten, ABC's leisurely *My Three Sons* and CBS's rural-oriented *Andy Griffith Show*. *My Three Sons* was just a routine family comedy featuring Fred MacMurray, while CBS's show effectively reunited the "No Time for Sergeants" movie team of Andy Griffith and Don Knotts. Their roles were essentially continuations of their film characters, grown a bit older and relocated in the small town of Mayberry, North Carolina. Andy played an understanding and mature good ol' boy who served as the town's sheriff, and Knotts was the hysterically bug-eyed paranoiac deputy, Barney Fife, who constantly tried, and failed, to fit his own image of the traditional tough cop. Barney never understood that big city high pressure tactics were unnecessary in Mayberry because it was virtually crime free. The program's tempo reflected the slow-as-molasses life of a small rural town and a good deal of time was devoted to warm family segments featuring Andy as a gentle widower trying to raise his young son, Opie (Ronny Howard), with the help of his aunt, Bee Taylor (Frances Bavier). These vignettes followed *The Rifleman* pattern of a father-son relationship as Opie learned homey lessons about life either on his own or from his dad. The comedic foundation of the show, though, rested with the contrast between this very normal family life and a handful of Mayberry's citizens who could be set off on some crackpot notion in a matter of moments. Aside from occasional outbreaks of hysteria caused by Barney, the show's stories often involved some of the town's other colorful characters such as Otis, the town drunk; Floyd, the barber; and the two personifications of country naiveté, Gomer and Goober Pyle. Through it all, Andy was never ruffled and did not bother to carry a gun. He knew that nothing had ever happened in that town and that nothing ever would. The calm hominess of the program, combined with the balance between sanity and insanity, proved very popular with viewers and they followed the story of Mayberry for eleven years.

There were also a few outstanding dramatic shows that season, including an expanded hour version of *Naked City* (with a new leading man, Paul Burke), the surprisingly serious private eye drama of *Checkmate* (with Sebastian Cabot as a portly professional

criminologist who was the guiding genius behind prettyboy detectives Anthony George and Doug McClure), and the offbeat character studies of *Route 66*. George Maharis and Martin Milner played a pair of wandering anti-heroes who set out on U.S. highway 66 "in search of America" and some direction for their lives. Milner played a clean-cut college boy who had lost his family fortune with the death of his father and Maharis portrayed a reformed juvenile delinquent from the ghetto. The two had pooled their funds, purchased a Corvette (the show was sponsored by Chevrolet), and become drifters who cruised the country, inevitably drawn along the way into the lives of people who were facing some crisis. The wide open format allowed the series' chief writer, Stirling Silliphant, the opportunity to introduce a varied assortment of offbeat personalities and place them into modern morality plays. These people were good at heart, if slightly warped, and it was up to Maharis and Milner (acting as unofficial social workers and psychoanalysts) to help them face the consequences of their actions and reassert their goodness. Filmed on location, *Route 66* was a good show due to its strong cast, good writing, and flexible format. The only aspect that made no sense was how episodes taking place in Butte, Montana, or in rural Mississippi could be part of a series named after a road that ran from Chicago to Los Angeles.

These series provided a few moments of high quality entertainment in an otherwise depressingly mediocre season. Effluvia such as *Peter Loves Mary, National Velvet, The Tab Hunter Show, Pete and Gladys,* and *Guestward Ho!* filled the airwaves. Westerns reached a new level of sadism with the gory vengeance killings and intrafamily homicides of *Whispering Smith,* and the sadistic white slavers and threats of brutal mutilation in *The Westerner* (produced and directed by Sam Peckinpah). Even two former

The pride of Mayberry: *(from left)* Deputy Barney Fife (Don Knotts), gas station attendant Gomer Pyle (Jim Nabors), and sheriff Andy Taylor (Andy Griffith). *(CBS Photo Archive © 2003 CBS Worldwide, Inc. All Rights Reserved.)*

television greats, Jackie Gleason and Milton Berle, turned up in roles that were embarrassing and demeaning to their tremendous talents.

Gleason returned to television as the host of an insipid quiz show, *You're in the Picture*. Contestants behind a large picture canvas stuck their faces through cutouts in the scene and tried to identify the situation in the picture, using clues provided by Gleason. This format lasted one week. Gleason scrapped it and took over the show himself, announcing on the second program that the premiere had, "laid, without a doubt, the biggest bomb in history." He devoted the entire program that week and the next to a thirty-minute comedy monologue based on the frantic meetings by the show's producers as they desperately tried to salvage something from the venture. They finally wrote it off as a total loss and Gleason used the two remaining months of the program's run to feature whatever friends he could talk into helping him out. Even though Gleason's show was an obvious loser, it remained on the air for two more months because, at that time, the networks did not bother with wholesale mid-season schedule changes and replacements. They felt that a show doing poorly in January could not possibly improve dramatically before the season ended, so to try to promote and improve it would be a waste of time and money. It was much wiser to write off the bad shows, let them finish their run, and concentrate instead on assembling the new fall schedule by the end of February.

Milton Berle's reappearance was not a great public flop like Jackie Gleason's, but it was no less degrading. Mr. Television, the man whose talents had enticed many Americans into purchasing their first sets, was relegated to providing patter for *Jackpot Bowling*. Each week, sportscaster Chick Hearn did the play-by-play and Berle appeared at the beginning, middle, and end of the show to tell a few jokes and hand out a few thousand dollars in prize money. The comedown of Gleason and Berle was staggering but representative. The previously respected geniuses of television's early years were being reduced to cheapened pawns whose name value was callously exploited. Where would it all end? Would Sid Caesar turn up as a carnival clown on a kiddie show? Would Fred Coe begin producing laxative commercials? Would Pat Weaver wind up running a UHF station in Arkansas? Would Tony Miner start working for Soupy Sales? No esthetic genius appeared invulnerable. Television seemed hell-bent on eradicating any reputation for quality it had developed. Though the networks pointed with justifiable pride to their highly praised documentaries and news shows, programs such as *Jackpot Bowling*, *Surfside Six*, and *The Flintstones* more accurately reflected the true state of the industry.

Television's critics had all but given up complaining that the networks had gone too far in sacrificing program quality to viewer quantity, realizing that their protests would be brushed aside with the latest statistics indicating that viewing totals were up again. After all, the network chiefs responded, the public cast its vote of support every day by tuning in whatever they churned out. Among themselves, though, even broadcasters admitted that the 1960–61 season was less-than-exceptional, and there were plans to tinker with a few programs and perhaps introduce a few new programming wrinkles; but there was no hurry. Improvements might take place eventually, but in laying out the schedules for the 1961–62 season the emphasis remained on gaining a competitive edge, not upgrading quality. A few mundane programs were accepted as a necessary part of broadcasting along with the desperate rating battles and unstable program formats. It was all business as usual. Each of the networks totaled their profits and losses for the season and prepared for the annual convention of the National Association of Broadcasters.

Every year broadcast executives met to discuss the state of the industry, pat themselves on the back, and listen to a bland speech by an important government figure (usually from the FCC) who did little to dispel the convention euphoria or the notion that everyone there was doing a great job "serving the public interest." Newly appointed FCC chairman Newton Minow was scheduled to deliver the address on May 9, 1961, before that year's NAB gathering in Washington. Coming only two months after he took office, Minow's speech would be his first chance to express his ideas about broadcasting directly to its important executives and leaders. Though the thirty-five-year-old former law partner of Adlai Stevenson was an unknown quantity, it was assumed that he would probably follow the usual pattern of praise tempered with vague exhortations that the industry do even better in the future. All of the bigwigs of network TV were in the audience: Robert Sarnoff and Robert Kinter of NBC, Leonard Goldenson and Ollie Treyz of ABC, and Frank Stanton and James Aubrey of CBS. They were not prepared for what Minow chose to say:

> I invite you to sit down in front of your television set when your station [or network] goes on the air and stay there without a book, magazine, newspaper, profit-and-loss sheet, or ratings book to distract you-and keep your eyes glued to that set until the station signs off. I can assure you that you will observe a vast wasteland. You will see a procession of game shows, violence, audience participation shows, formula comedies about totally unbelievable families, blood and thunder, mayhem, violence, sadism, murder, Western badmen, Western goodmen, private eyes, gangsters, more violence, and cartoons, and, endlessly, commercials, many screaming, cajoling, and offending, and, most of all, boredom. True, you will see a few things you enjoy, but they will be very, very few, and if you think I exaggerate, try it.

At this point, the trade journal *Variety* later reported, Sarnoff's brow (always perpetually wrinkled) showed a few more furrows. Treyz's face had turned white, while Stanton's was red. The faces of Kinter and Aubrey were frozen in masks, and Goldenson's had iced into a Mona Lisa smile. Minow went on:

> Is there one person in this room who claims that broadcasting can't do better? Is there one network president in this room who claims he can't do better? Why is so much of television so bad? ... We need imagination in programming, not sterility; creativity, not imitation; experimentation, not conformity; excellence, not mediocrity.

The members of the NAB were stunned. No one had ever talked to them that way before. What's more, Minow, as head of the FCC, might actually do something to implement his suggestions and seriously affect the industry. Consequently, no one dared to openly rebuke him as he delivered his speech, though the convention was filled with behind-the-scenes grumbling.

Newspapers picked up Minow's "vast wasteland" phrase and critics used it as a quick condemnation of the entire industry. Though broadcasters grudgingly came to the general consensus that in some respects Minow was right and the 1960–61 season had been exceptionally weak, they were in a bind. Despite the expectation that something should be done immediately to improve television programming after the adverse publicity directed toward it, the 1961–62 schedules had been locked up and sold since March and could not be changed in May. The best the networks could do was slot a few more public affairs shows, paint rosy pictures for 1962–63, and prepare to endure the barrage of criticism they felt certain would greet the new season.

21. I Still Have the Stench in My Nose

NETWORK CZARS WERE BRACED FOR DISASTER following FCC chairman Newton Minow's roasting of the industry in his "vast wasteland" speech. Lavish reforms were promised by network potentates for the 1962–63 season, but as the 1961–62 season progressed the need for such dramatic action faded. Though some truly terrible television aired in the new season, Minow's speech, almost by accident, marked the rock bottom end of a decline rather than the identification of a permanent, insoluble situation. Ever since the rise of the big money quiz shows in 1955 and 1956, the quality of TV had been eroding steadily as the industry put aside many high quality drama, comedy, and news shows which drew only adequate ratings in favor of programs that offered the promise of flashy, but unstable, instant success. In searching for possible new hit formats for the 1961–62 season, network executives had developed, by chance or instinct, several concepts that revived some of television's best work, updated for the 1960s. Major breakthroughs took place in legal, medical, movie, and sitcom formats with programs that set the pattern television shows of both high and low quality would follow for the remainder of the decade. There were only a handful of these new shows that fall, but they provided enough good new television to take some of the immediate sting from the vast wasteland description and to convince people that, after one of the most uninspired seasons in TV history, something was being done to improve programming.

The legal drama of *The Defenders* came directly from the so-called golden age of television. Back in February 1957, *Studio One* had presented a two-part story of a father-and-son legal team that had to overcome both intrafamily disagreements and judicial obstacles. Written by Reginald Rose and produced by Herb Brodkin, "The Defenders" offered a situation far more complex than the average TV crime show. As lawyer *pere,* Ralph Bellamy found himself torn between his distaste for the defendant, a repulsive young hoodlum played by Steve McQueen, and his responsibilities to the legal profession. His bright but idealistic son, played by William Shatner, insisted that their client receive the best defense possible, even though he was probably guilty. The story received high critical acclaim and, four years later, with *Perry Mason* a successful series, Brodkin and Rose teamed up again to produce a new lawyer series based on the play. They brought their high dramatic standards to *The Defenders* and treated it like the drama anthology shows of old, with one important difference.

Drama anthologies such as *Studio One* had demanded that viewers accept a whole new world every week, without offering any identifiable continuing characters to provide a much-needed personal link. Even if the shows were first rate and dealt with themes and issues that hit home, many viewers felt it just was not worth the constant effort required to follow the maze of new faces and settings. Instead they turned increasingly to continuing series with familiar central characters or, at best, anthology series with stable, well-known hosts such as Alfred Hitchcock and Rod Serling. In the waning days of the drama anthology genre, producers used big name Hollywood guest stars in an attempt to overcome the continuity gap, but the tactic was not very successful because the format problem still remained: in the intimate world of television, the public preferred familiar characters and settings.

In *The Defenders,* Brodkin and Rose tied together their high quality writing, production, and selection of guest stars with a strong pair of central characters: E. G. Marshall as trial lawyer Lawrence Preston and Robert Reed as his son, Kenneth. Within the very accessible framework of courtroom drama, they presented tight character studies as well as the public debate of controversial topics television normally never dealt with. Nonetheless, it still looked for all the world like just another good lawyer show and CBS slotted it on Saturday night following *Perry Mason.* The placement was perfect because the two programs complemented each other. *Perry Mason* was a well-directed murder melodrama while *The Defenders* focused on characters and issues. The treatment of touchy subjects was never obvious and overbearing because Brodkin and Rose carefully incorporated it into each week's case. The trial process became a full-scale debate presenting both pro and con arguments through Marshall, Reed, and the supporting characters and guest stars as they planned the best ways to handle the legal strategy. Through all the topical discussions, however, the program still maintained the basics of good drama with strong characters and entertaining scripts.

The Defenders was the first TV series to examine the effects and implications of entertainment blacklisting. Jack Klugman portrayed a John Henry Faulk-type character who found his broadcasting career ended after his sponsor was frightened by a small pressure group. Another episode, "Voices of Death," scrutinized the flaws in the judicial system itself and raised the possibility that an innocent person could be sentenced to death. The first episode

Day	Net	7:00	7:30	8:00	8:30	9:00	9:30	10:00	10:30
MON	ABC	Expedition	The Cheyenne Show (Cheyenne; Bronco)		The Rifleman	Surfside Six		BEN CASEY	
MON	CBS	local	To Tell The Truth	Pete And Gladys	WINDOW ON MAIN STREET	Danny Thomas Show	Andy Griffith Show	Hennesey	I've Got A Secret
MON	NBC	local		National Velvet	The Price Is Right	87th PRECINCT		Thriller	
TUE	ABC	local	Bugs Bunny Show	Bachelor Father	CALVIN AND THE COLONEL	THE NEW BREED		ALCOA PREMIERE	Bell And Howell Close Up
TUE	CBS	local	Marshal Dillon	DICK VAN DYKE SHOW	The Many Loves Of Dobie Gillis	Red Skelton Show	ICHABOD AND ME	Garry Moore Show	
TUE	NBC	local	Laramie		Alfred Hitchcock Presents	DICK POWELL SHOW		CAIN'S HUNDRED	
WED	ABC	local	STEVE ALLEN SHOW		TOP CAT	Hawaiian Eye		Naked City	
WED	CBS	local	THE ALVIN SHOW	Father Knows Best	Checkmate		MRS. G. GOES TO COLLEGE	U.S. Steel Hour / Armstrong Circle Theater	
WED	NBC	local	Wagon Train		JOEY BISHOP SHOW	Perry Como's Kraft Music Hall		BOB NEWHART SHOW	DAVID BRINKLEY'S JOURNAL
THR	ABC	local	Adventures Of Ozzie And Harriet	Donna Reed Show	The Real McCoys	My Three Sons	MARGIE	The Untouchables	
THR	CBS	local	FRONTIER CIRCUS		NEW BOB CUMMINGS SHOW	THE INVESTIGATORS		CBS Reports	
THR	NBC	local	The Outlaws		DR. KILDARE		HAZEL	Sing Along With Mitch	
FRI	ABC	local	STRAIGHTAWAY	THE HATHAWAYS	The Flintstones	77 Sunset Strip		TARGET: THE CORRUPTORS	
FRI	CBS	local	Rawhide		Route 66		FATHER OF THE BRIDE	The Twilight Zone	Eyewitness
FRI	NBC	local	INTERNATIONAL SHOWTIME		Robert Taylor's Detectives		Bell Telephone Hour / Dinah Shore Show		FRANK McGEE'S HERE AND NOW
SAT	ABC	Matty's Funday Funnies	The Roaring Twenties		Leave It To Beaver	Lawrence Welk Show		Fight Of The Week	Make That Spare
SAT	CBS	local	Perry Mason		THE DEFENDERS		Have Gun, Will Travel	Gunsmoke	
SAT	NBC	local	Tales Of Wells Fargo		The Tall Man	NBC SATURDAY NIGHT AT THE MOVIES			
SUN	ABC	Maverick (from 6:30)	FOLLOW THE SUN		Lawman	BUS STOP		Adventures In Paradise	
SUN	CBS	Lassie	Dennis The Menace	Ed Sullivan Show		General Electric Theater	Jack Benny Program	Candid Camera	What's My Line
SUN	NBC	The Bullwinkle Show	Walt Disney's Wonderful World Of Color		CAR 54, WHERE ARE YOU?	Bonanza		DuPont Show Of The Week	

of the series thrashed out the issue of mercy killing while another installment, "The Benefactor," dealt openly with abortion, then illegal and barely acknowledged. This episode, in which a doctor spoke out in favor of the practice, caused a public controversy in which eleven of the 180 stations that normally carried the program, as well as the regular sponsor, pulled out for that week. Despite such a daring (yet generally evenhanded) approach to important issues, *The Defenders* was an immediate ratings winner for CBS. Throughout its four-year run it maintained high standards of production quality while attracting a large and faithful audience that did not seem to mind "serious drama" on a weekly basis.

NBC and ABC turned to a different profession, medicine, in their pursuit of ratings success. Aside from *Medic* (Worthington Miner's 1954 series for NBC starring Richard Boone), doctors had been largely ignored by television until those two networks realized that the medical profession offered the opportunity to present romantic, good-looking heroes in situations that were literally matters of life and death. For its medical drama, NBC reached back two decades with *Dr. Kildare,* based on an old MGM film series that starred Lew Ayres and Lionel Barrymore. For the TV update, Raymond Massey portrayed the Barrymore character of crusty but compassionate Dr. Leonard Gillespie, the senior medical guru at Blair General Hospital, and Richard Chamberlain played the young idealistic intern, James Kildare. The two central characters established a relationship similar to the father-and-son lawyer team of *The Defenders*, in which they consistently disagreed on operating policy for each week's patients. Gillespie, the experienced veteran, preached patience and understanding while the impetuous Kildare put principle before tradition, often making the innocent mistakes of youthful inexperience. Unlike *The Defenders,* though, the stories emerging from their conflicts were not in-depth discussions of complex issues but rather high class soap opera. While a very good soap opera, *Dr. Kildare* was still just a sugar-coated view of life with inordinately good-looking people experiencing one heightened dramatic crisis after another. There always seemed to be some beautiful woman with a fatal who fell in love with Kildare, or a visiting specialist who threatened to have Kildare suspended over some minor procedural infraction. Chamberlain, while a fine dramatic actor, projected a choir-boy image of goodness in these situations. He was almost too good. He never seemed to have an impure thought or a desire to do anything in life other than cure disease. The steady stream of guest stars, as the patients and visiting doctors, suffered from the same inherent limitations of the soap opera plots. All the characters and situations were neatly wrapped up in a structure that was ridiculously constant: each episode featured three patients suffering different maladies, while an in-house controversy raged among the doctors.

ABC's medical drama, *Ben Casey,* was structured almost identically to *Dr. Kildare.* It had the same soap opera-ish conflicts and diseases, a parade of guest stars as the tormented patients, and the interaction between the handsome young neurosurgeon, Ben Casey (Vincent Edwards), and his crusty but compassionate mentor, Dr.

A portion of President John Kennedy's press conference on July 23, 1962, was carried on the first live TV program transmitted to Europe using AT&T's *Telstar I* satellite. *(Property of AT&T. Reprinted with permission of AT&T.)*

Zorba (Sam Jaffe). The chief difference between the two programs was that Casey was a more rugged character than Kildare. Casey's image was that of a man torn by his conscience as he faced important decisions at the hospital. In contrast to Kildare's choirboy goodness, Casey was once described as "the grim doctor who must be cruel to be kind." Despite the minor differences, both *Dr. Kildare* and *Ben Casey* were exactly the same in one important area: both programs seemed designed to appeal specifically to women. The love and death medical themes that had kept housewives entranced for decades on the daytime soap operas were moved, intact, to the nighttime medical soapers. The characters of Kildare and Casey were enticing and charismatic, with Chamberlain appealing primarily to older mothers and young girls, while Edwards attracted more worldly women in their twenties and thirties. Both programs offered competent drama and conflict in addition to the suds and sex, thus extending the appeal to the entire family. Both programs also turned into the smash hits of the season, which was welcome news to both NBC and ABC.

The two networks had faced the 1961–62 season in a depressed state and were moved to innovation out of a desire to dramatically change their situations. ABC was fading rapidly following the collapse of its action-adventure format, and NBC was trying hard to rise from the unfamiliar number three slot. Besides developing the successful new medical dramas, the two competitors also revived the idea of prime time feature films and this, too, provided both with welcome ratings boosts.

Films had been regularly aired in network prime time before 1961, but no network had ever presented relatively recent domestic feature films in the slots. When network television began, the major Hollywood studios had been very reluctant to release their old films to television because they feared this would destroy the market for rerelease and would offer, free on television, competition to their new material then at the theaters. Consequently, the *CBS Film Theater of the Air* in the 1940s had run ancient two-reelers more to fill empty hours than to attract an audience. In the 1950s, ABC's *Famous Film Festival* was forced to belie its title by featuring moldy unknown British product rather than well-known American films. The network's *Hollywood Film Theater* managed to secure American material from RKO, but the films were largely stale and forgettable. By 1957, the major American studios had changed their policies and released most of the pre-1948 films to

the home viewing market. By then, the networks feared that these high quality films would make their weekly series look bad, so they did not pick up the available films; instead, these became the private cache of late afternoon and late night local programmers.

In 1961, NBC decided to take a shot at scheduling movies in

September 17, 1961
DuPont Show of the Week. (NBC). After four years as a series of floating dramatic specials for CBS, the DuPont program switches to NBC, changing formats as well. The weekly series now includes drama, documentary, and variety presentations ranging from "The Wonderful World of Christmas" (with Carol Burnett and Harpo Marx) to "Hemingway" (narrated by Chet Huntley).

September 24, 1961
Walt Disney's Wonderful World of Color. (NBC). Robert Kinter, who signed Disney to television when he was with ABC, brings the popular family program with him to NBC. For the first time, the show airs in color (which ABC shied away from), beginning with the premiere episode, "Mathmagic Land," featuring Donald Duck and a new animated character, Professor Ludwig Von Drake.

September 30, 1961
Gunsmoke expands to sixty minutes, while the cream of six years of the half-hour shows are rerun on Tuesday nights under the title *Marshal Dillon.*

October 2, 1961
Calendar. (CBS). Harry Reasoner hosts a thirty-minute morning show combining hard news and soft features. Reasoner's wry essays, co-written with Andrew Rooney, are a high point of the program.

October 3, 1961
Calvin and the Colonel. (ABC). One year after the death of *Amos 'n Andy* on radio, Freeman Gosden and Charles Correll again bring their characters to television, but in the less controversial animated animal adventures of Col. Montgomery J. Klaxon (a fox, voiced by Gosden) and Calvin Burnside (a bear, voiced by Correll).

December 11, 1961

The Mike Douglas Show. The former band singer starts a ninety-minute afternoon talk show on Westinghouse's KYW in Cleveland. By October, 1963, the show is syndicated nationally.

February 20, 1962

After ten postponements, John Glenn becomes the first American in orbit and part of television's first big space spectacular. Jules Bergman (ABC) and Roy Neal (NBC) do well, but the earthbound star is CBS's Walter Cronkite.

March 17, 1962

Benny "Kid" Paret dies at the hands of Emile Griffith in a Madison Square Garden boxing match carried on ABC's *Fight of the Week.* Using special replay equipment, the network reruns the mortal blow in slow motion, over and over.

March 26, 1962

ABC Evening Report. (ABC). Revamping its nightly news, ABC brings in Ron Cochran as anchor.

June 14, 1962

Steptoe and Son. (BBC). Following a successful one-shot comedy special in January, the junkyard duo of crusty old Alfred Steptoe and his restive son, Harold, are brought back for a regular sitcom series.

June 25, 1962

The Steve Allen Show. Westinghouse replaces Mike Wallace's *P.M.* with a traditional talk show hosted by a net vet.

July 10, 1962

"World television" becomes more than just a publicity catch phrase with the launching of the *Telstar I* satellite. For the first time, live television transmission across the Atlantic Ocean is possible.

prime time as part of its effort to raise itself from the doldrums of last place. The network paid Twentieth Century Fox $25 million for fifty post-1950 films to be aired in prime time on Saturday night, though the network protected itself against the possibility of a major with a clause in the contract that gave it the right to cancel the agreement after sixteen weeks if the film series proved unsuccessful. Unlike every previous prime time film effort, *NBC Saturday Night at the Movies* quickly established itself as a ratings contender, though it did not come to dominate Saturday night for several more years. The series succeeded where previous efforts had failed for two reasons: The films were relatively new and the package contained a fair portion of outright box office hits. What's more, nearly half of the films were in color, and with color set sales continuing a slow but steady advance, such an attraction was beginning to have some meaning.

ABC noted NBC's success, quickly purchased fifteen post-1948 films from United Artists, and in April 1962, premiered its own prime time movie slot, *Hollywood Special* (soon renamed *The ABC Sunday Night Movie*). After years of bitter rivalry between network television and the Hollywood studios, the two now looked to each other as important partners in the entertainment industry. The battle was over and their marriage was nearly complete.

As the power at the top, CBS did not have to chase every program fad and unproven concept, but could develop shows at a more leisurely pace in its traditional strengths such as drama and situation comedy. The network had been the home of high quality situation comedies since the early 1950s with programs such as *I Love Lucy, The Honeymooners,* and *The Phil Silvers Show,* but as the decade progressed it had turned from this format to emphasize other forms such as Westerns, quiz shows, and sixty-minute adventure series. Consequently, CBS had not actively searched for successors to the great sitcoms of the decade and had been content with keeping the top ten vehicles of its established stars such as Jack Benny and Danny Thomas. When the other formats faded, the network turned again to comedy for new material. With the obvious success of such programs as *Dennis the Menace,* network president James Aubrey reemphasized this network strength and, in the fall line-ups for 1960 and 1961, one-half of CBS's new programs were situation comedies. Aubrey also encouraged the development of ideas and pilots for additional sitcoms, feeling that the potential for tremendous success rested in this format.

In the summer of 1960, CBS aired *Comedy Spot* which, like many summer filler series, served as a dumping ground for pilot films that had failed to win network support. Occasionally one of the rejected pilots struck a nerve and was picked up for production after all, but most faded away, with the summer broadcast serving as a sad postscript to an aborted idea. The few that were picked up on the rebound sometimes faced special difficulties in production because very often by that time the cast and crew had already committed themselves to other ventures and were no longer interested in the proposed series. One pilot from the summer of 1960 that managed to overcome its initial rejection and find a place in the 1961–62 schedule was a pet project of Sid Caesar's old cohort, Carl Reiner, called *Head of the Family,* which depicted the home and office life of Rob Petrie, the head writer for a television comedy show. It was, in effect, Reiner's own professional story.

In the pilot episode aired on *Comedy Spot,* Petrie (played by Reiner) and his wife Laura (Barbara Britton) had to convince their son Ritchie (Gary Morgan) that his father's job was as interesting and important as those of the other kids' fathers. To prove his point, Rob brought Ritchie to the office to see firsthand how valuable he was to the other two writers, Sally Rogers (Sylvia Miles) and Buddy Sorrell (Morty Gunty), and the show's host, Alan Sturdy (Jack Wakefield). The format seemed workable, the cast adequate, and the writing clever, but it just did not click. Reiner refused to give up on the idea after the initial rejection (drafting additional scripts beyond the pilot), and reworked the series, keeping the format intact but assembling a new cast. He remained an occasional performer as the Alan Sturdy character (renamed Alan Brady), but concentrated on writing and production, relinquishing the lead role of Rob Petrie to Dick Van Dyke (who had bounced about CBS for five years as a host of cartoon and morning programming). Mary Tyler Moore (the leggy, sexy-voiced phone operator "Sam" on *Richard Diamond*) assumed the part of Laura, and Larry Matthews played Ritchie. In a stroke of genius, veteran comics Morey Amsterdam and Rose Marie, who had labored for years in the wilderness after some success in the early days of broadcasting, were cast as the new Buddy and Sally. Amsterdam had been a frequent performer in network television's early days and Rose Marie had begun singing on the NBC radio network when she was three years old (as Baby Rose Marie), and both brought an essential sharp comic edge to their characters. CBS was convinced and scheduled the new series, renamed *The Dick Van Dyke Show,* to begin in October 1961. The new cast lifted the program's highly workable format far above its original promise. Although the series took a few seasons to truly catch on, *The Dick Van Dyke Show* became a worthy successor to *Lucy* and

Bilko, building its own large and loyal audience. The program also had an all star team behind the scenes including executive producer Sheldon Leonard and directors John Rich and Jerry Paris. Reiner penned half the scripts for the first two seasons himself, but also added writers such as Bill Persky, Sam Denoff, Garry Marshall, and Jerry Belson who understood the series dynamic perfectly.

The Dick Van Dyke Show set its action in both the Petrie home in suburban New Rochelle (Reiner's home in real life) and Rob's office in Manhattan. The home scenes were solid and grounded, with support for the domestic situations provided by next door neighbors, Millie and Jerry Helper (played by Ann Morgan Guilbert and director Jerry Paris), but the office scenes were bits of inspired brilliance that gave the show its drive. Reminiscent of another Sheldon Leonard program, *The Danny Thomas Show*, Reiner and his fellow writers set Dick Van Dyke in a world they knew well. Van Dyke, the star of a TV sitcom, portrayed a writer for a TV comedy series, in a part written for him by writers of a TV sitcom. By working with a setting they faced every day (writing for a TV comedy show), they infused the office scenes with sharp, animated humor as Rob, Buddy, and Sally tossed quips back and forth in a rapid-fire style reminiscent of an old vaudeville stage show. The writers also directed some effective barbs against television itself in scenes that involved the show's vain star, Alan Brady (Reiner), and the flunky producer, Brady's brother-in-law, Mel Cooley (Richard Deacon). Whether the comedy was set at work or at home, the situations were always humorous and exaggerated, but still basically identifiable and real. The stories were not a grand satire on the times, but the presentation of comic crises and complications that someone who worked as a New York television writer might face.

Series such as *I Love Lucy* and *Leave It to Beaver* had symbolized life in the 1950s, and *The Dick Van Dyke Show* did much the same for the first half of the 1960s, perfectly capturing the feeling and sense of the Kennedy years. (With her bouffant hairdo, Mary Tyler Moore even looked a little like first lady Jackie Kennedy in those days.) The series presented a range of characters living in a world not very different from the one that many viewers faced. Rob and Laura lived in a real middle class town in which real people commuted to and from real jobs. He was a decent, intelligent, hard-working father and she was a helpful and clever wife who was neither wacky, gorgeous, nor conniving. They were true partners in marriage. The program effectively replaced the interchangeable blandness of the 1950s with a generally believable view of successful middle class life of the early 1960s.

The Dick Van Dyke Show, The Defenders, Dr. Kildare, Ben Casey, and prime time movies were important signs that television was improving and had begun to break out of its mediocre state of the 1960–61 season. Nonetheless, they were only a handful among the new shows that premiered in the fall. Most of the new entries were weak vehicles for talented performers, mindless fluff, or just very bad television. For the most part, the 1961–62 season still carried the unmistakable marks of a vast wasteland.

Several new sitcoms merely maintained the mold of late 1950s blandness: *Window on Main Street* reactivated Robert Young in his favorite role as thoughtful patriarch; *Room for One More,* starring Andrew Duggan, continued television's fascination with families enlarged by adoption or remarriage; *Hazel* (based on the long-running *Saturday Evening Post* cartoon) cast Shirley Booth as maid to possibly the dumbest family in TV history; and *Mrs. G. Goes to College* provided an awkwardly improbable swan song for Gertrude Berg as a newly enrolled student.

Two promising young comics, Bob Newhart and Joey Bishop, made misdirected, undistinguished debuts as comedy headliners. Newhart, whose comedy album *The Button Down Mind* had been a 1960 sleeper hit, was miscast as a genial host of a half-hour variety show. Bishop, who had made a name for himself with his ad-lib witticism on TV panel and talk shows, found himself playing a public relations man in a ploddingly scripted sitcom that wasted his quick wit.

Nat Hiken, the creator of Sergeant Bilko, tried unsuccessfully to duplicate the formula of that series with *Car 54, Where Are You?* Two excellent character actors, Joe E. Ross and Fred Gwynne,

The Dick Van Dyke Show home setting: *(from left)* Dick Van Dyke as Rob Petrie, Larry Matthews as son Ritchie, and Mary Tyler Moore as Laura Petrie. *(CBS Photo Archive © 2003 CBS Worldwide, Inc. All Rights Reserved.)*

were cast as the bumbling policemen who cruised the Big Apple in squad car 54, but it was *Bilko* without Bilko. Ross, as Gunther Toody, faithfully duplicated his bumbling oo-oo-ooing *Bilko* character of Mess Sergeant Rupert Ritzik, but it was not enough. Though he and Gwynne, as the drab, earlobe-pulling Francis Muldoon, provided hilarious caricatures of the Jack Webb lookalikes that appeared to populate nearly every cop show, the two worked best as supporting actors. They could not match the mad energy of Phil Silvers, whose domineering personality had held the *Bilko* show together, and *Car 54, Where Are You?* seemed constantly in search of a main character. Hiken had slipped up on the basics of a good sitcom and as a result the program provided merely adequate diversion, rarely matching the energy of its catchy opening theme song.

One new sitcom, though, managed to top all these minor artistic flaws with a premise that seemed designed to epitomize the term "vast wasteland": The *Hathaways,* one of the worst series ever to air on network TV. The show marked the last step in television's vilification of American parenthood, presenting Jack Weston and Peggy Cass as surrogate parents to three chimpanzees, Enoch, Charley, and Candy. Weston and Cass treated the three chimps as human children, dressing them in children's clothes and encouraging them to imitate human actions such as dancing, eating, and playing. The scripts, acting, and production were horrible, and the premise itself was utterly degrading to both the audience and the actors. (Weston often wore an expression that made him look like a befuddled monkey.) *The Hathaways* more than justified the network executives' early apprehension about the new season and, though it lasted only one year, it stood as an embarrassing example of the depths programmers had reached in their desperate search for a chance hit in any format or premise.

At the office in *The Dick Van Dyke Show*: *(from left)* Dick Van Dyke, Morey Amsterdam as Buddy Sorrell, and Rose Marie as Sally Rogers. *(CBS Photo Archive © 2003 CBS Worldwide, Inc. All Rights Reserved.)*

Despite the total worthlessness of sitcoms such as *The Hathaways,* the programs that attracted the heaviest criticism in the 1961–62 season were the so-called "realistic" crime shows. These programs presented violence that was at best merely gratuitous but at its worst sordid, morbid, and gruesome. Among the merely gratuitous shows were *Cain's Hundred* and *Target: The Corruptors,* two inferior permutations of *The Untouchables* set in the present. In *Cain's Hundred,* Mark Richman portrayed Nicholas Cain, a former mob lawyer who came over to the side of the law and helped track down his former employers, the nation's one hundred top mobsters. Though the series bore some surface resemblance to *The Untouchables* (Richman's Cain personality was very similar to Robert Stack's Eliot Ness; and Paul Monash, executive producer of *Cain,* had worked on the pilot for "The Untouchables"), it lacked high quality supporting characters and any feel for realism. The series focused on little else but gunplay. *Target: The Corruptors* set its violent gunplay under the respectable guise of uncovering modern crime by featuring the adventures of an intrepid newspaper reporter who worked with federal agents to weed out and expose corruption. No matter what area of modern life they investigated, though, violence was inevitable. The series began with a dramatization of crime in the field of garbage collecting and within the first twenty seconds of the premiere episode, a garbage man was shot.

87th Precinct went beyond violence into morbidity and sexual overtones. It was a bad version of *Naked City,* focusing on the daily grind of New York City law enforcement. Detective Steve Carella (Robert Lansing) led a squad of plainclothes cops who were all morose, shoddy, and dense. The plots emphasized cheap thrills and titillating violence. One episode featured the pursuit of a sadistic murderer who first tattooed, then poisoned, his female victims. After a particularly gruesome chase, he was somehow detained by Carella's beautiful deaf-mute wife and then captured. Such individuals and plots cast an appropriately somber pall over the entire series.

Of all the exercises in violence, ABC's drama anthology *Bus Stop* provided the most graphic, brutal, and controversial episode, and the one that touched off a wave of outraged reaction among network affiliates as well as in the halls of Congress. Loosely based on the 1956 movie of the same name, *Bus Stop* set a small central cast in a tiny Colorado town where they awaited the weekly guest stars who inevitably began each story with their arrival at the town's bus depot. At first, the Twentieth Century Fox series dealt in light Hollywood fluff such as an errant father returning to defend the honor of his wrongly accused son. To spice up later episodes, the show turned to more sensationalist tabloid material, culminating in "A Lion Walks Among Us" (directed by Robert Altman). *Bus Stop* used pop singer Fabian as its guest star draw. Though really a very clean-cut young man, Fabian was cast as a degenerate drifter capable only of deceit, betrayal, and murder. To win acquittal of one charge of murder in the town, he had an affair with the D.A.'s alcoholic wife and then used that to blackmail the D.A. Once released, he killed his own lawyers. In a perverse "balance of justice," the D.A.'s wife then killed him.

This sordid episode was labeled "rancid" by one critic and twenty-five stations refused to air it. They claimed it was obscene and that it glorified violence and perversion while deliberately using a teen favorite to entice young viewers. Senator John Pastore of Rhode Island, who was rapidly becoming a vocal new watchdog of television, agreed. He happened to be holding hearings on the very topic of TV violence when the episode aired and he could not get it out of his mind. He brought it up in congressional debate

Both on-screen and as a producer, Ernie Kovacs was a groundbreaking, innovative force in television comedy. *(Courtesy Edie Adams Trust)*

again and again for months as the perfect example of the terrible excesses he was fighting. "I looked at it," he said, "and I haven't felt clean since. I still have the stench in my nose."

In spite of the *Bus Stop* brouhaha, network television weathered its first season following Newton Minow's vast wasteland speech rather well. Westerns no longer saturated each evening's line-up. Action-adventure gave way to medical soap opera. Serious drama returned in the guise of a continuing series. Situation comedy experienced a rebirth. And public affairs programming increased substantially. Overall, television had steered itself away from the mediocre excesses of the immediate past and pulled itself out of the rut it had fallen into after the quiz shows. In the process, TV managed to restore some of the luster to its tarnished respectability. What's more, the public's perception of television quality had risen as well. Consequently, executives planning the 1962–63 season felt no compulsion to implement the full scale changes they had vaguely pledged immediately following Minow's speech. Instead, they slipped back into business as usual and worked at developing imitations and spinoffs of the respectable and successful new doctor, sitcom, and movie formats. At the same time as the networks began seriously considering exactly what to copy for the new fall schedules, television lost one of its true originals, Ernie Kovacs, who died on January 12, 1962, in a car crash.

Kovacs had been the first true *television* comedian. Even back in the *Three to Get Ready* days on a local Philadelphia station, he seemed to understand the visual possibilities inherent in television better than any other performer on the air. Though other comics such as Milton Berle and Sid Caesar were visual performers (that

is, their acts had to be seen to be appreciated), they we[re] doing vaudeville in front of a camera. Kovacs understood potential for humor in the tricks and effects that were possible on[ly] on television. Since his brief stint as a part-time host of the *Tonight* show in the 1956–57 season, Kovacs had been offered few opportunities to perform on network television. He made a few movies in Hollywood while being wasted as host of several low-level ABC series such as *Take a Good Look* (a panel quiz show that used his characters and skits as game clues) and *Silents Please* (in which he supplied funny voice-over comments to cut-downs of old silent films).

In early 1961, Kovacs talked his sponsor, Dutch Masters, into allowing him to produce, write, and act in a series of monthly specials in the company's regular Thursday night *Silents Please* slot. The cigar makers enjoyed having the cigar-chomping Kovacs as host to that show and agreed to support the experiment. On an absurdly small budget for the project he envisioned ($15,000 per show), Kovacs launched his series. From the very first special in April, he totally departed from the then-established form of TV comedy (monologues followed by skits) and presented instead short unconnected bits of humor (blackouts) with an emphasis on visual, often abstract, tricks of TV technology. One thirty-minute program consisted of the visual interpretation of sound, with no narration whatsoever. For instance, instead of showing an orchestra playing "The 1812 Overture," Kovacs used snapping celery stalks and slamming desk drawers as visual accompaniment to the music. He also directed digs at his regular show, *Silents Please,* by taking the logical next step in his manipulation of the old films. Instead of providing just voice-over comments, he used a special effect to physically step into the picture as a frustrated director calling out humorous and absurd orders to the performers.

The program also featured Kovacs's cast of his own continuing characters he had developed over the years, who were quite funny even without the aid of his technological tricks. The most familiar was Percy Dovetonsils, an effeminate, permanently soused poet who read nonsense verse with ludicrous titles such as "Ode to an Emotional Knight Who Once Wore the Suit of Medieval Armor Now in the Metropolitan Museum of Art While Engaged to One of Botticelli's Models." Others included Miklos Molnar, a Hungarian chef also "under the influence," who presented cooking tips; Auntie Gruesome, a dolled-up host to a creature features-type TV show, who ended up scaring himself with his long and gruesome descriptions of the horror stories; and Wolfgang Sauerbraten, a German radio DJ who introduced the latest hits in gibberish German-English clearly aimed at lampooning American broadcasters. Even such sacred objects as the closing credits fell to Kovacs's wit: Once they appeared as writing in a sink and were washed down the drain after each name.

Kovacs turned out eight such specials on ABC before he died and, though hampered by a meager budget, he nevertheless tried to do something different with television. Many viewers were frankly befuddled by what they saw because it departed so dramatically from their expectations for television comedy-variety. Yet that did not matter. What was vitally important was that in an industry content with blandness and imitation, Kovacs dared to challenge the limits of TV technology and steer it into previously unexplored territories. He pioneered a style that would completely alter television comedy, but that would not occur until years later, when his approach and technique were used to form the basis of *Rowan and Martin's Laugh-In* and *Monty Python's Flying Circus.* Long after his ABC specials were aired and forgotten, the world at last understood just what he had been trying to accomplish, and applauded.

22. CBS + RFD = $$$

DESPITE ALL THE PROMISES of programming reform made by television executives in May 1961, the 1962–63 schedule turned out to be business as usual. The improvements during the 1961–62 season had blunted Newton Minow's vast wasteland charge and diffused criticism by the government and the public. Profits and ratings once again became the chief concerns of network programmers and they began to cast a critical eye at the overabundance of news and public affairs shows which had proliferated chiefly as a public relations device to shore up television's respectability. By the 1962–63 season, six prime time programs, two on each network, provided a total of four hours of this type of material weekly: *Howard K. Smith News and Comment* and *Bell and Howell Closeup* on ABC; *CBS Reports* and *Eyewitness* on CBS; and *David Brinkley's Journal* and *Chet Huntley Reporting* on NBC. Nonetheless, several hard-hitting news reports reached prime time in the process, giving the network news departments the opportunity to flex their muscles.

CBS, with a sideways glance at the *cinema verite* style of ABC's *Closeup* documentary series, had hired Jay McMullen in 1961 as its own roving *verite* reporter. Even though at the time the networks had serious reservations about investigative news reporting for television (preferring traditional public affairs documentaries and discussions instead), McMullen was assigned to dig for unusual and controversial material. His first (and best) piece for CBS, "Biography of a Bookie Joint," managed to overcome most network objections to the form and demonstrated the effective impact of investigative TV journalism. McMullen found a key shop in Boston's Back Bay area that was visited by nearly 1,000 people each day, including many policemen. Further investigation revealed that the key shop was actually a bookie joint. He set up an observation post in a room across the street from the shop and, over a period of months, watched and filmed the comings and goings of the key shop's customers and even managed to shoot (admittedly jerky) footage of the shop's interior using an 8mm camera hidden in a false lunch box. Federal agents were informed of the illegal operations by McMullen and they, in turn, apparently tipped off the crew with the time of their impending raid on the shop, giving McMullen the opportunity to film it. "Biography of a Bookie Joint" emerged as an engrossing, real life crime thriller, complete with a dramatic sweep by the Feds as a climax, and it was widely acclaimed by viewers across the country.

In the city of Boston itself, the report caused immediate and long lasting convulsions. The local affiliate did not air it for one and one-half years, while legal wrangling took place. The city's police commissioner was forced to resign, and the Massachusetts legislature censured one member for the disparaging remarks he made on the program about his colleagues. In the ensuing trial, the police, tarnished by the evidence on film of their participation in the illegal gambling joint, tried to disprove the facts and dates contained in the story. Others contended that the show revealed blatant news mismanagement and biased reporting. The accuracy and objectivity of McMullen's story was proved correct at every step, though the charge of bias would be leveled with increasing frequency as investigative TV journalism developed through the decade.

In 1962, NBC presented its own real life dramatic news adventure, "The Tunnel," a ninety-minute war story set in Berlin. Most foreign-oriented documentaries of the time were generic formula pieces that inevitably settled for fluff travelogue visits like "This Is Monaco" and innocuous insights like "Mouamba: Land in Conflict," but "The Tunnel" presented the desperate scheme of some brave heroes in conflict with clear-cut bad guys. The program followed the daring escape of fifty-nine East Berliners through a 450-foot tunnel dug by twenty-one West Berliners. The constant fear of exposure and capture hung over everyone until the exciting climax of the story when the joyful East Berliners successfully made their way under the Berlin wall to freedom. So potent was this story that, due to the international tensions resulting from the Cuban missile crisis in October, "The Tunnel" (originally scheduled to air in October) was delayed two months. When it played in December, it earned critical acclaim, registered surprisingly strong ratings, and proved to be far more dramatic than the artificial action shows that usually filled prime time.

Besides offering a crime expose and war drama, the networks also displayed more daring in traditional documentaries and news reports. *CBS Reports* tackled such previously taboo subjects as birth control and teenage smoking as well as new concerns such as ecology. In "The Silent Spring of Rachel Carson" (broadcast in April 1963), CBS presented an evenhanded examination of the heavy use of pesticides and their possible disruption of the balance of nature, which Carson described in a book she had written. Because the issue was not familiar to most Americans, exposure in a network documentary tremendously aided Carson's side, much as the great debates in 1960 had helped relative unknown John Kennedy achieve an equal footing with Richard Nixon in the eyes of the public. Simply by acknowledging and interviewing advocates of a cause, television could inadvertently aid one side or another and make it almost impossible to ignore an issue or personality. One of the season's major TV controversies, in fact, developed when ABC's Howard K. Smith examined the personality and then-fading career of former Vice President Richard Nixon.

Smith had quit CBS, his long-time home, at the end of 1961 after a phrase comparing Southern bigots to Nazi storm troopers had been blipped from one of his occasional commentaries on the network's nightly TV news (oddly, the comment was left in the radio version). CBS said that Smith had crossed the line between analysis and editorial opinion, so Smith said *adios*, signed with ABC in the beginning of 1962, and immediately received his own program, *Howard K. Smith-News and Comment*. Unlike *David Brinkley's Journal, Chet Huntley Reporting*, and *Eyewitness* (with Walter Cronkite and Charles Kuralt), which all mixed feature reports and in-depth news reviews, Smith attempted to revive the spirit of the radio news commentators of the 1930s and 1940s. Other respected commentators including Quincy Howe and Drew Pearson had tried to bring that style of news analysis from network radio to television in the late 1940s and early 1950s, but the format always seemed too static for television. Smith set his program in a homey living room and embellished the commentary with charts, maps, occasional film clips, and interviews. Despite all the window dressing, it remained essentially just "talking heads" with little visual impact for television. Nonetheless, the program created quite a fuss in November 1962 with "The Political Obituary of Richard Nixon."

Only two years after his unsuccessful bid for the presidency, Nixon had lost a bitter campaign for the governorship of California, and it appeared that he was, in fact, through with politics (or vice versa). Following his latest defeat he proclaimed to the reporters gathered in California that they would not "have Nixon to kick around any more because, gentlemen, this is my last press conference." Smith took Nixon at his word and devoted his program on November 11 to a review of the man's political career, presenting observations from both supporters and detractors. Among those critical of Nixon was Alger Hiss, a former state department official who had been labeled a "Red subversive" in the late 1940s by then Representative Nixon and who eventually served time for perjury. In a one-minute film interview, Hiss said that Nixon's main motivation for doggedly pursuing him had been pure personal and political ambition. Hiss's charges were immediately followed by four minutes of filmed praise for Nixon by Representative Gerald Ford. Despite the careful balance of opinions, the very appearance of Hiss ignited a firestorm of protest. One of the show's sponsors, Kemper Insurance, pulled out. Conservative politicians and some publications, particularly the *Chicago Tribune*, kept the story alive for months, constantly issuing shocked statements asking how a TV network such as ABC could allow a convicted liar on the air. "Mr. Hiss is news," Smith replied, "and we're in the news business. I'm not running a Sunday school program." Other sponsors stuck by the program and ABC sued Kemper for violating its contract (the network eventually won its case). In spite of ABC's vigorous defense, though, it did not appreciate the trouble Smith had stirred up and the veteran newsman was by-passed for major assignments for the next year, and his *News and Comment* disappeared in the summer.

Smith's program joined most of the other public affairs shows that were dropped or lost their regular prime time slot as the networks modified their commitments to news throughout 1963. Executives pointed out that there had been too many shows appearing at once and the reduced frequency would loosen budgets and allow higher quality presentations. Though these programs were

generally well done, there were too many of them and their sheer number diluted the audience and stretched resources far too thin to allow quality productions each week. Besides, the special public affairs programs had already served their chief function very well by contributing to the overall prestige of television and apparently proving to the FCC that the medium was no longer a vast wasteland. No new government regulations had been imposed and none appeared on the horizon. There was therefore no overwhelming reason to continue to carry too many unprofitable shows with generally unspectacular ratings in prime time, though the networks insisted that they strongly supported the continuing growth of their individual news departments.

Even at the season's high water mark in prime time public affairs, many of television's critics saw a network retreat from the form as inevitable. Though they applauded the material carried by ABC, CBS, and NBC, they began searching for some way to break the iron grip of network influence and control over programming. The UHF system and educational television were two potential tools to that end and both exhibited long overdue development in the 1962–63 season. They had both been created by the FCC in 1952 as the freeze on TV station construction was lifted, but had remained catatonic for nearly a decade.

The commission launched educational television in 1952 with a bold stroke, setting aside 242 station allocations specifically for noncommercial broadcasting. Despite this promising beginning, educational broadcasting experienced very little growth over the next ten years. By 1960, there were only forty-eight educational stations on the air. All but four of them were associated with the fledgling National Educational Television (NET) network, but that only produced eight hours of programming each week. What's more, expensive coaxial cable connections were out of the question, so the filmed shows were sent to the affiliates through the mail. Such cost-cutting measures were necessary because, in setting up noncommercial stations, the FCC had left one important problem unresolved: funding. If the stations were to be noncommercial but also independent of the government, where was the money for operational expenses to come from? A few private corporations, particularly the Ford Foundation, stepped in from the beginning and contributed millions, but it was nowhere near the amount necessary to launch a national chain of stations that could be taken seriously by viewers.

There was an additional problem. Viewers. Many of the frequencies so generously earmarked by the FCC for noncommercial use were on the UHF band. None of the eighteen million television sets in use in 1952 were capable of receiving UHF signals. Stations in a few markets such as KQED in San Francisco and WGBH in Boston were lucky enough to receive VHF allocations, but for the most part viewers could not tune in the educational stations, so there was virtually no audience. More important, by the end of the 1950s, major markets such as New York, Los Angeles, Cleveland, and Washington still had no educational station at all. The near invisible status of noncommercial television reduced it to a very expensive laboratory and made it impossible to stir any interest in improving the situation. Until the important figures in broadcasting and government living in New York, Los Angeles, and Washington could see educational television in operation, a solution to the funding problem would never be worked out.

In order to provide a noncommercial outlet in New York City, a group of New York-based forces (calling themselves Educational Television for the Metropolitan Area) decided to buy an existing commercial VHF station and set it up as a showpiece for educational TV. After protracted delays and legal challenges, the group purchased Newark's WNTA, channel 13, for $6.2 million. One-

	Net	7:00	7:30	8:00	8:30	9:00	9:30	10:00	10:30
MON	ABC	local	Cheyenne		The Rifleman	STONEY BURKE		Ben Casey	
	CBS	local	To Tell The Truth	I've Got A Secret	THE LUCY SHOW	Danny Thomas Show	Andy Griffith Show	NEW LORETTA YOUNG SHOW	Stump The Stars
	NBC	local	IT'S A MAN'S WORLD		SAINTS AND SINNERS		The Price Is Right	David Brinkley's Journal	local
TUE	ABC	local	COMBAT!		Hawaiian Eye		The Untouchables		Bell And Howell Close Up
	CBS	local	Marshal Dillon	LLOYD BRIDGES SHOW	Red Skelton Hour		Jack Benny Program	Garry Moore Show	
	NBC	local	Laramie		EMPIRE		Dick Powell Show		Chet Huntley Reporting
WED	ABC	local	Wagon Train		GOING MY WAY		OUR MAN HIGGINS	Naked City	
	CBS	local	CBS Reports / CBS News Specials	The Many Loves Of Dobie Gillis	THE BEVERLY HILLBILLIES	Dick Van Dyke Show		U.S. Steel Hour / Armstrong Circle Theater	
	NBC	local	THE VIRGINIAN			Perry Como's Kraft Music Hall		THE ELEVENTH HOUR	
THUR	ABC	local	Adventures Of Ozzie And Harriet	Donna Reed Show	Leave It To Beaver	My Three Sons	McHALE'S NAVY	Alcoa Premiere / Fred Astaire Presenting	
	CBS	local	Mr. Ed	Perry Mason		THE NURSES		Alfred Hitchcock Hour	
	NBC	local	WIDE COUNTRY		Dr. Kildare		Hazel	ANDY WILLIAMS SHOW	
FRI	ABC	local	THE GALLANT MEN		The Flintstones	I'M DICKENS, HE'S FENSTER	77 Sunset Strip		local
	CBS	local	Rawhide		Route 66		FAIR EXCHANGE		Eyewitness
	NBC	local	International Showtime		Sing Along With Mitch		DON'T CALL ME CHARLIE	JACK PAAR SHOW	
SAT	ABC	Beany And Cecil	ROY ROGERS AND DALE EVANS SHOW	MR. SMITH GOES TO WASHINGTON	Lawrence Welk Show			Fight Of The Week	Make That Spare
	CBS	local	JACKIE GLEASON SHOW		The Defenders		Have Gun, Will Travel	Gunsmoke	
	NBC	local	SAM BENEDICT	New Joey Bishop Show	NBC Saturday Night At The Movies				
SUN	ABC	Father Knows Best	THE JETSONS	The ABC Sunday Night Movie				Voice Of Firestone	Howard K. Smith: News And Comment
	CBS	Lassie	Dennis The Menace	Ed Sullivan Show		The Real McCoys	General Electric True	Candid Camera	What's My Line
	NBC	ENSIGN O'TOOLE	Walt Disney's Wonderful World Of Color	Car 54, Where Are You?		Bonanza		DuPont Show Of The Week / # Dinah Shore Show	

third of the money was donated by CBS, NBC, and ABC, who saw educational television as an excellent way to answer the criticisms leveled at the commercial networks. They could point to their generosity in supporting the noble project even as they continued to concentrate on more profitable popular appeal entertainment. As long as educational television stuck to classroom type programming aimed at the egghead fringe, they knew it would never provide any real competition for the mass audience.

WNTA was renamed WNDT (later changed to WNET) and it hit the New York airwaves on September 16, 1962, as the sixty-eighth educational station in the country. Newton Minow and Ed Murrow hosted the gala opening festivities which were attended by representatives from all three commercial networks. Yet there were conflicting priorities and philosophies among the many divergent interests that had united to establish the new station and these immediately surfaced during the chaotic two-and-one-half-hour premiere broadcast. The networks were most upset by an eighty-three-minute British film which extolled the BBC and labeled American television as 80% junk. They felt the film was a stab in the back after all the support they had given the new station and CBS, NBC, and ABC executives went away angry. The station also faced union problems and had to shut down for two weeks immediately following the premiere telecast in order to resolve them.

When WNDT returned, New Yorkers had an opportunity to see, at last, the wonders of noncommercial television. It was a direct throwback to the very early days of commercial television. Aside from the expected educational fare for children, there were boring discussion shows (*Books for Our Times, Invitation to Art*), attempts at educational fare for adults (*Russian for Beginners, Face of Sweden*), an overload of British films, and the inevitable, excruciatingly detailed thirty-minute studies of esoteric subjects such as Japanese brushstroke painting. All were numbing and not very entertaining, but channel 13 was new to broadcasting, short of money, and uncertain which tricks of the trade would work in the world of noncommercial television.

The increased visibility of educational television did bring about important changes, though. The federal government began handing out small yearly subsidies and the Ford Foundation increased the amount of its support. Educational stations started broadcasting (though on UHF) in Washington and Los Angeles, and the NET network developed its first quasi-hits. *International Magazine* was a weekly news feature program put together by foreign broadcasters (chiefly from the BBC) who covered world events as well as reporters on the commercial networks, and sometimes surpassed them. In February 1963, WGBH in Boston began producing *The French Chef* which featured Julia Child demonstrating elaborate cooking techniques. Within a few months, she became the network's first star as her imposing figure and distinctive voice appeared on NET stations across the country.

Despite these impressive gains, the fate of educational television ultimately rested with the development of UHF, because that's where most of the educational stations were located.

The UHF system had also begun in 1952 and it faced a long struggle to win support among set manufacturers, viewers, and sponsors. From the beginning, manufacturers saw no reason to spend extra money to include UHF capabilities unless their customers demanded it. The public would not demand UHF until there was something worth watching on the system. Until there were enough sponsors to pay for exciting new programs, there could not be anything worth watching, and with so few viewers, what sponsor would make the investment? For more than two years the status of UHF remained unchanged. In September 1954, following government and industry pressure on the FCC to do something to help the system, the commission amended its rules and increased the number of owned and operated stations a network could possess from five to seven, as long as two were UHF stations. It was assumed that if a network affiliate in a major city were on UHF, there would be sufficient demand by the public to push set manufacturers into beginning production of sets capable of receiving both UHF and VHF signals, thus breaking the stagnant situation. Within two years, CBS and NBC had purchased two UHF stations each and began offering their shows on UHF only to viewers in Milwaukee, Wisconsin and Hartford, Connecticut (CBS), and New Britain, Connecticut, and Buffalo, New York (NBC). This did not cause any increased demand for UHF sets. Instead, a few interested people purchased expensive special converters that allowed their old sets to pick up both UHF and VHF signals while most simply tuned to another network.

The FCC then decided to attempt a much more sweeping change and announced that it would suggest ordering cities throughout the country to be designated as either all-UHF or all-VHF markets. The problem with "deintermixture" (as the proposed policy was labeled) was that no city wanted to be converted to an all-UHF market, rendering every television set in town useless. The FCC faced intensive lobbying for and against deintermixture, and wavered back and forth throughout 1956 and 1957, though Peoria, Illinois; Madison, Wisconsin; Evansville, Indiana; and Hartford, Connecticut were actually designated as deintermixture test cities. In late 1957, the commission, in effect, opted for "undeintermixture" and allowed the UHF situation to remain unchanged, thus ending any serious efforts for expansion. By 1959, NBC and CBS had sold their UHF stations and the problem remained unsolved for nearly three more years.

In February 1962, the FCC took up the question again and decided to aim directly at the chief stumbling block to the growth of the UHF system, the home receivers themselves. Instead of counting on the subtle pressures of supply and demand to motivate television set manufacturers into including UHF reception capabilities on their sets, the commission proposed to Congress that a law be passed *requiring* the feature on all new American televisions. Throughout the spring, FCC chairman Newton Minow

The Clampett clan: *(from left)* Jed (Buddy Ebsen), Granny (Irene Ryan), Jethro (Max Baer), and Elly May (Donna Douglas). *(CBS Photo Archive © 2003 CBS Worldwide, Inc. All Rights Reserved.)*

September 10, 1962

Hugh Downs replaces John Chancellor as major domo of *Today*.

September 10, 1962

Mal Goode becomes the first black network correspondent, covering the United Nations for ABC.

September 19, 1962

The Virginian. (NBC). The first ninety-minute television Western and, like *Bonanza*, it is broadcast in color. Though the series has a strong central cast (Lee J. Cobb, James Drury, and Doug McClure), the stories frequently focus on the weekly guest stars.

September 23, 1962

The Jetsons. (ABC). ABC at last airs its *first* program in color, the premiere of another Hanna-Barbera cartoon series. Essentially *The Flintstones* backwards, the new show is a simple animated family sitcom with the setting moved from the Stone Age to the twenty-first century.

September 27, 1962

The Andy Williams Show. (NBC). Mr. Easy Listening enters the limelight in a series produced by Bud Yorkin and Norman Lear. Andy's television "family" includes the four singing Osmond Brothers (ages seven through twelve) who open with "I'm a Ding Dong Daddy from Dumas."

September 29, 1962

Phase two of *The Avengers* in Britain. Patrick Macnee continues his role as a dapper adventurer, but he is now identified as government agent John Steed, and teamed up with a beautiful woman, the ultra-cool widow Mrs. Catherine Gale (played by Honor Blackman). The writing for the revamped format is much sharper and more innovative: On the first new episode, a double agent is killed while appearing on a television talk show.

carried on an effective lobbying effort, with help from the White House, and salvaged the bill after most observers had given it up for dead. To underscore its strong belief that the proposed law offered the best possible solution to the UHF problem, the FCC announced that if the bill were not passed, it would deintermix eight major markets—immediately. A few days later, Congress passed the bill and the commission set April 30, 1964, as the day the law would take effect. Due to manufacturing production schedules, this meant that the 1965 model sets would be the first with both VHF and UHF capabilities.

Though it would take years for the full ramifications of the new law to be felt, it was obvious that changes in American broadcasting would be monumental. Eventually, most television sets in the country would be capable of receiving UHF signals, thus allowing many more independent commercial stations, as well as most of the country's educational stations, the opportunity to survive and grow. The slow but steady growth of UHF in the late 1960s would also help solve ABC's long-standing problem of not having enough affiliates. By the end of the decade, ABC, for the first time, would have stations carrying its programming into every major American city. Newton Minow's work with the "all-channel" bill would change the shape of American television far more than his vast wasteland speech. Its passage provided a satisfying conclusion to his tenure as commissioner and he resigned from the FCC in

1963, having set into motion forces in television that would continue to grow through the next two decades.

After the period of uncertainty that culminated in the 1960–61 vast wasteland season, the commercial networks themselves were at last coasting into the new decade·with confidence, several hit formats, and a sense of control. The 1962–63 season presented a nod toward medical drama (following the success of the previous season's *Ben Casey* and *Dr. Kildare),* several series set in World War II, a surprise revival in variety formats, and an incredibly successful new sitcom. These were added to a schedule that already included strong holdovers in several different formats and some outstanding individual news programs, producing what was, overall, a very good season.

After ABC's performance in the 1961–62 season sent the network back into the cellar, action-adventure whiz Ollie Treyz was forced to walk the plank in March 1962, and the new president, Tom Moore, continued the search for another successful format to bring ABC back into contention. He brought in a revamped schedule for the 1962–63 season which contained the usual ABC potpourri of gimmicks, adding one new one: war. With World War II nearly two decades in the past, it seemed safe for television to restage the conflict, so ABC presented *Gallant Men, Combat!,* and *McHale's Navy. Gallant Men* from Warner Bros. was pure grade-B movie pap that followed the 1943 battle for Italy through the eyes of an American war correspondent who accompanied an infantry squad on vital "suicide" missions that never seemed to endanger him or any other members of the regular cast. The Robert Altman-directed series *Combat!* was more realistic, focusing on the continuing struggles of average soldiers in an infantry unit winding through Europe after D-Day, rather than on supposedly momentous battles that could decide the outcome of the entire war. *Combat!* drew on a consistently good cast of regulars, guest stars, and a first class production unit to develop the personal conflict of men at war into tight drama. The war setting also allowed a good deal of violence and ABC knew that could not hurt in the ratings.

McHale's Navy offered an entirely different view of the same war in a "briny *Bilko*" situation comedy set on an island in the South Pacific. In the true *Bilko* style, the members of the crew under Lieutenant Commander Quinton McHale (Ernest Borgnine) spent most of their time bickering among themselves, gambling, and hatching money-making schemes rather than facing the enemy. Of course, Bilko's adventures had been set in a peacetime Army but McHale's were close enough. The Japanese were usually presented as an unseen threat or convenient plot device rather than a dedicated, visible foe. Borgnine was cast as a lovable conniver, Joe Flynn as the perpetually befuddled C.O., and Tim Conway as the head of McHale's crew of flunkies. Unfortunately, the show suffered from weak scripting and, as if to compensate, most of the characters seemed to be trying too hard to be funny, and their antics paled in comparison to their obvious *Bilko* counterparts. Nonetheless, the series did excel at physical humor and many of the Borgnine-Conway interactions bordered on classic slapstick, often saving the program. The inspired moments of *McHale's Navy* made it funnier than many comedies then on the air (two other new military sitcoms, NBC's *Don't Call Me Charlie* and *Ensign O'Toole,* could barely muster a laugh between them), and the crew managed to survive four seasons, a transplant to the European front, and two theatrical feature films ("McHale's Navy" and "McHale's Navy Joins the Air Force").

As usual, ABC drew on this new programming theme for several more seasons, eventually exploiting nearly every theater of conflict from World War II. Surprisingly, though, the network all but ignored the successful medical format of the previous season and left it to NBC and CBS to produce predictable imitations. *The Nurses* (on CBS) brought the familiar sudsy style of romantic serials to such topical issues as syphilis, thalidomide babies, and drug abuse as well as the struggles of black nurses attempting to make it in medical profession. Naturally, there was an idealistic student nurse and the crusty but compassionate head nurse. For NBC, MGM sent medical drama down the road taken by Warner Bros. in the late 1950s (when it produced a Western that was not a Western, *77 Sunset Strip)* by offering a doctor show that was not quite a doctor show, *The Eleventh Hour.* Though they did not stray far from the operating room, the stories of psychiatrist Theodore Bassett (Wendell Corey) demonstrated that the life, death, and romance found in television's hospitals could be presented within the structure of other occupations in so-called career dramas. The new series managed to incorporate topical and titillating angles such as a frigid woman and her unfaithful husband, illegitimate teenage pregnancy, abortion, and the murder and rape of a girl by a young boy with taints of homosexuality. It was obvious that the format of career drama could be just as soapy as straight medical fare and the studios made plans to develop other spinoffs in the future.

Perhaps the season's biggest surprise was the successful revival of Jackie Gleason's old variety show after several misfired comebacks over the previous five years. It was virtually the same program Gleason had brought to CBS from DuMont a decade earlier (even Art Carney dropped by occasionally) and there was no reason for its revival to work this time. More than likely, the almost total absence of such material from TV for several years, combined with the position Gleason had achieved as one of the medium's immortals, generated enough energy and interest to make the show appear fresh and new again. In any case, there were a few new wrinkles: Most of the skits were placed within the so-called "American Scene Magazine"; and Gleason's Joe the Bartender character was joined every week by comedian Frank Fontaine as the slightly smashed Crazy Guggenheim, whose slurred speech and halfwit manner gave way to a deep operatic voice when he was asked to sing a song. Gleason once again registered high ratings on Saturday night and, within two years, used his clout to move the entire show to "the sun and fun capital of the world," Miami Beach.

Another TV veteran, *Tonight* host Jack Paar, decided the daily routine was too much and moved his variety format intact from his late night slot to prime time on Friday night. During his five years on the *Tonight* show, Paar had cultivated a peculiarly ambivalent image and, in an era of very predictable leading men, was practically the only unpredictable character on TV. He fluctuated between images of a "good-little-boy-who-loves-everybody" and a snarling, slightly blue, cobra that was liable to lash out at enemies, real and imagined, forever prompting the gossip columns to wonder: "What is Jack Paar *really* like?" During his heyday at the turn of the decade, he carried on innumerable public feuds on the air, insulting nationally known entertainers and columnists that had crossed him, even walking off his own show once after an NBC censor had arbitrarily blipped a mildly risqué joke from the day's tape. He made the NBC brass come begging for his return and thereafter he seemed ready and willing to walk off again over other issues, such as his salary and work schedule. Paar had clout with NBC and he knew it. Though his move to prime time left a gaping hole in a slot the network had always found difficult to fill, NBC agreed to it. In prime time, Paar continued his successful approach to variety and interviews, which included a bevy of showbiz celebrity guests (Zsa Zsa Gabor, Jayne Mansfield), up-and-coming young talent (such as writer-turner-comic Woody Allen), nation-

ally known public figures (Richard Nixon was a frequent guest), and home movies depicting his travels to exotic locales of the world. NBC was left with the problem of finding a late night successor.

The network chose Johnny Carson, the host of an ABC daytime game show, *Who Do You Trust?,* for the difficult job of maintaining NBC's lock on late night viewing. Though he had substituted for Paar on the *Tonight* show a number of times, Carson had a very different style and the network was not sure that he could maintain the program's consistently high ratings. NBC brass realized that Paar himself had been in a similar situation in 1957 when he took over the program, and had responded by shaping it to his own style and taste, and into a ratings winner. They felt that Carson probably had the right instincts for the tough job and hoped for similar success. There was one important complication, however. Jack Paar had scheduled his departure from *Tonight* for April 1962 and Carson's contract with ABC did not expire until October. Though he had been allowed to moonlight as host on a part time basis in the past, ABC refused to let him start a permanent stint on another network before his contract ran out. This resulted in a five-month interregnum that provided a golden opportunity for anyone else to attempt to snatch the late night audience from NBC. The network hung tight with guest hosts joining Paar's number two man, Hugh Downs, who remained on hand to provide some continuity. The expected challenge to the *Tonight* show came, ironically, from a former host of the program, Steve Allen, whose latest variety show

---

September 30, 1962
  The Saint. Former Maverick cousin Roger Moore portrays yet another Anglican spy, the very handsome Simon Templar a.k.a. The Saint, for Britain's ATV network.

October 1, 1962
  The Merv Griffin Show. (NBC). The former singer and game show host tries his hand at an hour-long afternoon talk show, with help from such writers as Pat McCormick and Dick Cavett. This daytime version of *Tonight* fades by April.

April 1, 1963
  Twenty-six-year-old Fred Silverman, who, during the late 1950s, did his masters thesis at Ohio State on ABC's programming schedule, becomes chief daytime programmer for CBS.

May 12, 1963
  CBS bars twenty-one-year-old Bob Dylan from singing "Talkin' John Birch Society Blues" on *The Ed Sullivan Show*, even though Sullivan approved it. Dylan takes a hike and refuses to appear at all.

May 14, 1963
  Newton Minow resigns as FCC chairman.

May 15, 1963
  Gordon Cooper sends the first live television pictures from an American astronaut in orbit, but NASA refuses to allow the networks to show them.

August 30, 1963
  The final weekday appearance of *American Bandstand.* Beginning September 7, the program will appear only on Saturday afternoons.

for ABC had been foundering. Allen was signed by the Westinghouse (Group W) stations to host a pre-taped late night talk show that was syndicated throughout the country and run in direct competition with NBC. With a few months head start on Carson, Allen's new show, produced by Allan Sherman, managed to maintain respectable ratings even without his old familiar family of supporting performers. It was clear that Carson's task would not be easy.

Carson took over *Tonight* on October 1, 1962, bringing along his game show cohort, Ed McMahon, as his number two man. (Hugh Downs left the show in September to become the host of the morning *Today* program.) Like Paar, Carson grew comfortably into the job and tailored the show to fit his style, shifting the emphasis from variety to light talk. He carefully limited his involvement as a central performer to his daily monologue and occasional sketches, preferring instead the role of overall program manipulator whose main job was to keep up the pace by steering guests into productive areas of conversation (interesting, funny, ribald) and injecting humorous barbs. By not overextending himself, Carson was able to maintain viewer interest in his personality (a mixture of Midwestern farm boy naiveté and Hollywood brashness), even without a familiar family of guests (McMahon and the band were the only regulars). He brought a relaxing charisma to the late night slot and was soon known to all simply as "Johnny." The *Tonight* show withstood challenges mounted both in syndication (Mike Douglas and Merv Griffin) and on the other networks (Les Crane and Joey Bishop), and Carson remained as host of the slot longer than Jerry Lester, Steve Allen, and Jack Paar combined, giving NBC unquestioned supremacy in late night programming into the 1990s.

For the rest of the broadcast day, though, CBS ruled the ratings. At one time in the 1962–63 season, CBS had all of the top ten daytime shows and eighteen of the top twenty prime time shows. Network president James Aubrey's decision to develop CBS's traditional strength, situation comedy, paid off far beyond his expectations. Though there were a few flops such as *Fair Exchange* (an attempt to expand sitcoms to a sixty-minute format) and the transplanted *Real McCoys* (with only Luke, Grandpa, and Pepino left), the new vehicle for Lucille Ball was an outright smash. In *The Lucy Show* she was reunited with Vivian Vance and played yet another TV widow trying to raise her children, outfox her boss (the omnipresent Gale Gordon), and earn extra money. Lucy quickly returned to the top ten alongside Jack Benny, Andy Griffith, and Danny Thomas. By February, the increasingly popular Dick Van Dyke joined their ranks. And then there were the Clampetts.

The Beverly Hillbillies opened to some of the worst reviews in TV history. Critics tore the show apart for its many obvious faults: The plots were abysmal, the dialogue childish, and the production Hollywood-to-the-core. What they failed to recognize or perhaps refused to accept was that the program was extremely funny. Viewers apparently had no difficulty detecting the comic strengths of the show because, within six weeks of its premiere, it became the number one show in the nation. Not since *The $64,000 Question* had a new program risen to the top so fast.

Like *Lucy, Bilko,* and *The Honeymooners, The Beverly Hillbillies* respected the basics of situation comedy. It contained both a humorous premise and central characters that had the potential for continuous exploitation week after week. Another product of the mind of Paul Henning (from *The Real McCoys),* the show presented a family of Ozark hillbillies who moved to California after striking oil on their property and becoming fabulously wealthy. The dichotomy of a hillbilly clan living in a sumptuous Beverly Hills mansion provided two important sources of humor: the naiveté of the Clampetts as they persisted in their backwoods

manners and morals in posh Beverly Hills, and the specious sham of Beverly Hills itself as snobby rich people put aside their exclusive standards and bowed to the Clampett fortune. A careful mixture of craziness and sanity in the cast of characters allowed this setup to work perfectly as Henning took the make up of *I Love Lucy* and turned it on its head. In *I Love Lucy,* the generally realistic premise set Lucy as the "zany but lovable madcap" in a normally sane world. *The Beverly Hillbillies* was just the opposite. The premise was implausible, so Henning placed one rational mind in an otherwise madcap, lunatic world.

Jed Clampett (Buddy Ebsen) provided the oasis of reason among the loco characters. Jed was a simple backwoods man who possessed most of the admirable traits connected with rural folks: he was decent, unpretentious, and sagacious. More than anyone else in the show, Jed understood not only his immediate family but the strange breed of people living in Beverly Hills as well. He quickly figured out how the big city folks operated, but he never assimilated, keeping his mountain clothes and downhome drawl despite his new-found wealth. Only Jed, the family and neighborhood peacemaker, kept his head while everyone else engaged in heated spats and irrational flights of fancy. Without him, the Clampett house and the program itself would have collapsed into anarchistic rubble.

With Jed as a central hub of normality, the lunatic characters of the show could take off, as the philosophies and manners of Beverly Hills met those of the Ozark Mountains head on. Jed's mother-in-law, Granny (Irene Ryan), was an unreconstructed Confederate always ready to fly into a rage against the forces of modern America. She never accepted her new surroundings as her real home, remaining convinced that nothing in California would ever come close to what she had left behind in the hills. Granny made no attempt to hide her disdain for the city folks and waged a never-ending war with anyone she saw attempting to upset her way of life. That included practically everybody.

Elly May (Donna Douglas), Jed's beautiful but unmarried daughter, was also off in a world of her own, though she had no quarrel with normal society as long as it played by the rules she was familiar with. Consequently, she continued to act the way she felt any normal girl should act, perpetually dumbfounding potential suitors by ignoring the traditional shy demure pose of young debutantes and persisting in her tomboyish independence. Elly May loved animals, from homed toads to goats, and was also proud to display her physical strength, easily outwrestling any prospective husband. She never appreciated the fact that she had moved into an entirely new world and she could never understand why she had so little success in finding a mate in the wilds of Beverly Hills.

Elly May was a clarion of clarity compared to her cousin, Jethro Bodine (Max Baer, son of the former heavyweight champ). He was the quintessential country rube, a refugee from the sixth grade who had no difficulty understanding the big city: it was one huge playground. Very much a ten-year-old mind in a twenty-year-old body, he engaged in childish mischief playing with such Beverly Hills toys as hot rods, swimmin' pools, and movie stars. More than anyone else, Jethro needed the constant attention of his Uncle Jed for discipline and guidance, so that he would not be swept away by the distractions and excitement of the city and lose his hillbilly roots.

Trying to uphold the reputation of Beverly Hills were Jed's banker, Milburn Drysdale (Raymond Bailey), and his secretary, Jane Hathaway (Nancy Kulp). The pair provided an upper class mirror of the Clampetts, funny in their own marvelously lampooned world and even funnier when they tried to imitate the hillbilly ways of their clients. Drysdale filled the traditional sitcom image of a business executive: He was a dimwitted, amoral schemer driven totally by the possession and acquisition of money. Beyond that, Drysdale constantly humiliated himself to satisfy every whim of the Clampetts. He could not risk the possibility that they might move their boodle elsewhere, so he willingly bent every rule of genteel conduct for them. Miss Hathaway was a stuck-up, overeducated snobbish big business secretary who was as totally dedicated to pleasing the Clampetts as her boss and she effectively bullied anyone who dared cross her path. The two were models of self-serving dedication and they stood at the center of high society's world as it fell to the hillbillies.

In spite of all the reviewers who told viewers *The Beverly Hillbillies* was a stupid show, the audience laughed. It really did not matter that the plots were innocuous and the dialogue quite silly. The characters were genuinely amusing and it was a joy to see them go through their paces. The program was an exaggerated farce, in the tradition of television's most cherished comedy shows. And it was funny.

The overwhelming success of *The Beverly Hillbillies*, and comedy in general in 1962–63, propelled CBS to an astounding lead in nighttime ratings. On the average, CBS's prime time schedule earned higher ratings that year than any other network schedule in television's past. Added to its total domination of daytime programming, the season's prime time success made CBS appear invincible, and most of the hit shows looked as if they could last for years. More important, the success of *The Beverly Hillbillies* and veteran *Andy Griffith* convinced not only CBS, but the industry at large, that rural-based situation comedies were the new key to the public's heart. Once again, the networks stood ready to give the public exactly what it wanted. In abundance.

23. Hands Across the Ocean

CBS REIGNED AS THE UNDISPUTED KING of television entertainment programming in 1963 and network president James Aubrey aimed to consolidate that position in the new fall line-up. He shifted the time slots of a few veterans, added several new drama and variety programs, and began the seemingly endless procession of country clones from the wildly successful *Beverly Hillbillies.* As Aubrey was fine-tuning the prime time schedule, CBS News moved to regain its preeminence in the nightly news race, one of the few program periods where the network was not number one. Though CBS was the acknowledged leader in producing news documentaries, the much more commercially lucrative nightly news slot was then consistently dominated by NBC's *Huntley-Brinkley Report.*

The perpetual battle between the CBS and NBC news departments had begun on the radio in the late 1930s. In an era dominated by a reliance on outside wire services for the latest headlines, CBS had taken the lead in developing its own news-gathering operation. During World War II, Edward R. Murrow's live on-the-spot reports from England allowed the entire country to share the dramatic events in Europe, and put CBS far out in front of NBC in news prestige and ratings. As the networks set up their television news operations in the 1940s, CBS took the lead in this new medium by using a constant, familiar figure as its nightly news anchor-young Douglas Edwards. By 1950, NBC's slick professional newsreel show, *Camel News Caravan* with John Cameron Swayze, had passed Edwards and had remained at the top for several years, fading from number one in the mid-1950s as the public tired of Swayze's overly theatrical style. In 1956, NBC replaced him with Chet Huntley and David Brinkley, a news team that had proved very popular covering the political conventions that year, and by 1958 it was on top once again with *The Huntley-Brinkley Report,* retaining that lead into the 1960s.

Despite the strong competition between the two networks, their fifteen-minute TV news programs were remarkably similar and stuck to the simple formula of a news anchor reading the headlines for major news items and covering a few stories in moderate detail, possibly with accompanying film. The network news departments could cover scheduled special events such as presidential elections quite well, but were limited to a handful of cities for breaking stories. The two news giants had only recently begun acting like independent news organizations at all by setting up their own camera crews and bureaus in their New York, Washington, and Chicago locations, but it remained virtually impossible for them to cover adequately events in most other American cities. The networks still had to rely on local affiliates for film footage and reports from out in the hustings. In December 1961, CBS announced a major change in its news-gathering operation as it established four additional domestic bureaus—in Los Angeles, Denver, Atlanta, and Dallas—to give the network the capability of covering, on its own, almost any news event in the United States. The expansion allowed the CBS nightly news program to shift from the leisurely newsreel style of the past to a roving reporter format that encouraged its bureau heads, such as Dan Rather in Dallas (newly hired from Houston's KHOU), to dig for stories and move immediately on major events. Accompanying this reorganization behind-the-scenes was an important on-camera substitution. After sixteen years as anchor, Douglas Edwards was deftly deposed by CBS and replaced by Walter Cronkite, a newsman who had been CBS's man at political conventions, elections, and space shots for more than a decade and who had already become, in the public's eye, Mr. CBS News. Cronkite took over the show in April 1962, and CBS hoped that his proven ability to engender public trust would attract more viewers than the effective but somehow distant Edwards. These changes set the stage for the most important move of all: expanding the length of the nightly news show, which had remained at fifteen minutes since its inception in the 1940s. With the number of network bureaus more than doubled, fifteen minutes was not enough time to present all the stories they could turn out. Though affiliates were reluctant to surrender lucrative local news time to an expanded national newscast, after intensive lobbying by the network, the locals agreed.

On September 2, 1963, CBS launched its expanded news program with a new set, a new regular feature, a special opening night interview, and an intense publicity campaign usually reserved only for fall premieres of entertainment programs. In a departure from the traditional sparse studio news set, CBS placed Cronkite at a desk directly in the newsroom itself, with other people working at their own desks visible in the background, and the noise of the news teletype machines audible as well. He was joined by Eric Sevareid, who began fourteen years of nightly commentary and analysis that evening. As a special opening night attraction, CBS aired a lengthy, exclusive interview Cronkite had conducted with President Kennedy, in which they discussed Vietnam, civil rights, and the 1964 election—topics that the expanded news programs could begin to cover with regularity and depth never before possible on television. One week later, NBC expanded *The Huntley-Brinkley Report* to thirty minutes (including its own exclusive interview with President Kennedy), and joined the shift to the more comprehensive approach to the news. Network news had done more that double in length; its quality had improved tremendously in the process.

When the fall's new entertainment programs appeared, though, news once again receded into the background and viewers began selecting their favorites for the season. To no one's surprise, CBS continued its domination of prime time television with *The Beverly Hillbillies* again in the number one spot and situation comedy in general thriving. There was also considerable interest in variety because two major entertainment figures who had for years avoided television series commitments signed up for new weekly programs: Judy Garland and Jerry Lewis. Neither show survived the season.

Judy Garland had triumphed the previous season in a low-key, easy-going special with friends Frank Sinatra and Dean Martin, and she had agreed to try the weekly grind for CBS by continuing that same style of program with Norman Jewison as producer. Unfortunately, this mood was not successfully transplanted to her series which suffered from some inconsistent writing and inappropriate casting. Jerry Van Dyke (younger brother of Dick) was given the "show-within-a-show" role of Judy's teacher in TV technique. The boisterous Van Dyke personality was completely at odds with Garland's and the hoped-for humorous interactions between the two fell flat. Occasionally particular guest star segments of the show worked well, such as Garland's numbers with her young daughter, Liza Minnelli, and up-and-coming young singer Barbra Streisand, but the success of the program rested on the weekly scripts and Garland's overall performance, and both were far too erratic. Against the steadily increasing strength of NBC's *Bonanza,* the show brought in embarrassingly low ratings, despite the strong lead-in provided by Ed Sullivan. Garland went through several producers before her program quietly expired in the spring.

ABC took the biggest variety gamble of the season by providing a 120-minute vehicle for TV's *enfant terrible,* Jerry Lewis. The network invested nearly $9 million in the project, including a share of the expensive, extensive remodeling of the El Capitan theater in Hollywood (scene of Richard Nixon's Checkers speech) to serve as the locale for the show. Besides being live (in an era when nearly every other show was on film or tape), the series violated several unwritten laws of prime time television. Variety shows were usually given a one-hour block to fill; Lewis's new live show was two hours every week. Network prime time schedules normally ended at 11:00 P.M.; Lewis's show ran from 9:30 P.M. until 11:30 P.M. Most variety shows stocked themselves with a family of secondary comics and singers to help ease the pressure on the host; Lewis tried to carry the whole show by himself, relying only on guest appearances by his well-known showbiz friends for support. Lewis was certainly funny enough to carry his own television show but, in this case, he tried too many innovations at once, and the program fell flat in its premiere. Everybody appeared tense. Camera shots and mike cues were off. A huge screen set up so that the studio audience could see the show just as it was seen by the home audience failed to work and ended up blocking their view. With the audience blinded, Lewis's timing was thrown off. Worst of all, the skits were bad. Reviewers labeled it a "tasteless flop" and the program never recovered. The harder Lewis worked, the more frantic the show seemed to get, never settling down to acquire any style, pace, or direction. Instead of being an "informal two hours of fun, entertainment, discussion, and interviews in a spontaneous atmosphere" it took on the appearance of a weekly Jerry Lewis telethon containing a few entertaining performances by superstar guests amid extended stretches of clumsy filler. Perhaps *The Jerry Lewis Show* might have had a chance if it had been only one hour long so that the writers would not have been so desperate for material, or if it had been prerecorded on tape so that some of the more complicated bits could have been staged several times and reworked. Even against such tough competition as *Gunsmoke* and the NBC movie, Lewis might have then triumphed instead of being clobbered by them. In December, ABC, making the best of a bad situation, paid Lewis $2 million to tear up the contract for forty shows. Lewis closed his final show in anger, blaming his failure on the networks and sponsors who, he said, did not like his "non-conformist ideas." "I don't like to do like I'm supposed to!" he explained.

Though Lewis was gone, ABC was still stuck with the remodeled El Capitan theater. In a surprise move, the network decided to replace the flopped Jerry Lewis variety show with another variety show from the same theater. What's more, *The Hollywood Palace* (as both the series and theater were rechristened) did not even have a regular host. Instead, the program used guest stars as hosts to what was essentially a sixty-minute vaudeo show straight out of the *Toast of the Town* mold, featuring eight different acts that were presented in the lavish, almost garish, setting of the cavernous Hollywood Palace. Although originating in Hollywood, the show brought the look and feel of Las Vegas-style revues to network television. Apparently, the absence of such material on other networks and the wide range of guest hosts (from Bing Crosby to Phyllis Diller) made the show appear fresh and exciting because, against all odds, it caught on and lasted until the end of the decade.

The Hollywood Palace was another case of a classic format being revived and updated for a new generation of viewers, just as sitcoms such as *The Dick Van Dyke Show* and drama programs such as *The Defenders* had successfully brought these forms into the 1960s. Though some mourned the passing of the originals, especially in live drama, it was necessary and inevitable for television to move on. In June of 1963, the *U.S. Steel Hour* and the *Armstrong Circle Theater* were axed, and at the end of the 1963–64 season, the last of the New York-based drama series, David Susskind's *DuPont Show of the Week,* was also canceled. The concept of weekly live drama (or live-on-tape) had fit well with television's early years but seemed an anachronism in an age of mass entertainment shows and high pressure ratings races. More important, though the golden age of television produced many priceless moments, it had been elevated, in memory, to a higher position than it ever deserved. There were, after all, many very bad live dramas, and the productions were often not really the thrilling challenge many people fondly looked back on. Upon the demise of his *DuPont Show,* David Susskind, who had carried on live drama almost single-handedly for the past few years, candidly acknowledged that the excitement of staging such drama was mostly "hallucinatory; like the kicks induced by cocaine, it's not worth the hangover." With the avenues opened by filmed series, it seemed ridiculous to endure the physical limitations of the studio, the omnipresent feeling of claustrophobia, and the occasional minor but distracting fluffs of live productions. Film was easier to work with, cost about the same, and, if handled with discipline and skill, could rival the best work from the golden age of television.

Susskind's Talent Associates achieved artistic success in a filmed series that very season with *East Side, West Side,* a career drama modeled somewhat after *The Defenders.* The series was shot in New York City and dealt with contemporary social problems faced by a Manhattan social worker, Neil Brock (George C. Scott) and his secretary, Jane Foster (Cicely Tyson). Each week's episode

Day	7:00	7:30	8:00	8:30	9:00	9:30	10:00	10:30	
MON	local	THE OUTER LIMITS			Wagon Train		BREAKING POINT		ABC
	local	To Tell The Truth	I've Got A Secret	The Lucy Show	Danny Thomas Show	Andy Griffith Show	EAST SIDE, WEST SIDE		CBS
	local	NBC Monday Night At The Movies				HOLLYWOOD AND THE STARS	Sing Along With Mitch		NBC
TUE	local	Combat!		McHale's Navy	THE GREATEST SHOW ON EARTH		THE FUGITIVE		ABC
	local	Marshal Dillon	Red Skelton Hour		PETTICOAT JUNCTION	Jack Benny Program	Garry Moore Show		CBS
	local	MR. NOVAK		Redigo	RICHARD BOONE SHOW		Andy Williams Show / Bell Telephone Hour		NBC
WED	local	Adventures Of Ozzie And Harriet	PATTY DUKE SHOW	The Price Is Right	Ben Casey		CHANNING		ABC
	local	CBS Reports / CHRONICLES		GLYNIS	The Beverly Hillbillies	Dick Van Dyke Show	DANNY KAYE SHOW		CBS
	local	The Virginian			ESPIONAGE		The Eleventh Hour		NBC
THR	local	The Flintstones	Donna Reed Show	My Three Sons	JIMMY DEAN SHOW		Sid Caesar Show / EDIE ADAMS SHOW	local	ABC
	local	Password	Rawhide		Perry Mason		The Nurses		CBS
	local	TEMPLE HOUSTON		Dr. Kildare		Hazel	KRAFT SUSPENSE THEATER / # Perry Como's Kraft Music Hall		NBC
FRI	local	77 Sunset Strip		BURKE'S LAW		THE FARMER'S DAUGHTER	Fight Of The Week	Make That Spare	ABC
	local	GREAT ADVENTURE		Route 66		The Twilight Zone	Alfred Hitchcock Hour		CBS
	local	International Showtime		BOB HOPE PRESENTS THE CHRYSLER THEATER / # Bob Hope Show		HARRY'S GIRLS	Jack Paar Show		NBC
SAT	local	Hootenanny		Lawrence Welk Show		JERRY LEWIS SHOW (to 11:30)			ABC
	local	Jackie Gleason Show		NEW PHIL SILVERS SHOW	The Defenders		Gunsmoke		CBS
	local	THE LIEUTENANT		Joey Bishop Show	NBC Saturday Night At The Movies				NBC
SUN	local	THE TRAVELS OF JAMIE McPHEETERS		ARREST AND TRIAL			100 GRAND	ABC News Reports	ABC
	Lassie	MY FAVORITE MARTIAN	Ed Sullivan Show		JUDY GARLAND SHOW		Candid Camera	What's My Line	CBS
	BILL DANA SHOW	Walt Disney's Wonderful World Of Color		GRINDL	Bonanza		DuPont Show Of The Week / NBC Specials		NBC

focused on a particular aspect of the seamy side of the big city such as prostitution, juvenile delinquency, and inadequate housing, and often developed into something of a social docudrama on the injustices of American life, with Scott and Tyson sometimes used only peripherally as part of the discussion. In spite of such a potentially dry format, many episodes were gems of insight and warmth (such as James Earl Jones's portrayal of an enraged but powerless Harlem father whose baby had died of a rat bite) and the series emerged as one of the best attempts ever to combine dramatic entertainment with social commentary. Nonetheless, there was not very much latitude in the show's premise; as a mere social worker Scott could do little but offer words of advice when confronted with yet another problem. In a mid-season attempt to remedy this shortcoming, Scott's character went to work for a local congressman so that possible solutions could be presented. Despite the first class writing and production, and the variation in format, the show never succeeded in shaking off its generally maudlin tone and vanished after only one season.

The most successful new drama of the season was ABC's *The Fugitive,* a Quinn Martin production. Rather than dealing with all the social ills of the country, it focused on the struggle of one man, Dr. Richard Kimble, an outlaw that society was out to destroy. Created by former *Maverick* producer Roy Huggins, the series was loosely inspired by the real-life 1950s murder case of Dr. Sam Shepard, with elements of Victor Hugo's *Les Miserables* and

Route 66 thrown in. *The Fugitive* followed the flight of Dr. Kimble (David Janssen), who had been unjustly accused and convicted of murdering his wife, but who had managed to escape his police guard and execution in the confusion following the wreck of the train carrying him to the death house. Though free, Kimble faced the twin tasks of finding a mysterious one-armed man he had seen leaving the scene of the crime (but who could not be found at the time of the trial) and evading the pursuit of police Lieutenant Philip Gerard (Barry Morse) who was "obsessed with his capture."

In a TV world populated almost exclusively by winners, Kimble was a loser, free to go anywhere he wanted in the United States, but living in constant fear of capture. He was a prisoner of the entire country because anyone, even those he befriended in his travels, could turn him in, wittingly or unwittingly. Whenever Kimble found himself becoming too involved in people's lives, he would "clam up" and attempt to fade into the background, unnoticed. As a convicted murderer under a death sentence, any move that made him stand out, however briefly, was literally a life-and-death gamble. Yet despite the risks, he was inevitably drawn into other people's lives because he needed them in order to evade the law, track the one-armed man, and escape his own loneliness. Janssen's low-key acting style captured perfectly the behavior of a man on the run, down to the guarded mannerisms and nervous tics of a fugitive. His sad, quick smile (a brief rise in one corner of his mouth while the rest of his face remained immobile) said it all: Dr.

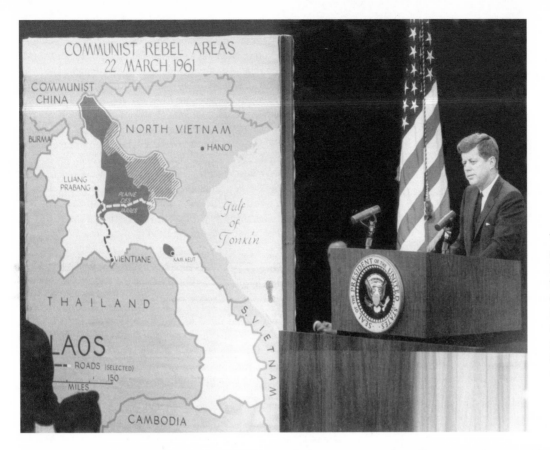

Throughout his time in office, President John Kennedy regularly held televised news conferences that covered both domestic issues and international issues. *(National Archives Photo by Abbie Rowe/National Park Service)*

Kimble could never find true peace, even if he met people who believed in his innocence; he had to keep running and to find the one-armed man because the alternative for him was death. No amount of human kindness could change that cold, hard fact. The tension created by this setup gave the series an underlying dramatic edge that was skillfully underplayed but constantly present.

In many ways, *The Fugitive* was a program ahead of its time, presenting the intense struggle of a truly alienated American years before the phrase became popular. Other characters such as Maverick and Paladin had operated on a different moral plane than traditional society, but they had chosen that life, thrived on it, and could one day probably settle somewhere without much difficulty. Richard Kimble could never let down his guard, relax, and rejoin normal society. He had been forced outside its boundaries by its legal machinery even though he was innocent, and his only chance for survival rested with his own individual strength and determination. Until he could find a man the police forces had been unable to locate, even while dodging these same forces himself, Kimble was an outcast, a hunted man as well as a hunter. In the late 1960s, television and movies tried to exploit the feeling of alienation that seemed to grip many people in the country then, but most of those vehicles were shallow and failed to grasp the scope of emotions involved. *The Fugitive* managed to handle the concept of alienation with considerably more success and at the same time treat more complex themes of justice, guilt, and justified paranoia as well. Though such themes had previously appeared on TV, chiefly in the extinct drama anthologies, *The Fugitive* developed them over time in a well produced weekly series. It took four years for Richard Kimble to come face-to-face with the one-armed man. Through it all, the series maintained strong ratings (it was frequently in the top ten) and a loyal audience that found itself caught up in both the characters and the premise, as the series seemed to touch an almost hidden vein of American sympathies.

The refinement of themes and formats from television's early days was not limited to entertainment programs. One of the devastating issues of the 1950s, blacklisting, popped up again, even though it had been assumed that the triumph of John Henry Faulk in 1962 had marked the end of the odious practice. It had not.

In early 1963, ABC decided to latch onto the latest teen music fad, folk music, with *Hootenanny,* a weekly series taped on various college campuses. For the April premiere program, the reigning queen of American folk music, Joan Baez, was slated to appear with Pete Seeger, the man who had invented the word "hootenanny" along with Woody Guthrie. Then ABC announced that it would not accept Seeger because of his well-known leftist politics and, in particular, because on August 18, 1955, during the height of blacklisting, he had refused to answer questions put to him by the House Un-American Activities Committee on his Communist Party ties. Blacklisting was not dead, and ABC was not alone in its apprehension over Seeger. In January 1962, NBC had vetoed a scheduled appearance by Seeger on *The Jack Paar Show* and, in early 1963, CBS had done the same to his planned participation in a folk music special. The networks were still wary of controversial figures and allegations of subversive activities, and now relied on a policy of "network censorship" (the phrase seemed less McCarthyesque than blacklisting) to protect themselves. Though the controversy over Seeger and the issue of his blacklisting soon faded, the issue of censorship remained and, six years later, Seeger would once again bring it to a head.

Hootenanny's premiere went on without Seeger. And without Joan Baez, the Greenbriar Boys, Tom Paxton, and Ramblin' Jack Elliott, who all refused to perform on the program in protest. Despite this inauspicious beginning, the show recovered and became a surprise hit, hanging on through the spring and summer to earn a niche in ABC's fall schedule for 1963. *Hootenanny* was an effective outlet for folk music and introduced many performers

September 15-21, 1963

ABC, which premiered its new shows late the previous season, experiments by unveiling all of its new fall shows in one "sneak preview" week. In the process, the number three network beats NBC and CBS out of the starting block.

September 15, 1963

100 Grand. (ABC). Live, from New York, an attempt to bring big money quizzes back to television after four years of exile. Emcee Jack Clark directs grimacing contestants through the "new" but all-too-familiar formula (instead of isolation booths there are big soundproof bubbles). It is the biggest flop in years and the show is axed on September 29.

September 15, 1963

Arrest and Trial. (ABC). The gimmick: Tie two forty-five minute shows together with a common plot. In the "arrest" portion, Ben Gazzara plays the cop who tracks down and captures the accused criminal. Chuck Connors plays the defense counselor in the courtroom *denouement.* Problem: One of the stars has to be proved wrong!

September 16, 1963

The Outer Limits. (ABC). A well-written science fiction anthology series with a distinctive flair for frightening monsters and scary plot twists. After building a respectable following on Monday night, the program is torpedoed in its second season when ABC moves it opposite CBS's Saturday night powerhouse, *The Jackie Gleason Show.*

September 17, 1963

The Fugitive. (ABC). The day the running starts.

September 24, 1963

Petticoat Junction. (CBS). Paul Henning begins spinning off successful series from *The Beverly Hillbillies.*

September 24, 1963

Mr. Novak. (NBC). James Franciscus plays a Dr. Kildare of the classroom, with Dean Jagger in the mentor-principal Dr. Gillespie style role.

---

previously unknown to the American public, including Canada's Ian and Sylvia (Tyson), Ireland's Clancy Brothers, and natives such as the Simon Sisters (Carly and Lucy), the Smothers Brothers, and the very all-American Chad Mitchell Trio. At the same time, the show displayed little musical and emotional connection with the new wave of folk protest then in vogue. It was the folk equivalent to the Dick Clark *Beechnut Show,* presenting a new form of music in an antiseptic forum. Host Jack Linkletter (Art's son) was, like Dick Clark, more a clean-cut announcer than someone in tune with the spirit of the music. He and the producers were content with the happy-go-lucky song-around-a-campfire style of such safe singers as Glenn Yarbrough and the Limeliters, the Rooftop Singers, and the New Christy Minstrels, and they tried to avoid the controversy inherent in protest figures like Bob Dylan, Phil Ochs, and Pete Seeger. Though *Hootenanny* lasted the season, it, and the entire folk music boom, was soon outdistanced by a seemingly brand new musical style that slipped in from over the horizon.

In October 1963, *The Ed Sullivan Show* featured British singer Cliff Richard, who had been the reigning king of rock'n'roll in Britain for five years, but had never made a dent in the American charts. Then, in November, Sullivan met with young British impresario Brian Epstein, who managed that country's hottest group, The Beatles. Something was up. Sullivan, a man who had made his name in television being one step ahead of the public's mood, was devoting attention to the British brand of rock'n'roll, a form then often ridiculed, if not completely ignored, in the U.S.

Ed Sullivan had actually been a little late in picking up on the previous major teen phenomenon, Elvis Presley, so he might have been more attuned to reports in the British press about a new generation of successful homegrown rockers. A frequent traveler to Europe, Sullivan was struck by the frantic reception teenagers there had given The Beatles, a reaction the British press had already dubbed "Beatlemania." Brian Epstein's subsequent pitch to feature The Beatles on Sullivan's show was perfectly timed, coming just a week after the group had stolen the show at Britain's annual Royal Command Performance variety show. The two men agreed that The Beatles would be headliners on *The Ed Sullivan Show* in February 1964. At that point, in American music circles, The Beatles were considered just another British act that had been successful in England but were unable to stir any interest in the United States, and the first class treatment accorded the band by Sullivan seemed highly unusual. After all, they had never performed in America and three singles released in the U.S. in 1963 had gone nowhere. By the time Sullivan introduced The Beatles to his audience on February 9, 1964, his agreement seemed nothing short of brilliant. They were the number one group in the nation with records topping both the single and album charts. In just over two months, an extensive push by their new American record company, Capitol, had helped to turn The Beatles into a national mania, and their song "I Want To Hold Your Hand" had become one of the fastest selling records ever released. Millions of Americans were eager to see the group perform live for the first time.

It was a peculiar evening. More than sixty percent of the American television audience (almost twenty-five million homes) tuned to CBS, driven both by eager kids and curious adults. The Beatles opened and closed the show and in the space of one hour were transformed from motionless publicity photos to real live human beings with distinct individual personalities: Ringo Starr, the plain one with the big nose, sat in the back, "pounding them skins." George Harrison, the quiet mysterious one, played lead guitar while Paul McCartney and John Lennon handled (respectively) bass and rhythm guitars as well as the lead vocals. Paul was the cute one while John ("Sorry girls, he's married") projected more of a tough guy image. Just as Presley had his hip swivel, The Beatles displayed their own distinctive symbol, a mop-top hair style that shook as they sang, "Yeah! Yeah! Yeah!" during another big hit song, "She Loves You." Besides seeing and hearing the group perform, viewers were also exposed to their first direct dose of Beatlemania in the U.S. as the studio cameras focused on hundreds of teenage girls in the audience weeping, screaming, and even fainting. Parents did not know whether to laugh at the group and the screaming fans or condemn them, but kids across the country drank it all in. In that one night, as television allowed millions to share an experience as one, the medium helped to establish a musical and cultural phenomenon.

Ironically, despite their British persona, The Beatles were essentially bringing American music back home, filtered and refined through their fresh eyes. They drew on rock'n'roll from the Presley era, rhythm and blues, rockabilly, and even a touch of Broadway. Nonetheless, their distinctive accents and dress and powerful sound made them appear totally new, and their overnight exposure to millions of Americans helped create an instant interest in other British rock groups such as The Dave Clark Five and The Rolling Stones, who soon turned up on shows such as Sullivan's and *The Hollywood Palace.* In addition, the desire for *anything*

English, which had been building with an increasingly successful series of theatrical films on British secret agent James Bond, exploded into nearly every aspect of American culture with the coming of The Beatles. Television executives now took a closer look at adapting British material for the American market. This was a distinct change from the image British television had carried throughout the 1950s.

Under the watchful eye of the British government, the noncommercial British Broadcasting Corporation had always followed a philosophy that steered away from the pure entertainment programs that shaped American television. In September 1955, after much wrangling, commercial television came to Britain and began to compete with the BBC. At first, the newcomers relied heavily on imported American filmed series, turning out only a few of their own that made the return trip to the States. (Shows such as *The Adventures of Robin Hood* and *Ivanhoe* dealt with traditional American views of England: knights, castles, feudal lords, and the like.) By 1960, British television began producing its own programs that equaled, and sometimes surpassed, American fare.

Britain's first major homegrown commercial hit was Granada TV's *Coronation Street,* a soap opera which debuted in 1960. Instead of dealing with beautiful rich people, as traditional American soapers did, the program centered on the exploits of just plain folk in the working class city of Manchester, the sort that might be found in America in *The Honeymooners.* Gleason's show was an exception, though, to the general American view of TV heroes. In Britain, *Coronation Street* quickly became the top-rated show and working class settings became commonplace in other series.

One and one-half years later, the BBC (aiming to meet its commercial competition head-on) presented a sitcom take on the world of *Coronation Street, Steptoe and Son,* starring Wilfrid Brambell (later cast as Paul McCartney's grandfather in the Beatles' film "A Hard Day's Night") and Harry Corbett. The two portrayed Albert and Harold Steptoe, father and son junk dealers who were forever squabbling over money and the future. As the elder Steptoe, Brambell played to perfection the garrulous and possessive aging father determined to prevent his son from leaving the homestead; he often resorted to underhanded tricks to break up Harold's budding romances or inclinations to venture into a new business on his own. He always succeeded as Harold inevitably decided to remain in the junk business, at home, with his dad, despite the constant interference. The vibrancy of Brambell and Corbett in their characters, as well as the unique nature of the setting, quickly caught on with the British public and by late 1963 *Steptoe and Son* replaced *Coronation Street* for a while as the country's most popular program. It was one of the first important British programs to catch an American network's attention and NBC showed a few *Steptoe and Son* clips on *The Jack Paar Show* in April 1964, while subcontracting with Embassy Pictures to produce a pilot for an American version of the show. The pilot, however, was rejected and plans for the series were eventually shelved. Even adapted for American tastes, the "life among the lowly" concept did not seem quite right for Stateside audiences weaned on solid middle-class heroes.

British television's first major success in the American market was with its own particular brand of spy adventures, a field that had been remarkably unsuccessful in the U.S. Throughout the 1950s, American producers had insisted on presenting stereotyped cold war clashes between square-jawed Americans upholding democracy and Communist forces made up of unbelievably stupid agents with heavy foreign accents, in such vehicles as *I Led Three Lives* (starring Richard Carlson), *Biff Baker, USA* (starring Alan Hale, Jr.), and *The Hunter* (starring Barry Nelson). None of these were very successful and the networks were convinced that spy

shows just did not sell. Ironically, James Bond, the smooth, sophisticated spy whose adventure novels launched the British passion for international intrigue, was nearly made into an American television series several times during the decade.

In 1954, shortly after the publication of the first James Bond novel, *Casino Royale,* CBS paid author Ian Fleming $1,000 for the rights to do a special one-hour live TV drama production of the story. The network cast veteran TV spy Barry Nelson as agent-playboy James Bond (a role almost identical to Nelson's U.S. agent/playboy character from the old *Hunter* series) and Peter Lorre as Le Chiffre (a ruthless Soviet operative) and on October 21, 1954, presented the adaptation on its *Climax* anthology series. CBS was not interested in any further adventures, so Fleming sold the theatrical film rights to that story and turned out two more novels. The next year, working with NBC producer Henry Mor-

November 18, 1963
Prior to their U.S. pop success, The Beatles are the subject of a pair of light network news feature reports about British Beatlemania, starting with a piece from NBC correspondent Edwin Newman for that night's *Huntley-Brinkley Report.* Four days later (November 22), on *The CBS Morning News*, London bureau chief Alexander Kendrick offers his take, but his story does not reach Walter Cronkite's *CBS Evening News* until December 10.

November 23, 1963
Doctor Who. (BBC). The premiere of a serialized science fiction adventure series about a mysterious "Doctor" (William Hartnell), who flies through time and space in what looks like a big blue phone booth. Although the program becomes a British hit by its second story arc (which introduces the villainous, robotic Daleks), it does not catch on in the U.S. until the late 1970s via public television, with Tom Baker in the lead role.

December 30, 1963
Let's Make a Deal. (NBC). Monty Hall begins exploiting basic human greed every weekday afternoon.

January 21, 1964
Ed Murrow resigns as director of the U.S. Information Agency due to poor health.

March 2, 1964
Fred Friendly replaces Dick Salant as president of CBS News. Salant moves to a more amorphous position, CBS vice president for corporate affairs.

March 25, 1964
Live trans-Pacific television begins, via the *Relay II* satellite.

April 30, 1964
UHF Day. From this point on, all new television sets must be capable of receiving channels 14 through 83.

August 13, 1964
CBS buys the New York Yankees.

September 11, 1964
After twenty years, boxing vanishes from weekly network television as ABC's *Fight of the Week* expires in Cleveland. Don Dunphy calls the last fight: Dick Tiger beats Don Fullmer in ten rounds.

ganthau III, he began writing a new half-hour TV adventure series to be filmed on location in Jamaica, *Commander Jamaica.* James Bond served as a model for the main character in the pilot script, but the project fell through so Fleming used the script as a basis for the next book in the Bond series, *Dr. No,* instead. Several years later, in 1958, CBS decided to try a TV series featuring the actual Bond character (titled, appropriately, *James Bond, Secret Agent*), and Fleming wrote plot outlines for six episodes. Once again, the planned series was shelved, so he adapted three of the TV treatments for his anthology of James Bond short stories, *For Your Eyes Only,* and concentrated his energies on using the character as the basis for a series of theatrical films. (The *Casino Royale* film project had never materialized.) Fleming at last succeeded in selling the options to his remaining Bond novels in 1961 to producers Harry Saltzman and Albert Broccoli who, in turn, convinced United Artists to finance the project, and in 1962 the first James Bond film, "Dr. No," appeared. It earned over $1 million in Britain alone and the 1963 followup, "From Russia With Love," was released at the height of the spy craze in Britain, and became a major box office success in the U.S.

British television had begun to cash in on the increasing interest in spies and international espionage at the turn of the decade, and each of its three major spy programs (*Danger Man, The Saint, The Avengers*) eventually made it to American television. In September 1960, ATV, a British commercial network, produced its own version of James Bond, secret agent John Drake (Patrick McGoohan) in *Danger Man.* Unlike America's old spy vehicles, the series showed the enemies of democracy as intelligent equals to the government's agents, and their elaborate plans of subversion unfolded in well-written, engrossing adventures. (Specific politics were, of course, downplayed.) McGoohan's punchy independent persona gave the show an extra lift that attracted American attention and CBS picked it up for a brief run in the summer of 1961, when it attracted critical acclaim but few viewers.

One year later, another series featuring global intrigue began in Britain, Leslie Charteris's *The Saint,* starring Roger Moore as Simon Templar. Templar was presented as a handsome, wealthy, sophisticated playboy in the Bond mold, but the program was really quite bland. The villains were usually involved in moderately elaborate but routine crimes and, very often, Templar emerged as nothing more than a vintage private eye updated for the 1960s. Nonetheless, Moore was already a familiar figure to American audiences from his stint in several Warner Bros. action-adventure series and *The Saint* was picked up for the American market rather quickly: first through syndication to individual stations in 1963 and, four years later, by NBC for a network run. The more traditional approach of the program made it much more attractive to American programmers interested in exploiting the spy craze with a fairly safe product. A more unconventional British spy series, *The Avengers,* had to wait until 1966 for its extraordinary style and premise to reach American viewers.

The Avengers began in January 1961 as a moderately straightforward spy show featuring Patrick Macnee and Ian Hendry as dilettante men-about-town involved in solving crimes and avenging evil. In October 1962, the premise was revamped and the show began displaying a distinctively different tone that turned it into a British cult favorite with a small but rapidly growing legion of fans. Macnee was identified as government agent John Steed and joined in his adventures by Mrs. Catherine Gale, a widow (played by Honor Blackman). The two were thrust into complicated plots hatched by peculiar villains and the series began adopting a subtle, tongue-in-cheek approach that produced bizarre yet intriguing stories. Not only were the cases highly unusual, but the relation-

ship between Steed and Mrs. Gale was completely unheard of. They operated as a team and she was his equal in every way. They both defended themselves with skill and finesse, never losing their British cool and sly smiles even in the most dire situations, and neither was dependent on the other for constant rescue. What's more, the romantic connection between the two was kept deliciously unclear; there were hints of *amour* but the viewer was left to decide whether there was, in fact, a liaison or not.

Only a few months after *The Avengers* shifted to its more offbeat style, full-bodied satire came to the BBC with *That Was The Week That Was.* Premiering in December 1962, *TW3* (as it was known) marked a major step forward in British broadcasting because it was the first show to poke fun at, and actually ridicule, well-known politicians and office holders. A stock company of players, hosted by David Frost and featuring singer Millicent Martin, performed generally irreverent skits to press their points, occasionally even indulging in shock tactics (such as name calling) to catch viewers' attention. The writers based the words and music of the show on the events of the previous week, giving *TW3* a feeling of immediacy akin to a cabaret comedy ensemble. The program was biting, controversial, very funny, and alternately admired and resented by viewers, depending on who was the latest target of abuse. Nonetheless, while a shock to Britain, such satire seemed unthinkable for American television. If any series was unlikely to appear in the United States, *That Was The Week That Was* was it. Yet on Sunday, November 10, 1963, NBC presented a one-hour special-pilot for an American version of *TW3.* Obviously, something had changed.

The mood of the country had grown less somber and less paranoid since 1960. The new spirit was due partly to the reduction in cold war tensions and also to the youth and humor of the Kennedy administration. People simply felt more like laughing. In this atmosphere, NBC decided to take a chance on satire in America. Produced by Leland Hayward and hosted by Henry Fonda, the pilot for *TW3* was not as flip or as rough as its British cousin, but it presented some of the freshest, funniest material to hit U.S. TV in years. The guests on the special were traditional humorists including Mike Nichols and Elaine May, Henry Morgan, and Charly Manna, but their humor was much more topical than usual. In one hour they directed barbs at President Kennedy, Richard Nixon, Barry Goldwater, Nelson Rockefeller, crime leaders, dirty books, funeral costs, and left-wing folk songs. The reaction was so strong and positive that NBC called for immediate production of the series, which it had originally considered as a possible new entry in the fall of 1964. Instead, the network planned on a premiere in January. All that remained was to convince skeptical sponsors that the public was ready for such humor. Then something happened.

CBS was in the midst of *As the World Turns* on Friday afternoon, November 22, when Walter Cronkite broke in to announce that President Kennedy had been shot in Dallas. Within a few minutes, all three networks suspended regular programming and began what became four days of noncommercial television (at a loss of $40 million in advertising revenue). By presenting, live, all the far-flung events of that weekend at a moment's notice, television news proved itself truly deserving of both serious attention and popular acclaim. People throughout the country looked to television for news of the tragedy. They saw the official announcement that Kennedy was dead, as well as the first appearance of the new president, Lyndon Johnson. They followed the return to Washington and the formal ceremonies of the state funeral. Many newsmen on each network distinguished themselves throughout the long hours on the air and several new faces became instant "news celebrities."

Television brought the funeral ceremonies for President Kennedy from Washington to the nation's living rooms. Jacqueline Kennedy *(center)* with daughter Caroline and son John. *(National Archives White House Photo by Abbie Rowe)*

On CBS, Dan Rather, who scooped all others in reporting Kennedy's death, became unofficial anchor of the Dallas reports, while Roger Mudd and Harry Reasoner, two veteran network reporters who had worked largely unnoticed for years, came to the forefront with their handling of the events in Washington. On ABC, Howard K. Smith returned from oblivion and teamed up with a new addition to the ABC news staff, Edward P. Morgan. They were so effective together that they became the regular ABC anchor team for the political specials of 1964. Through it all, television treated the events of the Kennedy assassination with a dignity and style many had thought impossible. For the first time, people throughout the country began to appreciate how much television really meant to them and just what it was capable of.

Even well-known critics such as former FCC chairman Newton Minow marveled, "Only through television could the whole country grasp the tragedy, and at the same time the strength of the democratic process that passed the administration from one president to another within two hours. Television's treatment was sensitive, mature, and dignified. We always hear that television is a young medium. If so, it grew up in a couple of days."

More than any other event to that point, the Kennedy assassination cemented television's role as national information source and national unifier.

As disturbing as the assassination was, television faced an even more unsettling event two days after the president had been shot,

as the medium immediately discovered the dangers and conflicts of its increased stature. Lee Harvey Oswald, the accused assassin, was to be transferred from one jail to another on Sunday morning, November 24, and the press, especially television, demanded to witness the event. It was no longer sufficient to merely report that something had happened, the activity had to take place before the cameras. Dallas police complied with the request by making their plans public so that reporters, or anyone, could see Oswald leave the city jail. At 11:20 A.M., at the end of a memorial service for Kennedy in Washington, NBC cut live to Dallas just in time to show the first real-life murder on television as it occurred: A man in a dark suit and hat came out of the crowd, there was a pop, and Oswald dropped from sight, fatally shot. CBS and ABC both just missed also telecasting the event live, but a new device developed for TV sports coverage allowed all three to show the murder again and again with the added impact of slow motion video tape replay.

In demanding access to Oswald, a man who had become an instant media figure, television had focused attention and publicity on what should have been a routine procedure, the prison transfer. Unknowingly, television and television news had crossed a line into a new situation in which it would become increasingly difficult to view the medium as just another reporter. Television was beginning to affect the course of events, transforming seemingly inconsequential actions into important moments in history merely by its presence.

24. The Unloved Messenger

TELEVISION BECAME THE OBJECT of increasing vilification throughout 1964 for both its entertainment and news programming. The more effective and complete coverage of developing issues and special events by the network news departments upset people of every ideology. They resented the growing encroachment by TV news upon their personal lives and beliefs as well as the unsettling nature of the news itself, often equating the bearer of bad tidings with the disturbing events it reported. At the same time, a move to pure escapism in entertainment programming triggered by the huge success of CBS's rural-based comedy line-up offended the sensibilities of many viewers who found the tube pandering more and more to the lowest common denominator. In contrast to the fondly remembered high drama of TV's golden days, the networks' fall schedules offered country bumpkins, ridiculous settings, childish plots, witches, Martians, and pure soap opera. It all seemed deliberately designed to appeal to viewers who looked at television as a mindless escape tool. Critics pointed to the continuing number one status of *The Beverly Hillbillies* as irrefutable evidence that quality television had fallen on hard times.

The Beverly Hillbillies never deserved all the public defilement it received, but the program was a symbol of the direction television entertainment had taken under the guidance of CBS president James Aubrey. His rural comedy philosophy had kept CBS number one in the ratings and it cleared the path for a host of inferior successors launched by all three networks, with CBS leading the way. Most of the new programs lacked the comic energy of the hillbilly original and were responsible for generally humorless TV. As parent to the trend, though, *The Beverly Hillbillies* received its share of the blame for the sins of its offspring. Even though imitations of successful formats were expected as a normal part of the industry, the blatant, almost incestuous, development of the new sitcom spinoff shows struck many as going too far.

Spinoffs had been an accepted practice in broadcasting for decades, especially in the field of variety. Popular personalities such as Phil Harris and Dennis Day (from *The Jack Benny Program),* Julius La Rosa and Pat Boone (from Arthur Godfrey's shows), and Gisele MacKenzie (from *Your Hit Parade)* had all been promoted from second string status to programs of their own because their association with an established hit gave them an instant advantage over the competition. Situation comedies had certainly followed program trends in the past (wacky housewives, talking animals, showbiz widowers) but in courting the rural themes television developed a very systematic approach to the spin-off process. A specific character or gimmick from a successful sitcom was carefully eased into a new setting and show, as close to the original as possible. Sometimes there were even crossover cast appearances from the established hit. Unfortunately, many of the new series failed to develop past the surface gimmicks and did not deliver the strong secondary characters and good scripts necessary for support. Yet with the momentum provided by familiar hooks and faces, simple-minded escapist fare prospered.

Beverly Hillbillies producer Paul Henning had started the cloning process in the 1963–64 season with *Petticoat Junction,* which presented the adventures of the folks "back in the hills." Henning took veteran character actor Bea Benaderet, who played cousin Pearl Bodine, Jethro's widowed mother (a minor role in *The Beverly Hillbillies),* rechristened her Kate Bradley (also a widow), and put her in charge of the Shady Rest Hotel in the mythical backwoods town of Hooterville. Though *Petticoat Junction* had the outward trappings of *The Beverly Hillbillies,* there were no creative crazies or charged conflicts in it. The setting was much too restrictive. Gone was the incongruity of the progenitor between rich and poor, socialite and hillbilly. Hooterville was a one-horse town. Even occasional invasions by city slickers such as Homer Bedloe (Charles Lane as a railroad executive determined to scrap the town's ancient train, the *Cannonball)* were doomed from the start. The aseptic peace of 1950s TV had been transported to the hills and nothing could disturb it. Worst of all, the characters were far too bland to be funny. While Benaderet was usually an excellent supporting character (in roles such as Blanche Morton, the crazy neighbor to George Burns and Gracie Allen), her warm mother figure of Kate Bradley was not credible either as a comic center or cagey manipulator. Her three daughters were as interchangeable as their names: Billie Jo, Bobbie Jo, and Betty Jo. Gravelly voiced Edgar Buchanan tried his best in the role of a scheming moneymaker, Joe Carson (the hotel's self-proclaimed manager), but Uncle Joe's ventures usually produced little more than a few jokes about him being a scheming loafer. In short, the series was harmless fluff, not at all offensive, but not very funny either. It was pure escapism, a sort of "chewing gum for the eyes and mind," not only far removed from the everyday grim reality of the big city, but also a world apart from rural reality as well.

Nonetheless, the hillbilly connection worked and *Petticoat Junction* was an instant hit. Its premiere episode came in as the number five show of the week. Hooterville was undeniably popular and the program lasted seven seasons. In 1965, the show spawned its own calculated clone, *Green Acres*. For that series, Henning took the spinoff formula one step further by keeping the same setting (Hooterville), using many of the same characters (there were frequent crossovers with *Petticoat Junction)*, and introducing a premise that was a mirror image of *The Beverly Hillbillies:* two city slickers (Eddie Albert and Eva Gabor) moved to the country. That incongruity brought the series much closer to *The Beverly Hillbillies* in quality and, once again, home viewers were entranced as *Green Acres* clucked on for six years.

Following the success of *Petticoat Junction* in the 1963–64 season, CBS turned to another popular series, *The Andy Griffith Show,* for a spinoff in the fall of 1964, *Gomer Pyle, U.S.M.C.* The Gomer Pyle character of a halfwit gas station attendant (played by Jim Nabors) was drafted by Uncle Aubrey, taken from Mayberry, North Carolina, and placed in a Marine base in California. There, under the tutelage of the often infuriated Sergeant Vincent Carter (Frank Sutton), the simple country rube repeatedly exasperated yet outwitted the military minds. The setting and premise were nearly identical to Andy Griffith's first major vehicle, "No Time for Sergeants," in 1955. To complete the circle (and to make certain the spinoff was properly launched) Andy accompanied Gomer from Mayberry, taking him into his new setting, and keeping a watchful eye on him throughout the first episode. Gomer clicked and the series stood as further proof that spinoffs from established hits were a valuable tool that, if handled properly, could produce another equally potent program. Gomer's success was especially impressive because the show not only outscored the direct competition of veteran Jack Benny (who had moved to NBC that year following a contract dispute) but also easily outperformed the very same premise on ABC. As a very familiar character, Gomer stood out among the fall premieres and found it much easier to gain a toehold and build an audience than did the unknowns (Sammy Jackson and Harry Hickox) of the ABC version, which even took the *No Time for Sergeants* title. The country took Gomer to heart in his new job, making Nabors a star in his own right as the series remained in the top ten through the 1960s. Gomer's wide-eyed innocence also presented a reassuring view of the military in an era when people were beginning to become aware of the presence of real Marines in a real war. Gomer Pyle was always the all-American country boy.

Some critics, however, found the character to be the personification of everything objectionable about the rural slant being pursued by CBS. Gomer was a naive country bumpkin who obviously read and enjoyed nothing more challenging than *Captain Marvel* comic books (as his cry of "Shazam!" indicated), yet he was one of television's new heroes. His character might have been acceptable as a second banana but as a lead his effusive manner and familiar expressions such as "Sur-*prise!* Sur-*prise!* Sur-*prise!*" and "Gaul-lee Sergeant Carter!" were particularly discordant and grating to some. Nonetheless, the program was well done and often funny, and such reactions more likely reflected deep resentment at the near total domination by escapist fare in entertainment programming. The style seemed as pervasive as Westerns and quizzes had been at their saturation points, but it looked as if the spinoff potential and continued high ratings earned by the silly gimmicks and simpleton heroes would assure them spots in the network schedules for years. While some viewers were upset, most people clearly enjoyed the programs. They were light, uncomplicated, and a welcome haven from bad news.

Just as action-adventure shows in the late 1950s had given the networks Westerns that were not Westerns, the escapist sitcoms quickly expanded beyond strictly rural settings. Though not direct spinoffs from any established hit, the premises of these new shows

were just as unlikely as millionaire hillbillies and included such hooks as Martians, monsters, and witches. Of these, the program that showcased Aubrey escapism at its worst was *Gilligan's Island,* which followed the adventures of the passengers and crew of a sight-seeing charter boat that was shipwrecked on an uncharted South Pacific island. The show literally went to the ends of the earth to avoid reality in a premise that seemed to overwhelm the writers with its limitations. Though the castaways were confined to a tiny island and could never be rescued (or the show was over), someone from the outside world was always finding the way to their doorstep, then departing without them after going through the same sort of obvious jokes and misunderstandings. It was like repeating one skit from a comedy variety show over and over and over again. Yet even with this strained set-up and repetitious scripts, the cast might have been able to overcome these limitations by developing a sharp comic sense in each of their characters. Instead, most just settled into the plastic caricatures they had been given: the hard working skipper (Alan Hale, Jr.), his well-meaning but bumbling first mate (Bob Denver), a dumb but beautiful movie star (Tina Louise), a pretty homespun Midwestern girl (Dawn Wells), a brilliant research professor (Russell Johnson), a multimillionaire (Jim Backus) and his pampered wife (Natalie Schafer). Hale, Backus, and Denver made valiant attempts to bring life to their roles, but even they usually fell short. Denver brought the spacey, naive innocence of his Maynard G. Krebs character to first mate Gilligan, but what had worked well in a supporting role to Dobie Gillis could not carry an entire series. He was just another lost child on the island. Backus and Hale flashed moments of wit, but it was a losing battle. Overall, the show resembled nothing so much as a kiddie cartoon and it seemed designed to capture the interest of young children by presenting cardboard adults who acted like children in grownup bodies. This strategy attracted a fair size audience and allowed the program to survive for three seasons, though it rarely elicited more than an audible groan from most of the nation's adults.

Other new gimmicks might have appeared as silly as *Gilligan's Island* on the surface, but the better ones kept a tighter rein on the initial premise. Rather than building a sweeping but all-too-limiting setting that could prematurely strangle the series, other producers settled for a slight wrinkle to reality that could be continuously exploited. In this vein, a Martian and a witch were incorporated into moderately normal situations and acceptable, if not outstanding, TV fare resulted. Both *My Favorite Martian* (starring Ray Walston as a Martian shipwrecked on Earth) and *Bewitched* (Elizabeth Montgomery as a suburban housewife who happened to be a witch) used their zany hooks primarily as an excuse to display entertaining visual tricks in that week's situation. Once the complications were introduced, the actors and scripts, not the gimmicks, carried the episodes.

Still, a totally bizarre setting could succeed as long as it stuck to the basics of comedy. If the characters and atmosphere on *Gilligan's Island* had been developed beyond dull caricature and cheap tropical sets, the program might have been able to transcend its limitations. ABC proved it could be done that season with the hilarious adventures of an entire family that came directly out of the world of late night creature features, *The Addams Family* (based on the characters created by cartoonist Charles Addams). Though the plots for the series were usually just adequate, the characters and setting were devilishly sharp. Gomez (John Astin) and his wife Morticia (Carolyn Jones) headed the freaky family that lived in an appropriately spooky old family mansion just outside of town. Rather than limiting the program to predictable monster jokes or half-hearted attempts to make the characters appear a

	7:00	7:30	8:00	8:30	9:00	9:30	10:00	10:30	
M O N	local	VOYAGE TO THE BOTTOM OF THE SEA		NO TIME FOR SERGEANTS	WENDY AND ME	BING CROSBY SHOW	Ben Casey		**ABC**
	local	To Tell The Truth	I've Got A Secret	Andy Griffith Show	The Lucy Show	MANY HAPPY RETURNS	SLATTERY'S PEOPLE		**CBS**
	local	90 BRISTOL COURT (KAREN; HARRIS AGAINST THE WORLD; TOM, DICK AND MARY)			Andy Williams Show / # JONATHAN WINTERS SHOW		Alfred Hitchcock Hour		**NBC**
T U E	local	Combat!		McHale's Navy	TYCOON	PEYTON PLACE	The Fugitive		**ABC**
	local		WORLD WAR ONE	Red Skelton Hour		Petticoat Junction	The Doctors And The Nurses		**CBS**
	local	Mr. Novak		THE MAN FROM U.N.C.L.E.		That Was The Week That Was	Bell Telephone Hour / NBC News Specials		**NBC**
W E D	local	Adventures Of Ozzie And Harriet	Patty Duke Show	SHINDIG	MICKEY	Burke's Law		ABC Scope	**ABC**
	local	CBS Reports / CBS News Specials		The Beverly Hillbillies	Dick Van Dyke Show	CARA WILLIAMS SHOW	Danny Kaye Show		**CBS**
	local	The Virginian			NBC Wednesday Night At The Movies				**NBC**
T H U R	local	The Flintstones	Donna Reed Show	My Three Sons	BEWITCHED	PEYTON PLACE	Jimmy Dean Show		**ABC**
	local	THE MUNSTERS	Perry Mason		Password	THE BAILEYS OF BALBOA	The Defenders		**CBS**
	local	DANIEL BOONE		Dr. Kildare		Hazel	Kraft Suspense Theater / # Perry Como's Kraft Music Hall		**NBC**
F R I	local	JONNY QUEST	The Farmer's Daughter	THE ADDAMS FAMILY	VALENTINE'S DAY	TWELVE O'CLOCK HIGH		local	**ABC**
	local	Rawhide		THE ENTERTAINERS		GOMER PYLE, U.S.M.C.	THE REPORTER		**CBS**
	local	International Showtime		Bob Hope Presents The Chrysler Theater / # Bob Hope Show		Jack Benny Program	Jack Paar Show		**NBC**
S A T	local	The Outer Limits		Lawrence Welk Show		Hollywood Palace		local	**ABC**
	local	Jackie Gleason Show		GILLIGAN'S ISLAND	MR. BROADWAY		Gunsmoke		**CBS**
	local	FLIPPER	FAMOUS ADVENTURES OF MR. MAGOO	KENTUCKY JONES	NBC Saturday Night At The Movies				**NBC**
S U N	local	Wagon Train		BROADSIDE	The ABC Sunday Night Movie				**ABC**
	Lassie	My Favorite Martian	Ed Sullivan Show		MY LIVING DOLL	Joey Bishop Show	Candid Camera	What's My Line	**CBS**
	PROFILES IN COURAGE (from 6:30)	Walt Disney's Wonderful World Of Color		Bill Dana Show	Bonanza		THE ROGUES		**NBC**

normal part of society (in spite of their background), the producers accepted the members of the family for what they were and stretched the premise to the limit. The Addams family were ghoulish eccentrics and proud of it. They flaunted their behavior in characters that were bristling with energy. Morticia and Gomez cultivated man-eating plants, stayed in on sunny days, and reveled in hurricane winds. To relax, family members enjoyed stretching each other out on the basement rack and, at play, the children experimented with dynamite. The household also included live-in relations Uncle Fester (Jackie Coogan), Grandmamma Addams (Blossom Rock), and cousin Itt (a four-foot-tall ball of hair), as well as the ultra basso butler, Lurch (Ted Cassidy), and the ultimate right hand helper, Thing. For all of them, the question of conforming to normal society never came up; the most important task was maintaining family traditions and an awareness of the Addams family roots, which stretched back hundreds of years. They were aristocrats with highly unusual tastes and no doubts about their proper station in life. Gomez and Morticia were passionate, but proper, and their strict adherence to traditional upper class role models resulted in a marvelous caricature of the aristocratic lifestyle. Ever the ardent lover (just a word of French by Morticia sent him into an uncontrolled fury), Gomez often found himself frustrated by his wife's insistence on abiding by the rules of public decorum ("not now dear; it wouldn't be right"). They were ghoulish in their preferences, but always socially correct.

Such a rich collection of characters, added to the colorful household accouterments, gave the program a comic verve which was even more striking when contrasted with the mundane monster fare of CBS's family of freaks, *The Munsters.* Unlike the Addams household, the Munster family looked like classic horror film creatures: Fred Gwynne played a Frankenstein father; Yvonne De Carlo, the vampire mother; and Al Lewis, Count Dracula. Unfortunately, the attempts at humor in the show never rose above the physical incongruity of the Munsters as they tried to act like an average, if somewhat odd, middle-class family. Once the "shock value" of a collection of monsters had worn off, the routine nature of the scripts became painfully evident. Visitors from the outside world would leave the Addams home in a terrified daze; intruders in the Munster mansion merely faced grownups in Halloween costumes. Both series lasted only two seasons, but *The Addams Family* brought a touch of class to escapist television.

Escapism was certainly not limited to situation comedy or new to television under Aubrey, but rarely had the networks pursued the concept with such a vengeance. TV critics, upset at the trend to rural settings and mindless heroes, were positively aghast at the move by ABC to bring daytime soap opera, intact, to prime time. Television's cultural slide seemed undeniable and complete in the fall of 1964 with the premiere of *Peyton Place.*

Actually, pseudo-soap operas had been appearing in prime time for years in the guise of drama anthologies *(Lux Video Theater)*, situation comedies *(Ozzie and Harriet),* epic Westerns *(Bonanza* and *Wagon Train),* and career dramas *(Dr. Kildare* and *Ben Casey),* so much of the disgust was in reaction to the term "soap opera" itself. The networks had found that the label carried a certain stigma that turned off large segments of viewers, so they generally kept the soapy aspects of their prime time programs discretely in the background and adhered to an unwritten rule limiting blatant soap operas to the afternoon "housewife" hours. ABC's move marked a major break from this policy. *Peyton Place* was a regular soaper following characters through a continuing story line, rather than the usual self-contained episodes of other prime time series. The program brazenly displayed the sudsy staples of life, love, and scandal.

For the number three network, the soap opera strategy made a great deal of sense. After all, CBS had made a fortune in daytime TV with such long running classics as *Love of Life, As the World Turns, Search for Tomorrow,* and *The Guiding Light,* and ABC saw no reason to limit its assault on the field to the daytime. Potential ratings points were just sitting there and, if *Peyton Place* caught on, the network would have two hit shows at once because the series was on twice each week. ABC boldly ballyhooed the show as a novel for television (it was based on a successful book as well as a movie), ignored the cries of anguish from outraged critics, and launched the series with high hopes. It was a smash, though its individual success didn't alter the bias against soaps. *Peyton Place* was the exception that gave soap opera fans a chance for an evening dose of bathos.

The program was a classic soaper with the usual conflicts stemming from guilt associated with extramarital and premarital sex. Though such themes were bold and titillating for prime time, they were familiar stuff to afternoon viewers who studied the cast and conflicts in the New England town of Peyton Place and nodded their approval. Constance MacKenzie (Dorothy Malone) feared the devastating humiliation she felt would occur if anyone discovered her dark secret: Eighteen years before she had "made a terrible mistake" and, nine months later, given birth to an illegitimate child, Allison MacKenzie (Mia Farrow). Now, Dr. Rossi (Ed Nelson), who had delivered the baby (and who probably knew "the secret"), was in love with Constance while Rodney Harrington (Ryan O'Neal) was in love with Allison (only he probably *did not* know "the secret"). There was much, much more and the story continued with ripening teenagers, broken marriages, adultery, more illegitimate kids (the *ne plus ultra* development in soap opera scripts), and an endless string of coincidences.

In its first season, *Peyton Place* often landed in the top ten, and in the summer of 1965 ABC launched a third night, which lasted through the following summer. At the same time, CBS gave *Our Private World,* an off shoot of *As the World Turns,* a twice-each-week prime time tryout, but this ran only for one summer. In the fall of 1965, NBC converted *Dr. Kildare* into a twice-each-week serial, recognizing that the program easily matched the sudsiest of daytime soaps. After one year in this guise, *Kildare* also disappeared. Obviously, *Peyton Place* was a one-of-a-kind hit, at least for the moment. TV viewers were apparently unwilling to devote themselves to several prime time soaps simultaneously, though they followed *Peyton Place* for nearly five years.

A much more imaginative form of escapist entertainment was the spy craze, led by the phenomenally successful James Bond films and books. Americans had been a bit slower than the British in embracing such larger-than-life international adventures, but by 1964 they, too, were hooked and the networks responded with a parade of Bond-like TV spies. Spies had never been handled very well by American television and the task of bringing the delicate

balance of refined wit, cruel violence, desirable women, expensive gimmicks, and occasional self-parody to television seemed especially difficult. NBC was the first to jump on the bandwagon, enlisting James Bond's creator, Ian Fleming, for a very Bond-ish proposed TV spy series, originally titled *Mr. Solo.* Fleming had to drop out of the project due to ill health, but the show made it to the air in the fall of 1964 as *The Man from U.N.C.L.E.*

Though obviously working with a substantially smaller budget than the multimillion-dollar Bond film epics, the series was a very good television equivalent, comfortably adopting many of the most attractive Bond gimmicks. The *U*nited *N*etwork *C*ommand for *L*aw and *E*nforcement was a powerful CIA-type organization headquartered in the bowels of New York City, with a secret entrance hidden at the innocent-looking Del Floria's tailor shop (behind the fake wall of a changing room). U.N.C.L.E. deployed a world-wide network of agents and an arsenal of elaborate gadgets, specially designed guns, and exotic electronic gear including miniature communicators, tiny listening devices, and coded identification badges. Concerns over world domination, the balance of power, and freedom were bandied about, but this was a cosmetic device to give the scripts a topical flavor for what amounted to a weekly battle between good and evil. Just as Bond's British secret service squared off against SPECTRE, U.N.C.L.E. faced the highly skilled forces of Thrush. (Its acronym was never revealed in the series, but an authorized tie-in paperback novel, *The Dagger Affair*, revealed it as the *T*echnological *H*ierarchy for the *R*emoval of *U*ndesirables and the *S*ubjugation of *H*umanity). The two organizations were engaged in a never-ending struggle that appeared more like a high-powered chess game between two superpowers than a fight for world domination. Particular schemes assumed important propaganda value and served as arenas for a perverse, sportsmanlike competition between the best agents from both sides.

Napoleon Solo (played by Robert Vaughn) was U.N.C.L.E.'s top agent. Like Bond, he was a company man who flaunted the rules of discipline to pursue his own pleasures, placing more trust in his instincts than in standard operating procedures. Solo was a highly refined, highly educated boy-next-door type who fell somewhere in between the aristocratic aloofness of Sherlock Holmes and the gritty earthiness of Sam Spade. He was an excellent Bond surrogate who always got the job done for agency head Alexander Waverly (Leo G. Carroll).

The chief difference between the man from U.N.C.L.E. and James Bond was that Bond operated solo but Solo had a partner. At first, Illya Kuryakin (David McCallum) was little more than a right-hand flunky to Solo. (He was featured for all of five seconds in the pilot episode for the series.) In February, however, McCallum was sent on a promotional tour of eight major cities with low *U.N.C.L.E.* ratings, during which he earned the right to become an equal partner to Solo. Not only did the ratings go up in the cities he visited, but to the surprise (and delight) of the producers, it became obvious by the enthusiastic response of female fans that the Kuryakin character had become a teen heart-throb. From then on, McCallum's sensitive, intellectual, continental allure was used as an excellent complement to Vaughn's middle-American goodness.

In contrast to the James Bond films, *The Man from U.N.C.L.E.* downplayed cynical sadism and violence in favor of a stronger emphasis on tongue-in-cheek humor and character interaction. An innocent bystander (usually a beautiful woman) was always introduced to the plot to bring the high-level conflict down to a less abstruse level. If the future of mankind did not mean anything to viewers, then a damsel in distress certainly did. More important, with the increased visibility of Kuryakin, the men from U.N.C.L.E.

The arrival of U.S. marines in Vietnam in March 1965 brought about an increase in TV coverage of the war. *(U.S. Army)*

developed a natural repartee, very much in the style of John Steed and Kathy Gale in Britain's *The Avengers.* Because the world of international intrigue all too often involved plots that threatened "the fate of the entire Western world," such an approach was vital to prevent overkill and made the weekly life-and-death perils much easier to take. Though occasionally the program went overboard and turned the entire episode into one long joke (as in the "My Friend, the Gorilla Affair"), when kept in check the lighter touch lifted *The Man from U.N.C.L.E.* far above the level of mundane TV melodrama into a first class escapist spy adventure.

ABC and CBS did not get their spy programs out until the next season, though in April CBS, perhaps spurred by *U.N.C.L.E.*'s mid-season surge, brought back the British spy series, *Danger Man,* under a new title, *Secret Agent* (featuring a catchy new theme song by Johnny Rivers). The new hour-long version of the program had begun in Britain in October with Patrick McGoohan still in his role of agent John Drake, though he had softened the character a bit to emphasize a wry sense of humor. It proved only slightly less successful than U.N.C.L.E. and confirmed that TV spies were a viable commodity.

One marvelous tongue-in-check series somehow lost in this season of escapist fare was *The Rogues.* Produced by Four Star Television, the program was developed as a sophisticated, high quality vehicle for a troupe of veteran performers led by two of the company's star-owners, Charles Boyer and David Niven. (They had also participated in the 1950s drama anthology series, *Four Star Playhouse,* the company's first venture.) Set in London, *The Rogues* presented the complicated schemes and crimes of an international family of con artists, led by Niven (as Alec Fleming), who rotated the lead each week with Boyer (as French cousin, Marcel) and Gig Young (as American cousin, Tony). Occasionally, all

three would join forces for exceptionally challenging plots, and they often enlisted the aid of British cousins Timmy (Robert Coote) and grande dame Margaret (Gladys Cooper). Naturally, the Fleming family only chiseled victims that deserved it (bad guys such as a South American dictator played by Telly Savalas), often leaving them embarrassed and humiliated as well as fleeced. Despite rave reviews and a strong lead-in (the number one rated *Bonanza*), the program failed to register high ratings and was dropped by NBC after only one season. To those disgusted by what they saw as the abysmal level of entertainment programming, such a decision was not surprising. *Gilligan's Island* and *Petticoat Junction* lived on, but a witty, sophisticated program was not even given a second chance.

The critical blasts labeling TV's entertainment programming as childish and unimaginative were ironic because, at the same time, the medium was also being lambasted for its aggressive (some said intrusive) approach to the news. In either direction, television faced outraged viewers, though objections to the news were far more serious. Television entertainment was a matter of taste and tastes differed and changed. Television news touched deeply held and long-standing personal beliefs, and it was becoming increasingly apparent that some people would have been pleased to see TV network news completely disappear from their lives.

Resentment of the news had grown out of its increased visibility and the exposure it gave to developing controversial issues. Some of the additional coverage was merely a function of time: Over fifteen years viewers had grown accustomed to fifteen-minute nightly newscasts. In 1963 the programs had doubled in length. The number of bureaus and correspondents had also increased substantially. Resources available for normal coverage of an average news event allowed much more depth and detail than before, so by just following everyday procedures correspondents produced more extensive reports. Though the reporters were not "fighting for" a particular cause, some viewers felt that the additional attention made certain issues seem much more important than ever before.

It was also true, however, that the network news departments had been specifically devoting portions of the additional nightly news time to an examination of social and political issues previously left undiscussed. That was one of the reasons they had fought for the longer news time in the first place: to win the opportunity to deal, at length, with important issues. Viewers did not necessarily want to face some of these issues, though, and many resented what they saw as an intrusion on their lives. There were always countless special interest newspapers and magazines catering to every ideological slant (not everyone had to read the *New York Times)*, but if people chose to watch network news at all they had a choice of only three similar programs. Each one tried to present a survey of all the important national news events of the day. The structure of the network news programs made it all but impossible to skip disturbing news items; they came unpredictably into the home before an irked viewer could stop them. Despite the networks' efforts to take an unbiased stance in the reporting, what seemed cool and objective in one region of the country could touch a very sensitive spot in another. It was not like radio either. That had permitted the individual listener to form a picture to fit preconceived notions based merely on sounds and narration. Television, with its increasing emphasis toward "on the spot" news film, brought profoundly disturbing sounds and pictures into the home and these were difficult to ignore. The period of the mid-1960s was one of volatile social change anyway and many people resented being forced to confront so many different issues each night in their own living rooms. More and more, they linked their growing resentment of the changes in the country with television, television news, and the networks. The messengers that had, at first, merely carried the word of a new order soon became interchangeable with it. As in the old story of the king who punished the messenger who brought him bad news, viewers reacted to the alterations in their lives by turning on the tube and attacking it. One of the first events to spark the wave of such negative viewer reaction was the mass protest march on Washington led by Dr. Martin Luther King, Jr., on August 28, 1963.

The protest was the largest such assembly in Washington since impoverished World War I veterans (dubbed the "bonus marchers") had gathered in 1932. The networks, which had been slowly increasing the amount of their civil rights coverage through the early 1960s, treated the assembly as a major national event, equivalent to a space shot or presidential election. There were special live reports throughout the day, prime time specials, and late night wrapups. The coverage showed more than 200,000 civil rights supporters as peaceful, reasonable people gathered together in support of a righteous cause. Reverend King's impassioned and eloquent "I Have a Dream" speech in favor of civil rights and integration served as the emotional high point to the day and it was carried live to people throughout the nation. Favorable public reaction to the presentation provided a tremendous boost to civil rights legislation before Congress. Legislators began to think that, perhaps, passage of a civil rights bill would not be political suicide. Defenders of segregation, however, saw the changing mood as disastrous and television's participation as unforgivable.

In a three-hour NBC prime time special on civil rights, broadcast five days after King's speech, Mississippi Governor Ross Barnett said that television was to blame for civil disorder in America. By raising the expectations of America's blacks too

rapidly, he said, the medium had created the climate that allowed "rabble rousers" such as King to gain power. Though Barnett might have been somewhat biased, having felt the sting of bad TV publicity in his own moves against civil rights activities (his efforts to block the admission of a young black man, James Meredith, to the University of Mississippi in 1962 had received extensive TV coverage), he was by no means alone in his beliefs. In the spring and summer of 1964, Alabama Governor George C. Wallace, in his first run at the presidency, pointed very specifically to the extended civil rights coverage by CBS, NBC, and ABC, as well as the *New York Times* and the *Washington Post*, as "unnecessary." Publicity given to civil rights activities, he contended, not any underlying social injustice, was responsible for the civil rights problem.

On July 18, 1964, the problem of minor disorders resulting from the push for civil rights exploded into a much more dramatic confrontation as the first major inner city race riot in decades erupted in New York City's Harlem. TV crews rushed to the scene and were shocked to discover that both sides hated reporters. Police, sensitive to the possibility of bad publicity for the force, did not welcome the presence of the news crews, but neither did the rioters. To them, television, with its fancy remote trucks and equipment, was just another arm of what they saw as a white power structure, which was ready to distort their viewpoint and the meaning of their actions. Both sides, during the night, beat up reporters. For the remainder of the summer, thoughtful documentaries and discussions filled the airwaves, as people bravely searched for the complex, underlying causes of the problem, but they usually reached the predictable general conclusion that difficult slum living conditions and police brutality had touched off the violence. In this light, "Harlem: Test for a Nation" (on NBC) naively cited two cities as models of how to avoid riots: Detroit and Los Angeles. Detroit had an integrated police force; and the black section of Los Angeles, Watts, did not even look like a slum, it was almost a heavenly suburb. One year later, this "suburb" erupted into violence that totally overshadowed the Harlem riot of 1964. Two years after that, much the same occurred in Detroit.

In the summer of 1965, all three networks picked up dramatic and mildly sensationalist overhead shots of the riot in Watts from a helicamera devised by the crew from an independent Los Angeles station, KTLA (whose grimly appropriate news motto had been: "If hell breaks loose, turn to KTLA!"). Helicopter pilot Hal Fishman provided a blow-by-blow description of the rampaging mobs, audacious looters, burning buildings, and police-civilian confrontations. Thirty-five people died and more than $200 million in property damage took place. At the same time, the news crews were stoned by the mob, equipment was stolen, and a number of $10,000 mobile vans were torched. The beleaguered police displayed little concern for representatives of a medium many felt was glorifying violence with its reporting anyway. In covering Watts, television was once again caught in a no-win situation.

TV conveyed the terror of a volatile situation in a way no other news medium could. The expanded scope of network news had dovetailed almost exactly with the rapidly developing issue of civil rights, in both its peaceful and violent forms. In general, TV failed to satisfy anyone with its coverage. Many people saw it as an all-too-willing forum for anti-establishment figures out to win converts and propagate violence, while many frustrated blacks found it insensitive and ignorant.

With the country reeling from racial tensions and the aftereffects of the Kennedy assassination, it took a great deal of guts for NBC to go ahead with its plans for an American version of the popular British satire program *That Was The Week That Was*. The BBC had, in fact, dropped its version of the program at the end of

September 16, 1964

Shindig. (ABC). Britain's pioneer of television rock'n'roll, Jack Good, shows America how it's done. His fast-paced showcase for rock talent not only features top artists such as The Beatles, but also presents up-and-coming performers such as Billy Preston and Bobby Sherman.

September 19-25, 1964

"NBC Week." Following ABC's lead, NBC puts all of its fall premieres into one easy-to-publicize week. NBC also emphasizes the fact that it is the first network to have more than 50% of its prime time fare in color.

October 5, 1964

90 Bristol Court. (NBC). An experiment in program packaging. NBC presents three standard sitcoms as part of one ninety-minute show. The hook? All the characters in *Karen, Harris Against the World,* and *Tom, Dick, and Mary* live in the same apartment complex: 90 Bristol Court. Only *Karen* survives past January.

October 7, 1964

NBC and Universal Studios present the first two-hour made-for-television movie, "See How They Run," starring John Forsythe and Jane Wyatt. This film—and a few others like it aired this season—receives very little publicity and registers mediocre ratings.

November 8, 1964

Profiles in Courage. (NBC). Robert Saudek, former *Omnibus* guru, presents a series of twenty-six historical dramatizations inspired by John Kennedy's 1956 Pulitzer Prize winning book.

1963 because, it explained, 1964 was to be an election year in Britain and it would not be right for the BBC to make fun of politicians. Despite the fact that the U.S. also faced elections that year, NBC did not follow suit and instead set about convincing both Madison Avenue and the American public that topical, political humor could be entertaining and profitable.

One fortunate result of the cancellation of the British *TW3* was that it allowed David Frost to join the American version when it premiered in January 1964 (though at first he remained in the background as just another member of the *TW3* family). Elliott Reid originally acted as the host and he was joined by Frost, Henry Morgan, Phyllis Newman, Buck Henry, puppeteer Burr Tillstrom, and Nancy Ames (the singing "TW3 Girl"). At first, the writers were unsure of their ground (satire was certainly new to American television) and settled for standard TV jokes with topical names plugged in. By the late spring, they began to find their mark and the show picked up noticeably in both pacing and overall quality. The writers developed satirical approaches to topical issues and events while also poking fun at television itself, especially its commercials. Variety shows had been doing sendups of over-played, all-too-familiar commercials for years (at the time, Danny Kaye's were among the best), but *TW3* did them one better. In one instance, a silly but genuine catsup commercial was run as scheduled. It featured talking hamburger buns that, at the spot's end, joyfully threw their tops into the air when they heard the brand of catsup to be used. When the show resumed, the cast added an unexpected coda: As David Frost began talking to the audience, dozens of hamburger bun tops fell from above and covered him.

The program was at its best, though, in its semi-serious and topical moments. Guest comics Sandy Baron and Alan Alda appeared as a pair of singing segregationist plumbers. Puppeteer Tillstrom staged an award-winning detente of East and West hand puppets that met atop the Berlin wall. President Lyndon Johnson's infamous beagle episode (in which the president lifted one of his pet dogs by its ears) inspired a sendup featuring handpuppet HBJ (Him Beagle Johnson) being snatched by giant presidential hands before it could reveal LBJ's choice for his vice presidential running mate. Johnson was a godsend to the writers because he had so many easily caricatured qualities: he was tall, earthy, and a Texan with an obvious accent. As humorous a target as Johnson was, Barry Goldwater, a Republican presidential candidate in 1964, was even more tempting. One of the most effective (and disturbing) putdowns of Goldwater came in the form of a puppet reading various quotes from the candidate's public statements.

In its first half season (January through June of 1964), *TW3* did fairly well as a Friday night lead-in to Jack Paar. When David Frost took over as host in the fall of 1964, however, NBC moved the program to perhaps the toughest spot on its schedule, Tuesday night against *Petticoat Junction* and *Peyton Place.* Besides facing two top ten shows, *TW3* came into direct conflict with the 1964 presidential campaign. Just as the elections in Britain had caused the end of the BBC version of *TW3*, the American presidential elections effectively doomed the U.S. counterpart, though in a very unusual way. The fate of *TW3*, however, was just one minor skirmish in a running battle over the proper role of television in the contest. As in its civil rights reporting, the medium's own actions were as severely scrutinized as the candidates' campaign strategies. Once again, a deep resentment of television reporting was revealed.

The competition between the network news departments (especially between CBS and NBC) was particularly fierce that year as *The Huntley-Brinkley Report* found itself at the start of a yearlong deadlock with Walter Cronkite for nightly news supremacy. Traditional wisdom in broadcasting circles held that the network which won the convention and election coverage would carry the momentum into the lucrative nightly news shows and probably remain on top for the next four years. An increased interest in the early spring primaries provided a convenient warm-up arena, and all three networks took the opportunity to roll out their latest gimmick, computers, to help them make "instant vote projections." John Kennedy's dramatic primary victories in 1960 had alerted reporters to the potential importance of these local contests and, with larger staffs and new technological tricks available, it seemed strategically wise to cover them. As the votes in these elections came in that spring, CBS, NBC, and ABC raced with each other to be the first to declare a winner, using their fancy new equipment. The speed techniques did more than impress the regular viewers and politicians watching; it left them flabbergasted. How could the networks declare a winner with only a minuscule percentage of the vote totals in? CBS, for example, declared Senator Barry Goldwater the victor in the crucial California primary in June with only 2% of the state's vote totals listed on the tote board.

Actually, the feat was illusory. The network computers did not rely on the official vote tallies for the projections because these not only took hours to trickle in, they were often quite misleading as well (an area strongly supporting one candidate might report in first and show a huge lead that would be wiped out by subsequent reports). Instead, each of the networks employed statistical analysis techniques using the results from a handful of key precincts that had been targeted (from past voting patterns) to provide a highly educated projection of what the final totals for the state would be.

Stringers were placed in these precincts and they called the networks directly as soon as the votes were counted, allowing television to call a race often within two hours after the polls closed, compared to a turn-over time of six hours in the past. Instant vote projection was really the result of long hard work and calculated preparation, but the shorthand label stuck and the audience saw the final product in that light. Though there was nothing dishonest about the technique, it nonetheless irked people and raised vague suspicions and resentments. With instant vote projections, the networks had taken away much of the fun from election night with its ever-changing see-saw totals that hinged on every vote. In fact, they also seemed to reduce the importance of each individual vote by using just a sample to pronounce an election decided. To some this was TV news at its most arrogant and intrusive, appointing itself national election judge and showing off its influence on the perception of politics and current events, reducing everything to just more programming fodder.

Anger at the network news operations surfaced unexpectedly at the Republican National Convention at San Francisco's Cow Palace in July, during a speech by former president Dwight Eisenhower, the grand old man of the GOP. In the course of a traditional pep talk address, Eisenhower touched off a spontaneous roar when he unexpectedly condemned "sensation seeking columnists and commentators" (an ironic generalization because Eisenhower was serving as a commentator for ABC at the time). The phrase had been inserted at the last minute and the delegates eagerly took the opportunity to express their deep distrust (even hate) for TV news to the nation at large. For five minutes they jeered and screamed, shaking their fists at Huntley and Brinkley who were encased in the NBC glass booth high above the arena floor, looking down. Many supporters of Senator Goldwater, whose conservative forces controlled the convention (as the result of a brilliant state-by-state primary and caucus strategy), honestly felt that TV news was a disrupting influence on America. If there were any doubters among them, they were convinced by a report carried by CBS while the convention was still in progress. The CBS correspondent in Germany, Daniel Schorr, reported that Goldwater had plans to visit West Germany after the convention and meet with his "counterpart" right wingers. Very few people missed the Nazi allusion, intended or not, and Goldwater was forced to cancel the trip to prevent the negative association from sinking in any deeper. He was rightly incensed and CBS was properly embarrassed.

CBS also lost in the ratings race at the Republican convention, with Huntley and Brinkley clobbering Walter Cronkite by a wide margin. In a desperate move to improve the ratings at the Democratic convention in Atlantic City the next month, CBS executives replaced Cronkite (CBS's sole anchor at special events since 1952) with the team of Robert Trout and Roger Mudd. Though Cronkite insisted he did not take the action as an insult, people throughout the nation did. "We Want Cronkite" buttons popped up all through the Democratic gathering and viewers across the nation complained. CBS reinstated him for the election coverage in November, apparently deciding that it was best not to tamper with a national personality so obviously loved and admired. Besides, the Trout-Mudd team had fared no better than Cronkite anyway.

The campaign in the fall between Goldwater and President Johnson was one of the most bitter and vicious races in years, and television was the forum for one of the major battles: imagery. Using some campaign commercials that bordered on being downright unethical, the Democratic Party subtly (and not so subtly) painted Goldwater as a man likely to kill little children by irresponsibly and indiscriminately using nuclear power. In September, the message relied on subtle implication: A cute little girl was shown gathering daisies in a field and counting to herself as she picked the petals from the flowers. Her counting blended with and was replaced by the countdown to an atomic bomb explosion. At detonation, the fiery blast replaced the little girl on the screen. Then, Lyndon Johnson was heard saying: "These are the stakes—to make a world in which all of God's children can live, or to go into the dark." An announcer then urged viewers to vote for Johnson on election day, saying that "the stakes are too high for you to stay at home." Not voting for Johnson apparently would lead to nuclear disaster. This commercial was considered so outrageous that it was withdrawn after only one official appearance (during a movie on NBC on September 7), but it was then picked up in news reports and played so often there that its message reached an audience far beyond its single play.

Another commercial aired soon after this and left less to the imagination. Another cute little girl was shown licking an ice cream cone as a voice-over announcer calmly explained that the girl could be in serious trouble. The ice cream could contain some dangerous strontium 90 radiation from nuclear fallout because Barry Goldwater had opposed the nuclear test ban treaty. If he were elected, there was no telling how long the little girl might last. Though the Democrats pulled this spot after Republican complaints, the damage had been done. Millions had seen it.

The Republicans, through the Mothers for a Moral America, presented their own lapse in taste, a thirty-minute film, "Choice." The movie painted a picture of the U.S. on the edge of moral collapse with images of topless bathing suits, pornographic book

November 9, 1964
The Les Crane Show. (ABC). Johnny Carson at last faces some network competition in the late night talk show game. Thirty-year-old Les Crane generally steers his ninety-minute show towards substantive issues rather than celebrity chit chat, using an "in the round" setting and a shotgun microphone to take questions from the audience.

January 1, 1965
After four years, ABC gives up its Monday-through-Friday fifteen-minute late night news program and instead institutes a similar format on weekends only.

January 12, 1965
Hullabaloo. (NBC). A glitzy copy of ABC's *Shindig*, emphasizing scantily-clad, wildly gyrating "go-go" dancers and using mainstream pop stars such as Annette Funicello and Frankie Avalon as guest hosts.

February 1, 1965
Twenty-six-year-old Canadian newsman Peter Jennings replaces Ron Cochran as the anchor of ABC's nightly fifteen-minute news show.

April 27, 1965
Edward R. Murrow, 57, dies of lung cancer.

May 10, 1965
The Merv Griffin Show. Group W revamps its syndicated late night talk show, installing Merv Griffin and his sidekick, Arthur Treacher.

June 7, 1965
Sony introduces the first commercial home video tape recorder. Price: $995.

covers, and frenzied black rioters as illustration. It was scheduled to run on NBC on October 22, but at the last minute Goldwater repudiated the production as "nothing but a racist film" in its portrayal of blacks and canceled it.

Goldwater's personal TV presentations were remarkably traditional in comparison to such titillating fare, largely relying on the old style of buying thirty-minute blocks of time to plug his campaign rather than using the already well-established technique of presenting thirty- or sixty-second ads. Nonetheless, he did manage to stage his own bit of subtle media manipulation. He arranged for his thirty-minute programs to be scheduled, as often as possible, on Tuesdays at 9:30 P.M. on NBC, preempting *That Was The Week That Was*, which constantly ribbed the senator in its skits. The September 22, 1964, season premiere of *TW3* was replaced by Goldwater's program. The September 29 episode would also have been preempted but NBC had already agreed to sell a sixty-second spot on the show to the Democrats, so *TW3* began its new season only a week late. However, the Republicans managed to buy out the October 6, October 13, and October 27 slots. When they were unable to preempt the show on October 20, they bought a half-hour

of time on CBS, to compete with *TW3*. Tuesday, November 3, was election day, so NBC's election coverage wiped out the evening's regular programs. At last, on November 10, a week after the election and President Johnson's landslide victory, *TW3* responded to Goldwater's shenanigans by beginning that week's episode with a film of his concession speech, adding a voiceover announcer who substituted the words, "Due to circumstances beyond control, the regularly scheduled political broadcast scheduled for this time is pre-empted."

It was an appropriate, very funny response, but *TW3* had already been mortally crippled in its quest for even passable ratings. In the vital first weeks of the season, it had rarely been on. *Peyton Place* and *Petticoat Junction* were top ten hits and it was doubtful that many viewers would turn to NBC instead, except perhaps by accident. By spring, *TW3* was gone, a victim of low ratings and a change in attitudes. In the seventeen months since the enthusiastic reception given the *TW3* pilot, the mood in the country had changed. There were deep feelings of confusion, frustration, and resentment among viewers. Fewer and fewer people felt like laughing at anything so close to home as the news.

25. The Second Season

IN THE FALL OF 1965, FOR THE FIRST TIME in television history, all three networks presented their entire set of new season premieres in one week. For seven nights, beginning September 12, viewers were faced with a staggering selection of thirty-five new programs, and more than sixty returning shows. This insane competition marked a complete turnaround from the previous network practice of stringing out the season premieres from late September through mid-October, a procedure that had been in effect for nearly two decades. The reason for the change was quite simple: the CBS ratings romp of the early 1960s had turned into a tight, three-way race and none of the networks could afford to allow their competitors the slightest advantage.

ABC, which had fallen back to last place after a brief fling at the number two spot in the early 1960s, had initiated the practice of a single week for the premieres of its new shows in the fall of 1963. When the network repeated the strategy in the fall of 1964, it scooted to the number one position for the first two ratings reports of the 1964–65 season. Even though CBS regained the lead by November, ABC remained in its best position in years. Building on the advantage provided by its strong early returns, ABC nosed out NBC as the number two network for the season. NBC and CBS had no intention of allowing ABC to repeat that success in the 1965–66 season and both entered the September melee with their own premiere weeks.

The practice of scattering the premieres of new programs over one month, starting in late September, had begun in the early days of network radio and had been automatically carried over to TV. It was said that such a leisurely pace gave viewers plenty of time to notice and tune in new shows while continuing to follow their old favorites. Consequently, the best way to launch a new show was to slot it either before or after a proven hit in order to catch the spillover audience. Such a policy obviously favored the network with the greatest number of established hit shows and left most of the new programs on the others unwatched and unnoticed. An industry rule-of-thumb developed: The network with the greatest number of new shows in the fall would probably be the network that came in last. Since the early 1960s, ABC had been in the position of changing nearly one-half of its schedule every fall, and, more than any other network, it had to constantly combat viewer indifference to its unfamiliar new programs. As a result, the network had become locked in the number three position and was desperate for a way to break out. The experimental premiere weeks in 1963 and 1964 were just another ploy in its search for a solution.

ABC's placement of all its new shows in one eye-catching dramatic seven-day sweep made a great deal of sense. With NBC and CBS still in summer reruns, viewers were more inclined to give ABC a chance. As a result, several of its new shows such as *Twelve O'Clock High, The Addams Family, Bewitched, Voyage to the Bottom of the Sea,* and *Shindig* became hits early in the 1964–65 season. Some programs even managed to maintain their momentum once the other two networks unveiled their own new offerings. For example, *Peyton Place,* ABC's experiment in prime time soap opera, received an invaluable boost when viewers tuned in the first week "just to see what all the fuss was about" and became hooked by the dramatic complications and character conflicts. Returning ABC programs benefited as well. *Ben Casey,* for instance, had nearly been canceled after a very weak performance against *The Dick Van Dyke Show* and *The Beverly Hillbillies* in the 1963–64 season but, with the head start provided by the premiere week in 1964, it found its old audience and became a hit again in a new time period. In short, ABC's plan worked and the network broke the vicious cycle that had helped condemn it to last place.

The quick lead and continued strength of ABC during the 1964–65 season were a dramatic slap to CBS and its president, James Aubrey. Though, technically, a number of specials and preemptions (for the Summer Olympics and presidential election campaign) had provided the extra boost that took ABC to the top in its premiere week, there was no denying that the unchallenged king of TV had been seriously shaken. Worse yet, of CBS's own new programs for the 1964–65 season, only *Gomer Pyle* and *Gilligan's Island* were major successes. Drawing on the strength of its veteran hits, CBS regained the ratings lead by Thanksgiving, but by a very slim margin. Faced with the very real possibility of presiding over the network's first losing season in more than a decade, Aubrey boldly broke another industry tradition himself and began a major mid-season overhaul of the CBS schedule.

For years, the networks had operated under the assumption that it was meaningless to tamper significantly with their schedules once the season had begun. It was felt that viewing patterns for the year were formed and set by late November and would not change until the summer break and the next fall. Certainly there had been alterations in the network schedules between January and March in the past, but they were usually a stop-gap maneuver and not part of an overall programming strategy. Aubrey's actions were a calculated effort to repair the damage suffered in the fall and to steer CBS back to undisputed control of first place.

Day		7:00	7:30	8:00	8:30	9:00	9:30	10:00	10:30	
M O N		local	Twelve O'Clock High		THE LEGEND OF JESSE JAMES	A MAN CALLED SHENANDOAH	The Farmer's Daughter	Ben Casey		ABC
		local	To Tell The Truth	I've Got A Secret	The Lucy Show	Andy Griffith Show	Hazel	STEVE LAWRENCE SHOW		CBS
		local	Hullabaloo	JOHN FORSYTH SHOW	Dr. Kildare	Andy Williams Show / # Perry Como's Kraft Music Hall		RUN FOR YOUR LIFE		NBC
T U E		local	Combat!		McHale's Navy	F TROOP	Peyton Place	The Fugitive		ABC
		local	Rawhide		Red Skelton Hour		Petticoat Junction	CBS Reports / CBS News Specials		CBS
		local	MY MOTHER THE CAR	PLEASE DON'T EAT THE DAISIES	Dr. Kildare	NBC Tuesday Night At The Movies				NBC
W E D		local	Adventures Of Ozzie And Harriet	Patty Duke Show	GIDGET	THE BIG VALLEY		Amos Burke, Secret Agent		ABC
		local	LOST IN SPACE		The Beverly Hillbillies	GREEN ACRES	Dick Van Dyke Show	Danny Kaye Show		CBS
		local	The Virginian			Bob Hope Presents The Chrysler Theater / # Bob Hope Show		I SPY		NBC
T H R		local	Shindig	Donna Reed Show	O.K. CRACKERBY	Bewitched	Peyton Place	THE LONG HOT SUMMER		ABC
		local	The Munsters	Gilligan's Island	My Three Sons	CBS THURSDAY NIGHT MOVIES				CBS
		local	Daniel Boone		LAREDO		MONA McCLUSKEY	DEAN MARTIN SHOW		NBC
F R I		local	The Flintstones	TAMMY	The Addams Family	HONEY WEST	Peyton Place	Jimmy Dean Show		ABC
		local	THE WILD, WILD WEST		HOGAN'S HEROES	Gomer Pyle, U.S.M.C.	SMOTHERS BROTHERS SHOW	Slattery's People		CBS
		local	CAMP RUNAMUCK	HANK	CONVOY		MR. ROBERTS	The Man From U.N.C.L.E.		NBC
S A T		local	Shindig	The King Family Show	Lawrence Welk Show		Hollywood Palace		ABC Scope	ABC
		local	Jackie Gleason Show		TRIALS OF O'BRIEN		THE LONER	Gunsmoke		CBS
		local	Flipper	I DREAM OF JEANNIE	GET SMART	NBC Saturday Night At The Movies				NBC
S U N		Voyage To The Bottom Of The Sea		THE FBI		The ABC Sunday Night Movie				ABC
		Lassie	My Favorite Martian	Ed Sullivan Show		Perry Mason		Candid Camera	What's My Line	CBS
		Bell Telephone Hour / NBC News Sp. (fr. 6:30)	Walt Disney's Wonderful World Of Color		Branded	Bonanza		THE WACKIEST SHIP IN THE ARMY		NBC

The underlying assumption of Aubrey's mid-season revamping was that the new CBS shows were good, but the schedule had not been put together quite right. He made eleven changes for the winter of 1965, focusing his efforts on shifting time slots rather than introducing new shows. For example, *Slattery's People,* a traditional lawyer drama starring Richard Crenna and featuring Ed Asner, was shifted from Monday night opposite the resuscitated *Ben Casey* to Friday night following *Gomer Pyle,* replacing the weak newspaper melodrama of *The Reporter.* The reasoning was simple: *Slattery's People* had received good critical reviews and should have been able to develop into a hit against a fading veteran, but the show had faltered when *Ben Casey* experienced its surprise revival. With Gomer as a new lead-in, *Slattery's People* could benefit from his spillover audience and slow down the progress of *Twelve O'Clock High,* a new but increasingly popular ABC show. Aubrey discarded the mediocre *Reporter* series and, with a clever trick, even managed to reduce the ratings damage on Monday night. Though he conceded the slot to *Ben Casey* and ABC by moving in *CBS Reports,* he stripped the news program of all national advertising, realizing that the Nielsen company did not count unsponsored shows in the ratings. Other shifts followed a similar pattern and involved such "deserving" programs as the sitcom *My Living Doll* (Julie Newmar as a gorgeous female robot).

Aubrey's frantic mid-season changes worked no miracles, though CBS's ratings improved slightly and it managed to eke out a slim victory for the 1964–65 season. At the end of February 1965, Aubrey was fired. Rarely in television history had any executive fallen so far, so fast. Yet there were suggestions that Aubrey had undercut his own position by allowing three very weak programs (*The Reporter, The Baileys of Balboa,* and *The Cara Williams Show*) onto CBS's 1964–65 schedule because he had a financial interest in their production outfit. What's more, the poor showing by all three was seen as the central reason CBS had begun to slip in the fall of 1964. When Aubrey's winter tinkering failed to magically restore the network to its previously unquestioned supremacy, he became a marked man under a cloud of suspicion. Aubrey was replaced by Jack Schneider, whose main background was in sales and administration, rather than programming. He faced the task of keeping CBS on top for the 1965–66 season in what promised to be another tight race.

With all three networks launching the 1965–66 season the same week in head-to-head competition, any small advantage was seen as potentially decisive. NBC and CBS focused on color as the gimmick that could provide the edge necessary for victory because, a decade after color TV sets first went on sale, consumers were buying them in great numbers at last. The long-hoped-for color boom had begun with set sales and color broadcasting growing dramatically in just two years. During 1964 there was a 77% increase in color set purchases. In the fall of 1964, NBC launched the first major color season, with more than 50% of its programming in full tint. During the summer of 1965, the networks began covering live news events such as space shots in color. In the fall of 1965, NBC became the first nearly all-color network with only two of its shows, *I Dream of Jeannie* and *Convoy,* in black and white. At the same time, CBS reached the 50% color mark in its schedule. ABC lagged far behind both and felt the pinch immediately as the ratings for the 1965 fall premieres came in. Not only had it lost the advantage of having the only premiere week on television, it also had not moved fast enough on color. For the first time ever, all of the top ten shows were in color. Six percent of American TV homes had color sets and, not surprisingly, people with color sets watched color shows more than the national average. ABC found its black and white stalwarts such as *Peyton Place* and *Ben Casey* sliding lower and lower in the ratings.

CBS and NBC took a strong lead in the new season and once again ABC was in the cellar, facing the grim prospect of a major overhaul of its schedule for the 1966–67 season. Driven by desperation, the network decided to discard another industry tradition in the hope of salvaging the 1965–66 season. After the fall premieres, the networks usually focused their attention on setting up the next season's schedule, locking it up by February, and letting unsuccessful shows run their course. If Aubrey had achieved moderate success for CBS in 1964–65 with his mid-season tinkering, why not go one step further: treat January like a new season, with both new programs and major time shifts. A house cleaning would be necessary anyway, so why wait until the next fall? Thus, in January 1966, ABC launched "the second season."

The early September premiere week made a so-called second season possible. In the early 1960s, the bible of network TV, the Nielsen ratings book (published twice each month), took almost a week to compile, print, and distribute. For example, the book covering the period of September 5 through September 19 (called the "first September" book) would not be in the hands of eager executives until the last days of the month. The book covering September 20 through October 3 (called the "second September" book) would arrive in mid-October. Each month contained a "first" and "second" book with similar delays, so that when the fall premieres stretched from mid-September through October, the first Nielsen book to take into account all of the new shows for the fall was the second October report, which was not in print until the first week of November. Now, with the new season completely launched by mid-September, the second September ratings book could function as the first true gauge of a program's popularity, and thus reliable information on program performance was available an entire month earlier than before. There was enough time to plan and select shows for a second season that could begin in January.

The obvious ramification of a formal second season was that more programs were given a chance to air. This was a double-edged development because, at the same time, a potentially popular show with low ratings at the start might be yanked off the air before it had a chance to build an audience. In the process, having a second season start in January delayed until March final decisions on the next fall's line-ups because programmers wanted to see how well second season entries performed.

ABC unveiled its second season amid great fanfare ("The excitement of the fall starts all over again!"), but most of the new shows bombed, which was not surprising because most new ABC shows at the time bombed. Despite the additional month available to prepare, many of ABC's new shows were thrown together at the last minute or quickly imported from England. Nonetheless, some of the time shifts worked well. *Peyton Place,* for instance, changed from a Tuesday-Thursday-Friday rotation to a Monday-Tuesday-Friday arrangement, and its ratings returned to the level of the 1964–65 season. In addition, the network increased its percentage of color programming. Most important, though, ABC came up with a smash hit to revitalize its schedule, the camp heroic adventures of *Batman.*

Critics had often complained that television was filled with comic-book-type characters. *Batman* accepted the comic book roots of its hero not as a putdown but an inspiration, and proudly flaunted them, though in a very different manner from its fraternal crime stopper, Superman. The syndicated *Adventures of Superman* television series of the 1950s had the trappings of the comic book adventures (the man of steel's colorful costume, invulnerability, power to fly, and super-strength), but ultimately it was just a traditional kiddie-cop adventure presenting Superman as an exceptional, but in many ways typical, stalwart crime fighter. He usually faced the same faceless hoods and routine crimes encountered by his colleagues in the police force and private detective agencies. Batman (billed in the comics as "the world's greatest detective") could have easily fit into the same mold, but producer William Dozier realized that such a formula would probably not work in an age of superhero-type spies and secret agents. Instead, he looked not so much at the character of Batman but at the gimmicks surrounding him and, most important, at the style of the comic book medium itself with its flashy colors, impossible gadgets, and unusual action sequences. Dozier decided to stage the series as a television comic book, but with one important difference: all the comic book elements were grossly exaggerated and the program turned into one huge tongue-in-cheek joke. After all, could two adults in leotards and capes really be taken seriously?

Adam West (as Batman and the caped crusader's alter ego,

Gourmet food was often the order of the day for Colonel Hogan (Bob Crane, *left*) at Stalag 13 on *Hogan's Heroes,* aided here by guest star Hans Conried as Major Bonacelli. *(CBS Photo Archive © 2003 CBS Worldwide, Inc. All Rights Reserved.)*

September 12, 1965

After building a following for five years on ABC, the American Football League jumps to NBC.

September 14, 1965

My Mother the Car. (NBC). Jerry Van Dyke plays a suburban hubby who discovers his dead mother reincarnated as a decrepit automobile on a used car lot. Ann Sothern supplies the voice for "mother," who speaks to her son through the car radio.

September 15, 1965

Green Acres. (CBS). Eddie Albert and Eva Gabor play backwards Clampetts (city slickers that move to the country) in a third-generation Paul Henning hillbilly spinoff.

September 16, 1965

The Dean Martin Show. (NBC). Martin returns to television in an easy-going variety hour carried almost completely by his relaxed, slightly naughty personality.

September 16, 1965

CBS Thursday Night Movies. (CBS). The number one network becomes the last to add prime time movies, beginning with Frank Sinatra in "The Manchurian Candidate" from 1962.

September 18, 1965

I Dream of Jeannie. (NBC). Barbara Eden plays a beautiful 2,000-year-old magical genie who attaches herself to an American astronaut (played by Larry Hagman). As "lord and master," he gets as many wishes as he wants.

September 19, 1965

The FBI. (ABC). Quinn Martin presents Efrem Zimbalist, Jr. in a series based on actual cases from the FBI's files.

October 24, 1965

With the debut of Saturday's *Scherer-MacNeil Report* (anchored by Ray Scherer and Robert MacNeil) and Sunday's *Frank McGee Report* (in addition to the weekday *Huntley-Brinkley Report*) NBC becomes the first television network to offer thirty minutes of nightly news seven days a week.

aristocrat-goldbrick Bruce Wayne) and Burt Ward (as Robin the Boy Wonder and Dick Grayson, Wayne's young ward) played the heroes as marvelous caricatures of the gung-ho, power of positive thinking super patriots that had dominated comics since World War II. Batman and Robin were very, *very* serious about fighting crime in Gotham City but, though they never cracked jokes, much of what they said was hilarious. With a perfectly straight face, Batman would wax prosaic on the evils of crime and the importance of good citizenship, even while struggling to escape from a seemingly foolproof trap. Robin greeted every challenge with boyish enthusiasm and shamelessly displayed his perception of the obvious with such phrases as "Holy ice cubes, Batman! It's getting cold!" It was too ridiculous to be true; so naive that it was preposterous; so bad that it was good. That was Dozier's trump card. By hopelessly exaggerating every aspect of the show, he fashioned an environment that re-created the comic book world for children but also offered "camp" humor for the teenagers and adults. The style touched every aspect of the show, from the full-screen comic book

captions that adorned every fight (matching each punch to some "Crunch!," "Pow!," "ZAP!," or "Ka-zonk" type graphic superimposed on the scene) to the dramatically hokey voiceover announcer-narrator (Dozier himself) who solemnly posed the inevitable question in each episode: "Is this the end of Batman and Robin?" The series, in color, ran twice each week, on Wednesday and Thursday nights, and Dozier ended the Wednesday episodes with absurd cliff-hangers designed to lure even the most incredulous audience back for part two: "same bat-time, same bat-channel!" The exaggerated perils were a direct sendup of the many kiddie serials that had run on the radio and in the movie theaters during the 1930s and 1940s, using the cliff-hanger come-on to coax fans back for the next episode. At various mid-week climaxes, Batman and Robin were on the verge of being frozen, fried, eaten by lions, unmasked, or turned into postage stamps. The two heroes used a ludicrous arsenal of "bat" gimmicks in their weekly skirmishes including the batmobile, batcopter, batcomputer, batpole, and batarang; all housed, of course, in the batcave.

At the beginning of each story, Police Commissioner Gordon (Neil Hamilton) would solemnly summon Batman and Robin by using a special batphone "hotline," or by switching on a rootop batsignal searchlight. The reason was always the same: Some dastardly villain had appeared. That might have been cause for alarm in Gotham City, but it was good news for viewers because a wide range of Hollywood performers donned the garb of Batman's most popular comic book opponents. Unlike the dynamic duo, the villains in the series obviously were having a great time and relished the opportunity to taunt their hated adversaries with clues to their impending crimes. For them, the thrill of battle mattered more than the cold hard cash. Burgess Meredith (Penguin), Cesar Romero (Joker), and Frank Gorshin (Riddler) were the most popular guest stars, though others such as Art Carney (Archer), Vincent Price (Egghead), Maurice Evans (Puzzler), George Sanders (Mr. Freeze), David Wayne (Mad Hatter), Victor Buono (King Tut), and, at various times, Julie Newmar, Eartha Kitt, and Lee Ann Meriwether (Catwoman) were equally entertaining. Each performer brought a frenzied lunacy to the role (mad laughter was the most common trait among them) and their antics were the effective balance to the mock-deadpan of Batman and Robin.

Dozier's comic book for television combined superb guests, camp humor, colorful costumes, unusual camera work (emphasizing weird angles), and pure imagination. The result was an instant hit that justified ABC's second season gamble and gave viewers something unusual to laugh at beyond the thick-headed antics of Gomer Pyle and Gilligan. *Batman* relied on the traditional battle between good and evil, but treated the melodramatic conflict as a very silly game in which the villains were the most appealing characters. (Batman and Robin were far too serious and the police were incredibly dumb.) Though by no means the only tongue-in-cheek program that season, *Batman* was undoubtedly the most distinctive. It launched a nationwide bat-craze, inspired countless parodies in every medium (most never matching the original), and revealed a willingness among viewers to laugh at square-jawed heroics and pillars of authority.

The late-blooming success of *The Man from U.N.C.L.E.* the previous season had set the stage for the influx of tongue-in-cheek heroes starting in the fall of 1965, as all three networks rushed to follow the lead of Napoleon Solo and Illya Kuryakin. Not since ABC's overdose of action-adventure clones from *Maverick* and *77 Sunset Strip* had so many flippant characters appeared. Unlike the uninspired knockoffs at the turn of the decade, this new wave of programs contained first class writing, clever situations, and very talented performers.

Foremost among these programs was Britain's *The Avengers* which ABC brought to America as part of its second season lineup. By this time, Honor Blackman had departed from the series and Patrick Macnee (as John Steed) had a new cohort, the lovely, leggy Diana Rigg (as Mrs. Emma Peel), who picked up the saucy, flippant interplay and the deliciously ambiguous relationship with Steed. Like Mrs. Gale, she was a strong, sexy, independent woman who could fight crime as well as any man. Such a notion was practically unheard of at the time in American television (the best the Stateside networks could offer was Anne Francis as a female private eye, *Honey West*), and *The Avengers* began building a strong American cult following and winning high critical praise.

Homegrown productions included both tongue-in-cheek spy thrillers and sharp sitcom spoofs that marked a return to the quality of such classics as *Sergeant Bilko*. The two adventure series that came directly out of the *U.N.C.L.E.* mold were NBC's *I Spy* and CBS's *The Wild, Wild West*, which both featured pairs of witty, resourceful agents. *I Spy* presented Robert Culp and Bill Cosby as U.S. government agents (posing as an international tennis star and his trainer) roaming the world in search of Russian, Asian, and mobster bigwigs. Though eschewing the Bond-U.N.C.L.E. device of a fictional super-secret non-aligned organization of evil in favor of more realistic foes and dramatic situations, the program's location shots and humorous edge were its chief attractions. Cosby, a veteran black comic and nightclub entertainer, worked in some hilarious dialogues with Culp (often about Cosby's ghetto youth in Philadelphia) as they engaged in typical spy shenanigans throughout the world. At first it had been feared that Cosby's co-starring status would be a possible trouble spot for the show, but the mere presence of a black performer on television was no longer automatically a major risk. Only three NBC affiliates refused to air the series (in Albany, Georgia; Savannah, Georgia; and Daytona Beach, Florida). Television was improving its attitude toward blacks and, in fact, the industry felt comfortable enough to award Cosby an Emmy for his *I Spy* role.

CBS's *The Wild, Wild West* offered a unique combination of espionage and Western adventure by reaching all the way back to the *Maverick* roots of flippant cowboys for its unlikely premise of two spies operating in the American West of the 1870s. President Ulysses S. Grant personally assigned special U.S. government agents James T. West (Robert Conrad) and Artemus Gordon (Ross Martin) to the Western frontier, though it was never made quite clear exactly who or what menace inspired fears of such threats out amid the sagebrush and tumbling tumbleweeds. The producers and writers never let that bother them, nor did they feel obligated to explain what some of the best electronic gadgets of the twentieth century were doing in the 1870s (thinly disguised as "contemporary" inventions of the time). Instead, they used the unique hook provided by the combination of genres to gently spoof both Westerns and spy formats while, at the same time, developing exceptionally off-beat and intriguing stories. Conrad and Martin displayed the required light banter in the face of danger and even managed to "save the Western world" (of the nineteenth century) from the schemes of crazed madmen such as their most frequent foe, Dr. Miguelito Loveless (Michael Dunn), a dwarf with grand ambitions. With its fabulous cast and crew, *The Wild, Wild West* became a solid, entertaining hybrid and a CBS Friday night staple for four seasons.

Action and humor had teamed up earlier in television history in such series as *Maverick*, but in the new programs the line between adventure and comedy grew increasingly fuzzy. The season's best adventure shows were tongue-in-cheek while the best new sitcoms were spoofs of familiar dramatic settings. In the comedies the

stories were certainly exaggerated and silly, but they still retained enough action, mock-horror shootouts, and plot complications to function as adequate, though absurd, dramatic adventures. Among the most resilient of the new comedy-adventures was the marvelously mad put-on of *Get Smart*, which managed to outlast all of the other new video spies.

A product of the collective dementia of Buck Henry, Mel Brooks, and Howard Morris, *Get Smart* featured Don Adams as the bumbling, over-confident klutz, Maxwell Smart, secret agent 86 for a CIA-type organization, Control. *Get Smart* used the passion for absurd spy gimmicks as the launching pad for its gags and built from there. U.N.C.L.E. headquarters was hidden behind a false wall in a dry cleaning store, so to gain entrance to Control, Smart had to drop through the false floor of a phone booth. While Solo and Kuryakin used sophisticated communication devices the size of a ballpoint pen, Smart had to dial a telephone that was hidden in his shoe. Adams's hilarious portrayal of Smart, though, was the strong comic hub for the show. He was the classic bumbling idiot that won important battles in spite of himself (a character type Adams had developed on the short-lived *Bill Dana Show* in which he played an incompetent hotel detective, Byron Glick). With a superb sense of timing year after year, Adams milked laughs from

---

October 29, 1965
ABC throws in the towel on late night television, axing Les Crane's show, which had been renamed *ABC Nightlife* in March.

November 15, 1965
NBC's *Huntley-Brinkley Report* goes to color. Walter Cronkite's news show on CBS follows suit on January 31, 1966.

December 9, 1965
"A Charlie Brown Christmas." (CBS). Charles Schulz brings the "Peanuts" gang to television for the first time, in an animated family special.

December 20, 1965
The Dating Game. (ABC). Former ABC program executive Chuck Barris updates the 1940s *Blind Date* premise of eager bachelors trying to win a date with an eligible woman.

January 1, 1966
Robert Kinter, president of NBC-TV since 1958, is forcibly "kicked upstairs" to the position of chairman of the NBC board (a largely figurehead position he resigns a mere three months later). At the same time, "The General," David Sarnoff, gives up his day-to-day control of RCA, but remains as RCA chairman of the board.

June 6, 1966
Till Death Us Do Part. (BBC). Alf Garnett (Warren Mitchell) is television's first humorous bigot in this sharp-tongued but insightful working class sitcom set in a rundown area of London.

July 11, 1966
The Newlywed Game. (ABC). Chuck Barris takes the logical next step from *The Dating Game* and brings newlyweds together to blush over intimate details of their married life.

Robert Conrad *(right)* and Ross Martin played government agents operating in *The Wild, Wild West* of the 1870s. *(CBS Photo Archive © 2003 CBS Worldwide, Inc. All Rights Reserved.)*

such phrases as "Sorry about that, Chief!" (a deadpan apology to his superior following a major foul-up) and "Would you believe?" (a transparent attempt to bluff a hidden back-up force when his opponents had the upper hand).

At first, series regulars Edward Platt, as the chief of Control, and Barbara Feldon, as agent 99, often found themselves acting as "straightman" to the buffoonery of Smart, though as the program developed, their roles were expanded. *Get Smart* managed to survive even as interest in spies waned in the late 1960s because it never lost its comic touch and sense of imagination. As programs such as *The Man from U.N.C.L.E.* began reaching for cheap, obvious gags to pump new life into the spy format, *Get Smart* turned to other fields for humor and began using its "family" of players in parodies of classic films, other TV shows, and even its own ridiculous conventions and gag lines—while staying within the spy motif. *Get Smart* became an excellent, flexible vehicle for Adams and an effective parody of larger-than-life espionage adventures through all of its stories. By the time the series ended in 1970 and Smart had inadvertently saved the world countless times, he and agent 99 were happily married with two children, a humorous reminder that spying could fall into a nine-to-five routine just as easily as any profession.

Two other exceptional new sitcoms, *F Troop* and *Hogan's Heroes,* maintained the high standards of *Get Smart*'s lampoon style, but shifted the focus to the military life. *F Troop* was a Western *Bilko* ripoff that worked, turning the traditional John Wayne-frontier scout-cowboys and Indians story on its head. Situated in the wilds of Kansas after the Civil War, both the Indians and the men of F Troop were far more interested in drinking, sleeping, gambling, and turning a profit than in fighting each other. Bilko surrogates Sergeant Morgan O'Rourke (Forrest Tucker) and Corporal Randolph Agarn (former *Cavalcade of Stars* headliner Larry Storch) managed most of the money-making illegal activities in the area, including a moccasin concession turned out by the local Indian tribe, the "ferocious" Hekawis (as in "where the heck-ah-we?") Most of the plots revolved around O'Rourke and Agarn's constant search for profitable new ventures. The commander at

Fort Courage, Captain Wilton Parmenter (Ken Berry), was in a perpetual fog and posed no threat to the O'Rourke-Agarn enterprises. As a member of a family with a distinguished military history, Captain Parmenter had earned his commission by sneezing —and accidentally leading a Union charge to victory in one of the last battles of the Civil War. He was content to let fate guide his career at the fort as well, and O'Rourke and Agarn were only too happy to oblige. In true Bilko style, the only major threats to the happy profitable life of F Troop and the Hekawis came from outsiders, either visiting military brass that insisted the men at the fort go "by the book" (drills! exercise! reveille!), or wandering Indian tribes with the foolish notion of teaming up with the Hekawis for a raid on the fort. ("Hekawis not fighters, we lovers," the chief explained.) The series was a total farce with a heavy emphasis on physical humor and marvelous caricatures. Besides the conniving O'Rourke and Agarn and the spacey Parmenter, there was Melody Patterson as Wrangler Jane (a sharpshooting woman with marriage on her mind and an eye on Captain Parmenter), Edward Everett Horton as Hekawi medicine man Roaring Chicken, and Frank De Kova as Wild Eagle, the cowardly Hekawi chief. Even the men of F Troop maintained the Bilko tradition, resembling a collection of refugees from the Bowery rather than Civil War veterans. Whatever the background, they each carried the Bilko banner of deception, double-dealing, and self-interest proudly, and the show demonstrated that fresh comedy could still be found in the perennial TV staple of the old West.

Hogan's Heroes broke new territory in the field of military comedy as it made fun of the theretofore sacrosanct topic of World War II prisoner of war camps. Spoofing such film and stage productions as "Bridge on the River Kwai" and "Stalag 17," the series presented the inmates of Stalag 13 in total control of their environment. They had a complete system of tunnels under the prison camp and could escape at any time, but they did not. Why should they? There was practically a mini-Pentagon of supplies and services beneath the camp, including custom tailoring, munitions, direct radio contact with the Allies, and gourmet food. They could do more to sabotage the Nazi war machine from the prison camp than anywhere else. Obviously, the premise required a tremendous suspension of belief and some people, seeing no humor in either World War II in general or a group of POWs in particular, were taken aback at first. Actually, the series was a put-on of modern war films (with their super-human somewhat miraculous heroics behind enemy lines) rather than a rewrite of World War II, and in that light the program was eventually seen as very funny and very harmless. As with *Get Smart,* the stories were straightforward adventure yarns, only with absurd twists. The elaborate Allied operations, usually sabotage or aiding fugitives, were run from the POW camp by Col. Robert Hogan, the senior officer (played by Bob Crane, most recently seen as an affable suburban doctor in *Donna Reed*). In the tradition of hundreds of typical war films, Hogan was assisted by a perfectly integrated staff of comrades: one Frenchman, Cpl. LeBeau (Robert Clary); one cockney Englishman, Cpl. Newkirk (Richard Dawson); one American black, Sgt. Kinchloe (Ivan Dixon); and one naïve American kid, Sgt. Carter (Larry Hovis). The missions for the Allies were presented rather straight, but life at Stalag 13 was a completely different story. The Nazis were shown as either bumbling incompetents who really meant well or strutting loudmouths easily duped by Hogan. It was never revealed exactly how the prisoners had managed to set up such a complete battle station in Stalag 13, but the ineptness of camp commandant Wilhelm Klink (Werner Klemperer) and the simpleminded cooperation of porcine prison guard Sgt. Hans Schultz (John Banner) suggested that the task had not been *too* difficult. In fact, the two Germans were considered vital to the continued success of Hogan's operation and many episodes of the series focused not only on Allied missions but on the difficult task of keeping Klink in power and Schultz away from the Russian front. As time went on, Hogan and Klink developed an unconscious, guarded partnership similar to the relationship between the Hekawis and soldiers of *F Troop.* Neither wanted to be bothered by outsiders and both realized that, in a very strange way, they needed each other for survival.

The fall premiere week of 1965–66 and the second season which followed really did generate more excitement over the new shows than usual and, for once, network hype was not totally removed from reality. Though still strongly influenced by Aubrey's philosophy of mindless escapist programming, television had produced some clever variations and intelligent parodies. It even had room for some short-run off-beat series that attracted small cult followings if not high ratings, including *The Trials of O'Brien, Hank,* and second season entry *Blue Light.* At the same time it was displaying new life in entertainment programming, though, the medium was also experiencing painful growth as it faced the increasing complexity of covering events in the real world. There, real military activity was bringing network news departments into conflict with both the government and their own corporate brass.

In the spring of 1965, the independent judgments of network correspondents proved an embarrassment to the government with reports filed on the American intervention in the Dominican Republic. President Johnson had announced that American Marines were being sent to the island merely to protect American civilians from possible harm during the civil disturbances following a government *coup d'etat.* Within a few days of the action, network reporters on the scene began filing stories that the American troops were openly and blatantly aiding the take-over bid of the military faction friendly to the United States government, directly contradicting the president's publicly stated objectives. At first, American officials flatly denied the reporters' statements, but when films arrived showing the troops engaged in combat, the

truth became clear. Unlike stories by members of the print medium (even with photographs), the dramatic evidence provided by the network films was all but impossible to dismiss with just a few blustery denials. CBS's Harry Reasoner stated on the evening news that there had been "an apparent shortage of candor" at the White House, the closest a network reporter had ever come to calling a president an outright liar. Nonetheless, this was only a minor irritant for the government compared to the potential havoc such bluntness could cause in a far more important theater of U.S. military intervention, the conflict in Vietnam.

Through 1964 and 1965, ABC, CBS, and NBC steadily increased the size of their staffs in South Vietnam because, as CBS News president Fred Friendly explained, "We are covering this as a war, for that's what it is." The war-type status had developed in August 1964, when the American government announced that two U.S. destroyers had been attacked by North Vietnamese torpedo boats in the Gulf of Tonkin. In response, Congress had passed, almost unanimously, the "blank check" Gulf of Tonkin Resolution giving President Johnson virtual wartime powers to "take all necessary measures to repeal any armed attack against the forces of the U.S. and to prevent further aggression." In March 1965, the first U.S. combat Marines landed in South Vietnam as the American Air Force began continuous bombing raids throughout the North. Without ever having declared it, the United States was at war with a country most Americans could not even pronounce. The networks, however, were ready to apply their growing technical expertise to the difficult challenge of covering the overseas jungle conflict.

It was assumed that the American intervention would last only a few months, so much of the reporting in 1965 reflected an excited, almost adventurous spirit. Unlike the Korean War, with its clumsy battle footage (often provided by the U.S. government itself), the Vietnam conflict offered a unique opportunity for television to place its correspondents in an exotic jungle setting as they filmed their stories for the nightly news programs. CBS's Walter Cronkite took a three-week tour of Vietnam in July of 1965 and filed reports of the visit that focused on the sophisticated hardware and know-how of the American forces. One segment featured Cronkite aboard a plane zooming through the sky while the American pilots aboard proudly explained the bombing apparatus as if it were some shiny new car. For the most part, though, network reports of battle action usually consisted of film of a squad of Marines slogging through some jungle and firing at an unseen enemy somewhere in the bush. Secretary of Defense Robert McNamara had stated that the troops would be home by Christmas, and the need to dig deeper into the story did not seem that pressing.

Though many newsmen (like most other Americans) were slow to realize the ramifications of the steadily growing American involvement in Vietnam, the truly remarkable aspect of the coverage was that, despite some government pressure and secrecy, the networks were largely free to cover the venture as they wished. For the first time in history, a government conducting an overseas war relinquished control of the way the war was perceived back home. Vietnam became a true "television war" as many people in the country received most of their information on it from the nightly news coverage and occasional specials on the three networks. Such reports rarely examined the underlying purposes of the war and mostly emphasized very popular and visual aspects such as superficial combat footage, the American GIs adjusting to life overseas, and trivial battle statistics and graphs. Still, the fact was that the power of government rhetoric had been usurped and replaced by pictures brought directly into the privacy of individual homes across the country.

It was inevitable that such power over forming public opinion on a foreign policy matter would eventually upset the government. In August 1965, just a few months after the Dominican Republic conflict, CBS aired a dramatic film report by Morley Safer that deeply disturbed officials. On the August 5 edition of the *CBS Evening News,* viewers were shown the story of an American outfit destroying some huts in the small Vietnamese village of Cam Ne. It was not so much what was said in the report that bothered the government, but rather the impression the film left behind. While the residents of the village stood by meekly, crying and begging for a reprieve, the Marines methodically set the huts on fire, many using Zippo cigarette lighters to ignite the straw roofs. The image left by the film was potent and needed no elaboration: The United States, a powerful mechanized society, had sent its Marines into a backward rural country and, with apparently no provocation, was systematically destroying it. Whether there had been any enemy activity (by the Viet Cong) in Cam Ne was not really discussed. The chilling efficiency and lack of moral qualms displayed by the Marines (who were obviously in no immediate danger from the civilians) could not help but raise doubts among puzzled citizens as to what the U.S. was really doing there. Other people reacted with anger at CBS, criticizing the network for distorting the story, putting sensationalism above patriotism, and undermining morale. Safer even received mysterious threats on his life. Fred Friendly observed, in response to the protests, "As the power of the [news] medium increases, the power used to suppress it will increase."

The government began to exert more and more pressure on network reporters to "go along with the party line" on war dispatches. Such pressure was usually indirect and couched in appeals for teamwork, patriotism, and common sense understanding that were filtered through the networks' own channels to be conveyed by immediate superiors. This was not very difficult because many top broadcast officials had direct ties to the government and were actually "on the same team." Yet the pressure applied through influential company men rarely came in the form of some heavy-handed demand for the suppression of information, but usually appeared as a polite request to be more restrained, balanced, and sensitive to the possibly damaging repercussions of adverse war reports. Nevertheless, the "reasonable desire" for a more "evenhanded" approach to the news merely added to the tension that was always present between the network news departments and the profit-minded network executives who often viewed the news as an extravagant loss leader necessary merely for prestige.

In spite of the pressure from the top, all three networks presented competent but generally uninsightful war specials throughout 1965. These usually consisted of carefully balanced panel discussions between supporters of the war (such as Harvard professors Henry Kissinger and Zbigniew Brzezinski) and anti-war critics (usually foreign war correspondents because there were not very many homegrown critics available). In a perverse way, TV's evenhandedness in these debates served to help the anti-war cause the most because in 1965 many viewers had never heard arguments against the government's policy expressed at all. As the war intensified, though, the networks began putting more emphasis on the government's side of the story.

In response to the storm of protest over Safer's Cam Ne report, CBS, later that August, aired *Vietnam Perspective,* a series of four hour-long specials that examined several different viewpoints on the war, though it generally presented the government line as basically correct. NBC also began a weekly war program (on Sunday afternoons, hosted by Garrick Utley), *Vietnam Weekly Review,* but this was merely a well produced yet essentially meaningless review of the week's battle reports, focusing on ultimately pointless jungle skirmishes and hill assaults.

The reality of the ongoing war for those on the front lines meant constant vigilance. A converted armored personnel carrier showers flame on anti-personnel mines in January 1967.
(U.S. Army)

Surprisingly, ABC, the network with the weakest news department, provided the best overall coverage of the war within its weekly public affairs series, *ABC Scope.* This program had run, under a variety of titles, in odd hours since 1963. Starting in February 1966, it devoted all of its time to the Vietnam War. Realizing that the weekly battle statistics were given more than enough coverage on the nightly news (they were as familiar and as meaningless to most viewers as the stock market reports), the producers of *ABC Scope* concentrated instead on one particular aspect of the war each week. Using filmed reports usually produced on location in Vietnam, they tried to make sense of the increasingly perplexing conflict. Some of the programs included: a study of the role of blacks in Vietnam (comparing the views of black militants such as Stokely Carmichael with the views of blacks doing the fighting); film of North Vietnam itself, shot by a French crew on location; and thoughtful, on-the-spot analysis by Howard K. Smith, one of the most eloquent supporters of the war. These programs offered an important perspective to the jumble of general war news available and provided the opportunity for viewers to form intelligent and informed opinions on the issue.

Nobody watched these shows. All of the Vietnam specials regularly turned up at the very bottom of the ratings charts and *ABC Scope* in particular registered the worst ratings of any network program in modern television history. In September 1965, before it changed formats to become a weekly Vietnam show, only 28% of the more than 150 ABC affiliates aired the program. By 1966, only 27 affiliates bothered to show it at all and not one ABC station in the top fifty markets carried the program at its scheduled slot in prime time (Saturday night at 10:30 P.M.). Most of the ABC stations in major cities stuck the program in some obscure corner of the weekly schedule. WABC in New York aired it Sunday afternoon at 2 P.M. WFAA in Dallas aired it Sunday morning at 9 A.M. WNAC in Boston topped them all; it aired each episode eight days after its scheduled broadcast date, at 1 A.M. Sunday morning. Viewers never complained about the ridiculous time slots because they did not care. Whether for or against the war, a majority of viewers found any coverage of Vietnam generally upsetting and they fervently avoided anything more than the short clips on the nightly news.

Keenly aware of the public's disinterest in special coverage of the Vietnam War, the networks faced the difficult policy question of how to balance the guaranteed low ratings of Vietnam specials with their unwritten obligation to adequately present such a major story. The question came to a head in early 1966 when it became necessary to decide the best way to cover the public hearings that were being held by Senator William Fulbright's Foreign Relations Committee on the government's handling of the war. Fulbright had become one of the best known congressional war critics and had turned the hearings into the first high level public discussion of the real aims and ultimate goals of the Vietnam conflict. In late January he began by publicly roasting top administration witnesses such as Secretary of State Dean Rusk in days of long, tough questioning. The early sessions were briefly covered on the nightly news but, as the hearings progressed, it was clear that they deserved more extensive airtime. The event was certainly newsworthy, but in what manner would most people prefer to follow it? Live coverage of the actual testimony during the day? The familiar two-or three-minute reports on the nightly news? A special late night half-hour wrap up? A weekend special reviewing the events of the entire week, featuring a discussion panel to analyze the significant developments?

Network executives argued that live coverage preempted the most profitable part of the day and would be wasted anyway; most people interested in the hearings would not be able to watch them. As head of CBS News, Fred Friendly strongly supported blanket live coverage, feeling that the hearings were important and that TV had a responsibility to present them to the millions of viewers who would "bother" to tune in. With NBC's president and longtime supporter of extensive news coverage, Bob Kinter, recently deposed, Friendly was virtually alone among top brass in advocating complete live coverage. He grudgingly agreed to follow a compromise "day-to-day decision process" that called for live coverage on days important witnesses testified and evening highlights for the rest. Without too much trouble, both NBC and CBS followed this course in early February, but on February 10, while NBC went ahead with its planned broadcast of the testimony of George Kennan, former ambassador to Russia, CBS coverage plans were vetoed by network president Schneider. With that action, Schneider saved CBS $175,000 but lost the most respected name in contemporary TV journalism. Friendly quit CBS in protest and was replaced by the man he had succeeded in the first place, Richard Salant.

Though both CBS and NBC wound up carrying two days of hearings live the very next week, an important turning point had been reached in television's handling of the Vietnam War. Friendly's resignation marked the beginning of a swing away from extensive coverage and, while American involvement in the war rapidly increased over the next year, the number of Vietnam specials dropped sharply. Investigative reporting and discussions including advocates for "all points of view" were also downplayed. It was not worth the trouble, both internally and with the government, to follow a story viewers did not seem to want to hear about anyway. So even as the United States committed more than 100,000 additional troops to the war effort, the chief source of information on the war for most Americans became nothing more than short repetitive news clips dished out nightly at suppertime.

26. Same Is the Name of the Game

VARIETY, THE ENTERTAINMENT INDUSTRY'S own weekly trade magazine, labeled 1966 and 1967 as the era of "no guts journalism" in television. Though ABC continued to produce the rarely seen *ABC Scope* and CBS offered the *CBS News Hour* in prime time, the number of documentaries based on hard news events was down drastically. For example, between September 12 and November 22, 1966, NBC broadcast only three prime time news documentaries of any sort, and ABC offered only two. The news departments at the commercial networks seemed afraid to turn out anything that might possibly provoke official displeasure or viewer indifference.

All three networks largely ignored a new round of hearings on the Vietnam War held in early 1967 by Senator William Fulbright's Foreign Relations Committee. Only the noncommercial NET network gave the discussions extensive coverage, instituting a highly practical policy of presenting one-hour cutdowns of the day's live hearings for prime time viewing each night. NBC chose puff travelogue-type features such as "The Royal Palace" and "Thoroughbred." ABC featured some gung-ho material sponsored by major defense contractors such as the 3M corporation for "Our Time in Hell" (the Marines at war) and B. F. Goodrich for "War in the Skies" (with actor and retired Brigadier General James Stewart as narrator for the exploits of the Air Force in Southeast Asia). CBS came up with "The People of South Vietnam: How They Feel About the War," in which the network attempted to analyze the effects of the war in Vietnam by conducting an on-the-spot public opinion poll. Such a technique was safe, noncontroversial, and hopelessly misdirected, treating the problems facing uneducated peasant farmers in the war-torn country like political or fashion trends in middle class American suburbs.

Yet the "no guts journalism" label was not only limited to the apparent non-inflammatory policy toward the Vietnam War. The commercial networks seemed to be ignoring a wide range of controversial subjects, once again leaving NET as the only force apparently willing to produce incisive programs. On shows such as *At Issue* and *NET Journal,* the noncommercial network tackled such topics as misleading advertising, defects in American medical care, the manipulation of the press by President Johnson's administration, and overcharges levied against the poor by supermarkets, credit unions, and the phone company. Serious questions began to be raised on the integrity and independence of the commercial networks' news operations. Was the toning down of controversy deliberate? Were the networks fearful of reprisals by government and industry? Were they somehow too closely aligned to those same forces in government and industry? Or was all this just a comparative cooling off of coverage in contrast to the dramatic news events of 1963, 1964, and 1965?

In January 1966, ABC brought the discussion to a very concrete level when it announced its desire to be absorbed by International Telephone and Telegraph Company (ITT), one of the nation's largest communications conglomerates, and one with extensive government ties. In its petition to the FCC, the network effusively promised that the proposed merger would be a tremendous benefit to broadcasting. With the new corporate money that would be available, ABC could, for instance, expand its public affairs programming. In addition, the increased stature of the network could only help the still struggling UHF system because ABC had the greatest number of UHF affiliates. Thus, as the fortunes of ABC improved, the status of UHF would have to rise as well. At first, the commission appeared to accept all the grand promises at face value and the merger seemed destined for a quick approval. Then, unexpectedly, serious opposition from within both the FCC and the Department of Justice developed and the matter grew more complicated. Asked by the commission for a legal opinion on the case, the Justice Department pointed out that the merger would quite probably lead to some violations of the anti-trust laws and would also discourage ITT from going ahead with a backburner notion to start a new television network on its own. Within the FCC, newly appointed commissioner Nicholas Johnson put aside the traditional FCC policy of giving big business the benefit of the doubt, cut through the self-serving posturing and vague promises dished out by ABC, and stated quite bluntly that he saw the merger as motivated solely by economic self-interests that had nothing to do with better serving the public. Johnson also raised the disturbing possibility that ITT, with its extensive government war contracts, might attempt to influence the ABC news department. Though ITT pledged a three-year "hands off" policy in changing the ABC executive personnel, there were serious doubts that this would be sufficient restraint. In the course of the public hearings on the case, newspaper reporters testified that ITT had pressured their papers to kill stories considered detrimental to the proposed merger. Critics quickly pointed out that if ITT would attempt to distort the news in outlets over which it had no control, what would it do to a wholly owned subsidiary?

In spite of all the objections, the FCC voted to approve the merger by a 4 to 3 margin, twice (December 1966 and June 1967). Miffed that its warnings had been dismissed so cavalierly, the Department of Justice took the ruling to the U.S. Court of Appeals, further delaying the procedure that by then had dragged through nearly two years of hearings. On January 1, 1968, ITT called off the merger, citing the extensive opposition within the government as the reason for its pullout. Some observers, however, said that the continued mediocre ratings performance by ABC had as much to do with the withdrawal as the expensive, embarrassing legal delays.

As the usual number three network, ABC was constantly searching for gimmicks to attract attention and boost its ratings. Such innovations as the second season premieres of January 1966 usually brought a brief burst of success, but the glow soon faded as people returned to their old favorites. Nonetheless, ABC's gimmicks kept the overall network race tight for a while each year and forced CBS and NBC to seriously consider the latest ABC flash and decide whether or not to adopt it for their own schedules. For the fall of 1966, ABC's strategy hinged on two stunts: First, the network moved up its fall premiere week to begin just after Labor Day, giving the shows a week's head start against the premieres on the other networks. Second, ABC slotted blockbuster films such as "Bridge on the River Kwai" for the first weeks of the new season, thereby "front loading" its new schedule with exceptionally attractive specials. The strategy worked and ABC ran away with the psychologically important first ratings period. "Bridge on the River Kwai" was especially potent and captured an impressive 60% of the audience, making it the most popular film then ever seen on television. Though ABC's ratings once again faded as the 1966–67 season progressed, another weapon had been discovered in the battle for ratings success throughout the season: hit movies.

All three networks had been pursuing a growing love affair with prime time movies since 1961, but "Bridge on the River Kwai" underscored the dramatic ratings boost a box office smash could provide in a week's competition. Even moderate box office hits could be counted on to score rather well against the more limited formats of weekly series because they were, in comparison, high-budget specials. By early 1967, each network had two nights of movies per week, leaving only Monday without a theatrical production. At the same time, the growing popularity of feature films began to alter the face of network programming in more subtle ways. Though the three other celluloid smashes of the 1966–67 season were "The Robe," "Lillies of the Field," and "PT 109," network purchases for future broadcast included such films as "Tom Jones," "Cat on a Hot Tin Roof," and "Never on Sunday." Even edited for television, they formed the vanguard of a movement to present more "mature" themes (usually of a sexual nature) on TV, dealing with them in a manner no regular series then dared to try. In addition, the continuing success of two-hour films offered solid evidence that the home audience would accept longer programs on a regular basis and the networks increased the number of extra-length series, which sometimes ran up to ninety minutes.

There were some drawbacks in the ratings bonanza, though. The spectacular performance by "Bridge on the River Kwai" guaranteed that the price tags on future film purchases would begin to increase substantially, because there were only so many blockbuster movies available. Facing the prospect of filling six movie slots each week, it was only natural for the networks to search for a guaranteed source of future films. Logically, the search led back to Hollywood and this resulted in the long-postponed consummation of the marriage between television and the major film studios, with NBC and Universal leading the way.

Actually, since the fall of 1962, NBC and Universal had been presenting feature length material each week with the epic Western, *The Virginian*. The ninety-minute series used a core of continuing cast members, but the extra length provided the time for both the stories and guest star performers to develop. Consequently, *The Virginian* was much closer in feel to an anthology of Western films rather than a regular Western TV series. Audiences obviously accepted feature length television shows and enjoyed seeing movies on TV. There was not much difference between a ninety-minute Western and a two-hour melodrama, so the next step was practically inevitable. NBC contracted with Universal to begin producing feature length films that were not part of a series but meant to stand on their own in the regular network movie slots, bypassing any traditional theatrical release. The first batch premiered on NBC in the fall of 1964, but failed to generate either viewer or critical enthusiasm. After more than a year, NBC and Universal came back with new films, but this time backed them with higher budgets and more elaborate publicity.

The first of these new made-for-TV movies was "Fame Is the Name of the Game," which aired on NBC's *Saturday Night at the Movies* during the Thanksgiving weekend of 1966. It was not a major motion picture event by any means. Tony Franciosa played a wise-cracking investigative reporter with a soft heart beneath his cool exterior (a role almost identical to his character in the short-lived *Valentine's Day* series) and Susan Saint James played his wise-cracking cynical gal Friday with a soft heart beneath *her* cool exterior. It was very similar to Universal's other TV productions, only with a bigger budget. Though well produced, the film was a typical TV action-adventure story with the same gimmicks, characters, and plot twists found in dozens of television series and grade B pictures. (In fact, the plot displayed a remarkable similarity to the 1949 reporter saga, "Chicago Deadline.") Nonetheless. "Fame Is the Name of the Game" stood out as a special event, a "world premiere" movie, and did very well. Three months later, the second new Universal made-for-TV film, "Doomsday Flight," topped those ratings.

"Doomsday Flight" was a much better film, a TV thriller with a clever premise and effective pacing. Written by Rod Serling, the story focused on the ever-increasing sense of hysteria among the crew members (led by Van Johnson), passengers, and ground personnel of a flight from Los Angeles to New York City upon the discovery that a bomb had been planted aboard the plane. A mad bomber (Edmund O'Brien) had hidden the device before takeoff and perversely armed it with an altitude-sensitive explosive set to detonate whenever the plane dropped below a height of 4,000 feet. Luckily, Denver, the "mile high" city (5,280 feet above sea level) was on their flight path, so … It was not Academy Award material either, but the film was certainly a cut above the average TV adventure stories of the time. The presence of Rod Serling served as an appropriate reminder that made-for-TV movies were really a combination of several familiar TV formats: drama anthology, high-budget special, feature length film, and television melodrama.

Both "Fame Is the Name of the Game" and "Doomsday Flight" turned up among the ten most popular films on TV that season, assuring made-for-TV movies a firm spot in plans for the future by all three networks. NBC was happy with new material from an old friend and Universal, in turn, was pleased to have the jump on its competition in a lucrative new market. Viewers, too, were treated to something special that was, at the same time, very familiar. By

	7:00	7:30	8:00	8:30	9:00	9:30	10:00	10:30	
MON	local	IRON HORSE		THE RAT PATROL	FELONY SQUAD	Peyton Place	The Big Valley		ABC
	local	Gilligan's Island	RUN, BUDDY, RUN	The Lucy Show	Andy Griffith Show	FAMILY AFFAIR	JEAN ARTHUR SHOW	I've Got A Secret	CBS
	local	THE MONKEES	I Dream Of Jeannie	ROGER MILLER SHOW	THE ROAD WEST # Perry Como's Kraft Music Hall		Run For Your Life		NBC
TUE	local	Combat!		THE ROUNDERS	THE PRUITTS OF SOUTHAMPTON	LOVE ON A ROOFTOP	The Fugitive		ABC
	local	Daktari		Red Skelton Hour		Petticoat Junction	CBS News Hour		CBS
	local	THE GIRL FROM U.N.C.L.E.		OCCASIONAL WIFE	NBC Tuesday Night At The Movies				NBC
WED	local	Batman	THE MONROES		THE MAN WHO NEVER WAS	Peyton Place	ABC STAGE '67		ABC
	local	Lost In Space		The Beverly Hillbillies	Green Acres	Gomer Pyle, U.S.M.C.	Danny Kaye Show		CBS
	local	The Virginian			Bob Hope Presents The Chrysler Theater # Bob Hope Show		I Spy		NBC
THR	local	Batman	F Troop	TAMMY GRIMES SHOW	Bewitched	THAT GIRL	HAWK		ABC
	local	JERICHO		My Three Sons	CBS Thursday Night Movies				CBS
	local	Daniel Boone		STAR TREK		THE HERO	Dean Martin Show		NBC
FRI	local	THE GREEN HORNET	THE TIME TUNNEL		MILTON BERLE SHOW		Twelve O'Clock High		ABC
	local	The Wild, Wild West		Hogan's Heroes	CBS FRIDAY NIGHT MOVIES				CBS
	local	TARZAN		The Man From U.N.C.L.E.		T.H.E. CAT	Laredo		NBC
SAT	local	SHANE		Lawrence Welk Show		Hollywood Palace		ABC Scope	ABC
	local	Jackie Gleason Show		PISTOLS 'N' PETTICOATS	MISSION: IMPOSSIBLE		Gunsmoke		CBS
	local	Flipper	Please Don't Eat The Daisies	Get Smart	NBC Saturday Night At The Movies				NBC
SUN	Voyage To The Bottom Of The Sea		The FBI		The ABC Sunday Night Movie				ABC
	Lassie	IT'S ABOUT TIME	Ed Sullivan Show		Garry Moore Show		Candid Camera	What's My Line	CBS
	Bell Telephone Hour NBC News Sp. (fr. 6:30)	Walt Disney's Wonderful World Of Color		HEY LANDLORD	Bonanza		Andy Williams Show		NBC

the end of the decade, with popular TV movies as a base, Universal became one of the most important individual sources of prime time material on television. Its high percentage of programs on the networks marked the ironic triumph of the Hollywood studios over the upstart television and assured viewers a never-ending flow of standard West Coast productions.

While NBC was experimenting with feature length made-for-TV movie specials, ABC launched its own showcase for special programming, *ABC Stage '67*. This series was considerably more ambitious than NBC's movies, embracing the spirit of Pat Weaver's mixed-bag spectaculars of the 1950s. Under producer Hubbell Robinson, *ABC Stage '67* presented a one-hour drama, comedy, variety, or documentary program each week. The opening episode, "The Love Song of Barney Kempinsky," was a comedy with Alan Arkin (fresh from his comic lead in the hit movie "The Russians Are Coming, The Russians Are Coming") as a scheming, amoral New Yorker trying to raise money by any means possible for his vacation. In the field of drama, Truman Capote wrote and narrated a recreation of his youth in Alabama, "A Christmas Memory." Former comedy writer Dick Cavett presided over a variety format, "Where It's At," a schizophrenic mix of songs, standard jokes, dance, and parody. Documentaries stuck to safe topics such as the death of Marilyn Monroe and the wit of John Kennedy.

Nonetheless, ABC's attempt to revive the one-hour anthology structure with *ABC Stage '67* failed. Critics, perhaps secretly hoping for a program totally dedicated to serious drama (Bob Hope's *Chrysler Theater* hardly qualified), were only lukewarm in their support of the unpredictable anthology approach that was as likely to showcase Rick Nelson as William Shakespeare. More important, though, *ABC Stage '67* was crippled at birth by the network affiliates, many of which did not bother to carry the program at all, fearing that it was too "highbrow." It was almost mathematically impossible for a show to become a ratings hit unless at least 90% of the television audience could tune in. With so many local defections, *ABC Stage '67* came in well below the 90% mark and was doomed before its first telecast. Slotted against the very popular *Danny Kaye Show* and *I Spy,* the program was gone within a year. As Pat Weaver had discovered with his spectaculars the decade before, the format demanded patience, fine-tuning, and gradual viewer acceptance, as well as entertaining material. Eventually his spectaculars clicked in such triumphant broadcasts as "Peter Pan." ABC, too, would prosper with the format, but not until the early 1970s when it packaged the eclectic mix in the more accessible made-for-TV movie setting.

Pat Weaver himself was back in network television on CBS (following an aborted pay television venture in California and an ill-conceived attempt at a fourth network) as executive producer for the revived Garry Moore show. Moore, returning to TV after a two-year absence, was set in a format identical to his successful, long-running variety show of the early 1960s: music, sketches,

Durward Kirby, and a fresh family of supporting players including Jackie Vernon, John Byner, Chuck McCann, Lily Tomlin, and Ron Carey. The program was fairly good, but it failed to make a dent in the ratings of its competition, the number one show on television, *Bonanza*. CBS brass, eager for instant success, refused to give the show time to build a following and instead, in November, they fired the supporting players and replaced Weaver. A new format, in which Moore presented tired retreads of old Broadway musical comedies such as "High Button Shoes," was an even bigger flop and the program was axed in January.

To replace the veteran Moore, CBS brought in a pair of young comics who had failed in a situation comedy the previous season, the Smothers Brothers. Tom and Dick Smothers were successful nightclub performers and recording artists who had been given a dumb permutation of *My Favorite Martian* to work with in their 1965–66 sitcom. Tom played Dick's dead brother (lost at sea) who returned to Earth as an inept apprentice angel assigned to aid people in trouble. Even before the show's premiere, CBS wanted to scrap the silly sitcom and use the pair to host a half-hour youth-oriented comedy-variety program instead, but the sponsor owned the program and refused to change formats. *The Smothers Brothers Show* opened to strong ratings, then collapsed. To CBS, this was proof that viewers liked the Smothers Brothers but could not stand the nonsense premise. The network canceled their sitcom but planned to use them in the variety format as soon as possible. The rapid demise of Garry Moore provided the opportune, though unenviable, slot: against number one *Bonanza*.

The Smothers Brothers Comedy Hour began as a very traditional comedy-variety show that just happened to be geared to younger viewers. The team's laid-back style was first described as similar to Dean Martin's: casual to the point of apparent sloppiness, but masking a very deliberate, controlled approach to comedy. They were the fresh new kids of television, bringing along youth-oriented acts such as Harry Nilsson, The Doors, The Who, Mason Williams, and John Hartford, and it was expected that they would slowly build a strong young audience as a base while continuing the variety show traditions of such veterans as Danny Kaye, Red Skelton, and even the recently departed Garry Moore. The unassuming Smothers surprised everyone. Within a few weeks of their February premiere they had drawn away enough viewers to knock *Bonanza* out of the number one slot. A large number of youthful viewers who normally stayed away from variety shows tuned in to catch the Smothers Brothers. Almost immediately the Smothers demanded, and received, more latitude in the show and began to adopt a decidedly controversial, anti-establishment, politically topical tone that was appropriate to the new audience but quite different from anything else on television. It turned into the closest thing to satire on American TV since *That Was The Week That Was* but, unlike *TW3*, *The Smothers Brothers Comedy Hour* was a ratings smash.

Tom and Dick had built their routines on their never-ending sibling rivalry and personal caricatures: Tom was the "dumb" one and Dick was his level-headed, understanding brother. Their monologues had always consisted of Dick trying to straighten out one of Tom's misconceptions, but the source of Tom's confusion now began to shift from family frustrations ("Mom always liked you best!") to the government's war policies. Though Dick would eventually "set the record straight," it was clear that Tom's foolish misunderstandings were considered closer to the truth. Supporting cast members Bob Einstein and Pat Paulsen provided additional digs at authority figures through their own deadpan exaggerations. Einstein played a narrow-minded, atonal Los Angeles policeman, Officer Judy, who sauntered on stage whenever the barbs against

lawful authority went too far, and callously warned the Smothers that they were under suspicion, arrest, or both for violating some rule of society, usually "abusing" the privilege of free speech. Paulsen mocked much of the foolishness that passed for public debate by solemnly backing absurd notions and supporting familiar issues with ridiculous arguments, usually in the form of program "editorials." He assumed everyone, including himself, was a deliberate liar and not to be trusted; he often paused momentarily and gave a sly smile over particularly blatant distortions in his speeches.

CBS did not quietly accept everything the Smothers wished to present, hit show or not. The network allowed the rarely seen Pete Seeger to appear on the program, but cut out the performance of his new song, "Waist Deep in Big Muddy," a thinly veiled criticism of President Johnson and his Vietnam War policy. Though the Smothers were very angry, they could not do anything about this particular decision. Nevertheless, they continued to stretch the limits of their expression at every opportunity and slowly developed a strong adversary relationship with CBS. The Smothers were not certain how far they could push their own network, but it seemed that as long as they continued to be funny and successful, they were safe.

In contrast to the new ground being broken by the Smothers Brothers in comedy-variety, the new situation comedies had slipped back into the same well-worn plots, gags, and themes of the early 1960s. More than a dozen new sitcoms premiered in the fall of 1966 and many, such as *Pistols 'n' Petticoats, It's About Time,* and *The Tammy Grimes Show,* were still in the grip of the mindless escapist philosophy of humor. They were worlds apart from the Smothers Brothers and even the clever sitcom parodies of the previous season.

The most popular new sitcom was CBS's *Family Affair,* which featured the tried-and-true formula of a bachelor father adopting and raising orphaned children. Brian Keith played the father figure (he was their uncle, actually) and Sebastian Cabot was his manservant, French. In a very predictable format, the two portrayed refreshingly believable level-headed adults. Keith, as a construction company executive, enjoyed a life apart from his new-found family, and Cabot, despite proper huffing and puffing, grew to love his new charges. The two men were not endowed with a magic instinct for raising children perfectly but, rather, made mistakes, yelled, and were sometimes baffled by the process. Unfortunately, the children, Buffy, Jody, and Cissy, were as mechanical and cardboard as the adults were real. They were children that fulfilled an adult's view of the perfect child: sweet, heartwarming, and innocently profound. No self-respecting kid would ever identify with them. Yet in the same way that *Leave It To Beaver*'s realistic children saved the program from its cardboard adults, *Family Affair*'s adults rescued it from the children. Though occasionally overloaded with saccharine plot twists, the series had its heart in the right place. CBS seemed to acknowledge that the show was geared to adult fantasy rather than children's by slotting it rather late in the evening (9:30 P.M.).

Family Affair was the latest example of CBS's continued reliance on traditionalist sitcoms that had kept the network number one, in spite of momentary spurts by the competition, for more than a decade. In the 1966–67 season, CBS had fifteen thirty-minute situation comedies on its schedule and, though many of the shows were beginning to age, the network saw no reason to abandon an approach that still worked well. Even if most of the new comedies did not catch on, the veterans would stay on top until the right successors could be found.

ABC and NBC were also top-heavy in sitcoms, launching ten

September 17, 1966

Mission: Impossible. (CBS). Producer Bruce Geller turns out an action-packed formula espionage show. Each week, an "impossible missions" force (led by Steven Hill as Daniel Briggs the first season and thereafter by Peter Graves as Jim Phelps) tackles a covert operation too sensitive for even the CIA.

September 17, 1966

Jackie Gleason revives the Honeymooners skit in his variety show, bringing back partner Art Carney as Norton and casting Sheila MacRae in the role of Alice Kramden.

October 17, 1966

The Hollywood Squares. (NBC). Peter Marshall hosts a daytime game show that places nine celebrities in a three-level tic-tac-toe seating formation.

January 9, 1967

ABC at last extends its nightly news to thirty minutes and begins televising the show in color.

January 9, 1967

Mr. Terrific. (CBS). and *Captain Nice.* (NBC). Two virtually identical *Superman* takeoffs appear on the same night, one after the other. Both feature mild mannered heroes played strictly for laughs, but neither catches on.

January 15, 1967

"Super Bowl I." (CBS & NBC). The titans of television and professional football clash, with the CBS-NFL combination easily beating the NBC-AFL challenge. The Green Bay Packers outscore the Kansas City Chiefs 35 to 10, and CBS tops NBC in the Nielsen ratings, 24.6 to 17.4. Beginning with the second Super Bowl, the two networks will take turns each season carrying the game.

new comedies of their own that season. A small number of these broke away from the focus of most situation comedies of the past: middle age, middle class families, with preteen or just-teen children. Instead, they attempted to portray an age group usually left out of the equation completely: young adults, some without any children at all!

NBC's most obvious attempt to reach the youth market came in the form of a comedy about a group of struggling rock musicians, *The Monkees.* Michael Nesmith, Micky Dolenz, Davy Jones, and Peter Tork were cast as surrogate Beatles to act and sing amid the thinnest of plots. Most stories were simple, exaggerated melodramas usually carried by a handful of mildly clever camera tricks and special effects. Director Jim Frawley won an Emmy for his work in the show, often borrowing techniques used in the obvious models for the series, the Beatles' own films "A Hard Day's Night" (1964) and "Help!" (1965). While particular segments in the program were quite funny, the most talked about aspect of the series was its effectiveness as a promotional tool for rock music. Each episode was, in effect, a half-hour plug for the Monkees' latest disc and their TV image as rock stars became self-fulfilling. Throughout the two-year prime time run of the series, they produced an unbroken string of top ten singles and albums, outselling even the Beatles. When the series ended in 1968, though, their fortunes took an immediate nosedive and the group soon split up. The brief, but intense, success of *The Monkees* was still a minor breakthrough for youth-oriented sitcoms. Even though it was mass consumption TV at its most blatant and commercial, *The Monkees*

was the first youth sitcom to directly tap the ever-growing rock'n'roll generation. The comedy was often just traditional slapstick, but the very premise and tempo of the show were a dramatic contrast to the sub-juvenile plodding of such programs as the prehistoric time travel setting of *It's About Time* and the much-visited but still uncharted desert island of *Gilligan's Island.*

ABC presented the best of the emerging new style of young adult sitcoms with *Love on a Rooftop,* which depicted the first year struggles of young marrieds Julie and Dave Willis. The program featured an excellent mix of personalities with a fine sense of comedy: Judy Carne, as Julie, played her character as a 1960s variation of Lucy, slightly wacky but also intelligent and level-headed. Julie was the daughter of a wealthy car salesman but she gave up her life of luxury to marry Dave (Peter Duel), a young apprentice architect. Duel portrayed the husband as a likable average guy (real world average, not TV average) who was good looking (but not handsome) and funny (without resorting to cheap slapstick). He just wished that Julie's rich dad (Herbert Voland) would believe that the couple could be happy with his minuscule salary and their tiny rooftop apartment, because they were in love. Rich Little, as their downstairs neighbor, offered his personal support that alternately helped and further complicated the couple's lives. *Love on a Rooftop* stood apart from the childish humor of rural escapist fare and the exaggerated farce of larger-than-life spoofs. It delivered very human, very funny characters in mildly realistic situations that many young adults could identify with. In doing so, the program was years ahead of its time. The series was also totally eclipsed in the ratings by the more familiar competition of NBC's movies and CBS's *Petticoat Junction.* ABC brought the series back five years later for a brief summer rerun and it weathered the test of time well.

Love on a Rooftop might have been the best of the young adult comedies, but *That Girl* was the most successful. Marlo Thomas (Danny's daughter), who had played a stage struck young girl in *The Joey Bishop Show* five years before, played Ann Marie, a stage struck young woman determined to break into showbiz and become an actress. In order to support her single life in New York City, she assumed different odd jobs while searching for that lucky break. A young single working woman trying to fulfill a personal dream offered marvelous possibilities though there were rarely adequately exploited in this series.

Several elements in the stories undercut the premise. For easy laughs, the writers frequently included slapstick scenes that not only shattered the mood and motivation, but also did not work because Thomas was no Lucille Ball and broad physical humor was not her strength. Ted Bessell played her boyfriend, Don Hollinger, as the epitome of the sexless, dumb males that had populated sitcoms in the 1950s and his character further tarnished Ann Marie's credibility. Worst of all, the series paid only lip service to the premise of an intelligent working woman. Ann Marie was too much the TV textbook daffy woman who succeeded in spite of herself. If Ann was a sharp, sensitive woman who relied on her wits and self-motivation to survive, the scripts hid those qualities very well. Instead, *That Girl* relied on Thomas to carry the show as a safe heart-tug comedy set in the comfortable myths of idealized television romance, with an all-American sweetheart at the center. In this guise, it lasted five seasons. Even though *That Girl* compromised an innovative premise, its success and its touted image demonstrated that a different type of sitcom *could* work. ABC, NBC, and even CBS soon began tinkering with a slant toward young adults and more realistic settings, but it would not take hold until early in the next decade.

Another concept that would not reach mass acceptance until the

1970s was the peculiar science fiction brainchild of producer Gene Roddenberry, *Star Trek*. Roddenberry had worked on undistinguished series since the mid-1950s, including an obscure Western in 1960, *Wrangler* (as a writer), and a competent military career drama in 1963, *The Lieutenant* (as its producer). In 1964 he turned his attention from the trials and tribulations of young Marines to a more imaginative project he had been toying with for years, a science fiction show. Science fiction had never been handled very well by television, which treated it either as strictly kid stuff such as *Captain Video, Tom Corbett, Space Cadet,* and *Rod Brown of the Rocket Rangers* or in pedantic anthologies such as *Science Fiction Theater, Men into Space,* and *Tales of Tomorrow*. Classier anthologies such as *The Twilight Zone* captured the audience's fancy for a while but suffered from a lack of identifiable continuing characters. In 1963, while Roddenberry was still busy with *The Lieutenant,* ABC launched *The Outer Limits,* a series with substantially better writing than most previous science fiction programs, but it was still mired in the anthology format and it placed too strong an emphasis on frightening, unearthly creatures (bug-eyed monsters). Roddenberry envisioned his project as something different; he called it a "*Wagon Train* to the stars." A small central cast, always on the move, would encounter people with problems (the weekly guest stars) and attempt to resolve them. This was a simple format that had worked well in series such as *Wagon Train, Route 66, The Virginian,* and *The Fugitive*. The only difference was that *Star Trek* would take place in outer space.

By presenting his proposed science fiction show as a saleable adventure series with continuing characters and a slightly different, but exciting, locale, Roddenberry made it easier for the networks to overcome their preconceived notions of science fiction formats as kid stuff and consider the series on its own merits. In April 1964, the Desilu studios agreed to work on the project and CBS began making favorable noises. The network, though, instead decided to stay with science fiction as children's fare and took on Irwin Allen's *Lost in Space* (an average American suburban family of the future launched into the cosmos, but hopelessly lost soon after take-off). Undaunted, Roddenberry continued work on his program and in December 1964 a one-hour *Star Trek* pilot episode ("The Cage") was completed. It featured Jeffrey Hunter as Christopher Pike, captain of the starship *Enterprise,* and Leonard Nimoy as his chief assistant, Spock, an alien from the planet Vulcan with dark raised eyebrows and pointed ears. They encountered an alien race, humanoid in appearance, with the ability to project illusions so strong that they seemed real. Pike discovered how to sort the truth from illusion, learned the aliens' master plan, and escaped from their planet. NBC expressed interest in the concept, looked at and liked the pilot, but still had some reservations about the series, specifically the cerebral subject matter and the casting. The network was especially bothered by the presentation of the captain's chief assistant as a pointy-eared alien. NBC was sufficiently intrigued with the premise, however, to ask for another pilot, a second shot few producers ever received. Roddenberry took no chances with the new pilot, making the conflicts more obvious and using an almost entirely new cast. William Shatner (who had been playing in the unsuccessful CBS lawyer series *For the People* when the first pilot had been filmed) was recruited as the new captain of the *Enterprise,* James T. Kirk. Leonard Nimoy was kept on as Spock, with his ears intact but the eyebrows softened. Roddenberry finished his revised pilot episode ("Where No Man Has Gone Before") in November 1965 and presented it to NBC. This time, the network gave him the go-ahead to begin production, setting the series premiere for the fall of 1966.

Actually, Roddenberry had veered somewhat from his promised

"*Wagon Train* of the stars" in "The Cage." The story *had* been a bit "too cerebral," especially for a pilot. With the series in production, though, he set out to prove that science fiction could be accessible, entertaining, and a limitless source of continuing adventures. He imposed strict standards on himself and his production crew, determined to avoid the pitfalls of past TV science fiction ventures by presenting a well thought out, orderly universe for his characters. He had made a very good start in the pilot episodes by eliminating the usual space adventure hardware: space suits, landing craft, and launching pads.

The *Enterprise* had been assembled in space and was not designed to ever land on any planet (gravity and heat friction would have destroyed it), so the ship merely locked into orbit each week around some new planet. This replaced boring and repetitious lift-off sequences with brief, attractive shots of the ship circling a colorful new world. Kirk and his crew were also assigned to visit only class "M" type planets, those with an atmosphere and inhabitants not very different from Earth. This eliminated bulky space suits and also kept the number of weirdly shaped aliens to a minimum. To transport members of the crew from the spaceship to the planet's surface, some mumbo jumbo about instantaneous matter transfer was devised and an ingenious special effect was used to avoid cumbersome landing vehicles. A landing party would simply stand in the "transporter" device and, within a matter of seconds, their atoms would be broken down, sent to the planet's surface via radio waves, and reassembled with no ill effect. Besides breaking

---

April 17, 1967
The Joey Bishop Show. (ABC). Making a return to late night television, ABC teams *Tonight*'s regular substitute host, Joey Bishop, and former California talk show host Regis Philbin for a familiar Monday through Friday desk-and-sofa show. Bishop's first words, after the applause dies down: "Are the ratings out yet?"

May 1, 1967
The Las Vegas Show. (United Network). The one-and-only offering in an unsuccessful attempt to launch a fourth commercial network. Bill Dana hosts a late night celebrity talk show that, like the proto-network, lasts only one month.

June 25, 1967
"Our World." (NET). The first truly world-wide television show, consisting of live broadcasts from twenty-six countries on five continents, including a Beatles recording session in London for "All You Need Is Love."

August 27, 1967
After six years as a first run prime time series, two years as a rerun in prime time, three summers as a warm weather prime time fill-in, eight years as a Monday through Friday daytime rerun, two years as a weekend afternoon rerun, and one year as a Saturday morning rerun, *I Love Lucy* is taken off CBS and put into local syndication where it begins rerunning all over again.

August 29, 1967
The Fugitive. (ABC). The day the running stops.

September 3, 1967
What's My Line? ends 17½ years on CBS. The final "mystery guest" is the show's moderator, John Charles Daly.

away from the traditional approach to interplanetary exploration, there was a very practical reason for these innovations: money. Weird aliens, space suits, landing gear, and associated hardware involved steep costs in makeup, design, and construction. The technical process used in the transporter sequences was the most expensive continuing device, but it was a bargain compared to the alternative costs. Roddenberry realized that viewers would not be tuning in for a guide to twenty-third-century hardware, so he did not spend much time explaining them in any great detail. Warp drive engines were just like steam engines; overworked they would overheat and explode. Machines were machines, circuits were circuits, weapons were weapons. They broke down, overloaded, and misfired. The technical details did not matter. Roddenberry focused his energies instead on telling the story.

He quite firmly dismissed a frequent trash can device of hack science fiction: the unexplained mystery of the future. All too often such stories presented the universe of the future as filled with temperamental villains, heroes who could single-handedly overcome astounding odds, and technical innovations that violated all laws of twentieth-century mechanics. To Roddenberry, it did not matter that the show took place several hundred years in the future; the audience existed in the present, so everything that happened in *Star Trek* took place for a reason. Aliens required a reason to attack the *Enterprise*. Planets were saved or destroyed for a reason. If the captain and crew embarked on a particular mission, there had to be a reason. The lack of distracting technical gear and jargon, as well as the strict adherence to understandable motivation for each conflict and action, gave the writers and performers the comfortable setting necessary for a solid, dramatic story.

Star Trek operated under the premise that, in the twenty-third century, human nature remained unchanged, even though technological breakthroughs of astounding scope had taken place. Consequently, the outer galaxy appeared no more foreign than a World War II battalion headquarters or a frontier outpost in the American West of the 1880s. In this tradition, Kirk's immediate supporting crew was a perfect blend of racial and ethnic personalities: a young and impetuous Russian navigator, Ensign Pavel Chekov (Walter Koenig); a two-fisted drinker from the Highlands, Lieutenant Commander Montgomery "Scotty" Scott (James Doohan); a beautiful Nubian communications officer, Lieutenant Uhura (Nichelle Nichols); and the efficient, soft-spoken Asian navigator, Sulu (George Takei).

Kirk stood at the helm, a handsome American man of action, respected by his enemies and loved from afar by women throughout the galaxy. His first love, of course, was the *Enterprise*. Shatner brought just enough lightness and humor to his portrayal of the strong commanding officer to save himself from the horrid clichés inherent in the role. As captain, he constantly faced decisions that required a choice between humanism and official procedure and his two top aides, science officer Spock (Nimoy) and chief medical officer Doctor Leonard "Bones" McCoy (De Forest Kelley) personified his inner struggle. Spock was half Earthling and half Vulcan (an alien race motivated totally by logic), and he calmly analyzed situations based on facts and precedent. He wasn't a cold computer (his human side certainly prevented that), but he would not allow normal human emotions to determine his decisions. On the other hand, McCoy was a country boy from Georgia who put his faith in intuition and man's fallible but essentially generous nature above all rules, logic, and analysis. People came first. Spock and McCoy were constantly at odds with each other, but together they formed a perfect advisor to Kirk as he dealt with each new situation by weighing the two usually conflicting points of view.

By stripping away the peripheral traits of science fiction that other TV presentations had concentrated on, Roddenberry opened up *Star Trek* to the best strain of the sci-fi genre: speculative, symbolic stories. In the guise of an alien setting, *Star Trek* could deal with real twentieth-century Earth problems such as racial antagonism, uncontrolled war, systematic cultural domination, and individual freedom, while not appearing heavy-handed, obvious, or dated. Problems facing humanoid creatures in the far flung future and on distant planets were not as threatening or offensive to people as the same stories in a contemporary setting. The stories became timeless studies of human struggles, often based on familiar folk tales, Biblical stories, and even classical literature. For instance, one of the continuing themes that ran through many *Star Trek* plots was the necessity of a free will and the dangerous illusion of paradise. Though Kirk and his crew usually accepted the fact that each civilization had its own unique style, they were profoundly suspicious of so-called "Garden of Eden" planets and deeply disturbed by any force (man or machine, oppressive or benign) that systematically denied its people the right to exercise their free will. Systems that combined paradise with the removal of all complications and conflict were presented as the most tyrannical of all. Freedom without hard choices and responsibility turned a blissful paradise into a very pretty prison. No matter what the theme, however, the scripts were superbly executed. The energy of the cast usually managed to overcome occasional rough spots in the dialogue and plots, and *Star Trek* attained the high standards Roddenberry had set for it.

Unfortunately, the program's ratings never matched this level of artistic success. They were adequate, but never outstanding. NBC tried to cancel the program after the second season, but an outpouring of viewer support won the series a third go-round. This turned out to be merely a brief reprieve and, following the third season, *Star Trek* was canceled, after airing seventy-nine episodes.

Like many other network series, *Star Trek* was put into syndication soon after its axing. Unlike nearly every other syndicated series, *Star Trek* became more popular in off network repeats than in its network run. Most series actually needed a good syndication stint to turn a profit (the network run usually only paid for initial production costs), but *Star Trek* went beyond this. Its popularity steadily increased throughout the 1970s and by 1979, ten years after its cancellation, the continued public interest in the program moved Paramount studios to reassemble the entire cast for the first of a series of feature-length theatrical films. Not since *The Honeymooners* had any series achieved such success so long after it had been dismissed by the networks as past its peak. The themes, production, and characters remained popular long after the "five year mission" of the *Enterprise* had run out.

With *Star Trek, ABC Stage '67, Love on a Rooftop,* and the Smothers Brothers, the 1966–67 season was filled with new shows that were slightly ahead of their time. Appropriately, one of the season's dramatic highlights was the conclusion of a four-year-old series that had once been ahead of *its* time, Quinn Martin's *The Fugitive*. It was an amicable cancellation as Martin, ABC, and David Janssen agreed that, while a fifth season might still be profitable, it was time to move on, but not without resolving the conflicts and questions viewers had been following for over three years. Throughout early 1967, a well-coordinated publicity drive built up suspense over the closed filming sessions for the program's finale. The two-part episode ("The Judgment") was held in secrecy until August, after the full cycle of summer reruns had played. No details were given out prior to air time. No reviewers were allowed to prescreen the show. The final episode was shown the same day throughout the world wherever *The Fugitive* was broadcast.

Part one provided the setup. Police in Los Angeles captured the one-armed man and Lieutenant Gerard knew the publicity would draw Kimble to the area, so he set a trap. Throughout the episode, spurious clues suggested that perhaps the one-armed man was really innocent and that someone else had committed the murder. Perhaps a neighbor, perhaps Gerard, or perhaps even Kimble himself. For seven days the world waited. On August 29, the final episode aired, capturing over 70% of the American viewing audience (making it the most-watched program of the decade). Baseball games were delayed. Bars stopped business for one hour. In New Zealand, the International Rugby championship game was delayed as television shared with the world the story of one desperate man in his bid for freedom.

In the final episode, the one-armed man managed to escape police custody, only to be pursued by Kimble and Gerard. At the conclusion of a dramatic chase through a closed amusement park, Kimble and the one-armed man both climbed a high tower where the two stood face-to-face, alone. With nowhere else for either man to run, the one-armed man confessed his guilt, but then lunged, determined to kill Kimble. Back on the ground, Gerard, armed with a high-powered rifle, looked up and faced an agonizing choice. He then shot the one-armed man, saving Kimble's life. Only this apparently left Kimble in worse shape than before. No one else had heard the confession, the killer was dead, and Dr. Kimble was now back in the hands of the law, a doomed man. Then, shamefully, a chicken-hearted neighbor who had seen the murder take place stepped forward. He had fearfully kept silent for deeply personal reasons over the years, even as he watched Richard Kimble receive a death sentence. Now, given a second chance, he offered to do the right thing and testify.

Kimble was exonerated. The final scene showed a triumphant Dr. Kimble leaving the courthouse a free man, accompanied by a good-looking new girlfriend. Narrator William Conrad religiously intoned, "Tuesday, August 29, 1967. The day the running stopped." Real police departments broadcast orders to end the search for both Kimble and the one-armed man. For both men, the running was over. Richard Kimble had found peace at last. Justice and freedom had finally triumphed, at least on television.

There was, however, a postscript. Later that night, on ABC's late night talk show hosted by Joey Bishop, there was a live interview with David Janssen, who was working in Georgia on a new movie. Bishop asked Janssen whether he had anything to say now that he was a free man and beyond the reach of the law. "Yes," Janssen said. "I killed her, Joey. She talked too much."

27. The Whole World Is Watching

IN THE FALL OF 1967, TV'S TOP TEN LIST included such venerables as Red Skelton, Ed Sullivan, Jackie Gleason, Lucille Ball, Andy Griffith, *Bonanza, Gunsmoke,* and *The Beverly Hillbillies.* Most had been around for over a decade, some nearly twenty years. Though still popular, they could not last forever. Yet programmers were having trouble coming up with a formula to produce durable new replacements and the only bona-fide hits that had emerged from the previous season's new shows were the very traditional *Family Affair,* a revival of *Dragnet,* and the youth-oriented *Smothers Brothers Comedy Hour.* For the 1967–68 season premieres, the networks included a nod to the young adult audience, but for the most part continued to emphasize familiar TV veterans in new but very safe and predictable variety, sitcom, crime, and Western vehicles. Viewers were generally unexcited by it all and, after the flurry of fall premieres passed, they turned back to their old favorites. Though a number of the new shows eventually caught on, none of them became an instant smash. By Christmas, the bucolic saga of *Gentle Ben* (a lovable bear in a Florida game preserve) was the only new program in the top twenty.

As part of the second season revamping in January, another new variety show appeared, hosted by a pair of very familiar showbiz veterans, Dan Rowan and Dick Martin. For years, the two had brought their straightforward routines to numerous traditional comedy-variety shows and, in the summer of 1966, had served as competent hosts to one of Dean Martin's summer replacement series. They were unlikely candidates to be pioneers in a new wave of television comedy, yet their new show was truly different. Within four months, *Rowan and Martin's Laugh-In* exploded into a national hit, bringing to mass popularity the innovative television comedy techniques developed years before by Ernie Kovacs.

In the early 1960s, Kovacs had put together a monthly comedy program for ABC in which he replaced the traditional comedy-variety structure with bizarre visuals, off-the-wall sketches, and short unconnected bits (blackouts). The program had fallen short of its innovative premise, though, because Kovacs had been severely limited by a minuscule budget. In 1967, producer George Schlatter, armed with much more money and the latest TV technology, produced a pilot for NBC called "Laugh-In," which aired on September 9, 1967. The show reworked and updated the Kovacs approach to humor, incorporating new video tape tricks and techniques, expanding the crew of writers and performers, and providing

viewers with familiar characters to guide them through the maze of images. Blackout bits in the special were edited into a frenzied, machine-gun pace. A gaggle of talented but generally unknown comedians including Ruth Buzzi, Henry Gibson, Arte Johnson, Jo Anne Worley, and Judy Carne delivered the punch lines, catch phrases, puns, and clunkers. The material went by so fast that if there were three good jokes in ten, the laughter from these blotted out the memory of the seven flops. If none of them clicked, there would soon be more flashing by anyway. All the electronic madness was held together by Rowan and Martin, who served as the essentially "square" hosts of the "Laugh-In" special. They had the very important role of anchoring the flights of fancy with their familiar presence and humor. Confounded by everything else, viewers could turn to them for reassurance.

"Laugh-In" was colorful, innovative, and far more exciting than any of the new fall shows premiering that month. When the CBS heavyweights of *Gunsmoke* and *Lucy* swamped the languishing *Man From U.N.C.L.E.* on Monday nights, NBC quickly slotted *Laugh-In* as a mid-season replacement series, though the network feared that the program's unique style might hurt acceptance. Instead, it helped. *Laugh-In*'s frantic structure, slightly risqué jokes, and many running gags set the show apart from everything else on television, injecting life into an ossified format that too often settled into the same dull routine. Viewers grew to enjoy the unexpected twists, surprise guest shots, and fresh new characters of *Laugh-In.*

On the first episode in January, Rowan and Martin introduced viewers to the unlikely figure of Tiny Tim, a singer who looked like a cross between a Bowery bum and Tinker Bell. He had a large hook nose, a death-white complexion, and an Arthur Godfrey-type ukulele that he used to accompany his high, lilting falsetto on such traditional ballads as "Tip Toe through the Tulips." Such a bizarre guest was clear evidence that *Laugh-In* was willing to break from the staid and safe traditions of TV variety shows, though even Rowan and Martin acknowledged his extreme peculiarity and turned his presence, actual or threatened, into a running gag ("You're not going to bring back Tiny Tim, are you?").

Other, more traditional, celebrities also appeared on the show, usually delivering quick one-liners in brief cameo shots. Viewers had to be alert to catch such guests as Bob Hope, Sonny Tufts, John Wayne, Zsa Zsa Gabor, and then presidential candidate Richard Nixon, who publicly pondered, "Sock it to *me*?" (the show's main punch line). Frequent guests Sammy Davis, Jr. and Flip Wilson revived the old Pigmeat Markham routine that used the hook line: "Here come de' judge."

Though the guests kept viewers on their toes, the regular cast developed the program's popular continuing bits. A weekly "cocktail party" and the many-shuttered "joke wall" served as the launching pads for timely one-liners by the entire crew, who soon became familiar figures with well-known characterizations. Arte Johnson was a dirty old man repeatedly pestering a spinsterish Ruth Buzzi; Judy Carne was a bikinied go-go dancer with pithy sayings painted on her body; Goldie Hawn was the similarly adorned dumb blonde incarnate; Henry Gibson was a poetry-spouting "flower person"; and announcer Gary Owens was an ear-cupping caricature of radio's deep-voiced announcers of the 1930s. These characters popularized a lexicon of punch lines that soon wound their way into the national language. From Johnson, who also played an unreconstructed Nazi soldier, came the intonation at the end of each show, "Verry interesting." Whenever Carne was tricked into saying "Sock it to me" she found herself hit by pies, drenched in water, or falling through a trap door. Rowan and Martin themselves added such phrases as "You bet your bippy,"

"the fickle finger of fate," and "beautiful downtown Burbank." After the show had been a solid hit for more than a year, some cast members moved on and a second generation of *Laugh-In* supporting players arrived including the hippy-dippy Alan Sues; the very English Richard Dawson (moonlighting from *Hogan's Heroes*); and Lily Tomlin, as the caustic, chest-scratching telephone operator, Ernestine.

Like any truly different TV show, *Laugh-In* had to overcome initial uncertainty among viewers, but once they became familiar with the program's style, they found it easy and fun to follow. In one hour, *Laugh-In* squeezed together slapstick, vaudeville, satire, clever visuals, an air of current hipness, and even a few normal guests. The program had everything the other comedy-variety shows had-just more of it, presented with fresh faces and sophisticated technical discipline. By May, *Laugh-In* was a solid top ten hit and frequently ended up the number one program on television. Its enormous popularity, along with that of *The Smothers Brothers Comedy Hour*, was tangible evidence that the American TV audience seemed ready for more experimental, sophisticated, and even controversial fare than had been available week in and week out over the previous decade. For still further proof, there was the continuing success of prime time movies.

Number 6 (Patrick McGoohan) makes a speech to the residents of the Village as part of his campaign for the post of Number 2 in *The Prisoner*. (© *ITC Entertainment, Inc.*)

Day		7:00	7:30	8:00	8:30	9:00	9:30	10:00	10:30	Net
M	local	COWBOY IN AFRICA		The Rat Patrol	Felony Squad	Peyton Place	The Big Valley			ABC
O	local	Gunsmoke		The Lucy Show	Andy Griffith Show	Family Affair	CAROL BURNETT SHOW			CBS
N	local	The Monkees	The Man From U.N.C.L.E.		DANNY THOMAS HOUR		I Spy			NBC
T	local	GARRISON'S GORILLAS		The Invaders		N.Y.P.D.	Hollywood Palace			ABC
U	local	Daktari		Red Skelton Hour		GOOD MORNING WORLD	CBS News Hour			CBS
E	local	I Dream Of Jeannie	JERRY LEWIS SHOW		NBC Tuesday Night At The Movies					NBC
W	local	THE LEGEND OF CUSTER		THE SECOND HUNDRED YEARS	The ABC Wednesday Night Movie					ABC
E	local	Lost In Space		The Beverly Hillbillies	Green Acres	HE AND SHE	DUNDEE AND THE CULHANE			CBS
D	local	The Virginian			KRAFT MUSIC HALL # Bob Hope Show		Run For Your Life			NBC
T	local	Batman	THE FLYING NUN	Bewitched	That Girl	Peyton Place	GOOD COMPANY	local		ABC
H	local	CIMARRON STRIP			CBS Thursday Night Movies					CBS
R	local	Daniel Boone		IRONSIDE		Dragnet 1968	Dean Martin Show			NBC
F	local	OFF TO SEE THE WIZARD		HONDO		THE GUNS OF WILL SONNETT	JUDD, FOR THE DEFENSE			ABC
R	local	The Wild, Wild West		Gomer Pyle, U.S.M.C.	CBS Friday Night Movies					CBS
I	local	Tarzan		Star Trek		ACCIDENTAL FAMILY	Bell Telephone Hour / NBC News Specials			NBC
S	local	The Dating Game	The Newlywed Game	Lawrence Welk Show		Iron Horse		ABC Scope		ABC
A	local	Jackie Gleason Show		My Three Sons	Hogan's Heroes	Petticoat Junction	MANNIX			CBS
T	local	MAYA		Get Smart	NBC Saturday Night At The Movies					NBC
S	Voyage To The Bottom Of The Sea		The FBI		The ABC Sunday Night Movie					ABC
U	Lassie	GENTLE BEN	Ed Sullivan Show		Smothers Brothers Comedy Hour		Mission: Impossible			CBS
N	local	Walt Disney's Wonderful World Of Color		THE MOTHERS-IN-LAW	Bonanza		THE HIGH CHAPARRAL			NBC

While most of the new network series struggled near the bottom of the ratings charts, all four movie nights on CBS and NBC rested safely in the top forty. Viewers accepted and supported the more realistic, adult themes in such features as "Never on Sunday," "Tom Jones," "Splendor in the Grass," "Dr. Strangelove," and "King Rat," with such films as "The Birds," "Cat on a Hot Tin Roof," "The Great Escape," and "North by Northwest" racking up extremely high ratings. At mid-season, NBC decided to add a third night of movies in the fall of 1968 so that, for the first time ever, there would be a network movie every night of the week.

Yet over the entire television schedule such changes were taking place slowly, with both viewers and the networks generally moving with caution in shaking up different formats. CBS made a few moves to modernize both its image and schedule for the 1967–68 season, but met solid viewer resistance or indifference in the process. The network had attempted to cancel the oldest oater of them all, *Gunsmoke,* at the end of the 1966–67 season, but an outpouring of public support (and the direct intervention of CBS's William Paley) saved the show, though it was moved to a new early time slot (Monday at 7:30 P.M.), assumed to be an impossible position for an adult Western. Fooling everybody, *Gunsmoke* bounced back into the top ten with even higher ratings than before. However, this did not signal a revival of interest in the overall Western format and new shows such as *Custer* and *Dundee and the Culhane* quickly faded from view. At the same time, CBS hesi-

tantly experimented in the field of situation comedy with a moderately realistic young adult show, *He and She,* but it met the same fate as ABC's *Love on a Rooftop* from the previous season. *He and She* starred the real life husband and wife team of Richard Benjamin and Paula Prentiss, who filled admirably the roles of slightly befuddled, misunderstood husband and slightly wacky, often incomprehensible wife. Paula Prentiss's character (like Judy Carne's in *Love on a Rooftop*) was a genuine step forward in the presentation of women in sitcoms. Though slightly daffy, Paula clearly had a head on her shoulders and was not totally dependent on her husband. They had no children so she was free to pursue her own interests while he worked at his realistic, though certainly uncommon, job as a cartoonist. The two displayed a deep and genuine affection for each other so that even the usual sitcom schemes and complications seemed a reasonable part of being in love.

Besides the strong leads, *He and She* was blessed by a fantastic group of supporting players who should have made the program a smash hit on their talent alone. Former folk singer Hamilton Camp portrayed a gnomish, klutzy apartment superintendent; the venerable Harold Gould was Dick's boss; and Kenneth Mars was a thickheaded but friendly neighborhood fireman who often entered the firehouse by climbing through Dick and Paula's kitchen window. Best of the best, Jack Cassidy was Oscar North, a TV star who played Jetman, the lead character in a television series adaptation of one of Dick's cartoon heroes. Cassidy looked as if he had stepped directly from the comic page and his narcissistic, self-centered manner demonstrated that he truly believed he was a superhero. Creator and character frequently faced off, with Dick's dry drollery serving as the perfect antidote to North's insatiable appetite for self-aggrandizement. Nothing could ultimately shake the star, though, and he thrived on compliments. He instantly responded to one adoring fan's delight at meeting him with the heartfelt observation, "It was worth waiting for, wasn't it?"

He and She was given the advantageous Wednesday night slot that *Gomer Pyle* had recently held (following *The Beverly Hillbillies* and *Green Acres*), but the new sitcom bombed out in the ratings and was canceled after its first season. While very similar programs such as *The Mary Tyler Moore Show* would catch on in another four years, *He and She,* like *Love on a Rooftop,* was guilty of being ahead of its time with a mix of realistic and satirical characters. The most successful new sitcom of the 1967–68 season featured the childish adventures of *The Flying Nun.*

With the failure of *He and She,* and the implied failure of sophisticated sitcoms in general, CBS canceled plans to develop (with American filmmakers Norman Lear and Bud Yorkin as producers) a Stateside version of the relatively daring BBC working class sitcom, *Till Death Us Do Part.* For two years that program had been both shocking and delighting the British audience as the openly bigoted Alf Garnett (Warren Mitchell) violated all known rules of TV decorum. He hurtled epithets at his wife and son-in-law, constantly dropped racial slurs, and called well-known political figures names such as "grammar school twit." Though Britons accepted this behavior in a situation comedy, CBS saw it as obviously too strong for American consumption.

One format that managed a mix of traditional characters and settings with more contemporary concerns was the cop show. With real urban crime on the public's mind and on the nightly news shows, it was often a very short step to the world of fictional police work. The TV crime revival had begun in the 1966–67 season with the return to television of the old *Dragnet* duo of Jack Webb and Ben Alexander, though they appeared in two different programs. Alexander arrived first, in the fall of 1966, with *Felony Squad* for ABC. The program was a very routine crime exercise set in Los Angeles, and its proclivity for scenes of spurting blood ("going heavy on the ketchup") was its only distinguishing feature. Jack Webb, though, made a very conscious effort to appear topical in his revival of *Dragnet* for NBC.

As producer-writer-narrator-star, Webb brought his tight-lipped "just the facts, ma'am" style of drama to a new decade, first in a successful made-for-TV movie, then as a mid-season replacement series, *Dragnet '67* (the year was added to make certain the audience knew this was no rerun). Following its spine-chilling theme song, *Dragnet* had always assured viewers that the story to follow was true and that only the names had been changed to protect the innocent, so the format was the perfect front for stories that could be consciously topical. In the first episode, Webb (as Joe Friday) and his new sidekick, Harry Morgan (as Bill Gannon), relentlessly pursued a crazed LSD pusher who died dramatically of an overdose at the end of the show. Despite the topical trappings, though, *Dragnet*'s chief strengths continued to be its painstaking methodical style and dedicated support for the average cop on the beat. Yet by focusing on crazed peaceniks and deranged dope fiends, *Dragnet* and other crime shows such as *The FBI* could pass off standard cop show material as hip, modern drama.

The mid-season success of *Dragnet* brought several new crime shows to the 1967–68 line-up. Though they reflected touches of TV topicality, the programs generally presented well produced, high quality stories and conflicts. *N.Y.P.D.* (produced by David Susskind's Talent Associates) was filmed on location in New York City and featured a black and white police duo (played by Robert Hooks and Frank Converse), but the series managed to resist any heavy-handed sociology. *Mannix* (created by Richard Levinson and William Link) cast Mike Connors in the role of the old faithful private eye. At first, the plots in the series centered on the conflict between the lone investigator and the increasingly mechanized job of crime detection. By its second season, though, *Mannix* dropped

Though *Laugh-In* and the Smothers Brothers were ushering in a new generation of comedy-variety, veterans Ed Sullivan *(center)* and Bob Hope *(right)* still remained two of television's top draws. Both received Peabody Awards in 1967, presented by Dean John E. Drewry *(left)* to honor, respectively, twenty and thirty years of broadcast success. (*Courtesy Peabody Awards Collection*)

September 14, 1967

Ironside. (NBC). One year after the end of *Perry Mason*, Raymond Burr switches sides and resumes the fight against crime in California—this time as a determined police detective. Though paralyzed from the waist down (by a would-be assassin) and confined to a wheelchair, chief Robert Ironside is always at the scene of the crime, aided by a special support team that does his legwork.

November 6, 1967

The Phil Donahue Show. Donahue, a radio newsman in Dayton, Ohio, begins an hour-long weekday television interview and call-in show there on the Avco Corporation's WLWD. In June, 1969, the program goes into national syndication.

January 1, 1968

Bob Young replaces Peter Jennings as ABC's nightly news anchor.

January 9, 1968

It Takes a Thief. (ABC). Robert Wagner stars as Alexander Mundy, an unreformed cat burglar released from prison to work for the U.S. government as an undercover agent-thief. The adventures are played tongue-in-cheek, combining the charming sophistication of the short-lived *Rogues* series with the spy shenanigans of *The Man from U.N.C.L.E.* Fred Astaire adds a further touch of class in the program's third season by assuming the recurring role of Alister Mundy, father of Alex and a master thief in his own right.

the computer-and-society angle and slipped into the more familiar rock'em sock'em two-fisted detective mold popular since the days of Mickey Spillane. Raymond Burr settled for a less violent gimmick premise and portrayed a disabled San Francisco police chief in the slickly produced *Ironside.* Though confined to a wheelchair by a sniper's bullet, Robert Ironside could still track down criminals and often used his dominant, snarling personality to intimidate them into surrendering.

As the urban action police shows returned in strength to television, the more fantasy-oriented world of the spies was fading. Over just a few years, the form had been hopelessly diluted in every medium: film, print, and television. For the most part, gimmicks and humor had completely supplanted the stories, character development, and dramatic confrontations. Even the granddaddy of them all, James Bond, fell victim to gimmick overkill, prompting Sean Connery's departure from the theatrical Bond role after the well-panned "You Only Live Twice." The weekly TV spy series were especially vulnerable to the constant overexposure and had practically become parodies of themselves with conflicts that could no longer be taken seriously. In Britain, where the spy craze had begun, Diana Rigg (the delectable Mrs. Peel) left TV's best spy series, *The Avengers,* and her replacement, Linda Thorson (as Tara King), adopted a more helpless demeanor that robbed the show of its dramatic tension and unique point of view. Even worse, the series was revamped so that both John Steed and Tara King lost their free-wheeling independence and were forced to report directly to Mother (Patrick Newell), an oddball superior in a wheelchair. Yet as super-sleuth TV was in its death rattle, Britain came up with one final spy masterpiece that successfully combined numerous strains of entertainment into one of the best television programs ever devised, *The Prisoner.*

Since 1960, Patrick McGoohan had been portraying secret agent John Drake (a.k.a. Danger Man) and, after seven years, Drake had been involved in almost every possible spy plot. McGoohan felt it was time to take the spy motif one step further and present some concepts that were often lurking just under the surface in the *Danger Man/Secret Agent* series. Working under heavy security wraps and backed by Sir Lew Grade's British television network conglomerate, McGoohan, acting as executive producer and star, turned out the seventeen-episode *Prisoner* series. It was the most dazzlingly produced program then on British television and also one of the most expensive, running $168,000 per episode. Such high costs for individual episodes would have been impossible to bear in the open-ended world of American television. There, producers developed ideas into series they hoped would run for years, yet faced the very real possibility of being canceled within weeks. Most British series were designed to end after a set number of weeks anyway, so the total cost of a program was much easier to project. The limited run also allowed more time to concentrate on pacing both in particular episodes and in the entire series. McGoohan constructed each segment of *The Prisoner* with the same care and complexity usually reserved for one-shot feature films and live theatrical productions. As a result, the series achieved a level of artistic success on a par with high quality literature, films, and theater.

The Prisoner took the audience from the supposedly real world of John Drake, the spy, into the symbolic world of The Village, a very pretty prison-resort in which everyone was known only by a number. McGoohan, once again portraying a government agent (similar to Drake), found himself in The Village following his abrupt resignation from the British spy service. He had planned to leave Britain (with a good deal of sensitive security information in his head) and take a soul-searching vacation, but was rendered unconscious and spirited away to the mysterious seaside village before he could finish packing. Once there, he was placed in an apartment and given his own number, Six. Number Six faced constant scrutiny and interrogation by Number Two, in charge of the day-to-day operations and security. The contest was simple: In each episode Number Two tried to discover the reason for Number Six's resignation while Number Six tried to thwart him and escape.

This was merely the setup, the logical explanation for the conflict in each episode. The real focus of the series was the concept of independence and free will forever battling authority and submission. Most of the private eyes, spies, and cops presented over the years had been waging the same battle as Number Six, but it had never been so vividly expressed. Philip Marlowe, Sam Spade, Boston Blackie, Martin Kane, Peter Gunn, James Bond, John Drake, and Richard Kimble (on the other side of the law) had been inside-outsiders trying to cope with the encroachments of an increasingly impersonal world. Their unending struggle, though, had always been presented within the convenient and easily identifiable framework of crime and justice. In such a setting, the loner-hero might be insubordinate and a rebel but, in the long run, he still worked for the "legitimate" authority. In reality, the inside-outsider often had more in common with those he pursued than with his superiors. It was just a matter of which side of the fine line of the law one happened to fall on. Ultimately, the most important battle these heroes ever waged was the fight to keep their independent, idiosyncratic ways and not be forced to become average citizens.

In *The Prisoner,* this conflict was laid bare and the dichotomy revealed. Number Six had spent his adult life tracking down and capturing agents just like him. In The Village he had to face the consequences of his actions and experience first hand the effects of the system he had been working for. The possibility of freedom and escape was constantly dangled as an inducement for him to reveal his real reasons for resigning, but this was an illusion. His personal identity had always come from his own skill and instincts and if he ever dropped his guard, gave in, and accepted such an offer, he would be a beaten man, totally indistinguishable from the faceless, nameless populace at large.

It was never made clear who ran The Village. At various points in the series Soviet, British, and even joint control was suggested. Easily definable good guys and bad guys were thereby eliminated and it was possible that the good guys (the British) were not so good after all. There might not be any difference between them and the supposed bad guys (the Russians). Perhaps both, as important world powers, were inherently bad. Capitalism and Communism lost all meaning and the real, underlying division became clear in *The Prisoner:* control from above or personal free will.

Throughout the fall of 1967 in Britain (and the summer of 1968 in the United States, when CBS presented the series), a surprisingly large number of viewers kept tuning in to observe both McGoohan's splendid performance as a frustrated, but intelligent, caged rat, and the complex plots and elaborate sets that gave the show a level of sophistication far above normal TV fare. The beauty of *The Prisoner,* though, was its simultaneous success on many levels. While a rich, deep program that delved into complex psychological questions, it never ignored the basic rules of good action-adventure television. There was a standard fist fight in almost every episode and, if nothing else, *The Prisoner* could be viewed as an exciting escape story with elaborate gadgets and interesting characters to tickle the imagination. In fact, one episode effectively presented the entire philosophy of the program in the more familiar form of a Western. McGoohan portrayed Number Six as a loner-gunfighter former lawman who refused to become the flunky sheriff in a small town under the thumb of an all-powerful, corrupt judge. In this guise, Number Six seemed almost the same as Matt Dillon and Paladin, and the inside-outsider theme of *The Prisoner* was revealed as a universal one which had already been used by that most basic and durable American morality play, the Western.

The series ended in a tour de force, two-episode finale that revealed still another level of meaning. At the dramatic climax, Number Six discovered that Number One (the boss of all bosses), for whom he had been searching from the beginning, was none other than himself. He was both jailer and prisoner. Hunter and hunted. Persecutor and persecuted. As the characters in the comic strip "Pogo" once explained, "We have met the enemy and he is us."

For a show so different, *The Prisoner* did remarkably well. It became a minor mania in Britain and registered a more than respectable 34% share of the audience in America. The program also received enough critical acclaim to be rerun by CBS the following summer and it later turned up in syndicated reruns (sans commercials) on public television.

With the appearance of *The Prisoner,* many American TV observers at last admitted that Britain was outshining America in quality television production on several levels: sitcoms (*Steptoe and Son* and *Till Death Us Do Part*), adventure (*The Prisoner* and *The Avengers*), soap opera (the ever-present *Coronation Street*), and high-class soaps, called historical dramas (such as *The Forsyte Saga,* which was a hit in its first BBC airing during the 1966–67 season). America had few equivalents. For all their good points, programs such as *Ironside* and *Mannix* were not seen as profound expressions of television art. One reason for Britain's superior product was that British television was guided by a looser set of rules which allowed characters and plots to maintain a more

realistic and earthy nature. Another very important reason was the existence of the government-funded, noncommercial BBC that could afford to experiment with forms considered too volatile for commercial broadcasters.

America had nothing to compare with the BBC. For more than ten years, NET had served as a quasi-network for more than one hundred educational stations in the United States, but it operated under a severely limited budget and was usually forced to send its programs through the mail. Instructional shows such as *The French Chef,* children's shows such as *Mr. Rogers' Neighborhood,* and "talking head" public affairs shows such as *Washington Week in Review,* while excellent programs, all reflected very frugal production techniques that pointed up the lack of available funds. The programs looked low budget and could never seriously compete with commercial fare for viewer support.

In early 1967, a commission funded by the Carnegie Corporation issued a report suggesting a radical rethinking of the basics behind educational television. It offered a blueprint for a new concept, public television, that would emphasize entertainment and information, not merely instruction. Congress would provide the major funding for public television, but an independent corporation would be established to dispense the money to the local stations in the NET network and act as a buffer between them and Congress. This would allow governmental support but, hopefully, preclude governmental control. President Johnson's strong support of the Carnegie commission's proposals helped push a bill through Congress that made most of the recommendations law. In November

---

March 4, 1968
The Dick Cavett Show. (ABC). Former gag writer Dick Cavett conducts a ninety-minute talk show on weekday mornings, with a twist: Not only does he include "serious" non-showbiz guests such as Buckminster Fuller, he brings them out first!

May 21, 1968
"Hunger in America." (CBS). Producer Martin Carr turns out an old-fashioned hard-hitting CBS documentary for *CBS Reports.* Carr focuses on malnutrition among Indians in the Southwest and tenant farmers in Virginia, in the style of Ed Murrow's 1960 "Harvest of Shame." The agriculture industry is quick to criticize the report and even the Secretary of Agriculture, Orville Freeman, finds it necessary to defend the department's hunger policy from the embarrassing footage.

May 27, 1968
After only five months as anchor for *The ABC Evening News,* Bob Young is replaced by Frank Reynolds.

August 5, 1968
The Republican National Convention opens in Miami Beach. ABC opts for "selected coverage" and sticks with regular entertainment fare for the first ninety minutes of prime time.

September 6, 1968
The era of fifteen-minute soap operas, once a staple of daytime radio and television, comes to an end with the final quarter-hour broadcasts of CBS's *Search for Tomorrow* and *The Guiding Light.* Three days later, the two shows return in expanded thirty-minute formats.

1967 Johnson signed the Public Broadcasting Act of 1967, which set up the fifteen-member buffer organization called the Corporation for Public Broadcasting (CPB). Immediately, CPB ran into the first of many governmental road blocks. Congress was to grant $9 million for CPB's first year of operation but, in early 1968, both the White House and Congress delayed the actual transfer of funds, stalling governmental support for the new system. Instead, as in the past, the largess of many private organizations kept public television afloat until a lower compromise figure could be agreed to by the government. Such haggling over congressional money became a yearly ritual that repeatedly left the CPB on unsure footing. Even with all its complications, though, the institution of government funding was an important step for the future of public television.

The first program to incorporate the concept of public television was *PBL* (the *Public Broadcast Laboratory*), a weekly, two and one-half hour live news magazine program. The Ford Foundation, which had been channeling money to educational television since NET's inception in 1952, donated $10 million in 1967 for the creation of the program at the urging of former CBS News president, Fred Friendly, who had become the foundation's advisor on television. With the exception of the *CBS News Hour,* the networks had largely given up weekly, hard-hitting news shows, preferring instead safe specials such as "Discover America with Jose Jimenez." *PBL* promised to be unlike anything else then available on television and certainly unlike anything ever seen on NET. It would be live, in color, and use some well-known, highly professional talent drawn from commercial television itself. Edward P. Morgan was granted a two-year leave of absence from ABC to act as *PBL*'s anchorman. Tom Pettit of NBC became head of one of the regional bureaus that produced pieces for the program. CBS News veteran Av Westin was named executive producer. Advance publicity touted the show as a "revolution in broadcasting" and Westin explained the need for it, declaring, "The time has come to put an end to what I call 'music up and under documentaries' in which, as we head into the final commercial, we are reminded that there is a problem and certainly something ought to be done about it—but, please don't ask what."

The premiere of *PBL* in November 1967 was not quite a revolution, but it was an important landmark in American TV. The first program was a cross between *See It Now* and *Omnibus,* using a mixture of documentary and drama segments all devoted to an overall theme, race relations. The documentary reports examined the Cleveland and Boston mayoral contests, which centered on race; a traditional panel discussion presented appropriately antagonistic extremists (from Chicago); and a dramatic production, "A Day of Absence," showed a fantasy world in which all the blacks in America decided to leave, and white society found itself unable to cope with their absence. *PBL* also incorporated sixty-second spots (dubbed "anti-commercials"), placing them at points in the show where their counterparts on a regular commercial program would normally appear. The messages revealed that all the competing brands of aspirin *were* alike, and that the long-longer-longest fad among cigarette manufacturers only resulted in more-most-mostest tar for the suffering consumer.

The most important aspect of *PBL* was that it successfully adopted the methods and formats used by the commercial networks, signaling a sharp break from the pure educational slant of NET's past. In place of the many drab and deadly boring pseudo-lectures, *PBL* brought in well-known commentators, slick production, and elaborate graphics and sets. It showed that American television could have it both ways, offering programs that were informative and classy as well as entertaining and appealing.

Unfortunately, *PBL* lasted only two seasons and never became a hit on its own.

PBL was debilitated from its inception by a series of internecine battles as people at both the Ford Foundation and NET tried to mold the program to fit their own expectations. The thinly veiled anti-white viewpoint of the nearly all black theatrical troupe in the premiere episode rankled a few corporate nerves, so "A Day of Absence" was the only important drama presentation *PBL* ever offered. The anti-commercials were also judged too controversial and dropped after a few weeks, as the program settled into a more traditional documentary format. Even in this approach there was continued disagreement among the *PBL* overseers throughout its first season as the traditional educational faction (led by the dean of the Columbia school of journalism) fought the progressive public wing (headed by Av Westin) for total control of the program. After a showdown in June 1968, Westin's side retained control, but bitter feelings remained. Money shortages during the second season forced a drastic cutback of in-house production and, after a gallant but losing struggle, *PBL* died on May 18, 1969. Most of its top staff members moved to ABC's news department.

In spite of its troubled history, *PBL* served as an important force in broadcasting. While the commercial networks remained mum, *PBL* examined such issues as a proposed anti-ballistic missile system (ABM), community antenna television (CATV), health care, and the possibility of a second Northeast blackout. It offered independent documentary producers such as Frederick Wiseman invaluable exposure, airing individualistic views of Vietnam, Martin Luther King, Jr., cancer, law and order, and country music. The very existence of *PBL* spurred NBC and CBS to increase their own output of real news documentaries, and the program served as the direct model for NBC's *First Tuesday* and CBS's *60 Minutes,* two newsmagazine shows which premiered in the 1968–69 season.

Despite the prodding from public television in 1967, the commercial networks were still caught in the cautious doldrums of "no guts journalism," especially in their reports on the Vietnam War. Even as American troop strength neared one-half million, network coverage of the war continued practically unchanged, reaching a symbolic low point from late 1967 through January 1968. Largely due to lobbying by CBS, all three networks tacitly agreed to devote very little attention to the October peace march on Washington by thousands of war protesters, which ended in hundreds of arrests when the group stormed the Pentagon. In January, ABC, accepting the inevitable, canceled its excellently produced, objectively balanced, but rarely seen weekly Vietnam show, *ABC Scope.* In contrast that same month, public television displayed its guts and aired a frankly pro-Viet Cong documentary by Felix Greene, "Inside North Vietnam." Actually, CBS had originally paid for the film but, upon seeing the footage, decided to use only brief excerpts on the nightly news. *NET Journal,* however, presented more than half of the ninety-minute documentary which, though biased, provided a rare look at the North Vietnamese in their homeland.

The film was followed by a one-hour hawk and dove debate but, even so, NET received a great deal of flak for airing the material at all. In April, however, CBS sent its own Charles Collingwood directly to Hanoi for a series of filmed reports. In just a few months, the commercial networks had drastically altered their coverage of the war. The Tet offensive in early February provided the dramatic rallying point for the change and the end of the era of "no guts journalism."

For years, network correspondents had been generally accepting the official government line that the United States was, in fact, winning the war and that the Viet Cong were growing weaker and weaker. Suddenly, this supposedly weakened enemy found the strength to launch a major, well-coordinated offensive throughout South Vietnam. After innumerable evenings of generally pointless jungle combat scenes, Tet gave the networks exciting, street-by-street fighting footage that dramatized the war as never before. The Viet Cong occupied a number of provincial capitals for a few days and the American embassy in Saigon itself for a few hours. Eventually, the U.S. pushed the Viet Cong back while inflicting heavy casualties, but an important image had been shattered. It was clear that the American government was either ignorant of the Viet Cong's real strength or lying to the American public. For the first time in years, network reporters aggressively and openly questioned the government's position.

The Tet offensive also provided one powerful photographic moment that would come to symbolize the Vietnam War itself. During the height of the offensive, while NBC cameras rolled, the Saigon chief of police calmly raised a small revolver to the temple of a Viet Cong prisoner and pulled the trigger. The prisoner dropped to the ground and blood spurted from his head. It was a quick, passionless act without any great emotions or dramatic words. None were necessary. Though the prisoner was no doubt guilty of something, the real-life execution, taking place without even the niceties of a legal conviction, seemed the final outrage to many Americans. Following the Tet offensive, more and more people joined the reawakened press in publicly questioning the credibility of the government's war policy and the promise of eventual victory.

Network news attention quickly shifted back to the domestic front, as the growing skepticism on the war turned the campaign for the Democratic presidential nomination into a race in which the incumbent president might actually lose. On March 31, in a special television speech, President Johnson announced a reduction in the American bombing of Vietnam, then dramatically withdrew himself from the campaign. Robert Kennedy, Eugene McCarthy, and Vice President Hubert Humphrey were left to vie for the nomination. Among the Republicans, Richard Nixon was well on his way to completing a long personal comeback struggle.

Both parties staged their nominating conventions in August. For the first time, ABC decided to depart from traditional gavel-to-gavel television coverage of the event and opted for ninety-minute "selected coverage" (9:30–11:00 P.M.). This allowed the network to air some of its regular entertainment programs while NBC and CBS vied for the attention of those wrapped up in the convention's developments. The Republican convention in Miami in early August (where Nixon received his party's nomination) turned out to be a tedious affair with very few interesting moments anyway. The Democratic convention in Chicago in late August, however, proved an entirely different matter.

A strong feeling of enmity between the press and politicians developed in Chicago even before the convention opened. There was exceptionally tight security due, in part, to the genuine fear which developed after the assassination of Robert Kennedy in June. Beyond that, however, Chicago Mayor Richard J. Daley seemed determined to prevent anything or anyone, especially the press, from spoiling the traditional convention euphoria. A protracted union dispute (which many network executives felt Daley could have settled if he had really wanted to) wreaked havoc on the networks' plans for live coverage of events throughout the city. Daley and the Democrats also tried to impose strict reductions on the number of press people allowed on the convention floor. What's more, there was obvious tension between pro-administration and antiwar factions, both in the convention hall and gathered on the streets outside. When the convention itself began, the barely contained antagonism broke out into the open.

The press openly referred to Chicago as an armed camp, even a police state, evoking memories of the Soviet invasion of Czechoslovakia only days before. Despite the security (or because of it), violence broke out both outside and inside, with parts of the convention floor sometimes resembling a wrestling ring as frustrated anti-war Democrats (while numerous) were out-voted at every turn. (Vice President Humphrey wound up as the Democratic nominee.) At the height of the melee inside the convention hall, CBS's Dan Rather was shown being punched and dragged from the floor by security forces, prompting Walter Cronkite to proclaim, "I think we've got a bunch of thugs here, Dan." Outside, an eruption of violence between demonstrators and police resulted in vivid and graphic TV footage of pitched battles, flying objects, and brutal beatings. Ironically, the limited technical connections for live coverage throughout the city delayed delivery of some of these images just enough so that when they hit the air, they were in direct competition with the main portion of the convention session. The result was an eerie counterpoint of outside riot footage juxtaposed against convention hall platitudes, touching a sensitive nerve in those watching at home.

In the many post-convention inquiries by the FCC and independent organizations, the networks were acquitted of taking a biased point of view in covering the Democratic convention. Nevertheless, television was once again cast in the role of the messenger with the bad news, punished for telling what it knew. The whole world might have been watching, as the street protesters chanted, but the whole world was not getting the same message. People of every point of view were infuriated by what they saw at the Chicago convention, but they adjusted the television images to fit their own preconceived beliefs. Anti-war forces called the outside confrontations a police riot, driven by instances of deliberate police brutality. They angrily viewed the mayor of Chicago as responsible for their treatment, considering him a heavy-handed despot who directed the convention from his delegate seat, heckling speakers like a common street hood. Many others, viewing the same scenes, saw a gang of unruly riotous protestors who taunted and attacked police, provoking officials into reacting. Yet, they still received free publicity, even open support, from the news media.

No matter how the Chicago convention was seen, however, television was accused of a much worse sin: forcing millions of Americans to witness the outrageous events and choose sides.

28. The One Punch Season

THE CHICAGO CONVENTION SOURED Americans not only toward television news but also toward the Democratic Party. As a result, Democratic nominee Hubert Humphrey began his campaign in September far behind Richard Nixon, the Republican candidate. Unlike the 1964 presidential campaign, the 1968 race never appeared openly vicious and cutthroat. Nonetheless, behind the scenes there was a great deal of intense activity to foster positive, effective images, especially through television.

Remembering his experience against John Kennedy in 1960, Nixon turned down Humphrey's incessant requests for a series of televised debates. Nixon's strategy hinged instead on maintaining complete control over his television environment with the help of a TV-savvy team (including twenty-eight-year-old talk show producer Roger Ailes). As depicted by Joe McGinnis in his book *The Selling of the President, 1968*, their strategy successfully bypassed Nixon's traditional foes, the working press. When Nixon arrived in a town, he would take part in a staged press conference-discussion program with a supposedly typical cross section of local citizens. Participants in these carefully arranged and highly formatted discussions were gathered in each city by the Nixon advance team as part of its preparation for the candidate's appearance there. Former college football coach Bud Wilkinson traveled along and hosted the local broadcasts. In settings reminiscent of real press conferences, the selected citizens would lob softball questions at Nixon who sharply handled each one, resulting in the appearance of frank and open debate without any of the risks.

Humphrey slowly began fighting his way back, gathering sympathy from home viewers who saw the vice president shouted down by anti-war protesters at rally after rally. In an effective Salt Lake City speech broadcast nationwide on September 30, Humphrey broke, ever so slightly, from President Johnson's Vietnam policies, giving him his long-sought image of independence.

Throughout October the gap between the two candidates narrowed and, by November 1, it was a dead heat. On election eve, Monday, November 4, both candidates held separate two-hour national call-in programs on which average citizens phoned in questions to either Nixon (on NBC) or Humphrey (on ABC). Humphrey, ever anxious to debate, had aides monitoring the Nixon broadcast and often took time to respond to charges his opponent had made moments earlier.

Election night itself proved to be a marathon, the longest election coverage in TV history at that time. Near noon of the following day, Nixon was declared the winner, just barely edging out Humphrey in the popular vote. Six years after his supposed "last press conference," Nixon had completed a remarkable political comeback. Hoping to start fresh, both the President-elect and the press agreed to an initial "hands off" phase, but many doubted the honeymoon would last very long.

With public interest in news events at an election year high, in September CBS launched *60 Minutes*, its version of *PBL*. The new show, which alternated with the *CBS News Hour* on Tuesday nights, used the "magazine for television" design quite effectively, even down to the graphics and set. The program was broken into several distinct segments that mixed both hard news and soft feature stories, with veterans Harry Reasoner and Mike Wallace serving as hosts and *See It Now* veteran Don Hewitt as executive producer. On the first show of the series, they presented the views of Italian, German, and British journalists on the American presidential campaign along with an interview with Attorney General Ramsay Clark on American police as the hard news items. These were balanced with warm, homey film essays showing Nixon and Humphrey on the nights they were nominated, and an animated short, "Why Man Creates."

NBC retaliated in January with a similar show, hosted by Sander Vanocur, the two-hour *First Tuesday*, which ran once a month on Tuesday nights. It had a generally softer tone than *60 Minutes*, offering such features as a report on Philip Blaiberg, one of the first successful heart transplant patients; a portrait of Rita Hayworth at fifty, and an in-depth look at the baton industry. It was *First Tuesday*, however, that came up with the TV news scoop of the year on its second program (February 4, 1969). In a story on the American military's use of chemical warfare, Vanocur reported that in March 1968 there had been an accident in Dugway, Utah, which resulted in the death of a large number of sheep. *60 Minutes* had done a two-part story on chemical warfare four months earlier, but had allowed the government to review the final product before airing, and its story produced no such revelations. When the Defense Department offered to help NBC (with the stipulation that it would be able to review the final product), the network turned down the agency and pursued the story on its own. New York Congressman Richard McCarthy saw the February 4 piece and, wondering why he had never heard of the sheep incident, launched an investigation. Because of the television report and the subsequent congressional action, the Department of Defense not only admitted that it had caused the death of the sheep, but also ended all in-air tests of chemicals and gasses for biological warfare.

Congress and television were interacting in a very different way in the upper body as Senator John Pastore of Rhode Island again began beating the TV violence drum. The upsurge in crime shows in the previous two years had once again raised the issue of excessive TV violence and fostered another inconclusive round of debate on its possibly harmful effects upon children. The networks feared that in the atmosphere of public outrage following the assassinations of Martin Luther King, Jr. and Robert Kennedy (in April and June of 1968), Senator Pastore might suggest some form of special federal regulation if they did nothing about television violence themselves. Therefore, the networks sent out the word in the middle of 1968 to tone down the level of violence in productions planned for the fall.

Assuming this to be just another passing furor, some producers tried to keep their cop and Western formats essentially intact by merely limiting the length and severity of the gun play and fist fights until the congressional heat passed. A star in a new Western series complained that, under the new rules, after an Indian was shot and fell one hundred feet from a cliff, clutching his chest, a follow-up scene had to be added with the gunman leaning over the cliff saying, "He'll live." Even the veterans had to adapt, and the season premiere of *Felony Squad* contained exactly one punch. What's more, there was only one instance of police gunfire and, following that, detective Sam Stone (Howard Duff) leaned over the victim and said, "He's still alive." These strange new rules and illogical twists for action stories gave the 1968–69 season the derogatory nickname of the "one punch season."

With violence out, at least for a while, cop shows had to scrounge for a different type of distinctive hook. *Hawaii Five-O* opted for beautiful travelogue-like scenery, much like *Hawaiian Eye* and *Adventures in Paradise* in the early 1960s. There, lantern-jawed Steve McGarrett (Jack Lord) headed a team of plainclothes detectives who used all the legal and extra-legal measures necessary to foil any criminal schemes that threatened to disturb the tranquility of their island paradise. Jack Webb, whose police shows had always deemphasized violence, capitalized on the swing away from action and turned out the first in a series of *Dragnet* clones, *Adam-12*. The new program featured a pair of tight-lipped young policemen (played by Martin Milner and Kent McCord) who became involved in three or four unrelated and not very violent crimes each week while on patrol in Los Angeles.

NBC's *Name of the Game* brought the flippant hero back to the forefront in the old but reliable premise of journalist-as-cop. The ninety-minute weekly series, based on the made-for-TV movie "Fame Is the Name of the Game," presented the story of Howard Publications and the exploits of its publisher and reporters who all worked tirelessly to expose the fetid world of organized crime in such magazines as *Crime*. The show sometimes borrowed the ploy used by *Dragnet* and *The FBI,* grafting a few topical characters onto a well-worn crime story, but the glib-talking performers were the chief draw of the series. Gene Barry, Tony Franciosa, and Robert Stack rotated in the starring role each week, with all three receiving assistance from the company's girl Friday, played by Susan Saint James. In spite of occasional plots based on contemporary issues, at heart *Name of the Game* was pure pulp fiction, with just a few surface trappings of reality. Early in one episode, for instance, Tony Franciosa received a bruise in a fist fight and—violating television's unwritten rule of instantaneous regeneration—he kept that bruise through the rest of the episode.

The prime exponent of 1968 television reality, however, was ABC's *Mod Squad* (produced by Aaron Spelling). The series marked the first full-fledged attempt by a network to absorb the look and lingo of the self-proclaimed counterculture and turn them into a standard TV action show. In the face of the deemphasis on violence, ABC wanted a gimmick to keep the action-adventure type format functioning almost undisturbed. With an eye on attracting the younger audience that was boosting the ratings of the youth-flavored comedy-variety shows, the network hoped to create a new sort of TV hero in *Mod Squad.* The three main stars in this cop show were not only young, they were young outcasts. Pre-season ads identified the mod squad as: "One black, one white, and one blonde." Pete Cochran (Michael Cole) was a troubled reject from a wealthy Beverly Hills family, driven to committing petty crimes while racked by the existential angst then so fashionable. Underneath his denim garb, though, lurked the soul of a three-piece suit. Julie Barnes (Peggy Lipton) was a poor white girl who had run away from her prostitute mother. Reflecting the changing times in the world of television, she was a very pretty young woman, but no dummy. Linc Hayes (Clarence Williams III) was an intensely brooding, beautiful black rebel, a veteran of Watts who perpetually wore dark sunglasses. With black consciousness then undergoing a revolution in America, television was beginning a 180-degree turn in its portrayal of blacks. They were no longer bumbling, easy-going po' folk like Beulah, but rather articulate neo-philosophers just descended from Olympus, though still spouting streetwise jargon.

September 16, 1968
Richard Nixon says "Sock it to *me?*" on *Laugh-In.*

September 17, 1968
The Doris Day Show. (CBS). The singer-actress begins a hectic five years adapting to a changing television world. In the first season, Day's Doris Martin character is a city widow who moves to the country with her two children. She begins commuting to a job in the city (as a working mother) during the show's second season, moving back to town with her clan in the third. Finally, in the fall of 1971, the family disappears and she becomes a swinging single woman working for a powerful news magazine in San Francisco.

September 23, 1968
Here's Lucy. (CBS). Lucille Ball again uses her durable formula of wacky redhead against the world. Gale Gordon continues as her blustery boss, but, in a special addition to the cast, Lucy's real-life children, Lucie Arnaz and Desi Arnaz, Jr., play her fictional children, Kim and Craig.

November 17, 1968
The Heidi Incident. To begin on time a heavily promoted new made-for-TV version of "Heidi," NBC opts to cut from a Sunday afternoon football game in progress (with the New York Jets holding a comfortable lead over the Oakland Raiders, and only one minute left to play). Though the children's special airs intact, East Coast viewers miss a stunning football comeback as Oakland scores twice to win.

December 3, 1968
"Singer Presents Elvis." (NBC). The king of rock'n'roll makes his first television appearance in eight years, headlining a one-hour special that is a ratings smash, with both the TV soundtrack album and a single from the show ("If I Can Dream") becoming big hits. Quickly dubbed "The Comback Special," the program's musical show stopper is an intimate in-the-round performance with Presley at center stage, recapturing his 1950s rocking swagger.

	7:00	7:30	8:00	8:30	9:00	9:30	10:00	10:30	
M	local	The Avengers		Peyton Place	THE OUTCASTS		The Big Valley		**ABC**
O	local	Gunsmoke		HERE'S LUCY	Mayberry R.F.D.	Family Affair	Carol Burnett Show		**CBS**
N	local	I Dream Of Jeannie	Rowan And Martin's Laugh-In		NBC MONDAY NIGHT AT THE MOVIES				**NBC**
T	local	THE MOD SQUAD		It Takes A Thief	N.Y.P.D.		THAT'S LIFE		**ABC**
U	local	LANCER		Red Skelton Hour	DORIS DAY SHOW		CBS News Hour / 60 MINUTES		**CBS**
E	local	Jerry Lewis Show		JULIA	NBC Tuesday Night At The Movies				**NBC**
W	local	HERE COME THE BRIDES		Peyton Place	The ABC Wednesday Night Movie				**ABC**
E	local	Daktari		THE GOOD GUYS	The Beverly Hillbillies	Green Acres	Jonathan Winters Show		**CBS**
D	local	The Virginian			Kraft Music Hall / # Bob Hope Show		THE OUTSIDER		**NBC**
T	local	THE UGLIEST GIRL IN TOWN	The Flying Nun	Bewitched	That Girl	JOURNEY TO THE UNKNOWN		local	**ABC**
H	local	BLONDIE	HAWAII FIVE-O		CBS Thursday Night Movies				**CBS**
R	local	Daniel Boone		Ironside	Dragnet 1969		Dean Martin Show		**NBC**
F	local	Operation: Entertainment		Felony Squad	DON RICKLES SHOW	The Guns Of Will Sonnett	Judd, For The Defense		**ABC**
R	local	The Wild, Wild West		Gomer Pyle, U.S.M.C.	CBS Friday Night Movies				**CBS**
I	local	The High Chaparral		THE NAME OF THE GAME			Star Trek		**NBC**
S	local	The Dating Game	The Newlywed Game	Lawrence Welk Show		Hollywood Palace		local	**ABC**
A	local	Jackie Gleason Show		My Three Sons	Hogan's Heroes	Petticoat Junction	Mannix		**CBS**
T	local	ADAM-12	Get Smart	THE GHOST AND MRS. MUIR	NBC Saturday Night At The Movies				**NBC**
S	LAND OF THE GIANTS		The FBI		The ABC Sunday Night Movie				**ABC**
U	Lassie	Gentle Ben	Ed Sullivan Show		Smothers Brothers Comedy Hour		Mission: Impossible		**CBS**
N	NEW ADVENTURES OF HUCK FINN	Walt Disney's Wonderful World Of Color		The Mothers-In-Law	Bonanza		THE BEAUTIFUL PHYLLIS DILLER SHOW		**NBC**

The three young demigods had each been arrested on minor charges. Then, middle-aged middle-American police captain Adam Greer (Tige Andrews) talked the reluctant troika into a strange deal. They could do something positive and work within the system as undercover agents who would take on special youth-oriented assignments, possibly even hunting down criminals among their former colleagues. It was a cumbersome, strained premise, but it worked. The three hip, "with it" juvenile detectives were easier for America's teens to identify with than either the square-jawed heroes of *Dragnet* and *The FBI* or the high-living aristocrats of *Name of the Game*. The fact that the trio was secretly working for the establishment mollified the oldsters. With Pete, Julie, and Linc involved in cases as timely as the evening's headlines, ABC could exploit current issues such as youth rebellion, drug abuse, and racial tension while making sure the legitimate authority always triumphed in the end. Now *this* was TV reality.

NBC and CBS, feeling they had been left behind, quickly turned out a number of soapy "with-it" drama specials that were equally facile at incorporating then current issues into traditional TV plots. The occasional drama series, *CBS Playhouse*, presented a string of stories dealing with ostensibly rebellious young men who pounded their chests and questioned society but, after a talk with a learned elder, saw the light and got a haircut. This symbolic shearing became TV's new happy ending as youth and maturity were reconciled and the prodigal son looked nice for the holidays.

The sudden urge to "tell it like it is" and thus appear "relevant" also began to take hold in the traditional sitcom format as well. NBC patted itself on the back and presented the first modern situation comedy to focus directly on blacks, *Julia*. As if to make up for lost time, though, the series shared the *Mod Squad* approach of raising its black characters to nearly divine heights. Julia (Diahann Carroll) was a registered nurse who possessed every possible positive human attribute: she was kind, sweet, forgiving, thoughtful, obedient, and reverent. Befitting the times, her husband had been killed in Vietnam, leaving her to care for their young boy, Corey (Marc Copage). However, this meant that the head of television's first black family in years was actually a single mom, a setup then nearly as rare as a black lead. (On television, sitcom widows with kids were quickly remarried.) There was little chance that either image would really upset viewers, though, because Julia ended up nearly indistinguishable from dozens of white counterparts such as the Andersons, living in the same aseptically clean expanse of bland suburbia as they did. She, too, faced predictable family complications, and had a child too adorably cute to be believed. In an odd way, then, *Julia* really did bring true racial equality to the era's television lineup because it was just as realistic and relevant as any other sitcom then on the American airwaves.

What actual relevancy there might have been was still found only on *The Smothers Brothers Comedy Hour* and *Laugh-In*, both of which had blossomed throughout 1968. The Smothers were feeling their oats, having squeezed *Bonanza* from the number one spot on television while remaining comfortably in the top twenty themselves. Drawing on their hit status, they pushed to include more and more material that was considered unacceptable to the CBS censor, achieving mixed success. Pete Seeger was at last permitted to sing "Waist Deep in Big Muddy," but Harry Belafonte was not allowed to sing "Lord, Don't Stop the Carnival" as accompaniment to video tapes of the 1968 Democratic convention's street confrontations. Local CBS affiliates grew increasingly nervous over the Smothers' antics, fearing incensed complaints from viewers and possible government reprimands. To mollify them, CBS instituted a closed circuit preview screening of *The Smothers Brothers Comedy Hour* for affiliates, allowing them several days to decide whether they wanted to air that week's program. Yet while the nitpicking by the locals and the CBS censor continued week after week, the Canadian commercial network (CTV) regularly aired the show Sunday nights and never registered any complaints; in fact, it often included the segments excised from the U.S. transmission.

The first showdown between the Smothers and CBS came in March 1969 when the network substituted a Smothers' rerun for that week's scheduled show, claiming the program had been delivered too late for the affiliate preview. The Smothers said that the CBS censor was waging a vendetta against them and demanded that the network change its censorship policy or they would quit. After all, they pointed out, it had been censorship changes that delayed delivery of the program in question. The network had objected to some remarks by Joan Baez about her husband David (who was then serving a three-year jail sentence for draft evasion), insisting the Smothers delete her line, "Anybody who lays it out in front like that generally gets busted, especially if you organize, which he did." Tommy Smothers had agreed to the cut under protest but, at the last minute, the censor had raised some additional objections, making it impossible for the Smothers to meet the affiliate preview deadline with the completed show. After heated behind-the-scenes meetings, the Smothers capitulated and

the canceled show was aired (as edited by CBS) on March 30. The next week, the two sides reached the breaking point again, and this time the Smothers lost both the battle and the war. On Thursday, April 3, CBS notified the Smothers Brothers that the final-cut tape of the program scheduled for broadcast April 6 had not yet arrived in New York for review. During production, CBS had objected to two segments: the ribbing of Senator Pastore by Tommy and guest Dan Rowan (should the senator receive the Fickle Finger of Fate award?) and the double entendre monologue by comedian David Steinberg, who interpreted the Biblical story of Jonah and the whale with lines such as "Then the Gentiles grabbed the Jew by his Old Testament." So on April 6, as the controversial episode aired as scheduled in Canada, U.S. viewers were shown a repeat of the November 10 program.

The next morning, the Smothers held an impromptu press conference in the screening room of the Four Seasons restaurant in New York City. TV critics from New York, Boston, and Philadelphia viewed the controversial program and heard an angry outburst by the Smothers against CBS. As far as CBS was concerned the war was already over. The Smothers Brothers were fired. Walter Cronkite's news show on Friday had already carried the story that *The Smothers Brothers Comedy Hour* had been terminated. Recalcitrant stars could hold out for more money, but calling out CBS in public and repeatedly refusing to toe the network line was something the top brass would not tolerate. CBS never aired the April 6 episode, filling the time slot with the last two shows that had already been taped, then playing reruns until a replacement was ready. (In September, the censored show did air through local syndication by Metromedia.) The Smothers filed an extensive lawsuit against CBS charging breach of contract, trade libel, and infringement of copyright, and eventually (1973) won a court judgment. But their *Comedy Hour* was gone.

They had hoped their success would provide them with enough clout to take their fight for principles to the limit, but the truth was that with the national political mood increasingly polarized and

Hawaii Five-O's tried-and-true crime formula ran for twelve years on CBS. Series star Jack Lord *(right)* and guest villain George Lazenby. *(CBS Photo Archive © 2003 CBS Worldwide, Inc. All Rights Reserved.)*

On October 13, 1968, the crew of the *Apollo* 7 sent a live television transmission back to viewers back home. *(From left)* Command module pilot Donn F. Eisele and mission commander Walter Schirra, Jr. *(NASA)*

watchdogs such as Senator Pastore breathing down broadcasters' necks, none of the networks felt the extra trouble caused by such volatile figures as the Smothers Brothers was worth it. By 1970, the Smothers Brothers wanted to return to network television, and they turned up in a bland special that won them a brief summer series on ABC. In all their subsequent appearances, though, they seemed noticeably subdued, especially in contrast to their reputation for generating exciting controversy on their old show.

NBC's *Laugh-In*, though, remained where it was. In spite of occasional political needling, *Laugh-In*'s most revolutionary aspects were its format and pacing. Once the show had become a hit, both were easily accepted and, with the exception of a few ticklish double-entendre jokes, the program was comparatively safe for the network. After its slow start in 1968, *Laugh-In* overtook Lucille Ball and became the top rated TV show on television through most of 1969. Then, surprisingly, nothing happened.

Normally all the networks eagerly jumped on the bandwagon of a new hit format and began turning out numerous formula copies. In the early 1960s, the success of such country hits as *The Andy Griffith Show* and *The Beverly Hillbillies* led to dozens of similar shows throughout prime time and to a strong rural orientation by CBS that remained the backbone of the network's programming even in 1969. *Laugh-In*'s intricate format and image of topicality, however, proved a difficult mixture to match. The networks made several attempts to clone the series, but only one caught on.

In early 1969, ABC launched two *Laugh-In* lookalikes: *What's It All About, World?* and *Turn-On,* which were both complete failures. *What's It All About, World?* was a sorry copy that was lost in the netherworld between a standard comedy-variety format and *Laugh-In*'s zaniness. Dean Jones was the program host, but his image was far too straight-laced for the task. The troupe of comedy unknowns could never quite find their mark either, even aided by veteran newsman Alex Dreier. The show tried to be titillating without offending anybody. *Turn-On* was even worse.

Turn-On (Get it? *Laugh-In. Turn-On.*) earned the dubious honor of having the shortest network run in television history: one show. Though it used *Laugh-In*'s own producer, George Schlatter, *Turn-*

On showed little of the humor and ingenuity of the original, concentrating instead on the mere mechanics of the hit format. Even the human host was eliminated and replaced by a computer, though it was assisted by a guest celebrity (Tim Conway in the first-last episode). The pacing in the program was nothing short of frenetic, modeling itself after the incessant tempo of television commercials: three hundred separate bits were crammed into the half-hour premiere, with the show's credits interspersed randomly throughout. Even with *Laugh-In* an established hit and its fast paced format accepted by the public, *Turn-On* still appeared to many as an incomprehensible mishmash. What's worse, almost every joke fell flat. Two policemen holding Mace cans intoned, "Let us spray." Draft dodgers were shown hitchhiking to Sweden. Maura McGiveney played the slinky, painted Body Politic (à la Judy Carne). "Topical" political comments included such gems as: "The capital of South Vietnam is in Swiss banks!"; "Down with Haya Education!"; and the exchange "I just bought the Washington Senators." "Oh, all I could afford was a Congressman!" The strongest viewer reaction was touched off by several questionable jokes concerning Pope Paul VI and by the sight of a young woman eagerly pulling the lever of a machine dispensing "the pill."

Even before *Turn-On* was aired on Wednesday night, February 5, a number of ABC affiliates expressed their uneasiness over the show, with some either refusing to carry it at all or shifting its local broadcast time to an obscure slot (the type formerly warmed by *ABC Scope*). Though many people missed seeing the show, *Turn-On*'s alleged sacrilegious tenor immediately turned it into a national controversy. An executive of ABC affiliate WEWS in Cleveland sent a wire to the network which stormed, "If you naughty little boys have to write dirty words on the walls, please don't use our walls." This angry missive received a great deal of publicity, though it was later pointed out that the man who sent the wire had not seen the program. While ABC's position of last place in the network ratings race gave it more freedom to experiment with new ideas in the hope that one might turn into a hit show, it was, at the same time, in the weakest position to withstand intense public criticism. On February 7, two days after *Turn-On*'s premiere, the program was axed. Three additional shows, already in the can, were never aired. ABC padded the Wednesday night movie to fill *Turn-On*'s slot until it could find a substitute. Taking no chances, the network replaced *Turn-On* with the wholesome musical-variety of *The King Family*.

Laugh-In's George Schlatter had no better luck on NBC. In October 1968 he produced "Soul," a pilot for a series that NBC planned to slot as a black version of *Laugh-In*. The "Soul" special starred veteran entertainers Lou Rawls, Redd Foxx, Nipsey Russell, and Slappy White, and received acceptable critical reviews, but NBC was unable to sell the projected series to sponsors.

Strangely enough, the only successful copy of *Laugh-In* was one that avoided the liberal-urban slant of the original and settled instead for deep-fried country corn, CBS's *Hee-Haw*, the network's replacement for the canceled Smothers Brothers. While few fans of *Laugh-In* would ever consider watching *Hee-Haw*, both shows were two peas from the same pod, featuring virtually identical formats. *Hee-Haw* merely substituted rural trappings. Familiar country music stars Buck Owens and Roy Clark acted as hosts and they were supported by celebrity guest stars and a comedy troupe of proficient unknowns which soon developed its own familiar characters. Like *Laugh-In*, the pace was rapid, the catch phrases redundant, and the dialogue filled with sexually oriented double-entendres. Ironically, *Hee-Haw* turned out to be the most resilient of all the clones, even outlasting *Laugh-In* itself. At first *Laugh-In* had displayed more wit but, by 1970, the program found itself practically a prisoner of its own catch phrases and format. Even the very name *Laugh-In* seemed anachronistic. *Hee-Haw* suffered from some of the same problems but it was able to maintain a more consistent, if somewhat lower, strain of humor during its twenty-three years on the air (all but the first two as an independent syndicated series).

Hee-Haw was originally intended to serve as only summer filler, but it was such a success that CBS brought it back at the first opportunity. In mid-December of 1969, *Hee-Haw* took the time slot of another successful, but more traditional, down-home comedy-variety show, *The Glen Campbell Goodtime Hour*. That, in turn, switched back to Sunday, taking the old Smothers time period, where it had also begun life (as the Smothers 1968 summer replacement). The Smothers Brothers were gone and these two new hits merely reinforced CBS's decade-old image (going back to the James Aubrey days) as the rural network.

Despite occasional gestures to other forms, CBS inevitably turned to rural-appeal fare for both new season programs and emergency substitutions. Even its copy of the innovative *Laugh-In* followed the same pattern. What's more, the network continued to carry the largest stable of aging veterans which, while still successful, could not last indefinitely. CBS needed some fresh faces and formats to maintain viewer loyalty should some of the old favorites begin to fade during the increasingly tight ratings race. For this season, only some key mid-season shifts allowed CBS to beat a strong challenge from NBC and maintain its long streak of season wins. Nonetheless, CBS continued essentially unchanged into the 1969–70 season, even picking up a sitcom discarded by NBC (*Get Smart*) for the fall of 1969. After all, though NBC and ABC continued to tinker with unproven formats such as the more topical urban slant of the *Mod Squad* series, CBS still remained number one thanks to its established hits. Though probably inevitable, a major overhaul did not seem at all urgent to the network brass.

Just as CBS constantly went back to the farm to shore up its programming, ABC, the perennial third network in ratings, also turned to past strengths such as game shows whenever its latest gimmicks failed. With the exception of an occasional summer re-placement, game shows had been largely absent from the networks' prime time schedules since the quiz show scandal of the late 1950s. This policy began to change in the fall of 1966 when, faced with replacing an instant flop (*The Tammy Grimes Show*), ABC promoted one of its daytime winners, *The Dating Game*, into the nighttime fold to act as a stop gap. Surprisingly, the show earned respectable ratings and, with its low production costs, proved a bargain for advertisers. *The Dating Game* was the first production effort of game show impresario Chuck Barris (a former ABC programming executive), and its prime time success was a breakthrough of sorts in the field. The program dispensed with the all-too-familiar Hollywood celebrity angle of other game shows and instead used nubile young women and handsome young men who were unknowns both to each other and to the audience. The premise was simple: One contestant tried to choose a perfect date from a trio of suitors hidden behind a stage wall by asking a series of specially prepared, slightly suggestive, questions. Though almost a direct copy of the ancient ABC Arlene Francis vehicle, *Blind Date*, the loosened moral standards since the late 1940s allowed *The Dating Game* to maintain a fairly blatant risqué tone. Barris immediately copied his own gimmick and produced the equally successful *Newlywed Game*, which had an even stronger

---

January 5, 1969
NET totally discontinues its use of the U.S. Postal Service to send shows to its affiliates, instead relying full time on the coast-to-coast coaxial cable for live transmissions.

February 17, 1969
Robert Wood becomes president of the CBS television network.

March 5, 1969
Ralph Roberts, who entered the cable TV business in 1963 by buying American Cable Systems Inc. (a Tupelo, Mississippi, system of 1,200 subscribers) reincorporates his company in Pennsylvania as Comcast Corporation (a mix of the words "communications" and "broadcast").

March 31, 1969
The CBS Morning News with Joseph Benti becomes the first hour-long daily network news show.

May 26, 1969
After receiving great reviews but low ratings for Dick Cavett's daytime talk show, ABC moves it to prime time, three days a week, for a three-month summer run.

May 26, 1969
Av Westin, former *PBL* boss, becomes executive producer of ABC's nightly news. Howard K. Smith is promoted from commentator to co-anchor with Frank Reynolds.

July 7, 1969
The David Frost Show. Group W brings in David Frost to replace CBS-bound Merv Griffin on its syndicated talk program.

August 18, 1969
The Merv Griffin Show. (CBS). With the inauguration of Griffin's talk show on CBS, all three networks have nearly identical ninety-minute gabfests running opposite each other late night, Monday through Friday.

Walking on the moon, *Apollo 11* mission commander Neil Armstrong took this photo of fellow astronaut Edwin "Buzz" Aldrin, Jr., the lunar module pilot. *(NASA)*

base in double-entendre. The two games became back-to-back brothers on the ABC schedule.

In November 1968, ABC scored a major game show coup by luring the four-year-old *Let's Make a Deal* from NBC. Although the show was a long-time smash in the daytime, NBC was reluctant to grant it prime time exposure, allowing only a brief summer run in 1967. When the network refused to give the show a second prime time run, its producers defected to ABC. Desperately in need of hit programs to build up its daytime strength, ABC was more than happy to place *Let's Make a Deal* in one of its many open slots in the evening as part of the deal. Though never much of a hit at night, *Let's Make a Deal* carried its loyal daytime audience to ABC and within months the network became number two behind CBS during the daytime.

Let's Make a Deal was a masterpiece in greed, dispensing with challenging questions and specialized knowledge in favor of pure luck. Otherwise respectable citizens stood in line for hours, dressed in ridiculous costumes, hoping for a good seat and the chance to catch host Monty Hall's attention. Hall chose the most oddly attired people in the studio audience as contestants and gave them the chance to wheel and deal their way to big bucks. He awarded them a small prize and then played on their natural greed in a series of increasingly valuable trades, offering visions of untold riches at the end if they would only deal the pittance they had for what lurked behind door number one, door number two, or door number three. Unlike programs such as *Twenty-One,* contestants took all their winnings to each new deal; one bad trade and they could lose everything. Nonetheless, *Let's Make a Deal* tapped the barely subconscious wish to strike it rich quick, and the series

became a symbol of the successful excesses of the game show genre. It might not have been great art, but it was pure popular entertainment.

American commercial television has always been the embodiment of both crass and class. In 1969, the gelt gaucherie of *Let's Make a Deal* was the runaway hit of daytime TV, yet at the same time television delivered some of the most historic and poetic moments in its history as it presented the climax to the story of the conquest of space and the race to the moon. ABC's Jules Bergman, NBC's Frank McGee, and CBS's Walter Cronkite had been dutifully reporting the exploits in America's space program since the early 1960s, from the first sub-orbital flights to the launching of the behemoth *Saturn V* rocket. At first, the space launches produced very long programs that had very few visual highlights once the rocket had been launched. There were only voice transmissions and network mockups to fill the remaining hours. In late 1965, NASA began to allow live transmission of the splashdown and recovery procedure (starting with *Gemini 6*), but it was not until October 1968 that Americans were treated to the sight of their astronauts, live and in orbit, through signals sent from *Apollo 7.* The ever-improving technology that permitted live broadcasts from space, even from the capsule itself, at last allowed television to present the full impact and wonder of space exploration.

On the cold and snowy Christmas Eve of 1968, as millions gathered to celebrate Christmas, television shared with the nation, and the world, the excitement and the drama of the flight of *Apollo 8,* the first manned spaceship ever to orbit the moon. As the ship completed its first lunar orbit and emerged from the far side of the moon, mission control in Houston announced that contact had been reestablished with *Apollo 8.* Within seconds, an eerie but peaceful black and white image of the moon, close up, appeared on television. It was a sight never before witnessed by human eyes. Later that night, astronauts Frank Borman, Jim Lovell, and Bill Anders presented another panorama of lunar landscape while reading from the book of *Genesis,* closing with, "God bless all of you on the good Earth."

Six months later, the three commercial networks followed the journey of the *Apollo 11* team of Neil Armstrong, Michael Collins, and Edwin "Buzz" Aldrin, Jr., remaining on the air over thirty continuous hours in order to show the first astronauts landing on the moon. On July 20, 1969, in preparation for the decent to the lunar surface, Armstrong and Aldrin entered the lunar module (dubbed the "Eagle"), which then separated from the command module and headed to the surface. At touchdown in the Sea of Tranquility Armstrong reported, "Houston, Tranquility Base here. The Eagle has landed."

The actual landing of the lunar module was not televised but, shortly before 11:00 P.M. (Eastern time), Armstrong pulled a string as he began to climb down the ladder of the module to the surface of the moon. A panel opened and a small TV camera followed his descent. The signal was transmitted to the orbiting command module, from there to an Earth-based antenna, then to NASA in Houston, and finally to the networks, thus allowing millions of people to see Armstrong descend the stairs and take the first step on the moon milliseconds after it actually occurred.

If those who struggled in the early part of the century to create television were to come back to life and ask how their invention was used, it would be wise to ignore every entertainment program ever broadcast and show them instead these moments from space. It has been estimated that between 300 million and three-fourths of one billion people either saw or heard Armstrong's descent, live. If ever there was a time that television fulfilled its creators' dreams and brought the world together in peace, this was it.

29. Effete and Impudent Snobs

SEX AND VIOLENCE: the twin tar babies of American television. No matter how much the public moralists decried what they saw as an excess of sex and violence on TV, as soon as their clamor died down network programmers once again returned to these two familiar standbys. Most of the outraged critics faded after a short time in the public spotlight, while the home audience continued to be drawn by the lure of programs that included healthy doses of sex and violence. So for nearly twenty years, through each cycle of outraged criticism, the networks and producers tried to sneak in as much as possible without disturbing too many vocal viewers or politicians with clout. However, Rhode Island's powerful senator, John Pastore, proved to be one of the more persistent in the long line of television critics. He chaired a series of well-publicized hearings in 1969 and demonstrated that he had no intention of just fading away. Consequently, the new fall schedule for 1969 turned into a schizophrenic mix of strategies devised to bypass governmental intrusion yet still produce hit shows.

Violent police sagas were an easy target for criticism, so the wave of new cop shows was stopped cold. Not one new policeman, spy, private eye, or reporter-as-cop appeared in the fall schedule. There were no new Westerns, either. What's more, even veteran shoot'em-ups such as *The Virginian* continued the one-punch mentality of the previous season, replacing the traditional bar room brawl with nonhuman violence such as turbulent cattle stampedes. The freezing of these two forms still left the networks searching for new ways to present the same sort of emotions. Crime shows and Westerns, with all their violent tendencies, were the perfect vehicles in which to depict basic human crises (love, hate, life, death, greed) in showcases that allowed a natural, dramatic climax of capture and justice. To replace the cowboys and the cops the networks turned to two formats that had flourished on TV in the early 1960s after the demise of ABC's Warner Bros. action-adventure fad, the doctors and the lawyers. Both professions also dealt with intriguing law breakers and heartbroken beauties, but the drama usually began immediately after the violence had taken place, so the action was verbal rather than physical, often resembling soap operas.

The soapiest of them all were the doctors, presented in three new shows: *Marcus Welby, M.D., Medical Center,* and *The Bold Ones.* These sudsy dramas were aimed directly at young adults and middle-aged women in the desirable 18 to 49 age demographic group. Each of the new series maintained the inviolable Casey-Zorba/Kildare-Gillespie arrangement of a young handsome medico for sexual interest and a sage mentor to serve as a voice of reason. The standard operating procedure in each episode also remained unchanged from the Casey-Kildare days as the angels in white sought to overcome the illnesses that had struck that week's celebrity guest stars in several unrelated cases. What had changed, though, was the by-then prerequisite injection of a hip with-it touch to make the series appear bold and modern. Even the traditional TV doctor conflict between brash youth and experienced elder was viewed as a convenient hook to use in exploiting the then current interest in the "generation gap."

CBS's *Medical Center* had young stalwart Dr. Joe Gannon (Chad Everett) champing at the bit placed on him by the chief surgeon, Dr. Paul Lachner (James Daly). Both men worked together, though, in dealing with the complex and exotic disorders that came their way, usually in the form of a beautiful, but troubled, woman. *The Doctors* segment of *The Bold Ones* cast E. G. Marshall as a chief neurosurgeon, considered a liberal innovator by his colleagues, who had to keep in check his even more headstrong protégés (John Saxon and David Hartman). On ABC, Marcus Welby, played by the consummate TV parent, Robert Young, fought to control the hot-blooded youthful exuberance of his dashing young aide (who even rode a motorcycle), Dr. Steven Kiley (James Brolin).

Young, a proven hand at dispensing philosophical TV homilies, played Dr. Welby as a father-confessor figure who operated from his own home rather than from a large, impersonal hospital. (The show could have easily been called "Doctor Knows Best.") Though the standard TV doctor illnesses such as amnesia, temporary blindness, and brain tumors received their usual exposure, previously taboo subjects such as abortion and venereal disease were added to the plots. The insertion of controversial issues was an ingenious ploy to lure the young audience and seemed to allow frank discussions of complex issues, though in reality the presentations were stacked in advance and the character of Welby was used to spout the established catechisms on the topics. The pregnant woman in the abortion program came to Dr. Welby only after she was almost killed by a sloppy back-alley butcher. Welby, of course, took the injured woman under his care, but was quick to point out that he felt an abortion had been the wrong choice to make in the first place. In facing the problem of sexually-transmitted diseases, Welby played the consummate guidance counselor, delivering frank but comforting lectures to the young-

Day	7:00	7:30	8:00	8:30	9:00	9:30	10:00	10:30	
M	local	THE MUSIC SCENE	THE NEW PEOPLE		THE SURVIVORS		LOVE, AMERICAN STYLE		**ABC**
O	local	Gunsmoke		Here's Lucy	Mayberry R.F.D.	Doris Day Show	Carol Burnett Show		**CBS**
N	local	MY WORLD AND WELCOME TO IT	Rowan And Martin's Laugh-In		NBC Monday Night At The Movies / # Bob Hope Show / # NBC Specials				**NBC**
T	local	The Mod Squad		MOVIE OF THE WEEK			MARCUS WELBY, M.D.		**ABC**
U	local	Lancer		Red Skelton Hour		THE GOVERNOR AND J.J.	CBS News Hour / 60 Minutes		**CBS**
E	local	I Dream Of Jeannie	DEBBIE REYNOLDS SHOW	Julia	NBC Tuesday Night At The Movies / # First Tuesday				**NBC**
W	local	The Flying Nun	THE COURTSHIP OF EDDIE'S FATHER	ROOM 222	The ABC Wednesday Night Movie				**ABC**
E	local	Glen Campbell Goodtime Hour		The Beverly Hillbillies	MEDICAL CENTER		Hawaii Five-O		**CBS**
D	local	The Virginian			Kraft Music Hall		THEN CAME BRONSON		**NBC**
T	local	The Ghost And Mrs. Muir	That Girl	Bewitched	This Is Tom Jones		It Takes A Thief		**ABC**
H	local	Family Affair	JIM NABORS HOUR		CBS Thursday Night Movies				**CBS**
R	local	Daniel Boone		Ironside		Dragnet 1970	Dean Martin Show		**NBC**
F	local	Let's Make A Deal	THE BRADY BUNCH	MR. DEEDS GOES TO TOWN	Here Comes The Brides		JIMMY DURANTE PRESENTS THE LENNON SISTERS HOUR		**ABC**
R	local	Get Smart	The Good Guys	Hogan's Heroes	CBS Friday Night Movies				**CBS**
I	local	The High Chaparral		The Name Of The Game			BRACKEN'S WORLD		**NBC**
S	local	The Dating Game	The Newlywed Game	Lawrence Welk Show		Hollywood Palace		local	**ABC**
A	local	Jackie Gleason Show		My Three Sons	Green Acres	Petticoat Junction	Mannix		**CBS**
T	local	Andy Williams Show		Adam-12	NBC Saturday Night At The Movies				**NBC**
S	Land Of The Giants		The FBI		The ABC Sunday Night Movie				**ABC**
U	Lassie	TO ROME WITH LOVE	Ed Sullivan Show		LESLIE UGGAMS SHOW		Mission: Impossible		**CBS**
N	Wild Kingdom	The Wonderful World Of Disney		BILL COSBY SHOW	Bonanza		THE BOLD ONES (THE DOCTORS; THE LAWYERS; THE PROTECTORS)		**NBC**

sters and their parents. They, in turn, responded with appropriate lines like "Who, me?" and "What? *My* child??" Thus, the show was able to reassure one side with the dead certainty of a Sunday school lesson while luring the other with the appearance of presenting progressive drama.

Though not at all violent, the new doctor shows could sneak in underlying sexual themes in the same way as the afternoon soap operas, by being all talk and no action. Other series, which could not wrap their titillation in the white robes of professional respectability, fared far worse. One of the major victims of the more stringent limitations on TV sex was an elaborately planned ABC series, *The Survivors,* another of the network's forays into the world of novels-for-television (succeeding *Peyton Place*, which faded from view in 1969). Produced by Universal and created by Harold Robbins, a master in the genre of broad-based sexy pulp fiction, the new series proposed to bring to television exciting sex-drenched dramas of the rich and playful jet set. ABC promised that Robbins would be closely involved in the production of the series and that the program would be a true television novel, presenting a different chapter of a continuing story each week. None of this ever happened. Just as the show was about to begin production in mid 1968, the sex and violence controversy flared and *The Survivors* was delayed until the fall of 1969. With the toned-down standards still in effect, the series was turned into a traditional television suspense thriller with soap opera touches. Consequently,

the exploits of a powerful banking family were mixed with such sudsy daytime staples as pregnant unmarried damsels trying to hide their shame. The network also abandoned the concept of a TV novel storyline and settled for a stable, celebrity-studded continuing cast (Ralph Bellamy, Lana Turner, Kevin McCarthy, and George Hamilton), but the program did not survive its forced neutering. The show quickly went through three producers, lost its head star (Bellamy), and, by mid-season, was written off as a full-fledged flop. Despite ABC's major financial investment, the project was quickly disposed of, with an equally unsuccessful spinoff series, *Paris 7000* (starring the only cast holdover, George Hamilton, as an American playboy in Paris), fulfilling certain contractual arrangements between ABC and Universal Studios.

Another victim of the tighter production code was an NBC project with Twentieth Century Fox, *Bracken's World,* which ostensibly presented the behind-the-scenes lives and loves at a major Hollywood studio but was actually an excuse to expose as much of the nubile young starlets (including Karen Jensen, Linda Harrison, and Laraine Stephens) as the censors would allow. By the time *Bracken's World* began production in the spring of 1969, the stricter rules required the beautiful women to keep most of their clothes on. Though they flitted to and fro complying with the orders given by the off-camera unseen head of the studio, John Bracken (Leslie Nielsen), the stories were quite weak. Forced to rely on its dramatic content without maximum exposure of the aspiring but compliant female characters, *Bracken's World* folded after only one-and-a-half seasons.

The only new show to succeed with up-front sex in spite of such production limitations was ABC's *Love, American Style,* the first hit comedy anthology program on network TV. Since the early 1950s, the ratings domination by situation comedies in the *I Love Lucy* mold had convinced the networks that stable, familiar characters were essential in order to capture the fickle TV audience. *Love, American Style* broke from this assumption and presented three unconnected playlets that used guest stars exclusively. The only group of regulars turned up in the short comedy "quickies" that appeared between the individual playlets. The omni-present theme of love, as portrayed in the different humorous vignettes, held the program together.

Love, American Style did indeed display a freedom in topic and treatment above the traditional situation comedies and it worked hard at cultivating a risqué image. At heart, though, it was *very* respectable. There was talk of affairs, sleeping together, and premarital sex, but the Puritan ethic always triumphed and nothing salacious ever occurred either on or off camera. The program was a successful and effective transplant to TV of the Doris Day-Rock Hudson bedroom comedy films of the 1950s, with the same simple underlying premise: The courting rituals in America are in themselves hilarious and will seem so to the viewers when presented in a slightly exaggerated style. With an emphasis on rituals and games over the sex act itself, *Love, American Style* was the most representative example of permissible 1969 TV sex: Not only was it just all talk and no action, even the talk was not meant to be taken seriously. Occasionally the sugar-coated view of life became a bit too rich, but the program was generally funny and a genuinely successful innovation by ABC.

ABC and NBC were the only two networks actively experimenting with new forms in the 1969–70 season because CBS had decided to stand pat a while longer with its veteran sixty-minute variety shows and thirty-minute sitcoms. CBS had barely won the previous season and, in fact, had experienced noticeable difficulty in coming up with new hits during all of the late 1960s. Instead of trying much that was new, the network ended up relying on years of viewer loyalty to familiar formats and stars, assuming that people would come back to CBS after sampling the competition. In the fall of 1969, it looked as if this strategy was going to fail for the first time in more than a decade. CBS still had its hits, but there were enough successful regular series, movies, and specials on NBC and ABC to tip the balance in the overall ratings. NBC jumped into first place at the start of the season and remained there until New Year's, while ABC's new *Movie of the Week* occasionally hit number one in the weekly ratings. The new *Bill Cosby Show* sitcom and *The Bold Ones* career drama gave NBC a powerful Sunday night line-up. ABC turned out an intelligent new sitcom of its own, *Room 222,* and it received both critical praise and surprisingly good ratings against *The Beverly Hillbillies.*

Room 222 was a sharp break with both the rural slant of CBS's sitcoms and ABC's own trademark of mindless escapism. The series was topical and humorous while being only slightly sentimental in its portrayal of an integrated middle class urban high school. A largely unknown cast acted out believable stories with the focus on three excellent characters: a daffy white student-teacher (Karen Valentine), an understanding but much put-upon Jewish principal (Michael Constantine), and a black teacher of American history (Lloyd Haynes) whose classes were held in Room 222. They dealt with such dramatic issues as student rights and racial tension, but faced them with humor and more credibility than characters in such series as *The Mod Squad* or *Marcus Welby,*

M.D. With its successful showing in the ratings, *Room 222* at last proved that more up-to-date settings could work very well in sitcoms, too.

In contrast to this successful momentum, all of CBS's new sitcoms failed, and even variety stalwarts such as Ed Sullivan and newcomer Jim Nabors were in the dumps. In January, NBC felt strong enough to order no changes in its prime time schedule and, by February, it looked as if CBS might actually lose the season to NBC. Faced with this awesome prospect, CBS's new president, Bob Wood, decided to take drastic steps to stay on top. The first phase was a full-court press to win the season in progress with a game plan designed by veteran CBS programming chief Mike Dann, and dubbed "Operation 100."

During the one hundred days remaining in the regular season (which ended in April), Dann countered NBC's regular programming and previously announced specials, slot by slot, night by night. He preempted weak shows such as *Get Smart* as often as possible, realizing that even a moderately successful special would probably register better ratings. The most striking aspect of Dann's counter-programming was that he used some very unusual material: previously run movies such as "Peyton Place" and "The African Queen," specials that had played years before (sometimes on competing networks), and documentary films from National Geographic. By packaging and promoting them as special events, CBS beat NBC at its own game. NBC had aired most of its blockbuster movies in building its fall lead and was unable to effectively counter the CBS moves. Dann's strategy violated CBS's traditional reliance on the strength of its regular series for success, but the plan worked. CBS managed to win by enough each week during the one-hundred days to boost the network's overall season average past NBC's, though just barely.

With his mission accomplished, Dann quit while he was ahead and went to work for the new noncommerical Children's Television Workshop. To replace him, CBS promoted its thirty-two-year-old wunderkind, Fred Silverman, head of the network's daytime programming since 1963. For seven years, Silverman had kept CBS so far ahead in daytime ratings and revenue that the network could afford a few close calls in the nighttime ratings.

The second phase of Wood's plan to retain the number one spot was the surprise axing of three still successful CBS series at the end of the 1969–70 season: *The Jackie Gleason Show, Petticoat Junction,* and *Red Skelton.* (Skelton moved over to NBC for one last season.) The rationale for these cancellations lay in the new shibboleth of TV programming: demographics. The total number of people viewing a program was no longer the most important consideration, but rather the kind of people watching. While Gleason, Skelton, and *Petticoat Junction* had maintained adequate ratings, they also served to reinforce the image of CBS as the network appealing primarily to old people and country folk rather than the advertisers' favorite segment of society: young marrieds in the 18 to 49 age bracket, preferably women because they made most of the domestic purchases. For the sin of appealing to the wrong types of Americans, Gleason, Skelton, and the gang at Hooterville became the first of the CBS veterans to walk the plank.

Though CBS was just coming to grips with the changing reality of television, the other two networks had begun to tinker with some firmly established traditions of prime time TV years before. Since the early 1960s, in fact, a number of network programmers (at NBC in particular) had been sliding back toward the all-but-abandoned anthology format to the extent that even some of the features of the British system, which emphasized limited run series, began turning up on American TV. Ninety-minute Westerns such as *The Virginian* and *Wagon Train* marked the first tentative

September 22, 1969

Music Scene. (ABC). David Steinberg hosts a rock version of *Your Hit Parade* (with some comedy thrown in), featuring on the first show James Brown, Three Dog Night, and a film of The Beatles with their latest hit, "Ballad of John and Yoko." The program is one of two back-to-back forty-five-minute shows, but the packaging strategy fails and both vanish by January.

September 26, 1969

The Brady Bunch. (ABC). A vapid suburban sitcom straight out of the 1950s. Robert Reed plays a widower (with three cute sons) who marries a widow (played by Florence Henderson) with three cute daughters. The combined family lives in a typical Los Angeles suburban house, complete with a dog, a cat, and a smart-aleck maid (played by Ann B. Davis).

October 5, 1969

Monty Python's Flying Circus. Meanwhile, back in Britain, the BBC uncovers five *David Frost Show* graduates (and one American) who take the *Laugh-In* formula beyond the fringe.

December 29, 1969

Dick Cavett becomes ABC's late night replacement for the slumping Joey Bishop.

January 1, 1970

Robert Sarnoff becomes chairman of the board at RCA as his father, seventy-nine-year-old David Sarnoff, is named honorary board chairman.

February 4, 1970

After seven years as CBS's daytime programming boss, Fred Silverman is promoted to the nighttime division, as an assistant to chief programmer, Mike Dann.

moves in this direction because the programs were, in effect, Western anthologies that primarily showcased weekly guest stars while carrying a few continuing characters. NBC's 1964 effort at a situation comedy anthology, *90 Bristol Court,* attempted to incorporate three half-hour sitcoms under one banner, with each segment dealing with that week's particular topic in a different way. It was an intriguing concept, but it turned out to be clumsy, poorly connected, and a total failure.

In the middle and late 1960s, the success of both prime time movies and made-for-TV movies (which were, after all, anthology series) provided the strongest impetus to break from the standard weekly format. *Name of the Game,* a spinoff from the successful made-for-TV movie, used its setup of three major characters alternating in the lead role to have, in effect, three different shows with the same general setting running in the same time slot. NBC extended this concept in 1969 with *The Bold Ones,* a series that alternated separate, totally unrelated segments in the same time slot (*The Doctors, The Lawyers,* and *The Protectors,* the last one eventually replaced by *The Senator*). NBC discovered that major stars such as Gene Barry, Tony Franciosa, Robert Stack (*Name of the Game*), E. G. Marshall (*The Doctors*), Burl Ives (*The Lawyers*), Leslie Nielsen (*The Protectors*), and Hal Holbrook (*The Senator*) were much more likely to agree to do a television series if they did not have to maintain the grueling production pace that a weekly sixty- or ninety-minute TV show required. This very practical consideration resulted in series with both a healthy diversity and

many top stars, giving NBC potent programs to capture and keep an audience.

ABC took the almost inevitable next step with made-for-TV movies and gave the format its own ninety-minute weekly slot without any continuing segments at all, the Tuesday night *Movie of the Week* (the brainchild of twenty-seven-year-old ABC programming executive Barry Diller). Though not quite a return to *Studio One,* the program in effect brought the full-length weekly anthology format back to television several years after the death of the last limp remnants of the form, the *U.S. Steel Hour, Armstrong Circle Theater,* and *Chrysler Theater.* The move in the mid-1950s toward presenting series with popular, continuing characters had, by 1958, marked the end of the TV drama anthologies as an important creative force, but the success of made-for-TV movies demonstrated their renewed viability.

Actually, ABC's *Movie of the Week* more closely resembled the old *ABC Stage '67* show as it incorporated comedy and traditional specials, as well as adventure and drama, under its banner. Thus, material such as David Wolper's documentary film "The Journey of Robert F. Kennedy" joined bread-and-butter adventure-drama features such as "Seven in Darkness," which presented the struggle to safety by seven blind survivors of a jungle plane crash. In addition, the *Movie of the Week* slot served as an excellent showcase for thinly disguised pilot films of proposed regular series; *The Immortal* and *The Young Lawyers* were two such series given the go-ahead for the 1970–71 season following their successful feature film debuts.

NBC also increased its made-for-TV showcases, which the network labeled "world premieres" and inserted in its regular movie slots. Among the presentations were some fairly serious dramas that pulled off the very elusive TV trick of garnering both high ratings and strong critical praise. "Silent Night, Lonely Night," a Christmastime TV adaptation of Robert Anderson's Broadway play, was a tasteful and sensitive study of the pangs of desire between two married people (played by Lloyd Bridges and Shirley Jones) who decided to have a brief affair after one chance meeting. The two lovers were actually shown in bed together and, though they returned to their respective spouses at the end, neither was struck by some divine punishment for the transgression. Outside of the daytime soaps (which had been dealing with such encounters, and much more, for years), adultery had never received such favorable treatment in a work for television.

One month later, NBC presented "My Sweet Charlie," a novel-turned-play produced and adapted for television by Richard Levinson and William Link (the creators of *Mannix*). The story was a sensitive portrayal of a chance encounter inter-racial romance – an even more precedent shattering situation than "Silent Night, Lonely Night." Patty Duke played a runaway unwed teenage mother driven by a hurricane to seek shelter in a deserted house. There she encountered a fugitive black activist (Al Freeman) and the two outsiders lovingly shared each other's burdens, discovering that they had a great deal in common. With the passing of the storm, though, their utopia evaporated and the real world entered, breaking them apart. As a sign of the changing times, the kind portrayal of an unwed teenage mother (a very controversial concept only a few years before) was all but overlooked as attention focused on the first black-white romance in TV history. "My Sweet Charlie" won three Emmys and, more important, both it and "Silent Night, Lonely Night" did surprisingly well in the ratings. "My Sweet Charlie," in fact, emerged as the highest rated movie on television that year. The message from the ratings success of these innovative stories was that the television audience was evidencing a noticeable rise in the level of its tolerance and sophistication, a development many TV detractors had claimed would never take place.

Accompanying this change was an increase in the number of viewers tuning in programs on public television's NET network. NET had learned from *PBL* that its success as a network rested with shows that were at least structured like commercial network programs so that the audience would give them a chance. In the 1969–70 season it clicked with two such well-produced series, *Sesame Street* and *The Forsyte Saga*. *Sesame Street* was a product of the new Children's Television Workshop and began life as an eight million dollar, twenty-nine week television "head start" program aimed at preschool children, especially those in the urban ghettos. The program attempted to teach basic concepts of letters and numbers by using the technique of exciting, constant repetition pioneered by TV commercials. Program headliners such as Jim Henson's colorful muppet characters including the Cookie Monster, Big Bird, and Bert and Ernie elaborated on the basic lessons, adding their own humorous interpretations of the facts. *Sesame Street* was entertaining, educational, and an instant success with adults as well as children, lasting far longer than the originally planned twenty-nine weeks. (It was still going strong after twenty-nine *years*.) The show brought invaluable attention to the other less frenetic features of the NET schedule and boosted the ever-present funding drives as well.

The twenty-six-week *Forsyte Saga* began a Sunday night run on NET in October 1969, following its smash hit appearances in England in 1967 and, again as a rerun, in 1968. *The Forsyte Saga* was an expensive adaptation of John Galsworthy's novels, following the lives, loves, and losses of a respectable upper class Victorian family over fifty years and three generations. Production and acting in the series were first rate and the historical setting was quite impressive. At heart, though, the series was really just a high-gloss soaper, containing all the ingredients of a period soap opera: dashing young men, beautiful young women, a scheming old skinflint, extra-marital affairs, and a complicated continuing storyline. Nevertheless, American viewers who would never be caught dead watching *As the World Turns* considered *The Forsyte Saga* classy and morally uplifting because it was British and on "educational" TV. They bragged about following the weekly Sunday night exploits of the Forsyte family, encouraging their friends to tune in as well. Consequently, the 167 NET stations carrying the program noticed a sizable increase in their Sunday night audiences and they began looking for programs with the same type of attraction. In the fall of 1970, *Masterpiece Theater* was created (with the help of substantial grants from the Mobil Oil Corporation) to present British-made historical dramas on a regular basis, every Sunday night. The program, hosted by *Omnibus* alumnus Alistair Cooke, began with *The First Churchills* and then moved on, in subsequent years, to other Anglophile sagas such as *Elizabeth R* and *Upstairs, Downstairs*. The limited-run imported series brought the individual NET stations large audiences and projected an air of classy success. They also made the expense and bother of producing similar domestic programs seem less and less worthwhile, thus beginning NET's extended parasitic dependence on British television.

In 1969, though, NET was still producing several excellent programs of its own, including *The Advocates, NET Playhouse,* and *Hollywood Television Theater. The Advocates* presented a debate of controversial issues argued courtroom-style by knowledgeable experts from both sides. *NET Playhouse* turned out dramatic productions such as "The Trail of Tears," an unflinching portrait of American persecution of the Cherokee Indians in the 1830s, starring Johnny Cash and Jack Palance. Perhaps NET's best

dramatic production of the year appeared on the May 17, 1969, premiere of *Hollywood Television Theater,* the lavishly funded successor to *NET Playhouse.* George C. Scott directed a new production of "The Andersonville Trial," a 1959 Saul Levitt play that dramatized the Nuremberg-like post-Civil War trial of the commander of an inhuman prisoner of war camp. Scott himself had starred in the original Broadway production but for the new television version, recorded live on tape, Richard Basehart, Jack Cassidy, and William Shatner took the leads in the thought-provoking debate on moral responsibility.

NET's production style was much closer to the fondly remembered live drama of such vehicles as *Playhouse 90* than the generally action-oriented made-for-TV movies on the commercial networks. Though such programs as *Hollywood Television Theater* were not going to spark a revival of *Studio One* on commercial television, NET's programming was at last providing something of a real alternative to the lock-step TV world of CBS, NBC, and ABC. NET's programming wound up having an effect on long-range planning by the commercial television executives. With public television viewing on the rise, they began using NET as a test ground for formats and ideas they feared might not yet be ready for a commercial run. NET had truly become a force to reckon with, not only by the commercial networks but by the government itself.

May 8, 1970
The FCC adopts the Financial Interest and Syndication rules (the "Fin-Syn" rules). These severely limit the networks from retaining any financial interest in the rerun syndication rights of programs they air and prohibit them from maintaining in-house syndication divisions. The Fin-Syn rules do not fully go into effect until 1973.

June 22, 1970
Fred Silverman succeeds Mike Dann as programmer #1 at network #1.

July 8, 1970
The Smothers Brothers Summer Show. (ABC). The brothers sneak back onto television for a summer series with some of their old crew and a few new faces (including Sally Struthers). They avoid becoming embroiled in topical controversies but also fail to rekindle their popularity with viewers. As a result, their program is not picked up for a regular fall season run.

July 16, 1970
Nearly ten years after Ed Murrow's "Harvest of Shame" documentary, Martin Carr's "Migrants" shows how little has changed for American migrant workers.

July 31, 1970
Chet Huntley says "goodnight" to David Brinkley for the last time, with the hope that "there will be better and happier news, one day, if we work at it." On August 3, John Chancellor and Frank McGee join Brinkley for the new *NBC Nightly News* format.

September 27, 1970
Ted Mack's Original Amateur Hour, television's longest running entertainment show, gets the gong. Age: 22 years. During its last ten years, the show had been relegated to a Sunday afternoon slot on CBS.

President Richard Nixon announced the U.S. invasion of Cambodia in a prime time television speech on April 30, 1970. *(National Archives)*

Since the mid-1960s, NET had been the boldest network in producing public affairs programs and documentaries. During that time, it managed to avoid most governmental interference because of its minuscule audience and minor budget requirements. As the network became more influential and more dependent on government funding, this began to change. The Corporation for Public Broadcasting (CPB) began to feel pressure from the Nixon administration to reduce clearly anti-administration material. A number of public TV stations became very nervous about airing any possibly inflammatory programs at all. In February 1970, WETA in Washington refused outright to show "Who Invited Us?" on *NET Journal*. This program was a heavy-handed portrait of U.S. foreign policy as a strategy strongly influenced by the CIA and private corporations in order to further their own interests (a theme certain to irk the Nixon administration). With governmental funding becoming a major factor in NET finances, it seemed foolish to antagonize the people who had a strong say in just how much money Congress voted for public television. Though home viewers and private corporations such as the Ford Foundation and Mobil Oil still donated freely to NET, the network faced mounting costs such as AT&T line charges as it began to operate more and more like a real network and to distribute some of its shows via the national coaxial cable connections. With the Nixon people sorting out friends from enemies, the CPB began noticeably kowtowing to the administration in a manner reminiscent of the commercial networks at the height of President Johnson's influence.

In contrast to public television's pullback, the commercial networks, which had been rebuilding their commitment to hard-hitting news after the "no guts journalism" era of a few years before, regained the courage to air a few truly controversial documentaries. The Black Panthers, a prime target of J. Edgar Hoover's FBI, became the subject of reports on both CBS and ABC in the 1969–70 season. CBS's story led the network into an aggravated battle with the Justice Department, which issued a subpoena for the outtakes from the filmed interviews with Panther leaders. Under protest, CBS surrendered the leftover film, though it's doubtful the FBI found any nefarious plot or revealing off-the-cuff remark in the scraps from the cutting room floor. Nonetheless, when ABC

did its report a few months later, the network could not guarantee that the same thing would not happen to its films, so only Panther boss David Hilliard agreed to speak on camera. As a final frustration for the network, the Justice Department then refused to provide anyone to give the government's side of the Panther issue. Despite these limitations, the ABC report was an effective overview of the group and it served as a high point of the network's short-lived new prime time public affairs series, *Now* (hosted by Edward P. Morgan).

NBC, which was usually content to cover safer subjects such as "The Great Barrier Reef," tackled the politically volatile story of migrant farm workers in an *NBC White Paper* produced and directed by Martin Carr, "Migrants." The program was an effective followup to Carr's own previous report (on CBS) in 1968, "Hunger in America," which itself had been a followup to Ed Murrow's 1960 "Harvest of Shame." The most amazing aspect of the new reports was that so little had changed since Murrow's first story on the agricultural workers, both in the fields and behind the scenes. Like its predecessors, "Migrants" took a tough stand and named some major American corporations as being responsible for keeping the migrant workers close to starvation in the world's most bountiful land. It showed a representative of the Coca-Cola company, which owned a large citrus farm, physically breaking up an interview with a tenant who lived in one of the company's filthy shanties. As in the past, the crop growers cried "foul" and exerted intense pressure on NBC to keep the show off the air, labeling it "sneaky journalism." Despite the pressure, the report aired, albeit in the middle of July, without any commercial time sold, and with some affiliates refusing to show it anyway.

In spite of these incidents of bravery, network journalism was forced to take a step backwards in the 1969–70 season as the networks and the Nixon administration locked horns on the most troubling issue of all, the Vietnam War. On October 15, 1969, antiwar forces throughout the country held rallies as part of what was called Moratorium Day. As with the march on the Pentagon two years earlier, CBS was reluctant to devote much coverage to the protests. For Moratorium Day, however, NBC took the initiative and scheduled an 11:30 P.M. wrapup, so CBS did the same. Even this small dose of publicity given to the demonstrators irked Nixon and the president seemed convinced that the press, particularly the television press, was out to sabotage his administration. The next month he saw even further evidence that the "hands off" honeymoon with the news media had certainly come to an end.

On Monday, November 3, Nixon delivered an appeal directly to the viewing public in a half-hour speech that outlined his new Vietnamization policy and asked for support from "the great silent majority of my fellow Americans." Nixon promised his new strategy would eventually lead to the withdrawal of all American ground combat forces and leave South Vietnam to fight the ground war on its own. The speech ended at 10:05 P.M. As usual, the networks had received advance texts of the address a few hours before airtime, and their correspondents stood by for the traditional post-speech commentary and analysis. NBC and CBS devoted ten minutes each to the discussion and then returned to their scheduled programming. One CBS reporter observed that the President's Vietnamization program really offered nothing new and would simply mean an intensification of the American air war. ABC, which ran its report until 10:30, called on other political figures, as well as its own correspondents, for comments, reactions, and analysis. Veteran Democrat Averell Harriman, a former chief negotiator at the Vietnam peace talks, took the opportunity to delivery some harsh criticisms of Nixon's handling of both the war and the ever-stalled peace talks.

This public disagreement and criticism immediately following his own speech seemed to be the final straw for Nixon. He decided to launch a strong counter-attack before the networks had a chance to give the protesters any more free air time during the Moratorium II activities scheduled for November 15. The networks were

In late 1969, Vice President Spiro Agnew launched a strong attack against the networks, criticizing the slant of their news broadcasts. *(National Archives)*

warned that "it would be wise" to cover, live, a speech by Vice President Spiro Agnew at a Republican party conference in Des Moines on November 13. They did. At 7:00 P.M., speaking on CBS, NBC, and ABC, Agnew launched a vituperative attack on these same networks. Before the highly partisan crowd, he criticized the fact that "a small group of men, numbering perhaps no more than a dozen anchormen, commentators, and executive producers" decided what appeared on the nightly network news shows. They comprised, he said, an "unelected elite," an "effete corps of impudent snobs," primarily based in the East, who held a monopoly on the national dissemination of news and opinion. Agnew specifically criticized the "instant analysis" that followed President Nixon's November 3 speech, implying that, coming immediately after the President's address, the remarks were inadequately prepared and therefore of less value to the public. (He did not point out, of course, that the networks had received advance texts of the speech hours before airtime.) Significantly, Agnew exempted the local affiliates from blame because they merely found themselves in the position of broadcasting whatever the networks sent down the line.

The Agnew speech, largely authored by presidential speechwriter Patrick Buchanan, was a deliberate declaration of war by the Nixon administration against the networks. The administration realized that, aside from limited behind-the-scenes pressure, there was very little it could do to force the networks to toe the line. Instead, in a brilliant divide-and-conquer strategy, it aimed for the networks' Achilles' heel. By appealing to the American public and, in particular, to the local affiliates, the administration sought to polarize vague anti-TV news feelings and resentments that had developed throughout the decade, sharpening them into a clear-cut "us versus them" conflict. The networks were thereby outnumbered. If local affiliates began demanding a softening of network tone, then the three majors would have to listen. At the end of Agnew's speech, NBC and ABC immediately returned to regular programming. CBS read a short prepared reply and then pulled out as well. Two days later, there was no special coverage of the Moratorium II activities on any of the networks. On November 20, in Montgomery, Alabama, Agnew added two more names to his enemies' list, identifying the *New York Times* and *Washington Post* as part of the same "Eastern liberal establishment."

For the administration, Agnew's Des Moines speech was a tremendous success. Not only had the networks' tone softened immediately in its aftermath, but the tenor of public debate had turned around. Agnew's speech had touched a responsive nerve in the American public and the networks were on the defensive, trying to prove their innocence while the government called the shots. In January 1970, the president ended the practice of supplying advance texts of his speeches and distributed them just before air time instead to ensure a reduction in instant analysis. In addition, Nixon aides began leaking stories suggesting that several network reports that placed either the American war effort or the South Vietnamese government in a bad light were trumped up. Richard Salant, president of CBS News, said, "there is an official smear campaign under way to dissuade us from telling the truth as we see it." To counter charges of distortion leveled against one particular story on South Vietnamese atrocities, CBS was fortunate enough to have interviews with the soldiers involved, corroborating the network's story on prisoner mutilation. Nonetheless, the attacks continued and, on another front, individuals with strong ties to the administration (and President Nixon personally) filed a challenge with the FCC to take away a Miami television station owned by the *Washington Post.*

On April 30, Nixon delivered a prime time address announcing an American invasion of Cambodia. Following the speech, the networks offered almost no commentary at all. A wave of student protests (punctuated by the killing of four students at Kent State University) could not be ignored for long, though, and all three networks did prime time wrapups of a major Washington demonstration on May 9, which marked the culmination of the reaction to the invasion. The TV reports presented speakers from both sides and went to extraordinary lengths to appear balanced and non-biased. However, as if to "balance" the very coverage of such an event, CBS (after some outside pressure) agreed to also do a similar prime time wrapup of a pro-administration rally held in Washington on Honor America Day, July 4. NET, also feeling pressure from the White House, gave Honor America Day extensive air time. During all the public reaction to the invasion, both the electronic and print press generally accepted the administration's assertion that the invasion be referred to as the Cambodian "incursion."

Nearly two years after he had vowed to bring the country together, Richard Nixon presided over a highly divided nation, torn apart by the war in Indochina. The television networks were also in a very difficult position, facing pressure from all sides. The government wanted them to "go along" with the official line and was not hesitant to use its muscle. Affiliates were critical and nervous. Yet there was a reawakened conscience in the network news departments and, even in the face of general viewer apathy, they produced incisive news specials and daily reports on the war which only further piqued the administration's anger.

The born-again news team at CBS was especially effective, gathering first hand reports from the war front itself. John Laurence's sixty-minute portrait of an American infantry unit (called C-Company) revealed that there were clear anti-war feelings present even among America's fighting men. Another CBS special, "Where We Stand in Indochina," presented unflattering interviews with Vietnamese generals as CBS's correspondents concluded that, at best, the American invasion of Cambodia was a mistake. Yet in spite of the networks' attempts to reassert their journalistic integrity in covering the important events of the year, all of the season's Vietnam and public affairs specials found their usual place at the very bottom of the ratings tabulations, with the special "Ethics in Government" coming in, somehow appropriately, dead last.

30. Totally Committed and Completely Involved

"WE'RE PUTTING IT ALL TOGETHER this fall on CBS!" "Let's get together on ABC!" "It's happening on NBC!" That's what the networks told their viewers again and again through the summer of 1970. Campus revolt and the rock generation were reaching a high water mark and youth-oriented shows, which had been bubbling under the surface for about four seasons with increasing success, seemed to hold the key to the new ratings emphasis on audience demographics. The type of person watching had become increasingly important because the total television audience often included a great number of viewers who were judged to be too old or too rural for advertisers' tastes. Determined to win the attention of those in their late teens and twenties, all three networks decided to cast their lot with the kids and they proclaimed the arrival of the new season as heralding something completely different. Everything would be "Now"! Variations on phrases from then-current teen slang such as "getting it all together" and "what's happening" filled the networks' ads and show descriptions. This effusive commitment to "telling it like it is" led to one of the shortest format cycles in television history, "relevancy."

Despite all the rhetoric, the networks' self-proclaimed dedication to relevancy in programming really meant TV relevancy, a far cry from anything in the real world. It consisted of grafting the head of topical issues onto the body of standard grade-B drama and restocking familiar forums such as hospitals and court rooms with different, preferably youthful, characters. ABC had attracted lightning with this formula in *The Mod Squad* and *Marcus Welby, M.D.* and each of the networks rushed to include as many hip phrases, committed characters, and timely conflicts as possible. CBS in particular pursued the trend with a vengeance, apparently out to prove that it was no longer the network of the fuddy-duddies. To the god of youth it offered *Headmaster, The Interns,* and *Storefront Lawyers.* All three received "thumbs down."

Headmaster was a well-intentioned but poorly executed comedy-drama that cast veteran Andy Griffith as Andy Thompson, headmaster at a small private high school in California. In many ways, Griffith was a perfect choice for making relevancy work. He had spent eight years cultivating an image as a warm, level-headed folksy sheriff who was respected by old and young alike, and it was a short step to his new role as a Welby-ish father-confessor. In a setting reminiscent of ABC's moderately successful high school sitcom of the previous season, *Room 222,* Griffith took on the timely concerns of his troubled wards, trying to guide them through brewing campus revolt and drug overdoses. Unfortunately, the scripts and supporting cast generally lacked the control and subtlety of *Room 222* and the relevant problems clashed with the stock sitcom humor of such characters as the school's athletic coach, played by the slapstick-oriented Jerry Van Dyke. As a result, *Headmaster* emerged as a mish-mash of emotion that made the program appear a cheap vehicle simply attempting to cash in on "today's headlines."

The Interns presented the lives, loves, and labors of five sparkling clean doctors-in-training (three white, one black, one blonde) at a major Los Angeles hospital, and brought the relevancy angle to a format that was quite well suited for soapy topical melodrama. The program religiously adhered to the traditional *Ben Casey-Dr. Kildare* structure including a wise elder statesman and three guest patients each week, but the new divinities of youth and relevance raised their unwieldy influence at every turn. As a result, the show was not merely heavy-handed, it was often ludicrous in its emphasis. In their spiffy attire and perfectly set *coiffures,* the interns looked more like hairdressers than medicos. Their supposedly wise mentor (played by that old highway patrolman, Broderick Crawford) was presented as being no match for the wisdom of youth and he alternated between sagacity and surliness. Above all, the patient ailments were absurd. On one show, they included: a go-go dancer who was bedridden with a twisted foot; a former girlfriend of one of the wavy-haired interns who begged for the mercy killing of her sick husband; and a meditative monk who not only needed his physical illness cured but his political consciousness reawakened (a task handled by the black intern). For added topicality, this very same episode included a subplot that focused on a bearded orderly who was arrested for peddling pornographic movies. Through it all the happy-go-lucky interns, like their comrades in the Mod Squad, stood by the traditional rules and routine, determined to help trendy youth come to grips with the flawed but ultimately manageable establishment.

The mixed bag of topical drama, youth, and good old American tradition in these relevant shows aimed at scoring the TV hat trick of *The Mod Squad:* Bring in the oldsters with exciting all-American action; win praise for presenting topical drama; and capture the youth market with stories the kids could relate to. In this approach, *Headmaster* and *The Interns* were merely indelica-

	7:00	7:30	8:00	8:30	9:00	9:30	10:00	10:30	
M O N	local	THE YOUNG LAWYERS		THE SILENT FORCE	ABC NFL MONDAY NIGHT FOOTBALL (to 12 Midnight)				**ABC**
	local	Gunsmoke		Here's Lucy	Mayberry R.F.D.	Doris Day Show	Carol Burnett Show		**CBS**
	local	Red Skelton Show	Rowan And Martin's Laugh-In		NBC Monday Night At The Movies				**NBC**
					# Bob Hope Show		# NBC Specials		
T U E	local	The Mod Squad			Movie Of The Week		Marcus Welby, M.D.		**ABC**
	local	The Beverly Hillbillies	Green Acres	Hee-Haw		To Rome With Love	CBS News Hour		**CBS**
							60 Minutes		
	local	DON KNOTTS SHOW		Julia	NBC Tuesday Night At The Movies				**NBC**
					# First Tuesday				
W E D	local	The Courtship Of Eddie's Father	Make Room For Granddaddy	Room 222	Johnny Cash Show		DAN AUGUST		**ABC**
	local	STOREFRONT LAWYERS		The Governor And J.J.	Medical Center		Hawaii Five-O		**CBS**
	local	The Men From Shiloh			Kraft Music Hall		FOUR-IN-ONE (McCLOUD; S. F. INT'L AIRPORT; NIGHT GALLERY; THE PSYCHIATRIST)		**NBC**
T H R	local	MATT LINCOLN		Bewitched	BAREFOOT IN THE PARK	THE ODD COUPLE	THE IMMORTAL		**ABC**
	local	Family Affair	Jim Nabors Hour		CBS Thursday Night Movies				**CBS**
	local	FLIP WILSON SHOW		Ironside		NANCY	Dean Martin Show		**NBC**
F R I	local	The Brady Bunch	Nanny And The Professor	THE PARTRIDGE FAMILY	That Girl	Love, American Style	This Is Tom Jones		**ABC**
	local	THE INTERNS		THE HEADMASTER	CBS Friday Night Movies				**CBS**
	local	The High Chaparral		The Name Of The Game			Bracken's World		**NBC**
S A T	local	Let's Make A Deal	The Newlywed Game	Lawrence Welk Show		THE MOST DEADLY GAME		local	**ABC**
	local	Mission: Impossible		My Three Sons	ARNIE	MARY TYLER MOORE SHOW	Mannix		**CBS**
	local	Andy Williams Show		Adam-12	NBC Saturday Night At The Movies				**NBC**
S U N	THE YOUNG REBELS		The FBI		The ABC Sunday Night Movie				**ABC**
	Lassie	Hogan's Heroes	Ed Sullivan Show		Glen Campbell Goodtime Hour		TIM CONWAY HOUR		**CBS**
	Wild Kingdom	The Wonderful World Of Disney		Bill Cosby Show	Bonanza		The Bold Ones (The Doctors; The Lawyers; THE SENATOR)		**NBC**

cies. *Storefront Lawyers*, however, was downright rude and insulting. It epitomized the glaring and obvious contrast between the relevant, realistic world touted in the network ads, and the sugar-coated Neverland in the programs themselves. The series presented Robert Foxworth, Sheila Larkin, and David Arkin as three young pretty white kids from the safe, liberal suburbs who worked for a law firm uptown but who also set up a storefront office in the ghetto ("where the action is") to aid the poor there for free. The hackneyed scripts never ventured beneath the Naugahyde surface of these 100% plastic kids or into anything even resembling the more sordid side of life among the lowly. Instead, the three legal Samaritans remained oblivious to even the hint of evil or a shred of characterization. In the show's opening credits they blissfully skipped hand-in-hand into the halls of justice, accompanied by a sorry excuse for a contemporary rock theme. Though they battled the establishment, the only motivation ever suggested for their actions came from CBS's incessant plugs that presented the members of the trio as "totally committed and completely involved." Or was it "completely committed and totally involved"?

Storefront Lawyers was easily the worst of the relevancy shows though, ironically, many of the problems with the series reflected problems of the 1960s youth movement itself. Both were based on a philosophy that merely bringing together "nice" people with "nice" ideas could solve everything: Powerful, entrenched bogeymen of the establishment would roll over and die and some hip

jargon would topple a decade of fantasy on television. To this end, *Storefront Lawyers* deliberately oversimplified any complex problems and created a sanitized version of the ghetto populated by evil ogres, helpless po' folk, and noble youth. However, CBS was not alone in the pursuit of relevancy, with both NBC and ABC also offering their own exercises in revolutionary fantasy. To varying degrees, though, nearly every entry suffered from the same problems as *Headmaster, The Interns,* and *Storefront Lawyers.*

NBC's two major relevant offerings were segments in rotating series: *The Senator* in *The Bold Ones* and *The Psychiatrist* in *Four-in-One. The Senator,* starring Hal Holbrook as Senator Hays Stowe, was a commendable effort to treat topical and controversial issues that became bogged down in television's mugwump philosophy on most issues: everybody to a degree is guilty, therefore nobody in particular is guilty. Stowe had won his seat by taking a bold and forthright stand against pollution but, once in office, he emerged as a fuzzy-thinking middle-of-the-road befuddled moderate. The stories therefore could not hold together because it was hard to understand why unscrupulous radicals of both the left and right would bother attacking him. Even treatment of issues such as a Kent State-type incident was nothing more than calculated, camouflaged ambiguity.

The Psychiatrist was similar to *The Interns,* presenting a premise that was traditional Hollywood melodrama featuring forced relevant angles that were almost laughable. Roy Thinnes played a young, semi-hip psychiatrist who used controversial new techniques to bring the day's strung-out acid heads to their senses and guide them to the barber shop for that inevitable haircut. As proof of his success, he was assisted by a former patient-junkie, played by Peter Duel. ABC's *Young Rebels* was even sillier. It modestly rewrote American Revolutionary War history as if it were a free-speech revolt at Berkeley. The youthful members of the Yankee Doodle Society (two white, one black, one gal) acted as spies behind the British lines, specializing in sabotage and harassment.

Of all the relevant shows presented that fall, ABC's *Young Lawyers* came closest to reaching the touted goal of dealing with contemporary themes through moderately realistic characters. Though its premise was virtually the same as *Storefront Lawyers,* the scripts avoided the tired murder-arson-dope trilogy and centered solely on the learning pangs of two young barristers trying to deal with people caught in the era's uncertainties. For example, in one episode they fought a malpractice suit filed against a young medical intern who had decided to "get involved" and help an auto accident victim. To add further credibility to the series, the team (one white guy, one black gal) received sound but not condescending advice from their mentor, played by veteran Lee J. Cobb. Overall, the stories were much more believable than the fairy tales usually dished out by the other relevant shows and, in a departure from the typical vast expanse of clichéd California adventureland, the action was set in historic Boston.

Ultimately, though, even *The Young Lawyers* fell victim to the essential deception of the entire television relevancy movement. Though ads for the new shows implied the presentation of strongly pro-radical positions, the networks had no intention of taking bold and forthright stands on controversial issues every week in a time of genuine national division; and certainly not on their entertainment programs. This was the soft white underbelly of TV relevancy. Important social problems and contemporary jargon were simply churned into standard television format drama wrapped in love beads. Stories and issues were stacked in advance so that the establishment, aided by clear-thinking moderates, always won. At heart the establishment was right, though occasionally it needed a slight kick to uncover one or two bad apples. Anti-establishment figures usually had some axe to grind and, even if their points were justified, their methods were all wrong. Consequently, the villains in the stories were inevitably demonic bearded hippies or corrupt, longhaired radicals who were, at best, overzealous reformers. The new breed of hero was the former outsider won over to help the establishment correct its own shortcomings in dealing with overly suspicious communities and individuals. Such characters dressed respectably, worked on the side of justice, and, most important, had gotten that haircut.

There was certainly nothing new about presenting fantasy as reality on television, nor was there anything morally wrong with exploiting news events and popular fads in television entertainment programming. Such policies had been pursued for years in both good and bad shows. In promoting the 1970–71 season, though, network flaks had presented wholly unrealistic claims that their relevant shows were to be truly different from the past in both substance and image, knowing full well that was not to be the case. By promising a new era in television realism after nearly a decade of escapism and fantasy, but then delivering the same old goods, the networks' new shows had to be judged, however harshly, by a different set of rules. By these rules, the half-hearted almost schizophrenic programs of television's relevancy craze were artistic failures.

More important, the structure of the "relevant" programs demonstrated that even with an interest in young adult demographics,

the networks had not decided to alienate the silent majority of older viewers overnight. Grownups were still the bread-and-butter of the Nielsen ratings points, so relevancy had been tempered for establishment consumption. By mid-season, it became clear that, in trying to attract two opposite segments of society, the watered-down relevant programs had failed to excite anyone. The ratings were dismal. In January 1971, ABC dropped its *Young Rebels,* and CBS hurried in face-saving format changes on *Headmaster* and *Storefront Lawyers. Headmaster* became *The New Andy Griffith Show* in which Griffith played a town mayor who was a former sheriff, a carbon copy continuation of his old Mayberry series. The storefront lawyers gave up the ghetto, got haircuts, and moved uptown permanently, becoming *Men at Law.* Under the tutelage of sagacious Devlin McNeil (Gerald S. O'Loughlin), they defended more affluent clients such as innocent collegians under attack from the lawyers for the nasty radicals in the Students for a Free America (a barely concealed copy of the real-life Students for a Democratic Society). Both of these permutations, as well as *The Young Lawyers, The Senator, The Interns,* and *The Psychiatrist,* expired at the end of the season.

Television's loud and sloppy foray into contemporary drama was a total flop. Yet, almost lost amid the ballyhoo of the 1970 fall premieres, there appeared a saner and more realistic solution for the medium's sudden desire to update its own image. In September of 1970, after half a decade of bland sitcoms that became hits, good sitcoms that flopped, and horrible sitcoms that just hung on, CBS introduced a worthy successor to its comedy classics of the past, *The Mary Tyler Moore Show.* The program was the first out and out hit in a new wave of situation comedies that effectively combined more contemporary attitudes and outlooks with the basic elements of the *I Love Lucy, Honeymooners,* and *Dick Van Dyke* schools. These past sitcoms had used good writing, tight central and supporting casts, and the simplest of sets to present memorable, hilarious comedy. To this strong base, *The Mary Tyler Moore Show* added an important new element: The lead character was an intelligent, unmarried career woman who faced humorous complications and situations that real people often faced.

Mary Tyler Moore played Mary Richards, a small-town girl who came to the big city (Minneapolis-St. Paul, not Los Angeles) to make it on her own. She landed a job in a local TV station (WJM) as an associate producer for the evening news, working behind the scenes in the newsroom with producer Lou Grant (Edward Asner), newswriter Murray Slaughter (Gavin MacLeod), and anchorman Ted Baxter (Ted Knight). There she began to build her confidence and skills as a single woman on her own with a responsible job and personal career goals. The mix of characters and personalities in the office, ranging from generally realistic to broad stereotype, balanced almost perfectly and gave the "young working woman" hook the opportunity to catch on. Very quickly viewers accepted both the novel premise and the first rate cast because they combined to produce a very funny show.

Lou Grant and Mary Richards were presented as the two most realistic characters. Mary obviously took her job as newsperson-producer seriously and was very conscious of her professional manner, though she was often a bit too straight, soft-hearted, and trusting for her own good. In some respects, Lou Grant began as the typical blustery sitcom boss who was really soft as Jello inside, but he soon developed into the nearest thing to a real life boss that might be expected in a television comedy. His bravado character was tempered and became a more complex mix of emotions so that he tossed in funny cracks even when he was sad and radiated genuine warmth through his anger. Both Lou and Mary certainly delivered their share of punch lines, but overall they usually carried off

The six main performers of *The Mary Tyler Moore Show*: *(from left, front)* Valerie Harper, Mary Tyler Moore, and Cloris Leachman; *(back)* Ted Knight, Ed Asner, and Gavin MacLeod. *(The Mary Tyler Moore Show © 1970 Twentieth Century Fox Television. All Rights Reserved.)*

their humor as people trying to deal with realistic but confusing situations.

Ted Baxter and Murray Slaughter served as the focus of the more traditional office sitcom barbs. Murray delivered sharp one-liners and putdowns that were primarily directed at Ted, though he departed from these often enough to develop his character beyond the quick-witted wisecracker type in the style of *Dick Van Dyke*'s Buddy Sorrell. Ted, on the other hand, was all stereotype, but a perfectly marvelous stereotype. Only in Jack Cassidy's Jetman role (in the all-too-brief run of *He and She*) had television ever poked fun at itself so openly. In an era that elevated the blow-dried "happy talk" local newscaster to the forefront (making him the rule, not the exception, in the major markets), the self-obsessed Baxter was a wonderful lampoon of the trend. His rich silver hair and deep-voiced resonance barely camouflaged the near vacuum behind his empty grin.

In the program's third season, a new character was added to the office setting, WJM's "Happy Homemaker," Sue Ann Nivens (Betty White), and she provided yet another frontal attack on television's glossy self-image. White, drawing on her background of playing goody-two-shoes characters over the years, portrayed the sweet-talking pure-as-gold "woman's show" star as a forked-tongued dirty old lady who merely used her bill-and-coo voice to mask the venom of her pointed remarks.

Such a corps of performers would have been the envy of any sitcom but, just as *The Dick Van Dyke Show* had been staged as essentially a two-set series (the Petrie home and the office), the

action in Mary Tyler Moore's program was also split between two settings: the office and Mary's bachelorette apartment. At home, two other strong supporting characters, Rhoda and Phyllis, helped to carry a wide range of domestic plots. Rhoda Morgenstern (Valerie Harper) was Mary's upstairs neighbor, a New York City transplant and a fast-talking putdown artist whose barbs were often self-directed. Like Sally Rogers in *Dick Van Dyke* and nearly all other female sidekicks in sitcom history, Rhoda was on the prowl for a husband. Unlike most, though, she was not presented as a de-sexed spinster but as a young, attractive woman who was no dummy. Rhoda was not about to fall for the first clichéd line that came her way and was too intelligent to honestly expect Mr. Right to suddenly walk into her life, but she had not given up hoping, either. Though Mary also went out on dates and vaguely planned on marriage, she was in no hurry. Rhoda looked to Mary as a close friend and confidante (practically a sister) and the two shared their feelings on the hopes and frustrations of single life. Rhoda's sharp wit was frequently directed at the manager of their apartment house, Phyllis Lindstrom (Cloris Leachman). Though Rhoda's character was in the more realistic spirit of Lou and Mary, Phyllis was presented as an effective homebody caricature, the epitome of style conscious egoism, who never hesitated to impose on Mary. She eagerly latched onto the latest trends and, while not really evil, usually acted kind and considerate only when she needed something and could not just take it.

Lou, Murray, Ted, Sue Ann, Rhoda, and Phyllis were just as much *The Mary Tyler Moore Show* as Mary herself and particular episodes sometimes featured a member of this supporting group as the central character, with Mary stepping more to the sidelines. As a true sign of the depth of the individual cast members, it must be noted that all six went on from *The Mary Tyler Moore Show* to star in programs of their own, a feat unmatched by any other sitcom.

Even though the talented cast was the driving force behind the success of *The Mary Tyler Moore Show,* the high level of sophistication in the show's scripts lifted the series above the restrictive confines TV sitcoms were proscribed into during the 1960s. While the writers generally avoided obviously topical issues and fads, they managed to capture the feeling of the 1970s in much the same way as *The Dick Van Dyke Show* had done during the 1960s. The three chief characters—Mary, Lou, and Rhoda—were often given the types of problems that real people of the era faced.

Rhoda was caught in the position of many young women at the time: She never tried to hide the fact that she was talented, aggressive, and certainly just as intelligent as many of the men she went out with (probably more so). Though fully aware of the complications in husband hunting that resulted from such a stance, Rhoda had no intention of changing. When she found her ideal candidate for marriage he would have to accept her as she was or not at all. Over the course of the series, Lou became divorced and, as a chunky, middle-aged man whose children had already grown and left home, he really did not feel like starting to date again. This development added a sensitive edge to his sometimes cantankerous office demeanor because Lou was just as lonely as any former family man, but he did not want to expose his feelings to strangers or in public.

Mary's image as an unmarried career woman with a responsible job other than a secretary or a teacher was a major break from television tradition. She was not a widow, had no children, and was working because she wanted to build her own life and career. While by no means a diatribe on women's liberation, the program presented, without fanfare, women as being capable of interests beyond housework, marriage, and crazy sitcom schemes. As a true professional, Mary prized her own honesty and integrity very highly. In one episode she even went to jail in order to protect a news source.

Unlike the heavy-handed plots of the flopped relevancy dramas, these serious, sometimes even topical, aspects of *The Mary Tyler Moore Show* never stood out as preachy or phony, but were instead quietly incorporated into the funny scripts and characters, presenting a reality that was tempered by a light and gentle touch that could render it painless, but not forgotten. From the very first episode, the series displayed exceptional production skill and care that set it apart from its competition.

The Mary Tyler Moore Show provided exactly what CBS president Bob Wood had wanted: a new hit show in the traditional CBS groove (a thirty-minute sitcom) that also pulled the network from its old rural rut into new settings that were right for the new decade. Working hand-in-hand with newly chosen program chief Fred Silverman, Wood had made it clear his renovation plans for CBS were serious, including not only a search for new hits, but also the display of new attitudes and strategies in the process of network scheduling as well. In a move considered nothing short of blasphemy for an era that still chiseled network fall schedules in stone in the early spring, Wood approved Silverman's last-minute schedule changes in July 1970, less than six weeks before the season premieres. This gave Silverman the opportunity to display his later renowned talent for counter-programming and thematic flow, and the new *Mary Tyler Moore Show* emerged with a better time slot than originally planned. *The Beverly Hillbillies* and *Green Acres* were moved to Tuesday, logically preceding *Hee-Haw,* and *Mary Tyler Moore* was shifted to Saturday, joining the company of the more sophisticated *Mission: Impossible, Mannix,* and another new "urban" sitcom, *Arnie* (starring Herschel Bernardi). There was more to come. In January 1971, the second major program component in Wood's modernization drive arrived, *All in the Family.*

For three years, filmmakers Norman Lear and Bud Yorkin had been trying to sell the networks an American version of the BBC hit, *Till Death Us Do Part.* The British series had been on since 1966, offering an irreverent and boisterous view of a working class family that hinged on a crafty old bigot who dominated his wife and daughter while constantly arguing with his liberal son-in-law. In February 1968, Yorkin and Lear produced a pilot for CBS based on *Till Death Us Do Part,* but CBS turned them down when some moderately innovative domestic sitcoms bombed. Even with the success of the Smothers Brothers and *Laugh-In,* the concept of a lovable bigot tossing off racial epithets and political insults proved too much for the old brass at CBS. In the fall of 1968, Yorkin and Lear approached ABC with a second pilot for the proposed series, called "Justice for All," starring Carroll O'Connor and Jean Stapleton. ABC liked it and scheduled it for January 1969, but then got cold feet and postponed the series to the fall of 1969. The network at last gave up the idea completely, labeling it too controversial. Sensing failure at marketing the concept as a television series, the two producers prepared to turn it into a film instead but, at the last minute, CBS, under new management, extended some positive feelers. In March 1970, a revised pilot, "Those Were the Days," was secretly tested on a random audience at the CBS studios in New York City. The reaction was favorable, if somewhat guarded. In July 1970, in spite of considerable negative pressure from within the CBS hierarchy, network president Bob Wood scheduled the series, renamed *All in the Family,* to premiere in January 1971. He said in a press release, "It's time to poke fun at ourselves."

Nonetheless, CBS was quite uncertain how to treat *All in the Family.* Was it satire? Comedy? Social comment? Fearful of a public outcry similar to the one that followed the still not forgotten *Turn-On,* CBS gave the series practically no publicity. It was stuck in a perverse time slot, directly following *Hee-Haw* but right before *60 Minutes.* In either case, pro or con, the network expected a huge reaction the night of the show's debut (January 12, 1971). It never came. Only a few calls were received and most of them were favorable. With so little fanfare, the first ratings for *All in the Family* were naturally quite low.

TV critics and the general public were as confused as the network by the program, uncertain how to react because, in many ways, *All in the Family* was unlike anything Americans had ever

With all his faults, Archie Bunker (Carroll O'Connor) never became totally unbearable and could even be kind and considerate, especially to his wife, Edith (Jean Stapleton). *(Sony Pictures Television)*

September 17, 1970

The Flip Wilson Show. (NBC). Young black comic Flip Wilson, for years a frequent guest on variety and talk shows, receives his own comedy-variety hour. Armed with such characterizations as the sassy Geraldine Jones and the hustling Rev. Leroy (from the Church of What's Happenin' Now), Wilson turns his new program into an immediate top ten smash.

September 21, 1970

ABC's NFL Monday Night Football. (ABC). Roone Arledge brings professional football back to prime time after nearly two decades. The Cleveland Browns beat "Broadway" Joe Namath and the New York Jets 31 to 21 in Cleveland. Howard Cosell and Keith Jackson do play-by-play while "Dandy" Don Meredith supplies color.

September 24, 1970

The Odd Couple. (ABC). After successful treatments as a hit Broadway play and a feature film, Neil Simon's story of two divorced men sharing an apartment in New York City becomes a hit sitcom for ABC. Under producer Garry Marshall, the show displays consistently good writing and outstanding character acting, led by Tony Randall as the ultra-clean Felix Unger and Jack Klugman as the incurably sloppy Oscar Madison.

October 5, 1970

PBS, the Public Broadcasting System, takes over the non-commercial functions of NET, National Educational Television. New York's WNDT becomes WNET.

December 7, 1970

After defecting from CBS, Harry Reasoner replaces Frank Reynolds as co-anchor of ABC's nightly news, teaming up with Howard K. Smith.

January 1, 1971

A federally imposed ban on television cigarette ads goes into effect.

---

seen before. It successfully transferred the spice and life of the controversial British original to an American setting. Archie Bunker (O'Connor) was a "hardhat" racist who disdainfully referred to "Yids, Polacks, Spades, and Spics," with his only comeuppance being the protests of his long-haired son-in-law, Mike (Rob Reiner, son of Carl), derisively nicknamed "Meathead" by Archie. The program also dealt with sex, including both blatant verbal references and, for a change, implications of physical activity. Archie and his wife, Edith (Stapleton), who he referred to as "Dingbat," were shown walking in on their daughter, Gloria (Sally Struthers), and her husband, Mike, just as the two were clearly on the way up to bed to make love. Archie admonished the mini-skirted Gloria, "When you sit down in that thing, the mystery is ended." Because Mike and Gloria lived with Archie and Edith, such ideological and theological clashes were frequent and inevitable. How were viewers to take the racial and sexual references? Blacks in the media were openly split on the *All in the Family* question. Tony Brown, producer of public television's *Black Journal,* called it "shocking and racist," while Loretta Long, Susan the schoolteacher on *Sesame Street,* said it was "unoffensive and realistic," and Pamela Haynes of the black-oriented *Los Angeles Sentinel* said, "His rantings serve a purpose."

The truth dawned slowly. *All in the Family* was not racist, but it

was not *The Life of Riley,* either. It was a well-written, superbly acted contemporary farce that painted broad stereotyped characters in the best *I Love Lucy* tradition. The difference was that the producers based the stereotypes on real down-to-earth personalities who argued about topics that real people argued about, using words and phrases real people used. After decades of TV shows populated exclusively with stars who were *very* nice, confronting a central character who was not completely lovable came as a shock to many Americans. The Archie Bunker character, in fact, often was not lovable at all. Nonetheless, the producers of *All in the Family* did not allow Archie to become totally unbearable, operating under the assumption that everybody has his reasons. He might have been a reactionary stick-in-the-mud spouting a perverse sort of malapropism, but there was another part of him that was genuinely likable. Archie was an honestly simple man who talked about his bigotry but rarely did anything else with it. What's more, it soon became clear that Archie never won the arguments. He might remain titular king of his castle (retaining sole rights to his favorite easy chair), but his world of male-WASP domination, simple verities, and America-first-ism was crumbling all about him. Archie fumed and sputtered but always had to concede to the inevitable changes thrust before him by his liberal son-in-law, his feminist daughter, and his black neighbors.

The most amazing aspect of *All in the Family* was that its architects succeeded at what the relevancy show producers had seemed to be trying to do: explaining new attitudes in the country to older Americans. TV reviewers were flabbergasted, though, to see such attempts at social realism in the least likely of all formats for national controversy: the television sitcom. The *Mary Tyler Moore* formula had been taken one step further with current issues injected into the very funny, well-written scripts. The combination worked because the producers never forgot the prime rule of showmanship: keep the audience entertained. By carefully mixing the humor and politics, *All in the Family* avoided heavy-handed preaching and became an almost subliminal national self-examination. Producer Norman Lear explained the program's approach, saying, "[*All in the Family*] holds a mirror up to our prejudices ... We laugh now, swallowing just the littlest bit of truth about ourselves, and it sits there for the unconscious to toss about later."

Though *All in the Family's* underlying premise and lively flavor came from its British roots, the show also drew on important American sitcom basics previously used in series such as *The Honeymooners.* The program was essentially a one-set show, with the action taking place in the Bunker living room (with occasional huddles in the kitchen). In a radical departure from then-current TV scripture, *All in the Family* returned to the concept of recording its episodes before a live audience, just as in *The Honeymooners.* The laughs heard at home were actual laughter by live human beings watching the performance as it was being videotaped. This literal liveliness, combined with the Kramden-like working class atmosphere and the inclusion of topical references, served to create a refreshing sense of reality and to make *All in the Family* an actual revolution in American TV. Yet, it was also a revival (in the literal sense of the word) bringing back the basics that had made previous classics so memorable and, at the same time, updating the content for modern consumption.

All in the Family had a very slow start and, like most out of the ordinary TV shows, had to build an audience gradually. By mid-February it sneaked into the top thirty. The first set of episodes ended in March and Silverman wisely chose to begin a full cycle of reruns immediately in order to hook the growing number of new viewers that had only discovered the series in the previous month. It was during this rerun cycle that the show took off. By late May, just before it went off for the summer, *All in the Family* hit number one. The expected viewer reaction to the innovative, controversial program had developed, but the show had also become a big hit. Its characters were accepted and absorbed into everyday language, even appearing in New York City graffiti. "Archie Bunker for President" somebody scrawled on a subway wall, to which another wit added, "He is."

All in the Family marked a turning point in American television programming and it appeared at a time of major change throughout the industry in both commercial and noncommercial broadcasting. In October 1970, the noncommercial television network structure was reorganized, changing NET into PBS, the Public Broadcasting System. More important, public television continued to move away from original domestic productions, increasing its reliance on imports from Britain. That fall, PBS presented the thirteen-week BBC series, *Civilisation,* hosted by Kenneth Clark and funded by Xerox. The program took viewers on a world-wide tour of Western culture tracing its development over 400 years by focusing on great works of art and architecture. In January, *Masterpiece Theater* picked up where *The Forsyte Saga* left off and offered British-made historical dramas every Sunday night. As delightful as these British imports were, they began to spark complaints that PBS was showing signs of practically becoming a BBC subsidiary. Though British programs meant instant class they also discouraged efforts at homegrown productions. In the winter, PBS presented its last major domestic program for years to come, *The Great American Dream Machine,* hosted by the corpulent Marshall Efron. *Dream Machine* was similar to *PBL,* but humor and satire were added to the "straight" segments (such as a report on FBI-paid provocateurs in radical groups) and, under Efron's guidance, the show reached great heights of wit and irreverence. Levity had always been noticeably absent on public television and this infusion of humor was welcomed by many, though it made the series unpopular with both the Nixon administration and Congress. Poking fun at commercials for frozen pies and Kool-Aid was all right but, when guests such as Woody Allen began ribbing Henry Kissinger, and regular contributor Andy Rooney parodied Nixon's volunteer Army proposal, *Dream Machine* became a walking target for the government. It was shot down in mid-1972. Efron departed with a stinging blast at PBS and New York's WNET, calling them, "A tight club of relatively rich guys, putting cameras on the poor and asking the middle class for money. What do they say when the middle class asks what channel 13 [WNET] is doing for them? 'We've got some wonderful acquisitions from the BBC!'"

The commercial networks were also happy to soak up the prestige from British imports. In the summer of 1971, CBS took the unusual step of slotting the six-part British miniseries, *The Six Wives of Henry VIII,* into its Sunday night schedule. It was the only program to eventually air on *Masterpiece Theater* that first found its way to America through a commercial network. NBC previewed and promoted the *Civilisation* series when it ran on PBS in the fall of 1970. At the same time, the network also gave the British limited run series concept a thorough testing in its *Four-in-One* program from Universal Studios. Unlike *The Bold Ones,* in which three separate series alternated in the same time slot, *Four-in-One* ran all six episodes of each series before moving on to the next. This was just the style adopted by *Masterpiece Theater* in its presentations.

British limited-run series were usually just that: one premise carried over a set number of episodes and then ended. *Four-in-One* was set up as an extended pilot program for testing new series ideas in prime time against regular shows. At the time, studio pilots were usually aired as single episodes stuck into the movie

nights during the spring lull and so rarely faced any strong competition. *Four-in-One* provided a more challenging but realistic face-off. Two of the series failed their tryouts, the silly relevancy of *The Psychiatrist* and the "Airport"-type melodrama of *San Francisco International Airport* (starring Lloyd Bridges and Clu Gulager). *Night Gallery,* a watered down version of *The Twilight Zone,* caught on and became a regular series in 1971 that lasted two seasons. Rod Serling was the host and occasional writer, though he actually had very little control over the choice of material used. The most successful of the miniseries was *McCloud,* starring Dennis Weaver as a Western sheriff somehow assigned to the New York City police force. This series survived for six years, though always remaining a segment in some permutation of *Four-in-One.* Beginning in the 1971–72 season, *Four-in-One* changed to the rotating segment style of *The Bold Ones* and was retitled *The NBC Mystery Movie.*

Though the testing of British concepts from *All in the Family* to miniseries signaled the possibility of important new developments in programs and programming, the government was responsible for the most dramatic changes facing broadcasters. In early 1970, after pressure from Congress, the networks accepted a plan to ban all TV cigarette advertisements. Beginning January 1, 1971, the largest single source of revenue in broadcasting was cut off and television profits were squeezed. To further complicate the situation, a 1970 FCC ruling was put into effect and, starting in the fall of

---

April 19, 1971

National Public Radio (NPR), a national non-commercial radio network set up by the Corporation for Public Broadcasting, begins with live coverage of a U.S. Senate committee hearing on the Vietnam War. Two weeks later, on May 3, *All Things Considered,* a daily news and features program, becomes the network's first hit. In the beginning, NPR has ninety affiliates in thirty-six states.

June 6, 1971

After twenty-three years of "really big shows," Ed Sullivan is axed. Guests on the final program: Sid Caesar, Carol Channing, Robert Klein, and Gladys Knight and the Pips. "Say goodnight, Eddie."

July 26, 1971

Apollo 15, America's fourth lunar landing mission, sends back the first color television signals from space, using the CBS "spinning disk" system the FCC discarded eighteen years before.

August 16, 1971

John Chancellor becomes the sole anchor on *NBC Nightly News* as Frank McGee leaves the show to replace Hugh Downs on *Today* while David Brinkley is reduced to the post of commentator.

August 29, 1971

After one final season on NBC, Red Skelton ends eighteen years of network television, wishing all "Good health, good life, and may God bless. Goodnight."

September 4, 1971

ABC pulls the plug on Lawrence Welk's bubble machine. The sixteen-year television veteran has the last laugh, though, as his program shifts effortlessly into syndication, continuing with new episodes for another eleven years on a strong line-up of local stations.

1971, the networks were required to slice thirty minutes from prime time each night of the week.

Since the mid-1950s, the FCC had conducted hearings on ways to decrease, if not eliminate, the networks' legal and financial control over programs. Over the years, the networks had voluntarily cut back on the degree of such lucrative control temporarily in order to mollify the FCC, though they returned to near total control as soon as it seemed the commission would not notice. In March 1965, the FCC drafted a proposed rule that would have limited the networks to 50% control of their prime time schedule, and also virtually banned their profits from domestic and foreign syndication of old shows. This 50–50 proposal was roundly criticized by the networks and bandied about for five years until, in May of 1970, the FCC embraced compromise proposals suggested by Westinghouse's Group W stations and issued a series of rules that boldly reshaped the TV business landscape. One set of rules, the Financial Interest and Syndication Rules ("Fin-Syn" rules) nearly eliminated network profit from the rerun syndication of programs. Another new rule flatly limited to three hours the amount of prime time broadcasting a network could do in one evening. This rule was labeled the "access rule" because it proposed to grant access to the airwaves to independent producers who would be able to go directly to the affiliates to slot their programs in what had previously been network prime time.

The networks, naturally, were aghast at the new FCC rules and CBS filed suit to block the access rule. The Justice Department and the courts, however, upheld the FCC, thus giving legal sanction to the first major inroad in direct governmental control of programming in television history. The FCC's aim, greater access, was quite commendable and the commission no doubt believed the access rule served a wholesome purpose, but the fact was that the rule represented direct governmental control of programming, something the FCC was specifically forbidden to engage in by law. With the precedent set, it was feared that additional interference could only follow.

The Fin-Syn rules did not fully go into effect until 1973, but then they wound up cutting off one formerly significant source of network revenue. CBS, for example, was forced in 1973 to spin off its successful TV syndication division, which took the new name

Viacom International. The money that had previously rolled in from the reruns of series such as *I Love Lucy* and *The Andy Griffith Show* now went to the independent Viacom company, not to CBS. In time, it was Viacom rather than CBS that became one of the first to invest significantly in the developing field of cable TV.

On the other hand, the FCC's new access rule was set to go into effect in the fall of 1971. Faced with the reality of having to cut three and one-half hours of prime time each week, the networks tried to make the best of it. ABC, which had always had more than its share of dead weight, found the access rule a godsend and in, January 1971, jumped the gun by adding two and one-half hours to the half-hour of prime time it already ceded to the local affiliates each week. Freed of the albatross of some of its losers, including remnants of the relevant cycle (*Young Rebels*) and a few flopped crime shows (*Silent Force* and *Most Deadly Game*), ABC's ratings shot up and, in mid-January, the network won one week of the ratings war. It was ABC's first such victory in more than six years.

The second season surge by ABC further tightened the network competition. CBS had been unable to break away from the incessant challenge by NBC and the two had spent the season locked in a see-saw ratings battle. At the end of the 1970–71 season, CBS and NBC were in a dead heat, with both claiming victory. To the CBS leadership, it was clear that more drastic measures had to be taken to ensure supremacy. With the success of two new "urban" sitcoms, president Wood swallowed hard and in one swoop canceled eight stalwarts of the CBS zodiac: *The Ed Sullivan Show* (23 years), *Lassie* (17 years), *Mayberry RFD* (11 years), *The Beverly Hillbillies* (9 years), Jim Nabors (5 years as Gomer Pyle, 2 years as a variety host), *Hogan's Heroes* and *Green Acres* (6 years each), and *Hee-Haw* (2 years). Many of these shows were still very successful but some slots had to be cleared and this was as good a time as any to complete Wood's previously stated plan to steer CBS away from the oldster-yokel image. Wood's purge of so many net vets was the symbolic confirmation that, with the public's acceptance of new shows such as *Mary Tyler Moore* and *All in the Family,* the government's forced ban on cigarette commercials, and the appearance of the access rule, 1971 would mark a seismic shift in the equilibrium of American television.

31. Not Just Another Pretty Face

ON SEPTEMBER 13, 1971, PRIME TIME SHRUNK. The FCC's access rule had taken effect and the nightly schedules of all three networks reflected a shakeup far greater than the usual fall season reorganization. The new rules stipulated that the networks could not present more than three hours of prime time fare between 7:00 P.M. and 11:00 P.M. However, the FCC had not specified which three of the four available hours should be used, leaving the choice to the networks themselves. As the traditional domain of news shows (except on Sunday), the 7:00–7:30 P.M. slot was sacrosanct, so the network programmers had to decide between a prime time that would run 7:30–10:30 P.M. or 8:00–11:00 P.M. Though such a minor shift might have seemed a trivial difference at first, the choice was vitally important because it would determine the tone of network schedules not only for the 1971–72 season but for many seasons to come. If 7:30–10:30 P.M. were selected as prime time, the networks would place even more emphasis on kiddie-oriented productions, and the independent producers would have to develop adult material to fill the resulting late night access time (10:30–11:00 P.M.). The situation would be reversed with 8:00–11:00 P.M. as prime time; the networks would lose a half-hour of kidvid and the earlier access time could be filled with less somber fare such as frothy game shows.

Throughout the spring of 1971, the programming chiefs at CBS, NBC, and ABC engaged in a perverse form of high-level "chicken," using compliance with the access rule as a means to psyche out their competitors and to gain some slight advantage in what promised to be a tight ratings battle in the fall. At first, NBC and ABC seemed to be set on an 8:00–11:00 P.M. prime time so CBS, seeing an irresistible chance for a head start on its competitors, said it would opt for a 7:30 P.M. starting time in which it would schedule sixty-minute shows to kick off every evening. Such a move would have forced the other two to follow suit and change their schedules in order to prevent CBS from nailing down a large audience at the start of each night's viewing. Rumors, tentative plans, and revised proposals filled the air as the networks jockeyed back and forth for two months. Then CBS, which said it really favored the choice of the 8:00–11:00 P.M. slot all along but had suggested 7:30 P.M. only out of competitive zeal, asked the FCC to "suggest" that the networks consider 8:00 P.M. as the start of prime time. The commission went along, issued the proposal, and all three quickly complied. This did not end the pre-fall wrangling, however.

NBC applied for and received a waiver of the access rule so that it could continue sending out three and one-half hours of programming every Sunday night. This exception was granted so that *The Wonderful World of Disney* could continue to provide high quality family entertainment at its usual time. The FCC agreed that *Disney* deserved special treatment, though as penance NBC agreed to cut an extra half-hour from its Friday night schedule. ABC applied for and received a similar waiver for Tuesday night, based on the convoluted reasoning that because Tuesday was its strongest night, cutting part of it out would render the network impotent. In return for an untouched Tuesday line-up, ABC gave up another half-hour on Monday.

Following these Byzantine negotiations, which placed an inauspicious reliance on federal umpiring and even invited governmental judgments on program quality, the fall schedules were set. The new boundaries for prime time were from 8:00 P.M. to 11:00 P.M. Wednesday through Saturday and on Monday, and from 7:30 P.M. to 11:00 P.M. (with appropriate gaps) on Sunday and Tuesday. In one final exercise of network brinkmanship, CBS's chief programmer, Fred Silverman, upset the networks' plans again in August, just before the start of the season, by announcing another of his infamous last-minute schedule shifts. *All in the Family,* which had done well in an abominable slot the previous winter, was to be tucked away at 10:30 P.M. Monday, against an NBC movie and ABC's pro football coverage. Playing his trump card, Silverman shifted the proto-hit to the lead-off slot on Saturday night, against very weak competition, in the hope that it would help build Saturday into a CBS sitcom blockbuster night. It worked. *All in the Family* quickly returned to the number one slot in the Nielsen ratings, becoming a solid fall smash and not just a spring fad hit.

Though the boundaries of prime time, and therefore access time, had been established, the question of just what would fill the newly liberated slots was still left up in the air. In announcing the access rule, the FCC had conjured up visions of locally produced public affairs shows, programs offering something nice and wholesome for the kiddies (perhaps a commercial version of *Sesame Street*), and even independently produced serious drama that the networks would not dare touch. Instead, there were game shows. Lots of game shows. Old game shows. Syndicated game shows. Cheap game shows.

Actually, game show producers had begun sliding into syndication five years earlier as they found prime time on the networks, for the most part, closed to them. In September 1965, *Truth or Consequences,* a veteran of both daytime and nighttime network

Day		7:00	7:30	8:00	8:30	9:00	9:30	10:00	10:30	
M O N		local		Nanny And The Professor	local	ABC NFL Monday Night Football (to 12 Midnight)				**ABC**
		local		Gunsmoke		Here's Lucy	Doris Day Show	My Three Sons	Arnie	**CBS**
		local		Rowan And Martin's Laugh-In		NBC Monday Night At The Movies				**NBC**
T U E		local	The Mod Squad			Movie Of The Week		Marcus Welby, M.D.		**ABC**
		local	Glen Campbell Goodtime Hour			Hawaii Five-O	CANNON		local	**CBS**
		local	Ironside			SARGE	THE FUNNY SIDE		local	**NBC**
W E D		local		Bewitched	The Courtship Of Eddie's Father	The Smith Family	SHIRLEY'S WORLD	THE MAN AND THE CITY		**ABC**
		local		Carol Burnett Show		Medical Center		Mannix		**CBS**
		local		Adam-12	NBC Mystery Movie (McCloud; COLUMBO; McMILLAN AND WIFE)			Night Gallery		**NBC**
T H R		local		Alias Smith And Jones		LONGSTREET		OWEN MARSHALL, COUNSELOR AT LAW		**ABC**
		local		BEARCATS		CBS Thursday Night Movies / # 60 Minutes		# CBS News Hour		**CBS**
		local		Flip Wilson Show		NICHOLS		Dean Martin Show		**NBC**
F R I		local		The Brady Bunch	The Partridge Family	Room 222	The Odd Couple	Love, American Style		**ABC**
		local		CHICAGO TEDDY BEARS	O'HARA, U.S. TREASURY		THE NEW CBS FRIDAY NIGHT MOVIES			**CBS**
		local		THE D.A.	NBC World Premiere Movie / # Chronolog				local	**NBC**
S A T		local		GETTING TOGETHER	MOVIE OF THE WEEKEND			THE PERSUADERS		**ABC**
		local		All In The Family	FUNNY FACE	NEW DICK VAN DYKE SHOW	Mary Tyler Moore Show	Mission: Impossible		**CBS**
		local		THE PARTNERS	THE GOOD LIFE	NBC Saturday Night At The Movies				**NBC**
S U N		local	The FBI			The ABC Sunday Night Movie				**ABC**
		local	CBS Sunday Night Movies			CADE'S COUNTY		local		**CBS**
		local	The Wonderful World Of Disney	JIMMY STEWART SHOW	Bonanza / # Bob Hope Show		The Bold Ones (The Doctors; The Lawyers)			**NBC**

TV runs, was booted from NBC. One year later, the producers turned down an offer from ABC to revive the show and instead decided to return the program to the air by syndicating new episodes to local stations throughout the country. Most of these stations were not affiliated with a network, had the time to fill, and were more than happy to broadcast new, first run-episodes of a proven hit in place of their usual diet of reruns of old network series. *Truth or Consequences* was soon back in the groove, reuniting long-lost sisters and the like on a jerry-rigged chain of stations throughout the country. Other former network quizzers such as *What's My Line* (fall 1968), *Beat the Clock* and *To Tell the Truth* (September 1969), and *This Is Your Life* (January 1971) followed the lead of *Truth or Consequences* and were resurrected, usually with the word "new" stuck in front of the old title. The appearance of access time in the fall of 1971 opened new vistas for the syndicators as hundreds of network affiliates searched for programs to plug the new gaping holes in their schedules. To serve the expanding market, *Let's Make a Deal* and *Hollywood Squares,* still enjoying successful daytime network runs, joined the fray and began producing additional episodes for evening syndication.

For the most part, local stations chose the syndicated game shows to fill the Monday through Friday access slots. Other material was available such as new syndicated episodes of former network series including *Lassie, Lawrence Welk, Wild Kingdom,* and *Hee-Haw,* but these did not offer the quick, cheap solution to the weeknight program gap that the quizzes provided and so were usually scheduled for the weekends. Nonetheless, as shows that had been dumped by the networks merely for appealing to the wrong audience (either too rural or too old) they were eventually picked up because, like the quiz shows, they supplied familiar entertainment. (*Hee-Haw,* in fact, thrived in syndication.) Completely new shows, however, faced an almost insurmountable barrier. Group W, which had pressed the concept of local access with the FCC in the first place, offered a number of its own new entertainment shows in syndication including the satirical *David Frost Revue* and *The Smothers' Organic Prime Time Space Ride,* only to see them die. These programs required larger budgets which made them more expensive to the locals. Consequently, neither the Frost program nor the Smothers show was ever ordered by enough stations to justify the costs involved and both ceased production by the end of the year. More important, they could not compete for a mass audience with the plebian appeal of the ever-resilient game show format. With the broadcast day largely filled with network programs, the local stations were not about to sacrifice a potentially lucrative new local time period for material that might not turn a maximum profit. They were even less receptive to innovative concepts than the three networks, a commercial reality that had escaped the FCC's planners. Creative high-quality television might emerge in the long run from the FCC's access rule, but in the short run it just brought more junk.

While the individual stations were filling local access time with game shows, the networks were filling prime time with gumshoes. The most recent movement against television sex and violence had brought to the forefront the less violent figures of doctors, lawyers, and legislators who could act as cop surrogates until the wave of public and governmental pressure lost momentum. While two new Marcus Welby clones did turn up in the fall of 1971, the heat from Washington had sufficiently abated to allow real cops and private eyes to make a comeback. They still avoided violence as much as possible, though, with watered-down settings either in traditional Jack Webb-produced sagas or in equally nonviolent gimmick series featuring a new wave of inside-outsiders.

The Welby imitations came from the good doctor's own executive producer, David Victor, who adapted the soapy but successful doctor format twice, emerging with one failure, *Man and the City,* and one success, *Owen Marshall: Counselor at Law.* The pilot episode for *Man and the City* cast Anthony Quinn as the mayor of a medium-sized Southwest desert city in a gritty setting that contained innovative touches of reality as part of the mayor's life: a tacky office, an estranged wife, and a devil's advocate for an aide. Once the regular series began, however, the unique desert feel and realistic setting were eliminated and the aseptic Welby world of spiffy offices and beautiful people was substituted instead. Quinn, one of the best tough guy actors of the era, ended up fighting soapy emotional causes such as the right of deaf parents to adopt a child who could hear. As a result, the program became merely a lame attempt to create a governmental *Father Knows Best* with pat answers and silly caricatures. *Owen Marshall: Counselor at Law,* with Arthur Hill as a widower-solicitor, was far more successful. Like Welby, Marshall was an idealized professional who lived in a fancy town and who dealt with problems of the upper middle class, assisted by such gorgeous "hunks" in the supporting cast as Lee Majors and David Soul. The series was awash in bathos as it joined its companion professions in bringing topics previously considered "for soaps only" into prime time. In contrast to the others, though, *Owen Marshall* sometimes attempted a more evenhanded treatment of its subjects, such as lesbianism.

The new cops and detectives dispensed with such indulgences and resumed the clear-cut direct pursuit of justice in the never-ending war against crime, albeit still without the physical gusto of the past. Jack Webb's two new entries for the fall continued to follow his standard nonviolent format, emphasizing tight-lipped personalities and the mechanics of crime detection, but neither *The D.A.* nor *O'Hara, U.S. Treasury* proved successful. In an unusual move, Webb used two celebrities that were known for exuding emotion on the screen in the series (Robert Conrad in *The D.A.* and David Janssen in *O'Hara*), but their animated character traits put them in direct conflict with the basis of Webb's unyielding dour format. Consequently, in both shows, the lead character seemed to be visibly straining against the role of tight-lipped hero. Neither program survived the season. Webb was much more successful with a mid-season replacement, *Emergency,* which returned to his standard character types while increasing the instances of urban style visual action. In fact, *Emergency* could be considered the perfect Jack Webb program, taking his philosophy of routine, but real-life, crime and crime detection and stretching it to the limit. For one hour each week, a succession of unrelated gas explosions, helicopter crashes, arson blazes, bomb threats, and even mundane car crashes bombarded the viewer. It resembled nothing so much as a sixty-minute compilation of short film clips from the very visual disasters local television news directors inevitably featured in their nightly news programs. The show's premise tying the events together was simple: A squad of paramedics from the Los

Angeles fire department's rescue division was dispatched to aid the victims, and in each show they drove from disaster to disaster. As with all Jack Webb productions, interspersed in this mayhem were a few moments of everyday personal conversation among the hard-working public servants (including paramedic regulars Robert Fuller, Bobby Troup, Julie London, Kevin Tighe, and Randolph Mantooth). Though the personalities of the paramedics were usually lost in the deadly inferno of disasters each week, *Emergency* was generally well done, entertaining, and its success in the spring of 1972 began to put the "action" back into crime adventure shows. The program also added immeasurably to the image of Los Angeles as the setting of every horrendous natural or manmade cataclysm ever conceived.

The networks' attempts to be hip the previous season had proven an abysmal failure, so no true outsiders turned up among the new crop of law enforcers in 1971. Instead, there was a collection of characters more acceptable to TV viewers; characters only slightly out-of-synch with mainstream society, usually personified as loner cops. Lone guns had thrived in the 1950s (Martin Kane, Peter Gunn, Paladin) but the advent of *77 Sunset Strip* signaled the advance of a more conformist troika-type system. For a decade, law enforcers worked in well-polished teams, sometimes borrowing from the medical format of a young man and his veteran mentor. The success of *Mannix* in the late 1960s began to bring the loner back into vogue and, in the fall of 1971, more than a half dozen such law enforcers appeared. Following in the footpath of the TV Westerns of the late 1950s, many of the new cop shows seemed almost laughable in their desperate search for attractive gimmick characters. George Kennedy played a policeman turned activist-priest on *Sarge;* James Garner was a cowardly sheriff in the Old West on *Nichols;* and James Franciscus was a blind crusading insurance investigator on *Longstreet.* Several other programs with equally gimmicky characters, though, managed to catch on with viewers and develop into finely crafted adventure series. *Cannon* and the three rotating segments of *The NBC Mystery Movie* (*McCloud, McMillan and Wife,* and *Columbo*) had slightly stronger setups which allowed a wider set of story lines, better scripts, and more effective humor. They could present touches of reality within the ever present fantasy world of television lawmen. At heart, these series were identical in purpose to *Nichols* or *Longstreet,* only they happened to be more successful in overall execution and ratings.

McCloud (a holdover from the previous season's segments of *The NBC Mystery Movie,* then called *Four-in-One)* featured Dennis Weaver as a straight-talking, horse-riding marshal from New Mexico attached to the New York City police force. By using his Western sagacity and common-sense knowledge of people, McCloud regularly broke cases that stumped the locals, thereby exasperating yet amazing his Manhattan precinct chief, played by J. D. Cannon. Weaver was already familiar to viewers as a Western hero from his long stint as Chester, the sidekick in *Gunsmoke,* so he brought some credibility to the task of showing up the smart aleck city bureaucrats (always an appealing notion to beleaguered urban dwellers). Astride his horse and wearing a cowboy hat, McCloud was a literal outsider to the urban New York setting, but his shrewd perception of people's motivations made him a law enforcement insider to be reckoned with. The program thus emerged as a very clever mix of Western and cop formats.

Another segment in *The NBC Mystery Movie* slot, *McMillan and Wife,* drew on the old *Mr. and Mrs. North* stories for inspiration. The series presented a pleasant combination of mystery, humor, and police action by the unusual team of Stu McMillan (Rock Hudson), the police commissioner of San Francisco, and his

In the 1968 made-for-TV movie "Prescription: Murder," Peter Falk *(left)* first portrayed Lieutenant Columbo. Gene Barry played Dr. Roy Flemming, a suave psychiatrist who murdered his wife. *(Courtesy of Universal Studios Licensing, LLLP)*

wife, Sally (Susan Saint James). Saint James transferred her wisecracking character from *Name of the Game* to the new setting, mixing her domestic detective work with lighthearted household antics, usually planned with the couple's busybody housekeeper, played by Nancy Walker. Hudson's McMillan was also down-to-earth and, even though he was the top cop in San Francisco (about as "inside" as possible), he inevitably took to the streets himself in the best loner cop tradition. He and his wife generally discovered and solved most cases themselves with only nominal help from the San Francisco police department, usually represented by McMillan's good-natured aide, Sergeant Enright (John Schuck). *McMillan and Wife*'s emphasis on likable characters and humor was a carefully planned technique used by each of the successful gimmick series. It allowed them to deemphasize violence and also to stand apart from the more traditional police shows which took themselves so seriously in the war against crime.

Still, McCloud and McMillan and his wife were only slight deviations from traditional crime fighters compared to the unlikely characters of Cannon and Columbo, the season's biggest (and sloppiest) successes. *Cannon* brought to the forefront the long-deserving William Conrad, whose rich deep voice had served him well in radio (playing Marshal Dillon in the radio version of *Gunsmoke*) and as a voice-over announcer for television (as in Quinn Martin's *The Fugitive*), but whose stout appearance relegated him to playing criminal heavies on camera. As detective Frank Cannon, Conrad starred in a new series by Quinn Martin that broke two unwritten rules about television heroes: Cannon was fat and he was old. Obviously pushing fifty (if he had not already pushed it over), Cannon could never win the hearts of the much-sought-after female audience in the same way as the svelte heroes portrayed by stars such as Craig Stevens, Efrem Zimbalist, Jr., Dennis Weaver, and Rock Hudson. With his heavy gait, Cannon was also not quite the ideal candidate for a frenzied police chase. Since the inception of television cops, such traits were, at best, left to the self-deprecating sidekick and never featured in a leading character. Nonetheless, Conrad, like most of the year's wave of loner cops, played his character strongly but with a slightly humorous touch,

keeping the focus on personalities over incidents and appearance. He, too, never let the war on crime overshadow the people most affected by it.

The most visibly eccentric inside-outsider crime fighter introduced that season was Columbo, played by another veteran character actor, Peter Falk, who had been working for years to gain public acceptance for such a hero. In the fall of 1965, Falk starred in the CBS crime show, *The Trials of O'Brien*. In an era of pretty boy heroes (populated by such good lookers as Richard Chamberlain and Robert Vaughn), Falk's interpretation of attorney Daniel O'Brien as a seedy-looking disheveled little man proved an enigma to most television viewers, who were unable to take the character seriously. When he was not in the courtroom, O'Brien was more than likely to be found at the race track playing the horses. How could such a man be a counselor at law? He was even divorced! The mix of humor and drama in *Trials of O'Brien* found little appreciation, and the series was canceled at mid-season, a good show that was unfortunately ahead of its time.

A year later, Universal Studios began producing made-for-TV films for NBC, many of which served as pilots for projected new series. In February 1968, NBC-Universal presented "Prescription: Murder," written by Richard Levinson and William Link. The story traced the elaborate scheme of a wealthy psychiatrist (played by Gene Barry) who murdered his wife, but was eventually unmasked by a polite and deceptively deferential detective from the Los Angeles police department, Lieutenant Columbo. That character had previously been used by Levinson and Link in a 1960 NBC summer anthology, then in a stage play, and they had first envisioned Bing Crosby for the TV movie, but Peter Falk instantly made it his own. With a creditable rough-hewn style, Falk's Columbo appeared to be little more than a sloppy, unsophisticated gumshoe who chewed on cheap cigars, sported a well worn raincoat, and drove a beat up old car. A supremely self-confident murderer would easily dismiss the lieutenant as no threat at all. In fact, Columbo was actually an alert, perceptive investigator whose meticulous eye for detail helped him spot the guilty party quickly. Then, it was a matter of building a case, step by step, with an ingratiating manner that even invited the suspect to offer explanations for particularly nagging points. This approach to a murder mystery seemed appealing and a second film, a full-fledged pilot, "Ransom for a Deadman," was produced in 1971.

In the fall of 1971, the *Columbo* series was quietly added to the *Mystery Movie* rotation, offering about half a dozen stories each season. Slowly, very slowly, the program built a following, though it did not achieve wide public acceptance until well into its second season. Times had changed, though, since *The Trials of O'Brien* and the television audience now seemed willing to accept a short fuzzy man in a wrinkled raincoat as a detective capable of cracking schemes conceived as the "perfect murder." The series attracted a wide range of guest stars as the murderers (Richard Kiley, Donald Pleasence, and Patrick McGoohan were among the best), usually casting them as rich, powerful, and influential, occupying social circles far above Columbo. As in the two TV movies, each episode followed an "inverted murder" structure: At the beginning of the story the audience was shown the crime as it was committed, so there was never any question of who was guilty. Rather than being a traditional "whodunit," *Columbo* was a "howzecatchem," focusing on *how* the lieutenant would trap the guilty party, and it played out as an elaborate cat-and-mouse game between the shuffling detective and the overconfident suspect. Every episode of *Columbo* adhered to this formula but, as in the old *Perry Mason* series, the repetition increased viewers' involvement by making them think, alertly searching for the inevitable fatal error by the villain and the casual, but oh-so-devastating, off hand remark by Columbo, who inevitably returned to each suspect to ask "just one more thing."

The success of these slightly off-beat new shows, as well as the steady number one status of CBS's *All in the Family*, was more tangible economic proof that the American television audience was willing to embrace programs that were somewhat out of the ordinary. Mindful of this, NBC offered at mid-season the first follow-up attempt to the successful style of *All in the Family, Sanford and Son*, another Norman Lear and Bud Yorkin production with British roots and a long history.

In January 1962, the BBC anthology program *Comedy Playhouse* presented "The Offer," a situation comedy featuring the antics of Albert Steptoe (Wilfrid Brambell), a garrulous and possessive curmudgeon who ran a junk dealership with his son, Harold (Harry Corbett). Albert Steptoe was the archetypical lovable grouch who spent most of his time scheming to break up any plans (such as marriage) his son might have to leave the family business. The public response to the two characters was so strong that in June 1962, a *Steptoe and Son* series began on the BBC and, by early 1964, it was the number one show in Britain. That same year, excerpts from the program were shown in the United States on *The Jack Paar Show* and NBC and Embassy Pictures put together a pilot for an Americanized version of the series that was intended to begin in 1965. The pilot, however, was rejected and plans for the series shelved. The British original itself went off the air in November 1965. Though *Steptoe and Son* was still a highly rated show, its producers admitted frankly that they had run out of ideas and decided to quit while on top. Four and one-half years later, giving in to public demand, the original cast was reassembled and *Steptoe and Son* returned to the BBC with new episodes. Though the series did not reach the number one slot in this new run, it was successful enough to once again attract American attention. In March 1971, Norman Lear and Bud Yorkin, who had just finished a long struggle to bring *All in the Family* to television, acquired the rights to produce an American version of *Steptoe and Son*. In September, NBC agreed to put the show into its schedule in January 1972. By this time, Lear and Yorkin had ceased working

as a pair, so while Lear kept his eye on *All in the Family*, Yorkin took control of the new series, called *Sanford and Son*. Like *All in the Family, Sanford and Son* was essentially a one-set show recorded on tape before a live audience. In transferring the junkyard world of *Steptoe and Son* to an American setting, Yorkin kept everything the same as in the original with one major exception: father and son (Fred and Lamont Sanford) were black.

Just as the Bunkers liberated television from the bland stereotypes of white suburbia, the Sanfords led the way in upsetting television's then-current stereotypes of blacks as middle class whites in blackface (such as *Julia*) and Olympian supermen (such as Linc in *The Mod Squad*). Instead, *Sanford and Son* presented blacks in a working class situation set in the ghetto, and used race as a peg for a number of jokes. And yet, just as *All in the Family* was highly derivative of *The Honeymooners, Sanford and Son* was, in many ways, a modern version of *Amos 'n Andy*, which in the 1950s had cast blacks in a standard wacky *I Love Lucy* style of comedy. Both *Amos 'n Andy* and *Sanford and Son* presented comic characters who happened to be black living in an essentially all-black world. Within such a setting, the presence of whites was more an emotional feeling than an everyday reality so the programs could put aside any awkward preaching and instead thrive in the all-black world with the strengths, stereotypes, and outlandish humor of any other first class American sitcom. Redd Foxx, a patriarch of black vaudeville halls (the so-called chitlin' circuit), portrayed the hypochondriac scheming bumbler, Fred Sanford. Foxx was a master at overacting and, since this was exactly what the character called for, it seemed as if he had spent his entire

---

September 18, 1971
The New Dick Van Dyke Show. (CBS). Dick Van Dyke returns to television in a new, but familiar, sitcom setting, directed by Carl Reiner and slotted immediately before the increasingly successful *Mary Tyler Moore Show*. Van Dyke plays Dick Preston, host of a local television talk show in Phoenix, Arizona.

October 1, 1971
Frank Stanton, president of CBS, Inc. since 1946, moves up to become vice chairman of the CBS board of directors.

October 6, 1971
This Week. (PBS). Bill Moyers, former press secretary to President Lyndon Johnson, begins a weekly documentary essay series. In its second season, the program is renamed *Bill Moyers' Journal*.

October 10, 1971
Upstairs, Downstairs. Britain's London Weekend Television network begins an extended drama series focusing on the social life of Edwardian England. The action is centered at the Bellamy townhouse in a well-to-do district of London. Upstairs: the rich Bellamy family. Downstairs: their servants. The show makes it to the U.S. on *Masterpiece Theater* beginning in January 1974.

October 13, 1971
The Pittsburgh Pirates beat the Baltimore Orioles 4 to 3 at Pittsburgh in the first World Series night game. NBC urged the later starting time in order to register higher ratings for the contest in prime time and, within a few years, most of baseball's championship games are staged "under the lights."

December 12, 1971

Brig. General David Sarnoff, the father of American television and honorary chairman of the board of RCA, dies in New York at the age of eighty. He worked at the company for sixty-five years.

February 14, 1972

The CBS Late Movie. (CBS). After failing to catch Johnny Carson with Merv Griffin, CBS switches late night formats from talk shows to movies (beginning with "A Patch of Blue"). On March 13, Griffin, still headquartered in Los Angeles, returns to television in afternoon syndication for Metromedia.

April 30, 1972

Arthur Godfrey Time goes off CBS Radio after exactly twenty-seven years.

May 1, 1972

After making numerous West Coast trips over the years, NBC's *Tonight* show moves permanently to Los Angeles.

July 1, 1972

Facing tough new afternoon competition from Merv Griffin's return to syndication, David Frost's syndicated talk program for Group W goes off the air.

July 8-9, 1972

"The Democratic National Telethon." (ABC). On the eve of its nominating convention, the Democratic Party stages an 18½ hour telethon to help cut the party's debt.

July 12, 1972

Thirty-seven-year-old Arthur Taylor becomes president of CBS, Inc., taking Frank Stanton's old job.

career preparing for the role. Son Lamont (Demond Wilson) served the role of believable straightman who, like Jed Clampett in *The Beverly Hillbillies,* was an oasis of sanity necessary to bring the flights of fancy back from the stratosphere. Foxx and Wilson were perfect needles to each other and their love-hate relationship gave the show a secure foundation of humor. The usual sitcom supporting characters rounded out the cast, including a dull-witted accomplice (Whitman Mayo as Fred's pal, Grady) and a female battleaxe (LaWanda Page as Fred's sister-in-law, Esther). At heart, then, *Sanford and Son* was not so much a racial show, but rather a very basic, well-produced contemporary sitcom set in a black ghetto. In fact, all but one of the first year's episodes were simply rewritten *Steptoe and Son* scripts, though in later years Yorkin made a determined effort to use black writers. Fred Sanford might assert his blackness but, more often than not, it was only as part of some scheme or con using his race in much the same way as he used his feigned heart attacks. This television portrayal of working class blacks who were conscious of their race and the problems of ghetto life, but who were also strong humorous characters facing funny situations, was the most important aspect of the success of *Sanford and Son.*

With the American audience softened up after a year of *All in the Family, Sanford and Son* found it much easier to shoot to the top of the Nielsen ratings and managed to place sixth in the compilation of the season's top shows, even though it first appeared in January. Viewers were beginning to understand that *All in the Family* and *Sanford and Son* were not revolutionaries per se, but rather up-to-date continuations of great sitcom traditions of the

past. Noting the public's acceptance of the innovative new series, producers and the networks grew bolder both in pursuing new formats and reworking old ones. In the process, the formulas for success in the 1970s seemed to be falling into place. Phasing in more contemporary adult concerns, CBS managed to stay on top in the ratings, closely followed by NBC. As usual, ABC was bringing up the rear, though it also joined the movement toward more experimental network ventures.

Miniseries appeared on all three networks, following the success of the CBS presentation of *The Six Wives of Henry VIII* the previous summer. NBC broadcast the BBC's six-part *Search for the Nile,* ABC imported a four-part adaptation of *War and Peace* (produced in Russia), and CBS presented the five-part Italian production of *The Life of Leonardo da Vinci.* Overall, the emphasis on special network programming increased and even the Pat Weaver notion of regularly scheduled specials made a comeback with NBC devoting most of Tuesday night to specials and ABC offering the weekly *Monday Night Special.* ABC also registered impressive success with its expanded schedule of made-for-TV movie presentations. Of the top twenty-three movies aired in the 1971–72 season, eighteen came from ABC's made-for-TV *Movie of the Week* slot. (In fact, only nine of the year's top thirty-two films were traditional theatrical features.) ABC's made-for-television hits included such blockbusters as the spooky crime-tinged "Night Stalker," and the solidly sentimental black-white sports camaraderie of "Brian's Song."

This boldness in entertainment programming was slowly sliding into the news departments as well, especially at CBS. With occasional, but dramatic, bursts of independence even in the face of government irritation and affiliate uneasiness, the network became the unquestioned leader in brave news presentations, particularly after its early 1971 *CBS Reports* episode, "The Selling of the Pentagon." The report examined the American military's public relations efforts that ranged from Pentagon propaganda films (some narrated by nationally known news commentators such as Chet Huntley and CBS's own Walter Cronkite) to elaborate and costly fireworks displays of new battle weapons shown to junketing VIPs. Though the Pentagon claimed the cost of these activities was only $30 million per year, CBS implied that $190 million of the taxpayers' money was a more accurate estimate of the yearly expenses. "The Selling of the Pentagon" did not follow the "on the other hand" tradition of television reporting, adopting instead the best aspects of the subjective muckraking style of journalism newspapers had long practiced. Produced and written by Peter Davis (who later won an Oscar in 1974 for "Hearts and Minds," an admittedly subjective view of the war in Vietnam), the program did not claim to be an objective study, but rather a hard-nosed TV expose that examined an issue and reached a conclusion. The program directed criticism not so much at the concept of Pentagon public relations, but at the incredible waste of taxpayer funds on extravagancies. The military and its congressional friends blasted the show as a "vicious piece of propaganda." Representative Harley O. Staggers, chairman of the House Investigations Subcommittee, kept the issue alive for months by attempting to have CBS executive Frank Stanton cited for contempt because he refused the committee's demand for outtakes from the program. In July 1971, though, the full House turned its back on Staggers and refused to press the contempt issue, and even President Nixon supported CBS in the battle. A few months later, however, the president and CBS were again at loggerheads, this time over a CBS report, "Under Surveillance," that documented FBI spying and wire tapping on domestic radicals.

At the same time, in the fall of 1971, the simmering warfare

Some of the top names in broadcasting (including CBS's Walter Cronkite and Eric Sevareid) were part of the press corps reporting on President Nixon's February 1972 trip to China. *(National Archives)*

between the White House and public television at last broke into the open as officials from the Corporation for Public Broadcasting (CPB) publicly complained that Clay Whitehead, chief of the White House's Office of Telecommunications Policy, was trying to inject partisan political considerations into the administration of American public television. In January 1972, Whitehead went on record as saying that, "there is a real question as to whether public television . . . should be carrying public affairs, news commentary, and that sort of thing." With an election year beginning, the White House preferred a weak, unobtrusive public broadcast system and Whitehead's statement virtually corroborated the charges of administration pressure on public TV. The battle intensified in the summer and, in July, President Nixon vetoed the CPB funding bill that would have granted public television $155 million over the next two years. In August, Nixon forces staged a coup d'etat and the chairman and president of CPB, both appointed by President Johnson, agreed to resign. Public television was rapidly becoming, in effect, the Nixon network. As a result, it offered no commentary at all in its gavel-to-gavel coverage of the August Republican convention in Miami Beach. The cameras simply focused on the podium and followed the scheduled activities, one after another. Recently hired PBS newsmen Robert MacNeil and Sander Vanocur (both formerly of NBC) refused the meaningless wooden role of convention anchor (though they did participate in the nightly convention wrapups), so the job fell to former Johnson press secretary, Bill Moyers. The convention itself, however, was

so well planned (it was literally scripted) that only a few aspects stood out anyway: the fanatically cheering young Nixon supporters and the one vote cast for David Brinkley for vice president.

In contrast, the Democratic convention, held a month earlier in Miami, was extremely disorganized, even for Democrats. Long, rancorous debates on controversial issues such as Vietnam and gay rights filled prime time television and constantly forced the sessions to run overtime. Even on nomination night the delegates failed to restrain themselves and presidential nominee South Dakota Senator George McGovern was forced to deliver his acceptance speech at 3:00 A.M., when all but the most ardent supporters had already gone to bed.

On the eve of the convention, however, the Democrats managed to coordinate and stage a unique political fund-raising event, an eighteen and one-half hour national telethon, carried on ABC. It was a novel way to erase part of the party's outstanding $9 million debt (from the 1968 campaign) and at the same time reduce the image of dependence on the traditional "fat cats" of politics by appealing directly to millions of "little people." The program was packed with stars and, as such events go, reasonably well produced and entertaining. It contained humorous partisan "commercials" including a *Mission: Impossible* take-off with a self-destructing tape that instructed Republican agents to bug the Democratic headquarters in Washington. By the end of the telethon, the Democrats had raised $4 million, enough to pay for the network time and still leave a profit of $2 million.

President Nixon, however, was clearly headed for a second term and, all year, the networks were very wary of crossing him. His February trip to China received heavy coverage, but the May protests to his mining of Vietnam's Haiphong harbor were given minimal exposure. Yet despite this generally cautious manner, Nixon and Nixon supporters continued to be irked at even occasional probing by CBS News. At the Republican convention, for instance, Mike Wallace bravely interviewed Nixon campaign money man Maurice Stans on possible connections to a June burglary at the Democratic National Committee headquarters in Washington's Watergate hotel. Previous reports by Daniel Schorr apparently angered the administration enough that an FBI investigation of Schorr was ordered by White House staffer Chuck Colson. When news of this leaked, the government released the patently absurd story that the FBI was checking into Schorr because he was under consideration for an environmental job in the administration. Following the May protests to the Haiphong mining, CBS, the only network to air a prime time special on the activities ("Escalation in Vietnam: Reasons, Risks, and Reactions"), was chastised by the Republican National Committee's publication, *Monday,* which claimed in a headline that: "CBS News accentuates the negative, distorting the facts in reporting Vietnam action." Shortly thereafter, CBS calmly aired films made by Anthony Lewis from the *New York Times* who showed North Vietnamese hospitals, homes, and schools destroyed by American bombs. Ironically, the films were very similar to the Felix Greene footage turned down by the network four years earlier. CBS newsman Don Webster, returning from the war front, said that ever since the American invasion of Cambodia and Laos (which had resulted in some negative comments and reports), the American military displayed open animosity to the press, "especially the radio-TV press and, even more, CBS News."

It was not the Vietnam War, however, that produced the season's most gripping combat coverage but, rather, the Summer Olympics in Munich, Germany, broadcast on ABC. In 1968, ABC had carried both the Summer and Winter Olympic Games, earning merely satisfactory ratings but demonstrating remarkable professionalism in its handling of the events. NBC's coverage of the 1972 Winter Olympics in Japan registered the same "just adequate" Nielsen figures. For the Summer Olympics in late August and early September of 1972, the well-trained ABC *Wide World of Sports* production crew, headed by producer Roone Arledge and announcers Jim McKay and Howard Cosell, again turned the often scattered Olympic events into a tight, comprehensible show.

Making extensive use of satellite transmissions, ABC scheduled many segments for prime time viewing. The network once more won critical plaudits but this time, surprisingly, very high ratings as well, averaging a 52% share of the audience on Olympic nights.

On Tuesday morning, September 5, the Olympics were dramatically transformed from a highly rated sporting event to an important news story as Palestinian terrorists captured a group of Israeli athletes inside the Olympic compound and held them as hostages. ABC, of course, had a large, professional staff already on the scene to provide extensive day-long coverage of the Munich events, but the network's coverage of the hostage story went beyond being fortunately at the right place at the right time. ABC displayed a strong professional manner and discipline that suddenly made many Americans aware that ABC was a network to be taken seriously. Jim McKay displayed a depth of insight and emotion he had never revealed on *Wide World of Sports* as the events unfolded, live, before the cameras. Newsman Peter Jennings reported from within the cordoned-off compound itself. The terrorists were shown brandishing their weapons and sticking their heads out the window while German paratroopers surrounded the compound and prepared for a possible assault. The possibility that open warfare could erupt at any moment was painfully clear, and undeniably exciting. Both sides waited, tensely, all day. Near 5:00 P.M. (New York time), the terrorists emerged from the compound with their hostages in tow, stepped into the fuzzy street light, then entered a special bus they had demanded be brought to take them all to the local airport. As the bus disappeared, both the ABC commentators and the home audience could only wait and speculate. At about 9.00 P.M. McKay wearily but joyfully announced that, according to the first reports from the airport, all the hostages had been freed. Soon he had to retract this premature happy ending with the ominous phrase, "There will be bad news from the officials." Near 10:30 P.M. McKay, visibly exhausted after his twelve-hour marathon job of anchoring, presented the bad news: All the hostages had died in a violent shoot-out between police and the terrorists. Memorial services were held for the slain athletes and then the games were resumed and completed amid extremely tight security.

ABC's Munich coverage marked an important turning point in the network's image. Not only had it displayed innovation and skill in its excellent production of the Olympic events themselves, it also revealed tremendous adaptability in facing unexpected developments with its presentation of the hostage story. The events in Munich served as a highly visible "coming of age" for what had been derisively labeled for years as "the third network."

32. Ideological Plugola

IN 1973 THE FCC AT LAST got around to holding hearings on the first complaints registered against implementation of the 1970 prime time access rule. Despite the howls of protest that had originally greeted the proposal three years earlier, when the hearings began no one spoke out in favor of scrapping the new system. The three networks privately confessed that it would take them years to develop a new batch of 7:30 P.M. lead-in programs should the time be returned to them. Independent syndicators and local station owners, who were prospering with profitable game shows in the access slots, had no intention of giving up their newfound bonanza without a fight. In a very short time, a new status quo had taken hold in television. The exemptions granted to ABC and NBC for the 1971–72 season expired and were not renewed. ABC broke up its Tuesday night block while NBC shaved an additional thirty minutes from its Sunday night schedule. For the 1972–73 season, each network adhered to the prescribed three-hour limit on prime time broadcasting every night. At the FCC hearings, NBC publicly conceded that access might actually be a good idea, while ABC had no qualifications; it was ecstatic about the plan. Though still number three, ABC had used the access rule to cut dead weight from its schedule and found itself in a good competitive position, registering a small but healthy ratings jump in the 1971–72 season. Even number one CBS had weathered the storm well, dropping the last of its rural-based programs in its compliance with the commission's access rule.

At the same time, CBS looked to its new smash hit, *All in the Family,* to set the style of comedy for the new decade, and had begun to cultivate the development of similar programs. The network had drawn on sitcoms for ratings success throughout the 1950s and 1960s and prepared to exploit the rejuvenated format again for the 1970s. *All in the Family* was fresh, exciting, provocative, and a rich source to tap for the new wave of humor. The series had expanded its scope from racial themes to deal with other controversial topics such as menopause, impotency, homosexuality, and the Vietnam War. Producer Norman Lear did not just milk the topical issues for a few cheap laughs, but used them as realistic complications faced by generally believable character types. (Lear, in fact, said that he had modeled the Archie Bunker character after his own father.) The popular success of Lear's sitcom style had, within a very short time, effectively changed the focus of situation comedy from the silliness of pure escapist fare to the presentation of human mini-dramas that had a strong base in comedy.

Irwin Segelstein, one of CBS programmer Fred Silverman's top aides, described this approach to comedy in *Variety*, calling it the first major change from the *I Love Lucy* "obstacle course sitcoms." Those had presented lovable and wacky characters in absurd situations such as trying to fly a plane without a pilot or falling down a laundry chute. In contrast, Segelstein said, "The new comedy always grows out of an identifiable situation, and it involves realism in both life style and dialogue style. It still involves jokes, but the jokes are being made on a different level than before … Where it really departs from the old is that the comedy grows out of the characters themselves rather than out of plot or farcical incidents. The writers start with a serious theme and then develop a comedy about it."

Television drama series had long before melted into a panoply of cops and doctors in soap opera-type action-adventures, so sitcoms had unexpectedly become the driving force in the examination of real-life issues by the medium. Such a development worked because the framework of comedy defused the omni-present stench of exceeding seriousness and glib solutions that had too often pervaded and ultimately undercut attempts to deal with real life in the so-called relevant dramas such as the defunct *Storefront Lawyers.* In those series, current headlines had merely been grafted onto cliché-ridden plots, shallow characters, and cardboard settings in order to appear up-to-date and topical. Though the characters in sitcoms such as *All in the Family* often fell into stereotypes themselves, the world they were placed in was very real. Consequently, controversial, topical, and realistic issues did not appear as heavy handed intrusions but, rather, as reasonable developments in that particular setting.

All in the Family had opened its second season with Archie trying to wiggle out of paying for the funeral of a bothersome relative who had died (off camera) in his house. Such a plot twist was unique to television because characters in traditional TV sitcoms simply did not die. It worked because the Bunker family faced the situation in character and handled it with humor. This was the key to the continuing success of the series as Norman Lear constantly updated *All in the Family* to reflect the shifts of popular controversy in the 1970s, duplicating the arguments that took place in many homes across the country throughout the decade. Originally Archie and son-in-law Mike had passionately disagreed on religious morals, race, and the conduct of the Vietnam War. This expanded to include the ethics of President Nixon's reelection campaign and the investigation into the break-in at the Democratic headquarters in the Watergate. Some episodes went even further

FALL 1972 SCHEDULE

	8:00	8:30	9:00	9:30	10:00	10:30	
M	THE ROOKIES		ABC NFL Monday Night Football (to 12 Midnight)				ABC
O	Gunsmoke		Here's Lucy	Doris Day Show	THE NEW BILL COSBY SHOW		CBS
N	Rowan And Martin's Laugh-In		NBC Monday Night At The Movies				NBC
T	TEMPERATURE'S RISING		Tuesday Movie Of The Week		Marcus Welby, M.D.		ABC
U	MAUDE		Hawaii Five-O		The New CBS Tuesday Night Movies		CBS
E	Bonanza		The Bold Ones (The Doctors)		NBC REPORTS / # First Tuesday		NBC
W	PAUL LYNDE SHOW		Wednesday Movie Of The Week		JULIE ANDREWS HOUR		ABC
E	Carol Burnett Show		Medical Center		Cannon		CBS
D	Adam-12		NBC WEDNESDAY MYSTERY MOVIE (BANACEK; COOL MILLION; MADIGAN)		SEARCH		NBC
T	The Mod Squad		THE MEN (ASSIGNMENT:VIENNA; DELPHI BUREAU; JIGSAW)		Owen Marshall, Counselor At Law		ABC
H	THE WALTONS		CBS Thursday Night Movies				CBS
R	Flip Wilson Show		Ironside / # Bob Hope Show		Dean Martin Show		NBC
F	The Brady Bunch	The Partridge Family	Room 222	The Odd Couple	Love, American Style		ABC
R	Sonny And Cher Comedy Hour		CBS Friday Night Movies				CBS
I	Sanford And Son	THE LITTLE PEOPLE	GHOST STORY		BANYON		NBC
S	Alias Smith And Jones / # KUNG-FU		STREETS OF SAN FRANCISCO		The Sixth Sense		ABC
A	All In The Family	BRIDGET LOVES BERNIE	Mary Tyler Moore Show	BOB NEWHART SHOW	Mission: Impossible		CBS
T	Emergency		NBC Saturday Night At The Movies				NBC

	7:00	7:30	8:00	8:30	9:00	9:30	10:00	10:30	
S	local		The FBI		The ABC Sunday Night Movie				ABC
U	local	ANNA AND THE KING	M*A*S*H	Sandy Duncan Show	New Dick Van Dyke Show	Mannix		local	CBS
N	local	The Wonderful World Of Disney	NBC Sunday Mystery Movie (McCloud; Columbo; McMillan And Wife; HEC RAMSEY)			Night Gallery		local	NBC

and shifted the primary emphasis from comedy to drama. In one such story, the Bunkers and a "Hebrew Defense Association" activist spent the final third of the episode arguing the pros and cons of using violence as a political tool. Neither side convinced the other. At the conclusion of the argument, the HDA member left the Bunker house and (off camera) stepped into his car, turned the ignition key, and was instantly killed by a bomb planted under the hood. The episode ended with a silent shot of the stunned Bunkers looking through their doorway at the wreckage.

By 1973, with direct American involvement in the Vietnam War ending, the series slowly shifted to playing up the cause of women's liberation. The conflicts between Archie and Gloria, his feminist daughter, were obvious and practically unavoidable. Even though she was a grown woman in her twenties with a job and a husband, to Archie, Gloria would always be his "little girl." It pained him to see her display the independence that signaled not only her rejection of his traditional values but also her inevitable departure from the home roost. A less expected but equally important development was the change in the largely decorative character of Edith. She came forward to demonstrate that older women deserved respect as well. Previously used as a squeaky-voiced butt of all the dumb-Dora housewife jokes ("Stifle it, Dingbat!" Archie would admonish), Edith was emboldened enough to demand consideration of her own needs for love and self-fulfillment. Edith truly cared for Archie and consequently wanted not only his

respect for her daily activities but also a little more of the affection he thought years of married life had made unnecessary.

By the mid-1970s the national mood had returned to one of practicality, leaving polemics behind, and *All in the Family* changed again as well. In a television world then filled with *All in the Family* style imitations, it stood as almost a traditional sitcom that focused on such familiar themes as parenthood and grandparenthood. Gloria had a child and she and Mike at last moved out of the Bunker house and set up housekeeping next door. There was still controversy, though it was usually much less strident than in the past. Over the objections of Mike and Gloria, for instance, Archie took their baby, Joey, to a church and baptized him. Lear also kept up the topical flavor of the series with such realistic developments as Archie's getting laid off from his plant (he eventually quit anyway) and Edith fending off a rapist. Archie himself even became a small businessman, mortgaging his house in order to buy his neighborhood bar (allowing the eventual change of the series name to *Archie Bunker's Place*). Eventually, a mellower and shorter-haired Mike Stivic, like much of his generation, "settled down." He accepted a teaching job in California, taking Gloria and Joey to the other end of the country and leaving Archie and Edith alone in New York. Like much of *their* generation, Archie and Edith carried on in a greatly altered world with their own new interests. To the end, even after Edith's death, Archie still colorfully griped about whatever was in the headlines.

All in the Family became an American institution of the 1970s, yet at the beginning of the decade its success in dealing with controversy was viewed with amazement. Still, its acceptance should not really have been a complete surprise because over the years viewers had been growing accustomed to seeing more sensitive themes on television through the increasing number of adult-oriented prime time movies. The all-too-obvious double standard between movies and weekly series had to crack eventually as the public became more tolerant of such material. In the fall of 1972, CBS, embracing this new form of sitcom as the key to its continued primacy, launched its first major followups to *All in the Family*: *Maude* and *M*A*S*H*

Norman Lear's *Maude* was a direct spinoff from *All in the Family* and, on the surface, appeared to be merely a vehicle for an archliberal version of Archie Bunker. The character of Maude Findlay (Beatrice Arthur) had been presented in several episodes of *All in the Family* as Edith's cousin whose left wing slant and abrasive manner put her in direct opposition to the outspoken Archie. Maude was quick tempered, rich, and an ardent believer in the right of women to control their own lives. She defended all the planks of liberal dogma and strongly supported freedom of action, freedom of speech, and a big benevolent government that helped others to help themselves. Archie hated her and she despised him. Maude was the perfect focus for a spinoff series and the character was awarded her own program for the 1972–73 season, set in her home environment of a liberal, worldly, upper middle class New York suburban neighborhood. It immediately hit the top ten, joining *All in the Family* and *Sanford and Son,* which had become ensconced at the top of the Nielsen ratings lists (occasionally taking the number one and two slots together). Unlike series such as *Petticoat Junction* in the 1960s, *Maude* was not a bland cash-in on a successful hit formula. Lear used the different setting and liberal characters to tackle a whole new range of topics in treatments that matched *All in the Family* in daring and sensitivity.

Perhaps the most revolutionary aspect of *Maude* was that it freed middle-aged women from the TV stereotype of addlebrained spinsters, just as Mary Tyler Moore's program had upset the traditional TV image of a young woman. Though certainly not a raving beauty, Maude was an attractive woman with an active sex life and apparently boundless self-confidence. Despite three unsuccessful marriages that had ended in divorce, she had married again. Her latest husband, Walter (Bill Macy), possessed an intelligent pragmatism and he recognized that Maude needed not only love and reassurance but the opportunity to assert herself, so he usually bowed to her wishes. Walter's business was successful enough that Maude did not have to work, so she devoted her time to myriad liberal and women's causes, leaving basic household chores to her maid, Florida (Esther Rolle). Carol (Adrienne Barbeau), Maude's daughter from a previous marriage, and her son, Phillip (Brian Morrison), also lived with Maude and Walter.

Maude was one of the first programs to take advantage of the networks' grudging acceptance of divorce as a fact of life and to successfully incorporate it into a series premise. In 1970, ABC's *The Odd Couple* (produced by Garry Marshall), featuring a pair of divorced men living together, had marked the beginning of the end of television's parade of widows and widowers, but Maude outdid them both. She had been divorced three times herself and daughter Carol had been divorced once as well.

Despite her exaggerated liberal tendencies and loud-mouthed caricature, Maude was a strong complex character who faced very difficult and very realistic problems. When the issue of personal freedom hit her in areas close to home (such as the possible involvement in premarital sex by her grandson and some obvious affairs by her daughter), she found herself falling into the traditional role of overbearing suspicious mother. She tried to control her instincts, often to no avail. When a series of business mishaps pushed Walter, a normally heavy drinker anyway, into a fling with alcoholism, she fought her own panic and his depression to help them both weather the crisis. Perhaps the most painful personal decision she ever faced took place in one of the first episodes of the series, a two-part story on abortion, shown in November 1972. Maude discovered that she was pregnant at an age in which she had no intention of becoming a mother again, and had to decide whether or not to have an abortion. After an agonizing soul search, she concluded that an abortion was the only realistic alternative open to her, but despite her liberal philosophies, this was not presented as an easy choice. The program was the strongest pro-abortion statement made on network TV at the time and it set off a brief public controversy in which a number of CBS affiliates refused to air the episodes. Such actions had formerly been taken only in reaction to documentaries, dramas, or an occasional topical variety format. The Maude protests were a symbolic confirmation of the full-fledged serious status being accorded sitcoms.

CBS's other new wave hopeful, *M*A*S*H,* also successfully combined drama with comedy, though it took several years to refine and develop its presentation. The series was based on the popular 1970 Robert Altman film that followed the adventures of two merry playboy combat surgeons (played by Elliott Gould and Donald Sutherland) assigned to an overseas American *Mobile*

In *Maude*, Beatrice Arthur played a strong and independent middle-aged woman. *(Sony Pictures Television)*

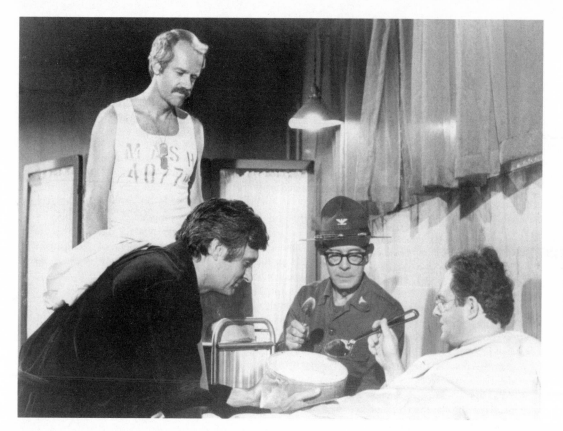

The "second generation" of *M*A*S*H* included: *(from left)* Mike Farrell as B. J. Hunnicutt, Alan Alda as Hawkeye Pierce, Harry Morgan as Sherman Potter, and Gary Burghoff as Radar. (M*A*S*H © 1973 Twentieth Century Fox Television. All Rights Reserved.)

Army Surgical Hospital (MASH) unit during the Korean War. Altman used the twin shock tactics of excessive blood and explicit language to set his film apart from typical war comedies and to stress the cruelty of combat. The television adaptation toned down both the language and obvious bloodletting but, within the limits of television, kept both the gore of war and the joy of sex as major themes. In its first season, though, TV's *M*A*S*H* was, for the most part, a traditional war-is-funny comedy that owed as much to *Hogan's Heroes* and *Sergeant Bilko* as Altman's film. Alan Alda (as Hawkeye Pierce) and Wayne Rogers (as Trapper John McIntyre) emphasized the playboy-surgeon aspect of their characters, drinking too much and perpetually chasing nurses. They were excellent medicos (and knew it) who constantly manipulated their nominal commander, Lieutenant Colonel Henry Blake (McLean Stevenson), while thumbing their noses at military regulations and discipline. Such themes and characters were basic to every war comedy film since World War II, and the initial TV treatment offered little evidence that the series was in the same league as Norman Lear's comedies.

M*A*S*H did very poorly in the fall of 1972. It was stuck in a hell-hole of a slot: Sunday, between the anemic *Anna and the King* and *The Sandy Duncan Show*, and against ABC's *The FBI* and NBC's *Wonderful World of Disney*. Yet, premiering as it did at the tail end of the Vietnam War, its mocking of military regimentation and futile war strategies were timely and close to home. The program's demographics indicated that while the overall ratings were terrible, *M*A*S*H* was very popular among young adults. CBS executives therefore decided to allow the show time to build an audience. In January, *M*A*S*H* was given slightly more respectable company (*Dick Van Dyke* and *Mannix*), and it broke into the top thirty, winning renewal for a second season. CBS program chief Fred Silverman gave it the royal treatment in the fall of 1973 and placed *M*A*S*H* between two comedy blockbusters on Saturday, *All in the Family* and *The Mary Tyler Moore Show*. The series rocketed to the top ten and remained there until it ended in 1983.

Along with its new ratings success, *M*A*S*H* began displaying a remarkable improvement in content. Alan Alda took on added duties such as occasional script writing and directing, and members of the supporting cast began to develop their characters into more complex individuals. The image of merry doctors on the loose was replaced by the intricate relationships among people thrown together in a unique war situation. The writers began shifting the focus of the scripts from straight sitcom into the world of comedy-drama. By the third season, they hit their stride as *M*A*S*H* developed a dramatic style similar to, yet distinct from, Norman Lear's programs.

While the Bunkers and Maude very often grappled with topical headline issues, the individuals in *M*A*S*H* faced intimate, personal conflicts of a more timeless nature that were set against the equally real backdrop of a hospital unit trying desperately to save as many lives as possible in a war zone. Very often, particular episodes replaced the traditional sitcom structure of rapid-fire punch lines leading to a hilarious denouement with three occasionally interweaving plot threads, of which one or two were usually serious. A device sometimes used to tighten these stories was the composition of a letter home. In effect, this allowed a member of the cast to act as narrator of recent developments at the base, which were shown in flashback as the note bound for the States took shape. Besides serving as a convenient plot hook, these "letters" also allowed the individual cast members to tell the story from their own point of view, adding depth to the character traits already familiar to the viewers.

Character development became the most impressive feature of *M*A*S*H* and the cast soon raised the TV series far beyond the meat-axe humor and caricatures of the feature film, in a rare instance of the TV copy surpassing the film original. Gary Burghoff, the only performer from the film that made the crossover to television, fleshed out his role of Corporal Radar O'Reilly, Colonel Blake's young aide with an extraordinary sixth sense. (He anticipated events moments before they took place.) Though Radar possessed an instinctive understanding of the intricate twists in military bureaucracy, and his knowledge of procedure actually kept the base running, in many respects he remained the terribly naive Iowa farm boy who sometimes found himself a bit jealous of the swinging lifestyle of Hawkeye and Trapper. Larry Linville and Loretta Swit assumed the roles of Major Frank Burns and chief nurse Major Margaret "Hot Lips" Houlihan, two officers carrying on a torrid affair with each other but determined to follow "proper procedure" whenever possible in the meatloaf surgery world of Korea. They both suffered mercilessly as foils to Hawkeye and Trapper, but they also displayed more humanity and depth than their feature film counterparts (Robert Duvall and Sally Kellerman). Two characters substantially upgraded in the move to television were Father Mulcahy (William Christopher), the company chaplain, and Henry Blake. As camp commander, the TV Henry Blake realized that it was not worth the aggravation involved to try to stop the pranks of Hawkeye and Trapper, so he wisely chose to ignore them in the interests of company harmony (and his own peace of mind). The TV Blake was a pushover but he realized it and knew when it was really important to draw the line. Altman's Blake had been just plain stupid. His Mulcahy had been even worse, set up as an ignorant sissy priest. Christopher portrayed the character as a realistic Army chaplain, just as likely to be found in an all-night poker party as in a formal chapel setting. Each of these characters could step in with complications, conflicts, and problems of their own, thus breaking up the strain of constantly focusing on Hawkeye and Trapper.

Good as this cast and the show were by 1974, both aspects improved even further in the fourth season as M*A*S*H revitalized itself with two important cast changes. McLean Stevenson decided to quit the program and move into the comedy-variety field on his own, so his character was written out of the series. The final episode of the 1974–75 season featured a happy farewell party for Henry Blake, who had received his orders shipping him back to the States. A short postscript ended the episode: the death of Henry Blake. In one brilliant stroke, the simple departure of a series regular was transformed into a tragic, ironic twist of war – one of the main themes of the show anyway. After months at the front lines, Blake was killed on the way home in an offshore crash as his plane was struck by random enemy fire. A tearful Radar announced the news in the operating room and, between stitches, the doctors and nurses cried.

Before production for the next season began, Wayne Rogers also decided to depart. He had found himself trapped in a character almost identical to Alda's and had been severely limited by the duplication (there was room for only one super-intelligent Yankee anarchist in Korea). As a result, in the fall of 1975, M*A*S*H was practically a brand new program with two-thirds of its central cast altered. Both replacements turned out to be even stronger characters than their predecessors and the quality of the series once again increased dramatically.

Veteran series actor Harry Morgan portrayed the new C.O., Colonel Sherman Potter, an experienced soldier, surgeon, and a much more creditable Army figure than Colonel Blake. Unlike Blake, Potter not only grew angry at his charges, he occasionally disciplined them. This made his role as benign ruler, inclined to overlook harmless pranks and unnecessary procedure, much more believable. Mike Farrell played Hawkeye's new sidekick, Captain B.J. Hunnicutt, a pure product of the San Francisco way of life. Unlike Trapper, B.J. was different from Hawkeye, yet the two still became fast friends. B.J. was a cool West Coast high-liver with a wife and family and no desire to upset his stable home with promiscuous behavior in Korea. Their personalities complemented each other perfectly, giving both characters plenty of room to shine.

With its basic cast further strengthened, M*A*S*H grew even bolder in its departure from standard sitcom structure. One episode centered solely on the crew trying to watch a film (the old horse opera, "My Darling Clementine") that constantly jammed in the camp projector. To continue the entertainment while the projector was being fixed, they launched an impromptu sing-along talent show. The program reached no dramatic climax; the party simply ended with the inevitable arrival of the new wounded. Another episode brought the series to a level of visual, lyrical poetry as it recreated Ed Murrow's legendary 1952 *See It Now* show from Korea. The performers were allowed to ad-lib in character when responding to questions from the traveling "newsman" and never was their grasp of their roles more evident. Radar blushed at the opportunity to say "hello" to the folks back home. Colonel Potter called the whole Korean escapade stupid. Hawkeye nearly broke down trying to explain how he dealt with keeping a measure of sanity through the war. Father Mulcahy gasped at the recollection of doctors fighting the cold Korean air by subconsciously warming their hands from the heat of open body wounds.

With such powerful descriptions, complex characters, and the very real terror of dealing so closely and continuously with death, M*A*S*H became one of the best sitcom-drama combinations ever on television. It joined *All in the Family* and *Maude* in focusing dramatic interest on character development, not slam-bang action and cheap slapstick.

In the fall of 1972, along with the appearance of M*A*S*H, CBS applied this same respect for characters to a new dramatic program as well, in an attempt to revive the moribund format of family drama with *The Waltons.* Series such as *Mama* and *One Man's Family* had flourished in the early 1950s, but had vanished with the development of filmed series and Westerns. With film, action became the goal and Western drama had led to crime drama, adventure drama, war drama, and so forth. In these, "drama" really meant "action" (itself a euphemism for "violence"), and producers saw no place for what they regarded as the comparatively dull, extremely limited action in family drama. After a numbing decade of cops, cowboys, and killings, the simple peace of personal family conflict began to appear quite attractive, at least for an occasional contrast. CBS gave *Playhouse 90* graduate Martin Manulis and writer Earl Hamner the go-ahead in 1969 to try such a theme and, in October 1969, *CBS Playhouse* presented "Appalachian Autumn." The story was set in modern times but focused on the experiences of a government agency volunteer working with a close-knit family in a poor Virginia mountain town. Watching the family deal with a devastating coal mine disaster, the volunteer learned that even though they were poor, the members of the mountain clan still retained enough strength and dignity to refuse to beg for help. Reviewers at the time praised the play and its theme, but pointed out that the dialogue was somewhat hokey. The criticism was tempered with encouragement; one reviewer observed, "All it needs is practice."

Just before Christmas 1971, CBS presented another play with a strong Appalachian family theme, "The Homecoming." Earl Hamner was again the writer and another live drama great, Fielder Cook, served as the director. Hamner based the play on his own autobiography and set the scene in the time period of his own boyhood, the day before Christmas, 1933, in the home of a large poor family from rural Virginia, the Waltons. John Boy (Richard Thomas), the oldest son in the clan, acted as narrator for the story, which took the form of his personal reminiscence of that Depression-era Christmas. The gathering was very important to his own

September 16, 1972

Bridget Loves Bernie. (CBS). Meredith Baxter is Bridget, a rich Irish-Catholic. David Birney is Bernie, a poor New York Jew. The two fall in love, get married, and have to overcome opposition from both sides of the family. Placed between *All in the Family* and *The Mary Tyler Moore Show,* the program registers good ratings, but also stirs the ire of some religious groups objecting to the positive portrait of inter-marriage. As a result, CBS axes the show after only one season. Life, however, triumphs (temporarily) over art. Baxter and Birney later marry each other in real life, but then are divorced.

November 8, 1972

Time-Life's Home Box Office (HBO) cable television network begins operations with a New York Rangers hockey contest from Madison Square Garden followed by a movie, "Sometimes a Great Notion." At first, HBO is limited to just 365 cable subscribers in Wilkes-Barre, Pennsylvania.

November 24, 1972

In Concert. (ABC). Don Kirshner produces a late Friday night special of live rock acts, taped in concert. First up is shock-rocker Alice Cooper. After about twenty minutes of Cooper's mock horror tactics and gyrations with a snake, WPRC in Cincinnati pulls out of the show, saying, "This stopped being music and art and had turned into pornography." On January 19, *In Concert* becomes a regular, once-every-other-week ABC late night series.

January 4, 1973

CBS sells the New York Yankees to George Steinbrenner.

personal growth because it was the first time the family members faced the real possibility of losing John Walton (Andrew Duggan), the head of the family, who was the provider for seven children, his wife Olivia (Patricia Neal), and his own parents (Edgar Bergen and Ellen Corby). John had been caught in a bus wreck fifty miles from home, but that was all the news the rest of the family had received. As the play unfolded, each member came to grips with the significance of the potential tragedy and its far-reaching aftershocks. If the father was dead or even badly injured, it would be more than just the loss of a loved one; already financially pressed, the family would be pushed into a severe economic pinch. John Boy became acutely aware of his own responsibilities as the oldest son and went to the site of the accident to see if he could help his father, while the rest of the family waited, gripped by fear and trepidation. The story ended happily with the father, safe and sound, reunited with the family in a tearful, heartfelt welcome.

The straightforward, unembarrassed sentimentality of "The Homecoming" touched a responsive nerve in the American psyche and the play was judged successful enough to be turned into a series. In spite of several major cast changes (Ralph Waite took the role of John Walton, Michael Learned the role of Olivia, and Will Geer the role of Grandpa Walton), *The Waltons* retained the strength of the Christmas special. The program was sometimes overly sentimental, but the characters carried their emotions well and a strong strain of reality woven through each episode tempered this tendency. Rather than degenerating into a maudlin tear-jerker soap opera, *The Waltons* emerged as a nostalgic re-creation of a much simpler era. Within this world, the strong cast presented their characters as proud, realistic people struggling through hard times.

Even the Walton children were believable and, during the long run of the series, they grew up, became young adults, and began to move out on their own as America turned from a depression to a world war.

At its premiere in the fall of 1972, *The Waltons* was nearly buried by the competition. The program contained no action-packed gunplay, screeching tires, crime czars, or murder. Few viewers gave it a chance, preferring instead the flashy humor of black comedian Flip Wilson on NBC and the popular but routine gunplay of ABC's *Mod Squad.* Encouraged by some ecstatic reviews and hopeful demographic data, CBS stuck with *The Waltons* even though the program barely nudged the top fifty through the fall. Then slowly, very slowly, it began to catch on. By the spring, it beat Flip Wilson's show for the first time. Just before it went into reruns, the program reached the top ten.

Both *The Waltons* and *M*A*S*H* had been saved by demographics. With the networks beginning to focus on the makeup of the audience that a program attracted rather than merely the total number of viewers, they allowed some shows more time to develop a following. Though shows that appealed to the *wrong* audience (too old, too rural) faced the prospect of a much quicker cancellation than before, the new priorities opened up television to the whims of affluent young adults and allowed the introduction of more daring themes to network entertainment programming. Previously, trying to reach the greatest number of people possible had precluded shows containing anything that anyone might have found offensive. The networks now dared to risk a few unusual themes designed to appeal to a particular segment of the audience. They were surprised to discover that sometimes these gambles paid off in high ratings as well.

On November 1, 1972, ABC's *Wednesday Movie of the Week* offered one of these innovative programs, the first straightforward, sympathetic portrayal of homosexuality on American television, the made-for-TV film, "That Certain Summer." Hal Holbrook played a building contractor and Martin Sheen a sound engineer, two very masculine figures, who became homosexual lovers. "That Certain Summer" avoided all the usual clichés and stereotypes of homosexual behavior and focused instead on the personal struggle of Holbrook's character as he tried to explain his lifestyle to his teenage son (by his former wife). Despite the complications the father decided to follow his own feelings and, while his son tried very hard to understand the radical alteration in his father, he could not quite accept it. There were no simple solutions offered nor glib putdowns presented. The program was simply a sensitive slice of life featuring normal people caught in a difficult situation yet trying to make the best of it. The program was also a ratings smash.

The networks could "get away" with such innovative entertainment fare because, as the ratings indicated, the public seemed more willing to accept it. At the same time, governmental watchdog Senator John Pastore had faded from view so, for the moment, there was no major anti-sex and violence advocate on the public scene to crusade against the networks. However, the situation was far different in the realm of public affairs. There, the Nixon administration carefully monitored the output from all the networks and was ready to pounce on any item that presented something disturbing to the White House. Such situations seemed to occur more and more often as the Nixon administration, fresh from a landslide victory over Senator George McGovern in November 1972, stepped up its attack on both commercial and public television. Richard Nixon was at the peak of his power and appeared ready to make the most of the situation.

Just one month after the election, Nixon aide Clay Whitehead delivered a stinging anti-network speech to the executives of local TV stations, spelling out the theories Vice President Spiro Agnew had only implied in his attacks three years before. Whitehead called for more pressure by local affiliates against the networks, especially in the area of news, urging them to delete the segments of the network feed that they did not care for (which would, presumably, be the same segments the administration did not like). He labeled the networks' news and public affairs presentations as consisting chiefly of "elitist gossip" and "intellectual plugola." In exchange for more aggressive action, Whitehead dangled the prospect of affiliate station licenses that would be much more difficult to take away and also remain valid for five years (two years more than the law then allowed). Even ABC's Howard K. Smith, long a supporter of President Nixon, began to worry, saying, "It begins to look like a general assault on reporters."

With such a concerted campaign against them, it was understandable that the networks began to retreat from their aggressive pre-election news style. Nixon was clearly playing for keeps. Consequently, CBS announced the elimination of the well-publicized practice of "instant analysis" that usually followed presidential addresses and delayed its commentary until the next regularly scheduled news program. All three networks failed to present any news specials at all on the controversial Christmas bombings of North Vietnam that took place just a few weeks after Whitehead's speech.

Early in 1973, the administration negotiated a face-saving treaty with the North Vietnamese which ended direct American involvement in the war and secured the release of American prisoners of war. Yet the end of the combat did not mark an end to the pressure on the networks. Almost immediately, both the government and the public indicated that they wanted to put the memories and effects of the war behind them, instantly. Responding to this mood, CBS postponed the television adaptation of a timely new Broadway play concerning the return to the States of a blinded Vietnam veteran, David Rabe's "Sticks and Bones." The production was a flawed but well-crafted and effective treatment of the gap between the returning soldier (ruined both mentally and physically by the war) and his peaches and cream family (unable to accept the way the war had changed him). Despite his desperate need for help and understanding, the soldier's family chose to virtually ignore him, vainly hoping that he would just disappear from their lives.

"Sticks and Bones" had been scheduled for Friday, March 9, as the second production in a series of thirteen specials for CBS by Joseph Papp's New York Shakespeare company (the first, "Much Ado About Nothing," had played in February), but then the network realized in horror that the program would air in the middle of the return of the real-life POWs from Vietnam. The drama was a far cry from the image the administration had cultivated for the men coming home and CBS decided its placement was inappropriate and rescheduled it for a later date. After all, President Nixon had billed the return of the POWs as a joyful celebration of the conclusion to the war and it seemed foolish to risk antagonizing him with the downbeat theme of the play. Papp was furious at the delay and canceled his four-year agreement with CBS, charging the network with censorship. CBS did air the play months later, stuck in the summer viewing ghetto (August 17) and without any commercials. Only 94 of the usual 200 CBS affiliates chose to air it and some delayed their telecast until late at night.

The situation was even worse over on public television, which found itself almost swallowed whole by the Nixon administration. The top two posts in public TV were held by Nixon appointees after the previous officials had been forced from office. Former Representative Thomas Curtis of Missouri was installed as chair-

man of the Corporation for Public Broadcasting, the organization that served as the liaison between the Public Broadcasting System and Congress, and Henry Loomis, a former deputy director of the U.S. Information Agency, was appointed president of CPB. Loomis seemed particularly insensitive to the concept of an activist approach to public broadcasting. During Congressional confirmation hearings, Loomis acknowledged that he had never seen an episode of *The Great American Dream Machine,* PBS's most important recent production, and could not even pick up the PBS affiliate in Washington because his set could not receive its UHF signal. His concept of "vital programming" topped even the uninterrupted coverage of the Republican convention in 1972. He announced that PBS would offer twenty-one hours of live coverage of the *Apollo 17* moonshot in December of 1972, an expensive project that could only duplicate network broadcasts of a fairly dull expedition and would probably serve as nothing more than a good source of pro-administration publicity. Loomis was talked out of this particular proposal, but it was clear that public broadcasting's priorities had been hopelessly distorted as it was placed firmly under the thumb of the administration. It was at this stage that the Watergate scandal broke into the news and things began to change.

The break-in at the Democratic National Committee's Washington offices in the Watergate building had taken place back in June 1972, but through the summer and beyond election day, most people had accepted the administration's dismissal of it as a "third rate burglary." Although Democratic presidential candidate George McGovern had tried to make it a campaign issue by contending

---

January 8, 1973
Wide World of Entertainment. (ABC). Revamping its late night schedule after failing to catch Johnny Carson with Dick Cavett's talk show, ABC institutes a complicated new format arrangement and brings in a former late night giant, Jack Paar. Each month, *Jack Paar Tonight* appears for one week, Cavett runs for one week, and the remaining two weeks are filled with movies, specials, and concerts.

February 2, 1973
The Midnight Special. (NBC). Network television's first late late night show, running from 1:00 A.M. till 2:30 A.M. Friday nights. Hosted by legendary rock DJ Wolfman Jack, the program is NBC's answer to the ABC *In Concert* show.

March 31, 1973
Frank Stanton, president of CBS, Inc. for twenty-five years and, since 1971, vice chairman of the CBS board, retires upon reaching the age of sixty-five.

May 4, 1973
Bruce Jay Friedman's play "Steambath" is shown on PBS's *Hollywood Television Theater,* but only a few stations are brave enough to carry it. The story offers an unusual portrayal of the afterlife, with God presented as a Puerto Rican steambath attendant. Bill Bixby plays a man who refuses to admit that he has died, and Valerie Perrine becomes one of the first women to display her nipples on American network television.

August 6, 1973
Following a tremendous publicity campaign, CBS unveils its new morning news line-up consisting of veteran television newsman Hughes Rudd and newspaper reporter-TV neophyte Sally Quinn.

that the Nixon administration was tied in with the burglars, most people dismissed that as a desperate political ploy by a candidate hopelessly behind in the polls. *Washington Post* reporters Bob Woodward and Carl Bernstein had turned out a steady stream of stories also suggesting a tie-in between the White House and the burglary but, without substantial documentation, no one cared. Television virtually ignored the story. CBS was the only network to do anything important with Watergate before the election, scheduling two fifteen-minute reports on the topic for Walter Cronkite's evening news show during the last week of the campaign. Most Americans were indifferent to the story but, after viewing the first report, presidential aide Charles Colson tried to pressure CBS chairman William Paley into canceling the second report. The second story aired anyway, despite Colson's efforts, though it was cut in half.

In March 1973, the Senate set up a select committee, under Senator Sam Ervin of North Carolina, to look into the numerous charges of impropriety that had been raised by then. The committee scheduled public hearings for the spring and summer and the networks were faced with a familiar, perplexing problem: What was the best way to cover congressional hearings on a topic that was suddenly very important? They feared that the procedure might drag on for months and gavel-to-gavel coverage would cost a small fortune in lost revenue, estimated at $300,000 per network per day. All three broadcast the opening week's sessions in May and then they agreed to a simple but practical solution: They would rotate coverage. Each day, one network would take its turn showing the hearings while the other two maintained their normal schedules-though they both had the option to carry the session as well if they wished to. This wonderfully obvious solution satisfied nearly everybody. People who did not care about Watergate could find a soap opera or game show on another network. No one network was backed into a corner and forced to carry the burden alone. Viewers who were interested in the hearings were guaranteed that one network (at least) would have the story. For public television, however, the problem was not so easily resolved.

As soon as the hearings were announced, the administration put strong pressure on PBS stations, discouraging live coverage. For a while it looked as if the tactic might succeed, but the audacity of the action struck some of the larger stations as going too far. WETA in Washington, WGBH in Boston, WNET in New York, KCET in Los Angeles, and KQED in San Francisco staged their own counter-revolution and formed the so-called salvation network, a group determined to oppose White House efforts to control public television. In April, forces from the salvation network seized control of the PBS board and immediately launched an attack on the Nixon-controlled CPB parent organization. This counter-pressure led to an attempt to reach a compromise, with Tom Curtis acting as chief negotiator, but the CPB board rejected the truce proposal. Curtis resigned as CPB chairman, charging that his efforts had been undermined by administration interference. Board member James Killian, who had been appointed by President Johnson, assumed the post of CPB chairman as an official with no obvious ties to the White House. In spite of continued administration pressure to prevent coverage of the hearings, the newly rejuvenated PBS decided instead to provide extensive coverage, using its Washington-based production agency, NPACT, the National Public Affairs Center for Television (responsible for such programs as *Washington Week in Review*). Via NPACT, PBS sent out both gavel-to-gavel daytime coverage and, more important, taped replays in prime time. The evening rebroadcasts, hosted by Robert MacNeil and Jim Lehrer, allowed millions of working people the opportunity to see the actual hearings virtually intact and to judge for themselves the importance of what had taken place that day.

Just as in the Army-McCarthy hearings of 1954, interest in the Watergate hearings was low at first, but picked up as the public became familiar with the personalities involved and began to appreciate the gravity of the charges. All through the summer, major figures from the administration appeared before the committee. Some confessed to minor infractions while others "stonewalled" and denied any wrongdoing whatsoever. At the end of June, former Nixon counsel John Dean testified for five consecutive days, laying out the most detailed, damaging charges of the summer in which he stated his belief that President Nixon had not only known of the cover-up, but had probably directed it. All three commercial networks chose to cover his testimony and the public was inundated with Watergate stories. The continuing characters of the Ervin committee became national celebrities, with the Bible-quoting Southern drawl of Senator Ervin himself the biggest hit of all. Catch phrases such as "At that point in time," "To the best of my recollection," and "Deep-six" wound their way from the witnesses' testimony to become common slang across the nation.

Much to the amazement of the networks, the usual drop-off in summer TV viewing never took place. People could not seem to get enough of Watergate. In response, NBC began to include a weekly two-hour Watergate wrapup in prime time every Friday. CBS averaged three sixty-minute prime time wrapups each week, covering the days the other networks handled the daytime rotation. The prime time PBS coverage brought in staggeringly high ratings for public television stations across the country, with some almost reaching the level of a low-rated commercial network show. Daytime coverage regularly topped the game shows and soap operas offered by the other networks, which turned out to be no competition to the real-life drama unfolding every day as the committee (and the public) tried to answer the question: What did the President know and when did he know it? On July 16, the investigation reached a dramatic high point as former Nixon aide Alexander Butterfield revealed that an elaborate secret taping system had been set up in the White House and that there were probably recordings of the many meetings and conversations that had been cited throughout the committee's hearings. The committee requested access to the tapes. President Nixon refused to release them. One month later, after hearing from almost everyone involved in White House affairs, the Ervin committee adjourned for a fall vacation. The networks returned to their normal broadcasting schedules and prepared to launch the 1973–74 season.

Technically, the months of testimony had produced no tangible results or hard evidence. Those who ardently believed in Nixon's innocence remained unconvinced by the testimony. Even those who felt that the entire administration, from Nixon on down, had been proved guilty many times over acknowledged that there did not appear to be enough clear evidence that could be used to support a vote for impeachment by the House and a trial by the Senate. In reality, though, the testimony resulted in a monumental change in attitude among the American people. Public confidence in the president had plummeted during the televised hearings. The Ervin committee had presided over a struggle for the hearts and minds of the American public similar to the Army-McCarthy hearings two decades before. Once again, television had expanded the forum and allowed the entire nation, as one, to examine a vital issue. Though it still seemed that Nixon would be around for "four more years," he had lost his most powerful tool, the confidence of the nation. He might still be President of the United States, but he was no longer in a position to make the press jump.

33. The New Centurions

THE TIMING OF THE SENATE Watergate hearings in the summer of 1973 had been perfect for the networks. Not only did the proceedings end just in time to avoid interfering with the fall premieres, they also helped fill the void in a summer schedule that was leaner than usual. As the result of a three and one-half month strike by television writers in the spring of 1973, program production had ground to a halt. There was an obvious absence of new material for the summer months, and the networks relied on news specials and reruns of old series to carry them through to the fall. The major effect of the strike, though, was felt in September.

Most programs airing in September normally began preproduction work in March, immediately after the networks announced the next fall's schedule. Filming followed in June and most series were ready well before the early September premiere week. The writers' strike did not end until June, so the entire process was thrown off. Despite the frantic work by the writers and crews all through the summer of 1973 once the strike was settled, there just was not enough time. Consequently, the networks were forced to ease into the 1973–74 season and, for the first time in a decade, their season premieres had to be strung out over a month. The new series and new episodes of returning programs were aired as they came in. Hastily assembled specials and more reruns filled the remaining gaps. Amid this confusion, CBS was pleasantly surprised with the high ratings scored by *Dan August,* a loner cop series starring Burt Reynolds, which had flopped on ABC in 1970. CBS had picked it up as just another writers' strike filler for the summer, but the program outscored not only the other summer reruns but even some new fall series as well. *Dan August* remained on the air long enough to serve as a strong warmup for the program that was delayed the longest by the writers' strike, another cop show, *Kojak,* which did not premiere until October 24, the last new series of 1973–74 to arrive.

There were high hopes for *Kojak* among critics and programmers, based in large part on the quality of the feature-length pilot that had aired the previous March, "The Marcus-Nelson Murders." The three-hour TV film, based on the real life Wylie-Hoffert murder case in New York City, introduced Telly Savalas as Lieutenant Theo Kojak, a radiantly bald, fiercely independent Greek plainclothes detective on the New York City force who fought the establishment he worked for, and lost. Savalas had spent the better part of his career playing an assortment of criminal roles, and he brought a gritty edge to his portrayal of the tough realistic cop. In the pilot, Kojak saw the methods the police had used to railroad a black Brooklyn kid, falsely accused of rape, into confessing to a completely unrelated crime, a double-murder, and he set about to prove the confession baseless. After tedious legwork by Kojak and a lengthy trial, the youth was exonerated of the murders and Kojak joined the happy family to celebrate. Their triumph was short lived. Determined to salvage some "law and order" publicity, the police and prosecutors resurrected the original rape charge and forced the boy back into court to defend himself. Though technically a different case, it was really the same trial all over again, only the prosecution had refined its presentation while the boy, shocked at the turn of events, had lost his confidence and composure. Stunned, Kojak watched helplessly as a new jury delivered a verdict of guilty. The boy was sent to jail and, this time, there was no last minute reprieve. Kojak had been outmaneuvered and could not do anything to change things. Even his own resignation would have been meaningless. He remained at his post, keenly aware of his own limitations but determined to continue the sometimes hopeless fight for justice.

"The Marcus-Nelson Murders" set very high standards for the series and it soon became apparent that the exceptionally late premiere date reflected time well spent in production. Though it made concessions to the reality of the weekly TV grind (Kojak usually *won* his new cases), the program was the best scripted, directed, and acted cop show on TV, and it maintained the spirit of the highly praised pilot. Kojak remained the people's champion, confident, tough, and willing to defend neighborhoods and individuals battered by crime and injustice. In addition, the writers expanded on some themes implicit in the pilot: In the 1970s, the easily understood and clearly identified mobsters and crime czars of the past had been replaced in the public's mind by more amorphous, but equally frightening, forces. Criminals were often violent delinquents or madmen with no stake in society, who attacked randomly for no discernible reason. Even worse, the machinery of justice itself seemed to break down with increasing frequency, often looming as a greater threat than the criminals it was supposed to punish. Kojak was presented as a reassuring figure capable of taking on both of these elements. He was cool under pressure, streetwise, and always in control. At the same time, he was too smart to let his distrust of the bureaucracy blind him to the most effective ways to use it. Kojak could confront a self-serving bureaucrat and a trigger-happy punk with the same unflinching determination, never wasting his anger on meaningless macho stunts. He out-maneuvered his opponents, waited for the perfect moment,

	8:00	8:30	9:00	9:30	10:00	10:30	
M O N	The Rookies		ABC NFL Monday Night Football (to 12 Midnight)				**ABC**
	Gunsmoke		Here's Lucy	New Dick Van Dyke Show	Medical Center		**CBS**
	LOTSA LUCK	DIANA	NBC Monday Night At the Movies				**NBC**
T U E	New Temperature's Rising Show	Tuesday Movie Of The Week			Marcus Welby, M.D.		**ABC**
	Maude	Hawaii Five-O		The New CBS Tuesday Night Movies / SHAFT / HAWKINS			**CBS**
	CHASE		THE MAGICIAN		POLICE STORY		**NBC**
W E D	BOB & CAROL & TED & ALICE	Wednesday Movie Of The Week			Owen Marshall, Counselor At Law / # DOC ELLIOT		**ABC**
	Sonny And Cher Comedy Hour		Cannon		KOJAK		**CBS**
	Adam-12	NBC Wednesday Mystery Movie (Banacek; TENAFLY; FARADAY AND COMPANY; SNOOP SISTERS)			LOVE STORY		**NBC**
T H R	TOMA		Kung-Fu		The Streets Of San Francisco		**ABC**
	The Waltons		CBS Thursday Night Movies				**CBS**
	Flip Wilson Show		Ironside / # Bob Hope Show		NBC FOLLIES		**NBC**
F R I	The Brady Bunch	The Odd Couple	Room 222	ADAM'S RIB	Love, American Style		**ABC**
	CALUCCI'S DEPARTMENT	ROLL OUT	CBS Friday Night Movies				**CBS**
	Sanford And Son	THE GIRL WITH SOMETHING EXTRA	NEEDLES AND PINS	Brian Keith Show	Dean Martin Comedy Hour		**NBC**
S A T	The Partridge Family	ABC SUSPENSE MOVIE / # THE SIX MILLION DOLLAR MAN			GRIFF		**ABC**
	All In The Family	M*A*S*H	Mary Tyler Moore Show	Bob Newhart Show	Carol Burnett Show		**CBS**
	Emergency		NBC Saturday Night At The Movies				**NBC**

	7:00	7:30	8:00	8:30	9:00	9:30	10:00	10:30	
S U N	local	The FBI		The ABC Sunday Night Movie				local	**ABC**
	local	NEW ADVENTURES OF PERRY MASON		Mannix		Barnaby Jones		local	**CBS**
	local	The Wonderful World Of Disney		NBC Sunday Mystery Movie (McCloud; Columbo; McMillan And Wife; Hec Ramsey)				# NBC News Presents (10:00-11:00)	**NBC**

and then exploded. When Kojak let loose, his personal energy crackled. He obviously enjoyed both his verbal and physical confrontations because they sometimes provided the only opportunity for justice to triumph. Savalas infused Kojak with a saucy independent personality that dominated the program and gave the scripts added punch. His portrayal of the confident bald man who brandished a lollipop instead of a cigar turned him into a very unlikely national sex symbol and attracted viewers that otherwise had only mild interest in cop shows.

The most controversial aspect of *Kojak,* however, was its use of violence, and some people brushed aside the excellent acting, writing, and directing to denounce the show as dangerous and harmful. Actually, there was a noticeable upswing in violent action throughout the networks' crime formats this season, reflecting the popularity of violent theatrical cop films such as "The French Connection." *Kojak* admittedly contained its share of violence, but the writers and producers handled it well. Just as *The Untouchables* had used violent shoot-outs to underscore the brutality of gangland activity in the 1930s, *Kojak* used violence as an artful illustration of the frustration of the 1970s. The entire program was as carefully controlled as Kojak himself, with violent interludes used to punctuate the conflicts and emotions. To ignore violence in a program that attempted to present a gritty, realistic picture of New York City urban crime contradicted its very premise. Nonetheless, over the years the level of violent action in the program

was reduced somewhat in response to protests from organized pressure groups strongly opposed to TV violence in any form, no matter how artistically effective. In order to restore some of that lost energy in later years, the producers tried to compensate in other ways, such as filming on location in New York City to accentuate the urban atmosphere of the program.

Kojak became an immediate hit in the fall of 1973 and the newest star in a solid line-up of crime programs on all three networks. For decades, such shows had served as basic bread-and-butter programming, occasionally slumping due to overexposure or claims of excessive violence, but inevitably returning with some slight twist, unusual setting, gimmick hero, or outstanding performer as a new draw. Network number one, CBS, for instance, always liked to mix in a few crime dramas with its sitcom strategy because while hit sitcoms scored very well, flopped sitcoms were equally big losers, landing at the very bottom of the ratings charts. Crime shows usually hugged the middle positions in the ratings, turning in a generally stable if not outstanding performance. There were ten new crime shows in the fall of 1973 and, as evidenced by *Kojak,* the loner cop format was still on the upswing that had begun in the 1971–72 season. Many of the new entries were obvious imitations of the latest gimmick variations to the form. In the 1972–73 season, veteran Buddy Ebsen had taken his down-home country charm into the fight against urban crime in Quinn Martin's *Barnaby Jones,* and the show had become a second season CBS hit. In the fall of 1973, veteran low-key charmers Jimmy Stewart and Lorne Greene tried their hands in, respectively, *Hawkins* (a common sense criminal attorney) and *Griff* (an L.A. private eye), but they both flopped. *Banacek,* another hit show from the previous season, had featured a confident ethnic hero, a dapper Polish insurance company detective played by George Peppard. In the usually WASP world of TV cops, such a character was a rarity and, sure enough, several other ethnic detectives appeared along with Kojak in the fall of 1973. With the exception of *Kojak,* however, most of these programs had serious inherent flaws and floundered in the ratings despite the ethnic hook.

There was already an obvious model for the new black TV detectives in the wildly successful black Superman-type that appeared in such theatrical films as "Superfly" and "Shaft." NBC's *Tenafly* consciously avoided this image while CBS brought Shaft himself to network television. Both interpretations left viewers with the uncomfortable feeling that something was missing. In the case of *Shaft,* it seemed obvious. Despite the fact that the film's star, Richard Roundtree, repeated the title role of New York City private detective John Shaft for the TV series, he had to leave his violent, sexy world behind. Instead, *Shaft* was given a carbon copy of *Columbo's* structure in which, at the beginning of each episode, the crime was shown as it took place and the rest of the story focused on Shaft's investigation. Unlike Columbo, who talked the villains to death, Shaft had always depended on direct, explicitly violent, methods of persuasion, with an undercurrent of legitimate distaste for manipulative whites in positions of power. Revenge and retribution were acceptable options through the three theatrical features ("Shaft," "Shaft's Big Score," and "Shaft in Africa"), but all the tough talk, blazing gun battles, and beautiful women had to be sanitized for television. As a result, TV's *Shaft* seemed a pale imitation of the real thing.

NBC's *Tenafly* tried so hard to avoid the image of a black superdude that it went too far in the other direction. Richard Levinson and William Link, the team responsible for *Columbo,* presented private detective Harry Tenafly (James McEachin) as just a regular Joe, an average family man with few exciting or distinguishing characteristics. Each episode of the series devoted nearly as much time to his middle class home life and family (a wife and two children) as to the case at hand. It ended up as just plain dull.

One ethnic series that did manage to bring the world of violent exploitation movies to television with some success was ABC's *Toma,* loosely based on the exploits of Dave Toma (played by Tony Musante), an actual undercover Italian policeman from Newark, New Jersey. Though the stories made superficial nods to real life drama (Toma had a home life and was shown in bed with his wife), they had none of the class of *Kojak* and instead embraced some of the worst features of the era's violent films by focusing on violence, brutal sex, and Toma's foul mouth. This was accomplished within the confines of television through implication; the audience was shown everything except the violent acts themselves. For example, one episode featured a kinky rapist with a talcum powder fetish. His frenzied attacks were conveyed by vivid closeups of each victim's face, flashes of talcum powder, and screams, grunts, and gasps which built to a ferocious climax. Without focusing on anything more explicit than the look of terror on the woman's face, these scenes could satisfy a viewer's voyeuristic fantasies nearly as well as the more explicit brutality of the theatrical films. *Toma* also captured the spirit of the abusive language of these films with snarling putdowns such as "If that hooker of yours doesn't shut her mouth, I'll stuff it full of dead fish." *Kojak* proved that television violence could be done artistically and used it to reinforce generally realistic themes and settings. *Toma* did not

bother with such complexities and lasted only one season, though some of its core elements would be revamped and handled more effectively the following season with *Baretta*.

Ethnic detectives were, of course, just another strain in the continuing crime format boom. As in most fads, a rash of them appeared over a few seasons, a few outstanding ones survived, and then another gimmick surfaced. The crime genre was so resilient because, within the gimmick setups, countless minor variations could be incorporated into the same plots. Innovations that led to an entirely new approach to crime were rare. Jack Webb's presentation of policemen as intricate professionals using brains, not brawn, had been such a dramatic departure in the 1950s. Its aftereffects were still being felt in television twenty years later when it stood as a television staple. In 1973–74, a successful innovation away from the Jack Webb school of policework arrived from the hands of Joseph Wambaugh, a Los Angeles policeman who moonlighted as a very successful writer. (His police novel, *The New Centurions,* had been turned into a feature film.)

Over the years, the incessant repetition of Webb's stock characters had turned his innovation into a cliché of its own. Cops in programs such as *Adam-12* had become monotonous automatons that talked in clipped phrases and never seemed to entertain an evil thought. Wambaugh knew better. There were bad cops, good cops who made terrible mistakes in judgment, and outstanding officers who performed brilliantly under tremendous pressure. He felt each of the categories offered the potential for rich drama, so he created an anthology series for NBC, *Police Story,* in order to exploit these possibilities. By adopting the anthology format, Wambaugh freed himself from the limitations of one central character that could not possibly incorporate every nuance of police action and remain creditable. Instead, he used different guest celebrities in weekly stories that dealt with every aspect of policework. They all shared a sharp, realistic style of dialogue (in contrast to Webb's officialese) as well as an affection for the common cop on the beat who, despite his faults, was usually presented as doing the best job possible. *Police Story* opened a rich new field of police drama that focused on more realistic characters who also faced personal problems that sometimes affected their on-the-job performance. As with many innovative series, *Police Story* caught on very slowly. Though it never became a big hit, it continued in the tradition of TV's best cop shows, delivering dependable ratings in its time slot while inspiring a number of spinoffs and imitations such as *Police Woman, Joe Forrester,* and *David Cassidy: Man Undercover.*

Even as he launched his anthology series, Wambaugh was hard at work on another innovative project, a four-part miniseries focusing on the career of one cop, Bumper Morgan (William Holden), who was rapidly approaching retirement age. *The Blue Knight* ostensibly traced the investigation following the murder of a prostitute, but the crux of the story was Morgan's battle with advancing age. He painfully acknowledged that he was too old to do all the legwork necessary to the case, but he insisted that, mentally, he was just as sharp as ever. In any case, he feared retirement because he knew he was not ready to cope with such a drastic change in his life. The program was an extended display of Wambaugh's cop philosophy and could have easily played on consecutive weeks of *Police Story* as a series within the series. Instead, NBC ran the four-hour drama on four consecutive nights beginning Tuesday, November 13, in a bold experiment that marked a breakthrough in television programming. Reactions ranged from mild surprise to outright ridicule. Some snidely suggested that such a schedule demanded too much attention from home viewers to succeed. The ratings from the miniseries proved inconclusive. *The Blue Knight* averaged a 30% share of the audi-

August 15, 1973

Man About the House. Britain's Thames Television network presents a new sitcom featuring Richard O'Sullivan as a young man who moves into an apartment with two cute young women (played by Paula Wilcox and Sally Thomsett). Though the set-up sounds racy, the three actually maintain a very innocent household, which puzzles their apartment landlord (played by Brian Murphy) and his sex-starved wife (played by Yootha Joyce).

September 8, 1973

Star Trek. (NBC). With syndicated reruns of the old series more popular than the show ever was on NBC, the original *Star Trek* crew is reunited to supply voices for a Saturday morning animated cartoon series that continues the "five year" mission of the starship *Enterprise* for another two years.

September 10, 1973

Diana. (NBC). Diana Rigg breaks from her adventurer image and stars in a sitcom about a gorgeous young British divorcee trying to make it in the New York fashion world, but the program folds within a few months. One highlight: a guest appearance by former *Avengers* cohort Patrick Macnee.

October 15, 1973

Tomorrow. (NBC). With *The Midnight Special* scoring well Fridays in the late late night slot, NBC brings Los Angeles TV newsman Tom Snyder to New York to host an hour-long late late talk show Monday through Thursday.

November 16, 1973

After slipping badly following his great opening ratings in his occasional ABC late night slot, Jack Paar departs network television again.

---

ence which, while respectable, was no vindication of the concept. It was left to ABC with its two-part presentation of *QB VII* at the end of April to prove the concept could be very successful.

QB VII was a six-hour adaptation of the lengthy Leon Uris novel that followed the post-war life of a Polish doctor who had performed experiments on inmates in a Nazi concentration camp. Part one focused on the war trial of the doctor while part two examined his life through 1972. The first episode attracted a healthy 38% share and the following night's wrap-up did even better, winding up the fifth highest rated show of the week. Buoyed by this success, ABC announced plans for the presentation of multi-part adaptations of other major works such as *Rich Man, Poor Man, Eleanor and Franklin,* and the as-then unpublished *Roots.* The network had been talking about "novels for television" ever since *Peyton Place* and the 1969 Harold Robbins series *The Survivors,* but the success of *QB VII* and *The Blue Knight* convinced ABC that the development of several miniseries could provide occasional boosts to ratings in much the same manner as blockbuster movies such as "Bridge on the River Kwai" and "Airport."

ABC was still patching together a prime time schedule that included practically anything that might hype ratings, even on a one-shot basis, because it had once again begun slipping from contention. In many ways, the situation was reminiscent of ABC's woes in the mid-1960s when it instituted the attention-grabbing concepts of an early premiere week and the second season. The

major difference was that few such tactics were left. Even the "third season" (beginning in the spring) that was made possible by the Nielsen company's new "overnight" ratings service did not have the popular impact of the previous gimmicks.

ABC had again repeated one of its most frequent programming sins, loading its schedule with too many spinoffs of a hit gimmick, thus diluting its strength. Made-for-TV movie slots occupied the greater part of three nights of the network schedule, but they were no longer sure-fire ratings winners; the network regularly peppered them with tabloid-style stories on such topics as prostitution, homosexuality, bigamy, and rape. Attempts to exploit the new strain of sitcoms pioneered by CBS flopped in such series as *Adam's Rib* and *Bob and Carol and Ted and Alice.* ABC's highest rated show (18th) was its *Monday Night Football* broadcast (now in its fourth season). For the season, ABC's greatest individual successes came with comic book–type heroes and by grafting a topical hook onto an otherwise routine sports event.

ABC realized very early in the season that it might be possible to exploit one of the few areas in which the network was a respected leader, sports, and so it filled one of the writers' strike gaps in September with "Tennis—The Battle of the Sexes." This silly "confrontation" between fifty-five-year-old over-the-hill tennis boor Bobby Riggs and up-and-coming twenty-nine-year-old Billie Jean King was no contest (King won easily), but ABC treated the match with the same intense coverage television usually reserved for such events as the World Series or political nominating conventions. The fluff contest was set, appropriately, in the 100% artificial Houston Astrodome, in prime time, and ballyhooed as the monumental resolution of the perpetual battle between men and women. In order to insure a "balanced" presentation of such an important event, the network assigned one male and one female to serve as color commentators. They supplemented the "play-by-play" reporting by ABC's front line team of Frank Gifford and Howard Cosell, whose convoluted phraseology (such as "making assurance doubly sure") was particularly humorous that night. Despite strong counter-programming by CBS, the tennis special registered lovely ratings for ABC and demonstrated the viability of sexual hooks and pseudo sports events. The show also pointed to a general formula that the network had decided to exploit.

With CBS cornering the audience for programs with more adult, real-world concerns, ABC chose to concentrate on the fantasy world of tabloids and pulp adventure. In that, the network's brightest hopes were two larger-than-life heroic caricatures, Kwai Chang Caine and Steve Austin.

Caine's adventures had begun in the 1972–73 season on a once a month series, *Kung–Fu.* David Carradine played a half Chinese, half American martial arts master who roamed the American West of the 1870s as a veritable Jove of Justice in a premise that mixed bits of *The Fugitive,* "Lost Horizon," and "Billy Jack." Like *The Fugitive* he was on the run, having fled China after deliberately (but in his eyes, justifiably) killing a member of the royal family. His thoughts frequently returned to the rigorous training of his youth in far away China as he attempted to serve the cause of justice in the lawless West. Caine took himself very, very seriously, spouting Oriental wisdom and platitudes of peace (in the preachy self-righteous style of Tom Laughlin's Billy Jack character) and was a bona-fide priest within his obscure religious sect. He preached non-violence and could overwhelm his foes by the sheer force of his character. However, Cain usually did not stop there. Despite his "best efforts" to avoid violent confrontations, Cain was inevitably forced to draw on his physical fighting skills, leading one reviewer to describe the show as "pacifist vegetarian priest beats the holy bejeezus out of frontier bullies." These battles were

On April 29, 1974, President Nixon presented his most effective speech dealing with Watergate, using as background props bound volumes of transcripts from his secretly taped conversations. *(National Archives)*

presented in slow motion, reinforcing a comic caricature style to the program. In early 1973, *Kung-Fu* was promoted to a weekly slot, though it did not become a hit until late in the year. The program displayed enough promise in its first season, however, to encourage ABC to approve development of a somewhat similar project for the 1973–74 season, *The Six Million Dollar Man.*

Like *Kung-Fu,* the new series began in the fall as a once a month offering and, as part of a reshuffling of ABC's schedule in January 1974, it was awarded weekly status. The show moved the slow motion battle scenes from the past to the immediate future, featuring the exploits of Steve Austin (Lee Majors), an astronaut who had been horribly crushed in an Air Force jet crash. Rescued from the rubble, he was reconstructed at great government expense (six million dollars) and outfitted with nuclear powered limbs that gave him powers and abilities far beyond those of most mortal men, in an effective update of the ever-popular Superman legend. Unlike *Kung-Fu,* the scripts for *The Six Million Dollar Man* were not burdened with excessive simplistic philosophical preaching. Austin willingly joined the government's Office of Strategic Operations (a CIA-style organization) and fought America's enemies at home and abroad in the best tradition of such wartime comic book patriots as Captain America. The show delivered exciting fantasy and demonstrated that airy comic book television could be done well. When ABC moved Austin into a weekly slot as part of the 1973–74 mid-season shakeup, *The Six Million Dollar Man* became the network's top rated show.

The second season shuffling also resulted in another welcome hit for ABC, the nostalgic *Happy Days* (produced by Garry Marshall, who had adapted *The Odd Couple* for television). As its name implied, *Happy Days* turned from the grim reality of the turbulent early 1970s to the simple rituals of teenage life in the already legendary 1950s. *Andy Griffith Show* veteran Ron Howard played cute-but-shy Richie Cunningham, a very average, very bland teenager living in the very bland city of Milwaukee with his nondescript family: a kind and bumbling father (Tom Bosley), a cheerful and understanding mother (Marion Ross), and a cute-but-devilish younger sister, Joanie (Erin Moran). The sitcom usually focused on the escapades of Richie and his bosom buddy, Potsie

Weber (Anson Williams), two struggling high school innocents who shared teenage fantasies about sock hops, girls, and hot rods. The *Happy Days* pilot episode had run on *Love, American Style* in February 1972, and the show's premise was far removed from the new wave of comedy of CBS. Nonetheless, *Happy Days* immediately entered the top twenty, right behind *The Six Million Dollar Man* in the ratings.

Happy Days owed much of its initial success to momentum from the theatrical film "American Graffiti" (the surprise blockbuster of 1973), in which Howard (the only cast member also in the TV series) had played Steve Bolander, a character very similar to Richie Cunningham. Unlike the film, though, the TV series lacked a strong central character (such as Richard Dreyfuss's Curt Henderson). Howard's Richie was made far too weak and Potsie was a klutz. There was a token hood, Fonzie (Henry Winkler), similar to the John Milner character of the film (played by Paul LeMat), but unlike LeMat, Winkler had only a minor role in the stories.

At the same time *Happy Days* offered itself as an entertaining look back at the 1950s, two key figures from the era were passing from the scene. They both owed their success to television and both had continued to use it successfully for two decades. Only one went out in triumph.

After twenty-three years of almost continuous production, Lucille Ball retired from the weekly TV grind. She had taken her character through several different settings, but the format had remained the same for all of them: wacky redhead against the world. The final permutation, *Here's Lucy,* featured her real life children as co-stars (Lucie and Desi Arnaz, Jr.) and it was a highly appropriate way for the original queen of television to depart, alongside the young man whose birth had marked the beginning of modern TV. Lucy ended her sitcom run with style and class. Her contemporary, Richard M. Nixon, had experienced an equally long (though considerably rockier) television career, but he left his profession in shame and disgrace.

The Ervin committee had adjourned in August of 1973 and it appeared that President Nixon would have a breathing spell after months of public inquiry. Instead, a new unrelated scandal rocked

January 31, 1974

"The Autobiography of Miss Jane Pittman." (CBS). Richard Rosenberg and Robert Christiansen adapt a successful novel into a powerful television drama special spanning black American history from slavery to the civil rights marches. Cicely Tyson portrays Jane Pittman, a proud black woman, in four stages of her life: from young womanhood to the age of 110. The highly praised program wins nine Emmy Awards.

February 1, 1974

Sally Quinn quietly departs *The CBS Morning News,* confessing that she was not really prepared for the job.

April 17, 1974

Frank McGee, fifty-two, host of NBC's *Today,* dies of cancer.

July 4, 1974

Bicentennial Minute. (CBS). The first sixty-second program in television history. Once each night, for more than two years, a celebrity reports on "the way it was" in American history on that date 200 years earlier.

July 29, 1974

Jim Hartz becomes the new host of *Today.*

September 2, 1974

After starring in a CBS television series for twenty-one of the previous twenty-three years, Lucille Ball takes a breather. *Here's Lucy* joins *The Lucy Show* and *I Love Lucy* in the never-ending world of reruns.

---

his administration, touching the one man who had gone through Watergate unscathed, Vice President Spiro Agnew. An investigation into general corruption in Maryland led to allegations of bribery payments to Agnew going back to the days when he had served as the Baltimore county executive. Determined to meet the challenge to his integrity head on, Agnew embarked upon a nation-wide speaking tour in the hope of stirring his supporters into pressuring the Maryland prosecutor to call off his dogs. An old hand at manipulating television, Agnew knew his rhetoric would make news and he convinced NBC to carry, nationwide, a speech before a group of Republican women in California on September 29. Looking straight into the camera without batting an eye (as only an honest person could), Agnew proclaimed, "I will not resign if indicted! I will *not* resign if indicted!" On October 10, Agnew resigned, pleading *nolo contendere* ("no contest," virtually equivalent to admitting the charges were true by not challenging any of them) to charges of tax evasion on the bribery payments made to him by Maryland contractors. He was sentenced to three years' probation and fined $10,000. Five days after Agnew's resignation, all three commercial networks, for the first time in history, gave thirty minutes of free prime time to a felon charged with extortion, bribery, and conspiracy. In this last appearance before the public, Agnew ignored his *nolo contendere* plea and pronounced himself innocent. NBC's legal correspondent, Carl Stern, was incredulous. In the network analysis immediately following the speech, Stern compared Agnew's courtroom admissions of guilt with his TV plea to be judged innocent and pointed out that the facts did not support this stance. CBS allowed Agnew's speech to stand on its own, though, as the network continued to exclude instant analysis from its news operations.

Agnew's case had nothing to do with Watergate, but it furthered the perception of total corruption waiting to be unearthed in the Nixon administration. Ten days after Agnew's resignation, Nixon fired Archibald Cox, the special Watergate prosecutor. This touched off the first serious calls for the president's impeachment.

In mid-November, following publication of an old memo in which Nixon aide Charles Colson bragged of intimidating CBS chairman William Paley, CBS announced it would immediately resume providing analysis following presidential addresses. PBS also exhibited a renewed independence and presented some new public affairs programming such as the excellent "Essay on Watergate" on *Bill Moyers' Journal,* a fair but opinionated one-hour primer on the complex and sometimes confusing events of Watergate. On the evening news shows, new sources of suspicion continued to appear before the public. Seven top White House aides were indicted for their role in the coverup. One of the tapes Nixon was pressured into releasing contained a mysterious 18½ minute gap during a key conversation. The possibility was even raised that Nixon had deliberately claimed illegal deductions on his income tax.

As he had done so often throughout his career, Nixon turned to television as a means of appealing directly to the people and possibly blunting negative sentiment building against him. President Nixon went on a nation-wide speaking tour and the networks covered, live, his appearances before sympathetic audiences and he scored a few minor points. Nixon was obviously feeling the pressure, however, and openly sniped at reporters and the commercial networks during the tour. At one televised press conference he nervously exclaimed, "I am not a crook." At another, he pointed out that he was not really angry at the press because "you can only be angry at those you respect." On April 29, 1974, Nixon at last delivered his first truly effective television speech on Watergate. Pleading with the nation to move on to more important business and put Watergate aside ("One year of Watergate is enough"), he proudly displayed a huge stack of notebooks which contained hundreds of pages of edited transcripts from most of the White House tapes that had been requested by the courts and by the House impeachment committee. Nixon explained that the unprecedented disclosure of private presidential conversations demonstrated his willingness to cooperate in the various investigations and proved he had nothing to hide. It was a very successful speech, but its positive effects quickly dissipated as people examined the text of the transcripts.

Television's treatment of the mountain of material proved particularly devastating. Instead of being overwhelmed by the sheer volume of the release, the network reporters who had been covering Watergate for months zeroed in on several very important conversations and all three networks presented specials featuring oral readings of transcript excerpts. The results were devastating to Nixon's image. Even heavily edited, the transcripts revealed Richard Nixon as a petty, self-centered man with little concern for justice and an obvious contempt for those he regarded as his enemies. After carefully studying the conversations, even previously friendly newspapers such as the *Chicago Tribune* (which had rushed to print the transcripts verbatim for free distribution to its readers) sadly but firmly called for the president's resignation. Others called for impeachment, convinced that Nixon would never succumb to the calls that he should step down.

After months of deliberation behind closed doors, the House Judiciary Committee opened its formal impeachment hearings to the public, including television, on July 24 and the reality of impeachment hit everyone in the country. As with the Senate hearings the previous year, the mid-summer timing was perfect for the

Before they boarded the helicopter waiting to take them to Air Force One, President Richard Nixon and Pat Nixon shared parting words with Vice President Gerald Ford and Betty Ford. *(National Archives)*

Saturday, July 27, the debate reached a dramatic climax, the formal vote on the first article of impeachment. In a scene reminiscent of *Studio One*'s "Twelve Angry Men," the TV cameras focused on each member's face for the roll call voice vote. Throughout the country, viewers shared the drama and tallied the score as the camera panned from member to member, each speaking only one word: "yes" or "no." The motion passed, 27 to 11.

Two additional articles of impeachment were voted and it appeared almost certain that the full House would approve the resolution of impeachment, which would lead to a trial in the Senate in the fall unless Nixon stepped down voluntarily before then. At first, it looked as if he would "tough it out" and the networks nervously stood by, ready to cover the lengthy procedure live, fully aware that the process would seriously disrupt their new fall programming.

On August 5, Nixon released an additional tape transcript which served as the long-sought smoking gun and proved to nearly everyone that he had participated in an obstruction of justice. Three days later, Richard Nixon announced his resignation in a prime time address carried live by the networks. They canceled all regular programming for the evening and devoted four hours to the resignation and reactions to it. Nixon's speech was rather restrained and, though lacking both an adequate explanation for his decision to step down and any admission of guilt, it was remarkably free of recrimination. It was so straight that in the analysis that immediately followed, CBS correspondent Dan Rather, a frequent target of Nixon's ire, gushed that the speech contained "nobility" and "a touch of class," before colleague Roger Mudd began to pick it apart. Some die-hard Nixon supporters such as South Carolina Senator Strom Thurmond went even further and described Nixon's tenure as president in glowing terms, dismissing Watergate as a minor aberration. Roger Mudd pointedly responded, "Well, Senator, if he was so wonderful, why did he have to resign?"

The next morning Nixon was anything but classy. Before leaving the White House he could not resist allowing the TV cameras in for one last time as he delivered a farewell speech to his staff. With tears in his eyes, he spoke of his family and middle class background. He pleaded for understanding and forgiveness, but never acknowledged that he had done anything wrong. It was the 1952 Checkers speech all over again and, by sharing it via television, Nixon seemed to be offering it as a counterpoint rebuttal to his own resignation remarks the night before. He had come full circle, and, perhaps instinctively, he welcomed television once again as the means to help fix a tough situation. Only that strategy no longer worked. The man who had reached fame and power through a very personal medium could no longer use it to draw support from the people. Nixon still knew the right words but they no longer touched the emotions of the American public in the same way. They had supported him with the greatest popular mandate in American history and he had betrayed their trust and consistently lied to them. The people no longer believed Richard Nixon and in his final TV speech he appeared as an empty, broken man who was not worthy of their support, only their pity.

One-half hour later, President Richard M. Nixon flashed the "double V" victory symbol one more time to the cameras, climbed into a helicopter, and flew away.

networks and they once again set up rotating coverage while PBS (through NPACT) presented prime time replays. The sense of jocularity that had often lightened the mood of the Ervin committee's activities was absent. The House Judiciary Committee was engaged in a serious debate that could well lead to the impeachment of the President of the United States.

For three days, the members of the committee debated the pros and cons of the articles of impeachment, and television carried it all. It became clear that the members of the committee were not engaged in the partisan rhetoric that usually marked such televised hearings. Each committee member displayed a deep personal anguish in trying to determine the truth of the charges and the proper course of action. Lacking clear evidence of a specific crime ("a smoking gun"), they were forced to examine cumulative impressions, general attitudes, strategies, and policies of the president. On

34. Affirmative Access

RICHARD NIXON'S RESIGNATION SAVED the networks from a lengthy impeachment trial that would have thrown their fall schedules into disarray. This reprieve was a welcome relief to executives who had been forced to rip up and redraw their schedules once already that summer in response to official rulings from Washington. Government bureaucrats had decided it was again time to do something that would raise the standards of television and promote the kinds of programs they felt were in the public's best interest. In January 1974, the FCC unveiled Access II, targeted to take effect with the 1974 fall season.

The commission had emerged looking quite foolish following implementation of its 1970 prime time access rule. With a great deal of ballyhoo about increasing the quality of television, it had taken the potentially dangerous step of instigating backhand controls over some prime time programming, only to see an embarrassing proliferation of cheap game shows emerge as a result of Access I. Not taking any chances with its new rule, the FCC moved from merely hoping that producers would gear their new efforts to the commission's taste to a system that demanded it. Two hours each week (7:00–8:00 P.M. Saturday and Sunday) would be returned to network control, but only if the time were filled with news, public affairs, and FCC-approved kidvid. The offer was too tempting for ABC, CBS, and NBC to resist. Even though the networks had frankly admitted in 1973 that it would probably be impossible for them to resume control of all seven nights of access time, they were perfectly willing to attempt to fill the lucrative weekend slots. They quickly agreed to the commission's ground rules and in the spring announced line-ups for the fall that included the necessary quota of FCC sanctioned programs. The independent producers were furious and they took the FCC to court. In June, a U.S. District Court ruled in their favor, declaring Access II illegal on the grounds that the new rule did not allow program producers enough time to prepare for its implementation. (The 1970 access rule had provided sixteen months for industry adjustment.) The court also strongly implied that there were other entire sections of the rule it did not like. Rather than offer to extend the lead-in time to meet the court's stated objection, the FCC took the opportunity to reexamine its entire strategy and to prepare a completely new proposal. In the meantime, with Access II declared illegal, the original access rule was once again in force. Ironically, this left producers and local stations facing an even tighter situation than before. They had only ninety days to fill the two hours suddenly returned to their control. In order to make the

September deadline, everyone turned to the quickest, cheapest programs available: more game shows.

The networks faced the opposite task. Each one had to reshuffle its schedule in order to absorb the loss of two hours of programming. The weekend public affairs, news, and kidvid material was all excised. Additionally, six new thirty-minute sitcoms (two on each network) were temporarily shelved, though all of them eventually aired in one form or another later in the season. They included: NBC's *Sunshine* and *The Bob Crane Show*, CBS's *We'll Get By* and *The Love Nest*, and ABC's *Where's The Fire?* and *Everything Money Can't Buy*.

In spite of the last minute legal wrangling and the across the board program purge, the overall tone of the new season's prime time line-up remained unchanged. Though a half dozen sitcoms had been cut from the September schedule, there were still six left among the new fall shows as situation comedy continued to experience a renaissance that had begun in the early 1970s. Success in this "new wave" of comedy, however, eluded all but a handful of producers. Some of the best minds in American TV comedy had already tried and failed to ride this upswing, and the major casualties included Alan King's *The Corner Bar*, Carl Reiner's *A Touch of Grace*, Rob Reiner's *The Super*, and Sam Denoff's *Lotsa Luck*. Many of these vehicles had started with promising concepts, but few had the necessary accompaniment of standout actors and top notch writing to make the premises come alive. They also relied too heavily on all too obvious *All in the Family* production traits such as a live audience, British origin, and proletariat struggle to cover their weaknesses. Most of the producers cited the difficulty of finding good writers for the shows as the major reason for their failure.

Though there was an increasing demand for new wave-style comedy programs, an entire generation of TV sitcom writers had grown up on obstacle-course comedy of the 1950s and 1960s, never dealing with situations such as a lead character's decision to have an abortion. Consequently, when they were asked to deliver scripts for series that were conceived in the Norman Lear-Bud Yorkin mold, the writers drew on the superficial elements of the new shows and inserted as many racial putdowns and topical references as possible. They failed to realize that the so-called new wave of sitcoms was based on the same strains of humor that had worked for decades, from the vaudeville stage to *I Love Lucy*. Though the subject matter and settings might be more realistic than in the past, clever plot twists, funny situations, sharp dialogue, and interesting characters were still essential. Abandoning these in favor of a half-hour of cheap putdowns and racial slurs underscored the fact that many people in the industry still failed to understand the subtle interplay of traditional humor and realistic settings at work in the shows. This combination was very difficult to handle, even by those who championed the trend, and, at first, Lear and Yorkin had found it necessary to write most of their scripts themselves. Yorkin explained, "You can't take those young guys off shows like *Doris Day* and expect them to do this kind of comedy."

By 1974, Lear had groomed an entire stable of writers proficient in this new form of sitcom and he was able to fuel an amazingly successful string of spinoffs and new shows, most of which wore the distinct stamp of *All in the Family*. Though even he could not guarantee a winner every time (Lear's adaptation of the off-Broadway hit "The Hot 1 Baltimore" flopped on ABC in the spring of 1975), he had worked out a very reliable formula for the success that had eluded so many others. Lear carefully selected supporting characters from his established hits and placed them in their own vehicles, building a chain of ratings champs for CBS in the process. Just as CBS president James Aubrey had directed a parade of rural spinoffs from *The Beverly Hillbillies* and *The Andy Griffith Show* in the early 1960s, Lear took race, topicality, and forays into serious issues and ran with them through the 1970s. His techniques were just as blatant as Aubrey's, but a steady supply of top notch scripts maintained a generally high level of quality with each succeeding series. While perhaps not quite as good as the *All in the Family* original, his new programs were certainly well done and, to his credit, Lear tried to give each one its own special focus.

First out of the *All in the Family* mold was *Maude,* begun in the fall of 1972 as a spinoff series for the character of Edith Bunker's cousin, played by Beatrice Arthur. In February 1974, Lear launched *Good Times,* which showcased Maude's black maid, Florida Evans (Esther Rolle), who left New York and settled with her family in the projects of Chicago. As something of a black "heart" comedy in the tradition of *Mama* from the 1950s, *Good Times* emphasized the warm goodness of the hard working parents, Florida and her husband James (John Amos), as they struggled to raise their three children, James Junior "J. J." (Jimmie Walker), Thelma (BernNadette Stanis), and Michael (Ralph Carter). In his update of this once popular form, Lear presented the characters originally as a generally believable realistic black family. There were the obligatory putdowns and insults, but most of these were handled by the children, especially J. J., the oldest son. Florida and James saved their energy for the never-ending problem of family survival in the white man's world.

For his next spinoff (in January 1975) Lear presented the problems faced by a middle class black family that actually "made it," Archie Bunker's next door neighbors, the Jeffersons. The Jefferson family had been introduced in *All in the Family* as a black equivalent to the Bunkers, so a spinoff series was almost inevitable. After all, every important element was already there. George Jefferson (Sherman Hemsley) was a self-centered snob and bigot who intensely disliked whites, Louise (Isabel Sanford) was his long-suffering but forgiving wife, and Lionel (Mike Evans) was his tolerant son who outraged his father (and Archie) by becoming close friends with Mike and Gloria. To launch the new series, the Jeffersons moved from Queens to a fashionable East Side apartment in Manhattan. Though peppered with topical references and characters (an inter-racial couple lived just down the hall), for the most part this new series was far less serious than *All in the Family* and placed more emphasis on the energetic give-and-take and blustery confrontations of its characters. George Jefferson was an even more pigheaded "head of the household" than Archie Bunker, though he was constantly deflated by his business associates and neighbors, the rest of his family, and Florence (Marla Gibbs), their flippant black maid. Nonetheless, as a self-made black businessman he faced racial problems from a perspective totally different from Archie, Maude, and Florida, and the series effectively made use of his particular point of view.

It was no accident that Lear's two new hit sitcoms focused on blacks. Perhaps the one aspect of new wave comedy that everyone agreed on was that it had strong ethnic and racial themes. Unfortunately, some writers and producers frequently used the mere presence of minorities as a lazy shortcut that allowed them to sidestep complicated issues and complex drama and settle instead for stories that were "automatically topical" because they featured blacks. Worse yet, their treatment of ethnic groups frequently degenerated into a string of very old stereotypes. For instance, an Archie Bunker type would be set up as a lovable strawman to be torn down after delivering "unintentionally" funny lines that demonstrated what a close-minded bigot he was. This was a crafty combination that allowed warmed-over racial clichés to be used in the inevitable exchange of putdowns, turning what might have been labeled as racist or insulting in the past into an unmistakable sign that the program was "up to date" and "with it." The line between a sophisticated sitcom and a plastic exercise in name calling was often a fine one and, even on the better shows, it was sometimes unclear whether the scripts drew on the putdowns of the bigot or the cheap racial caricatures for the laughs.

One offender in this regard was, surprisingly, Norman Lear's *Good Times* which, by its second season, began shifting the focus more and more to J. J.'s antics. Walker portrayed J. J. as a hip-talking wisecracker, but when he rolled his eyes and exclaimed "Dyn-o-mite!" it sounded an awful lot like "Holy mackerel, Andy." The original scripts had kept his antics in check, with J. J. appearing as nothing worse than a problem child with an enormous ego (certainly a realistic problem) who even poked fun at himself and his shortcomings. However, J. J. soon became a cult figure among pre-teen youth and the writers began playing up his comic caricature more and more. By the end of the third season, John Amos quit the series in disgust, citing his personal frustration at the degeneration in writing and characterization. One year later, Esther Rolle also quit. Both characters were written out of the series (James was killed in an accident in Mississippi while Florida remarried, "temporarily" relocating in Arizona for her new husband's health) so that, ironically, for one season a warm "family" comedy functioned with no parents at all. Rolle returned in the fall of 1978 when the producers promised to shift back to the original thrust of the show and downplay J. J.'s antics. Even with Rolle back, though, the program could not recapture its initial spirit and it was canceled only a few months after her reappearance.

Jimmie Walker's sudden rise to cult status was the perfect example of the shaky status of television's newly found social conscience. Here was a young black comic who became a national celebrity, especially among black children, by portraying a smart-mouthed, irresponsible hustler—exactly the sort of media character blacks had been complaining about for years. Just because a series centered on a minority group did not guarantee that the characters would necessarily be given enviable and uplifting traits, even within the supposedly sophisticated sitcoms.

No matter what shape they took, though, minority groups were firmly established as the strong hook for television in the 1970s. Despite the many horrible scripts and one-dimensional characters that had appeared in the wake of *All in the Family,* television was slowly absorbing them. After several years of scrutiny, other

	8:00	8:30	9:00	9:30	10:00	10:30	
MON	The Rookies		ABC NFL Monday Night Football (to 12 Midnight)				**ABC**
	Gunsmoke		Maude	RHODA	Medical Center		**CBS**
	BORN FREE		NBC Monday Night At The Movies				**NBC**
TUE	Happy Days	Tuesday Movie Of The Week			Marcus Welby, M.D.		**ABC**
	Good Times	M*A*S*H	Hawaii Five-O		Barnaby Jones		**CBS**
	Adam-12	NBC World Premiere Movie			Police Story		**NBC**
WED	THAT'S MY MAMA	Wednesday Movie Of The Week			GET CHRISTIE LOVE		**ABC**
	SONS AND DAUGHTERS		Cannon		MANHUNTER		**CBS**
	LITTLE HOUSE ON THE PRAIRIE		LUCAS TANNER / # Bob Hope Show		PETROCELLI		**NBC**
THR	The Odd Couple	PAPER MOON	The Streets Of San Francisco		HARRY O		**ABC**
	The Waltons		CBS Thursday Night Movies				**CBS**
	SIERRA		Ironside		MOVIN' ON		**NBC**
FRI	KODIAK	The Six Million Dollar Man	THE TEXAS WHEELERS		KOLCHAK: THE NIGHT STALKER		**ABC**
	PLANET OF THE APES		CBS Friday Night Movies				**CBS**
	Sanford And Son	CHICO AND THE MAN	THE ROCKFORD FILES		POLICE WOMAN		**NBC**
SAT	THE NEW LAND		Kung-Fu		NAKIA		**ABC**
	All In The Family	PAUL SAND IN FRIENDS LOVERS	Mary Tyler Moore Show	Bob Newhart Show	Carol Burnett Show		**CBS**
	Emergency		NBC Saturday Night At The Movies				**NBC**

	7:00	7:30	8:00	8:30	9:00	9:30	10:00	10:30	
SUN	local		Sonny Comedy Revue		The ABC Sunday Night Movie				**ABC**
	local	Apple's Way		Kojak		Mannix		local	**CBS**
	local	The Wonderful World Of Disney		NBC Sunday Mystery Movie (McCloud; Columbo; McMillan And Wife; AMY PRENTISS)				# NBC News Presents (10:00-11:00)	**NBC**

writers and producers at last began to adapt the Norman Lear formula successfully in their own efforts. In the process, TV completely reshaped its portrait of the world from the aseptic white suburbs of the 1950s, to the new ideal of the 1970s: a totally integrated society with a perfect mixture of every race, color, and creed. This merely reflected changes in the real world, where assorted minority groups were becoming increasingly vocal, demanding additional participation in such diverse fields as politics, labor, and education through programs of "affirmative action" (a term that replaced the buzz word "quotas"). Though such profound social changes might take generations in real life and require government legislated mathematical mixes, for network television it meant that the WASP world was suddenly junked in favor of a new money maker, the increasingly popular world of colorful ethnics who promised high ratings and increased profits. By the 1974–75 season, this new order seemed practically a *fait accompli* (on TV at least) as viewers welcomed *Chico and the Man* and *Barney Miller*. Neither of these shows came from Norman Lear, but both were up to his standards and they signaled that successful, high quality, generally realistic ethnic humor was no longer Lear's exclusive domain.

James Komack's *Chico and the Man* literally followed in the footsteps of *Sanford and Son* and, riding on the strength of such an enviable lead-in, catapulted straight into the top ten. It was a perfect companion show to the story of a father and son junk dealership in the Los Angeles ghetto. In the new show, Ed Brown (Jack Albertson) and his Chicano assistant Chico Rodriguez (Freddie Prinze) operated a run down garage in a decrepit section of East Los Angeles.

Though one of the first programs to slant itself toward Hispanic viewers, *Chico and the Man* was just as much a generation gap comedy as a racial show. Ed ("The Man") was a dyspeptic old coot who one day let a cheerful young Chicano talk him into a job as his assistant at the garage. Very quickly he and Chico became friends, though Ed never publicly dropped his image as a hardnosed quasi-Bunkerish bigot. (He claimed that he did not like anybody, but it was obvious he really loved everybody.) Unlike the structure in many of the other ethnic-based shows, Ed and Chico were not so much characters in conflict as two sides of the same character: one was a buoyant optimistic dreamer who believed anything was possible, and the other was an unreconstructed cynic who had seen too many such hopes turn sour. Neither was set up as an obvious bad guy and both delivered funny one-liners that were closer to vaudeville routines than spiteful putdowns. The energy between the two characters turned merely adequate scripts into highly entertaining encounters as grumpy Ed found himself growing increasingly fond of the enthusiastic Chico, secretly hoping that he would succeed in working his way out of the ghetto.

One reason for the strong chemistry between Ed and Chico was that there seemed to be a touch of real life magic to the setting.

Prinze was only twenty when he moved from a brief career as a nightclub stand-up comic to share the lead in a top ten TV show. He seemed remarkably successful at keeping up with veteran trouper Albertson and well on his way to fulfilling his character's optimistic dream of becoming a Chicano superstar. This fusion of images made Prinze's subsequent suicide in January of 1977 especially shocking, and it punctured the show's premise with a grim dose of reality. Though the producers attempted to continue the series by using twelve-year-old Gabriel Melgar as a new Chicano character (orphan Raul Garcia), Prinze's death had robbed the show of its comic tension. The revamped format lasted only one season, unable to duplicate the special energy that had first propelled the series.

If the champions of affirmative action could have selected the cast for a TV sitcom, they could not have done better than the crew of New York City's 12th police precinct as presented in Danny Arnold's *Barney Miller.* Set in the appropriately diverse district of Greenwich Village, the program showcased a kaleidoscope of distinctive character types: Captain Barney Miller, a level-headed Jewish chief of detectives (Hal Linden); Detective Harris, a cool confident black (Ron Glass); Sgt. Wojciehowicz, a beefy hard-working Pole (Max Gail); Sgt. Yemana, a soft-spoken reliable Asian (Jack Soo); Sgt. Chano Amengual, a voluble Puerto Rican (Gregory Sierra); Sgt. Fish, an aging but dedicated man on the verge of retirement (Abe Vigoda); and Inspector Luger, a pure Hollywood B-movie type complete with fedora and raincoat (James Gregory). Each performer drew on the accepted stereotypes of his character but, for the most part, snide putdowns were kept in check and the group evolved into a close knit company facing realistic, if often warped situations. These were a mix of conflicts from the everyday world of New York City (such as an exuberant lottery winner causing a riot by tossing money from a window) to more personal station house situations (such as dealing with the effects of unintentionally consuming brownies spiked with hashish). Despite the very funny plots, *Barney Miller* was a far cry

from the pure farce and physical pratfalls of previous "station house sitcoms" such as *Car 54, Where Are You?* Its humor grew out of the characters themselves placed in believable, though exaggerated, situations, rather than from outlandish plots or silly misunderstandings. The program was one of the best new-wave sitcoms to evolve outside the Norman Lear stable, combining topical themes and ethnic concerns with the basics of comedy: a simple set, good acting, and well-written scripts. It was not, however, an instant smash, premiering as part of ABC's second season schedule in January of 1975, slotted against *The Waltons.* Over the years, though, it went through a number of time shifts and became one of the network's steady, reliable shows, even inspiring a short lived spinoff series, *Fish* (featuring Sgt. Fish after his retirement).

CBS was quite pleased with the success of Norman Lear's spinoffs and eagerly looked to its other hot sitcoms for more winners. The network had slated a program created and produced by *M*A*S*H*'s* Alan Alda, *We'll Get By,* for the fall of 1974, but postponed it as part of the cutbacks resulting from the Access II mess. When it finally aired in the late spring, *We'll Get By* proved a disappointment. Audiences expecting the mixture of madcap humor and serious themes of *M*A*S*H* were let down by the low-key premise of a middle class lawyer and his family living in a New Jersey suburb. The series simply never caught fire. Viewers, as well as the CBS brass, were much happier with the first spinoff from *The Mary Tyler Moore Show, Rhoda,* the most successful new sitcom of the season.

Fans of *The Mary Tyler Moore Show* had become quite fond of Mary's wisecracking neighbor with a heart of gold, Rhoda Morgenstern, and they eagerly followed her move from the frozen Midwest back to her home turf of New York City. She was giving it "one last chance." Valerie Harper handled the transition from plumpish second banana to slim, glamorous lead character quite well. She softened Rhoda's slightly out-of-synch personality a bit, giving the character more stability and providing the new supporting crew with opportunities to shine on its own. Rhoda's sister

After splitting with her husband, Rhoda (Valerie Harper) once again became an eligible single woman, often double dating with her sister, Brenda (Julie Kavner). *(From right)* Harper, Ray Buktenica, Kavner, and Ron Silver. *(Rhoda © 1974 Twentieth Century Fox Television. All Rights Reserved.)*

September 10, 1974

NBC presents "Born Innocent" as a *World Premiere Movie.* Linda Blair plays a fourteen-year-old who goes through a rough time in a juvenile detention home.

September 13, 1974

The Rockford Files. (NBC). James Garner and his producer on *Maverick,* Roy Huggins, update their successful adventure formula by one century.

October 6, 1974

Monty Python's Flying Circus begins an unexpectedly successful run on a handful of U.S. public television stations.

October 19, 1974

Weekend. (NBC). Lloyd Dobyns hosts a once-each-month late Saturday night news magazine show. The program wields a much lighter touch than CBS's *60 Minutes,* mixing solid reporting with off-beat features and humorous epigrams.

October 22, 1974

Fred Pierce becomes president of ABC-TV.

January 1, 1975

Dick Cavett, reduced to infrequent appearances in ABC's revamped late night schedule, does his last show for the network after signing with CBS for a brief summer variety show.

January 6, 1975

A.M. America. (ABC). Twenty-three years after the advent of *Today,* ABC at last tries its own early morning version, hosted by Bill Beutel and Stephanie Edwards. Peter Jennings reads the news.

Brenda (Julie Kavner) assumed Rhoda's old role as an over-intelligent but somewhat insecure, chubby young woman, traditional enough to spend much of her time talking about men and dating, but modern enough to joke about it. Their mother, Ida Morgenstern (Nancy Walker), played the perfect Jewish mother: pushy, overbearing, self-deprecating, but with the required heart of gold beneath her tough exterior.

Perhaps the most important change in Rhoda's life was that in the first episode of her own series she met a man and fell in love. Though not Jewish, Joe Gerard (David Groh) was a handsome guy and an eminently respectable young business man on the way up. In short, a "good catch." On October 28, after four years of frustrated single life in Minneapolis, Rhoda got married in a one-hour special that featured the entire crew from *The Mary Tyler Moore Show* as wedding guests. The program was the top-rated special of the season and *Rhoda* stayed in the top ten for two years straight. Yet, there were some Rhoda fans who were unhappy.

Critics complained that marriage had taken the edge from Rhoda and trapped her in stories that were severely limited by the dull character of Joe Gerard. In the fall of 1976, the writers took the critics' advice and began to work Joe out of the series. He and Rhoda were first separated, then, a year later, divorced. Joe admitted that he had only consented to marriage because he knew that Rhoda would never have agreed simply to live together (which was all he had really wanted). During the messy transition year between the separation and divorce, the writers were very uncertain what to focus on for the humor. Consequently, *Rhoda* became

more a soap opera than a sitcom and the show's ratings dipped dramatically. It was not until well into the 1977–78 season that the program began to regain some of its old stature as viewers discovered that the show once again was funny. Rhoda had returned to the role of an attractive, eligible single woman. She and Brenda (who had lost her chubbiness) were set in the very workable premise of independent young women trying to make it on their own, which was what many people had expected of the show from the very beginning.

With such a strong line-up of freshmen, TV comedy was at a peak virtually unmatched in network history. Nearly a dozen excellent sitcoms aired each week, from veterans such as *All in the Family, M*A*S*H, The Odd Couple,* and *The Mary Tyler Moore Show* to newcomers *Rhoda, Chico and the Man,* and *Barney Miller.* American television had successfully absorbed the British television style of working class humor while it redeveloped some of its best sitcom characters and settings for the 1970s. Appropriately, it was at this point that British television provided a *new* "new wave" style of comedy that made the American Norman Lear type of sitcom seem almost old hat. It was in 1974 that Americans discovered *Monty Python's Flying Circus.*

The program had begun its run on the BBC in October 1969, as British TV humor began to move away from working class comedy (which had flourished there in the mid-1960s) to its own interpretation of the Ernie Kovacs style of television. *Rowan and Martin's Laugh-In* was the obvious catalyst for the show, as the BBC gathered a group of talented graduates from a variety of British comedy series (including David Frost's many comedy programs) and offered them the opportunity to write and perform in their own weekly half-hour comedy. Graham Chapman, John Cleese, Terry Gilliam (an American), Eric Idle, Terry Jones, and Michael Palin responded with a mad collection of blackouts, outrageous skits, old fashioned physical humor, and rapid-fire editing that surpassed even *Laugh-In* in bringing the Kovacs style to high-quality realization. Sketches were interrupted by other sketches as well as by flashes of music, phony "program announcements," reactions by "outraged government officials," and animated cartoon cutout characters (designed by Gilliam). Being on the BBC, each episode ran without commercials so the dizzying pace never let up. It appeared to be total anarchy, but was actually a very careful mixture of bread-and-butter physical comedy with high class word play, shock-tactic humor, and parodies of television itself. Within the same half-hour, punch lines and sketches were reworked several times, presenting different approaches to the same jokes. As writers and editors as well as performers, the Python crew understood the necessity of setting up contrasts to punctuate the comedy and to help the pacing.

The physical humor was loud and flashy, in the best tradition of Milton Berle burlesque. Characters walked funny, donned ridiculous costumes, dressed in drag, and screamed. Word play ranged from slightly restrained vulgarity ("filthy bastard") to complicated allusions to great works of literature. The animated cutouts included a variety of unlikely subjects: nude women, government leaders, nude men, cricket players, and giant animals. Just for variety, "taboo" subjects such as death, sex, and cannibalism were discussed as casually as royal pronouncements. Biting its own BBC hand, the crew lampooned the mainstays of noncommercial British television: pretentious documentaries and boring talk shows. Participants in the Python permutations were either perversely handicapped (unable to speak English or, worse, simply dead) or stuck in the wrong panel ("Che Guevara" was questioned about obscure cricket championship matches). Documentary narrators inevitably missed the obvious and focused on ridiculous subjects such as flying sheep. The BBC was quite uncertain about the monster it had unleashed, convinced that only a lunatic fringe could possibly enjoy such an eclectic mess. Instead, the program went beyond the fringe and became a big enough success for the BBC to call the Python crew back for three more seasons.

American television would not touch *Monty Python's Flying Circus* at first. Not only was it a censor's nightmare, the humor seemed too idiosyncratic. (Who outside Britain *cared* about cricket?) The initial reaction by the American public seemed to confirm this judgment. Two record albums and a film ("And Now for Something Completely Different"), consisting of selected sketches from the series, flopped in the early 1970s. Members of the cast made a few U.S. TV appearances but they failed to have any impact on the American market, and *Monty Python* seemed destined for the same obscurity in the United States as Britain's *Goon Show* in the 1950s. In 1974, Time-Life Films sold the Python series to the Eastern Educational Network (a consortium of East Coast PBS stations) and, that fall, five years after its British premiere, *Monty Python's Flying Circus* appeared on a handful of public TV stations. Much to the surprise of everyone, the show took off and became one of public TV's highest rated programs. Viewers simply ignored the occasional inscrutable allusions to obscure British interests and enjoyed the show's fresh, daring style. As a British import on public television, *Monty Python* aired intact the outrageous treatment of topics that American performers would have been booted off the air for even suggesting (such as eating your dead mother). By mid-1975, the group's second film ("Monty Python and the Holy Grail") opened to an enthusiastic Stateside reception. By then, the TV series itself was on 120 stations throughout the country, including KPRC, Houston, the first commercial station to carry it (complete with commercials). *Monty Python's Flying Circus* provided a lively change of pace from the equally funny but fervently realistic sitcoms then on American network television. It allowed viewers the opportunity for a direct dose of a completely different style and the program became a long-running staple of public television. Over the next few years, *Monty Python*-style humor would turn up in some American television shows, most notably in a 1975 venture outside of network prime time, NBC's *Saturday Night Live*.

Though situation comedy served as the networks' primary component for the 1974–75 season, the crime show format was close behind. In exploiting the form, the networks relied on the most successful gimmicks of the previous season: loner ethnic cops and violence. The plots in many of the new shows, however, rarely progressed beyond the obvious and failed to generate much excitement. In fact, most of the new "individualistic loners" were practically dead on arrival. *Archer* (Brian Keith as a 1930s Sam Spade-style investigator) and *Khan!* (featuring perennial *Hawaii Five-O* villain Khigh Dhiegh as an Oriental private eye in San Francisco) ran only four weeks each. *Nakia* and *Caribe* lasted a few months. *Get Christie Love* (Teresa Graves as a sassy, sexy black undercover police agent) eked out nearly one complete season. *Petrocelli* (a Harvard-educated Italian working as a defense attorney in Arizona) and *Harry O* (David Janssen as a disabled former cop turned private eye) managed to hold on for two dull seasons each.

The only instant hit among the new crime shows really was not a new crime show at all. James Garner simply dusted off his old Maverick-style character, moved from the amorphous West of the 1870s to the amorphous West Coast of the 1970s, and became Jim Rockford, a smart-talking ex-con with a wry sense of humor who worked as a private investigator. *The Rockford Files* followed the *Maverick* formula to the letter, downplaying life-and-death con-

frontations in favor of lighter, less wearisome complications between Rockford and his clients, his dad (played by Noah Beery), and various collection agencies. (He always seemed on the verge of bankruptcy.) It was one of the smoothest crime shows in years, as the writers tailored the scripts to match Garner's relaxed character perfectly, and the program remained one of NBC's most consistent ratings winners for half a decade.

Three other crime shows also became hits that season, but unlike *The Rockford Files,* NBC's *Police Woman* and ABC's *Baretta* and *S.W.A.T.* each took more time to build an audience, not catching on until the spring rerun cycle. They were different from *The Rockford Files* in one other important respect: each was very violent.

Police Woman (which followed *The Rockford Files*) was a spinoff from Joseph Wambaugh's *Police Story* anthology series, but it was not very faithful to the original's concept of focusing on more realistic, human aspects of police work. The "unflinching look at the real world of police women" devoted much of its attention to gratuitous violence such as savage death scenes or closeups of traumatized rape victims. Pepper Anderson (Angie Dickinson) was played up primarily as a titillating sex symbol, with frequent shots of her in revealing costumes, legs apart, pistol pointed. One reviewer described the show as the epitome of the crime genre's new excesses, saying its motto was, "Shoot now, talk dirty later." *Kojak* had demonstrated that violence could be used very effectively in order to underscore the grim reality of urban crime, but the writers on that program generally turned in scripts that gave Telly Savalas excellent material to work with. *Police Woman* rarely offered Dickinson the same opportunity.

January 6, 1975

NBC's eleven-year-old daytime hit, *Another World,* becomes the first soap opera to expand to one hour, five days a week.

January 24, 1975

Hot l Baltimore. (ABC). Norman Lear's first major flop, an offbeat sitcom based on a popular off-Broadway play by Lanford Wilson. Set in a seedy Baltimore hotel (with a permanently burned out light behind the *e* of the "hotel" sign), the program focuses on a wide range of controversial character types (from pimpless hookers to a pair of male homosexual lovers). Some people object to the treatment of such risqué topics in prime time, but, unlike Lear's other ventures, the show does not generate any great following from the protests. One reviewer observes that the so-called "adult" series is really just bad caricature and "as shocking as last week's bread."

April 29, 1975

To mark the fall of Saigon, all three commercial networks present documentary reports. CBS: "Vietnam: A War That Is Finished"; NBC: "7,382 Days in Vietnam"; and ABC: "Vietnam: Lessons Learned, Prices Paid."

August 6, 1975

NBC News Update. (NBC). NBC begins inserting a sixty-second news summary into prime time.

September 1, 1975

The oldest oater of them all, *Gunsmoke,* fades from CBS after twenty years, leaving prime time virtually devoid of Westerns.

Baretta was even worse, presenting stories that could be accurately summarized as: Smash! Bang! Crash! Boom! Screech! Zoom!

Baretta was a new attempt by the producers of *Toma* to cash in, more gracefully, on the violent cop show trend. Robert Blake was cast as an out-of-the-ordinary cop who was streetwise and ready to defend the little people from hardnosed police harassment as well as from violent urban criminals. Blake's interpretation of the role was the high point of the show as he hammered Tony Baretta into an intriguing offbeat character. He took the gimmicks of the premise—Baretta was a master at disguise and owned a talking cockatoo for a pet—and transformed them into engaging traits of the little fellow's personality. Occasionally some interesting plot twists surfaced, but it was usually Blake's energy that carried the overall production, raising *Baretta* to the level of a good, straight-forward cop show. This helped to smooth over the excessive violence that formed the nucleus of nearly every episode. Though Tony Baretta might have been engaged in a constant battle against urban crime, he still took the time to care for individual victims and was not afraid to show honest, gut emotions. *S.W.A.T.,* ABC's other late-rising cop show of the season, took a completely differ-ent approach, carrying the theme of urban guerrilla warfare to its extreme, depersonalized conclusion.

Producers Aaron Spelling and Leonard Goldberg (of *The Mod Squad* and *The Rookies)* set up *S.W.A.T.* as the ultimate crime-action program, portraying Los Angeles (where else?) as a battle-ground populated by raving lunatics, crazed maniacs, and helpless citizens. To protect the populace from those poised to ravage the city, a five-man Special Weapons And Tactics (S.W.A.T.) squad stood ready, led by Lieutenant Hondo Harrelson (Steve Forrest). Every week, just when it appeared as if the city were doomed, an ominous green truck would come howling into view. As the truck screeched to a halt, a small army of faceless men in flak suits threw open its doors and leaped out, ready to face a threat no average citizen or normal police department could handle. It was a perverse combination of grade-B war and Western films, with the S.W.A.T. team riding in like the cavalry of old to overwhelm the enemy. However, instead of using six-shooters, they rode in with an arsenal of bazooka-type weapons that could demolish a small country. The enemy was not beaten, it was blown away.

Such total war completely eliminated the chance for a slice of humanity and left little room in the field for the personal one-to-one confrontations of such Sam Spade surrogates as Columbo, Cannon, and Mannix or of such hard working outsiders as Kojak and Baretta. *S.W.A.T.* literally turned the war on crime into an all-out war between society and its enemies. In such a war, anything was allowed. Even Jack Webb's fiercely pro-cop series, from *Dragnet* to *Emergency,* had shown more restraint. *S.W.A.T.* cele-brated overkill and massive retaliation, briefly touching a sensitive nerve among viewers. The program flashed into the top ten in the summer, but disappeared after its second season. As its legacy, the series left behind an unmistakable sign of television's ability to influence taste and modify values of separate communities across the country simultaneously. In dozens of small, previously peace-ful towns such as Bloomington, Indiana, local officials began setting aside huge sums of local revenue to finance their own smartly dressed S.W.A.T. teams. After all, there was more glamour to be found in training for such a squad than merely concentrating on humdrum, routine police work.

S.W.A.T. marked a symbolic peak in television violence, coming as it did at the end of more than a decade of real life uncontrolled violence that television had brought into everyone's living room. Americans had viewed graphic confrontations on the home front and on the war front with increasing frustration at their inability to do anything about them. S.W.A.T., in effect, restaged the Vietnam War and the riots in the streets, but returned ultimate control to the righteous forces of law and order for a satisfying conclusion. It was a bitterly ironic contrast to the confusion and desperation that marked the end of the real war that seemed to have caused so many of the problems in the first place.

Following the 1973 treaty ending direct American involvement, the United States had rushed to sweep the Vietnam War under the carpet. American combat troops were withdrawn by the fall of 1973, and the South Vietnamese army assumed responsibility for keeping order in the countryside and maintaining security. They faced a series of widespread guerrilla attacks which kept the war percolating at a low but constant level. In the spring of 1975, the South Vietnamese forces collapsed, and the American public was given a visual jolt more shocking that the years of combat footage and bombing statistics. As Communist forces swept through the country and assumed control over village after village, the network cameras focused on the stream of refugees fleeing to the south for safety. By the end of April, uncontrolled panic had set in. Suppos-edly safe enclaves protected by the South Vietnamese forces had fallen in rapid succession and the Communist drive south became a rout. A Communist takeover of the countryside seemed inevitable. Bureaucrats, soldiers, merchants, and thousands of average people who had built their lives around the American presence in Vietnam feared for their own survival. Everyone began scrambling for the apparent safety of the capital city of Saigon itself, determined to get there by any means possible. Near the end, the only way out was by American airplanes.

On the last flight out of DaNang, a CBS camera crew captured the incredible scene. Frightened men (chiefly South Vietnamese soldiers) shoved women and children aside in a desperate bid to climb aboard an already overcrowded airplane. The plane was so jammed with refugees that it had to take off with the stairway ramp still hanging out, open, and the crew had to push people off as the craft taxied down the runway. Some of those who could not make it aboard began shooting at the plane in anger and frustration. Others clung to the stairs even after takeoff, with most falling off once the plane was airborne. Soon after their arrival in Saigon, those who had made it discovered that their escape to freedom was short lived. The collapse of Saigon itself was imminent. Once again, there was a hectic evacuation, starting at the U.S. embassy. Once again, the TV crews focused on the desperate crowds trying to reach safety. At the embassy, they clawed at the gates while helicopters took the last of the staff and press to boats waiting offshore. At the harbor, thousands pressed to climb aboard one of the departing ships. South Vietnamese pilots hijacked expensive American-built Army helicopters and ditched them in the sea near the American carriers, hoping to make it on board. The final hours at the Saigon airport were a repeat of the desperation of DaNang.

No matter what position they had taken on the war, individual Americans found the news clips a sobering, gut-wrenching experi-ence. The United States was leaving behind, defenseless, a great number of people who had staked their lives on America's ultimate success in South Vietnam, either on the battlefield or at the nego-tiating table. In return, they had been abandoned. The graphic television reports were something of an emotional penance for the country, as Americans watched the traumatic mess of Vietnam conclude right before their eyes, forced to confront at their dinner tables the reality of what their country had done to a small group of people half a world away.

35. Freddie or Not?

ON TUESDAY, SEPTEMBER 10, 1974, NBC kicked off a new series of made-for-TV movies for the 1974–75 season with "Born Innocent," a tough presentation of the effects of reform school on a naive teenage girl. It was produced by Richard Rosenberg and Robert Christiansen, the team responsible earlier that year for the highly acclaimed civil rights drama, "Autobiography of Miss Jane Pittman," a successful vehicle for Cicely Tyson. In "Born Innocent" they cast Linda Blair, the young star of the hit theatrical horror film "The Exorcist," as fourteen-year-old Chris Parker, a gentle and confused child placed in a juvenile detention home by her parents for being an incorrigible runaway. Though Chris had run away six times in two years, it was clear that, with an alcoholic mother and a weak, sadistic father at home, she was an unfortunate victim needing help and understanding, not punishment. Instead, she was made a ward of the state and locked up with drug addicts and child prostitutes in the women's section of a state reform school. There, Chris was cruelly and insensitively handled by the authorities and mercilessly taunted by the other girls. For the most part, the producers managed to handle the entire story with a minimum of graphic horror. The film did not set up any easily identifiable devils or angels but rather concerned itself with the deadend hopeless condition of the prison and its dehumanizing influence on everyone there. At the climax of the story, the innocent Chris was gang raped in the shower by a group of girls using a wooden plunger. They triumphantly cried, "Now you're one of us!"

"Born Innocent" was practically swallowed up amid the fall premiere hoopla. It did not receive much on-air promotion and, up against the season premieres of CBS's hit *Good Times* and ABC's mildly successful *Happy Days,* it registered only fair ratings. Afterward, many TV critics did not bother to review it, though those who did tended to be largely complimentary. Ron Powers of the *Chicago Sun-Times* praised the program as "courageous, honest, and intelligently crafted television drama." The *Hollywood Reporter* called it "a massive, brutal indictment of the juvenile justice system." A few years earlier, the serious topic and brutal setting of "Born Innocent" might have sent shock waves throughout the industry but, by the fall of 1974, even rape scenes were almost passé on television. Still, the clearly adult-oriented film had been particularly accessible to a young audience, airing relatively early in the evening (8:00–10:00 P.M.) and appearing at the start of the new fall season when youthful viewing levels were high.

A few days after the "Born Innocent" telecast, a San Francisco teenage girl was assaulted on a deserted stretch of California beach by a gang of girls, who used a coke bottle to rape her. The parents of the attacked girl sued NBC, claiming the violence on the tube had been the instigator of the violence on the beach. NBC denied any connection or responsibility, but the legal wrangling lasted four years. (NBC eventually won the case.) Even before it ever reached the courts, though, the real life incident of rape provided a very visible rallying point for the small but vocal group of viewers who, for years, had protested what they saw as excessive levels of sex and violence on television. At last, they said, here was proof of the harmful effects of unrestrained television on impressionable minds.

Throughout the previous cycles of public protest that had accompanied the heydays of Western, crime, and action-adventure shows during the 1950s and 1960s, the networks had been able to blunt the criticism and avoid any serious threats of anti-network legislation. In the 1970s, the anti-gore groups grew more sophisticated and organized their scattered interests into a number of dedicated lobbying groups, moving beyond outraged letters to the editor and appearances at inconsequential congressional hearings. They took careful aim at lawmakers, television moguls, and the news media in general. As a result, the protests that followed the "Born Innocent" case could not be brushed aside with a few vague promises by the networks. In the fall of 1974, the intensified protests reached the House and Senate committees that controlled the FCC's purse strings and they ordered the commission to take some sort of action on the complicated matter of the influence of television sex and violence on children.

The FCC was hesitant to impose an outright ban. Access rules that "encouraged" quality programming (however heavy-handedly) were one thing, but an out-and-out veto of sex and violence in programming ventured onto very shaky legal grounds that the commission preferred to avoid. Instead, it passed the buck to the networks, urging them to solve the problem for everyone by coming up with strong self-imposed guidelines to mollify the public protesters. In the meantime, the FCC continued to work on its revised prime time access rules and in January 1975 it unveiled Access III, a complicated set of specific guidelines loaded with exemptions and clarifications, and scheduled to take effect that fall. On a practical level, the complex new rules translated into the return to network control of one hour of prime time each week (Sunday, 7:00–8:00 P.M.), as long as it was filled with FCC-approved kidvid or public affairs. There were the expected chal-

	8:00	8:30	9:00	9:30	10:00	10:30	
M O N	BARBARY COAST		ABC NFL Monday Night Football (to 12 Midnight)				**ABC**
	Rhoda	PHYLLIS	All In The Family	Maude	Medical Center		**CBS**
	THE INVISIBLE MAN		NBC Monday Night At The Movies				**NBC**
T U E	Happy Days	WELCOME BACK, KOTTER	The Rookies		Marcus Welby, M.D.		**ABC**
	Good Times	JOE AND SONS	SWITCH		BEACON HILL		**CBS**
	Movin' On		Police Story		JOE FORRESTER		**NBC**
W E D	WHEN THINGS WERE ROTTEN	That's My Mama	Baretta		STARSKY AND HUTCH		**ABC**
	Tony Orlando And Dawn Show		Cannon		KATE McSHANE		**CBS**
	Little House On The Prairie		DOCTORS HOSPITAL		Petrocelli		**NBC**
T H R	Barney Miller	ON THE ROCKS	The Streets Of San Francisco		Harry O		**ABC**
	The Waltons		CBS Thursday Night Movies				**CBS**
	THE MONTEFUSCOS	FAY	ELLERY QUEEN		MEDICAL STORY		**NBC**
F R I	MOBILE ONE		The ABC Friday Night Movie				**ABC**
	BIG EDDIE	M*A*S*H	Hawaii Five-O		Barnaby Jones		**CBS**
	Sanford And Son	Chico And The Man	The Rockford Files		Police Woman		**NBC**
S A T	SATURDAY NIGHT LIVE WITH HOWARD COSELL		S.W.A.T.		MATT HELM		**ABC**
	The Jeffersons	DOC	Mary Tyler Moore Show	Bob Newhart Show	Carol Burnett Show		**CBS**
	Emergency		NBC Saturday Night At The Movies				**NBC**

	7:00	7:30	8:00	8:30	9:00	9:30	10:00	10:30	
S U N	SWISS FAMILY ROBINSON		The Six Million Dollar Man		The ABC Sunday Night Movie				**ABC**
	THREE FOR THE ROAD		Cher		Kojak		BRONK		**CBS**
	The Wonderful World Of Disney		THE FAMILY HOLVAK		NBC Sunday Mystery Movie (McCloud; Columbo; McMillan And Wife; McCOY)				**NBC**

lenges to the new regulations, but the courts were more receptive than they had been to Access II the previous year, not even objecting to the mere nine months lead time allowed for industry adjustment. By the spring, the arguments against the new formula for prime time had been turned down and the FCC had a legally approved right to sit as judge and censor over a specific slice of network prime time programming.

That was only one hour from the schedule, hardly enough to assuage the critics of sex and violence. In the face of the tremendous pressure from the FCC, Congress, and the public, the networks needed to do something specific to blunt the criticism and take the sting from the continuing accusations.

In late December 1974, nearly four months after "Born Innocent" aired, CBS president Arthur Taylor proposed that all three networks agree to observe a "family hour" between 8:00 P.M. and 9:00 P.M. each night, during which they would air only material suitable for the entire family. Taylor promised that CBS would lead the way and urged the other networks to follow. One month later, the NAB, the National Association of Broadcasters (the self regulating organization of the television industry), voted overwhelmingly to make the family hour quasi-legal, revising its general code of practices established in the 1950s to include adherence to the concept. Its new rules required that "programming inappropriate for viewing by a general family audience" not be aired in the family hour and, beyond that, shows which "contain material that could be disturbing to significant segments of the audience" would have to be preceded by a warning that the program was intended for mature viewers—no matter what time of day it aired.

Other TV executives were furious but helpless. What network could dare openly say, "No, we are not going to adhere to the family hour. We'd rather fill our time with gratuitous sex and violence." That would be public relations suicide. So ABC and NBC joined CBS in setting up their schedules for the fall of 1975 in light of both Access III and the family hour. Congress was happy. The FCC was happy. Sponsors felt relieved. Adoption of the rule diffused the most intense public pressure, though it did not lay the issues to rest. With the family hour in effect, watchdog groups had very specific criteria by which to judge eight of each network's twenty-two prime time hours every week, as well as the encouragement to scan the remaining time for other offenses. Far from being a final solution, then, the rule created a host of other production and planning problems.

One question was obvious: Just what was appropriate for a general family audience? When dealing with the Sunday night kidvid slot in its access rules, the FCC specifically cited *The Wonderful World of Disney* as the kind of programming it wanted. *Disney,* however, was in a unique situation that really did not offer much help in planning other series. Its producers could draw on more than forty years of studio material, from beautifully photographed nature films to dozens of hit movies specifically aimed at kids to some of the best cartoon animation ever done. For twenty years the networks had tried and failed to generate just one program in this style; they certainly could not produce eight each in one season. A more practical model was CBS's *The Waltons* which offered an obvious hook: programs in the family hour could focus on … families! Consequently, *Joe and Sons* (the struggles of a widower-sheet metal worker trying to raise his two teenage sons), *Three for the Road* (the travels of a widower-photographer who roamed the country in a motor home with his two young sons), *Swiss Family Robinson* (Irwin Allen's suburban-family-lost-in-space motif shifted back to a desert island), and *The Family Holvak* (the struggles of the Holvak family in a small Southern town during the Depression) appeared in the fall line-up. They were simple, sanitized, and saccharine with obvious heavy-handed morals handed down by preachy adults. None of these programs even made it to January. In fact, the only successful family hour copy of *The Waltons* was NBC's *Little House on the Prairie,* which had begun the previous fall.

Though *Little House on the Prairie* also presented a sentimental view of life (here, in the plains states in the 1870s), the cast was strong and the stories were interesting character studies of the individual members of the Ingalls family, told from the perspective of the second oldest daughter, Laura (Melissa Gilbert). The series was based on the *Little House* books written by the real life Laura Ingalls Wilder and, overall, the program downplayed violent action, presenting it as an aberration rather than the main thread of family life in the Old West. Unlike *The Waltons,* which had started out slowly in its first season, *Little House on the Prairie* popped into the top ten within weeks of its fall premiere and remained a consistent winner for NBC into the early 1980s. The program was given a strong boost from the very beginning by the credibility of Michael Landon in the lead role of Charles Ingalls, the young father. He eased his Little Joe persona from *Bonanza* into the new role of a struggling homesteader in the Minnesota frontier who was loved by his family and respected by his fellow pioneers. Like the Waltons, the Ingalls family had to adapt to the changing demands of life in an uncertain period of American history. They also faced difficult personal crises such as the sudden blindness of daughter Mary in the show's fourth season. Though it had been conceived well before the family hour concept was developed, *Little House on the Prairie* was an ideal show for the time period.

For the most part, however, the networks were extremely unsuccessful not only with new family-oriented programs for the family hour, but with practically all their other new offerings in those slots. Nineteen of the twenty-six new family hour programs from the 1975–76 season were axed by the next fall. Actually, this percentage was not that much worse than the failure rate for most new shows, but these were spectacular failures with extremely low ratings and uninspired episodes. CBS and NBC were particularly uncertain of just what sort of show was suitable for the family hour, and they groped for guidelines that would help sort through the maze of inconsistency. *All in the Family* was moved to a later slot, but *The Jeffersons* was kept in place. The family humor of *Good Times* remained in the family hour, but so did the realistic comedy-drama of *M*A*S*H*. Sex was to be downplayed, yet Cher wore low-cut, revealing outfits on her variety show.

Against such a mish-mash of contradictory interpretations of the new rule, writers and producers struggled to turn out their programs. Some managed to roll with the punches, such as the ever-resourceful crew of *M*A*S*H* who used the de-emphasis on sex as a plot springboard to end the overplayed torrid love affair between Major Burns and Major "Hot Lips" Houlihan. Other shows found their concepts crippled beyond repair, and many in the industry

pointed to *Fay* as the best example of a potentially good show done in by the family hour.

Fay was created by Norman Lear graduate Susan Harris, who had written a number of episodes for *All in the Family* and *Maude,* including the two-part story of Maude's abortion. She conceived *Fay* as a free-wheeling realistic comedy about a middle-aged divorcee (Lee Grant) attempting to adjust to life after marriage. Instead, the program was stuffed into the family hour and Fay's adult concerns (such as the pursuit of an active sex life) were reduced to adolescent pap. Grant angrily lashed out at NBC for the change and for supporting the family hour in general, saying that, "they all think the American people have no intelligence whatsoever…the family hour is a form of childish censorship." Following the family hour guidelines, *Fay* became a hopeless bland mess that was canceled by NBC programming chief Marvin Antonowsky after only three weeks. Grant, appearing on the non-family hour *Tonight* show, heard the news backstage and, once on camera, labeled Antonowsky "the mad programmer" and then proceeded to symbolically "give him the finger."

Other people were just as outraged, but they expressed their anger through the courts, hoping to get the rule declared illegal. Right after the family hour took effect, the Writers Guild, the Directors Guild, the Screen Actors Guild, and top producers such as Bill Persky, Sam Denoff, and Norman Lear filed suit, claiming the family hour violated the First Amendment to the Constitution by infringing on free speech and setting up governmental intervention in programming. They pointed to the pressure from Congress and the FCC that had led to the "voluntary" inception of the rule and argued that it was created illegally. More important, they said it "chilled the creative activity" of TV and threatened to "set back television's move toward realism and social importance." They held these goals as more important than "protecting" impressionable children by shielding them from the slightest whiff of controversy. In fact, if violent shows were to be judged as dangerous because they fostered distorted concepts among children (such as violence being an acceptable solution to life's problems), then overly sentimental idealized programs could be accused of the same sin; they, too, presented goals and values out of synch with real life. While filming *Fay,* Lee Grant had touched on this concept: "I think it's dangerous and cruel to tell people that such a [sweet sentimental] world exists. It's simply not true."

In addition to these lofty motives, there was a very important financial threat perceived. The lucrative post-network syndication rerun value for shows such as *Kojak* and *Baretta* would most likely be greatly reduced by the tone set in the family hour rule. If such material was unsuitable in the early evening, could it possibly survive public scrutiny in the later afternoons when many children would certainly be watching?

The family hour case lasted until the end of May 1976, but Judge Warren J. Ferguson withheld ruling immediately, hoping that an out-of-court settlement could be worked out in the meantime. He feared that if he ruled against the family hour, the court would be compounding the problem by sticking its nose into programming decisions. In November 1976, when it became clear that an out-of-court compromise would never be reached, Judge Ferguson issued his ruling. He blasted the FCC, CBS, NBC, ABC, and the NAB for walking all over First Amendment rights, but he did not overturn the family hour rules. Instead, he issued a stern warning to the government to stay out of program control and urged the networks to dismantle the family hour if they wanted to. Despite the strong condemnation of the family hour by the court, the networks were still in the same bind: They could not eliminate the family hour without a great deal of embarrassing negative public-

September 8, 1975

Harry Reasoner becomes the sole nightly news anchor on ABC, as Howard K. Smith is relegated to occasional commentaries.

September 19, 1975

Fawlty Towers. (BBC). John Cleese (as innkeeper Basil Fawlty) and his real-life wife Connie Booth (as parlormaid Polly) create and star in an intricately plotted comic farce set at a small town British seaside guest house, with Prunella Scales as Basil's domineering wife, Sybil, and Andrew Sachs as the hapless Spanish waiter, Manuel. The six-episode run is an instant hit, but the perfectionist creators take until 1979 to turn out an additional half-dozen. All twelve episodes later come to the U.S. via public television.

September 20, 1975

Saturday Night Live with Howard Cosell. (ABC). Roone Arledge and Howard Cosell team up for a weekly variety hour that unsuccessfully attempts to duplicate the successful Ed Sullivan formula.

September 21, 1975

Space: 1999. A British outer space series rejected by the American networks begins its U.S. run in syndication. Martin Landau, Barbara Bain, and Barry Morse play Earth scientists set adrift in space after a lunar explosion blows their base into the inky deep. After a strong start, the program falters as viewers complain about its wooden characterizations and weak storylines.

September 30, 1975

Home Box Office goes national via a satellite hook-up to cable systems throughout the country.

October 2, 1975

"Fear on Trial." (CBS). Twenty years after firing John Henry Faulk, CBS airs a two-hour docudrama on the famous blacklisting case. William Devane plays Faulk, George C. Scott plays lawyer Louis Nizer, and David Susskind and Mark Goodson appear as themselves. The *real* John Henry Faulk, meanwhile, has returned to television as a storyteller on the syndicated *Hee-Haw.*

October 2, 1975

ABC Late Night. (ABC). In a new move to compete with Johnny Carson, ABC begins airing repeats of old network series, beginning with episodes from its own *Movie of the Week* program and CBS's *Mannix.*

---

ity. For the rule to disappear, it would have to do so quietly, just fading away due to a lack of public and network interest (which was exactly what eventually happened). For the immediate future, however, the family hour became part of the network status quo, despite its obvious flaws and inherent contradictions.

Perhaps the most noticeable by-product of the family hour was its effect on the remainder of the schedule. Both old and new programs that were deemed too violent, sexy, or controversial for the family slot were all squeezed into the 9:00–11:00 P.M. period every night, prompting one TV critic to label it "Slime at Nine." This was more than just a cute phrase; it served as a cutting reminder of the ludicrous fallacy behind 8:00–9:00 P.M. as an off limits area to supposedly noxious adult fare. Many children were not ushered off to bed at 9:00 P.M. (8:00 P.M. in the Central time

zone). The Nielsen audience figures revealed that the number of children that watched *Baretta* was greater than the number that watched *The Waltons.* Before long, the self-appointed guardians of public morality concluded that the family hour was inadequate protection for impressionable children and they began to search for a more effective solution, though for the time being their intense public pressure on broadcasters eased.

Ironically, CBS, the network that had proposed the family hour concept, suffered the most from it. In one swoop, CBS president Taylor had undermined the philosophies and formulas of the sophisticated, generally realistic programs such as *Kojak, All in the Family, M*A*S*H,* and *Maude* which had kept CBS number one through the 1970s. In doing so, he stopped the network's momentum cold and, in effect, completely changed the direction of television for the remainder of the decade. Rather than flourishing with further developments of adult themes, the networks had to redirect one-third of their efforts to kidvid programming. CBS and NBC were caught unprepared for that form. ABC, however, was ready.

Kidvid had been an important cornerstone of ABC strategy for more than twenty years, from *Disneyland* to *The Six Million Dollar Man.* While NBC and CBS foundered trying to devise programs suitable for the entire family for the fall of 1975, ABC quickly realized that its kidvid fare would be perfect for the family hour.

Taylor's tactical blunder had given ABC the opportunity to excel in a format that drew on one of its proven strengths. He then compounded his mistake by letting Fred Silverman, his chief programmer, slip away to ABC. This double stroke of good fortune could not have come at a more opportune time for the perennial third place ABC. In the fall of 1974, Fred Pierce had become president of the ABC network and he immediately launched a shakeup designed to pull ABC from its doldrums. He overhauled the fall schedule only a month after it began, determined to build on traditional ABC strengths and expand the network's horizons.

In the second season reshuffling, Pierce reduced the frequency of made-for-TV movies (which were no longer sure-fire blockbusters), brought forward one of the network's rare new-wave sitcoms (*Barney Miller*), and placed a renewed emphasis on the urban action-adventure format with *Baretta* and *S.W.A.T.* There was no immediate dramatic rise in ABC's fortunes, but Pierce clearly demonstrated that he had strong programming instincts. In the spring of 1975, he and his chief programmer, Martin Starger, put together one of the strongest ABC fall schedules in years. They placed their popular crime-action shows (*S.W.A.T., The Rookies, Baretta, Streets of San Francisco*) in the pivotal post-family hour 9:00–10:00 P.M. swing shift and built around them: crime and medical drama at 10:00 P.M.; variety, kidvid adventure, and sitcoms at 8:00 P.M. It was a solid schedule in theory, but many ABC master plans of the past had looked good on paper, only to fail in the field. Perhaps this one would have failed as well, but, in June 1975, Fred Silverman joined ABC and the new schedule was placed in the hands of one of television's sharpest programmers.

Silverman had written his master's thesis at Ohio State University in the late 1950s on ABC's prime time programming strategy. At age twenty-five he had become the wizard behind CBS's daytime programming success, and in the early 1970s had helped keep the network number one by modernizing its prime time line-up. In early 1975, with his contract about to expire, Silverman asked for an increase in official power at CBS, feeling he deserved the recognition. CBS president Taylor disagreed over this relatively modest request and let Silverman take his talents to ABC instead. One network insider observed that "giving Freddie just one more limousine might have kept him home."

Silverman did not make a single change in ABC's fall 1975

schedule, but his manipulative skills were put to the test immediately. ABC had scheduled its new season premieres for late September while both NBC and CBS had targeted their push to begin right on the heels of Labor Day with special "sneak preview" episodes, so it was possible for ABC to fall behind before one of its programs ever aired. In order to prevent NBC and CBS from developing runaway hits against weak ABC rerun competition, Silverman slotted clusters of flashy specials against these previews. His strategy worked. ABC held on until its own premieres and turned in its best ratings performance in more than a decade. The network jumped into second place, right behind CBS.

Of course, there were some immediate failures, including shows that had "looked good on paper." Mel Brooks had interrupted a string of red hot genre parodies in film to create a TV parody of Robin Hood, *When Things Were Rotten,* but his combination of broad comedy and mild obscenity was forced to fly on television without the obscenity and flopped. Howard Cosell tried to revive the Ed Sullivan combination of a non-performing host and a mixed bag of live variety acts, but he lacked the savvy and restraint to pull it off. And despite the continued popularity of *Star Trek* in syndicated reruns, William Shatner failed to attract a sufficiently large audience to carry the kidvid Western adventure yarns of *Barbary Coast.* For a change, though, ABC found good news mixed with the bad, and its new *Welcome Back, Kotter* and *Starsky and Hutch* joined the revitalized *Happy Days* as new season hits.

Very often in the past, ABC had stumbled upon good programming ideas, but was unable to slot them effectively or cultivate them into major hits. One of Fred Silverman's talents was spotting sometimes hidden potential in marginally successful shows and bringing it out into the open. For the fall of 1975, producer Garry Marshall's *Happy Days* was given a complete body job and began its third season sporting a new, more up-to-date theme song, flashier production, and a live audience. More important, the theretofore minor figure of Arthur "Fonzie" Fonzarelli was promoted to co-star status. When the series had begun in early 1974, ABC had been wary of focusing too much attention on a proto-hoodlum wearing a leather jacket, so Fonzie had been restricted to brief appearances in the stories. When on-camera, he was shown with his motorcycle-which somehow served as an acceptable excuse for the menacing leather jacket. In the revised premise for *Happy Days,* Fonzie was liberated from his bike and moved into the garage apartment of the Cunningham home, becoming, in effect, a member of the family. Fonzie's expanded role provided the series with a sorely needed strong central character to contrast with the bland world that had been set up. To stand out in this setting, Henry Winkler played his Fonzie character as a more exaggerated macho-bravado hero, who was not merely the toughest, sharpest teenager around, but also protector, counselor, and guru to both adults and teenagers in the neighborhood. They naturally turned to him because "the Fonz" always appeared to be on top of things and in control; he was "cool" in the face of virtually any challenge. This dichotomy between cool control and witless confusion charged the series with new energy and gave both the bland teens and hapless adults the motivation to assert themselves in order to win Fonzie's respect and approval. (Ron Howard's character of Richie improved the most in this manner.)

Setting up a dropout auto mechanic as the smartest guy in town was patently absurd, but the show needed such a larger-than-life caricature. The 1950s nostalgia hook that had first served as the basis for the series had worn thin very quickly. There was not any reason to be interested in the unexciting, slightly nerdish characters of Richie and Potsie, nor in the bumbling good intentions of Mr. and Mrs. Cunningham. Besides, *Happy Days* had never been a

very good representation of teenage life in the 1950s anyway; it had merely imitated the bland world of 1950s TV sitcoms. With the elevation of Fonzie to the driving force in the *Happy Days* world, the series became the past as people wished to remember it, whether it was the 1950s, 1940s, or even the 1970s. In such memories, Fonzie was the perfect hero: He drew on his natural wits rather than formal schooling and could handle any situation better than stuffy, over-educated adults. Fonzie also became a hero to contemporary teens who were entranced by his cool control, and they turned Henry Winkler into a heart-throb of the 1970s.

The revitalized *Happy Days* registered a strong upsurge in ratings and served as an unexpectedly potent lead-in to a new teen sitcom, *Welcome Back, Kotter.* Stand-up comic Gabe Kaplan played a young teacher (Gabe Kotter) who accepted a post at his old high school in Brooklyn to teach a special remedial class of disruptive juvenile delinquents, nicknamed "the sweathogs." They consisted of an appropriately diverse group of ethnic types, including: Vinnie Barbarino, a dumb but handsome Italian (John Travolta); Juan Epstein, a Jewish-Chicano muscleman with a head full

---

October 20, 1975
Robert MacNeil Report. Former NBC newsman Robert MacNeil presents a thirty-minute in-depth study of a top news story of the day. The program begins on the East Coast public television stations, then goes to the full PBS network early the following year (January 5). Later in 1976, Washington co-anchor Jim Lehrer receives co-billing.

November 3, 1975
Good Morning America. (ABC). A complete facelift for ABC's version of *Today,* including new hosts (David Hartman and Nancy Dussault) and a new newsman (Steve Bell).

November 5, 1975
End of the Sarnoff era at RCA as fifty-seven-year-old Robert Sarnoff is deposed as RCA's chairman of the board and chief executive officer.

February 2, 1976
Jackie Gleason brings back the Honeymooners, on ABC, as an occasional special. Audrey Meadows returns to the role of Alice Kramden as she and Ralph celebrate their 25th wedding anniversary.

April 12, 1976
ABC takes over Monday night baseball from NBC.

June 7, 1976
David Brinkley is promoted back to co-anchor (with John Chancellor) of *NBC Nightly News.*

June 14, 1976
The Gong Show. (NBC). Game show whiz Chuck Barris steps in front of the cameras as the last-minute choice for hosting his latest daytime project: a zany update of the *Original Amateur Hour* format. Aspiring amateur talent perform for a panel of celebrity judges, any of whom can eliminate the would-be stars by "giving them the gong."

July 10, 1976
Time-Life's Home Box Office network gets a competitor in the pay-cable television field in the form of Viacom's Showtime.

of get-rich-quick schemes (Robert Hegyes); Frederick "Boom Boom" Washington, a confident, jive-talking black (Lawrence-Hilton Jacobs); and Arnold Horshack, a naive, ingratiating kid with a high pitched, squeaky voice (Ron Palillo). Kotter recognized their antics from his days as a class troublemaker ten years before and realized that the special class was their last chance; if he failed to win their trust and cooperation, they would probably leave high school without the basic skills for survival.

Welcome Back, Kotter had all the trappings of an insightful, topical study of ghetto education, only the producer (Chico and the Man's James Komack) had no desire to take the series in that direction. It was intended as light family hour humor aimed at the kids, so the conflicts and crises at James Buchanan High School owed much more to Our Miss Brooks than Norman Lear. Occasionally there were a few serious message episodes on such topics as the dangers of drugs, the importance of a high school diploma, and sex education but, for the most part, the show consisted of stand-up comedy exchanges between Kotter and the sweathogs, very loosely tied together by minor plot complications. Of course, Kotter never seemed to teach anything, rarely asking questions much harder than "Who discovered America?" Instead, the sweathogs were always involved in "special educational activities" outside the classroom. The program fulfilled every child's secret fantasy of the perfect class: field trips, a comedian for a teacher, and no work. Yet despite the ancient jokes and simple plots, the series worked. The cast members had an excellent sense of timing and their personal interaction covered the many obvious flaws of the series quite well. After awhile, Welcome Back, Kotter produced its own teen idol, as Travolta's sexy Vinnie Barbarino began competing with Winkler's Fonz for pinup space in the teen magazines. Travolta parlayed this attention into an unusually successful transition to feature films, a feat rarely accomplished by TV stars.

With Welcome Back, Kotter, ABC showed how an old fashioned kidvid sitcom could handle the family hour requirements quite nicely, leaving the high-gloss violence to thrive after nine. ABC's big new success in this style of post-family hour programming was Starsky and Hutch, placed immediately after the increasingly popular Baretta. In order to breathe life into the familiar setting of two plainclothes detectives (Paul Michael Glaser as Dave Starsky and David Soul as Ken "Hutch" Hutchinson), producers Aaron Spelling and Leonard Goldberg took the Maverick formula of witty camaraderie under fire and mixed it with the 1970s world of urban crime and violence. Starsky and Hutch needed to be near Supermen to survive the endless car chases and shoot-outs that filled each episode, so their light banter, personal putdowns, and sly sideways glances at beautiful women were necessary to keep viewers interested in their lives. This obvious scenario had been in the ABC schedule for years in various action-adventure series, but it represented a major change by Spelling and Goldberg. They toned down their reliance on the Jack Webb style of super-efficient, flawless, gung-ho cops (their S.W.A.T. had been a souped-up version of Webb's Emergency) in favor of more casual characters that did not necessarily adhere to the law themselves. Thus, Starsky and Hutch resembled the street punks they fought more than other members of the police force. Though the program proved to be quite popular with many viewers, some critics pointed to the sleazier aspects of the package as the perfect example of "Slime at Nine" programming.

Nonetheless, with Starsky and Hutch, Welcome Back, Kotter, and Happy Days, ABC coasted through the early fall in second place, well behind CBS but far ahead of NBC. In a panic, NBC tore up its schedule and began making plans for wholesale changes in January. In mid-October, however, it received a welcome but unexpected boost from the World Series. The dramatic battle between the Boston Red Sox and Cincinnati Reds extended over seven games, most played in prime time, and brought in the highest sports ratings in television history at the time. On the strength of those two weeks of baseball competition, NBC jumped back into contention in the cumulative ratings contest. By December, less than one ratings point separated the three networks.

At this critical juncture in the season's ratings competition, Fred Silverman's instincts and expertise came into play as he analyzed ABC's position. Silverman reasoned that with the three networks virtually even, implementing successful mid-season changes was more important than planning the next fall's line-ups. The network that jumped ahead in January would have the momentum to carry it through the next season. After all, finishing first in 1975–76 meant starting the next season at number one. Consequently, Silverman treated January 1976 like a brand-new season. He not only introduced a cluster of second season hopefuls, he also slotted special programming designed to keep the competition constantly off balance.

CBS executives chose to follow the strategy that had worked for twenty years: wait out the competition. They felt that ultimately viewers would return to their old favorites on CBS after the novelty of the new programs wore off. The public had remained loyal to CBS for over two decades; the network still had more than half the shows in the top ten; and there was no reason to assume that ABC, even with Fred Silverman, could keep pace through the winter and spring. Therefore, CBS made only a few minor adjustments in its schedule for the second season. By early February, it was clear that CBS had underestimated the competition, as ABC began winning week after week of the ratings battle.

Silverman fine-tuned the ABC schedule, building strong lead-in shows perfect for the family hour. The biggest new hit of the second season was a spinoff from Happy Days featuring two young women, friends of the Fonz, Laverne (Penny Marshall, sister of the show's producer, Garry Marshall) and Shirley (Cindy Williams), who had graduated high school and were striking off on their own. They were aggressive working class characters employed at a Milwaukee brewery, but with a very active social life that frequently put them in conflict with snotty upper-class types. Like Fonzie, they drew on their natural instincts and know-how rather than formal education in successfully facing these situations. Though set in the late 1950s (like Happy Days), Laverne and Shirley presented women in a role unheard of in television twenty years before: They were strong, self-sufficient, and in control of their lives—as well as being lovable, wacky, and searching for eligible men. They were just as likely to pull their klutzy male co-workers, Lenny (Michael McKean) and Squiggy (David Lander), from some dumb misunderstanding as to need rescuing themselves. At the same time, the series also marked a return to the 1950s I Love Lucy style of physical comedy and slapstick humor, continuing the move from realism precipitated by the family hour.

Practically overnight, the thrust of new comedy shows had changed. Though Welcome Back, Kotter, Happy Days, and Laverne and Shirley had serious moments, their humor was straightforward, physical, and not very sophisticated or overly concerned with relevant social issues. Comic caricatures and "cool" heroes such as the Fonz and Barbarino became the important new hooks for the plots and laughs. This marked the beginning of the end of the dominance of Norman Lear's style of comedy, and his new entry for CBS, One Day at a Time, was his last new network series to become a top ten hit. Laverne and Shirley was placed in the hot slot following Happy Days (Welcome Back, Kotter was moved to lead into Barney Miller on Thursday), and both series immediately jumped into the top ten. They were joined there by another ABC clone, *The Bionic Woman,* who was literally raised from the dead and given her own show.

In the spring of 1975, a two-part story on *The Six Million Dollar Man* introduced Jaime Sommers (Lindsay Wagner), an old flame of Steve Austin's who, after an accident, was also given nuclear powered limbs. The ratings for the episodes had been extremely high and the public obviously wanted to see more of the Bionic Woman; however, she had been killed at the end of that story. Such minor considerations had never stopped comic book writers in the past, so she was brought back in the fall of 1975 in another two-part episode of *The Six Million Dollar Man.* In January, *The Bionic Woman* became a weekly family hour series of its own. In order to help boost the new program's ratings, both Steve Austin and Jaime Sommers occasionally appeared in each other's stories, and both series were plugged in the coming attractions at the end of every episode. Anyone who was interested in one of the shows would end up watching both. Just to be sure, Silverman also flip-flopped the two series a few times, running *The Bionic Woman* in *The Six Million Dollar Man's* time slot, and vice versa.

ABC had unlocked the secret of the family hour, going straight for the motherlode: kids from two through seventeen. The kids responded and turned ABC's family hour fare into certified hits on five of the seven nights of programming. Suddenly, ABC was dominating most nights of the week, combining its family hour success with solid action-adventure shows that aired later in the evening.

In the past, ABC had blown ratings leads by finding one program type and working it to death. Silverman did not let this happen and seemed determined to develop winning programs in many directions so that ABC could build its own well-rounded stable of hits and draw viewer loyalty similar to the support that had taken CBS through season after season of success. Even as the new ABC hits became familiar to more and more people, Silverman began inserting special programming to lure new viewers who would then hopefully stick around for the regular series.

In early February, ABC devoted thirty and one-half hours of prime time to coverage of the Winter Olympics in Innsbruck, Austria. NBC's coverage of the Winter Games four years earlier had bombed, so many television insiders regarded this as a foolhardy risk, but it paid off. Roone Arledge's *Wide World of Sports* crew, led by Howard Cosell, Frank Gifford, and Chris Schenkel, clearly explained each event. They produced "up close and personal" profiles of standout performers (filmed in the athletes' home towns before the formal competition) to give viewers human background information in addition to the usual endless statistics. Bewildering events such as a cross-country ski and shoot competition became comprehensible and exciting contests with heroes the home audience could cheer on. The Winter Olympics coverage won most of its time slots, even up against established entertainment hits.

Immediately after the Winter Olympics, ABC introduced its first major followup to the successful 1974 novel-for-television,

QB VII, a twelve-hour adaptation of Irwin Shaw's *Rich Man, Poor Man.* Like the British historical dramas presented on public television's *Masterpiece Theater, Rich Man, Poor Man* was a high-gloss soap opera. It traced the lives, loves, and intrigues of the members of a high-class family over the span of one generation, focusing on two fiercely antagonistic brothers (played by Peter Strauss and Nick Nolte). Like the Olympics, this miniseries also cracked the top ten.

In the spring, Silverman gave producers Aaron Spelling and Leonard Goldberg the chance to move from the cop mold to more serious themes in *Family.* The concept of the series had been kicked about at ABC for three years but landed nowhere because the network had been afraid that the average viewer would not be able to identify with the Lawrence family: they "lived too well, dressed too well, and spoke too well," one executive said. In short, they were portrayed as real people who talked about serious matters such as death, divorce, alcoholism, and homosexuality without wrapping the discussions in vicious putdowns or simpleminded caricatures. Silverman had enough faith in the series to give it an extended tryout against first-run competition in early March, rather than waiting for the late spring and summer rerun season. With practically no publicity, it replaced the ailing *Marcus Welby, M.D.* and captured a 40% share of the audience against CBS's gimmicky "Sting" rip-off, *Switch,* earning a spot in the fall lineup.

The Olympics were supposed to bomb. *Rich Man, Poor Man* was not supposed to be a big hit. *Family* was not even noticed at first. But they all clicked. CBS and NBC executives had felt certain that once the flashy specials were out of the way, ABC's new viewers would melt away. They did not. For eleven weeks in a row, through the winter and into the spring, ABC won the weekly ratings race, not just with its specials, but with growing viewer loyalty to its regular series. During the second season, ABC had four of the top five shows, nine of the top twenty, and thirteen of the top thirty. It was steadily chipping away at the cumulative ratings lead CBS had built at the start of the season.

In the summer, after the regular season had ended, ABC carried the Summer Olympic Games in Montreal and these proved more successful than the incredible 1972 Olympics in Munich. For two weeks, the network junked its prime time schedule and presented the Olympics all night, every night. It won every time slot every night, with an average 49% share of the audience. With this sports blockbuster, ABC matched and passed CBS's average over the previous twelve months. In one amazing season, ABC had become the number one network, ending years of programming frustration.

Fred Silverman appeared to be a miracle man, with everything he touched turning to gold. Actually, he still had not proved himself in creating new programs from scratch; he had relied on spinoffs and series already under development before he came to ABC. However, there was no denying his ability to program the material at hand into the best possible slots. Fred Silverman had taken his new network to the top and there was no one in the industry better equipped to keep it there.

36. The Big Event

DESPITE ABC'S INCREDIBLE PERFORMANCE from January to August of 1976, the network had just barely edged out CBS in the cumulative ratings for the entire twelve months of the 1975–76 season. CBS, in fact, had technically won the "regular" season (September to April), losing only when the summer rerun period was averaged in to the total. The fall of 1976 was therefore expected to mark the beginning of a very tight season-long ratings battle. To counter the revitalized ABC, NBC turned to special event programs while CBS eased in a handful of new shows, still convinced that, in the new season, viewers would return once again to their old favorites. As the network temporarily on top, ABC planned to build on the momentum of last season's dramatic come-from-behind victory, confident that it had won viewer loyalty with its new hits and frequent specials.

Just as he had done in keeping CBS on top earlier in the decade, Fred Silverman carefully arranged ABC's series, stars, and special events for the fall, yet he remained flexible enough to make last minute changes to counter the competition with the strongest possible line-up. He shifted a variety series featuring the musical duo of the Captain and Tennille from a scheduled summer tryout period directly into the fall line-up, where it could serve as both an ideal family hour program and an ABC promotional device. Then, at the end of August, he changed the announced time slots of five series, including new episodes of the popular *Rich Man, Poor Man* story. He rescheduled that series (labeled *Book II*) from a Saturday night slot to the frontlines on Tuesday at 9:00 P.M., right after *Laverne and Shirley*.

Counting on the strength of its familiar veterans, CBS held firm. NBC, however, juggled its own schedule in response, changing the announced time slots of six shows, eliminating *Snip* (a situation comedy based on the film "Shampoo"), and postponing the John O'Hara-inspired drama *Gibbsville* until an appropriate second season slot opened. These changes took place so close to the opening of the new season that the special annual fall preview edition of *TV Guide* (which hit the stands in mid-September) still contained profile background information on these two NBC proto-series. The editors apologized and explained that the text, graphs, and writeups in that issue reflected the new season as it stood at press deadline time, but that everything could change at any moment. Even the once sacrosanct fall schedules had succumbed to the increasingly common last-minute network brinkmanship aimed at scoring the season's first ratings blow.

Attempting to gain an additional edge, each of the networks also jammed September with special events such as blockbuster films, extended length series premiere episodes, TV movies, and celebrity-studded variety shows. The previous fall Silverman had used such "stunting" and "frontloading" techniques extensively in order to keep the other networks from building an insurmountable ratings lead over then number three ABC. This season, all three networks stressed such programming both to pump up their ratings on particular nights and also to tout their overall schedules by using regular series stars as special headliners and guests. Such cross-pollination encouraged viewers to follow a network's entire line-up to see their favorite series stars in action.

During premiere week, variety star Sonny Bono played a ruthless rock manager and record promoter on CBS's *Switch,* while the casts of both *Switch* and *One Day at a Time* appeared on the season opener of *The Tony Orlando and Dawn Rainbow Hour.* Freddie Prinze, from *Chico and the Man,* played a character similar in spirit to his fast-talking Chico in a new NBC made-for-television movie, "The Million Dollar Ripoff." On ABC, stars such as Penny Marshall and Cindy Williams from *Laverne and Shirley* and the sweathogs of *Welcome Back, Kotter* appeared throughout the week. They ushered in the new Captain and Tennille variety show as well as new series from Bill Cosby (*Cos*) and *Kotter*'s producer, James Komack (*Mr. T and Tina*). To plug the one-hour season premiere of *Happy Days* featuring Roz Kelly as Pinky Tuscadero (a tough-talking woman with her eyes on the Fonz), Kelly also appeared the night before as a special guest on *The Captain and Tennille.*

Once viewers had sampled the many new offerings and specials, they did just as CBS had predicted and returned to their old favorites. However, these favorites now included Lee Majors, Henry Winkler, John Travolta, Robert Blake, Peter Strauss, Lindsay Wagner, Penny Marshall, Cindy Williams, and Gabe Kaplan—all stars of series on ABC. Fred Silverman had analyzed the network situation perfectly the previous season. The special events and flashy changes in the early months of 1976 had lured viewers and introduced them to the regular ABC stars and series. As these shows began winning week after week in the ratings, more and more people fell into the habit of looking in on the programs presented by the new number one network. These new viewer habits carried over into the fall and the expected tight three-way race never developed. Instead, ABC quickly jumped out in front and stayed there, dominating four or five nights a week. It was soon clear that ABC had solidified its position as the number one network and would win the 1976–77 season with ease. CBS's two-decade string of season victories was at last at an end. The real fight this season became the contest for the number two spot.

Of course, ABC had its share of clunkers including *Holmes and Yo Yo, The Nancy Walker Show,* and *Mr. T and Tina*; these never caught on even with all the hype. Overall, however, the network did extremely well with its returning shows and managed to come up with the only new regular series to break into the top ten, *Charlie's Angels.*

Produced by crime show veterans Aaron Spelling and Leonard Goldberg (of *Starsky and Hutch* and *The Mod Squad*). *Charlie's Angels* featured a trio of beautiful women taken from routine police work and assigned to special undercover detective duty by a man known only as Charlie (John Forsythe). He dubbed them his squad of "angels" and used them for dangerous undercover missions suited to their particular talents. Charlie never appeared in person, but gave his instructions over a speaker phone, outlining the details of each high-priority mission. When not near a phone, the angels took orders from Charlie's flunky, John Bosley (David Doyle). Despite the familiar cloak and dagger trappings, *Charlie's Angels* was far more than a routine detective-adventure show. It was an excuse to show sixty minutes of suggestive poses by walking, talking pin-up girls.

Each of Charlie's angels waged her battles in form-fitting clothes, a bikini, or nightgown, soundly thrashing international spies, deranged maniacs, and other strawmen-villains, yet barely worked up more than a mild, sexy sweat. Yet they also willingly responded to the orders from their off camera male superior, creating the perfect male sexual fantasy with a dream woman for every man: Sabrina (Kate Jackson) was the low-key intelligent type that combined brains and beauty; Kelly (Jaclyn Smith) symbolized the traditional high society charmer who was always in style; and Jill (Farrah Fawcett) brought up images of torrid back-street passion with her windswept coiffure and knowing smile.

Television critics gasped in horror when they realized that the most popular new series of the season had such titillation at its soft, suggestive core. They rushed to point out the obvious flaws of *Charlie's Angels,* panning the show as "dreadful," "schlock" and "stupid." Yet just as the general public had ignored the critical lambasting of *The Beverly Hillbillies* the decade before, viewers (male and female) eagerly followed the adventures of the three scantily clad glamour lovelies despite the knocks. The threadbare plots, papier-mâché characters, and wooden dialogue did not matter. Women were pleased to see a team of female adventurers more than hold their own in a standard television setting. The men were more than happy to ogle. Besides, nothing explicit ever took place on the screen.

The sex on *Charlie's Angels* was really just suggestive, squeaky clean TV sex. Even with their bra-less wardrobe, Sabrina, Kelly, and Jill were, in truth, just like previous television glamour girls such as the genie (Barbara Eden) of *I Dream of Jeannie,* the perfectly constructed female robot (Julie Newmar) of *My Living Doll,* and the aspiring starlets of *Bracken's World.* They never appeared in scenes of torrid physical passion, just in revealing costumes. The active imaginations of the viewers filled in the rest with whatever fantasy seemed appropriate.

With *Charlie's Angels,* ABC had once again struck ratings gold and the reality of the network's competitive position at last hit home at CBS. After the first month of the new season, though CBS still had twelve of the top forty shows (including the very successful *All in the Family* and *M*A*S*H*) the former number one found itself in the cellar. With the exception of a new blue collar working sitcom, *Alice (*based on the hit movie "Alice Doesn't Live Here

Anymore"), all the new CBS shows bombed. More important, many previously solid CBS hits such as *Phyllis, Kojak,* and *Sonny and Cher* were dropping even as the ABC line-up soared.

Part of CBS's problem could be traced directly to the family hour, which CBS president Arthur Taylor had originally proposed and championed. Overnight it had shifted the emphasis in prime time programming away from relatively adult fare such as *Kojak* to the types of teen-oriented material that ABC had specialized in for years. While ABC rolled on with shows such as *Laverne and Shirley,* CBS was unable to develop new programs that could adapt its strengths to the demands of a television world less interested in topical issues and realistic violence.

A more important cause of CBS's downfall, however, was that while on top the network had become complacent and overconfident. Instead of developing a wide range of pilots and new shows as back-up inventory, the network had stagnated. Since the fall of 1974 CBS had come up with only three new hit shows (*Rhoda, The Jeffersons,* and *One Day at a Time*) to step in and share some of the load. As a result, CBS's success depended almost entirely on an increasingly old line-up. ABC, in contrast, had only one program (*The Streets of San Francisco*) that had been on before the fall of 1973.

In the late 1960s, CBS management had committed the same sin with an over-reliance on aging rural series, but then-network president Bob Wood and his chief programmer Fred Silverman had been able to snap CBS back to life by pruning the schedule and ushering in the Norman Lear-*All in the Family* era. That action had come just in time. Now, it was too late to save the 1976–77 season. As one CBS insider put it, "We're running out of gas."

In October, CBS's Arthur Taylor walked the plank and the

Less than a year after the premiere of *The Robert MacNeil Report*, Washington-based anchor Jim Lehrer *(left)* received official co-billing with the New York-based MacNeil *(right)* and *The MacNeil/Lehrer Report* was born. *(Courtesy of MacNeil/Lehrer Productions)*

	8:00	8:30	9:00	9:30	10:00	10:30	
M O N	THE CAPTAIN AND TENNILLE		ABC NFL Monday Night Football (to 12 Midnight)				ABC
	Rhoda	Phyllis	Maude	ALL'S FAIR	EXECUTIVE SUITE		CBS
	Little House On The Prairie		NBC Monday Night At The Movies				NBC
T U E	Happy Days	Laverne And Shirley	Rich Man, Poor Man: Book II		Family		ABC
	Tony Orlando And Dawn Rainbow Hour		M*A*S*H	One Day At A Time	Switch		CBS
	BAA BAA BLACKSHEEP		Police Woman		Police Story		NBC
W E D	The Bionic Woman		Baretta		CHARLIE'S ANGELS		ABC
	Good Times	BALL FOUR	All In The Family	ALICE	The Blue Knight		CBS
	The Practice		NBC Movie Of The Week		THE QUEST		NBC
T H R	Welcome Back, Kotter	Barney Miller	TONY RANDALL SHOW	NANCY WALKER SHOW	The Streets Of San Francisco		ABC
	The Waltons		Hawaii Five-O		Barnaby Jones		CBS
	THE GEMINI MAN		BEST SELLERS (CAPTAINS AND THE KINGS; ONCE AN EAGLE)		VAN DYKE AND COMPANY		NBC
F R I	Donny And Marie		The ABC Friday Night Movie				ABC
	SPENCER'S PILOTS		CBS Friday Night Movies				CBS
	Sanford And Son	Chico And The Man	The Rockford Files		SERPICO		NBC
S A T	HOLMES AND YOYO / MR. T AND TINA / # NEW ORIGINAL WONDER WOMAN		Starsky And Hutch		MOST WANTED		ABC
	The Jeffersons	Doc	Mary Tyler Moore Show	Bob Newhart Show	Carol Burnett Show		CBS
	Emergency		NBC Saturday Night At The Movies				NBC

	7:00	7:30	8:00	8:30	9:00	9:30	10:00	10:30	
S U N	COS		The Six Million Dollar Man		The ABC Sunday Night Movie				ABC
	60 Minutes		Sonny And Cher Show		Kojak		DELVECCHIO		CBS
	The Wonderful World Of Disney		NBC Sunday Mystery Movie (McCloud; Columbo; McMillan; QUINCY, M.E.)				THE BIG EVENT		NBC

network began a top-to-bottom executive housecleaning. The new management team, led by Gene Jankowski, faced both the long-term task of rebuilding the network's schedule and the immediate challenge of trying to salvage the current season by at least moving ahead of NBC into the number two spot.

NBC found itself in a much better competitive position going into the fall of 1976. Not only did the network have high hopes for two special prime time vehicles (dramatic miniseries and "big event" specials), it had also developed a new comedy-variety show the previous season that had become the talk of television: *Saturday Night Live.*

Since the early 1950s, NBC had consistently turned to comedy-variety as an important television programming strategy. Stars such as Bob Hope, Dean Martin and Jerry Lewis, Sid Caesar, Flip Wilson, and Dan Rowan and Dick Martin had headlined some of the network's most successful programs. Though Bob Hope and Dean Martin continued to do occasional specials, NBC had been unable to find successful new headliners for a weekly series going into the mid-1970s. The network had brought in the Smothers Brothers as mid-season replacements in 1974–75, but, after strong opening ratings in January 1975, their series failed. Despite fresh talent such as Steve Martin, Don Novello (as Vatican correspondent Father Guido Sarducci), and writer Chevy Chase, the Smothers seemed unable to adapt to the new decade. They fluctuated between familiar rehashes of bits from their late 1960s show (with

Pat Paulsen and Bob "Officer Judy" Einstein) and bland new skits with guests such as Ringo Starr.

For the fall of 1975, the network turned to former *Laugh-In* writer Lorne Michaels to supervise a new comedy-variety show. (Over the previous two seasons Michaels had worked on two successful comedy-variety specials starring another *Laugh-In* graduate, Lily Tomlin, first as a writer, then as a producer.) Because the proposed new NBC series was viewed as somewhat experimental, it was slotted to appear late night on Saturdays, 11:30 P.M. to 1:00 A.M., three times a month. This placement was also aimed at tapping the young adult audience, a long-ignored but growing group of viewers that the networks had begun to pursue during the 1972–73 season.

The initial shows targeted for this demographic group featured rock music. ABC was first in November 1972 with a late Friday night special, *In Concert.* The program soon became a twice-monthly fixture and NBC followed in early 1973 with its own weekly late night series, *The Midnight Special* (hosted by legendary rock disk jockey Wolfman Jack). That program also broke new ground by becoming the latest-starting network show in television history, beginning after the Friday night *Tonight* show (1:00 A.M. Saturday morning). Though rock had rarely been able to capture sufficiently high ratings to succeed in prime time, the late Friday night exposure attracted a solid audience consisting primarily of young adults that shunned prime time (going out for the evening instead) but who returned to catch their favorite acts before turning in.

In the fall of 1974, NBC slotted a monthly news and public affairs program, *Weekend,* in the Saturday night slot of 11:30 P.M. Its slightly tongue-in-cheek style catered toward this same young adult crowd. For the fall of 1975, NBC's new Saturday night comedy-variety show was to fill in the remaining three Saturday nights of each month.

In setting up the new program, Michaels was determined to develop *Saturday Night Live* as a special entity, different from standard prime time network variety. Like NBC's *Your Show of Shows* from the early 1950s, there would be guest stars, but they would be generally limited to a guest host that would work with a continuing company of writers and supporting players. Like the late night rock shows, the musical guests (rock, jazz, and folk-oriented) would be presented straight, performing one or two songs without engaging in banal "transition" patter. Like *Laugh-In* and the original *Smothers Brothers Comedy Hour,* there would be topical references and satirical jabs, as well as parodies of television, movies, and commercials. And, like the fondly remembered golden age of television, the program would be presented *live,* from New York City, before a real studio audience.

The decision to do the program as a live New York production immediately gave the project a distinct flavor and generated high expectations, while the late night weekend slot provided the much needed time to work out the rough spots. The first broadcast of NBC's *Saturday Night Live* took place on October 11, 1975, with veteran comic George Carlin as host and Billy Preston and Janis Ian as the musical guests. It was very uneven. Singer-songwriter Paul Simon hosted the second show and, in effect, turned it into a Paul Simon musical special. (He had three guest singers and together they performed nearly a dozen numbers.) Yet in just a few months, working with subsequent hosts such as Rob Reiner, Lily Tomlin, Candice Bergen, Richard Pryor, Buck Henry, and Dick Cavett, the program's crew gelled and the show began to develop its style, a reputation, and a following.

High school and college students were among the first to latch on to the show, partially because the program was deliberately outrageous, sometimes even tasteless, in the style of the increasingly popular BBC import, *Monty Python's Flying Circus,* and the homegrown radio, stage, and magazine efforts of the *National Lampoon.* The opening joke on the very first show involved the Python-ish premise of two men dying of heart attacks, capped with the punchline: *"Live,* from New York, it's *Saturday Night!"*

As with *Your Shows of Shows,* the company of regular performers evolved into the real stars of the series. Dubbed "The Not Ready for Prime Time Players," Dan Aykroyd, John Belushi, Chevy Chase, Jane Curtin, Garrett Morris, Laraine Newman, and Gilda Radner each developed their own distinctive character types and caricatures. Chase was the first to attract a following, based chiefly on his mock newscasts ("Weekend Update") and his portrayal of a bumbling, dull-witted President Gerald Ford.

Aykroyd, Belushi, and Chase also served as program writers, joining *National Lampoon* co-founder Michael O'Donoghue, Lorne Michaels himself, and nearly a dozen others including Al Franken, Tom Davis, Anne Beatts, Rosie Shuster, and Alan Zweibel. They produced the expected excellent movie and television parodies, including a remake of "Citizen Kane" (revealing Kane's last words to be: "Roast Beef on Rye with Mustard"), *Star Trek*'s final voyage, and a "Jaws"-like urban killer, the "Land Shark." Political and topical subjects ranged from President Richard Nixon's final days in office to Claudine Longet's "accidental" shooting of a number of helpless skiers on the slopes. (The latter

prompted an on-the-air apology.) Yet there were also very effective mood pieces such as a chance coffee shop encounter between a young man and a woman he had admired from afar years before, in high school. By the spring of 1976, *Saturday Night Live* had gained such a following that even Gerald Ford's press secretary, Ron Nessen (a former NBC news correspondent), agreed to serve as host, bringing along film inserts of President Ford himself.

For the next four years, *Saturday Night Live* grew in popularity and quality. Though the very nature of a live weekly show meant that any particular episode might be weak, overall the series emerged as the most daring and innovative television program of the late 1970s. Hosts such as consumer advocate Ralph Nader, football star O. J. Simpson, and rock star Frank Zappa, as well as more traditional Hollywood actors such as Cecily Tyson, Richard Benjamin, and Elliott Gould, turned in excellent performances as headliners. Though Chevy Chase left the cast in the program's second season to pursue a solo career in films (he was replaced by another of the show's writers, Bill Murray), the rest of the players remained, further developing their stock of characters and routines. Skits became increasingly complex and sophisticated with such presentations as "The Pepsi-Syndrome" (based on the nuclear accident at Three Mile Island and the film "The China Syndrome") running nearly twenty minutes.

After five seasons, all the players as well as Lorne Michaels himself left the show. A completely new cast took over in the fall of 1980 but it was a chaotic transition; by 1985, Michaels was lured back to the helm. After leaving the show, most of the original cast attempted solo film projects, with Chevy Chase and John Belushi scoring the biggest initial successes: Chase in "Foul Play" and Belushi in "National Lampoon's Animal House" and "The Blues Brothers" (with Dan Aykroyd). Through many up-and-down cycles (in both ratings and creativity), *Saturday Night Live* carried on into the twenty-first century, serving as the launching ground for wave after wave of comedians including Eddie Murphy, Dennis Miller, Phil Hartman, Mike Myers, Chris Farley, Chris Rock, Adam Sandler, Will Ferrell, Amy Poehler, Jimmy Fallon, and Tina Fey.

Unlike *Your Show of Shows,* all *Saturday Night Live* episodes were preserved on video tape and could be rerun during the summer or during the regular season to give the cast a few weeks off. In the show's fifth season, NBC took highlights from these tapes and turned them into a brief prime time series, *The Best of Saturday Night Live.*

NBC's 1975 late night comedy-variety experiment was quickly recognized as an unqualified success and, for the fall of 1976, the network hoped for similar success in prime time with another traditional NBC programming strength, blockbuster special events.

Ever since the Pat Weaver days of the early 1950s when NBC had last been on top, the network had done very well with special programming. In the 1975–76 season, for instance, the prime time World Series broadcasts had kept NBC in contention for number one through December. For the 1976–77 season, NBC set aside a specific weekly slot for prime time sports extravaganzas, blockbuster movies, special dramatic presentations, and even nostalgic retrospectives. Dubbed *The Big Event,* this Sunday night series was designed to expand or shrink to accommodate different types of programs. Some nights it ran ninety minutes; on others it filled the entire Sunday night prime time block. Occasionally *The Big Event* extended to other nights as well. This was the most flexible, extensive use of irregularly scheduled programming any network had attempted in years.

The Big Event got off to an inauspicious start with "The Big Party," a boring collection of live and taped clips from a number of

August 30, 1976

Tom Brokaw replaces Jim Hartz as host of *Today.*

September 20, 1976

The Muppet Show. Jim Henson's muppets get their own program, a high-quality syndicated half hour aimed at the access slots.

September 21, 1976

The Toronto branch of the improvisational theater troupe Second City brings its satirical skewering to TV with *Second City Television* on Canada's Global network. John Candy, Joe Flaherty, Eugene Levy, Andrea Martin, Catherine O'Hara, Dave Thomas, and Harold Ramis are the core performers (later joined by Rick Moranis and Martin Short), playing multiple roles at a fictional low-budget TV station in "Melonville." The series is syndicated to the U.S. in 1977 and lands a late night network slot on NBC in 1981 as *SCTV Network 90.*

September 23, 1976

Televised debates between presidential candidates return after a sixteen-year hiatus as Democratic challenger Jimmy Carter takes on incumbent Republican Gerald Ford.

October 3, 1976

Quincy, M.E. (NBC). Jack Klugman stars in a new segment of *The NBC Mystery Movie,* featuring television's first coroner-as-cop.

October 4, 1976

Barbara Walters, television's first million-dollar newswoman, joins Harry Reasoner as co-anchor of *The ABC Evening News.*

October 18, 1976

Four months after Barbara Walters left, twenty-six-year-old Jane Pauley debuts as her replacement on *Today.*

October 19, 1976

The New Avengers. (Thames). The popular adventure series of the 1960s returns in top form in Britain with Patrick Macnee continuing his role as government agent John Steed, aided by two new young partners: Joanna Lumley as Purdey and Gareth Hunt as Mike Gambit. The updated Avengers arrive in the States on CBS in a late night slot for the fall of 1978.

"exciting and glamorous showbiz parties" throughout New York City. Rather than perform, most of the celebrities merely plugged their latest projects before waving the camera on. Dick Cavett, host of the confusing, fractured event, said at one point, "I'm absolutely humiliated because I don't know what I'm supposed to be doing." Shortly thereafter, he began doing impromptu hand shadows.

Subsequent *Big Event* presentations were much better shows, offering viewers many exciting television programs, from the annual World Series contest to the American network debut of the 1939 movie classic, "Gone With the Wind." The *Saturday Night Live* cast made its first prime time appearance in February with "Live from the Mardi Gras-It's *Saturday Night* on Sunday!" Among the special dramatic presentations were several docudramas including "Raid on Entebbe" (the Israeli commando rescue mission to Africa), "Tail Gunner Joe" (a silly and self-righteous review of McCarthyism), and "Jesus of Nazareth" (a special Easter

presentation of the life of Christ, directed by Franco Zeffirelli). There were also well produced retrospectives that gave producers and writers the chance to rummage through movie studio and network archives and to share, on the air, the nostalgic treasure trove they uncovered. Two of the best of this type were the three-hour "*Life* Goes to the Movies" (a dandy review of cinematic history hosted by Shirley MacLaine, Liza Minnelli, and Henry Fonda) and the four-and-one-half-hour "NBC: The First Fifty Years" (NBC's own history presented through the eyes of Greg Garrison, Dean Martin's producer, and hosted by Orson Welles, the era's consummate voice of history).

The Big Event gave NBC a tremendous weekly ratings boost that pushed it past CBS and into brief head-to-head competition with ABC, largely due to the record-breaking audience for "Gone With the Wind," telecast over two nights in early November. At the time, the film won the distinction of being the highest rated program in television history.

The chief problem with *The Big Event* was the one that always followed such special series, from Pat Weaver's spectaculars to ABC's made-for-TV movies: There were only so many special events. What's more, each episode had to stand on its own with less carryover than for a regular series with returning characters and a consistent situation. Viewers did not automatically follow *The Big Event* but rather tuned in special programs that had caught their attention. In subsequent seasons, then, the emphasis of *The Big Event* shifted somewhat to more frequent use of theatrical features, special made-for-TV movies, and miniseries, mixed in with occasional specials.

Even with its shortcomings, *The Big Event* was a welcome success for NBC and became one of the top ten shows during the 1976–77 season. It demonstrated that viewers would tune to special events, even those carried over an entire evening or running several nights. Lacking many regular series hits, NBC frequently billed special events on other nights as "Big Events" and began to further develop this "event programming" strategy as its answer to ABC's success. This dovetailed perfectly with the network's increasing interest in miniseries, begun that season with the *Best Sellers* anthology.

Best Sellers was an obvious attempt to cash in on the success of ABC's novel-for-television hit *Rich Man, Poor Man* by using the approach taken by public television's *Masterpiece Theater* to present several "novels" in one season. Since 1970, *Masterpiece Theater* had served as the weekly slot for such miniseries as *The Pallisers* and *Upstairs, Downstairs,* running one entire work before moving on to the next title. These sweeping, romantic dynasty epics (chiefly British series, usually set in the 1800s) pulled in surprisingly high ratings for PBS and had even inspired CBS to attempt an Americanized version in 1975–76, *Beacon Hill.* That series, however, quickly became bogged down by its period production and stilted storyline and lasted for only half a season.

NBC planned to avoid those problems with *Best Sellers* by taking the attractive soap opera hooks of lust and intrigue and wrapping them within the works of slick pulp fiction in the style of Harold Robbins, Jacqueline Susann, and Irwin Shaw. The network turned to Universal Studios for production of the series and the studio brought in big name stars as special secondary and cameo players to support the very beautiful but generally unknown newcomers cast in the lead roles. In addition, each story was structured to follow the style of the drawn-out British epics that spanned generations, though these American versions usually focused on World War II.

Best Sellers consisted of four miniseries: Taylor Caldwell's *Captains and the Kings,* Anton Myrer's *Once an Eagle,* Norman

Bogner's *Seventh Avenue,* and Robert Ludlum's *The Rhinemann Exchange.* They all did fairly well in the ratings, though overall *Best Sellers* was not a blockbuster, averaging just a 27% share of the audience. This was quite a letdown and far below the top ten performance of *Rich Man, Poor Man* the previous season. One other NBC novel-for-television, however, did much better. Upton Sinclair's *The Moneychangers,* which ran in four parts on *The Big Event* in December, scored a 35% share of the audience presenting exactly the same type of soapy drama as *Best Sellers.* Apparently the weekly *Best Sellers* slot was not the most effective commercial format for these novels for television. In fact, a weekly series seemed to reduce the impact of the programs as special events. Incorporating such miniseries within *The Big Event* format, though, seemed to offer the best of both worlds. Not only could each one be touted as a special presentation, there was also no need to churn out "a chapter each week" because other material appeared in the slot as well. NBC therefore dropped the weekly *Best Sellers* after only one season and merged subsequent miniseries into various *Big Event* and movie slots.

Although NBC had made the most substantial commitment to special events and miniseries for the 1976–77 season, it was number one ABC that scored with the show that was both the season's most successful miniseries and television's biggest big event.

Following the high ratings of one of television's first multi-part docudramas, *QB VII* (presented in April 1974), ABC had begun work on other historical-type dramas, based both in pure fiction *(Rich Man, Poor Man)* and real life *(Eleanor and Franklin).* One of the books selected for miniseries treatment was *Roots,* a work in progress by black writer Alex Haley, who had distinguished himself with his assistance on the autobiography of black activist Malcolm X in the mid-1960s. At that time, Haley had become increasingly interested in his own black heritage and, at age forty-four, set about reconstructing his family genealogy, determined to trace his personal roots back to Africa, if possible. His search consumed nearly twelve years and was financed chiefly through the advance sale of every possible permutation of the story he hoped to tell, including an adaptation for television.

Plans for the David Wolper production of *Roots* were already well under way before Fred Silverman came to ABC, but it was Silverman who had to decide the most effective way to present the finished product. Haley's incessant probing had resulted in a story that was potential ratings dynamite, tracing the struggle for freedom by Kunte Kinte, an African hunter brought to America as a slave in colonial days, and his descendants. The twelve-hour adaptation took Haley's story from the kidnapping of the young Kunte Kinte (LeVar Burton), through several generations of slavery to the family's post-Civil War independence on their own farm. Subtitled "The Triumph of an American Family," *Roots* was an epic drama of love, war, and death in the soapy style of the successful *Rich Man, Poor Man.* It was assumed that ABC would place *Roots* in a weekly slot (two or three hours at a time) for a month or two, just as it had done with *Rich Man, Poor Man.* Instead, Silverman chose to transform *Roots* into a special television event and he scheduled it for eight consecutive nights, from Sunday, January 23, through Sunday, January 30, 1977, running one or two hours each night. Such treatment had never been given to an entertainment program before, though it was not unprecedented. In its coverage of the Olympics the previous season, ABC had junked its entire prime time schedule for two straight weeks in order to present special sports coverage. The packaging of *Roots* was a simple variation on that strategy.

Silverman was taking a chance with the eight nights of Roots,

facing either overkill from too much exposure at once on a sensitive topic, or indifference to the entire subject, especially by whites. Of all the networks, though, ABC was in the strongest position and had the most room to maneuver. The continued high ratings of ABC's regular series had given the network a comfortable lead in the cumulative ratings race so it could have absorbed even a mediocre performance. Just to be safe, though, Silverman made certain that *Roots* ended its run before the vital February ratings sweeps period began.

Naturally, ABC gave *Roots a* tremendous buildup on the air, emphasizing the star-studded cast that included O. J. Simpson, John Amos, Leslie Uggams, Cicely Tyson, Ben Vereen, Ed Asner, Chuck Connors, Lloyd Bridges, and Lorne Greene. It also encouraged schools and civic groups to participate in special courses and discussions based on the program. Haley himself was already working the lecture-and-talk-show circuit hyping the book, so he started including plugs for the television adaptation as well. Just before the miniseries aired, the hardcover edition of *Roots* topped the bestseller charts. Yet despite all the promotion, no one was prepared for the tremendous surge of interest that exploded across the nation.

Roots began with an unexpectedly large number of viewers on opening night and the interest just kept growing. By the time the series concluded, it had broken practically every ratings record in TV history. One-hundred-thirty million people saw some part of

November 11, 1976
 "Network," Paddy Chayefsky's prophetic film fantasy of television network strategy taken to a deadly extreme, opens in New York. Peter Finch plays Howard Beale, news anchor for the mythical UBS network, who angrily denounces American broadcasting and American life in general, shouting, "I'm as mad as hell and I'm not going to take it anymore!" Instead of firing him, the network uses "the mad prophet of the airwaves" to build an audience. When his ratings drop, Beale is assassinated by the network's hired guns.

December 17, 1976
 WTCG, Ted Turner's Atlanta UHF independent station carried by cable in six Southern states, becomes a "super station" by sending its signal, via satellite, to cable systems nationwide.

March 19, 1977
 After seven successful seasons, *The Mary Tyler Moore Show* goes out with a sly twist: In the final episode, the new management of WJM-TV fires the entire staff except for the incompetent Ted Baxter.

May 4, 1977
 After being paid one million dollars, former President Richard Nixon comes out of nearly three years of hibernation to be interviewed by David Frost in the first of five hour-long programs syndicated nationally.

May 11, 1977
 CBS chairman William Paley relinquishes his other job, chief executive officer, to CBS president John Backe.

June 1, 1977
 Roone Arledge, president of ABC Sports, becomes president of ABC News as well.

Roots, more than any other entertainment program ever aired, topping even the spectacular ratings of NBC's presentation of "Gone With the Wind" two months earlier. ABC won every night *Roots* aired and its ratings average for the week (35.5%) was the highest any network had ever registered. The eight episodes of *Roots* held the top eight ratings positions of the week, boosting all twenty-one of ABC's shows into the top twenty-six as well. The concluding segment snared a 71% share of the audience and was, at the time, the highest rated entertainment show in TV history. (The other seven segments placed fourth, fifth, sixth, eighth, ninth, tenth, and thirteenth in the all-time ratings compilation, as of 1977.) The first post-*Roots* issue of the showbiz weekly *Variety* epitomized the entertainment industry's reaction to the program as it bluntly headlined: "Roots Remakes TV World in Eight Nights!"

The more impulsive analysts and executives went even further, declaring that thirty years of programming tradition had been exploded practically overnight, and that *Roots* marked the passing of regular weekly TV fare in favor of diversified miniseries that placed an extra emphasis on reality. Some people even asserted that *Roots,* and *Roots* alone, had made ABC number one for the 1976–77 season. Such contentions conveniently ignored both the merely adequate ratings of other miniseries that season, as well as the strength of ABC's regular line-up.

In reality, ABC had been safely ensconced at the top before *Roots* aired and its ratings never slumped once *Roots* was gone. Regular weekly series were still the backbone of television and *Roots* did not mark the end of that format. It was merely an exceptionally successful special event. Nonetheless, *Roots* had passed beyond being viewed as merely a very successful TV show to the status of a national phenomenon, and the nation's pundits felt obligated to explain every aspect of its success. *Time* magazine confidently labeled its story: "Why *Roots* Hit Home." Other magazines, newspapers, and talk shows rushed to present their own sweeping observations, identifying *Roots* in terms such as "the ultimate admission of white guilt" and "the beginning of a new era of racial harmony."

There was certainly a good deal to analyze. Millions of people had rearranged eight days of their lives in order to follow *Roots* on television. Restaurants, social clubs, and movie houses reported sharp drops in attendance during the broadcast, while bookstores faced mobs of buyers who depleted their stockpiles of the book. Places such as drug stores and newsstands, which normally never touched hardcover editions, sold *Roots.* Beyond that, people from every ethnic group began to take an interest in their own personal roots and thousands followed Haley's lead in digging through state birth records, newspaper files, and old shipping logs. It was obvious that *Roots* had touched Americans in every walk of life, but in their zeal to come to grips with a very special event, people ignored many simple, obvious aspects of the *Roots* phenomenon.

Ethnic pride and interest in U.S. history had been on the upswing for years, reaching a peak during the 1976 American bicentennial celebrations. Haley, in fact, dedicated the book as his bicentennial gift to the nation. *Roots* was therefore presented to an exceptionally receptive audience which was generally familiar with the highlights of the country's developments. The program was also handed a built-in base audience of sorts: An extended cold weather snap throughout the East and Midwest forced many people to remain home, so television viewing was slightly higher than usual anyway.

Above all, *Roots* attracted and kept its audience because it contained the basics of entertaining television: excellent writing, first rate acting, effective violence, strong relationships, tantalizing sex angles, a clear-cut conflict between good and evil, and an upbeat ending. Although race was its central theme, in structure *Roots* was actually more like a Western in the tradition of *Bonanza* and *Wagon Train* only with blacks as the heroes and whites as the villains. The willingness of whites to identify with the black characters did not reflect an admission of racial guilt as much as the usual desire of the audience to side with the good guys on TV. Their allegiance was perfectly consistent with twenty years of television adventure yarns.

Of course, the presentation of blacks as the good guys was a very important change. Over the eight nights of *Roots,* millions shared the black perspective on very familiar events, seeing the old story of the struggle for personal freedom and the fulfillment of the American dream from a new vantage point. "The triumph of an American family" cheered by the nation was, for the first time, the triumph of black Americans. In a way no lecture, preacher, or textbook ever could, *Roots* conveyed the essence of black pride and black culture to millions of Americans. *Roots,* in that sense, *did* become far more than just a successful television show. It came to serve as a respected national rallying point for all black Americans, transforming Alex Haley's own personal "obsession" into a symbol of ethnic pride.

37. T & A TV

IN EARLY 1975, DESPITE THE SUCCESS of *All in the Family, Sanford and Son, Maude, The Jeffersons,* and *Good Times,* producer Norman Lear found himself unable to convince any of the three commercial networks to pick up one of his new program projects: a spoof of soap operas. Even CBS, which had financed the pilot, declined to exercise its option on the material. Lear was convinced he had another potential hit on his hands, so he decided to use his contacts and prestige to deal directly with local television programmers, by-passing the networks completely in order to syndicate the show. He met with nearly two dozen of the country's top station managers in late summer 1975, offering them rights to *Mary Hartman, Mary Hartman.*

Pitching a show too hot for the networks directly to the locals went against the conventional programming wisdom. Traditionally, local programmers were viewed as even more fearful of controversy than the networks. Yet local executives were also interested in getting the larger slice of the television advertising pie possible when the "middle men" (the networks) were eliminated. Earlier that year more than 100 stations had purchased an original science fiction series, *Space: 1999,* directly from a British production company that had offered it to them following rejection by all three networks. Lear was then one of the most successful program producers in television, so the locals gave his proposal serious consideration. After viewing a few sample episodes, several stations agreed to sign on, though Lear did not woo everyone. WNBC and independent WPIX from New York City turned down *Mary Hartman, Mary Hartman* before Metromedia's WNEW bought it. Chicago's top VHF independent, WGN, decided to pass on the offer as well, so the series went to a low-rated UHF station instead. By *Mary Hartman's* premiere in January 1976, though, Lear had assembled a complement of fifty-four stations to run the series, five days a week.

At first, many stations placed *Mary Hartman* in the afternoon, the time when other television soaps played. Other programmers discovered that *Mary Hartman* worked quite well in a late night slot and many placed the show just after prime time. It was there that, unexpectedly, the series took off and became a national hit. For the first time, a syndicated program became the most talked about series on television.

Mary Hartman, Mary Hartman built a following by walking the delicate line between reality and farce in presenting the adventures of characters from the mythical town of Fernwood, Ohio. The program was funny, clever, satirical, sometimes outrageous, and sometimes touching. In form, it played more like a regular soap opera than a sitcom: There was a complicated continuing storyline, no laugh track, and an absence of typical comedy one-liners. Yet the pacing was faster than the usual soaper and the expected plot complications of illicit sex, love triangles, and dreams of showbiz success were set slightly but effectively askew by exaggerating both the soap opera style and soap opera plot twists.

Mary Hartman (Louise Lasser) was a typical middle class housewife and mother, only she wore a little girl's Pollyanna housedress and pigtails. Her husband Tom (Greg Mullavey) was temporarily impotent, her young daughter Heather (Claudia Lamb) was ready to run away, her promiscuous sister Cathy (Debralee Scott) was suicidal, and her grandfather Raymond (Victor Kilian) had been identified as the neighborhood flasher. Mary's deepest concern in the opening episode, however, was over the waxy yellow buildup on her kitchen floor.

In subsequent weeks as the storyline evolved, viewers found themselves hooked on the characters of Mary, her family, and her friends, as well as on the program's quickly won reputation for unusual plot twists. At the end of the first season, Mary was chosen the year's "average American housewife" and invited to appear on television on *The David Susskind Show.* As the definitive consumer housewife who had accepted and modeled her real life on the commercial images of the perfect television household, she found herself unable to cope with actually crossing over to become a part of the world of television. Susskind himself appeared as a guest on that episode and, in the studio, Mary suffered a mental breakdown on the air.

With such stories, *Mary Hartman, Mary Hartman* regularly topped its competition, often at the expense of the lucrative local news shows running against it on the network affiliates. In March, Metromedia found itself doing so well with *Mary Hartman* that the company ripped up its contract with Norman Lear and wrote a new one for a higher rate.

While *Mary Hartman, Mary Hartman* never duplicated its frantic first year following, the show did last for two more seasons, never losing its feel for outlandish plot twists. Mary began her second season in a mental hospital, recuperating from her on-the-air breakdown. This facility turned out to have another function: It was one of the "average TV households" selected by the Nielsen television ratings service for estimating national viewing habits. Back home, Mary's friend Loretta Haggers (Mary Kay Place) achieved her dream of recording a hit Country and Western record

	8:00	8:30	9:00	9:30	10:00	10:30	
MON	THE SAN PEDRO BEACH BUMS		ABC NFL Monday Night Football (to 12 Midnight)				**ABC**
	YOUNG DAN'L BOONE		BETTY WHITE SHOW	Maude	RAFFERTY		**CBS**
	Little House On The Prairie / # Laugh-In		NBC Monday Night At The Movies / # Columbo				**NBC**
TUE	Happy Days	Laverne And Shirley	Three's Company	SOAP	Family		**ABC**
	THE FITZPATRICKS		M*A*S*H	One Day At A Time	LOU GRANT		**CBS**
	RICHARD PRYOR SHOW		MULLIGAN'S STEW		Police Woman		**NBC**
WED	Eight Is Enough		Charlie's Angels		Baretta		**ABC**
	Good Times	Busting Loose	CBS Wednesday Night Movies				**CBS**
	The Life And Times Of Grizzly Adams		THE OREGON TRAIL		BIG HAWAII		**NBC**
THR	Welcome Back, Kotter	What's Happening!!	Barney Miller	CARTER COUNTRY	REDD FOXX		**ABC**
	The Waltons		Hawaii Five-O		Barnaby Jones		**CBS**
	CHIPS		THE MAN FROM ATLANTIS		ROSETTI AND RYAN		**NBC**
FRI	Donny And Marie		The ABC Friday Night Movie				**ABC**
	New Adventures Of Wonder Woman		LOGAN'S RUN		Switch		**CBS**
	Sanford Arms	Chico And The Man	The Rockford Files		Quincy, M.E.		**NBC**
SAT	Fish	OPERATION PETTICOAT	Starsky And Hutch		THE LOVE BOAT		**ABC**
	Bob Newhart Show	WE'VE GOT EACH OTHER	The Jeffersons	Tony Randall Show	Carol Burnett Show		**CBS**
	The Bionic Woman		NBC Saturday Night At The Movies				**NBC**

	7:00	7:30	8:00	8:30	9:00	9:30	10:00	10:30	
SUN	The Hardy Boys / Nancy Drew Mysteries		The Six Million Dollar Man		The ABC Sunday Night Movie				**ABC**
	60 Minutes		Rhoda	ON OUR OWN	All In The Family	Alice	Kojak		**CBS**
	The Wonderful World Of Disney				The Big Event / # Police Story				**NBC**

("Baby Boy"), but was tricked into signing over her career management from her husband Charlie (Graham Jarvis) to a slick con man, Barth Gimble (Martin Mull). Neighbor Merle Jeeter (Dabney Coleman) managed to stage a successful campaign for mayor by proving that he had nothing to hide: He stood before a town assembly wearing only a raincoat. Mary's father, George Shumway (Philip Bruns) topped them all. Much to the confusion (but eventual delight) of his wife Martha (Dody Goodman), George came out of necessary plastic surgery following a plant accident looking exactly like movie star Tab Hunter, from head to toe. (Tab Hunter himself took over the role.)

Louise Lasser decided to leave the show at the end of the second season, so the title changed to *Forever Fernwood* in the fall of 1977. To set up her departure, Mary abandoned her family and left Fernwood to elope with a handsome policeman, Sergeant Dennis Foley (Bruce Solomon). The final episode with Lasser showed Mary's new life as a virtual replay of her old, even down to concern over the waxy yellow buildup on her floor.

The message of *Mary Hartman, Mary Hartman* went out loud and clear to both local station programmers and program producers: Popular new programs could be successfully sold and promoted without any involvement by ABC, CBS, or NBC. In 1977, Lear himself launched two other syndicated ventures, *All That Glitters* (a humorous soap opera on sexual role reversal) and a *Mary Hartman* spinoff/summer substitute that spoofed late night

talk shows, *Fernwood 2-Nite* (later called *America 2-Nite*). Universal Studios and Mobil Oil were even more successful with their respective first-run projects: Operation Prime Time (OPT) and the Mobil Showcase Network. These ad-hoc networks were set up for a limited but effective penetration of prime time, including placement on network affiliates. The first OPT presentation, a six-hour miniseries (*Testimony of Two Men*), scored well on ninety stations during the May 1977 sweeps. Mobil's first series, a ten-part program the company purchased from the BBC (*The Explorers*, which Mobil retitled *Ten Who Dared*), ran over ten weeks on forty stations, twenty-five of which were network affiliates. Each success guaranteed that there would be further challenges to the established networks' hold on programming, even in prime time.

While all three networks had been embarrassed by the acceptance of *Mary Hartman* in syndication after they had turned it down, ABC was the only one to try a similar format in prime time, slotting its own soap opera spoof for the fall of 1977. Thirty-five-year-old Susan Harris (a veteran writer for such Norman Lear shows as *Maude* and *One Day at a Time*) was the creator and chief writer for this new program, called *Soap*. The series setup was simple: the trials and tribulations of two sisters and their families, one wealthy (the Tates) and one middle class (the Campbells). The plots would focus on the usual grist of soaps, with a heavy emphasis on sex.

Even with the acceptance of *Mary Hartman,* ABC was nervous

about *Soap* and held a private screening of two episodes for affiliate executives at an ABC convention in May 1977. While the reaction was generally favorable (much to the relief of the network), the affiliate programmers convinced ABC to allow stations in the Central time zone to delay the show an hour so that it would not appear before 9:00 P.M. The network also promised to add a "viewer discretion" warning at the beginning of each episode identifying the series as more adult-oriented. Then something strange happened. Months before an episode of *Soap* hit the air, the series became the subject of heated criticism across the country.

Advance word about the show clearly conveyed the point that *Soap*, like *Mary Hartman*, would be a sexually oriented comedy, but no one seemed to know just how far it would go. Speculation based on plot summaries and hearsay touched off a wave of charges and counter-charges. *Newsweek* magazine, given an advance synopsis of one of the episodes already produced, reported that *Soap* would present the seduction of a priest in church. This set off alarms in Catholic parishes throughout the country, and letters began pouring in to ABC demanding that the network take the show off the air, even before it aired one episode. *The Tiding*, the official weekly of the Los Angeles archdiocese, observed that ABC's decision to schedule *Soap* showed little respect for the audience and that the network's initials really stood for "Absolutely Brazen Contempt." Citizens of Memphis, Tennessee, picketed local ABC affiliate WHBQ with placards that read: "Protect our children from evil!" and "We don't want *Soap!*" The U.S. Catholic Conference labeled *Soap* "morally reprehensible," saying the program would be "publicly challenged" and should be "removed from television."

Even some of those select few that had already seen *Soap* joined in the criticism. Westinghouse's only ABC affiliate (WJZ in Baltimore) decided not to air *Soap* because "it presented a variety of subject matter which does not lend itself to comedic episodic form." The executive vice president of WOWK in Huntington, West Virginia, called it, "one long dirty joke."

As public protests mounted through the summer, ABC and its chief programmer, Fred Silverman, began to fight back. The network described *Soap* as more than just a soap opera: It was "an adult character comedy with a continuing storyline." More important, Silverman stressed that "no character in *Soap* is ever rewarded for immoral behavior, and, in the final analysis, there will be retribution for such behavior."

Regarding the controversy over the show itself, Fred Silverman pointedly remarked in *Variety*, "The summer of 1977 may well go down in television history as the summer of *Soap*. Never have so many words been written about a television pilot which so few people have actually seen."

The Reverend Bob Spencer, an Atlanta Baptist minister, explained the validity, in his eyes, of the protests against the program before it aired, saying, "We don't have to see the show to know it's indecent. We believe what we have read in national and local publications. I believe in the Bible and I don't have to see certain things to know they are wrong."

By August, fifteen ABC affiliates said they would not show the program, and two advertisers had pulled out. In early September, both the *New York Times* and the *Washington Post* ran editorials on the *Soap* controversy. The *Times* backed the protesters, asking how else could people object. The *Post* defended the right to object but said that people should wait until the show was on before registering their complaints. Through the entire rumpus, ABC held firm. On the day before the premiere, the *ABC Evening News* covered the *Soap* controversy as a news story and, on September 13, the special one-hour first episode aired. It was quite a letdown.

People expecting a sophisticated sexy show that would upset the traditional television taboos were given instead a series of silly slapstick scenes and sophomoric one-liners. Unlike *Mary Hartman, Mary Hartman*, everything in *Soap* was played for cheap laughs. The characters were one-dimensional and relegated to delivering leering putdowns on such topics as homosexuals, extramarital affairs, impotency, transvestites, and sex-change opera-

Louise Lasser as Mary Hartman and Greg Mullavey as her husband, Tom, in Norman Lear's humorous soap opera, *Mary Hartman, Mary Hartman*. *(Sony Pictures Television)*

September 5, 1977

Laugh-In. (NBC). Producer George Schlatter revives the *Laugh-In* format as a monthly special for NBC, but without Dan Rowan and Dick Martin. Instead, guest hosts perform with a group of comedy unknowns, including Robin Williams.

September 13, 1977

Richard Pryor Show. (NBC). The daring and imaginative black comic is perversely stuck in a family hour slot with his new comedy-variety hour. Following some censorship feuds with NBC, Pryor himself calls it quits after four shows.

September 15, 1977

Cheryl Ladd steps in as Kris, a new member of Charlie's Angels, following the departure of Farrah Fawcett in a contract squabble.

September 16, 1977

Sanford Arms. (NBC). After Redd Foxx and Demond Wilson quit *Sanford and Son,* NBC bravely tries to keep the series going, explaining that Fred and Lamont have moved to Phoenix. In their place, Phil Wheeler (Theodore Wilson) operates a rooming house next to the junk yard. The revamped show lasts only one month.

September 20, 1977

Starting the fifth season of *Happy Days,* Fonzie is in California for a Hollywood screen test and, as part of a beachside challenge, jumps over a shark while on water skis. In the 1990s, the "Jump the Shark" Internet website uses this event to symbolize the moment when any good TV series begins to fade in quality.

October 10, 1977

The Dick Cavett Show. (PBS). ABC's former talk show host reappears on public television, hosting a half-hour weeknight interview show that lasts four years.

October 11, 1977

After twenty-six years as an NBC exclusive, the World Series comes to ABC in the beginning of a new yearly rotation with NBC.

November 4, 1977

The end of the Lucy era at CBS. Twenty-six years after the premiere of *I Love Lucy,* the third of Lucille Ball's sitcoms, *Here's Lucy,* ends its weekday morning network rerun cycle and goes off CBS.

tions. Even the much-discussed seduction of the priest turned out to be just a double-entendre proposition which produced a few moments of embarrassment for the cleric but no violation of his vows. *Soap* was not the promised outrageous adult satire, just a tiresomely childish program.

Nonetheless, with all the advance publicity, *Soap* became the season's first big hit, immediately landing in the top ten. As the season wore on, it slipped a bit in the ratings, but several important revisions also took place. The scripts moved away from being a collection of scandalous topics and innuendo to focus instead on developing both the comic characters and plotline. Though still more joke-oriented than *Mary Hartman, Soap* began to mix in less boisterous, more human moments. There was still a tremendous emphasis on sex, but the characters began to care for each other.

With this new approach, *Soap* began to build solid audience support presenting likable characters in funny situations. The highlight of the first season was the trial of Jessica Tate (Katherine Helmond) for the murder of her tennis-pro lover (played by Robert Urich). Certain of her innocence, she spent most of the time trying to cheer up her household, including her promiscuous husband Chester (Robert Mandan), their daughters Corinne (Diana Canova) and Eunice (Jennifer Salt), son Billy (Jimmy Baio), and their sharp-tongued black butler Benson (Robert Guillaume). Though pronounced guilty, Jessica was saved from imprisonment at the start of the second season when Chester confessed to the crime, explaining that he had been temporarily out of his mind when he did it. Jessica's sister, Mary Campbell (Cathryn Damon), spent much of the first season trying to prevent the murder of her new husband, Burt (Richard Mulligan), by her son, Danny (Ted Wass), who had become involved in organized crime.

The best example of the improvement in *Soap* could be found in the character development of Mary's other son from her first marriage, Jodie Dallas (Billy Crystal), a homosexual. At the start of the series, Jodie served chiefly as the focus for every "gay" joke the writers felt they could get away with. Then Jodie's character was fleshed out and softened. He decided against a sex-change operation, had an unsuccessful affair with a football player, and, to his own amazement, found himself involved with a woman, even becoming a father. This eventually led to an emotional legal battle at the close of the third season in which Jodie gave a powerful, impassioned courtroom speech in defense of his attempt to win custody of the child. By then, all that remained of the original *Soap* controversy was ABC's continued policy of airing the summer reruns of the show in late night slots instead of its usual prime time period. The network had quietly dropped both the time delay feed to the Midwest and the viewer discretion warning in December 1977, as *Soap* shifted focus.

Perhaps the most important aspect of the public controversy surrounding the premiere of *Soap* was that it served as a dramatic illustration of the networks' increased emphasis on sex as a replacement for violence; it also became a rallying point for reaction against this policy. This new wave of sexual hooks had begun with the success of *Charlie's Angels* for ABC in the fall of 1976 and the number one network had the most success in exploiting it in other shows for the 1977–78 season, especially in comedies. As with *Charlie's Angels,* these programs took an ogler's approach to sex, emphasizing well-built bodies and suggestive comments over any real sex. The perfect example of this ABC formula for sexual comedy was *Three's Company,* a carry-over hit that had begun in the spring of 1977.

Three's Company presented three young singles living together in the same apartment: Jack Tripper (John Ritter), an easy-going part-time professional cook; Janet Wood (Joyce DeWitt), a level-headed brunette florist; and Chrissy Snow (Suzanne Somers), a sexy "dumb blonde" office secretary. Despite the scandalous setup, nothing ever happened between them. The three were "just good friends" sharing the apartment in order to split the rent. To assure Stanley Roper (Norman Fell), their apartment landlord, that their activities were perfectly harmless, they convinced him that Jack was gay and had no interest in either woman.

As a matter of fact, Jack would eye both, and practically any other pretty woman that crossed his path. In addition, everyone else in *Three's Company* was always thinking about and talking about sex, so a typical program would consist of some simple complication (usually resulting from a misunderstanding involving Chrissy) giving the men a chance to leer and deliver risqué lines, and the women a chance to strike suggestive poses and deliver risqué lines. The series was an obstacle course sitcom right out of the all-talk-no-action mode of *Love, American Style* from the 1960s and the Rock Hudson-Doris Day "pillow talk" theatrical comedies of the 1950s, playing it squeaky clean but hinting dirty while dishing up malapropisms, double takes, and pratfalls.

While *Three's Company* merely carried on the *Love, American Style* philosophy, two other of the season's new hit ABC series actually followed that program's format. Produced by Aaron Spelling and Leonard Goldberg (of *Charlie's Angels*), both *The Love Boat* and *Fantasy Island* (a mid-season replacement) were mildly titillating anthologies, interweaving several light romantic tales to make an hour show. Unlike *Love, American Style*, though, there were also series regulars that appeared each week to tie the individual segments together as part of the same overall story: *Mary Tyler Moore* alumnus Gavin MacLeod acted as the skipper of the *Pacific Princess, Love Boat's* romantic cruise ship, while Ricardo Montalban played the mysterious Mr. Roarke, owner of the tropical island resort where fantasies seemed to come true.

ABC was comfortably on top, propelled by the tremendous performance of its sitcoms, both the established series such as *Happy Days* and the new hits including *Love Boat, Soap,* and *Three's Company.* Even against this competition, former number one CBS still had solid top ten performances from *M*A*S*H, All in the Family, One Day at a Time,* and newcomer *Alice,* but the network was very eager to develop new shows itself as part of a concerted rebuilding effort. One of the companies it placed strong hope in was Mary Tyler Moore's production company, MTM (headed by her husband, Grant Tinker). Like Norman Lear's company, MTM had developed a specific approach to comedy that could be used to spawn other shows. For seven years, *The Mary Tyler Moore Show* and its immediate spinoffs (*Rhoda* and *Phyllis*) stood as the base of the company, but when Moore decided to end her show after the 1976–77 season, the company needed to work in earnest to create series successors to these hits.

MTM had developed *The Mary Tyler Moore Show* as the model of an adult-oriented ensemble comedy for the 1970s, with very strong supporting players and excellent writing. While Norman Lear usually set his stories in a formal family situation (such as the Bunkers or the Jeffersons) and would "do a show on rape" (or some other topical issue), Moore's ensemble formed a "professional family" of individuals that worked together and grew to love, respect, and depend on each other. Such an approach, however, needed time for the writers and performers to develop the pacing of the series and for the audience to become familiar with the characters.

MTM's first attempt at a new companion comedy was *The Bob Newhart Show,* which began in the fall of 1972, slotted immediately after Moore's show. This placement gave it a spillover audience that found another good show similar to but distinct from *Mary Tyler Moore.* Developed by David Davis and Lorenzo Music, *The Bob Newhart Show* focused on the home and office life of a low-key Chicago psychologist, Bob Hartley (Bob Newhart), and his loving but strongly independent wife Emily (Suzanne Pleshette), an elementary school teacher. The excellent supporting cast included Bill Daily as neighbor-sidekick Howard Borden, Marcia Wallace as office receptionist Carol, Peter Bonerz as orthodontist Jerry Robinson, and Jack Riley as Elliott Carlin, an incurable neurotic. Like *The Mary Tyler Moore Show,* Newhart's series improved each season as the cast members developed their characters and personalities.

Besides *Bob Newhart* and the two direct *Mary Tyler Moore* spinoffs (*Rhoda* and *Phyllis*), MTM had found that the ensemble comedy formula, while easy to outline in theory, was very tricky to

successfully duplicate with totally new characters and settings. Three promising MTM shows flopped, hurt chiefly by either unfamiliar characters or a difficult premise to develop: *Paul Sand in Friends and Lovers* (a bass violinist with the Boston Philharmonic), *We've Got Each Other* (a husband who did the housework while his wife worked downtown) and *Texas Wheelers* (Jack Elam, Gary Busey, and Mark Hamill as fun-loving ranch hands in modern rural Texas). Yet at the same time the ensemble approach was still working quite well in non-MTM shows such as *M*A*S*H* and *Barney Miller,* which both survived major cast changes by drawing on the strength of their respective companies of players. Obviously, the formula was resilient once a show got off the ground. The difficulty was in trying to quickly acquaint viewers with a totally new world. For the 1977–78 season, MTM had tremendous hope for a careful combination of the old and the new in what looked like a sure-fire comedy winner: *The Betty White Show.*

The new program carefully drew basic elements from *The Mary Tyler Moore Show,* including two former cast members, Betty White and Georgia Engel. White played Joyce Whitman, a sweet-

---

November 14, 1977

Walter Cronkite interviews both Egyptian President Anwar Sadat and Israeli Prime Minister Menachem Begin, via satellite, on his nightly news show. Sadat says he might visit Jerusalem. Cronkite asks Begin if that would be all right with Israel. Begin says yes. Five days later, Sadat flies to Israel with Cronkite, NBC's John Chancellor, and ABC's Barbara Walters in tow.

November 30, 1977

Eric Sevareid, a thirty-eight-year CBS veteran, retires upon reaching age sixty-five.

January 22, 1978

Sportsworld. (NBC). A new weekend afternoon sports anthology, modeled after ABC's Wide *World of Sports.*

March 10, 1978

The Incredible Hulk. (CBS). Bill Bixby plays Dr. David Banner who, when angered, turns into Lou Ferrigno as the big green Hulk. The series is loosely based on the Marvel Comics hero.

March 19, 1978

Mike Stivic, wife Gloria, and baby Joey leave Archie and Edith Bunker and Queens for a new home in California.

April 10, 1978

America 2-Night. Norman Lear's satiric view of late night television moves intact from Fernwood, Ohio, to Alta Coma, California (the unfinished furniture capital of the world). Martin Mull is Barth Gimble, the self-centered host; Fred Willard plays the Ed McMahon role of sidekick Jerry Hubbard; and musical veteran Frank DeVol is band leader Happy Kyne, director of the off-key Mirth-makers.

July 10, 1978

World News Tonight. (ABC). ABC News President Roone Arledge breaks up the Harry Reasoner-Barbara Walters anchor team and creates a new style (and name) for ABC's nightly news show. Frank Reynolds, Peter Jennings and Max Robinson share the anchor chores in the new format.

Though CBS's Walter Cronkite initiated a moment of TV diplomacy in November 1977 by inviting the leaders of Egypt and Israel to talk, it was U.S. President Jimmy Carter *(center)* who brokered the 1979 agreements between Egyptian President Anwar Sadat *(left)* and Israeli Prime Minister Menachem Begin *(right)*. *(National Archives / Photo by Bill Fitz-Patrick, The White House)*

faced woman with a biting tongue (just like Sue Ann Nivens) and Engel was Mitzi Maloney, Joyce's dumb but kind-hearted apartmentmate (just like Georgette Franklin, her similar supporting character on *The Mary Tyler Moore Show*). Like *Mary Tyler Moore,* the series included a show-within-a-show. Joyce was the star of a new CBS television cop show called *Undercover Woman* (a take-off on the popular NBC series *Police Woman* starring Angie Dickinson) and the stories focused on both her home life and behind-the-scenes production activity, including anxious reports on the show's ratings. Included in the support cast were John Hillerman as acerbic show director John Elliot, Joyce's former husband; Caren Kaye as Tracy Garrett, a sexy young actress on the make; and Alex Henteloff as Doug Porterfield, the insecure liaison from the network.

The Betty White Show started strong in a tough slot (against *Monday Night Football* and an NBC movie), but then collapsed and was gone by January. Even with so many "surefire" hooks, the mixture had failed to gel, hurt chiefly by two flaws in the setup: White's caustic character, while a good foil in a supporting role, did not provide a very likable lead; and the angle of Joyce's former husband being the director of *Undercover Woman* was a silly gimmick that just got in the way of the inevitable conflicts between the two working on opposite sides of the camera.

The failure of *The Betty White Show* was a great disappointment to MTM, which had pegged the series as its front line comedy successor to Moore's show. It was also more bad news for CBS, which wanted some quick success to counter ABC's increasing number of successful comedies. With this latest failure, the prospect for quickly regaining the top spot looked increasingly bleak. Neither Norman Lear nor Grant Tinker of MTM, who had been the main sources of CBS's sitcom success in the early 1970s, seemed able to come up with new hits to replace their successful older shows when they inevitably ended their runs.

As ABC continued securely in its number one spot, NBC and CBS went on the offensive and became more openly critical of ABC's programming. This dovetailed perfectly with the protests by pressure groups which had suddenly realized that their crusades against violent television had ushered in the increased emphasis on sex. As the top network with the top shows, ABC was the obvious target for their renewed protests. CBS and NBC just joined in the

chorus. Robert Wussler, president of CBS television, said during the height of the *Soap* controversy that his network would *never* have aired the program, and then went on to call ABC's shows "comic book stuff, cartoon style without the cartooning, and I say it is junk … they're all clever and well done, but they're like junk food." NBC's new programming boss, Paul Klein, offered the shorthand reference "jiggling" to describe ABC programming that prominently featured females in revealing tight tops, often with no bra underneath, and an emphasis on shots of bouncy breasts.

What neither network pointed out, of course, was that both were scrambling for that same audience and were looking for ways to adapt such ABC hooks as comic book adventures, teen comedy, and sexual-orientation to their own schedules. When ABC's Fred Silverman decided in early 1977 to cut the still successful *Bionic Woman* and *Adventures of Wonder Woman* from the ABC schedule (feeling they had probably peaked), NBC and CBS (respectively) were more than willing to pick them up for the fall of 1977. Besides *The New Adventures of Wonder Woman,* CBS also added another comic book series to its schedule, *The Incredible Hulk.*

NBC was even more blatant in playing up sexual hooks. The World War II adventure series *Black Sheep Squadron* (a revival of the previous season's *Baa Baa Black Sheep*) introduced four nubile nurses to the cast, dubbed "Pappy's Lambs" (a dig at *Charlie's Angels* which ran opposite the show). A relatively straightforward drama series, *James at 15,* pumped up the scripts with sex angles, culminating with the day James turned sixteen and lost his virginity. There was even a male equivalent to the beauties of *Charlie's Angels* with *CHiPs,* which featured two gorgeous California police "hunks" (Larry Wilcox and Erik Estrada) for the women to admire.

NBC's sex angle surfaced most often, however, in the network's schedule of miniseries, which formed the cornerstone of its programming strategy. One insider said, only partly tongue-in-cheek, "If ABC is doing 'kiddie porn,' NBC will give the audience 'adult porn.'" The soapy drama of *The Moneychangers* had done well the previous season taking such an approach, so the network touted *79 Park Avenue, Aspen, Loose Change,* and *Wheels* as spicy special events. These "novels for television" usually ran over consecutive nights on NBC's Saturday movie, the Sunday *Big Event,* and the Monday movie, and all featured steamy TV sex (frequent thrashing in bed), seamy characters, and unbridled ambition.

Though not actually showing much more than ABC's sex comedies, the presentation in these pulpy stories was far more direct in its underlying assumption: Illicit sex was just another requirement for success and advancement in corporate America.

These programs did well in the ratings, to an extent proving that the success of *Roots* and *Rich Man, Poor Man* was no fluke. Nonetheless, the grand pronouncements regarding miniseries toned down considerably from the euphoria following *Roots.* NBC was the only network committed to miniseries on a continuing basis. The other networks regarded them more as extended specials to be used sparingly as blockbuster lures during the ratings sweeps or to open the season. ABC, for example, slotted the six-part *Washington: Behind Closed Doors,* a political drama loosely based on John Ehrlichman's Watergate-themed book *The Company,* as its premiere week lure. That series did all right, but was not an exceptional blockbuster like *Roots.*

NBC scored much better in November with *The Godfather Saga,* a combination of the two theatrical "Godfather" films plus nearly an hour of previously unused footage. "Godfather" director Francis Ford Coppola himself supervised the entire project, including the necessary adjustment of particularly violent scenes to the limitations of television. The finished product ran nine hours over four nights and was dubbed: *Mario Puzo's "The Godfather": The Complete Novel for Television.* By presenting the saga of the Corleone family in chronological order, the chilling evolution of gangland power from young Vito Corleone's first kill to Michael Corleone's calculated murder of his own brother clearly emerged. For once, the television version of a theatrical feature was more effective and powerful than the original presentation.

NBC's success with such special events helped the network cover the fact that it had very few hit series. *Little House on the Prairie* was the network's only top ten entry, and *CHiPs,* its highest rated new show, did not even make the top twenty. NBC was in even worse shape than CBS, which was at least trying its best at a concerted rebuilding effort.

As the season wore on, the problems with NBC's event strategy became increasingly apparent as did the problems of miniseries. Miniseries were much more expensive to produce than regular series, yet generally they did not do well in reruns. Unlike the interchangeable segments of a regular series, the episodes of a miniseries had to be shown in order, preferably over consecutive nights. Yet this meant either setting aside weekly slots for miniseries—thus reducing their "specialness" by making them part of the weekly program routine—or constant preemption (which undercut attempts to develop strong regular series).

The most dramatic flaw in the miniseries scheme was that the best time to slot a series could instantly become the worst. A new story had to do well on opening night or the network was stuck with a multiple-night failure because it was hard to convince people to join the events in mid-run. NBC's biggest miniseries bomb took place during the February sweeps when ABC's *How the West Was Won* and CBS's Sunday movie, "Gator," soundly defeated an episode of *King,* a highly touted three-part story on the life of Dr. Martin Luther King, Jr.

King became the symbol of an unsuccessful miniseries. It was well-written and featured excellent performances (Paul Winfield as Martin Luther King, Jr.; Ossie Davis as Martin Luther King, Sr.; and Cicely Tyson as Coretta Scott King). Nonetheless, it lacked the sexy hooks of shows such as *79 Park Avenue* or the built-in violence of *The Godfather Saga.* Consequently, NBC was very careful with its final miniseries of the season, *Holocaust,* scheduling it before the spring sweeps and against chiefly rerun material on CBS and ABC. Network programming boss Paul Klein even downplayed network expectations because *Holocaust* seemed the perfect candidate for a ratings flop. It was a depressing story of the persecution and systematic murder of six million Jews by the Nazis in World War II. There was no happy ending and nearly all the heroic characters were gassed or shot by the end of the story.

Despite all these apparent handicaps, the four nights of *Holocaust* became the most-watched entertainment show in NBC's history to that point, drawing nearly 120 million viewers. It became the number two miniseries in television, right behind *Roots.* And, like *Roots,* it used the basics of good television drama to hit home in a very special way.

Holocaust transformed a nearly incomprehensible crime against humanity into a personal war drama, focusing on an ambitious young German lawyer, Erik Dorf (Michael Moriarty), and on an upper-middle-class Jewish doctor in Berlin, Josef Weiss (Fritz Weaver), and his family (Rosemary Harris as his wife Berta; Joseph Bottoms as their younger son, Rudi; Blanche Baker as their daughter, Anna; James Woods as their son, Karl; and Meryl Streep as Karl's Aryan wife, Inga). Both were caught up in the rise of Nazism: Dorf as a legal henchman for the party and Weiss as an innocent man fighting to hang on to his family, his dignity, and his life. Over the four nights of *Holocaust* he was stripped of them all.

Like *Roots, Holocaust* acted as a catalyst for ethnic pride and even anger. Throughout the country, millions watched the re-creation of events that had been a frightening part of their lives. For another, much younger, generation, *Holocaust* conveyed the horror of events they had never really thought about as anything more than another page of history.

Despite the surprising performance of *Holocaust,* NBC's basic programming problems remained unchanged. The network's decision to commit itself to developing expensive miniseries over weekly shows locked it into that "longform" pattern. Without strong new series to plug in, NBC would have to continue to stress "event programming." This, in turn, seemed to guarantee a long stint by NBC at number three and the beginning of a long reign by ABC as number one.

ABC's formulas ruled the airwaves.

CBS continued to arrange and rearrange its old hits.

NBC produced great special events, but was a prisoner of its abysmal lack of strong regular series.

Then, in one bold move, this network equation changed.

On January 20, 1978, the man who had guided ABC to the top, Fred Silverman, announced his defection to NBC. The broadcast industry wondered: Could Silverman pull the TV hat trick and make NBC his third number one network?

38. Born Again Broadcasting

THE ANNOUNCEMENT OF FRED SILVERMAN'S jump from ABC to NBC not only sent shock waves through the broadcast industry but also attracted a great deal of coverage by the general news media. Like his move from CBS to ABC three years before, the story made good copy. Once again, Silverman was leaving a number one television network and taking his tremendous programming expertise to the last place competition. In 1975 that had marked the beginning of a changed television world that soon found ABC at the top of the heap. Comparisons and speculation were inevitable: Could "Freddie" work his magic once again?

Actually, Silverman faced a far more difficult task coming to NBC. ABC in the mid-1970s had been on the verge of breaking out with its kid-oriented shows and was only waiting for a deft hand to guide it. NBC in 1978 had only a handful of popular prime time shows: *The Big Event, Little House on the Prairie, The Rockford Files, Quincy,* and the moderately successful *CHiPs.* More important, NBC was heavily committed to a big-event-miniseries strategy, which placed great reliance on what had proved to be a very unpredictable form.

There were also other weak spots. Late night ratings king Johnny Carson was showing increasing signs of wanting to end his seventeen-year stint on *Tonight.* The previously unassailable *Today* show found its ratings lead being whittled away by ABC's *Good Morning America.* In the nightly news race, ABC's new *World News Tonight* format threatened NBC in the contest for the number two spot behind CBS's Walter Cronkite. And as a result of such overall slippage, NBC was even losing affiliates.

NBC was the perfect new challenge for Fred Silverman, offering him something more important than a hefty salary and fringe benefits: an impressive boost to his professional pride. Instead of simply moving over to become NBC's prime time programmer, Silverman was hired as president of the entire NBC broadcast corporation, including television, radio, and special projects.

Beyond that, there was the undeniable challenge of once again playing the part of miracle man. Almost single-handedly Silverman had built up the image of a network programmer to someone just as important as the programs and stars themselves. With ABC almost routinely continuing as number one, his day-to-day decisions there seemed far less crucial. Now, at NBC, he was instantly the most important man at the network.

Silverman's contract with ABC ran until June 8, 1978, and the network held him to it. As a result, between January and June, Silverman was forced into a management limbo of sorts. He could not communicate with NBC personnel yet was no longer part of the ABC team. For five months he vacationed while his new network put together the schedule for the fall of 1978 with absolutely no input from him. This heightened the dramatic effect of Silverman's arrival in June: Who or what would remain?

NBC's emphasis on event programming under chief programmer Paul Klein ran in direct opposition to Silverman's philosophies. Though he was master at slotting special events, Silverman's base of success at ABC and CBS was regular series, especially sitcoms. NBC did not have one hit sitcom going into the fall of 1978, so it was expected that when Silverman took over there would be an all-out campaign to beat ABC at its own game with teen sitcoms and suggestive sex. Yet when Silverman actually assumed control in June, just the opposite occurred: Fred Silverman suddenly became the champion of "quality" programming. Three days after assuming office, he told NBC affiliates, "I want NBC not only to be the audience leader, but also the most respected network." He also pledged a stronger commitment to news, cultural specials, and family programming.

Obviously, some of this was standard public relations rhetoric, but Silverman also backed such talk with action. During the summer he made several changes in the announced NBC fall schedule, replacing *Coast to Coast* (a sexy adventure-comedy featuring two airline stewardesses and a handsome steward) with *Lifeline* (a *cinema-verite*-style documentary series about real life doctors operating on real patients in real hospitals), and transforming *Legs* (a Garry Marshall sitcom about the backstage life of sexy Las Vegas showgirls) into *Who's Watching the Kids?,* an apartment house sitcom emphasizing Jim Belushi (brother of John) and *Happy Days* alumnus Scott Baio rather than the glamour girls. Though NBC could not cut back overnight on miniseries well into production, Silverman did axe plans for thirty hours of steamy Universal miniseries that he labeled as too exploitative. These included a sequel to the successful *79 Park Avenue* and a Taylor Caldwell story about a prostitute in ancient Rome.

Such moves seemed quite surprising from the man who had recently presided over a schedule that included *Three's Company, Charlie's Angels,* and *Love Boat.* In a sense, though, this "born again" commitment to quality was about the best counter-programming hook available. Practically speaking, there was little chance of changing NBC's competitive position for the 1978–79 season, so while planning for the future Silverman focused attention on something other than instant ratings success. He ordered at least

On March 19, 1979, Speaker Thomas "Tip" O'Neill gaveled the U.S. House of Representatives into the television age as C-SPAN (the Cable-Satellite Public Affairs Network) began live coverage of its sessions. *(Courtesy of C-SPAN)*

thirty new pilot concepts to be ready in January, when he could begin to phase in shows more in tune with the long-range Silverman plan for NBC supremacy. Silverman also felt that ABC's approach to television had peaked and it was only a matter of time before viewers grew tired of the ABC schedule as a whole, so he instructed producers to stay away from "jiggling" themes in the new NBC pilot projects.

Following Silverman's schedule adjustments, NBC opened the season a strong number two, temporarily buoyed by good opening ratings for the mammoth twenty-five hour miniseries *Centennial* (running as a *Big Event*) and the usual boost provided by the World Series. By November, NBC had begun to slide. *Centennial* fell out of the top twenty and all nine of the network's new fall series flopped. During the November ratings sweeps, NBC finished a distant third with only four programs among the top forty shows.

Though he had promised in June to cut down on last-minute program shuffling, Silverman decided he could not wait any longer to act. At the start of December, he wiped the slate clean and canceled nine of NBC's nineteen series in one day, including all of the new fall shows that had survived until then. Silverman fell back on the thirty pilots he had ordered and pulled out nine new shows, including three sitcoms. Soon thereafter, holdover programming boss Paul Klein was deposed as part of the network shakeup. It was clear the Silverman era at NBC had begun in earnest.

Despite these moves, the rest of the season was a shambles for NBC. From January until May, the network's schedule was a revolving door for new shows that premiered, quickly shifted time slots, and then disappeared. NBC tried virtually any concept for a series, including: a weekly slot for miniseries (*NBC Novels for Television*); a revival of *Columbo* without the Columbo character (*Mrs. Columbo*); a land-locked *Love Boat* (*Supertrain*, produced by NBC itself and featuring a very expensive model train set); an update of the *Millionaire* format (*$weepstake$*); a cash-in on the fraternity humor success of the film "Animal House" (*Brothers and Sisters*); serialized melodramas (*Cliffhangers*); and even the

old *Stand by for Crime* setup of a crime drama mixed with a game show-type panel (*Whodunnit?* with Ed McMahon as host and famed criminal lawyer F. Lee Bailey as a regular panelist). None of these shows made it to 1980.

Even the high-priority search for new hit NBC sitcoms produced only two marginal successes, *Diff'rent Strokes* and *Hello Larry,* back-to-back offerings from Norman Lear's TAT/Tandem company. *Hello, Larry* was a male version of *One Day at a Time,* starring McLean Stevenson as a divorced radio talk show host with two teenage daughters. *Diff'rent Strokes* served as a black-infused *Family Affair,* featuring Conrad Bain (of *Maude*) as a wealthy Manhattan millionaire-widower who adopted two black orphans from Harlem, thirteen-year-old Willis Jackson (Todd Bridges) and his eight-year-old brother, Arnold (Gary Coleman). Both series offered warm lessons on growing up and occasionally the two combined for special one-hour joint episodes. Silverman also treated them as a matched set; even during NBC's many schedule shifts the two moved in tandem. Silverman saw Coleman as a potential new network star and he hoped that *Diff'rent Strokes* would help *Hello, Larry* build its audience as well. *Hello, Larry* eventually flopped (surviving for little more than a year), but *Diff'rent Strokes* caught on, lasted eight seasons, and Coleman became a frequent guest star on other NBC series.

NBC wound up finishing the 1978–79 season deep in third place, a full rating point lower than its 1977–78 showing. Silverman eventually admitted that his frantic mid-season juggling was the wrong strategy, saying that a slower transition would have worked better. Most of the chosen pilots had been forced into the weekly schedule far too quickly and suffered from the lack of production time. Still, Silverman carried over into the next season a few shows that had done moderately well and continued with his reorganization plans, aiming for the 1980 Olympic Games in Moscow. NBC had purchased exclusive television rights for them in February 1977 at a price tag of $100 million, and Silverman knew from his ABC success with the 1976 Olympics that the games provided the perfect launching pad for the new season. If NBC had a strong line-up to promote during the Olympics, the network could, with a little luck, be back on top by Christmas 1980. Informally, that became Silverman's deadline for success.

For the present, however, ABC continued to reign as number one. Silverman had left his former network in very strong shape and ABC president Fred Pierce and Tony Thomopoulos, Silverman's replacement as chief programmer, pursued a vigorous fall campaign, determined not only to keep ABC far ahead of the pack, but also to prove that the network's success had not been due totally to Silverman. Besides touting all the returning ABC hits, they used a rerun of *Roots* to open September and then promoted a championship boxing rematch between Muhammad Ali and Leon Spinks into the number one slot the first week of the new season. Through October ABC continued comfortably on top with eight of the top ten shows and nineteen of the top thirty. Unlike NBC, ABC had little trouble with its new fall shows: Four of the five were in the top fifteen. The only thing close to a ratings disappointment for ABC was the late fall collapse of *Battlestar Galactica,* the network's attempt to cash in on the spectacular success of George Lucas's film for Twentieth Century Fox, "Star Wars."

Opening in May 1977, "Star Wars" quickly became the top-grossing movie in history at that time, appealing to both children and adult audiences. It took a simple space war adventure yarn, reminiscent of the popular Buck Rogers and Flash Gordon film serials of the 1930s and 1940s, and effectively updated it with a witty script and spectacular special effects. Its success led to a host of imitations and a revival of interest in science fiction adventures.

	8:00	8:30	9:00	9:30	10:00	10:30	
M O N	Welcome Back, Kotter	Operation Petticoat	ABC NFL Monday Night Football (to 12 Midnight)				**ABC**
	WKRP IN CINCINNATI	PEOPLE	M*A*S*H	One Day At A Time	Lou Grant		**CBS**
	Little House On The Prairie		NBC Monday Night At The Movies				**NBC**
T U E	Happy Days	Laverne And Shirley	Three's Company	TAXI	Starsky And Hutch		**ABC**
	THE PAPER CHASE		CBS Tuesday Night Movies				**CBS**
	GRANDPA GOES TO WASHINGTON		The Big Event				**NBC**
W E D	Eight Is Enough		Charlie's Angels		VEGA$		**ABC**
	The Jeffersons	IN THE BEGINNING	CBS Wednesday Night Movies				**CBS**
	DICK CLARK'S LIVE WEDNESDAY		NBC Wednesday Night At The Movies				**NBC**
T H R	MORK AND MINDY	What's Happening!!	Barney Miller	Soap	Family		**ABC**
	The Waltons		Hawaii Five-O		Barnaby Jones		**CBS**
	Project U.F.O.		Quincy, M.E.		W.E.B.		**NBC**
F R I	Donny And Marie		The ABC Friday Night Movie				**ABC**
	New Adventures Of Wonder Woman		The Incredible Hulk		FLYING HIGH		**CBS**
	THE WAVERLY WONDERS	WHO'S WATCHING THE KIDS	The Rockford Files		THE EDDIE CAPRA MYSTERIES		**NBC**
S A T	Carter Country	APPLE PIE	The Love Boat		Fantasy Island		**ABC**
	Rhoda	Good Times	THE AMERICAN GIRLS		Dallas		**CBS**
	CHiPs		NBC SATURDAY SPECIALS		THE SWORD OF JUSTICE		**NBC**

	7:00	7:30	8:00	8:30	9:00	9:30	10:00	10:30	
S U N	The Hardy Boys Mysteries		BATTLESTAR GALACTICA		The ABC Sunday Night Movie				**ABC**
	60 Minutes		MARY		All In The Family	Alice	KAZ		**CBS**
	The Wonderful World Of Disney		The Big Event				LIFELINE		**NBC**

The first "Star Wars"-inspired television series was NBC's *Quark,* a space comedy (created by Buck Henry) that had just missed earning a spot on the network's fall schedule in 1977. Though *Quark's* May 1977 pilot was set up as a parody of *Star Trek,* the revived series added appropriate "Star Wars" touches and opened in February 1978 with an effective take-off on the hit film, down to a "Force"-like power known as "The Source" (actually the voice of Hans Conried). The series regulars included Richard Benjamin as commander Adam Quark, skipper of a garbage ship in the United Galaxy Sanitation Patrol; Conrad Janis as Palindrome, Quark's home base superior; Richard Kelton as Ficus, Quark's Spock-like logical assistant (he was really a plant that looked human); and former Doublemint chewing gum identical twins Cyb and Tricia Barnstable as Betty I and Betty II, the ship's radio crew (one was a clone of the other). Subsequent episodes featured parodies of other popular space tales (including Flash Gordon, "2001: A Space Odyssey," and *Star Trek*), but the premise was far too limited and the series failed to catch on.

For the fall of 1978, Universal came up with *Battlestar Galactica,* a flashy big-budget space effort that took the essential "Star Wars" plot hook of a space war and combined it with other familiar science fiction touches for the program premise of a small army of humans (led by Lorne Greene as Commander Adama) fighting the Cylons, a race of robots out to destroy all human life. *Battlestar Galactica* opened with a three-hour premiere that so effec-

tively captured the "Star Wars" techniques and rhythm that Twentieth Century Fox sued Universal for copyright infringement. *Galactica's* early episodes landed in the top ten and easily defeated its competition, especially CBS's highly touted new variety hour starring Mary Tyler Moore. This produced a sigh of relief at both ABC and Universal because, in order to duplicate the technical effects audiences had come to expect after "Star Wars," the program's budget for the first few episodes was several million dollars. This success, however, was short-lived.

The scripts for subsequent episodes of *Battlestar Galactica* were far below the quality of the season opener, shifting the emphasis to simple kiddie adventures closer to *Lost in Space* than *Star Trek* or "Star Wars." In November, CBS juggled its Sunday schedule, dropped Moore's show, and placed veteran *All in the Family* against *Battlestar Galactica.* Within one month, Archie and Edith had knocked the space saga out of the top thirty. By the end of the season, ABC dropped the program as an expensive failure. Both the network and Universal attempted a bit of additional mileage from their investment the following season with a short run revival (*Galactica: 1980*) and an update of *Buck Rogers,* but neither registered impressive ratings.

Though *Battlestar Galactica* turned out to be a flop, ABC scored spectacular success with a very different sort of space hero, Mork from Ork, in another spinoff from Garry Marshall's *Happy Days.* Marshall explained that one of his children (no doubt inspired by "Star Wars") suggested it would be fun to do *a Happy Days* episode involving aliens from outer space, so he had the adventure take place in a dream. Dozing off one night, Richie Cunningham dreamt that he met Mork (Robin Williams), a nutty alien with strange powers, who decided to take him back to his home planet, Ork. To save Richie, the Fonz challenged Mork to a duel and then—Richie woke up. Naturally, neither Richie's friends nor family took his story seriously, yet the episode ended with a knock at the door and the reappearance of Robin Williams, playing a country hick, asking Richie for directions.

The "Mork" episode ran in February 1978 and went over extremely well, so Williams was given his own series for the fall, set in the present. For *Mork and Mindy,* he continued the role of alien Mork, this time sent on a long term fact-finding mission to Earth, landing in Boulder, Colorado, and taken in by a young single woman, Mindy McConnell (Pam Dawber). On the surface, *Mork and Mindy* was just *My Favorite Martian* updated and it should have been primarily for kids, but instead it managed the "Star Wars" trick of appealing to all ages. Williams's Mork had a crazy unpredictable manner (he often talked and operated at very high speed) and at any moment could spout lines (in the appropriate voices) from old movies, TV shows, and even political speeches. These off-the-wall improvisations appealed to young adults, while the physical humor (such as hanging upside down in a closet or drinking orange juice from a pitcher using only his index finger) attracted the kids. Parents found the program good family entertainment because, despite his powers, Mork was very much a little boy exploring a strange new world. Dressed in baggy jeans and suspenders, he innocently wandered into situations and each week learned some basic lesson of life.

Even though Mork lived with Mindy (staying in the attic of her apartment), the two were like brother and sister, with Mork running to her arms for a hug whenever he was afraid or confused. In a similar manner, Mindy's father (played by *Quark* veteran Conrad Janis) and grandmother (played by Elizabeth Kerr), who ran a music shop in town, acted as homespun surrogate parent figures, casting a stern but loving eye on Mork's crazy actions, even after they learned he was an alien.

Though the supporting cast was good, Williams and his manic energy were the obvious focus of the series. He was regularly allowed to draw on his improvisational background and ad-lib some bits during the filming before a live audience. As a result, when Mork broke into one of his wild spurts of rapid-fire jokes, allusions, and body movements, the show revved up to a pace reminiscent of *Laugh-In.* No one, not even the writers and other performers, knew exactly what was coming next.

Mork and Mindy was launched with a special one-hour episode featuring guest appearances by Henry Winkler and Penny Marshall in a new "flashback" sequence showing how the Fonz and Laverne had met alien Mork in the 1950s. With this tie-in from ABC's top superstars, *Mork and Mindy* became an instant smash, adding to ABC's chain of sitcom hits. The network's continuing ratings success, though, prompted cries of anguish by television critics, even those that liked *Mork and Mindy,* because it seemed to guarantee that teen-oriented shows would continue to dominate programming at the expense of more adult fare for years to come. In particular, critics pointed to the failure of a prestigious new CBS drama series, *The Paper Chase,* as a sure sign that in this ABC-dominated era of television, a quality show did not stand a chance.

The Paper Chase was based on the 1973 theatrical film of the same name starring Timothy Bottoms as James Hart, a Harvard law student who fell in love with the daughter (played by Lindsay Wagner) of his tyrannical law professor, Charles Kingsfield (John Houseman). For the series, Houseman continued his role of Kingsfield with a new cast of students, but the same focus: the struggles of first-year law students in a study group trying to develop the necessary discipline to become lawyers. The series tackled such abstruse subjects as legal ethics, personal discipline, and legal methodology, as well as flashier matters such as sexual harassment of students and prison reform.

CBS slotted *The Paper Chase* directly opposite *Happy Days* and *Laverne and Shirley* which, at first glance, seemed "suicidal" scheduling. Actually, though, it made sense as potentially perfect counter-programming. *The Waltons,* for instance, had proved to be Flip Wilson's undoing in a similar match-up earlier in the decade. With high quality writing and good characters, *The Paper Chase* could slowly but steadily build an audience and perhaps pull a similar upset. Its placement against the top teen humor shows of television, however, turned the series instead into a symbolic rallying point that was regarded somehow as a barometer of whether, in the short run, the American public wanted quality drama or familiar comedy. Not surprisingly, the public chose familiar comedy.

As a result, *The Paper Chase* found itself pulled in opposite directions throughout the season. Though it wore the mantle of serious drama, there was constant pressure for more accessible hooks aimed at more broad-based success. John Houseman was very effective in the lead role of Professor Charles Kingsfield, completely dominating the screen with his presence. James Stephens, who took over the role of James Hart for the TV series,

With *WKRP in Cincinnati*, MTM again turned the premise of an unsuccessful Midwest broadcast operation into a top-notch sitcom: *(from left)* top: Frank Bonner and Gordon Jump; middle: Richard Sanders, Gary Sandy, Jan Smithers, and Tim Reid; bottom: Loni Anderson and Howard Hesseman. *(WKRP in Cincinnati © 1979 Twentieth Century Fox Television. All Rights Reserved.)*

September 10, 1978

Return of the Saint. ATV in England brings back suave adventurer Simon Templar a.k.a. The Saint with a new lead, Ian Ogilvy. CBS airs the revival in a late night slot beginning in December 1979.

September 13, 1978

W.E.B. (NBC). Lin Bolen, a former NBC programmer who served as the role model for Faye Dunaway's Diane Christensen character in the film "Network," produces a TV series patterned after the movie. Appropriately, this is the first show canceled in the 1978-79 season.

October 14 & 21, 1978

"Rescue from Gilligan's Island." (NBC). After fourteen years on the "uncharted desert isle," the seven shipwrecked refugees from the *Minnow* are rescued at last. This two-part special ends with everyone shipwrecked again on the same island, but the program does well in the ratings so they are rescued once more in a May 1979 sequel. After one final TV movie in 1981 (when the island becomes a resort), the series at last fades to black.

October 16, 1978

Sneak Previews. (PBS). After one year on local Chicago public TV, Roger Ebert and Gene Siskel (film critics for the *Chicago Sun-Times* and *Chicago Tribune*, respectively) go national with their weekly critiques of new film releases. The duo moves to commercial syndication in 1982 with a new series, *At the Movies.*

November 18, 1978

California Congressman Leo Ryan, NBC correspondent Don Harris, and two others are ambushed and killed at the air strip near the religious commune run by Jim Jones in Guyana.

was also good as the hardworking kid from the Midwest waiting tables to earn his law degree. However, too often potentially effective themes were sabotaged with hokey, heavy-handed subplots. In two of the best episodes (one on moot court and another on understanding contract law), key characters were inexplicably struck by puppy love halfway through the story. Even more basic, the scripts often seemed to be fighting the central setup of focusing on a small group of law students, who spent most of their lives studying and going to complicated classes. It was also sometimes awkward attempting to involve Kingsfield in every story of their lives.

Still, these flaws might have been overcome by fleshing out all the characters. Instead, apart from Hart and Kingsfield, *The Paper Chase* too often settled for stiff stereotypes that made most of the "first year" characters downright unlikable. Hart's study group included a strident feminist, the son of a prominent lawyer, and a smart-aleck jock. They were all clever kids studying at a prestigious law school to be rich and successful lawyers, and it was sometimes very difficult to feel much sympathy for characters whose greatest fear was not finishing at the top of the class. Even Hart, who had to work nights to earn money for school, was exactly the type of student the average person grew to resent: He studied hard, always had the right answers, and held down a job to boot. Stephens, fortunately, was given the opportunity to soften and develop his character. The others were not so lucky. The fact that *The Paper Chase* often managed to overcome so many obstacles for some effective episodes was a tribute to the determination of the cast and the powerful figure of Houseman. CBS did not let *The*

Paper Chase die without a fight. When it appeared obvious that the program was not going to siphon viewers from the ABC comedy blockbusters running against it, the network moved the show for a few weeks to later Tuesday night against much weaker competition (the fading *Starsky and Hutch*). However that was hardly enough time for new viewers to discover the program, nor for the production team to work out some of the rough spots in the show's pacing and scripting. Fans of the series insisted that with a little more time and some breathing space, *The Paper Chase* could build on its strengths and develop into a solid and successful offering. Instead, when the program's ratings did not change significantly after its time shift, the series was canceled, becoming the most glorious television failure in years.

Despite the well publicized flop of *The Paper Chase,* the state of quality programming on television was actually quite healthy. Besides established hits such as CBS's *M*A*S*H,* ABC's *Barney Miller,* and NBC's *Saturday Night Live,* there were several strong newcomers, including four high quality shows from the MTM production family: *Lou Grant, The White Shadow, WKRP in Cincinnati,* and *Taxi.*

Lou Grant had premiered in the fall of 1977, starting very slowly in the ratings and barely hanging on through the winter. The show was a somewhat risky approach to one of the most obvious successors to *The Mary Tyler Moore Show.* Instead of placing Ed Asner's Lou Grant character in another sitcom, MTM used him as the basis for its first hour-long drama program. The premise was simple: After being fired from his management position at WJM-TV in Minneapolis, Lou Grant returned to the newspaper business, becoming city editor of the *Los Angeles Tribune.* Each episode revolved around the investigation and preparation of stories for the daily paper.

MTM applied its comedy ensemble approach to the new drama series, building a large supporting cast behind Asner and a wide range of topical, sometimes controversial, subject matter for the stories. This was a tricky combination and everyone involved needed the opportunity to work out the bugs. Asner's Lou Grant character had been a popular part of *The Mary Tyler Moore Show* for seven years and his presence helped buy the time necessary for development.

At first, the stories and character development focused primarily on Asner. This allowed him some very effective scenes as a middle-aged man suddenly taking on a whole new career in a brand new city, but it left the supporting characters less clearly defined. They seemed more like character types straight out of such theatrical "newspaper film" hits as "The Front Page" and the more recent "All the President's Men" (about the Watergate investigation by Bob Woodward and Carl Bernstein). There was an irascible editor-in-chief (Mason Adams as Charlie Hume), a long-haired photographer (Daryl Anderson as Dennis "Animal" Price), a young woman reporter (Rebecca Balding as Carla Mardigian, soon replaced by Linda Kelsey as Billie Newman), an intense Bernstein-like investigative reporter (Robert Walden as Joe Rossi), a handsome assistant city editor (Jack Bannon as Art Donovan), and an older woman as owner and publisher (live TV drama veteran Nancy Marchand as Margaret Pynchon). In addition, some of the scripts ended up a bit preachy and self-conscious while others tried to cover too many aspects of some "burning issue" and emerged as just a series of interviews ending in some dramatic headline. For example, in one of the first season's episodes (Billie Newman's investigation into the background of an American Nazi), an otherwise effective drama was undercut at the end by the melodramatic news of the Nazi's suicide as a result of the *Tribune's* story. (Billie had discovered that the Nazi actually was Jewish.)

City editor Lou Grant (Ed Asner) frequently ended up at the office of newspaper owner Margaret Pynchon (Nancy Marchand) on *Lou Grant*. *(Lou Grant © 1977 Twentieth Century Fox Television. All Rights Reserved.)*

One of the best episodes of the first season was more restrained and realistic in tackling its problem: Should an aging, possibly senile, judge be removed from the bench? It could have been a flashy expose, but instead turned into an intense interpersonal confrontation, reaching a dramatic peak during a discussion between the judge, Mrs. Pynchon, Lou Grant, and Charlie Hume in the *Tribune's* editorial offices. After some serious soul-searching, the judge decided on his own to retire. The *Tribune's* only story from the events was a short item in the back of the paper.

This was the heart of the matter: Most newspaper stories are not Watergate-style headliners that help topple governments, but rather consist of small slices of life from the news of the day. Throughout the first season both the writers and the performers sharpened their skills and moved into a more difficult style: tackling issues that often had no flashy ending, glib solution, or obvious bad guys. To do so, the focus shifted away from the expose orientation to how shades of problems affected people. In the process, the *Lou Grant* ensemble graduated from being merely reporter types to full-fledged interesting characters that just happened to work at a newspaper. The show became an effective equivalent to the legal drama of *The Defenders* from the early 1960s, providing entertaining dramatizations of current topical issues within the framework of a standard TV series.

By the 1978–79 season, *Lou Grant* had stretched, found its style, and flourished. Though Asner's Grant remained the solid rock at the helm of the city desk, more and more time was turned over to the other performers. With this more controlled approach emphasizing characters, *Lou Grant* was able to mix in stories that went beyond merely dealing with controversy, including quiet mood pieces, straightforward character conflicts in the office, and even a sly tribute to 1930s-style Hollywood detective movies (complete with a Sam Spade-type voiceover narration by Asner). At the same time, particular episodes that did take a strong stand were that much more effective.

In a story dealing with Vietnam veterans, Lou tried to help an unemployed black vet find a job, discovering in the process that there were dramatic differences in the after-effects of World War II (Lou's war) and the Vietnam War on the men who fought. While this naturally led to a *Tribune* series on Vietnam veterans, it also

---

January 28, 1979

Sunday Morning. (CBS). Charles Kuralt comes off the road to host a low-key, informative ninety-minute news show on early Sunday morning.

February 18-25, 1979

Roots: The Next Generations. (ABC). For twelve hours over seven nights, Alex Haley's search for his family history moves from Reconstruction to Africa in 1967. James Earl Jones plays Haley and Marlon Brando, in a rare TV role, plays American Nazi leader George Lincoln Rockwell.

March 5, 1979

NBC's *Another World* becomes the first ninety-minute soap opera.

March 11, 1979

Mr. Dugan. (CBS). The scheduled premiere for the show that never was. Although promotional clips have already aired, at the urging of prominent black leaders, Norman Lear cancels his new sitcom about a black Congressman.

April 1, 1979

William Leonard succeeds Richard Salant as president of CBS News. Salant, forced to retire from CBS upon reaching age sixty-five, moves to NBC where he becomes vice chairman in charge of news.

April 20, 1979

Howard K. Smith quits ABC after seventeen years. Angered that his nightly news commentaries had been cut to about three-per-week, Smith leaves his resignation on the ABC bulletin board in Washington and goes on vacation.

September 7, 1979

Bankrolled by Getty Oil and headquartered in Bristol, Connecticut, the Entertainment and Sports Programming Network (ESPN), an all-sports cable network, begins. By its first anniversary, it is on twenty-four hours a day, seven days a week.

In *Diff'rent Strokes*, Conrad Bain played a millionaire-widower who raised both his daughter and two orphaned brothers (played by, *from left*, Dana Plato, Gary Coleman, and Todd Bridges). *(Sony Pictures Television)*

helped Lou to understand the personal pressures affecting a Vietnam veteran on his staff, Animal. The program also made effective use of the *60 Minutes* style of intercutting between separate interviews to underscore points. While Rossi asked officials from a local Veterans Administration office about the unique problems facing those who had fought in Vietnam, Billie posed similar questions to representatives from an organization of Vietnam vets. As each person raised an issue, there was an appropriate comment from the other interview inserted, illustrating how very different the perceptions of the same situation really were. The episode ended with mixed results: Animal solved his problem, the unemployed veteran did not get a job, and all the frustrations discussed in that hour remained unresolved.

A sure sign that *Lou Grant* had inherited the mantle of the golden age of television drama came when a pressure group tried to stop the airing of an episode on nursing homes. The program not only presented an effective look at older Americans, it stirred the ire of the nursing home industry which tried to get the sponsors and CBS not to include the episode in the summer reruns. The story in question focused at first on the shoddy treatment in one particular nursing home where Billie took an undercover job as a nurse's aide. It quickly expanded to the larger issue of growing old with dignity and, on that subject, the program took a clear, unequivocal stand: Nursing homes were not the answer. One character, a seventy-year-old woman, explained that she would rather spend one day at home than ten years in a nursing home, *any* nursing home. Another declared that "even the best of 'em is just a place to wait to die." To its credit, CBS stuck by the series and reran the episode.

Like the MTM ensemble comedies, *Lou Grant* had needed time to grow. Once in the groove, the show managed to pull off the difficult task of presenting thoughtful, well-written, and entertaining drama with class and consistency. It also provided a sharp reminder to CBS that some of its biggest hits had needed time to catch on. From barely adequate ratings early in its first season, *Lou Grant* slowly inched up the charts. It cracked the top thirty by early spring, winning renewal. By the summer of 1978, it took off, consistently finishing in the top ten. Thereafter it scored well enough to be considered both a solid ratings performer and one of the most respected series on television.

Lou Grant's success gave MTM credibility in the drama field and the company followed with another hour-long series, *The White Shadow*, which CBS plugged into the 1978–79 schedule in late November. Produced by Bruce Paltrow and Mark Tinker (son

of MTM's boss Grant Tinker), *The White Shadow* presented Ken Howard as Ken Reeves, a former professional basketball player who was forced to retire following an injury. In order to stay with the game, he took a job as basketball coach for Carver High, a largely black Los Angeles ghetto school. The stories focused on the white coach's efforts, on and off the basketball court, to build the talented but unsuccessful team members into winners by helping them develop self-respect, discipline, responsibility, and a spirit of teamwork. Actually, these goals were quite similar to the ideals behind the ill-fated *Paper Chase,* only in *The White Shadow* everything clicked. The writing, dialogue, and characters at Carver High were solid and believable, especially the students. As a result, the series was able to tackle a wide range of themes in a manner distinct from but every bit as good as *Lou Grant*. Some stories dealt with broad topical issues such as venereal disease, drugs, and teenage pregnancy, while others concentrated on small slices of life such as the team's first airplane flight or each senior's decision whether or not to try college. At the end of the second season, the team won the city basketball championship and, in violation of television's usual taboo against anyone ever aging, all but four of the players graduated. Like any real high school coach, Reeves had to start all over again the next school year, which proved to be the show's last.

MTM's new-found success in the field of drama was welcome news to CBS, but the network was even more pleased when the company at last came up with a sitcom successor to *The Mary Tyler Moore Show*, *WKRP in Cincinnati.*

Another story of broadcasting in the Midwest, *WKRP* began with Andy Travis (Gary Sandy), a hot-shot program director, being brought in to boost the ratings of a "beautiful music" radio station, WKRP. He immediately changed its format to rock'n'roll, receiving only grudging approval from station manager Arthur Carlson (Gordon Jump), who was worried what his mother might think. ("Mama" Carlson owned WKRP.) Andy discovered that one of the station's disc jockeys was a West Coast rock radio legend, Dr. Johnny Fever (Howard Hesseman) and instituted the format change during the "Doctor's" morning show. Fever dragged the needle across the instrumental record then playing and kicked into a hard-driving rock song, punctuating the format announcement with the word "Booger!" (He had lost his job in Los Angeles for saying that on the air.) Travis then brought in another rock pro for the evening shift, Venus Flytrap (Tim Reid), a hip but mellow black disc jockey.

The changes in WKRP upset sales manager Herb Tarlek (Frank

Bonner) and news director Les Nessman (Richard Sanders), both of whom did not like rock'n'roll. Les was a straight-laced newsman who took his job very, very seriously, especially the hog reports. (He proudly displayed the Silver Sow award he had won prominently on his desk.) Herb spent most of his time making unsuccessful passes at Jennifer Marlowe (Loni Anderson), the station's beautiful receptionist. Yet they both decided to give the new format a try. It might catch on and possibly boost the station's ratings from dead last in the market.

WKRP's premise and ensemble were MTM's strongest since *The Mary Tyler Moore Show* and the series won high praise (especially from radio disc jockeys). Like *The Mary Tyler Moore Show*, *WKRP* got in some effective digs at the world of broadcasting. For instance, as a Thanksgiving promotion, Carlson decided to release a load of wild turkeys from a helicopter above a shopping mall where Les was stationed to do a live remote broadcast. Carlson failed to realize until it was too late that turkeys cannot fly. Les described the results in a horrified voice, using lines exactly like those in the live radio report of the crash of the German Zeppelin *Hindenburg* in 1937.

In spite of such inventiveness, *WKRP*'s ratings were quite low through September and October, and it seemed doomed to die just a popular cult program. CBS, however, came up with an innovative new strategy to give the show a second chance. Instead of canceling *WKRP*, the network pulled the program from the schedule for a few months. This break gave MTM time to fine-tune the show and when *WKRP* returned in January, CBS gave it the royal treatment, slotting it between *M*A*S*H* and *Lou Grant*. *WKRP* registered the expected better ratings in its new slot and then took off. During the summer, it shot into the top five, outscoring even *M*A*S*H*.

WKRP was a near-perfect execution of the MTM philosophy of sitcoms, which may be why CBS gave it a second chance. The show had a funny situation with many obvious hooks, yet it also used the setting as a backdrop for developing the humanity of its characters. Jennifer looked like a typical "dumb blonde" but was totally in control of her situation at all times. Leering Herb played up to her but when she called his bluff, he backed down and the two actually became friends. Venus hid behind his on-the-air name because he was AWOL from the Army, yet conservative Arthur Carlson stood by him when that news came out and helped negotiate a compromise settlement with the government. Johnny Fever loved rock music, but admitted that he felt embarrassed living and looking like a college kid when he was almost forty. Les was an insecure, shy man who hid behind a male supremacy view, yet he learned to accept assistance in his private turf, news gathering, from a woman, Bailey Quarters (Jan Smithers).

The other MTM-family newcomer for the fall of 1978 had a similar high quality set up and cast, but unlike *WKRP in Cincinnati*, ABC's *Taxi* became an immediate hit. Technically, *Taxi* was not an MTM show, but the series had the MTM company style stamped all over it. In early 1977, as *The Mary Tyler Moore Show* ended its run on CBS, ABC signed four veteran MTM producers to turn out a similar style show. James L. Brooks (co-creator of *Mary Tyler Moore* and *Rhoda*), Ed. Weinberger and Stan Daniels (co-producers of *Mary Tyler Moore*), and David Davis (producer of *Rhoda* and co-creator of *The Bob Newhart Show*) came up with a series set in a New York City taxi company's dispatch garage.

Alex Reiger (Judd Hirsch) was the lead cabbie on *Taxi*. While he was perfectly happy driving a taxi as his life's work, the other "hacks" dreamed of grand success in other areas and claimed that the taxi job was just temporary: Bobby Wheeler (Jeff Conaway) wanted to be an actor, Tony Banta (Tony Danza) a boxer, and

Elaine Nardo (Marilu Henner) an art dealer. In the meantime, they shared the less glamorous life at the Sunshine Cab Company working with each other, an immigrant mechanic who barely spoke English (Andy Kaufman as Latka Gravas) and a surly, diminutive dispatcher (Danny DeVito as Louie DiPalma). As in every good MTM show, the group developed into a strong ensemble, fleshing out the characters while facing a wide variety of funny situations. Unlike the many other ensemble shows, though, *Taxi* was an immediate top ten smash, given a tremendous boost by the lead-in of *Happy Days, Laverne and Shirley,* and *Three's Company.*

Adding the strong performance of newcomers *Taxi, Mork and Mindy,* and (in the early fall, at least) *Battlestar Galactica* to its returning hits, ABC jumped out to a commanding lead at the start of the 1978–79 season. It was painfully obvious to CBS and NBC almost immediately that ABC would walk away with its third straight winning season in the overall ratings. Yet there was still a chance to score an upset victory in a more limited contest, the brief but highly competitive race to win the "sweeps" months.

Throughout the year, the Nielsen ratings service measured how well the networks were doing each week, using its sample of some 1,200 "metered" families across the country. Four times each year, for an entire month, the company conducted a much more detailed survey (called a "sweep") that encompassed the performance of more than 700 commercial stations nationwide, which then used the results to determine their local advertising rates that would apply until the next sweeps period. In order to calculate these ratings, Nielsen used a much larger sample (several hundred thousand homes) for the four sweeps periods of November, February, May, and July (representing typical months for their respective seasons).

Because the prime time programming on the network affiliates was in the hands of the networks, the locals pressured them to air the most saleable shows possible during the sweeps. The increasingly fierce ratings wars in the mid-1970s led to the practice of stacking these months (especially the heavy-viewing fall and winter months of November and February) with blockbuster movies, specials, and flashy gimmicks—in the process, of course, making these supposedly typical months very untypical.

The February 1979 sweeps were the most intense to that point. The month became a merry-go-round of time shifts, stunts, and specials. One night viewers had to decide between one episode of ABC's *Roots: The Next Generations* and the network television premieres of two major movies: "American Graffiti" on NBC and "Marathon Man" on CBS. On another February evening, the choice was between "Elvis," ABC's docudrama on the life of Elvis Presley, "Gone With the Wind" on CBS, and "One Flew Over the Cuckoo's Nest" on NBC. There were expanded editions of some series while others completely disappeared. It was an expensive, confusing month that left both viewers and executives unhappy. The concentration of so many blockbuster events running against each other and disrupting the regular weekly schedule frustrated and annoyed viewers. At the same time, counter-programming moves and stunts were very expensive for the networks. (One night, February 11, was reported to have cost them $13 million.)

Ironically, after all the moves and countermoves, the February sweeps produced no surprises and seemed only to confirm the obvious: ABC was on top with CBS and NBC far behind fighting for the number two spot. Media analysts regarded these results as clear evidence of a television network status quo that would be around for a long time to come. ABC's number one position looked unassailable.

They were wrong.

39. Gleam in the Eye

IN MAY 1977 ABC MADE AN UNUSUAL personnel shift and appointed Roone Arledge, then president of the network's sports operations, to an additional post: president of ABC News. Though ABC had successfully taken a commanding lead in entertainment programming, it desperately wanted similar triumphs in the less profitable but more prestigious area of news. Arledge had built ABC Sports into a highly respected and tremendously successful arm of the network; and while continuing at that post, he was to do the same in news.

Since coming to ABC from NBC in 1960, Arledge had demonstrated a sharp sense for packaging and presentation, overseeing such operations as ABC's live coverage of the Olympic Games and weekly shows such as *Wide World of Sports* and *Monday Night Football*. His news responsibilities required him to apply his expertise to another area of network programming that involved both live on-the-spot events and reports from all over the nation and the world.

One of the key areas for improvement was ABC's nightly news program. In 1976, the network had attracted a great deal of attention by signing away Barbara Walters from NBC for $1 million and making her co-anchor of the evening news with Harry Reasoner. That match-up never gelled, leaving Reasoner unhappy and the ratings virtually unchanged. When Arledge took command of ABC News he realized that trying to find a personality mix to outdraw Walter Cronkite was the wrong strategy. Instead, Arledge concentrated on completely reworking ABC's nightly news format to give the program a distinctly different feel and appearance from the competition.

Arledge's primary goal was to reduce the incessant focus on the anchor position in the nightly news and, at the start of 1978, *The ABC Evening News* began to change. Two former ABC news anchors, Frank Reynolds and Peter Jennings, appeared more often, acting as "mini-anchors" for stories from their respective beats: Washington (for governmental stories) and London (for foreign news). ABC's news ratings went up, so Arledge decided to develop his concept further. The result was *World News Tonight*.

The new format, which premiered in July 1978, was slick and fast moving. There was less patter between stories, more use of graphic material (including teasers for upcoming reports) and catchy electronic stinger music going into the commercials. Arledge moved the anchors into a newsroom setting and incorporated the control room bank of monitors into the open and close of the program. Moreover, he broke from a hoary news tradition and

eliminated the New York anchor position. Frank Reynolds, still in Washington covering the federal government, became the "first among equals" in an anchor triumvirate: Reynolds usually opened and closed the show, with the necessary transition comments divided between him, Peter Jennings (in London, at the foreign desk), and newcomer Max Robinson (in Chicago, handling domestic reports outside Washington). Barbara Walters remained in New York, but shifted to special assignments and interviews, her real strengths, while Harry Reasoner returned to CBS, the network he had left for ABC back in 1970.

World News Tonight did improve in the ratings, but that represented only a first step. If ABC was going to tout itself as a leader in news programming, it needed some dramatic action to build its credibility. The most obvious move was to expand the nightly news slot, but such a proposal had been fiercely resisted for years by affiliates from all three networks, even when championed by Walter Cronkite himself. Local programmers knew that an hour of network news, or even forty-five minutes, would take time from their own lucrative newscasts or access slot series. It was unlikely that ABC would have any better luck with a proposal to expand the evening news. There was, however, another way for the network to increase its news programming: use a different slot, such as late night (11:30 P.M.) immediately following the late local news. This was the time all the networks generally used anyway for either their "instant news" special reports on late-breaking developments in big stories or the obligatory obituaries on major political and entertainment figures. The chief problem with the late night slot was that it faced formidable competition: Johnny Carson. Since the mid-1970s, CBS and ABC had garnered respectable, if not spectacular, ratings against the *Tonight* show with reruns of movies and old network series. No one thought that a regular late night news show would stand a chance against such solid entertainment fare. Then on Sunday, November 4, 1979, Iranian militants seized control of the U.S. embassy in Teheran and, in the process, took more than fifty Americans hostage.

NBC aired the first TV report on the events in Iran, showing pictures of the embassy takeover during halftime of its Sunday afternoon football game. All three networks immediately rushed correspondents and crews into the country, while drawing on film from European broadcasters in the meantime. In the special late night reports, network correspondents attempted to sort out the events, and their initial explanation of the situation was rather straightforward: Iranian militants had seized the American embassy in angry reaction to the decision by the United States government to admit the exiled Iranian Shah, Mohammed Reza Pahlavi, for medical treatment in New York City. They demanded the extradition of the former Shah in exchange for the hostages.

All three networks did their best to report every available detail on the hostage crisis and, on November 18, each one broadcast its own filmed interview with Iran's religious and secular leader, Ayatollah Ruhollah Khomeini (conducted by Mike Wallace for CBS, John Hart for NBC, and Peter Jennings for ABC; all of whom had to submit questions in advance). After a flurry of late night reports following the embassy seizure, though, both CBS and NBC pulled back, scheduling a late night wrapup only if there were some dramatic developments that day. ABC, however, committed itself to a broadcast at least fifteen minutes long each weeknight "for the duration" (beginning November 8), under the title *The Iran Crisis: America Held Hostage* (anchored first by Frank Reynolds, then by Ted Koppel). In the process, the network not only attracted a huge audience (sometimes outdrawing the entertainment offerings on both CBS and NBC), but also found itself in a position to deal with the story in much greater depth. Instead of merely repeating what had been reported on the nightly news, *The Iran Crisis* featured longer and more detailed presentations on all aspects of the story. At first, the reports covered the obvious questions: What happened today? What do Americans think about it? What can the United States do now? These soon led to a far more difficult question: Why did it happen? In trying to answer that, each evening's report became, in effect, a mini-lesson in basic foreign policy and Mideast history.

The *Iran Crisis* reports served as an all-around unexpected bonus for Roone Arledge and ABC News. The show attracted a large, steady audience and helped viewers to become accustomed to a late night news program. It also established ABC as *the* network with complete coverage of the situation. This boost in credibility and viewership spilled over into other programs. *Good Morning America,* which had been gaining on *Today* for a while, at last pulled ahead with the bonus carryover audience of people who had gone to bed watching ABC and who then woke up with the TV dial still set there. *World News Tonight* also rose in the ratings, moving into a virtual deadlock with NBC for the number two news position behind CBS.

The hostage situation lasted far longer than anyone first imagined. Through November, December, and early January, reporters filed hundreds of stories on virtually every movement, rumor, and protest in and around the captured embassy. Media coverage, in fact, became an issue itself both in the United States and in Iran. American correspondents complained that often the "spontaneous" demonstrations against "Western imperialism" probably took place because the Western camera crews stationed outside the embassy were ready and eager to film. Officials in Iran, on the other hand, grew increasingly frustrated at their inability to control the image of their own country sent back by the journalists. In mid-January, Iran ordered all American reporters out of the country, so subsequent stories had to be filed from "listening posts" in nearby countries or through other foreign reporters allowed to remain.

By March, though there was still no end to the hostage situation at hand, ABC decided to change its late night *Iran Crisis* "special reports" into a permanent nightly news show that would cover other stories as well. The show was extended to twenty minutes each night and retitled *Nightline*. The revamped program followed the *Iran Crisis* format, though, concentrating on in-depth coverage of a few items rather than a recap of the earlier nightly news (much like PBS's *MacNeil-Lehrer Report).* While *Nightline* was not as big a draw as the Iran wrapups, four months of late night reports

had built a solid base audience for ABC, and the show was able to compete successfully in the slot. ABC News emerged from the crisis with stronger news credibility, an expanded news schedule, and higher ratings overall for its *World News Tonight* program. Arledge had done his job well and now focused on beating CBS. Even the nightly news lead would be up for grabs soon because Walter Cronkite was nearing retirement.

Despite ABC's improved news performance, CBS was still considered the leader in news, based on the tremendous public respect for Cronkite as a credible source, the quality of CBS's own special reports, and its increasingly successful news magazine, *60 Minutes,* which had actually become a top ten show.

60 Minutes had been around since 1968, attracting little attention at first with its deft mix of hard-hitting investigative reporting and softer, entertaining feature pieces. It ran for three seasons in prime time, but was exiled in 1972 to the fringe period of very early Sunday evening where it was preempted every fall by professional football. During the summer of 1975, the show ran in a Sunday prime time slot and managed to land in the top thirty. When it returned in December, following the football season, *60 Minutes* was placed at the beginning of prime time against *The Wonderful World of Disney,* allowing it to be on the air year round. At the same time, correspondent Dan Rather joined Mike Wallace and Morley Safer as one of the program's co-anchors.

Through 1976 and 1977, the program's ratings rose steadily, benefiting from the hefty audience of its new fall sports lead-in,

Reflecting accomplishments in both sports and news, Roone Arledge received the Peabody Award in 1966 (for *ABC's Wide World of Sports*), 1968 and 1976 (for network coverage of the Olympic Games), and in 1984 (honoring his entire career). *(Courtesy Peabody Awards Collection)*

	8:00	8:30	9:00	9:30	10:00	10:30	
M	240-ROBERT		ABC NFL Monday Night Football (to 12 Midnight)				**ABC**
O	The White Shadow		M*A*S*H	WKRP In Cincinnati	Lou Grant		**CBS**
N	Little House On The Prairie		NBC Monday Night At The Movies				**NBC**
T	Happy Days	Angie	Three's Company	Taxi	THE LAZARUS SYNDROME		**ABC**
U	CALIFORNIA FEVER		CBS Tuesday Night Movies				**CBS**
E	THE MISADVENTURES OF SHERIFF LOBO		NBC Tuesday Night At The Movies				**NBC**
W	Eight Is Enough		Charlie's Angels		Vega$		**ABC**
E	THE LAST RESORT	STRUCK BY LIGHTNING	CBS Wednesday Night Movies				**CBS**
D	Real People		Diff'rent Strokes	Hello, Larry	The Best Of Saturday Night Live		**NBC**
T	Laverne And Shirley	BENSON	Barney Miller	Soap	20/20		**ABC**
H	The Waltons		Hawaii Five-O		Barnaby Jones		**CBS**
R	BUCK ROGERS IN THE 25th CENTURY		Quincy, M.E.		Kate Loves A Mystery		**NBC**
F	Fantasy Island		The ABC Friday Night Movie				**ABC**
R	The Incredible Hulk		The Dukes Of Hazzard		Dallas		**CBS**
I	SHIRLEY		The Rockford Files		EISCHIED		**NBC**
S	The Ropers	Detective School	The Love Boat		HART TO HART		**ABC**
A	WORKING STIFFS	The Bad News Bears	BIG SHAMUS, LITTLE SHAMUS		PARIS		**CBS**
T	CHiPs		B.J. And The Bear		A MAN CALLED SLOANE		**NBC**

	7:00	7:30	8:00	8:30	9:00	9:30	10:00	10:30	
S	OUT OF THE BLUE	A NEW KIND OF FAMILY	Mork And Mindy	THE ASSOCIATES	The ABC Sunday Night Movie				**ABC**
U	60 Minutes		Archie Bunker's Place	One Day At A Time	Alice	The Jeffersons	TRAPPER JOHN, M.D.		**CBS**
N	Disney's Wonderful World		The Sunday Big Event				Prime Time Sunday		**NBC**

NFL football. In April 1977, the CBS news division announced an unheard-of development: Due to the success of *60 Minutes,* it was showing a profit. This was a dramatic change from the long-standing image of news programs as prestigious loss leaders, and for the 1977–78 season CBS made every effort not to have its Sunday afternoon football coverage run overtime and thereby shorten *60 Minutes.*

Going into the fall of 1979, *60 Minutes* was an established top ten show and, by October, it ranked as the number one network show overall. This proved to be no fall ratings fluke as *60 Minutes* hung on through the winter and spring, eventually finishing as the number one program for the 1979–80 season, the first television news show ever to reach this rarefied height. Such ratings success sent a clear message to all the networks' programming departments: *60 Minutes* was the biggest bargain in television. Not only did *60 Minutes* now offer both prestige and high ratings, but, as a news show, its budget was only a small fraction of most entertainment series, thus allowing a tremendous profit margin. Both NBC and ABC joined the bandwagon and reinstituted prime time news shows, with mixed results.

ABC launched *20/20* in the summer of 1978, but its June premiere at times seemed almost a bad parody of *60 Minutes.* A pair of ill-at-ease hosts, Harold Hayes and Australian Robert Hughes (two print journalists) introduced an investigative report by Geraldo Rivera on the training of vicious greyhound racing dogs (including gory footage of the animals attacking and eating rabbits); a piece by Sander Vanocur on the threat of homemade nuclear bombs; and puff piece interviews with California governor Jerry Brown, his sister, and his mother. Hayes and Hughes were canned after the first show and veteran Hugh Downs assumed the hosting chores. The program ran weekly through the remainder of the summer and as a monthly series during the regular season, hammering out its weak spots and moving away from the much-criticized sensationalist style of the opening episode to a more controlled and focused approach. By the time *20/20* returned as a weekly series in May 1979, the show had developed its own distinctive weekly magazine format, which was generally more feature-oriented than *60 Minutes.* As with the nightly news race, ABC gave up trying to beat CBS at its own game and tailored its program to a different style of appeal.

NBC decided to use an existing series for its prime time magazine, promoting *Weekend* (with Lloyd Dobyns) from a late Saturday night monthly show to a weekly prime time slot beginning in January 1979. *Weekend*'s mix of serious subjects and light, satiric features did not transfer well to the demands of weekly prime time exposure, and the show bombed in its new time period, coming in as the lowest rated program on prime time television. In June, NBC brought in another late night star, *Tomorrow*'s Tom Snyder, to host the more serious *Prime Time Sunday.* Though scoring better than *Weekend,* this series was also unable to duplicate the success of *60 Minutes* or even *20/20.* In the fall of 1980, NBC revamped the show again as *NBC Magazine with David Brinkley,* adding to the usual feature reports a round table discussion between NBC correspondents (much like PBS's *Washington Week in Review).* However, like its predecessors, *NBC Magazine* was a ratings flop.

Even CBS had difficulty when it tried to create its own feature-oriented spinoff to *60 Minutes.* Back in January 1977, the network launched *Who's Who* (hosted by Dan Rather and Barbara Howar), built around personalities in the news, much like the weekly feature magazine *People.* Each program included extended profiles of or interviews with famous writers, performers, and politicians, mixed with short gossipy anecdotes delivered by Rather and Howar. To contrast with these high-powered celebrities, the program also incorporated reporter Charles Kuralt's popular "On the Road" feature from the evening news in which he turned attention to unusual, amusing, and talented non-celebrities throughout the country. Though individual segments of *Who's Who* occasionally worked (Kuralt's features were consistently the most entertaining), the program never gelled and was gone by June.

For the fall of 1978, CBS went directly to Time-Life, the publisher of *People* magazine, for a celebrity-oriented feature program called (what else?) *People.* With David Susskind as executive producer, the half-hour show (hosted by former Miss America Phyllis George) faithfully duplicated its slick, glitzy magazine namesake. That, too, flopped, chiefly because *People's* print style of dozens of super short articles and picture captions did not adapt well to television. TV's *People* played like a series of thirty-second commercials sandwiched between title graphics and upbeat disco music.

Ironically, while all three networks had great difficulty trying to successfully copy *60 Minutes,* another type of news magazine was catching on locally in the prime time access slot. This Monday-through-Friday program began in August 1976 on Group W's KPIX in San Francisco, which axed the syndicated *Concentration, Dealer's Choice, The Price Is Right, The New Treasure Hunt,* and *Name That Tune* from the 7:30–8:00 P.M. access slot in order to run the new locally produced show. Three of the five canceled series had been beating their competition, so the move was not out of desperation at poor ratings. Rather, it reflected a desire by KPIX program manager Bill Hiller to do something different with access time, possibly even developing a program that could itself be profitably syndicated. He made himself executive producer for *Evening: The MTWTF Show* (for Monday, Tuesday, Wednesday, Thursday, and Friday), soon simplified to *Evening Magazine.*

The format for the new show consisted of a nightly celebrity profile (subjects the first week included Paul McCartney, Bill Cosby, Valerie Perrine, and John Ehrlichman), brief helpful "tips" (such as how to exercise while watering your plants), and a "wild card" feature piece. After only two months, the program was a hit, registering better ratings than the game shows it replaced. Within a year, the Group W stations in Boston, Philadelphia, Pittsburgh, and Baltimore added the program to their schedules. Each followed the basic format, with their own local production crews and hosts, and each was also responsible for doing one piece each week that was offered to the other stations. This gave each show both a local and a national slant. By the fall of 1979, the *Evening Magazine* format was on forty-five stations (running as *PM Magazine* on non-Group W stations) and had become the number one access show in the country.

Television critics, of course, loved *Evening Magazine* and pointed to it as the program that at last fulfilled the ideal of the FCC's much maligned access rule. While *Evening Magazine* was certainly much more informative than most syndicated game shows, it was not exactly an overnight commitment to educate viewers with hard-hitting public affairs. In essence, all *Evening Magazine* did was take generally non-controversial "soft" features that were typically part of many local newscasts anyway and package them with similar features from other local stations. Yet this familiar feel probably helped account for the program's popularity, especially with its use of local hosts to read transition material and introduce each story. (Most stations that carried the show did at least one or two local pieces each week.) While *Evening Magazine* was born and bred in local access syndication, there was no reason that its basic format could not work in network prime time as well. NBC, in early 1979, became the first network to come up at last with a workable feature and personality-oriented program, *Real People.*

Former *Laugh-In* producer George Schlatter developed *Real People* as a stage for non-celebrities, "real people" who were presented to be as amusing, talented, and entertaining as any showbiz figures. This was the same world of American backroads visited by such reporters as Charles Kuralt, whose stories usually served as an off-beat closing feature for the network news. *Real People* strung together a series of such reports and anecdotes on unusual individuals in strange situations, focusing as much on the personality of the visiting correspondents as on the "ordinary folks" being interviewed. Schlatter enlisted a large cast of entertaining personalities to act as co-hosts, correspondents, and regular guests, including (for the first season) Fred Willard, Jimmy Breslin, Mark Russell, John Barbour, Sarah Purcell, Bill Rafferty, and Skip Stephenson. He also took a cue from Allen Funt's old *Candid Camera* series and set up the show itself as the playback stage for the films and tapes of their stunts and interviews, presented to a studio audience for laughs and applause. These feature reports included such subjects as an all-male swimsuit competition judged by women, a man in San Francisco named Sherlock Bones who

The *60 Minutes* team: *(clockwise from top)* Dan Rather, Harry Reasoner, Mike Wallace, and Morley Safer. *(CBS News Photo/CBS Photo Archive © 2003 CBS Worldwide, Inc. All Rights Reserved.)*

September 10, 1979

Tinker, Tailor, Soldier, Spy. (BBC-2). Alec Guinness is outstanding in this seven-hour miniseries as low-key spy master George Smiley, brought back from a forced retirement to find a "mole" in the British intelligence service (dubbed the "Circus"). Produced by Jonathan Powell, it arrives in the U.S. in September 1980 on PBS's *Great Performances* series.

September 12, 1979

Shelley Hack, who appeared in commercials for "Charlie" perfume, replaces Kate Jackson as one of Charlie's Angels.

September 13, 1979

Benson. (ABC). Robert Guillaume takes his butler character, Benson, from *Soap* to the household of a bumbling governor.

September 23, 1979

Archie Bunker's Place. (CBS). A revamped *All in the Family,* set at Archie's tavern. Martin Balsam joins as Murray, Archie's Jewish partner, and Anne Meara plays the new chef, Veronica.

September 23, 1979

The Associates. (ABC). James L. Brooks, Stan Daniels, and Ed. Weinberger (from *Taxi*) create an engaging ensemble sitcom set at a powerful Wall Street law firm. Even with a cast including Martin Short, Tim Thomerson, Joe Regalbuto, and Wilfrid Hyde-White (and a theme song played by B. B. King), the show is a ratings flop.

September 29, 1979

Paris. (CBS). James Earl Jones stars as Woody Paris, a black police detective in an unnamed urban setting. At night, Paris moonlights as a professor of criminology at the local university. While earning good reviews, this series, produced by Steven Bochco for MTM, is axed in January.

October 8, 1979

David Brinkley gives up his co-anchor chores on *NBC Nightly News* and is again reduced to only occasional commentary.

November 4, 1979

Three days before Senator Edward Kennedy announces his candidacy for president, "Teddy" airs on *CBS Reports.* Roger Mudd's extended interview catches the "last Kennedy son" surprisingly unclear as to why he even wants to be president, damaging his image at the start of his campaign.

December 6, 1979

World premiere of "Star Trek—The Motion Picture," first in a series of theatrical films based on the 1960s TV show.

---

upward and by Christmas of 1979, the show had sneaked into the top thirty, occasionally beating ABC's *Eight Is Enough* in the time slot. As *Real People* caught on, all three networks were quick to launch copies, turning the format into a programming fad labeled "reality shows."

Alan Landsburg, creator of the pseudo-scientific syndicated access show *In Search Of* (which examined such topics as witchcraft and UFOs), produced *That's Incredible* for ABC. This mid-season entry harkened back to Robert Ripley's *Believe It or Not,* showing "incredible" occurrences that affected real people such as a forest ranger hit by lightning seven times, a woman who allowed herself to be covered with bees, and a Minnesota policeman who reported seeing a UFO. Hosts John Davidson, Cathy Lee Crosby, and Fran Tarkenton presented the stories in an upbeat casual style of wide-eyed amazement ("That's incredible!"). *That's Incredible* turned in incredible ratings, placing in the season's top ten shows, even ahead of *Real People.* Landsburg followed up *That's Incredible* with *Those Amazing Animals,* a similar series for ABC that focused on "incredible" events in the animal kingdom, and *No Holds Barred,* a brief late night CBS show that copied the *Real People* formula but aimed it toward the *Saturday Night Live* audience. CBS also turned to veteran game show producers Mark Goodson and Bill Todman for a reality show update of *What's My Line* called *That's My Line.* The refurbished program did away with the original's celebrity panel and presented instead on-the-scene reports of real people with oddball occupations.

In spite of the success of *Real People,* NBC had disappointing results with its subsequent follow-up reality shows. The in-house *Games People Play* lasted just four months, presenting real people participating in so-called "trash sports" such as beer chugging, tug-of-war, and bar bouncer competition. George Schlatter's outlet for the *vox populi, Speak Up, America,* ran only a few episodes with a format that offered real people throughout the country the opportunity to speak up on the issues of the day. However, the deliberate mix of news, public affairs, and entertainment inherent in such a show stirred unease among the network's affiliates.

Even with such problems, NBC embraced the reality formula because the network needed some kind of breakthrough in its campaign to climb from the ratings cellar. Nonetheless, going into the fall of 1979, it was still no match for the powerhouse line-up at ABC, which looked as if it would continue to roll right over the competition. Not only were there such returning top ten hits as *Happy Days, Three's Company, Laverne and Shirley, Taxi, Mork and Mindy,* and *The Ropers* (a successful spring spinoff from *Three's Company*), but the network also had the World Series in October and the Winter Olympic Games in February. There seemed no way ABC could lose.

Buoyed by such assumptions, network president Fred Pierce and chief programmer Tony Thomopoulos confidently decided to go for the kill and move some of ABC's big hits (*Mork and Mindy, Laverne and Shirley, Fantasy Island,* and *The Ropers*) to other nights in order to spread ABC's ratings strength over all seven nights, and obtain an even larger ratings lead. Though this tactic went against the traditional network strategy of not tampering with established successes, it was not really regarded as that much of a risk. After all, the programs could always be moved back.

The poor performance of some of CBS's unsuccessful new fall sitcoms (*Working Stiffs, The Last Resort,* and *Struck by Lightning*) only seemed to underscore the security of ABC's position. Yet in the first week of the new season, NBC finished on top due to Fred Silverman's front-loading with blockbuster movies and specials. NBC also won the third week, due to the baseball playoffs and the prime time broadcast of Johnny Carson's 17th anniversary on the

---

searched for lost pets, and even a *Candid Camera*-type skit featuring real shoppers being asked their opinion of a foul-tasting "new" drink as if they were part of a commercial. (When they thought the camera was on, they praised the drink; when they thought the camera was off, they made faces and admitted it was awful.)

Real People represented one of NBC's few moderate successes from its 1978–79 "revolving door" season, capturing just enough viewers during a six-episode spring run to win renewal for the fall of 1979. Without much fanfare, the ratings for *Real People* crept

Tonight show. At the same time, ABC's former hits were slipping in their new time slots, sometimes dropping completely out of the top twenty. ABC recovered somewhat and pulled into the lead for the season by the fifth week as NBC used up its blockbuster specials and faded. CBS, however, quickly cut off some of its dead weight new shows and bounced back as well, moving ahead of NBC by mid-November and breathing down ABC's neck by Christmas. Part of the reason for this immediate rebound by CBS was the sudden surge by the network's Friday night Southern soul mates, *The Dukes of Hazzard* and *Dallas.*

Dallas began as a little-noticed spring series in April 1978, a product of the Lorimar company (which also turned out *The Waltons*). The program was a high-powered classy soap opera, presenting the oil-rich world of the burgeoning sunbelt as the locale of the Ewing clan, owners of a powerful energy empire. Though each episode of *Dallas* could stand on its own, the series also played like a spicy soap opera, with continuing story threads winding in and out all season. Aging John "Jock" Ewing (Jim Davis) was the nominal boss of the company, but he was being steadily usurped by his crafty oldest son, John Jr., better known as J. R. (Larry Hagman.) J. R. was determined to keep as much control as possible over the family business, and he was more than willing to use anyone and anything to increase his personal power and Ewing Oil's profits. In fact, he rather enjoyed stepping on other people. He blithely ignored his high-strung wife, Sue Ellen (Linda Gray), and boldly carried on an affair with Kristin (Mary Crosby), Sue Ellen's sister. Yet, when Kristin tried to turn the tables and have her own affair on the side, J. R. barged into the bedroom, smiled at the couple in bed, and coolly telephoned the boss of Kristin's lover, having the interloper fired on the spot.

Jock's younger and more principled son, Bobby (Patrick Duffy), was married to Pamela Barnes (Victoria Principal), the daughter of "Digger" Barnes (David Wayne, and later, Keenan Wynn), Jock's former partner turned arch-enemy. Pamela's brother, Cliff (Ken Kercheval), carried on the family feud by waging a war against the Ewing empire from his post in Texas state government. The youngest Ewing, Lucy (Charlene Tilton), Jock's granddaughter (and daughter of the exiled Ewing son, Gary), spent her time seducing Ewing ranch hands and flirting with any other men who passed by. Only the Ewing matriarch, "Miss" Ellie (Barbara Bel Geddes), held no grudge against another main character, and she always acted as confidante and peacemaker.

What made *Dallas* stand out from other soap operas (including recent prime time failures such as *Executive Suite* and *Big Hawaii*) was its Texas locale (where myths of the old West clashed with the reality of modern day business morals) and the character of J. R. Most glossy soap operas focused on admirable, if somewhat flawed, heroes. J. R. was bad and mean and no good and he knew it. He was a villain people loved to hate, and his personal manipulations added an electricity to *Dallas* that attracted viewers who kept tuning in just to see what J. R. would dare try next.

At first CBS did not quite know what to do with *Dallas,* shifting the show a few times before settling on a Friday night slot beginning in January 1979. There it was teamed with another new Southern-based CBS show, *The Dukes of Hazzard,* a slick television equivalent to the popular 1977 Burt Reynolds film, "Smokey and the Bandit."

The Dukes of Hazzard presented life in the rural South as just good fun with fast cars, beautiful women, and moonshine whiskey. Plots for the shows were simple: Cousins Luke Duke (Tom Wopat) and Bo Duke (John Schneider) and their curvaceous female kin Daisy Duke (Catherine Bach) were out to have a good time in Hazzard county, despite constant run-ins with the corrupt local power boss, J. D. Hogg (Sorrell Booke) and his bumbling police force, sheriff Rosco Coltrane (James Best) and deputy Enos Strate (Sonny Shroyer). The two Duke boys were on probation (from some trumped-up charge) so they had to watch their step, and they never did anything really bad. They were what country singer and program narrator Waylon Jennings described as "good ol' boys fightin' the system." *The Dukes of Hazzard* pulled off its simple, good-timey premise with light-hearted scripts, a colorful cast, up-beat country music, and non-stop car chases and car crashes.

Dallas and *The Dukes of Hazzard* complemented each other well and made a perfect back-to-back Friday night double feature. One month into their partnership, both shows were into the top thirty. By the end of the 1978–79 season, both were in the top twenty. In the fall of 1979, the team kept rising, and both shows broke into the top ten. CBS had already built winning lineups on Sunday and Monday going into the new season, so the *Dallas-*

March 4, 1980
The Big Show. (NBC). Nick Vanoff, who produced *The Hollywood Palace*, flops with more old style vaudeo, featuring ninety minutes of singing, dancing, swimming, skating, and comedy.

March 11, 1980
United States. (NBC). Larry Gelbart, the co-creator of *M*A*S*H*, tries a unique thirty-minute comedy on marriage (starring Beau Bridges and Helen Shaver) reminiscent of Ingmar Bergman's "Scenes from a Marriage" for Swedish TV. The program runs without an opening theme or laugh track, devoting most of each episode to conversations about life, death, and sex.

March 15, 1980
Sanford. (NBC). Redd Foxx returns as Fred Sanford, sans son, but with a rich girlfriend.

April 11, 1980
Fridays. (ABC). In a blatant copy of NBC's *Saturday Night Live,* ABC brings together nine young unknowns (including Larry David and Michael Richards) to serve as the troupe for a seventy-minute live comedy show from Los Angeles.

May 8, 1980
CBS chairman William Paley fires John Backe, his heir apparent. Thomas Wyman is named the new president and chief executive officer of CBS, Inc.

June 1, 1980
Ted Turner's Cable News Network begins twenty-four hours a day of television news.

June 23, 1980
David Letterman Show. (NBC). Frequent *Tonight* show substitute host David Letterman receives his own ninety-minute morning variety show. His off-the-cuff esoteric humor does not click in daytime, though. After trimming the show to sixty minutes on August 4, NBC drops it entirely at the end of October.

June 30, 1980
John Davidson Show. Group W dumps Mike Douglas as host of its syndicated talk show for the younger Davidson. Douglas keeps his show going by syndicating it himself.

Dukes of Hazzard combination gave the network three consistently strong nights. This was one of the main reasons CBS rebounded so fast from its weak fall start.

For ABC, something was wrong. The network's seemingly invulnerable position had crumbled practically overnight. Boosted by the World Series and hit movies such as "Jaws," ABC held on to first place in the cumulative ratings through January, though CBS won the November ratings sweeps. A season that was supposed to be a rout for ABC had turned into a neck-and-neck race.

Fred Silverman had observed, going into the 1979–80 season, that he expected ABC to fade soon because the network was repeating its most frequent sin, overworking hit formulas. When he had been with ABC, Silverman had stressed diversity in programming (from *Three's Company* to *Family*) and even raised a few eyebrows by canceling shows that were still ratings winners (*The Bionic Woman* and *Wonder Woman*) because he felt they had peaked. Now ABC seemed determined to produce as many teen-oriented sitcoms as possible, while banking on the success of all its older series to continue undiminished. Even the homespun *Mork and Mindy* found itself tinted with titillation in episodes featuring Mork as a Dallas Cowboy cheerleader and Raquel Welch as a sexy alien. Silverman explained that when viewers at last tired of ABC, they would not so much tire of particular shows as of the approach taken by the entire schedule.

Equally important to ABC's slippage, though, was the miscalculation by Fred Pierce and Tony Thomopoulos on the drawing power of particular hit shows. Viewers did not automatically follow them to different nights and different times, so all the programs dropped in their new slots, some immediately, some after a few weeks. (*Mork and Mindy* dropped as low as 41st in the ratings one week; in another, *Laverne and Shirley* sank to 51st.) ABC shifted *Fantasy Island* back to its previous Saturday slot almost immediately and the show regained much of its ratings strength. The network doggedly stuck with its other shifts awhile longer, and that was a fatal mistake.

CBS had made similar scheduling moves in the 1978–79 season, rearranging several moderate hits in mid-season to build strength on other nights. In the process, *The White Shadow*, *One Day at a Time*, and *The Incredible Hulk* lost their audience and practically dropped from sight. CBS quickly saw its mistake and, within a month, moved them all back to their previous slots, thereby saving the shows.

In the fall of 1979, CBS yanked its fall flops from the schedule right away (in addition to its three unsuccessful sitcoms, that also included three hour-long series, *Paris, California Fever,* and *Big Shamus, Little Shamus*). Some were gone by the beginning of October. ABC, on the other hand, took until February to finish its moves. By then, shows such as *Laverne and Shirley* and *Mork and Mindy* had lost much of their ratings luster and needed time to rebuild even in their old slot. To have former top five shows occasionally in the Nielsen basement dragged down the entire ABC schedule and CBS pulled ahead in January.

One important reason for ABC's inability to move quickly, cut its losses, and bring in new shows was that the network had failed to develop adequate back-up strength. Earlier in the decade, CBS had fallen from first place for much the same reason: While comfortably on top, it had not built up a solid inventory of replacement shows. CBS, however, had also learned its lesson. In the 1978–79 season, the network was ready with *The White Shadow* and *The Dukes of Hazzard* as early winter replacements. This season, CBS displayed more of its valuable "bench strength" at the end of 1979 by quickly replacing failed series with two strong new shows:

Knots Landing (a *Dallas* spinoff set in California, with Ted Shackelford as Gary Ewing, the exiled son) and *House Calls* (a hospital comedy starring Wayne Rogers and Lynn Redgrave and based on a hit movie of the same name). Both series became solid hits and kept up the CBS momentum. In April, CBS temporarily replaced *House Calls* with yet another strong series, *Flo* (a spinoff from *Alice*), which immediately jumped into the top ten as well.

ABC, in contrast, had only one big new mid-season hit, *That's Incredible. Tenspeed and Brownshoe,* a well produced new cop show, flashed into the top ten after an intense publicity boost surrounding its premiere, but then faded before the characters had time to catch on. *240-Robert* (a pale copy of *CHiPs* and *Emergency*), *B.A.D. Cats* (worse than *240-Robert*), and a condescending blue collar sitcom, *When the Whistle Blows* (worst of them all), were tremendous flops.

Still, ABC planned to hang on for the season by riding the Winter Olympics ratings boost, then heavily promoting its key series as they returned to their previous hit slots and plugging in special blockbuster movies. The February Olympics did put ABC back in the lead, but, by March, CBS was rolling with solid performances on Sunday, Monday, and Friday. Veterans such as *Archie Bunker's Place* (the renamed *All in the Family*), *Alice,* and *The Jeffersons* were once again top ten hits. MTM shows such as *Lou Grant*, *WKRP in Cincinnati,* and *The White Shadow* were also doing well. And then CBS's Friday night headliners exploded.

As the battle for the top spot in network television moved into the spring, *Dallas* and *The Dukes of Hazzard* became the hottest shows on the air, sometimes finishing first and second in the weekly ratings. *Dallas* pumped up fresh viewer interest by closing out its new episodes for the season with the shooting of the dastardly J. R. by a mysterious assailant. Reruns began the following week and many new *Dallas* viewers, lured by the closing episode, stayed put to fill in character background and catch up on the plot lines and setups they had missed from earlier in the season.

Armed with this line-up of hits, CBS closed the gap on ABC and the two were in a dead heat going into the final week of the regular season (which ended April 20). The cumulative ratings victory rested on the performance of a few blockbuster specials. ABC opened strong on Monday, April 14, with the number one show of the week, the annual Academy Awards program hosted by Johnny Carson. CBS neutralized this by scoring big on Tuesday and Wednesday with the surprisingly well-done miniseries, *Guyana Tragedy: The Story of Jim Jones.* On Friday, ABC put in "The Best of *That's Incredible,*" a special edition of its only new big hit. It all came down to the last day, Sunday, April 20. ABC pulled out one of its champion theatrical films, "The Sting," for an encore performance. CBS countered with a special new two-hour episode of *The Dukes of Hazzard.* The downhome Hazzard County crew beat the con men from Chicago. CBS won the night, the week, and the season. The final seasonal averages for the networks were CBS: 19.6; ABC: 19.5; and NBC: 17.4. CBS held a party to celebrate its first regular season win since the 1975–76 season, and network chairman William Paley called it one of his "sweetest victories."

In one season, CBS had outscored and outmaneuvered the competition with a varied, versatile schedule ranging from the high gloss soap of *Dallas* to the serious character drama of *Lou Grant.* Yet, this dramatic turnaround also underscored how volatile the network standings had become. Even with one of CBS's strongest line-ups in years, there was little chance that victory in the 1979–80 season, however sweet, marked the beginning of another twenty-five year reign at the top by CBS.

40. The Strike

FOR MORE THAN THREE YEARS, NBC's strategy for becoming the number one network hinged on the 1980 Summer Olympic Games. In February 1977, even before luring Fred Silverman from ABC, NBC had won the rights to the contests (the first to be held in the Soviet Union) by committing a record-breaking $100 million in its bid. This broke down to approximately $22.4 million for the actual television rights, $50 million for the production facilities in Moscow, $12.6 million to the International Olympic Committee, and $12–$15 million for such miscellaneous items as talent and transportation.

There was a very good reason for this expenditure: The 1976 Olympics had helped push ABC to the number one slot. Even though the Summer Games took place before the annual ratings battle began for the regular season, they had provided a tremendous opportunity for ABC to promote its upcoming fall schedule. NBC counted on doing the same in 1980, while also treating its overall Olympic coverage as an on-going "big event" with frequent on-the-air promotions. When Fred Silverman joined NBC in 1978, he paced his plans toward the summer and fall of 1980, aiming to have ready a strong program line-up that could ride the momentum of the Olympics and bring NBC to the top by Christmas 1980.

To coincide with its huge investment, NBC signed ABC's 1976 Olympics producer, Don Ohlmeyer, to supervise both the actual coverage in 1980 and the necessary preparations by NBC's sports department. Ohlmeyer's first NBC project was *Sportsworld,* a weekend afternoon sports anthology modeled after ABC's *Wide World of Sports,* that arrived at the start of 1978. This new program gave NBC's sports production crews the opportunity to sharpen their technical skills while providing the network with the perfect on-air promotional forum to talk up Olympic-type competitive events.

As 1980 drew nearer, NBC also scheduled a host of other tie-in programs, ranging from specials such as the animated "Animalympics" to the NBC-financed movie "Goldengirl" featuring Susan Anton as an American track star at the Moscow games. Ohlmeyer himself produced a four-hour made-for-TV movie on the Summer Olympics, "The Golden Moment." NBC announced plans for 152½ hours of Olympic coverage in 1980, pre-empting most of its prime time schedule from July 18 through August 5. Then, on Christmas day 1979, the entire NBC Olympics project was put in jeopardy as the Soviet Union invaded Afghanistan.

The Russian invasion shocked and angered many Americans who were already frustrated by the continuing stalemate over the hostages taken in the seizure of the American embassy in Iran the previous month. Looking for some way (short of war) to protest the Soviet move, many people focused on the Summer Olympic Games in Moscow as a symbolic rallying point and they began to call for a boycott of the event. On January 20, 1980, President Jimmy Carter appeared on NBC's *Meet the Press* and expressed his support for such a move. He said that unless the Soviets withdrew their forces from Afghanistan by February 20, he would formally request the U.S. Olympic Committee to officially sanction a boycott. Many athletes, who had been training years for the games, disagreed with that course of action, saying that it unfairly mixed sports and politics in violation of the true spirit of Olympic competition.

While everyone watched for the next move by the Soviets, the 1980 Winter Olympics went on as scheduled in Lake Placid, New York, running from February 12 through 24 and carried by ABC. The ratings were even better than ABC's successful 1976 Winter Olympics coverage, culminating in a dramatic face-off between the Soviet Union and the United States, on ice. There, for the first time in twenty years, the U.S. hockey team beat the Russians, eliminating them from the Olympic championship series. A video tape replay of the game placed as the number four program of the week and, two days later, the U.S. team went on to beat Finland for the gold medal in hockey.

In the jubilation over the American victory, many people opposed to the boycott were quick to point out that the Winter Olympics seemed a perfect illustration of why the United States should participate in the Summer Games: Confrontations could take place in the sports arena rather than on the battlefield. Nonetheless, the Soviet troops remained in Afghanistan into the spring and, on April 22, the U.S. Olympic Committee voted 1,604 to 797 in favor of the resolution calling for a boycott. Though individual athletes were not specifically ordered to stay home, the committee's vote meant that there would be no official U.S. team sent to Moscow and, therefore, no funds available to defray the tremendous cost of participating.

Throughout the months of public debate on the boycott, NBC found itself in a difficult position and deliberately kept a low profile. Because the Soviets said that the Olympics would go on even without U.S. participation, NBC could still carry them. Realistically, however, such a move would have been a public relations fiasco. The network's financial investment in the games had been widely reported and to go through with coverage while the athletes

	8:00	8:30	9:00	9:30	10:00	10:30	
MON	That's Incredible		ABC NFL Monday Night Football (to 12 Midnight)				**ABC**
	Flo	LADIES' MAN	M*A*S*H	House Calls	Lou Grant		**CBS**
	Little House On The Prairie		NBC Monday Night At The Movies				**NBC**
TUE	Happy Days	Laverne And Shirley	Three's Company	TOO CLOSE FOR COMFORT	Hart To Hart		**ABC**
	The White Shadow		CBS Tuesday Night Movies				**CBS**
	NBC Tuesday Night At The Movies				STEVE ALLEN COMEDY HOUR		**NBC**
WED	Eight Is Enough		Taxi	Soap	Vega$		**ABC**
	ENOS		CBS Wednesday Night Movies				**CBS**
	Real People		Diff'rent Strokes	The Facts Of Life	Quincy, M.E.		**NBC**
THR	Mork And Mindy	BOSOM BUDDIES	Barney Miller	IT'S A LIVING	20/20		**ABC**
	The Waltons		MAGNUM, P.I.		Knots Landing		**CBS**
	GAMES PEOPLE PLAY		NBC Thursday Night At The Movies				**NBC**
FRI	Benson	I'M A BIG GIRL NOW	The ABC Friday Night Movie				**ABC**
	The Incredible Hulk		The Dukes Of Hazzard		Dallas		**CBS**
	MARIE		NUMBER 96		NBC MAGAZINE WITH DAVID BRINKLEY		**NBC**
SAT	BREAKING AWAY		The Love Boat		Fantasy Island		**ABC**
	WKRP In Cincinnati	Tim Conway Show	FREEBIE AND THE BEAN		SECRETS OF MIDLAND HEIGHTS		**CBS**
	BARBARA MANDRELL AND THE MANDRELL SISTERS		NBC Saturday Night At The Movies				**NBC**

	7:00	7:30	8:00	8:30	9:00	9:30	10:00	10:30	
SUN	THOSE AMAZING ANIMALS		Charlie's Angels		The ABC Sunday Night Movie				**ABC**
	60 Minutes		Archie Bunker's Place	One Day At A Time	Alice	The Jeffersons	Trapper John, M.D.		**CBS**
	Disney's Wonderful World		CHiPs		The Sunday Big Event				**NBC**

themselves were forced to stay home would have appeared to be the height of cynical self-interest.

In May, NBC announced that its far-flung summer Olympics programming would be drastically cut back. Because the U.S. Olympic Committee decided to go through the formality of naming an Olympic squad, NBC did cover those team trials in the spring and early summer. For the actual games in Moscow, though, NBC limited itself to short feature reports (running about ninety seconds each) during the nightly news. This was virtually indistinguishable from the short clips and summaries offered by ABC and CBS as well as other news organizations. A few individual stations went even further and specifically ignored *any* Olympic news, refusing even to mention winners in major events or new world records. Though most news organizations did not go to that extreme, for most television viewers it was as if the 1980 Summer Olympics never took place.

NBC lost more than $50 million in ad revenue as well as money already spent in preparations. There was not even a chance to rebound four years later. ABC had already won the bidding for the rights to both the Summer and Winter Olympic Games in 1984. Above all, NBC had lost the promotional vehicle it had counted on for more than three years. Fred Silverman and NBC had been done in by events totally outside their control.

Just a few days after the Moscow Olympics began, though, there was another development outside network control, but this one disrupted all three networks. On July 21, 1980, the members of the American Federation of Television and Radio Artists and the Screen Actors Guild went out on strike. This halted production on theatrical films, made-for-TV movies, and most prime time filmed and taped series. The central issue of the strike was a desire by the unions to win for their members a share of the money earned by producers upon the distribution of programs via pay television systems and prerecorded video cassettes and video discs.

Everyone involved recognized the precedent-setting importance of the negotiations. At the time, actors received nothing from cable, cassette, or disc sales, yet, since the mid-1970s, use of these alternate television systems had begun to grow. Any new contract would serve as a model for future arrangements both by the actors and other craft unions. Both sides therefore approached the contract talks very carefully and, as a result, an immediate settlement was unlikely. Negotiations dragged on through the remainder of the summer while celebrities walked the picket lines.

When the strike began, the companies supplying program material for the networks were just a few weeks into production for the 1980–81 season and had only a handful of shows "in the can." As September approached, it became clear that, for the first time in television history, the networks would have to begin the new season without most of their regular series.

Though the strike virtually shut down Hollywood, there were a number of areas unaffected. Performers appearing in commercials, news programs, game shows, sports broadcasts, afternoon soap operas, and variety shows all operated under different contracts. Programs such as *Tonight, 60 Minutes, Monday Night Football,* and *Real People* could go on as usual. The networks were forced to improvise with what was available for the fall, carefully mixing variety specials, theatrical films, sports events, selected reruns, and the few series episodes completed before the strike began.

By chance, number three NBC appeared to be in the best shape to handle the strike season, which seemed a perverse form of justice to balance its Olympic disaster. NBC had a backlog of both old and new miniseries and "big event" presentations to draw from, including the twenty-five hour *Centennial* from 1978, the combined *Godfather Saga* from 1977, and a new twelve-hour miniseries, an adaptation of James Clavell's novel, *Shogun.* In addition, the network's "reality shows" such as *Real People* were unaffected, and it even had ready a good number of completed episodes from popular series (including four of *CHiPs* and six of *Little House on the Prairie*). NBC also had the World Series and, if the strike dragged into 1981, the Super Bowl.

With such strong inventory, Fred Silverman went into September very aggressively, touting the NBC schedule as being 75%–80% new material through October. CBS and ABC, more reliant on weekly sitcom and drama series than NBC, were not as fortunate. Though ABC featured its own reality shows (*Those Amazing Animals* and *That's Incredible*) and reran its 1978 miniseries of *Pearl* during the usual September premiere period, the network essentially continued its summer rerun schedule, occasionally using episodes that were several years old. CBS was squeezed even tighter. Though the network had a few new "pre-strike" episodes of *Lou Grant* and *The White Shadow,* some of its other top series such as *M*A*S*H* and *Archie Bunker's Place* had already parceled out all but the preceding season's shows into rerun syndication. In addition, short-run winter and spring replacement hits such as *Flo* and *House Calls* had only a handful of episodes at all, and those had already been rerun in the summer. Thus, CBS had to scrap most of its schedule and rely instead on elongated movie presentations and reruns of specials.

NBC sensed the potential for a big victory. Even before the strike, Silverman had planned to open the 1980–81 season with a week of *Shogun.* He stood by that timetable, figuring that the miniseries could be practically unbeatable without front line series competition from the other networks. Silverman's calculations were correct. The five episodes of *Shogun* ranked as the top five shows of the first week of the "new" season, giving NBC the highest rated week in its history. *Shogun* became the second highest miniseries ever at the time, right behind *Roots.*

Unlike *Roots* or *Holocaust,* which focused on generations and families, *Shogun* was the story of one man's personal struggle. Richard Chamberlain played the hero, an English sea pilot named John Blackthorne, who found himself shipwrecked in Japan during the early 1600s. Facing vast cultural differences, as well as complex political and religious intrigue, Blackthorne slowly adapted his Western instincts to the Eastern traditions. The Englishman befriended Toranaga (Toshiro Mifune), a Japanese warlord aspiring to be the supreme military dictator (or "shogun") of the country, and fell in love with his translator, the beautiful Mariko (Yoko Shimada). Along the way, Blackthorne also proved himself in combat and won acceptance in his new land, becoming the first non-Japanese samurai warrior. *Shogun* was an entertaining combination of exotic settings, beautiful photography, a love triangle, and bursts of violence. The program was challenging, effective, and, much to NBC's delight, an overwhelming success, giving the network a big lead to open the season.

The week after *Shogun,* the striking unions reached a tentative settlement with the producers. However, there still remained two or three weeks for ratification by the rank and file, and then about three or four more weeks before the first new shows would be ready to air. So the ad hoc strike schedule continued until the beginning of November, with new shows, new specials, sports, and theatrical films generally outdrawing rerun competition. ABC's NFL *Monday Night Football* had the best opening ratings in its history. Both the baseball playoffs (on ABC) and the World Series (on NBC) also earned record-high ratings. CBS's highly publicized made-for-TV movie about a Jewish woman in a Nazi concentration camp, "Playing for Time" (starring Vanessa Redgrave), scored as the number one show of its week, giving CBS its only weekly win during the strike.

At the beginning of October, the actors ratified the tentative agreement and, on October 6, series production resumed. For the immediate future, the settlement provided actors with a pay rate boost of 33% for prime time reruns. In the developing new video fields, there were important precedents established: Performers were granted 4.5% of the distributor's gross for the first year of a show's play on pay TV, and 4.5% of the producer's gross on prerecorded video disc and video cassette sales above 100,000 units. Though such provisions did not result in any immediate cash, they promised performers a share in the expanding video industries that could eventually prove lucrative. Looking even further ahead, the new pact acknowledged the likelihood that as more and more material was required by cable services, cable programmers would have to follow the route taken by the commercial networks years before and begin to develop original movies, variety specials, and even continuing dramatic, adventure, and comedy series to supplement their basic late 1970s schedule of uncut movies and sporting events. All that was years away, though. The immediate focus following the settlement was to turn out new material for the season already in progress as quickly as possible.

The networks' post-strike schedules in October, November, and December were almost as confusing as the strike period because not every returning series followed the same production timetable. Half-hour videotaped programs were ready much faster than hour-long filmed series, so the networks had to continue to improvise, plugging the holes in their schedules as the shows became available. There were other disruptions as well, including election coverage, the November sweeps, and holiday specials for Thanksgiving and Christmas. As a result, some season premieres were practically buried and did not produce the expected instant jump in the ratings. It was not until January 1981 that the schedules settled down at last. Despite NBC's success during the strike season, though, it was CBS that came out on top, once again propelled by *Dallas.*

CBS had done the worst of the networks during the strike because it did not have as extensive a backlog of flashy "event" programming as NBC. More important, this weak start threatened to scuttle CBS's game plan for the entire season because it diffused the momentum of the network's strong come-from-behind victory in the 1979–80 season. CBS had planned to start the 1980–81 season with its winning schedule in place and quickly build its previous razor-thin victory into a healthy lead. The strike nullified those plans and gave NBC the initiative instead. CBS could only sit on the side and wait.

Once the strike ended and program production resumed, CBS set out to quickly win back the audience. Its first move, in mid-October, was to rebuild interest in *Dallas* by rerunning episodes from the show's initial tryout as a 1978 spring series. This innovative ploy worked. Few current *Dallas* fans had followed the series

September 9, 1980

The FCC creates "secondary stations," a new technical classification that sets up the possibility for thousands of new low-powered local television stations.

September 16, 1980

As part of Johnny Carson's new contract with NBC, *Tonight* shrinks to sixty minutes. Tom Snyder's *Tomorrow* expands to ninety minutes to take up the half-hour slack.

October 25, 1980

ABC's *Love Boat* and *Fantasy Island* are the first series to get new episodes on the air after the strike settlement.

October 28, 1980

President Jimmy Carter debates Republican challenger Ronald Reagan in Cleveland before a television audience of forty-six million.

November 2, 1980

In the season premiere of *Archie Bunker's Place,* Archie comes to grips with the death of his wife, Edith. This realistic plot development evolved from Jean Stapleton's desire to leave the series for good.

November 4, 1980

NBC's use of strategic exit polls helps it to call Ronald Reagan the winner in the presidential election at 8:15 P.M. Eastern time, beating ABC's announcement by more than ninety minutes and CBS's by more than two hours.

November 15, 1980

Under new producer Jean Doumanian, the "next generation" of *Saturday Night Live* debuts with a new cast of six unknowns, but the refurbished program fails to gel. After only four months, NBC installs another producer (Dick Ebersol) and revamps both the crew and format, with only two cast holdovers: Joe Piscopo and Eddie Murphy.

November 17, 1980

Roger Mudd, passed over by CBS as Walter Cronkite's successor, defects to NBC News.

---

in its original run and the ratings for the program remained strong. Then, going into November, CBS began to rekindle the "Who shot J. R.?" mania that had started with the season finale of *Dallas* the previous spring. Since then, the program had turned into a worldwide sensation. In Britain there was spirited betting on the identity of the assailant, with odds quoted at 20 to 1 that J. R. shot himself.

To open November, CBS staged "*Dallas* week," airing four episodes of the program in one week (one on Thursday, two on Friday, and one on Sunday). The first two were reruns of the final episodes from the previous season, featuring some of J. R.'s dirtiest deals and culminating in his shooting. This effectively set the stage for the two-part season premiere in which doctors rushed to save J. R.'s life. All four episodes finished in the top ten (coming in at number one, two, four, and nine for the week). The regular Friday episode the following week continued the story, dangling spurious clues and suspects. This also finished number one. With interest once again at a peak, the answer to the burning question "Who shot J. R.?" came at last on Friday, November 21. In the closing moments of the program, Kristin, J. R.'s mistress and personal secretary, confessed that she had done it.

A record number of viewers tuned in to find out the answer,

sending *Dallas* through the ratings roof. With a 53.3 rating and a 76 share, it became the highest rated individual show in television history to that point, topping such sports events as the Super Bowl and World Series and previous TV milestones including the birth of Little Ricky on *I Love Lucy,* the final episode of *The Fugitive,* and even the concluding segment of the original *Roots.*

Dallas stayed at the front of the television ratings pack for the remainder of the season as its many new viewers stuck around to follow the plot complications introduced while J. R. recovered. As CBS's other regular series fell into place, the network wiped out its ratings deficit from the strike period and by mid-December passed both ABC and NBC in the cumulative ratings race, eventually winning the entire 1980–81 season with relative ease.

One reason that NBC, which had taken the ratings lead during the strike, fell so quickly from the top was that the network could not match CBS's line-up of established hit series. Yet, for a while, it looked as if NBC at least had a chance at making a respectable showing for second place overall by following an innovative three-phase post-strike plan. First, in November, Fred Silverman quickly set in place NBC's strongest night, Wednesday, bringing back *Facts of Life*, *Diff'rent Strokes,* and *Quincy* to follow the hit *Real People.* For phase two, he held back most of NBC's other returning shows and new series while ABC and CBS slotted theirs, filling in with short-run series instead. One of these, a variety hour starring country singer Barbara Mandrell, proved successful enough to win instant renewal in January.

At the beginning of January, Silverman launched phase three and brought in the remainder of NBC's regular series. Because CBS and ABC had just finished their delayed fall premieres, NBC had a second-season type limelight all to itself. For the first five weeks of 1981, the NBC strategy seemed to be working as the network beat out ABC and came in second four times. Returning (and revamped) programs such as *Lobo, BJ and the Bear,* and *Buck Rogers* all did well in elongated two-hour openers, and new series such as *Flamingo Road* and *Harper Valley P.T.A.* turned in respectable ratings.

NBC's three-phase post-strike strategy gave Fred Silverman a chance to demonstrate his greatest strength: effectively juggling hit programs on a schedule in order to entice viewers to give the other shows on the network a chance. However, though such Silverman favorites as *Real People* and *Diff'rent Strokes* had caught on, NBC still had not developed a sufficient number of solid series to fill the entire schedule. In many cases, once viewers were lured to NBC, they found little to keep them there. Instead, NBC still had to depend on big events and specials both to buy time for shows to catch on and also to fill between hits. Here, ironically, Silverman's successful strike strategy took its toll.

In presenting a mostly new schedule during the actors' strike, NBC had not only drawn from its backlog of material, it had also aired many blockbuster movies and specials normally kept until the ratings sweeps periods. This tactic put NBC in a very vulnerable position, particularly during the February sweeps. While CBS had such top theatrical movies as "Hooper" (with Burt Reynolds) and "The Amityville Horror," and ABC aired "Norma Rae" and "Jaws 2," NBC was left with tepid made-for-TV films such as "Kent State" and "Elvis and the Beauty Queen." Worse yet, with a shortage of attractive event programming, NBC was forced to throw its regular series against such ABC specials as the three-part, eight-hour sexy miniseries *East of Eden* and the flashy made-for-TV movie "Miracle on Ice" (recreating America's 1980 Olympic hockey triumph). As a result, Fred Silverman presided over his third consecutive losing season at NBC, with the network's ratings for the 1980–81 season exactly the same as the year before. On

"The most trusted personality in America," Walter Cronkite, ended nearly nineteen years as anchor of *The CBS Evening News* on March 6, 1981. *60 Minutes* correspondent Dan Rather took over the post three days later. *(CBS News Photo/ CBS Photo Archive © 2003 CBS Worldwide, Inc. All Rights Reserved.)*

June 30, new RCA board chairman Thornton Bradshaw announced that Silverman had been removed from NBC and was being replaced by Grant Tinker, president of the MTM studios. Silverman's dream of being the first person to take all three TV networks to number one had to remain unfulfilled.

The two and one-half month actors' strike made the 1980–81 season one of the most confusing programming periods in television history. The strike, however, had a much more significant meaning than merely messing up network plans for that one season. It also marked the first time ABC, CBS, and NBC were forced to confront head-on the changing reality of television technology and to acknowledge the rapidly growing influence of cable TV and home video attachments. For years, the networks had steadfastly ignored or dismissed advances in these fields, but in 1980 this could no longer be done. On the surface, the industry in 1980 looked much as it had for decades. The three networks, combined, averaged 86% of the TV viewing audience. Less than 2% of American homes owned video cassette recorders. About 20% of the country subscribed to cable TV service (more than doubled from 1970), but original programming on cable was still minimal, at best. Nonetheless, many established television production outfits had begun to diversify in order to be ready to fill the programming needs that were just now starting to emerge with the new video outlets. The demands by the actors (and other craft unions) for a share in these new sources of profit reflected the increasing confidence in their inevitable growth. At last, the networks began to deal with these changing times as well. Near the end of 1980, first ABC, then CBS, established new cable television divisions to develop programs exclusively for the new video industries. ABC's were the first to hit the air.

At 9:00 P.M. on Sunday, April 12, 1981, ARTS, ABC's cultural cable service (the *A*lpha *R*epertory *T*elevision *S*ervice) debuted with three hours of original cable TV programs three nights each week (rebroadcasts filled the other four nights). Like the sparse schedule of network television four decades before, the ARTS offerings represented only a modest start in a new market. Yet they were an important first step, signaling that a seismic change was coming to the television world.

November 30, 1980

Tanya Roberts joins *Charlie's Angels* as Julie Rogers, replacing Shelley Hack who lasted only one season.

December 8, 1980

While watching ABC's *Monday Night Football*, millions learn of the fatal shooting in New York City of former Beatle John Lennon, with announcer Howard Cosell clearly upset by the news. Six years earlier, Cosell had interviewed Lennon on air during a Monday night game in Los Angeles.

December 20, 1980

As an experiment, NBC airs a televised football game between the New York Jets and Miami Dolphins without any play-by-play announcers.

January 12, 1981

Tomorrow Coast-to-Coast. (NBC). Rona Barrett, formerly of ABC's *Good Morning America,* joins Tom Snyder as co-host of NBC's revamped late late night talk show.

January 15, 1981

Hill Street Blues. (NBC). MTM presents a critically acclaimed series on police life in an urban setting.

January 20, 1981

After twenty-nine years as CBS's chief anchor for special events, Walter Cronkite reports his farewell news spectacular: the inauguration of Ronald Reagan as president and the release of the American hostages from Iran.

April 11, 1981

TV writers begin a three-month strike against TV and film producers in another dispute over how to divide profits from the new video technologies. The fall 1981 premieres are delayed somewhat as a result.

April 12, 1981

Anne Baxter hosts opening night for ARTS, ABC's cultural cable service. The initial offerings include performances by flutist Michel Debost, a concert by the Israel Philharmonic, and a feature on painter Gustav Klimt, kicking off the first week's theme: "Paris: The Dream and the Reality."

May 8, 1981

SCTV Network 90. (NBC). Nearly five years after the Toronto branch of Second City launched its uniquely warped TV satire series, the program moves from syndication in the U.S. to a network slot. Despite a starting time of 12:30 A.M. (following *Tonight* on Friday), it quickly becomes a late night comedy favorite.

September 1, 1981

Milton Berle's thirty-year ("$200,000 per year") contract with NBC expires.

41. Stop and Start It All Again

BY THE EARLY 1980s, THE PUBLIC ATTENTION directed toward which network was number one and what shows were in the top ten had fostered the image of television competition as a wide-open free-for-all. The reality was completely different.

From the beginning, network television bore the stamp of a surprisingly small number of people. Milton Berle inspired millions to buy their first TV sets in the late 1940s. During the early 1950s, *I Love Lucy* launched the Desilu studios and began the domination of filmed sitcoms. Throughout that decade, Louis G. Cowan presented one quiz show after another on all the networks. In the late 1950s, ABC drew more than one-fourth of its schedule from the Warner Bros. film studios. NBC carried a similar reliance on Universal Studios through the 1960s and 1970s. CBS's president James Aubrey presided over programming geared toward rural America in the early 1960s, building on the success of Paul Henning's *The Beverly Hillbillies*. Ten years later, producer Norman Lear developed a style of television comedy with *All in the Family* that was more urban-oriented, topical, and controversial. Garry Marshall supplied ABC with a string of hit sitcoms that made the network number one in the mid-1970s. Ace programmer Fred Silverman directed strategy at all three networks during the 1970s, moving from CBS to ABC to NBC.

Though tens of thousands of people worked toward the finished products, over the decades access to television remained limited. Ultimately, program material was funneled through just a few networks, studios, and producers. As a result, the race for the top spot was more accurately a contest among those who had already staked out a share of the television pie. Placing a show on television meant the opportunity to earn huge profits. It also afforded a vast pulpit to present a particular point of view. So from the beginning, the constant battle in broadcasting was between those who had power and influence, fighting to keep it, and those without such status, fighting to attain it.

From its creation in 1927, the Federal Communications Commission recognized the special limited nature of the broadcast medium and set up rules that called for use of the airwaves for the public's "interest, convenience, and necessity." The FCC tried to include avenues of access by calling on stations (first radio, then television as well) to incorporate a wide range of programming aimed at serving their communities. Though often compliance with the commission's rules consisted only of token religious, public affairs, and educational programs, these were important precedents because, from the start of American television until the mid-1960s,

most cities had only a few stations. On these, for the most part, access to the viewing public was largely limited to those within the New York-Hollywood entertainment-production axis.

Besides fighting for time on existing channels, others in search of a television forum tried to find new outlets, attempting to multiply choices for viewers and available markets for producers. Over the years, a frequently proposed scheme to enhance access was the creation of a fourth commercial network that might organize stations into a force equivalent to ABC, CBS, and NBC.

American television had, in fact, begun with four networks, but that situation lasted only a few years. By the mid-1950s, the DuMont television network had foundered and died—a victim of politics, financial constraints, and a lack of affiliates. The same problems almost killed ABC as well.

By the mid-1960s, the number of stations throughout the country had grown. Many major cities had at least three TV stations, and UHF reception had been mandated for all TV sets. More viewers were capable of picking up ABC's signals and, as that network grew, serious discussions once again began on the possibility of starting a new fourth commercial network.

One 1967 effort, the United Network, actually hit the air. It lasted all of one month with just one program, *The Las Vegas Show,* a virtual clone of the *Tonight* show on NBC, hosted by Bill Dana (a *Tonight* show regular himself under Steve Allen in the 1950s). But the problem remained finding affiliates. Though there were many more stations operating than there had been in the early 1950s, when both ABC and DuMont were floundering, they were still not in the right places to follow the existing network model.

In order to reach 90–95% of the homes with TV sets, a network needed broadcast affiliates in about two hundred cities. However, most of the stations unaffiliated with ABC, CBS, and NBC were bunched in only the largest cities, thereby leaving out significant sections of the country. Even with more than seven hundred commercial TV stations on the air nationwide, every fourth network model still faced a daunting task trying to reach a sufficiently large audience (90% of the viewing public) to attract major advertisers.

Until the problem of audience penetration could be dealt with, there would be no viable fourth network. So program producers turned to another form of access: syndication, creating an ad hoc network of stations for individual programs. During the late 1940s and early 1950s independent producers such as Jerry Fairbanks and companies such as Ziv began selling programs to individual stations to slot during time periods not used by the networks. These efforts stalled in the late 1950s as the networks increased the amount of their programming and the locals began using a greater number of readily available old movies as well as reruns of network filmed series. So syndication producers then joined forces with the networks to produce the new wave of filmed Westerns and action-adventure series that were starting to dominate prime time. These, in turn, wound up as syndicated reruns.

Original material for syndication increased in the 1960s, when powerful groups of stations such as the Westinghouse, Metromedia, and Avco chains struck gold with talk shows. They supplied member stations and other interested locals with videotaped gabfests hosted by Mike Douglas, Merv Griffin, and Phil Donahue for use in the brief non-network time slots of later afternoon and late night. The government expanded the potential syndication market even further with the "all-channel" bill, which required all televisions sets manufactured after 1964 to include UHF reception capabilities.

As UHF grew through the decade, independent producers again ventured into the realm of producing entertainment series, though at first they just turned out new versions of old game and quiz shows. The government entered the field again with the FCC's 1971 "access rule," which mandated that all three networks return thirty minutes each night to be filled locally by their affiliates. The commission also forbade the use of off-network reruns in this "prime time access" slot, so independent producers stepped in with more game shows, new versions of canceled network programs, and even a few original series.

Through the 1970s, producers grew bolder in their access ventures, producing new comedy, adventure, and drama programs. Many of these had been rejected by the networks, so they were placed on individual stations, by-passing the networks. In 1975, the British-made *Space: 1999* gave local programmers big-budget space drama with familiar television stars (Martin Landau and Barbara Bain from the successful *Mission: Impossible* series). In 1976, Norman Lear supplied five episodes weekly of the adult-oriented *Mary Hartman, Mary Hartman* comedy soap opera.

Universal Studios, then television's largest supplier of prime time network programming, took the next step in 1977 when it set up Operation Prime Time (OPT), a short-lived attempt to compete with prime time network programming. For a few years, the studio successfully slotted a handful of first-run drama miniseries directly with individual stations, beginning with *Testimony of Two Men*.

Both Universal's OPT formula and Lear's *Mary Hartman, Mary Hartman* went to the heart of *alternative* access. Instead of trying to build and maintain a full-time network, they wisely concentrated on small slices of time. They allowed subscribing local stations flexibility in airing this flashy material against their competition. However, the success of Universal and Lear only underscored the frustration experienced by "outsiders" trying to gain access to prime time television. Ultimately, Universal and Lear merely offered minor variations on what they were, at the same time, supplying to the networks. Yet the resemblance of their shows to familiar network offerings probably accounted for their success in syndication.

Ironically, for all the talk (especially by the government) of seeking alternatives to the major commercial networks, there already was such a system in place. This system had been created by the government itself and was designed with a different motivation from the commercial networks. It was public television.

Noncommercial television began in the United States in 1952, but due to a lack of funding the system was limited to low-budget "educational" fare. Access to public television was almost a joke because there were very few people watching the cheap-looking,

deadly dull programs. In the late 1960s, after passage of the Public Broadcasting Act of 1967, public television began acting more like a full-fledged network as its member stations gained production savvy and the federal government awarded it a yearly stipend. During the administration of President Richard Nixon, public television was strong enough as an alternative network power to pique the government with its public affairs analysis of war and domestic policies. As a result, the administration forced the PBS network to decentralize and return more power to the local stations. Oddly, the complicated system that emerged worked.

The PBS schedule was set up by a convention of local affiliates that bid on shows and pledged support for new series. Local stations usually did not air PBS shows at a set time, instead fitting them into their own schedules as they chose. The affiliates in larger cities such as New York, Chicago, Washington, Boston, and Los Angeles often produced programs and offered them to the entire network, but anyone who could navigate the funding bureaucracy could produce a show.

Once a show was picked up, it was treated far differently than it would be by the commercial networks. Philosophically, PBS was meant to co-exist as an alternative to commercial television, not as a replacement for it. As a result, programs were treated as something special. Even a one-shot program might be aired multiple times during the same week as its original broadcast, then offered additional times during the same season and periodically revived over the years. Limited-run series could also receive the same treatment. Movies would often be aired without any interruption. Though public television had less consistent success with comedy (apart from a handful of British imports such as *Monty Python*), it excelled with dance, drama, variety, and documentary shows.

Yet even with all these offerings, public television was still not the all-encompassing answer to American television's closed nature. The stations were still constrained by the same limited number of frequencies available for broadcast. They had merely been earmarked by the government for this specific purpose.

The chief stumbling block to practically any major change in television access and selection remained the very nature of the commercial television setup. A fixed number of outlets were in competition with each other. Even more limiting, they all had to cater to a huge audience.

In addition, because commercial television was beamed to homes indiscriminately, nervous executives tended to remove whatever might be perceived as offensive by some people—even though others might consider the same material to be high quality, mature, adult entertainment. Popular theatrical movies were edited to soften language and to remove violent and sexual content. Series were created for the largest possible audience. Because commercial television advertising rates were based on the relative standings of the programs against each other, the networks selected entertainment formulas that had proven popular and successful in the past and might "knock off" the competition.

By the dawn of the 1980s, however, there was a glimmer of potential for change, coalescing around ideas that had been around for decades.

As soon as television caught on with the public in the 1950s, various production outfits pressed to get "pay TV" started as a competitor to free TV. Hollywood studios, losing box office business to television, were especially interested in a system that would allow charges beyond commercials and the one-time purchase price of the TV set. A few such experimental systems got off the ground in the 1950s and early 1960s, using individual TV stations that broadcast signals that were coded and could only be picked up by viewers with a decoding box attached to their home sets. Zenith

September 27, 1977

Madison Square Garden Sports Network (MSG), owned by United Artists/Columbia, begins programming via cable. It is the first attempt at an all-sports cable network.

April 1, 1979

Warner/Amex's Nickelodeon cable network, aimed at children, begins operations.

April 26, 1979

Weekly Major League Baseball comes to cable via the Madison Square Garden network, with the beginning of twenty-three weeks of Thursday night games. Generally games are blacked out within fifty miles of the home team's city. Jim Woods, the regular announcer for the Boston Red Sox telecasts, handles the games from cities in the East, while Monte Moore (who does Oakland Athletics games) handles those from the West Coast.

September 15, 1979

TV Guide adds listings for pay cable services such as HBO and Showtime to its New York City edition.

had an experimental pay TV station in Chicago; pay TV stations stayed on the air for a few years in California and Connecticut. The stations ultimately failed for the same reason that various fourth networks had flopped to that point: They could not compete with the selection on the established commercial networks.

Advances in the concept of pay television took place from another angle during the 1950s with "cable television." Rural residents who lived in fringe reception areas that could only receive over-the-air signals from one or two stations (if that many) willingly signed up to pay for clear reception of the closest free TV stations. Cable companies plugged a cable connection directly into the home sets, delivering a signal that even a rooftop antenna could not supply. In addition, the cable wires even had capacity for some extra channels, though not a great number at first, beyond those needed to present the nearby local stations.

At first, the FCC seemed uncertain how to handle such signals which, technically, were not using the broadcast airwaves at all. Eventually it claimed jurisdiction and issued rules such as the "must carry" requirement specifying that local cable services had to carry all local broadcast stations, not just the more popular channels. In the 1970s, several legal cases brought by the cable industry successfully staked out cable's identity as being different from the broadcast networks and more akin to print publications. There would be rules, but the rules would begin with a different set of assumptions about scope, coverage, and content. They were not, in general, as restrictive as the rules that applied to broadcasters.

As the market for rural cable service grew, urban over-the-air local stations soon realized that they could expand their total audience by arranging to feed their signals to the nearby cable systems. In the mid-1970s, Atlanta entrepreneur Ted Turner revolutionized cable TV by taking this process a step further and transforming his low-profit non-network UHF station into America's first "superstation," WTCG (later renamed WTBS). Though the programming on WTBS generally consisted of old movies, syndicated reruns, and local sports events, Turner worked to get cable TV systems throughout the Southeast to add his station to their service.

Turner realized that, unlike many city dwellers, rural viewers had rarely been offered a choice beyond network affiliates because

there were few independents operating in their areas. As more and more local cable systems added WTBS to their cable service, Turner's station became available throughout the South. Using TV relay satellites to bounce his signal to cable systems throughout the country, Turner eventually transformed WTBS into a virtual national TV station. Other non-network stations (such as WGN in Chicago) followed Turner's lead and began sending their signals to cable systems throughout their regions.

Though these independent superstations offered their viewers a new choice on the dial, their programming was hardly revolutionary television. The movies, sports, and series reruns were even peppered with plenty of commercials. However, Turner's idea of aggressively using cable connections was revolutionary.

While they reached a relative handful of viewers compared to ABC, CBS, and NBC, these cable connections could by-pass the limited number of available over-the-air frequencies. In addition, the fact that viewers were willing to pay for such connections (even with commercials) opened up a whole new revenue stream. Once households went from paying *zero* to paying *something* for television, there was the potential to add other charges.

In 1972, Time-Life set up Home Box Office (HBO), a program service carried over various cable systems, but one with an important difference. Cable subscribers had to pay an *additional* fee above their regular costs in order to receive HBO. This income allowed HBO to be noncommercial and still be profitable, succeeding with an audience of thousands rather than millions. At first HBO was distributed (via microwave transmitters) to just a few systems in the East, and its programming was restricted to recent box office films not yet farmed out to network television, R-rated films considered too racy to air intact on the commercial networks, and sporting events that the networks had by-passed. By the mid-1970s, HBO was using TV relay satellites to distribute its signal to cable systems coast-to-coast and also had developed a number of original programs to drop in between the films, including concerts, comedy-variety acts taped in nightclubs, and independently produced entertainment shows.

Though the initial audiences were miniscule (HBO's premiere night reached a mere 365 subscribers), cable systems soon learned that adding HBO as another channel in their service resulted in a higher number of subscribers. By 1976, HBO had a competitor, Viacom's Showtime, which also charged a premium fee for its own package of uncut movies, original programs, and special events. The potential business was there, even if nobody yet knew exactly what programming mix would convince cable subscribers to ante up an additional fee.

Even more challenging was the question: How could viewers who had no problem receiving the networks over the air for free be convinced to *pay* for television? What could lure members of this audience into becoming cable subscribers? There was no obvious answer, but there was also no shortage of those trying to find one.

With ABC, CBS, and NBC offering one-stop "department store" shopping for a mix of mainstream comedy, drama, news, and sports, those attempting to emulate Ted Turner's success needed concepts that were both distinctive and cost-effective. Because the superstations were already the surrogate local stations in their markets, there was little room for others in that format. New cable services had to be even more specialized, though taking a cue to offer potential viewers something reassuringly familiar.

The quickest route was one that involved existing material or program models. Television preachers had been a broadcasting mainstay for decades, and the Reverend Pat Robertson had been particularly successful since the early 1960s with his syndicated program, *The 700 Club*, which packaged religion within a comfortable talk show format. In 1977, Robertson used that program as the foundation for the Christian Broadcast Network (CBN), which began feeding *The 700 Club* and other religious programming to cable systems via satellite.

The Madison Square Garden (MSG) network had local (New York) production roots from years of in-house coverage at one of the country's premiere sports arenas. For its national cable service, MSG offered selected hockey (New York Rangers) and basketball (New York Knicks) games, along with a handful of special events such as an annual dog show competition.

In 1979, Nickelodeon brought programming for kids to cable, taking what had started in 1977 as a local Ohio offering (*Nick Flicks*) and expanding it nationally. Nickelodeon represented a break from many past local children's shows by eschewing familiar old cartoons in favor of its own original creations. A modest daytime schedule allowed these new features nurturing time.

The halls of government provided the programming material for another new 1979 service, C-SPAN (the Cable-Satellite Public Affairs Network), a noncommercial offering funded by the cable industry itself. The brainchild of thirty-seven-year-old journalist Brian Lamb, C-SPAN was a savvy corporate venture that allowed the nascent cable industry to display a commitment to public affairs by providing a daily civics lesson for home viewers.

Initially, the main focus for C-SPAN was live gavel-to-gavel coverage of the U.S. House of Representatives, but it quickly added other features to fill its off-session hours, including videotapes of recent congressional meetings and hearings and other public events involving political figures. Because many of these events had already been routinely open to the press, C-SPAN needed only to bring its camera crews. However, in contrast to other news organizations that rarely aired more than a few words from the events, C-SPAN carried every minute. Even more attractive to those appearing on camera, the network took the approach of being an "observer of record" and did not inject any critical commentary during the coverage. Instead, that was handled on separate viewer call-in shows.

Sports was another ready-made programming hook with events already taking place that did not require much in the way of scripts, sets, and original production. The challenge, though, was to find sports not already claimed by ABC, CBS, and NBC. In September 1979, ESPN (the Entertainment and Sports Programming Network) took on the mainstream networks with a service that assembled a mix of the available, the obscure, and the otherwise ignored. Sports of every sort were carried from virtually anywhere around the world, then repeated (and repeated) on tape.

Such repetition was necessary because cable services interested in luring new customers were realizing that one strong selling point was constant availability. While the commercial networks and even most locals aired individual programs only once and usually signed off in the wee hours of the night, cable services realized there was no good reason not to keep on playing and replaying their material throughout the day. It did not cost them much to do so and it helped solidify their identity on the cable dial.

A pattern began to emerge. Because these cable services could not afford to be all encompassing, they had to define themselves by the type of programming they were offering. Because they also could not afford non-stop original material, they plugged in reruns as often as necessary. In the process, having a succession of original episodes became less important. For the specialized cable services, it was most important to emphasize their brand identity: Government. Sports. Kids. Movies.

This resulted in a subtle, gradual, but significant change in cable viewer expectations. Instead of tuning in at a specific time for a specific show, viewers turned to a channel virtually anytime for a specific *type* of program. It almost did not matter that, at any particular moment, the program on that service might be a rerun.

The development of these specialized services occurred completely under the radar screen of most television viewers. For one thing, there were large areas of the country that did not have cable franchise setups, so residents of cities as large as Chicago could not order cable if they wanted to. There also remained the question: Why would they want to? Cable services for the most part still offered little in the way of original programming that could be considered on a par with that of ABC, CBS, NBC, or PBS. Probably the biggest lure of cable was the opportunity to see uncut and uncensored theatrical films, but that was more a substitute for going to a movie theater than an alternative to commercial television.

It was Ted Turner who again upped the ante.

In 1979, Turner announced that his next cable venture would be an all-news service, CNN (the Cable News Network). It was to begin the following year, just in time to cover that year's political conventions and fall presidential campaign.

While on the surface "all-news" appeared to be yet another in a growing list of specialized cable networks (like "all-sports"), the idea of a full-time on-air television news service was staggering in its audacity. In the early days of television, the three networks had regarded news as a loss leader. Later, when the evening news programs and prime time series such as *60 Minutes* and *20/20* became bona fide successes, they were still just one element of a network's revenue stream.

CNN would be a news operation that would stand on its own, twenty-four hours a day. Unlike all the other specialized cable

---

January 25, 1980

Black Entertainment Television (BET), the first U.S. television network aimed at black audiences, commences programming on cable with a limited schedule of two hours per day. BET's founder is black businessman Robert L. Johnson.

April 9, 1980

Cable's MSG network is renamed the USA Network, as it begins to move away from an all-sports schedule to a more diversified general entertainment format.

August 1, 1980

Cinemax, a sister channel of Time-Life's HBO, debuts on cable with an eighteen-hour per day schedule of movies, movies, and nothing but movies.

December 7, 1980

Bravo, a pay cable service focusing on the arts, debuts with a tribute to Aaron Copland taped at Carnegie Hall in New York.

August 1, 1981

MTV (Music Television), Warner/Amex's latest cable venture, brings rock music videos to TV twenty-four hours per day, beginning with The Buggles' "Video Killed the Radio Star" and Pat Benatar's "You Better Run." Some of the other artists featured in MTV's first hour include Rod Stewart, The Who, Todd Rundgren, Split Enz, and .38 Special. The original five "veejays" are Martha Quinn, Nina Blackwood, Mark Goodman, J. J. Jackson, and Alan Hunter.

formats to that point, a creditable television news operation would cost money. Big money. That was because, in contrast to the congressional sessions typically carried by C-SPAN or the scheduled sports events on ESPN, major news stories could take place anytime, anywhere in the world, at a moment's notice. If CNN was to be a respected news source, it would have to be ready to go where the news was.

Turner made it clear that CNN would be such a major player doing things his way, even down to locating the CNN news headquarters in Atlanta, Georgia, rather than in the traditional network turf of New York or Washington. (Both cities would contain bureaus.) Such pronouncements added to Turner's maverick reputation (which had earned him the nickname "the mouth from the South"), but they also followed in the tradition of previous stubborn visionaries, such as NBC's David Sarnoff and CBS's William Paley. Ted Turner had previously transformed his family's successful billboard-advertising business into a wide-ranging communications company. Now he was expanding that vision further, in the process taking original cable programming to a new level.

At 6:00 P.M. on June 1, 1980, CNN debuted as promised. After a filmed presentation of "The Star Spangled Banner" (just like a "regular" TV station might run when signing on every morning), anchors David Walker and Lois Hart in Atlanta began presenting the news as if this was just another day of a service that had always been there.

Even then, CNN was not automatically accorded parity with the existing network news operations. For example, at the Democratic Party's August presidential nominating convention in New York's Madison Square Garden, ABC, CBS, and NBC were allowed to build huge anchor booths immediately adjacent to the floor of the convention. CNN, by contrast, was allocated much smaller space in the nosebleed level along with local TV stations and other independent broadcast news groups. It still had to prove itself.

Within the broadcast news establishment, the attitude in some circles was to dismiss the fledgling news service with a condescending sneer, calling it "Chicken Noodle News." For the future, then, CNN would have to build its own news tradition, one twenty-four-hour day at a time, as people became accustomed to the concept of tuning in the latest news anytime they wanted.

CNN was joined about one year later (in August 1981) by another groundbreaking cable service, this one aimed at quite a different niche audience: MTV (Music Television).

While some cable concepts such as all-sports seemed obvious and inevitable, the same could not be said for the premise behind MTV. It was designed to be a video radio station, playing "music videos" (self-contained rock music performances on film and tape, provided by the artists themselves). These were not lengthy concerts but, rather, individual songs that were introduced by hip and stylish young "veejays" such as Martha Quinn and Nina Blackwood. MTV played these music videos again and again, twenty-four hours a day. Such promotional music films had been around for years, proving especially popular on European television. In the U.S., only a handful ever hit the networks, usually in a one-time broadcast on some music or variety show such as *American Bandstand* or *Ed Sullivan*.

Unlike sports, news, movies, and kids programming, music videos were not a proven format with a hit track record on U.S. network TV. Yet teens soon transformed the slogan "I Want My MTV" into a national catch phrase and put the desire for a home cable TV connection on the family shopping list. There was no equivalent to the non-stop MTV music video lineup anywhere on network TV.

So even though ABC, CBS, and NBC entered the fall of 1981 with ratings numbers that continued to dwarf those of cable, the networks were actually already engaged in the opening skirmishes of a battle for the hearts and souls of the viewing public.

42. Freddie's Blues

WHEN GRANT TINKER ASSUMED CONTROL of NBC in July 1981 as chairman and CEO, he brought a significant change to the public face of that network.

As former head of the MTM production company, Tinker had built a reputation as a leader in quality television, primarily in comedy (*Mary Tyler Moore*, *The Bob Newhart Show*, *WKRP in Cincinnati*) but also in drama (*Lou Grant*, *The White Shadow*). These were shows that won high critical praise and also registered good ratings.

This track record was contrasted to that of the departing chairman, Fred Silverman, who (despite championing such series as *M*A*S*H*, *The Waltons*, and *Roots*) remained inexorably linked to his big (but more lowbrow) hits on ABC (including *The Love Boat*, *Three's Company*, and *Charlie's Angels*). For NBC to put forth Tinker as its new front man guaranteed a wave of positive critical PR. It suggested that as the number three network NBC might be considering something a little daring as a competitive strategy: quality programming. After all, could the network do much worse?

Tinker's presence also sent a signal to the creative community (and its many MTM alumni and friends) that they might find sympathetic ears in the NBC network offices.

Tinker did make a few changes to the 1981–82 season schedule, which had been planned during Silverman's regime, but NBC's fall lineup was still largely Silverman's creation. More significantly, Tinker kept in place the man that Silverman had made his programming chief, thirty-one-year-old Yale graduate Brandon Tartikoff.

Like Silverman, Tartikoff was a programmer who truly enjoyed television. During his ABC days, Silverman had spotted Tartikoff working at ABC's Chicago O&O (WLS) and pulled him to the network. Soon after Silverman became president at NBC, he lured Tartikoff to that network as well, installing him as head of the entertainment division. In that role, Brandon Tartikoff had the opportunity to use his "TV generation" sensibilities to seek out viable concepts that appealed to him as both a programmer and a viewer. He understood that, in some cases, new programs needed awhile to find their niche, and he was ready to fight for that opportunity for the shows he truly believed would eventually thrive.

Appropriately, the 1981–82 schedule Tartikoff had developed toward the end of Silverman's regime already included its share of quality offerings. There was Merlin Olsen in *Father Murphy* (a warm Western period piece from *Little House on the Prairie*'s Michael Landon), James Garner in *Bret Maverick* (a revival of one of the best 1950s Westerns), and—as a centerpiece of high-class television—the MTM-produced police drama *Hill Street Blues*.

A mid-season entry in the strike-delayed 1980–81 season, *Hill Street Blues* had registered high critical praise but extremely low ratings during that first go-round. In fact, the program was ranked in the bottom 20% of all series for the 1980–81 season (eighty-third out of ninety-seven shows). Nonetheless, in his closing days at NBC, Fred Silverman had signed off on Tartikoff's renewal of the program, making it one of the lowest-rated prime time series ever brought back for a second season.

There were practical elements to the decision. NBC did not have a deep bench of sure-fire replacements waiting in the wings. Having been the number three network for a few years, NBC was also more inclined to try practically anything in search of a potential hit. Though *Hill Street Blues* had not yet registered with the general public, it had developed a passionate following among critics. That was exactly the type of scenario that had worked in the past for such series as *All in the Family* and *M*A*S*H*, so NBC was willing to give this one more time to catch on. The 1981–82 season would make it or break it.

Going into the fall, *Hill Street Blues* received a tremendous boost from the Emmy awards. First, in August, it received twenty-one nominations (including multiple citations in several categories). At the Emmy telecast itself in early September, *Hill Street Blues* walked away with wins in eight of its twelve nominated categories, including Best Drama, Lead Actor, Lead Actress, Supporting Actor, Directing, Writing, Cinematography, and Sound Editing. Boosted by these numbers, NBC found itself unexpectedly with more Emmy wins than anyone else.

NBC ran promotional clips from the Emmy show incessantly leading up to the new season, which had a later than usual start due to a spring-summer strike among writers. Though not as disruptive as the previous season's labor dispute, this year's strike once again stretched the unveiling of new series past the traditional September premiere dates. Because NBC was airing baseball's World Series that October (and so delayed the premieres of most of its shows until early November), it had a perfect promotional platform leading up to its premiere week. After all the press coverage, on-air promos, and word-of-mouth attention, *Hill Street Blues* at last managed to attract a larger audience. What viewers found when they tuned in was something truly different, a worthy successor to previous MTM dramas such as *Lou Grant* and *The White Shadow*.

Hill Street Blues had the sharp writing and attention to charac-

	8:00	8:30	9:00	9:30	10:00	10:30	
M O N	That's Incredible		ABC NFL Monday Night Football (to 12 Midnight)				**ABC**
	Private Benjamin	The Two Of Us	M*A*S*H	House Calls	Lou Grant		**CBS**
	Little House On The Prairie		NBC Monday Night At The Movies				**NBC**
T U E	Happy Days	Laverne And Shirley	Three's Company	Too Close For Comfort	Hart To Hart		**ABC**
	SIMON AND SIMON		CBS Tuesday Night Movies				**CBS**
	FATHER MURPHY		BRET MAVERICK		Flamingo Road		**NBC**
W E D	The Greatest American Hero		THE FALL GUY		Dynasty		**ABC**
	MR. MERLIN	WKRP In Cincinnati	Nurse		SHANNON		**CBS**
	Real People		Facts Of Life	LOVE, SIDNEY	Quincy, M.E.		**NBC**
T H R	Mork And Mindy	BEST OF THE WEST	Barney Miller	Taxi	20/20		**ABC**
	Magnum, P.I.		Knots Landing		JESSICA NOVAK		**CBS**
	Harper Valley	LEWIS AND CLARK	Diff'rent Strokes	GIMME A BREAK	Hill Street Blues		**NBC**
F R I	Benson	Bosom Buddies	DARKROOM		STRIKE FORCE		**ABC**
	The Incredible Hulk		The Dukes Of Hazzard		Dallas		**CBS**
	NBC Magazine		McCLAIN'S LAW		NBC Specials		**NBC**
S A T	MAGGIE	Making A Living	The Love Boat		Fantasy Island		**ABC**
	Walt Disney		CBS Saturday Night Movies				**CBS**
	Barbara Mandrell And The Mandrell Sisters		NASHVILLE PALACE		FITZ AND BONES		**NBC**

	7:00	7:30	8:00	8:30	9:00	9:30	10:00	10:30	
S U N	CODE RED		TODAY'S F.B.I.		ABC Sunday Night Movie				**ABC**
	60 Minutes		Archie Bunker's Place	One Day At A Time	Alice	The Jeffersons	Trapper John, M.D.		**CBS**
	The Flintstones	Here's Boomer	CHiPs		NBC Sunday Night At The Movies				**NBC**

ters typical of MTM offerings. It went further, however, adding the soapier style of continuing storylines and doses of steamy sensuality that might be found in shows such as *Dallas.* There was also occasional violent action that would not have been out of place in a series such as *S.W.A.T.* Yet *Hill Street Blues* brought a fresh take to all these elements, mixing them with a gritty inner-city sensibility. Judiciously placed handheld camera shots (quite unusual for mainstream TV in the early 1980s) conveyed the sense that viewers were really peeking in on the day-to-day life of cops on the front lines, from morning roll call to the end of another exhausting shift.

The program put identifiable and believable faces to the very real challenges of contemporary police work, showing men and women serious about their jobs yet also able to see the humor and absurdity of life that came with it. For example, at times during the opening roll call the cops seemed almost like restless students being addressed by a patient teacher, but that was just one way of coping with the unknown that lay ahead. The daily warning "Let's be careful out there" was the understated acknowledgment of the dangers they faced. With its deft combination of quality production style, writing, and character development, *Hill Street Blues* reenergized the police show format and helped set the standard for TV dramas for the next decade.

Created by Steven Bochco (producer of *Delvecchio* and *Paris,* two innovative but overlooked CBS police shows from the late

1970s), *Hill Street Blues* was set in a shabby downtown police station in an unnamed rust belt city. There, Capt. Frank Furillo (Daniel J. Travanti) tried to keep some semblance of order and justice in the often crazed world of urban law enforcement at his precinct. He was supported by a well-rounded cast of characters both at the station house and on the street. These included the quiet and considerate roll call sergeant, Phil Esterhaus (Michael Conrad); the hyper and militaristic S.W.A.T. leader, Lt. Howard Hunter (James B. Sikking); the bleeding-heart liberal crisis negotiator, Sgt. Henry Goldblume (Joe Spano); the borderline manic undercover cop, Mick Belker (Bruce Weitz); the uncouth but cunning Lt. Norman Buntz (Dennis Franz); and three great teams of street cops. Reflecting the diversity of the force, one was the male-female team of Lucy Bates and Joe Coffey (Betty Thomas and Ed Marinaro) and two were black-white pairings: Bobby Hill and Andy Renko (Michael Warren and Charles Haid) and Neal Washington and J. D. Larue (Taurean Blacque and Kiel Martin).

Furillo's former wife, Faye (Barbara Bosson, Steven Bochco's wife in real life), was constantly turning up at the station to talk with him about money, their young son, and the tribulations of going back into the dating world. He provided a sympathetic ear without revealing that he was involved in an intense secret romance of his own with headstrong public defender Joyce Davenport (Veronica Hamel). That steamy affair provided some of the key sexual tension at the beginning of the series because the two

Every morning at roll call, Sgt. Phil Esterhaus (Michael Conrad) warned the officers at the *Hill Street Blues* station to "Be careful out there." (Hill Street Blues © 1980 *Twentieth Century Fox Television. All Rights Reserved.*)

were always in conflict at work, but passionate lovers after hours. Eventually almost every major character was involved in a romantic sub-plot, with some of the sex scenes rather daring for the era. For example, the audience did not just see Furillo and Davenport together in bed; there were also erotic settings such as a steamy shared bubble bath. There were also kinky daytime precinct house trysts between Sergeant Esterhaus and his sex-obsessed widowed girlfriend, Grace Gardner (Barbara Babcock).

With a strong core cast, *Hill Street Blues* came up with years of intriguing stories that were realistic, gripping, and entertaining. The continuing storylines, often overlapping dialogue, and complex themes required a fair level of attention from viewers, but the reward was a near-perfect mix of TV drama elements.

Despite all the critical attention lavished on *Hill Street Blues* following its Emmy triumph, NBC still languished in last place during the 1981–82 season. In fact, the network's overall ratings for the year dropped in comparison with those of the previous season (although *Hill Street Blues* managed to jump to twenty-eighth place among all the season's programs). This had been Fred Silverman's final NBC schedule, leaving him far short of a network "hat-trick." Number one CBS and former number one ABC still had the programs that filled the weekly top ten, building on familiar formats and stars, many of which had been nurtured during Silverman's earlier days at both networks.

ABC, in fact, was still mining *Happy Days* with the short-run success of mid-season spinoff *Joanie Loves Chachi.* The network also turned to familiar faces William Shatner and producers Aaron Spelling and William Goldberg for its own new police show, the mid-season entry *T. J. Hooker.* Though including slices of off-duty life and earnest plots involving the rights and wrongs of the police world, the series was a far cry from *Hill Street Blues* and generally stuck to a standard crime action formula over its run. Shatner played the title character, a veteran cop who chose to go "back on the street" to guide such fresh-faced officers as Vince Romano (Adrian Zmed) and Stacy Sheridan (Heather Locklear).

The most popular crime fighter on CBS was private investigator Thomas Magnum (Tom Selleck) on *Magnum, P.I.* The series was in the spirit of *The Rockford Files,* but in a far more comfortable setting: Hawaii. Less than six months after Steve McGarrett (Jack Lord) had booked his last case on *Hawaii Five-0, Magnum*'s producers Donald P. Bellisario and Glen A. Larson brought viewers back to that luscious island setting for one of the best set-ups a TV detective could hope for.

In exchange for providing security for the lavish island estate of Robin Masters, Magnum was given lodging in a comfortable guesthouse, access to a snazzy $60,000 red Ferrari, and the time to pursue his own cases. Masters, in fact, was never there at all, though his very proper and officious British aide Jonathan Quayle Higgins III (John Hillerman) attempted to keep in check the flip and casual Magnum. The sparring between Higgins and Magnum (perfectly executed by Hillerman and Selleck) provided a core of camaraderie to the series. It was clear that the two men deeply respected each other and, after a while, Magnum became convinced that, in fact, Higgins himself was the never-seen Robin Masters. (Of course he denied it.)

Overall, *Magnum, P.I.* was lighter fare, buoyed by Selleck's charm and good looks (his smile while he raised his eyebrows was truly disarming). Yet the series did not go over the comic edge. Magnum was a Vietnam vet and two of his war buddies helped on his cases: helicopter pilot T. C. (Roger E. Mosley) and nightclub owner Rick (Larry Manetti). This carefully developed serious side to the characters emerged just often enough to keep the series and the stories grounded for eight seasons.

CBS's most innovative police drama of the 1981–82 season was *Cagney and Lacey.* Though stylistically worlds apart from *Hill Street Blues,* the series had its own unique point of view and its own protracted quest for ratings success. The project had first been pitched as a feature film by two female writer-producers, Barbara Avedon and Barbara Corday, but it eventually ended up as a TV movie (co-produced with Corday's husband, Barney Rosenzweig).

The premise was groundbreaking in either medium: female buddies. Over the years, there had been solo female cops (*Police Woman*), male-female couplings (*McMillan and Wife*), plenty of teams (*The Mod Squad*), and male buddies (*Starsky and Hutch*).

November 15, 1981

This Week with David Brinkley. (ABC). Six weeks after leaving NBC, David Brinkley lands as host of a one-hour Sunday morning news and interview show at ABC.

November 16-17, 1981

ABC's *General Hospital*, TV's number one rated daily soap, sets a new daytime ratings record with the ultra-hyped wedding of Luke (Tony Geary) and Laura (Genie Francis). Soon enough, they are split up, when Laura is kidnapped (and presumed drowned) and Luke barely survives an avalanche.

December 21, 1981

HBO at last expands its schedule to twenty-four hours a day, seven days a week.

January 1, 1982

Ted Turner launches his second all-news cable network, called CNN-2. Unlike CNN, CNN-2 simply runs forty-eight consecutive self-contained half-hour live newscasts daily, with each updated for the latest developments. By August, the network is renamed CNN Headline News.

January 4, 1982

Sports announcer Bryant Gumbel replaces Tom Brokaw as co-host (with Jane Pauley) of NBC's *Today* show.

Cagney and Lacey offered television's first female buddies, two women elevated to the rank of police detective, working closely together on high-profile cases.

The TV movie aired in October 1981, with Loretta Swit (in between filming for *M*A*S*H*) as Chris Cagney and Tyne Daly as Mary Beth Lacey. That film scored well and earned the premise a series tryout in the spring of 1982, with Meg Foster stepping into Swit's role for further cases with the groundbreaking pair. Cagney was single, highly competitive, and determined to prove herself the best on the force. Lacey was equally dedicated to her career, but was also committed to her home life, where she had a husband and two children. Together, the two women were determined to show that they were not only as good as "the boys," they were better.

Unfortunately, the spring tryout did not do spectacularly well. While the network brass contemplated possible renewal, stories circulated that perhaps there were second thoughts about exactly how the premise was being executed, with nervous executives reportedly concerned that the series was "too feminist."

Cagney and Lacey was at last given the green light to return in the fall of 1982. However, the character of Cagney was recast with Sharon Gless, fresh from replacing Lynn Redgrave for the final run of episodes in the CBS hospital sitcom *House Calls*. It was left to see whether that change to a "softer" and more accessible Cagney would make a difference to viewers in the fall of 1982.

Sexual identity was still one of those areas the networks approached with caution and apprehension. Whenever anything slightly daring was attempted, there was sure to be controversy. For example, programmers were still extremely careful about gay characters in regular series. Yet, because placing a gay character on a prime time television series was so rare, it also offered the opportunity for some extra publicity.

NBC walked that line early in the season when it unveiled *Love, Sidney*, which featured Tony Randall as Sidney Shorr, a middle-aged commercial artist who happened to be gay. Almost. In the TV movie pilot that aired in early October ("Sidney Shorr: A Girl's Best Friend"), Sidney made no secret of his homosexuality as he helped a young single pregnant woman, Laurie, deal with the decision of whether to have the child or to have an abortion. However, when the regular sitcom series started a few weeks later, Sidney may still have been gay but he was not reminding anybody about it. Instead, it was a few years later and he and Laurie and her daughter, Patti, shared his large Manhattan apartment in a perfectly platonic relationship. Randall brought his usual comic timing to the character and Swoosie Kurtz was effective enough as Laurie, but even at its funniest, the series was haunted by the unaddressed "big issue" just out of sight and still hanging in the closet.

ABC had a much less volatile take on non-traditional sexual roles in *Bosom Buddies*, a low-rated carryover from the previous season. The original premise was highly convoluted and deeply in debt to the 1959 film "Some Like It Hot." Henry and Kip, two offbeat young advertising agency employees newly arrived in Manhattan, found their bargain-rent apartment building demolished one morning. With no other affordable housing available, they jumped at their co-worker Amy's idea of moving into her apartment building. One problem: It was a women-only residence. The solution? Henry and Kip decided to dress in drag as Hildegarde and Buffy, their respective "sisters," when they were in the apartment building. Only Amy (who had a crush on Henry) knew their secret.

Naturally, this premise not only called for plot complications revolving around keeping their double lives straight, it also meant that beautiful women (often in skimpy nightgowns) were regularly dropping by "Hildegarde" and "Buffy's" apartment for "girl talk" (allowing ABC a few promotional titillating moments). This premise was too complicated to sustain a series for long, and the show largely dropped the "boys in drag" emphasis in the midst of the program's second (and final) season. Henry and Kip "came out" to their women friends in the apartment building and set up their own small production company. By then, *Bosom Buddies* could emphasize what had been its *real* strength all along, sharp writing and an outstanding pair of leading actors: Peter Scolari as the cute, smallish, and shy Henry, and twenty-four-year-old Tom Hanks as the lanky and bolder Kip.

While the networks tended to shy away from dealing with controversial sexual issues, viewers certainly were not automatically outraged by sexual matters. That was reflected in the ratings; the most popular format on television was now clearly the sex-drenched prime time soap opera, with *Dallas* comfortably ensconced at the top of the ratings. In the 1981–82 season, it had plenty of company.

Everywhere, even in everyday life, conspicuous consumption was celebrated, with success in the boardroom and the bedroom seen as a badge of honor. Larry Hagman's J. R. Ewing might be presented on *Dallas* as a villainous manipulator, but he also came across as the sly one you'd like to see on your team. J. R. managed to put a smiling face on greed.

That allure of wealth, sex, and crafty manipulators was not lost on Lorimar, the *Dallas* production company, which set in motion similar conflicts on *Knots Landing* (its direct *Dallas* spinoff), *Flamingo Road* (an NBC series based on a 1949 movie of the same name), and its newest hit series, CBS's *Falcon Crest*. (No surprise there. *Falcon Crest* was placed in a choice slot immediately after *Dallas*, which moved up an hour). *Falcon Crest* was set in the wine country region outside San Francisco and centered on the schemes of powerful matriarch Angela Channing (Jane Wyman, who had been the real-life first wife of newly inaugurated President Ronald Reagan). She would do anything to consolidate and extend her vineyard holdings while crushing her enemies, real or imagined. The series quickly established its own ardent following and ran for nine seasons.

And then there was *Dynasty*, which brought Aaron Spelling (a veteran TV producer of extravagant fluff) to the prime time soap opera world in a big way. Set in the breathtaking natural beauty of the Rocky Mountains near Denver and the man-made beauty of opulent mansions and offices, *Dynasty* presented the story of the Carrington business empire and its far-flung cast of backstabbing, self-centered, amoral beautiful people living luxurious lives or aspiring to them. Despite such a winning formula, the series had a slow start as a midseason entry for the 1980–81 season. It began promisingly with the wedding of company head Blake Carrington (John Forsythe, the voice of Charlie in Spelling's *Charlie's Angels*) and his former secretary Krystle Jennings (Linda Evans), but then meandered through complicated business and family plots. These culminated with Blake standing trial for murder and, at season's end, a mysterious veiled woman entering the courtroom.

In the fall of 1981, viewers learned the woman's identity: Alexis Carrington (Joan Collins), Blake's former wife. Once Alexis entered the *Dynasty* world, the program took off. Deliciously played by Collins, Alexis was the ultimate manipulator, determined to once again sit with Blake at the seat of corporate and personal power, or destroy him and everything he had built. (At times it appeared she would do both, just for the fun of it.) Alexis saved her strongest vitriol for Krystle, whom she regarded as a rank pretender for Blake's love. Over the course of the series, the two women became entwined in a series of bitter confrontations, including outright physical battles (most dramatically, a knockdown fight in an artificial lily pond).

Dynasty had its share of complicated plots and a long list of supporting characters (including Krystle's daughter, played by Heather Locklear, at the same time she was collaring criminals on *T. J. Hooker*). The series even had several gay characters, including Blake's own son, Steven. Yet, first and foremost, *Dynasty* was all about style. No matter their sexual orientation, both the men and the women of *Dynasty* were strikingly attractive and inevitably wrapped in sartorial splendor. This was a glitterati world in which viewers spent most of their time admiring the scenery, over time generally ignoring the details of stories that often resembled daytime soaps at their most self-indulgent, with kidnapping, amnesia, and characters undergoing plastic surgery so new actors could assume the roles. Real-life Washington power broker Henry Kissinger and former U.S. President Gerald Ford appeared in cameos, further blurring the line between the real world and the make-believe world of Hollywood.

Though stargazing had been a part of American pop culture for decades, at the time there was an increasing emphasis on celebrities and their associated lifestyles, even up to the White House. President Reagan had served eight years as governor of California, but he had first spent decades as a star in feature films and television. So as president he seemed perfectly at ease in front of the cameras, easily connecting with people back home yet also comfortably mixing with celebrities of all sorts. He and his wife Nancy were not products of elite family backgrounds like that enjoyed by President John F. Kennedy, but they nonetheless brought to the White House a Hollywood-trained sense of style and gloss not seen in Washington since the early 1960s.

In this context, *Entertainment Tonight* premiered during the fall of 1981 as a syndicated show (distributed via satellite) devoting a half hour each day to the world of showbiz. It became a hit by treating glitzy film openings and entertainment industry announcements as news—*celebrity* news. Inevitably, such stories focused on luxurious homes, fancy cars, and lavish lifestyles. In essence, these

were real-life versions of people like the Carringtons of *Dynasty* and the Ewings of *Dallas*.

Dynasty did well enough in the 1981–82 season, landing in the top twenty overall. Still, *Dallas* remained television's number one series, letting CBS easily ride to another victory in the annual battle for network ratings superiority. With CBS at the top of its ratings game, the network looked to make its mark in the emerging world of cable. What could be easier?

Unlike ABC (and its lukewarm investment in the ARTS cable channel), CBS affixed the network's own brand name to its cable identity. This identification helped CBS Cable to better stand out in the crowd and could be used to help attract new viewers to sign up for cable service. ABC's ARTS service was almost exclusively filled with programs purchased from outside suppliers. CBS Cable, on the other hand, emphasized its own productions (which made up 60% of its schedule).

On October 12, 1981, CBS Cable began with style. In the first program, *Signature*, host Gregory Jackson spoke with musician Isaac Stern, but the camera never cut away to Jackson. Instead it remained focused only on Stern, demonstrating that this was a show that put the interview subject first.

There was much more. Respected journalist and documentarian Patrick Watson, from the Canadian Broadcasting Corporation, served as the original on-air host for the cable network's schedule. Author-producer Norris Chumley offered a special on Gene Kelly. Emmy-winning editor Alan Miller worked his magic on the program *Mixed Bag New Wave*. Charles Kuralt hosted *I Remember*, a weekly one-hour examination of a news story from the past thirty years. Bill Moyers hosted a lavishly produced twenty-part documentary series, *A Walk Through the 20th Century*. There were concerts, operas, and a weekly one-hour drama anthology.

It was as if television's critics had at last been given their own network to program. CBS Cable embraced the buzzword "narrowcasting" and seemed tailor-made for the upscale, well-educated viewers that potential advertisers wanted to reach. It was a high-class operation that seemed determined to show this upstart cable industry just how the seasoned professionals did the job.

February 1, 1982

Late Night with David Letterman. (NBC). NBC replaces Tom Snyder in the post-Johnny Carson late late night slot with a sixty-minute program hosted by cool young gap-toothed comic David Letterman, who recently flopped with an equally hip show that NBC weirdly slotted at 10:00 A.M.

March 4, 1982

Police Squad! (ABC). In Color. The creators of the hit film spoof "Airplane!" present an equally crazed send-up of TV cop shows. Leslie Nielsen plays the dense but deadpan Det. Frank Drebin. While a flop on TV, this idea succeeds six years later with the first of three "Naked Gun" films.

March 15, 1982

ABC teams up with the Hearst television chain for a new cable service called Daytime, aimed at women. At first, it only runs from 1:00 to 5:00 P.M. Monday through Friday.

April 5, 1982

Tom Brokaw (in New York) and Roger Mudd (in Washington) replace John Chancellor as anchor of *NBC Nightly News*. Chancellor still provides occasional commentaries.

For longtime CBS boss William Paley, this was the vision of television he had preferred to tout from the beginning of his network. Yet ever since TV had become a mass medium in the mid-1950s, pandering to the broad American populace had been the guiding principle at all three networks. As time went on, there were fewer and fewer slots available on CBS's own competitive schedule for the more "refined" (some would say "elitist") programming that Paley wanted to have associated with his network.

Yet clearly Paley had not forgotten those days; he became one of the biggest boosters of CBS Cable. So what if the commitment to the cable service cost a great deal of money? William Paley had started CBS on its road to riches back in the 1920s. He had certainly earned the right to spend some of his company's money to recapture the stature that had once given CBS its nickname as the "Tiffany" network. If CBS Cable succeeded in this new medium by being the best, that success would be one more jewel in Paley's crown.

However, that hoped-for renaissance in television never took hold. Instead, after just fourteen months, CBS Cable signed off as a costly failure. The service never drew enough subscribers or advertising dollars to prosper. Instead, it produced a loss of about $50 million for CBS. As a result, the network essentially wrote off cable as part of its corporate plans for more than a decade. It was not worth the bother and yielded little immediate bottom-line return. Cable was in barely a quarter of the country's households. The percentage of homes with video recorders was in the single digits. Together ABC, CBS, and NBC still dominated television viewing, day in and day out, with their over-the-air broadcasts.

Besides taking CBS out of the cable game, the failure of CBS Cable marked the end of an era for the network. The press release disclosing the demise of CBS Cable came out (not coincidentally) just one week after William Paley announced his plan to resign as chairman of the board of CBS, thus relinquishing his day-to-day control over the network. Paley would remain as one of the company's directors (and its major stockholder), but the last of the original broadcasting pioneers no longer had the final say at the network he had created.

In an odd way, CBS Cable had tried to do too much, bringing a traditional network emphasis on specific content to the fractured world of cable choice. Even the familiar network brand name did not help, particularly because it had virtually nothing to do with the CBS identity people had come to know from its top-rated shows. Instead of J. R. Ewing, Thomas Magnum, and Hawkeye Pierce, viewers were offered Isaac Stern and Patrick Watson.

The real direction cable was heading was far less splashy than the glittering CBS Cable line-up. Down the street, Paramount, Time-Life, and MCA/Universal were buying up Madison Square Garden's cable network and renaming it the USA Network, changing its programming to a more mainstream "superstation"-like mix of movies, TV reruns, and sports. WTBS was buying the rights to begin airing live NCAA college football in the fall of 1982, while ESPN joined the USA Network in obtaining the rights to air some NBA basketball games.

In May 1982, *Good Morning America* weatherman John Coleman launched the Weather Channel, a twenty-four-hour-a-day cable service that only reported … the weather. Just a few years before, such an idea might have been the basis for a *Saturday Night Live* skit. Now, it was cable reality.

As the number of cable networks continued to grow, most local cable system operators upgraded their systems to gain the capacity to provide more than just a handful of strictly cable channels along with retransmissions of local over-the-air stations. In addition, many cable channels continued to expand their hours of operation, moving in the direction of twenty-four-hour-a-day programming.

Clearly, a process of profound change had begun in television, but it was the type of change that would unfold over decades, not just a season or two. It would not come about because of any one show or any one event, though there would be important milestones. Instead, the change would be cumulative, as households began to respond to the additional television choices being presented to them. New generations were growing up seeing more than just ABC, CBS, and NBC as the sources of television entertainment. Even though viewers still tuned in the major networks for most of the big shows, they were also becoming aware that there might be something else, just down the dial.

43. Send in the "A" Team

ON JULY 5, 1982, NBC VENTURED INTO late late news with *NBC News Overnight*, hosted by Linda Ellerbee and Lloyd Dobyns. The program aired even later than ABC's *Nightline*, running Monday through Thursday from 1:30 to 2:30 A.M., and Friday nights from 2:00 to 3:00 A.M. The program was remarkable in its simplicity and elegant in its execution. Recognizing that NBC's network correspondents worldwide sent in far more reports than could ever be used by the nightly news, *NBC News Overnight* offered those reporters a chance for air time—not only presenting pieces that had never made the regular news cut, but also including longer versions of stories that had been trimmed for time.

Consequently, *Overnight* was cost-effective, using resources the network already had in place, including feeds from international news services. As anchors, Ellerbee and Dobyns were not afraid of irony and often used the odd juxtaposition of stories to make subtle points without sacrificing the integrity of the overall presentation. It was perfectly appropriate for the wee hours and, with the emphasis on world news and in-depth pieces, *Overnight* was a newshound's newscast.

A few months later (October 1982) CBS launched its own overnight service (*CBS News Nightwatch*) digging even deeper into the late hours (broadcasting from 2:00 to 6:00 A.M. late Sunday through Thursday nights) and making similar use of resources already in place. That same month, ABC replaced its late night entertainment series reruns with *The Last Word*, a flashy followup to *Nightline*, featuring Gregory Jackson and daytime interview impresario Phil Donahue providing news analysis and interviews.

The networks also expanded their news coverage at the other end of the broadcast day. On July 5, ABC placed a one-hour newscast, *ABC News This Morning* (with Steve Bell and Kathleen Sullivan), before *Good Morning America*. That same day, NBC extended its *Today* show an extra thirty minutes, using the regular *Today* cast for *Early Today*. In October, CBS also added a thirty-minute early edition of the news, *The CBS Early Morning News*.

Cumulatively, these new programs added some forty hours of news per week to the networks' schedules. Because the overnight shows and the early morning shows practically overlapped, they effectively extended network feeds for their affiliates to nearly twenty-four hours a day, just like some cable services. This represented a spectacular recommitment by the networks to one of their most respected areas of programming, and resulted in nearly ninety hours each week of news, information, public affairs, and interview shows across ABC, CBS, and NBC. Not coincidentally, this expansion also served as a strategic response by those networks to a new venture by cable magnate Ted Turner.

In January 1982, Turner had launched CNN-2 (later called Headline News), a companion service to CNN that could make further use of the material already being gathered for the all-news cable channel. Headline News packaged its stories into self-contained thirty-minute news programs that were repeated (with updates) twenty-four hours a day. These programs could be plugged into virtually any time slot, using a news format very familiar to viewers: a half-hour survey of national and international news, features, and sports. Just like a network newscast.

What made ABC, CBS, and NBC take notice, however, was the fact that Headline News was not offered only to cable services; it was also pitched to over-the-air broadcasters, including network affiliates, for use in filling whatever slot the local station might choose. This was a direct encroachment on network turf, not only in content but also in servicing their affiliates.

The relationship between the networks and their affiliates had always been complex, with affiliates, in theory, retaining considerable flexibility in deciding what network shows they slotted and when. Practically speaking, it made good business sense to run network programs exactly as scheduled to take advantage of viewer familiarity and national publicity. However, there were exceptions, as when stations chose to insert local sports events or decided to avoid controversial network programs they felt might offend local sensibilities.

Affiliates had always looked to programming sources apart from the networks for early evening and post-prime time shows (generally game shows and talk shows), so in that sense Headline News was just another potential program provider. However, by offering news programming, Headline News was aggressively staking out new territory. ABC, CBS, and NBC did not want longtime relationships ruptured, even in the empty overnight hours (where many stations slotted Headline News). In theory, such a change could set a bad precedent from the networks' point of view. If the affiliates became accustomed to turning to Headline News, they might by-pass other network programs elsewhere in the broadcast day. So the networks moved in with their own news offerings for late night, overnight, and early morning to try to nip this affiliate "rebellion" in the bud.

Though CNN's Headline News marked the first time there was such an identifiable and direct challenge to the broadcast networks from cable, there were skirmishes on other fronts as well.

	8:00	8:30	9:00	9:30	10:00	10:30	
MON	That's Incredible		ABC NFL Monday Night Football (to 12 Midnight)				**ABC**
	SQUARE PEGS	Private Benjamin	M*A*S*H	NEWHART	Cagney And Lacey		**CBS**
	Little House: A New Beginning		NBC Monday Night At The Movies				**NBC**
TUE	Happy Days	Laverne And Shirley	Three's Company	9 To 5	Hart To Hart		**ABC**
	BRING 'EM BACK ALIVE		CBS Tuesday Night Movies				**CBS**
	Father Murphy		GAVILAN		ST. ELSEWHERE		**NBC**
WED	TALES OF THE GOLD MONKEY		The Fall Guy		Dynasty		**ABC**
	SEVEN BRIDES FOR SEVEN BROTHERS		Alice	Filthy Rich	TUCKER'S WITCH		**CBS**
	Real People		Facts Of Life	FAMILY TIES	Quincy, M.E.		**NBC**
THR	Joanie Loves Chachi	STAR OF THE FAMILY	Too Close For Comfort	IT TAKES TWO	20/20		**ABC**
	Magnum, P.I.		Simon And Simon		Knots Landing		**CBS**
	Fame		CHEERS	Taxi	Hill Street Blues		**NBC**
FRI	Benson	THE NEW ODD COUPLE	The Greatest American Hero		THE QUEST		**ABC**
	The Dukes Of Hazzard		Dallas		Falcon Crest		**CBS**
	POWERS OF MATTHEW STAR		KNIGHT RIDER		REMINGTON STEELE		**NBC**
SAT	T.J. Hooker		The Love Boat		Fantasy Island		**ABC**
	Walt Disney		CBS Saturday Night Movies				**CBS**
	Diff'rent Strokes	SILVER SPOONS	Gimme A Break	Love, Sidney	THE DEVLIN CONNECTION		**NBC**

	7:00	7:30	8:00	8:30	9:00	9:30	10:00	10:30	
SUN	RIPLEY'S BELIEVE IT OR NOT		MATT HOUSTON		ABC Sunday Night Movie				**ABC**
	60 Minutes		Archie Bunker's Place	GLORIA	The Jeffersons	One Day At A Time	Trapper John, M.D.		**CBS**
	VOYAGERS!		CHiPs		NBC Sunday Night At The Movies				**NBC**

With music videos on MTV continuing to generate "teen buzz," NBC became the first broadcast network to attempt a regular slot for such programming. In the summer of 1983, NBC unveiled its response, *Friday Night Videos.*

For ninety minutes late Friday night into Saturday (12:30 to 2:00 A.M.), *Friday Night Videos* brought the MTV video world to mainstream television. At first, there was only an off-screen announcer (Nick Michaels) to introduce the videos, but soon the network used its clout to vie with MTV for the latest video premieres and celebrity guests to spice up the program's format.

Friday Night Videos developed into a respectable program by network standards, but it could never hope to compete for teen loyalty with MTV's twenty-four-hour video lineup. Instead, it was more like Music Videos 101 for those who had heard about this new form of TV and now could see some of it for themselves. Nonetheless, slotting *Friday Night Videos* was a tacit admission that in this case the over-the-air networks were playing catch-up with cable, attempting to lure the young audience for a hot programming form that had been created totally outside their system.

ABC, CBS, and NBC were much more comfortable viewing cable as the pricey home for network castoffs, reruns, and a limited number of movies that were repeated ad nauseam. Broadcasters were still the only ones that could afford the original, high-gloss professional productions that viewers had come to expect from commercial television. Still at no additional charge.

Yet even here, the first chinks were appearing in the network armor. In the spring of 1983, the premium cable service Showtime added to its schedule a network "castoff," *The Paper Chase.* The series had originally played for a single season on CBS in 1978–79, and more recently had been rerun on PBS. Showtime was the program's third home. However, Showtime was doing something unprecedented with the series: It was paying for the production of additional new episodes, marking the first such commitment by a cable service. This was a warning that another exclusive network area could be challenged: the production of original series.

The Paper Chase was the perfect vehicle for such a venture. During its CBS run, the series had been well regarded as a strong adaptation of the 1973 feature film, due primarily to Oscar-winning star John Houseman continuing his role as Professor Charles Kingsfield. Houseman was riveting as the no-nonsense contract law professor who demanded the best from his classes, winning the immediate and undying admiration of first-year student James T. Hart (James Stephens), the epitome of Midwestern integrity, optimism, and hard work.

Houseman and Stephens formed the nucleus of the series and both were back for *The Paper Chase: The Second Year.* These new episodes not only gave Showtime the chance to show off a new production that looked as good as any network series, they also allowed a glimpse of what premium cable could do that the commercial networks could not (or would not).

From first year to graduation, the relationship between Professor Charles Kingsfield (John Houseman, *right*) and his top student, James Hart (James Stephens), was at the center of *The Paper Chase*. (The Paper Chase © 1979 Twentieth Century Fox Television. All Rights Reserved.)

The CBS *Paper Chase* episodes had seemed buffeted by the demands of playing in a television world dominated by the likes of *Laverne and Shirley* and *Charlie's Angels*, so that for every plot about integrity and moot court there were also riffs about romancing a mobster's daughter or helping a defecting Russian gymnast. The result was hit and miss, never luring the *Three's Company* crowd but often annoying the quality crowd. Nonetheless, *The Paper Chase* still stood out as an exceptional offering for the time and its quick cancellation on CBS became a rallying point for those who found little to watch on commercial television. Its revival on cable was a chance to support quality television by pointedly subscribing to an alternative.

Showtime's viewers were not disappointed. On the new episodes, the pacing was less frenzied and the plotting more character- and issue-driven. There was a greater willingness to let the stories flow at their own pace, even if they were less flashy. One episode ("My Dinner with Kingsfield") found Kingsfield and Hart unexpectedly sharing dinner and conversation as the result of a snowstorm. In another story, Kingsfield quietly disappeared for one day, forcing both students and faculty to make important decisions on their own, without having him there for guidance.

The new *Paper Chase* episodes did not air each week. Instead, Showtime took three years to present thirty-six new episodes,

treating each one like a special mini-movie that was repeated and promoted throughout the schedule. Eventually, the series took Hart and Kingsfield through the three years of law school to graduation. For his part, Houseman refined and polished the nuances of his character, giving cable subscribers the opportunity to see performances that went far beyond the original film portrayal.

The Paper Chase showed that, in addition to offering movies, cable could use the right series to attract subscribers. That was exactly what had lured viewers to commercial television in the first place back in the 1950s: regular series with strong, identifiable characters. The trick was to use familiar formats with hooks that differentiated the cable shows from those of the over-the-air networks. After all, while people regarded watching movies on cable as saving the cost of going to the theater, there were already series on commercial TV for free. A series on cable had to be something special. As competition to land hit films increased, such original productions would become a key element in defining the cable landscape.

The overall television landscape, however, remained the province of ABC, CBS, and NBC. Among the three, CBS maintained its reign at the top of the ratings with a mix of soaps led by *Dallas*, adventures led by *Magnum, P.I.,* comedy led by *M*A*S*H*, and television's number one show, *60 Minutes*. In second place, ABC had its soapy mainstay (*Dynasty*), a handful of aging comedies (*Three's Company, The Love Boat*), and *Monday Night Football* (hurt that fall by a players' strike). NBC remained a distant third. Overall CBS had a comfortable lead in the competition, and the new shows for the fall of 1982 did little to change that equation.

Yet amid a fall lineup on the three networks that included such disposables as *Bring 'em Back Alive* (a knockoff of Indiana Jones), *The Powers of Matthew Star* (a teen-hero science fiction tale), and *Matt Houston* (a generic male hunk detective), there came almost unnoticed an astonishing number of high quality comedy and drama offerings. Most were from writers and producers weaned on the MTM production company style, and a few were from MTM itself. Nearly all were on the third place network, NBC. Only one registered respectable ratings that season: Bob Newhart's new sitcom on CBS.

Newhart placed Bob Newhart's resilient deadpan everyman persona in the setting of a small Vermont country inn. He played Dick Loudon, a transplanted big-city writer of how-to books (and, after awhile, the host of a local TV talk show), who bought and ran the Stratford Inn with his wife, Joanna (Mary Frann). Throughout the eight-season run of the series, Dick and Joanna remained perpetual "newcomers" to old Vermont, continually puzzled by the town's otherworldly situations that brought a never-ending parade of odd characters through their door as guests, neighbors, or employees. These included the slow but countrywise handyman George Utley (Tom Poston), shallow and self-absorbed local TV producer Michael Harris (Peter Scolari), pouty and self-absorbed hotel maid Stephanie (Julia Duffy), and backwoods siblings Larry (the only one who spoke), his brother Darryl, and his other brother Darryl (William Sanderson, Tony Papenfuss, and John Volstad, respectively). All of them gave Newhart plenty of opportunities to do what he did best: React. Slowly. Cautiously. Hilariously.

Newhart was a comfortable fit with CBS, giving the network a new yet very familiar program from one of its comedy mainstays of the 1970s. As part of the CBS Monday-night lineup (following *M*A*S*H*), the series got the time it needed to properly establish itself and easily landed in the top twenty for the season

Of course, even the CBS clout did not guarantee that every new series from the network would be a hit, especially those shows that ventured too far from the familiar CBS groove. *Square Pegs*, also slotted on Monday night, was a high school comedy created by former *Saturday Night Live* writer Anne Beatts, focusing on the in-out social crowds at Weemawee High School. Tracy Nelson (daughter of Rick Nelson) was one of the "in" Valley Girls while Sarah Jessica Parker played Patty Greene, a tall, awkward "plain Jane" with glasses. The program was clever but inconsistent, displaying a hip swagger more appropriate to an MTV audience. With fractured storylines and jarring "new wave" musical riffs (including a theme song by The Waitresses and such guest acts as Devo), the series did not seem to belong on CBS and disappeared after one season. That was the downside of a slot at the number one network. While a show would get a built-in audience, it also faced expectations that it would fit in and deliver solid ratings.

There was little pressure of that type over at NBC. Despite the critical success and decent ratings of *Hill Street Blues*, the network still did not have any big hit shows. Nonetheless, programming chief Brandon Tartikoff continued to try a wide variety of offerings, in the process building a true A-list of programs for the network. That fall, the new shows on the NBC schedule included *Family Ties, Silver Spoons, Cheers, Remington Steele,* and *St. Elsewhere.* None of them caught on in their first season, but Tartikoff judged the shows to be worth nurturing. They each had a distinctive premise, good writing, and a solid cast. All they needed was the opportunity to connect with viewers.

Family Ties was the creation of Gary David Goldberg, who had been a writer on such MTM series as *The Bob Newhart Show* and *Lou Grant,* and who had created the short-lived 1979 sitcom *The Last Resort* (college students working in the Catskills). Goldberg took his ear for strong dialogue, character nuance, and believable situations and applied it to a 1980s twist on generational conflict. He set *Family Ties* in the heart of middle America (Columbus, Ohio), though instead of having the World War II generation cross swords with the Swinging 1960s crowd (as had been the case with the previous decade's *All in the Family*), this series presented as its *older generation* a pair of idealistic baby boomers who had come of age in the 1960s and now had to deal with their own kids.

Mom and dad (Elyse and Steven Keaton, played by Meredith Baxter Birney and Michael Gross) were appropriately earnest (especially Steven), constantly asking themselves whether they were being true to their starry-eyed past. As responsible adults with three children, they had respectable jobs (she was an architect, he was manager of a local public TV station), made a comfortable living, and hoped to pass on their liberal values to the next generation. Teenage daughter Mallory (Justine Bateman) and nine-year-old Jennifer (Tina Yothers) were polite and respectful of these efforts, but were frankly far more interested in their own growing up concerns than in nostalgia-tinged music and tales from an era that was just so much history to them. Son Alex (Michael J. Fox), the oldest, was equally respectful but far more engaged in the political side of life. He was an intelligent and articulate conservative, a firm believer in the wonders of free market capitalism, and an admirer of such U.S. presidents as Richard M. Nixon and Ronald Reagan.

Despite this setup, *Family Ties* never settled for a formula of shrill shouting matches on the issues of the day. Instead, Alex and his family agreed to disagree, talking forcefully but not constantly about liberal and conservative values. The series quickly showed its strength as a genuinely affectionate family comedy, with the members always there for each other, working through conflicts, and inevitably embracing after disagreements. The real focus was on growing up, not only by the three children, but also by the parents. Alex even opened doors by bonding with his similarly conservative grandfather Jake (Steven's dad, played by John

Randolph) as the two tried to figure out how a guy as good-hearted as Steven could be so wrong in his world view. For all the characters, especially the parents, family life was a blessing, representing the best thing that ever happened to them.

Over time, Michael J. Fox's Alex emerged as the program's most popular character, with his ingratiating smile, nervous self-confidence, and puppy-dog charm. Though always remaining true to his conservative leanings, Alex also learned to explore his emotions in greater depth. One pivotal moment took place when he illogically lost his heart to Ellen Reed (Tracy Pollan), an art student at his college. Uncertain how to express himself, he watched tongue-tied as she boarded a train to visit her current boyfriend at another college (with marriage likely to follow). A short time later, on the way to a prestigious college party, Alex impulsively turned the car away from campus and frantically drove hundreds of miles to meet Ellen at the destination train station. There, in the early morning hours, Alex finally uttered the words, "I love you" and she reciprocated. Though the character of Ellen was written out of the series after only a season, in real life Pollan and Fox followed through on that declaration and were soon married.

Family Ties did not keep its characters frozen in time but took Alex and Mallory from high school through college and Jennifer into her teen years. Steven survived a heart attack and bypass surgery, while Elyse had a late-in-life fourth child (son Andrew). Appropriate to the generations theme of the series, conservative Alex soon won the heart of his younger brother, though the series blatantly jumped character time-line continuity to help this along. The season after Andy was born, he was suddenly a walking and talking child (played by four-year-old Brian Bonsall) who was much easier to integrate into the stories than the eight-month-old baby he should have been. As a result, Andy could engage in verbal give-and-take, especially enjoying the attention of his older brother. Together the two scanned such publications as the *Wall Street Journal* and watched such television shows as *Wall Street Week in Review.* Alex knew it was never too early to develop important family values.

NBC's other new generational sitcom that fall, *Silver Spoons*, was hatched by producers from *The Jeffersons.* In this series, there was no doubt as to which was the most mature and intelligent character: It was twelve-year-old Ricky Stratton (Ricky Schroder), who had just moved in with his wealthy dad, thirty-five-year-old Edward Stratton III (Joel Higgins), owner of a fabulously successful toy company. The two had never spent time together before then (as the result of a divorce, Ricky had been raised by his mom and then sent to military school), so Ricky was amazed to see that his dad was more of a kid than he was: sunny, optimistic, and taking great delight in playing with toys, not just selling them. The household included a miniature railroad train system that ran throughout the mansion, with cars just big enough for Edward to ride in. Edward's secretary, Kate (Erin Gray), kept his life in order and hoped for adult romance one day; while his business manager, Dexter (Franklyn Seales), and his lawyer, Leonard (Leonard Lightfoot), made sure he remained solvent. Grandfather Edward Stratton II (John Houseman, in an occasional role) scowled at his son's childish (though successful) behavior, but Ricky helped bridge that generation gap. Not surprisingly, Ricky and his dad taught each other aspects of life they had missed by going their separate ways. Edward learned to let go of some of his extended childhood tendencies (marrying Kate in the third season) while Ricky found it was all right to relax and enjoy being a kid while he was still a kid.

In contrast to the family settings in *Family Ties* and *Silver Spoons, Cheers* used the "workplace family" hook that had worked so well on *Mary Tyler Moore* and, more recently, on *Taxi*. In fact, not only did some of the same talents behind *Taxi* serve as the creators of *Cheers* (director James Burrows and writers Les Charles and Glen Charles), but also the new program began its network run on NBC coupled with the cabbies. Upon hearing the news that ABC had canceled *Taxi* in the spring of 1982 (and of reported overtures by HBO to continue the series), Brandon Tartikoff had stepped in and picked up the program. For the fall of 1982, NBC placed *Cheers* at 9:00 p.m. Thursday, followed by *Taxi* in its old 9:30 P.M. time slot, with accompanying promos by Danny DeVito in his Louie De Palma persona sneering, "Same time, better station." Unfortunately, the new network home did not improve *Taxi*'s soft ratings (the reason ABC cited for the cancellation in the first place), so the program ended five years of high quality production with this one final season on NBC. That left *Cheers* on its own, but the series was up to the challenge. Just as *Taxi* could have virtually anyone turn up as a passenger in one of the cabs, *Cheers* had a setting (a neighborhood bar in downtown Boston) that allowed virtually anyone to come through the front door.

Cheers had all its key elements in place starting with the first episode, and never looked back. It all began when a well-educated but somewhat starry-eyed graduate student, Diane Chambers (Shelley Long), stopped at the Cheers bar with her paramour, literature professor, Sumner Sloan, for a celebratory drink before he made good on his promise to whisk her away to a tropical island (leaving his wife behind). Before the end of the evening, though, he had disappeared, flying off instead with his wife and leaving Diane behind. Realizing she could never return to the school, a distressed Diane accepted a job offer by bar owner Sam Malone (Ted Danson) to work as a cocktail waitress, rationalizing it as an opportunity to help her writing by getting to know the "common people." Sam, in turn, needed a new waitress, felt sorry for her situation, and knew that with her lack of real-world experience she was not qualified for much else.

Sam also wanted to have sex with Diane. It was his natural reaction to any attractive woman. (Sam's long list of lovers was legendary at the bar.) She would not admit it (at first), but Diane was attracted to Sam from the start as well. Initially, Sam and Diane hid their feelings for each other with quips and putdowns. She made fun of his lack of formal education, and he mocked her pretentious mannerisms. By the end of the first season, though, they admitted their true feelings and at last embraced after a passionately angry argument in Sam's office (with the entire bar listening at the door). They then carried on an intense affair for one season, but it was a stormy arrangement and their barroom comments were still peppered with quips and putdowns. That sharp edge continued through every subsequent phase of their relationship as they split, continued to work together, and flirted with other people (Diane nearly married her psychiatrist, Frasier Crane). Sam and Diane eventually became engaged, but called off the marriage at the last minute. The give-and-take between the couple gave the series a continuing sexually charged lure, with Long and Danson particularly adept at keeping the sparring familiar yet fresh.

The on-going relationship also gave the writers the freedom to develop the comic possibilities in all the other characters, using the flexibility of the premise to take the stories anywhere. This turned *Cheers* into one of the best written and best executed situation comedies ever, with parallel subplots and throwaway background comments that were as funny as the main punch lines. The main bar lineup included a logically illogical bartender, Ernie "Coach" Pantusso (Nicholas Colasanto), who had coached Sam during his time as a baseball pitcher with the Boston Red Sox; a sharp-tongued waitress who hated Diane and loved kinky sex, Carla Tortelli (Rhea Perlman); a deadpan intellectual psychiatrist, Frasier Crane (Kelsey Grammer), who hung out at the bar even after Diane left him at the altar; a know-it-all yakker, Cliff Clavin (John Ratzenberger), a U.S. postal worker who still lived with his mother; and a rotund, beer-drinking schlub, Norm Peterson (George Wendt), an accountant who spent as much time as possible at his Cheers barstool and whose entrance was always greeted with a chorus of "Norm!" from the patrons. When Colasanto died after the third season, Woody Harrelson stepped in as Woody Boyd, a wisely innocent young farm boy come to the big city.

These characters were all clearly defined and remained true to type, even if that meant coming off as selfish, slovenly, or obnoxious. Personal flaws and all, they were dead-on hilarious. They also ended up providing a truly supportive family for each other, in the tradition of the best workplace ensembles.

Though many of the people behind these three new NBC comedy series had roots back in the MTM production company, the only new programs for the network that were actually from MTM were a pair of dramas: *Remington Steele* and *St. Elsewhere*.

With *Remington Steele*, MTM ventured into the lighter fare of detective adventure with a clever take on a romantic male-female team. Private investigator Laura Holt (Stephanie Zimbalist) had been frustrated at the unwillingness of potential clients to take seriously a female detective, so she created an imaginary boss

---

September 26, 1982
Gloria. (CBS). Archie Bunker's little girl, now a single mom after her husband left her for a flower child, briefly gets her own TV show. She is an assistant veterinarian in upstate New York.

December 17, 1982
Just fourteen months after its debut, CBS Cable dies. Its final offering is *Mixed Bag*, which presents highlights of the service's brief history.

March 6, 1983
A new attempt at spring football, the United States Football League (USFL), begins with the first of sixteen Sunday-afternoon telecasts on ABC. Keith Jackson and Lynn Swann are behind the microphones as the Los Angeles Express defeats Herschel Walker and his New Jersey Generals 20 to 15 at the Los Angeles Coliseum. The league lasts only three seasons.

March 19, 1983
"Still the Beaver." (CBS). The surviving cast members of *Leave It To Beaver* reunite for a two-hour made-for-TV movie. Things have not gone well for the Beaver in the past twenty years. He is now thirty-three, overweight, in the middle of a divorce, and the father of two sons who largely ignore him. Still, high ratings for the movie lead to *The New Leave It To Beaver*, a regular series that runs on cable from 1985 to 1989.

March 31, 1983
After months of criticism for not featuring videos by black artists, MTV presents the world premiere of Michael Jackson's innovative "Beat It" video. Eight months later, Jackson's fourteen-minute big-budget mini-movie (directed by Hollywood's John Landis) for "Thriller" also has its world premiere on MTV.

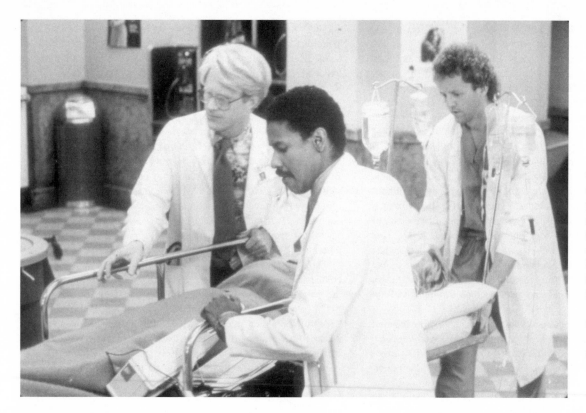

Strong characters and literate scripts put *St. Elsewhere* in a class by itself. The cast included *(from left)* Ed Begley, Jr., Denzel Washington, and David Morse. (St. Elsewhere © 1983 Twentieth Century Fox Television. All Rights Reserved.)

named Remington Steele (who preferred to be "behind the scenes" whenever her agency was on the job). In the pilot, a professional thief and con man (played by Pierce Brosnan) discovered the deception and found the opportunity to step into the role of Remington Steele irresistible—primarily because he found himself attracted to Laura Holt. She, in turn, agreed to the setup because she was attracted to him as well. All they had to do was figure out how to take that next step to commitment. It would take Holt and Steele five years to successfully work out their relationship and, unlike Sam and Diane in *Cheers*, this did not involve falling into bed with each other on a first date.

Instead, while getting to know each other, Holt and Steele constantly sparred, as he grew to enjoy and embody the character of Remington Steele and she constantly probed, looking for hints about his mysterious past. Unlike such series as *Hart to Hart* (which featured an already comfortably married couple), there was a sense of seduction and mystery to the repartee between Holt and Steele because the two did not know a lot about each other. Each episode provided the opportunity to fill in a few more lines in their respective portraits.

That was the central romantic premise, but the additional genius of the series was its clever mystery writing. Every episode was a genuine puzzle executed with the right balance of humor, adventure, and personal panache worthy of the classic *Avengers* days of John Steed and Emma Peel. Because Steele was established as a movie buff, the stories were inevitably filled with cinematic allusions; some episodes were even structured like particular films, such as Alfred Hitchcock's "The Trouble with Harry" or the appropriately manipulative "The Sting."

In the program's second season, Holt and Steele were joined by Mildred Krebs (Doris Roberts), a former IRS auditor who became their office manager, dogged researcher, and unofficial "mom." Over the course of the series, Steele also searched for details of his own past that even he did not know, at last learning the answers from his lifelong mentor, con man Daniel Chalmers (played by Efrem Zimbalist, Jr., real-life father of Stephanie).

MTM's other new drama, *St. Elsewhere*, was, in essence, largely *Hill Street Blues* set in a hospital. Even though it had no direct connections to that Steven Bochco drama, *St. Elsewhere* shared many of its best traits. *St. Elsewhere* had an equally strong creative team behind it, including MTM veteran writers Joshua Brand and John Falsey, producer Bruce Paltrow, and director Mark Tinker, who had all worked together on *The White Shadow*. *St. Elsewhere* also had a rich acting ensemble and, like *Hill Street Blues*, a similarly bleak urban setting. Located in a run-down neighborhood in Boston, St. Eligius Hospital was the place you ended up if you could not afford one of the fancy downtown medical facilities, thus earning it the nickname "St. Elsewhere." Sometimes the sobriquet seemed particularly well earned because, just like in real life (and unlike typical television medical dramas), some patients brought to St. Eligius did die. Nonetheless, the hospital staff was clearly top-notch, and so was the program's storytelling.

A large regular cast allowed for a wide range of plot threads on different levels of hospital life, from administrators to orderlies. Donald Westphall (Ed Flanders) and Daniel Auschlander (Norman Lloyd) were the administrators charged with the task of keeping the institution open, despite the fact that St. Eligius was always on budgetary life support. Mark Craig (William Daniels) was the highly honored chief of surgery, a demanding taskmaster to the rest of the hospital staff, especially to his protégé Victor Ehrlich (Ed Begley, Jr.). Many of the doctors and nurses were there for the duration of the series, including Jack Morrison (David Morse), Wayne Fiscus (Howie Mandel), Helen Rosenthal (Cristina Pickles), and Phillip Chandler (Denzel Washington), with each one experiencing personal and professional ups and downs. Others had shorter but no less dramatic stints. Peter White (Terence Knox) was a confessed rapist who was executed in the hospital morgue by vengeful nurse Shirley Daniels (Ellen Bry). Robert Caldwell (Mark Harmon) and, years later, Seth Griffin (Bruce Greenwood) both departed the series as separate victims of AIDS. Among the support staff, orderly Luther Hawkins (Eric Laneuville) eventually became an emergency medical technician while his buddy Warren Coolidge (Byron Stewart) showed the turns life could take after high school basketball. (Stewart's character had originated on *The White Shadow*.)

Because St. Eligius was a teaching hospital with a front line emergency room, *St. Elsewhere* could work in the expected life-and-death struggles of any hospital drama, but with a more gritty and immediate feel. Yet the series offered much more. Throughout its run, there was a liberating sense that *anything* could happen on *St. Elsewhere* with scripts that were literate, philosophical, and downright playful. One episode was staged much like the Thornton Wilder drama "Our Town"; another sent Mandel's Dr. Fiscus up to heaven to meet God; others showed liver cancer victim Auschlander donning superhero garb and accomplishing impossible tasks. Such dramatic fantasies were usually (but not always) explained as dreams or medical hallucinations. Other moments simply reflected a whimsical sense of humor. When one character said that it's not over "until the fat lady sings," it was no surprise that an opera singer under treatment at the hospital burst into song before the end of the episode. Being located in Boston, members of the St. Eligius staff eventually wandered over to the *Cheers* bar for a drink. After all, it was the same city and the same network, if not the same production company. In turn, when Carla on *Cheers* gave birth, it was at St. Eligius.

St. Elsewhere never achieved hit status, but the series managed to hang on for six seasons by successfully appealing to a young, upscale demographic. Even so, the program's year-to-year fate was always in doubt. That uncertainty, though, perversely added to *St. Elsewhere*'s appeal because every season unfolded as if it were the last, with the program's writers approaching their stories with abandon. Anything could happen, even if it was not high ratings for NBC.

In fact, about the only time NBC and ABC had the chance to score big in the 1982–83 season was with specials such as sports events or miniseries. ABC did just that under its Novels for Television umbrella (used for *Roots*) with two miniseries: *The Winds of War* (in February) and *The Thorn Birds* (in March). They quickly succeeded each other as the number two miniseries behind *Roots*.

In May, NBC did well with the miniseries *V,* an allegorical science fiction adventure that likened a subtle and insidious alien invasion of Earth to the rise of Nazi power in Europe that led to World War II. The four and one-half hour presentation took the story up through the first underground resistance efforts against the triumphant aliens, leaving the all-out confrontation for a planned miniseries sequel the following year.

NBC's most predictable special-event success was the annual football Super Bowl in January, which rotated each year between CBS and NBC, the two primary football networks. Determined to make the most of that one-time audience, NBC undertook a tremendous promotional campaign for *The A-Team,* with the program premiere scheduled to follow the game. For weeks the network peppered its schedule with mock recruitment messages that continued through the Super Bowl itself. These featured high-powered wrestling personality Mr. T, who practically demanded that viewers tune in *The A-Team*. They did, sending the two-hour pilot into the top five for the week. Even more important, viewers stayed around for the regular series, giving NBC its first big hit in years.

Created by Stephen J. Cannell (who had recently scored a minor hit on ABC with *The Greatest American Hero,* a gentle send-up of superheroes), *The A-Team* was a canny mix of broadly drawn characters, exaggerated adventures, and countless vehicle crashes. The members of the A-Team were veterans of the Vietnam War who had been falsely convicted of a major theft during the closing days of battle in that country. They promptly escaped from maximum security and fled to the Los Angeles underground, where they kept one step ahead of the military law and occupied their time as soldiers of fortune taking on impossible missions at $100,000 a crack. (Typical of TV heroes, they waived the fee if you were broke but had a truly hopeless cause.)

The A-Team was gleeful in its audacious sense of fun, especially at the expense of such TV mainstays as *Mission: Impossible,* turning the well-ordered and orchestrated world of meticulous government missions into a wide-open guerrilla warfare free-for-all. Though team leader and part-time actor Col. John "Hannibal" Smith (George Peppard) inevitably declared, "I love it when a plan comes together"; in fact it rarely did without some unexpected improvisation (much like combat missions back in Vietnam). Simply assembling the team itself was sometimes a challenge. Capt. H. M. "Howling Mad" Murdock (Dwight Schultz) often had to be sprung from a mental hospital. Ace mechanic Sgt. B. A. "Bad Attitude" Baracus (Mr. T) was paranoid about flying, so he had to be tricked into taking a sleeping injection. That was assuming the smooth-talking Lt. Templeton "Face" Peckman (Dirk Benedict) could con someone out of the cash or materials necessary for their transport. Once on the job, the A-Team eschewed the latest

April 10, 1983
Casablanca. (NBC). TV's second attempt to turn the classic 1942 film into a TV series. This time, David Soul (of *Starsky and Hutch*) plays American émigré Rick Blaine, the proprietor of Rick's Café.

April 18, 1983
Just two months after Disney's weekly TV series temporarily shuts down, the studio trailblazes a new medium for promoting its product, with the debut of cable's Disney Channel.

April 20, 1983
William Paley formally steps down as chairman of the board of CBS; he is replaced in that post by Thomas Wyman. Paley retains the title of chairman of the executive committee of the CBS Board of Directors.

May 16, 1983
"Motown 25: Yesterday, Today, and Forever." (NBC). Michael Jackson and his "moonwalk" dance steps steal the show in a two-hour special honoring the twenty-fifth anniversary of the Detroit-based R&B record label.

August 9, 1983
Two weeks after the death of ABC news anchorman Frank Reynolds, his temporary replacement (Peter Jennings) is given the post on a full-time basis, as *World News Tonight* adopts a solo anchor format. Fifteen years earlier, Jennings had given up the very same position.

September 5, 1983
Roger Mudd is removed as co-anchor on the *NBC Nightly News*, leaving Tom Brokaw the sole anchor.

September 5, 1983
The MacNeil-Lehrer NewsHour. (PBS). After nearly eight years as a thirty-minute show, public television's *MacNeil-Lehrer Report* expands to sixty minutes nightly, with Robert MacNeil and Jim Lehrer continuing as co-anchors.

electronic gadgets and generally used whatever was available, from spare machine parts to boxes of toilet paper. The plots were not particularly complex and usually depended on cartoon-style explosions and car crashes. Typically, a car might fly through the air, tumble, and crash, but at the last minute, just before it exploded, the occupants would pop out and flee.

The A-Team was admittedly pure fluff, but it was also a hit, giving NBC its first wedge for building word-of-mouth awareness for its other series. For a network hungry for any success, that was welcome news.

Appropriately, just as *The A-Team* was beginning to present renegades from the Vietnam War as heroes, another series was wrapping up its portrayal of an unorthodox group of military characters.

By the 1982–83 season, *M*A*S*H* had been on the air for ten years, nearly three times as long as its Korean War setting, and it had lasted nearly six years after the end of the Vietnam War (the implicit target of many of its initial jibes). *M*A*S*H* had maintained that rare balance of high ratings and high critical praise. Over the years, the program had morphed from a comedy with dramatic overtones into a drama with comic overtones. While some episodes played almost as experimental short films (a *Twilight Zone*-style tale told by the spirit of a dead soldier, or a surrealistic collection of dream images), the program could also be consistently counted on for well-polished jokes, especially when delivered by Alan Alda's droll Hawkeye Pierce.

As with any long-running series with a familiar central cast, the program was starting to show the strain of searching for stories it had not already done. Led by Alda (who by then was also a creative consultant, a regular writer, and an occasional director) the cast and crew were ready to go out in style at the end of its eleventh season. The last round of regular episodes for the season were confidently reenergized, ending with a time capsule story that allowed for references to such departed characters as Radar O'Reilly, Trapper John, and Henry Blake. With all that out of the way, there remained the final sendoff.

The *M*A*S*H* finale aired Monday, February 28, 1983, as a heavily promoted must-see sweeps event. News outlets vied for leaks on plot details; magazines and newspapers devoted special features to the show; and broadcasters covered it as the major pop culture event it had become. Directed by Alan Alda and running two and one-half hours (which, minus commercials, was about as long as the original theatrical film), "Goodbye, Farewell and Amen" almost managed to live up to all the hype in its first forty-five minutes.

Viewers expecting merely an extra-long episode of a popular comedy were immediately surprised to see the story beginning at an Army psychiatric hospital, with Hawkeye Pierce at last driven over the edge by the war and now a patient under the care of Dr. Sidney Freedman (Allan Arbus). But how? When? Why? Layer by layer, the details came forth along with plot complications facing the other characters. Unlike past *M*A*S*H* episodes in which Freedman sometimes made what amounted to miraculous insights, the premise here was perfect. *Everybody* knew what had driven Hawkeye over the edge—everybody except Hawkeye and the viewers. It was up to him to face his demons. When that moment came, it was a gut-wrenching payoff, an out-pouring of anger, sorrow, and contrition that left Hawkeye cursing Freedman for making him face himself. Hawkeye felt he had been responsible for the death of a child and that fact had destroyed his self-image as a healer, driving him into deep denial and into the hospital.

This was *M*A*S*H* completely crossing the line from sitcom to drama and it left some viewers puzzled. What had happened to that perfect balance between comedy and drama? Though the rest of the episode offered some deliberately comic moments, they were routine in comparison to the high drama surrounding Hawkeye in the first forty-five minutes. Over the course of the finale, the other characters also faced some dramatic complications before the 4077th was decommissioned and its members sent home because the interminable peace talks had finally produced a truce that ended the fighting. Some of these plots were touching, as when the imperious Charles Winchester (David Ogden Stiers) took a group of Korean musicians under his wing. Others were ironic, as when Max Klinger (Jamie Farr) stayed behind with his new Korean wife, after spending the entire series attempting to convince the Army to send him home. Some were just silly (Father Mulcahy failing to report an accident that left him nearly deaf). On departure day, Hawkeye was given the book-ending series closer, flying away in an evac helicopter scene that mirrored the arriving helicopter sequence that had opened each episode since the series began in 1972.

The *M*A*S*H* finale was a tremendous ratings success that easily eclipsed the previous champion, the "Who Shot J. R.?" episode of *Dallas*. More than three-quarters of all television viewers were tuned to *M*A*S*H* that night, making it the most-watched episode of a series ever.

Over its entire run, *M*A*S*H* demonstrated that a commercial television series could be groundbreaking, critically acclaimed, and a smash hit. Its heavily promoted finale represented the high-water mark of viewer loyalty to the already fading TV world that simply assumed viewers would automatically turn to one of three places for television entertainment. That night, for one last time, more than 100 million viewers tuned in to confirm that *M*A*S*H* was the best show in town.

44. After *M*A*S*H*

WHAT COULD FOLLOW *M*A*S*H*?

Even before the characters from *M*A*S*H*'s fictional 4077th unit folded up their tents and headed back to U.S. civilian life (circa 1953), CBS had selected what it saw as the perfect sitcom successor. It would follow some of the same characters from the fictional 4077th back to U.S. civilian life (circa 1953).

Production people from the final season of *M*A*S*H* came along for the new series, including executive producer Burt Metcalfe and producer Dennis Koenig. Old hand Larry Gelbart also returned as one of the writers and directors. (Gelbart had written the *M*A*S*H* television pilot and had later co-produced the series for three seasons.) They slyly dubbed the new program *AfterMASH* and set it in Col. Sherman Potter's home turf, Missouri, where he took the job of chief of staff at General Pershing Veterans Administration Hospital. This setting provided the opportunity to see Potter's much-talked-about home life (at last meeting his wife, Mildred) as well as giving him the chance to hire two old friends: Max Klinger (as his administrative assistant) and Father Francis Mulcahy (as the hospital chaplain). Klinger also brought along his new wife, Soon-Lee (Rosalind Chao). After some first-episode surgery, Mulcahy had his hearing restored, correcting an annoying plot contrivance from the *M*A*S*H* finale. All three were determined to adjust to life after war and to fit in as civilians.

AfterMASH premiered in the prize *M*A*S*H* Monday night slot in September and its first episode was the number one show of the week. Viewers were obviously curious about "what happened next" with the characters and were also ready for more of the high quality entertainment they had come to enjoy over the eleven-season run of *M*A*S*H*.

Yet within weeks the new series had dropped out of the top ten and by the spring it had been banished from its Monday night slot. While *AfterMASH* was renewed for a second season, the program barely lasted a few months into that second round.

What happened?

Though Twentieth Century Fox went so far as to label *AfterMASH* (in the closing titles) as "a continuation of *M*A*S*H*," the question was, which version of *M*A*S*H* was it continuing? By the end of its run, *M*A*S*H* was more than just a sitcom and had moved beyond such plots as fighting over a pair of long underwear in winter or dealing with the body of a pompous general who died while having sex with Margaret Houlihan. More often than not, *M*A*S*H* in its later years led with dramatic elements, supported by comedy. With his rapid-fire Groucho Marx-style delivery, Alan

Alda was particularly adept at meeting viewer expectations for laughs, adding just the right injection of humor in each story and allowing the series to successfully walk the line between comedy and drama.

AfterMASH did not have Alan Alda or any strong equivalent to his humorous but commanding Hawkeye Pierce character. Instead, the program seemed oddly off balance from the start, never able to find the right mix. It began confidently, indeed acting just like a continuation of *M*A*S*H*. But even with three returning characters, *AfterMASH* was more akin to a brand new comedy that had to prove itself funny, especially with its stateside setting far from the inherent contradictions and pathos of a war zone. This made the combination of comedy and drama particularly difficult to achieve. What might have come off as a heartfelt observation back in Korea too easily veered toward heavy-handed preaching in a civilian setting. For example, about halfway through the first episode Klinger made a dramatic speech on veterans' rights and dreams. Rather than resonating, it brought the episode to a screeching halt. It seemed too much. Railing against military authority in a war zone was one thing; there was no option to leave. Complaining about bureaucrats in a booming peacetime U.S. setting was a different matter. No one was holding a gun to their heads and forcing them to stay.

There were other problems with *AfterMASH*. Bringing three out of the seven main characters from the final *M*A*S*H* season was too much. Following just one (such as Harry Morgan's Sherman Potter) with occasional guest appearances by the others would have been a wiser strategy with more flexibility. Jamie Farr and William Christopher also had to face the problem encountered by any supporting performer stepping into a lead role. What worked beautifully as comic relief (Klinger) or inspiring fortitude (Mulcahy) did not automatically translate to the expanded status of co-star, especially when their characters were already best known as supporting players.

Yet being senior to all the other performers, Morgan, Farr, and Christopher ended up with the lion's share of each episode, leaving too little time to develop the other characters. That was a major problem because to work as its own series, *AfterMASH* needed new faces to do more than just the equivalent of a walk-on role. Though the production crew did an excellent job attempting to make the series an authentic slice of 1950s America, it needed to show more of that world through different sets of eyes.

New characters such as Dr. Gene Pfeiffer (Jay O. Sanders), Dr.

	8:00	8:30	9:00	9:30	10:00	10:30	
MON	That's Incredible		ABC NFL Monday Night Football (to 12 Midnight)				**ABC**
	SCARECROW AND MRS. KING		AFTERMASH	Newhart	EMERALD POINT N.A.S.		**CBS**
	BOONE		NBC Monday Night At The Movies				**NBC**
TUE	JUST OUR LUCK	Happy Days	Three's Company	OH MADELINE	Hart To Hart		**ABC**
	The Mississippi		CBS Tuesday Night Movies				**CBS**
	The A-Team		Remington Steele		BAY CITY BLUES		**NBC**
WED	The Fall Guy		Dynasty		HOTEL		**ABC**
	WHIZ KIDS		CBS Wednesday Night Movies				**CBS**
	Real People		Facts Of Life	Family Ties	St. Elsewhere		**NBC**
THR	TRAUMA CENTER		9 To 5	IT'S NOT EASY	20/20		**ABC**
	Magnum, P.I.		Simon And Simon		Knots Landing		**CBS**
	Gimme A Break	Mama's Family	WE GOT IT MADE	Cheers	Hill Street Blues		**NBC**
FRI	Benson	WEBSTER	LOTTERY		Matt Houston		**ABC**
	The Dukes Of Hazzard		Dallas		Falcon Crest		**CBS**
	MR. SMITH	JENNIFER SLEPT HERE	MANIMAL		FOR LOVE AND HONOR		**NBC**
SAT	T.J. Hooker		The Love Boat		Fantasy Island		**ABC**
	CUTTER TO HOUSTON		CBS Saturday Night Movies				**CBS**
	Diff'rent Strokes	Silver Spoons	THE ROUSTERS		THE YELLOW ROSE		**NBC**

	7:00	7:30	8:00	8:30	9:00	9:30	10:00	10:30	
SUN	Ripley's Believe It Or Not		HARDCASTLE AND McCORMICK		ABC Sunday Night Movie				**ABC**
	60 Minutes		Alice	One Day At A Time	The Jeffersons	Goodnight Beantown	Trapper John, M.D.		**CBS**
	First Camera		Knight Rider		NBC Sunday Night At The Movies				**NBC**

Boyer (David Ackroyd), and Mike D'Angelo (John Chappell) tried gamely to make their marks, but there was an overwhelming sense that this was not so much a new series as an old favorite hanging around too long. Rather than being cutting-edge, *AfterMASH* seemed almost nostalgic. In that sense, it was appropriate that the second season highlights included the birth of Klinger and Soon-Lee's child and a visit by Radar O'Reilly on his wedding day. Then it was time to truly say goodbye and farewell to the last remnants of the 4077th.

The failure of *AfterMASH* also seemed to confirm a growing sense that the television sitcom was spent. Viewers had seen one too many. While the genre still had a few successes, most of the programs regularly in the top twenty were in some other format. Prime time soaps. Various adventure series. Police and detective dramas. Even news.

Once-popular sitcoms were aging and fading fast. In the 1982-83 season, shows such as *Archie Bunker's Place, Laverne and Shirley,* and *Taxi* had tumbled in the ratings and been axed. This season, *One Day at a Time* and *Happy Days* also faded. By the close of the season, even Jack Tripper's "scandalous" eight-year living arrangement on *Three's Company* ended when both his female roommates moved out. (No, nothing *ever* happened between Jack and any of the women sharing that flat.)

NBC continued to nurture a handful of sitcoms (including *Cheers, Family Ties,* and newcomer *Night Court*), but given their place on the number three network, they generated comparatively limited interest. In fact, NBC's biggest success in comedy came in the form of *TV's Bloopers and Practical Jokes*, a variety show featuring comical outtakes from movies and TV programs, hosted by Dick Clark and Ed McMahon. The series was an outgrowth of occasional specials produced by Clark.

Even more troubling, with just a handful of exceptions, most new sitcoms seemed terribly derivative and were not connecting with viewers. Failures among the new series sitcoms in the fall 1983 included *Just Our Luck* (a magical genie), *Oh Madeline* (Madeline Kahn as a bored suburban housewife), *It's Not Easy* (life among the divorced and remarried), *We Got It Made* (two bachelors and their sexy live-in maid), and *Jennifer Slept Here* (Ann Jillian as a knockout ghost haunting a Beverly Hills mansion). Mid-season sitcom entries did not fare much better, with such failures as: *Suzanne Pleshette Is Maggie Briggs* (a hard-news reporter writes soft features), *Domestic Life* (Martin Mull as a TV commentator about humor in family life), and *The Duck Factory* (Jim Carrey in an MTM production about a tiny animation studio). Even the Alan Alda-produced adaptation of his hit movie *The Four Seasons* did not catch on as a mid-season series.

About the only recent sitcom success was CBS's low-key *Newhart*, which was joined in March by another comfortably relaxed comedy, *Kate and Allie*. Susan Saint James and Jane Curtin played the respective title characters, two divorced women while Tyne Daly continued as Mary Beth Lacey. Amazingly, the chemistry between the two characters worked better than ever and the program continued its groundbreaking portrayal of two strong women as New York City police detectives. This was a truly different series that managed to juggle a multitude of elements. Though the cases were treated seriously, *Cagney and Lacey* was not as grim as *Hill Street Blues*. Neither was it structured as a soap opera. The scripts were not a weekly feminist diatribe, though the dialogue and subject matter frequently dealt with issues important to women. Cagney and Lacey were considered every bit as good as "the guys," yet they were also consciously different from the guys, and they knew it. They regularly took advantage of the fact that no men could follow them into the women's bathroom by having their one-on-one conversations there.

Though the series execution was tremendously successful (Tyne Daly won an Emmy for best actress), its ratings still fell short. CBS canceled *Cagney and Lacey* at the end of the 1982-83 season. That touched off organized protests that resulted in the return of the series as a midseason replacement for the 1983-84 season, with one caveat: This time, the program had to deliver strong ratings or it was gone for good. By then, *Cagney and Lacey* had achieved enough public awareness that its return was a genuine high-profile TV event. Its spring run registered as one of the top ten series for the entire season. It was back and a hit, eventually running seven seasons, with both Gless and Daly picking up multiple Emmy awards during that time.

sharing a Greenwich Village apartment along with their children (Kate's daughter and Allie's son and daughter). Each episode began with a quiet conversation between the two leads, usually in some outdoor New York setting. The plots were creditable complications facing intelligent women attempting to balance children, career, love, and friendship. *Kate and Alley* also marked the first success by a *Saturday Night Live* alum (Curtin) in prime time, and did well filling the vacated *AfterMASH* slot adjacent to *Newhart*. Appropriately, the program also benefited from proximity to the highly promoted return of another pair of independent women, Chris Cagney and Mary Beth Lacey.

The road for *Cagney and Lacey* had not been easy. The series had won its initial renewal by replacing one of its two leads and for the fall of 1982 Sharon Gless stepped into the role of Chris Cagney

The baseball drama *Bay City Blues* combined a love of the game with steamy off the field encounters. The program's lineup included *(clockwise from top)* Bernie Casey, Dennis Franz, Kelly Harmon, and Michael Nouri. (Bay City Blues © *1983 Twentieth Century Fox Television. All Rights Reserved.*)

The success of *Cagney and Lacey* was more good news for CBS, which won virtually every key ratings contest that season. The network led in prime time, daytime, the nightly news, and late night. CBS won all three sweeps periods and its shows dominated the top ten. The network's only concern was the age of some of its series, which would have to be replaced soon. But by carefully adding a few successful new performers each year, CBS had no reason to think its lock at the top would be broken anytime soon.

The other two networks had to settle for more modest successes.

ABC did send into the top ten the most luxurious-looking new series, *Hotel*, starring James Brolin and Connie Sellecca (looking their best). Inspired by the Arthur Hailey novel and using the real-life Fairmont Hotel on Nob Hill in San Francisco for its exterior, the series was a combination soap opera and drama anthology, a five-star *Love Boat* with accommodations that would please even the characters in *Dynasty*.

As usual, however, ABC's biggest successes came from its miniseries and TV movie specials. In January, Glenn Close and

Ted Danson (from NBC's *Cheers*) starred in the racy tale of incest, "Something About Amelia." To cap the February sweeps, the network offered the shamelessly trashy miniseries *Lace,* the story of Lilli (Phoebe Cates), a movie sex star who went in search of her real mother (who had put her up for adoption at birth) in order to extract revenge. Lilli stopped at nothing in her quest, finally confronting three suspected moms with the scathing question: "Which one of you bitches is my mother?"

Lace brought ABC very close to CBS in the February sweeps, but the sports events during the season that were expected to be blockbusters proved disappointing. ABC scored lower than expected ratings with the World Series, a fairly lackluster set of just five games out of a possible seven. The ratings for the Winter Olympics (in Sarajevo, Yugoslavia) were down significantly compared to 1980, primarily because there were no strong U.S. team stories this time around.

Still, the disappointments at ABC and CBS were nothing compared to the frustration at NBC. There, programming chief Brandon Tartikoff continued to try a variety of programming types in an intriguingly varied schedule: some parts deliberately highbrow, others as mainstream as possible, still others deliberately off-beat. Yet despite a couple of legitimate hits (*The A-Team, TV's Bloopers*) the total package still had not gelled. In fact, NBC was doing as badly as ever in the overall ratings for the season. A pair of new Friday night "animal" series (*Mr. Smith* and *Manimal*) seemed to symbolize the network's desperate willingness to try anything. Both were easily mocked, sight unseen. *Mr. Smith* featured a talking genius orangutan (played by C.J., best known from Clint Eastwood's film "Every Which Way But Loose"). *Manimal* presented a criminology consultant (played by Simon MacCorkindale) who could magically turn himself into various animals (a hawk, a bull, a horse), usually in a series of disconnected close-ups or, more often, in some dark corner or behind closed doors. Neither show made it past December.

Other NBC failures were painful in different ways. *The New Show*, a mid-season prime time comedy-variety package from *Saturday Night Live* maestro Loren Michaels, felt old and tired and quickly faded. The soapy *Yellow Rose* (with Cybill Shepherd and David Soul) could not make a dent against the *CBS Saturday Night Movie*, even with fading competition from *Fantasy Island* on ABC. *Bay City Blues*, Steven Bochco's long-awaited followup to *Hill Street Blues,* held great promise with the lovingly executed story of a minor league baseball team (the Bluebirds) in Bay City, California. The program had a true all-star lineup of writers and performers, including Dennis Franz, Ken Olin, and Michele Greene, but it was gone in less than a month.

It was a disappointing cycle. Sometimes a series had great performers but a flawed premise. Sometimes there were great production people behind the concept, but things never fell into place. Most disappointing, sometimes everything worked perfectly, but still large numbers of viewers did not find the programs. Highly praised comedies such as *Cheers* and *Family Ties* and dramas such as *St. Elsewhere* still had not caught on. Already NBC's best show, *Hill Street Blues,* seemed to have passed its modest ratings peak after four seasons.

Would time pass the rest of the NBC lineup as well?

45. We Are the World

BILL COSBY AND TELEVISION first discovered each other in the 1960s. As a rising young comic with a series of hit record albums, Cosby had made successful appearances on variety and talk programs such as *Ed Sullivan* and the *Tonight* show. Cosby's first signature bit (included on his 1963 debut album *Bill Cosby Is a Very Funny Fellow, Right!*) was a series of conversations between God and Noah about building the Ark before the Great Flood. It quickly became clear that Cosby's strong suit went beyond simple punch lines to the fine art of storytelling. With a relaxed, matter-of-fact style, he was especially effective mining humor from the details of everyday life, equally comfortable with childhood memories of growing up in Philadelphia and with observations about being a parent himself. In these routines, his expressive face and versatile vocal delivery made each character come alive, especially colorful neighborhood kids such as Fat Albert.

While playing Alexander Scott on the mid-1960s adventure series *I Spy*, Cosby occasionally hinted at such stories as part of that character's background. He brought more of that comic persona to the character of athletic teacher Chet Kincaid in the 1969 *Bill Cosby Show*, even staging one of his classic bits ("Rigor Mortis") about freezing up while running on the track field. However, that series had lasted only two seasons. Cosby's other prime time efforts in the late 1960s and 1970s were comedy-variety shows. The stand-alone specials did well, but series such as *The New Bill Cosby Show* and *Cos* were unable to last more than a few episodes. During this period, Cosby did have considerable success outside prime time, turning his stories and characters into a Saturday morning cartoon show, *Fat Albert and the Cosby Kids* (beginning in 1972). He also lent his support to other educational children's programming, most notably *The Electric Company* on public television.

Through all these ventures, Bill Cosby himself came across as a very likable person, everybody's best friend or favorite uncle. He parlayed that positive persona into a lucrative career in commercials, being particularly at ease interacting with children for such sponsors as Jell-O. By the early 1980s Cosby appeared to have found a very comfortable niche: effective commercial spokesman, talk show guest (and occasional substitute host), and education advocate (he had earned a Ph.D. in his spare time). Then, NBC's programming chief Brandon Tartikoff happened to see Cosby on the *Tonight* show and was reminded of the comic's long-time appeal, and of his potential to once again front a series.

Turning to a familiar face for a new series was perfectly consistent with the wide net Tartikoff had been casting for several years in search of prospective hits. In previous seasons he had already tried ventures with former *Vega$* star Robert Urich (in *Gavilan*), former *McMillan and Wife* lead Rock Hudson (in *The Devlin Connection*), and former *Medical Center* star (and one-time pop music pinup) Chad Everett (in *The Rousters*). However, none of those shows had caught on. Clearly, familiarity alone was not enough to guarantee a hit, especially on the number three network.

Tartikoff's interest in Cosby coincided with the comedian's own discussions with producers Marcy Carsey and Tom Werner about developing a new series. However, because Carsey and Werner had an existing relationship with ABC (where they had both been network executives), that network was offered the show first, but passed on it. That left Tartikoff the opportunity to pursue the project with them for NBC and the network made a guarded commitment for an initial half dozen episodes of *The Cosby Show*.

Part of Cosby's motivation for taking on the new series was that he was at the ideal time of his life to play a perfectly tailored alternate version of his own happy home life. So Bill Cosby, the successful entertainer and educator with a savvy professional wife (Camille) and five children (daughters Erika, Erinn, Ensa, and Evin, and son Ennis), portrayed Cliff Huxtable, a successful obstetrician with a savvy lawyer wife (Clair, played by Phylicia Rashad) and five children: daughters Rudy (Keshia Knight Pulliam), Vanessa (Tempestt Bledsoe), Denise (Lisa Bonet), and Sondra (Sabrina Le Beauf), and son Theo (Malcolm-Jamal Warner). The Huxtables lived in a comfortable Brooklyn townhouse with a living room that closely resembled the one in Cosby's own Massachusetts home. Cliff operated from a home office that allowed him to always remain just a few steps from family life. In short, *The Cosby Show* was like a Bill Cosby comedy routine brought to life. Just like his monologues, the series was deliberately low-key, following the simple premise that family life has its own gentle good humor and there was no need to resort to silly caricatures, painfully dumb misunderstandings, or demeaning insults. More so than any of his previous series, *The Cosby Show* captured the heart and soul of his warm family tales, with the entire cast quickly making these characters their own.

Cosby's material had always successfully connected across ethnic lines, but that did not mean that he ignored being black. In fact, he fashioned the series to reflect a diverse world view beyond the usual television trappings. The decorations in the kids' rooms included black pop stars and anti-apartheid posters. The girls

	8:00	8:30	9:00	9:30	10:00	10:30	
MON	CALL TO GLORY		ABC NFL Monday Night Football (to 12 Midnight)				**ABC**
	Scarecrow And Mrs. King		Kate & Allie	Newhart	Cagney And Lacey		**CBS**
	TV's Bloopers And Practical Jokes		NBC Monday Night At The Movies				**NBC**
TUE	Foul-Ups, Bleeps & Blunders	Three's A Crowd	PAPER DOLLS		JESSIE		**ABC**
	AfterMASH	E/R	CBS Tuesday Night Movies				**CBS**
	The A-Team		Riptide		Remington Steele		**NBC**
WED	The Fall Guy		Dynasty		Hotel		**ABC**
	CHARLES IN CHARGE	DREAMS	CBS Wednesday Night Movies				**CBS**
	HIGHWAY TO HEAVEN		Facts Of Life	IT'S YOUR MOVE	St. Elsewhere		**NBC**
THR	PEOPLE DO THE CRAZIEST THINGS	WHO'S THE BOSS	GLITTER		20/20		**ABC**
	Magnum, P.I.		Simon And Simon		Knots Landing		**CBS**
	THE COSBY SHOW	Family Ties	Cheers	Night Court	Hill Street Blues		**NBC**
FRI	Benson	Webster	HAWAIIAN HEAT		Matt Houston		**ABC**
	The Dukes of Hazzard		Dallas		Falcon Crest		**CBS**
	V		HUNTER		MIAMI VICE		**NBC**
SAT	T.J. Hooker		The Love Boat		FINDER OF LOST LOVES		**ABC**
	Airwolf		Mickey Spillane's Mike Hammer		COVER UP		**CBS**
	Diff'rent Strokes	Gimme A Break	PARTNERS IN CRIME		HOT PURSUIT		**NBC**

	7:00	7:30	8:00	8:30	9:00	9:30	10:00	10:30	
SUN	Ripley's Believe It Or Not		Hardcastle And McCormick		ABC Sunday Night Movie				**ABC**
	60 Minutes		MURDER, SHE WROTE		The Jeffersons	Alice	Trapper John, M.D.		**CBS**
	Silver Spoons	PUNKY BREWSTER	Knight Rider		NBC Sunday Night At The Movies				**NBC**

consciously sported stylish international fashions. When Cliff and Clair dug out one of their favorite old songs, it was the rhythm and blues hit "(Night Time Is) The Right Time" by Ray Charles. Even daughter Sondra's decision to name her twins Winnie and Nelson carried a special meaning, honoring South Africa anti-apartheid activists Winnie and Nelson Mandela. These details were not delivered in some smug, preachy manner but, rather, were presented as a natural part of everyday life. Cosby also deliberately played against television's clichés about black family life and family life in general. Clair and Cliff Huxtable were professional, upper middle class, in love with each other, and clearly in charge of the household. The kids might be cute and clever, but mom and dad still had the last word.

Though this was a strong package, there was no guarantee of success. Nonetheless, Tartikoff put *The Cosby Show* on the front lines, leading off Thursday nights against CBS's powerhouse *Magnum, P. I.* As a further vote of confidence in Cosby's across-the-board appeal, Tartikoff did not pigeonhole the show as a companion to other NBC series featuring black characters (such as *Gimmie a Break* or *Diff'rent Strokes*). Instead, he slotted it as the lead-in to three highly regarded but underperforming NBC comedy series: *Family Ties*, *Cheers*, and *Night Court*. It worked. From the beginning, *The Cosby Show* connected with audiences and quickly became the unexpected hit of the season, a buzz-generating across-the-board success. The series was not just a top ten show, it was a popular program that people made a point to remember to watch. It was "appointment television."

Equally important, the spotlight shining on *Cosby* reflected onto other shows in NBC's schedule that had been quietly toiling in comparative obscurity. The most immediate beneficiary was the program slotted after Cosby's show, *Family Ties* (in its third season), which followed the lead-in hit right into the top ten. The rest of the NBC Thursday night lineup moved up in viewer awareness as well. In the general television landscape, *The Cosby Show* also restored the credibility of sitcoms as a ratings draw, less than a year after the form had been written off in some circles as being past its prime.

The Cosby Show was the linchpin that NBC had been looking for, drawing viewers to the network in record numbers. Once they were there, they could find their way to other offerings in a surprisingly varied lineup of adventure, comedy, and drama shows, such as *Knight Rider*, *Cheers*, and *St. Elsewhere*. Among other new shows, NBC found itself with two other surprise hits that were poles apart: *Miami Vice* and *Highway to Heaven*.

Miami Vice was the first successful marriage of the music video world with prime time television, a concept Brandon Tartikoff succinctly described as "MTV cops." With Michael Mann (director of the theatrical film "Thief") as executive producer and *Hill Street Blues* writer and producer Anthony Yerkovich authoring the pilot, *Miami Vice* set its tone from the opening episode. The series took

Bill Cosby and Phylicia Rashad were at the center of *The Cosby Show*, portraying a loving, affectionate couple that handled raising a large family with humor and style. *(*The Cosby Show *Photo Courtesy of the Carsey-Werner Company, LLC/NBC)*

the familiar elements of crime-fighting detective stories and washed them through the aural and visual trappings of music video production. It was all about style, fashion, and attitude. Miami police detectives Sonny Crockett (Don Johnson) and Ricardo Tubbs (Philip Michael Thomas) were not only the usual rebel outsiders they were also cutting-edge hip. Crockett was white, often unshaven, drove a Ferrari, lived on a boat with a pet alligator, and dressed in a casual combination of t-shirts, loose pants, and European jackets. Tubbs was black, urbane, drove a Cadillac, came from New York, and sported silk shirts and double-breasted designer jackets.

The hip look extended to the film presentation, which was richly cinematic with sweeping camera angles, rapid-fire cuts, and, above all, music. As in a theatrical feature film, music helped set the tone with a combination of original pieces and showcases for contemporary performers. Some program segments looked for all the world like mini versions of the better MTV music videos—allowing snatches of the latest chart-bound songs to move the story along (or to comment on the plot) without any dialogue, presenting images related to the tone of the song. In the first episode, for example, the Phil Collins hit "In the Air Tonight" accompanied shots of a speeding car in the night, focusing as much on close-ups of the tires as on the driver. Other episodes included music by such artists as Glenn Frey ("Smuggler's Blues"), Chaka Khan ("Own the Night"), Tina Turner ("Better Be Good to Me"), and Gladys Knight ("Send It to Me"), with the series generating a pair of hit soundtrack compilations.

The Florida setting completed the effect, emphasizing splashy tropical colors, exotic birds, and sun-drenched waters. But this was not the theme park Florida of the tourist brochures. Beginning with the staccato riffs of the program's Jan Hammer opening theme, the message was clear: This was a supercharged, pulsating world with wholly different assumptions. Drugs and drug money were everywhere, ready to ensnare both the innocent and the ambitious. In this world, people lived to get high and party, to flaunt their wealth, and to show off their power. This was not mere street-corner drug traffic. There were powerful individuals behind these activities with far-flung international operations and networks of connections that infiltrated society at all levels. Crockett and Tubbs might snare their share of bigwigs (and, more often, mid-level operators) but the series left the clear impression that over the long haul they were unlikely to win the war.

Despite such a downbeat setup, the overall package worked. *Miami Vice* looked and felt cutting edge, with Don Johnson and Philip Michael Thomas as likely to appear on the cover of *Rolling Stone* as on *TV Guide*. Though the series was not an instant hit like *The Cosby Show*, the program's reputation grew throughout the year and in its second season it reached (and peaked) in the top ten.

Highway to Heaven could not have been further from the world of *Miami Vice*, though it, too, reflected a distinct, individual vision. Michael Landon served as a writer, producer, creator, and star, playing Jonathan Smith, an angel on a mission to help people in trouble. He and his companion, Mark (Victor French), did not necessarily solve each person's specific earthly problem, but they

September 14, 1984

MTV presents its first annual MTV Music Video Awards live from Radio City Music Hall in New York. Bette Midler and Dan Aykroyd are the hosts, with performances from Madonna, Huey Lewis & the News, Rod Stewart, and Tina Turner. Video of the Year award goes to "You Might Think" by the Cars.

September 25, 1984

Three's a Crowd. (ABC). John Ritter and ABC eke out one more year of the saga of Jack Tripper after his *Three's Company* platonic female roommates move out. In the retitled format, Jack falls for a stewardess named Vicky (Mary Cadorette) and proposes marriage, but she prefers to just live together. They do and this time there really is plenty going on behind the bedroom door, much to the intense dismay of her father (played by Robert Mandan), who turns up as landlord of their apartment building.

October 8, 1984

"The Burning Bed." (NBC). Tired of being typecast as just another blonde-haired pretty face, Farrah Fawcett takes a gamble by playing a decidedly unglamorous battered wife who, after years of abuse from her husband, sets him on fire while he sleeps.

October 26, 1984

V. (NBC). Five months after the miniseries wrap-up showed resistance forces using a homegrown virus to thwart the efforts of the extra-terrestrial "Visitors" to Take Over The World, the lizard-like aliens-disguised-as-humans get their own weekly series. Aided by treacherous human collaborators, they are engaged in Cold War tactics to win the planet piecemeal. TV newsman Mike Donovan (Marc Singer) again leads the freedom forces.

December 8, 1984

After almost thirty years (the last two in obscure early morning weekend slots), *Captain Kangaroo* is mustered out of the CBS schedule.

January 1, 1985

Warner/Amex launches VH1 (Video Hits 1), a new music video cable service aimed at the already-graying baby boomers, who prefer their old favorites to the wild kids making noise over on sister service MTV.

---

did manage to remind individuals of their own inner strength and good souls. The program further solidified Landon's long-standing image as champion of wholesome family entertainment (such as *Little House on the Prairie*) that could also deliver strong ratings.

Going into the fall, nobody had expected NBC to have multiple hits, especially in such a variety of formats. Yet because Tartikoff had been trying for four years with so many different types of shows, when some at last began to connect the success was not just in one area (such as prime time soaps), but across the board. Of course, there were also outright flops, including *Berrenger's* (a soap opera about a department store), *Hot Pursuit* (a husband-and-wife fugitive pair), and *Partners in Crime* (veterans Loni Anderson and Lynda Carter failing to gel as a private eye team). Yet when weighed against the success of *The Cosby Show*, these were only minor disappointments. In fact, NBC suddenly found itself a contender for top ratings honors. Though CBS won the November and February sweeps, NBC was a strong second. By the spring

NBC had built sufficient momentum to win the May sweeps. It was NBC's first sweeps win since November 1974.

NBC's success was a big surprise to the number one network, CBS, which had been treating its successful lineup of prime time soaps, adventure shows, and *60 Minutes* as a well-oiled machine that just needed annual tuning. For the new season it had trimmed a few old series and introduced a handful of new shows, including one instant hit, *Murder, She Wrote* (created by Peter Fisher and *Columbo* mavens Richard Levinson and William Link). Angela Lansbury played mystery writer Jessica Fletcher, a successful author who solved murders in between writing novels. It was akin to raiding PBS's *Mystery!* series and casting its featured authors such as Agatha Christie or Dorothy L. Sayers as the lead character. The clever premise was executed as a perfectly paced whodunit, complete with enough time for viewers to guess the murderer before Jessica's narrated flashbacks revealed the solution.

None of CBS's other new series matched the performance of *Murder, She Wrote.* The misfires included the medical comedy *E/R* (Elliott Gould as a divorced doctor working in a Chicago emergency room), the family comedy *Charles in Charge* (Scott Baio as a college student boarder taking care of a busy couple's three kids), and the spy adventure *Cover Up* (which lost its co-star Jon-Erik Hexum in a real-life fatal accident on the set). Nonetheless, CBS still won the ratings race for the 1984–85 season although by its end NBC was close behind.

That left ABC as the number three network for the season, though hardly without bragging rights. ABC had the number one show on television, *Dynasty*, which created an international stir with a story arc featuring Rock Hudson in his last TV role. (He died later in 1985 from AIDS-related illnesses.) The series capped the season with a particularly far-fetched cliffhanger involving the long-lost daughter of Alexis marrying the prince of Moldovia (a tiny European kingdom) in a ceremony that climaxed with *Dynasty*'s main characters facing armed revolutionaries attacking the wedding party, guns blazing. While viewers waited over the summer to learn who had survived, ABC confidently planned a *Dynasty* spinoff, *The Colbys*, for the following fall, featuring Charlton Heston as business magnate Jason Colby, father of *Dynasty*'s Jeff Colby.

Though most of ABC's new fall programming flopped, the network did score with *Who's the Boss?*, a family comedy that cast Tony Danza (from *Taxi*) as a widower working as a live-in housekeeper in Connecticut and raising a young daughter. His boss, played by Judith Light (from the daytime soap *One Life to Live*), was a divorced woman living with her young son and her free-spirited mom (played by Katherine Helmond, from *Soap*). As usual, ABC also did well with flashy miniseries, including *Lace II*, which picked up from the original's "Which one of you bitches is my mother?" and offered the scathing companion question, "Which one of you bastards is my father?"

In the spring, ABC also managed to steal the sexy detective couple crown from NBC's *Remington Steele* and CBS's *Scarecrow and Mrs. King* with *Moonlighting*. Created by former *Remington Steele* writer Glenn Gordon Caron, *Moonlighting* featured a pair of bickering detectives, Maddie Hayes (Cybill Shepherd) and David Addison (Bruce Willis) at the Blue Moon detective agency. Maddie was a successful former model who owned the agency (probably as a tax loss) but had never bothered to visit it until she discovered her manager had absconded with her fortune, leaving it as one of her few saleable assets. Addison was its number one slacker, a fast-talking charmer who convinced her to keep the agency open. Maddie agreed, but also insisted on being an active participant in the cases—partially out of boredom, partially because there was an instant energetic chemistry between them. The verbal sparring between Maddie and David quickly evolved into a deliciously entertaining mating ritual, with the dialogue taking on an almost lyrical quality filled with clever puns, rhymes, and pop culture allusions (with asides to the audience).

Moonlighting was rarely about the cases (sometimes the mystery, if any, was not apparent until halfway through the story) and some of the best episodes completely abandoned the regular format. In one, all the characters appeared in a full-costume adaptation of William Shakespeare's "The Taming of the Shrew." Another episode offered a film noir period piece hosted by Orson Welles, who patiently explained why the episode was in black and white. Even the regular cases, though, were handled with style and humor, usually ending with a slapstick chase scene. About midway through the series (March 1987), the two did "get horizontal" (as Addison described having sex) but the writers then seemed flummoxed over where to go next. They later attempted to work Shepherd's real-life pregnancy into the scripts, but the resulting story arcs were surprisingly leaden, with visual tricks (such as a claymation sequence) appearing more forced than clever. Eventually, Maddie's pregnancy ended in a miscarriage, and the two characters were never able to reestablish that same balance of energetic sparring and deep affection.

Ultimately *Remington Steele* proved to be the better executed series over the long run, keeping its plots coherent and its leads out of bed until the last episode, while *Scarecrow and Mrs. King* showed that it was possible for a couple to get married and still have exciting adventures. But neither of these series ever reached the giddy, self-confident highs of *Moonlighting* at its best. During its brief and glorious run, *Moonlighting* gave ABC one of the truly hip and sophisticated shows on television.

ABC also showed off its hip credentials during the summer of 1985 when it signed on as the U.S. prime time network showpiece for a unique international entertainment event, the Live Aid fund-raising concerts. Live Aid was the culmination of more than eight months of extraordinary humanitarian efforts by some of the biggest pop music icons in the world, all to raise money and awareness for a disastrous situation in Africa. Appropriately, this plight had been driven into the world's consciousness as the result of international television news coverage.

In October 1984, Michael Buerk of the BBC reported on famine conditions in the country of Ethiopia, sending back heart-breaking television footage. *NBC Nightly News* picked up Buerk's report on its October 23, 1984, edition. Those pictures instantly transformed the story from just another event "out there" into a portrait of personal pain and suffering. While various relief agencies worked on aid plans, in Great Britain Bob Geldof (leader of the pop group The Boomtown Rats) hatched a plan to jump-start donations by tapping the small fortune he knew came with a hit record. He wrote a pair of songs with musician Midge Ure and on November 25, 1984, assembled an impromptu collection of about forty performers in Britain to record a benefit single under the banner Band Aid. In short order, "Do They Know It's Christmas?"/"Feed the World" became the best-selling single release in British history, capturing some of the millions spent on holiday gift giving and directing those proceeds to help Ethiopia. Sufficiently wise in the arcane ways of music business accounting (and determined to avoid legal and financial problems that had plagued previous well-intentioned benefit projects by other people), Geldof structured each stage of the distribution to capture every penny possible for the cause, even arguing (unsuccessfully) that the British government should contribute the taxes collected on the sale of each record.

The artists performing on the disc were not all household names in the U.S., but they were well known to fans of MTV, whose playlist regularly featured their videos (including work by Boy George, George Michael, Phil Collins, Duran Duran, U2, and Bananarama). Not to be outdone, U.S. performers Lionel Richie and Michael Jackson wrote their own song for a U.S. benefit disc. After the January 28, 1985, American Music Awards telecast on ABC, they gathered their own star-studded supergroup with producer Quincy Jones to record "We Are the World" under the moniker USA for Africa. Apart from Richie and Jackson, about forty performers participated, including Stevie Wonder, Kenny Rogers, Bruce Springsteen, Dionne Warwick, Ray Charles, and Bob Dylan. The single (and a companion album of solo songs donated to the cause) topped the charts that spring while the video played incessantly on MTV (and its new sister service, VH1).

To keep the fund-raising momentum going, Geldof spearheaded plans to gather an international lineup of artists for one gigantic telethon-style benefit, harnessing the power of television and radio throughout the world. Under the banner Live Aid, they staged an

---

January 20, 1985
Almost fifteen years after the debut of *Monday Night Football*, ABC is at last allowed by the NFL to join CBS and NBC in the annual rotation of telecasting the Super Bowl. In ABC's first title game, the San Francisco 49ers defeat the Miami Dolphins 38 to 16 at Stanford Stadium in California.

April 9, 1985
Television. (ITV). Britain's Granada Television produces a thirteen-hour documentary on the history of the medium, narrated by Ian Holm. An eight-hour U.S. version (revised to present a more stateside focus), narrated by Edwin Newman, appears on PBS in February 1988.

June 3, 1985
Larry King Live. (CNN). Mutual radio's popular late night interviewer brings his successful format to cable, as host of a Washington-based weekday prime time hour.

June 14, 1985
Michael Nesmith in Television Parts. (NBC). The ex-Monkee, who was producing music videos before there was an MTV, presents a decidedly esoteric and eclectic mélange of music video and comedy that is soundly ignored by the viewing public. Comics Garry Shandling and Whoopi Goldberg are among the featured performers.

June 17, 1985
Debut of cable's Discovery Channel, which focuses on science-based documentaries.

July 1, 1985
One month after expanding from thirteen hours each day to twenty-four hours, the Nickelodeon cable channel begins filling the prime time evening hours with reruns of old network series such as *Dennis the Menace* and *Route 66* in a programming block dubbed "Nick at Nite."

July 1, 1985
After four years as a local Tampa, Florida, cable service, the Home Shopping Network (HSN) goes national with twenty-four hours a day of selling merchandise to cable viewers who can order via telephone. A competing shop-at-home cable channel, QVC, appears in November 1986.

all-day concert on July 13, 1985, at two large outdoor venues: London's Wembley Stadium (starting at about noon British time) and Philadelphia's JFK Stadium (starting at about nine in the morning Philadelphia time). There were also cut-ins for videos from Australia, Japan, Belgrade, Moscow, Austria, Cologne, and the Hague. To avoid potential business complications, there was no companion album, video, or even a rerun at the time. The only way to see Live Aid was to share in the event as it happened that day. In the U.S. this was a perfect opportunity for cable's MTV to promote itself as *the* premiere music outlet on television, so the four-year-old service outdid itself with all-day live coverage of the proceedings on both continents. The bubbly MTV veejays were on screen as much as possible providing chatter between acts. Throughout the broadcast, viewers were urged to call in their pledges.

Because most of the U.S. was not yet wired to MTV, there was also a special syndication network created just for the event, offering local stations as much of the all-day extravaganza as they wished to carry. At 8 P.M. Eastern time, while MTV's coverage continued, ABC stepped in with an exclusive three-hour U.S. network prime time special (produced by Dick Clark). In that broadcast, ABC presented highlights from the entire day interspersed with live performances still in progress. There were separate finales (originally hours apart) from England and the U.S. with Paul McCartney on stage in London singing The Beatles song "Let It Be," while in Philadelphia Bob Dylan wrapped up the night with Keith Richards and Ron Wood from The Rolling Stones. When ABC aired its prime time package, it served to confirm that Live Aid was more than just a pair of rock concerts for the MTV generation. It was an event worthy of placement on a major television network and worthy of support.

Live Aid was a tremendous fund-raising success, a once-in-a-lifetime event that raised more than $80 million and was seen by approximately 1.6 billion people in 170 countries. The Live Aid broadcast structure in the U.S. also showed the approach to cable the broadcast networks had apparently settled on. They would keep the cream of any programming event for their prime time show-cases. If cable wanted to devote endless hours to what led up to "the good stuff," that was fine with them. Network time slots were there for maximum return aimed at the widest possible audience. After all, network television was first and foremost a business.

Network news had taken that approach the previous summer while covering the 1984 political conventions. Breaking a decades-old tradition, all three broadcast networks chose not to carry the proceedings gavel-to-gavel in San Francisco (for the Democrats) or Dallas (for the Republicans). Instead, they pointed to cable services such as C-SPAN and CNN (disdainfully dismissed only four years before) as sources for those who wanted such non-stop coverage. ABC, CBS, and NBC would each deliver their comprehensive highlights packages in prime time. It made perfect economic sense. After all, *most* viewers did not care about every procedural moment at a political nominating convention any more than they cared about every act on the Live Aid stages.

In taking that approach, the networks were choosing a logical bottom-line strategy. They were also sending a subtle but signifi-cant message to viewers, especially younger audiences: Network television was there for the important highlights. If you wanted the complete presentation, you went elsewhere. The networks were no longer the source of record they had been in the past, not even for unique political and pop culture events. Instead, they were handing off that role. Ironically, cable was not stealing the networks' thunder. They themselves were giving it away, one event at a time.

46. Isn't That Amazing?

STEVEN SPIELBERG BEGAN HIS DIRECTING CAREER in the late 1960s in television, working for Universal Studios. One of his first assignments was "Darker Than Dark," a segment in the 1969 made-for-TV movie pilot for Rod Serling's *Night Gallery* anthology. Written by Serling and starring Joan Crawford, Barry Sullivan, and Tom Bosley, it was a creepy tale of a wealthy blind woman who bought the eyes of a gambler in debt so she could see for half a day. Spielberg also directed "Make Me Laugh," a first-season episode of the subsequent *Night Gallery* series, which played in the 1970–71 season as part of *Four-in-One* (NBC and Universal's unusual experiment to alternate four different series under one umbrella title). In addition, he directed a pair of episodes for one of the other series in the rotation, *The Psychiatrist*, created by Richard Levinson and William Link.

By then, that duo had already scored with two successful made-for-TV movies featuring the character of Columbo, and for the fall of 1971 they turned to Spielberg as director (and Stephen Bochco as writer) for "Murder by the Book," the first episode in the regular *Columbo* series. While never getting in the way of the already-established style of a Columbo mystery, Spielberg showed an uncanny ability to manipulate visual images, sound, and shot sequences to maximum effect. For example, instead of using some "mysterious music" during the otherwise wordless opening exposition, Spielberg punctuated the story of a writer planning to murder his partner with the thundering rat-a-tat sound of typewriter keys. Just two months later, during the November 1971 sweeps, Spielberg's reputation as a director was nailed when ABC aired the made-for-TV movie "Duel," in which Dennis Weaver played a traveling salesman driving on a lonely Western highway who was being "stalked" by a mysterious ten-ton truck with no visible driver. It was a superbly executed suspense premise straight out of *The Twilight Zone* and *Alfred Hitchcock Presents,* and the TV film earned release as a theatrical feature in Europe.

Spielberg stuck with television for a few more directing assignments, the last being "Savage," a 1973 Levinson/Link made-for-TV movie starring Martin Landau and Barbara Bain as a pair of investigative reporters. In 1974, Spielberg moved on to his first theatrical feature, "The Sugarland Express." With the worldwide success of "Jaws" in 1975, he never had to look back to television.

Only he did. Serving as executive producer, Spielberg brought back Rod Serling's signature series as a theatrical feature film in 1983 with "Twilight Zone—The Movie." The film was actually an anthology of four *Twilight Zone* stories, one new and three re-makes of tales originally presented as part of the television series. Burgess Meredith served as narrator (Serling had died in 1975), adopting a soft, understated style and remaining discretely off-screen, wisely avoiding any visual comparisons with Serling's distinctive on-camera series persona. Spielberg himself directed one segment in the movie ("Kick the Can") and landed top-drawer names for the others: "Blues Brothers" director John Landis for "Time Out" (from a previously unfilmed Serling story), "Gremlins" director Joe Dante for "It's a Good Life," and "Mad Max: Road Warrior" director George Miller for "Nightmare at 20,000 Feet." "Twilight Zone—The Movie" did reasonably well, demonstrating some commercial viability for the anthology format.

Meanwhile, Spielberg himself was in top form as a box office force. He had directed five films that were among the all-time highest grossing movies to that point: "Jaws," "Close Encounters of the Third Kind," "Raiders of the Lost Ark," "E.T., The Extra-Terrestrial," and "Indiana Jones and the Temple of Doom." He had also served as a producer for many other hits, including the summer 1985 blockbuster "Back to the Future." So when NBC announced that Steven Spielberg would be returning to television in the fall of 1985, the hype was understandable and network expectations were sky high. Without seeing a pilot, NBC made a commitment for two years (forty-four episodes) of the new series, a half-hour anthology called *Amazing Stories*, with Spielberg serving as executive producer.

The series setup offered considerable flexibility: The stories could be about anything in virtually any style, allowing Spielberg to lure a who's who of actors and contemporary directors, both famous and obscure, many of whom normally "did not do TV." They welcomed the opportunity to try something different that would be seen quickly, thanks to the fast turnaround time of television production. For NBC, the anthology format meant that each episode would offer opportunities to promote different big-name performers. It all began on September 29.

The nifty opening sequence for the series celebrated storytelling, reaching back to primitive caveman days and the warm glow of the campfire. There, all eyes were fixed on the storytellers spinning their tales. Then, sweeping through the ages and technologies, there was a montage of images from storytellers and stories from those eras, all leading up to another warm, glowing campfire. This one was on a living room television screen, with a typical American family gathered to watch and listen. The opening was the kind of dazzling presentation viewers had come to expect

	8:00	8:30	9:00	9:30	10:00	10:30	
M	Hardcastle And McCormick		ABC NFL Monday Night Football (to 12 Midnight)				**ABC**
O	Scarecrow And Mrs. King		Kate & Allie	Newhart	Cagney And Lacey		**CBS**
N	TV's Bloopers And Practical Jokes		NBC Monday Night At The Movies				**NBC**
T	Who's The Boss	GROWING PAINS	Moonlighting		OUR FAMILY HONOR		**ABC**
U	Hometown		CBS Tuesday Night Movies				**CBS**
E	The A-Team		Riptide		Remington Steele		**NBC**
W	THE INSIDERS		Dynasty		Hotel		**ABC**
E	STIR CRAZY		CHARLIE & COMPANY	GEORGE BURNS COMEDY WEEK	THE EQUALIZER		**CBS**
D	Highway To Heaven		HELL TOWN		St. Elsewhere		**NBC**
T	The Fall Guy		LADY BLUE		20/20		**ABC**
H	Magnum, P.I.		Simon And Simon		Knots Landing		**CBS**
R	The Cosby Show	Family Ties	Cheers	Night Court	Hill Street Blues		**NBC**
F	Webster	Mr. Belvedere	Diff'rent Strokes	Benson	SPENSER: FOR HIRE		**ABC**
R	The Twilight Zone		Dallas		Falcon Crest		**CBS**
I	Knight Rider		MISFITS OF SCIENCE		Miami Vice		**NBC**
S	HOLLYWOOD BEAT		LIME STREET		The Love Boat		**ABC**
A	Airwolf		CBS Saturday Night Movies				**CBS**
T	Gimme A Break	Facts Of Life	THE GOLDEN GIRLS	227	Hunter		**NBC**

	7:00	7:30	8:00	8:30	9:00	9:30	10:00	10:30	
S	Ripley's Believe It Or Not		MacGYVER		ABC Sunday Night Movie				**ABC**
U	60 Minutes		Murder, She Wrote		Crazy Like A Fox		Trapper John, M.D.		**CBS**
N	Punky Brewster	Silver Spoons	AMAZING STORIES	Alfred Hitchcock Presents	NBC Sunday Night At The Movies				**NBC**

from one of the movie industry's most successful directors, and they were looking for the show itself to live up to the title.

At their best, the stories that followed delivered on the promise of bringing a real mix of talent to a weekly television showcase. In "Fine Tuning," Bob Balaban (from the cast of "Close Encounters of the Third Kind") directed the hilarious Steven Spielberg story of alien visitors that came to Earth (specifically, Hollywood) with the hope of meeting their favorite stars from old TV broadcasts they had picked up in space. (Best moment: A great cameo by Milton Berle.) In "Secret Cinema," Paul Bartel ("Eating Raoul") remade his own 1969 short film about a woman whose whole life was being secretly filmed and shown in theaters as a slapstick serial. Peter Hyams ("Running Scared") directed "The Amazing Falsworth," with Gregory Hines as a mind-reading magician who uncovered a murderer in the audience. Clint Eastwood directed "Vanessa in the Garden," with Harvey Keitel as a painter looking to reconnect with his deceased wife through his portraits of her. John Lithgow starred as a lonely bachelor entranced by a hand-made doll and its real-life model in "The Doll," written by Richard Matheson (author of Spielberg's breakout TV movie "Duel").

There were many others. Yet, just like the classic anthologies of the past (including *The Twilight Zone*), for every successful entry there were also episodes that did not quite gel. Ironically (given the program's title), while the visual presentation was generally good, the stories themselves often turned out to be the weak link, in need

of another round of polishing and rewriting. That shortcoming might have been minimized had the series found a way to capitalize on its greatest strength, the amazing array of talent behind the productions, rather than merely getting that angle out to potential viewers through press coverage. Had Spielberg personally introduced the episodes, explaining why a particular story was being done with certain people or incorporated chats with the talent into the program, the series could have emphasized its assets the moment viewers tuned in. Instead, most viewers simply saw the stories in a vacuum, judging them instantly without any context, sometimes coming away with the question, "What was *that* all about?" As a result, *Amazing Stories* ended up as a particularly difficult sell from week to week, despite the tremendous hype that had preceded it.

The series also faced an unexpected problem: it did not have the anthology format all to itself. Amazingly, after years of absence from network television, *three other* anthologies were also introduced that fall.

One series was also on NBC, a revival of the half-hour *Alfred Hitchcock Presents*, which the network placed immediately after *Amazing Stories* to create what it saw as a logical programming flow. This new version of the Hitchcock series continued the presentation of "stories with a twist" that had worked so well in the original run (1955–65) but with a twist of its own. Recognizing that Alfred Hitchcock's on-screen presence delivering humorously

Only CNN covered live the lift off of the *Challenger* (the twenty-sixth U.S. space shuttle launch) on January 28, 1986. An explosion seventy-three seconds later destroyed the vehicle and claimed the lives of schoolteacher Christa McAuliffe and her six astronaut partners. *(NASA)*

deadpan comments had been essential to the program's original success, the new production brought him back from the grave (he had died in 1980) by colorizing and reusing his original black-and-white clips. The technique had worked well in a two-hour TV movie the previous spring, when Hitchcock's comments were coupled with newly filmed versions of four stories from the original series. For the new weekly anthology, Hitchcock's remarks were carefully chosen so that it was not necessary to always redo the old stories – the comments could fit any drama. Unfortunately, that's exactly how the program then played: as a collection of remarks by Hitchcock sandwiching stories that might best be described (in his cold, measured tones) as "irrelevant."

The two anthology series on CBS were, in their own ways, unexpectedly effective. *George Burns Comedy Week* once again cast Burns in his favorite role (playing George Burns), with the nearly ninety-year-old performer acting as host to a variety of humorous tales bearing the unmistakable off-beat touch of producer Steve Martin. Throughout the series there was a nice mix of veteran comedy faces (including Don Knotts, Harvey Korman, and Don Rickles); the *Saturday Night Live/SCTV* crowd (including Laraine Newman, Catherine O'Hara, and Eugene Levy); and a host of others (including Martin Mull, Fred Willard, Bronson Pinchot, Sandy Baron, Howard Hesseman, Patrick Duffy, and Tim Matheson). The stories ranged from silly mock adventure ("Home for Dinner," in which a fishing trip was turned into a rescue mission in a foreign country) to downright surreal (Telly Savalas and Elliott Gould in 1940s Africa searching for a supposedly extinct animal in "The Assignment"). One of the best was "Christmas Carol II: The Sequel," in which Ebenezer Scrooge (James Whitmore) was once again visited by Marley's ghost, this time to tell him that his newfound generous nature had turned him into a patsy.

The most quietly impressive anthology was the one-hour CBS revival of *The Twilight Zone*. Apart from a brief flash of Rod Serling's face in the program's opening montage, this series made no attempt to revive the dead. Instead, it stood on its own in the spirit of the original *Twilight Zone*. There was new theme music (by the Grateful Dead), a soft-spoken off-screen narrator (actor Charles Aidman), and, most important, original new writing (and only a few remakes of stories from the original series), with science fiction writer Harlan Ellison serving as a story consultant. The first presentation was "Shatterday" (written by Ellison), in which Bruce Willis played the dual role of a man confronting himself in a separate body with a separate personality. "A Little Peace and Quiet" followed, featuring Melinda Dillon as a woman who gained the power to stop time in its tracks and then start it again. During the temporal hiatus, she was the only one who could move around because everyone and everything else was frozen. However, that power soon left her with an impossible choice when she stopped time as a nuclear missile headed toward her town. She could see it frozen in the sky, about to strike, but everyone else (including anyone who might help) was also frozen. Should she live that way for the rest of her life, alone? Or should she unfreeze the world and die a second later? On a less cataclysmic level, "Wordplay" cast Robert Klein as a man who discovered one day that everybody else was speaking a different language and that he needed to learn to talk, read, and think from scratch.

Despite the many intriguing, entertaining, and sometimes thought-provoking stories offered on all these anthology series, none of them connected with viewers. Though several decades had passed since the networks had abandoned the form, the programs were still haunted by the same problems that had led to their demise by the mid-1960s. Anthologies had no regular characters, no familiar settings, and no reassuringly consistent approach to storytelling. Even the most effective presentations played for one night only. Viewers had to deal with entirely new elements in every episode. As a result, anthologies were unable to perform well in the competitive network ratings environment. Even though the latest group of anthology series presented some very good TV, viewers just could not get into the habit of checking them out, week after week. It was simply too much trouble.

September 15, 1985

"Death of a Salesman." (CBS). The 1984 Broadway revival of Arthur Miller's classic play is brought to TV for a three-hour adaptation, with Dustin Hoffman as salesman Willy Loman and John Malkovich as his son Biff.

November 15, 1985

Viacom International acquires control of the Warner Amex cable holdings, giving it complete ownership of Showtime and The Movie Channel and majority ownership of MTV and Nickelodeon.

December 1, 1985

"Perry Mason Returns." (NBC). Almost thirty years after the popular lawyer drama faded from CBS, Raymond Burr revives his Perry Mason role in the first of a series of popular two-hour made-for-TV movies. Barbara Hale also returns as Della Street, with her real-life son William Katt added as Paul Drake, Jr., Perry's investigator. The TV movies run until Burr's death in 1993 and come from former network executive Fred Silverman's production company.

December 6, 1985

Radio program production company Westwood One buys the Mutual Broadcasting System, the radio network that never expanded into television. Over the next decade, MBS is folded into Westwood One's expanding radio programming empire and no longer operates independently. By April 1999, Westwood One at last kills off the Mutual network after almost sixty-five years of broadcasting.

January 3, 1986

Capital Cities Communications closes on its acquisition of ABC.

George Burns Comedy Week was gone after Christmas, though there was a spinoff series (*Leo & Liz in Beverly Hills*) that followed characters introduced in one episode ("The Couch"). *Amazing Stories* finished its two-year commitment and also spawned a spinoff series, the animated *Family Dog*. Later, groups of *Amazing Stories* episodes were packaged for use by local stations in their TV movie slots. As anthology *films*, the touts usually focused on *film* stars (such as Kevin Costner in "The Mission" episode) who had appeared in the series. *Alfred Hitchcock Presents* lasted only one year on NBC, then shifted to the USA cable network with a handful of new episodes and repeats from the initial run.

The Twilight Zone did return for a second season, but it aired only sporadically. Eventually CBS (which co-produced the series) struck a deal to turn out enough additional half-hour episodes (produced in Canada) for the program to go into syndication. (The first-run syndication strategy had worked well for the off-network suspense anthology *Tales from the Darkside*, which turned out original scary tales on a modest budget from 1984 to 1988.) *The Twilight Zone* ended up with nearly one hundred half-hour episodes, splitting up the segments of the one-hour network shows and redubbing the voiceovers with new narrator Robin Ward. Somehow, syndication seemed to be the best venue for the form, outside the intense glare of the network ratings race. There, the program came full circle, returning to the original *Twilight Zone*'s roots as a low-budget series that did not try to do more than take a good story and tell it well, with few pretensions to grandeur.

Though the highly touted anthologies fizzled for the networks in the 1985–86 season, there was no doubt what did connect with

viewers. It was sitcoms. A format that had been dismissed as past its prime just two seasons earlier was not only back, it was dominating television. NBC was the greatest beneficiary of the trend. It had the greatest number of newer hit sitcoms, led by *The Cosby Show*, which began its second season as the number one show on television and maintained its momentum. (For the 1985–86 season, thirteen out of the fifteen highest rated individual programs were episodes of *The Cosby Show*, with only the Super Bowl and its post-game show breaking the streak.) Yet NBC's comedy success did not end with Bill Cosby.

Family Ties had already become a top ten hit, buoyed by *The Cosby Show* as a lead-in, but it was further boosted by the successful launch of Michael J. Fox's film career in the summer smash "Back to the Future." These two Thursday night shows, in turn, were luring viewers to *Cheers* and *Night Court*, the comedies that followed, both of which were invigorated with fresh supporting characters for the new season. *Cheers* introduced Woody Harrelson as naive barman Woody Boyd, while *Night Court* added Markie Post as legal-aid defense lawyer Christine Sullivan. (Later on Thursdays, *Hill Street Blues* also got new blood when Dennis Franz joined the cast as Lt. Norman Buntz.)

NBC's comedy success was not limited to its powerful Thursday night lineup. The network also had the most successful new show of the season, *The Golden Girls*, in the process establishing a comedy beachhead on Saturday night. Once again, NBC programming chief Brandon Tartikoff had given the go-ahead to a new showcase for some familiar names and it paid off. Bea Arthur (from *Maude*), Betty White (from *Mary Tyler Moore*), Rue McClanahan (Maude's best friend), and Estelle Getty (fresh from playing a mom in Cher's theatrical feature "Mask") showed that life in Miami consisted of more than the drug lords of *Miami Vice*. The four played active single women over fifty living together in a retirement community, who acted anything but retiring. All four performers were in top form (over the course of the series each won an Emmy), playing their characters with almost giddy enthusiasm. *The Golden Girls* also provided a strong lead-in for another familiar face, Marla Gibbs (from *The Jeffersons*), and her new ensemble sitcom, *227* (set at an apartment building in Washington, D.C.). Still later on Saturday night, producer Lorne Michaels was back in charge of *Saturday Night Live* after an absence of five years. Among the faces in his new troupe were Joan Cusack, Robert Downey, Jr., Jon Lovitz, Damon Wayans, and Dennis Miller doing the news.

Of course, NBC still had its share of disappointments for the season. Apart from the lower-than-hoped-for ratings registered by *Amazing Stories*, there was the silly *Misfits of Science,* the volatile *Hell Town* (with Robert Blake as a Catholic priest), and an unsuccessful attempt to hitch a promotional wagon to the theatrical James Bond films. In the spring of 1986, amid rumors that Pierce Brosnan was in line to succeed Roger Moore in the role of 007, NBC unexpectedly announced the renewal of *Remington Steele*, exercising its contractual option for a fifth season despite soft ratings. It would have been a priceless cross promotion for the network, but after the announcement Brosnan was immediately dropped from the short list for Bond. Lacking that tie-in, NBC ended up dumping a truncated four-episode *Remington Steele* season into "special" time slots the following fall, giving the series a less than royal sendoff. (Brosnan did assume the Bond role a decade later, beginning with the film "Goldeneye.")

Nonetheless, for the 1985–86 season, NBC had rarely looked better. The network owned Thursday and Saturday nights, won the November sweeps, tied for the lead in the February sweeps, and ended up with five of the top ten shows of the season. When the final numbers came in, NBC had won the 1985–86 season. It was not even close. The wide-ranging mix of program types, performers, and styles had paid off for CEO Grant Tinker and ace programmer Brandon Tartikoff.

For NBC, this was a momentous achievement. It had been a "respectable" number two during CBS's long years of TV dominance in the 1950s and 1960s, but then had mostly languished in third place since ABC's glory days in the late 1970s. While rarely thought of as a failing enterprise, the harsh reality was that NBC had not clearly won a TV season since 1951–52, back when Milton Berle was still in his heyday and *I Love Lucy* was brand new.

NBC's success did not mean that the other networks were locked out of the top ten or that they did not have some very good and successful shows of their own. ABC, for example, had the lock on Tuesday night with a new comedy, *Growing Pains*, joining the already established *Who's the Boss?* and *Moonlighting*. The network also added a pair of high quality adventure series, the classy *Spenser: For Hire* (based on detective novels by Robert B. Parker, with Robert Urich as a literate Boston detective and Avery Brooks as his mysterious streetwise comrade); and *MacGyver* (with Richard Dean Anderson playing a private agency special operative who knew how to skillfully use science and everyday objects to thwart the bad guys). CBS had its own shadowy force for justice in *The Equalizer*, with Edward Woodward as former government agent Robert McCall, a classy one-man version of *The A-Team* who stepped in to help people in seemingly hopeless situations.

Still, the lackluster ratings performance of CBS and ABC that year was symbolized by the weak seasons turned in by their two primary prime time soaps, *Dallas* and *Dynasty*. Though both shows remained in the top ten, they both had particularly bad years. *Dynasty* had to deal with the fact that its much-touted Moldovian wedding cliffhanger in the spring of 1985 had been a washout. When the smoke cleared in the fall, all the major characters were still alive, though facing particularly silly plots even by *Dynasty* standards. (For example, Krystle was kidnapped and replaced by a lookalike, also played by Linda Evans). A few interconnected episodes to launch *The Colbys* spinoff series further complicated *Dynasty*'s storylines.

Dallas had its own problems. Patrick Duffy had quit the long-running program at the end of the 1984–85 season, so his character of Bobby Ewing was deliberately struck and killed by a murderous hit-and-run driver. Unfortunately, the writers soon discovered that removing Bobby from the series totally upset the balance of conflicts. Larry Hagman's J. R. Ewing had no one else who could stand up to him, and other characters such as Bobby's widow Pam no longer had much reason to exist on the show at all. Worse yet, the stories lost focus and the series became a nightmarish caricature of itself, including silly foreign intrigues more appropriate to *Dynasty* than *Dallas*. These included Pam Ewing in a South American jungle and J. R. venturing overseas with a sexy international executive (played by Barbara Carrera). In a startling admission of failure, the final scene of the final episode of the 1985–86 season had the effect of throwing the entire season's scripts into the trash can. Pam, who had just remarried, woke up alone in her bed, but heard the sound of water running in the bathroom shower. In a daze, she walked over and opened the bathroom shower door. There was Patrick Duffy, who turned and said simply: "Good morning." Freeze frame for the season, with closing credits that teased: "Patrick Duffy as ?."

That cliffhanger became the talk of television over the summer. Everyone knew that *Dallas* wanted Patrick Duffy back on the series, preferably as Bobby Ewing, but was that Bobby in the shower? If so, how did he get there? In the fall of 1986, *Dallas*

revealed the answer in its very first scene. It was, in fact, Bobby Ewing. He was back because his death had really been Pam Ewing's nightmare. And, by the way, so had the entire 1985–86 season. Pam had dreamed it all. Bobby was not dead. She was not remarried. Everything was as it had been before the car struck Bobby. Though some purists were outraged at such a blatantly corny turn, series fans knew that if ever there had been a *Dallas* season that should have been erased, the 1985–86 season was it. They were perfectly happy to watch the characters follow a "road not taken," somehow wiser in the new choices they made. The "Bobby-in-the-shower/It-was-all-a-dream" stunt helped pump new life into *Dallas*, which ran for five more years. However, it was also the last gasp of the prime time soaps, the last time they would be the subject of such intense national discussion. None of them could ever match the audacity of that *Dallas* move. Nor could they ever completely recapture total credibility in their storylines. After all, if some plot thread did not quite work out, couldn't any soap just declare, "It was all a dream"? Later, other series apart from prime time soaps would be tempted to play with season-ending or series-ending dream sequences. Only a few, notably *Newhart* and *St. Elsewhere*, would pull it off.

Turning an entire season into a discarded dream was a reminder that television's business side had the ultimate control over what appeared on the screen. The people behind *Dallas* (including Larry Hagman, who personally appealed to Duffy to return) had concluded that they needed to fix a problem, and so they did. Story continuity had to adjust to business reality. Yet this was nothing compared to changes that were beginning to occur in the overall

---

March 6, 1986
Fox acquires six Metromedia television stations, forming the basis for its new TV network.

March 25, 1986
Ted Turner's Turner Broadcasting System acquires MGM's massive film library (including "Gone With the Wind") to provide programming for Turner's cable services.

April 13, 1986
"Return to Mayberry." (NBC). Most of the cast of the 1960s *Andy Griffith Show* reunite in what turns out to be the top-rated TV movie of the season, providing a comfortable sense of series closure as Andy returns home and once again becomes town sheriff.

May 30, 1986
Almost five years after its birth, MTV makes its first change in veejays. Nina Blackwood and J. J. Jackson are out, "Downtown" Julie Brown is in.

June 2, 1986
Live television coverage of the U.S. Senate begins with the debut of a second C-SPAN cable channel, C-SPAN 2.

June 9, 1986
GE closes on its acquisition of RCA and its subsidiary, NBC.

September 5, 1986
Merv Griffin ends twenty-one years of hosting a daily talk show by shutting down his syndicated Metromedia series.

television industry, reshaping the status quo of U.S. broadcasting that had been in place in for decades.

Network ownership had been remarkably stable over the years, a situation that was reinforced by the fact that commercial broadcasters operated by special rules set by the U.S. government through the FCC. These rules called for certain actions in the public interest, especially related to news, community service, and children's programming. They also imposed limitations on station ownership such as a cap on the number of stations a network could own, forbidding simultaneous ownership of a newspaper and a television station in the same market, and not allowing foreign ownership of stations. As long-time participants in this process, the established networks appeared to be uniquely qualified to thrive in a business that allowed only a few players due to the limited number of broadcast stations in the country. CBS and NBC had remained part of the same corporate ownership structures virtually since their foundation in the 1920s. During the 1950s, the DuMont network had gone under, while ABC had held on after several lean years only by merging with a division of Paramount. Since then, ABC, CBS, and NBC had been in place as the only successful commercial television networks.

Suddenly in 1985, that began to change. Rapidly.

In March 1985, Capital Cities Communications, the nation's second-largest independent chain of TV stations, announced it was buying ABC for a reported cost of about $3.5 billion. Just like that, after thirty years, one of the three U.S. television networks was suddenly under new ownership. Though the Capital Cities move did not result in any obvious changes to ABC's on-air offerings, it served as notice that networks were just like any other business in a world where big businesses were increasingly falling under the control of even larger conglomerates. The TV networks were simply one more valuable commodity that could be bought and sold, bringing in new players to the network world.

At the same time, there was also action on a different front as fifty-four-year-old Australian media mogul Rupert Murdoch began a series of striking moves into the U.S. entertainment industry. Murdoch had started his career in 1952, turning a family inheritance of Australian newspaper properties into a major corporate concern. He took over two British newspapers (*News of the World* and *The Sun*) in the late 1960s and made inroads into the U.S. in 1974 with the similarly styled *Star* tabloid. He added the *New York Post* in 1976. Murdoch was renowned for his ruthless financial efficiency and his unashamed emphasis on tabloid journalism and titillating sensationalism to attract and maintain readership.

In April 1985 Murdoch's News Corporation bought 50% of Twentieth Century Fox (an established producer of both feature films and television series) and, eight months later, purchased the remaining 50%. In May 1985, News Corporation announced its intention to buy six TV stations from the independent Metromedia group (the living remnant of the long-defunct DuMont network) for a reported cost of about $2 billion. These included stations in New York, Los Angeles, Chicago, Dallas, Houston, and Washington, D.C., covering some of the top media markets in the U.S.: a perfect lineup of potential network O&Os. In order for the station purchase to receive the necessary legal approvals, Murdoch became a naturalized U.S. citizen (effectively dealing with the FCC requirement forbidding foreign ownership of TV stations). The station purchase finally closed in March 1986 and, two months later, Murdoch boldly announced the formation of what advocates of TV diversity had long hoped for, a fourth commercial television network. Murdoch's network was to be called Fox (after the famous film studio he had just purchased) and it would carry Murdoch's traditional bold "in your face" style.

Fox was to be based on the six O&Os purchased by Murdoch, and the proto-network's first important task was to line up affiliates in other major cities in time for its planned launch during the 1986–87 season. For its programming, Fox would rely on the talents of veteran television executive Barry Diller, who had developed the flashy "made-for-TV movie" concept for ABC back in the 1970s and had gone on to head up first Paramount Pictures and then the Twentieth Century Fox studio just before it was acquired by Murdoch. Although Diller wisely decided that the new network would start slowly with a limited schedule of shows, from the beginning Fox clearly intended to become a significant player in the world of television networks. Unlike DuMont, the last fully functioning fourth commercial network, the Fox ownership had deep pockets.

As if that was not enough of a seismic shift in the TV world for one year, General Electric announced, in December 1985, that it was buying RCA (including its subsidiary, NBC) for $6.28 billion. Unlike the situation with Capital Cities and ABC, GE was not another broadcaster. In fact, television was not even its primary business. Instead, GE drew its revenue from such diverse areas as military contracts, financial services, and manufacturing. The targeting of RCA was strictly a matter of aggressively pursuing a profitable company. The acquisition process was completed in June 1986, giving new ownership to the number one television network at the peak of its prestige and popularity. GE moved quickly to install its own people at the upper echelon of NBC network operations. (Clearly GE had not gone after RCA for its line of television sets.)

Sixty-year-old Grant Tinker was unceremoniously shown the door by GE. To replace Tinker, Jack Welch, chairman of GE, was named chairman of the board of NBC, while forty-three-year-old Robert Wright was named president and CEO. Wright had most recently served as head of GE Financial Services. Tinker's departure from NBC, even coming so soon after the network had at last won a season, was really no surprise. Though he had a lifetime career in all aspects of television (including time at Universal Studios and founding the MTM production company), the network's future was now in the hands of new owners with a far different viewpoint on the business of broadcasting. Before the acquisition, NBC had been responsible for more than 40% of RCA's profits. Now, the network was just one division of a much, much larger company.

This was the evolving new reality of American television.

47. Finally a Fourth

GE'S NEW CORPORATE OWNERSHIP of NBC had no immediate effect on the network's continued ratings success. The 1986–87 season was not even close. It was clear by the November sweeps that NBC had the momentum to win the entire season. In February 1987, the network notched its eighth consecutive sweeps victory. By the end of the season in April, NBC had won twenty-seven of the thirty weeks, including every Thursday and Saturday night. Even though both ABC and CBS still had their share of hits, NBC had an unquestioned claim as the number one network.

Though Grant Tinker was gone, programming ace Brandon Tartikoff remained in place at NBC, keeping an eye on returning hits, shepherding new programs, and maintaining existing relationships with the creative community. Meanwhile, new NBC head Robert Wright embarked on a strategic reshaping of the network that reflected his strong business orientation. Apart from serving as head of GE Financial Services, Wright previously had been in charge of the GE division handling cable TV and, years earlier, had been on the corporate management side of Cox Communications (which encompassed not only cable concerns but also a strong group of independent TV stations). With GE now in the network television business, it looked to diversify, expand, and rework NBC for an even greater return on its investment. With the percentage of U.S. households wired for cable nearing 50% (and the total share of viewers tuned to the three networks dropping slowly but steadily each year), Wright also pursued possible opportunities in cable alliances.

Yet there were key unanswered questions that hung over the new GE ownership. What would be the long-term effects? Grant Tinker's presence had served as a welcoming beacon to producers. Would that continue? Though GE was an extremely successful corporation, could the company adjust its ingrained bottom-line approach to handle the more intangible aspects of an entertainment property? There were early signs that it would not be a perfectly smooth transition. An attempt by *Late Night* host David Letterman to deliver a tongue-in-cheek welcoming gift to the new GE bosses (only to be rebuffed by security) produced a hilarious taped bit that underscored a huge corporate culture gap. Rather than basking in a golden public relations moment courtesy of the network's own hip star, the image that emerged was that of a company annoyed by one of its own employees. Nonetheless, as long as NBC continued to perform well, such considerations just seemed to be a minor glitch in the changing of the guard.

The reality of NBC's solid leadership position hit hard at former ratings champ CBS. Clearly this was not a one-season fluke and there was nothing to suggest that CBS was likely to bounce back soon. Even with its existing stable of hits, profits at CBS dropped and that turn could not have come at a worse time. With ABC and NBC already sporting new corporate owners (and the Fox network just starting up), there was a sense that CBS needed an infusion of new blood (and more cash would not hurt, either). There were rumors of possible corporate takeovers or mergers with the likes of Time Inc., Gannett, and Ted Turner. What emerged instead in the fall of 1986 was an unexpected "palace coup" that represented a change, for all practical purposes, in control of the network.

Just as the 1986–87 season was getting under way, the CBS Board of Directors suddenly voted to make major changes in senior management. Out went Chairman of the Board and Chief Executive Officer Thomas Wyman, who had succeeded William Paley upon his retirement in 1983. Coming in as CEO was Laurence Tisch, CBS's new primary stockholder (and chairman of Loews Corporation, a financial holding company), who had only joined the CBS Board of Directors the previous year when his accumulation of company stock had grown. In an effort to give the power shift more of a sense of continuity, Paley (on the verge of his eighty-fifth birthday) was brought out of retirement and returned to the largely figurehead position of chairman of the board. While at first these new titles were deemed temporary, by January 1987 they were made permanent, confirming that a new era had begun at CBS. However, it was not the aged Paley who was to run the network but, rather, financial wheeler-dealer Tisch. While this was technically not a corporate takeover in the same way as Capital Cities and ABC or GE and NBC, the change had virtually the same effect as a takeover. That meant all three networks had undergone significant ownership upheavals within twelve months. Within a year of the CBS power shift, Tisch had instituted a host of corporate changes large and small, including installation of a new head of CBS News (veteran producer Howard Stringer) and the sale of CBS's publishing and record divisions for some $3 billion as CBS became far more fiscally conservative.

The most controversial cost-cutting moves involved the news division. On March 6, 1987, CBS News laid off some 220 staffers, including thirteen on-air correspondents such as Ike Pappas and Fred Graham. Coming just two years after a round of belt-tightening moves by the now-departed Thomas Wyman, this left CBS's news division reeling. Those who were left pressed on, dealing with this new tighter budgetary world. Though new man-

	8:00	8:30	9:00	9:30	10:00	10:30	
MON	MacGyver		ABC NFL Monday Night Football (to 12 Midnight)				**ABC**
	Kate & Allie	MY SISTER SAM	Newhart	DESIGNING WOMEN	Cagney & Lacey		**CBS**
	ALF	Amazing Stories	NBC Monday Night At The Movies				**NBC**
TUE	Who's The Boss	Growing Pains	Moonlighting		JACK AND MIKE		**ABC**
	THE WIZARD		CBS Tuesday Night Movie				**CBS**
	MATLOCK		CRIME STORY		1986		**NBC**
WED	Perfect Strangers	HEAD OF THE CLASS	Dynasty		Hotel		**ABC**
	TOGETHER WE STAND	BETTER DAYS	Magnum, P.I.		The Equalizer		**CBS**
	Highway to Heaven		Gimme A Break	You Again?	St. Elsewhere		**NBC**
THR	OUR WORLD		The Colbys		20/20		**ABC**
	Simon & Simon		Knots Landing		KAY O'BRIEN		**CBS**
	The Cosby Show	Family Ties	Cheers	Night Court	Hill Street Blues		**NBC**
FRI	Webster	Mr. Belvedere	SLEDGE HAMMER	SIDEKICKS	STARMAN		**ABC**
	Scarecrow And Mrs. King		Dallas		Falcon Crest		**CBS**
	The A-Team		Miami Vice		L.A. LAW		**NBC**
SAT	LIFE WITH LUCY	ELLEN BURSTYN SHOW	HEART OF THE CITY		Spenser: For Hire		**ABC**
	DOWNTOWN		The New Mike Hammer		The Twilight Zone		**CBS**
	Facts Of Life	227	The Golden Girls	AMEN	Hunter		**NBC**

	7:00	7:30	8:00	8:30	9:00	9:30	10:00	10:30	
SUN	Disney Sunday Movie				ABC Sunday Night Movie				**ABC**
	60 Minutes		Murder, She Wrote		CBS Sunday Night Movie				**CBS**
	OUR HOUSE		EASY STREET	Valerie	NBC Sunday Night At The Movies				**NBC**

agement at all the networks was scrutinizing news budgets, it was CBS that seemed to be leading the way in downsizing.

Even though all the networks had always operated for the purpose of making money, news generally had enjoyed a special status. Sometimes it was there for prestige, for public service, or to assuage governmental and community watchdogs. At its best, though, news had become a source of network pride (especially at CBS) because it was one extraordinary way to show off U.S. broadcasting at its best, following a tradition that stretched back to World War II.

Yet, as more finance-based management put news under the magnifying glass at all the networks, tradition became less important than the bottom line. The success of *60 Minutes* (a huge money machine for CBS) almost inevitably led to the observation that the rest of the news industry could learn a fiscal lesson from that show's success. News did not have to be a loss leader; it could, in fact, make money.

The fact remained, however, that most news coverage did not lend itself to easy cost control. To fully function as a news organization, there was always the need to dispatch correspondents to exotic locations or to devote precious airtime to important (but less lucrative) public discourse (such as, in this season, the congressional hearings from May to August on allegations of illegal arms sales to the country of Iran).

Ironically, all three networks (including CBS) had been trying

for years to duplicate the ratings and financial success of *60 Minutes* (a steady top ten hit for years), with generally disappointing results. While the programs themselves might have been well done, they all faced a difficult time drawing audience numbers that could match a successful entertainment series. In 1983, NBC, which had been struggling for nearly twenty years to develop its own version of a successful news magazine, boldly tried running its latest effort (*First Camera*) on Sundays directly opposite *60 Minutes*, but that attempt had failed. This season, NBC tried again but on Tuesday night with *1986*. That series did not last long enough to have to deal with a name change in January. ABC had achieved reasonably consistent performance from *20/20* on Thursdays against *Hill Street Blues*, but when the network slotted a wonderfully conceived weekly documentary series, *Our World* (hosted by Linda Ellerbee and Ray Gandolf), earlier that night against the one-two ratings hits *The Cosby Show* and *Family Ties,* the news show ended up as the lowest-rated series of the season. It was only CBS with *West 57th* that seemed to find some success in copying and updating its own formula. Beginning with its brief summer run in 1985, *West 57th* was squarely aimed at younger audiences, featuring younger correspondents and shorter stories on trendy topics such as "designer drugs" and cosmetic surgery.

CBS did have some good news in the ratings for the 1986–87 season, but there just was not enough of it. Patrick Duffy's return to *Dallas* (following the infamous "shower" resurrection) rejuvenated that old favorite, besting the no-longer-trendsetting *Miami Vice*, while *Magnum, P.I.* knocked off *Dynasty*. The strong Monday night regulars of *Kate and Allie*, *Newhart*, and *Cagney and Lacey* were joined by the moderately successful *My Sister Sam* (with former Mork and Mindy co-star Pam Dawber) and a brassy slice of Southern charm, *Designing Women*. Produced by Linda Bloodworth-Thomason (who wrote the original pilot for *One Day at a Time*) and her husband, Harry Thomason, *Designing Women* focused on four strong-willed, independent women running their own design business in Atlanta. Delta Burke, Dixie Carter, Jean Smart, and Annie Potts each played a distinctly defined character and the energetic sharp-tongued give-and-take among the four formed the core of each episode (with occasional kibitzing from their in-house male handyman/assistant, played by Meshach Taylor). This loud and saucy "girl talk" served as the perfect lead-in to *Cagney and Lacey*. CBS might have lost its ratings crown, but it still had good performers on Sundays, Mondays, and Fridays.

Number three ABC also had its strong slots, especially on Tuesdays with *Growing Pains*, *Who's the Boss?*, and *Moonlighting*. Even more promising for the future, ABC seemed particularly open to a range of series ideas (much as NBC had done earlier in the decade, when it was in the ratings basement). In the winter, for example, ABC offered *Max Headroom*, a sardonic (but prophetic) science fiction peek "twenty minutes into the future" at a world essentially controlled by media organizations totally obsessed with profit and ratings. The title character existed only on television, hopping from set to set. Matt Frewer played the dual role of muckraking reporter Edison Cater and his video doppelganger, Max.

ABC also had the dubious distinction of airing two of the season's bigger flops, both of which had arrived with great expectations: *Life with Lucy* and the miniseries *Amerika*. *Life with Lucy* was one of the most highly touted ventures for the fall, reuniting Lucille Ball with her long-time foil, Gale Gordon. Unfortunately, the program did not follow the successful path of *The Golden Girls* (which put its over-fifty characters in a savvy contemporary setting). Instead, *Life with Lucy* settled for familiar physical shtick (already decades-old by her 1970s *Here's Lucy* series), even though Ball herself had broken from her standard character type the previous season when she starred as a bag lady in the successful made-for-TV movie "Stone Pillow." The new series merely trotted out shopworn routines, set them in a hardware store, and waited for the magic. It never came, though the seventy-five-year-old Ball was in surprisingly good physical shape and gamely tackled every bit. The problem was that *Life with Lucy* had to compete with the Legend of Lucy, ingrained in the national consciousness through daily *I Love Lucy* reruns. That legend was from another era and it was a mistake to try to do exactly the same thing one more time. Critics were merciless and ratings were tepid. Despite a commitment for a full slate of episodes, there was no great fuss when only eight aired before cancellation.

ABC's other highly touted disappointment, the miniseries *Amerika*, would have been perfect airing during the Cold War 1950s because it had a premise that had haunted the era: What if the U.S.S.R. somehow took over the U.S.? Set in the near future of 1997, *Amerika* never bothered to explain how the Russians assumed control of the country, only that it had happened ten years earlier. (A tie-in novel's back story pointed to an electromagnetic pulse weapon that destroyed all U.S. communication operations.) It was an intriguing, if far-fetched, premise. The miniseries had a strong cast (including Kris Kristofferson, Robert Urich, Sam Neill, Christine Lahti, and Mariel Hemingway), but at fourteen and one-half hours the story went on far, far too long. What might have made a truly powerful made-for-TV movie played out as a diffuse

and tedious miniseries that registered respectable but ultimately disappointing ratings, considering its cost and length. This was particularly bad news for ABC because for a decade such expensive long-form drama had proven to be a reliable draw, especially during sweeps periods. If that was no longer the case, the network's resources would have to be directed elsewhere.

There were few such doubts for number one NBC. Led by its Thursday night comedy line-up, the network enjoyed spectacular success, making GE's pricey purchase appear to be a wise investment. The hit shows not only provided a stable base, they also served as lead-in launching pads or cross-promoting platforms for new programs. Though not every one became a hit, there was no denying they had plenty of opportunities for exposure.

One year after *The Jeffersons* ended, lead Sherman Hemsley slipped easily into the post-*Golden Girls* slot with *Amen*, bringing his blustery style to the role of Ernest Frye, deacon at the First Community Church of Philadelphia. *ALF* offered a brand new face, following the misadventures of a fluffy three-foot-tall Alien Life Form who was adopted (and hidden) by a suburban family (headed by Max Wright) after crash-landing his spaceship into their garage. The family's biggest challenge? Keeping ALF from dining on the family cat (considered a delicacy on his home planet Melmac). It was perfect prime time kids' TV.

In addition, that season NBC had a particularly good batch of new crime and law dramas, including successful new turns by several veteran performers. Michael Mann, still basking in the glow of his previous hit *Miami Vice*, came out with *Crime Story*, a wonderfully executed tale of mob activities during the 1960s. (It featured a well-chosen opening theme, an effective remake by Del Shannon of his 1961 hit "Runaway.") The key figures in the story were Lieutenant Mike Torello (Dennis Farina, a one-time Chicago cop in real life) and mobster Ray Luca (Anthony Denison), who sparred throughout the run, first in Chicago, then in Las Vegas, where Luca established a legitimate casino business as a front for

---

September 2, 1986
"48 Hours on Crack Street." (CBS). A two-hour news special that provides something of a *cinema-verité* look at drug addicts in New York City serves as the impetus for a weekly documentary series (*48 Hours*) using the same basic style the following season.

September 8, 1986
After a few years as a local daily talk program, *The Oprah Winfrey Show* begins Monday-through-Friday national daytime syndication from its Chicago locale.

September 10, 1986
It's Garry Shandling's Show. (Showtime). Standup comic Garry Shandling updates the old George Burns sitcom idea of a TV star playing himself and talking directly to the home audience during the show.

December 16, 1986
The Singing Detective. (BBC). Michael Gambon plays bed-ridden detective-story writer Phillip Marlow, whose thoughts, dreams, and boyhood memories mix with his written plots, resulting in a convoluted, hallucinogenic masterpiece. Authored by the prolific Dennis Potter, the six-part series features characters breaking into song, akin to his previous miniseries-turned-Hollywood movie, "Pennies from Heaven." This eccentric new series comes to the U.S. via PBS in February 1988.

February 23, 1987

Newsman Charles Gibson replaces David Hartman as the host of ABC's *Good Morning America.*

May 5, 1987

Television coverage begins of congressional hearings into charges that the Reagan administration diverted funds from covert arms sales to Iran in order to fund the anti-Sandinista "Contra" rebels in Nicaragua.

June 9, 1987

National Amusements Inc., a movie theatre chain controlled by Bostonian Sumner Redstone, closes on its $3.4 billion acquisition of Viacom Inc., whose holdings include the cable channels Showtime, The Movie Channel, MTV, Lifetime, and Nickelodeon.

September 5, 1987

After thirty years, *American Bandstand* ends its run on ABC, with Dick Clark still serving as host. Two weeks later, the show returns to TV via weekly syndication. Eighteen months later, the program briefly switches to the USA cable network, where it at last dies in the fall of 1989.

his underworld operations. In contrast to the more style-oriented *Miami Vice*, the *Crime Story* plots were complex, understandable, and engaging; the characters were authentic and believable; and the overall package was retro yet still cutting edge.

Working with Fred Silverman's production company, NBC also brought a genuine 1960s figure back into the crime-fighting game: Andy Griffith. Following an eye-catching turn as a prosecutor in the 1984 miniseries *Fatal Vision*, Griffith was cast as disarming Atlanta-based defense attorney Ben Matlock in a TV movie pilot that played in the spring of 1986 (about a month before the highly touted "Return to Mayberry" aired, also on NBC). The fall *Matlock* series was an immediate hit, with Griffith effectively retailoring his familiar Southern character into a crafty but charming courtroom persona. The success of *Matlock*, along with the continuing revival of Raymond Burr's *Perry Mason* (also from Silverman's company), demonstrated once again that viewers would welcome their old favorites, in the right vehicles. Eventually, *Matlock* ended up running longer than the original *Andy Griffith Show* itself.

With *Hill Street Blues* rolling into its seventh (and final) season, producer Steven Bochco brought in a worthy successor, *L.A. Law.* Created with *Cagney and Lacey* writer-producer Terry Louise Fisher (a former lawyer from the office of the L.A. district attorney), *L.A. Law* examined a wide range of contemporary issues from the comfortable perspective of a prestigious downtown law firm (the opening sequence, showing the license plate "LA LAW" on the back of a fancy Jaguar, immediately let you know you were in a world of conspicuous consumption). The firm's original lineup included crusty senior partner Leland McKenzie (Richard Dysart), high-strung managing partner Douglas Brackman, Jr. (Alan Rachins), good-looking litigation partner Michael Kuzak (Harry Hamlin), sleazy domestic relations partner Arnie Becker (Corbin Bernsen), levelheaded litigation partner Ann Kelsey (Jill Eikenberry), nebbish tax partner Stuart Markowitz (Michael Tucker, in real life married to Eikenberry), eager associate Abby Perkins (Michele Greene), and suave litigation attorney Victor Sifuentes (Jimmy Smits). In court, they often faced off against icy assistant district attorney Grace Van Owen (Susan Dey, formerly Laurie in *The Partridge Family*). Because the characters in *L.A. Law* (unlike

those in *Hill Street Blues*) did not begin every episode wondering if they would still be alive by the end of the day, there was time to discuss nuances and implications of legal strategies. In doing so, the series displayed a knack for making legal issues understandable, more like engaging puzzles rather than dull discourses.

Each episode of *L.A. Law* followed multiple cases, ranging from divorce and taxes to fraud and murder. This variety allowed the different characters time in court in their special areas. Jimmy Smits was particularly strong on this stage, with his Victor Sifuentes character providing the true heart for the series. At the same time, his portrayal also deftly shook up the complacent casting cliché that all too often seemed to relegate ethnic characters either to the police line-up or to their own self-referential circles. Without surrendering a bit of his ethnic identity, the Hispanic Sifuentes confidently and successfully walked the establishment corridors of power, knowing full well that he was always under scrutiny. In one episode, such scrutiny was literally true as Kuzak asked Sifuentes to act as the plaintiff's attorney in a consulting firm's videotaped mock trial for a liabilities case the firm was defending. Taking one look at Sifuentes (sporting an earring), the consulting firm thought it had an easy win, but by the end of the presentation it was Victor who had won over the mock jury (with one of the consultants shedding a sympathetic tear).

L.A. Law also included large doses of soapy interpersonal developments, beginning with Kuzak wearing an ape suit courting Van Owen, and Markowitz wowing Kelsey in bed with a technique he called the Venus Butterfly (the specifics of which were never revealed). Over time, particularly as the show underwent many cast changes during its eight-year run, these personal plots grew to be at least as important as the cases themselves, and often more so.

If there was any programming uncertainty at NBC, it was the realization that one day the current big draws (especially *Cosby*) would run their course. Would the network be sufficiently nimble (and lucky) to find equally strong successors? The increasingly popular *Cheers* was even a cause for concern because the series finished the 1986–87 season with the departure of Shelley Long, thus breaking up the show's key character relationship. Though the season finale was a spectacular success (Diane Chambers left Sam Malone and the Cheers bar to go write a novel), could the series continue to draw the next fall without the on-again/off-again relationship between Diane and Sam? Would such a change work?

Such concerns were part of the cycle of success. It was often easier for a network to develop a varied and innovative line-up outside the spotlight of being number one. Practically speaking, a network carrying a full complement of hit shows had fewer open slots for new ventures. There was also greater corporate pressure to continue turning out more of whatever formula was working. Ironically, this tension between the familiar and the fresh often meant that viewers, critics, and producers looking for something a little bit different might find more opportunities at the lower-rated networks. Starting in the 1986–87 season, they had one more such venue when the Fox network took to the airwaves.

Following its spring 1986 unveiling announcement, Rupert Murdoch's Fox network began easing into programming at a slow and deliberate pace. With only ninety-five stations to start (far fewer and less prominent than those affiliated with ABC, CBS, and NBC), Fox strove to project its own distinctive "attitude" to help make its mark. This meant that, even while working within familiar genres, Fox programs would be deliberately different. The network's first offering embodied that spirit: *The Late Show* (starring Joan Rivers), a one-hour Monday-through-Friday entry into the late night talk show game that began October 9, 1986 (with guests Cher, David Lee Roth, Pee-Wee Herman, and Elton

John). Though comedian Joan Rivers had been the permanent guest host for Johnny Carson's *Tonight* show on NBC since 1983, their styles were worlds apart. In contrast to the relaxed and affable Carson, Rivers was a non-stop talker with an "in your face," gossipy style. She not only took her own act "to the edge," she also egged on her guests. In short, she was the perfect fit for Fox. Having Rivers leave *Tonight* for this new show gave Fox the best of both worlds: a familiar face with credibility from her association with Carson, yet also a clear alternative to that same competition.

Fox did not begin prime time programming until six months later, near the end of the regular 1986–87 season, starting with just one day (Sunday). The first Fox prime time shows included four comedies (*Married ... with Children, The Tracey Ullman Show, Duet*, and *Mr. President*) and a cop show (*21 Jump Street*). Even then, all the series did not arrive on the first day (April 5). Instead, the premieres stretched out for a month (*Mr. President* had its debut May 3), with the new series easing in week by week using such gimmicks as repeating the same episode multiple times in the same night or in subsequent weeks. This scheduling was itself in radical contrast to the routine of the established networks and was more akin to cable's approach. In addition, these repeats helped deal with the fact that Fox did not yet have all that much programming. Yet from the beginning, Fox, when it could, deliberately attempted to do something different from the competition.

21 Jump Street was aimed squarely at teens, with producer Stephen J. Cannell deftly combining elements of *The Mod Squad* and *Miami Vice* with flashy editing and a rock music soundtrack. A youthful squad of performers (including Johnny Depp, Holly Robinson, and, later, Richard Grieco) played undercover cops dedicated to helping teens in difficult situations (drugs, sex, violence). They operated out of an abandoned chapel at 21 Jump Street in Los Angeles, working under the tutelage of Capt. Richard Jenko (Frederic Forrest) and, later, Capt. Adam Fuller (Steven Williams). The characters were designed to connect with kids, and the actors even delivered sincere public service announcements as part of the show. Naturally, the music used on the series was consciously aimed at teens and, not surprisingly, also turned up in a compilation record album.

The Tracey Ullman Show took the traditional mainstays of a comedy-variety sketch show and then added a sly new twist to the entire proceeding. It was a brassy, confident stance for someone who was a virtual unknown (at least, to U.S. television audiences). Actually, the thirty-two-year-old Ullman was an established star on British television. There she had demonstrated her versatility in variety with a pair of BBC sketch shows (*Three of a Kind* and *A Kick Up the Eighties*), excelling not only at character types and accents but also in singing; she landed three top ten songs in the British music charts, with one ("They Don't Know") becoming a U.S. top ten hit in 1984. In the viciously manipulative comedy series on Britain's ITV network, *Girls on Top,* Ullman played a pathological liar and pseudo-hypochondriac sparring with her equally devious London flatmates (played by Ruby Wax, Dawn French, and Jennifer Saunders).

As Ullman began appearing in feature films (including Paul McCartney's "Give My Regards to Broad Street" and Meryl Streep's "Plenty"), she connected with *Cheers* producer James L. Brooks. In developing the variety series for Fox, they assembled a versatile support troupe of comparative unknowns: Dan Castellaneta, Joe Malone, Sam McMurray, and Julie Kavner (who, from her stint as younger sister Brenda on *Rhoda*, was the only truly familiar face). They also added short, irreverent, self-contained drop-in animation bits, many featuring the Simpson family (the brainchild of artist Matt Groening, creator of the off-beat weekly comic strip "Life in Hell"), with Castellaneta providing the voice for dunderhead father Homer Simpson and Kavner as the voice of his wife, Marge. The entire package was wrapped with a catchy rock theme and an anything-goes attitude.

The skits each stood on their own and allowed Ullman to display her amazing ability to totally inhabit a character, whether it was a shy spinster still living with her "mum" or a confidently self-centered Yuppie having her way with the world. The program also had an ingrained rock and roll sensibility far beyond the usual approach of including musical performers as guest stars. Songs would become part of the routines. Ullman herself usually tackled the vocals, sometimes using the entire sketch as a setup to the song as a punch line. (For example, a sketch about painting led to the 1965 hit by The Rolling Stones, "Paint It, Black.") In a final dig at the established variety format, Ullman replaced the usual obsequious concluding "thank you" to the audience with a quick ending bit, coming out in her bathrobe to thank the unseen studio audience and to tell them to "Just go home!"

By far the longest lasting of the new Fox shows was the sitcom *Married ... with Children,* which followed the woeful life of the working-class Bundy family. Though each episode began with the

Though Tracey Ullman became totally immersed in many different characters in her skits, she closed each show as herself. (The Tracey Ullman Show © 1988 Twentieth Century Fox Television. All Rights Reserved.)

cheery Frank Sinatra recording of "Love and Marriage" set against scenes of the Chicago skyline, the series took to heart the song's warning that love led to marriage. It then reached some unpleasant conclusions: Marriage wrecked your dreams, saddled you with children, and then it was all downhill. This was the epitome of Fox "attitude," and also the setup for a wickedly funny program.

Married ... with Children consistently skewered familiar situations, starting with the warm and fuzzy view of families that had come to dominate television in the wake of *Cosby* and *Family Ties*. In contrast, Al and Peg Bundy (Ed O'Neill and Katey Sagal) felt stuck in a dead-end life. (He was a shoe salesman and she was a dysfunctional housewife.) They especially resented their kids, Kelly and Bud (Christina Applegate and David Faustino), who, in turn, could not believe they had been dealt such a loser life. None of them made any attempt to hide their feelings and, in fact, they came to pepper their ritual exchanges with zingers that only family members could direct at each other. In that spirit, a send-up of the film "It's a Wonderful Life" had Al looking at his own life with his guardian angel (played by burly comic Sam Kinison) after a brush with death. Ultimately, Al chose to live, but not because the world would be a better place if he was there. Rather, Al discovered that everyone would be happier if he was *not* there and he knew his family did not deserve that.

The only thing the Bundy family found worse than their lives was dealing with the rest of the world. They suspected that everyone was deliberately out to get them and they were absolutely right, suffering at the hands of government bureaucrats, inflexible corporate types, and incompetent service people. Worst of all were their neighbors, Marcy and Steve Rhoades (Amanda Bearse and David Garrison), who were well off, not burdened by children, and had a great sex life. *Married ... with Children* consistently took its characters to exaggerated extremes, yet in doing so the series ultimately made them more identifiable and, oddly, more believable. Anyone at any age who was ever frustrated by life could easily identify with these characters.

Sex was a constant in the series, but it was usually presented as just one more conflict in a non-stop battle between men and women. Al hated the drudgery of his tired sex life with Peg and much preferred to look at gorgeous models at the local "nudie bar" or in the latest pinup magazine. Peg dreamed of great sex (but was stuck with Al), Bud fantasized about it (often with an inflatable model), and Kelly successfully used her jail-bait sex appeal in her high school social circles. Though Marcy and Steve enjoyed sex, that did not stop them from splitting. When Marcy later took a trophy second husband, Jefferson D'Arcy (Ted McGinley), it was just for the sex. This sophomoric attitude toward sex was admittedly crude but it also served to tear through Hollywood's mystique about "making love." It was just sex.

This brash, ribald, often crude tone offended some viewers, but it attracted many as well. While sexual innuendo and sexual themes were a staple of many shows on the existing networks, it was only on Fox that sex was treated in such an up-front and matter-of-fact manner.

None of the Fox shows were bona fide hits that season. The network did not yet have a sufficiently strong lineup of affiliates to reach the same viewer levels as the established networks, so Fox's programs were more ratings footnotes than real competition. Many of its early series came and went quickly and quietly, without garnering much attention. *The Late Show* fizzled after the initial curiosity phase passed, and Joan Rivers herself was gone from that program by mid-May 1987. Black comic Arsenio Hall was one of several replacements that stepped in as host for several months, and *The Late Show* began to take on a more hip, urban feel. But that change came too late and continued low ratings killed the show in 1988.

Yet, for all its early failures, Fox was able to connect with some parts of the viewing audience. Average viewers of *Murder, She Wrote* might not have cared for (or even been aware of) *21 Jump Street*, but teens noticed. Hollywood's creative community quickly took note of Tracey Ullman's show (nominating it for an Emmy in its first season), while *Married ... with Children*'s growing reputation for crude humor soon made it a target for TV watchdogs that launched an unsuccessful boycott of the show's sponsors. Three talked-about series in one month was not bad for any network.

By the end of the 1986–87 season, Fox had established a beachhead in the highly competitive TV network landscape. Compared to the already-existing networks, it was barely a network at all. Fox offered no sports. No news. No morning or afternoon programming. Even when it added a second night (Saturday) in the summer of 1987, Fox still seemed more a high-powered syndication service than a fully functioning network on a par with ABC, CBS, NBC, or even PBS. In some ways, that was a conveniently helpful limitation, winning the network exemptions from having to adhere to FCC rules on program ownership imposed on the full-fledged networks. Yet this gradual ramp-up also made business sense because it kept Fox from spreading itself too thin by expanding its programming too quickly.

The key point was that Fox had managed to do what had previously been regarded as virtually impossible. It got on the air as a fourth commercial broadcast television network. Not via cable or through some special coded satellite dish, but as free TV, just like the established networks. Though the FCC had certainly not pictured Al Bundy, Joan Rivers, and Johnny Depp when it worked for decades to encourage alternative television offerings, in fact that was exactly what it had received. Alternatives. A new network. A different attitude, with all of its consequences.

48. The Boomer Years

MEMBERS OF THE POST WORLD WAR II baby boom generation had spent virtually their entire lives accompanied by television. From their earliest days they had been pitched to and courted by programmers and advertisers, who were eager for their loyalty and influence on family spending. Yet while the shows aimed at this generation might feature young on-screen performers, the behind-the-scenes writing and producing talent was often from older, established generations whose experiences growing up drew on memories of vaudeville in the 1920s, the Great Depression in the 1930s, and World War II in the 1940s.

By the 1980s, enough writers, producers, and executives from the baby boom generation had come of age within the entertainment industry to be in positions of authority, and they were able to project their view of the world onto the screen. Rather than looking back to the big band era, Little Orphan Annie radio serials, World War II battle reports, and U.S. President Franklin Roosevelt, they cast their memories to The Beatles on *Ed Sullivan*, the "Summer of Love," Vietnam War body counts, and U.S. President John Kennedy. In viewer demographics, members of the baby boom generation were also now sufficiently established in jobs and households to be the ones to spend the money. They did not have to ask mom and dad to buy a product. They *were* mom and dad.

Baby boomer Brandon Tartikoff's successful lineup on NBC had done well with this lucrative advertising demographic. In part, this success came from having hugely popular series that drew audiences of all types. However, it also extended to particular series such as *St. Elsewhere*, which drew advertising support more for the upscale quality of its audience rather than for its total ratings numbers. For the new season, ABC, the third-place network, took deliberate aim at this audience with the self-reflective drama of *thirtysomething*.

Created by Edward Zwick and Marshall Herskovitz (who had written for the low-key 1970s series *Family*), *thirtysomething* aimed to mine the inherent drama in everyday life. No screeching car chases. No exploding oil rigs. No international intrigue. Instead, the two creators looked at their own lives and immediate concerns and translated them into characters and situations that felt familiar and accessible. They even set the show in their old hometown of Philadelphia. The stories centered on two couples and three singles in their thirties (the prime baby boomer age in the 1980s). Friends Michael Steadman and Elliot Weston (Ken Olin and Timothy Busfield) had left lucrative positions at a large advertising agency to start their own company, balancing long hours on the job with family life. Michael's wife, Hope (Mel Harris), was a Princeton graduate who "temporarily" put aside her high-powered career aspirations to raise their new baby. Elliot's wife, Nancy (Patricia Wettig), was an aspiring artist with "flower child" sensibilities who also stayed at home, taking care of two school-age children. The families were comfortable but not super wealthy, sharing their everyday concerns with singles Ellyn Warren (Polly Draper), Hope's "career woman" friend; Gary Shepherd (Peter Horton), Michael's college professor friend; and Melissa Steadman (Melanie Mayron), Michael's sex-obsessed cousin and an expert photographer. These characters were simultaneously confident yet uncertain, upwardly mobile yet nostalgic, focused on career yet endlessly introspective. They wondered about every decision, no matter how mundane, and constantly compared their actions with each other's. The result was an emphasis on the routine moments of life (working late, time with the kids, looking for love) mixed with a touch of soap opera (inevitable relationship tensions) and punctuated by occasional dramatic turns (such as Nancy facing the prospect of cancer).

For some viewers, the package worked perfectly. They easily identified with the sentiment behind the ABC print ad for the series that observed,: "Happiness is envying your single friends less than they envy you." Others found the angst of the characters whiney and self-indulgent—after all, they were not exactly scrubbing floors and digging ditches. What was their problem? No matter the response, though, it was clear that *thirtysomething* had chosen a distinctive point of view for its stories, giving TV-savvy baby boomers something a little different with very familiar elements.

Surprisingly, *thirtysomething* was not alone in such ambitions. Throughout the schedule there were a number of high quality dramas and comedies that took innovative approaches to their subjects. At CBS, Stephen J. Cannell went from the undercover teens of *21 Jump Street* even deeper into the world of organized crime with *Wiseguy*. Ken Wahl played Vinnie Terranova, a tough, street-smart undercover government agent who infiltrated criminal organizations by posing as "one of them." Even Vinnie's own family believed that he had "gone bad" after he served time in prison (arranged as a necessary cover by the government's O.C.B., the Organized Crime Bureau). With such street credibility, Vinnie could do serious damage to the criminal organizations he infiltrated with some carefully timed moves. However, if he was discovered, he was dead. That left Vinnie in constant peril, with only limited backup from the O.C.B. He was really on his own.

	8:00	8:30	9:00	9:30	10:00	10:30	
MON	MacGyver		ABC NFL Monday Night Football (to 12 Midnight)				ABC
	FRANK'S PLACE	Kate & Allie	Newhart	Designing Women	Cagney & Lacey		CBS
	local						FOX
	Alf	Valerie's Family	NBC Monday Night At The Movies				NBC
TUE	Who's The Boss	Growing Pains	Moonlighting		THIRTYSOMETHING		ABC
	Houston Knights		JAKE AND THE FATMAN		THE LAW AND HARRY McGRAW		CBS
	local						FOX
	Matlock		J.J. STARBUCK		Crime Story		NBC
WED	Perfect Strangers	Head Of The Class	HOOPERMAN	THE "SLAP" MAXWELL STORY	Dynasty		ABC
	THE OLDEST ROOKIE		Magnum, P.I.		The Equalizer		CBS
	local						FOX
	Highway To Heaven		A YEAR IN THE LIFE		St. Elsewhere		NBC
THR	Sledge Hammer	The Charmings	ABC Thursday Night Movie				ABC
	TOUR OF DUTY		WISEGUY		Knots Landing		CBS
	local						FOX
	The Cosby Show	A DIFFERENT WORLD	Cheers	Night Court	L.A. Law		NBC
FRI	FULL HOUSE	I MARRIED DORA	Max Headroom		20/20		ABC
	BEAUTY AND THE BEAST		Dallas		Falcon Crest		CBS
	local						FOX
	Rags To Riches		Miami Vice		PRIVATE EYE		NBC
SAT	ONCE A HERO		Ohara		Hotel		ABC
	My Sister Sam	EVERYTHING'S RELATIVE	LEG WORK		West 57th		CBS
	Werewolf	Beans Baxter	SECOND CHANCE	Duet	local		FOX
	Facts Of Life	227	The Golden Girls	Amen	Hunter		NBC

	7:00	7:30	8:00	8:30	9:00	9:30	10:00	10:30	
SUN	Disney Sunday Movie		Spenser: For Hire		DOLLY		BUCK JAMES		ABC
	60 Minutes		Murder, She Wrote		CBS Sunday Night Movie				CBS
	21 Jump Street		Married...With Children	WOMEN IN PRISON	Tracey Ullman Show	Mr. President	local		FOX
	Our House		Family Ties	MY TWO DADS	NBC Sunday Night At The Movies				NBC

Such a setup meant that it would not have been creditable to put Vinnie into a different assignment each week—surely even typically dumb TV bad guys would catch on eventually. Instead the series was structured into a limited number of story arcs of five to ten episodes each, following the same assignment over an extended period. (There were fewer than a dozen such arcs over the three-year run of the series.) Apart from giving individual stories time to develop, this also allowed a particularly strong lineup of guest performers. They could turn in virtuoso performances more detailed and expansive than in a feature film without the potential typecasting of being a television series regular. Some of these included Ray Sharkey as Atlantic City mobster Sonny Steelgrave; Kevin Spacey and Joan Severance as demented international smugglers Mel and Susan Profitt; and Jerry Lewis and Ron Silver as garment industry merchants Eli and David Sternberg, entangled with mobster Rick Pinzolo (played by Stanley Tucci). Vinnie dealt with them, and many others, as part of a highly charged duplicitous world where betrayal could come at anytime from anywhere. From his own government. From his own family. Even from himself. It was an engrossing presentation and a surprisingly dark slice of American life, especially for prime time television.

Another new CBS drama offered a completely different take on battling crime. *Beauty and the Beast* was a shamelessly romantic fairy tale, with New York City attorney Catherine Chandler (Linda Hamilton) discovering love and another world deep beneath the streets of Manhattan. Her paramour was named Vincent (Ron Perlman), a powerful man-beast with the facial features of a lion and the soul of a poet. He first spotted Catherine left for dead after an attack in Central Park, took her to his underground world to recover, and then, in the best romance novel tradition, they fell in love. Over the course of the series they protected each other from evil forces both above and below ground while dreaming of an eventual happy life together. With its romantic and poetic atmosphere, *Beauty and the Beast* was unlike anything else on television.

CBS also slotted one of the first TV war dramas in years, *Tour of Duty*, breaking through apprehensions about revisiting Vietnam (a painful episode for baby boomers). The series followed the exploits of Bravo Company in 1967 as its men (including Terence Knox as Sergeant Zeke Anderson) attempted to deal with the peculiar challenges of fighting that controversial war. The series was gritty and honest (with the dark Rolling Stones song "Paint It, Black" as the opening theme), though its earnest portrayal of the era sometimes seemed to be a throwback to such 1960s series as *Combat*. It was ABC later in the season that best captured the complicated nuances of the first television war with *China Beach*.

Premiering as a late spring 1988 series, *China Beach* followed the Vietnam War from a very different perspective, that of the women at a hospital and recreational facility near the U.S. base at Da Nang, on the South China Sea. Conscientious nurse Colleen McMurphy (Dana Delany) and manipulative hooker K. C. Koloski

(Marg Helgenberger) were the key characters, living in two very different worlds yet both constantly facing situations that took them through a roller coaster of conflicting emotions and choices. Though McMurphy was responsible, she also did not hesitate to pursue the joy of sex. K. C.'s life revolved around sex, but she also knew how to maximize other wartime opportunities for profit. As with *M*A*S*H*, the hospital setting allowed for life-and-death situations and a constant stream of guest characters. The entertainment environment of the recreational facility, which featured personalities such as radio star Wayloo Marie (Megan Gallagher), fit perfectly into the media-rich texture of the series. Equally important, *China Beach* was capable of moving effortlessly from straight drama to evocative mood piece to symbolic juxtaposition to comic relief – all in the same episode. Rather than play out all the character threads in strict chronology, the series sometimes skipped forward. "Fever" (directed by Diane Keaton) jumped to the 1970s. Other stories zipped straight into the contemporary 1980s. They then flashed back to the past, filtering events in Vietnam through the knowledge of what was to come. One of the most effective episodes ("Vets") incorporated on-camera observations by real-life Vietnam veterans into "flashbacks" from the fictional storylines. If *M*A*S*H* had been done as an hour show, it might have turned out close to the deft mix of character, narrative, style, and experimentation in *China Beach*.

M*A*S*H, of course, had shown how the half-hour form could regularly shift the balance in particular episodes from a comedy with dramatic elements to a drama with comic elements. Though the show had a laugh track, even that was banned from the operating room and from particularly intense scenes. Since *M*A*S*H*'s heyday, there had been a number of attempts to push sitcoms even further from their traditional domain, such as *United States*, a darkly grim 1980 marriage comedy from former *M*A*S*H* producer Larry Gelbart. More recently (May 1987), NBC had turned over the post-*Cheers* slot to veteran producer Jay Tarses (*The Bob Newhart Show*) for a spring and summer run of *The Days and Nights of Molly Dodd*. Blair Brown played the title character, a thirty-something divorced woman living solo in a rent-controlled Manhattan apartment and dealing with the everyday details of life, love, family, and career. The program was a quirky blend of low-key musings, odd occurrences, and simple complications. Though the series dispensed with a laugh track, *Molly Dodd* was humorous, earning it a return spot in the spring of 1988.

By then, *Molly Dodd* was joining a handful of other half-hour sitcoms attempting to redefine the balance between comedy and drama. Generally running without a laugh track, these "dramedies" (as they were dubbed) were among the distinctive series of the 1987–88 season that were willing to take a chance on executing visions that were just a little bit different.

On CBS there was *Frank's Place*, with Tim Reid as star and executive producer (along with Hugh Wilson from *WKRP in Cincinnati*). Already familiar to viewers from roles in two previous CBS series (Venus Flytrap on *WKRP* and Downtown Brown on *Simon and Simon*), Reid brought a sense of comfortable credibility to the role of Bostonian Frank Parrish, a professor of Renaissance history who unexpectedly found himself owner of a small New Orleans Creole restaurant, the Chez Louisiane, when he inherited it upon the death of his estranged father. A Northern Yankee in the Deep South, Frank was both puzzled and fascinated by this exotic new world, so much so that by the end of the first episode he was ready to believe that perhaps it was a touch of voodoo magic that kept him from successfully returning home to New England. Maybe head waitress Miss Marie (Frances E. Williams) had cast a spell and that was why suddenly his Boston home was wrecked,

his girlfriend left him, and his office burned. Or, maybe what really kept him in town was his attraction to Hannah Griffin (Daphne Maxwell Reid, his real-life wife), a mortician and embalmer at the neighborhood funeral parlor. The series followed Frank's subsequent attempts to fit in, not only as a fish-out-of-water big-city single guy, but also as a son trying to make sense out of his dad's world after a lifetime of separation.

Frank's Place also built upon Bill Cosby's powerhouse sitcom success that had broken the long-time TV stereotype of black characters too often placed in lower class or domestic "housekeeper" settings. In fact, *The Cosby Show* was now the television series that offered the era's snapshot of the American dream perfectly fulfilled (1980s style), much as programs such as *Father Knows Best* and *Leave It to Beaver* had done in the 1950s. Yet while *The Cosby Show* remained focused on upscale Manhattan family life, *Frank's Place* ventured into adult single life, drawing from a variety of different social and economic circles. As with *The Cosby Show*, *Frank's Place* proudly displayed a deep and detailed sense of black history, but with a funkier New Orleans flavor. In particular, the New Orleans setting allowed for some unusual storylines that were different from the tried-and-true New York or California settings of most sitcoms (white or black oriented). The series also dared to get into some touchy issues, such as racial prejudices among some blacks. For example, in one story Frank found himself courted for membership in an exclusive black men's social club, only to discover he was being used as the "token" dark-skinned black in a group dominated by blacks with fairer skin. Yet even with such topical angles, *Frank's Place* always remained anchored in basic entertainment and human insight by Reid's superb sense of comic timing. The ultimate draw in *Frank's Place* was Frank, as he attempted to loosen up and strike a balance between trying to run his own establishment and allowing it (and New Orleans) to run him.

ABC also used this season to dive into experimentation with half-hour dramedies. The network had lured hit drama producer Steven Bochco with an exclusive multiple-series deal, and one of his first new offerings was a police show dramedy, *Hooperman*. Former *Three's Company* lead John Ritter played the title character, a San Francisco cop who had a demanding boss (played by Barbara Bosson, a former *Hill Street Blues* regular) and a quirky home life (Hooperman managed a rundown apartment building left to him by his former landlady), and who loved to play the saxophone (allowing for jazzy interludes). ABC also looked to the dramedy form as the ideal fit for Dabney Coleman, who excelled at selfish, manipulative, and self-centered characters (as in the film "9 to 5" and in his previous short-lived NBC series, *Buffalo Bill*). *The 'Slap' Maxwell Story* cast him as an egocentric sportswriter at a second-rate newspaper.

The Wonder Years, ABC's most effective dramedy that year, arrived midway in the season. After a heavily promoted premiere in the choice post-Super Bowl slot, *The Wonder Years* followed up with a short six-episode spring run. The series returned for its first full season in the fall of 1988 and, over the course of 115 episodes, presented the story of white, suburban, middle-class family life in the U.S. from 1968 to 1973. It was all seen through the eyes of Kevin Arnold (Fred Savage), who went from junior high to his high school junior year during the series run, observing not only his own concerns but also the dynamics of his family, his friends, and the world around him. What set the series apart was the use of an off-screen narrator, Kevin as an adult (voiced by Daniel Stern, uncredited). This technique allowed the series a remarkable level of insight and perspective that did not come off as forced. It was really the adult Kevin remembering what had happened, filling in nuances that he might have observed but not really understood as a

August 16, 1987

An exhibition match between the Chicago Bears and the Miami Dolphins inaugurates ESPN's new three-year, $55 million contract with the National Football League, the last of the major U.S. sports leagues to expand its TV coverage to cable. The deal includes eight regular-season Sunday night NFL games during the second half of the football season, along with the usually ignored Pro Bowl all-star game and four pre-season contests.

August 25, 1987

For $50 million, NBC agrees to sell its radio network to burgeoning radio program producer Westwood One (which previously purchased the Mutual radio network in 1985). Westwood will lease the use of the NBC name as it takes over operations. Within a year, NBC also sells its radio O&Os in New York, Chicago, Boston, San Francisco, and Washington, D.C., effectively ending its sixty-two-year radio history.

September 11, 1987

The CBS network goes dark for seven minutes. First, the network's live coverage of the U.S. Open women's tennis semi-finals runs two minutes into the scheduled time for Dan Rather's live evening newscast. Then Rather (steamed that sports would intrude on his air time) is down the hall attempting to reach his boss by telephone to complain when the tennis coverage ends. With Rather off the set, the news could not begin, so CBS sends blank air to its affiliates. Finally, Rather returns to begin an abbreviated edition of the *CBS Evening News*.

September 20, 1987

NBC adds a ninety-minute version of *Today* to its Sunday morning schedule, hosted by Boyd Matson and Maria Shriver.

December 7, 1987

Remote Control. (MTV). Sliding away from being a twenty-four-hour music video service, six-year-old MTV offers its first game show, an irreverent quizzer that looks at television and pop culture trivia through a rock fan's eyes. Ken Ober hosts, with sidekick Colin Quinn.

---

child. This years-later distance also made dwelling on the mundane details of everyday life appear less self-indulgent than it did on *thirtysomething*. Such details were touchstones to the past and, seen through adult eyes, they could be viewed with a more knowing sense of humor. One narrative device was to have the adult Kevin eloquently describe a situation with what he had *wanted* to say at the time, then the scene would play out with what the young Kevin blurted out back then, in words far less profound or poetic. The use of nostalgic period music also worked, as part of associated memories from days that were simultaneously in the distant past, yet as fresh as yesterday.

Stories in *The Wonder Years* covered the expected topics of growing up: school, friendship, siblings, learning to drive, and, of course, girls. Winnie (Danica McKellar) was Kevin's first love, Paul (Josh Saviano) was his best buddy, and the three of them experienced together the ups-and-downs of youthful discovery. Kevin's older sister, Karen (Olivia d'Abo), went through "all that hippie stuff" (protests and love beads), even moving in with her boyfriend Michael (David Schwimmer) before they were married. Kevin's older brother, Wayne (Jason Hervey), "tortured" Kevin

---

mercilessly (or so he remembered it), but was also eager to make his own mark, landing a job out of high school at their dad's company. Kevin's parents, Jack and Norma (Dan Lauria and Alley Mills), were a believable combination of concern and authority, with the family confrontations (especially involving Karen) perfectly epitomizing the "generation gap" of the era. Kevin's observations about his parents benefited the most from the "looking back" perspective. He could see how frustrated his dad was with his own life, which had not turned out the way he had hoped it would. Even at angry moments, Kevin could see, in retrospect, the conflicting emotions of love, fear, and disappointment in his dad's eyes. In a rarity for television, the final episodes of the series wrapped up the story, with the voice-over narration explaining what happened to everybody.

Ultimately, there was nothing extraordinary about the life of the Arnold family during this era, and that was the point. Variations of the same sort of stories had unfolded in many other U.S. households in the late 1960s. The grown-up Kevin acknowledged as much in the opening episode, noting that the relatively stable and secure suburban setting led many to think that nothing of interest occurred there. But, the adult Kevin pointed out, that was not a fair observation. Those living in the suburbs had their own crises to deal with, which seemed as real and difficult to them as anyone else's might be. By keeping such concerns close to the heart, *The Wonder Years* truly succeeded in capturing the inherent human drama of daily living in that era, presenting an "inside" view of the much-vaunted 1960s from those who had gone through it.

Of all the innovative and creative shows that arrived during the 1987–88 season, only *The Wonder Years* landed in the final top ten listing for that season. Or in any subsequent season. Though these dramas and comedies collectively had shown that television was still capable of high quality production, these products did not translate into chart-topping ratings. At best, they were more akin to such series as *St. Elsewhere*, prestige productions capable of reaching more limited though desirable niche audiences. That was fine if network programmers would be satisfied with such performance. In some cases they were, at least for a few seasons. However, if they were seeking the next *Cosby Show* or *Cheers*, they were doomed to disappointment. Most of the year's innovative series only lasted about three seasons. *Frank's Place* and *'Slap' Maxwell* were gone after one. After its second spring run on NBC, *The Days and Nights of Molly Dodd* was banished to cable, appearing now and again for two additional seasons on Lifetime. Though *thirty-something* managed to last four seasons, it changed part of the central dynamic during its second year, adding a more mainstream *Dallas*-type villain (David Clennon as Miles Drentell).

For most viewers, though, television for the 1987–88 season was business as usual as they returned to their long-running favorites. *The Cosby Show. Cheers. Growing Pains. Who's the Boss? 60 Minutes. Murder, She Wrote. ALF.* For many, the biggest question of the new season was how the new female lead on *Cheers* would fit in after Shelley Long's departure. New bar owner Rebecca Howe (Kirstie Alley) did just fine, providing a new type of male-female interaction with former owner Sam Malone, who was now just another Cheers employee. *Cheers* remained a top-five hit, usually landing just behind *Cosby* and also behind the most successful new show of the season in the ratings, *A Different World*.

There was no doubt as to why *A Different World* was an instant success. The program occupied the choice time period immediately after *The Cosby Show*, replacing *Family Ties* (which was moved to Sunday). There was also no doubt why the series had landed that golden slot. *A Different World* was a direct spinoff from *The Cosby Show*'s production company, following Huxtable daughter Denise

(Lisa Bonet) to her dad's alma mater, the predominantly black Hillman College. Some of the other Huxtables visited in the first few episodes and, like *The Cosby Show*, the stories themselves offered a wide variety of positive and uplifting black role models. Yet, unlike *The Cosby Show* (which had instantly gelled as a Bill Cosby monologue come to life), *A Different World* was not built around a seasoned stand-up comic. Instead Bonet faced the familiar problems of a supporting character thrust into the lead spotlight, and the series drifted into an ill-defined ensemble form. It was not a good fit. As the number two show on television, though, *A Different World* was given the time to right itself. In its second season, the series took shape under new producer Debbie Allen who reworked the cast and stories with a snappier style. Lisa Bonet left and eventually returned to the well-defined ensemble mix of *The Cosby Show*. This allowed Whitley Gilbert (Jasmine Guy), who had stolen the show from day one, to officially became the main focus. The series ran for six seasons, though its ratings success continued to depend on its coupling with *The Cosby Show*. When that program ended its run, *A Different World* spent its final year far from the top.

Because its success was so closely linked to *Cosby*, *A Different World* did not offer the networks any clues for future hit formulas. In fact, overall, there were no new breakout network hits, merely hints at what might work. Series such as *thirtysomething* and *The Wonder Years* simply confirmed what they already knew: A small number of such quality programs could succeed on a limited basis. A highly touted vehicle built around country singer Dolly Parton flopped, confirming the belief that prime time variety was still dead. In the spring Fred Silverman's production company once again succeeded in bringing a familiar face to a new setting with *In the Heat of the Night* (based on the 1967 film), casting Carroll O'Connor in Rod Steiger's role as a small-town Southern sheriff. The sitcom *My Two Dads* raised eyebrows (but little viewer interest) with its premise of an odd couple pair of young men (played by Paul Reiser and Greg Evigan) raising a twelve-year-old girl left to their care by the child's deceased mother, who had slept with them both back in college but who had no idea which was the dad. *Full House* offered a far less tawdry-sounding premise and connected with a very young Friday night audience. A cute widower (played by Bob Saget) talked his two buddies into moving in with him to help raise his young girls (including the precocious Michelle, played by twins Mary-Kate and Ashley Olsen).

In a completely different direction, the Fox network connected directly with viewers in *America's Most Wanted,* hosted by John Walsh (who had come to prominence when his young son had been kidnapped and murdered a few years before). The program started in February 1988 on local Fox O&O stations, recreating real-life crimes in short vignettes, packaging them along with background conversations with victims and law enforcement officials, and then inviting viewers to call a toll-free number with information to help apprehend the perpetrators. A few days after the first episode, viewer calls led to the capture of one of the FBI's ten most wanted. A few months later, the program was on the entire Fox network.

As all the networks searched for and tinkered with formats aimed at new generations of viewers, an old baby boomer favorite made a triumphant return. For the fall of 1987, Gene Roddenberry brought back *Star Trek*. In the eighteen years since NBC had pulled the plug on the series after only three seasons, *Star Trek* had become its own cottage industry. The original 79 episodes played endlessly in rerun syndication. There had been four theatrical features, with the most recent ("Star Trek IV: The Voyage Home," directed by Leonard Nimoy) one of the most successful films of 1986. For Roddenberry, the time seemed right for another run at

television, but on his terms. Rather than subject himself to the capricious scheduling decisions of an established network (which would treat his project as just another fungible commodity), Roddenberry and Paramount created an ad hoc network pitching *Star Trek: The Next Generation* directly to individual stations for first-run syndication. In a canny business arrangement that maximized the value of the new series and the old, stations signing up for *Next Generation* also got the rights for the original *Star Trek* episodes for their market (when next available). After just one season of *Next Generation*, the total *Star Trek* package would reach 100, the preferred episode total for syndication. It was a modest goal. *Star Trek: The Next Generation* far exceeded it. The series ran seven seasons (178 episodes), more than double the run of the original.

Next Generation found clever ways to reconstitute the elements that had worked before. Stories still took place on a ship called the *Enterprise*, but it was now set in the 24th century, seventy-eight years after Captain Kirk. That shift allowed for creditable advances in technology and also established a respectful distance from the

January 25, 1988
During a live interview on the *CBS Evening News,* anchor Dan Rather and Vice President George Bush get into a shouting match over Bush's role in the Iran-Contra scandal. Bush says that judging him just on that one issue would be like judging Rather only on his seven-minute absence from the news anchor chair the previous September.

February 15, 1988
Tanner '88. (HBO). Film director Robert Altman ("MASH") and *Doonesbury* comic strip creator Garry Trudeau team up to produce an innovative and off-beat short-run cable series taking pot shots at American presidential campaigns. Michael Murphy plays Democratic presidential candidate Jack Tanner, with Cynthia Nixon as his daughter, Alex.

February 21, 1988
"Bring Me the Head of Dobie Gillis." (CBS). Twenty-five years after leaving prime time, the cast of *Dobie Gillis* reunites for a two-hour TV movie. Dobie, now married to Zelda, still has a hankering for Thalia Menninger, now a wealthy widow who actually wants Dobie: dead or alive.

March 7, 1988
Television writers begin a strike against the program production companies, which lasts five months.

April 1, 1988
Douglas Edwards, anchor of a daily CBS newscast since 1946, hosts his last news show before retirement. It is in his regular slot, a sixty-second newsbreak at 11:58 A.M.

May 25, 1988
The final episode of *St. Elsewhere* ("The Last One") concludes with the bizarre implication that all the stories in the series might have been figments of the imagination of Donald Westphall's autistic son, Tommy.

August 1, 1988
The Reverend Pat Robertson's Christian Broadcasting Network changes its name to the Family Channel, highlighting the cable channel's move from a full-time religious schedule to one that combines preaching with wholesome "family" entertainment such as reruns of *Bonanza* and *The Waltons*.

original's characters. Kirk had been something of a loose cannon, so new Captain Jean-Luc Picard was cast as someone more in control. Patrick Stewart, with impressive stage credentials that included Britain's Royal Shakespeare Company, was perfect for the role. He not only projected a true air of authority and had a commanding presence, but he was also erudite and literate. In contrast to Kirk, Picard was perfectly comfortable letting his number one officer, William Riker (Jonathan Frakes), lead the various away teams. Humanoid android Data (Brent Spiner) filled the Mr. Spock role of logical advisor haunted by human emotions—though in Data's case, he wanted to be more human, not less. Picard's other counselors included Deanna Troi (Marina Sirtis), who could read emotions; Tasha Yar (Denise Crosby), head of security; Worf (Michael Dorn), a Klingon advisor who later took over security; and Guinan (Whoopi Goldberg), the ship's mysterious bartender. The ship's technical crew included Beverly Crusher (Gates McFadden), head of the medical team; Geordi La Forge (LeVar Burton), a blind helmsman-chief engineer who could see when aided by a special visor; and Miles O'Brien (Colin Meaney), the transporter chief. Unlike the original *Star Trek*, all the members of the support crew were given story showcases that developed their individual characters.

Next Generation also greatly expanded the mythos of the Star Trek universe, adding new alien races including the ruthless Borg, which wiped out entire civilizations by absorbing them into a "collective," and the virtually omnipotent Q (John Delancey), who delighted in toying with the *Enterprise* crew by putting them through various tests (much to the annoyance of Picard). The *Enterprise* also contained a wonderful plot innovation called the holodeck, which created a computer-generated environment aboard the ship, allowing the show's writers to set particular stories anywhere in time or space (as when Data played Sherlock Holmes).

Most important, the quality and variety of the stories on *Next Generation* outshone the inconsistent nature of the 1960s original. There were character studies, interstellar battles, moral fables, and pure speculative science fiction. Patrick Stewart was at the center of many of these delivering truly sublime performances. For example, in "The Inner Light" Picard collapsed on the bridge when an alien mind probe took over his brain. Though still unconscious aboard the ship, in his mind Picard began living an alternative life on another planet. In about twenty minutes (from the point of view of the *Enterprise* crew), he experienced a full life on that other planet, was happily married, had children, then grew old and approached death. When he revived he found himself still on his own starship, but with a second lifetime of memories. That was a story that could not be found anywhere else on television.

Even more than the original, *Star Trek: The Next Generation* embodied Gene Roddenberry's positive vision of the future. Its success opened the doors for many other *Star Trek* ventures, winning viewer support and affection by turning a television treasure from the past into an even more satisfying new experience.

It was the ultimate in baby boomer wish fulfillment.

49. The Goddess

ROSEANNE BARR WAS NOT a household name going into the fall of 1988. Though she had achieved success in stand-up comedy circles (including appearances on Johnny Carson's *Tonight* show and her own 1987 special on HBO), Barr was a comparative unknown to the general public. Her comic persona—a chunky, unglamorous woman getting by on pointed barbs and biting observations (she sarcastically referred to herself as "the domestic goddess")—set her miles apart from the cool, folksy style of fellow stand-up comic Bill Cosby. Still, Barr was chosen by *Cosby Show* executive producers Marcy Carsey and Tom Werner to star in a new TV sitcom, simply titled *Roseanne*. Like *The Cosby Show*, the focus was on family. Like *The Cosby Show*, traits for the fictional lead character were drawn from the star's stand-up act. And like *The Cosby Show*, the new series was an immediate hit. In its first season, *Roseanne* ended up number two in the overall ratings, right behind *Cosby* and just ahead of *A Different World*. This success gave Carsey and Werner television's top three series, and reemphasized the appeal of casting a stand-up comic as centerpiece to a sitcom.

Yet from the beginning *Roseanne* proved to be anything but a *Cosby* clone. This was family life with all the frayed edges. Barr and John Goodman played Roseanne and Dan Connor, a beefy working-class couple living in Lanford, Illinois, a world quite different from the upscale Manhattan life of Cosby's Huxtables. She was stuck in a boring manufacturing job and he worked as a small-time construction contractor with seasonal cycles of employment. They needed both paychecks to barely stay ahead while maintaining their midwestern bungalow and raising thirteen-year-old Becky (Lecy Goranson), eleven-year-old Darlene (Sara Gilbert), and six-year-old D. J. (Michael Fishman). Roseanne and Dan's big night out typically involved bowling or penny-ante poker, and for their anniversary they might head to a cheap neighborhood restaurant (preferably with a two-for-one coupon). Though love existed in the Connor family, conversations between family members were usually laced with putdowns and dark humor. (For example, after the kids had left for school, Roseanne suggested changing the locks so they could never get back in.) Dan usually played good cop and let Roseanne's flat-voiced sarcasm set the family boundaries, recognizing that she was going to rule the home roost anyway so there was no point in fighting it.

Life imitated art as the real-life Roseanne quickly established that she was the one in charge of *her* program, on and off stage, leading to the first-season departure of Matt Williams, the official series creator. Producers Carsey and Werner soon opted to take a "hands off" attitude toward the hit show (and its mercurial and temperamental star). Fortunately, though Barr quickly became the unquestioned production force of the series as well as the star, she was also smart enough to let her strong supporting cast shine. Goodman and Gilbert were particularly effective, with the level-headed Dan acting as a calming force in the household and the headstrong and independent Darlene clearly taking after her sharp-tongued mom. That family resemblance also extended to Roseanne's sister, Jackie Harris (Laurie Metcalf), who brought the trials and tribulations of adult single life to the stories. Though already a thirty-something, Jackie was still unmarried and uncertain what she wanted to do when she grew up. She had a long string of disastrous relationships and unfulfilling jobs to illustrate her frustrations. Barr and Metcalf played the sibling connection between Roseanne and Jackie so effectively it seemed as if they really were sisters, alternately sniping and supportive, knowing each other's best and worst sides. Over the course of the series, the two characters ended up running a small business together, a local diner.

Roseanne's world was not pretty. There was hard work. Low pay. Deferred dreams. Serious limitations on the future. And yet the series connected with large numbers of viewers who found its blue collar vision authentic, accessible, and funny. The audience recognized situations from their own day-to-day lives and enjoyed the Connors' minor victories over bosses and bureaucrats. Best of all, the family exchanges had bite and were almost like eavesdropping on real kids and real adults as they argued, teased, bluffed, lied, and occasionally almost hugged. The series was often unflinchingly topical, but the creditable characters made such storylines both believable and humorous. For example, a "just say no to drugs" harangue directed at Darlene's boyfriend David (Johnny Galecki) was tempered by Roseanne's realization that some marijuana she found in the house was actually her own from years back, not his. When the series dealt with gay characters such as Leon Carp (Martin Mull) and Nancy Bartlett (Sandra Bernhard), they received the same sarcastic jibes as anyone else. When Darlene went off to art school (on a scholarship), boyfriend David moved into her off-campus apartment, but only until mom showed up. And when Jackie found herself single and pregnant, the entire Connor clan backed her, and the episodes included shots of Metcalf's own real-life pregnant form, conveying an impending mom's outright pride at the new life inside her. Bringing such moments to the series enhanced the credibility of the characters and

Day	8:00	8:30	9:00	9:30	10:00	10:30	Network
MON	MacGyver		ABC NFL Monday Night Football (to 12 Midnight)				ABC
	Newhart	Coming Of Age	MURPHY BROWN	Designing Women	ALMOST GROWN		CBS
	local						FOX
	Alf	The Hogan Family	NBC Monday Night At The Movies				NBC
TUE	Who's The Boss	ROSEANNE	Moonlighting		thirtysomething		ABC
	HIGH RISK		CBS Tuesday Night Movie				CBS
	local						FOX
	Matlock		In The Heat Of The Night		MIDNIGHT CALLER		NBC
WED	Growing Pains	Head Of The Class	The Wonder Years	Hooperman	China Beach		ABC
	THE VAN DYKE SHOW	ANNIE McGUIRE	The Equalizer		Wiseguy		CBS
	local						FOX
	UNSOLVED MYSTERIES		Night Court	BABY BOOM	TATTINGERS		NBC
THR	KNIGHTWATCH		Dynasty		ABC Specials		ABC
	48 Hours		PARADISE		Knots Landing		CBS
	local						FOX
	The Cosby Show	A Different World	Cheers	DEAR JOHN	L.A. Law		NBC
FRI	Perfect Strangers	Full House	Mr. Belvedere	Just The Ten Of Us	20/20		ABC
	Beauty And The Beast		Dallas		Falcon Crest		CBS
	local						FOX
	Sonny Spoon		SOMETHING IS OUT THERE		Miami Vice		NBC
SAT	MURPHY'S LAW		Police Story				ABC
	DIRTY DANCING	RAISING MIRANDA	Simon & Simon		West 57th		CBS
	The Reporters		BEYOND TOMORROW		local		FOX
	227	Amen	The Golden Girls	EMPTY NEST	Hunter		NBC

Day	7:00	7:30	8:00	8:30	9:00	9:30	10:00	10:30	Network
SUN	Incredible Sunday		Mission: Impossible		ABC Sunday Night Movie				ABC
	60 Minutes		Murder, She Wrote		CBS Sunday Night Movie				CBS
	21 Jump Street		America's Most Wanted	Married... With Children	It's Garry Shandling's Show	The Tracey Ullman Show	Duet	local	FOX
	The Magical World Of Disney		Family Ties	Day By Day	NBC Sunday Night At The Movies				NBC

also showed a savvy awareness of the off-screen world. *Roseanne* consciously played on the notoriety associated with pushing TV boundaries and deftly walked a fine line. Even while incorporating such topics as child abuse (which Barr cited from her own early life), the series was careful not to sacrifice the credibility of its characters. The program even survived her short-lived marriage to Tom Arnold, another stand-up comic, who then joined the show as an occasional character (Dan's buddy, Arnie) and as a behind-the-scenes business partner. After the marriage ended (and Arnold's own series, *The Jackie Thomas Show*, was canceled), Roseanne dropped the character, the business relationship, and the married name of Arnold. Thereafter she was known simply as Roseanne.

The only series remotely like *Roseanne* was Fox's *Married … with Children*, which previously had taken up the darker side of family life. Yet there was a key difference between the Connor family and the Bundy family. The Bundys seemed to take perverse pleasure in their woeful lot, while on *Roseanne* the characters actually tried to do something to improve their lives. Often the plans did not work out, but it was easy to see why viewers would welcome them in. The Connors might not be an ideal family unit, but over the nine-year run of the series they never stopped trying.

Roseanne was not the only new series to feature a strong female force on and off camera. At CBS, producer Diane English (with husband Joel Shukovsky) created *Murphy Brown*, which revisited the *Mary Tyler Moore* hook of an independent woman at a televi-sion newsroom, but through 1980s eyes and in a major market, Washington, D.C. Candice Bergen played the title character, an ace correspondent for the TV newsmagazine *F.Y.I.* Murphy was aggressive, overbearing, sarcastic, a ruthless competitor, an unreconstructed liberal, and, in the opening episode, was just coming out of rehab at the Betty Ford clinic, where she had quit smoking and drinking. She was an uncontainable fury who (in a running gag) blew through personal secretaries at about one per episode. Yet Murphy was also the consummate professional, respectful of and respected by her *F.Y.I.* colleagues, including straight-laced anchor Jim Dial (Charles Kimbrough); dogged investigative reporter Frank Fontana (Joe Regalbuto); perky correspondent and former Miss America Corky Sherwood (Faith Ford); and a new program producer in his twenties, Miles Silverberg (Grant Shaud), so young that he did not recognize some of Murphy's favorite old Motown songs. They formed a classic workplace family with intertwined lives and moments of genuine affection. At home in her private townhouse, Murphy (unlike Mary Richards from the 1970s) had no upstairs neighbors to drop in, but she was hardly alone. Eldin Bernecky (Robert Pastorelli), hired to paint the interior of her home, remained on the job day and night (for more than half a decade) and was always ready to talk. He was philosophical, patient, and clearly a perfectionist.

Generally, though, after hours the *F.Y.I.* gang hung out at Phil's Place, a longtime Washington bar whose owner (played by Pat

Roseanne Barr was the driving forced behind the authentic working class comedy of *Roseanne*, with John Goodman rock solid as her husband, Dan. (Roseanne *Photo Courtesy of The Carsey-Werner Company, LLC/Don Cadette*)

Corley) had tactfully shared sage moments with politicos of every stripe. Murphy Brown, in contrast, was no diplomat (she made no secret of her liberal political preferences), but she was a terrific reporter and interviewer in the *60 Minutes* mode. Her high-profile comments carried weight and she was on a first name basis with her fictional network honchos (including Alan Oppenheimer as Gene Kinsella and Garry Marshall as Stan Lansing). The show also regularly dropped in real-life names from both political and broadcast circles and featured cameos from the likes of Walter Cronkite, Linda Ellerbee, and Larry King. Though the series did not instantly land in the top ten like *Roseanne*, within a few seasons *Murphy Brown* became one of television's most successful series, right beside *60 Minutes*.

The debuts of both *Roseanne* and *Murphy Brown* came during a particularly disjointed fall premiere season. Beginning in the spring of 1988, a five-month strike by the TV writers' union had disrupted the annual TV production routine. This process usually involved preparing scripts for fall shows in the spring so production could begin in the summer and the first finished episodes could arrive in time for the fall premieres. Though the spring writers strike was settled by August, this still meant that this season's new shows would appear only as each series was able to get up to speed with its production schedule, and new episodes for some programs did not arrive until November. Some fall series (including a revival of *Columbo* on ABC) were delayed until mid-season. *TV Guide* did not issue its traditional fall preview until the beginning of October.

As luck would have it, number one NBC was in the best posi-

tion after the strike ended. A few of its series (including *The Cosby Show*, *A Different World*, and *Highway to Heaven*) had managed to arrange separate deals with the writers' union before the general settlement, so they were ready to air in early October, giving them a head start over most other series, which were delayed by the effects of the strike. The network had plenty of extraordinary back-up material in the form of special event programming: the Summer Olympics in Seoul, South Korea, in September, and baseball's World Series in October. So NBC was perfectly content unveiling its new and returning series during October and November, after heavily promoting them throughout both sports events. Given that lead-off boost, NBC once again had an easy win for the entire season, which was anchored by its solid Thursday and Saturday night lineups. The network won all thirty weeks of this strike-affected season and had thirteen of the top twenty shows.

NBC was particularly adept at creating new hits by carefully slotting them to follow established successes. Thus, *Cheers* led to *Dear John* (Judd Hirsch playing a divorced husband attending a singles support group), while *The Golden Girls* ushered in *Empty Nest* (Richard Mulligan as a widowed physician in Florida keeping a fatherly eye on two grown daughters). Apart from such direct ratings jumpstarts, NBC also was able to use its lineup of hits in general to promote the rest of the schedule. Of course, that was still no guarantee that every NBC program would connect, with series such as *Baby Boom*, *Something Is Out There*, and *Sonny Spoon* quickly fading. The former producers of *St. Elsewhere* also flopped with *Tattingers*, an hour drama set at a tony Manhattan eatery. Despite a strong cast (including Stephen Collins, Blythe

October 3, 1988

Ted Turner unveils a new cable network, TNT (Turner Network Television), which initially serves as an outlet for the hundreds of old films he had acquired from the MGM studio. (The first offering is "Gone With the Wind.") By 1989, Turner moves to TNT the NBA basketball games previously showcased on his WTBS superstation.

October 23, 1988

Mission: Impossible. (ABC). Fifteen years after shutting down operations on CBS, the IMF crew returns in an Australian-produced series. Peter Graves is back as Jim Phelps, directing an otherwise new (and younger) crew. ABC uses the series to fill gaps while awaiting the programs delayed by the writers' strike.

November 13, 1988

War and Remembrance. (ABC). Picking up where the 1983 miniseries *The Winds of War* left off, this eighteen-hour sweeps presentation follows Herman Wouk's World War II novel from Pearl Harbor to 1943. During the May sweeps, another eleven-and-one-half hour stretch at last brings the saga to the war's end in 1945.

January 9, 1989

The Pat Sajak Show. (CBS). After eleven years of filling its late night slot primarily with reruns of old series, CBS takes a stab at cloning Johnny Carson's success. Amiable *Wheel of Fortune* host Pat Sajak aims for the same cool detachment as Carson, but his tame program fails to catch on. After fifteen months, the network concedes defeat and cancels it.

February 5, 1989

Lonesome Dove. (CBS). Larry McMurtry's engaging novel of a Texas-to-Montana cattle drive in the 1870s turns into a February sweeps success for CBS. The eight-hour adaptation stars Robert Duvall, Tommy Lee Jones, and Robert Urich and is the season's highest rated miniseries.

Danner, Jerry Stiller, and Rob Morrow), they quickly discovered that, no matter how well written, the woes of wealthy restaurateurs did not entice the public.

Overall, though, NBC seemed to be on the right track for the long run by continuing to place a few new hits into its lineup each season. In addition to *Dear John* and *Empty Nest,* there was *Midnight Caller* in the fall (Gary Cole as a former cop hosting a late night radio call-in show) and, at mid-season, *The Father Dowling Mysteries* (Tom Bosley as a sleuthing priest, with Tracy Nelson as a nun). In the spring, NBC, which since the start of the Brandon Tartikoff era had often tried but always failed to develop new hit fantasy series (such as *Manimal* and *Something Is Out There*), at last came up with a successful science fiction series in *Quantum Leap,* from producer Donald P. Bellisario. In *Quantum Leap,* Scott Bakula played Dr. Sam Beckett, a time traveler leaping through the recent past (his lifetime) and temporarily assuming the physical appearance of a person in trouble at each stop (although to viewers Dr. Beckett still looked like Scott Bakula). Beckett's only guide through his journeys was Al (Dean Stockwell), a wisecracking hologram projection from Beckett's time. Bakula's likable and accessible persona helped make the outlandish premise seem perfectly believable.

NBC also nimbly picked up on the growing viewer interest in Fox's real-life crime-stopper series *America's Most Wanted,*

(which had premiered the previous season) and, for the fall of 1988, turned its own *Unsolved Mysteries* from a string of occasional specials into a weekly series. Robert Stack stepped in as host (Raymond Burr and Karl Malden had served that role in the specials), taking viewers through stories of unusual "unsolved" cases. These cases included not only confirmed crimes (as on *America's Most Wanted*) but also personal mysteries such as a lonely person's disappearance after a date or reports concerning UFO encounters or paranormal activities. For most of these tales there was no actual footage, so the program staged reenactments of the incidents, clearly labeling them as such. At the end, the screen showed an 800 phone number to call for viewers with any information. The combination worked and *Unsolved Mysteries* easily landed among the season's top-twenty series.

With all these successes, NBC still faced the usual problems of any network with a strong lineup of hits. NBC had fewer available slots to try out new ideas, and at the same time the network was reluctant to give new programs a great deal of time to prove themselves. It was also a calculated gamble to rely so much on mildly successful series that depended primarily on the strength of their established hit lead-ins, some of which were already half a decade old. When programs such as *The Cosby Show* and *The Golden Girls* faded, would the new shows have built enough of a following by then to stand on their own? On top of that, NBC, like ABC and CBS (the other "Big 3" networks), had to fight harder than ever to maintain viewer attention as other forces nipped away at the edges of the network audience, including more aggressively promoted syndication and cable offerings.

The previous season's success of the first-run syndication package of *Star Trek: The Next Generation* had invigorated hopes for similar original syndication fare, especially because some affiliates occasionally chose to slot that space adventure in place of particularly weak prime time network fare. For the 1988–89 season, Paramount (home studio for *Star Trek*) launched *War of the Worlds,* a one-hour series that served as a continuation of the 1953 feature film based on the H. G. Wells novel. Other companies offered such programs as *Freddy's Nightmares* (a horror anthology based on the "Nightmare on Elm Street" feature films), *Superboy* (from the producers of the "Superman" feature films), and *The Munsters Today* (a dreadful revival of the 1960s series). Though none of these attempts succeeded, there was a new groundbreaking syndication smash that season when black comic Arsenio Hall entered the late night talk show world in January 1989 with *The Arsenio Hall Show.* Fresh from co-starring with his friend Eddie Murphy in the feature film "Coming to America," Hall brought a completely different attitude to the talk show genre, with consciously hipper guests, a funkier musical tone, and a vocal studio audience that seemed more like a basketball game crowd than one at a talk show. Hall easily bested the more traditional Pat Sajak (moonlighting from hosting the game show *Wheel of Fortune*), who launched his own late night talk show at the same time for CBS.

Cable tweaked the networks in several areas as it continued its slow but steady penetration into more U.S. households (more than 50% by 1988). Apart from showing recent feature films uncut and (on the premium services) commercial free, cable increasingly cashed in on viewer familiarity with network shows by buying cable rerun rights. This trend was extending beyond golden oldies to include such recent hits as *Miami Vice* (just canceled at the end of the 1988–89 season) and *Murder, She Wrote* (still running on CBS). Even more significant, starting with the ceremony held in August 1988, television's Emmy awards began including original cable offerings in its competition. (One of the first awards went to HBO for a special featuring stand-up comic Jackie Mason.) This

February 28, 1989

Coach. (ABC). Craig T. Nelson shows his comic side playing Hayden Fox, the divorced football coach of Minnesota State University. His sitcom sidekicks include TV veterans Jerry Van Dyke as a dense but well-meaning assistant coach and Shelly Fabares as a local newscaster who is Hayden's new love.

March 7, 1989

Anything But Love. (ABC). Jamie Lee Curtis (fresh from the film "A Fish Called Wanda") and Richard Lewis (a stand-up comic with a borderline-neurotic persona) star in the premise that opposites attract, eventually. Set largely in the offices of a Chicago magazine, this sitcom takes two years and multiple time-slot shifts before the two admit they are in love.

April 17, 1989

NBC launches its first cable network, CNBC (Consumer News and Business Channel), featuring business news all day and talk shows in the evening.

April 26, 1989

Lucille Ball, age seventy-seven, the first lady of TV sitcoms, dies.

July 5, 1989

The Seinfeld Chronicles. (NBC). Stand-up comic Jerry Seinfeld plays himself in this half-hour sitcom pilot, which he created with fellow comic Larry David. Jason Alexander plays Jerry's not-quite-bald pal George, while Michael Richards is Jerry's very odd neighbor, named Hoffman.

August 3, 1989

Prime Time Live. (ABC). Diane Sawyer defects from CBS (and her post as a *60 Minutes* correspondent) to join ABC as co-host with Sam Donaldson for this hour-long news magazine. Her opening night interview is with ABC star Roseanne Barr.

---

marked an important perception change. Up until then, "television" had meant offerings by broadcast stations, while "cable" was considered programming outside this mainstream. Including cable in the Emmy categories carried the suggestion that the two might be far more equal than previously thought—adding credibility to cable services and chipping away at the networks' status as the only showcase that really mattered for original programming.

The Big 3 networks were also facing the rising force of the new Fox network. Though Fox was still losing tens of millions of dollars annually on its television operation, in the increasingly cost-conscious network world, nobody was better at coming up with eye-catching innovations, especially on the cheap. In early 1988, Fox found a quick way to land a highly regarded comedy for its schedule. Striking a deal with the Showtime cable service, it began to air episodes of *It's Garry Shandling's Show*, no less than one month after their initial cable presentation. Created by stand-up comic Garry Shandling and former *Saturday Night Live* writer Alan Zweibel, the program began on Showtime in the fall of 1986, following the everyday life of stand-up comic Garry Shandling. In an effective update of the *George Burns and Grace Allen* TV set-up, Shandling regularly broke the "fourth wall" between the audience and the performers, delivering asides on the story in progress and also gleefully manipulating the action for maximum effect. Unlike *Burns and Allen*, the other characters also knew they were part of a television show, but just accepted that fact. The series was an instant critical hit, not only because of the storytelling gimmick, but also because it was perfectly in tune with comic Shandling's personality, a hilarious combination of media savvy, social insecurity, and an obsession with the most trivial details of life. Though the series never became a big ratings hit for Fox, the broadcast airing allowed viewers without cable to see what all the fuss was about. It also let Fox tout one of the best programs on television as one of its own.

In January 1989, Fox took reality programming to the next level with *Cops*. The premise behind this series was simple. With permission, crews armed with portable video cameras traveled with local police and taped their pursuits and arrests. This was real front line footage, which took advantage of advances in video technology that had reduced camera sizes and required lighting levels. The program began in January on the Fox O&Os, and by March it was on the entire Fox network. There were no reenactments, no somber narratives, and no expensive actors and scripts.

Even with its still-minuscule ratings (only about one-third of NBC's total), Fox had shown the ability to win viewers and influence the television landscape with its self-proclaimed in-your-face style. *Married ... with Children* helped set the stage for *Roseanne*. *America's Most Wanted* showed the viability of a weekly *Unsolved Mysteries*. Arsenio Hall had gotten his start as a substitute host in the waning days of the Joan Rivers late night talk show on Fox. The Big 3 networks at last seemed to be realizing that they just might have to make some changes in their programming styles in order to stay ahead.

50. Mmmm ... Doughnuts

DESPITE CONTINUING BOTTOM-LINE budget concerns, network spending on sports rights escalated rapidly at the end of the 1980s, in the process changing that landscape for the new decade just beginning. CBS made the first move, capturing exclusive broadcast network rights to Major League Baseball for four seasons (1990 through 1993), for the then-astounding price of $1 billion. In that deal, CBS became the sole outlet for the World Series, the League Championship Series, and the All-Star game, along with the long-running Saturday afternoon game of the week, an NBC staple since 1966. ESPN soon followed this move by paying $400 million for exclusive national cable baseball rights for those same four years, with an ambitious schedule of 175 games per season, highlighted by a national game of the week on Sunday nights.

NBC retaliated by stealing away professional basketball from CBS, which had televised the NBA for seventeen years. Beginning in the fall of 1990, NBC would pay $150 million a year for four years of NBA broadcasts, more than triple the $47 million per year CBS had been paying. In response, CBS agreed to yet another $1 billion sports rights package, capturing exclusive rights to the annual March NCAA college basketball tournament for seven years (1991 through 1997), also almost tripling the then-current rate paid between CBS and ESPN (which had aired some of the tournament's early round games for several years).

CBS's NCAA contract, eliminating cable from the college basketball tournament picture, went against the latest trend among sports organizations, which was to foster parallel deals covering both broadcast networks and cable. This policy of multiple outlets increased revenues from the sale of TV rights, allowed the cable networks to fill their schedules with newsworthy sports events, yet still left the broadcast networks with the principal sports events, such as the World Series and the NBA championship games.

The prices paid in these new sports contracts were truly astonishing, especially when, at the same time, the networks were otherwise scrutinizing every penny. How could they possibly recoup such expenditures? There were several justifications. It was a partially preemptive move, keeping specific sports away from the competition. It was also proactive, landing distinctive events that helped set the network (and its affiliates) apart from the competition. Most important, the price tags were justified by judging sports in a new way. Sports events were not to be seen merely as sports events. They were now positioned as a key part of an overall promotional effort. In that light, sports contests did not have to

make back through the sale of commercial time all the money spent on the rights because, as marquee showcases, they were offered as the perfect vehicle for promoting the entire network schedule. Viewers for basketball or baseball games would be bombarded with information about the network's other offerings, from morning news to late night programs. This would be an especially effective way to launch new shows, providing the network a short cut to rejuvenating its lineup. With sports as the promotional billboard, viewership and associated ad revenue would increase throughout the rest of the schedule. Overall, the network would make money.

That was the theory. Of course, this assumed that sports broadcasts would actually deliver a sufficiently large number of new viewers to the rest of the network schedule. Even more basic, it assumed that the rest of the schedule contained programming that was worth promoting. After all, it would do little good to lure potential viewers if they immediately went away disappointed.

It seemed CBS would have the toughest task exploiting such promotions in the near future. For the 1989–90 season it was still struggling with comparatively few hits (*60 Minutes*, *Murphy Brown*, and *Murder, She Wrote*) and an assortment of long-running leftovers from its previous glory days (including three prime time soaps: *Falcon Crest*, *Dallas*, and *Knots Landing*). More troubling, the network was having only limited success with its new programs. *Rescue 911* (host William Shatner chronicling real-life disasters) garnered respectable ratings when it became a regular weekly series that fall after successful specials the previous spring. CBS's only other new fall series hit was *Major Dad*, with Gerald McRaney playing a career Marine who fell for and married a liberal reporter (played by Shanna Reed) with three daughters. Otherwise, most of CBS's new series did not catch on, even with good casts, including Jon Cryer and Alex Rocco in *The Famous Teddy Z* (a mailroom gofer lands a top spot in a talent agency), Lindsay Wagner and Tom Wopat in *Peaceable Kingdom* (life at the L.A. County Zoo), and the affable husband-and-wife acting pair of Tim Reid and Daphne Maxwell Reid in *Snoops* (in which they played a husband-and-wife sleuthing pair). Perhaps incessant sports promotions might have helped. CBS would find out soon enough.

NBC hardly needed multi-million dollar sports programs to remind viewers of such continuing hits as *The Cosby Show*, *Cheers*, and *The Golden Girls*. Nonetheless, while remaining in the top ten, those shows were no longer the fresh new hits of television. *Cheers* was already in its eighth year, while *The Cosby Show* found itself edged out as the top show of the season by ABC's *Roseanne* (in only its second year). NBC needed fresh blood in its fall lineup, but, like CBS, none of its new shows were particularly successful. *The Nutt House* (from Mel Brooks) was set at a one-time ritzy New York hotel, but seemed tired rather than manic. *Mancuso, FBI* (with Robert Loggia) was intense but bland. *Sister Kate* seemed incongruous, casting Stephanie Beacham (who had played *Dynasty* vixen Sable) as a nun managing a home for adorable but scheming orphans (led by Todd Mahaffrey, played by Jason Priestley). Even *Baywatch*, a new offering from the production company of former NBC head Grant Tinker, flopped, despite a familiar name (David Hasselhoff) and a premise (lifeguard adventures in sunny California) that placed dozens of good-looking men and women on the beach wearing revealing swim wear.

Though *Baywatch* disappeared from NBC after one season, a reconstituted version returned one year later in first-run syndication. Combined with strong international sales, the series eventually laid claim as one of the most watched programs in the world. The fact that number one NBC had let *Baywatch* slip through without success seemed oddly symbolic. NBC had some of television's most popular series, but was unable to generate any "buzz" for its new offerings. In fact, the most talked about new shows for the season were elsewhere, most often on ABC and (surprisingly) Fox.

In the summer of 1989, Fox once again found a cheap-to-produce format with *Totally Hidden Video*. Borrowing a page from Allen Funt's *Candid Camera*, the series used the compact portable equipment that worked so well on programs such as *Cops* to stage and tape stunts catching average people in embarrassing moments. A few months later, ABC launched its own inexpensive video program, *America's Funniest Home Videos*, starting with a special in November and beginning a regular series in January 1990. Recognizing that many people had video cameras at home, the program invited viewers to send in their best clips – that is, those that captured silly moments in everyday life. Bob Saget served as the comic host (while continuing with his Friday night sitcom *Full House*), introducing the videos in front of a studio audience, which voted for each week's favorite entry and awarded its creator a $10,000 prize. That was a strong lure for amateur video participants but a pittance on the network budget sheets. The makeshift quality of the material was oddly appealing and *America's Funniest Home Videos* lasted more than two decades for ABC.

The network had a far less satisfying experience with *Chicken Soup*, a highly touted new sitcom from Marcy Carsey and Tom Werner. It began in the fall with extraordinary ratings in the post-*Roseanne* slot, but then was almost immediately canceled. The series had seemed a perfect continuation of Carsey and Werner's *Cosby Show/Roseanne* formula, once again building a premise around a distinctive stand-up comic performer by casting wisecracking borscht-belt comic Jackie Mason as a middle-aged New York Jewish man in love with an Irish Catholic woman (played by Lynn Redgrave). Using his trademark comedy monologues, Mason would stand on the roof of his building and talk to God about the latest turns in life. Unfortunately, the comic monologues were the only part that worked. The mixed-religion coupling seemed forced, with virtually no romantic chemistry generated between Mason and Redgrave. Though viewers had shown an increasing willingness to follow distinctive characters such as Roseanne and Murphy Brown, *Chicken Soup* lacked their authenticity. Instead, the series just felt awkward. Determined not to squander such a prime programming slot, ABC canceled *Chicken Soup* and in November replaced it with *Coach*, a mid-season hit from the previous spring.

By righting itself so quickly, ABC was able to maintain a sense of momentum for the season, not only building on *Roseanne*'s success, but also adding a mixed bag of fresh new series. In addition to *Coach* and *America's Funniest Home Videos*, the network had *Doogie Howser, M.D.*, a Steven Bochco comedy-drama series following a sixteen-year-old wunderkind (played by Neil Patrick Harris) who found that being a licensed M.D. still did not spare him the usual challenges of growing up. In a nod to the growing presence of personal computers, each episode ended with Howser typing his reflections about life into an electronic diary. ABC also continued to build its strong Friday night franchise of sitcoms aimed at younger viewers (dubbed the "TGIF" lineup) with *Family Matters* (following a working-class black family in Chicago). Though that series was quickly hijacked by the nerdy next-door-neighbor character of Steve Urkel (Jaleel White), *Family Matters* still proved an ideal companion to *Full House*, *Perfect Strangers*, and *Just the Ten of Us*. ABC also found appropriate counter-programming to *60 Minutes* on Sundays with the sentimental *Life Goes On*, casting Christopher Burke (who had Down Syndrome in real life) as Corky Thatcher, a high school student similarly affected. And there was the ABC equivalent to CBS perennial *60 Minutes,* with the twenty-year-old *Monday Night Football* still landing among the season's top ten series.

October 17, 1989

Just four minutes into ABC's pre-game coverage of game three of the World Series (the Oakland Athletics hosting the San Francisco Giants), an earthquake rocks the Bay area, temporarily knocking ABC off the air. When power is restored, ABC's Al Michaels switches roles from sports to on-the-spot news reporting to cover the calamity.

November 8, 1989

NBC, which had been late in covering the San Francisco earthquake story the previous month, is the first broadcast network to have its nightly news anchor (Tom Brokaw) report live from Berlin, Germany, as the wall dividing the city is opened and knocked down.

December 18, 1989

CBS, stuck in third place in the ratings, hires Jeff Sagansky as its new president of entertainment, the executive in charge of scheduling.

January 8, 1990

Deborah Norville, thirty-one, who had been reading the news on the *Today* show since September, replaces Jane Pauley, thirty-nine, as the show's co-host.

January 10, 1990

Time-Life merges with Warner Communications to form Time Warner, the world's largest entertainment conglomerate.

January 21, 1990

MTV Unplugged. (MTV). The video music channel begins a series featuring rock acts performing acoustically. First up: Squeeze, Syd Straw, and Elliot Easton of The Cars.

February 7, 1990

Ralph Roberts, founder of cable's Comcast Corporation, names his thirty-year-old son Brian to succeed him as president. The elder Roberts remains as Comcast's chief executive officer and chairman of the board.

		8:00	8:30	9:00	9:30	10:00	10:30	
MON		MacGyver		ABC NFL Monday Night Football (to 12 Midnight)				ABC
		MAJOR DAD	PEOPLE NEXT DOOR	Murphy Brown	FAMOUS TEDDY Z	Designing Women	Newhart	CBS
		21 Jump Street		ALIEN NATION		local		FOX
		Alf	The Hogan Family	NBC Monday Night At The Movies				NBC
TUE		Who's the Boss	The Wonder Years	Roseanne	CHICKEN SOUP	thirtysomething		ABC
		RESCUE 911		WOLF		ISLAND SON		CBS
		local						FOX
		Matlock		In The Heat Of The Night		Midnight Caller		NBC
WED		Growing Pains	Head Of The Class	Anything But Love	DOOGIE HOWSER, M.D.	China Beach		ABC
		PEACEABLE KINGDOM		Jake And The Fatman		Wiseguy		CBS
		# Fox Night At The Movies				local		FOX
		Unsolved Mysteries		Night Court	THE NUTT HOUSE	Quantum Leap		NBC
THR		Mission: Impossible		THE YOUNG RIDERS		Prime Time Live		ABC
		48 Hours		TOP OF THE HILL		Knots Landing		CBS
		local						FOX
		The Cosby Show	A Different World	Cheers	Dear John	L.A. Law		NBC
FRI		Full House	FAMILY MATTERS	Perfect Strangers	Just The Ten Of Us	20/20		ABC
		SNOOPS		Dallas		Falcon Crest		CBS
		local						FOX
		BAYWATCH		HARDBALL		MANCUSO, FBI		NBC
SAT		Mr. Belvedere	LIVING DOLLS	ABC Saturday Mystery (Kojak; CHRISTINE CROMWELL; B.L. Stryker; Columbo)				ABC
		Paradise		Tour Of Duty		SATURDAY NIGHT WITH CONNIE CHUNG		CBS
		Cops	The Reporters		Beyond Tomorrow	local		FOX
		227	Amen	The Golden Girls	Empty Nest	Hunter		NBC

		7:00	7:30	8:00	8:30	9:00	9:30	10:00	10:30	
SUN		LIFE GOES ON		FREE SPIRIT	HOMEROOM	ABC Sunday Night Movie				ABC
		60 Minutes		Murder, She Wrote		CBS Sunday Night Movie				CBS
		BOOKER		America's Most Wanted	Totally Hidden Video	Married...With Children	OPEN HOUSE	The Tracey Ullman Show	It's Garry Shandling's Show	FOX
		The Magical World Of Disney		SISTER KATE	My Two Dads	NBC Sunday Night At The Movies				NBC

Of all its offerings in the 1989–90 season, ABC won the most praise for two diametrically different slices of American life: *Elvis* and *Twin Peaks*. Twelve years after the death of Elvis Presley at age forty-two, the mythology around the singer had come to focus primarily on his decline. The *Elvis* series set out to recapture the singer's roots, focusing exclusively on the 1954–55 era, when the future icon was still a teen dealing with small-town Southern life, just beginning his recording career, and discovering the power of his music. Michael St. Gerard was Elvis (a role he first played in a 1989 theatrical film about Jerry Lee Lewis, "Great Balls of Fire"), though singer Ronnie McDowell supplied most of the singing vocals, as he had previously done in the TV movies "Elvis," "Elvis and the Beauty Queen," and "Elvis and Me." Nonetheless, *Elvis* was a true TV innovation—a biographical portrait that was inspired by real-life incidents but that freely adapted them for a weekly series (under the watchful eye of executive producer Priscilla Presley, Elvis's widow). Though not a big ratings hit, *Elvis* successfully transported viewers to another era, offering a genuine insight into what made the earthshaking emergence of this young man from Memphis such a deeply personal event.

Twin Peaks also looked at small-town America, but with a far darker vision and far greater ratings success. (The series was in the top twenty-five for the 1989–90 season.) Theatrical film director David Lynch (from "Blue Velvet," a 1986 cult hit starring Dennis Hopper and Kyle McLaughlin) and veteran *Hill Street Blues* writer Mark Frost teamed up to transform what could have been merely a typical TV murder story into a moody peek into the eerie and duplicitous corners of the American psyche. Set in the Pacific Northwest town of Twin Peaks (just a few miles south of the Canadian border), the series followed special FBI agent Dale Cooper (Kyle McLaughlin) as he investigated the circumstances surrounding the death of teenager Laura Palmer. Working with local sheriff Harry S. Truman (Michael Ontkean), Cooper encountered a wide range of local residents including Catherine Martell and Josie Packard (Piper Laurie and Joan Chen), the competing half-owners of the local sawmill; Laura's emotionally sensitive dad, Leland (Ray Wise); Laura's "good girl" best friend, Donna Hayward (Lara Flynn Boyle); Audrey Horne (Sherilyn Fenn), the manipulative daughter of a local hotel owner; and eccentric characters such as the Log Lady (Catherine Coulson), who received messages through the small log she carried. They all seemed to have some personal or professional secrets to hide and, while those may or may not have had anything to do with the death of Laura Palmer, the locals were not happy to have a federal agent poking about.

Yet it quickly became obvious that this was not a traditional whodunit. *Twin Peaks* was part soap opera, part murder mystery, and part journey to the outer limits. Cooper consistently spoke in oblique dialogue and seemed as intensely interested in the quality of the town's pie, hot coffee, and doughnuts as in the latest leads. He was also open to psychic inspiration, dreams, and visions,

In Matt Groening's *The Simpsons,* each family member was voiced by a different performer *(from left)*: Homer (Dan Castellaneta), Marge (Julie Kavner), Maggie (silent, with pacifier), Lisa (Yeardley Smith), and Bart (Nancy Cartwright). (The Simpsons © *1990 Twentieth Century Fox Television. All Rights Reserved.*)

which took the series down increasingly quirky paths that eventually suggested (among other things) ancient contact with an alien race from outer space. Cooper's work also brought into the picture other agents, including his half-deaf boss (hilariously played by David Lynch himself), his vindictive one-time partner (Ken Welsh as Windom Earle), and drug enforcement agent Dennis/Denise Bryson (David Duchovny) fresh from a change in sexual orientation. Ultimately, though, none of the particular plot details mattered as much as the style, tone, and individual set pieces of the series. With these, *Twin Peaks* demonstrated that television could go places far beyond typical mainstream entertainment. Viewers were caught up, at first, with Lynch's kinky theatrical style as they focused on the "who killed Laura Palmer" angle. When Lynch deliberately took the series to an even higher level of weirdness, abandoning logic and apparent interest in explaining the Laura Palmer mystery, viewers began deserting in droves—left cold by such sequences as dreamy interludes featuring a backward-talking dwarf. Though the series self-destructed within a year, the fact that it made such an impression during its brief run demonstrated that there was an audience to tap for such distinctive fare.

The Fox network also had a pair of innovative series, including one with its own ardent doughnut lover. After three years as a short feature on *The Tracey Ullman Show*, the animated Simpsons graduated to a full-fledged mid-season series (beginning with a December 17 Christmas special). While the shorts for Ullman had essentially been one-liner gags, the half-hour *Simpsons* series was a full-fledged situation comedy that happened to be an animated cartoon. The premise was deceptively simple: the everyday life of a middle American family in the typical U.S. town of Springfield. Homer was a dim-witted safety control engineer at the town's nuclear plant (the thought of a doughnut, or of any rich and fattening food, would send him into a state of bliss); Marge was a stay-at-home-mom; their ten-year-old son, Bart, was the terror of the fourth grade; daughter Lisa was a sweet and sensitive second grader; and baby Maggie just looked on, sucking her pacifier.

The Simpsons took full advantage of the animation format. There were dozens of other characters created and drawn without a casting call, often voiced by the same handful of performers (especially Dan Castellaneta, Hank Azaria, and Harry Shearer). These included Krusty the Clown (foul-mouthed host of Bart's favorite TV show), Montgomery Burns (Homer's megalomaniac boss), Waylon Smithers (Burns's excessively devoted assistant), Seymour Skinner (stressed-out principal at Bart and Lisa's school), and Kwik-E-Mart owner (and frequent robbery victim) Apu Nahasapeemapetilon. Set budgets were irrelevant because everything had to be drawn anyway. Guest stars could be either soundalike caricatures or real celebrities offering their own voices.

Most important, by design the characters never aged (though they might be involved in flashbacks or flash-forwards). Therefore, it was impossible to treat the series as a linear chronological narrative. In effect, all the stories were taking place during the same time period. This approach was tremendously liberating, allowing the writers to treat each episode of *The Simpsons* as a fresh pallet, capable of going anywhere, with the assurance that the next episode would start all over again from essentially the same point. With such creative freedom, *The Simpsons* became one of the best

April 9, 1990

ESPN begins coverage of Major League Baseball with an opening-day tripleheader: the Orioles vs. the Royals, the Padres vs. the Dodgers, and the Blue Jays vs. the Rangers.

April 13, 1990

CBS shuts down its late-night *Pat Sajak Show* and resumes airing reruns of action-adventure series in the slot.

April 19, 1990

Wings. (NBC). Producers from *Cheers* move that concept to the cozy lounge of a small airport on Nantucket Island off the Massachusetts coast. Timothy Daly and Steven Weber play brothers who work as pilots for Sandpiper Airlines.

May 21, 1990

Bob Newhart wraps up eight seasons of *Newhart* by tying it back to his previous hit series. In the last scene of this final episode, he wakes up as Bob Hartley (his character from his 1970s series) and tells his wife, Emily (Suzanne Pleshette, his co-star from that show), about his nightmare of running a Vermont inn. It is the definitive dream finale.

May 31, 1990

Seinfeld. (NBC). Almost a year after its pilot aired, stand-up comic Jerry Seinfeld's sitcom debuts, with Michael Richards's character's name changed to Kramer, and Julia Louis-Dreyfus added as Jerry's ex-girlfriend, Elaine.

July 12, 1990

Northern Exposure. (CBS). The producers of *St. Elsewhere* offer a successful summer series that returns in the spring of 1991 for a four-year run. Rob Morrow plays a young New York doctor required to practice in Cicely, a small town in Alaska, to pay off his medical school loans. The cleverly written show contains a wry collection of characters and a tastefully eclectic soundtrack.

comedies ever on television, with multi-layered plots suffused with references to pop culture, literature, art, and historical events. Though cut from the same skeptical cloth as *Married ... with Children* and *Roseanne*, *The Simpsons* contained an even greater sassy subversive streak that tweaked everybody. Yet while characters were lazy, selfish, manipulative and greedy, they could also be generous, caring, and surprisingly wise. Even the adults.

Fox never touted *The Simpsons* as just a children's show and, in fact, the series proved popular with adults, especially young adults. This demographic fact was vital for the still-fledgling network because, while it could not yet hope to win the ratings race outright, Fox could still thrive by selling itself as a popular destination for the more youthful viewers increasingly prized by advertisers.

Just a few months after *The Simpsons* series began, Fox introduced yet another innovative take on a familiar format with the comedy-variety series *In Living Color*. Created by Keenan Ivory Wayans, this was a fast-paced half-hour sketch show starring comparative unknowns. There were musical guests, commercial parodies, original characters, and pop culture send-ups. Wayans had scored a theatrical hit in 1988 with his canny spoof of black exploitation films, "I'm Gonna Git You Sucka," and he brought this satirical sense to the new show, along with a few of the film's performers (David Alan Grier and siblings Kim and Damon Wayans). They formed the core of performing regulars along with Jim Carrey, Kelly Coffield, Tommy Davidson, Kim Coles, and T'Keyah

"Crystal" Keymah. (Later years added Wayans brothers Shawn and Marlon, as well as Jamie Foxx and Chris Rock.)

In Living Color had an energetic beat that began with its distinctive opening theme and continued throughout, courtesy of its sexy dancers (dubbed The Fly Girls) and its musical DJ—initially Shawn Wayans (a.k.a. SW-1) before he became a regular skit performer. The cast was racially mixed and displayed a sassy self-confidence tweaking ethnic, racial, and gender stereotypes. There were gleeful double entendres throughout the show, along with deliberately contrarian characters and grossly exaggerated authority figures. These included the downright nasty Homey the Clown, a pair of blatantly gay film critics ("Men on Film"), the pyromaniac Fire Marshal Bill, and a pair of jive-talking street hustlers operating their own shopping channel dealing in stolen goods.

Like *The Simpsons*, *In Living Color* was seeped in pop culture self-awareness, conscious of the conventions of its genre and constantly putting its own spin on the format. The program's racial humor was a particular departure, bringing a different perspective on how the world worked. For example, one of the show's first skits followed a runaway slave from the Civil War era as he emerged from a hidden cave into a downtown park in modern America. A confident black professional assured him that there was no need to automatically shuffle and bow to white passers-by because slavery was abolished and he was now free. But by the end of the skit, it was the professional who was hauled away by a pair of white cops (essentially for being "too uppity") as the former slave knowingly looked on. As with the Bundys on *Married ...with Children*, the Connors on *Roseanne*, and the cartoon *Simpsons*, *In Living Color* offered satirical snapshots of the American dream turned upside down. There was no confusing this with yet another of Bob Hope's mainstream variety specials, which were still regularly showing up on NBC's schedule.

In Living Color and *The Simpsons* once again demonstrated that Fox was truly bringing something different to the broadcast network picture. On the business side, though, the network was still struggling with its weaker lineup of affiliates and a schedule that only covered three nights a week. Fox needed to keep its total number of hours per week below fifteen so it would not be subject to the FCC's long-standing prime time access rule and its complicated requirements limiting network ownership and syndication of programming. However, that dual ability to create and distribute programs was precisely the type of synergy that had allowed Fox to financially get off the ground in the first place, as an outgrowth of the Twentieth Century Fox studios. If the network was to grow further, it had to deal with these restrictions that the older networks had chafed under for years. In May 1990, the FCC, which was beginning to question the continued need for the prime time access rule and the financial interest and syndication rules, granted Fox's petition for a temporary waiver from these rules. Fox immediately announced expansion plans for the 1990–91 season, and it soon began adding additional programming. In August, Fox added Thursday nights to its schedule. In September, it added Friday, nights, plus five and one-half hours of children's programming on weekends and weekday afternoons.

The big news, though, was how Fox planned to kick off its Thursday night lineup. The network announced that in the fall of 1990 it would move its most successful show, *The Simpsons*, from Sunday to Thursday, opposite *The Cosby Show*. This was a symbolic declaration that Fox was taking the next step as a competitive network, entering the ring to duke it out with the Big 3 by challenging the series that had dominated television for half a decade.

51. The Live Storm

BART SIMPSON VERSUS BILL COSBY was the marquee match-up for the fall of 1990, when Fox moved *The Simpsons*, its most successful series, to the Thursday night slot directly opposite NBC's *Cosby Show*. This was a brilliant strategic move that enhanced the visibility and credibility of the Fox network, playing as the perfect story hook for media coverage of the new season. Images of the cartoon Simpsons (usually represented by Bart) were inevitably juxtaposed with those of Bill Cosby, giving the newer network invaluable exposure. Because Bart had already become a symbol of youthful rebellion, the contrast with the mature and more staid Cosby perfectly suited the Fox pitch to younger viewers. In addition, Fox's weaker affiliate lineup meant that few expected *The Simpsons* to really beat *The Cosby Show* outright in the overall ratings, so the network could declare victory with almost any respectable showing. Finally, with *Cosby* entering its seventh season, there was the possibility of ratings slippage anyway (almost inevitable for a long-running series), and *The Simpsons* stood ready to claim credit. Though new episodes did not arrive until later than most other returning series, *The Simpsons* did very well in the slot, with ratings for its October 11 second-season premiere matching *Cosby*'s. Ultimately, *The Cosby Show* easily won the head-to-head contest, though it lost enough of its total audience to fall from number two in the previous season to number five this season in the annual series rankings. (*Cheers* ended up at the top.)

The Fox strategy had worked, up to a point. However, NBC's lineup still continued to dominate Thursday nights, with *The Simpsons* a single destination hit. (Few viewers stuck around Fox for the show that followed, *Babes*, a live-action comedy about three beefy Manhattan women.) The problem was that Fox did not have deep bench strength. Though the network had rushed to fill five nights of prime time for the new season (versus three the previous season), many of its new series were clearly second- or third-tier offerings. *Haywire* was a comedy anthology mishmash, *Good Grief!* dropped comedian Howie Mandel into a mortuary setting, and David Lynch's documentary series, *American Chronicles,* was too far off the beaten path. Clearly, Fox still had a long way to go to lose its image as the (distant) fourth network.

Nonetheless, with offerings such as *The Simpsons* and *In Living Color*, Fox had shown the viability of gearing series toward younger-skewing demographics, even if the total audience was less than the competition's. Those who tuned in were prime advertising targets. (For example, the Thursday night *Simpsons* was the perfect place to advertise teen-appealing theatrical feature films opening on Fridays.) For the fall, the other networks also joined Fox in adding a few new series aimed at younger viewers (usually telegraphed by a high school setting or goofy characters), though Fox continued to be most on-target with its offerings. *Get a Life* featured former David Letterman regular Chris Elliot playing a thirty-year-old slacker newspaper delivery boy still living at home with his parents (played by Elinor Donahue and his real-life dad, Bob Elliott). *Parker Lewis Can't Lose* cast Corin Nemec in the title role of a deviously charming teen and Melanie Chartoff as his exasperated high school principal. The concept was in the spirit of the hit 1986 film "Ferris Bueller's Day Off" and was far superior to the official TV series adaptation, *Ferris Bueller*, on NBC that fall.

The most impressive new Fox teen offering was from veteran producer Aaron Spelling, *Beverly Hills, 90210,* set in that posh California zip code. It opened with siblings Brenda and Brandon Walsh (Shannen Doherty and Jason Priestley) as sophomore transfer students from Minnesota dropped among the sons and daughters of the rich and famous at West Beverly Hills High School after their dad's company moved him to the West Coast. The series perfectly captured teenage self-confidence tempered with awkward self-awareness and social peer pressure, providing a slice of high school life grounded in reality but highly accelerated in the tony Beverly Hills setting. Over time, both Brenda and Brandon built a strong circle of friends, including status-savvy Kelly (Jennie Garth); Steve (Ian Ziering), a dedicated party animal; Dylan (Luke Perry), a brooding loner with a James Dean aura; Donna (Tori Spelling, daughter of Aaron), a "good" girl proud of her virginity; David (Brian Austin Green), a freshman music wiz interested in Donna; and Andrea (Gabrielle Carteris), the brainy editor of the school newspaper who was from the less affluent side of town (she lived with her grandmother so she could reside in the high school's district). Together they faced issues that resonated with teen viewers, including choosing the latest fashions; using fake IDs; dealing with academic and social pressures; resisting the lures of drugs, cheating, and gambling; pursuing an active sex life; and, most important, developing and treasuring friendships. Even teens who would never own a Porsche could identify with them.

On the Big 3 networks, about the only creditable new youthful personality in prime time was Will Smith, who had scored a mainstream pop music hit in 1988 (as half the duo D. J. Jazzy Jeff and the Fresh Prince) with the comic rap lament "Parents Just Don't Understand." NBC's *The Fresh Prince of Bel-Air* alluded to Smith's rap identity in the title, casting him as a teen from the

	8:00	8:30	9:00	9:30	10:00	10:30	
M	MacGyver		ABC NFL Monday Night Football (to 12 Midnight)				ABC
O	UNCLE BUCK	Major Dad	Murphy Brown	Designing Women	THE TRIALS OF ROSIE O'NEILL		CBS
N	# Fox Night At The Movies				local		FOX
	FRESH PRINCE OF BEL AIR	FERRIS BUELLER	NBC Monday Night At The Movies				NBC
T	Who's The Boss	Head Of The Class	Roseanne	Coach	thirtysomething		ABC
U	Rescue 911		CBS Tuesday Movie				CBS
E	local						FOX
	Matlock		In The Heat Of The Night		LAW & ORDER		NBC
W	The Wonder Years	Growing Pains	Doogie Howser, M.D.	MARRIED PEOPLE	COP ROCK		ABC
E	LENNY	Doctor, Doctor	Jake And The Fatman		WIOU		CBS
D	local						FOX
	Unsolved Mysteries		THE FANELLI BOYS	Dear John	Hunter		NBC
T	The Father Dowling Mysteries		GABRIEL'S FIRE		Prime Time Live		ABC
H	Top Cops	THE FLASH		(specials)	Knots Landing		CBS
R	The Simpsons	BABES	BEVERLY HILLS, 90210		local		FOX
	The Cosby Show	A Different World	Cheers	Grand	L.A. Law		NBC
F	Full House	Family Matters	Perfect Strangers	GOING PLACES	20/20		ABC
R	EVENING SHADE	Bagdad Café	OVER MY DEAD BODY		Dallas		CBS
I	America's Most Wanted		DEA		local		FOX
	Quantum Leap		Night Court	Wings	Midnight Caller		NBC
S	The Young Riders		China Beach		Twin Peaks		ABC
A	THE FAMILY MAN	The Hogan Family	E.A.R.T.H. FORCE		48 Hours		CBS
T	Totally Hidden Video	HAYWIRE	Cops	AMERICAN CHRONICLES	Comic Strip Live		FOX
	PARENTHOOD	WORKING IT OUT	The Golden Girls	Empty Nest	Carol & Company	AMERICAN DREAMER	NBC

	7:00	7:30	8:00	8:30	9:00	9:30	10:00	10:30	
S	Life Goes On		America's Funniest Home Videos	AMERICA'S FUNNIEST PEOPLE	ABC Sunday Night Movie				ABC
U	60 Minutes		Murder, She Wrote		CBS Sunday Movie				CBS
N	TRUE COLORS	PARKER LEWIS CAN'T LOSE	In Living Color	GET A LIFE	Married...With Children	GOOD GRIEF	AGAINST THE LAW		FOX
	HULL HIGH		LIFESTORIES		NBC Sunday Night At The Movies				NBC

rough side of town (West Philadelphia) sent to live with his wealthy uncle in the Bel-Air neighborhood of Los Angeles. Though the series itself was often standard-issue class comedy (the triumph of streetwise savvy over pompous wealth), Smith quickly established himself as a supremely confident comic performer. He even delivered the opening theme song, which turned a rap-style music video into a familiar weekly prime time tune.

Steven Bochco's *Cop Rock*, ABC's most-touted new series of the fall, went one better in its musical aspirations, offering four to five original songs each episode. These were not merely random music videos, but integrated elements in the storylines of a new police drama set in Los Angeles. The twist was that at any time in any episode (usually once each act) one or more of the characters might break into song, with appropriate (unseen) musical backing. It was an innovative premise, but not unprecedented. In the 1978 British TV miniseries *Pennies from Heaven* (set during the Great Depression), characters conveyed their emotions by lip-synching to familiar popular recordings of the time. More recently, on the live theater circuit, stage shows such as "Les Miserables" and "Evita" became huge international successes with original scores and barely a word of dialogue. Bochco's new series attempted to put these elements together for a weekly TV series. Veteran composer Randy Newman (best known for his hit record "Short People") wrote and performed the title song over the credits, surrounded by members of the main cast, as if to underscore that this was a theat-

rical company about to take the stage. The curtain rose for the first time on September 26, 1990, but in short order it became clear that the concept as a TV series was doomed by several inherent flaws.

Unlike *Pennies from Heaven* (which had used fairly well-known hit recordings), the songs in *Cop Rock* were unfamiliar originals that had to work quickly in the context of each episode's ongoing storylines. They played once and were never given a chance to grow on viewers. Even worse, the constant need for new material meant that there were far too many songs needed for the run of the series (several dozen over just three months). In contrast, an ongoing stage show such as "Evita" could use the same finely honed tunes night after night. As a result, most of the songs on *Cop Rock* generally ended up being unexceptional formula compositions (heartfelt love song; angry anthem; contemplative ballad), with most not even considered rock (belying the program's title). Yet even if all the songs had been perfect, viewers were not accustomed to seeing characters reveal their thoughts in musical soliloquies instead of standard dialogue. What might have worked on a grand opera stage ended up looking silly and unbelievable in the world of personal television drama. ABC quickly canceled the series, though it did let all thirteen episodes play out to Christmas.

That was a gutsy move that probably cost ABC valuable ratings points, but it reflected respect for Bochco's efforts. Oddly, apart from the music, *Cop Rock* showed him in top form, with a strong cast (including James McDaniel, Ronny Cox, Teri Austin, Peter

Onorati, and Bochco regular Barbara Bosson) and a deft mix of personal conflicts and political intrigues. One particularly daring plotline that began in the first episode focused on a likable but cocky detective, Vincent LaRusso (Onorati). Frustrated that a known drug dealer he was busting was likely to once again work the system and walk away, LaRusso tied him to a chair and, to the horrified surprise of the only other detective on the scene, unexpectedly executed the dealer. Then the truly dark journey began as LaRusso himself worked the system, in consort with a pricey attorney who took the case at a discount, with an eye on ancillary profits from its high notoriety. That story arc played out over the entire run of *Cop Rock*, as LaRusso watched his own partner (the only witness) eviscerated on the stand. Ultimately, LaRusso walked away clean because the prosecution was unable to prove its case. This was a view of the U.S. legal system rarely dealt with on television, acknowledging the inherent disadvantage in court of the prosecutor, who has to convince the jury of the plaintiff's guilt, as opposed to the defense attorney, who only has to establish reasonable doubt in order to win acquittal. In other words, when the defense does a good job, sometimes it lets its client get away with murder. Unfortunately, this dramatic departure from a typical TV law story resolution (in which the defense hands over the *real* guilty party complete with a roadmap for subsequent prosecution) went virtually unnoticed amid *Cop Rock*'s musical rubble.

Though ABC garnered positive press for backing such distinctively different series as *Cop Rock* and the returning *Twin Peaks*, the ratings for such fare proved problematic. In fact, the network's most successful shows were the far more mainstream *America's Funniest People* (a spinoff of the still successful *America's Funniest Home Videos*), *Monday Night Football*, and the innovative yet accessible *Roseanne*. Though there was clearly a cachet to edgy and distinctive offerings (Fox had demonstrated that), the need to draw significantly larger audiences meant that such programs were best used as supplements to a schedule with wider appeal.

CBS faced similar difficulties with its own high-profile entries that fall. Though Sharon Gless returned to her old Monday night *Cagney and Lacey* slot, her new show, *The Trials of Rosie O'Neill*, came off as annoyingly arty, with the title character inevitably at her analyst's office bemoaning life. *WIOU* (from Grant Tinker's production company) won critical praise but found few viewers interested in the machinations at a TV station with sagging news ratings. *Uncle Buck* (based on the 1989 John Candy film) pushed the broadcast standards envelope in a different way by including such terms as "You suck!" in the dialogue between the title character (played by Kevin Meany) and his three smart-mouthed wards. It still flopped. Even a well-done science fiction adventure, *The Flash* (based on a DC comics superhero who could run incredibly fast), proved to be too specialized for wide ratings appeal.

What worked better for CBS were more familiar and accessible series such as *Evening Shade*, from *Designing Women*'s Linda Bloodworth-Thomason. Set in the small town of Evening Shade, Arkansas, this family comedy featured veterans Burt Reynolds and Marilu Henner and, by November, it had slipped into the Monday night period vacated by *Uncle Buck*. In the spring, *Northern Exposure* took *Rosie O'Neill*'s slot. Though the engaging tales of small-town Alaskan life were offbeat compared to standard network TV dramas, *Northern Exposure* never let its quirky aspects overwhelm the stories and the characters (as had occurred with *Twin Peaks*). By the end of the season, CBS had a very strong Monday lineup in place, with four solid comedies and a popular drama, reminiscent of its glory days. The network also tapped such memories outright in the February sweeps, winning the month in part by staging "classic weekends" dominated by specials showcasing such past

hits as *Ed Sullivan*, *All in the Family*, and *Mary Tyler Moore*. Unfortunately for CBS, it could not run retrospectives every week.

NBC's most successful new show of the season was *Law & Order*, in which producer Dick Wolf found a perfect way to follow cases all the way from the street through the courtroom. In the 1960s, a series with a similar idea, *Arrest and Trial*, had imploded by focusing on apprehending a suspect in the first half, then switching the viewer's loyalties by emphasizing the suspect's defense during the trial that occupied the second half. *Law & Order* stuck with the state all the way, with the New York City police department and district attorney's office working together not only to arrest but also to convict a perpetrator. The result was disciplined and methodical, generally eschewing personal office intrigue and focusing instead on the well-crafted details of each case. It was a resilient formula that relied on a strong cast, but which also benefited from turnover in the cast over the years. (The police side at various times included Chris Noth, Paul Sorvino, S. Epatha Merkerson, and Jerry Orbach, while the D.A.'s side included Sam Waterston, Michael Moriarty, Jill Hennessy, Angie Harmon, Fred Thompson, and Steven Hill.) With different performers consistently bringing new blood to the stories, *Law & Order* lasted two decades and became a television franchise.

When the final ratings were tabulated for the 1990–91 season, there was both good and bad news for all the networks. On the positive side, Fox had successfully expanded, and the ratings race was so close that NBC, CBS, and ABC all had bragging rights in some area. Though the contest was the tightest it had been in decades, NBC once again emerged on top, for the sixth consecutive season. The win gave a positive send-off to Brandon Tartikoff,

---

October 26, 1990

William Paley, chairman of the board of CBS and last of the original broadcasting business pioneers, dies at age eighty-nine. In mid-December, Laurence A. Tisch, president and CEO of CBS and the real power at the network for the past four years, is also given Paley's old title of chairman.

October 27, 1990

NBA Inside Stuff. (NBC). As part of NBC's new contract with professional basketball, the network begins airing this weekly thirty-minute series late Saturday mornings, aimed at younger viewers. Actual games begin on November 3, starting with a Saturday afternoon match-up between the Los Angeles Lakers and the San Antonio Spurs.

April 1, 1991

Two struggling cable comedy networks, HBO's Comedy Channel (on since November 1989) and Viacom's HA! (on since April 1990), merge to form CTV: The Comedy Network, later renamed Comedy Central.

April 2, 1991

Crimetime After Primetime. (CBS). One year after dumping Pat Sajak and reverting to reruns of action series in late night, CBS now fills the time instead with five original hour-long low-budget crime dramas, one each week night. The new lineup consists of *Sweating Bullets* on Mondays, *The Exile* on Tuesdays, *Scene of the Crime* on Wednesdays, *Fly by Night* on Thursdays, and *Dark Justice* on Fridays.

April 4, 1991

Katie Couric, who had been filling in as co-host of *Today* since February when Deborah Norville went on maternity leave, is named as Norville's permanent replacement.

who had decided to leave NBC after eleven years as its programming boss to become head of the Paramount movie studios. His assistant, Warren Littlefield, moved up to fill Tartikoff's old job.

Over at CBS, the death of network patriarch William Paley in October 1990 meant that CEO Laurence Tisch at last became the undisputed boss of the network. Though the good news for Tisch was that his network actually improved its ratings a bit that year, he also had to confront the bad news that greeted all the networks. For the 1990–91 season, the economy was tight and so was advertising revenue. But CBS also had its own specific money problems. Already, after only one year, it was apparent that its billion-dollar baseball deal was not delivering the hoped-for increased ratings. Despite having exclusive rights to the baseball playoffs and the World Series, the network calculated a loss of some $55 million per year on the arrangement. And the season brought yet another escalating sports price tag, this time a new deal to carry professional football. Starting with the 1990–91 season, the collective fees paid by CBS, ABC, and NBC (along with ESPN and TNT) increased the NFL's annual income from television by about 90% compared to the previous deal, hitting $3.6 billion. All the broadcast networks were looking to trim costs, though CBS seemed most determined, announcing in April the intention to cut 400 jobs by the end of 1991.

Hanging over all these concerns were two new realities with major financial implications that could not be ignored: War and Cable. And the two were now becoming intimately interconnected.

In the early hours of Thursday, January 17, 1991 (late Wednesday in the U.S.), the United States and its allies launched Operation Desert Storm, sending waves of bombers over the country of Iraq. Though the start of the attack was news, it was hardly a surprise. Back in August 1990, Iraqi President Saddam Hussein had directed the invasion of Iraq's tiny neighbor, the oil-rich country of Kuwait. U.S. President George Bush had immediately responded

by stationing troops in nearby Saudi Arabia, then spent the balance of 1990 building a coalition to launch an international effort against Iraq. These actions meant that, in a time of tight network budgets, the respective news divisions had to gear up to cover a major overseas story, stationing personnel, placing support equipment, and leasing expensive satellite time. No one was certain that, at the last minute, there would not be some negotiated settlement. Just in case, the broadcast networks and CNN (which all maintained extensive international bureaus) set up special operations in the Persian Gulf area, including Iraq's capital, Baghdad. They wanted to be ready should the battle begin.

When the fighting did commence, it quickly became clear that this was to be war coverage of a very different nature. Though the Vietnam War in the 1960s had come to be known as the first television war, it had been, more accurately, the first time that filmed reports had come to television so quickly, so regularly, and so directly, without being filtered. But there still had been a significant time delay as film was developed and brought to transmission points. From the beginning, the Gulf War reports were mostly transmitted in real time, with sound and pictures going out live. These were quickly supplemented by highly graphic videos supplied by the military itself, showing the flight of its missiles from bomb bay doors to impact.

There was one other significant change from the past: The dominant coverage came not from the major broadcast networks but from CNN. When the first allied attacks began, CNN was able to outflank the competition by sending extensive live transmissions from the Al Rashid Hotel in Baghdad, where its correspondents Bernard Shaw, John Holliman, and Peter Arnett huddled while reporting on the battle being waged around them. While the U.S. public was trying to process the idea that it was engaged in a new conflict in some far-away corner of the globe, it was CNN that showed live images of the exploding allied bombs and illuminated anti-aircraft bullets lighting up the nighttime sky of Baghdad. At one point in the initial attack coverage, some broadcast affiliates (such as CBS's WAGA) took CNN's feed rather than transmissions from their own networks.

CNN's dominance did not end with the initial coverage because, as a twenty-four-hour news operation, it could stay with the story. Once the breaking news of the first bombings had passed, ABC, CBS, and NBC had to return to their regular entertainment schedules (with frequent news updates). They could not afford to do otherwise. CNN had all the time in the world for the story. Also, it turned out that, by January 18, CNN's Arnett was the only Western broadcast reporter left in Baghdad, giving CNN a short-term exclusive from the war's front lines until Arnett also had to leave. As a result, CNN essentially owned the story at the beginning, taking particular delight when the likes of Secretary of Defense Dick Cheney, Chairman of the Joint Chiefs of Staff Colin Powell, and Gen. H. Norman Schwarzkopf publicly referred to watching CNN reports to help stay fully informed. This was a stinging disappointment to the veteran news operations. At a time when they had been under pressure not only to deliver the news, but also to save money, CNN had outmaneuvered them. Equally significant, CNN's suddenly indispensable presence caused a major spike in subscriber interest in cable, with CNN's ratings up some 90%. (In the process, the cost of a typical thirty-second ad spot on CNN temporarily jumped from $3,500 to $20,000 by late January.) This also meant future trouble for the broadcast networks because, once cable had been established in new households, its myriad offerings would continue to chip away at the total network audience, even after the war ended.

The Gulf War effort was a rapid success for the U.S. and its

allies. On February 24, after six weeks of bombing, they initiated a ground attack. It lasted just one hundred hours. Three days later, with Kuwait secured, President Bush ordered a cease-fire. With this quick conclusion, the lingering TV images from the war ended up being the more distant and detached aerial shots of bombs and desert rather than individual soldiers in battle.

The war's brief duration and the intense pressure on reporters to provide late-breaking details left unexamined many issues raised by the change in news coverage. The underlying questions were simple and direct: Was "live" television war coverage a good idea? Did it give Iraq (or, in the future, any other targeted enemy) too much information too soon? Was there a point at which journalists might impede the safety and security of the military operation?

On the other hand, were journalists (especially from television) too willing to take at face value all military claims, as long as they were accompanied by snazzy visuals? Were the so-called "smart bombs" that seemed to practically knock on the door of their targets really that smart—or were the selected video releases from the military just that: *carefully selected* rather than truly representative of the campaign? Even more basic—despite the breathless enthusiasm of individual correspondents delivering reports against a skyline peppered with flashing lights and the sounds of bombs—did such coverage really convey helpful information? At times it seemed more akin to a local station covering a fire or a plane crash. There might be dramatic pictures, but someone who was not on the scene might actually have a better perspective.

Even twenty-four-hour coverage had its downside. Throughout the day there might be nuggets of hard news and opportunities for penetrating analysis, but these were usually overshadowed by up-to-the-minute official pronouncements or newly released bombing videos. There were also long stretches of repetitive recaps of recent events and, inevitably, long-winded "talking head" guest spots. The video sources and live hookups did indeed provide a new way to cover a war, but there often seemed to be far more flash than illumination.

Ironically, some of the best war coverage of the 1990–91 season did not involve smart bombs, infrared graphics, or continuous satellite hookups. It came in the form of *The Civil War*, an eleven-hour PBS documentary miniseries by producer Ken Burns. The program was an inspired undertaking that managed to breathe life into history simply by letting history speak for itself. Because this was from a pre-film era (1861 through 1865), the only first-hand reports available were photos and written observations. Burns used thousands of both to tell the story of the U.S. Civil War from all quarters, letting the camera linger on each picture as a variety of voices read from the past, accompanied by a tasteful musical score.

Though the series aired at the end of September amid the networks' fall premieres, it scored surprisingly high ratings for public television. Viewers were entranced. More than a century after the battles, these voices from the past provided perspective and analysis by real people trying to honestly understand the events unfolding around them. In the increasingly noisy twenty-four-hour news world, these were becoming truly precious commodities.

The air campaign of Desert Storm was accompanied by the strategic stationing of ground forces in the region, far from live television coverage. *(Left, top)* Cargo planes bring in key equipment, including *(second from top)* the "HMMMV" vehicle (popularly known as the "Humvee"). *(Bottom two)*: U.S. Army forces set up their camps, sometimes in the face of suddenly inhospitable conditions, such as sandstorms in the Saudi Arabian desert. *(Photos by Mark Abraham)*

52. The Sax Man

THE INCREASED PUBLIC STATURE OF CNN served as a daily reminder that cable offered something viewers seemed to increasingly feel was both essential and unavailable on the broadcast networks: non-stop news. Even after the end of the war in the Persian Gulf, a succession of other global and domestic stories seemed to prove the need for such saturation coverage.

In August 1991, Communist hard-liners attempted a coup against Soviet Union President Mikhail Gorbachev and actually played to the TV cameras hoping to stir support. However, the coup failed in less than thirty hours and negative public reaction in the Soviet Union to the televised events helped unleash a deep spirit of rebellion. By December, the individual Soviet republics (including Russia) had declared their independence and Gorbachev acceded to the dissolution of the Soviet Union. Suddenly the one-time superpower was gone, ending decades of cold war conflict.

On the home front in the fall of 1991, President George Bush's nomination of Clarence Thomas to the U.S. Supreme Court provoked allegations of sexual harassment by Anita Hill, a former aide. There was extensive television coverage of the highly charged and contentious congressional hearings that October, which in many ways boiled down to a "he said/she said" dispute of what transpired between Thomas and Hill. Though Thomas eventually was confirmed, it was only after lengthy questioning; that turned the judicial nominating process into hours of spicy viewing.

In April 1992, graphic street violence erupted in Los Angeles in response to a controversial jury verdict. In 1991, four white police officers had been charged with using excessive force in their arrest of Rodney King, a black man. An amateur observer had captured on videotape the actions of the arresting officers (shown beating, kicking, and clubbing King after a high-speed chase) and that had played endlessly in the news. Nonetheless, in reviewing the evidence, a jury acquitted the police officers of all but one count, touching off riots in the South Central area of Los Angeles. This unrest, in turn, ended up on television news reports, including eerie footage from a news helicopter showing a random mob assault on a white truck driver, Reginald Denny, who was inadvertently caught in the melee—pulled from his vehicle and smashed in the head with a brick, then kicked and trampled by the crowd. Eventually, the violence left fifty-two people dead.

All of the network news departments covered these events with frequent live shots and detailed special reports, but CNN, with plenty of time to fill and a commitment only to news, maintained its advantage. It was simply a case of the right format at the right

time. While the broadcast networks also maintained twenty-four-hour newsrooms, they could air their reports only in between entertainment offerings, in such venues as the nightly news, brief news windows throughout the day, occasional features on prime time news magazines, and the long overnight-early morning news programs. As all of these high-profile stories unfolded, they raised a familiar question that echoed the criticism of news coverage decades earlier in such areas as the civil rights movement and demonstrations against the war in Vietnam. Was the news coverage itself somehow fueling the stories? With the twenty-four-hour news cycle and the technical ability to show live footage instantly from almost anywhere, this question was even more troublesome. In addition, coverage now often extended from the street through the trial process itself (with live television cameras in some courtrooms) so that those intensely interested in a particular story might have their emotions stirred on a first-hand, daily basis for virtually the entire life of the news story.

The violence in the streets of Los Angeles also served as a stinging reminder that there were highly charged racial issues still unresolved in the U.S. more than a century after the Civil War and almost thirty years after the passage of major civil rights laws in the 1960s. Although broadcast television rarely dwelled on the historical past in its entertainment offerings, by coincidence the 1991–92 season had a handful of series that were set in the recent past. They provided a rare opportunity to gain perspective on the present by viewing entertaining, fictional snapshots of another era.

NBC had the prestige offering *I'll Fly Away*, from the *Northern Exposure* team of Joshua Brand and John Falsey. Set in the late 1950s in a small Southern town, the stories focused on the lives of local district attorney Forrest Bedford (Sam Waterston), his family, and their black housekeeper, Lilly Harper (Regina Taylor). Though the Bedfords were presented as pinups for enlightened racial sensitivity, even they were clearly products of their times, instinctively viewing society as divided by class and race. Only the youngest children (Forrest's and Lilly's respective six-year-olds) seemed to interact without self-consciousness, at least for a while.

This was a series with a serious mission, earnestly attempting to put character faces to images from history. Sometimes that aspect placed too great a burden on the main characters by inserting them at nearly every important news event of that era: lunch counter protests, voter registration confrontations, the use of gushing fire hoses against young black students, and even the outright murder of a young black man who made a wisecrack to a white woman

Extensive coverage of the hearings on the nomination of Clarence Thomas *(left photo)* to the U.S. Supreme Court included testimony by former aide Anita Hill *(right photo)*. C-SPAN alone carried 128 hours of hearings. *(Photos by Mark Abraham)*

(the equivalent of the real-life murder of Emmett Till). Yet placing these characters within such historical moments illuminated the contradictions of the era with devastating clarity, as when the Bedfords' perfectly likable neighbor was shown putting his young child to bed before proudly donning his white hood and heading out for an evening meeting of the local KKK. It was easy to see why change in this town (and, by implication, the entire South) would be a long, slow, and subtle process.

ABC's *Homefront* covered a slightly earlier era in U.S. history (the mid-to-late 1940s), but took a far less solemn approach, playing more as a comfortable soap opera. (The opening theme was the big bands tune "Ac-cent-tchu-ate the Positive.") This was giddy post-World War II America, with an authentic sense of the era and plenty of personal conflicts. Set in Cleveland, Ohio, it featured returning GIs eager to rejoin the workforce and women who had filled in at the assembly lines resentful at having to step aside. The wealthy Sloans (played by Mimi Kennedy and Ken Jenkins) were poised to cash in on the new economic boom, manipulating the laws and the system to their advantage at every opportunity, including union busting and anti-communist witch hunts. Their black domestic help, Abe and Gloria Davis (Dick Anthony Williams and Hattie Winston), had their own dreams, moonlighting as owners of a small diner. Jeff Metcalf (Kyle Chandler) landed a job as an outfielder with the Cleveland Indians, while doubling as a reluctant radio personality with the sweet but ambitious Ginger Szabo (Tammy Lauren). She even successfully lobbied for a show on the company's newest venture, television.

One of *Homefront*'s more unusual plot threads involved Jeff's buddy Charlie (Harry O'Reilly) attempting to join the Jewish faith upon learning that his girlfriend from Italy was Jewish. Coached by an activist Jewish friend, Charlie learned that it was not that simple to join a faith that did not, as a matter of course, proselytize and attempt to win converts. He did not just have to convince his local rabbi that he was a worthy candidate for the faith, he also had to work hard to convince the rabbi to even consider the *idea* of a grown man converting to Judaism. That was a rare TV moment, acknowledging the importance of religion and ethnic identity.

Brooklyn Bridge, on CBS, went even further, as producer Gary David Goldberg (of *Family Ties* fame) infused that series with his own warm memories of growing up Jewish in Brooklyn, New York, in the 1950s. The series was akin to Woody Allen's feature film "Radio Days," showing a very specific time period in loving detail and providing a sense of knowing recognition throughout.

September 2, 1991
In an effort to give its affiliates a few more minutes for their profitable local newscasts, NBC pushes back the start of Johnny Carson's *Tonight* show by five minutes. ABC and then CBS follow suit in 1993 with their late shows.

October 11, 1991
Redd Foxx dies of a heart attack during a rehearsal for the eighth episode of his new series, *The Royal Family*, a mildly successful sitcom (produced by Eddie Murphy) that premiered on CBS a month earlier. Though the episodes Foxx had already taped are aired and the death of his character is written into the new scripts, the show is canceled in the spring.

November 3, 1991
Nightside. (NBC). Eight years after the death of *NBC News Overnight*, NBC resumes providing late, late night news with this no-frills overnight news service, once again aiming to combat the growth of cable news. On January 5, ABC follows suit with the more lighthearted *World News Now*, while CBS replaces its ten-year-old *Nightwatch* with the straight news *Up to the Minute* on March 29.

February 28, 1992
Barry Diller abruptly quits as head of the Fox TV network and film studio. By the end of the year, Diller turns up as the new CEO of QVC, a cable shopping network, where he also becomes a part owner.

March 7, 1992
The Powers That Be. (NBC). Political satire flops on this Norman Lear sitcom, set in Washington, D.C. John Forsythe plays an empty-headed veteran senator with a suicidal congressman for a son-in-law (David Hyde Pierce) and a manic press secretary (Peter MacNicol).

March 31, 1992
Dateline NBC. (NBC). NBC at last develops a successful weekly hour-long news magazine. Anchored by Jane Pauley and Stone Phillips, the program adds a second night in June 1994 and by the fall of 1998 airs five nights a week.

	8:00	8:30	9:00	9:30	10:00	10:30	
MON	MacGyver		ABC NFL Monday Night Football (to 12 Midnight)				ABC
	Evening Shade	Major Dad	Murphy Brown	Designing Women	Northern Exposure		CBS
	# Fox Night At The Movies				local		FOX
	Fresh Prince Of Bel Air	Blossom	NBC Monday Night At The Movies				NBC
TUE	Full House	HOME IMPROVEMENT	Roseanne	Coach	HOMEFRONT		ABC
	Rescue 911		CBS Tuesday Movie				CBS
	local						FOX
	I'LL FLY AWAY		In The Heat Of The Night		Law & Order		NBC
WED	Dinosaurs	The Wonder Years	Doogie Howser, M.D.	SIBS	Anything But Love	GOOD & EVIL	ABC
	THE ROYAL FAMILY	TEECH	Jake And The Fatman		48 Hours		CBS
	local						FOX
	Unsolved Mysteries		Night Court	Seinfeld	Quantum Leap		NBC
THR	Pros & Cons		FBI: The Untold Stories	American Detective	Prime Time Live		ABC
	Top Cops		The Trials Of Rosie O'Neill		Knots Landing		CBS
	The Simpsons	DREXELL'S CLASS	Beverly Hills, 90210		local		FOX
	The Cosby Show	A Different World	Cheers	Wings	L.A. Law		NBC
FRI	Family Matters	STEP BY STEP	Perfect Strangers	Baby Talk	20/20		ABC
	PRINCESSES	BROOKLYN BRIDGE	THE CAROL BURNETT SHOW		PALACE GUARD		CBS
	America's Most Wanted		THE ULTIMATE CHALLENGE		local		FOX
	Real Life With Jane Pauley	Expose	Dear John	FLESH 'N BLOOD	REASONABLE DOUBTS		NBC
SAT	Who's The Boss	Growing Pains	The Young Riders		THE COMMISH		ABC
	CBS Saturday Movie				P.S.I. LUV U		CBS
	Cops	Cops	Hidden Video	THE BEST OF THE WORST	Comic Strip Live		FOX
	The Golden Girls	THE TORKELSONS	Empty Nest	NURSES	Sisters		NBC

	7:00	7:30	8:00	8:30	9:00	9:30	10:00	10:30	
SUN	Life Goes On		America's Funniest Home Videos	America's Funniest People	ABC Sunday Night Movie				ABC
	60 Minutes		Murder, She Wrote		CBS Sunday Movie				CBS
	True Colors	Parker Lewis Can't Lose	In Living Color	ROC	Married...With Children	HERMAN'S HEAD	The Sunday Comics		FOX
	THE ADVENTURES OF MARK & BRIAN	EERIE, INDIANA	MAN OF THE PEOPLE	PACIFIC STATION	NBC Sunday Night At The Movies				NBC

Danny Gerard effectively played fourteen-year-old Alan Silver, though the true rock of the program was Alan's grandmother, Sophie Berger, played by Marion Ross (looking quite different than she had as Mrs. Cunningham in the 1970s *Happy Days*). The series highlight was a delightful one-hour episode that had a "West Side Story" feel to the tense meeting at a local Chinese restaurant between Alan's family and the family of his Irish-Catholic girlfriend, Katie Monahan (Jenny Lewis).

At mid-season, ABC and George Lucas offered *The Young Indiana Jones Chronicles*, a history-adventure series on a grand (and expensive, for television) scale that served as something of a prequel to the three "Indiana Jones" theatrical films starring Harrison Ford. The most recent, "Indiana Jones and the Last Crusade," had included an extended flashback sequence with River Phoenix playing a teenage Indy. *Young Indiana Jones* turned this idea into its own full-fledged series, casting two different performers in the lead role to show the character at different ages: Corey Carrier was Indy at ten, while Sean Patrick Flannery played him at sixteen. A third actor (George Hall) played Indy at age ninety-three, launching the episodes by recalling the adventures of his much-traveled youth. With generous artistic license, Indy turned up anywhere in the world at key moments of the early twentieth century, meeting a host of historical figures ranging from Sigmund Freud to Pablo Picasso.

I'll Fly Away, *Homefront*, *Brooklyn Bridge*, and *Young Indiana Jones* were reminders of how effectively television could offer a slice of history when it presented that history within a well-crafted entertainment program. None of these series became big hits (each lasted only two seasons), but they did show that the broadcast networks were still capable of an imaginative array of offerings in their entertainment mix, despite increasing pressure on the bottom line. Even so, nearly 20% of the prime time schedule on all four networks that season was devoted to some form of the far less expensive reality- or news-based shows, ranging from the venerable *60 Minutes* to the lowbrow *Adventures of Mark and Brian* (silly stunts by two Los Angeles radio DJs). At the same time the networks were still touting their "one-stop-shopping" lineups as superior to specialized cable channels, they were undercutting their own credibility the more they cut corners, further blurring what were once obvious differences between broadcasters and cable. Though the networks were momentarily buoyed by the fact that the combined audience share for ABC, CBS, and NBC in 1991–92 was temporarily up (marginally) for the first time in years (hitting 63%), the fact remained that this share was still far lower than the near 90% level of two decades earlier.

Nonetheless, with nearly two-thirds of the television audience, the broadcast networks remained the starting point of reference for any discussion about television and the media in general. When Vice President Dan Quayle decided to speak about the "poverty of values" in U.S. culture in May 1992, he chose as an example the top ten series *Murphy Brown* and its season-long plotline. Murphy Brown not only had chosen to have casual sex with two different men (her current boyfriend and her former husband), she also had spurned marriage proposals from both men when she discovered she was pregnant, choosing instead to raise the baby on her own. Quayle strongly criticized what he viewed as the trivialization of a serious matter, with single motherhood defined as just another "lifestyle choice" in an "anything goes" culture. The speech generated immediate controversy, much to the bottom-line delight of CBS as the glare of attention boosted *Murphy Brown's* already strong ratings—it ended the 1991–92 season as television's number three show, right behind *60 Minutes* and *Roseanne*.

Amid all this historical and politicized programming, the season's most successful new series, ABC's *Home Improvement*, was far more traditional and non-controversial. Stand-up comic Tim Allen played Tim Taylor, host of *Tool Time*, a local home improvement TV show (akin to the PBS series *This Old House*), who dispensed practical advice with his carpenter partner Al Borland (Richard Karn) and gorgeous assistant Lisa (Pamela Anderson). Tim was a loving, well-meaning husband, devoted to his family, but his *Tool Time* success filled him with misplaced self-confidence about his ability to handle "real" problems in his own home. His wife, Jill (Patricia Richardson), was the voice of reality in the family, ever ready to contact the emergency room (or a professional) after one of Tim's home projects had gone awry. *Home Improvement* was a comfortably funny show that never took itself too seriously, becoming an immediate top ten hit and an ABC staple for the rest of the decade.

Though NBC won the November sweeps, as the 1991–92 season unfolded it became clear that the network had definitely lost its momentum after six years at the top. *The Cosby Show* (in its final season) at last slipped out of the top ten, and so did the rest of NBC's Thursday schedule, except *Cheers*. On other nights, aging NBC series such as *Night Court* and *The Golden Girls* were following *Cosby* into retirement. Though NBC still had hits, it no longer had a seemingly unassailable lineup. Together, CBS and ABC had eight of the top ten series of the season, with CBS easily winning the February sweeps propelled by the Winter Olympics held in Albertville, France. Even more important, CBS used its strong lineups on Monday and Sunday to build solid ratings week in and week out, going from the number three network the previous season to number one this season. Oddly, CBS accomplished this without introducing one new hit show that season, building instead on series that had been in place for several years. Though this coalescing of existing hits worked, for CBS to sustain its success it would have to eventually find successful new programs.

NBC did do very well with the 1992 Summer Olympic games in Barcelona, Spain, carrying 161 hours (74 in prime time) from July 26 to August 9, although those were outside the regular season rankings. However, the games were noteworthy on another level because NBC decided to use cable as a cash-generating companion to its free commercial-laden broadcast coverage, in order to help offset the increasingly expensive costs of obtaining the U.S. television rights to the Olympic Games. Working with local cable systems, the network set up an elaborate pay-per-view package that used three cable channels simultaneously to offer start-to-finish, commercial-free live coverage of about a dozen events each day (as opposed to the frequently taped coverage that aired on NBC along with many background pieces on the star athletes). For fans of Olympic sports, NBC's cable coverage was a dream come true, taking full advantage of the massive array of technical talent brought to the site to show what was happening, as it was happening. Though it was a hit with those who signed up (at $29.95 per

day or $125 for all fifteen days), the "Olympics TripleCast" did not attract anywhere near the number of subscribers needed and was deemed a financial flop. Nonetheless, the plan had at least recognized that the financial equation for TV coverage of major sporting events was changing and that the networks could utilize cable to their own advantage.

Nowhere was the changing face of TV clearer than on the political front. There, aspiring presidential candidates were actively working forums outside the traditional newspaper editorial pages and broadcast news programs, as well as adjusting their messages to deal with the round-the-clock news cycles created by CNN.

On January 26, Arkansas Governor Bill Clinton, running for the Democratic presidential nomination, made a strategic appearance on a special edition of *60 Minutes*, which aired in the highly visible slot right after the Super Bowl (which CBS carried that year). On the eve of the presidential primary and caucus season, Clinton was determined to deal with potentially damaging stories circulating about an affair he was alleged to have had with Gennifer Flowers. Clinton's wife, Hillary Rodham Clinton, joined him in facing correspondent Steve Kroft, and the two offered carefully worded ac-

May 21, 1992
The Real World. (MTV). Reality TV enters a new, more voyeuristic phase as the once all-music cable network brings together seven hip, attractive twenty-somethings (four men, three women, all strangers to each other, from a variety of locales). The program sets them up in a trendy Manhattan apartment, then turns on the cameras to record their lives in the big city over the next three months. The edited result is a thirteen-week series of half-hour shows that becomes an annual event, featuring a new cast (in a new city) each year.

June 19, 1992
Fox's three-month-old news department takes a public relations hit as Stephen Chao, the first president of the fledgling news unit, introduces a male stripper during a meeting with network executives (with Secretary of Defense Dick Cheney and his wife, Lynne, head of the National Endowment for the Humanities, also attending). Rupert Murdoch promptly responds by firing Chao.

June 26, 1992
CBS stops airing reruns of *Designing Women* as the lead-in to its mid-morning set of game shows. This change marks the end of the era (which began in 1956) when the networks regularly used reruns of prime time sitcoms as part of their daytime schedules.

July 8, 1992
Melrose Place. (Fox). Aaron Spelling takes the ritzy environment of *Beverly Hills 90210* past the school years to focus on attractive twenty-somethings living in an apartment complex at 4616 Melrose Place in Los Angeles. The series does not really take off until 1993 when Heather Locklear joins the cast as the scheming Amanda Woodward, who winds up buying the apartment building.

July 25, 1992
NBC ends thirty-four years of running animated cartoons on Saturday mornings, revamping its schedule to start with two hours of a new Saturday version of *Today* followed by live-action teen-oriented programming, such as the three-year-old sitcom hit *Saved by the Bell*.

knowledgments of past difficulties and finely worded assurances about the strength of their marriage. Though they were short on specifics, the fact that the Clintons had faced questioning on *60 Minutes* allowed them to say they had dealt with the issue. Most important, even though it had been a tough interview, Bill Clinton seemed to connect quite comfortably with the camera.

During the next few months of the campaign leading to the party's nominating convention, Clinton would need every bit of charm and on-screen likeability. At each stage he faced questions about a variety of personal matters, including how he had handled his draft notice during the Vietnam War, whether he had ever tried marijuana, and (constantly) rumors of sexual dalliances. Though on one level the race for U.S. president had always been a personal popularity contest as much as a political one, this seemed a test less of policy than of how well Clinton could hold up under media scrutiny, moving the campaign from the editorial pages to the tabloids. Yet it was a double-edged sword that he could also deftly wield. Clinton quickly demonstrated that appearances outside the mainstream news media could prove quite effective in reaching large audiences. He turned up on Oprah Winfrey's top-rated daytime talk show, and did a live call-in segment on the *Today* show. On June 3, Clinton appeared on Arsenio Hall's syndicated late night talk show, donning "cool" sunglasses and playing saxophone with the house band on "Heartbreak Hotel." By then, he had won several key primaries and had virtually locked up the Democratic presidential nomination.

Bill Clinton was not the only one with an eye for using television in new ways to campaign. In February 1992, millionaire businessman Ross Perot used Larry King's nightly talk show on CNN to launch his independent third-party candidacy for president. Perot hammered home his message (mostly criticism of incumbent President George Bush and the state of the economy) not only on King's show but also via blocks of airtime he purchased outright to present his own thirty-minute "infomercials" about himself. Perot had a personal fortune that allowed him to take full advantage of the communication opportunities afforded by the mass medium. He also had a distinctive personality and ear for quotable sound bites that won him consistent news coverage, elevating him from the status of a "fringe" candidate to that of a legitimate presidential contender. With his nasal, almost singsong delivery, Perot also quickly became easy fodder for TV humorists, with *Saturday Night Live*'s Dana Carvey doing a particularly popular caricature. Yet even though Perot's style and substance were often mercilessly mocked, such criticism often actually helped him, increasing Perot's growing name recognition. As a result, the presidential campaign of 1992 was driven by television into a three-way contest: Ross Perot and Bill Clinton versus George Bush. Going into the Democratic National Convention in July, some polls put Perot right behind Bush, with Clinton in third place.

As the press descended on the Democratic gathering in New York City, there was a greater emphasis than ever on those outside the three broadcast networks. Talk radio, local television, and cable services (including MTV and Comedy Central) placed correspondents at the site. Clinton's team (including James Carville and George Stephanopoulos) welcomed a film crew following the campaign into their strategy sessions (later included in the feature documentary, "The War Room"). The convention itself was a carefully orchestrated, formal introduction of Bill Clinton, capped by a slick biographical film ("The Man from Hope") produced by *Designing Women*'s creator, Linda Bloodworth-Thomason. Clinton emerged from the sessions with an unquestioned air of success.

The three televised presidential debates in the fall of 1992 used a variety of formats and Bill Clinton was particularly effective in

The first baby boomer president, Bill Clinton won reelection in 1996, taking the oath of office for a second time on January 20, 1997. *(Photo by Mark Abraham)*

the debate staged as a town meeting, which resembled a daytime talk show far more than the traditional debate setting. In that, the unforgiving camera happened to catch President Bush glancing at his watch, as if to indicate his impatience with "talking to the people." Clinton, in contrast, spoke easily and warmly with the crowd (and, by extension, with television viewers), at one point getting up from his stool and walking over to interact more directly with the audience. He was a candidate from the television generation who not only was comfortable on television, but thrived on it. This truly was a presidential campaign that hinged on a generational difference. George Bush had served with distinction in World War II. Bill Clinton was not born until the year after the war ended. Clinton was a baby boomer and, in the fall contest, he became the first of his generation to be elected president.

Appropriately, the 1991–92 season also had an on-air changing of the guard at another hallowed institution. In May, Johnny Carson ended thirty years as host of NBC's *Tonight* show with a pair of extraordinary farewell broadcasts. The penultimate show on May 21 was a star-studded extravaganza highlighted by some heartfelt love songs sung by Bette Midler and farewells from a host of celebrities. The final night, May 22, was just the opposite. Carson came on stage, alone, sat on a stool, and spent the rest of the evening sharing his favorite moments and memories directly with viewers. It was a classy exit, demonstrating his cool control in a demanding medium. Though off camera there had been frenzied competition to succeed him as host, on that final night Johnny Carson quietly demonstrated why he had been the undisputed king of late night TV for so long.

53. Nothing Much

NBC FACED AN UNUSUAL PROBLEM in naming a successor to Johnny Carson for the *Tonight* show. It had two well-qualified, popular candidates vying for the job: Jay Leno (Carson's permanent guest host since 1987) and David Letterman (host of *Late Night*, the program that, since 1982, immediately followed the *Tonight* show and came from Carson's own production company). This created a guaranteed win-lose situation for the network because the rejected candidate might well bolt elsewhere at the first opportunity.

Carson had publicly set the events in motion at a May 1991 NBC affiliates meeting when he announced that the 1991–92 season would be his last. Within a month, NBC officially anointed Jay Leno as the new *Tonight* host, to begin on May 25, 1992, the Monday following Carson's last show. Though the decision seemed to come quickly, the selection actually followed intense behind-the-scenes lobbying and high-level network maneuvering. After all, this was a decision about one of television's longest-running franchises. Not surprisingly, David Letterman was unhappy with the outcome, especially because he was expected to continue in the less prominent *Late Night* slot. After the Leno announcement, Carson teased Letterman when he was a guest on the *Tonight* show, wondering just how peeved he was. The answer came soon enough. In January 1993, Letterman signed a $42 million deal to host a new late show on CBS, to be scheduled directly opposite Jay Leno, beginning in the fall of 1993 (after Letterman's contract with NBC expired).

The competitive repositioning did not end there. Fox announced that it would reenter the late night talk circles in the fall of 1993 with a program hosted by former *Saturday Night Live* star Chevy Chase. NBC decided to also continue the *Late Night* program without David Letterman and named as its new host thirty-year-old Conan O'Brien, a former writer for *Saturday Night Live* and *The Simpsons*. He, too, was scheduled to begin in the fall of 1993. With the syndicated *Arsenio Hall Show* also remaining in place (as well as Ted Koppel's *Nightline* news program), fall 1993 promised to be a real battle of late night programming.

In the meantime, in the fall of 1992, as Jay Leno was just putting his own stamp on the *Tonight* show, a refreshingly different take on the entire late night TV talk show phenomenon was playing out on the HBO fictional series, *The Larry Sanders Show*. Deadpan comic Garry Shandling played the title character, a successful but neurotic late night TV talk show host. *Larry Sanders* was a brilliant blend of close-to-the-bone fantasy and reality, with real-life celebrities appearing as guests and interacting with the fictional characters just as if it was a real talk program. Shandling (a frequent *Tonight* show guest and pre-Leno substitute host) knew that world well and populated his fictional talk show with an obsequious sidekick (Jeffrey Tambor as Hank Kingsley), a savvy take-no-prisoners producer (Rip Torn as Artie), and a revolving door of ambitious writers, workaholic production assistants, and conniving network brass. Each episode contained scenes from the fictional *Larry Sanders* show-within-the-show (presented on videotape so they looked like part of a regular talk show) and combined those with behind-the-scenes action (presented on film so they looked like part of a regular sitcom). Protected by the veneer of fiction, the program was able to offer a glimpse of the strident, self-indulgent, and duplicitous side of show business, especially when the "off-camera" comments were juxtaposed with the "on-air" exchanges. With all the publicity surrounding the real-life late night competition, *Larry Sanders*, premiering in August 1992, was perfectly timed to offer viewers an inside peek on what they could imagine some private conversations really sounded like in show business circles, stripped of any pretense of public politeness. Sometimes, in reality, these people could not stand each other.

Because *Larry Sanders* was a premium cable offering, its dialogue was peppered with explicit language that could never appear in a broadcast series. However, there was little concern about offending viewers because, after all, the HBO signal remained scrambled to anyone not choosing to purchase it. There was also no need to attract the largest possible audience, just a sizeable slice of the pay-cable viewers. Just as important, *Larry Sanders* followed the shorter production schedule of an original cable series, with its first season consisting of only thirteen episodes. The series began just before the networks' fall premieres, won critical raves, played out its first batch of stories, then quickly went on hiatus for about a year. There was no need to stretch the material thin by producing two or three times as many episodes when the existing set could be rerun, multiple times, in between hit movies. The standards and expectations were simply different for cable.

On the other hand, the broadcast networks entering the fall of 1992 once again were expected to deliver all new material. Yet they found themselves increasingly interested in copying cable, especially the idea of aggressively rerunning episodes of a hit in multiple time slots. Fox did just that with *In Living Color*, but soon discovered that such a policy could be contentious. Creator Keenan Ivory Wayans split with the network and left the show, arguing

	8:00	8:30	9:00	9:30	10:00	10:30	
M	The Young Indiana Jones Chronicles		ABC NFL Monday Night Football (to 12 Midnight)				**ABC**
O	Evening Shade	HEARTS AFIRE	Murphy Brown	LOVE & WAR	Northern Exposure		**CBS**
N	# Fox Night At The Movies				local		**FOX**
	Fresh Prince Of Bel Air	Blossom	NBC Monday Night At The Movies				**NBC**
T	Full House	HANGIN' WITH MR. COOPER	Roseanne	Coach	GOING TO EXTREMES		**ABC**
U	Rescue 911		CBS Tuesday Movie				**CBS**
E	local						**FOX**
	Quantum Leap		Reasonable Doubts		Dateline NBC		**NBC**
W	The Wonder Years	Doogie Howser, M.D.	Home Improvement	LAURIE HILL	Civil Wars		**ABC**
E	THE HAT SQUAD		In The Heat Of The Night		48 Hours		**CBS**
D	Beverly Hills, 90210		Melrose Place		local		**FOX**
	Unsolved Mysteries		Seinfeld	MAD ABOUT YOU	Law & Order		**NBC**
T	DELTA	Room For Two	Homefront		Prime Time Live		**ABC**
H	Top Cops		Street Stories		Knots Landing		**CBS**
R	The Simpsons	MARTIN	THE HEIGHTS		local		**FOX**
	A Different World	RHYTHM & BLUES	Cheers	Wings	L.A. Law		**NBC**
F	Family Matters	Step By Step	Dinosaurs	CAMP WILDER	20/20		**ABC**
R	The Golden Palace	Major Dad	Designing Women	BOB	PICKET FENCES		**CBS**
I	America's Most Wanted		Sightings	LIKELY SUSPECTS	local		**FOX**
	FINAL APPEAL	WHAT HAPPENED?	THE ROUND TABLE		I'll Fly Away		**NBC**
S	COVINGTON CROSS		CROSSROADS		The Commish		**ABC**
A	FRANNIE'S TURN	Brooklyn Bridge	Raven		ANGEL STREET		**CBS**
T	Cops	Cops	Code 3	THE EDGE	Comic Strip Live		**FOX**
	HERE & NOW	OUT ALL NIGHT	Empty Nest	Nurses	Sisters		**NBC**

	7:00	7:30	8:00	8:30	9:00	9:30	10:00	10:30	
S	Life Goes On		America's Funniest Home Videos	America's Funniest People	ABC Sunday Night Movie				**ABC**
U	60 Minutes		Murder, She Wrote		CBS Sunday Movie				**CBS**
N	GREAT SCOTT!	THE BEN STILLER SHOW	In Living Color	Roc	Married...With Children	Herman's Head	FLYING BLIND	WOOPS!	**FOX**
	SECRET SERVICE		I WITNESS VIDEO		NBC Sunday Night At The Movies				**NBC**

that the additional reruns hurt his program's syndication resale value, where TV series producers earned most of their profits.

The broadcast networks also found cable affecting them in a much more basic way: content. While broadcasters still had far more viewers than cable, there seemed to be new viewer expectations of what was acceptable. As a result, the networks found themselves increasingly pushing the limits that were still in place for over-the-air signals, especially in the hope of satisfying young adults who had grown up watching the likes of HBO, MTV, and uncut feature films (on cable and on videotape).

Fox had been the first to embrace such an "in your face" approach to programming. That network had also focused more on the demographics of its audience rather than the total size. That was a practical strategy because, with its weaker lineup of affiliates, Fox could not yet match the total viewership of ABC, CBS, or NBC anyway. That targeting had already worked with such younger- and urban- skewing programs as *The Simpsons, Beverly Hills 90210*, and *In Living Color*, and the network attempted to replicate that formula throughout the new season. There was more youthful angst with *The Heights* (following an aspiring young rock band, which landed a real-life number one record, "How Do You Talk to an Angel") and *Class of '96* (college freshmen at an Ivy League school), while a pair of sketch comedy shows drew from new generations of performers. *The Edge* included former MTV veejay "Downtown" Julie Brown, Jennifer Aniston, and Wayne

Knight, while *The Ben Stiller Show* (produced by HBO) included Andy Dick and Janeane Garofalo. Host Ben Stiller (son of comics Jerry Stiller and Anne Meara) took this opportunity to polish his skills overall by serving as a writer, producer, and director, while also hanging out with guest stars such as Sarah Jessica Parker.

Perhaps the most blatantly sexual series of the season was Fox's *Flying Blind*, which pushed the boundaries of explicitness for broadcast television. It was truly all about sex, sex, and sex, wrapped in a steamy sensuality that took advantage of the fact that so much had to take place off camera (and therefore in viewer imaginations). Corey Parker played Neil Barash, a fresh college grad whose intended career path in marketing food products was permanently scuttled after a chance meeting with the sexy and uninhibited Alicia (Téa Leoni), who traveled the hip party circles of Manhattan. It was never clear why Alicia found Neil so incredibly sexy, but there was never any doubt how they spent most of their time together. Although *Flying Blind* quickly burned out in just one season, it illustrated the changing boundaries of prime time broadcast television. The pursuit of personal pleasure was simply assumed. That view of life (at least, life in a TV series) could be found throughout the schedule at each of the networks.

At number one CBS, for example, two of its top new Monday night comedies were suffused with sex. Though *Hearts Afire* (from *Designing Women* producer Linda Bloodworth-Thomason) was set on Capitol Hill, it was far more focused on the budding sexual

The tremendous success of David Letterman's *Late Show* at last allowed CBS to solidly establish itself in the late night talk show field. (*CBS Photo Archive © 2003 CBS Worldwide, Inc. All Rights Reserved.*)

relationship between its two lead characters (played by Markie Post and John Ritter) than on political humor. *Love & War* (from *Murphy Brown* producer Diane English) followed two opposites, an uptown socialite and a grubby newspaper columnist (played by Susan Dey and Jay Thomas, respectively) who fell madly in lust with each other. Later on Mondays, the respected drama *Northern Exposure* (which had always carried an on-going assumption of energetic sexual activity) brought new town resident Mike Monroe (Anthony Edwards) into the complicated relationship between Maggie O'Connell (Janine Turner) and Joel Fleishman (Rob Morrow). When the show's long-time May-December cohabitating couple of Shelly Tambo (Cynthia Geary) and Holling Vincouer (John Cullum) at last tied the knot that season, it seemed an odd throwback to a time when people in love actually got married.

At NBC, the new sitcom *Mad About You* embraced the daring proposition that marriage could be sexy and fun, with Paul Reiser and Helen Hunt playing a pair of young professionals living in Manhattan and thoroughly enjoying married life. Though the opening episode did include sex on the kitchen table before a dinner party, more typically the series focused on the inherent delight the two found in everyday life and each other. Reiser was a real-life

stand-up comic, yet the series went far beyond merely bringing his comedy routines to life. The two characters formed a believable young couple, and the series presented an evenhanded view of married life that meant sometimes she was the silly one, and sometimes he was.

Mad About You began the 1992–93 season slotted Wednesdays on NBC after another New York-based series, *Seinfeld*, which had been toiling in comparative obscurity since 1990. Both programs faced strong competition. *Seinfeld* was matched against ABC's returning hit, *Home Improvement*, one of the most popular programs on television. *Mad About You* was pitted against the long-running *Coach* (which ABC had quickly moved in after a new series, *Laurie Hill,* had flopped). By mid-season, NBC moved both to safer quarters, placing *Mad About You* on Saturday nights and *Seinfeld* on Thursdays after *Cheers.* The move was particularly important for *Seinfeld* because, at about the same time, *Cheers* announced this would be its final season. As a result, viewer interest was particularly high, with NBC counting down and heavily promoting each *Cheers* episode leading to the series finale. With such a strong lead-in, *Seinfeld* came into its own as a legitimate hit. In the Nielsen ratings for the entire 1992–93 season, it was number twenty-five (up from forty-two in the 1991–92 season), becoming NBC's comedy heir apparent to *Cheers.*

Created by stand-up comedian Jerry Seinfeld and writer Larry David (a regular on *Fridays*, ABC's late night comedy series from

September 20, 1992

NBC's *Meet the Press*, a forty-five-year-old interview show that is TV's longest-running program, expands its Sunday morning timeslot from thirty to sixty minutes, as the Sunday edition of *Today* shrinks from ninety to sixty minutes.

November 12, 1992

Absolutely Fabulous. (BBC). Jennifer Saunders and Joanna Lumley star in this celebration of drink, drugs, and sex in London's fashionable circles. *AbFab* becomes a U.S. cable hit in 1994 on Comedy Central.

November 17, 1992

Dateline NBC airs "Waiting to Explode," which includes fiery footage of test crashes conducted by the show's crew to illustrate allegations that some General Motors trucks exploded in crashes. After GM's in-house investigation reveals NBC installed incendiary devices on the demo trucks to make sure a fire erupted, Jane Pauley reads a three and one-half-minute apology on the show in February 1993.

January 3, 1993

Star Trek: Deep Space Nine. The Star Trek franchise expands, with this new hour-long weekly series joining the six-year-old *Star Trek: The Next Generation* in first-run syndication. The new show is set on an out-of-the-way space station orbiting the planet Bajor during the same era as *Next Generation.* Avery Brooks plays Benjamin Sisko, the first black *Star Trek* commander.

January 19, 1993

Fox expands to seven nights a week, beginning Tuesday night broadcasting with *Class of '96* and *Key West.* However, it is not until June 21, when Fox's Monday night movie shifts from once or twice a month to weekly, that Fox truly becomes a full-time prime time TV network.

January 31, 1993

Homicide: Life on the Street. (NBC). Film producer Barry Levinson ("Rain Man," "Diner") has the coveted post-Super Bowl time slot for the debut of his gritty police series, set in Levinson's hometown of Baltimore.

May 20, 1993

NBC's *Cheers* ends its eleven-year run with a ninety-six-minute finale that garners the highest ratings of any entertainment program this season. Shelley Long returns as Diane Chambers who ALMOST (but not quite) flies away with Sam Malone. Later that evening, Jay Leno hosts a loose, live episode of the *Tonight* show from Boston's Bull and Finch Pub, the inspiration for the *Cheers* setting, but finds that some cast members gathered there for planned on-air interviews are far more interested in real-life "last calls."

May 28, 1993

Major League Baseball owners vote to replace CBS's traditional TV rights contract (beginning in 1994) with The Baseball Network, a complicated joint venture arrangement with ABC and NBC. Rather than have the networks pay up front, this deal has them split the advertising profits from the game broadcasts with baseball. The traditional Saturday afternoon "game of the week" is also eliminated.

June 1, 1993

Connie Chung becomes Dan Rather's co-anchor on the *CBS Evening News.*

June 26, 1993

Front Page. (Fox). Fox's first attempt at a weekly news magazine show uses five correspondents (including Andria Hall, Tony Harris, and presidential son Ron Reagan) as rotating hosts. The series lasts less than a year.

---

the early 1980s), *Seinfeld* had a deceptively simple set-up: the everyday life of stand-up comedian Jerry Seinfeld. This was a break from *The Cosby Show* formula of using aspects of a stand-up act's persona to create a fictional alter ego in another profession. *Seinfeld* was more in the tradition of *The Jack Benny Show*, casting the star in a fictionalized version of himself. It was a perfect comedy role because, given the nature of his job, Jerry Seinfeld was left with plenty of off-stage time to do nothing in particular but hang out with his friend George Costanza (Jason Alexander), his former girlfriend Elaine Benes (Julia Louis-Dreyfus), and across-the-hall apartment building neighbor Cosmo Kramer (Michael Richards, another regular from *Fridays*), thus earning the show a reputation for "being about nothing."

In fact, the series was intricately plotted, weaving as many as three or four story threads into the same episode, following an exaggerated view of life among upper-middle-class singles in uptown Manhattan. Though stories were often based on such everyday activities as waiting for a table at a Chinese restaurant, collecting dry cleaning, or picking up a friend from the airport, all the characters were so totally self-involved that they inevitably introduced complications to the simplest acts. They were also never satisfied, so that, for example, the only thing worse than not having sex was having sex. There was always something to complain about. Yet somehow the four balanced each other collectively so that instead of coming off as obnoxious, they were hilarious. *Seinfeld* made fine comic art out of being judgmental, paranoid, mean-spirited, and distrustful when dealing with the world. As in *The Simpsons*

and *Roseanne*, the *Seinfeld* characters knew that the world itself could not be trusted, and they were right, as the series managed to milk engaging comedy out of its borderline neurotic characters.

Kramer was a lanky, wild-haired slacker who fancied himself a cool hipster but was actually easily agitated over the most mundane turns. He was constantly entangled in bizarre schemes either to right some perceived wrong or to make fast money. He once attempted to launch a Manhattan fleet of Hong Kong-style rickshaws, pulled by the city's available homeless population.

Elaine was a very attractive woman, remarkably self-centered, but with equal parts of chutzpa, aggression, and uncertainty. Her past affair with Jerry never stood in the way of her hanging around with "the boys" and she seemed to enjoy having the most active sex life of the four, even as she constantly bemoaned the shortcomings of her latest date. The most long-lasting in her line of boyfriends was the intently dense David Puddy (Patrick Warburton). Unlike Jerry, George, and Kramer, Elaine worked a succession of vaguely "real" jobs, including editor in a publishing house and copywriter for a clothes company's catalog. Yet she was also capable of her own misplaced self-confidence, as in her spastic dancing style, described by George as a "full body dry-heave set to music."

George was perhaps the most fascinating of the four, a bubbling cauldron of neuroses. Short, pudgy, and balding, he felt no shame at using any stratagem (usually bald-faced lies) when seeking to impress a beautiful woman or to snare a high-powered job. One of his few steady employment positions was at the offices of the New York Yankees, where George mastered the art of convincing almost everyone there that he was a workaholic. In fact, he did virtually no work. George's central traumas in life, though, came from his loud, nagging parents (played by Jerry Stiller and Estelle Harris), who constantly fed their son's raging self-loathing paranoia.

Jerry was the most successful of the four, because his stand-up comedy career provided him with a measure of respect and self-confidence. Still, he too was a bundle of anxiety, phobic about germs and, in fact, about any kind of personal interaction that was "too close." (Sex, apparently, was not considered "personal interaction.") Although easygoing and amiable on the surface, Jerry, at heart, did not really care for people ("I hate everybody!" he once happily proclaimed) and, like the rest of his friends, was really only interested in himself.

Apart from the central cast, *Seinfeld* also featured a wonderful assortment of quirky minor characters. Some appeared in numerous episodes, such as the portly Newman (Wayne Knight), an angry postal worker who viewed himself as holding a strategic job vital to the nation's welfare. (He and Jerry shared an intense dislike of each other.) Others flashed briefly in guest spots, such as Larry Thomas as the "Soup Nazi," a master chef who was responsible for the most delicious soups in Manhattan but who was also unmerciful in browbeating customers at his take-out shop, refusing to serve those who failed to follow his precise rules of ordering. All of these helped *Seinfeld* to cultivate a sense of the outrageous, constantly finding clever ways to tell gleefully embarrassing stories. The most talked-about episode in the 1992–93 season (airing several times) was "The Contest," involving a bet between Jerry, George, Elaine, and Kramer as to who could go the longest time without indulging in sexual self-stimulation. The cleverly written script conveyed every nuance of the competition without ever using the actual word for the off-limits practice, instead choosing terms like remaining "master of my domain." The topic itself would have been unthinkable a generation before, but in the increasingly explicit TV world it was considered a comic gem. NBC looked to series such as *Seinfeld* and *Mad About You* as possible models for future sitcom success for new generations of viewers.

That was the hope, though for the moment NBC was in a post-*Cosby Show* ratings plunge, dropping from number one just two seasons before to number three for the 1992–93 season. Only the departing *Cheers* remained in the top ten. Clearly, there was considerable rebuilding needed. In the meantime, number two ABC had some of the strongest-rated sitcoms (including *Roseanne, Home Improvement, Coach,* and *Full House)*, while CBS remained number one, carried by its strong Sunday and Monday lineups.

Once again, though, CBS had only limited success introducing potential new hits. *Love & War* and *Hearts Afire* simply gave their respective producers (Diane English and Linda Bloodworth-Thomason) the coveted Monday time slots after their own established hits (*Murphy Brown* and *Evening Shade)*. Unfortunately, that did not leave room for a new sitcom from Bob Newhart (*Bob,* in which he played a comic book cartoonist), which would have been perfect on Mondays in the old *Newhart* slot. Instead *Bob* was shuttled to Fridays with former Monday hits *Major Dad* and *Designing Women,* along with *The Golden Palace,* a reworking of *The Golden Girls* that followed its cancellation by NBC. All of these withered against ABC's TGIF kid-oriented lineup.

CBS did score a pair of unexpected spring hits with the Westerns *Dr. Quinn, Medicine Woman* (set in Colorado in the 1860s) and *Walker, Texas Ranger.* In *Dr. Quinn,* Jane Seymour played feminist physician Michaela "Mike" Quinn, who surprised the town residents who had hired her based on her masculine-sounding nickname. In *Walker,* Chuck Norris played a contemporary law enforcement officer who routinely surprised the bad guys with his quick fists and karate kicks (much like a typical Chuck Norris feature film). Even though both series became mid-level hits, as Westerns they seemed mildly old-fashioned in a TV world increasingly focused on more cutting-edge hooks. CBS's quirky, low-rated new drama series, *Picket Fences,* actually seemed easier to promote, following odd occurrences in small-town Rome, Wisconsin, such as a student bringing a severed human hand to "show and tell" or a town's "serial bather" surreptitiously entering people's homes to use their bathtubs. These incidents inevitably ended up in front of town sheriff Jimmy Brock (Tom Skerritt) and town judge Henry Bone (Ray Walston). The series was created by David E. Kelley, a real-life attorney (and *L.A. Law* writer), who structured *Picket Fences* as a mix of *L.A. Law*, and *Murder, She Wrote,* with a touch of *Twin Peaks.* Though the series attracted high critical praise, its sense of the outrageous was an equally viable promotional tool.

Both of these aspects were increasingly important to the broadcast networks. Each year, there were more and more new cable services competing for viewer attention. (This season launched the Cartoon Network and the Sci-Fi Network.) Each year, the pressure also seemed to increase to better match the eye-catching, explicit nature of cable (but still remain within broadcast boundaries). As a result, overall, television seemed to have an increasingly coarse, almost tabloid feel, both in its entertainment offerings and in its news and reality programs. This approach reached a symbolic moment at New Year's 1993, when, within the space of one week, all three major networks aired "instant" made-for-TV movies on the sordid real-life saga of seventeen-year-old Amy Fisher. The Long Island teen had been convicted of the attempted killing of her rival, the wife of her lover, thirty-eight-year-old Joey Buttafuoco. Though the tawdry tale had received ample coverage on the news, NBC, ABC, and CBS each felt it worthwhile to rush out their own take on the scandalous story, knowing full well it would not be the only one. NBC was first (on December 28) with "Amy Fisher: My Story" (starring Noelle Parker and produced in cooperation with Fisher herself); then (on January 3) ABC followed with "Beyond Control: The Amy Fisher Story" (starring Drew Barrymore), while CBS offered "Casualties of Love: The 'Long Island Lolita' Story" (starring Alyssa Milano) that same night. The reason for the rush was obvious: All three did reasonably well in the ratings.

Yet no matter how far broadcasters ventured, there always seemed to be something else more outrageous up the dial. For example, Court TV's well-intentioned commitment to showcasing the legal system with televised trials ended up finding its greatest following in scandalous cases such as the trial of the two Menendez brothers, accused of murdering their wealthy parents. And in March 1993, MTV gave animated lowbrow slackers Beavis and Butt-head their own show.

Created and voiced by cartoonist Mike Judge, Beavis and Butt-head first appeared on MTV's experimental *Liquid Television* series. Now featured in their own half-hour show, the crudely drawn duo was described in a network promo as "dumb, crude, thoughtless, ugly, sexist, self-destructive fools," yet ultimately they were seen as hilarious. They split their time between low-grade mischief and watching real MTV videos (which they instantly evaluated as "cool" or "it sucks"), punctuating their actions with an annoying laugh ("Heh-Heh-Heh-Heh"). Some of the initial episodes had the pair torturing small animals and starting small fires, but those actions were toned down after some viewer outrage arose in response to the program. Yet even such negative publicity ultimately helped, giving the characters more widespread name recognition. In truth, most television viewers never bothered to watch an episode of *Beavis and Butt-head,* but that did not matter. There were enough people from the right target demographic groups watching, and they turned the series into a cable hit, in the process underscoring the growing promotional dilemma facing the broadcast networks. *Beavis and Butt-head* demonstrated that the characters from a single, low-budget cable program could quickly win a spot on the popular culture stage, right alongside the most elaborate big-budget broadcast series. At a fraction of the cost.

54. The Truth That's Out There

THE ESTABLISHED BROADCAST NETWORKS offered an impressive show of force in the 1993–94 season. CBS scored its third consecutive season as the number one network, in particular registering extremely high ratings with its coverage of the Winter Olympics, far exceeding the numbers from its coverage of the previous winter contest. Each of the networks had strong returning shows as well as a surprisingly successful mix of new programs. The competitive face-off that fall in late night programming significantly raised the profile of everyone involved: Jay Leno, David Letterman, Arsenio Hall, Chevy Chase, Conan O'Brien, and *Nightline*'s Ted Koppel. In short, broadcast television still very much mattered.

Behind the scenes, the truth out there was far more complex, with business pressures building on a number of fronts. Nonetheless, those pressures did not change the fact that, for the 1993–94 season, viewers of ABC, CBS, NBC, and Fox were treated to an exceptional lineup of new drama and comedy series.

On ABC, *NYPD Blue* marked Steven Bochco's return to the gritty police format he had helped revolutionize twelve years before with *Hill Street Blues*. This time, he and co-creator David Milch set the stories in the rough-edged lower Manhattan area of New York City rather than some nameless urban zone, pushing the boundaries of broadcast drama closer to the more explicit levels of sex, violence, and language that could be found on cable. Based on advance word of such content, a handful of network affiliates declined to carry the program, even when a viewer advisory warning was added at the beginning of each episode. However, that notoriety ended up serving as an effective marketing tool, turning *NYPD Blue* into one of the most talked-about new series going into the fall. The program quickly demonstrated that it offered more than just hype: Bochco was back, in top form, with a solid mix of strong characters and street-smart stories. The main focus was on detectives John Kelly (David Caruso), a dedicated realist with fifteen years on the force, and his longtime partner, cynical alcoholic Andy Sipowicz (Dennis Franz), a one-man personal disaster. Kelly's former wife, Laura (Sherry Stringfield), still loved him, much to the discomfort of his current girlfriend, policewoman Janice Licalsi (Amy Brenneman), and the bedroom and shower scenes that highlighted that triangle provided much of the touted steamy content. The outspoken Sipowicz took care of pushing the envelope on language, even as he hit professional and personal rock bottom early on, nearly getting himself killed. Hardnosed (but even-tempered) precinct lieutenant Arthur Fancy (James McDan-

iel), rookie James Martinez (Nicholas Turturro), and veteran detective Greg Medavoy (Gordon Clapp) rounded out the main precinct squad. Each episode usually followed several cases to their conclusion, mixing street investigations with well-orchestrated interrogations back at the station house, where the volatile Sipowicz would effectively play the role of "bad cop." Yet it was Caruso's soft-spoken cold intensity that initially grounded the series, as he attempted to balance his conviction that police work really did make a difference with the almost endless succession of low-rent street criminals that were a part of his everyday life.

NYPD Blue became one of ABC's most reliable dramas, even surviving the quick departure of Caruso, who left during the second season for a feature film career. Former *L.A. Law* lead Jimmy Smits stepped in for a four-season run as detective Bobby Simone, bringing his own evenhanded sensitivity to balance Andy Sipowicz. Both characters found romance on the job, with Sipowicz marrying Sylvia Costas (Sharon Lawrence) from the D.A.'s office while Simone coupled with fellow detective Diane Russell (Kim Delaney). Between them, Smits and Franz won multiple Emmys, with Franz remaining as the central force when Smits moved on. *NYPD Blue* proved a worthy successor to *Hill Street Blues*, eventually reaching, then exceeding, that program's seven-season run.

The only other new police show to approach *NYPD Blue* in quality was Barry Levinson's *Homicide: Life on the Street,* though *Homicide* never achieved the same level of ratings success. The program premiered on NBC in the prize spot following the 1993 Super Bowl, but then the network aired it only sporadically (a few months during the winter of 1993, then again in February 1994), and it was not until the fall of 1994 that *Homicide* landed a regular slot (Friday nights). Nonetheless, whenever *Homicide* played, it garnered critical accolades for its believably realistic character interaction, devotion to authentic police detail, and edgy handheld camera techniques. The series followed ongoing murder investigations by an eclectic mix of Baltimore homicide detectives assigned to some of the city's roughest areas and working under the tough direction of Lt. Al Giardello (Yaphet Kotto). While some cases were wrapped up in a single taut episode, others stretched out over months, sometimes remaining permanently unsolved. Yet such resolutions were far less important than watching how the detectives got there, sometimes working well together, sometimes only grudgingly so. The series was a writer and actor's showpiece, with Andre Braugher (as Frank Pembleton) particularly riveting in one-on-one dialogue exchanges, especially those with suspects in the

X-Files creator Chris Carter turned out effectively chilling tales by tapping the popular sentiment that "official channels" were hiding what was *really* happening in the world. FBI agent Dana Scully (Gillian Anderson) brought healthy skepticism to her research efforts. (The X-Files © 1993 Twentieth Century Fox Television. All Rights Reserved.)

police station's interrogation room (known as "the box"). Comedian Richard Belzer did a surprisingly effective turn cast as the world-weary John Munch, while Daniel Baldwin's Beau Felton frequently sparred with Frank Pembleton. Levinson's cinematic credibility also landed him occasional high-profile guest stars including Robin Williams and Rosanna Arquette, as well as cameos by the likes of cult film director John Waters.

There was "cool" detective work of a different sort on Fox with *The X-Files,* which used as a fictional jumping-off point the public's fascination with unexplained phenomenon (the basis for such successful reality series as *Unsolved Mysteries*). In the hands of creator Chris Carter, subjects that might make the tabloid headlines were instead woven into truly scary tales in the tradition of *The Outer Limits* and *Kolchak: The Night Stalker*. FBI agent Fox Mulder (David Duchovny) was the driving force, firmly believing that there were kernels of truth behind even the most outlandish stories, ranging from hordes of killer bees to alien abductions. (He suspected his kid sister had been snatched by Visitors From Beyond.) Just as important, Mulder believed there were officials in government and business who were covering up such stories and

he was dedicated to investigating the bureau's "X-Files"—cases that could not, or would not, be solved—convinced that (as the series stated in each opening) "The Truth Is Out There." First, though, he had to convince his partner, the scientifically trained Dana Scully (Gillian Anderson), that the latest oddity could not be accounted for by rational means. She was the doubter who kept him in line and together they were a perfect investigating duo, consummate professionals attempting to explain the inexplicable. Refreshingly, sometimes Scully was right, finding sinister forces at work, only not quite the paranormal ones first suspected. At other times, the dark and deadly shadows were truly from "another place." This mix kept the series from being boxed into a predictable formula, as each tale revealed a portion of the truth in its own way, sometimes displaying a sly sense of humor in the process. (Scully and Mulder once posed as the perfect suburban couple, using the names Rob and Laura from *The Dick Van Dyke Show*.) The series also broke from the familiar cliché of casting a male-female team as a teasing romantic couple, instead allowing Scully and Mulder to act first and foremost as true professionals. Over time the series developed a complicated paranoid mythos that began to weigh down individual plots, but, at its best, *The X-Files* demonstrated that nothing could beat a good scary story, told well.

If *NYPD Blue*, *Homicide*, and *The X-Files* seemed too hip and intense for some viewers, there were more traditional TV crime fighters on the scene. With the venerable *Murder, She Wrote* still a top ten hit, CBS brought two other TV veterans to the murder mystery game: Gene Barry reprised his role as a millionaire cop in a mid-season revival of *Burke's Law* (from the 1960s), while Dick Van Dyke played a sleuthing coroner in *Diagnosis Murder* (from three made-for-TV movies that had run since 1991). Neither lead tried to hide his age, letting their TV sons do the heavy legwork (in Van Dyke's case, it was his real-life son, Barry). Though *Burke's Law* fizzled, *Diagnosis Murder* became a CBS staple.

The most successful new sitcom was ABC's *Grace Under Fire* (from producers Marcy Carsey and Tom Werner), built around stand-up comic Brett Butler as blue collar single mom Grace Kelly. Butler played Grace as a tough cookie (she worked at an oil refinery) who had seen far too much of the dark side of men and marriage, leaving her abusive husband to live on her own with their three children. Yet she could still wring humor from it all. There were also moments of poignancy because, while Roseanne Connor was deliberately frumpy, it was easy to see how, at one time, Grace Kelly would have been quite a "looker" with dreams of a storybook family life. Slotted after *Home Improvement*, *Grace Under Fire* was an instant hit, another working-class tale in the tradition of the still hugely successful *Roseanne*.

Rounding out its sitcom schedule, ABC also deftly reworked other proven comedy riffs. *Boy Meets World* cast Ben Savage (younger brother of Fred Savage from *The Wonder Years*) as Corey Matthews, following his life from junior high school to college. Because it was a contemporary setting, there was no nostalgic voiceover narrator, though teacher-neighbor George Feeny (William Daniels) was there throughout to offer perspective. The returning series *Hangin' with Mr. Cooper* (in its second season) combined elements of *Three's Company* with *Welcome Back, Kotter*, as Mark Curry played Mark Cooper, a former NBA player who returned to teach at his old high school, saving money by sharing a house with two beautiful women. Mid-season, that series took a break for *Sister, Sister,* featuring Tamera and Tia Mowry as twin sisters separated at birth and adopted by different parents (with Tim Reid as Tamera's dad and Jackee Harry as Tia's mom). The girls rediscovered each other as young teens and, as in the 1960s *Patty Duke Show*, took advantage of being able to switch identities.

	8:00	8:30	9:00	9:30	10:00	10:30	
MON	Day One		ABC NFL Monday Night Football (to 12 Midnight)				**ABC**
	Evening Shade	DAVE'S WORLD	Murphy Brown	Love & War	Northern Exposure		**CBS**
	Fox Night At The Movies				local		**FOX**
	Fresh Prince Of Bel Air	Blossom	NBC Monday Night Movie				**NBC**
TUE	Full House	PHENOM	Roseanne	Coach	NYPD BLUE		**ABC**
	Rescue 911		CBS Tuesday Movie				**CBS**
	Roc	BAKERSFIELD P.D.	America's Most Wanted		local		**FOX**
	Saved By The Bell: The College Years	Getting By	JOHN LARROQUETTE SHOW	THE SECOND HALF	Dateline NBC		**NBC**
WED	THEA	JOE'S LIFE	Home Improvement	GRACE UNDER FIRE	MOON OVER MIAMI		**ABC**
	Hearts Afire	THE NANNY	SOUTH OF SUNSET		48 Hours		**CBS**
	Beverly Hills, 90210		Melrose Place		local		**FOX**
	Unsolved Mysteries		NOW		Law & Order		**NBC**
THR	MISSING PERSONS		Matlock		Prime Time Live		**ABC**
	In The Heat Of The Night		Eye To Eye With Connie Chung		ANGEL FALLS		**CBS**
	The Simpsons	THE SINBAD SHOW	In Living Color	Herman's Head	local		**FOX**
	Mad About You	Wings	Seinfeld	FRASIER	L.A. Law		**NBC**
FRI	Family Matters	BOY MEETS WORLD	Step By Step	Hangin' With Mr. Cooper	20/20		**ABC**
	IT HAD TO BE YOU	FAMILY ALBUM	Bob	(specials)	Picket Fences		**CBS**
	THE ADVENTURES OF BRISCO COUNTY, JR.		THE X FILES		local		**FOX**
	AGAINST THE GRAIN		NBC FRIDAY NIGHT MYSTERY				**NBC**
SAT	GEORGE	Where I Live	THE PAULA POUNDSTONE SHOW		The Commish		**ABC**
	Dr. Quinn, Medicine Woman		HARTS OF THE WEST		Walker, Texas Ranger		**CBS**
	Cops	Cops	Front Page		Comic Strip Live		**FOX**
	THE MOMMIES	CAFÉ AMERICAIN	Empty Nest	Nurses	Sisters		**NBC**

	7:00	7:30	8:00	8:30	9:00	9:30	10:00	10:30	
SUN	America's Funniest Home Videos	The New America's Funniest People	LOIS & CLARK: THE NEW ADVENTURES OF SUPERMAN		ABC Sunday Night Movie				**ABC**
	60 Minutes		Murder, She Wrote		CBS Sunday Movie				**CBS**
	TOWNSEND TELEVISION		Martin	LIVING SINGLE	Married...With Children	DADDY DEAREST	local		**FOX**
	I Witness Video		SEAQUEST DSV		NBC Sunday Night Movie				**NBC**

It was NBC, however, that was truly rejuvenated by its comedy lineup. Though still the number three network for the season, on Thursday nights it vigorously touted itself as the home of "Must See TV," anchored by *Seinfeld* (which had successfully stepped into the old *Cheers* slot) and *Frasier*, the official spinoff from *Cheers*. Carefully mixing old and new, *Frasier* managed the rare feat of standing on its own as a successful sequel to a hit show. To freshen the title character after nine years on *Cheers*, psychiatrist Frasier Crane (Kelsey Grammer) was sent back to his hometown of Seattle (far from Boston), divorced from his wife Lilith (Bebe Neuwirth), and given a new job as a radio talk show host dispensing on-air psychiatric advice. Frasier also had a new apartment mate, his father, Martin (John Mahoney), a retired cop who had been shot in the line of duty. Feeling guilty, Frasier asked Martin to share his luxury apartment. Much to Frasier's annoyance, his dad also brought his dog Eddie and a ratty old easy chair. To help take care of Martin, who walked with a limp and a cane, Frasier hired a live-in physical therapist, the British-born Daphne Moon (Jane Leeves), who also claimed to have psychic powers. Her presence immediately bewitched Frasier's younger brother Niles (David Hyde Pierce), another psychiatrist, who fell in love with Daphne the moment he saw her. Unfortunately, Niles was already married to Maris, a wealthy Seattle socialite (and hypochondriac), so his feelings for Daphne had to remain hidden for years.

The program did not ignore its *Cheers* roots and brought along some proven elements. On *Cheers*, Norm's wife Vera had not been seen on camera, and on *Frasier* neither was Maris. Like Sam Malone, Frasier's radio producer Roz (Peri Gilpin) had a voracious sexual appetite and a seemingly endless list of lovers. Guest appearances by other *Cheers* characters were carefully parceled out (especially in the first season), but whenever anyone showed up (including Sam, Diane, and Woody) they also brought the latest gossip about the others. Because Lilith had custody of their son, Frederick, back East, she (and he) occasionally turned up as well.

Frasier was exceptionally well written and acted, with a clear comic vision and a wonderful balance of characters. The series trusted that combination to make the trials of the wealthy and sophisticated equally accessible and entertaining, even in a schedule filled with blue collar heroes. To that end, the relationship between Niles and Frasier was particularly effective, with Pierce and Grammer truly coming off as brothers. The character of Niles was as pompous, fastidious, and pretentious as Frasier had ever been on *Cheers*, allowing Grammer the room to refine his character. He developed an impeccable sense of comic timing akin to Jack Benny, and also adopted some of Benny's proven comic traits: Frasier was good-hearted but vain; unlucky in love; and despite his professional confidence, ultimately insecure. As in Benny's show, Grammer was confident enough for some of the best lines to go to the supporting cast. *Frasier* was a perfect addition to an NBC comedy lineup that touted its hip, youthful, and urban nature.

CBS, the number one rated network, did not have any of the talked-about new prime time comedies, but it did have considerable success in a different arena: the first round of the much-anticipated late night talk show wars. Ironically, after all the buildup, the contest played itself out quite rapidly that fall. The battle was joined on August 30, when David Letterman began his new *Late Show* for CBS while Jay Leno continued at NBC with the *Tonight* show. *The Chevy Chase Show* arrived on Fox in early September, but was gone in six weeks. Arsenio Hall found his syndicated show displaced or delayed in many cases as network affiliates (especially from CBS and Fox) made room for their network's new talk offerings. So the late night comedy face-off boiled down to a two-man affair between David Letterman and Jay Leno. Boosted by the publicity surrounding his jump from NBC to CBS, Letterman took the lead and remained consistently ahead of Leno for his entire first year. He also benefited from the lead-in provided by CBS's success in prime time, especially during the Winter Olympics. By transforming the long under-performing late night slot into a hip destination, CBS could claim success in yet another slice of the broadcast day. The network truly seemed at the top of its game.

In truth, however, CBS faced tremendous problems behind the scenes, as did all the broadcast networks to varying degrees. After years of warning rumblings, the broadcasting status quo was experiencing a seismic shift. For CBS, the end of its billion-dollar baseball contract offered a symbolic moment. Going into the fall 1993 premiere season, the network used its last World Series as a platform to promote its upcoming lineup, especially the new crime drama *South of Sunset* (starring Glenn Frey, of the rock group The Eagles). This was, after all, one of the reasons for spending all that money on a sports contract in the first place. Yet despite incessant plugging on baseball's premiere event, *South of Sunset* bombed, doing so poorly that CBS canceled the series after airing only one episode. This was a final reminder that the exclusive, expensive baseball deal had not worked as planned. Not only had CBS been unable to recover its costs with ads on the baseball broadcasts, it also had not been able to use baseball to significantly increase viewing in other parts of the schedule. (Ironically, as the number one network, CBS was already reaching most of those viewers anyway.) The network had learned an expensive lesson. However, a few months later, CBS found itself facing the opposite situation, with far more dire consequences.

In December 1993, Fox made its own billion-dollar sports deal and grabbed CBS's National Football League rights with a $1.58 billion bid (covering four years, 1994 though 1997). Starting the next season and for the three seasons to follow, the NFL would no longer appear on CBS, its home since 1956. It would be on Fox (while continuing on NBC as well). Soon afterward, Fox snared many of the familiar CBS play-by-play announcers (including Pat Summerall and John Madden) for its coverage team. With professional football gone from CBS, they had no reason to stay there.

For Fox, this billion-dollar deal made tremendous sense. Even though it probably would not be able to recoup its bid with just the commercial time sold on the NFL broadcasts, having the league on the network was invaluable. Unlike CBS, Fox still had plenty of room to grow and could benefit most from the increased exposure. In markets throughout the country, previously uninterested viewers would at last be motivated to find the Fox affiliate on their local dials. This was a huge boost to Fox's credibility. Six months later, Fox followed up with another bold move, this time boosting its own overall national market penetration by adding new affiliates in key cities. It did so by snatching them from the other networks, striking an affiliation deal with the New World Communications

station group for its twelve stations, including such major markets as Detroit, Atlanta, Dallas, Cleveland, and Milwaukee. Eight of the twelve stations would be moving to Fox from CBS. Clearly the prestige value of the NFL carried considerable weight. Although the new affiliation lineup would not take effect for more than a year, this direct assault on television's number one network showed just how far Fox had come in only seven years.

For much of that time, Fox had been playing by a different set of rules from the other broadcast networks. Because Fox had started out with so few hours each week, it was not subject to the same FCC requirements that applied to ABC, CBS, and NBC. Fox was considered a "second tier" network. Rather than being a limitation, such a designation allowed Fox time to gain its footing. As Fox increased the number of hours in its schedule, it always strategically remained just below the then-current "trigger point" number for the FCC, applying for specific temporary waivers when necessary. From the beginning, one of the most important issues for the network in this maneuvering was not being subject to the full force of the Financial Interest and Syndication Rules (Fin-Syn, for short). Without such latitude, the Fox network would not exist.

The Fin-Syn rules had been implemented by the FCC in 1970 as a way to put more players into the production process by limiting the amount of prime time programming the broadcast networks could produce themselves or hold a financial interest in, such as the right to syndicate the program's reruns. In the days before cable, the networks were seen as having a virtual monopoly over which programs aired. There was the fear that the networks would favor programs that they owned over those from outsiders, and would unfairly demand a percentage of ownership in those shows they did take from independent producers. Once the Fin-Syn rules went into effect, existing network syndication divisions such as CBS's Viacom had been spun off as independent companies. The Fin-Syn rules thus eliminated the possibility of network "vertical control" of both the production and distribution process, similar to the forced separation of the major film studios from ownership of

---

September 12, 1993

seaQuest DSV. (NBC). Steven Spielberg takes a deep dive as executive producer of the ultra-expensive (for TV) exploits of the *seaQuest*, a 1,000-foot-long "*deep submergence vehicle*" (better known as a submarine). Roy Scheider plays Capt. Nathan Bridger, commander of the ship, which prowls the oceans in the year 2018. After two seasons of weak ratings (and a time shift to 2032), the series tanks.

September 13, 1993

Though his main experience is in writing and not performing, the boyish, bookish Conan O'Brien steps in as host of David Letterman's old *Late Night* show. His early appearances are rough, but O'Brien confounds everyone (including NBC) by eventually growing into the role and winning over a new, younger generation of viewers.

November 3, 1993

The Nanny. (CBS). Fran Drescher plays Fran Fine, a loud, opinionated Jewish American Princess from Queens who winds up as the nanny for the three children of the very proper, very rich, and very handsome British widower Maxwell Sheffield (Charles Shaughnessy). Eventually, Fran gets Max to lighten up a little, Max gets Fran to straighten up (a little), and they get married (and have twins).

November 29, 1993

Little more than two months after Raymond Burr's death, NBC airs his final appearance as Perry Mason, the two-hour made-for-TV movie "The Case of the Killer Kiss."

June 17, 1994

Five days after the murder of Nicole Brown Simpson (and her friend Ronald Goldman), her ex-husband, former football star O. J. Simpson, is charged with the murders. Still at large (and declared a fugitive by the police), O. J. is driven by his friend Al Cowlings in Cowlings's white Ford Bronco. Police engage in "low-speed pursuit" of the Bronco through the freeways of southern Los Angeles for more than an hour, with Simpson reportedly holding a gun to his own head. ABC, CBS, NBC, and CNN air live helicopter footage of the chase, which ends with the Bronco parked for an hour in Simpson's driveway before he surrenders and is arrested.

June 20, 1994

Today unveils a new studio that harkens back to its past, showing program fans gathered in Rockefeller Plaza through large glass windows. Unlike the windows in the 1950s, these are made of two layers of bullet-proof glass.

July 7, 1994

For $10 billion, Sumner Redstone's Viacom purchases the Paramount corporation, resulting in the world's second-largest entertainment conglomerate (behind Time Warner).

---

movie theaters back in the late 1940s. The rules also removed the networks from the most profitable portion of a hit program's life cycle, the sale of syndication rights, and they were not happy to see this money go elsewhere. As they saw it, the successful sale of rerun rights was the direct benefit of strategic placement and promotion by the networks, which turned series into hits. Instead, just as the FCC had hoped, the production companies benefited, with such producers as Stephen J. Cannell and Steven Bochco becoming major moguls with programs on all the networks.

One of the strengths that the Fox corporation had brought to its network venture back in 1986 was program production. Though not everything on the Fox network came from Twentieth Century Fox, that ownership was a key component to its continued success (along with revenues from reruns of shows produced by Twentieth Century Fox). As a result, Fox pressed particularly hard to have the FCC Fin-Syn rules relaxed, if not completely eliminated. While ABC, CBS, and NBC had not been pleased to see Fox enter the broadcast business, they were perfectly happy for it to do the "heavy lifting" in the battle against the Fin-Syn rules. It paid off. Over time, from 1991 to 1995, the Fin-Syn rules (and other related governmental and judicial restrictions) were essentially eliminated, just as the last of the waivers granted to Fox expired. As a result, Fox could continue its steady growth, at last expanding its prime time schedule to all seven days in 1993. The other broadcast networks wasted no time in getting back into programming production, sometimes by pressing for at least a co-ownership production deal. This change also opened the door for film studios other than Twentieth Century Fox to own their own networks.

Fox's success had been noted by other movie studios. It had created a blueprint for starting a new network essentially from scratch by drawing on the resources of a major production studio. Fox not only had started small, but also had cleverly defined a different way of winning, focusing not on the total audience (which it

could not hope to match in comparison to the other networks) but on specific slices of highly desirable demographics, with particular emphasis on teens and young adults. In November 1993, two more studios, Paramount and Warner Bros., announced plans for new over-the-air networks, both to begin during the 1994–95 season.

The United Paramount Network (UPN) was a joint venture of the Paramount corporation (which owned some television stations) and the Chris-Craft group of stations. Many of these stations had been part of the ad hoc network for Paramount's *Star Trek: The Next Generation* and, not surprisingly, the first offering for the new network was to be another new *Star Trek* series (*Star Trek: Voyager*). The Warner Bros. network (quickly dubbed the WB) did not start with any stations at all, though within a month it had signed a deal with stations owned by the Tribune company (based in Chicago). Jamie Kellner, formerly of Fox, was hired to be its programming head. Both of the new networks planned to begin with about four hours each over two nights.

If Fox had faced a difficult situation in 1986 when it cobbled together affiliates to form a legitimate fourth broadcast network, UPN and the WB faced a seemingly impossible challenge. At the time, in about one-quarter of the country, all the viable over-the-air broadcast stations were already being used by ABC, CBS, NBC, Fox, and public television. There were no additional stations in some markets. In markets such as New York, Chicago, Los Angeles, and Washington, there were stations available, but they were often low-powered outlets on the UHF band. Nonetheless, with the FCC relaxing the Fin-Syn rules, the Fox model had shown a viable alternative to the business of doing business on television. Previously, studios would have to go hat-in-hand with their series to the networks, which might quickly slot, shift, and discard their product, tainting it for future sales. With their own networks, the studios would have their own primary showcases, with more control of both the production and the distribution of series. Just like Fox, Warner Bros. and Paramount would continue to sell original series to a variety of outlets, including competing networks, but they would now have a secure outlet for distributing their own shows.

By loosening the limitations on network ownership of programs, the FCC set into motion one of its most important policy changes. With networks venturing back into the program production business, and studios going into the network business, the two suddenly found themselves in increasingly similar pursuits. No one was certain whether this would lead to new alliances or more intense competition, but the television landscape had been profoundly altered. At the same time, there were also significant changes in cable.

In response to consumer protests over escalating cable costs, the U.S. Congress had passed the Telecommunications Act of 1992. The cable services quickly tweaked their pricing packages to technically comply with the law but, by carefully redefining what was included in each pricing tier, the net effect was little change in most bills. However, a far more significant development came out of this revisiting of cable pricing. Congress concluded that local broadcast stations were entitled to charge cable companies for retransmitting their signals, much like other program providers. This "retransmission consent" requirement was to go into effect on October 6, 1993, with the broadcasters and cable companies expected to arrive at appropriate fees by then. Otherwise, the broadcasters could pull their stations from the cable systems.

Led by John Malone, head of TeleCommunications, Inc. (the country's largest cable system), the cable companies flatly refused to pay any amount for what had once been "must carry" components to their systems. The message was clear: If the broadcast networks (through the O&Os and affiliates) wanted to withdraw their signals, that would be fine with the cable industry. They would get along without them.

This was a pure power play between the networks and the cable operators because it was unlikely that any cable service would drop the local stations for long without considerable complaints from its customers. Yet the networks could not afford to take that chance. A majority of television viewers now received the broadcast networks as part of their cable package. At a time when every ratings eyeball counted, the networks could not afford to blithely cede those viewers, taking the risk that they would go to the trouble of switching to over-the-air reception. In the end, both sides wanted a solution and, leading up to October 6, the networks and cable operators came up with creative packages that settled the issue, with the major cable operators agreeing to pay for some new cable services created by the networks. Cable operators could claim they were not paying for retransmitting over-the-air stations, and the networks could point to new revenues from cable (while waiving their right to demand payment for retransmitting their O&Os).

For its new offering, Fox created FX, a mix of series reruns, fluffy live interviews, and light news analysis. NBC created a low-budget talk-based service, America's Talking. ABC cloned its successful ESPN service by creating a secondary sports channel, ESPN2. Number one CBS had no cable channels to offer and eventually had to admit defeat, first granting a "waiver" and later acknowledging that it was never going to receive any cash. The days were over when the networks could pretend to ignore cable or dictate all the terms. Cable television was now strong enough to face the networks and wind up with, at worst, a tie. Ironically, in dealing with the newest challenge from cable, most of the networks decided that the best solution was to further embrace that medium.

There was good reason for the networks to be concerned about being dropped from cable lineups. Their programs might not be missed. Even though broadcast television had one of its best lineups in years, the truth was that cumulatively the cable lineup was also getting stronger and stronger. Individually, no cable show or cable service could yet come close to matching the broadcast networks. But that was the point of cable. Cumulatively, dozens of channels could offer viewers enough to fill a good portion of the day. And, individually, cable shows were winning fans and glowing reviews. Some of the same personalities who were hits on the broadcast networks were also on cable. Sometimes, they were simply in reruns of past or current hits (from *Dick Van Dyke* to *Murder, She Wrote*). More significantly, sometimes they appeared in series that were considered too edgy, racy, or just plain weird for broadcast television. HBO had some of the best programs with *The Larry Sanders Show, Dream On*, and the annual "Comic Relief" fund-raiser (hosted by Robin Williams and Whoopi Goldberg), but there were plenty of others catering to a wide range of tastes. Showtime had David Duchovny from *The X-Files* as host of the steamy *Red Shoe Diaries*. The animated *Duckman* (on USA) featured the voice of Jason Alexander from *Seinfeld*. Comedy Central offered *Mystery Science Theater* (wisecracking comments directed at awful old science fiction feature films), *Whose Line Is It Anyway?* (an improvisational comedy imported from Britain), and *Politically Incorrect* (an irreverent discussion program hosted by Bill Maher). There were even cable entries in the late night talk show wars, as the Cartoon Network edited old *Space Ghost* cartoons into a talk format, while MTV gave Jon Stewart an interview show.

Even with all the extraordinary challenges from cable, Fox, and a changing broadcast landscape, CBS could take solace in the fact that it won the 1993–94 season. Yet even here, there was an ominous underside. The margin of CBS's seasonal victory had been boosted primarily by its success with the Winter Olympics. Though this was often (but not always) the pattern for ratings during the Olympics, this time it was different. CBS scored extraordinarily high ratings, with one week coming in as the highest rated week since ABC's *Winds of War* miniseries in 1983. Significantly, it was not just sports fans watching.

Before the start of the Olympics, on January 6, 1994, American figure skater Nancy Kerrigan had been physically attacked by a club-wielding assailant while she was practicing. She recovered from the resulting knee injury in time to compete in the Winter Olympics the following month in Lillehammer, Norway, but in the meantime, investigators linked the attack to the former husband of another U.S. skater, Tonya Harding. That angle turned the figure-skating competition into something else: a juicy, scandalous, tabloid-style story that took on a life of its own. In the weeks leading up to the Olympics, the airwaves were filled with gossipy speculation as well as endless jokes from the late night talk show hosts. With Kerrigan and Harding both scheduled to compete on February 23, that contest became the symbolic payback setting to conclude the sordid tale. All CBS needed to do was remind viewers that it would be Kerrigan versus Harding going for the gold. Actually, neither took top honors; Kerrigan won a silver medal and Harding finished a disappointing eighth. The real gold went to CBS, which won the ratings competition that night hands down, walking away with more than double the combined ratings of ABC, NBC, and Fox. In the increasingly volatile and competitive television world, Olympic sports were a big draw, but tabloid stories were even bigger.

55. In the Blink of an Eye

FOOTBALL FANS SETTLING IN for a new season of contests found that some of their favorite NFL teams had a new home in the fall of 1994, the Fox network. Yet this change was not particularly jarring from decades of coverage on CBS. Once viewers located their local Fox affiliate, they were greeted with the reassuringly familiar faces of former CBS sports anchors John Madden and Pat Summerall as well as solid on-field coverage that was snazzy (faster cutting and more imaginative graphics than CBS) but not distracting. The National Football League had become a Sunday ritual for millions over the years, with CBS carrying the older and higher-rated National Football Conference (NFC) and NBC the newer American Football Conference (AFC). In landing the NFC, Fox was counting on this viewing routine to carry over, and, to a large extent, it did, although Fox's weaker lineup of affiliates meant that, for the first time in almost twenty years, NBC's ratings for the AFC topped the NFC. Fox was pleased to see that its football ratings were only 6% below where CBS had been in 1993, while the industry consensus had expected about a drop of 15% to 20%. The lesson was that football fans did not care which network carried the teams, they just followed their favorites.

As expected, CBS saw its Sunday prime time ratings drop after losing the NFL, though not as much as the network had feared. To CBS's relief, many football fans also continued to find their favorite shows after the game, automatically switching to CBS for *60 Minutes* (which had long benefited from following football coverage). That program remained in the season's top ten (only dropping to number six compared to number two the previous year), while viewers ignored the new post-football Fox show, *Fortune Hunter* (a gadget-equipped super-secret agent). Nonetheless, the billion-dollar NFL contract deal performed just as Fox had hoped, drawing new viewers to the network and giving it a tremendous boost in prestige and credibility. That, in turn, had helped Fox to sign deals with more powerful affiliates in a dozen markets and, at the end of 1994, those changes began to go into effect.

Because most of the new Fox affiliates previously had been with CBS, the changes hit that network hard, not just on Sundays but on every day, in every time period. In December 1994, Fox took the former CBS affiliates in Milwaukee, Atlanta, Detroit, Phoenix, and Tampa, while CBS was forced to move to far less powerful outlets in those markets (going to the UHF spectrum in three of the five cities). This one-two punch of losing football and losing several key affiliates within a few months threw the already-fragile CBS into a tailspin. By the end of the 1994–95 season, CBS

was down more than 20%, going from the number one network in prime time to number three. Even worse, CBS also found itself in a demographic squeeze.

One of the reasons landing David Letterman as its late night host had been such a coup for CBS was that Letterman was a top draw among the viewer demographics that advertisers prized the most (those aged 18 to 49). Because such viewers were seen as less set in their ways, more open to advertising messages, and in the age group most likely to spend money, programs that attracted that audience could charge higher rates for their commercial spots. This was a wholesale embrace of a distinction that the networks had previously trotted out only when they needed to, usually when a particular series did not score strongly enough in the overall ratings (for example, *St. Elsewhere* in the early 1980s). The difference now was that the "right" demographic ratings were touted more and more both by advertisers and some of the networks. One by-product of this emphasis was that most of the television industry essentially dismissed total audience figures and largely focused on the ratings among the 18 to 49 age bracket. Shows with high ratings among all ages could still find sponsors, but they were not able to charge the highest prices for advertising. In truth, of course, viewers past age forty-nine did not stop buying products, sampling different brands, or watching television. However, as broadcasters and advertisers increasingly treated such viewers as essentially irrelevant, they were becoming so by definition within the industry. This was a particularly troublesome change for CBS because, with respect to the 18 to 49 age bracket, it had, in some time periods, not just fallen to number three, but all the way to number four (behind Fox).

For years, CBS had relied on its past glory days, going again and again to old familiar faces either for series retrospectives or new series. This season, there were new series featuring (among others) Hal Linden and Suzanne Pleshette (*The Boys Are Back*) and Dudley Moore (*Daddy's Girls*), along with such returning faces as Dick Van Dyke (*Diagnosis Murder*) and Angela Lansbury (*Murder, She Wrote*). With this formula, CBS managed to win the November sweeps with nostalgic made-for-TV movie returns of *The Rockford Files*, *Cagney and Lacey*, and *The Bionic Woman*. Yet these specials were not only short-term solutions, they also reinforced CBS's image of appealing to older viewers not prized by advertisers. On top of that, CBS did not have a strong track record in developing new shows successful in attracting viewers in the prized demographics. This problem could not have come at a less opportune time for the network, because CBS was already struggling to deal with viewer erosion from its loss of football and affiliate turnover. There was no easy answer. Was it better for CBS to go after the audience that was attracted to *The Simpsons*, *The X-Files*, and *Seinfeld* or should it stick with the *Diagnosis Murder* crowd, even though that was increasingly considered irrelevant by the industry? CBS was not certain which path was best and this schizophrenic uncertainty would haunt the network for years.

Fox had no such conflicts. Youth and edgy series ruled. For example, its new drama *Party of Five* started with the premise that the parents of the main characters were dead (killed in a car accident) and that the five children had to get by on their own, with oldest son Charlie (Matthew Fox) the legal guardian. That left plenty of room for soapy romantic complications that touched them all, especially sister Julia (Neve Campbell), brother Bailey (Scott Wolf), and Bailey's girlfriend, Sarah (Jennifer Love Hewitt). The series even became a critical favorite, slotted after the romantic comings and goings of the young adults at *Melrose Place*. Elsewhere, on Fox's long-running *Beverly Hills 90210*, Tiffani-Amber Thiessen stepped into the program's "bad girl" role (after the departure of Shannen Doherty), playing Brenda and Brandon's cousin, Valerie. By the end of the season, the Walsh parents were shipped off to Hong Kong for business, conveniently leaving son Brandon in charge of the house. Naturally, he later invited his friends (and lovers) to move in.

In January 1995, Fox was officially no longer the newest broadcast network on the air, when both UPN and the WB began operations. Like Fox in the previous decade, both aimed at specialized audiences and started out very slowly (four hours a week over two nights for UPN, just two hours a week on one night for the WB). UPN reached about 80% of the country while the WB covered about 55% through its affiliates and reached the balance via cable through superstation WGN in Chicago, its lead affiliate. The logical centerpiece of the UPN network was its debut series, the new *Star Trek: Voyager*, which began January 16. It targeted the viewers who had turned both *Next Generation* and *Deep Space Nine* into strong syndicated hits. Though *Voyager* took place in the same future era as those two other shows, the series set its action 75,000 light years away so it could truly find "new worlds" to explore. It also broke ground by featuring *Star Trek*'s first female commander, Kate Mulgrew as Capt. Kathryn Janeway. The package worked as planned, and *Voyager* became UPN's dominant program, though the network still had to figure out what else it could slot. A dismal pair of sitcoms, *Platypus Man* (featuring stand-up comic Richard Jeni) and *Pig Sty* (twenty-somethings in Manhattan), barely lasted six months. At the WB, programming head Jamie Kellner (formerly of Fox) looked at what had worked for his old network and brought over a few of those ideas and personalities, including Shawn and Marlon Wayans (from *In Living Color*) in *The Wayans Bros.* (the network's first series, premiering January 11), Robert Townsend (from *Townsend Television*) in *The Parent 'hood*, and another woeful family (like the Bundys in *Married ... with Children*) in *Unhappily Ever After*. By the end of 1995, the WB also picked up *Sister, Sister* from ABC, hoping to better establish itself in the niche market of black ethnic programming.

There was no such concern about niche audiences at the top of the ratings competition, as NBC and ABC faced off with some of television's hottest shows, which were popular with the most-desired audience demographics. NBC had *Seinfeld* as its engine powering Thursday nights and, in the fall, the network successfully introduced two new programs to further boost that lineup, the comedy *Friends* and the drama *ER*. Created by David Crane and Marta Kauffman (producers of the HBO comedy *Dream On*), *Friends*

comfortably dropped into the slot between *Mad About You* and *Seinfeld*, focusing on six single twenty-somethings living in Manhattan. They were a careful mix of characters that allowed a wide range of plot threads. The first episode set the stage, introducing brother and sister Ross and Monica Geller (David Schwimmer and Courteney Cox); apartment buddies Chandler Bing and Joey Tribbiani (Matthew Perry and Matt LeBlanc); singer-massage therapist Phoebe Buffay (Lisa Kudrow); and runaway bride Rachel Green (Jennifer Aniston), who entered their neighborhood hangout (the Central Perk coffee house) in her wedding dress, having left her intended groom waiting at the altar. In short order, Rachel had cajoled a minimum wage job as a waitress, moved in with Monica, and stirred Ross's heart. Ross had loved Rachel from afar in high school and now, divorced from his pregnant wife (who had decided she was gay and left him for another woman), he wondered: Could the two of them end up together? Wisely, nothing much happened between Ross and Rachel in the first season, as the series instead allowed each of the characters time to establish themselves individually. The result was a true ensemble show with easy banter, a wonderful sense of timing, and performers who were perfectly believable as "friends." (In real life, they even negotiated contract renewals as a group.) *Friends* was a perfect fit for NBC's Thursday comedy block, even if no actual struggling twenty-something could afford to live in the characters' comfy Manhattan apartments.

To close prime time on Thursdays, NBC took the slot that had worked so well for *L.A. Law* and *Hill Street Blues* and launched *ER*, a medical drama created by Michael Crichton (fresh from his successful novel *Jurassic Park*). Set in a Chicago hospital emergency room, *ER* maintained a breathtaking frenetic pace, juggling a rapid-fire succession of medical situations, some resolved in a

August 25, 1994

My So-Called Life. (ABC). Fifteen-year-old Claire Danes plays fifteen-year-old Angela Chase, a high school sophomore going through the angst that comes with being a teenager in the 1990s. Produced by Marshall Herskovitz, Edward Zwick, and Winnie Holzman, all of *thirtysomething* fame, the program has that show's intense focus on personal self-scrutiny, which seems perfectly appropriate for a teen-based series. A critical hit with meager ratings, it is yanked by ABC in January 1995, but then does fairly well in cable reruns on MTV beginning in April.

September 18-28, 1994

Baseball. (PBS). Documentarian Ken Burns presents the history of America's national pastime in eighteen and one-half hours spread over nine "innings," narrated by former NBC newsman John Chancellor. Looking beyond the game, Burns shows how baseball reflected twentieth-century America's changing views on labor, race, and celebrity.

September 21, 1994

Touched by an Angel. (CBS). This uplifting one-hour drama stars Roma Downey as an apprentice angel and Della Reese as her mentor, both on Earth to help mortals in need. To the amazement of critics (who predicted its quick demise) and its own network, the show becomes a moderate hit and lasts for nine seasons.

January 1, 1995

The History Channel, a spin-off from the Arts & Entertainment channel, debuts on cable.

	8:00	8:30	9:00	9:30	10:00	10:30	
M	Coach	BLUE SKIES	ABC NFL Monday Night Football (to 12 Midnight)				**ABC**
O	The Nanny	Dave's World	Murphy Brown	Love & War	Northern Exposure		**CBS**
N	Melrose Place		PARTY OF FIVE		local		**FOX**
	Fresh Prince Of Bel Air	Blossom	NBC Monday Night Movie				**NBC**
T	Full House	ME AND THE BOYS	Home Improvement	Grace Under Fire	NYPD Blue		**ABC**
U	Rescue 911		CBS Tuesday Movie				**CBS**
E	Fox Tuesday Night Movie				local		**FOX**
	Wings	THE MARTIN SHORT SHOW	Frasier	John Larroquette Show	Dateline NBC		**NBC**
W	Thunder Alley	ALL-AMERICAN GIRL	Roseanne	Ellen	Turning Point		**ABC**
E	THE BOYS ARE BACK	DADDY'S GIRL	TOUCHED BY AN ANGEL		48 Hours		**CBS**
D	Beverly Hills, 90210		Models Inc.		local		**FOX**
	THE COSBY MYSTERIES		Dateline NBC		Law & Order		**NBC**
T	MY SO-CALLED LIFE		McKENNA		Prime Time Live		**ABC**
H	DUE SOUTH		Eye To Eye With Connie Chung		CHICAGO HOPE		**CBS**
R	Martin	Living Single	NEW YORK UNDERCOVER		local		**FOX**
	Mad About You	FRIENDS	Seinfeld	MADMAN OF THE PEOPLE	ER		**NBC**
F	Family Matters	Boy Meets World	Step By Step	Hangin' With Mr. Cooper	20/20		**ABC**
R	Diagnosis Murder		UNDER SUSPICION		Picket Fences		**CBS**
I	M.A.N.T.I.S.		The X Files		local		**FOX**
	Unsolved Mysteries		Dateline NBC		Homicide: Life On The Street		**NBC**
S	ABC Family Movie				The Commish		**ABC**
A	Dr. Quinn, Medicine Woman		FIVE MRS. BUCHANANS	Hearts Afire	Walker, Texas Ranger		**CBS**
T	Cops	Cops	America's Most Wanted		local		**FOX**
	SOMETHING WILDER	Empty Nest	SWEET JUSTICE		Sisters		**NBC**

	7:00	7:30	8:00	8:30	9:00	9:30	10:00	10:30	
S	America's Funniest Home Videos	ON OUR OWN	Lois & Clark: The New Adventures Of Superman		ABC Sunday Night Movie				**ABC**
U	60 Minutes		Murder, She Wrote		CBS Sunday Movie				**CBS**
N	FORTUNE HUNTER		The Simpsons	HARDBALL	Married...With Children	WILD OATS	local		**FOX**
	EARTH 2		Seaquest DSV		NBC Sunday Night Movie				**NBC**

matter of seconds, others carried through the entire episode. These were balanced with personal character complications (usually tangled relationships) that helped ground the series with more traditional plots, carried by a strong central cast that included George Clooney, Anthony Edwards, Sherry Stringfield, Noah Wyle, William Macy, Eriq LaSalle, Julianna Margulies, and Gloria Reuben.

ER was an instant hit and finished as the number two program for the entire season, the highest debut ever for a new drama. That success was just more bad news for CBS, which had the misfortune of scheduling its new hospital drama, *Chicago Hope*, directly opposite *ER*. Despite a stellar cast (including Mandy Patinkin, Adam Arkin, Hector Elizondo, and E. G. Marshall) and a hip producer (David E. Kelley, from *Picket Fences*), *Chicago Hope* seemed, in comparison, overly serious, stagy, and old fashioned. (The presence of Marshall, whose respected TV drama roots stretched back to the 1950s, also once again reinforced the CBS image as the "old" network.) Though CBS moved *Chicago Hope* up an hour (away from *ER*) after only three weeks, and then to a new night (Mondays) by Christmas, the series labored under the shadow of *ER* throughout its six-year run.

ABC had been laboring under the ratings shadow of both CBS and NBC for years, even though (for at least half a decade) it had offered some of the most talked about shows on television, including such comedy hits as *Roseanne* and *Home Improvement* and respected dramas such as *thirtysomething* and *NYPD Blue*. Before

Seinfeld moved to Thursdays, *Home Improvement* had regularly beaten it in head-to-head competition. ABC had a strong and varied lineup throughout the week, from its Friday night "TGIF" shows to *Monday Night Football* to *Nightline*. Though the network had no new breakout hits this season, it still ended up with half of television's top ten, in the process taking the crown as the number one network for the first time since 1979. Though technically ABC's overall ratings fell slightly compared to the previous season (NBC and Fox improved the most), there was no doubt that ABC was at a high point in prestige and popularity. As such, it also stood as an irresistible target for the growing potential synergy between the broadcast networks and production studios, which had been unleashed when the FCC had begun lowering previously erected barriers between the two, such as the Fin-Syn rules.

On July 31, 1995, the Disney corporation announced plans to purchase ABC (and its parent, Capital Cities) for $19 billion. What made the announcement especially dramatic was its surprise nature, taking about ten days from the proposal by Disney CEO Michael Eisner to execution of a sale agreement. (There had been no leaks or rumors about the impending action.) The deal represented a stunning combination of production, distribution, and exhibition forces and was widely regarded as an exciting move, creating the world's largest entertainment conglomerate (combining ABC, ESPN, and the Disney Channel, among others, under a single ownership). It was even historically appropriate. The Disney studio had been one of the main reasons ABC had survived as a network in the early 1950s, thanks to the success of the *Disneyland* series, which had marked the first significant foray into television by an established film studio. Now, forty years later, that same studio was buying the network outright. The only concern in some circles was how the two corporate cultures would mesh. Capital Cities, which had acquired ABC almost ten years before, had been a comparatively benign owner, generally giving its television executives considerable leeway in deciding how to run the network. Disney, on the other hand, was well known for exerting tremendous corporate control, with an eye on the bottom line. As the new owner, Disney (and its philosophy) would presumably be dominant.

The ABC announcement was also one final bit of symbolic bad luck timing for CBS that season. The next day, August 1, in a widely anticipated development, Michael Jordan, the chairman of Westinghouse, announced that his company would be purchasing CBS from Laurence Tisch and his Loews corporation for $5.4 billion. Coming just after the exciting buzz of the Disney story, this announcement seemed woefully anticlimactic. ABC had been purchased at the top of its game for top dollar. CBS, after years of stringent cost-cutting under the Tisch regime, had fallen from first to third, its station lineup was damaged, and previous corporate assets such as publishing and its record labels had long since been liquidated. In commanding a price two-thirds less than ABC's, this seemed less a sale for the future than the cashing out of investment. (Despite CBS's woes, Tisch's ownership group still managed to reap a $906 million profit on the sale.) Westinghouse, a company based in electrical appliances, had a long history in television through its Group W stations and productions but could not match the highly visible, aggressively innovative image of Disney. About the only immediate change for CBS was that Westinghouse at least dragged CBS back into the world of cable, because the company already owned interests in a few existing cable services (such as Country Music Television and The Nashville Network).

It was hard to miss the presence and influence of cable on the television industry this season because it was a key element in the most widely covered news story of the year, the case of O. J. Simpson, accused of killing his former wife Nicole and her friend, Ronald Goldman. Since Simpson's arrest in June 1994 (following a bizarre televised "chase" through the streets of Los Angeles), every aspect of the story had been followed by the media, especially television. On cable, the case was perfect for such services as Court TV and CNN, which placed cameras whenever they could at official public procedures, preferably for live transmission. Because the initial story unfolded in the summer rerun months, the broadcast networks also had plenty of venues available, especially their prime time news magazines. (The highest rated individual show that summer was an episode of ABC's *Turning Point* news magazine devoted to O. J. Simpson and hosted by Barbara Walters.) Some of this coverage offered helpful perspectives on the personalities involved and the workings of the legal system in an unfolding murder case. However, most stories (especially on cable) quickly moved beyond that to the far more salacious area of gossipy speculation. Although most reporters were generally careful not to declare the possible guilt or innocence of Simpson, the talk show commentators, guests, and armchair detectives at home felt no such restraint. Some felt Simpson was clearly guilty and feared that he was going to get away with murder. Others felt he was innocent, a convenient, highly visible figure tagged with the killings through tainted, circumstantial evidence. No matter how it turned out, everyone knew they were right.

In September 1994, jury selection began for the Simpson case, but the actual trial did not get under way until late January 1995.

By that time, the story had been a national obsession for nearly half a year, a cross between an episode of *Law & Order,* a sports contest, and a soap opera. As the trial unfolded, it kept viewers glued to their sets keeping track of the names, time lines, scenarios, and strategies playing out on live television. Ultimately, it became a contest between Simpson's high-profile array of defense lawyers (dubbed the "dream team"), led by Johnnie Cochran; and the prosecution team from the district attorney's office of Los Angeles, led by Marcia Clark. Presiding Superior Court Judge Lance Ito was seen as both referee and scorekeeper.

Court TV had demonstrated in previous televised cases that it was possible to position cameras unobtrusively in a courtroom setting. However, no matter the placement, there was no guarantee that the presence of the television cameras in the courtroom would not be disruptive in more subtle ways, as participants directed their comments as much to TV viewers as to those in court. For the O. J. Simpson trial, these pressures were all but impossible to ignore. Though the jury might have been kept from the barrage of press coverage, no one else was. Each day, attorneys, witnesses, and

---

January 9, 1995

The Late Late Show. (CBS). Tom Snyder returns to late, late night TV, directly from a two-year talk show stint on CNBC. His show follows David Letterman and replaces the last of CBS's *Crimetime After Primetime* series.

March 6, 1995

The syndicated daytime talk program *The Jenny Jones Show* tapes an episode on "Secret Admirers," during which the admirers confess their feelings to their crushes. Jonathan Schmitz, a heterosexual male, is shocked to learn that his secret admirer is his neighbor, Scott Amedure, a gay man. Three days later, still upset, Schmitz tracks down Amedure and shoots and kills him. The episode never airs; Schmitz is convicted of second degree murder; and, in 1999, the program's producers are found negligent by a Michigan jury and ordered to pay Amedure's family $25 million. (although that award is overturned on appeal in 2002).

March 21, 1995

NewsRadio. (NBC). Set at a fictional all-news radio station in New York (WNYX), this slyly playful sitcom features Dave Foley as Dave Nelson, a fresh-faced news director laboring under the intensely disengaged station owner Jimmy James (Stephen Root). Phil Hartman shines as pompous newscaster Bill McNeal, while Andy Dick steals scenes as overly sensitive reporter Matthew Brock.

March 26, 1995

The Outer Limits. (Showtime). Thirty years after its final fade out on ABC, the "control voice" again ushers viewers into the realm of scary science fiction with new episodes produced for cable (which, in edited form, are soon seen in syndication on over-the-air television stations).

May 26, 1995

After nearly two years as Dan Rather's co-anchor on the *CBS Evening News,* Connie Chung is unceremoniously relieved of her duties.

July 1, 1995

Leslie Moonves, president of Warner Bros. Television, becomes the new CBS Entertainment president, replacing Peter Tortorici, who had lasted only fourteen months.

Television carried the verdict in the O. J. Simpson trial, live, to a worldwide audience. *(Courtesy of ABC News)*

even the presiding judge were the subject of intense scrutiny by millions of viewers watching the proceedings live. On the air before and after, analysts and commentators picked apart every moment of the trial. Often, the courtroom itself seemed just a brief stop to and from some other television appearance. Even when Judge Ito warned people not to play to the cameras, that instruction itself seemed to be doing just that, directed as much to the world watching as to the courtroom.

There were hundreds of hours of testimony, ranging from the borderline comical ("Kato" Kaelin, house sitter to O. J. Simpson) to the charged and confrontational (Mark Fuhrman, from the Los Angeles Police Department). On June 15, 1995, in one of the defining moments of the proceedings, the prosecution had Simpson try on a pair of leather gloves that had been entered in evidence (the left one found at the murder scene, the right one at O. J. Simpson's estate). Simpson grimaced and struggled putting them on, then, in a dramatic visual, held up his hands showing that the gloves did not appear to fit snugly. They seemed too small for his hands. In the blink of an eye, there was suddenly a creditable moment of doubt. Johnnie Cochran alluded to that image in his closing summary, questioning not only the gloves as evidence but the entire case against Simpson by declaring, "If it doesn't fit, you must acquit." A more disquieting turn occurred on September 5, when the jury heard the voice of witness Mark Fuhrman on brief excerpts from an audio tape in which he repeatedly used racial epithets. (Transcripts and witness testimony accompanied the pres-

entation.) Back in March, Fuhrman had testified he had not used the word "nigger" in the past ten years, but this nearly ten-year-old tape contradicted that point, forcing Marcia Clark to denounce the offensive words of her own witness during her closing summary.

Technically, the tape had nothing to do with the murders. (It was a background interview with Fuhrman made by aspiring screenwriter Laura Hart McKinny back in 1985.) Yet its frank and explicit tone seemed to give credence to the defense charge that Fuhrman might have been racially biased in approaching the investigation of O. J. Simpson, a black man. If that was the case, then perhaps the evidence itself might have been tainted. The prosecution was caught in the difficult position of criticizing Fuhrman's racial remarks while urging the jury not to ignore a body of evidence that, it insisted, pointed to Simpson as the killer.

After the closing arguments and lengthy instructions from Judge Ito, the jury went into deliberation. At the same time, television prepared to report on the verdict. Oddly, it did not matter whether O. J. Simpson was found guilty or not guilty. In either case, there would be one more round of blanket coverage, which would be followed by a far greater challenge. For nearly sixteen months, both the broadcast networks and cable had enjoyed extraordinary ratings by following what was essentially a second-tier celebrity scandal. With that story coming to an end, would they find themselves irresistibly drawn in the future to similar fare, however tawdry and trivial, in the hope of finding "another O. J."?

56. Ready for Reform

THE JURY IN THE O. J. SIMPSON TRIAL reached its verdict after only four hours of deliberation. The next day, Tuesday, October 3, 1995, at 10:00 A.M. California time, Los Angeles Superior Court Justice Lance Ito had his law clerk, Deirdre Robertson, read the formal verdict aloud in open court, as an audience of more than 130 million watched the televised proceedings live (then the largest TV audience ever for a live news event). It took ten minutes to recite the specific language regarding the charges and the jury's decision, first regarding the murder of Nicole Brown Simpson, then the murder of Ronald L. Goldman. In both instances, O. J. Simpson was found not guilty. These verdicts pleased some and outraged others, with television immediately bringing both perspectives to center stage. The coverage then continued, as analysts and commentators dissected the jury's decision and, once more, the entire trial process. Nonetheless, nearly sixteen months after the double murder, the O. J. Simpson story had at last reached something of an endpoint, though there would be subsequent legal action on other fronts. Now, it was time to assess the aftermath.

While individual viewers had been caught up, to varying degrees, in the Simpson story, television itself had been completely upended and at times seemed practically addicted to the tale. Over the course of the trial, the three primary broadcast networks devoted a large part of the time on their nightly news programs to the story (10% on ABC, 14% on CBS, and 17% on NBC). The O. J. Simpson hook was a top draw on the prime time news magazines. On cable, it had been even more entrenched. At various points during the trial CNN and Court TV were practically wall-to-wall in their coverage, supplementing the courtroom sessions with specials and even more talk. E! Entertainment Television (a cable channel specializing in covering celebrities) wholeheartedly embraced the story, providing gavel-to-gavel trial coverage right beside CNN and Court TV, along with updates and discussions throughout the day. The reason for all this was obvious: ratings. CNN's audience during the trial period (January to October 1995) was about five times what it had drawn during the same period the previous year. Similarly, it was estimated that Court TV tripled its viewership during the trial. A nightly cable talk show hosted by Geraldo Rivera (*Rivera Live*, on CNBC) also increased its viewing five-fold by immersing itself in the Simpson story. And it did not stop there.

Though at heart the case was about the cold-blooded murder of two individuals and the accusation against a celebrity, the bizarre circumstances and attendant media circus had made the investigation and subsequent trial fair game for comedy. From the beginning, Jay Leno attacked the subject with particular vigor in his *Tonight* show monologues, at one point introducing the "Dancing Itos" novelty act. David Letterman held back at first, but then also added the subject to his repertoire. As the trial dragged on, TV's comedy references to the case became more wicked, sometimes carrying as the punch line not only the assumption that Simpson was probably guilty, but also that there was a good chance he was literally going to "get away with murder."

Yet even with scrupulously fair and conspicuously balanced reports, the virtual non-stop presentation across multiple channels could not help but affect the nature of the story. In the past, even intense television coverage would be limited to the event itself (if it was carried live), the nightly news, the Sunday morning news shows, and perhaps a special or two. The twenty-four-hour news cycle created in the 1980s by CNN and the overnight news shows on the broadcast networks upped the ante. Now, with even more all-day cable outlets in the equation, there was no relief—especially with the proliferation of talk, which too often emphasized opinion and speculation, sometimes focusing on the most mundane points in search of any new angle (and then repeating everything in taped reruns into the night). This television routine indiscriminately chewed through ideas (both helpful and outlandish), but it also offered the allure of a forum few seemed able to resist. Even Judge Lance Ito succumbed, taping a personal profile background interview in November 1994 with the local KCBS "Action News," which ran it over five nights during the sweeps. Clearly, any individual observations, however well intended, were almost inevitably swallowed up and turned into part of the ongoing media muck.

Perhaps the most troubling aspect of the ratings success of the O. J. Simpson coverage was that it blithely "justified" spending so much valuable airtime on the story in the first place. Though it surely warranted coverage (centering on a nationally known celebrity charged with a heinous crime), the Simpson case had become less a news story than just another TV programming fad (such as prime time soap operas in the 1980s), seized upon for a ratings fix. That might have been a legitimate rationale for chasing entertainment formats, but this was a real-life murder case, with coverage reflecting on the credibility of television news. Time devoted to this scandal meant that news venues had to leave out other issues, especially those that did not lend themselves to similar "instant news" coverage (such as complicated economic and international stories). Most important, after tasting this kind of tabloid story

	8:00	8:30	9:00	9:30	10:00	10:30	
MON	The Marshall		ABC NFL Monday Night Football (to 12 Midnight)				ABC
	The Nanny	CAN'T HURRY LOVE	Murphy Brown	IF NOT FOR YOU	Chicago Hope		CBS
	Melrose Place		PARTNERS	NED AND STACEY	local		FOX
	Fresh Prince Of Bel Air	In The House	NBC Monday Night Movie				NBC
	Star Trek: Voyager		NOWHERE MAN		local		UPN
	local						WB
TUE	Roseanne	HUDSON STREET	Home Improvement	Coach	NYPD Blue		ABC
	JOHN GRISHAM'S THE CLIENT		CBS Tuesday Movie				CBS
	Fox Tuesday Night Movie				local		FOX
	Wings	Newsradio	Frasier	PURSUIT OF HAPPINESS	Dateline NBC		NBC
	DEADLY GAMES		LIVE SHOT		local		UPN
	local						WB
WED	Ellen	THE DREW CAREY SHOW	Grace Under Fire	THE NAKED TRUTH	Prime Time Live		ABC
	BLESS THIS HOUSE	Dave's World	CENTRAL PARK WEST		COURTHOUSE		CBS
	Beverly Hills, 90210		Party Of Five		local		FOX
	Seaquest 2032		Dateline NBC		Law & Order		NBC
	local						UPN
	Sister, Sister	The Parent 'Hood	The Wayans Bros.	Unhappily Ever After	local		WB
THR	CHARLIE GRACE		THE MONROES		MURDER ONE		ABC
	Murder, She Wrote		NEW YORK NEWS		48 Hours		CBS
	Living Single	THE CREW	New York Undercover		local		FOX
	Friends	THE SINGLE GUY	Seinfeld	CAROLINE IN THE CITY	ER		NBC
	local						UPN
	local						WB
FRI	Family Matters	Boy Meets World	Step By Step	Hangin' With Mr. Cooper	20/20		ABC
	DWEEBS	THE BONNIE HUNT SHOW	Picket Fences		AMERICAN GOTHIC		CBS
	STRANGE LUCK		The X Files		local		FOX
	Unsolved Mysteries		Dateline NBC		Homicide: Life On The Street		NBC
	local						UPN
	local						WB
SAT	JEFF FOXWORTHY SHOW	MAYBE THIS TIME	ABC Saturday Night At The Movies				ABC
	Dr. Quinn, Medicine Woman		Touched By An Angel		Walker, Texas Ranger		CBS
	Martin	THE PRESTON EPISODES	Cops	America's Most Wanted	local		FOX
	JAG		The John Larroquette Show	THE HOME COURT	Sisters		NBC
	local						UPN
	local						WB

	7:00	7:30	8:00	8:30	9:00	9:30	10:00	10:30	
SUN	America's Funniest Home Videos	America's Funniest Home Videos	Lois & Clark: The New Adventures Of Superman		ABC Sunday Night Movie				ABC
	60 Minutes		Cybill	ALMOST PERFECT	CBS Sunday Movie				CBS
	SPACE: ABOVE AND BEYOND		The Simpsons	TOO SOMETHING	Married...With Children	MISERY LOVES COMPANY	local		FOX
	BROTHERLY LOVE	MINOR ADJUSTMENTS	Mad About You	Hope & Gloria	NBC Sunday Night Movie				NBC
	local								UPN
	PINKY & THE BRAIN	Sister, Sister	KIRK	SIMON	CLEGHORNE!	FIRST TIME OUT	local		WB

With his victory in the November 1995 sweeps, Jay Leno was back on top in the late night ratings race with his *Tonight* show, and never looked back. (*Photo Courtesy of NBC Studios/Photo by Paul Drinkwater*)

ratings success, both broadcasters and cable services would face similar programming lures again, sooner rather than later.

The coverage also prompted questions from the legal community about how the O. J. Simpson proceedings had unfolded. Should Judge Ito have been more aggressive in moving the trial along? Should he have barred both sides from talking with the press? Should he have been more stringent in his treatment of the media? While television continued to assert the positive value of carrying trials live, "after O. J." other judges in highly publicized trials would have to reexamine the role and degree of press coverage. Less than a year after the "not guilty" verdict in the O. J. Simpson criminal trial, Simpson was back in court to face civil (that is, non-criminal) "wrongful death" lawsuits brought by the families of Nicole Simpson and Ronald Goldman. For that trial, Judge Hiroshi Fujisaki was firm: There would be no TV cameras and no still photographers. He also imposed a gag order on all participants, prohibiting them from discussing the case-in-progress with the media. That trial attracted far less public attention, took about half the time of the criminal case (running from September 1996 to February 1997), and resulted in the opposite verdict: O. J. Simpson was found liable for the murders and ordered to pay $6.2 million in compensatory damages plus $25 million in punitive damages. Though the civil case operated under entirely different legal rules from the earlier criminal trial (making it much easier to reach a verdict against Simpson), the significantly toned-down coverage of the civil trial helped ensure that the case was settled more in the courtroom than on the international media stage.

In the meantime, television looked for different ways to further tap the public's apparent interest in the machinations of the legal system. CNN offered *Burden of Proof,* with Greta Van Susteren and Roger Cossack, discussing legal issues and specific trials on a daily basis. Court TV continued with its mix of cases (not all featured celebrities) and, in November, presented a commemorative retrospective on the post-World War II Nazi Nuremberg trials. ABC offered the highest profile venture, *Murder One*, an original legal drama series from Steven Bochco that followed a fictional murder case from beginning to end over an entire season. After all, viewers had tuned in the Simpson case daily for hours on end. Surely they would find a fictional show at least as interesting.

Bochco had previously traveled this road (following a murder and subsequent trial over the course of a series) in the short-lived *Cop Rock,* but *Murder One* clearly reflected the expectations and assumptions of the legal world after the O. J. Simpson trial. The main storyline followed the case of Neil Avedon (Jason Gedrick), a handsome but arrogant young movie star accused of beating and murdering a young woman. (She had been found dead in an apartment they had used for sex and drugs.) He sought the best defense money could buy and Theodore Hoffman (Daniel Benzali) was there to provide it, leading a team of ruthlessly ambitious, manipulative, and dedicated attorneys and investigators. They were experts not only in the law, but also in the art of managing the media. As in the O. J. Simpson trial, the plots and character connections were appropriately complicated and convoluted, with married millionaire Richard Cross (Stanley Tucci) (whose mistress was the murdered girl's older sister) having the most to hide. Also, as in the Simpson story, viewers did not know if Avedon had committed the crime, though they did get to see the strategy sessions for the case along with the courtroom presentations. In court, Hoffman was especially effective sparring with Miriam Grasso (Barbara Bosson, in one of her best roles ever for a Bochco series), recalling the male-female face-off at the Simpson trial between Johnnie Cochran and Marcia Clark. As the story arc reached its conclusion, *Murder One* did take a different path from real life: The jury found Avedon guilty. However, *Murder One* also managed to have it both ways by then introducing a newly found videotape from a hidden camera trained on the murder site. This not only exonerated Avedon but also showed that the real murderer was actually a relatively minor drug dealer character. Though that was a bit of a cheat on the premise of the series, it recognized the fact that while viewers might accept uncertainty in real life, when it came to fictional TV, they expected a clear resolution. That plot twist did not result in many viewer complaints, though, because by then *Murder One* did not have all that many viewers. It had been highly touted going into the fall but it ended the season as one of ABC's frustrating disappointments.

The network had slotted *Murder One* against NBC's *ER* on Thursdays, but that match-up was no contest, with *ER* drawing about three times as many viewers. ABC switched *Murder One* to Monday nights in January, but the damage had been done. *ER* had stolen *Murder One*'s thunder and, with so many viewers skipping the early set-up, it was extremely difficult to lure them into later episodes of the complex story-in-progress. That Thursday night clash of dramas captured the season in microcosm. Though ABC still had strong shows throughout the schedule and won the ratings competition on more than one hundred individual nights, NBC found itself with a ratings juggernaut on Thursdays, driven by *ER, Seinfeld,* and *Friends* (the first-, second-, and third-rated series of the season). NBC won only about sixty individual nights that season, but it won every Thursday by a great enough margin to essentially carry its entire schedule. NBC deftly used this strength to introduce new shows and to transplant former Thursday successes to other nights, in an attempt to establish "Must See TV" beachheads on Tuesdays (with *Frasier*) and Sundays (with *Mad About You*). As a result, ABC ended up ceding the prime time network ratings crown to NBC after only one season at the top.

NBC took full advantage of the cradles of space between *Friends* and *Seinfeld*, and then between *Seinfeld* and *ER*, to power new sitcoms to virtually guaranteed high ratings. Taking no chances, NBC blessed these slots with programs that were essentially variations on either *Seinfeld* or *Friends*, focusing on good-looking twenty-somethings hanging around together, facing mild complications, and, of course, dwelling on sex. *Caroline in the City* featured Lea Thompson as cartoonist Caroline Duffy (creator of a newspaper strip called "Caroline in the City"), who worked from her New York loft apartment, exchanging quips with her sardonic colorist, Richard (Malcolm Gets), her former boyfriend, Del (Eric Lutes), and her sex-obsessed neighbor from across the hall, Annie (Amy Pietz). *The Single Guy* dared to include *married* couples, though they seemed so annoying and unhappy it was easy to see why "single guy" Johnny Eliot (Jonathan Silverman), a Manhattan novelist, was in no hurry to wed, preferring instead a wide range of sexual partners. His most memorable was a guest shot by *Seinfeld*'s Julia Louis-Dreyfus (married to series creator Brad Hall), who played a woman obsessed with having sex in dangerous locations, such as on a bridge. *Boston Common* (a spring tryout

that temporarily took *The Single Guy*'s slot) did venture outside New York, only to follow lusting students and faculty at a Boston college. All three sitcoms ended up in the top ten for the season, though this performance was completely due to the company they kept. Unlike *Frasier* and *Friends* (and *Seinfeld* in its earlier days following *Cheers*), none of these were ready to stand on their own. Yet NBC seemed addicted to this formula, and acted as if the only programs that could work on its strongest night of television were programs that tried to ape selected traits of its established hits.

NBC did have one new sitcom, *3rd Rock from the Sun* (a mid-season offering) that broke from this mold, but the network did not nurture it in one of the golden Thursday night slots. Instead, NBC bounced it through no less than twelve time slots over six seasons. Even with that handicap, the series managed to lure a following and score multiple Emmy awards with a shameless mix of goofy slapstick, dizzy visuals, gross misunderstandings, and the willingness to do anything—anything—for a laugh. The premise was simple: Four alien visitors arrived on Earth and adopted human guises not quite matching their real forms. Sexy Sally (Kristen Johnston) was really a "male" alien, teenager Tommy (Joseph Gordon-Levitt) was actually older than the others, and Harry (French Stewart) *probably* was not as dumb as he seemed. Group leader Dick Solomon (John Lithgow) and Earthling Mary Albright (Jane Curtin) stood at the center of the series, carrying on an affectionate but puzzling romance, usually complicated by Dick's clueless takes on human customs. *Seinfeld*'s Wayne Knight fit right in, moonlighting to play Sally's cop-on-the-beat boyfriend. *3rd Rock* was anything but sophisticated urban humor, and was all the stronger for it.

Still, it was easy to see why NBC tried to find something familiar for its available Thursday slots. The need to use existing hits to create new hits was essential because the sheer volume of broadcast competition was greater than ever. With UPN and the WB adding more shows for their first full season, the fall of 1995 offered an astonishing forty-two new prime time series on the six broadcast networks, plus nearly seventy returning shows. Most new shows, no matter how good, faced an enormous challenge just getting noticed. Increasingly, that challenge was extending beyond specific shows to the need for the networks themselves to carve out a clear identity. The raft of pale *Friends* and *Seinfeld* clones on NBC might have been repetitious, but they also reinforced NBC's image as defined by its signature shows.

Fox had proven particularly adept at developing a strong network identity, not just tied to specific shows but also to its general approach, best described as "programming with attitude." This was open-ended enough to apply to anything from sports coverage to *The Simpsons* and was invaluable for a network that had torn through programs at a rapid rate since its inception, hoping to connect with specifically targeted audiences. For the 1995–96 season, Fox had a pair of successes. The increasingly popular *X-Files* was starting to take a bite out of ABC's hold on younger viewers Friday nights, while NBC's *Saturday Night Live* faced Fox's *MADtv,* its first creditable direct competition. Beginning a half-hour before *Saturday Night Live, MADtv* (based on *Mad* magazine) brought an aggressively irreverent style to the weekend sketch comedy stage (O. J. Simpson house guest Kato Kaelin was a guest on the first episode), with the series quickly establishing itself as the hungry alternative to NBC's twenty-year-old showcase.

Meanwhile, as the newest broadcast networks, the WB and UPN had different challenges. They just needed to get new programs on the air as they slowly expanded their respective schedules. Attempting to build on the draw of *Star Trek: Voyager,* UPN offered a number of adventure series (including *Deadly Games* and *Nowhere Man* in the fall and *The Sentinel* and *Swift Justice* when the network expanded to three nights per week at mid-season), then found surprising success with *Moesha*, a sweetly authentic sitcom premiering in January featuring black pop singer Brandy in the title role of a fifteen-year-old high schooler. The WB had already assembled several shows aimed at black ethnic audiences (including *The Wayans Bros.* and *Sister, Sister*), and for the new season (when it added a second night of programming) it presented *Cleghorne!* (with black comic Ellen Cleghorne, from the *Saturday Night Live* cast). That fall, the network also added three hours of Saturday morning cartoons and borrowed one of those programs, *Pinky and the Brain*, to run as part of the WB's prime time lineup as well. (The show followed two genetically altered lab mice determined to "take over the world.") Still, both UPN and the WB were far from set in their respective overall images.

ABC, which had a solid sitcom track record with working-class comedy, added a strong new spring season entry with *The Drew Carey Show*, featuring stand-up comic Drew Carey as an office grunt at a department store in Cleveland, Ohio (the antithesis of a twenty-something Manhattan setting). Carey had a solid workplace "family," including office nemesis Mimi (Kathy Kinney) and buddies Oswald (Diedrich Bader), Lewis (Ryan Stiles), and Kate (Christa Miller), but often the series used the work setup merely as a backdrop. The show was playfully innovative, sometimes more like a sketch comedy than a sitcom, with full-blown musical pieces, movie parodies, and "April Fool" episodes deliberately filled with mistakes. *Drew Carey* was a welcome new bright spot for ABC that season, even as the network watched NBC pass it in the overall ratings.

Of all the broadcast networks, CBS was in the most difficulty as it increasingly felt the loss of the key affiliates that had switched to Fox the previous year. In Detroit, for example, CBS went from a powerful VHF station to the obscure UHF channel 62 and found its ratings for that major market down 50%. The overall ratings erosion was affecting even CBS's hippest offering, David Letterman's *Late Show,* because the network's prime time lineup provided a weaker lead-in to the local news (if there even was a local news show on the new affiliate) and that, in turn, meant there were fewer viewers tuned in for late night. Meanwhile, NBC's powerhouse lineup on Thursdays had the opposite positive ripple for Jay Leno's *Tonight* show. Boosted by all these forces, in November 1995 Leno beat Letterman in a sweeps period for the first time, then moved ahead for the season to reclaim the late night crown.

In the prime time schedule, CBS was also attempting to increase its visibility and credibility among viewers in the increasingly targeted 18 to 49 age demographic group, looking especially to successes on Fox and NBC as models. It was an uncertain, at times awkward, effort. CBS's most touted venture for the fall was *Central Park West*, from producer Darren Star (one of the creative forces behind Fox's *Beverly Hills 90210* and *Melrose Place*), reaching back to the CBS staple of prime time soaps but recasting them in a more youthful mode. It was a spectacular flop and the network pulled the series after just two months. (A retooled version, called simply *CPW*, was ignored in a brief run in June.)

On Sundays, in a truly symbolic move, CBS lifted longtime hit *Murder, She Wrote* from its successful slot following *60 Minutes* and placed it instead on Thursdays, opposite *Friends*. In its place on Sunday the network dropped in a pair of hip urban series, *Almost Perfect* (with Nancy Travis as the only female writer on a hit Hollywood series) and *Cybill* (a mid-season addition from the previous year, starring Cybill Shepherd as a sharp-tongued fortysomething actress in Hollywood). The new combination could not begin to match the former Sunday ratings of *Murder, She Wrote*, though both sitcoms later continued for CBS on other nights.

On Friday nights, CBS aimed straight for the *X-Files* audience with *American Gothic*, slotting the program immediately after that Fox show. Created by former teen actor and pop singer Shaun Cassidy (with horror film director Sam Raimi as an executive producer), *American Gothic* was a mesmerizing combination of scary turns and steamy sexiness in the Southern gothic tradition of such writers as Anne Rice and William Faulkner. The stories were set in the small town of Trinity, South Carolina, where sheriff Lucas Buck (Gary Cole) reigned supreme. At times he seemed to be in league with the devil (if he was not the devil himself), and was so adept at playing on doubt, guilt, lust, and greed that he generally did not have to do most dirty deeds himself. He nudged people to the edge of temptation and let them hang themselves (sometimes, literally), creating spooky twists that were both psychological and physical (such as ravenous insects in the humorously titled "Meet the Beetles"). The sheriff's own deep secret was his paternal interest in a young orphan, Caleb Temple (Lucas Black), who was actually his son. (Lucas had raped Caleb's mother.) Caleb's half-sister Merlyn (Sarah Paulson) had been murdered by Lucas, though that did not stop her from appearing as a guiding spirit to Caleb. *American Gothic* was exactly the type of cutting-edge show CBS was looking for and it was a perfect companion to the *X-Files*. Unfortunately for the network, the only way to reach any *X-Files* fans

May 22, 1996
The "official" end of the 1995-96 television season. By consensus, the networks this year change the industry definition of a season (in effect since the mid-1950s) from 30 weeks (running from September until mid-April) to 35-36 weeks (running through the end of the May sweeps).

June 1, 1996
Fox Saturday Baseball. (Fox). After the collapse of The Baseball Network's two-year joint venture, Major League Baseball returns to a more traditional rights contract. As part of a new five-year deal, Fox revives the Saturday afternoon "game of the week," while also rotating coverage with NBC of the All-Star Game and the post-season playoff games (including the World Series).

June 10, 1996
The Rosie O'Donnell Show. Actress-comic Rosie O'Donnell hosts a warm and friendly syndicated daytime talk-variety program, positioned as an alternative to the many highly sensationalist, tabloid-style talk programs.

July 23, 1996
WRLD-HD in Raleigh, North Carolina, becomes the first U.S. commercial over-the-air high definition digital television station.

August 14, 1996
The FCC announces plans to end the current method of TV transmission ("analog" TV). All existing stations are to be assigned an extra channel (most between 7 and 59), which is to simulcast current programming with a digital signal over the air. After a transition period, the old analog channels are to be shut down and, eventually, used for other communication purposes.

August 30, 1996
With barely any fanfare, the FCC's twenty-five-year-old prime time access rule officially dies.

At the television-friendly setting of the Republican National Convention in San Diego, a video feed of Senator Robert Dole formed the backdrop to remarks by former president Gerald Ford. (*Photo by Mark Abraham*)

would have been to promote it on *The X-Files,* because Fox viewers would never imagine that CBS would carry something like that.

Ironically, despite CBS's efforts to cater to more youthful demographics, the network continued to score best with older-skewing fare. Though *Murder, She Wrote* promptly died against *Friends, Diagnosis Murder* continued to do well, as did the sentimental drama *Touched by an Angel* (reminiscent of Michael Landon's *Highway to Heaven*), and the old-fashioned breezy detective show, *Nash Bridges* (starring Don Johnson). In the changing television world, CBS was having a particularly tough time adapting. To varying degrees, so were the other networks.

While CBS had fallen the most dramatically due to the extraordinary circumstances of losing professional football as well as key affiliates, overall combined ratings for the Big 3 (ABC, CBS, and NBC) during the 1995–96 season were the lowest ever, reaching only 53% of television households. Though the numbers looked better when Fox, UPN, and the WB were added back into the mix, the truth was that decades of cable growth was taking its toll on the broadcast networks. More and more viewers were considering them just another choice from their cable company, which might be offering forty or more different channels. As a result, at any given moment, the networks were reaching fewer people than ever. This fact, in part, helped explain the increasing emphasis on demographics. The massive numbers were no longer there, so the networks had to show advertisers that the remaining numbers were exactly the people they wanted to reach. Simply being the number one network among total viewers was not what it used to be.

At the same time, further changes were affecting the industry, many stemming from revised broadcasting rules brought about by the Telecommunications Act of 1996, signed on February 8, 1996, by President Clinton. One aspect of the new law required the installation of "v-chip" technology in future television sets in response to growing criticism of the increasingly coarse and explicit nature of the medium. The v-chip would allow parents to filter out material they felt was inappropriate for their households. However, in order for any such system to work, each program had to carry some kind of rating to be electronically read by the v-chip system. Creating a ratings system and assigning a rating for every program represented an enormous undertaking. Nonetheless, if the networks did not do it, the alternative was a government-imposed system, so

the networks and program producers grudgingly joined forces to develop their own system for this "reform." However, there was much more enthusiasm in the industry about other "reforms" in the legislation, particularly those that granted some tremendously valuable new business opportunities.

For decades the government had imposed strict ownership limits on the number of radio and television stations a company could own, both within a particular market and collectively throughout the country. The 1996 legislation lifted all ownership limits on radio stations and relaxed the limits on television stations. Like the elimination of the Fin-Syn rules, this change allowed large media companies to become even larger, bringing more assets under the same corporate umbrella. For example, without the changes, the final approval of the Westinghouse purchase of CBS would have required the divestment of some properties because both companies owned stations and, combined, they would have gone over the previous limits. Practically overnight, then, the basic business model for television had to be reexamined for potential new opportunities, both on the air and behind the scenes.

In December 1995, NBC and the Microsoft corporation entered into a partnership to transform NBC's practically invisible cable service, America's Talking, into MSNBC, a new twenty-four-hour news venture crossing into different forms, forums, and formats. By linking with Microsoft (fresh from the successful launch of its Windows 95 operating system), NBC looked to have the strongest possible technology partner, especially in the rapidly emerging world of the Internet. The website component of MSNBC was designed to present online computer users with the latest news updates, expanded background text, and audio and video clips. The cable version began on July 15, 1996, with an equally ambitious combination of straight news (anchored by Brian Williams), talk, and archival material from NBC's news library (*Time and Again,* hosted by Jane Pauley). Yet, at any moment, MSNBC could devote itself entirely to one story, staying with it as long as necessary, much like CNN's lucrative coverage of the O. J. Simpson trial.

Though the presence of Pauley (as well as appearances by nightly news anchor Tom Brokaw) caused grumbling among affiliates concerned that this was competition for their own news programs, MSNBC actually represented a tremendous pressure relief valve for NBC's news operation. Ever since CNN had stepped in as a twenty-four-hour news service, the broadcast networks had been at a disadvantage, especially when covering breaking news stories such as the war in the Persian Gulf. They were always under pressure to return the network to its previously scheduled entertainment programming (with its pre-sold commercial time). With MSNBC, NBC now had its own twenty-four-hour service that had the luxury of staying with a story for as long as needed.

MSNBC could also follow developments in what might be considered marginal stories. For example, in early August, ABC's Ted Koppel caused a stir when he pulled his *Nightline* program from the Republican National Convention in San Diego, citing a lack of hard news at the event. Yet MSNBC could look at the same event in a completely different way, regarding the political convention hall as a perfect, television-friendly setting. There were thousands of potential on-screen guests, ranging from top party officials and interested business leaders to individual delegates and ardent political activists. There were even the formal programs and procedures of the convention itself, culminating in the acceptance speech by Kansas Senator Bob Dole, the party's nominee for president of the United States. For a cable service with all the time in the world, that combination was just fine.

57. All Around the Dial

VIEWING CHOICES FOR MORE THAN 60% of U.S. households in the 1996–97 season were not limited to the broadcast networks. With more and more people receiving television signals (including those of their local network affiliates) via cable, the thirty-nine new series and the eighty-one returning programs on ABC, CBS, NBC, Fox, UPN, and the WB were only the beginning for them. After nearly two decades of incremental growth, cable had reached a critical mass. It was now generally seen as part of the total television environment, not some esoteric add-on. Cable had effectively carved its own identity, attracting audiences either to specific theme channels (from sports to history) or to particular programs. While these still did not match the overall audience of the biggest hits on the broadcast networks (such as *ER* and *Seinfeld*), the gap between the lower-rated broadcast offerings and the top-rated cable series continued to narrow.

The September premiere season still belonged to the broadcast networks, though, driven by the annual publicity blitz surrounding that event, so the cable channels generally avoided launching their new series then. Any other time was fair game, particularly when broadcasters were likely to be in reruns. Summer was perfect (it had, for some years, been cable's favorite time to launch big series), but, lately, so were other periods throughout the year, especially since the networks were now working with a thirty-five to thirty-six week regular season (from September to May). With most network series having no more than twenty-two to twenty-four episodes, that meant there were numerous reruns outside the fall premiere period and the sweeps months of November, February, and May, when cable could air new episodes against fairly weak competition to help earn maximum viewership. Thus, cable services were now slipping in original programming at every opportunity to lure channel surfers, even though they still aired far more reruns than the broadcast networks.

Ironically, repeats on cable were not viewed in the same way as reruns by broadcasters. There was no stigma. Cable viewers had come to see cable reruns as multiple opportunities to view specific programs (much like multiple showings of feature films on the cable movie channels). That attitude effectively extended the programming reach of cable series, allowing fewer episodes to play again and again over a much more leisurely schedule than that of the broadcast networks. By the 1996–97 season, there was an impressive lineup of such series unique to cable, with standouts scattered throughout the dial, including many returning programs, just like the broadcasters.

American Movie Classics (a twelve-year-old cable network that primarily featured theatrical films from Hollywood's glory days) had *Remember WENN* (in its second season), a gentle period comedy created by songwriter Rupert Holmes and set at a small independent Pittsburgh radio station (WENN) during the golden age of radio. With its "behind the scenes" view of typical radio productions of the era (including comedies, soap operas, music shows, and dramas), the series meshed perfectly with AMC's nostalgic attitude that Hollywood stories were much better (certainly more civil) back "in the good old days."

Taking the opposite tack, HBO had its biting talk show satire *The Larry Sanders Show* (beginning a fifth season in November), as well as the cutting-edge sketch series from David Cross and Bob Odenkirk, *Mr. Show* (in its second season). A more routine show business comedy, *Arli$$*, began in August 1996, following a self-aggrandizing sports super agent, Arliss Michaels (Robert Wuhl). And in the summer of 1997, HBO launched *Oz*, a raw and brutal hour-long prison drama from film producer Barry Levinson (creator of NBC's *Homicide).*

On the E! Entertainment Television network, raucous New York morning radio personality Howard Stern (the self-proclaimed "King of All Media") was well into his third year of bringing cameras into the radio studio to package thirty-minute video highlights from his daily program. Another E! series, *Talk Soup,* also took video excerpts, drawing (with permission) from the many daytime talk programs across the dial to gleefully mock the excesses of the format. Greg Kinnear delivered the barbs when the program started in 1991, handing the job over to John Henson in 1995 after Kinnear replaced Bob Costas as host of NBC's late, late talk show, *Later.*

One of the most popular series on MTV was the year-old game show *Singled Out*, an aggressively hormone-driven take on matching up good-looking young men and women, with competition egged on by dream date co-host Jenny McCarthy (*Playboy* magazine's 1994 Playmate of the Year). By the spring of 1997, McCarthy had landed her own short-run MTV comedy skit show and then moved on to NBC for an equally brief sitcom (*Jenny*). At about the same time, MTV also introduced the animated series *Daria*, a spinoff from the four-year-old *Beavis and Butt-head*, featuring a sardonic schoolmate of the two slackers. Surprisingly, the new series eschewed the original's reliance on video clips and simple, endlessly repeated punch lines, playing instead as a multilayered, wickedly effective sitcom skewering of suburban teen life.

	8:00	8:30	9:00	9:30	10:00	10:30	
M	DANGEROUS MINDS		ABC NFL Monday Night Football (to 12 Midnight)				ABC
O	COSBY	INK	Murphy Brown	Cybill	Chicago Hope		CBS
N	Melrose Place		PARTY GIRL	LUSH LIFE	local		FOX
	The Jeff Foxworthy Show	MR. RHODES	NBC Monday Night Movie				NBC
	In The House	MALCOLM & EDDIE	GOODE BEHAVIOR	SPARKS	local		UPN
	7TH HEAVEN		Savannah		local		WB
T	Roseanne	LIFE'S WORK	Home Improvement	SPIN CITY	NYPD Blue		ABC
U	PROMISED LAND		CBS Tuesday Movie				CBS
E	Fox Tuesday Night Movie				local		FOX
	Mad About You	SOMETHING SO RIGHT	Frasier	Caroline In The City	Dateline NBC		NBC
	Moesha	HOMEBOYS IN OUTER SPACE	THE BURNING ZONE		local		UPN
	local						WB
W	Ellen	TOWNIES	Grace Under Fire	The Drew Carey Show	Prime Time Live		ABC
E	The Nanny	PEARL	Almost Perfect	PUBLIC MORALS	EZ STREETS		CBS
D	Beverly Hills, 90210		Party Of Five		local		FOX
	Wings	John Larroquette Show	Newsradio	MEN BEHAVING BADLY	Law & Order		NBC
	The Sentinel		Star Trek: Voyager		local		UPN
	Sister, Sister	NICK FRENO	The Wayans Bros.	JAMIE FOXX SHOW	local		WB
T	High Incident		Murder One		Turning Point		ABC
H	Diagnosis Murder		MOLONEY		48 Hours		CBS
R	Martin	Living Single	New York Undercover		local		FOX
	Friends	The Single Guy	Seinfeld	SUDDENLY SUSAN	ER		NBC
	local						UPN
	local						WB
F	Family Matters	SABRINA, THE TEENAGE WITCH	CLUELESS	Boy Meets World	20/20		ABC
R	Dave's World	EVERYBODY LOVES RAYMOND	MR. & MRS. SMITH		Nash Bridges		CBS
I	Sliders		MILLENNIUM		local		FOX
	Unsolved Mysteries		Dateline NBC		Homicide: Life On The Street		NBC
	local						UPN
	local						WB
S	Second Noah		Coach	COMMON LAW	RELATIVITY		ABC
A	Dr. Quinn, Medicine Woman		EARLY EDITION		Walker, Texas Ranger		CBS
T	Cops	Cops	Married...With Children	LOVE AND MARRIAGE	local		FOX
	DARK SKIES		THE PRETENDER		PROFILER		NBC
	local						UPN
	local						WB

	7:00	7:30	8:00	8:30	9:00	9:30	10:00	10:30	
S	America's Funniest Home Videos	America's Funniest Home Videos	Lois & Clark: The New Adventures Of Superman		ABC Sunday Night Movie				ABC
U	60 Minutes		Touched By An Angel		CBS Sunday Movie				CBS
N	BIG DEAL		The Simpsons	Ned And Stacey	The X Files		local		FOX
	Dateline NBC		3rd Rock From The Sun	Boston Common	NBC Sunday Night Movie				NBC
	local								UPN
	Kirk	Brotherly Love	The Parent 'Hood	THE STEVE HARVEY SHOW	Unhappily Ever After	LIFE WITH ROGER	local		WB

MTV's *Daria* effectively skewered both teens and adults for five seasons. The brainy but sardonic Daria Morgendorffer (*right*, voiced by Tracy Grandstaff) and her best friend, Jayne Lane (voiced by Wendy Hoopes) in class at Lawndale High School. *(Viacom International Inc. © 2003. All Rights Reserved.)*

Everything was a target, from high school teachers obsessed with political correctness to parents who were hopelessly clueless about life in this "Sick, Sad World" (Daria's favorite tabloid television feature).

The distinction of having cable's most controversial cartoon series passed, in August 1997, from MTV's *Beavis and Butt-head* to Comedy Central's *South Park,* which focused on four trash-mouthed third graders in the small Colorado mountain town of South Park. Created by Trey Parker and Matthew Stone (who also supplied the voices for many of the show's characters), the series was rated TV-M (for "mature" viewers) under the newly devised TV ratings system, due to its blasphemous, juvenile, mean-spirited (yet daring) tone that took aim at preachy know-it-alls of every political stance (for example, mocking both gun enthusiasts and gun control advocates). The artwork was deliberately basic (just a step above construction paper cut-outs) and the animated movements were simple, yet the satiric jabs were sharp and the imagery incongruous (such as a mountain creature with a leg that looked like actor Patrick Duffy). Embracing cartoon violence itself as a running joke, *South Park* killed one of the kids (Kenny) in virtually every episode, only to bring him back in the next story to be killed again. At the same time *South Park* made its debut, cable also reinforced its solid hold on more traditional kid-oriented animation as Nickelodeon unveiled the first new *Rugrats* episodes in four years. Reruns of the series' original seventy shows had been cable's top-rated program in 1996.

Cable's news and talk services found covering the 1996 presidential campaign the perfect way to showcase their own programming, though the contest between Bob Dole and incumbent Bill Clinton was a fairly dull affair (Clinton's reelection was never really in doubt). CNN had its fourteen-year-old *Crossfire* (liberals and conservatives arguing the issues) as well as the long-running Larry King (who frequently welcomed Ross Perot, who was again running for president, but on a third-party ticket). On CNBC, Chris Matthews conducted confrontational interviews on his new series, *Hardball*, while Mary Matalin (a former aide to George Bush) and Dee Dee Myers (a former press secretary for Bill Clinton) picked apart both sides on the three-year-old *Equal Time.*

On October 7, 1996, CNN and MSNBC got a new competitor in the cable news battle when Fox unveiled its all-news cable service, Fox News Channel. Under the stewardship of former Nixon and Reagan media advisor Roger Ailes (who previously had served as president of NBC's cable channels CNBC and America's Talking), Fox News displayed the company's trademark "attitude" with its self-defining mottos "Information without Opinion—News without Bias" and "We report. You decide." For prestige, the channel signed up respected ABC newsman Brit Hume as one of its lead anchors. Its biggest draws, however, ended up being strongly opinioned conservative-oriented talk segments, such as those hosted by Bill O'Reilly.

Comedy Central enthusiastically jumped into daily news coverage with *The Daily Show* (featuring Greg Kilborn), which followed real-life news events with a comically critical take. As a send-up of the many talk shows featuring debates by representatives "from the left and from the right," the program had liberal Al Franken and conservative Arianna Huffington hold their on-camera discussions dressed in pajamas and sharing a bed together.

One of Comedy Central's long-running series, *Mystery Science Theater 3000,* was canceled in 1996 after seven years, but then the program was picked up by the Sci-Fi Network for the fall of 1997.

September 4, 1996

Changing Rooms. (BBC-2). Two households swap redecorating opportunities on a set budget and, over two days with cameras rolling, both redo a selected room in the other's residence. The twist: Neither sees the other's handiwork until it is completed and unveiled to them on camera. This premise comes to the U.S. in October 2000 as *Trading Spaces* on cable's The Learning Channel.

October 10, 1996

Time Warner closes on its $6.5 billion acquisition of Turner Broadcasting System, creating the world's largest media company. Original cable maverick entrepreneur Ted Turner loses his independence and becomes Time Warner's vice chairman, under Chairman Gerald Levin.

October 20, 1996

The World Series airs on Fox for the first time, as the Atlanta Braves beat the New York Yankees 12 to 1 in the opening game of the fall classic.

October 29, 1996

Peter Chernin, Fox programming boss from 1989 to 1992 and lately head of Fox's film empire, is named president and chief operating officer of News Corporation, the number two man behind Rupert Murdoch.

November 1, 1996

Fox's latest cable venture, Fox Sports Net, is born as the network takes over several regional sports networks and begins to run them under the Fox name.

November 23, 1996

"Bob Hope: Laughing with the Presidents." (NBC). The 285th and final prime time TV special for NBC (Hope's network since 1935). The frail ninety-three-year old comedian recalls his associations with all the U.S. presidents from Franklin Roosevelt to Bill Clinton.

December 31, 1996

Westinghouse/CBS closes its $5 billion acquisition of Infinity Broadcasting Corp., one of the country's largest radio station groups. Infinity's chairman, Mel Karmazin, becomes head of Westinghouse's radio division and a significant Westinghouse stockholder. Due to the easing of radio ownership regulations from the Telecommunications Act of 1996, Westinghouse was previously able to add CBS's 21 radio O&Os to its 18 stations. Now, with Infinity's 44 stations, the conglomerate owns 83 radio stations, the most in the country. As a result of the acquisition, the CBS Radio Network is put under Infinity's control. Infinity appoints Westwood One to manage and operate CBS Radio.

The premise was an appropriate fit: a human imprisoned on a space satellite as part of an experiment, and forced to watch awful old films (such as "Attack of the The Eye Creatures" [*sic*] and "Manos, the Hands of Fate"). To help him keep his sanity, he built several robot companions from scrap, and they joined him in offering sarcastic comments about each movie as it played. Also taking aim at science fiction fans, Showtime offered its third season of new episodes of *The Outer Limits* and, in the summer of 1997, added an original space adventure series, *Stargate SG-1* (starring Richard Dean Anderson and based on a 1994 theatrical film with Kurt Russell), with characters traveling the universe simply by stepping through a stargate/wormhole "doorway."

The USA Network aggressively pursued new episodes of hour-long action and adventure series, picking them from a variety of sources. *Silk Stalkings* (crimes of passion in tony Palm Beach, Florida) had started in 1991 as a co-production with CBS that aired both on USA and in CBS's *Crimetime After Primetime* lineup until 1993, when CBS dropped the show and it began to air exclusively on cable. *Renegade* (a rebel cop on the run after being framed for murder) had begun in 1992 in first-run syndication, but moved to USA for the fall of 1996. USA's new *Pacific Blue* (cops on bicycles in California) and *The Big Easy* (jazzy cops in New Orleans) also began in the fall of 1996. In January 1997, USA introduced one of its most successful original series, *La Femme Nikita*, based on a 1990 French theatrical film (remade in the U.S. in 1993 as "Point of No Return"). Peta Wilson played Nikita, a young woman framed for murder and then sprung from jail by Section, an international counter-terrorist organization that offered her a take-it-or-leave-it deal: Work as one of its agents, or die. Nikita chose to live and proved to be a superbly effective operative, but she constantly looked for ways to escape her situation, keenly aware that Section's ruthless techniques were often little better than those of the people they fought. The series was simultaneously high-tech, darkly atmospheric, conspiratorial, violent, and sexually charged, particularly in the relationship between the leather-clad Nikita and fellow operative Michael Samuelle (Roy Dupuis). The two became lovers in the second season, and throughout its run *La Femme Nikita* remained a centerpiece of USA's stable of action series.

Having mom and dad (and an older brother) just next door provided *Everybody Loves Raymond* with comedy situations that were strikingly authentic and believable. The cast, *from left*: Ray Romano, Brad Garrett, Doris Roberts, Peter Boyle, and Patricia Heaton. (CBS Photo Archive © 2003 CBS Worldwide, Inc. All Rights Reserved/Photo by Monty Brinton)

In addition to their growing lineups of original programs, the cable channels also were saturated with reruns of series that had first played on the broadcast networks, benefiting from viewer familiarity with those shows. In some cases, there were still new episodes on the networks when the reruns began playing on cable, including such series as ABC's *America's Funniest Home Videos* (rerun on superstation WTBS), Fox's *Melrose Place* (rerun on E!), and NBC's *Law & Order* (rerun on A&E) and *Homicide: Life on the Street* (rerun on Lifetime). Mostly, though, cable now served as a comfortable rerun home for selected series from every corner of broadcasting's past, including first-run syndication. Some titles were familiar (the entire Nick at Nite and TV Land schedules), and some obscure (the Sci-Fi Network's lineup of ABC's maverick *Max Headroom*, CBS's *Flash*, and the syndicated *RoboCop*). Some filled a well-defined niche. A&E's reruns of mystery series drew not only from the commercial networks (with such hits as *Columbo* and *Quincy, M.E.*), but also snatched some of PBS's most popular *Mystery!* series such as the British productions featuring various Agatha Christie characters and *The Adventures of Sherlock Holmes* (starring Jeremy Brett). A&E also landed first U.S. runs of other British sleuths such as *Cracker* (starring Robbie Coltrane), which, prior to cable, would have been practically an automatic addition to PBS. Even the two most popular syndicated series on the current broadcast schedule, *Hercules: The Legendary Journeys* and *Xena: Warrior Princess* (with Kevin Sorbo and Lucy Lawless in the respective title roles, and both from *American Gothic* producers Sam Raimi and Rob Tapert), eventually aired reruns on cable (USA) while continuing first-run episodes in syndication.

This, then, was the competitive backdrop to the 1996–97 season, with enough full-fledged, high quality offerings throughout the cable spectrum to satisfy a casual channel surfer. Collectively, the broadcast networks still reached the most people, and, as usual, press write-ups about the September premieres focused on their new programs. Now, however, the broadcasters' task in selling themselves was much more difficult and the audiences for particular shows (especially new offerings) were far more elusive. It was not surprising, then, that for the 1996–97 season, ratings for the broadcasting Big 3 (ABC, CBS, and NBC) were off 22% from just three years before. Though NBC easily won the season (thanks to *ER*, *Seinfeld*, and *Friends*), it was the lowest-rated seasonal victory to that point. Winning the broadcast ratings crown was still important, but that was now just one aspect of successfully competing in a multi-channel world. The networks were no longer competing just among themselves. For each of them, it was more important than ever to clearly define their image, to find the programming with the greatest chance of attracting their target audience, and to keep a close watch on the bottom-line budget.

To those ends, recognizable names or familiar formats seemed vital. CBS landed two former *Cheers* stars as sitcom leads (Ted Danson in *INK* and Rhea Perlman in *Pearl*), but neither series ever quite gelled. As a sign of the increasing cost-consciousness among the networks, CBS went to great lengths tinkering with *INK*, scrapping several filmed episodes, changing producers, and delaying the premiere. Though this was a costly process, it was still less expensive to rework the material in the hope of saving it rather than to pull the plug and start over in the development process. There was even some reworking involved in the return of one of the biggest names in sitcoms, the godfather of "Must See TV," Bill Cosby. While his new program for CBS, *Cosby*, reunited him with his *Cosby Show* producers Marcy Carsey and Tom Werner, it was only at the last minute that they added former co-star Phylicia Rashad to once again play Cosby's wife, replacing the previously cast Telma Hopkins. That was a perfect bit of recasting and, as a result, the new series immediately felt familiar and comfortable. This could well have been Cliff and Claire (their *Cosby Show* characters), older and a little less wealthy, but together after the children had grown, still loving each other. In fact, though, it was a "new" premise, based on a 1990 British hit, *One Foot in the Grave*, with Cosby as a sixty-year-old airline worker forced into early retirement when his company downsized. Though the series was not a groundbreaking big hit, it did deliver consistent ratings for CBS. It was also a distinctive contrast to the urban single twenty-somethings of *Seinfeld, Friends*, and their many derivative copies. Though CBS still enviously eyed the lucrative 18 to 49 age demographic, the network could not afford to ignore the types of programs that still did well among its older viewers.

January 1, 1997
Faced with the threat of government-imposed ratings, the broadcasting industry institutes TV's first ratings system for content, with two sets of categories: one for shows aimed at children (TVY, for children of all ages; TVY7, for those over seven) and one for other entertainment shows (TVG, for general audiences; TVPG, for when parental guidance is suggested; TV14, for children over fourteen; and TVM, for those over seventeen, when there is mature content).

January 6, 1997
Three years after joining *Today* as its news reader, Matt Lauer is promoted to co-host (with Katie Couric), replacing Bryant Gumbel (a fifteen-year veteran of the show).

January 26, 1997
The Super Bowl airs on Fox for the first time, as the Green Bay Packers beat the New England Patriots 35 to 21 in New Orleans.

February 14, 1997
NBC launches *Homicide: Second Shift* on its NBC.com website, an "alternate" version of the *Homicide* series running in prime time. The online version follows a different set of detectives who come to work after the TV characters have gone home. Stories are told with text, photos, voices, and sound effects and are updated regularly, even through the summer while the TV series is off the air.

March 24, 1997
In the commercial launch of the DVD (digital video disc) system in the U.S., Panasonic unveils ads for its DVD players on TV's coverage of the Oscar awards, and several movie studios release film titles in the DVD format.

March 31, 1997
Three years after ABC, NBC, and Fox created new cable networks in order to resolve the "retransmission consent" dispute with cable systems, CBS at last tries to do the same by launching its Eye on People cable network.

April 30, 1997
On a heavily promoted episode of ABC's three-year-old sitcom *Ellen,* the character of Ellen Morgan (Ellen DeGeneres) publicly "comes out" as a lesbian to guest star Laura Dern. This revelation dovetails with the real-life acknowledgment by DeGeneres herself that she is gay.

August 7, 1997
Leslie Moonves, CBS's programming chief, is promoted to the post of president of CBS Television.

In that same vein, CBS also slotted *Everybody Loves Raymond* (produced by David Letterman's company), a warm family comedy featuring stand-up comic Ray Romano as a happily married newspaper sports reporter with three children. They lived on Long Island, across the street from Ray's parents, Frank and Marie (Peter Boyle and Doris Roberts), and his divorced older brother, Robert (Brad Garrett). Even though Robert had moved back in with mom and dad, he knew baby brother Ray was first in their affection ("Everybody loves Raymond," he deadpanned in the opening credits). Frank and Marie were shameless about constantly dropping in at Ray's house, much to the exasperation of his wife, Debra (Patricia Heaton), but Ray could never quite manage to turn them away. After all, it was mom and dad! The series effectively mined this back-to-the-basics domestic set-up for years, eventually becoming one of CBS's most successful comedies of the era.

The network also took a step back from its unsuccessful Sunday night coupling of brassy comedies after *60 Minutes* and instead moved in *Touched by an Angel* (in its third season), which was more akin to the previously displaced *Murder, She Wrote*. The uplifting series found a welcoming audience and once again won the time slot. Still, CBS had not given up on trying to find cutting-edge series aimed at a more hip audience. In October, the network launched the dark crime drama *EZ Streets*, starring Ken Olin as an undercover cop enmeshed in a deadly and duplicitous underworld setting. Unfortunately, the complex plot threads and character relationships were almost impossible to follow, even using the program's flashy online website, so CBS pulled the series after only two episodes. (It returned briefly and unsuccessfully the following spring.) Despite its best efforts, CBS just could not break from its more traditional programming image.

NBC was clearly defined by its biggest hits, which were also the top shows on television. *ER* was its lynchpin drama, but the gritty court and cop stories of *Law & Order* and *Homicide: Life on the Street* attracted a faithful following (if lower ratings), occasionally doing crossover episodes with each other. On Saturdays, the network tried to branch out into new areas, as it introduced a block of three dramas with themes straight out of *The X-Files*: *Dark Skies* (alien invaders), *Profiler* (solving murders with paranormal powers), and *The Pretender* (a maverick genius helping ordinary people while fleeing a top-secret government agency).

On the comedy side, NBC continued to follow its self-imposed comedy model for the Thursday night slots between *Friends, Seinfeld,* and *ER*: It kept airing programs involving groups of young urban characters amid plenty of sexual references. *Suddenly Susan* ventured to San Francisco with Brooke Shields as a single woman who left her groom-to-be at the altar (just like Rachel on *Friends*) before going to work for a local magazine run by the groom's brother (played by Judd Nelson). Midseason, the network brought two performers from ABC and stuck them with even more limited formulas. In *Fired Up*, Sharon Lawrence (from *NYPD Blue*) played a New York public relations maven who moved into the loft of her former assistant (played by Leah Remini) after both had been fired. With *The Naked Truth*, NBC took what had been a silly but amusing ABC vehicle for Téa Leoni (she played a star-chasing tabloid photographer-reporter) and recast it as yet another "friends at an office" comedy. Like their predecessors in these Thursday night slots, all three ended the season ranked in the top ten, but with considerable doubt about their ability to survive on their own. This was a major concern for the network because, even with seven of the season's top ten hits, its overall ratings went down 10% for the season.

Yet it was ABC that experienced the greatest ratings drop among the Big 3 broadcasters with only *Monday Night Football*

and *Home Improvement* in the season's top ten. Numbers were down significantly for its shows throughout the week, Numbers were down significantly for its shows throughout the week, including *Grace Under Fire* and *Roseanne*. In what was touted as *Roseanne*'s final season, the storyline began with the Connor family winning $100 million in the state lottery. Though that was certainly a common blue collar dream ripe for comedy, the resulting "life among the rich and famous" complications often seemed like they belonged on a different show, leaving long-time viewers puzzled. Not surprisingly, in the May 1997 season (and series) finale, the lottery plot was explained away as part of a complicated fantasy that essentially rewrote storylines and character traits from the entire series. In her final soliloquy, Roseanne explained what really happened to each character, providing her the last word on her series, which had been one of the bedrocks of ABC's schedule for nearly a decade.

With fewer successful veteran series, ABC had limited opportunities to help new shows with a powerful lead-in. *Home Improvement* did boost the reunion of Michael J. Fox and producer Gary David Goldberg in *Spin City*, a smart snapshot of New York life as seen from the mayor's office. In late night, ABC was able to use *Nightline* as the lead-in to *Politically Incorrect* (an irreverent topical discussion show hosted by Bill Maher), which the network brought over after a three-year cable run on Comedy Central. Back in prime time, Melissa Joan Hart, another cable performer, comfortably slipped into the schedule as part of ABC's TGIF Friday lineup. She went from three years of playing an energetic high school student on Nickelodeon's *Clarissa Explains It All* to playing a *magically endowed* energetic high school student on *Sabrina, the Teenage Witch* (based on the Archie comic book character), aided by her two loving aunts (played by Caroline Rhea and Beth Broderick) and Salem, a talking black cat.

Beyond the Big 3 broadcasters, Fox had the clearest vision and most distinctive image. It registered an increase in ratings for the year as it moved *The X-Files* to Sunday, joining *The Simpsons* and (mid-season) *King of the Hill*, a sharp new animated domestic comedy from *Beavis and Butt-head* creator Mike Judge. UPN still had its mix of action and adventure series (built around *Star Trek: Voyager*), but, following the success of *Moesha*, also began embracing programs featuring black characters. As a result, the UPN schedule included *Malcolm and Eddie, In the House, Sparks, Good News, Goode Behavior*, and a lame *Star Trek* parody, *Homeboys in Outer Space*. Both the WB and Fox previously had discovered this programming niche and their schedules featured (on the WB) *The Steve Harvey Show, Jamie Foxx, The Wayans Bros., The Smart Guy,* and *Sister, Sister* and (on Fox) *Martin, Living Single,* and *New York Undercover*. While this change was a commendable development in expanding diversity within the television lineup, it was less altruism than calculated counter-programming, filling in gaps left by the "major networks." That meant such urban-oriented shows (as they were dubbed) could easily fade when some other new programming fad came along.

That's just what was happening on the WB, which was finding its defining voice that season from two new series that, at first glance, seemed to be diametrically different: *7th Heaven* and *Buffy the Vampire Slayer*. *7th Heaven* (from veteran producer Aaron Spelling) was a wholesome family drama set in suburban Los Angeles, focusing on a strongly spiritual family led by the Reverend Eric Camden (Stephen Collins) and his wife, Annie (Catherine Hicks). They were loving parents and, as community leaders with five children, inevitably faced the contemporary issues of the day (such as drugs and teen pregnancy), yet never came off as pedantic or preachy. More important, though, the series sympathetically

With its smart dialogue and strong sense of character, *Buffy the Vampire Slayer* set the standard for a new generation of teen drama series. Buffy (Sarah Michelle Gellar) and her vampire lover, Angel (David Boreanaz). (Buffy the Vampire Slayer © 1997 Twentieth Century Fox Television. All Rights Reserved.)

barely one step from expulsion from school. Even Buffy's mom, Joyce (Kristine Sutherland), wondered why her daughter did not spend more time on homework and school spirit activities.

Fortunately, Buffy was not alone in her battles. After classes, she trained under the tutelage of Rupert Giles (Anthony Stewart Head), her mystic Watcher who also served as the school's librarian. The library was the perfect place for such training as well as for strategy sessions against the latest evil forces, because there was little chance any student would ever stop by looking for books. Most important, in her battles Buffy was backed by her classmates, Xander Harris (Nicholas Brendon), who was in love with Buffy, and Willow Rosenberg (Alyson Hannigan), who was in love with Xander. Though Xander was somewhat athletic and Willow was a computer whiz, all three were dismissed by the high school "in crowd," so taking on life-threatening situations seemed a perfectly acceptable way of hanging out together. Oddly, one of the most popular girls at the school, Cordelia Chase (Charisma Carpenter), frequently ended up drawn into their adventures as well. Over time, Buffy's support circle also included Oz (Seth Green), a teen werewolf who played guitar for a local band; Anya (Emma Caulfield), a one-time vengeance demon stuck in Sunnydale as a 1,100-year-old teenage girl; Tara (Amber Benson), a shy teen who dabbled in magic; and Dawn (Michelle Trachtenberg), Buffy's magically conjured fourteen-year-old sister. Informally, they were known as the Scooby Gang (a.k.a. the Scoobies), a reference to the crime-fighting kids who accompanied the title character canine in the 1970s animated series *Scooby-Doo*.

Buffy also developed complicated relationships with a pair of vampires, starting with Angel (David Boreanaz), a "good" vampire (he had a soul) who instantly won her heart. Angel was a true teen heartthrob, the embodiment of temptation: handsome and sexy, but forbidden (after all, Buffy was supposed to destroy vampires, not take one as her first lover). Later (when Angel went to his own spinoff show), Buffy became involved with "bad boy" Spike (James Marsters), a rakish vampire with a poet's heart and a wicked tongue, who was successively her foe, friend, and lover. Occasionally another Slayer, Faith (Eliza Dushku), showed up in Sunnydale. Streetsmart but impulsive, she was sometimes an ally to Buffy, other times a foe.

The cast fit very comfortably into these fantasy roles, aided by first-rate make-up, fight choreography, and special effects. The true heart of the series, though, was its writing. Each season was carefully constructed so that most episodes were self-contained and could stand alone, yet they also incorporated continuing elements that advanced character development without turning the series into pure soap opera. Equally important, the individual scripts were a wonderfully balanced mix of adventure and humor. There was a savvy awareness of storytelling conventions and genre expectations, and the dialogue was filled with clever allusions and self-effacing wordplay. The cast played these elements perfectly and made *Buffy the Vampire Slayer* truly fun to watch.

Above all, though, *Buffy* consistently stayed true to its central theme: the difficulty of growing up, going from the innocent confusion of high school to the more complex mystery of college to the even more imposing challenge of constructing lives as young adults. At each stage, there were intense moments of love, friendship, excitement, and deep disappointment—emotions that teens could readily understand.

Buffy the Vampire Slayer and *7th Heaven* offered the WB a readymade formula roadmap for connecting with a highly desirable teen audience, especially young women. In the increasingly fragmented world of television choice, that was like a personal message from God, impossible to ignore.

focused on the concerns of the kids, especially teenage brother Matt (Barry Watson) and sister Mary (Jessica Biel), taking their growing-up problems very seriously.

Mid-season entry *Buffy the Vampire Slayer* was a fantasy adventure, based on a 1992 feature film (written by Joss Whedon and starring Kristy Swanson, Luke Perry, and Donald Sutherland). Adapting the concept to a TV series could have been just another attempt to draw the *X-Files* crowd with scary monsters, but Whedon (serving as producer) made *Buffy* first and foremost about growing up and trying to fit in, from high school to young adulthood. Buffy Summers (Sarah Michelle Gellar) was the ultimate misunderstood teen, a high school sophomore transfer student who happened to be "the chosen one," a human born with incredible strength and reflexes, whose task as the Slayer was to dispatch vampires, demons, and other powerful forces of evil. There was no shortage of those because Buffy's new hometown of Sunnydale, California, happened to be located over the Hellmouth, a cosmic nexus of evil carving a subterranean path directly to hell. Consequently, Buffy was constantly (but secretly) saving the town, the world, and the universe from some foreboding doom. Nonetheless, that never stopped oblivious adults, especially school principal Snyder (Armin Shimerman), from labeling her a troublemaker

58. Devil with the Blue Dress On

TELEVISION HAD ALWAYS LOVED the story of Lady Diana Spencer. On July 29, 1981, she had, at age twenty, married Charles, Prince of Wales, heir to the British crown. Despite the trans-Atlantic time difference, millions of U.S. viewers had tuned in that day to the early, early morning live network coverage of their wedding at St. Paul's Cathedral in London, as Spencer officially became Her Royal Highness, Princess Diana. Correspondents gushed over every detail of the ceremony, which was cast as a modern-day fairy tale, with the prince and princess shown riding off in a gilded carriage presumably to live happily ever after. Subsequently, Diana proved to be a charismatic media personality whose every move was followed by the press, from the birth of two children (princes William and Harry) to appearances on behalf of a variety of charitable causes.

Over time, the reality of the marriage between Charles and Diana ended up closer to the grist of confessional daytime television talk shows. There were tales of personal unhappiness; family pressures (Diana's mother-in-law *was* the Queen of England); Diana suffering from bulimia; and Charles secretly pursuing the "true love of his life," Camilla Parker Bowles (also married at the time). All this led the pair first to a separation (in December 1992), then to a formal divorce (in August 1996). Yet Diana remained a much-loved celebrity, with her storybook-tale-gone-sour viewed as something with which fans could empathize, even after she confessed her own dalliances in a BBC interview. Though with the divorce Diana's title-by-marriage was gone, she departed the royal household with a $26 million settlement and soon resumed a more limited public profile, supporting such causes as the abolition of anti-personnel landmines. The press, however, continued to treat Diana as the ultimate media celebrity and hordes of photographers (referred to as the "paparazzi") constantly followed her everywhere, hoping to capture a private moment, especially if she found her new Prince Charming. When she was a member of the British royalty, being a celebrity had been part of her job but when she became a wealthy private citizen, she welcomed such constant coverage only when it helped her to promote a cause. Otherwise, she regarded it increasingly as an intrusive nuisance to be avoided if possible. Shortly after midnight (Paris time) on Sunday, August 31, 1997, Diana and her companion, forty-one-year-old millionaire Dodi Fayed, attempted to evade the paparazzi after a late gathering by being whisked away in their luxury car. That high-speed flight ended in a terrible accident (the vehicle hit a concrete divider in a tunnel) that left Diana, Fayed, and chauffeur Henri Paul dead.

The story broke overnight and, by Sunday morning U.S. time, television coverage was practically non-stop. There was a genuine outpouring of emotion from fans gathered outside London's Kensington Palace (Diana's former home) who left flowers, toys, and other tributes. Because Diana had been an international public figure for more than a decade, everybody had archival footage. There was also no shortage of friends, associates, and self-proclaimed experts available for interviews and commentary. Coverage continued throughout the week, leading up to the funeral service the following Saturday (September 6) in London, with news anchors Tom Brokaw, Peter Jennings, and Dan Rather among those on location. During the intervening week, the broadcast networks had quickly created instant prime time specials and devoted major portions of their news magazines to the story, including ABC's *PrimeTime Live*, NBC's *Dateline*, and CBS's *48 Hours* and *60 Minutes*. All scored impressive ratings. Naturally, the all-news cable channels embraced the Diana story with continuous coverage and specials. CNN more than tripled its daily viewer totals during the first few days. For the funeral itself, the fledgling Fox News Channel touted eight hours of commercial-free coverage, while A&E, Lifetime, E! Entertainment Television, and even C-SPAN joined in with a combination of live reports and taped replays.

Apart from some background stories on the car accident itself, there was no hard news, per se, over these hundreds of hours. Instead, though Diana was no longer Her Royal Highness when she died, the coverage was akin to reporting on the passing of a head of state, only it went far beyond what might have accompanied the death of an actual world leader. Television lingered for hours over every image, in effect honoring what it understood best: being a celebrity. The only pause came the morning of the funeral itself, when, in a moment of cosmic irony, news broke of the death of another much-admired woman, Mother Teresa. After a week of extolling Diana and her well-publicized exploits, anchors covering the lavish funeral ceremonies found themselves awkwardly searching for any remaining superlatives they could use for the eighty-seven-year-old Albanian-born nun who had renounced material possessions while helping the poor (chiefly in India) and traveling the world lobbying for human rights. In the end, both women were honored that day as different sorts of modern media celebrities, though Diana remained the top story.

Coverage of Diana's death allowed viewers a vicarious connection to a sad and accessible human-interest story. This was news as popular entertainment, but without the controversy of something like the O. J. Simpson investigation and trial. After the ratings bonanza of the O. J. Simpson trial, though, news organizations had seen that celebrity/tabloid-style stories were likely to generate higher viewing numbers and, consequently, higher ad rates. This, in theory, helped pay the costs of overall news operations, which could be very expensive in pursuit of far less sexy matters. The troubling question that remained was: Given the choice between a legitimate news story and a tabloid tale, which would win out?

In January 1998, television had the chance to show its commitment to covering an important political, religious, and cultural story when Pope John Paul II made a historic trip to the communist country of Cuba, meeting its leader, Fidel Castro. In preparation for the five-day visit (January 21–25), the networks and their news anchors descended upon the country, ready to transmit their news programs from Cuba throughout the visit. Setting up this coverage involved huge costs because the networks did not have full ongoing operations in Cuba. Yet despite their investment in the story, the networks practically abandoned their coverage after only one day. Instead, the lead anchors quickly headed back to the U.S. There, reports of a scandal surrounding the president of the United States had suddenly erupted. And this scandal involved sex.

Stories about Bill Clinton and his alleged extra-marital sexual escapades had circulated in the media since his first campaign for the U.S. presidency in 1992, but those incidents generally had been presented as vaguely acknowledged past indiscretions that were considered well behind him. Nonetheless, this past reputation continued to dog him as president, and not just as fodder for late night talk show jokes. In 1997, a U.S. Supreme Court ruling allowed Paula Jones, a former Arkansas state employee, to proceed with a sexual harassment suit against Clinton (concerning events during his days as Arkansas governor). That ruling required him to deal with accompanying legal procedures, including a deposition under oath that raised questions about his possible sexual relations with other women. It was here that Clinton's travails with Paula Jones intersected another on-going investigation, that of federal special prosecutor Kenneth Starr.

Back in 1994, Starr's office had been created and authorized to look into charges associated with Whitewater, a complicated land-development deal also from Clinton's Arkansas days. The inquiry had quickly expanded into a virtual dragnet of allegations into other areas (often raised by political critics), including some actions during Clinton's time as president. Investigations into every one of those proved inconclusive against Clinton. However, as the Jones case moved forward, Starr added aspects of that claim to his inquiry. By January 1998, Starr's attention was focused on twenty-four-year-old Monica Lewinsky, who had been an intern at the White House in 1995. Starr had reason to believe that Lewinsky had an affair with Bill Clinton at that time, and that the president may have lied about that fact under oath in his Paula Jones deposition. Further, Starr suspected Clinton might have pressured Lewinsky (who had also given a sworn deposition in the Jones case) to lie about it. Though it would be virtually impossible for Starr to build a case around just the affair itself (even if true), if Clinton had lied about it under oath, that would be perjury. If he had asked Lewinsky to lie about it, that would be subornation of perjury and obstruction of justice. If these could be proved, then Starr would at last have the basis for legal charges against the president.

At first, all of this took place out of the immediate public eye, but unconfirmed rumors began to circulate, starting at the Internet site of Matt Drudge on January 18. The story percolated over the next few days and broke into the mainstream media early on January 21. Driven by a mixture of public disbelief, anger, and outrage, the story was immediately sucked into the twenty-four-hour news cycle and its echo chamber of online discussions, talk radio call-ins, and television reports (which had drawn the networks from their coverage of the pope in Cuba). President Clinton chose to discuss the matter on January 21 in previously scheduled interviews on National Public Radio and on PBS's *NewsHour* (a program which continued to treat the pope's Cuban visit as its lead story). Clinton told *NewsHour* anchor Jim Lehrer, "I didn't ask anybody not to tell the truth. There is no improper relationship." Clinton was even more direct five days later (January 26) at a White House event. There he looked directly into the television cameras and, in the defining moment of the crisis for viewers, defiantly declared: "I want to say one thing to the American people. I want you to listen to me. I'm going to say this again. I did not have sexual relations with that woman, Miss Lewinsky."

For the moment, Clinton then left any further discussion of the

The day the Monica Lewinsky story broke, President Clinton still went ahead with a scheduled interview on *The NewsHour with Jim Lehrer* and used the opportunity to assert, "There is no improper relationship." *(Courtesy of MacNeil-Lehrer Productions)*

	8:00	8:30	9:00	9:30	10:00	10:30	
MON	TIMECOP		ABC NFL Monday Night Football (to 12 Midnight)				ABC
	Cosby	Everybody Loves Raymond	Cybill	GEORGE & LEO	BROOKLYN SOUTH		CBS
	Melrose Place		ALLY McBEAL		local		FOX
	Suddenly Susan	Fired Up	Caroline In The City	The Naked Truth	Dateline NBC		NBC
	In The House	Malcolm & Eddie	GOOD NEWS	Sparks	local		UPN
	7th Heaven		Buffy The Vampire Slayer		local		WB
TUE	Soul Man	OVER THE TOP	Home Improvement	HILLER AND DILLER	NYPD Blue		ABC
	JAG		MICHAEL HAYES		DELLAVENTURA		CBS
	Fox Tuesday Night Movie				local		FOX
	Mad About You	Newsradio	Frasier	Just Shoot Me	Dateline NBC		NBC
	Clueless	Moesha	HITZ	HEAD OVER HEELS	local		UPN
	local						WB
WED	Spin City	DHARMA & GREG	The Drew Carey Show	Ellen	Prime Time Live		ABC
	The Nanny	Murphy Brown	PUBLIC EYE WITH BRYANT GUMBEL		Chicago Hope		CBS
	Beverly Hills, 90210		Party Of Five		local		FOX
	THE TONY DANZA SHOW	BUILT TO LAST	3rd Rock From The Sun	WORKING	Law & Order		NBC
	The Sentinel		Star Trek: Voyager		local		UPN
	Sister, Sister	Smart Guy	The Wayans Bros.	The Steve Harvey Show	local		WB
THR	NOTHING SACRED		CRACKER		20/20		ABC
	Promised Land		Diagnosis Murder		48 Hours		CBS
	Living Single	BETWEEN BROTHERS	413 HOPE ST.		local		FOX
	Friends	UNION SQUARE	Seinfeld	VERONICA'S CLOSET	ER		NBC
	local						UPN
	local						WB
FRI	Sabrina, The Teenage Witch	Boy Meets World	YOU WISH	TEEN ANGEL	20/20		ABC
	Family Matters	MEEGO	THE GREGORY HINES SHOW	Step By Step	Nash Bridges		CBS
	THE VISITOR		Millennium		local		FOX
	PLAYERS		Dateline NBC		Homicide: Life On The Street		NBC
	local						UPN
	local						WB
SAT	C-16		TOTAL SECURITY		The Practice		ABC
	Dr. Quinn, Medicine Woman		Early Edition		Walker, Texas Ranger		CBS
	Cops	Cops	America's Most Wanted: America Fights Back		local		FOX
	The Pretender		SLEEPWALKERS		Profiler		NBC
	local						UPN
	local						WB

	7:00	7:30	8:00	8:30	9:00	9:30	10:00	10:30	
SUN	The Wonderful World Of Disney				ABC Sunday Night Movie				ABC
	60 Minutes		Touched By An Angel		CBS Sunday Movie				CBS
	THE WORLD'S FUNNIEST!		The Simpsons	King Of The Hill	The X Files		local		FOX
	Dateline NBC		Men Behaving Badly	JENNY	NBC Sunday Night Movie				NBC
	local								UPN
	Nick Freno: Licensed Teacher	The Parent 'Hood	The Jamie Foxx Show	Unhappily Ever After	THE TOM SHOW	ALRIGHT ALREADY	local		WB

topic to his lawyers and associates. The twenty-four-hour cable services lovingly embraced the story, which was the perfect melding of high-minded journalism and tabloid scandal. There was a very serious central issue. If the president of the United States had committed perjury and asked someone else to do the same, should he be impeached and removed from office? At the same time, it was hard to avoid the undercurrent of sensationalism. Despite the constitutional rhetoric, was this in reality all about sex? Was it simply being exploited by Clinton's political adversaries to sully his image? Did it matter if the subject of the perjury charge was a personal matter, far removed from the president's official duties? Would the country's news organizations have rushed to cover this as a crisis if the possible perjury had been regarding some arcane aspect of the Whitewater land deal? When anchors and correspondents repeatedly warned viewers they were about to hear something potentially shocking and offensive (describing the alleged sexual activity), was that also just as much a promotional tease?

Geraldo Rivera (on CNBC) offered the most spirited defense of Clinton on his nightly cable talk show, while other commentators such as radio's Rush Limbaugh were equally strong in their criticism. Across the dial, guests defending or criticizing the president inevitably followed party lines. As the story continued to unfold, it became entangled in a bizarre examination of exactly what type of activities Clinton had engaged in with Lewinsky, and whether these constituted "sexual relations." Lewinsky wound up testifying about her version of their "affair," but it all might have remained an unresolved "he said/she said" exchange except that she also turned over to the special prosecutor a blue dress she had worn during one of her private sessions with the president. After the FBI analyzed the dress, it confirmed that the DNA in the dress's telltale semen stain matched President Clinton's DNA.

Faced with this evidence, Clinton agreed to submit to closed-door questioning from Starr's office before a grand jury. Through four and one-half hours of a videotaped session at the White House on August 17, 1998, the president continued to insist that, technically, he had never lied under oath about his relationship with Lewinsky, taking an extremely limited reading of exactly what constituted a "sexual relationship." That evening, Clinton faced a much larger audience. In a tense, nationally televised address, he spoke uncomfortably again about his relationship with Monica Lewinsky, at greater length than he had seven months earlier. Contradicting his previous unequivocal denial, Clinton acknowledged, "I did have a relationship with Miss Lewinsky that was not appropriate. In fact, it was wrong." He also firmly insisted that the entire matter was, at heart, a family crisis to be faced by him with his wife and daughter and that, "It's nobody's business but ours. Even presidents have private lives."

If the story of Bill Clinton, his family, and Monica Lewinsky had been a fictional made-for-TV movie, the script could have ended there. His two public statements would have served as bookends to a straightforward, soapy tale: indiscretion, denial, discovery, admission, and personal punishment. However, this was the real world, and there were legal procedures already grinding forward to bring events to a very public conclusion. Acknowledging an "improper relationship" might have been embarrassing for the president, but the real fallout was how that admission would frame questions of perjury, obstruction of justice, and, potentially, impeachment. Congress prepared to deal with those issues in the fall of 1998, when Kenneth Starr was scheduled to present his report.

That meant the story would carry through well into the 1998–99 season, which was a godsend to the all-news cable channels. They had provided high-profile non-stop coverage since the Clinton-Lewinsky scandal broke at the start of 1998, to tremendous ratings

success. Once again, increased attention to cable programming resulted in more disappointment for the non-cable networks. For the overall 1997–98 season, the audience share for all six broadcast networks was down again, and cable viewing continued to rise. A symbolic turning point took place the week of June 22–28, 1998, when, for the first time, the combined ratings for the channels considered "basic cable" beat the combined ratings for ABC, CBS, NBC, and Fox (which were then mostly in reruns). As broadcasters faced the increasingly difficult challenge of standing out amid dozens of channels while still making a profit, they responded with a schizophrenic mix of cost-cutting and extravagant spending.

On the savings side, the broadcast networks were taking a page from cable and pulling back from so much first-run material. When the inevitable first round of cancellations followed the 1997 fall premieres, the networks did not rush in replacement series but generally filled in with specials and reruns, sometimes for the balance of the season. It was simply better to make deals for multiple runs of known quantities. So ABC slotted weekly "double runs" of such shows as *Home Improvement*, *Boy Meets World*, and *Sabrina, the Teenage Witch* to fill holes throughout the season. NBC topped them all, though, with *Seinfeld*, television's number one show for 1997–98. In addition to airing the full complement of twenty-one first-run episodes, NBC aired thirty-four rerun presentations of the show in various time slots during the regular season.

The networks also turned to less expensive programming whenever possible. At mid-season, ABC brought in *Whose Line Is It, Anyway?*, an improvisational skit series based on a ten-year-old British hit that had run six years on Comedy Central. With only a handful of props, four main performers, and Drew Carey as host, it was solid humor at a bargain price. Another obvious resource was the news department, which could turn out specials and news magazines at a comparatively modest cost. NBC, for example,

September 8, 1997
Joan Lunden, who served seventeen years as co-host of ABC's *Good Morning America*, is replaced by Lisa McRee.

September 16, 1997
Guests at the National Press Club in Washington watch the first U.S. major league sporting event telecast live via high definition digital TV, a baseball game between the Baltimore Orioles and the Cleveland Indians at Baltimore's Camden Yards.

September 25, 1997
NBC's *ER* presents its fourth season debut episode live. Once again, the series overshadows CBS's *Chicago Hope*, whose October 15 musical episode (with stars lip-synching to songs) seems tame in comparison.

September 28, 1997
After fifty-four years in broadcasting, David Brinkley retires from ABC. Since giving up the host position on Sunday morning's *This Week* the previous November, he had been limited to brief closing commentaries on the show.

October 1, 1997
All of the networks (except NBC) implement a second tier of program ratings in addition to the age-based ratings instituted nine months earlier, identifying shows according to sexual activity (S), violence (V), strong language (L), suggestive dialogue (D), and fantasy violence (FV).

October 21, 1997

Following a lengthy battle, MCA/Universal acquires total control over two cable networks, USA Network and the Sci-Fi Network, after squeezing out Paramount/Viacom, which had owned the other 50% of the networks.

December 1, 1997

Westinghouse spins off its broadcasting and media assets to a separate wholly owned subsidiary called CBS Corp.

February 13, 1998

Barry Diller's Silver King Broadcasting (which includes the Home Shopping Network) acquires control over all of Universal's U.S. TV operations, including cable's USA Network and the Sci-Fi Network. Diller's company is renamed USA Networks.

March 19, 1998

Major League Baseball owners approve Fox's $350 million purchase of the Los Angeles Dodgers from the O'Malley family.

April 7, 1998

Radio entrepreneur Mel Karmazin is named president of CBS Corp., the number two corporate post beneath that of Chairman of the Board Michael Jordan.

May 4, 1998

Charles Gibson, co-host of ABC's *Good Morning America* for eleven years, is replaced by Kevin Newman.

August 1, 1998

Linc's. (Showtime). A smart comedy (from producer Tim Reid) set at a neighborhood tavern in Washington, casting Pam Grier (fresh from Quentin Tarantino's film "Jackie Brown") as a liberal activist, Steven Williams as the conservative bar owner, and Georg Stanford Brown as high powered lobbyist Johnny B. Goode.

August 15, 1998

Fox, having purchased cable's Family Channel, renames the network the Fox Family Channel.

again increased the frequency of its *Dateline* news magazine, airing it four nights each week.

At the other end of the budget scale, the networks also found themselves paying ever-increasing amounts for material with a proven track record as "destination" television. Though the prices were high for such offerings, the returns were more certain. NBC in particular understood the dynamics, having embraced the phrase "Must See TV" to describe its various Thursday night lineups. Shows such as *Friends, Seinfeld,* and *ER* cut through the competition and brought people to NBC. There was no doubt about their drawing power because a succession of painful-to-passable comedies had managed to land in the top ten when cradled in the slots between these three shows. (This season, *Veronica's Closet* and *Union Square* were the beneficiaries.) So when Jerry Seinfeld announced in December 1997 that this would be *Seinfeld*'s final season, he sent a financial shockwave through the network. Not only was NBC unable to change his mind (even with lucrative new incentive offers), but it also found itself desperate to retain its other two Thursday night headliners. As a result, the network agreed to pay a record $286 million per year (about $13 million per episode) in order to renew its contract to air *ER*. At their next contract re-

newal, each of the six cast members of *Friends* ended up with $750,000 per episode. If there were any second thoughts about the power of those headline shows, though, NBC only needed to look at the disastrous Monday night ratings from former top ten hits *Suddenly Susan, Fired Up, Caroline in the City,* and *The Naked Truth,* which flopped outside their protected Thursday night slots.

Sports also continued to be an established, big-ticket draw, though the networks were being more selective in their commitments even as they continued to pay more. CBS, having been badly stung by the loss of professional football four years before, was ready to step in when NBC balked at the high price of renewal. As part of a massive new eight-year $18 billion series of contracts for rights to televise the NFL, CBS grabbed the American Football Conference from NBC (its home since 1964), while Fox kept the National Football Conference. ABC retained *Monday Night Football* (its highest rated show of the season), while expanding the Sunday night contests of its corporate stablemate, ESPN, to a full season (eliminating TNT's early-season telecasts).

For NBC, though, the expense of football did not justify the return from commercial time sold. Instead, the network previously had decided to put its major sports money into an unprecedented, multiple-year commitment to the Olympics. NBC struck deals to carry both the Winter and Summer Games for ten years (through 2008), later extending this to include the 2010 and 2012 Games as well, even without knowing where some of the contests would be held. The Olympics had the potential to recover costs from aggressive commercial sales and were a proven special event draw, as CBS demonstrated in February 1998, with the Winter Games in Nagano, Japan (the last contest before the NBC contract took effect). CBS offered 128 hours of coverage (50 in prime time) and easily dominated the ratings.

Nonetheless, by paying higher and higher prices for specific programs and events, the networks were cutting their own profit margins. This was pushing overall network operations (once a hugely profitable enterprise) closer to being almost a loss leader. Other income sources that had just recently become available were now becoming essential, most notably money from syndication and additional O&Os. Most limits on series ownership had been lifted with the end of the Fin-Syn rules, so the networks could now profit from series sold into syndicated reruns, which was where producers had always made the bulk of their money anyway. With the FCC allowing the networks to own additional stations, there were more opportunities to profit from station successes. This partially helped alleviate a particular sore point with the networks. While they spent ever-increasing sums on programming, the main beneficiaries ended up being the individual stations, which were able to sell more of their local ad time at higher rates. With more owned and operated stations, the networks could at least share a bit more in this growth.

This profit squeeze also helped further explain the emphasis on viewers in the coveted 18 to 49 age group. The networks had only so many commercial minutes available for sale, so it made sense to chase the audience that would command the highest prices paid by advertisers. Though being the number one network in total audience still provided bragging rights, viewer gains in the 18 to 49 demographic generally meant more money. On that scale, for the entire 1997–98 season, Fox scored the biggest improvement in ratings among viewers 18 to 49, ending up number two (for the first time) behind NBC with the continued success of such series as *Party of Five, The X-Files,* and *The Simpsons.* Fox also had the most talked-about new series of the season, *Ally McBeal.*

Created by David E. Kelley, *Ally McBeal* was a legal drama that deliberately played up its strong comic elements with a setting and cast of characters that seemed to embody the targeted 18 to 49 demographic: young, good looking, clever, likable, sexually active, and motivated for success. They worked at the Boston law firm of Cage/Fish & Associates, which specialized in highly creative (if quirky) legal strategies. Appropriately, the firm even made using the bathroom something unusual: It had a large unisex facility so everyone was always in everyone else's path. The primary focus of the stories, though, was on hardworking twenty-something attorney Ally McBeal (Calista Flockhart), who was trying to balance her career, friendships, romance, and, of course, sex life. She was extremely sensitive and somewhat neurotic, and the series often showed her projected fantasies. These ranged from an arrow tearing through Ally's heart to Ally's literally hearing her biological clock ticking while being taunted by the image of a dancing baby in her bedroom. The series and the character quickly became a hook for media stories about the concerns of contemporary working women and was extolled for capturing a strong female perspective, though it was Kelley himself who wrote nearly all of the scripts for the run of the series.

Kelley also managed to use the first season of *Ally McBeal* to promote another legal drama set in Boston that he had running on a different network, *The Practice* (a mid-season entry on ABC in the 1996–97 season). On that series, criminal attorney Bobby Donnell (Dylan McDermott) headed a small law firm that usually handled gritty murder cases. Kelley constructed a two-episode story arc that began on *Ally McBeal* and ended on *The Practice,* with characters from both shows crossing over. Though obviously a one-time stunt, this allowed Kelley to show the strengths of both series and to provide an awareness boost for *The Practice,* which had attracted far less media attention than *Ally McBeal*. With ABC continuing to slip in the ratings (even dropping behind Fox among viewers aged 18 to 49), that network was looking for any gimmick to help nurse its programs into full-fledged hits.

In that spirit, ABC took a chance with a pair of tough dramas (*Cracker* and *Nothing Sacred*) that were both placed in television's toughest slots: Thursdays against *Friends* and *Seinfeld*. *Cracker* was the U.S. adaptation of a successful British crime series that had recently played on A&E, with this new version taking the original's tone and playing it as an even darker drama. The series followed criminal psychologist Gerry "Fitz" Fitzgerald (Robert Pastorelli), a part-time homicide consultant to the Los Angeles Police Department. Though articulate and clever (he lectured at a local college and hosted a late night radio show), Fitz could barely manage his personal life. He was an alcoholic and a gambler, and he cheated on his wife. But all those dark qualities made him perfect for solving cases because, on a gut level, he truly understood the criminal mind. At the other end of the spectrum, *Nothing Sacred* took on the concept of translating positive, deeply held religious beliefs into everyday life. The stories focused on Father Francis "Ray" Rayneaux (Kevin Anderson), a young Catholic priest assigned to a large urban parish, where he faced such typical "inner-city" plots as maintaining a soup kitchen, fighting developers, dealing with teenage sex, and drug use. The series stood out, though, by offering a strong sense of the sacred among the characters, including creditable (if brief) sermons and services. The program did draw Catholic criticism for equivocating on the issue of abortion, but such protests never amounted to much and did not even provide a temporary ratings bump due to the controversy. Although both ABC dramas were commendable and entertaining alternatives to NBC's comedy block, neither lasted past spring. For a major ratings boost, ABC still needed something more.

As the 1997–98 season wound to an end, ABC joined NBC and HBO in turning to a proven gimmick: promoting the wrap-up of a long-running series. Ever since the 1983 *M*A*S*H* finale attracted more than 100 million viewers (as the most watched individual series episode ever, not counting Super Bowls), producers had looked for similar ways to turn the end of a show into a major event without spoiling future rerun syndication. It was a tricky balance. *M*A*S*H* had a dramatic endpoint built in: the end of the Korean War. Most other comedies had to create a somewhat artificial crisis to be dealt with at the end. They also had to resist the temptation to run too long with an overblown wrap-up that ended up as not very funny. This year's series finales achieved varying degrees of success.

NBC's *Seinfeld* led yet one more night of "Must See TV" with its highly publicized but ultimately disappointing May 14 wrap-up, still ending up number six in the all-time individual episode ratings list at 76.3 million viewers. The show's writers dusted off an old plot (NBC courting Jerry Seinfeld to do a series) that eventually led to Jerry, George, Elaine, and Kramer being put on trial in a small Massachusetts town for, essentially, being mean and selfish. (They had violated the town's Good Samaritan Law by doing nothing to help stop a crime they witnessed.) It was a strained concept to begin with that became further bogged down by a parade of guest stars from past episodes, as the trial was turned into a media circus parody (even including cable talk show host Geraldo Rivera). The final scene showed the four locked in a cell together to begin serving a one-year sentence, passing the time engaged in trivial conversation, about nothing in particular.

ABC's *Ellen* finale received far, far less attention, but marked a clever return to comic form for Ellen DeGeneres. After Ellen's "coming out" the previous season, the series had fallen into a rut of borderline preachiness, often coming off less a comedy and more a diatribe on gay rights. The one-hour conclusion was a clever stand-alone episode in which DeGeneres poked fun at her celebrity spokeswoman status, rewriting her own professional performing history as a fictionalized rags-to-riches tale, including "classic clips" from the golden days of sitcoms and celebrity panel shows.

Creatively, the most successful finale of the season came on HBO's *Larry Sanders Show*. Appropriately, the last batch of episodes followed Larry's departure from his late night program. Unlike the other series finales, this twist did not come in the final episode or two. The entire season played to that last episode. As with Johnny Carson back in 1992, Garry Shandling's character of Larry Sanders was the one who pulled the plug on his own series. Sanders was exasperated at "heavy handed" network interference and bad-faith negotiating, so he announced his retirement on the air and then "kissed off" the network rep backstage in a gloriously liberating "take this job and shove it" declaration. The balance of the series followed everyone's plans for the future, leading to the final show. That night was very much in the spirit of Johnny Carson's penultimate program, with a star-studded lineup of celebrity farewells including, appropriately, Jerry Seinfeld and Ellen DeGeneres. The episode also showed the usual candid off-camera exchanges, with angry words, score-settling, and blatant self-promotion. There was also a genuine sense of professional camaraderie, if not outright friendship, especially between Larry, producer Arte, and sidekick Hank. In a television world constantly looking for new ways to hook viewers, *Larry Sanders* showed that presenting authentic and believable characters and situations still remained one of the most effective and resilient lures.

59. Sex and Violence

SEXUALLY EXPLICIT MATERIAL had become, by the 1990s, one of the most quietly successful niche areas of television programming, generating billions in revenue for a variety of products. Before the early 1970s, the "adult entertainment" industry had largely been limited to cheesy movie theaters and seedy stores. The advent of videotape had been the first step in expanding the market into the home, allowing interested users to rent or to purchase increasingly explicit films for their own private viewing. With the growth of cable TV beginning in the late 1970s, specialty channels (such as the Playboy Channel, which debuted in September 1980) were created to provide more explicitly erotic sexual fare. Generally such signals were scrambled and required a separate payment for decoding, often on a pay-per-view basis. This system not only kept potentially offensive material isolated, but it also helped maximize financial returns, and soon additional outlets such as the Spice Channel and AdultVision arrived and thrived. In the 1990s, the slow but steady growth of direct satellite transmissions resulted in new outlets for even racier material that could be beamed directly and discreetly to hotel rooms and private homes. By the late 1990s, the Internet provided another channel through the proliferation of adult websites, including some that offered video images.

Although this niche represented a completely different world from both the mainstream broadcast networks and most of cable, the financial success of such sexually explicit material did suggest that, perhaps, general audiences might be open to more daring sexual fare, if it were done just right. For years, the premium cable services had experimented with late night offerings that included moderately explicit sexual fantasies, usually as part of some simple melodrama such as *The Red Shoe Diaries* or silly comedy such as *Beverly Hills Bordello* (both on Showtime). In 1991, HBO found a successful mix of the sensual and the explicit with the occasional documentary feature series *Real Sex,* in which typical segments included a Kama Sutra workshop for couples, a "fetish" costume ball, a "sex toy" sales party, and a co-ed nude mud bath.

Nonetheless, the mainstream cable networks were still reluctant to heavily promote such shows, in part to distance themselves from the "hard core" services. Instead, they quietly incorporated more explicit language and visuals into their original offerings, but did not push those aspects as the main draw. In HBO's office sitcom *Dream On* (which premiered in July 1990), daydreaming Manhattan book editor Martin Tupper (Brian Benben) often imagined exciting sexual encounters. However, his primary fantasy images,

and the promoted hook for the series, drew on memories of old black and white television shows (usually obscure drama anthologies from the 1950s). In October 1991, HBO's short run comedy *Sessions* (created by Billy Crystal) put sex talk and fantasies in the context of therapy sessions, with Michael McKean playing a patient facing a midlife crises and Elliott Gould as his therapist. In the mid-1990s, HBO's *Larry Sanders Show* successfully pushed the boundaries of explicit language further as part of its talk show parody setting, winning both critical praise and a strong following.

In the summer of 1998, both HBO and Showtime took the next step and put sex upfront and center in two new cable comedy series: HBO's *Sex and the City* and Showtime's *Rude Awakening.* Both aggressively pushed the boundaries of sexual themes in the sitcom format, with frank language, nudity, and the proposition that sex was, above all, recreational fun. Of the two, *Sex and the City* (which premiered June 6) was far more successful.

Created by *Melrose Place* producer Darren Star and based on a book collecting the sex-advice columns of Candace Bushnell, *Sex and the City* was a high-gloss ensemble series set and filmed in Manhattan. It followed four successful thirty-something women: newspaper sex columnist Carrie Bradshaw (Sarah Jessica Parker), the series narrator, who observed the dilemmas of her circle of friends as inspiration for her articles; attorney Miranda Hobbes (Cynthia Nixon), responsible and obsessive yet sexually insecure; high-end art dealer Charlotte York (Kristin Davis), a believer in true romance; and public relations agent Samantha Jones (Kim Cattrall), an energetic sex machine. They were all attractive, fashionable, unattached, and constantly looking for and talking about sex. Somewhat like *Seinfeld*, the show focused on four self-absorbed Manhattanites, but here there were four Elaines. The women's conversations were gossipy and explicit (on everything from various sexual positions to threesomes to Viagra), rendering devastating judgments on the men in their lives. These were stories told from a female perspective, so, for example, an episode that centered on getting a table at an exclusive night spot was resolved when Carrie bonded with the woman from the reservation station by providing her with a tampon when they were both in the ladies room. Yet the series also effectively played to male viewer fantasies with its "bad girl" image of beautiful women in the hedonistic New York scene who "talked dirty," looked fabulous, and were not afraid to misbehave in and out of the bedroom.

These characters also liked each other and that wonderful sense of camaraderie brought a surprising warmth to the series. For example, when Charlotte landed a trendy painter's new collection of original work for her gallery (a series of paintings based on women's vaginas), she told only Carrie, Miranda, and Samantha that she had posed for one canvas. Proud but blushing, Charlotte watched as her three friends found (and admired) that picture.

The four were especially supportive observing each other's roller coaster romances. Most of the relationships lasted only an episode or two, though there were exceptions. Miranda became a single mom. Charlotte thought she found the man of her dreams in Connecticut surgeon Trey MacDougal (Kyle MacLachlan), but that marriage quickly ended in divorce, due to disappointing sex. Ironically, Charlotte later married her divorce lawyer. Carrie herself had a long-term on-again/off-again relationship with a wealthy New York businessman (played by Chris Noth), whom she referred to simply as "Big." She also hooked up with other guys, most notably furniture maker Aidan Shaw (John Corbett) and Russian artist Aleksandr Petrovsky (Mikhail Baryshnikov). The sex, of course, was fabulous. Outside the bedroom, *Sex and the City* also embodied a self-fulfilling sense of hipness, with well-orchestrated media coverage of the show focusing on everything from Carrie's sipping a cold "Cosmo" martini to their individual fashion accessories.

Ultimately, such deft packaging was the key to the program's success. Taking language and behavior regarded in some circles as shocking, scandalous, and forbidden, *Sex and the City* slyly presented it all as elements of an accessible female "buddy" sitcom, reassuringly familiar and, ultimately, almost mainstream. Not surprisingly, in 2003 the show became the first original cable series to forge a high profile syndication rerun package for broadcast stations (with careful editing of its more explicit subject matter).

In contrast, *Rude Awakening*, Showtime's female-centered comedy that began in August 1998, demonstrated the limitations of being too bluntly "cutting edge." Sherilyn Fenn (Audrey on *Twin Peaks*) played actress Billie Frank, once part of a prime time soap opera cast, but now a young has-been, addicted to alcohol and sex. The opening credits showed Billie in a montage of "morning after" bedroom scenes with a variety of kinky partners, scolding herself for being so bad. It was easy to see the roots of Billie's behavior in her alternately soused-and-stoned mom, Trudy (Lynn Redgrave, in an over-the-top performance), yet by the end of the first episode Billie experienced her "rude awakening" and was grudgingly drawn into a rehab program. Her subsequent road to recovery from alcohol (sex remained a given) included romantic complications and family "sobriety rescue missions." There was also a high quotient of graphic language and angry confrontations, especially with other substance abusers, some of whom were just a heartbeat away from an overdose. Though plots were usually broad and farcical, the overall series tone was dark, loud, and often a bit *too* "rude."

Although *Rude Awakening* lasted three seasons, it was *Sex and the City* that established itself as the hot new "hip" series on TV (cable or broadcast), helping to earn HBO the reputation as the home for talked-about series, not just movies and specials. Only a few months later, HBO achieved yet another "brand identity" series success in the area of drama with *The Sopranos*, which followed the home and "office" life of a New Jersey mobster. A print ad for the January 10, 1999, premiere succinctly summarized the premise: "If one family doesn't kill him, the other family will."

Created by David Chase (a veteran writer and producer for such series as *The Rockford Files, Northern Exposure*, and *I'll Fly Away*), *The Sopranos* took an innovative approach to mob activities by placing the story in a respectable suburban community rather than the usual urban setting. Filmed on location in New Jersey and New York, the series focused on up-and-coming capo Tony Soprano (James Gandolfini). Thanks to his extremely profitable business interests as leader of his local crime "family," Tony lived very comfortably with his real family, wife Carmela (Edie Falco), daughter Meadow (Jamie-Lynn Sigler), and son Anthony, Jr. (Robert Iler). Much to his surprise, however, Tony found himself vaguely troubled. He suffered blackouts and panic attacks in his own backyard, and, in the first episode, those led him to the office of therapist Dr. Jennifer Melfi (Lorraine Bracco). Their conversations provided the central core for the series, as Melfi stood in for viewers, alternately fascinated and appalled by the world brought to her office.

Tony Soprano had plenty on his mind. There were pressures "at work" (including investigations by federal agents), which he kept deliberately vague so as not to encumber Melfi with too much information. Closer to home, Tony had a long history of cheating on his wife (despite claims that he loved her). He was also deeply

August 31, 1998
Pax Net, America's seventh national commercial TV broadcast network, debuts. Created by Lowell "Bud" Paxson, co-founder of cable's Home Shopping Network, Pax Net relies on more than seventy local television stations (mostly low-power UHF outlets) owned by Paxson's company. It presents itself as a family-oriented alternative network, beginning with non-controversial reruns such as *Touched by an Angel* and *Diagnosis Murder*, mixed with original programs such as the faith-based "reality" series *It's a Miracle* and the drama *Little Men*.

September 6, 1998
CBS resumes Sunday afternoon NFL telecasts, as it begins airing American Football Conference games.

September 8, 1998
Fox postpones its Tuesday night fall premieres for a week in order to air live coverage of a St. Louis Cardinals baseball game against the Chicago Cubs. In that, Cardinal Mark McGwire hits his sixty-second home run of the year, breaking the season record held by Roger Maris.

September 14, 1998
Total Request Live. (MTV). Carson Daly hosts a live weekday afternoon program featuring viewers' favorite current songs.

September 17, 1998
The WB network begins broadcasting Thursdays, its fifth night of programming. On October 8 and 9, rival UPN adds Thursdays and Fridays, its fourth and fifth nights.

September 20, 1998
NBC replaces its late, late, late night news show, *NBC Nightside*, with reruns of Jay Leno's *Tonight* show and the daytime soap opera *Sunset Beach*.

October 29, 1998
The era of digital high definition television ("HDTV") broadcasting comes to the U.S., as more than forty HDTV stations begin regular service by covering the space shuttle launch of a former astronaut, Senator John Glenn. For now, the HDTV schedule is sporadic, chiefly simulcasts of analog programming. That fall the first American digital TV sets go on sale, with Panasonic and Mitsubishi models (from 50 to 80 inches in diagonal size) costing about $7,000, including converters to allow reception of analog signals.

	8:00	8:30	9:00	9:30	10:00	10:30	
M O N	ABC MONDAY NIGHT BLAST	ABC NFL Monday Night Football (to 11:30 p.m.)					**ABC**
	Cosby	THE KING OF QUEENS	Everybody Loves Raymond	THE BRIAN BENBEN SHOW	L.A. DOCTORS		**CBS**
	Melrose Place		Ally McBeal		local		**FOX**
	Suddenly Susan	CONRAD BLOOM	Caroline In The City	WILL & GRACE	Dateline NBC		**NBC**
	GUYS LIKE US	DiRESTA	SECRET DIARY DESMOND PFEIFFER	Malcolm & Eddie	local		**UPN**
	7th Heaven		HYPERION BAY		local		**WB**
T U E	Home Improvement	THE HUGHLEYS	Spin City	SPORTS NIGHT	NYPD Blue		**ABC**
	JAG		CBS Tuesday Movie				**CBS**
	King Of The Hill	COSTELLO	Guinness World Records Primetime		local		**FOX**
	Mad About You	ENCORE! ENCORE!	Just Shoot Me	Working	Dateline NBC		**NBC**
	Moesha	Clueless	MERCY POINT		local		**UPN**
	Buffy The Vampire Slayer		FELICITY		local		**WB**
W E D	Dharma & Greg	Two Guys A Girl & Pizza Place	The Drew Carey Show	THE SECRET LIVES OF MEN	20/20		**ABC**
	The Nanny	MAGGIE WINTERS	TO HAVE AND TO HOLD		Chicago Hope		**CBS**
	Beverly Hills, 90210		Party Of Five		local		**FOX**
	Dateline NBC		3rd Rock From The Sun	Newsradio	Law & Order		**NBC**
	SEVEN DAYS		Star Trek: Voyager		local		**UPN**
	Dawson's Creek		CHARMED		local		**WB**
T H R	VENGEANCE UNLIMITED		ABC Thursday Night Movie				**ABC**
	Promised Land		Diagnosis Murder		48 Hours		**CBS**
	Wold's Wildest Police Videos		Fox Files		local		**FOX**
	Friends	JESSE	Frasier	Veronica's Closet	ER		**NBC**
	THURSDAY NIGHT AT THE MOVIES				local		**UPN**
	The Wayans Bros.	The Jamie Foxx Show	The Steve Harvey Show	For Your Love	local		**WB**
F R I	TWO OF A KIND	Boy Meets World	Sabrina, TheTeenage Witch	BROTHERS KEEPER	20/20		**ABC**
	Kids Say Darndest Things	Candid Camera	BUDDY FARO		Nash Bridges		**CBS**
	LIVING IN CAPTIVITY	Getting Personal	Millennium		local		**FOX**
	TRINITY		Dateline NBC		Homicide: Life On The Street		**NBC**
	LEGACY		Love Boat: The Next Wave		local		**UPN**
	local						**WB**
S A T	America's Funniest Home Videos		Fantasy Island		CUPID		**ABC**
	Early Edition		MARTIAL LAW		Walker, Texas Ranger		**CBS**
	Cops	Cops	America's Most Wanted: America Fights Back		local		**FOX**
	WIND ON WATER		The Pretender		Profiler		**NBC**
	local						**UPN**
	local						**WB**

	7:00	7:30	8:00	8:30	9:00	9:30	10:00	10:30	
S U N	The Wonderful World Of Disney				20/20		The Practice		**ABC**
	60 Minutes		Touched By An Angel		CBS Sunday Movie				**CBS**
	The World's Funniest	HOLDING THE BABY	The Simpsons	THAT '70s SHOW	The X Files		local		**FOX**
	(specials)		Dateline NBC		NBC Sunday Night Movie				**NBC**
	local								**UPN**
	7th Heaven Beginnings		Sister, Sister	Smart Guy	Unhappily Ever After	THE ARMY SHOW	local		**WB**

concerned about his children. After all, his deceased dad had been a crime boss and he had followed in those footsteps. Would they do the same? Most important, Tony "had issues" with his demanding mother, Livia (Nancy Marchand). She could appear frail and helpless but was really the embodiment of unrelenting, crafty manipulation. In a way, Livia was the most dangerous person in Tony Soprano's life. She had been "married to the mob" and knew all its secrets. In the first season she was even able to arrange an aborted "hit" on her son, slyly egging on her husband's old partner, Corrado "Uncle Junior" Soprano (Dominic Chianese). After all, Tony had dared move her to a nursing home.

At first, Tony kept the therapy sessions a secret from both his families, but eventually everybody learned and dealt with it. One of the most intriguing aspects of the conversations between Tony and Melfi was that many of the concerns raised could have come from any harried business executive. That was the point. Rather than portray the mob world as some glamorous larger-than-life grand opera, *The Sopranos* presented it matter-of-factly, as part of the grind of running a small business. Tony's Bada-Bing strip club served as his office, a dingy back room in an unassuming neighborhood. The difference was that Tony's business consisted of a host of illegal activities including prostitution, loan sharking, gambling, auto theft, money laundering, and drugs. Tony had a team at the club, including enforcer Paulie Walnuts (Tony Sirico); Tony's hot-headed nephew, Christopher Moltisanti (Michael Imperioli); street captain "Big Pussy" Bonpensiero (Vincent Pastore); and club manager Silvio Dante (Steven Van Zandt, better known in rock circles as a member of Bruce Springsteen's band). They were ready to use any means necessary to further their interests including bribery, blackmail, extortion, physical beatings, and cold-blooded murder.

Yet Tony Soprano himself emerged as sympathetic. He was generous, valued loyalty, and seemed as perplexed as anyone by modern life. Ultimately, this "naturalistic" view of a crime boss was a far more unsettling image than an easy-to-hate, heavy-handed kingpin. A likeable guy like Tony was far more effective in luring people (including viewers) into compromising their values, encouraging them to look the other way. Some compromises seemed comparatively harmless. At Christmas, for example, a local church happily accepted a station wagon filled with frozen turkeys that had "fallen off the truck." Sometimes Tony's actions seemed justified in response to personal or official arrogance. When a doctor treating Uncle Junior did not return phone calls, Tony and an enforcer visited the physician on the golf course in the middle of a game. They never struck the doctor, but he was so shaken that the next day he was suddenly available and caring. Such positive outcomes, though, obscured the dark and corrupt reality of Tony Soprano's world, which routinely played on people's worst tendencies, marking some for death. It posed a tremendous moral challenge for anyone caught up in its apparent largess.

In a powerful first-season episode ("College," which won an Emmy), Meadow confronted her dad about what he "really did" for a living, while they were driving together upstate to visit potential colleges. Much to her relief, Tony admitted that some of his activities were illegal and promised to be truthful with her. What she did not know (and what he did not tell her) was that, while on that trip, Tony committed murder at the same time Meadow attended a college interview session. Spotting a one-time mob informant who had been relocated to the area by a government witness protection program, Tony had found his house, ambushed him, and strangled him. Meadow remained innocently oblivious.

Carmela Soprano generally refrained from asking too many questions, about either Tony's work or his sexual affairs, appar-

ently content to be living the American dream. Yet by the third season even she was troubled enough to visit a therapist on her own, seeking guidance. He surprised her by not asking for any payment, explaining that since it was "blood money," he could not touch it and neither should she. He urged her to leave Tony and all their accumulated possessions and to start over again with the children. It was blunt advice that Carmela could not accept, and she was haunted by his parting warning: "One thing you can never say: That you haven't been told." Instead, afterward, she arranged for a generous financial gift to Meadow's college with some of that blood money. However, Carmella also began to worry seriously about the family's future, and her own. In the fourth season Tony's cheating pushed her too far, and Carmella's anger and resentment, long held in check, came out in full fury. She threw him out of the

December 24, 1998
CBS sells its foundering Eye on People cable network to Discovery Communications, which renames it Discovery People.

January 11, 1999
Jon Stewart takes over as anchor for the *Daily Show* news parody program on Comedy Central, following Craig Kilborn's departure to CBS.

January 18, 1999
After falling to third place in the morning show ratings for the first time since 1977, ABC's *Good Morning America* institutes major changes. Out go co-hosts Kevin Newman and Lisa McRee (on the job only eight and sixteen months, respectively). In come Charles Gibson (whom Newman had replaced) and Diane Sawyer.

February 23, 1999
Queer as Folk begins on Britain's Channel 4, following gay life in Manchester. The drama series immediately draws fire for graphic sex scenes between the characters of promiscuous twenty-nine-year-old Stuart (Aidan Gillen) and an underage schoolboy, fifteen-year-old Nathan (played by eighteen-year-old Charlie Hunnam). A U.S. adaptation begins on Showtime in December 2000.

March 9, 1999
AT&T closes its $52 billion acquisition of cable system operator Tele-Communications, Inc.

March 19, 1999
Farscape. (Sci-Fi). In this clever original series (co-produced by Jim Henson's company and Hallmark), Earth space explorer John Crichton (Ben Browder) is thrown through a wormhole into an interplanetary war in a distant galaxy. With such characters as Moya, a living space ship, the show quickly becomes a cult favorite.

March 30, 1999
Former *Daily Show* anchor Craig Kilborn replaces Tom Snyder as host of CBS's *The Late Late Show*.

July 17, 1999
SpongeBob SquarePants. (Nickelodeon). Stephen Hillenburg creates a delightfully cheerful Saturday morning cartoon that attracts young adults without straining to be too ironic or hip. Tom Kenny provides the voice for the hopelessly optimistic SpongeBob, a yellow sponge who lives in the undersea world of Bikini Bottom and works at the Krusty Krab, the local fast-food joint.

house and seriously considered divorce. Later Carmella relented and eventually reconciled herself to the life she had chosen.

It was Dr. Melfi who provided one of the strongest moments of adhering to personal integrity. In the episode "Employee of the Month," she was attacked and raped. Even though she identified the guilty party, he was released on a technicality. Melfi knew that all she had to do was mention this to Tony and, without her ever asking, the man who raped her would be "squashed like a bug." Instead, she struggled with that temptation for "justice" (Soprano style) and drew on her inner reserves during one session to assure Tony that her bruised face and limp were the result of a car accident and that she was jumpy but otherwise okay. Melfi knew that a moment of revenge would compromise a lifetime of integrity.

Such complex and deeply layered performances and scripts turned *The Sopranos* into an immediate critical hit. The well-paced mix of colorful characters, devious plots, and violent action made the series a top draw among premium channel subscribers.

The one-two punch of *The Sopranos* and *Sex and the City* lent credence to HBO's promotion of itself as the source of the best television programming *anywhere*, and it followed more than a decade of aggressive expansion of HBO's original productions. Though still primarily a premium theatrical movie service, HBO found it could attract additional subscribers by increasing its investment in its own original movies, documentaries, sports shows, miniseries, and, now, continuing series. An added benefit to the network was that, when these series were released to home video, HBO would benefit from those sales. In fact, because most viewers (including most cable subscribers) did not subscribe to HBO, that was how many would eventually see these exclusive offerings.

As a premium cable service HBO had several tremendous advantages over the broadcast networks. Because it had no commercials and virtually no restrictions on language or subject matter, HBO attracted both viewers and successful producers who resented the restrictions usually imposed by broadcasters. At the same time, HBO had a financial base of monthly income from its subscribers on top of the regular payment it received from cable systems for being part of their lineups (like any other cable network).

Another significant factor that helped HBO prosper was that, on any given day, most of its schedule consisted of reruns—chiefly feature films run multiple times. HBO could afford to lavish extra time, attention, and money on its original productions because it was not even close to filling an entire day (or seven days of prime time) with new material. On top of that, the original series it did have generally consisted of fewer episodes per season than the standard broadcast order of twenty-two. As a rule, *The Sopranos* had only thirteen episodes per season, while *Sex and the City* usually ran between twelve and eighteen. Sometimes there would be a gap of more than a year between "seasons." Even when they were in their first-run cycles, these episodes would be immediately rerun, playing (and filling) slots over multiple nights.

In a way, then, it was totally unfair to compare series on HBO with those on the broadcast networks. They were playing by different rules. (About the only downside to the HBO formula was that when it found a hit, HBO could not instantly benefit by raising ad rates.) Still, that did not change the fact that, in an increasingly fractured, competitive television market, HBO had found the best ways to maximize its particular assets. It was up to the competition, particularly the broadcast networks, to do the same, hatching new strategies for success, from production to scheduling to defining themselves and their audiences.

Such considerations also applied to the news departments for both broadcasters and cable outlets as they faced the denouement of their latest "story of the century," the investigation of President Bill Clinton for possible "high crimes and misdemeanors" that might lead to his impeachment. On Friday, September 11, 1998, Whitewater special prosecutor Kenneth Starr delivered his formal report to Congress. By then, his investigation had morphed far beyond its original scope and the 445-page document (with salacious details on exactly what had gone on between the president and the intern) was now regarded as a draft guide to possible impeachment proceedings against the president. In a nod to the growing interest in online communication, the report was also posted as a website beginning at 3:00 P.M. Washington time, so that viewers at home had the same access to the complete text as any media organization on Capitol Hill. As a result, viewers were treated to the sight of network news correspondents frantically trying to skim the lengthy report and commenting on its contents, live, at the same time.

On September 21, Starr released the videotape of Clinton's August 17 testimony before the grand jury. There was tremendous anticipation about the tape because, apart from the participants that day, no one knew exactly what had been said. Again, Starr's office did not provide news organizations with an advance copy nor did it provide an advance transcript. Instead, there was a single feed that went out, live, from Capitol Hill directly to broadcasters, who could immediately put it on the air, unedited. There was high interest in the testimony because it represented the only direct exchange between the president and the special prosecutor's office on the Monica Lewinsky affair. Unlike Clinton's public statements (in which he controlled the forum and did not face any questions), this was sworn testimony, under oath, subject to scrutiny and followup probing by a skeptical prosecutor. Over the course of the four hours, Clinton's responses frequently showed him relying on the same type of legalistic technical distinctions that he had used since the affair became public. At one point, he defended the accuracy of a statement from his Paula Jones deposition that "there is no sex of any kind" [with Lewinsky] with the convoluted statement that, "It depends on what the meaning of the word 'is' is."

The September 21 video playback of the previous month's grand jury deposition by President Clinton was carried in full by most news organizations, bringing his direct testimony via television to Capitol Hill offices and hearing rooms *(above)* and to viewers throughout the U.S. and the world. *(Photo by Mark Abraham)*

Airing the tape did not result in any great change in public opinions about the case, nor did it provide a "smoking gun" admission or a *Matlock* moment when the crafty attorney tripped up the smooth-talking witness. Instead, viewers saw that this was how Clinton was determined to present the situation. Whether they agreed with him or not, it was clear he was not changing his stance. Though he had gone on to "apologize" a half dozen times in public since the grand jury testimony, it was always about his "sin" or "letting people down," and never about the issue of lying under oath. When Clinton at last settled the Paula Jones sexual harassment case (she agreed to drop her lawsuit on November 13 in return for $850,000), he still did not admit guilt (nor did he apologize to her). Still, the Starr report removed any doubt about what had happened between Clinton and Lewinsky, with details that could have been the basis for an episode of *Sex and the City*. On the issues of perjury and obstruction of justice, though, it was up to Congress to bring the matter to an end, one way or another.

Throughout the fall, the U.S. House of Representatives (first through its Judiciary Committee and then as an entire chamber) debated the matter and whether the president's actions warranted removal from office. On December 19, 1998, for only the second time in U.S. history, the full House voted to impeach a president, with the vote essentially breaking down along party lines. The U.S. Senate then had to decide whether Clinton was guilty of the charges brought by the House and therefore should be removed from office. That formal process began on January 7, 1999, with U.S. Supreme Court Chief Justice William Rehnquist presiding in the Senate chamber. After an exhausting month of presentations by the "prosecutors" from the House and by Clinton's defense team, as well as long days of speeches by the senators, the whole matter ended on February 12 with a pair of votes. Both fell short of the two-thirds majority necessary for conviction. There was a fifty-fifty split on the charge of obstruction of justice; only forty-five of the one hundred senators voted to convict on the charge of perjury. (The perjury charge had been based on the August 17 grand jury testimony, not on the deposition from the Paula Jones case.)

Both the House and Senate proceedings were televised, though only the cable networks and PBS carried every moment of the sessions, with the commercial broadcast networks largely opting for selected coverage. There was surprisingly little sense of drama, especially in the Senate trial, because by then no one expected the president to be removed from office. There were forty-five Democratic senators and they appeared unwilling to convict, no matter what, leaving any charge short of the sixty-seven votes needed for removal. In addition, the trial itself was structured so that there were no live witnesses, only speeches and citations of evidence, so it seemed more like just another round of the discussions that had run practically non-stop in the media since the story had surfaced more than a year before. During that time, most of the public had long since made up its mind about Bill Clinton.

In a way, the twenty-four-hour television news cycle proved to be both Clinton's undoing and his salvation. The relentless coverage had exposed his attempts to cover up his actions, but, in the long run, viewers soured on the contentious, repetitive, and sometimes offensive nature of the story. By the time of the Senate trial, the public in general simply wanted it to end, preferably with some punishment other than removal from office. In a standard criminal trial such sentiments would have been irrelevant. In proceedings run by elected officials conscious of public opinion polls, such feelings were an inescapable part of the process. With a booming peacetime economy, Clinton remained popular, even though his personal ethical actions were generally held in low esteem.

Though Bill Clinton escaped removal from office, his public reputation took a severe beating. By the time Clinton's second term as president ended at the start of 2001, TV comics had permanently enshrined him in the lexicon of comedy as a punch line for irresponsible personal behavior.

The Clinton affair also left television news in low public esteem even though, on the surface, the medium had done just what it was supposed to do: cover the news with all available resources. The problem was, in a competitive twenty-four-hour news world, no one was willing to say "enough about that, for now," even when there was no new information. Changing the subject to another, less flashy, story risked sending viewers to another channel. (PBS's *NewsHour with Jim Lehrer* and ABC's *Nightline* with Ted Koppel were among the few shows to consistently take that risk.) The cable news channels wound up "solving" this problem by increasingly filling their schedules with opinionated talk shows that could continue dwelling on a subject without worrying about having to add anything new. The fact that such programs were also far less expensive to produce only made them more desirable.

Yet a basic central issue remained: In the non-stop news world, what constituted a newsworthy subject in the first place? At almost a moment's notice, television could bring to bear a small army of personnel and technical equipment. What was worthy of such an effort? Was the answer the same for the all-news cable channels as it was for the broadcast networks? What about entertainment news services such as E!? The online version of MSNBC? New players such as Matt Drudge, or anyone else with an opinion and access to the Internet? Most important, did viewers even make distinctions among all these sources anymore?

Just five months after the impeachment hearings ended, television news demonstrated how far it was from satisfactory answers to any of those questions. On July 17, 1999, there were reports that a small plane piloted by John F. Kennedy, Jr., might have crashed the night before near Martha's Vineyard off the Massachusetts coast. It was not until late on July 18 that Coast Guard officials said that Kennedy, his wife Carolyn, and sister-in-law Lauren Bessette had likely perished. (The bodies were recovered July 21.) In an earlier era, the accident reports might have warranted brief network news bulletins, later followed by short, but affectionate, obituary features about the son of assassinated president John F. Kennedy, probably including the 1963 salute by "John-John" (as he was referred to then) at his dad's flag-draped casket. Instead, both broadcast and cable news organizations descended upon the crash area, instantly providing nearly continuous coverage that stretched for days, even though for hours at a time the only video footage was, essentially, the water lapping off the shoreline.

On the one hand, the extent of the coverage before the wreckage was even located was puzzling. John F. Kennedy, Jr., had never run for elective office and, strictly speaking, his only official public activities at the time were with a few charities and as publisher of the financially struggling political magazine, *George*. Though a personal loss to his family, his passing had no direct personal consequences in the lives of most people. On the other hand, he was, without question, a modern American celebrity, akin to Princess Diana at the time of her death. Good looking. Wealthy. Best known for being well known. People did care. In the roiling waters of television news, that was enough to serve as the basis for a massive commitment of resources and air time by a news industry that had come to depend on regular fixes of this sort of easily promotable "event" to justify its very existence. Even if, in the big picture, the event was just not that important.

60. Not the Final Answer

WHO WANTS TO BE A MILLIONAIRE first made its mark as a surprise hit in Britain (on the ITV network) during the fall of 1998, bringing new life to the classic big-money quiz show format. Hosted by Chris Tarrant (a veteran British entertainment personality from morning radio and a variety of TV talk shows), the series took familiar elements of the quiz form and added some fresh twists. The game focused on individuals competing only with themselves in pursuit of big money. Each contestant had to answer a series of up to fifteen multiple-choice general knowledge questions (with four possible answers given). For each question correctly answered, the prize money doubled (roughly), up to one million. A contestant continued until either giving one wrong answer or deciding to stop with the money already won. Then the next contestant would step in and start the process all over again. In contrast to such past gimmicks as placing contestants in a soundproof isolation booth or having them anxiously race against time as a stern quizmaster counted down the clock, Who Wants to Be a Millionaire was open, friendly, and almost leisurely. Contestants sat center stage in a comfortable chair, facing the host, who was also seated. Though the show was taped before a live audience, episodes were edited down to their final running length, allowing contestants as much time as they liked to contemplate an answer. They could also ask for help in one of three ways: a "lifeline" phone call to a pre-selected friend, a survey of the studio audience, or a request that two of the choices be eliminated. (Each option could be used only once in the contestant's quest for a million.) Tarrant never offered a hint whether a possible answer was correct, but he was encouraging and reassuringly calm.

Even with all the comfortable trappings, though, there was a genuine sense of tension and excitement to the show, especially as the stakes increased. Producer David Briggs explained that, ultimately, the game was all about individual decisions by the contestants. Did they trust their own instincts? Would they dare risk their winnings by attempting to answer a question they did not know cold, or quit short of a million with the cash in hand? (Once they reached the 1,000 and 32,000 money levels, they were guaranteed that amount whether or not they were eliminated by a wrong answer.) To underscore the drama, for each question there was a moment of truth, a last chance to back out, as Tarrant asked: "Is that your final answer?"

The series also worked very well for viewers who did not care about the individual contestants. With the four potential answers to each question spelled out on the TV screen, it was easy to play along at home. Yet what truly helped set Who Wants to Be a Millionaire apart was that, initially, the program did not air as a weekly series. Instead, it ran as a special event, playing out over ten consecutive nights (beginning September 4), allowing viewers to follow contestants night after night. The series repeated that success with similar runs in January 1999 (thirteen days, beginning January 1) and March (eleven days, beginning March 5). The time in between helped to build excitement and anticipation for the next round. Millionaire was also a cost-effective show. Despite the prizes, it was still far less expensive to turn out than a typical comedy or drama series. (The UK series did not produce its first millionaire, garden designer Judith Keppel, until November 2000.) The show used real people, not actors, and (apart from the questions) was essentially unscripted. There was even a small revenue stream from people attempting to qualify as potential contestants, who had to answer automated questions via touch-tone phone elimination, paying a surcharge for each call. Within four years, more than 37 million calls had been made to this "recruitment line."

ABC executive Michael Davies spotted the British success of Who Wants to Be a Millionaire and the network licensed the series for the U.S., bringing the format intact. In a perfect bit of casting, ABC selected as its host Regis Philbin, a veteran TV talk personality whose daily Regis and Kathy Lee show was an established success in daytime TV syndication. The U.S. version of Who Wants to Be a Millionaire began on August 16, 1999, as a summer tryout, and, following the British model, ran eleven half-hour and two hour-long (Sunday) episodes over two consecutive weeks rather than in a weekly slot. The series won every time period in which it played. Philbin, already a familiar face, became television's newest superstar and the program was a hit in all demographics, even the sought-after 18 to 49 age group. Going into the 1999–2000 season, ABC had the strange luck of possessing the hottest series on television, even though it was not on ABC's fall schedule.

Continuing to follow the British strategy, ABC waited nearly three months before bringing the series back for the November sweeps, running it in hour-long segments on fifteen consecutive nights (November 7–21). Once again, Millionaire trumped the competition, with Internal Revenue Service worker John Carpenter becoming the first contestant to reach the $1,000,000 mark (on November 19). Suddenly, ABC found itself with its most powerful program in years, one that could provide a tremendous boost every few months during key ratings periods. Not surprisingly, the network was also tempted to turn the program into an hour-long weekly series for increased ratings all season. Rather than choose between the two strategies, ABC decided on both, departing from the British model in a major way. Beginning January 9, 2000, *Who Wants to Be a Millionaire* returned for eight consecutive nights. Then, on Tuesday, January 18, *Who Wants to Be a Millionaire* became a Tuesday night series. Two nights later it also became a Thursday night series. And three nights later it also became a Sunday night series, allowing viewers to follow contestants from episode to episode, three nights (and hours) per week. There was more. ABC ran *Millionaire* on nine of the last eleven nights in the February 2000 sweeps, which it won for the first time since 1993. For the May sweeps, it was the same story, and, with *Millionaire* as its driving force, ABC easily won the entire 1999–2000 season. *Who Wants to Be a Millionaire* was number one (Tuesday), number two (Sunday), and number three (Thursday) in the final season rankings, the first time ABC held the top three positions since the 1978–79 season (with *Laverne and Shirley, Three's Company*, and *Mork and Mindy*). In setting its schedule for the fall of 2000, the network penciled in a fourth night of *Millionaire* (Wednesday) as a weekly series.

This was an unprecedented reliance on just one program to carry a network's ratings hopes. (The closest comparison was NBC's heavy use of the newsmagazine *Dateline*, which aired up to five nights a week since fall 1998, but which drew from a variety of different available stories and was more of an easy programming "filler" than a show aiming for top ratings.) Yet this strategy with *Millionaire* showed a willingness by ABC to try something different in an increasingly challenging programming environment. Filling multiple slots with the same series was more akin to a specialized cable network schedule than a mass market broadcaster, but the nature of *Millionaire* made it possible. Due to its comparatively low production costs (in relation to its ratings return) the series could still have first-run episodes while playing multiple nights. The audience came pre-sold, clearly preferring another night of a popular hit formula over the competition. Though this schedule practically guaranteed that *Who Wants to Be a Millionaire* would soon suffer from overexposure, for the short run, ABC's strategy worked miracles. However, *Millionaire*'s total domination in the ratings was still not the long term "final answer" for ABC, which desperately needed to reinvent itself in the broadcast network marketplace.

ABC had been number one in the ratings at the time of the announcement of its acquisition by the Disney corporation in 1995, yet since then its performance had been disappointing. If there was going to be a much-touted on-screen synergy between the Disney brand and ABC, it still seemed surprisingly limited. ABC did bring back Disney's Sunday night showcase, placed Disney cartoons in its Saturday morning lineup, and found excuses for series plots to involve visits to Disney World, but there were no breakthrough events. Even more puzzling, ABC seemed determined to define itself more like a hip, cutting-edge cable network rather than the mass market arm of the quintessential family-friendly corporation. It had launched a sassy, irony-laced print campaign ("TV is Good") in the fall of 1997, offering such lines as "This may be the only action you get this Saturday." Garish yellow and black became the network's signature colors, with an on-screen graphics layout that looked a lot like an online website. Such promotions fit a handful of series (they were tailor-made for *Drew Carey*), but did not work for most others. While this might have been intended to win over more of the targeted group of viewers aged 18 to 49 (or younger), it ignored the fact that ABC's most successful recent prime time series were in the bread-and-butter mainstream formats

of family comedy (*Home Improvement*), crime drama (*NYPD Blue*), and sports (*Monday Night Football*). Under Disney, ABC was phasing out longtime successful strategies such as the family-friendly TGIF lineup in favor of more trendy comedy series such as *Seinfeld* wannabe *It's Like, You Know* (still nothing much happening, but now in Los Angeles), the Fox-like *Oh Grow Up* (three young Brooklyn buddies living together and loudly sharing jokes), and the HBO-style *Sports Night* (snappy dialogue from writer Aaron Sorkin, set at a nightly ESPN-ish cable sports program). In its quest to replicate NBC's urban chic, Fox's "attitude," and cable's studied hipness, ABC seemed to have lost some of its own identity. The success of *Millionaire* at least gave ABC time to "clean house" and focus on boosting existing series and introducing new ones with its powerful new lead-in. (*The Practice* became a top ten Sunday night hit this way.) Even as the network basked in its return to the top thanks to *Who Wants to Be a Millionaire*, it

---

September 7, 1999

Later Today. (NBC). To shore up its morning schedule, NBC clones "new" shows from its longtime success. After two hours of *Today*, the network presents a third hour, with the same basic set but with a different cast. NBC also replaces *NBC News at Sunrise*, its early, early half-hour news show, with *Early Today*, a business-oriented newscast produced by CNBC.

September 13, 1999

Seeing the popularity of *Today*'s window onto Rockefeller Plaza, ABC's *Good Morning America* unveils a new set with a large window looking onto Times Square.

September 16, 1999

NBC announces an agreement to acquire 32% of Paxson Communications Corp., the owner of Bud Paxson's Pax Net, for $415 million (with an option to acquire control of the company later). As part of the arrangement, Pax Net soon begins airing rebroadcasts of some NBC shows.

September 28, 1999

Ally. (Fox). Attempting to cheaply fill a prime time slot, Fox chops and condenses previously aired episodes of its hit *Ally McBeal* into "new" thirty-minute programs. This rerun-in-disguise is an instant flop.

November 1, 1999

The Early Show. (CBS). Bryant Gumbel returns to morning TV as host of yet another effort by CBS to compete with *Today*, Gumbel's old show. Jane Clayson serves as co-host.

November 2, 1999

The National Basketball Association launches the first major league-run U.S. cable channel exclusively focused on one sport, NBA.com TV. In 2002 it is renamed NBA TV.

November 29, 1999

President Clinton signs a law that lifts the long-standing rule prohibiting companies that distribute TV signals to homes via satellite from offering local TV stations (as opposed to national network feeds, which had been on satellite for years). The law provides that, after a six-month trial period when local stations can be added for free, the satellite companies must negotiate terms with local stations to pay for permission to retransmit their signals.

	8:00	8:30	9:00	9:30	10:00	10:30	
M O N	20/20		ABC NFL Monday Night Football (to 12 Midnight)				**ABC**
	The King Of Queens	LADIES MAN	Everybody Loves Raymond	Becker	FAMILY LAW		**CBS**
	TIME OF YOUR LIFE		Ally McBeal		local		**FOX**
	Suddenly Susan	Veronica's Closet	LAW & ORDER: SPECIAL VICTIMS UNIT		Dateline NBC		**NBC**
	Moesha	THE PARKERS	GROWN UPS	Malcolm & Eddie	local		**UPN**
	7th Heaven		SAFE HARBOR		local		**WB**
T U E	Spin City	It's Like, You Know…	Dharma & Greg	Sports Night	ONCE AND AGAIN		**ABC**
	JAG		60 Minutes II		JUDGING AMY		**CBS**
	ALLY	That '70s Show	Party Of Five		local		**FOX**
	Just Shoot Me	3rd Rock From The Sun	Will & Grace	THE MIKE O'MALLEY SHOW	Dateline NBC		**NBC**
	Dilbert	SHASTA McNASTY	THE STRIP		local		**UPN**
	Buffy The Vampire Slayer		ANGEL		local		**WB**
W E D	Two Guys And A Girl	Norm	The Drew Carey Show	OH, GROW UP	20/20		**ABC**
	Cosby	WORK WITH ME	CBS Wednesday Movie				**CBS**
	Beverly Hills, 90210		GET REAL		local		**FOX**
	Dateline NBC		THE WEST WING		Law & Order		**NBC**
	Seven Days		Star Trek: Voyager		local		**UPN**
	Dawson's Creek		ROSWELL		local		**WB**
T H R	Whose Line Is It Anyway?	Whose Line Is It Anyway?	WASTELAND		20/20 Downtown		**ABC**
	Diagnosis Murder		Chicago Hope		48 Hours		**CBS**
	World's Wildest Police Videos		Family Guy	ACTION	local		**FOX**
	Friends	Jesse	Frasier	STARK RAVING MAD	ER		**NBC**
	WWF SMACKDOWN!				local		**UPN**
	POPULAR		Charmed		local		**WB**
F R I	The Hughleys	Boy Meets World	Sabrina, The Teenage Witch	ODD MAN OUT	20/20		**ABC**
	Kids Say Darndest Things	LOVE & MONEY	NOW AND AGAIN		Nash Bridges		**CBS**
	RYAN CAULFIELD: YEAR ONE		HARSH REALM		local		**FOX**
	Providence		Dateline NBC		COLD FEET		**NBC**
	Blockbuster Shockwave Cinema				local		**UPN**
	MISSION HILL	The Jamie Foxx Show	The Steve Harvey Show	For Your Love	local		**WB**
S A T	ABC Big Picture Show						**ABC**
	Early Edition		Martial Law		Walker, Texas Ranger		**CBS**
	Cops	Cops	America's Most Wanted: America Fights Back		local		**FOX**
	FREAKS AND GEEKS		The Pretender		Profiler		**NBC**
	local						**UPN**
	local						**WB**

	7:00	7:30	8:00	8:30	9:00	9:30	10:00	10:30	
S U N	The Wonderful World Of Disney				SNOOPS		The Practice		**ABC**
	60 Minutes		Touched By An Angel		CBS Sunday Movie				**CBS**
	The World's Funniest	King Of The Hill	The Simpsons	Futurama	The X Files		local		**FOX**
	Dateline NBC		THIRD WATCH		NBC Sunday Night Movie				**NBC**
	local								**UPN**
	7th Heaven Beginnings		Felicity		JACK & JILL		local		**WB**

needed to plan for life after that show, especially in developing its own distinctive comedies.

In contrast, there was generally no mistaking a Fox series: fast-paced, loud, and—at its best—possessing a sense of savvy self-awareness. The new *Malcolm in the Middle* fit that description perfectly, bringing the spirit of *The Simpsons* to a live-action family sitcom. Characters were smart, weird, and everybody had their comic moments: middle child Malcolm (Frankie Muniz), his brothers Dewey (Erik Per Sullivan) and Reese (Justin Berfield), and their parents, Hal (Bryan Cranston) and Lois (Jane Kaczmarek).

Malcolm in the Middle debuted in January 2000 and joined the company of three other distinctive Fox sitcoms that had begun in the 1998–99 season. The live action *That '70s Show* (from the creators of *3rd Rock from the Sun*) looked at the disco decade from the vantage point of the small town Wisconsin home of Red and Kitty Forman (Kurtwood Smith and Debra Jo Rupp). Stories were usually anchored in the family basement (which functioned much like the bar at *Cheers*) where their responsible but dreamy teenage son Eric (Topher Grace) hung out with off/on again girlfriend Donna Pinciotti (Laura Prepon), "bad boy" Steven Hyde (Danny Masterson), foreign exchange student Fez (Wilmer Valderrama), hunky but naive Michael Kelso (Ashton Kutcher), and Kelso's off/on again girlfriend Jackie Burkhart (Mila Kunis).

On the Fox animated front, *Futurama* (from *Simpsons* creator Matt Groening) dropped twentieth century pizza delivery boy Phillip Fry (Billy West) into interstellar adventures in the year 3000 (via an accidental cryogenic freezing). Fry joined an interplanetary team that included eccentric professor (and distant relative) Hubert Farnsworth (West, again), caustic robot Bender (John DiMaggio), and sexy one-eyed alien Leela (Katey Sagal). The flexible planet-hopping premise allowed virtually any satirical setting, often using the thousand years' "hindsight" to skewer "ancient" Earth. *Family Guy* (from writer-cartoonist Seth MacFarlane) was set in contemporary times in Quahog, Rhode Island, following the dysfunctional Griffin family: lovably clueless dad Peter, talking dog Brian, and genius toddler Stewie (all voiced by McFarlane), along with teens Meg (Mila Kunis) and Chris (Seth Green), and the more practically grounded homemaker Lois (Alex Borstein). The series peppered each episode with pop culture allusions and send-ups, but also ambitiously targeted subjects in politics, business, and religion.

Overall these comedies brought new faces and talent to the mainstream broadcast network stage and seemed to put Fox ahead in the pursuit of "cutting edge" youth-oriented comedy programming. However, none were instant hits and, on the overall Big 4 network platform, even success in this important targeted niche still left Fox with only one program (*Malcolm in the Middle*) in the total audience top thirty for the 1999–2000 season.

NBC meanwhile demonstrated that its urban comedy style was still strong with *Will & Grace*, which had begun in the fall of 1998 and which the network was carefully nurturing for the long run. Though the premise dropped four characters into a Manhattan setting, like *Seinfeld*, there was an important twist: Will Truman (Eric McCormack) and Grace Adler (Debra Messing) were apartment mates who were *not* involved sexually. He was gay. They were creditable buddies, looking out for each other and hanging out with their friends Jack McFarland (Sean Hayes), who was also gay, and Karen Walker (Megan Mullally). In contrast to the controversy that followed the sitcom *Ellen* in 1997 when its main character revealed she was gay, *Will & Grace* simply established the sexual orientation of its characters and immediately moved on to the business of comedy. The result was a quiet revolution in mainstream television (calmly having an openly gay lead character of a major network sitcom) that was all the more effective because it was practically

beside the point. What mattered was the good character chemistry. *Will & Grace* became a hit and, in the fall of 2000, the series moved into the prestigious Thursday night "Must See TV" slot previously occupied by *Cheers* and *Seinfeld*.

Among drama offerings, the presentation of cutting edge shows and those geared primarily toward the highly sought younger demographic was also a priority, but a challenge as well. NBC's *Freaks and Geeks* illustrated the situation. Produced by Paul Feig and Judd Apatow, the series offered a lovingly (sometimes painfully) authentic portrait of high school life, circa 1980, set in Michigan (Feig's home state). There was Emmy-winning writing, a strong cast (including Jason Segel, Seth Rogen, Linda Cardellini, John Francis Daley, James Franco, Samm Levine, Busy Philipps, and Joe Flaherty), and a smart soundtrack (with such artists as Van Halen, Joan Jett, XTC, and The Who). Nonetheless, the series generated disappointing ratings on two different nights and was gone by March. In the eyes of the Big 4 broadcast networks, even a desirous audience still had to reach a certain size. Apart from cable channels, the broadcast networks that offered the best opportunities to succeed with a more limited or specialized audience were the WB and UPN.

In the wake of the success of *Buffy the Vampire Slayer* and *7th Heaven*, the WB had effectively split its identity, slotting its mostly black-oriented shows on one night and placing youthful, teen-oriented dramas everywhere else. That process had begun in January 1998 with the earnest and articulate teenage angst of *Dawson's Creek* (created by Kevin Williamson, writer for the hit feature film "Scream"). That was followed in the fall of 1998 with *Charmed* (Shannen Doherty, Holly Marie Combs, and Alyssa Milano as three sisters who were powerful witches) and *Felicity* (Keri Russell as Felicity Porter, a freshman enrolling in a New York City college to pursue her high school crush, Ben Covington, played by Scott Speedman, only to reach a four-year state of indecision upon meeting dreamy dorm advisor Noel Crane, played by Scott Foley).

New series for the fall of 1999 included *Angel* (a *Buffy* spinoff featuring her first vampire lover), *Popular* (the trials of good-looking, rich, and popular high school kids in Beverly Hills), *Jack & Jill* (Amanda Peet and Ivan Sergei as, respectively, runaway bride/wannabe journalist Jacqueline "Jack" Barrett and good-hearted toy designer David "Jill" Jillefsky), and *Roswell* (the ultimate alienated outsiders, teenagers from another planet). Though none of these series were anywhere near the top ten in the overall ratings, they did well enough with their target audiences, especially teenage girls, so that the WB replaced Fox as *the* place for teen and twenty-something viewers.

UPN, the WB's direct rival, found its own youth-oriented success with the campy wrestling contests of *WWF Smackdown!*, a series that strongly appealed to young males. Previously, matches staged by the World Wrestling Federation had played out on cable (*Raw Is War* had been on the USA network since 1995). A two-hour special on UPN in April 1999 scored some of the highest ratings ever for the network, so a broadcast series was inevitable. With its slick packaging, larger-than-life heroes and villains, and spicy mix of violence and sexual innuendo, *WWF Smackdown!* was an instant success and a perfect example of the leeway a smaller network such as UPN allowed. It could find and profit from a more limited television niche.

Thus, ironically, in a season in which the broadcast networks were all trying hard to find successful new generation, off-beat series (especially comedies), the programming forms that scored surprisingly well were two "retro" mainstays of 1950s television, the quiz show and wrestling. Another surprise was that, despite the attention being paid to the youth-oriented dramas, the scripted se-

December 31, 1999

Television welcomes the millennium in style. Both ABC ("ABC 2000") and PBS ("Millennium 2000") present live all-day coverage of the arrival of 2000 around the world. As usual, Dick Clark hosts ABC's coverage of the new year arriving in Times Square.

January 9, 2000

Following the success of ABC's *Who Wants to Be a Millionaire*, NBC revives *Twenty-One*, the 1950s game show that made Charles Van Doren a celebrity and was taken off the air during the quiz show scandals. Talk show personality Maury Povich serves as host of this new version.

February 15, 2000

"Who Wants to Marry a Multi-Millionaire." (Fox). Coyly cashing in on ABC's hit game show title, creator Mike Darnell and producer Mike Fleiss earn high ratings but bad publicity for Fox in this two-hour special. Fifty women compete to be chosen by wealthy bachelor Rick Rockwell as his bride. The "winner," registered nurse Darva Conger, actually marries Rockwell but quickly files for an annulment after second thoughts, an unhappy honeymoon in Barbados, and word that Rockwell's former fiancée had filed a restraining order against him in 1991. Fox cancels plans to air a repeat of the special and shelves any plans for a series.

April 3, 2000

Viacom buys the remaining 50% of UPN from its partner in the venture, the Chris-Craft group of TV stations, for a mere $5 million.

May 4, 2000

Viacom's acquisition of CBS closes. NBC is now the only network not affiliated with a film studio.

June 28, 2000

Soul Food. (Showtime). A slick adaptation (from executive producer Kenneth "Babyface" Edmonds) of the 1998 sleeper hit movie of the same name follows an extended black family that regularly gathers for boisterous Sunday dinners. The series continues the focus on grown siblings Teri (Nicole Ari Parker), Maxine (Vanessa Williams), and Bird (Malinda Williams), and their respective lives, loves, and ambitions.

ries that worked best for ABC, CBS, and NBC were adult-oriented programs, featuring characters that were well past puberty.

NBC brought back *Providence*, a surprise mid-season hit from January 1999, which followed Dr. Sydney Hansen (Melina Kanakaredes), a successful plastic surgeon who put aside her self-centered Hollywood clientele and returned to her home town and family in Rhode Island. In this second career, she worked at a downtown health clinic and, even more challenging, served as the voice of reason in her family (after the death of her mother), dealing with her single-mom sister, Joanie (Paula Cale); her kid brother, Robbie (Seth Peterson); and her easygoing but often inscrutable veterinarian dad, Jim (Mike Farrell). *Providence* was a mature, gently quirky drama that seemed more like a traditional CBS offering. Not surprisingly, for the fall of 1999, CBS unveiled the similar *Judging Amy*, which followed Amy Gray (Amy Brenneman), a newly separated corporate lawyer, as she left big city life to return to her home town and family in Connecticut, where she accepted a job as a juvenile court judge. At home as a single mom, Amy lived with her eccentric brother, Vincent (Dan Futterman), and her highly opinionated mom, Maxine (Tyne Daly), a former social worker. Both series offered a pleasing mix of issues, characters, and small-town charm.

For *The West Wing*, NBC went to a different sort of "small town," the insular, self-referential world of Washington, D.C., focusing on the president of the United States and his dedicated support staff at the White House (most located in that building's "west wing"). Produced by *ER*'s John Wells, Thomas Schlamme, and *Sports Night*'s Aaron Sorkin (who had written the somewhat similar 1995 theatrical feature "The American President"), *The West Wing* showed life in the world's most powerful office as a mix of grand issues, ideological conflicts, inner-office gamesmanship, sudsy personal complications, and constant jousting with a voracious press corps. Sorkin wrote nearly all the episodes and his sharp ear for dialogue helped convey the sense that viewers were truly peeking into the inner workings of the oval office, or at least an idealized version of it. (There were no actions leading to impeachment in this setting.) Fictional President Jed Bartlet (Martin Sheen) was a thoughtful and articulate liberal Democrat. First Lady Dr. Abigail Bartlet (Stockard Channing) was supportive, yet was a strong force in her own right. The staff included Chief of Staff Leo McGarry (John Spencer), Deputy Chief of Staff Josh Lyman (Bradley Whitford), Communications Director Toby Ziegler (Richard Schiff), Press Secretary "C. J." Cregg (Allison Janney), and Deputy Communications Director Sam Norman Seaborn (Rob Lowe). They conveyed just the right sense of high-strung anxiety driven by the rush of feeling that they were key players on the world stage.

In a more gritty setting, NBC expanded one of its most reliable drama successes, *Law & Order*, with a spinoff series, *Law & Order: Special Victims Unit*. Like the original, the new show's focus was on detailed criminal investigation procedures, but this series dealt with more violent, gruesome crimes, usually involving sex, though not in a titillating way. Here the lead investigating detectives were Elliot Stabler (Christopher Meloni) and Olivia Benson (Mariska Hargitay), and they were sometimes joined by John Munch (Richard Belzer), a character transferred from the recently canceled *Homicide: Life on the Street*. With its familiar structure and pacing, this new series quickly found a comfortable groove that was similar to the original, which had weathered multiple cast changes over the years and still thrived.

One of the most striking aspects of *Law & Order: Special Victims Unit* was on the business production side. Each original episode was rerun on the USA cable network only thirteen days after airing on NBC. Such "repurposing" (as it was dubbed) was seen as one way to deal with spiraling production costs, because the extra revenue from licensing the show to a second outlet right away supported the production company while holding down NBC's cost of airing the show. Not lost on the TV industry was the fact that this represented an important shift in the relationship between networks and affiliates. Airing quick reruns on cable effectively eliminated the affiliates' time as the exclusive source of a first-run network program, and the local stations resented the move. Nonetheless, the networks increasingly saw such a strategy as essential to controlling costs and promoting their programming. With so many cable channels out there, it only made sense to tap that audience, effectively promoting the airings on both outlets.

ABC followed the same concept with one of its new hour-long drama series, *Once and Again*, scheduling reruns of each episode only three days later on Lifetime, the cable channel partially owned by Disney/ABC that touted itself as "television for women." It was an appropriate placement because the series dealt very effectively with issues and emotions surrounding family, divorce, and new love. Created by Marshall Herskovitz and Edward Zwick, the series followed forty-something Lily Manning (Sela Ward) and Rick Sammler (Billy Campbell), both in the process of divorcing their respective spouses, as they found themselves attracted to each other. Their lives came with plenty of complications (spouses, children, interfering friends), yet they were genuinely excited at the prospect of finding love once again. The series effectively dealt with each step of their growing affection, including its effects on Lily's children, Grace (Julia Whelan) and Zoe (Meredith Deane), and Rick's children, Eli (Shane West) and Jessie (Evan Rachel Wood). In fact, for all of ABC's efforts to find youthful, cutting-edge vehicles, these characters were some of the most effective and believable on television. For any rebuilding by ABC and Disney, *Once and Again* was a good place to start.

If Disney was also going to look at ways to become more robust in its use of one-stop corporate synergy, Fox offered a practical example. There was the Twentieth Century Fox production studios, the Fox network, Fox cable services (FX, Fox Family Channel, Fox News Channel), Fox video, and, in newspaper publishing, such major holdings as the *New York Post* and for a while even *TV Guide*. The company actively used all of its platforms as means to reinforce each other, from tie-in books to the best place for reruns of current Fox hits. That top-to-bottom control brought its own problems and pressures, though, most notably in the area of syndicated rerun sales. Reruns for such Fox-produced series as *The X-Files* and *NYPD Blue* initially ended up on FX, and that led to legal action by participating partners such as David Duchovny and Steven Bochco. They questioned whether Fox the production studio had gotten the "best" possible deal from Fox's FX. (Bochco cited FX paying $400,000 per episode for *NYPD Blue* while TNT had paid $1.2 million per episode for *ER*.) There was also concern that playing older Fox-produced series such as *M*A*S*H* as often as ten times a day on FX might dilute future syndication sales. These were difficult questions that went to the heart of "vertical integration."

Yet even with such potential complications, there was greater motivation than ever to consolidate media assets because the FCC continued to revise rules and lower barriers that, previously, would have prevented such actions. For example, in August 1999, the commission announced that it would now allow some "duopolies," that is, the same corporation owning two TV stations within the same media market. Previously, a company could have only one. So any merger involving organizations with preexisting stations in the same geographic area had meant divesting some existing properties. There was a similar relaxation over the total number of owned and operated stations throughout the country that any one company could possess. Previously, the limit had been five. Now, there was no set number but, rather, the limitation was expressed as a percentage of national coverage (no more than 35% of the country for any company's lineup of owned stations).

It was in this atmosphere that giant media conglomerate Viacom (headed by Sumner Redstone) decided to add CBS (run by CEO Mel Karmazin), the country's second-oldest broadcast network, to its stable of assets. As a result of the acquisition (announced in September 1999), Viacom wound up with a strong, complementary mix that combined CBS with the Paramount movie studio, Simon & Schuster publishing, Blockbuster video, and cable mainstays such as MTV, Nickelodeon, and Showtime. There was some irony to the transaction. Viacom had begun life as the TV syndication division of CBS, which the network had been forced to divest in 1973 because of the adoption of the Fin-Syn rules. The offspring

was now taking over the former parent. This new vertical integration package put the combined Viacom/CBS media company assets just behind Time Warner and Disney, and just ahead of Fox's News Corp. (NBC's parent GE dwarfed them all, but broadcasting was only a small percentage of its assets.)

The merger was consummated in the spring, despite a pair of regulatory ownership issues. First, because Viacom/CBS's owned and operated stations would reach a total of 41% of the country, the FCC ruled that the combined entity would have to sell some of its stations. Second, because Viacom was already in the process of acquiring complete control of the much smaller UPN network, the combination meant that the company would now own two TV networks and the FCC still had a rule prohibiting that. The FCC eventually granted a temporary waiver of that rule to allow the merger to take place and, before the waiver expired, the commission amended its rule to allow a "big" network like CBS to also own an "emerging" network like UPN.

One result of the Viacom acquisition of CBS was that it helped the network to deal at last with its longtime concern about consistently attracting older viewers. That audience could now be viewed as one strong element of an overall company that could offer advertisers a portfolio of established "brand names" for all ages, starting with cable's Nickelodeon and MTV and then moving on. Of course, CBS still wanted to win the broadcast network competition for the lucrative 18 to 49 age demographic as often as possible, but now it had a greater range of potential resources to tap for partnerships. For example, in CBS's next turn to carry the Super Bowl (January 2001), MTV-style artists such as 'N Sync and Aerosmith ended up in the halftime show. Dan Rather now shared the same company as 'N Sync's heartthrob Justin Timberlake. That was quite a change.

However, the most dramatic corporate change of the season took place at the world's largest media conglomerate, Time Warner, the parent company of the WB network, HBO, and CNN. In January 2000, Time Warner CEO Gerald Levin and Steve Case, CEO of the Internet access company America Online (AOL), agreed to a media marriage. The truly stunning aspect of the deal was that, technically, AOL was the one buying Time Warner, with the entire deal driven by stock price value. Based on that, at the time, AOL's value was about $140 billion while Time Warner was valued at about $107 billion. Despite those numbers, this did not look like a merger of equals. Time Warner's assets included movie studios, TV production outfits, cable systems, magazines, book publishers, record labels, and sports teams. AOL was an Internet service provider that collected modest monthly subscriber fees (usually just over $20 each) and sold on-line advertising.

Though on paper there was a tremendous amount of money involved in this combination, at heart it really seemed more about dreaming. In less than a decade, the Internet had transformed itself from an obscure trivia question to a key part of everyday life. E-mail was replacing letter writing. Many major newspapers and magazines maintained web pages, offering their content electronically. More and more consumers were shopping on-line. New generations of music fans had found that their favorite songs could be sent along the Internet, almost like a text message. Would television signals soon be following the same route? There seemed to be endless opportunities (in theory) for cross-promotional synergy between the online world and traditional media outlets, especially television. To that point, though, no one had figured out how to fit all the pieces together into a solid, moneymaking plan. AOL touted itself as the answer, a perfect partner with Time Warner, selling itself as the savvy on-line insider on the cutting edge of this brave new media world.

61. Reality Is Bad Enough

AFTER ABC'S SUCCESS WITH REGIS PHILBIN at the helm of *Who Wants to Be a Millionaire* beginning in the summer of 1999, the other networks had gone shopping for their own quiz and game shows. A few series came and went quickly in the 1999–2000 season, including *Twenty One* on NBC, *Greed* on Fox, and *Winning Lines* on CBS. Once again, though, imports from overseas (like *Millionaire*) did the best.

NBC grabbed another British-based hit, *The Weakest Link*, which had scored well in England for the BBC in August 1999, at the same time that *Who Wants to Be a Millionaire* was hitting the U.S. airwaves. NBC's version of *The Weakest Link* arrived near the end of the 2000–01 season (April 16) attempting to lure viewers less with big prize money and more with a distinctive attitude. The show was a high-pressure, fast-moving, fiercely competitive contest that seemed designed to be the opposite of the contestant-friendly *Millionaire*. This was especially true of the program's host, Anne Robinson, who was brought from the British version of *The Weakest Link* as a virtual "anti-Regis." With her steel-rimmed glasses, proper black business dress, and icy stare, the fifty-six-year-old Robinson looked and acted like every student's dreaded nightmare of a school teacher from hell. A former British news reporter, she showed little tolerance for ill-informed flubs. Rather than reassure contestants, she mocked their shortcomings, saving her best putdowns for the "walk of shame" by the player eliminated at the end of a round, when she dismissed them with the declaration, "You *are* the weakest link. Goodbye."

The contest itself had far more complicated rules than *Millionaire* because contestants had to cooperate with, as well as compete against, each other. In each timed round, players had to answer questions round-robin style. Each correct answer added to a common prize bank. An incorrect answer would "break the link" and reset the total added in that round back to zero. At the end of each round, the group had to vote off one player (the "weakest link"), so the number of contestants kept dropping until there were only two left. Those two faced off for all the money accumulated in the prize bank, with only one going home a winner.

This setup meant that, each time the players had to vote someone off, the decision required considerations that went beyond simply determining who did the best (or worst) on the latest round. The trick was to remain in the competition while voting to keep on other players strong enough to build a big bankroll, yet not so strong that they would be the last ones standing. In short, winning required more than knowledge. It required "street smarts."

There was a similar emphasis on opportunistic cunning in a pair of series CBS introduced in the summer of 2000, *Big Brother* and *Survivor*. Though both were game shows in that they involved competition and the lure of big-money prizes, they drew more from the tradition of old television stunt shows such as *Truth or Consequences* and *People Are Funny*, along with newer voyeuristic reality shows such as MTV's *The Real World*.

Big Brother took the basic premise of *The Real World* (a group of people brought together to live under one roof), but then limited the action to just one location, placing cameras throughout the house to follow every move and not allowing the contestants to leave the premises. The program had begun in the Netherlands in 1999, and licensed versions quickly appeared in other European countries before coming to America. For the U.S. edition, ten strangers were locked in a comparatively cramped, specially constructed house on CBS's Hollywood studio lot for three months (from July to September), with Julie Chen (a news correspondent for CBS's *Early Show*) serving as host and egging them on as cameras recorded every move. Of course, the contestants were young and good-looking (allowing for plenty of possible sexual shenanigans) and, every other week, somebody was banished from the household. For the finale, home viewers voted on who should receive the prize of $500,000. CBS set aside large chunks of its summer schedule for *Big Brother*, airing thirty-minute episodes on Mondays, Tuesdays, and Fridays and one-hour episodes on Thursdays and Saturdays (with an extra sixty-minute Wednesday edition added soon after the show's debut). The Saturday episode recapped the previous week's developments, while the Thursday episode aired live. Otherwise, the program consisted of hastily compiled segments recorded since the preceding installment. Rather than turning the program into a titillating "must see" event, such extended exposure revealed that, even with all those cameras, much of the time "live" reality TV was, like real life, fairly boring. To be a successful TV show, life had to be carefully edited. *The Real World* consistently demonstrated this approach, usually generating only about a dozen episodes from months of taping.

CBS's other summer 2000 reality series, *Survivor*, handled the art of manipulating reality to perfection, airing only once a week but to far greater success than *Big Brother*. Originating in Sweden in 1997 (where it was known as *Expedition Robinson,* as in *Swiss Family Robinson*) and later playing on the ITV network in England, *Survivor* entered the U.S. market on May 31, 2000, shepherded by executive producer Mark Burnett. Part game, part travel

Contestant Richard Hatch *(far left)* and host Jeff Probst observed Kelly Wiglesworth and Rudy Boesch compete in the final immunity challenge of the first *Survivor* series. (*CBS Photo Archive* © *2003 CBS Worldwide, Inc. All Rights Reserved.*)

adventure, part intense sports competition, and part soap opera, *Survivor* had a deceptively simple premise: *The Real World* in a *Lord of the Flies* setting. Months before the program aired, sixteen competitors (along with the program's production crew) were deposited on the remote South Seas island of Palau Tiga, off the coast of Borneo, cut off from any contact with the outside world. They were split into two "tribal" groups, given exotic names (the Pagong tribe and the Tagi tribe), and then directed by program host Jeff Probst to set up housekeeping in these primitive conditions and try to make do with what few supplies they were given and whatever they could find or come up with. The contestants were also required to compete in a number of assigned "challenges," such as being the first to successfully build a fire, to swim to a certain point, or to run through a jungle rope maze. They were frequently pushed to demonstrate their individual mettle with food by eating worms or catching and roasting wild rats. In between the contests, they had time to themselves and were free to use it however they wished. (Contestant Richard Hatch, for example, celebrated his birthday on the island by walking around stark naked.) The players also took this personal time to form strategic alliances with each other. Those alliances were important because periodically the tribes were required to meet "in council" and to vote off a member (who would then be taken from the island). This was an intense decision for each person, involving not only the evaluation of who would be most useful to those remaining on the island, but also who might ultimately be less imposing in the quest to be the last survivor (and the winner of the $1 million prize).

All of these actions were caught on tape by the ubiquitous camera crew, then heavily edited over a few months and carefully orchestrated for the series presentation. *Survivor* may have been an unscripted reality show but there was precious little left to chance on how it played out for home viewers. After all, the producers knew how the actions were going to turn out by the time they edited the finished footage, so they selected scenes to maximize conflict, provide misleading impressions, and, generally, tease home viewers. Even the very premise of the series was an illusion: though the island location was physically remote, in many ways it could just as well have been taped in a closed set of some studio back lot, like *Big Brother*. For the sixteen participants, help in any

truly dangerous situation was always there just on the other side of the camera in the form of a huge, fully equipped production crew.

After twelve episodes, *Survivor* was down to four final contestants, the middle-aged Hatch, a consultant; tough-talking Susan Hawk, a truck driver; river guide Kelly Wiglesworth; and crusty retired Navy SEAL Rudy Boesch. In a dramatic two-hour finale that aired on August 23, the four were first narrowed down to two and then the previously ejected tribal members were involved in selecting the winner. Despite a snarling denouncement of Hatch by Hawk, Hatch walked away with the million-dollar prize check, in the process establishing an unsettling profile of a "winner" in reality TV. Throughout the series, Hatch had been manipulative, duplicitous, and self-centered (deliberately forming "alliances" with other contestants that he could utilize solely for his own ultimate advantage), but he was also undeniably charismatic. Despite such traits (or, perhaps, because of them), he won the competition, and *Survivor* became the highest-rated summer series in TV history, with the finale earning CBS's highest ratings since the equally melodramatic figure skating finals between Nancy Kerrigan and Tonya Harding at the 1994 Winter Olympics.

Like *Who Wants to Be a Millionaire* the previous year, *Survivor* still needed to prove that it was more than a mere summer success by playing against regular-season competition. CBS decided to next put the program on the front lines, slotting it Thursday nights against NBC's powerhouse *Friends*. However, that match-up did not start until January 2001 because, unlike *Millionaire*, *Survivor* (needing months for site preparation, contestant selection, filming, and editing) could not turn out an endless stream of episodes virtually overnight. Instead, CBS began a new round of the series (*Survivor: The Australian Outback*) on January 28, debuting after the Super Bowl and then moving to its regular Thursday slot. Despite the delay, the program delivered a ready audience, often topping *Friends*, all the way to its finale in the May sweeps. In the process, *Survivor* became the year's top-rated series and it helped CBS squeak by ABC in the overall ratings to win the 2000–01 season. Even more important for the network, *Survivor* did very well in the targeted 18 to 49 age demographic and, with careful advance planning, CBS was able to stretch out two new *Survivor* series over an entire season in 2001–02. It was a true "water cooler" program,

Day		8:00	8:30	9:00	9:30	10:00	10:30	Network
MON		20/20 Downtown		ABC NFL Monday Night Football (to 12 Midnight)				ABC
		The King Of Queens	YES, DEAR	Everybody Loves Raymond	Becker	Family Law		CBS
		BOSTON PUBLIC		Ally McBeal		local		FOX
		Daddio	TUCKER	DEADLINE		Third Watch		NBC
		Moesha	The Parkers	The Hughleys	GIRLFRIENDS	local		UPN
		7th Heaven		Roswell		local		WB
TUE		Who Wants To Be A Millionaire		Dharma & Greg	THE GEENA DAVIS SHOW	Once And Again		ABC
		JAG		60 Minutes II		Judging Amy		CBS
		That '70s Show	Titus	DARK ANGEL		local		FOX
		MICHAEL RICHARDS SHOW	3rd Rock From The Sun	Frasier	DAG	Dateline NBC		NBC
		UPN'S Night At The Movies				local		UPN
		Buffy The Vampire Slayer		Angel		local		WB
WED		Who Wants To Be A Millionaire		The Drew Carey Show	Spin City	GIDEON'S CROSSING		ABC
		BETTE	WELCOME TO NEW YORK	CBS Wednesday Movie				CBS
		Malcolm In The Middle	NORMAL, OHIO	THE STREET		local		FOX
		TITANS		The West Wing		Law & Order		NBC
		Seven Days		Star Trek: Voyager		local		UPN
		Dawson's Creek		Felicity		local		WB
THR		Whose Line Is It Anyway?	Whose Line Is It Anyway?	Who Wants To Be A Millionaire		Primetime		ABC
		48 Hours		City Of Angels		Diagnosis Murder		CBS
		Fox Thursday Night Movie				local		FOX
		Friends	CURSED	Will & Grace	Just Shoot Me	ER		NBC
		WWF Smackdown!				local		UPN
		GILMORE GIRLS		Charmed		local		WB
FRI		Two Guys And A Girl	TROUBLE WITH NORMAL	Norm	MADIGAN MEN	20/20		ABC
		THE FUGITIVE		C.S.I.: CRIME SCENE INVESTIGATION		Nash Bridges		CBS
		World's Wildest Police Videos		FREAKYLINKS		local		FOX
		Providence		Dateline NBC		Law & Order: Special Victims Unit		NBC
		FREEDOM		LEVEL 9		local		UPN
		Sabrina, The Teenage Witch	GROSSE POINTE	Popular		local		WB
SAT		ABC Big Picture Show						ABC
		THAT'S LIFE		Walker, Texas Ranger		THE DISTRICT		CBS
		Cops	Cops	America's Most Wanted: America Fights Back		local		FOX
		NBC Saturday Movie						NBC
		local						UPN
		local						WB

Day	7:00	7:30	8:00	8:30	9:00	9:30	10:00	10:30	Network
SUN	The Wonderful World Of Disney				Who Wants To Be A Millionaire		The Practice		ABC
	60 Minutes		Touched By An Angel		CBS Sunday Movie				CBS
	Futurama	King Of The Hill	The Simpsons	Malcolm In The Middle	The X Files		local		FOX
	Dateline NBC		ED		NBC Sunday Night Movie				NBC
	local								UPN
	The Jamie Foxx Show	For Your Love	The Steve Harvey Show	The PJs	HYPE	NIKKI	local		WB

with fans talking about the manipulations, double-dealings, and the latest outrageous stunts with the same enthusiasm once reserved for such fictional series as *Dallas* and *Dynasty*, or the number one series of the previous season, *Who Wants to Be a Millionaire*.

In fact, while ABC continued to bask in the total audience ratings strength for *Millionaire* (all four weekly editions ended up in the top twenty for the 2000–01 season, with three in the top ten), the show's ratings were down more than 30% from the previous season. More troubling for ABC, *Millionaire* was losing its cachet among viewers aged 18 to 49, who were not drawn to the quiz aspect of the series for the long run. Many of them had come, watched, and moved on. It appeared more and more that the big-money quiz show "fad" touched off by *Who Wants to Be a Millionaire* consisted of just one show: *Who Wants to Be a Millionaire*. By running it on multiple nights, ABC had essentially provided the viewing public with as many spinoffs of the form as it could take.

So for all the talk about "the return of quiz shows" in the wake of *Millionaire,* producers and programmers merely ended up using the artifice of a "game" as just another element in an already-developing new generation of reality shows. These proved to be a more viable and flexible formula that could put a contemporary spin on virtually any familiar program type, from talent shows à la the 1940s *Original Amateur Hour* (ABC's *Making of the Band*; the WB's *Pop Stars*) to the deliberately embarrassing moments of the 1960s *Dating Game* (UPN's *Chains of Love*). These shows continued to be less expensive to produce than original fiction series.

Reality shows also received a boost from fears that the entire Hollywood film and TV industry would grind to a halt in the middle of 2001, when contracts between the studios and the writers and actors unions were set to expire. With many open issues concerning the Internet and new methods of distributing product, most industry observers expected a prolonged strike by at least one of the unions, which would have effectively shut down production of scripted television series (and movies) set for the fall of 2001. Though both unions wound up agreeing to new contracts, thus avoiding any strike, in the meantime the networks had already given the green light to a wide range of reality shows that, for the most part, would let them avoid worrying about a walkout by writers and actors. There seemed to be no shortage of willing non-professionals ready to step into the spotlight and put themselves into funny, daring, embarrassing, and outrageous situations.

For years, daytime television and cable programs had emphasized, attracted, and nurtured such participants, putting them on stage or in the audience. Many of these programs were harmless fluff. At their worst, though, the images on such shows as MTV's *Jackass* were uncomfortably gross or disturbingly exploitative. Confrontational daytime talk shows such as those hosted by Jerry Springer and Jenny Jones had helped push the form to outrageous excess, essentially using the guests on stage and members of the studio audience as low-rent props for crude, titillating topics (like "Dating mom, and her daughter"). While the programs did not give formal scripts to the participants, there was little doubt that with minimal prompting they would perform exactly as expected. Having watched the shows, people came in knowing what was expected on camera, and acted accordingly. Each season seemed to push the boundaries a little further, with fewer and fewer actions considered out of bounds. The image of daytime television in particular grew so bad that in the late 1990s talk show personalities such as Oprah Winfrey and Rosie O'Donnell stood out by promoting the fact that they did *not* engage in such behavior. The difference in 2000 was that this crude, anything-goes attitude was also permeating the prime time broadcast schedule, going beyond summer fillers to become a strategic peg in year-round network pro-

gramming strategy at any time of the day. That was changing the perceived texture of television. The program from the 2000–01 season that epitomized this attitude was Fox's *Temptation Island*.

On the surface, the premise of *Temptation Island* (a mid-season series beginning January 10) seemed like a cross between *The Love Boat* and *Fantasy Island*, bringing eight extremely good-looking contestants (four couples) to a luxurious Caribbean beach resort. Though they were all still single, they were in various stages of developing relationships. *Temptation Island* was set up to test their resolve, splitting the men and women into separate groups and having them mix with twenty-six other attractive singles at the resort (half men, half women), whose "job" was to get as romantically involved with the contestants as possible, with all the "action" being recorded for replay. The "winners" would be the couple that strayed the least during their time at the resort. These rules offered everyone the lure of generating sparks with other people in an exotic setting and showing off with the cameras rolling, even if it meant jeopardizing an existing relationship. There was dancing, flirting, caressing, and, of course, moments of deceit and betrayal. Yet while *Temptation Island* was presented as just another "game" show, there were truly troubling aspects to it. If one of the draws of reality TV was that it involved real people, then that meant it affected real people as well. The *Temptation Island* setup seemed structured to take real people who might have found their partner for life and potentially ruin that real-life relationship, just for the sake of entertaining the viewing audience. It was one thing to catch and cook a rat in the self-contained world of *Survivor*. It was quite another to be a rat, as part of a series that

September 18, 2000
NBC drops the one-year-old *Later Today* and replaces it by simply expanding *Today* to a third hour.

September 25, 2000
After a bruising court battle, the World Wrestling Federation moves its cable contests from USA to TNN (owned by Viacom, the owner of UPN, home of *WWF Smackdown!*). At the same time, TNN changes its name from The Nashville Network to The National Network, shifts its headquarters from Nashville to New York City, and begins phasing out country-oriented programming.

October 15, 2000
Curb Your Enthusiasm. (HBO). *Seinfeld* co-creator Larry David plays a fictionalized version of himself that is hilariously abrasive, self-centered, and obsessive. The improvisation-based series also casts real life stars as themselves (first up: Richard Lewis). Cheryl Hines plays Larry's wife, Cheryl, and Jeff Garlin his manager, Jeff.

October 24, 2000
The Michael Richards Show. (NBC). The former co-stars of *Seinfeld* begin their quest for solo stardom with Michael Richards (a.k.a. Kramer) playing a bumbling private eye. This weak slapstick effort is gone by Christmas.

December 8, 2000
Dot Comedy. (ABC). Brothers Randy and Jason Sklar present "humorous" content from the Internet. With a feeble 1.7 rating for viewers aged 18 to 49, it lasts one episode.

January 11, 2001
AOL Time Warner is born, as the merger of Time Warner and America Online closes.

potentially involved real emotions and real relationships that could have real-life consequences long after the series had aired. This was a poor reflection on the standards of the people behind the program, on the contestants who willingly signed up to participate, and on the viewers drawn by the titillating setup. Nonetheless, by then the idea that people would do practically anything to end up on television was so deeply ingrained that viewers simply considered this as just another entertainment show and *Temptation Island* landed as one of the top fifteen programs for the 2000–01 season.

The drive to push TV into yet more outrageous territory met with a different reaction in the field of sports. After the success of prime time wrestling on UPN during the 1999–2000 season, World Wrestling Federation owner Vince McMahon aimed for a bigger broadcast stage in a deal with NBC to create a new football league, the XFL (an acronym for the "eXtreme" Football League). NBC was to be an equal partner in the new league and would provide the primary TV outlet by devoting its entire Saturday night prime time schedule to the XFL games from February through April. In addition, UPN signed on for a weekly Sunday night game and its sister cable network TNN took weekly Sunday afternoon contests.

As he had done with wrestling, McMahon planned for the XFL to take elements of an existing sport and exaggerate them in an alternative promoted as bolder, louder, and more audacious than the original. The XFL placed field-level microphones to catch raw comments by the players, enlisted a striking lineup of photogenic

scantily clad cheerleaders, and landed Minnesota Governor Jesse Ventura (a veteran wrestling personality) as a part-time color commentator. Such coverage trappings were straight out of McMahon's wrestling program playbook. It was harder to come up with noticeable differences that mattered much on the playing field, though the XFL touted its games as being faster moving and more physical. For NBC, which had dropped NFL football in 1998 when it found licensing rights too pricey, the XFL was an irresistible opportunity to once again carry the sport, but at a fraction of the NFL price. The XFL began on February 3, 2001, less than two weeks after the Super Bowl, attracting a sizable audience of 15.7 million viewers who sampled the first night's game. Once, apparently, was enough for most, and the audience dropped by about 60% the next week and 71% in the third week. By the end of the season, NBC's XFL coverage was registering some of the lowest ratings ever for a first run show on one of the Big 3 broadcast networks (a 1.6 rating one week), while UPN's Sunday night games came in 151st and last in the season's rankings. NBC quickly found a way out of its two-year contract, UPN and TNN also exited, and McMahon pulled the plug on the league after one season.

Oddly, the XFL probably failed because it was not outrageous enough. Regular WWF viewers no doubt expected the XFL to display the same kind of cutting-edge salacious violence that marked the weekly wrestling telecasts. Instead, all they saw were, in effect, minor league football games with some flashy visual effects and graphics, but no real sizzle. As the XFL experiment was quickly sinking into a ratings black hole, McMahon arranged for cameras to be placed in the cheerleaders' dressing rooms, but even the most gullible of viewers must have assumed that NBC was not really going to broadcast images of naked women in a desperate effort for ratings. NBC had not sunk that low. Yet.

Less than two months after the XFL faded from view, NBC, which had largely resisted the new reality show craze, wholeheartedly embraced the form with *Fear Factor*, which became *the* hot reality show for the summer of 2001 (beginning June 11). Produced by the same company that turned out *Big Brother*, *Fear Factor* presented six contestants (three men, three women) competing for a $50,000 prize by "confronting their fears" and performing three stunts for the cameras and audience. Some were simply physical challenges, such as jumping from one zooming speedboat to another. However, the most talked-about stunts were the "gross out" kind, with contestants allowing four hundred rats to crawl over them, or eating cockroaches, or sticking their heads in a box full of worms. In spring 2002, as one of its "stunts," *Fear Factor* had that week's contestants stand naked in front of the camera for three minutes, with the "naughty parts" fuzzed out electronically before the segment aired. In the year that NBC celebrated seventy-five years in the broadcasting business, this is what the network of Fred Coe, Pat Weaver, Sid Caesar, Dave Garroway, *Hill Street Blues*, and *The Cosby Show* had come to. Tellingly, these actions caused barely a ripple of outrage in the TV landscape. In fact, in the best spirit of cross-promotion, *Today* interviewed most of the contestants (one at a time, to spread out the number of times they could show the clips) discussing how they faced up to their fear of being naked in public.

Despite the mushrooming growth of every type of reality show during the 2000–01 season, the bulk of broadcast network programming in fall 2000 was still fictional comedy and drama. In an odd way, the reality shows began to serve a fill-in function for broadcasters similar to the use of feature film repeats and series reruns on cable channels. Broadcasters could not get away with that many reruns, so the less expensive reality shows filled the time perfectly (both during summer and to replace a canceled show). If they themselves became hits, so much the better. Reality series also helped offset the increasingly high prices attached to proven scripted series such as *ER* and *Friends* and allowed concentrated promotion on a comparative handful of new fictional shows.

For fall 2000, there were only thirty-one new series on all six broadcast networks (down about 25% from a few seasons before). CBS had the only breakout drama hit, the unexpectedly successful police show *CSI: Crime Scene Investigation,* with Marg Helgenberger and William Petersen as members of the forensic team in the Las Vegas police department. Produced by Jerry Bruckheimer (with feature film credits including "Top Gun," "Beverly Hills Cop," and, more recently, "Armageddon"), the series began on Friday nights following a heavily promoted glossy remake of *The Fugitive* series, but soon overshadowed its lead-in. Unlike *The Fugitive,* which had complicated on-going character conflicts and story arcs, *CSI* took an approach similar to NBC's successful *Law & Order* series, emphasizing self-contained stories that followed the painstaking process of each investigation. When *Survivor* began its second season at the start of 2001 in a Thursday time slot, CBS moved *CSI* to the adjacent slot (opposite *Will & Grace*). The network found itself with another solid, top ten hit on its way to winning the total audience ratings for the 2000–01 season.

CBS was still fourth in the competition for viewers aged 18 to 49, though it did show the most improvement in that category among the networks. In fact, the ratings race was so tight that less than one ratings point separated NBC, Fox, ABC, and CBS, making it the closest annual ratings competition in two decades. The rankings were so close that just one big hit show could completely change the standings, as had happened with ABC and *Who Wants to Be a Millionaire.* The key, though, was how well the winning network could take advantage of such a boost. With just a handful of exceptions, ABC had been generally unsuccessful in using the leverage provided by *Millionaire* to introduce other new shows.

More significantly, however, the lead by the broadcast networks over the cable services was rapidly evaporating. By now, more than two-thirds of all U.S. homes with TVs were wired to cable. In the summer of 2001, for the first time, the aggregate average rating of the basic cable networks topped the aggregate average ratings for all the broadcast networks. Clearly, the broadcasters were no longer competing just with each other but also with the dozens of cable channels they had once dismissed as statistically insignificant. To that end, the major corporate owners of the networks continued to build strength by acquisition and consolidation, not only of individual stations but also by investing in (or buying outright) cable outlets. Viacom/CBS acquired BET, Black Entertainment Television. Disney/ABC bought the Family Channel from Fox. NBC added an investment in the Pax network to its portfolio. Such moves not only helped the corporations capture particular niche audiences, but they also provided additional outlets for material. NBC, for example, reran episodes of *The Weakest Link* on Pax. This strategy also helped lessen the impact of the shift of viewers to cable. Disney, for example, would be far less concerned about fewer people watching ABC if those viewers simply switched to another Disney property, such as the Disney Channel or ESPN.

The networks had already applied a somewhat similar approach to news, with Fox, NBC, and CNN being particularly aggressive in showcasing material on multiple viewing venues. However, the key force in increasing news ratings continued to be the presence of a big news story. In the 2000–01 season, that came in the fall 2000 presidential contest between Democrat Al Gore and Republican George W. Bush (son of the former president). Ratings for the news networks were strong during the campaign and skyrocketed when a winner did not clearly emerge on election night. However,

viewers were also extremely critical of the performance by news organizations in reporting the close vote totals. Most of the networks called the key state of Florida for Gore at about 8:00 P.M. in the East on election night, then had to retract that two hours later, when they realized that state was too close to call. Four hours later, most put Florida in the Republican column and declared Bush the winner, only to sheepishly move the state back to the undecided column soon thereafter. The Florida count (and, therefore, the presidential race as a whole) then remained undecided for more than a month, during which time convoluted legal actions and local Florida recounts provided ample news fodder. At last, in mid-December, the U.S. Supreme Court ended the matter by letting stand the vote total that gave Bush a hair's breadth lead in Florida, earning him the necessary electoral votes to win the presidency.

Such extraordinary stories were, of course, the exception. Most days, as with regular entertainment programming, there were so many choices available that news shows often ended up stressing whatever hooks might lure potential viewers. In the process, the practice of maintaining distance between the news and the entertainment sides of a network sometimes completely disappeared. Though Julie Chen was a CBS news correspondent, her presence on the entertainment series *Big Brother* was treated as just another "network assignment." Even all-news CNN was changing its style to emphasize personality, stressing who was delivering the news as much as the news itself. This change was symbolized by the hiring of Andrea Thompson as an anchor for Headline News. Though she had a few months of recent on-air news experience (in Albuquerque, New Mexico), Thompson was best known for having been an actress on *NYPD Blue.* Overall, more and more news time (even on twenty-four-hour services) was filled with an increasingly loud, tabloid tone, or its antithesis: soft features and "popular" stories, often about celebrities. These trivialities received coverage beyond their objective news value. During the summer of 2001, two topics symbolized the situation. In the first, several shark attacks against swimmers near coastal areas led to a frenzy of stories filled with breathless detail and dire warnings. They treated the situation like a national emergency, even for landlocked areas miles away from the nearest shark habitat (which was most of the country).

On a more serious level, there was coverage of Chandra Levy, a twenty-four-year-old intern in Washington, D.C., who disappeared in May 2001. What transformed this simple missing person story into perfect summer tabloid fodder were rumors that she had been secretly involved in a relationship with U.S. Congressman Gary Condit, a Democrat from California. Talk show hosts, especially on cable, found the coupling of the words "intern" and "sex" impossible to resist, and they speculated endlessly on whether her disappearance (and possible death) might have resulted from that relationship. Although there was no evidence at the time that Condit had been involved with the disappearance, news organizations inevitably found the excuse to mention his name when covering the Levy case. One of the few dissenting voices came from Dan Rather, who made a point of not including such reports on the *CBS Evening News,* airing only one Levy-related story for months. But there was no stopping the tabloid tide when ABC's Connie Chung landed an exclusive prime time interview with Condit in August 2001. That interview was heavily hyped by the network though, in the end, Condit said little to Chung other than to assert that he had nothing to do with Levy's disappearance. The threads of this story played out in 2002 with Condit losing his bid for reelection (he was defeated in the primary) and the discovery of Levy's remains along a park pathway in Washington. By then, though, this story seemed far less important, even for cable news pundits.

In the intervening months, something else had happened.

62. Ground Zero

THE AIRPLANE ATTACK ON THE TWIN TOWERS of the World Trade Center in New York City on September 11, 2001, was a stunning television event. Because it took place in one of the most wired media cities in the world, the suicide assault was guaranteed a huge audience. The first plane hit without warning and in comparative obscurity at 8:46 A.M. Eastern time. Even so, there was a video camera that caught the action. Documentary filmmaker Jules Naudet, part of a team chronicling life at a New York City firehouse, had been taping members of the company in a routine call nearby when he heard the roaring sound of a plane. He instinctively turned toward it and, with his camera running, captured the moment of impact as American Airlines Flight 11 struck the North tower of the World Trade Center, instantly killing everyone aboard.

At the time, no one was certain that the crash had been deliberate. There was an almost eerie detachment to the network commentary that accompanied the initial pictures of the World Trade Center, smoke rising from a gaping black hole between the 96th and 103rd floors of the North tower. Had something happened to the pilot? Had there been trouble aboard? At 9:03 A.M., with cameras from all the networks trained on the scene, a second plane, United Airlines Flight 175, slammed into the South tower, creating a fireball and another gaping hole. Instantly, everyone knew that this was no accident. Network news correspondents who had been moving into position to follow a tragic aviation mishap suddenly found themselves covering a far more frightening story. This was a deliberate attack on the home soil of the United States.

With President George W. Bush far from the White House (visiting a school in Florida), news organizations automatically turned to other established sources of official information in Washington, primarily the Pentagon. Suddenly, correspondents on the air from that location reported that they were being told to leave. The Pentagon itself had been struck at 9:41 A.M. by another hijacked passenger plane, American Airlines Flight 77, though that crash had not taken place live on television.

The situation was unprecedented. It was the equivalent to being in a war zone, but not knowing where the battle lines were or the identity of the enemy. Clearly there was a coordinated attack aimed for maximum visual and symbolic impact. Network correspondents struggled to remain calm and informative, determined not to feed potential fears but to pass on the latest information as quickly and accurately as possible. They were also careful not to focus on (or show in identifiable close-ups) images of people in flames or those falling to their death from the World Trade Center towers. Still, the correspondents were haunted by uncertainty. How many more hijacked passenger planes were out there? Were there targets in other cities apart from New York and Washington? As the minutes ticked by, the story grew even more grim. At around 10:00 A.M., after burning for an hour, the South tower of the World Trade Center collapsed, live on television. Network anchors could barely contain their horror, while viewers at home sat stunned. Just before 10:30 A.M., the North tower fell as well. Everyone knew that rescue workers who had rushed to the scene to help save lives were in the towers and were now presumably gone.

In less time than it took to run a typical made-for-TV movie, television had shown a devastatingly effective act of real-life terrorism that had left thousands dead. By bringing these stark images of destruction, live, to viewers throughout the country (and the world), television had amplified the impact of the attack, transforming seemingly unassailable symbols of U.S. power into starkly vulnerable targets. These pictures were not after-the-fact images safely edited into a montage of distant smoldering ruins (often the case in coverage of virtually any disaster). This was a story that had unfolded in excruciating and uncertain detail in real time before millions of viewers. They had seen both towers of one of the world's tallest structures crumble before their eyes. In the television echo chamber of live reporting, the magnified impact of these actions was deafening.

Yet, at the same time, the non-stop television coverage also immediately saved lives. Most dramatically, it helped to stave off another attack by a fourth hijacked airplane. United Airlines Flight 93 had been seized after taking off from Newark, New Jersey, and was headed south, probably to another site in Washington (such as the U.S. Capitol). It was running later than the other three planes. More important, the passengers on board were armed with information. Soon after the hijacking, some passengers had telephoned the outside world and were immediately given a blow-by-blow description of the events at the World Trade Center from those watching the coverage. The passengers realized this was no ordinary hijacking and that they were probably destined for a similar fate and certain death. They quickly huddled together, settled on a strategy, and stormed the cockpit. The plane crashed in an empty field about eighty miles southeast of Pittsburgh, killing everyone aboard. Those passengers came to be honored as heroes who prevented an even greater number being added to the day's death toll.

Television coverage continued all day September 11, with the

As the events of September 11, 2001, unfolded, live, on television, network anchors such as ABC's Peter Jennings delivered their reports with deliberate, measured tones. (*Courtesy of ABC News*)

networks not only canceling all regular programming and all commercials, but also putting aside their normal competitive practices. Primarily at the urging of CBS's Don Hewitt, all the networks agreed to an almost unprecedented sharing of information for the rest of the day, sending feeds and stories back and forth as events unfolded. News reports also appeared all across the cable dial, even though most of the entertainment cable channels did not have their own news departments. In a snapshot of corporate ownership, network news reports were simultaneously fed to other properties controlled by the same companies, so that the CBS news coverage appeared on MTV, VH1, and UPN; ESPN picked up ABC; NBC fed Pax, MSNBC, and CNBC; Fox had FX, the Family Channel, and Fox News Channel; and TNT and TBS carried CNN's coverage. Other cable channels such as the Food Network, Home & Garden, and the shopping networks stopped their normal programming and instead displayed simple, respectful messages. A few channels, such as Nickelodeon (and Nick at Nite), deliberately stayed with their normal programming, serving as an alternative for both kids and adults to the frightening intensity of real life.

The television news coverage continued non-stop through the night of September 11, then into the next day, and the next, for seventy-two hours. This was the longest continuous period devoted to a news event in television history. (Previously, in November 1963, the networks had devoted four days to the assassination of President John F. Kennedy and its aftermath, but had signed off overnights.) Running commercial free, this cost the networks about $100 million per day in lost advertising revenue. On the first day, there were frequent replays of the second plane's crash into the World Trade Center's South tower and of the collapse of both buildings, but that was toned down significantly thereafter. Instead, the primary focus was on the dramatic rescue efforts, attempts to identify who was responsible for the attacks, and discussions of the possible U.S. response. There were countless individual stories of heroism and also of tragic final moments. As a group, New York's firefighters and police officers became the unquestioned heroes of the day. In searching for those behind the attack, the trail soon led to the international terrorist organization, al-Qaeda, and its leader, Osama bin Laden, based in the country of Afghanistan. Though neither name was a stranger to anyone closely following international news, for most viewers such information had been buried in a television world awash in increasingly trivial stories. The attacks of September 11 dramatically demonstrated that there was indeed a place for "real" news.

By September 15, though, it was almost a relief for viewers to see television edge back into an entertainment schedule, beginning with comedies and dramas produced long before September 11. On September 17, David Letterman was one of the first to face the recent events in a newly taped episode, opening his program with a heartfelt monologue that artfully balanced sadness, astonishment, and a determination to press on, even if he was not sure exactly what came next and how easy it would be to get back to comedy. He was not alone. No one was certain what would be appropriate and in good taste after the September 11 attacks. Still, by then President Bush had urged the country to begin a return to normal activities, and television was willing to lead the way. To open the September 29 first episode of *Saturday Night Live*, producer Lorne Michaels asked New York Mayor Rudy Giuliani, "Can we be funny?" prompting the ice-breaking response, "Why start now?"

The attack had occurred just as the broadcast networks were about to launch their fall premieres. As a result of the extended news coverage, most of the new shows and returning season debuts were pushed back at least a week. Even then, the networks as well as viewers had difficulty in focusing on entertainment programs, which gave an almost "who cares?" tone to the delayed season.

Aside from postponing the start dates for shows, the September 11 attacks also resulted in some last-minute adjustments to schedules and program episodes. Reality shows seemed particularly frivolous and self-indulgent, so most of those were quickly put on hold. (Being "brave" enough to eat exotic bugs on TV paled in comparison to stories of real-life heroics.) ABC found that viewers

FALL 2001 SCHEDULE

	8:00	8:30	9:00	9:30	10:00	10:30	
M O N	Who Wants To Be A Millionaire		ABC NFL Monday Night Football (to 12 Midnight)				ABC
	The King Of Queens	Yes, Dear	Everybody Loves Raymond	Becker	Family Law		CBS
	Boston Public		Ally McBeal		local		FOX
	The Weakest Link		Third Watch		CROSSING JORDAN		NBC
	The Hughleys	ONE ON ONE	The Parkers	Girlfriends	local		UPN
	7th Heaven		Angel		local		WB
T U E	Dharma & Greg	What About Joan	BOB PATTERSON	Spin City	PHILLY		ABC
	JAG		THE GUARDIAN		Judging Amy		CBS
	That '70s Show	UNDECLARED	24		local		FOX
	EMERIL	Three Sisters	Frasier	SCRUBS	Dateline NBC		NBC
	Buffy The Vampire Slayer		Roswell		local		UPN
	Gilmore Girls		SMALLVILLE		local		WB
W E D	My Wife & Kids	ACCORDING TO JIM	The Drew Carey Show	Whose Line Is It Anyway?	20/20		ABC
	60 Minutes II		THE AMAZING RACE		WOLF LAKE		CBS
	Fox Family Comedy Wheel	Grounded For Life	BERNIE MAC SHOW	Titus	local		FOX
	Ed		The West Wing		Law & Order		NBC
	ENTERPRISE		Special Unit 2		local		UPN
	Dawson's Creek		Felicity		local		WB
T H R	Whose Line Is It Anyway?	Whose Line Is It Anyway?	Who Wants To Be A Millionaire		Primetime		ABC
	Survivor: Africa		CSI: Crime Scene Investigation		THE AGENCY		CBS
	Family Guy	THE TICK	Temptation Island 2		local		FOX
	Friends	INSIDE SCHWARTZ	Will & Grace	Just Shoot Me	ER		NBC
	WWF Smackdown!				local		UPN
	Popstars 2	ELIMIDATE DELUXE	Charmed		local		WB
F R I	The Mole II: The Next Betrayal		THIEVES		Once And Again		ABC
	THE ELLEN SHOW	DANNY	That's Life		48 Hours		CBS
	Dark Angel		PASADENA		local		FOX
	Providence		Dateline NBC		Law & Order: Special Victims Unit		NBC
	UPN's Night At The Movies				local		UPN
	Sabrina, The Teenage Witch	MAYBE IT'S ME	REBA	RAISING DAD	local		WB
S A T	ABC Big Picture Show						ABC
	Touched By An Angel		CITIZEN BAINES		The District		CBS
	Cops	Cops	America's Most Wanted: America Fights Back		local		FOX
	NBC Saturday Movie						NBC
	local						UPN
	local						WB

	7:00	7:30	8:00	8:30	9:00	9:30	10:00	10:30	
S U N	The Wonderful World Of Disney				ALIAS		The Practice		ABC
	60 Minutes		THE EDUCATION OF MAX BICKFORD		CBS Sunday Movie				CBS
	Futurama	King Of The Hill	The Simpsons	Malcolm In The Middle	The X Files		local		FOX
	Dateline NBC		The Weakest Link		LAW & ORDER: CRIMINAL INTENT		UC: UNDERCOVER		NBC
	local								UPN
	Ripley's Believe It Or Not		The Steve Harvey Show	MEN, WOMEN & DOGS	Nikki	OFF CENTRE	local		WB

simply had no time to follow the return of its spring 2001 "find the imposter" mystery reality series, *The Mole*, and the network yanked the show after just a few fall episodes.

By coincidence, there were a number of new espionage dramas that had already been slotted in the fall lineup and, before some aired, adjustments had to be made quickly to specific scenes filmed before the attack in order to avoid offending viewers or treading too close to reality. The first episode of *24* (on Fox) was to show a passenger airliner exploding in flight from a bomb on board, so the scene was re-edited to eliminate images of the plane exploding. On CBS, the pilot episode of *The Agency* had shown CIA agents foiling a fictional plot by Osama bin Laden, so that episode was pulled. Later, another *Agency* episode had to be shelved when a story involving anthrax as a weapon proved too close to real-life events in October, when anonymous letters containing anthrax spores resulted in several deaths in the Eastern United States.

Much to the relief of programmers, viewers eventually seemed ready for a guarded return to entertainment offerings, with familiar forms and programs being the early favorites. Shows celebrating police, fire, and other rescue workers were particularly relevant, boosting the already-growing popularity of *CSI: Crime Scene Investigation* on CBS as well as NBC's *Law & Order* franchise. With the increased emphasis on the president of the United States as commander-in-chief, *The West Wing* on NBC also assumed added stature. Producer Aaron Sorkin quickly wrote a special episode ("Isaac and Ishmael") as the season opener. He obliquely dealt with the issues of September 11 by breaking from the series continuity and having the *West Wing* characters in a brief security lockdown, using that opportunity to discuss international issues with a group of high school students touring the White House.

The already-planned new espionage series packed extra punch in light of the September 11 attacks, as plots involving political duplicity, ruthless killers, and innocent bystanders seemed to possess added credibility. The two classiest new adventures were *Alias* on ABC and *24* on Fox. Conceived by *Felicity* creator J. J. Abrams, *Alias* cast Jennifer Garner as Sydney Bristow, a graduate student who was secretly a spy for the CIA. Unlike Felicity, who took four years to decide between two college boyfriends, Sydney made split-second decisions while on dangerous missions throughout the world, especially against the ruthless Arvin Sloane (Ron Rifkin), head of the SD-6 terrorist organization. Abrams also made the adventures personal by teaming Sydney with her estranged father, Jack (Victor Garber), and establishing romantic sparks between Sydney and her main CIA contact, Michael Vaughn (Michael Vartan). The stories were fast-paced and genuinely exciting, with Sydney (inevitably wearing a sexy disguise) constantly racing the clock to escape some complicated trap. Sometimes stories ended with a cliffhanger tease to the next episode.

The series *24* was even more consciously a cliffhanger because it was structured as a single story played out in twenty-four episodes, each one representing a single hour of a single day, unfolding in real time. Though admittedly a gimmick, the structure worked surprisingly well thanks to clever writing and a strong ensemble. The situation was deceptively simple: Special counter-terrorist agent Jack Bauer (Kiefer Sutherland) was trying to protect presidential candidate David Palmer (Dennis Haysbert) from an assassination plot on the day of the California primary. However, Bauer had to deal with one or more moles in his own organization, a kidnapping plot involving his daughter Kim (Elisha Cuthbert) and wife Teri (Leslie Hope), and a scheme to turn Bauer himself into the assassin, beginning with the shooting of his own deputy, Nina (Sarah Clarke). The series took full advantage of the drama inherent in a race against time and usually played out three or four

story arcs simultaneously, with a clicking digital clock often appearing on-screen to remind viewers of how compressed the story-line was. Cell phones and split screens tied the action together in what Bauer described as "the longest day of my life." Filled with complicated plot threads and character machinations, the intensity of *24* highlighted how intelligence, instincts, and luck were needed for any espionage mission to succeed. Though both *24* and *Alias* scored only moderate ratings in their first season, they attracted ardent fans, won renewal, and reassured viewers with the thought that sometimes the good guys won.

In the immediate aftermath of the September 11 attacks, though, it was sitcoms that emerged as television's true "comfort food" viewing, particularly those with positive, supportive ensembles. These ranged from the "mom and dad next door" setting of *Everybody Loves Raymond* (anchoring a CBS Monday night lineup of family comedies) to the extended social family of *Friends* (which scored its highest ratings in years with a storyline following the announcement by Rachel that she was pregnant). ABC found its greatest comedy successes with *My Wife and Kids* (a carryover from the previous spring, with Damon Wayans almost *Cosby*-like in dealing with his TV family) and *According to Jim* (a by-the-numbers family comedy pairing of Jim Belushi and Courtney Thorne-Smith as a lovable slob and his indulgent wife). On Fox,

---

September 26, 2001
Enterprise. (UPN). This fifth *Star Trek* series picks up the story thread from the 1996 "Star Trek First Contact" movie, with Capt. Jonathan Archer (Scott Bakula) commanding the first starship *Enterprise*, a century before Captain Kirk.

November 6, 2001
UPN extends the running time of *Buffy the Vampire Slayer* an extra ten minutes for a heavily promoted musical episode, "Once More, With Feeling," penned and directed by series creator Joss Whedon. The cast members do their own vocals on more than a dozen original Whedon tunes.

November 10, 2001
Two weeks after Disney/ABC's purchase of cable's Fox Family channel, the new owners rename it ABC Family.

December 19, 2001
AT&T announces that its Broadband division, the country's largest cable company (after acquiring Telecommunications Inc. and MediaOne), will be spun off and merged into Comcast Corporation, the number three cable company.

January 8, 2002
Last Call. (NBC). Carson Daly, host of MTV's hip *Total Request Live*, comes to NBC as host of a new post-Conan O'Brien late, late night interview show.

February 26, 2002
Watching Ellie. (NBC). Julia Louis-Dreyfus is the third *Seinfeld* alum to star in a solo sitcom. She plays a frazzled nightclub singer and, unlike her *Seinfeld* brethren, her show is renewed (though just barely), returning with a second batch of episodes in March 2003 before being canceled.

March 27, 2002
Milton Berle, hailed as "Mr. Television," dies at age ninety-three.

April 12, 2002

NBC buys Telemundo Communications Group, Inc., which operates the Telemundo Network (the number two rated Spanish-language TV network in the U.S.), for about $2 billion. Along with the network come ten new O&Os.

May 7, 2002

Barry Diller, who, in 1998, bought Universal's U.S. television operations (including the USA and Sci-Fi cable networks), sells virtually the same assets back to Universal's new owner, the French conglomerate Vivendi, for more than twice what Diller paid for them. Diller will continue to run the networks on behalf of Vivendi, under the name Vivendi Universal Entertainment.

May 16, 2002

Richard Parsons succeeds Gerald Levin as chief executive officer of AOL Time Warner. Eight months later, Parsons also gets the title of chairman of the board.

May 17, 2002

Bryant Gumbel leaves CBS's *Early Show*. Five months later, CBS installs Harry Smith, Hannah Storm, Julie Chen, and Rene Syler as the new anchors.

May 19, 2002

In the two-hour series finale of *The X-Files*, Fox Mulder learns that the final and complete alien invasion of the Earth will take place on December 22, 2012.

June 2, 2002

The Wire. (HBO). Former *Baltimore Sun* newspaper writer David Simon, whose nonfiction work had previously been adapted into *Homicide: Life on the Street*, returns to the Baltimore setting to create a series of demanding, complex, and thought-provoking stories of modern urban America. Each season's episodes focus on a different aspect of Baltimore life: government, law enforcement, education, the media, and the realities of "the street." The program offers no reassuring easy answers, but consistently delivers outstanding scripting and powerful ensemble performances.

September 7, 2002

In the first move growing out of the NBA's new six-year TV contract, *NBA Inside Stuff*, the league's weekly showcase, shifts from NBC to ABC, the broadcast network that will begin carrying the NBA finals in 2003.

The Bernie Mac Show put a less sentimental front to its family comedy setting, as successful black stand-up comic Bernie Mac (playing his fictional alter ego) found himself surrogate dad to his drug-addict sister's three children. While she entered rehab back in Chicago, they moved into "Uncle Bernie's" swank Los Angeles home. Unlike a typical squishy TV dad, Mac regarded this as a major disruption to his life that had to be kept under control. Frequently sharing his thoughts with direct-to-the-camera monologues, Mac explained that he and his wife, Wanda (Kellita Smith), loved the children, but he also regarded them as invaders to his kingdom, noting, "This is my house. *Mi casa es mi casa.*" His most important rule: "Don't touch my stuff without permission." Though such declarations were doomed to failure, Bernie Mac believed in and practiced "tough love," making the comic and sentimental moments more believable.

There were some shows that did seem particularly out of sorts immediately after September 11. *The Education of Max Bickford*

(Richard Dreyfuss as a college teacher and widower facing a mid-life crisis) and *Danny* (Daniel Stern as a newly divorced community service worker facing a mid-life crisis) came off as self-important and preachy. Off-beat or cutting-edge comedy (a tough sell anytime) also did not play well in the fall. The Fox series *The Tick* (Patrick Warburton as a dumb superhero) and *Undeclared* (a wry look at college life from Judd Apatow) drew modest audience support, while ABC's *The Job* (returning after a brief tryout in the spring of 2001, starring Denis Leary as a blunt, harsh, and troubled New York City cop) was the wrong attitude at the wrong time. The comedy bomb of the season, however, was *Bob Patterson*, starring Jason Alexander as a famous self-help/motivational speaker who, in his personal life, was whiney, insecure, and self-centered. Though these traits were just like Alexander's George Constanza character on *Seinfeld*, in this context they came off as plain obnoxious. ABC quickly canceled *Bob Patterson* and, as part of an early November program shuffle, moved in the long-running *NYPD Blue*, which found renewed audience interest in the exploits of hardworking New York City cops.

Though references to the September 11 attacks and the subsequent U.S. "war on terrorism" would continue to turn up throughout the season, by the end of 2001 viewers and programmers seemed to have regained their balance. While delayed, the fall premieres had played out. Major League Baseball had shut down for six days after the attacks, pushing back the rest of the season (and the playoffs). As a result, the World Series (on Fox) aired in the November sweeps and wound up going a full seven games as the Arizona Diamondbacks topped the suddenly much-beloved New York Yankees in the final inning of the final game. News programs, especially cable talk shows, had wrapped themselves in a new cloth of seriousness, with red, white, and blue graphics and a clear mission: Cover the war against terrorism. Even CBS's *Survivor* returned, first for another round beginning in October with *Survivor: Africa*, and then in February with *Survivor: Marquesas* (set on an island in French Polynesia). The program's continued ratings success showed that it might be safe for the other reality shows to begin reemerging. The Super Bowl on February 2 (also on Fox) provided a symbolic national transition "back to normal." It was the last major television event rescheduled in the aftermath of September 11 (like baseball, the National Football League had temporarily shut down, suspending all games for one week and delaying the rest of the season). The musical guests at the Super Bowl included Paul McCartney and U2, who both paid tribute to those who had lost their lives.

By mid-season, the on-air television atmosphere had become less self-conscious. In remarkably short order, programmers and viewers began to pick up where they had left off before September 11. The reality shows were proving particularly popular among 18-to 49-year-olds, so the networks were eager to bring them back, and not just as cheap summer filler. NBC's *Fear Factor* returned. ABC played the remaining episodes of *The Mole* that had been pulled from the fall schedule. That network also tapped producer Mike Fleiss to revive and revise the idea behind his ill-fated "Who Wants to Marry a Multi-Millionaire" with *The Bachelor*, featuring eager young women vying for the attention of a handsome and eligible guy as a potential husband. On March 5, MTV launched *The Osbournes*, a "family comedy" reality show edited from tapes made from multiple cameras placed at the home of veteran heavy-metal rocker Ozzy Osbourne and his family. Alternately goofy, antagonistic, warm, and incoherent, the Osbournes were part dysfunctional family, part guerilla theater. Their program became the most popular series in MTV's history to that point. Its April 30, 2002, edition drew enough viewers in the 18 to 49 demographic to tie with ABC's *NYPD Blue* for third place in the time slot among all television channels, both broadcast and cable.

The fact that ABC had a cable program breathing down its neck illustrated the depth the network had tumbled in just two seasons. In the final ratings for the 2001–02 season, ABC was down about 20% from the previous season (in both total audience and among viewers aged 18 to 49) and more than 30% since the recent heyday of *Who Wants to Be a Millionaire.* ABC had indeed ended up depending too heavily on that one program (which was taken off ABC's weekly schedule at the end of June), and it never developed a strong and coherent identity beyond that show. Apart from *Monday Night Football,* ABC's most successful series were, at best, in the middle of the overall ratings pack. For the future, the network looked to reestablish the family comedy identity that had worked so well in the past by developing more shows like *My Wife and Kids* and *According to Jim.* ABC also instituted much stronger cross-promotional ties with corporate parent Disney, even at the theme parks. At the same time, the network continued to look for short-term solutions. During the summer of 2002, ABC broadcast reruns of the new cable detective series *Monk* a few days after the program first played on the USA network. This was a dramatic and symbolic reversal of program migration: A broadcast network was now trying to cash in on the popularity of a cable offering.

Yet the changing relationship between broadcasters and cable was not limited to ABC. The success of *The Osbournes* as a popular programming choice signaled the fact that television itself had already crossed an important line. It was now generally assumed that, when people watched television, they were watching it through cable or satellite, rather than with an antenna limited to the local broadcast stations. Reflecting that change, April 2002 became the first non-summer month in which the aggregate average rating of the basic cable networks topped the aggregate average rating for all six of the major broadcast networks in prime time.

Even that understated the scope of the change. For more and more viewers, there was *no* practical distinction between one of the broadcast networks and one of the cable channels. The broadcast networks were there as part of basic cable, distinguished only by lower numbered channel positions. This point was underscored in microcosm by New Yorkers who were transfixed by television's coverage on September 11. Nearly every New York City-based broadcaster transmitted from the World Trade Center, so when those buildings were hit and then collapsed, the over-the-air signals were gone. Most Manhattan viewers did not notice. They were receiving their signals via cable. Statistically, only about 15% of the country still relied on over-the-air signals, while 85% was connected either to cable services or satellite transmissions. That threshold was so high, though, that the entertainment industry had simply started acting as if 100% of the country could receive cable channels. So did most viewers.

As a result, the expectations people brought to watching television reflected their cable experiences, especially among younger viewers who had grown up with cable much of their lives. Lists of favorite television series would inevitably include such broadcast favorites as *Survivor, Friends,* and *ER,* but also such cable hits as *The Osbournes* on MTV, *The Shield* on FX, *Trading Spaces* on The Learning Channel, *Soul Food* on Showtime, and such HBO series as *Six Feet Under, Sex and the City, The Sopranos,* and a classy new summer offering, *The Wire.* It was all part of the same world. So, when the NBA announced a new national television deal in January 2002 that sent the bulk of professional basketball games to cable, there was no great outcry among fans. It seemed perfectly sensible. The concept of multiple runs was also entrenched on cable, so a key component of Fox's strategy for *24*

was to air the series first on the Fox broadcast network, and then several more times each week on FX. After ABC took over the Family Channel in the fall of 2001, one of its first special features was a marathon rerun of all the episodes of *Alias* to that point.

This enhanced status for cable channels was also reflected in the perception of the broadcast "netlets," UPN and the WB. NBC and CBS might have dominated the top twenty ratings charts in overall viewers, but (like many cable channels) the smaller networks could tout their success in reaching the right slice of the targeted 18 to 49 age demographic. As a result, when UPN lured *Buffy the Vampire Slayer* from the WB in the fall of 2001, it was considered a major coup. In addition, new programs such as UPN's *Enterprise* (a *Star Trek* prequel) and the WB's *Smallville* (a retelling of the Superman legend that featured a cool teenage Clark Kent) were considered hits without ever landing near the top in the overall broadcast network ratings. With the increased emphasis on demographics and targeted audiences, some programs were being considered hits by using more nuanced views beyond the raw numbers.

Nonetheless, there was no mistaking the hard numbers that hit the broadcast networks throughout the summer of 2002, as cable continued to register stronger and stronger ratings. In part, this reflected the fact that the total viewing audience was distributed among more and more channels, resulting in shrinking numbers tuned to the broadcasters. However, the numbers for cable viewing were truly rising. MTV's annual video awards show in August won its time slot, beating the competition on both cable and broadcast channels. On September 5, for the first time, the NFL began its season with a game airing on cable (ESPN), and the prime time Thursday night telecast averaged more than 12 million viewers, enough to have been ranked tenth among network programs for that week, had cable been included on that list. Immediately topping that was the return of HBO's *The Sopranos* on September 15, 2002, at the cusp of the new fall season. There had not been a new episode of the series for sixteen months, and HBO hyped the event incessantly, from billboards to magazines to TV guest shots by members of the cast. It paid off. In the final summer weekend of mostly rerun programs and specials on the broadcast networks, the fourth season premiere of *The Sopranos* easily won its time slot and (had it been included in the weekly ratings list) placed sixth for the entire week against all other prime time programs, cable and broadcast. This was the first time that an original cable series beat all the broadcast competition in a prime time slot. Making the achievement even more impressive was the fact that, as a separate pay cable service, HBO started out with a built-in numerical disadvantage: it was seen in only about one-third of the 106.7 million homes with televisions in the U.S.

This was the new state of television. A pay cable service could outdraw all comers, including basic cable and free broadcast TV. What made this particularly troublesome for the competition was that while they depended on ratings success in selling commercials, HBO did not, collecting a monthly fee instead of selling ads. However, the commercial programmers had to deal with the long-term fallout of losing to pay cable competition. In essence, the underlying assumptions that had driven television for six decades were no longer in effect. The days of only a handful of broadcast television stations in most markets was over. Cable and satellite delivery systems were now entrenched, with generations of viewers knowing, and expecting, a wide range of channels. They would even pay outright for a handful of favorites, then channel surf for anything else.

The broad television status quo had changed and it seemed as if the FCC's long-sought goal of increased viewer choice had become a reality.

63. Go Pound Sand

SINCE 1999, A SUCCESSION OF warm-weather tryouts had transformed the summer months into *the* opportunity for introducing potential new reality show hits. Many of these were U.S. versions of British series and, in the summer of 2002, Fox launched *American Idol*, its adaptation of the 2001 U.K. hit *Pop Idol*. Created by Simon Fuller (former manager of pop music's Spice Girls), the show reached back decades to the tried-and-true formats of TV variety and talent shows, but wrapped them in a snazzy new setting with hooks aimed at fans of such reality series as *Survivor*. Rather than simply presenting a succession of unknown talent seeking to be named the best performer each week (like the 1980s syndicated show *Star Search*), *American Idol* was structured as a summer-long quest for the golden ring. There would be only one champion, who would earn the honor in a succession of live weekly performances, scrutinized by a panel of judges.

The series started on June 11, 2002, as potential stars were culled from tryouts throughout the U.S. A panel of three judges drawn from the music industry provided entertaining banter and often frank critiques of the performers as, over the first weeks, they selected the thirty who went on to the semi-final rounds. The credibility of the judges came from their real world professional experience. Paula Abdul had a string of top-selling singles, albums, and entertainment awards; Randy Jackson was a successful music producer and A&R executive with two decades of hits; and Simon Cowell (the only carryover from the U.K. version of the show) was also a record producer. These were exactly the sort of people any of the performers might have pestered with an audition tape. In evaluating the talent, Cowell proved the most caustic, Abdul the most forgiving, and Jackson (who tended to affectionately call everyone "dawg") right in the middle. As the show's popularity grew, Cowell's acerbic comments often were as big a draw as the talent itself. When the competition moved forward and the contestants were winnowed down to a more manageable ten finalists, the judges continued to offer their instant analyses of the performances, but the final weekly judgment was decided by phone-in votes from home viewers. Unlike reality shows such as *Survivor* or *The Weakest Link*, the process was not set up around voting to remove an unpopular contestant. Rather, viewers positively voted *for* their favorites. The contestant with the lowest vote total each week was the one cut.

American Idol also set itself apart by shamelessly celebrating itself and milking its popularity at every opportunity, offering tie-in merchandise, online features, blatant placement of its sponsors'

products, and two scheduled episodes each week (plus occasional "bonus" specials and elongated episodes). In the hour-long Tuesday episodes the remaining contestants each performed one song in line with the theme of the week (such as Motown or the 1960s), with their supporters urged to use a designated phone number displayed on the bottom of the screen to call in their votes. The half-hour Wednesday episodes announced who had been dumped, but only after presenting plenty of other features. Program co-hosts Brian Dunkleman and Ryan Seacrest kept the show moving with performance highlights, breezy banter, "up close and personal" profiles, and occasional chats with the studio audience, all the while urging viewers to phone in votes for their favorite performer.

Perhaps the most striking aspect of the series was the genuine talent it revealed; once the ten finalists were chosen, it quickly became clear that some of them were capable of winning legitimate success as artists. Viewers found and followed their favorites, cementing fan interest in the show as a whole. As the drama of who would survive each week unfolded, viewers became personally engaged in the fate of specific performers. For example, when soulful vocalist Tamyra Gray (considered by many to be the favorite to win it all) was voted out before the finals and wound up in only fourth place, her fans were genuinely shocked. During the summer of 2002, this personal viewer involvement boosted *American Idol* into the number one spot among viewers in the 18 to 49 age group and placed it third for viewers of all ages. In the September 4 finale, twenty-year-old Kelly Clarkson beat out curly-haired Justin Guarini to emerge as the series winner and, two weeks later, her official debut single ("A Moment Like This") was issued (by RCA records, of course). It quickly hit the charts and soon reached number one. A follow-up album, *Thankful*, topped the charts in April, while other *American Idol* compilation discs featuring all ten finalists also did well. Buoyed by the program's summer success, Fox slotted a new round of *American Idol* episodes to begin in January 2003.

In the meantime, attention turned to the new fall season, traditionally the primary annual showcase for the broadcast networks. However, in recent years the fall kickoff had begun to seem anticlimactic and almost routine. The previous fall season had been overshadowed by the trauma of the terrorist attacks of September 11 and had seemed practically irrelevant. But even before then, the fall premieres had begun to suffer in comparison to the pop culture buzz surrounding such summer hits as *Who Wants to be a Millionaire* and *Survivor*, as well as from incessant competition by cable.

420

The sheer number of cable channels continued to eat away at the broadcasters' collective share of the audience. In July 2002 broadcasters had only a 37% share while, for the first time over an entire month, basic cable accounted for more than 50% of viewership. Although the broadcasters' percentage always rose in the fall, they had trouble countering the focused promotability of cable series. HBO might have a dozen new and returning series spread throughout the year, but the six major broadcast networks had thirty-one new titles and more than twice that many returning series, all to sell to viewers at the same time in September. It was no surprise, then, when the easily promotable return of *The Sopranos* on HBO stood out as the major TV event of the fall of 2002.

Against this din of a hundred-plus stations, the networks trotted out their shows in the fall of 2002, stressing the return of longtime hits (such as *Everybody Loves Raymond* and *Friends*) and budding favorites from the previous season (such as *Alias* and *24*), along with their new titles. Among the newcomers were a few truly innovative offerings. NBC's *Boomtown,* reminiscent of the film "Rashomon," followed a new crime story each episode from the differing perspectives of various characters. *American Dreams*, a Dick Clark production also on NBC, set its drama in Philadelphia in the 1960s, where one main character became a regular dancer on *American Bandstand* (allowing the show to lovingly recreate segments from that old series). *Firefly* (on Fox) was an outer space ensemble adventure (from Joss Whedon, creator of *Buffy the Vampire Slayer),* that deliberately avoided high-tech heroics and concentrated instead on complex plots and character-driven drama. ABC's *Push, Nevada,* co-created by film star Ben Affleck, was a quirky combination of mystery and an interactive viewer game, offering the lure of a million-dollar prize. None of these new series became a big hit, and only the NBC shows survived the season. *Firefly* was gone by Christmas, while *Push, Nevada* never made it to Halloween and wrapped up its mystery in just seven episodes, with the final clue aired October 28 on ABC's *Monday Night Football.* (Twenty-four-year-old Mark Nakamoto claimed the prize of $1,045,000.)

Still, those series were the exception and they actually helped illustrate the reasoning behind the general approach taken by broadcasters for the new season: to embrace the familiar and the proven. There was safety in that strategy because, for the top hits, there was still no matching the big broadcast networks for reaching the greatest number of people at one time with one channel. Mainstream audiences did not seem to want quirky. They wanted reliable entertainment.

To that end, ABC aggressively embraced family sitcom settings (after the respectable success of *My Wife and Kids* and *According to Jim* the previous season). In *8 Simple Rules for Dating My Teenage Daughter* the network cast familiar faces John Ritter (from *Three's Company*) and Katey Sagal (from *Married … with Children*) as protective parents with three children at the prime dating age: a son played by Martin Spanjers and two daughters, played by Kaley Cuoco and Amy Davidson. *Life with Bonnie* followed the home and office life of a TV morning show host (played by Bonnie Hunt). At mid-season, the network bolstered its crime show line-up with a new version of *Dragnet* produced by *Law & Order*'s Dick Wolf and casting Ed O'Neill (another veteran of *Married … with Children*) as the new Sgt. Joe Friday.

Noting NBC's success with the *Law & Order* franchise (NBC had three successful shows under that umbrella title), CBS cloned its top drama series, *CSI*, to create *CSI: Miami,* the fall's most successful new show. Using a pair of familiar faces previously on *NYPD Blue,* David Caruso and Kim Delaney, the new series continued the successful *CSI* formula of a methodical crime investiga-

tion team in a trendy resort setting. As with the original (and the *Law & Order* titles), *CSI: Miami* generally wrapped up plots within each individual episode, rather than extending them over multi-episode story arcs so as to be less taxing for time-pressed viewers unable to commit to regular weekly viewing. CBS also did well with the similarly themed *Without a Trace* (slotted after *Survivor* and *CSI* on Thursday nights), changing what had once been easy victories for NBC's "Must See TV" lineup into a nip-and-tuck race. By season's end, *CSI* had beaten *ER* as television's most-watched drama for the second consecutive year.

In a previous era, the competition between NBC and CBS might have been the centerpiece story of the television season, but not any longer. For more than a decade the ratings race had been growing more complicated, driven by demographics. CBS, for example, had been number one in total viewers in two out of the previous four seasons, but for five of the previous six seasons NBC had been number one in the 18 to 49 age group (with CBS often an embarrassing fourth in that category). With the 18 to 49 ranking

---

September 14, 2002

CBS gives up independently programming its Saturday morning cartoon block and turns the three hours over to its sister channel, Nickelodeon, for reruns of popular cable series. On October 5, NBC follows suit by turning over its three-hour live-action teen-oriented Saturday block to cable's Discovery Channel.

September 15, 2002

The WB network expands its Sunday schedule by two hours just before prime time, adding reruns of two popular current series (*Smallville* and *Everwood*).

September 20, 2002

Firefly. (Fox). Joss Whedon's "outer space Western" follows the spaceship *Serenity* in 2517, with Nathan Fillion leading the ensemble cast. Though an instant fan favorite, the show is gone from Fox by December due to low ratings, finishing its only season in June on the Sci-Fi channel, followed by a one-shot 2005 theatrical film ("Serenity") .

October 30, 2002

ESPN begins regular season airings of NBA basketball, which, added to its on-going Major League Baseball, NFL football, and NHL hockey, makes ESPN the first network to televise all four major team sports in the same season.

November 18, 2002

The merger of AT&T's Broadband division into Comcast Corporation closes, making Comcast (with 21 million cable subscribers) the nation's largest cable TV system, almost twice its closest competitor (Time Warner cable). At the same time, Brian Roberts succeeds his father, Ralph, as chief executive officer. In May 2004 Brian will also replace him as Comcast's chairman of the board.

December 9, 2002

NBC purchases cable's arts-oriented Bravo channel for $1.25 billion.

January 26, 2003

Jimmy Kimmel Live. (ABC). Six months after the demise of *Politically Incorrect,* ABC fills its post-*Nightline* late-night slot with this new hour-long talk show based in Los Angeles. Kimmel previously was co-host of Comedy Central's *The Man Show.*

	8:00	8:30	9:00	9:30	10:00	10:30	
M O N	The Drew Carey Show	Whose Line Is It Anyway?	ABC NFL Monday Night Foootball (to 12 Midnight)				**ABC**
	The King Of Queens	Yes, Dear	Everybody Loves Raymond	STILL STANDING	CSI: MIAMI		**CBS**
	Boston Public		GIRLS CLUB		local		**FOX**
	Fear Factor		Third Watch		Crossing Jordan		**NBC**
	The Parkers	One On One	Girlfriends	HALF AND HALF	local		**UPN**
	7th Heaven		EVERWOOD		local		**WB**

	8:00	8:30	9:00	9:30	10:00	10:30	
T U E	8 SIMPLE RULES	According To Jim	LIFE WITH BONNIE	LESS THAN PERFECT	NYPD Blue		**ABC**
	JAG		The Guardian		Judging Amy		**CBS**
	That '70s Show	Grounded For Life	24		local		**FOX**
	THE IN-LAWS	Just Shoot Me	Frasier	HIDDEN HILLS	Dateline NBC		**NBC**
	Buffy The Vampire Slayer		HAUNTED		local		**UPN**
	Gilmore Girls		Smallville		local		**WB**

	8:00	8:30	9:00	9:30	10:00	10:30	
W E D	My Wife & Kids	George Lopez	The Bachelor		MDS		**ABC**
	60 Minutes II		The Amazing Race 3		PRESIDIO MED		**CBS**
	The Bernie Mac Show	CEDRIC THE ENTERTAINER	FASTLANE		local		**FOX**
	Ed		The West Wing		Law & Order		**NBC**
	Enterprise		The Twilight Zone		local		**UPN**
	Dawson's Creek		BIRDS OF PREY		local		**WB**

	8:00	8:30	9:00	9:30	10:00	10:30	
T H R	Monk		PUSH, NEVADA		Primetime		**ABC**
	Survivor: Thailand		CSI: Crime Scene Investigation		WITHOUT A TRACE		**CBS**
	Fox Thursday Night Movie				local		**FOX**
	Friends	Scrubs	Will & Grace	GOOD MORNING, MIAMI	ER		**NBC**
	WWE Smackdown!				local		**UPN**
	FAMILY AFFAIR	DO OVER	Jamie Kennedy Experiment	Off Centre	local		**WB**

	8:00	8:30	9:00	9:30	10:00	10:30	
F R I	America's Funniest Home Videos		THAT WAS THEN		20/20		**ABC**
	48 Hours Investigates		HACK		ROBBERY HOMICIDE DIVISION		**CBS**
	FIREFLY		JOHN DOE		local		**FOX**
	Providence		Dateline NBC		Law & Order: Special Victims Unit		**NBC**
	UPN Movie Friday				local		**UPN**
	WHAT I LIKE ABOUT YOU	Sabrina, The Teenage Witch	Reba	GREETINGS FROM TUSCON	local		**WB**

	8:00	8:30	9:00	9:30	10:00	10:30	
S A T	ABC Big Picture Show						**ABC**
	Touched By An Angel		The District		The Agency		**CBS**
	Cops	Cops	America's Most Wanted: America Fights Back		local		**FOX**
	NBC Saturday Movie						**NBC**
	local						**UPN**
	local						**WB**

	7:00	7:30	8:00	8:30	9:00	9:30	10:00	10:30	
S U N	The Wonderful World Of Disney				Alias		The Practice		**ABC**
	60 Minutes		Becker	BRAM AND ALICE	CBS Sunday Movie				**CBS**
	Futurama	King Of The Hill	The Simpsons	King Of The Hill	Malcolm In The Middle	Malcolm In The Middle	local		**FOX**
	Dateline NBC		AMERICAN DREAMS		Law & Order: Criminal Intent		BOOMTOWN		**NBC**
	local								**UPN**
	Gilmore Girls: Beginings		Charmed		Angel		local		**WB**

now seen as *the* key ratings scorecard for advertisers and programmers, CBS's victories among total viewers earned it precious little respect on Madison Avenue (the across-the-board success of *Survivor* being one of the exceptions). Instead, it was the younger-skewing networks that enjoyed the financial benefit of charging higher advertising rates for their shows.

On the other hand, members of this prized younger audience were especially elusive. Their early television points of reference had been dozens of channels, not just the three broadcast networks. In addition, they had spent a lifetime watching thousands of hours of scripted fictional stories (aided by reruns and video repackaging); many were as well versed in such stories as any Hollywood writer. Against this, even the best series could not help but carry an air of predictability after awhile. With a world of cable channels at their fingertips for most of their lives, these viewers were more inclined to move along the dial, looking for unexpected moments that might break free of familiar clichés and capture their attention. Increasingly, that meant non-scripted reality shows.

Although these had begun primarily as inexpensive first-run summer programming, *Survivor*'s staying power against regular season competition brought the genre more credibility. When it and other reality series regularly turned in strong ratings within the highly desirable 18 to 49 age demographic, the form became irresistible for regular season play, There was a wide variety of approaches to the genre including competitive quest series such as *The Amazing Race*, stunt shows such as *Fear Factor*, celebrity fluff such as *I'm a Celebrity, Get Me Out of Here*, crass flesh-fests such as *Are You Hot? The Search for America's Sexiest People*, and seductive searches for love and wealth in such series as *The Bachelor* and its distaff counterpart this season, *The Bachelorette*. As with any format, some of the reality series were well done; others were instantly forgettable. However, the sheer number of such shows had become an increasingly powerful programming force and, in January 2003, the non-scripted reality genre reached a new peak with the blockbuster return of *American Idol* and the premiere of *Joe Millionaire* on Fox.

A second round of success for *American Idol* was not really a great surprise. The series simply continued its formula with a new group of singing hopefuls, tweaking a few points (dropping co-host Dunkleman, increasing the number of finalists to twelve, and adding a different musical celebrity judge each week). *Joe Millionaire*, however, was a different story. During its winter run it surpassed even *American Idol* in the ratings, in the process demonstrating just how completely audiences had absorbed the reality genre.

The premise of *Joe Millionaire* was a wicked parody of the romantic quest for love and money in such series as *The Bachelor*. It was territory Mike Darnell, Fox's executive in charge of reality programming, knew well, going back to his special "Who Wants to Marry a Multi-Millionaire." In the January 6 *Joe Millionaire* premiere, twenty women arrived at a palatial setting and each one began her campaign to convince bachelor Evan Marriott (a self-described multi-millionaire) to select her as his bride-to-be. They knew they were being taped for later presentation on a television series, but they did not know that the entire set-up was a fraud: the mansion was not his home and he was not a wealthy bachelor. Marriott, a former construction worker earning $19,000 a year, had been hired to play the part. Although that twist was kept from the women during the series taping, it was gleefully played up in promotions for the program and throughout the series itself. In addition, the home audience had an on-screen confidant: estate "butler" Paul Hogan. He knew the truth and offered scathing commentary on all the participants. It was cruel TV, but viewers loved it.

Fox was quick to take advantage of the interest in both *Joe Mil-*

lionaire and *American Idol;* during the February 2003 sweeps, the network managed to fill 22% of its prime time schedule with just these two programs. This was possible because their formats made it fairly easy to repeat episodes, air elongated episodes, or stitch together additional episodes. Even the "new" episodes usually were filled with segments and clips from very recent past episodes. Viewers did not seem to mind. The weekly *American Idol* episode announcing the results of the voting from the previous night, for example, could have conveyed that one piece of new information in less than five minutes. Instead, the program was padded to fill a half hour—in some cases, even an hour. Nevertheless, fans still tuned in, eager to revisit the ongoing personal drama of their favorite performers. In some ways, reality shows were as good as prime time soap operas, but without the need for expensive writers. They presented the quest for personal triumph, pure and simple.

Thanks to the performance of *Joe Millionaire* and *American*

January 29, 2003
Ted Turner, no longer a key player in the management of AOL Time Warner, announces he will resign as vice chairman of the company.

February 2, 2003
NBC's coverage of the seventeen-year-old indoor Arena Football League begins with the Dallas Desperados beating the New York Dragons 60 to 56 in Dallas. Under an unusual two-year contract, NBC pays no rights fees for the five-month series of Sunday afternoon games, but will split revenue with the league after making back production costs.

February 21, 2003
Da Ali G Show. (HBO). Sacha Baron Cohen adapts his successful 2000 British satirical interview show for the U.S. Using one of his character guises (Ali G, Borat Sagdivev, or Bruno), Cohen talks with real political, business, and entertainment personalities (who think they are on a standard chat show), playing the exchanges for laughs by steering conversations into odd and embarrassing areas.

March 30, 2003
ESPN debuts a new sister cable channel, ESPN HD, which transmits twenty-four hours a day of high definition sports, beginning with the Major League Baseball season opener as the Texas Rangers beat the home town Anaheim Angels 6 to 3. Initially, most of the programming is standard ESPN material converted to a high definition signal, but the channel also features some original telecasts.

April 9, 2003
Rupert Murdoch's News Corporation signs an agreement to pay $6.6 billion to acquire a 34% controlling interest in DirecTV, America's largest satellite TV service, which has more than 11 million subscribers.

May 22, 2003
Viacom buys from AOL Time Warner the 50% of cable's Comedy Central that it did not own, for $1.2 billion.

August 11, 2003
Viacom's cable channel The National Network (TNN) is renamed Spike TV. Called "the first network for men," it emphasizes male-oriented programming such as wrestling, SlamBall (an "extreme" team sport), and *Striperella*, the animated adventures of a stripper (voiced by Pamela Anderson and created by comic book veteran Stan Lee).

In contrast to the hotel conference room backdrop used at briefings by Gen. Norman Schwarzkopf in the 1991 Gulf War, in 2003 the media center in Qatar had a specially constructed set designed, built, and shipped from the U.S. The briefings from there regularly turned up on the news, with C-SPAN carrying every one in its entirety. *(Courtesy of C-SPAN)*

Idol (along with other non-scripted reality series and specials added to its schedule), Fox won the February sweeps in the 18 to 49 demographic group for the first time ever. The network was not alone in its reliance on the reality format during that sweeps period. For example, Fox, ABC, and NBC together devoted ten hours in prime time that month to separate, juicy, behind-the-scenes exposees on eccentric pop celebrity Michael Jackson.

While there was no guarantee that Fox could build long-lasting ratings strength on this format alone, the strategy worked in the short run. It even boosted ratings for adjacent scripted series such as *24* and *The Bernie Mac Show*. An exciting season finish by *American Idol* in May, with hefty, soulful Ruben Studdard edging out the skinny but strong-voiced Clay Aiken, earned Fox its second straight sweeps victory among 18- to 49-year-old viewers. In the final season averages, CBS once again ended up as the top network in total audience ratings and NBC was able to stay ahead of Fox to again win the 18 to 49 category. But Fox clearly scored the prestige prize: The network had the most talked-about shows in what was still the hottest format.

Fox also did well in a very different reality setting: war news.

In the aftermath of the attacks on September 11, 2001, the network news departments had found themselves on high alert to cover the on-going "war against terrorism," but while it was easy to add red, white, and blue on-screen graphics, the story lacked obvious battle lines. Still, the twenty-four-hour news outlets (CNN, MSNBC, and Fox News Channel) embraced the story as the perfect fit for them. Unlike shark attacks and celebrity gossip, this was news truly worthy of extensive on-air examination. However, it was also a complex, long term international tale that resisted neat wrap-ups every twenty-four hours. Within those limitations, coverage often settled into a succession of official briefings and discussions over philosophical and political points. In that atmosphere, though, the Fox News Channel found itself surging ahead of CNN in the cable news ratings with a schedule that included a lineup of strongly opinionated talk show hosts such as Bill O'Reilly and Sean Hannity. Such personalities did not flinch from offering their self-professed "clear vision" on just what they thought should be done in the war against terrorism, and when, and to whom.

The first tangible battle action by the United States took place in October 2001, as it launched an attack against the country of Afghanistan (first by air, then with ground forces), aimed at destroying al-Qaeda forces located there as well as a national government viewed as sympathetic to that group. However, that effort offered only limited press access and television visuals. It also left the story unfinished because, while a new government was soon installed in Afghanistan, al-Qaeda's primary leader, Osama bin Laden, was neither captured nor confirmed dead.

Throughout 2002, though, it was clear that President George W. Bush and his administration were shifting the war on terrorism to focus more and more on Iraq and its leader, Saddam Hussein, who was still in power nearly a dozen years after the 1991 war in the Persian Gulf (launched by the first President Bush) had stopped short of removing him.

In 1991, Iraq's invasion of neighboring Kuwait had served as an international rallying point at the United Nations for sending a multinational coalition of troops into the region. By the start of 2003, the United States was pressing for a preemptive attack on Iraq without such overt provocation, arguing the case on a variety of levels at the United Nations. The main charge was that Iraq had not complied with earlier U.N. edicts to destroy its stock of weapons of mass destruction. This was a much more complex effort that stirred passionate debate both domestically and internationally, with television (especially the all-news channels) carrying key moments. These included addresses by both President Bush and Secretary of State Colin Powell before the U.N., as well as reports on demonstrations throughout the world against possible war action. CBS even arranged a one-on-one interview in Iraq between Dan Rather and Saddam Hussein.

Throughout all the debates over the possibility of military action, the U.S. methodically mobilized troops in the Gulf region and lined up its own coalition of allies (led by Great Britain), ready for engagement without the blessing of the United Nations. At the same time, on another front, the U.S. government undertook an unprecedented effort to deal with war coverage (when it began) by fashioning the means to effectively "bring the story home" through the press, especially television.

Coverage of the 1991 war in the Persian Gulf had started with a burst of dramatic live TV reports showing a dazzling display of bombs falling on Baghdad as the backdrop. Soon afterward, though, most correspondents had been forced to leave the country and their subsequent coverage of the aerial attacks drew from a far more limited selection of images: field briefings in a non-descript setting; aerial views of bomb runs (supplied by the military); and studio-bound discussions. The lightning attack by ground troops did not occur until shortly before the end of the campaign. Overall, despite its spectacular beginning, most of the coverage of the 1991 Gulf War was not particularly engaging TV. Victory had come quickly, but an odd sense of detachment accompanied the effort.

A dozen years later, the U.S. government pursued a very different strategy in its media planning for war coverage, looking at it as part of a news event being followed in a round-the-clock, multimedia world. The key was to convey a consistent, confident message in every way possible. In identifying the campaign, symbolic code names of the past such as "Desert Storm" were put aside in favor of the more image-conscious title "Operation Iraqi Freedom." Looking for a more impressive on-screen presence, the Pentagon contracted for a modern, television-friendly briefing area to use at command headquarters, turning to U.S. firms that normally did such sets for the networks. Most important, the government aggressively expanded a technique that had formerly been a common element of war coverage: making provisions for members of the press to travel with the troops as "embedded" correspondents, allowing them to report from the front lines. The difference was that they would now be reporting live. About five hundred members of the press were credentialed to travel with the ground troops. After a brief but intense training period together, they were shipped to their separately assigned units for the duration of any military campaign, if and when it began. On Wednesday, March 19, at about 9:45 P.M. Eastern time, it began.

Unlike the 1991 war, which had started with a sustained air campaign followed by a short ground assault, the initial 2003 attack was primarily a ground-based effort backed by strategically targeted but intense air support. What had not changed was the tremendous firepower at the command of the United States. Within three weeks, the U.S.-led coalition forces had occupied all of the major parts of Iraq and, on April 9, a U.S. tank helped yank down a towering statue of Saddam Hussein in downtown Baghdad, marking the regime's fall from power. On May 1, President Bush declared that the major "combat phase" in Iraq was over, though about 150,000 U.S. troops were still in the country and remained subject to a series of guerrilla attacks throughout Iraq.

The government's success at handling television coverage of the actual six-week war was especially impressive. Although previous wars had been called "television wars," this campaign truly lived up to the description. Using satellite hookups that could be accessed with portable transmitting equipment (in some cases, small enough to be handled by one person), correspondents could send back live reports straight from the field. These sometimes carried an almost giddy sense of excitement, and not just because of the impressive technology. Reporters found themselves the eyes and ears for viewers, allowing them to witness an on-going military campaign as it unfolded. They sent back to U.S. living rooms the ultimate reality show, with such images as overwhelming firepower pounding Iraqi forces in the desert or troops entering often-chaotic cities no longer under Hussein's control.

Equally important, having lived several weeks with the members of the individual units (eating, sleeping, and traveling together), the correspondents could not help but convey a new-found empathy and appreciation for the military. As a result, many of the reports sent back to the U.S. focused less on war policy than on putting human faces to the U.S. effort. This kept the campaign from being viewed in a more abstract, political context. Collectively, the sheer number of reports also had a more practical effect. They helped fill television news time with the numerous mundane details of on-going troop movements. If there was going to be a larger discussion of the war on television, it was not going to come from the field.

Back in their studios, each of the all-news cable channels kept the war coverage running around the clock. They combined the field reports with in-studio discussions (including an "army" of current and former high-ranking military officers brought in as experts), plenty of colorful maps, and cutaways to official briefings (back in Washington and at the coalition military's media center set up in Doha, Qatar, in the Persian Gulf). The broadcast networks had a similar mix of stories, though after their initial saturation live coverage of the opening salvos, they mostly left the on-going story to cable, returning to it in the nightly news shows and in a handful of specials. NBC and Fox benefited from having their cable news channels to draw from, though on a nightly basis ABC's *Nightline* had some of the most consistently cogent summary packages, combining Ted Koppel's reports as an embedded correspondent with focused context and analysis at home.

Overall, though, the war coverage once again demonstrated to the U.S. television industry the ability of cable news channels to turn over almost unlimited air time to a live, breaking story. The cable news ratings for the war period also showed the continued dominance of the Fox News Channel, which easily topped CNN and MSNBC with its quick-paced technical prowess and an overall tone that clicked with many viewers as unabashedly favorable to the Bush administration. It was the news channel that seemed to benefit most from the times it was covering.

From a more global perspective, however, the 2003 Gulf campaign presented an intriguing new aspect to the coverage that contrasted with that of the 1991 war: The U.S.-based news channels faced aggressive competition in the region to be the primary TV source for the story. The feisty Arab-language satellite news channel al-Jazeera, based in the free-wheeling Gulf emirate of Qatar, took them on in its own back yard with camera crews and reporters in Iraq, and beamed its signals throughout the Arab world. Playing toward regional anti-war sentiment, al-Jazeera adopted a blatantly negative attitude toward U.S. motives and policy behind the war. Its reports emphasized the human toll on Iraqi civilians far more than the stories running on the U.S. networks. Other news services throughout the world picked up many al-Jazeera reports, which angered U.S. officials. Still, when the U.S.-led troops entered Baghdad and encountered little Iraqi resistance, it was al-Jazeera that could most creditably convey to its Arab audience the harsh reality that the Iraqi army had virtually evaporated. For once, the world was not limited to watching a breaking global story primarily through the lenses of the U.S. news networks.

Even U.S. viewers found themselves plugged into some of these international reports, watching as other voices clamored to be heard in a global satellite news world that had truly become tied together by television. War, and war coverage, had provided a snapshot of that new interconnected reality. The astonishing new ability to peer over the shoulder of a reporter to see a military campaign unfold live quickly became a given, almost as routine as using a cell phone or sending an e-mail or watching the latest episode of *American Idol*. Returning soldiers and those back home did not need to be convinced that a new communications world was on the horizon.

They were already living it.

64. Game Change

FOOTBALL'S ANNUAL SUPER BOWL championship game had become one of television's premiere offerings, an over-the-air broadcaster exclusive, rotating among the networks with then current NFL deals. It was CBS's turn in 2004 for the faceoff between the Carolina Panthers and the New England Patriots at Reliant Stadium in Houston.

For sports fans, the Super Bowl was the final stop for that season's championship football teams in one winner-take-all game (unlike baseball's World Series, which could end unpredictably after four, five, six, or seven games). "Super Bowl Sunday," though, was a pop culture touchstone that reached far beyond a sports event audience. Over the years the networks had developed other features for casual viewers with no interest in football, including food and beverage tie-ins for Super Bowl party planning, prime time specials, celebrity watching, and, most notably, the celebration of commerce.

Commercial spots for the Super Bowl commanded a premium price ($2.25 million per 30 seconds in 2004), and that hook was promoted as its own informal scoreboard. Not everyone was steeped in football jargon, but viewers were experts at watching television and knew what they thought of particular product pitches. Saturday night CBS aired "Super Bowl's Greatest Commercials," looking back at such signature moments as the Budweiser croaking frogs from 1995 and the impossibly complex Michael Jordan-Larry Bird basketball shoot-out for McDonalds from 1993.

In 2004, for the first time, the NFL added an extra week between the conference championship finals and the Super Bowl, pushing it to February 1. This provided even more time for hype, ending with game day specials aimed at all ages, including "Nickelodeon Takes Over the Super Bowl," MTV's gossipy *Total Request Live* ("TRL at the Super Bowl"), and CBS's own four-hour pre-game show. After the national anthem (sung by Beyoncé Knowles) and the opening kickoff, the next major entertainment break came at halftime.

Oddly, until the 1990s, the Super Bowl halftime entertainment had been surprisingly routine, ranging from college marching bands to themed tributes such as honoring forty years of the comic strip "Peanuts" or celebrating a century of Hollywood history (with ninety-one-year-old George Burns as a guest). Even though the Super Bowl game itself was an automatic ratings powerhouse, such halftime offerings had provided opportunities for competitive counter-programming.

In 1992, Fox aggressively touted a special edition of its sketch comedy series *In Living Color* as a live no-holds-barred alternative to that year's halftime show on CBS, "Winter Magic" (featuring Olympic skaters and effectively serving as an early promotion for the network's 1994 Winter Olympic coverage). The *In Living Color* cast was in fine form, particularly Damon Wayans and David Alan Grier in their gay media critic characters ("Men on Film") offering double entendre game evaluations of ball handling and tight ends. Fox assured viewers that they would not miss a moment of the game and displayed an on-screen countdown clock to switch channels for the second half kickoff. The stunt successfully drew an audience of more than 20 million.

For the 1993 Super Bowl, the NFL and that year's host, NBC, attempted to recapture this prime spot inside their own event by recasting half time as a showcase for A-List, top-name performers. Michael Jackson was chosen as the first headliner, and he delivered an explosive performance of his song "Heal the World" (the fourth hit from his *Dangerous* album), backed by a children's choir of 3,500 and bathed in smoke and pyrotechnics. Some of the subsequent headliners through 2003 included Clint Black, Stevie Wonder, U2, and Sting. The staging also grew increasingly elaborate, as in the 2001 show on CBS, produced by Viacom corporate cousin MTV, which featured dueling swaggers by 'N Sync and Aerosmith. In 2003, Shania Twain walked onto an outdoor stage floor consisting entirely of video screens.

CBS once again turned to MTV to produce its halftime show for the 2004 Super Bowl. The lineup included P. Diddy, Kid Rock, Nelly, and Janet Jackson, accompanied by Justin Timberlake from 'N Sync. There was a provocative irreverence to their performances (Kid Rock wore an American flag as a poncho), with strong rhythms and suggestive body moves, particularly by Jackson and Timberlake. After a medley of Jackson's "All For You" and "Rhythm Nation," the pair concluded their segment with Timberlake's "Rock Your Body." At the last line of the song, viewers saw Timberlake "tear off" a portion of Jackson's costume, exposing her right breast (covered in part by a "nipple shield"). CBS immediately cut to a long shot, but the flash (cited as lasting "nine-sixteenths of a second") had been seen live by millions and captured for replay by millions more via home video recording.

The New England Patriots won the game (32 to 29), but it was the Jackson/Timberlake video moment that became an instant viral online phenomenon, with countless unauthorized postings via the Internet. The incident was dubbed "nipplegate" and the revealing moment described as a "wardrobe malfunction." It provided the late night comedy shows with irresistible material. CBS's David Letterman referred to it in his monologues and Top Ten list; NBC's *Saturday Night Live* not only referenced it in sketches but also as part of a direct spoof by Jackson herself (playing a "flashing" Condoleezza Rice). On these shows there was a light, almost dismissive tone on the subject, as if to say, "What's the big deal?" After all, there was far more explicit material on highly praised cable programs such as Comedy Central's *Chappelle's Show* and HBO's *Sex and the City*.

Yet for some viewers it was a big deal. The FCC eventually logged more than half a million comments, including thousands from self-identified decency watchdogs. At its most basic, the incident sparked dismay because it seemed a violation of trust, appearing in the wrong context, out of the blue, as part of a heavily promoted over-the-air television event popular with families. In a *TV Guide* follow-up analysis, editor-in-chief Michael Lafavore lamented that the stunt was "forced on us without so much as a 'parental discretion' warning."

Others extended the criticism to the tone of some of the program's commercial sponsors that day (including ads for products dealing with sexual dysfunction), and, even more broadly, to a coarsening of broadcast television beyond that one event. For example, there had been uncensored exclamations ("fleeting expletives"), but no FCC fines, at the Billboard Music Awards in 2002 (by Cher) and at the live Golden Globe telecast in 2003 (from U2's Bono), as well as uncensored postgame comments by sports figures such as Shaquille O'Neal. Within that wider context, the fallout from the Jackson/Timberlake incident had both short-term and long-term ramifications.

For the Super Bowl itself, the NFL reviewed its sponsorships (dropping some) and also immediately banned MTV from the show. The league tapped veteran producer Don Mischer (from its 1993 Michael Jackson halftime production) to help set the tone for future halftime entertainment, and later brought in Tony Awards telecast producer Ricky Kirshner as well. Beginning with Paul McCartney at the 2005 Super Bowl, halftime became a showcase for tightly paced performances by established rock acts that, over the years, also included The Rolling Stones, Prince, Tom Petty, Bruce Springsteen, and The Who. Each was presented as the sole headliner, steering clear of extraneous controversy and success-fully defining the segment as a smoothly integrated portion of the NFL's overall Super Bowl show.

The FCC for its part revisited its policies on airing objection-able material, targeting increasing fines tenfold in the future. That September, for the Super Bowl incident, the commission levied individual fines against twenty Viacom-owned stations totaling $550,000. CBS objected to the unprecedented nature of the penalty (then the largest in FCC history), especially given the unplanned nature of the incident. Individual stations were caught in the middle, punished after the fact for taking a network feed that contained a moment over which they had no control. That led to back-and-forth appeals for the remainder of the decade.

For the FCC, even this protracted process was useful, reminding broadcasters that over-the-air telecasts were still held to different standards than cable. It also gave the FCC a sexy populist topic to point to at the same time the commission was embroiled in public debates over station ownership limits and policies. While the corporate owners of the networks were interested in decency rules and penalties, they had far more at stake lobbying the FCC and the halls of Congress over lucrative ownership parameters.

Under FCC chair Michael Powell, in 2003 the commission had ruled 3 to 2 in favor of lifting a variety of limits on corporate media growth. With these changes, a company would be allowed to own TV stations that could reach, in the aggregate, 45% of the country (up from 35%). Companies could also own two TV stations in most major cities (three in the largest) and own daily newspapers as well as TV and radio stations in the same city. However, commissioners Michael Copps and Jonathan Adelstein not only dissented, they also participated in public information and outreach meetings throughout the country. Those attracted large numbers of vocal critics against the policy changes, and were accompanied by thousands of letters, calls, and emails, as well as legal challenges and congressional lobbying. At the end of that process, in June 2004, the station ownership limit was raised only slightly, to 39% (at which level the largest owners, Viacom and News Corporation, were not required to sell any existing stations). Otherwise, the previous caps continued as before.

September 8, 2003
The Ellen DeGeneres Show. Ellen DeGeneres hosts a "nice" syndicated daytime talk show, carried by her relaxed deadpan and friendly silliness, such as her daily dance step. First guests include Jennifer Aniston and singer Macy Gray.

September 13, 2003
TV Guide eliminates listings of programs airing between 5 A.M. and 5 P.M. Monday through Friday, replacing them with schedule grids for those time periods.

October 16, 2003
At last acknowledging the bursting of the dot.com bubble, AOL Time Warner reverts to its previous name, Time Warner. This clearly shows that the real dominant portion of the business is not AOL, but Time Warner's products.

November 2, 2003
Arrested Development. (Fox). Executive producer Ron Howard narrates the wickedly off-kilter comic tales of the Bluth family. In addition to a strong ensemble (including Jason Bateman, Jeffrey Tambor, Jessica Walter, Michael Cera, Portia de Rossi, Will Arnett, and David Cross), the series consistently draws top guest stars such as Liza Minnelli, Charlize Theron, and Henry Winkler.

November 4, 2003
The National Football League follows in the steps of the NBA with the debut of its own cable channel, the NFL Network. Beginning with football talk shows and archival films, the new network will not run a live NFL game for three years.

November 30, 2003
"The Reagans." (Showtime). This four-hour made-for-TV movie on the professional and personal life of President Ronald Reagan and wife Nancy (starring James Brolin and Judy Davis) had been scheduled to air on CBS during the November sweeps. Responding to outspoken charges from conservative groups that the film was unbalanced and inaccurate, CBS pulled the movie before its air date and instead ran it after Thanksgiving on its sister cable channel.

December 8, 2003
Battlestar Galactica. (Sci-Fi). This miniseries revival of the 1970s series thoroughly reimagines the battle between humans and their one-time robotic minions, the Cylons, as a dark and gritty epic. A full series launches in 2005.

	8:00	8:30	9:00	9:30	10:00	10:30	
M O N	Prime Time		ABC NFL Monday Night Football (to 12 Midnight)				**ABC**
	Yes, Dear	Still Standing	Everybody Loves Raymond	TWO AND A HALF MEN	CSI: Miami		**CBS**
	The Next Joe Millionaire		SKIN		local		**FOX**
	Fear Factor		LAS VEGAS		Third Watch		**NBC**
	The Parkers	EVE	Girlfriends	Half And Half	local		**UPN**
	7th Heaven		Everwood		local		**WB**

	8:00	8:30	9:00	9:30	10:00	10:30	
T U E	8 Simple Rules	I'M WITH HER	According To Jim	Less Than Perfect	NYPD Blue		**ABC**
	NAVY NCIS		The Guardian		Judging Amy		**CBS**
	The Next Joe Millionaire		24		local		**FOX**
	WHOOPI	HAPPY FAMILY	Frasier	Good Morning Miami	Law & Order: Special Victims Unit		**NBC**
	One On One	ALL OF US	ROCK ME BABY	THE MULLETS	local		**UPN**
	Gilmore Girls		ONE TREE HILL		local		**WB**

	8:00	8:30	9:00	9:30	10:00	10:30	
W E D	My Wife & Kids	IT'S ALL RELATIVE	The Bachelor		KAREN SISCO		**ABC**
	60 Minutes II		The King Of Queens	Becker	BROTHERHOOD OF POLAND, NH		**CBS**
	That '70s Show	A MINUTE WITH STAN HOOPER	The O.C.		local		**FOX**
	Ed		The West Wing		Law & Order		**NBC**
	Star Trek: Enterprise		JAKE 2.0		local		**UPN**
	Smallville		Angel		local		**WB**

	8:00	8:30	9:00	9:30	10:00	10:30	
T H R	THREAT MATRIX		Extreme Makeover		Prime Time		**ABC**
	Survivor: Pearl Islands		CSI: Crime Scene Investigation		Without A Trace		**CBS**
	TRU CALLING		SKIN		local		**FOX**
	Friends	Scrubs	Will & Grace	COUPLING	ER		**NBC**
	WWE Smackdown!				local		**UPN**
	STEVE HARVEY'S BIG TIME	Jamie Kennedy Experiment	What I Like About You	RUN OF THE HOUSE	local		**WB**

	8:00	8:30	9:00	9:30	10:00	10:30	
F R I	George Lopez	MARRIED TO THE KELLYS	HOPE & FAITH	Life With Bonnie	20/20		**ABC**
	JOAN OF ARCADIA		JAG		THE HANDLER		**CBS**
	Wanda At Large	LUIS	Boston Public		local		**FOX**
	MISS MATCH		Dateline NBC		Boomtown		**NBC**
	UPN Movie Friday				local		**UPN**
	Reba	LIKE FAMILY	Grounded For Life	ALL ABOUT THE ANDERSONS	local		**WB**

	8:00	8:30	9:00	9:30	10:00	10:30	
S A T	The Wonderful World Of Disney				L.A. Dragnet		**ABC**
	48 Hours Investigates		Hack		The District		**CBS**
	Cops	Cops	America's Most Wanted: America Fights Back		local		**FOX**
	NBC Saturday Movie						**NBC**
	local						**UPN**
	local						**WB**

	7:00	7:30	8:00	8:30	9:00	9:30	10:00	10:30	
S U N	America's Funniest Home Videos		10-8		Alias		The Practice		**ABC**
	60 Minutes		COLD CASE		CBS Sunday Movie				**CBS**
	King Of The Hill	Kimg Of The Hill	The Simpsons	The Bernie Mac Show	Malcolm In The Middle	ARRESTED DEVELOP-MENT	local		**FOX**
	Dateline NBC		American Dreams		Law & Order: Criminal Intent		THE LYON'S DEN		**NBC**
	local								**UPN**
	Smallville: Beginings		Charmed		TARZAN		local		**WB**

Although the FCC's proposed rule change did not take place as suggested, during the same period NBC initiated its own major business revamping. In October 2003, General Electric and French conglomerate Vivendi announced their agreement to merge GE's NBC (owner of NBC, CNBC, MSNBC, Bravo, and Telemundo) and Vivendi Universal Entertainment (owner of Universal Studios, theme parks, the Universal Television production company, and the USA and Sci-Fi cable networks). On May 12, 2004, the deal formally closed, splitting ownership of the new NBC Universal company 80% to GE and 20% to Vivendi.

This merger not only gave NBC Universal more cable platforms, it also connected television's oldest broadcast network with a major film studio, the last of the networks to do so. The significance of such a relationship was that it allowed for in-house one-stop shopping and packaging of product from beginning to end, from creation to screen.

Ironically, back in 1948, the U.S. government had successfully broken up the concentration of power by movie studios (in the "Paramount Case") because they had owned multiple stages of the feature film process: production, distribution, and exhibition. Through mergers and acquisitions, twenty-first-century media conglomerates had managed effectively to recapture such control with product distribution and exhibition piped directly into individual homes, adding to the mix the gathering and reporting of news. It remained to be seen how NBC Universal would position this new multifaceted company in that environment.

In the short run, for the 2003–04 season, competition by the broadcast networks mostly seemed to be business as usual, both in ratings performance and selecting types of new series.

CBS again won the ratings race for total viewers. It also successfully added a pair of new procedurals (*Cold Case* with Kathryn Morris and *Navy NCIS* with Mark Harmon) and the sitcom *Two and a Half Men* (with Charlie Sheen and Jon Cryer). The network's critical darling was *Joan of Arcadia* (Amber Tamblyn as a young girl who talked to God).

NBC again won the 18 to 49 demographic, although just barely ahead of Fox. While the network's successful new shows included Donald Trump's reality game *The Apprentice* and the drama *Las Vegas* (with James Caan), there were also major flops in drama (*The Lyon's Den* with Rob Lowe) and comedy (*Coupling*, a U.S. version of a British comedy inspired by *Friends*). Ominously for NBC's future planning, this season was the final one for both *Frasier* and *Friends*.

Fox was very close to matching NBC in the 18 to 49 demographic by once again following the formula of *American Idol*, dominating January to May, and combining that with a heavily promoted interchangeable reality show (this season, *My Big Fat Obnoxious Fiancé*) and anything else that worked (including the summer-fall soap opera *The O.C.*). Among its new shows, Fox won the hearts of critics, though not big ratings, with the dysfunctional family comedy *Arrested Development* and the Niagara Falls store clerk fantasy *Wonderfalls*.

Both UPN and the WB continued with their niche programming, with the WB successfully adding the teen soap opera *One Tree Hill*.

ABC, however, had a dismal season. None of its new comedies and none of its new dramas succeeded. Its best performance came from *Monday Night Football* and the *Bachelor* and *Extreme Makeover* reality series. Disney shareholders at a March meeting were extremely unhappy, voting 43% against Michael Eisner to continue as a member of the Board of Directors. Although Eisner remained CEO (and a member of the board), former Senator George Mitchell soon replaced him as chairman of the board.

Change was clearly in the works for ABC. Yet more generally, there were also fundamental challenges hanging in the air for all the broadcast networks, reminders that even if they could still pursue many of their familiar competitive routines, they were no longer the exclusive media status quo.

The broadcast networks had long ago lost their lock on viewers' time schedules with the growth of video recording. Now such home recording had become ingrained, which upset previously

February 22, 2004

HBO's *Sex and the City* series finale ("An American Girl in Paris") outscores the competition, including all but one broadcast network show, tying up loose ends but leaving the door open for a feature film sequel four years later.

March 21, 2004

Deadwood. (HBO). Executive producer David Milch (*NYPD Blue*) crafts a riveting Western from Hell, set in 1876 at the town of Deadwood, an illegal outpost located in the Black Hills Indian Cession, where no U.S. laws yet applied. For three seasons, the unflinching language, explicit violence, and complex characters (including settlers played by Ian McShane, Timothy Olyphant, Robin Weigert, and Keith Carradine) combine to form a portrait of greed, moral testing, and Machiavellian manipulation.

May 6, 2004

The final episode of NBC's ten-year-old *Friends* series ("The Last One") is watched by nearly 53 million viewers, ranking as the fourth-most-watched series finale in U.S. television history. Ross again confesses his love for Rachel and they get back together; Chandler and Monica adopt twins and move to the suburbs; Joey and Phoebe join them all turning in their keys and exiting the old apartment.

May 13, 2004

"Goodnight, Seattle" is the final episode of NBC's eleven-year-old *Frasier* series, as Frasier hosts his last Seattle radio show and contemplates departing for a San Francisco station. Before then, during an emergency visit to a veterinarian's office for the dog Eddie, brother Niles and wife Daphne have their first child (a boy), and dad Martin marries Ronee, former babysitter for Niles and Frasier.

May 18, 2004

CBS devotes one hour of prime time to a celebration of the career of Don Hewitt, the executive producer and creator of *60 Minutes*. At age eighty-one, Hewitt had recently reluctantly ceded control of the program to Jeff Fager (from *60 Minutes II*), to become producer-at-large for CBS News.

May 31, 2004

Mel Karmazin announces his resignation as chief operating officer of Viacom after losing a power struggle with his boss, Viacom chief executive officer Sumner Redstone. Karmazin is replaced by two executives, MTV's Tom Freston and CBS's Leslie Moonves.

July 18, 2004

Entourage. (HBO). An "inside showbiz" comedy with Adrian Grenier as Vince Chase, whose fictional film career is just successful enough to carry along hanging-out buddies Eric (Kevin Connolly), Turtle (Jerry Ferrara), and brother Johnny "Drama" (Kevin Dillon). Jeremy Piven plays his agent, Ari Gold, loosely based on real-life superagent Ari Emanuel, brother of Rahm (then an Illinois congressman).

Live presentation of the political nominating convention sessions by the commercial broadcast networks continued to be limited to just a few hours total across the four nights, leaving the more extensive coverage to PBS's *NewsHour* and to cable channels such as CNN *(above, left)*. As a result, during the 2004 Democratic National Convention in Boston, ABC, CBS, and NBC did not carry the Tuesday night keynote address by Barack Obama, then an Illinois state senator. *(Photos by Peter Sills, Digital Focus)*

assumed aspects of program promotion. For example, network reruns of series episodes during the same season (before programs went off to syndication) had lost their consistent viability to help fill out the schedule. Sometimes reruns still worked, sometimes they did not, but multiple network airings of first-run episodes could no longer be automatically counted on to help amortize annual production costs.

Unveiling new programs as part of the fall premiere season had also lost much of its luster. There were so many options and so many distractions through December that mid-season, rather than the fall, had become a prime platform for new shows. For the fall 2004 competition, the broadcast networks collectively spent hundreds of millions, yet their ratings were down 8% in the coveted 18 to 49 age category. Even with heavy promotion, there was no longer an automatic tune-in.

At one time, broadcast network television had been synonymous with popular culture in the U.S. Now there were many more players on the stage. ABC, CBS, Fox, NBC, and UPN and the WB were in the fray along with everyone else trying to grab the attention of the viewing audience, one event at a time.

Much of the new competition came from cable channels, which reached a symbolic milestone in the November 2003 sweeps: basic cable beat the broadcast networks in total households for the first time ever in that sweeps period. Cable also had practical advantages over broadcasters in viewer expectations and production requirements for series: there were fewer episodes needed each cable season; multiple runs (reruns) were accepted; there were fewer hours to fill with new material; a season could start and end virtually any time; there were fewer restrictions on subject matter; and cable channels received additional revenue from licensing fees from cable systems, apart from commercials.

But there was something more basic in play. Cable had become comfortably mainstream in its offerings, with drama, adventure, comedy, news, and reality programs that captured the Zeitgeist of American life every bit as well as the broadcasters did.

So in the mosaic of television in 2003–04, there were viable choices on both cable and broadcast television: gritty police drama in *The Shield* (FX) and *NYPD Blue* (ABC); superb comic timing on *Monk* (USA) and *Frasier* (NBC); high-class drama from *The Sopranos* (HBO) and *The West Wing* (NBC); stylish fashion on *Queer Eye for the Straight Guy* (Bravo) and *American's Next Top Model* (UPN); science fiction adventure with the *Battlestar Galactica* miniseries revival (Sci-Fi) and *Star Trek: Enterprise* (UPN); and best-buddy relationships on *Sex and the City* (HBO) and *Friends* (NBC), both of which ended their runs that season.

In fact, the farewell send-offs for *Sex and the City* and *Friends* illustrated the pop culture parity between cable and broadcast. As an over-the-air network offering, the *Friends* finale naturally drew far greater ratings numbers than *Sex and the City* on premium cable (about five times the audience), yet both were treated to massive media coverage as important pop culture events. Both offered a retrospective special before the wrap-up, providing a sense of closure with these friends from two different Manhattan neighborhoods. The stories left the respective characters looking forward, with marriage, children, and commitments to each other, yet still allowed the possibility for future visits.

Both series reminded viewers of television's ability to bring memorable characters into their everyday lives through engaging relationships fostered by repeated visits. It was a familiar and reliable formula as old as television itself.

What had changed, though, was that some of these fictional friends and neighbors had migrated to new TV homes. They were now as likely to be found through a cable set-top box as in the familiar haunts of the classic over-the-air broadcast channels.

65. ZigZag and JibJab

LOST BEGAN WITH THE CLOSE-UP of an eye, blinking open. Dr. Jack Shephard (Matthew Fox) awoke to take in the unexpected images around him: He was alone in a jungle, flat on his back and bleeding, dressed in a suit and tie, and looking up at the open sky through bamboo stalks and trees. He struggled to his feet, listened, then ran through the jungle toward what turned out to be a nearby beach with a wide expanse of shoreline, a bright blue horizon, and the dramatic backdrop of the burning wreckage of passenger plane *Oceanic 815*—his flight.

In the next six minutes, Shephard went into emergency medical triage mode at the site, moving from person to person in crisis—amid flames, debris, and a still-whirring jet intake engine that sucked in anyone standing too close. The meticulously staged scene ended when one of the plane's seventy-five-foot wings, which had been hanging precariously, still attached to the fuselage, broke away and hit the ground with an explosive crash.

It was a spectacular opening to the new series, tapping every airline passenger's worst nightmare. For authenticity, *Lost* used a real decommissioned Lockheed L-1011 plane, transporting it to the filming site at a remote island beach in Oahu, Hawaii. After that set-up, *Lost* could have played as a variant of the classic *Robinson Crusoe*, the 2000 Tom Hanks film "Castaway," or even as a scripted take on the reality show competition of *Survivor*. Those that survived the crash faced dealing with life on an island, awaiting rescue. Instead, by the end of the two-hour launch, it was clear that *Lost* offered far more.

Creators J. J. Abrams (*Alias*) and Damon Lindelof set up *Lost* as a suspenseful adventure story wrapped in mystery. This approach demanded characters who were more than accident survivors competing to build huts and find food. These were strong individuals caught in something bigger and more frightening, having to deal with the question "Where *are* we?" Their plane had crashed far off course en route from Australia to Los Angeles after encountering violent turbulence strong enough to tear off the cockpit and tail sections.

Literally lost, the passengers began to explore their surroundings and on the first night heard a menacing force loudly thrashing in the nearby jungle. They were further shaken the next day when they encountered a polar bear, discovered the bloody body of the plane's pilot high in a tree, and, most disquieting, intercepted a radio distress call, in French, from somewhere else on the island—a signal they concluded had been running continuously on a tape loop for sixteen years and five months. The

chilling reality: Not only had others been stranded on the island in the past, any rescue might be very long in coming (if at all).

Recognizing the potential limitations of just telling stories about survival on an island, the *Lost* writing team opened up the stage. Series episodes were structured to flash seamlessly back and forth through time and space. This technique allowed great flexibility, introducing each character's back story by shifting the scene as necessary from the island to the United States and other countries including Australia, Iraq, South Korea, and Great Britain. After a while, they also flashed back to earlier life on the island. The island arc unfolded at a creditable pace without rescue, as the entire first season covered just over a month since the crash. (Four seasons would barely pass one hundred days.) Most effectively, the island itself was treated as its own character, one that could unleash powerful forces at any time, including a shape-shifting black cloud of smoke, whispering voices in the jungle, and attacks by "the others" (a different group of people long stranded on the island). These forces provided a built-in dramatic tension: Would the passengers escape (or be rescued) before they were done in by the island?

As de facto leader of the *Oceanic* survivors, Jack Shephard quickly got to the heart of their situation: live together, or die alone. Although the number of survivors was pegged at about forty-eight in the first episode, the stories ultimately focused on a core group. In addition to Shephard these included survivalist John Locke (Terry O'Quinn), con man James "Sawyer" Ford (Josh Holloway), fugitive Kate Austen (Evangeline Lilly), former Iraqi military officer Sayid Jarrah (Naveen Andrews), English rock star Charlie Pace (Dominic Monaghan), big-hearted lottery winner Hugo "Hurley" Reyes (Jorge Garcia), pregnant single mom Claire Littleton (Emilie de Ravin), terminal cancer patient Rose Henderson (L. Scott Caldwell), step-siblings Boone Carlyle (Ian Somerhalder) and Shannon Rutherford (Maggie Grace), divorced father Michael Dawson and his young son Walt (Harold Perrineau and Malcolm David Kelley), and Sun-Hwa Kwon (Yunjin Kim), the daughter of a powerful South Korean businessman, and her husband, Jin-Soo Kwon (Daniel Dae Kim).

Later, other characters also entered the narrative, including manipulative island leader Benjamin Linus (Michael Emerson), reluctant scientist Juliet Burke (Elizabeth Mitchell), Rose's husband Bernard Nadler (Sam Anderson), inexplicably ageless Richard Alpert (Nestor Carbonell), and romantic suitor Desmond Hume (Henry Ian Cusick). This diverse cast introduced a breadth

	8:00	8:30	9:00	9:30	10:00	10:30	
M O N	THE BENEFACTOR		ABC NFL Monday Night Football (to 12 Midnight)				**ABC**
	Still Standing	LISTEN UP	Everybody Loves Raymond	Two And A Half Men	CSI: Miami		**CBS**
	North Shore		RENOVATE MY FAMILY		local		**FOX**
	Fear Factor		Las Vegas		LAX		**NBC**
	One On One	Half And Half	Girlfriends	SECOND TIME AROUND	local		**UPN**
	7th Heaven		Everwood		local		**WB**
T U E	My Wife & Kids	George Lopez	According To Jim	RODNEY	NYPD Blue		**ABC**
	NCIS		CLUBHOUSE		Judging Amy		**CBS**
	Trading Spouses: Meet Your New Mommy		THE NEXT GREAT CHAMP		local		**FOX**
	Last Comic Standing		FATHER OF THE PRIDE	Scrubs	Law & Order: Special Victims Unit		**NBC**
	All Of Us	Eve	VERONICA MARS		local		**UPN**
	Gilmore Girls		One Tree Hill		local		**WB**
W E D	LOST		The Bachelor		WIFE SWAP		**ABC**
	60 Minutes		The King Of Queens	CENTER OF THE UNIVERSE	CSI: NY		**CBS**
	That '70s Show	Quintuplets	The Bernie Mac Show	Method & Red	local		**FOX**
	HAWAII		The West Wing		Law & Order		**NBC**
	America's Next Top Model		KEVIN HILL		local		**UPN**
	Smallville		THE MOUNTAIN		local		**WB**
T H R	Extreme Makeover		LIFE AS WE KNOW IT		Prime Time		**ABC**
	Survivor: Vanuatu - Islands Of Fire		CSI: Crime Scene Investigation		Without A Trace		**CBS**
	The O.C.		North Shore		local		**FOX**
	JOEY	Will & Grace	The Apprentice		ER		**NBC**
	WWE Smackdown!				local		**UPN**
	Blue Collar TV	DREW CAREY'S BLUE SCREEN	One Tree Hill		local		**WB**
F R I	8 Simple Rules	COMPLETE SAVAGES	Hope & Faith	Less Than Perfect	20/20		**ABC**
	Joan Of Arcadia		JAG		DR. VEGAS		**CBS**
	THE COMPLEX: MALIBU		THE NEXT GREAT CHAMP		local		**FOX**
	Dateline NBC		Third Watch		MEDICAL INVESTIGATION		**NBC**
	Star Trek: Enterprise		America's Next Top Model		local		**UPN**
	What I Like About You	Grounded For Life	Reba	Blue Collar TV	local		**WB**
S A T	The Wonderful World Of Disney						**ABC**
	Crime Time Saturday		Crime Time Saturday		48 Hours Mystery		**CBS**
	Cops	Cops	America's Most Wanted		local		**FOX**
	The Apprentice		(specials)		Law & Order: Special Victims Unit		**NBC**
	local						**UPN**
	local						**WB**

	7:00	7:30	8:00	8:30	9:00	9:30	10:00	10:30	
S U N	America's Funniest Home Videos		Extreme Makeover: Home Edition		DESPERATE HOUSEWIVES		BOSTON LEGAL		**ABC**
	60 Minutes		Cold Case		CBS Sunday Night Movie				**CBS**
	King Of The Hill	Malcolm In The Middle	The Simpsons	Arrested Development	MY BIG FAT OBNOXIOUS BOSS		local		**FOX**
	Dateline NBC		American Dreams		Law & Order: Criminal Intent		Crossing Jordan		**NBC**
	local								**UPN**
	Steve Harvey's Big Time		Charmed		JACK & BOBBY		local		**WB**

of character-based stories that regularly reached back to pivotal moments in the past, like a drama anthology. They also illuminated such island threads as John and Jack in conflict as "the man of faith versus the man of science"; Jack, Kate, and Sawyer in a romantic triangle; and Hurley seeing his winning lottery numbers (14-8-15-16-23-42) repeatedly turn up on the island.

Although the individual episodes of *Lost* offered stand-alone twists and character revelations, the series quickly built a following with its mastery of "long form" storytelling—carrying through a narrative over multiple episodes, through an entire season, and ultimately through the whole run of the series. Along the way, each story added to an increasingly detailed program and character tapestry. Yet *Lost* stood out by offering even more, weaving in threads of philosophy, literature, pop culture, spiritual calling, the quest for personal redemption, and the consequences of choice at key moments in life. As part of a timeless battle between the forces of darkness and light, the series wore the trappings of classic mythology, mixing straight-ahead drama with the prospect of possibly understanding "life's big mysteries."

Lost attracted a devoted following from the start, and it became one of the most talked-about programs in the fall of 2004. The *Lost* pilot episode attracted more than 18 million viewers.

As a big-budget scripted series that ventured into science fiction and fantasy with complicated, season-long story arcs, *Lost* was an unexpected departure for the time, even more so coming from ABC. The network had suffered through a stretch of poor ratings through the previous few seasons, yet ABC programming boss Lloyd Braun gave the green light to *Lost* on a tight turnaround schedule for the fall, with the pilot cost alone reportedly about $12 million. Rather than placing ABC's hopes primarily on low-cost reality or a formula procedural show, Braun had instead invested in more expensive and demanding scripted fare. In effect, while others had zigged, ABC had zagged, going against conventional bottom-line wisdom. Though Braun was let go by ABC just before the fall 2004 schedule was announced, that strategy played out in the 2004–05 season to tremendous success, including two other high-gloss scripted series: *Desperate Housewives* and *Grey's Anatomy*.

Desperate Housewives was a smartly comic prime time soap premiering in a top Sunday night slot. Created by Marc Cherry (a former writer and producer for *The Golden Girls*), the program was set in what appeared to be a perfect slice of American suburbia, led by a strong cast of female characters: divorced mom Susan Mayer (Teri Hatcher), perfectionist homemaker Bree Hodge (Marcia Cross), career-on-hold-mom Lynette Scavo (Felicity Huffman), demanding professional model Gabrielle Solis (Eva Longoria Parker), and man-eater real estate agent Edie Britt (Nicollette Sheridan). The series started with a "bang" as seemingly happy homemaker Mary Alice Young (Brenda Strong) took a gun to herself (off camera) and committed suicide, sending shock waves and personal doubt among her friends. Why had she done it? The women of Wisteria Lane began looking for answers and, as in any good soap opera, that meant uncovering dirty little secrets including false identities, blackmail, and murder. Closer to home, though, they also had to acknowledge their own less-than-perfect situations and indiscretions involving sex, lies, money, theft, arson, rebellious children, straying partners, and unfulfilled dreams. Mary Alice herself commented on it all as the ultimate in omniscient narrators, speaking from the great beyond in voiceovers about her old neighborhood and her dear friends.

As a soap opera, *Desperate Housewives* naturally involved long form story threads, but with an overall humorous tone, turning it into more of a dramedy. In fact, for Emmy award consideration, *Desperate Housewives* was nominated in (and won in) the comedy categories. The program was an instant fall hit, giving ABC a strong Sunday night anchor show. Its good fortunes helped to boost the network's other shows that night: the lead-in reality program *Extreme Makeover: Home Edition* (a help-a-deserving-family home fix-it series led by Ty Pennington, former carpenter on TLC's *Trading Spaces*) and David E. Kelley's law drama *Boston Legal*, which plucked James Spader as Alan Shore and William Shatner as Denny Crane from *The Practice* and let them revel in their gleefully indulgent characters.

Midseason, *Boston Legal* stepped aside for ABC's third major new scripted series, the heart-throb medical drama *Grey's Anatomy*. Created by Shonda Rhimes, the series followed first-year intern Meredith Grey (Ellen Pompeo) pursuing a career at Seattle Grace Hospital in the shadow of her retired and departed, but still legendary, surgeon mother. Other members of the hospital team included fellow interns Cristina Yang (Sandra Oh), Izzie Stevens (Katherine Heigl), George O'Malley (T. R. Knight), and Alex Karev (Justin Chambers), who all labored under their demanding supervisor Miranda Bailey (Chandra Wilson) and hospital head Dr. Richard Webber (James Pickens, Jr.). Of course, sexy hook-ups and complicated affairs were inevitable in the intense soap-opera hospital setting. The premiere ad promised: "Operations. Temptations. Frustrations."

The central relationship of the series early on was between Meredith and surgeon Dr. Derek Shepherd (Patrick Dempsey), dubbed "McDreamy" for his striking good looks. Their connection was set from the first scene, which had Meredith sending him out after a one-night stand when they never learned each other's identities, only to meet him again right away as her boss on her first day at the hospital. It was a classic teasing couple match that waxed and waned over the years, even surviving the reappearance of Shepherd's former wife, Dr. Addison Forbes Montgomery Shepherd (Kate Walsh).

During its initial nine-episode spring 2005 run, *Grey's Anatomy* successfully built on its *Desperate Housewives* lead-in and became a major hit. During its second season, the program used a one-time post-Super Bowl slot for maximum promotional effect with a cliffhanger story that involved a live explosive device *inside* a surgical patient. Guest Kyle Chandler played bomb squad lead Dylan Young, who guided the hospital and Meredith through the crisis. *Grey's Anatomy* later shifted nights to become its own anchor series and remained one of ABC's consistent successes of the era, spawning the spinoff *Private Practice* (built around Kate Walsh's character).

By good timing, good instincts, and a bit of luck, ABC, which had been flailing, turned itself around in the 2004–05 season, even stealing some of the "hip quotient" from cable offerings. It was a reminder that, even after losing significant market share to the collective draw of dozens of cable channels, the Big 4 broadcast networks could still quickly reach a bigger and more broad-based audience. With the right programs, they could still drive pop culture buzz.

ABC's ability to leverage a strategically placed hit was also a reminder of how that could change a network's fortunes or help to maintain them. Connections to hits had long greased the path for any network. For the 2004–05 season ABC was not alone in successfully using such proximity and audience familiarity with a program or program type in promoting other series.

As the number one network in total audience ratings, CBS continued to rely on the strength of its procedural dramas, with crime cases that generally wrapped up in one- or two-episode stories. This season the network further expanded its most

September 29, 2004

On the fiftieth anniversary of the network premiere of the *Tonight* show, NBC announces that host Jay Leno (number one in late night ratings) will step down in 2009, to be replaced by *Late Night*'s Conan O'Brien.

December 1, 2004

After more than two decades of stability in the ranks of the three broadcast network nightly news anchors, Tom Brokaw is the first of the trio to leave, signing off from the *NBC Nightly News* after twenty-two years. On December 2 Brian Williams assumes the post.

January 3, 2005

Scottish comedian Craig Ferguson (late of *The Drew Carey Show*) takes over as host of CBS's *Late Late Show*, replacing Craig Kilborn, who had departed in August. Guest hosts had filled the gap.

March 9, 2005

Dan Rather anchors his last edition of the weekday *CBS Evening News* after exactly twenty-four years in the post. On March 10, fellow Texan Bob Schieffer steps in. Schieffer had previously replaced Rather in 1976 as anchor for the Saturday *Evening News* and then spent twenty years there.

March 13, 2005

A year after shareholders gave him a vote of no confidence, Michael Eisner announces that he will step down as Disney's chief executive officer on September 30, after twenty-one years as head of the company. Robert Iger, Disney's president since 2000, is named the new CEO. Former Senator George Mitchell says he will step down from the more ceremonial post of chairman of the board in 2006.

successful franchise with *CSI: New York* (starring Gary Sinise and Melinda Kanakaredes). That program joined *CSI: Crime Scene Investigation* (in its fifth season) and *CSI: Miami* (in its third), as well as *JAG* (the Judge Advocate General investigating military crimes) and its spinoff, *NCIS* (the Naval Criminal Investigative Service looking into naval crimes). There were also series that were not spinoffs: the second season of *Cold Case* (investigating officially closed cases) and the third season of *Without a Trace* (investigating missing persons). In comedy, CBS heavily promoted the final season of *Everybody Loves Raymond* on Monday night, and also effectively touted the program that followed, *Two and a Half Men*, in its second season and considered the network's future Monday night anchor show.

Fox once again used *American Idol* as its annual ratings linchpin to boost other shows and, for the very first time, the network won the season ratings race in the key 18 to 49 demographic. The chief beneficiary of the *American Idol* effect this season was the new medical series *House, M.D.*, created by David Shore. Set at Princeton-Plainsboro teaching hospital in New Jersey, *House* could have been just another procedural, but it quickly established itself as a character showcase built around Hugh Laurie as Dr. Gregory House, a brilliant diagnostic surgeon with a prickly, abrasive, and unsympathetic manner. He walked with a cane (owing to a painful leg condition), popped the strong prescription drug Vicodin to deal with that pain, and demanded the

professional best from his colleagues and himself. A mystery series about bizarre and "unsolvable" medical situations, it worked particularly well because of House's attitude: he took on cases for the sheer intellectual challenge, much as the classic character of Sherlock Holmes relished the chance to solve impossible puzzles. Everyone else served as House's Dr. Watson, at any moment providing the spark for an inspired insight. Naturally these often came from interactions with his medical team: Doctors Allison Cameron (Jennifer Morrison), Robert Chase (Jesse Spencer), and Eric Foreman (Omar Epps). They also flowed from House's informal repartee with his best friend, cancer specialist Dr. James Wilson (Robert Sean Leonard), and from charged face-offs with his boss, hospital administrator Dr. Lisa Cuddy (Lisa Edelstein), who ultimately had to approve his sometimes risky and unorthodox procedures. The emphasis on House and his character gamesmanship brought a lighter tone to the life-and-death drama, which helped it to soon build its ratings track record.

NBC's fortunes for the 2004–05 season illustrated the opposite side of the ratings equation: lacking a strong lineup to leverage. Although the network had its own procedurals in place (including three different *Law and Order* series) overall the schedule felt tired. The new dramas seemed generic and constricted (cops in Honolulu on *Hawaii*; a medical investigation team on *Medical Investigation*; *LAX*, a show set at the Los Angeles airport slotted after the returning *Vegas*, a show set in a Las Vegas casino). *Fear Factor* was no longer a hot reality show, and *The Apprentice* had yet to prove itself for the long run. The once formidable "Must See TV" comedy blocks had essentially disappeared with the departure of *Frasier* and *Friends* the previous season.

For the fall of 2004, NBC had hoped to replicate the formula used by *Cheers* (which had spun off *Frasier* by relocating that title character in a new city, with a new job, and with a new supporting cast). It led off Thursday night with a heavily promoted *Friends* spinoff, *Joey*, which dropped Matt LeBlanc's title character into a new city (Los Angeles), in a new but familiar job (struggling Hollywood actor), with a new supporting cast (including Drea de Matteo, from *The Sopranos,* as his sister). Joey was still Joey, but the overall package did not gel instantly, and its high-profile placement (the old *Friends* slot) did not allow time to work out the kinks. Curious *Friends* fans stopped by at first but did not stay. Although it hung around for two seasons, the series was unable to anchor the night for NBC and instead followed the path of *AfterMASH*, not *Frasier*, never becoming a ratings contender. Neither did NBC, finishing the season fourth in total audience and in the 18 to 49 viewer demographic.

That was the catch for the over-the-air networks. Even with so many broadcast series dominating the pop culture landscape in the 2004–05 season, the need for sufficiently high ratings to justify production on major comedy and drama series remained. Most programs had to reach their targets comparatively quickly, or face tweaking, schedule shuffling, or cancellation. There were some opportunities to let a program quietly grow, but those sometimes happened as much by chance as by planning. At mid-season, with little new working in its comedy lineup, NBC slotted a short run trial for a U.S. adaptation of a British comedy, *The Office*, but with modest expectations.

This was in contrast to the trajectory on cable, where a series could still be considered a success drawing far fewer viewers than broadcast series as long as it reached a large enough portion of its targeted audience and filled a niche for that channel. Over the summer of 2005, another *Friends* alum, Lisa Kudrow, starred in *The Comeback*, a wicked skewering of show business manipulations for HBO. *The Comeback* never approached *Joey*'s ratings numbers and lasted only one season, yet its short run did not carry the same sting of disappointment. It had served as a limited run prestige offering.

Besides, HBO had another entertainment industry comedy, *Entourage*, which premiered in the summer of 2004 and returned for its second season in the summer of 2005. Elsewhere on cable, the Sci-Fi network rolled out in January 2005 the first regular season of its new *Battlestar Galactica* series, more than a year after a well-received miniseries revival of the late 1970s program. Clearly, the pace of production for cable allowed for patience.

Among broadcasters, the WB and UPN were the closest kin to cable, drawing smaller audiences than the Big 4 networks. Consequently, in promoting their shows, both had to stress reaching targeted audiences, and rely on word-of-mouth and press coverage. Yet unlike the more focused programming approach of cable, both networks still had scattershot broadcasting schedules. UPN's returning lineup for 2004–05 included Friday night wrestling (*WWE Smackdown!*), science fiction adventure (*Star Trek: Enterprise*), fashion competition (*American's Next Top Model*), and a mix of comedies featuring black performers (including *Girlfriends, Half and Half*, and *All of Us*). The WB offered the fantasy adventures *Smallville* and *Charmed*, soap operas including *One Tree Hill* and *Everwood*, the mother-daughter drama *Gilmore Girls*, and comedies including *Reba, Blue Collar TV, What I Like About You*, and *Steve Harvey's Big Time.*

There were two new UPN showcase dramas for the fall 2004. *Kevin Hill* was a vehicle for Taye Diggs, who played a ladies' man entertainment lawyer who became an overnight dad when the death of his cousin left him inheriting an infant girl. *Veronica Mars* offered a different type of father-daughter combo: teen detective Veronica Mars (Kristen Bell), a high school student sleuth, and her detective dad, Keith (Enrico Colantoni). The series was set in the small oceanside California town of Neptune, an enclave of the super rich with a subculture of those barely getting by, joined at the public high school that served both worlds. Veronica provided a cleverly sardonic, world-weary film noir narrative tone. She had reason to be skeptical about fate: her alcoholic mom had abandoned the family after her dad had been squeezed out of his job as sheriff (into private detective work) when he drew uncomfortably close to Neptune's movers and shakers in the investigation of a high-profile murder case. The victim was Veronica's best friend (played in flashback by Amanda Seyfried). Keith's unofficial search for the killer remained an underlying arc throughout the first season, as did Veronica's efforts to that same end, along with her search for the identity of the person who had drugged and date-raped her the previous year.

Series creator Rob Thomas brought an unflinching sense of true teen angst to the scripting of the show yet also captured a strong and affectionate father-daughter bond between Veronica and Keith as two outsiders in the stubborn pursuit of justice. Their repartee was reminiscent of the clever give-and-take between Lorelai (Lauren Graham) and her daughter, Rory (Alexis Bledel), on the WB's long-running *Gilmore Girls*. In fact, *Veronica Mars* on UPN ran in the time slot immediately after *Gilmore Girls* on the WB in a cross-network perfect match.

The prestige new series on the WB, though, was *Jack and Bobby*, which focused on the teen years of two brothers, Jack and Bobby McCallister (Matt Long and Logan Lerman), one of whom was destined to become president of the United States—in 2040. Their first names conjured a connection to the real-life political Kennedy family and brothers Jack and Bobby (John and Robert), but these fictional stories were set in contemporary times, with flash-forwards to the future when Bobby would take the oath of office. In a Sunday night time slot against ABC's *Desperate Housewives*, the series illustrated the extraordinary challenges even a highly praised broadcast series faced, especially on one of the smaller networks. *Jack and Bobby* was a lovingly executed rendering of U.S. politics, premiering in a presidential election year cycle. Still that was not enough of a draw, and the program lasted only one season.

Jack and Bobby's view of the political process included behind-the-scenes moments of hardball maneuvering but was ultimately hopeful and positive. The real-life 2004 presidential election cycle, though, was a more difficult script, especially for established journalists. After decades of coverage, there was an all-too-familiar routine: a primary season with the nominees from both parties known by the spring, a long gap to the official nominating conventions, then a two-month sprint to election day. For the campaign teams, the trick was to control the story along the way.

It was a given that incumbent President George W. Bush would seek reelection, and there was no shortage of issues from his first term. These included the administration's general "war on terror" including the search for weapons of mass destruction in Iraq, domestic spying, Guantanamo prison, the Patriot Act, and, most important, progress in two theaters of overseas combat, Iraq and Afghanistan. Although President Bush had declared "mission accomplished" in Iraq on camera back on May 1, 2003, that effort was still far from over.

Yet reporters who covered all these stories also grappled with challenging questions: What was responsible journalism in an

May 1, 2005

Three years after cancellation because of low ratings, Fox's *Family Guy* returns with new episodes thanks to a persistent campaign by fans and strong DVD sales of earlier episodes. Creator Seth MacFarlane's opening bit cites by title twenty-nine flopped Fox series that came and went before the program was brought back.

May 13, 2005

UPN airs the final new episode of *Star Trek: Enterprise*, ending its fourth season. This marks the first time since the debut of the syndicated *Star Trek: The Next Generation* in 1986 that no new Star Trek series is running on television.

June 27, 2005

After fifty years as a fall broadcast television staple, organizers of the Miss America pageant announce that the show will move to cable in January 2006 on the CMT network. ABC had dropped the annual special after the low-rated September 2004 broadcast.

July 1, 2005

The Pax television network becomes i: Independent Television and changes formats from original programming (and rebroadcasts of some NBC shows) to a schedule of infomercials and reruns. On January 29, 2007, the struggling network changes names again to Ion Television.

August 7, 2005

Peter Jennings, sixty-seven-year-old anchor of ABC's *World News Tonight* since 1983, dies of lung cancer. He never returned to the show after taking a health leave of absence in April (with other ABC news anchors filling in) and was the last of the three nightly broadcast news anchors to depart within one year.

For Peter Jennings (ABC) *(left)*, Tom Brokaw (NBC), and Dan Rather (CBS), the 2004 race marked the last election cycle in their respective nightly news anchor chairs, which they had held for more than two decades. *(Photo by Peter Sills, Digital Focus)*

open-ended war that was still unfolding? What was appropriate criticism of the president, his policies, and the war effort itself? There were passionate critics as well as defenders of the administration's policies who were ready to weigh in on their judgments, often invoking the September 11 attacks and the shadow they still cast.

The White House team in place was not only media savvy but also determined to "right" what it saw as missteps with the media from past administrations. Among others, this team included Vice President Dick Cheney and Secretary of Defense Donald Rumsfeld, who had both worked in the administrations of Richard Nixon and Gerald Ford, and presidential advisor Karl Rove, who had guided George W. Bush's campaigns since Texas. Using every available resource to influence and control the narrative, the White House did not give ground easily. So, for example, the Bush administration continued the 1991 policy (from the Gulf War) that did not allow photos of coffins returning to the U.S. from war zones. Rumsfeld held regular lengthy press briefings, often carried live by cable news channels, and these war updates served as opportunities for pointed critiques of administration critics.

Press coverage of the 2004 election cycle began, as usual, with the focus on the "horse race" among candidates. With Bush a given on the Republican side, attention turned to the Democratic challengers. Early on in 2003, former Vermont Governor Howard Dean stood out when he launched a strong grassroots effort that tapped a growing number of Internet-savvy users to solicit contributions, to organize electronically organize, and to stoke support from online commentators ("bloggers"). Dean also challenged and criticized the administration's 2003 invasion of Iraq, and his campaign flourished in fund-raising and early polls.

However, his campaign began to come apart with the first round of voting at the Iowa Caucus on January 19. Dean placed third. More damaging, he lost control of his own story when, red faced and with a hoarse voice, he delivered a high-octane late-in-the-night speech to rally his supporters, ending with something resembling a rebel yell. Few people saw it that night, but it played repeatedly (hundreds of times in just a few days) on cable news,

local stations, the broadcast networks, radio talk shows, and the Internet. Outside its original context, Dean's animated exhortations came off to some as an odd rant that did not seem presidential (it was dubbed the "I have a scream" speech), and his fortunes tumbled. Very quickly, Massachusetts Senator John Kerry became the unquestioned front runner and locked up the nomination by March 2, Super Tuesday.

That left a nearly six-month gap until the respective party nominating conventions were completed (the Democratic convention in late July in Boston; the Republican convention in early September in New York City). During that time the Bush and Kerry teams pressed to define themselves and each other in the electoral landscape but avoided generating any real news. In addition to paid ads, they pursued "free media" on radio, broadcast television, cable, print, and online, often through surrogates. In addition, a host of special interest groups ran their own ads drawing on their own fund-raising apparatus.

Cable news channels were an obvious target for guests because those services needed to fill the entire day and devoted significant time to talk, analysis, and commentary shows. They aimed to grab channel surfing viewers with audience participation, combative exchanges, and strong personalities. An election cycle provided perfect fodder for such hosts as Bill O'Reilly and Sean Hannity on Fox; Paul Begala and Tucker Carlson (*Crossfire*) and Anderson Cooper on CNN; and Chris Matthews (*Hardball*) and Keith Olbermann (*Countdown*) on MSNBC.

Strangely, while there were many stories on the war in Iraq, the most passionate war-related media discussions focused forty years back—on both candidates' ties to the war in Vietnam. At first, that seemed to give an advantage to Kerry, who had been decorated for his service in Vietnam, while Bush had put in time at a stateside posting. Yet it played out just the opposite.

A group of "Swift Boat Veterans" critical of Kerry circulated their assertions questioning his Vietnam record. (Kerry had publicly criticized the war upon his return from service in the 1970s.) One key ad in August 2004 played in only three states for a limited time, but it extended its reach exponentially in the retelling, much like coverage of the Howard Dean "scream" speech. In various media settings, that was enough for the advocates of the cause to get their questions onto the table. Even if particular points were described as exaggerations, distortions, or outright lies, the assertions were still injected into the general discussion and, cumulatively, tarnished Kerry's public image. Although Kerry may have felt he was wronged, there seemed to be minimal consequences for those that had made the accusations in the media.

However, that was not the case a short time later in the campaign when Vietnam-era skepticism was directed at President Bush. Part of the difference was the venue. On the September 8 Wednesday edition of *60 Minutes*, CBS's Dan Rather, as a segment correspondent, reported on documents that seemed to confirm blatant favoritism and manipulation in the early 1970s on behalf of Bush's landing a cushy spot in the Texas Air National Guard (thereby avoiding service in Vietnam) and his failure to meet some of his required obligations. The problem was that some of the cited documents given to CBS from that era could not be definitively authenticated, a point quickly seized upon by Bush supporters, starting online. Whether the underlying charges were true and could be supported apart from the cited documents became irrelevant. Raising the question of the potential for forgery effectively took the entire issue of Bush's military history off the table for the balance of the campaign.

Instead, the onus fell on CBS, *60 Minutes*, and Dan Rather. After first defending the report, the network launched an investigation and issued a correction/apology less than two weeks after the program. (Final word on the veracity of the documents was not determined.) There were firings and resignations. Soon after the fall elections, Rather himself announced his retirement as anchor of the nightly news (effective in March 2005), followed by his departure from CBS in 2006 after forty-four years. It was an acrimonious end, and he later sued the network for breach of contract.

The quick about-face by CBS underscored the difficulty an established news organization faced trying to break through orchestrated narratives, spin, and the noise of advocacy groups: it had something to lose if there was a misstep. However, one type of political reporting and critical commentary was particularly well suited to navigate that landscape because it had virtually nothing to lose: comedy.

Earlier in the year, Evan and Gregg Spiridellis broke through the torpid and careful campaign season with "This Land," an equal time, online (JibJab.com) animated mocking of Bush and Kerry set to the tune of "This Land Is Your Land." More silly than topical, the short film was a viral online smash and also turned up on multiple cable and broadcast programs.

Other comedy outlets drilled deeper. NBC's *Saturday Night Live* once again included topical skits for the election cycle (including Will Forte as Bush and Seth Meyers as Kerry). Bill Maher timed the second season of his weekly HBO series *Real Time* to begin with the primaries, break briefly at summer, and end with election day. Michael Moore's satirical documentary "Fahrenheit 9/11" premiered in movie theaters in June. The film presented pointed criticisms of the Bush administration's actions before, during, and after the September 11 attacks, including television footage at the time.

By far, the most consistent and aggressive comedy commentary came from cable's Jon Stewart and *The Daily Show* team. The Comedy Central program had the advantage of airing multiple episodes each week looking just like a mainstream nightly news program, using real news clips and a team of field reporters. Yet it was freed of news conventions: Jon Stewart could say what some viewers (and, sometimes, news reporters) might be thinking about a story, mocking the subject and the spin. Stewart did not have to worry about accusations that the show did not tell both sides or that it distorted a story because there was a ready answer: It's comedy. Jokes. *Fake* news.

Although the program used its material for humor, *The Daily Show* was clearly well researched, carefully written, and reflected a profound interest in current events, earning kudos from real journalists such as Ted Koppel. In fact, the program often targeted the foibles of the news media itself, being especially critical of a lack of skepticism, the hesitation to ask hard questions, and the preference for noisy confrontation that looked hard-nosed but was all just theater. Stewart raised these points during a guest appearance on CNN's *Crossfire* on October 15, chastising co-hosts Paul Begala and Tucker Carlson for "hurting America" with their left/right routine rather than offering viewers real debate. Strikingly, though without citing Stewart, CNN canceled *Crossfire* early in 2005.

George W. Bush was reelected in November 2004, giving reporters and humorists four more years of material. *Time* named Bush "Person of the Year" and described him as essentially declaring the Death of Compromise, with the magazine quoting him directly as saying: "I've got the will of my people at my back" and "I'll reach out to everyone who shares our goals." Bush's team had taken him through a long election campaign and his political narrative appeared unassailable for another four years.

Until the rains came.

When Hurricane Katrina hit the New Orleans region on August 29, 2005, it set off one of the worst engineering disasters in U.S. history as protective levees were breached and entire towns and neighborhoods flooded. What started out as a weather story quickly turned into a heart-wrenching tale of human lives pushed to the brink. The statistics were stunning. More than 1,800 were confirmed dead. At one point, more than 10,000 refugees sought shelter in the New Orleans Super Dome. Numerous bodies floated in the flood waters. Government seemed very slow to respond to the gravity of the situation.

Television news rose to the occasion as witness to the destruction. CNN's Anderson Cooper came to epitomize the coverage, conveying the unthinkable at each step of the way and allowing his emotions to show—sorrow, shock, and even anger. When he dressed down an official falling into standard political spin, on camera, he set off a blaze of instant affirmation via the Internet.

As the story unfolded, it was clear that there were breakdowns beyond the levees: in communication, evacuation, rescue, food and shelter services, and federal and local rescue efforts. This was not some theoretical discussion about actions four decades old, nor stories from half a world away. This was a disaster in the country's backyard. In the end, no amount of spin control could hide what reporters, studio anchors, and home viewers could see for themselves.

Television could not change the forces of nature. Its coverage of Hurricane Katrina and the aftermath, though, once again demonstrated the power of TV news to tell compelling stories that could touch and stir a national audience, one person at a time.

66. Here's the Deal

WHAT COULD DUPLICATE the success of *American Idol*?

Over its first four seasons, *American Idol* had established itself as television's premiere ratings draw (reaching more than 27 million viewers in the 2004–05 season). In an increasingly uncertain media world, it was one of the few consistent hits. No knockoff was going to touch the program's performance and profitability, but that did not stop the time-honored television tradition of trying to cash in with something close.

The obvious elements to copy were some kind of competition and some kind of talent showcase. Cut-throat conflict and manipulation were already part of the reality show formula used by such series as CBS's *Survivor* and *Big Brother*. Those elements were successfully carried on by newer programs including NBC's *The Apprentice* and the Food Network's *Iron Chef* cook-off contests. However, there were also many flops of this type, including (in the 2004–05 season) a pair of boxing shows, *The Contender* (NBC) and *The Next Great Champ* (Fox), and disappointing numbers for Fox's *The Rebel Billionaire: Branson's Quest for the Best* (a globe-trotting business competition to become president of Richard Branson's Virgin Worldwide).

Talent shows were as old as television, and CBS had moved quickly in January 2003 down that path once the appeal of *American Idol* became clear. Arsenio Hall was tapped to helm a revival of the 1970s *Star Search* (originally hosted by Ed McMahon), which lasted for two seasons. In the fall of 2003, *Steve Harvey's Big Time* on the WB began its own two-year run, emphasizing an odd assortment of talent including jugglers, body benders, and "power" eaters. Harvey added a weekly $10,000 prize in his second season, and the acts grew even stranger (one winning contestant put nine rattlesnakes in his mouth). None of these prizes, though, could match *American Idol*'s lure as a proven stepping stone to show business success.

American Idol's Simon Cowell pursued his own talent show opportunities, crisscrossing between the U.S. and Great Britain with series that could easily translate from one international market to another. They included *X Factor* (beginning in 2004 in the U.K.) and, in 2006, *American Inventor* for ABC and *America's Got Talent* for NBC. These promised not only prizes but a degree of career-launching notoriety, albeit far less than *American Idol*.

By and large, the shows generally missed one of the more subtle aspects of *American Idol*, its carefully finessed pacing. Early rounds inevitably included aspirants with more heart than talent, leading to eye-rolling reactions by the judging panel and Cowell's scathing comments. Those performances, though, were really the entry barrier. Once the core dozen finalists were in place, the program became a true talent showcase, not only exciting and competitive but also ultimately positive and sometimes uplifting.

In the summer of 2005, both Fox and ABC found a formula that captured that same spirit in another form that harkened back to early television: dance competition. ABC's *Dancing with the Stars* began on June 1, and Fox's *So You Think You Can Dance* followed on July 20. Both became long-running hits with spirited competition, viewer voting, and performances that were pure entertainment.

Dancing with the Stars (hosted by Tom Bergeron and Samantha Harris) paired celebrities from different circles of fame with accomplished dancers as instructors, who put their famous partners through rigorous training. Rehearsals were recorded for use in "up close" profile segments. After each dance sequence there were tips and evaluations offered by a judging panel with strong backgrounds in the art, including Len Goodman (from Britain's *Strictly Come Dancing,* the BBC model for this series) and choreographers Carrie Ann Inaba and Bruno Tonioli. The celebrities were an eclectic lot, and part of the program's appeal was seeing them out of character, trying to shine in the world of tango, rumba, ballroom, and beyond. Over the years they included such acting, sports, music, tabloid, and political figures as Evander Holyfield, John O'Hurley, Kelly Monaco, Donny Osmond, Heather Mills, Jerry Springer, Tucker Carlson, and Tom DeLay.

So You Think You Can Dance was more directly a surrogate *American Idol*, from that program's creator, Simon Fuller, and producer, Nigel Lythgoe. Over each season, talented but unknown dancers embarked on a competitive training process, leading to a grand dance finale. Lythgoe (a former dancer and choreographer) led the judging, with ballroom dance champion Mary Murphy soon installed as a panel regular, along with a rotation of guest judges such as "Hairspray" director Adam Shankman and *Fame* star Debbie Allen. After the first season, lanky British TV personality Cat Deeley served as the show's host. Choreographers such as Mia Michaels and Mandy Moore developed artistic and imaginative dance productions that won the program several Emmy awards.

Both dance programs started in the summer but eventually shifted to include more competitive fall and mid-season slots. (*Dancing with the Stars* did so immediately). They were able to duplicate a number of *American Idol*'s scheduling strengths: they were live, non-scripted, and easily expandable, squeezing out extra episodes with results shows and recap specials that were not quite reruns. They were gently addictive, comfortable destination television, with a spirit of friendly, positive competition.

The dance programs were also part of a small cluster of "nice" reality shows that focused more on what participants could accomplish than on what they could do to undercut other people. ABC's returning *Extreme Makeover: Home Edition* (rebuilding people's homes) took that approach. NBC offered the second season of *The Biggest Loser*, a weight-loss competition that, despite the title, had a tough-love positive ethic.

NBC's greatest ratings success for the season came with its version of the European game show *Deal or No Deal*, hosted in the U.S. by Howie Mandel (formerly of *St. Elsewhere* and the animated *Bobby's World*). His personality had to carry perhaps one of the simplest contests ever. No qualifying questions. No spinning wheel. No competing teams. Each individual contestant would open the game by choosing one of twenty-six numbered metal suitcases (each held by a beautiful model), but not knowing the contents, which ranged in ascending cash value from $.01 to $1,000,000. The contestant would choose which of the other cases to open, one by one, to reveal its amount. Along the way, Mandel would talk with an unseen "banker" who would offer a cash payment for the originally chosen suitcase (which remained unopened to the end), reflecting the odds of its value based on amounts that still had not been uncovered. That led to the only question that mattered, as Mandel would ask the contestant: "Deal, or no deal?"

For NBC, the program was a very good deal, catching on quickly after its December 2005 premiere as a set of specials running five nights in a row. When the show returned as a regular series at the end of February, it aired three nights a week, and that Monday-Wednesday-Friday rotation did well for the rest of the season. Still, none of the game/competition reality shows could match the hold on the viewing public of *American Idol*, whose ratings for the 2005–06 season were its best yet, taking Fox to a second season win in the 18 to 49 demographic. (CBS again won the season in total viewers.) The program was the anchor for Fox's annual game plan: hold tight through the fall until the season *really* began, in January, with *American Idol*'s return.

Yet *American Idol* was not the only reason for a renewed emphasis on mid-season programming. After nearly a decade of increasingly aggressive promotion of cable series, viewers had come to see that a new "season" could begin virtually anytime and run any length. Among broadcasters, reality programs such as *Survivor* had embraced the cable concept of multiple seasons in the same programming year, treating each self-contained arc as its own "season." (In its fifth year, *Survivor* was on its eleventh contest sequence.) For years, mid-season had also been gathering strength as a preferred time to deploy a program strategically, far from the flurry of the fall premieres (as well as such disruptions as baseball's annual World Series, quadrennial presidential election coverage, the November sweeps, and holiday specials).

Most important, the willingness by the networks to break from the decades-old approach of placing their best hopes in the fall was an acknowledgment that they truly no longer controlled when and how viewers watched television. Seeds of this new relationship had first been planted in the 1980s with the advent of video tape recording, which allowed time shifting and preserving shows for later playback; when digital video recorders (DVRs) arrived at the turn of the century (led by TiVo, which was introduced in early 1999), such manipulations became even easier. By about 2005, individual control was in the DNA of viewers. Nielsen began to track DVR playback for its ratings calculations.

All that put new emphasis on the strategic airing of new episodes for maximum return. It was not that viewers objected to reruns per se; the cable schedules were filled with repeats, and some network shows still scored well in reruns (most consistently, single-episode procedurals). But with video recordings, viewers had seized control of content and could choose to rerun favorites any time *they* wished.

So, more than ever, viewers needed to be convinced to adjust their schedules to match television's. As a result, programs with

September 22, 2005

Everybody Hates Chris. (UPN). Chris Rock serves as executive producer and narrator (ala *The Wonder Years*) for a sitcom about his own teen years in the 1980s growing up in the tough Bedford Stuyvesant neighborhood in Brooklyn. Tyler James Williams plays the thirteen-year-old Chris, who is bused to an all-white junior high school and has to deal with two very different cultural settings.

October 5, 2005

The National Hockey League returns after losing the entire 2004–05 season to a lockout. Opening with the New York Rangers playing the Philadelphia Flyers, the NHL moves from ESPN to its new cable outlet, the much smaller Outdoor Life Network (renamed Versus eleven months later). On January 14, 2006, NBC begins the season's slate of weekend NHL games, taking over from ABC as hockey's U.S. broadcast TV home.

October 17, 2005

TV Guide undergoes the biggest change since its founding more than fifty years before. Gone is the 7.5-by-5-inch paperback book size, replaced by a magazine-style 10.5-by-8-inch format. Individual program listings are gone, leaving only evening schedule grids and feature stories. Previously, the magazine printed 150 editions each week (covering all major U.S. cities); now it has only 2 (east and west).

November 28, 2005

ABC's late-night news program *Nightline* undergoes a major revamp. Out is anchor Ted Koppel and the focus on one topic per night. In are a trio of anchors—ABC's White House correspondent Terry Moran, Martin Bashir (late of *20/20*), and Cynthia McFadden of *Primetime*—and a new three-story-per-night structure.

January 3, 2006

Less than six years after Viacom acquired CBS, the merger is undone. The "new" Viacom Inc. takes most of the cable networks (MTV, VH1, Nickelodeon, Comedy Central, CMT, Spike, TV Land, BET), plus the Paramount film studio. CBS Corporation takes the CBS television and radio networks, the owned and operated TV and radio stations, UPN, the Showtime cable channel, and the King World TV syndication group.

January 3, 2006

Almost nine months after Peter Jennings departed *World New Tonight*, ABC installs its new anchors: forty-four-year-old Bob Woodruff and forty-three-year-old Elizabeth Vargas, bypassing sixty-three-year-old Charles Gibson (of *Good Morning America*), the most frequent guest anchor since Jennings left. Tragically, just twenty-six days later, Woodruff (and his cameraman) are badly wounded in a bomb attack while reporting on the hostilities in Iraq. Guest co-anchors fill in for Woodruff as he recovers.

FALL 2005 SCHEDULE

	8:00	8:30	9:00	9:30	10:00	10:30	
MON	Wife Swap		ABC NFL Monday Night Football (to 12 Midnight)				ABC
	The King Of Queens	HOW I MET YOUR MOTHER	Two And A Half Men	OUT OF PRACTICE	CSI: Miami		CBS
	Arrested Development	KITCHEN CONFIDENTIAL	PRISON BREAK		local		FOX
	SURFACE		Las Vegas		Medium		NBC
	One On One	All Of Us	Girlfriends	Half And Half	local		UPN
	7th Heaven		JUST LEGAL		local		WB

	8:00	8:30	9:00	9:30	10:00	10:30	
TUE	According To Jim	Rodney	COMMANDER-IN-CHIEF		Boston Legal		ABC
	NCIS		The Amazing Race: Family Edition		CLOSE TO HOME		CBS
	BONES		House, M.D.		local		FOX
	The Biggest Loser		MY NAME IS EARL	The Office	Law & Order: Special Victims Unit		NBC
	America's Next Top Model		SEX, LOVE & SECRETS		local		UPN
	Gilmore Girls		SUPERNATURAL		local		WB

	8:00	8:30	9:00	9:30	10:00	10:30	
WED	George Lopez	FREDDIE	Lost		INVASION		ABC
	Still Standing	Yes, Dear	CRIMINAL MINDS		CSI: NY		CBS
	That '70s Show	Stacked	HEAD CASES		local		FOX
	THE APPRENTICE: MARTHA STEWART		E-RING		Law & Order		NBC
	America's Next Top Model		Veronica Mars		local		UPN
	One Tree Hill		RELATED		local		WB

	8:00	8:30	9:00	9:30	10:00	10:30	
THR	Alias		NIGHT STALKER		Prime Time		ABC
	Survivor: Guatemala - The Maya Empire		CSI: Crime Scene Investigation		Without A Trace		CBS
	The O.C.		REUNION		local		FOX
	Joey	Will & Grace	The Apprentice		ER		NBC
	EVERYBODY HATES CHRIS	Eve	Cuts	LOVE, INC.	local		UPN
	Smallville		Everwood		local		WB

	8:00	8:30	9:00	9:30	10:00	10:30	
FRI	Supernanny		Hope & Faith	HOT PROPERTIES	20/20		ABC
	GHOST WHISPERER		THRESHOLD		Numb3rs		CBS
	The Bernie Mac Show	Malcom In The Middle	KILLER INSTINCT		local		FOX
	Dateline NBC		THREE WISHES		INCONCEIVABLE		NBC
	WWE Friday Night Smackdown!				local		UPN
	What I Like About You	TWINS	Reba	Living With Fran	local		WB

	8:00	8:30	9:00	9:30	10:00	10:30	
SAT	ABC Saturday Movie Of The Week						ABC
	Crime Time Saturday		Crime Time Saturday		48 Hours Mystery		CBS
	Cops	Cops	America's Most Wanted		local		FOX
	NBC Saturday Movie				Law & Order: Special Victims Unit		NBC
	local						UPN
	local						WB

	7:00	7:30	8:00	8:30	9:00	9:30	10:00	10:30	
SUN	America's Funniest Home Videos		Extreme Makeover: Home Edition		Desperate Housewives		Grey's Anatomy		ABC
	60 Minutes		Cold Case		CBS Sunday Night Movie				CBS
	The Simpsons	King Of The Hill	The Simpsons	THE WAR AT HOME	Family Guy	American Dad	local		FOX
	Dateline NBC		The West Wing		Law & Order: Criminal Intent		Crossing Jordan		NBC
	local								UPN
	Reba	Reba	Charmed		Blue Collar TV	Blue Collar TV	local		WB

live contests such as *American Idol* and the dance competition shows became especially attractive because they unfolded in real time. Even with video playback options, there was a reason to tune in live because this was a special event.

Every program could not be a special event, however. To deal with the day-in and day-out demands to fill their schedules, the broadcast networks had to choose carefully. Generally, reality shows provided the least costly filler, and then scripted comedies and dramas could be plugged in. The previous season's success of ABC's *Lost* and *Desperate Housewives*, along with the ongoing performance of Fox's *24* (in its fifth season), opened the door for a rush of other long-form dramas for 2005–06. They were considered as potential promotable must-see shows.

First to launch in late August 2005 was Fox's *Prison Break*, an escape caper scheme that set architect Michael Scofield (Wentworth Miller) racing the calendar countdown to the death penalty execution of his brother, Lincoln Burrows (Dominic Purcell), falsely convicted of murder. To spring "Linc" from the inside, Scofield (who had taken his mother's last name when his father deserted the family) got himself arrested and sent to the same Illinois prison (Fox River), wearing details of an escape plan hidden in plain sight as an elaborate body tattoo. The premise was outlandish, but the implementation was superb, filled with clever twists, tricky puzzles, subtle manipulations, and unexpected alliances. These included a budding romance between Scofield and prison doctor Sara Tancredi (Sarah Wayne Callies), who happened to be the governor's daughter as well as a scared-straight former junkie. By season's end, the brothers (and a handful of inmate allies) were over the prison wall and on the run. It took four seasons to reach the day their running stopped.

Such long-form story arcs could create buzz, generate word-of-mouth speculation, and build fan interest. So Fox juggled *Prison Break* in the schedule from the start, running episodes during the fall (filling the *24* slot), taking a break, and confidently finishing the first season during the spring. This shifting schedule turned *Prison Break* repeats into helpful recaps and also allowed *24* to begin in January with a full slate of episodes and no repeats. Series with tightly interlocking continuity such as *24* and *Lost* had faced viewer complaints that their already complicated storylines were even more so when interrupted by reruns. By its third season *Lost* also looked to eliminate repeats, like *24*.

Nonetheless, long-form dramas were a particularly challenging proposition. While they could be addictive like *Lost,* they could also be off-putting to casual viewers. (And if a show tanked, programmers were left with a double dud: a ratings flop whose premature cancellation would annoy those still watching.) In fact, it was oddly daring that so many of the season's new scripted shows that followed ABC's breakthrough hits used the science fiction model of *Lost*, rather than the more accessible prime time soap structure of *Desperate Housewives*. As a result, there was an extraordinary swirl of densely complicated, otherworldly mysteries that unfolded in the fall.

CBS's *Threshold* (from producer Brannon Braga) featured a "first contact" team investigating alien sounds and images capable of seizing the human psyche. ABC's *Invasion* (from producer Shaun Cassidy and slotted after *Lost*) took the classic "Invasion of the Body Snatchers" theme to the Florida Everglades, where a hurricane may have been the cover for extraterrestrial activity. NBC's *Surface* (from producer brothers Josh and Jonas Pate) turned the pursuit of the unfathomable to the murky underworld of the earth's oceans. Apparently the planet was not big enough to contain all of these competing alien forces at once, and none of the series lasted beyond one season.

The only successful new otherworldly broadcast dramas were more spooky than spacey: *Supernatural* (UPN) was a cross between *The X-Files* and *Route 66*, with Jensen Ackles and Jared Padalecki as a pair of demon-hunting brothers who cruised the country in their 1967 Chevy Impala, and the sentimental *Ghost Whisperer* (CBS) cast Jennifer Love Hewitt as Melinda Gordon, a woman who could see ghosts trapped in this world with unfinished business and who helped them complete their journey. (One of her first mournful souls was a soldier played by Wentworth Miller.)

Otherwise, even with the misfires in long-form drama, the

January 20, 2006
"High School Musical." (Disney Channel). Zac Effron and Vanessa Hudgens star in a modern made-for-cable movie adaptation of the Romeo & Juliet story. As teens from rival high school cliques, they try out for the school musical and fall in love. The film's instant success leads to numerous repeat runs on Disney and, eventually, a TV sequel in 2007 and a theatrical movie follow-up in 2008.

March 12, 2006
Big Love. (HBO). Bill Paxton stars as a Utah home-improvement store owner who is father to seven children and who is also a polygamist, married to three women (played by Jeanne Tripplehorn, Chloe Sevigny, and Ginnifer Goodwin), living in adjacent houses.

May 29, 2006
Charles Gibson takes over after all as sole anchor of ABC's *World News Tonight*. With Bob Woodruff recuperating from his Iraq bomb injuries and co-anchor Elizabeth Vargas planning maternity leave in the late summer, ABC revamps its evening newscast again and installs the veteran Gibson. He will depart *Good Morning America* at the end of June, leaving that show to Diane Sawyer and Robin Roberts.

July 9, 2006
Forty-five years after feature films came to prime time TV, CBS ends its twenty-year-old Sunday night movie (with 2005's "Saving Milly"), the last of the first-run broadcast TV movie slots. All that remains for films in prime time are occasional rerun showcases that fill lesser-watched slots, such as Saturday night.

August 6, 2006
After a nine-year absence, NFL football returns to NBC, which takes over the Sunday night games from ESPN. The Hall of Fame exhibition game from Canton, Ohio, is NBC's opener, with the Oakland Raiders playing the Philadelphia Eagles. Al Michaels and John Madden, late of ABC's *Monday Night Football*, continue their announcing tandem, now on a new network and night. On August 14, *Monday Night Football*, an ABC staple for thirty-five years, shifts to sister cable channel ESPN, as the Oakland Raiders take on the Minnesota Vikings in a pre-season game.

September 17, 2006
For the first time in U.S. television history, a broadcast TV network promotes its own sign off. One day before the debut of the new CW network, the WB goes out with a bang, rerunning the pilot episodes of its defining shows: *Felicity, Angel, Buffy the Vampire Slayer,* and *Dawson's Creek.* UPN had ended with a whimper two nights earlier with a routine Friday night episode of the WWE's wrestling *Smackdown* show, which will continue on the CW.

broadcast networks could still point to individual successes for 2005–06, though these did not carry the same buzz of unexpected discovery from the previous season.

As number one in total audience, CBS continued its mix of major program types, successfully introducing a handful of new series. In addition to *Ghost Whisperer*, there was the procedural drama *Criminal Minds,* with Mandy Patinkin as the leader of an investigative team at the FBI's Behavioral Analysis Unit. Mid-season, David Mamet applied his signature style of terse dialogue and male camaraderie under fire to *The Unit*, a special operations assault squad shepherded by Jonas Blane, played by Dennis Haysbert (no longer a regular on *24*).

In comedy, CBS strengthened its Monday night lineup with the smartly delineated *How I Met Your Mother*, created by David Letterman writers Carter Bays and Craig Thomas. They set their romantic comedy in the present but (appropriate to the title) constructed the stories as voice-over flashbacks told to two kids by their dad, Ted Mosby (Josh Radnor, but voiced "in the future" by Bob Saget). Ted's quest for the love of his life was also the story of young adulthood friendships with Marshall (Jason Segel), Lily (Alyson Hannigan), Robin (Cobie Smulders), and Barney (Neil Patrick Harris). The series cleverly played its five leads as couples, potential couples, and best buddies, always there for each other.

Number one with the 18 to 49 demographic, Fox again had its ratings house successfully built around the power of *American Idol*. The network also reinforced Sunday by running *Family Guy* beyond its spring 2005 revival with new episodes through much of the summer and into the fall lineup. *24* also had a particularly strong season, with Jean Smart as the White House's new First Lady, and the dramatic opening twist of the assassination of Dennis Haysbert's character, former President David Palmer.

ABC's hits from the previous season continued to perform well, with *Grey's Anatomy* showing strong growth, but none of the network's new programs built on that momentum. One of the top prospects, *Commander in Chief* (Geena Davis as the first woman to be President of the United States), turned into a major disappointment. It started strong, ran into behind-the-scenes/network/production issues, slipped from sight, and never recovered.

NBC still struggled in the ratings, drawing its greatest numbers with the Winter Olympics in Turin, Italy, and the reality series *The Biggest Loser, Deal or No Deal,* and *America's Got Talent*. However, the network received its greatest critical praise for a pair of back-to-back comedies. The offbeat *My Name Is Earl* cast Jason Lee as a lottery winner rebalancing his karma by righting a lifetime list of his personal wrongs against others. Even more impressive, *The Office* (returning for its first full season) demonstrated perfect pitch in capturing work life in the Scranton, Pennsylvania, office of the Dunder Mifflin paper company. Steve Carell played regional manager Michael Scott, who acted as if he had all the business and personnel crises of the branch under his personal control but was really the textbook example of a clueless boss with poor interpersonal skills. His saving grace was that he desperately wanted to be liked and respected, even as he blundered into awkward situations of his own making. Michael's top assistant, Dwight Schrute (Rainn Wilson) was even worse at dealing with people, not concealing his fervent urge to do *anything* to advance himself. The pair provided a hilarious contrast to the more grounded (but quietly humorous) behavior of everyone else, especially young sales representative Jim Halpert (John Krasinski) and put-upon receptionist Pam Beesley (Jenna Fischer), who turned their office flirtation into a beautifully believable romance.

Even with such high-quality material, the broadcast networks still had to deal with a television world in flux from forces outside their control. It was more than cable and satellite competition; it was a matter of positioning their businesses for the future.

For some, this meant repositioning. In mid-2005, Viacom/CBS decided to untie its six-year-old merger of properties, finding that the entertainment behemoth was perhaps too large for maximum efficiency. The conglomerate split into CBS Corporation (with assets that included the CBS and UPN broadcast television networks) and a new Viacom (which kept most of the cable networks and the Paramount film studio). Even as separate entities, Viacom and CBS both continued to be controlled by media mogul Sumner Redstone, so this split did not reflect a real change of direction.

Soon after the Viacom/CBS split became official, CBS and rival giant Warner Bros. surprised the media world by announcing in January 2006 that their UPN and WB TV networks would merge at the start of the next fall season to create a new network, the CW ("C" for CBS, "W" for Warner Bros.). Not surprisingly, most of the local UPN and WB affiliates the CW chose to retain were WB- or CBS-owned stations. This left some remaining affiliates (many of which were owned by rival Fox) without a network connection. In February, Fox scrambled to offer the stranded affiliates an alternative new broadcast network, MyNetworkTV (MNT), for a fall 2006 debut alongside the new CW. That solved the immediate affiliate problem but avoided a deeper issue. It appeared that the television economy (and the number of locally known affiliates) could not support six national commercial broadcast webs, and so a combination of the two smallest chains had made business sense. Would this new Fox venture simply postpone the inevitable?

For all the networks, though, the essential bedrock issue was video control. It was not just that video recordings created a more convenient schedule for viewers. They streamlined the process of skipping commercials during playback, cutting to the heart of the advertiser-driven broadcast television business model. Without the ability to promise advertisers that viewers would see their commercials, broadcasters risked losing that revenue stream. Unlike cable networks, broadcasters received no direct payments from the fees paid by cable subscribers (a continuing sore point) even though they were carried on the same systems.

Yet there was no option to pull the plug on technology. Instead, broadcasters looked for other opportunities. They had seen TV show DVDs provide a new revenue stream, so they plugged into cable's Video on Demand (VOD) with TV reruns-on-demand. Working with the existing technology of rivals such as Comcast, the networks filled a home recording gap by selling viewers the opportunity to go back in time for series episodes they had not recorded. Initial offerings included *CSI: Crime Scene Investigation*, *Survivor*, and *Law and Order*, and pricing was modest.

Online access, however, represented an even more powerful challenge to the control of television content, especially through digital copies of shows created by DVRs (which grew to reach about 7% of U.S. households in 2006). The music industry had already seen the effects of digital music files shared, not sold, online. (Apple's iTunes store, not an existing record label, eventually emerged as the biggest authorized seller of digital music files.) Throughout the season, each of the networks tested using the Internet as an element of watching television.

Television-related websites had been around for more than a decade for specific programs and for general network information. News channels such as CNN and MSNBC and news programs such as PBS's Online *NewsHour* used sites to supplement stories. Because U.S. Internet connections were primarily slow dial-up services, these early sites were dominated by text and still images rather than full program video. By the fall 2005, the percentage of

Stephen Colbert *(right, at the podium)* delivered his remarks, in character, to President George W. Bush *(left)* at the April 29, 2006, White House Correspondents' Association dinner. *(Copyright C-SPAN)*

U.S. households with high-speed Internet had topped 40%, allowing for more emphasis on video streaming.

During the 2005–06 season, AOL partnered for a number of promotional stunts. AOL streamed an alternate ending to the November 30 episode of *Veronica Mars* ("My Mother, The Fiend") the same night it aired on UPN, inviting viewers to vote between the two outcomes. In March 2006, AOL ran online the entire first episode of a new WB college drama, *The Bedford Diaries,* the week before its broadcast premiere, including risqué dialogue and images not used on the air.

Apart from such one-shot gimmicks, the networks attempted to position themselves as online video destinations. They presented these services, though, as network-specific Internet channels, such as CBS's Innertube (launched in May 2006), which offered original content and selected CBS shows. NBC placed some of its shows online in December 2005. ABC.com tested downloading during the November 2005 sweeps and had streaming in place for the spring of 2006. Generally, these destinations had free streaming, limited selections, their own playback protocol, and some sponsorships. As with music, Apple also stepped in, selling authorized video from multiple sources at its iTunes store (at $1.99 per episode) and quickly reached a million sold by the end of 2005.

All the network efforts would need further refinement. Yet while the businesses tinkered, tech-savvy online users had already decided what they wanted: anything they could find. Fans snatched bits from digitally recorded television, created their own edited packages, and posted them online, generally ignoring questions of ownership rights. Many took advantage of the platform created by YouTube (begun in 2005, officially launched in 2006), designed to display user-generated original home videos. Soon the site was also host to "original" postings of captured television moments.

The increasing technical options for users meant a new deal in the decades-old relationship between established media companies and consumers. Television viewers could not only control when they accessed recorded content, they could also push it out onto the Internet, effectively declaring what *they* considered worthwhile and important, no matter what any official channels had decided.

Those forces were in full view surrounding the April 29, 2006, comic performance by guest speaker Stephen Colbert at the annual White House Correspondents' Association dinner, attended by the media elite and President George W. Bush.

Colbert had been a correspondent and writer on Comedy Central's *Daily Show* since 1997 before scoring the spinoff *Colbert Report* (both words pronounced without the final "t") in October 2005. Slotted immediately after *The Daily Show*'s satirical newscast, Colbert's show took aim at host-centered cable news commentary programs such as those helmed by Bill O'Reilly on the Fox News Channel. On *The Colbert Report,* Stephen Colbert played the character of Stephen Colbert, a supremely confident expert on everything, who based his analysis on "gut feelings" of what *ought* to be true rather than being tripped up by inconvenient facts (an approach he defined as "truthiness"). Colbert delivered deadpan zingers not by putdowns but by declaring himself an enthusiastic supporter (usually of conservative causes), stubbornly determined to press his points even when they led to embarrassing conclusions. He stayed in that character for his dinner speech.

Prior to Colbert's remarks, President Bush staged a skit of his own. He stood side-by-side with presidential impersonator Steve Bridges, who provided Bush's "inner voice" on issues. It was a gently mocking routine. Colbert's was not. He played the event just like his show, enthusiastically declaring his affection and support of Bush, and then delivering scathing criticisms of administration policies by praising them. This included such areas as Iraq, Hurricane Katrina, allegations of prisoner torture, domestic wire taps, global warming, sinking popularity poll numbers, and Bush's refusal to budge from particular positions. Colbert said with a tone of admiration, "He believes the same thing Wednesday that he believed on Monday, no matter what happened Tuesday."

Colbert also directed his "praise" at the Washington press corps for going along for so long not asking tough questions, but then chided them for now beginning to dig. He reminded them that the White House reporting process was simple: type out the decisions of the president, as announced by the press secretary, file them, and go home. That would give reporters time to do other things, like write a novel about "an intrepid Washington reporter with the courage to stand up to the administration. You know, fiction."

At the time, President Bush was accused of being in a White House "bubble," rarely confronted with direct and pointed criticism of his policies, even by the press. Colbert's remarks were seen by administration critics as a long-overdue calling to task. Others saw it as an inappropriate breach of etiquette. Initial media coverage of the dinner treated it as an "inside the Washington Beltway" event, with the Colbert remarks sometimes barely noted, or dismissed as not evoking much laughter in the hall. In an earlier era, that would have been the end of the story.

However, the event was carried on cable by C-SPAN and was rerun multiple times. More important, it was available as streaming video at C-SPAN's online site. Colbert's portion was quickly hijacked and spread through links and postings, becoming a viral hit. Viewers could judge for themselves the audience response, not by reading someone's opinion but by looking at people laughing on the playback itself. Nearly two weeks after the dinner, the widespread, often unauthorized, sharing of the video pushed the story back into the mainstream press, this time definitely focusing on Colbert's remarks. News reports might be the first draft of history, but there was now the means to instantly call for a rewrite.

This was the new media world the television industry now occupied. Their once exclusive pipelines of video distribution were broken. Even as the networks continued program planning for the immediate future, they also had to consider the fast pace of technological and social change. Clearly whatever happened next threatened to be a completely different business deal.

67. What *Else* Is On?

THERE WAS SERENDIPITOUS timing in ABC's fall 2006 launch of the fashion-world-based comedy-drama *Ugly Betty*. The series came on the heels of a hit theatrical film from the summer, "The Devil Wears Prada" (based on a best-selling book by Lauren Weisberger), which followed a young woman (played by Anne Hathaway) working as the assistant to a cut-throat fashion magazine editor (played by Meryl Streep).

ABC's *Ugly Betty* was similarly situated in the no-holds-barred fashion magazine world, following plain, plump, fashion-challenged, braces-wearing Betty Suarez (America Ferrera) swimming with the sharks as the assistant to Daniel Meade (Eric Mabius), the new young editor-in-chief of stylish *Mode* magazine. Betty landed her dream job because the head of the company, Daniel's dad (Alan Dale as Bradford Meade), wanted an assistant whom his womanizing son would not be tempted to bed. After initial pilot-episode skirmishes, Daniel and Betty found they formed a strong professional duo as she became the organizational handler he needed. They both had to fend off the glamorous creative director Wilhelmina Slater (Vanessa Williams), the publication's rejected heir apparent, who felt she had been robbed of the magazine's top position. To undercut her rival Daniel, Wilhelmina worked devious interoffice schemes backed by her fawning aide, Marc St. James (Michael Urie), who also administered her Botox injections. Wilhelmina found other in-house allies, including receptionist Amanda Tanen (Becki Newton), who had wanted Betty's job. In turn, Betty found everyday support from company seamstress Christina McKinney (Ashley Jensen) and accountant Henry Grubstick (Christopher Gorham), for whom Betty quickly developed a romantic crush.

At home, Betty was the glue who held that world together as well, watching out for her good-hearted immigrant dad, Ignacio (Tony Plana), her nephew, Justin (Mark Indelicato), her sister, Hilda (Ana Ortiz), and her (sometimes) boyfriend, Walter Tabachnik (Kevin Sussman). The series played all of these conflicts with a touch of humor, but no laugh track, similar to *Desperate Housewives*. *Ugly Betty* drew from far different roots, the Spanish-language telenovelas. Backed by an international producing team including Salma Hayek, Ben Silverman, Silvio Horta, Jose Tamez, and Joel Fields, *Ugly Betty* was a U.S. adaptation of the Spanish-language 1999–2001 telenovela *Yo soy Betty, la fea (I'm Betty, the ugly one),* from Columbia, South America (which had already been adapted, in numerous languages, into local TV series in countries throughout the globe). *Ugly Betty*

mixed a strong sense of female empowerment with a knowing awareness of Hispanic culture, starting with that TV genre.

The telenovela was a major program type in such countries as Mexico, Chile, and Columbia and was also a mainstay of Spanish-language television stations in the U.S. Part soap opera, part miniseries, a telenovela story generally played out in daily episodes, with a predetermined end point (generally 100+ episodes). There were clear conflicts, personal aspirations, powerful villains, and plucky heroes. Each year, hundreds of episodes unfolded in multiple telenovela stories throughout the world. *Ugly Betty* expertly shaped its source material to fit the weekly English language prime time television world for ABC. In doing so, it also provided the general viewing public a glimpse into an immensely popular form. Sometimes the television in the background at Betty's house showed whatever Spanish-language telenovela her immigrant dad watched. Hayek even appeared as one of the on-screen characters, as an appropriate inside joke.

Drawing Spanish-language households in real life was no joke, though, as media companies looked for footholds in that segment of the fractured TV universe. ABC had started to offer a Spanish-language audio translation for all of its prime time programs in the 2004–05 season. NBC, which had purchased the Telemundo Spanish-language network in 2002, began running both English-language and Spanish-language closed captioning on that network's programs in 2004, including newscasts and telenovelas. In March 2007, a new Spanish language network, V-me, launched as a public-private partnership that included Thirteen.org (PBS's WNET-TV in New York City), and featured selected public television shows in Spanish. V-me was offered via basic cable and satellite services as well as over-the-air, often on one of the digital subchannels of PBS affiliates in major markets.

The Spanish-language Univision broadcast network was the most successful in reaching more Spanish-language households in the U.S. than anyone else, building on more than four decades of growth. It had begun as the Spanish International Network (SIN) in the 1960s with stations in Texas, California, and New Jersey and became Univision in the 1980s.

During 2005 Univision marked important ratings milestones. In April, the three-hour special "Selena ¡VIVE!" (celebrating the career of one of the most popular Spanish-language pop singers of the era) scored record high ratings for the network, winning its time slot not just in Spanish-language households but in some markets against all competition. In January 2006 Nielsen officially began to include Univision in the company's ratings reports for all the major broadcast networks. (Previously Univision's programs had been tracked for specialized reports focused on Spanish-language stations.) Through the balance of the 2005–06 season, the newly listed Univision audience ratings sometimes ranked fifth, behind ABC, CBS, Fox, and NBC, and ahead of both UPN and the WB—some nights, even higher.

Serving a specific identifiable audience, Univision stood out in the media landscape. Nonetheless, to the general non-Spanish-speaking viewing public, such a competitive showing seemed to come out of nowhere, even though Univision's stations (and those of the other Spanish-language networks) had been there all along. Now they were a recognized force with a hit program type to copy.

In addition to ABC's *Ugly Betty*, the telenovela format was also embraced this season by Fox's MyNetworkTV, one of the two "new" broadcast networks launched in the fall. When CBS and Warner Bros. had formed the CW, they brought along the most successful shows from the WB and UPN schedules. Rival Fox had to start from scratch programming its new venture, but it had the resources. Fox had already been developing a syndication package of English-language telenovela programs when news of the CW's formation broke, so the company redeployed and expanded the material to play daily on MyNetworkTV, back-to-back, in prime time. The first two shows adhered to the genre's structure of a set duration (with plans to rotate in new titles after thirteen weeks) amid stories of passionate intrigue. *Desire* featured two handsome brothers (played by Zack Silva and Nate Haden) on the run from the mob while tearing at the heart of a beautiful woman (played by Michelle Belegrin). *Fashion House* touted the name recognition of Bo Derek and Morgan Fairchild, cast as archrivals in the unscrupulous, ruthless, yet fabulous and glamorous fashion world.

Neither title succeeded. The new network's next two telenovelas (*Wicked, Wicked Games* and *Watch Over Me*) did even worse. By April, MyNetworkTV all but dropped the telenovela format and reworked its strategy, moving to cheaper reality-based series (*Celebrity Exposé*, *Jail*, and *Meet My Folks*), "extreme" sports such as the International Fight League's mixed martial arts competitions, and several nights of nondescript recent theatrical movies. No matter the programming choices, MyNetworkTV faced a tough challenge because its affiliates were generally the least prominent broadcast stations in their respective markets.

Not surprisingly, the CW did better, but not much better than the old WB. Combining the stronger affiliates and most popular shows from two former struggling networks did not automatically bring along all of their viewers. The mix also made the CW "brand identity" hard to pin down. Was it the mother-daughter relationships of *Gilmore Girls*? The *femme noir* mysteries of *Veronica Mars*? Wrestling *Smackdown!* contests? The soapy *One Tree Hill*? Super heroics on *Smallville* and *Supernatural*? Chris Rock's autobiographical sitcom *Everybody Hates Chris*? Or, based on the name, was it a channel that offered County and Western programs?

Perhaps the greatest disadvantage for both new networks was that they were in pursuit of success with an advertiser-supported broadcasting model that itself was under siege. In 2006, broadcasters still held advantages with their overall reach and long-time brand familiarity and still commanded a significant share of media advertising dollars. However, changing viewing habits were eating away at this status quo because broadcast television no longer represented the total TV experience for most households. Dozens of cable channels and hundreds of their specific shows had been absorbed into the pop culture mainstream. Half a decade into the twenty-first century, these destinations had built their own history. MTV, for example, was already twenty-five years old in 2006.

Cable and satellite viewers (more than 85% of the U.S television audience) saw everything delivered through the same wired connections, with all of the channels part of the same overall television universe. Depending on the service package, that could include CNN, ESPN, USA, TNT, FX, TBS, Sci-Fi, Comedy Central, A&E, Disney, Nickelodeon, C-SPAN, BBC America, Lifetime, AMC, Fox News, HBO, Showtime, and many others. On remote controls, on digital video recorders, and in *TV Guide* program listings, they were on a par with the channels that originated as broadcast networks. Viewers would seek out specific shows and events as destinations, going to whatever source offered them.

That was a reasonable viewer perspective as channels elbowed each other for attention, sometimes to provide the same programs. While CBS aired new episodes of *CSI: Crime Scene Investigation*, cable's Spike carried the reruns. A&E did the same with CBS's *CSI: Miami*. NBC carried new episodes of *Law and Order: Special Victims Unit* and cable's USA offered reruns. SOAPnet brought

September 5, 2006
Katie Couric, after spending fifteen years as co-host of NBC's *Today*, takes over as anchor and managing editor of the weekday *CBS Evening News*, becoming the first woman to solo anchor a broadcast nightly news show. Couric supplants Bob Schieffer, who was always seen as a temporary replacement for Dan Rather. Schieffer remains as host of *Face the Nation*.

September 5, 2006
Fox's new broadcast network, MyNetworkTV, debuts with the premieres of its two five-nights-a-week hour-long telenovelas, *Desire* and *Fashion House*.

September 13, 2006
With Katie Couric gone to CBS, NBC installs Meredith Vieira as the new co-host of *Today*. Vieira previously worked at both CBS (as a *60 Minutes* correspondent and then co-anchor of the *CBS Morning News*) and ABC (as co-host of daytime's *The View*).

September 16, 2006
Fox expands its late night Saturday night programming by thirty minutes, with the debut after *MadTV* of *Talkshow with Spike Feresten*, starring a former writer for *Saturday Night Live* and David Letterman's late night shows.

September 18, 2006
Created in a "forced marriage" of UPN and the WB, the "new" CW television network debuts with a rerun of last season's finale of *7th Heaven*. Two nights later, the first new episode of a CW program airs, the season premiere of *America's Next Top Model*.

November 13, 2006
Internet search engine company Google Inc. acquires barely one-year-old Internet video sharing website company YouTube LLC for Google stock valued at $1.65 billion.

November 23, 2006
Live NFL regular season football at last comes to cable's NFL Network, with the first of a series of eight games in the second half of the football season (five on Thursday nights, three on Saturday nights). In the opener, the host Kansas City Chiefs defeat the Denver Broncos 19 to 10.

MON

	8:00	8:30	9:00	9:30	10:00	10:30	
	Wife Swap		The Bachelor: Rome		What About Brian		ABC
	THE CLASS	How I Met Your Mother	Two And A Half Men	New Adventures Of Old Christine	CSI: Miami		CBS
	Prison Break		VANISHED		local		FOX
	Deal Or No Deal		HEROES		STUDIO 60 ON THE SUNSET STRIP		NBC
	7th Heaven		RUNAWAY		local		CW
	DESIRE		FASHION HOUSE		local		MNT

TUE

	8:00	8:30	9:00	9:30	10:00	10:30	
	Dancing With The Stars			HELP ME, HELP YOU	Boston Legal		ABC
	NCIS		The Unit		SMITH		CBS
	House, M.D.		STANDOFF		local		FOX
	FRIDAY NIGHT LIGHTS		Law & Order: Criminal Intent		Law & Order: Special Victims Unit		NBC
	Gilmore Girls		Veronica Mars		local		CW
	DESIRE		FASHION HOUSE		local		MNT

WED

	8:00	8:30	9:00	9:30	10:00	10:30	
	Dancing With The Stars		Lost		THE NINE		ABC
	JERICHO		Criminal Minds		CSI: NY		CBS
	Bones		JUSTICE		local		FOX
	30 ROCK	TWENTY GOOD YEARS	The Biggest Loser		KIDNAPPED		NBC
	America's Next Top Model		One Tree Hill		local		CW
	DESIRE		FASHION HOUSE		local		MNT

THR

	8:00	8:30	9:00	9:30	10:00	10:30	
	UGLY BETTY		Grey's Anatomy		SIX DEGREES		ABC
	Survivor: Cook Islands		CSI: Crime Scene Investigation		SHARK		CBS
	TILL DEATH	HAPPY HOUR	CELEBRITY DUETS		local		FOX
	My Name Is Earl	The Office	Deal Or No Deal		ER		NBC
	Smallville		Supernatural		local		CW
	DESIRE		FASHION HOUSE		local		MNT

FRI

	8:00	8:30	9:00	9:30	10:00	10:30	
	Grey's Anatomy		MEN IN TREES		20/20		ABC
	Ghost Whisperer		Close To Home		Numb3rs		CBS
	Nanny 911		CELEBRITY DUETS		local		FOX
	1 VS. 100		Las Vegas		Law & Order		NBC
	WWE Friday Night Smackdown!				local		CW
	DESIRE		FASHION HOUSE		local		MNT

SAT

	8:00	8:30	9:00	9:30	10:00	10:30	
	Saturday Night College Football						ABC
	Crime Time Saturday		Crime Time Saturday		48 Hours Mystery		CBS
	Cops	Cops	America's Most Wanted		local		FOX
	Dateline NBC		(specials)		Law & Order: Special Victims Unit		NBC
	local						CW
	DESIRE		FASHION HOUSE		local		MNT

SUN

	7:00	7:30	8:00	8:30	9:00	9:30	10:00	10:30	
	America's Funniest Home Videos		Extreme Makeover: Home Edition		Desperate Housewives		BROTHERS & SISTERS		ABC
	60 Minutes		The Amazing Race		Cold Case		Without A Trace		CBS
	The Simpsons	TILL DEATH	The Simpsons	American Dad	Family Guy	The War At Home	local		FOX
	FOOTBALL NIGHT IN AMERICA			Sunday Night Football					NBC
	Everybody Hates Chris	All Of Us	Girlfriends	THE GAME	America's Next Top Model		local		CW
	local								MNT

same-day airings of new episodes of daytime soap operas including ABC's *All My Children* and *General Hospital*.

Cable channels were also landing the first rights to air syndicated reruns of past network series, once just the province of local broadcast affiliates. Viewers searching for reruns from any era could find them throughout the schedule, from *Everybody Loves Raymond* and *Friends* on TBS to *Golden Girls* and *Reba* on Lifetime to *M*A*S*H* and *Andy Griffith* on TV Land. These reruns from broadcast channels were important to the operations of the cable channels because they helped fill much of the daily schedule with proven shows that were familiar to the general public.

On the business side, the connections were even deeper. Apart from deals for reruns, individual cable channels and broadcast networks were often under the same corporate ownership, which had diversified its video distribution holdings over the years. Disney, for example, owned the ABC broadcast network and cable channels ESPN, Disney, and ABC Family. In addition, with the 2003 merger of NBC and Universal, each of the Big 4 broadcast networks (ABC, CBS, Fox, NBC) was part of a larger media conglomerate that included a major film studio.

The studio divisions added another connection by producing programs that aired on competing outlets, such as Fox Studios turning out *My Name Is Earl*, which played on NBC. There were also corporate connections back to the cable distribution system itself, with Time Warner cable in the same conglomerate family as HBO and the CW. The Comcast cable system operation also owned several cable channels (including E! Entertainment and shopping channel QVC) as well as regional sports and news services; however, it had no broadcast network connections.

In this total communication context, cable channels were not just an add-on to the broadcast networks. As programming options, they were full competitors who had built their own history, followings, and track record. For viewers with cable or satellite connections (more than four-fifths of U.S. television households) it was all one world—in sports, comedy, drama, news, and reality.

When a new NFL television contract for *Monday Night Football* moved that show from Disney's ABC broadcast side (after thirty-five years) to its ESPN cable side, that was major news, but not earth-shaking. Most fans could still watch the Monday night game. (However, with no other slots for NFL games on the network, this program departure did leave ABC out of the mix for a future Super Bowl, which remained one of the few broadcast exclusive events.) At the same time, in a related move, the NFL brought NBC back into the pro football mix with the weekly Sunday night prime time contest that had run on ESPN since 1987.

On the adventure side, after a 2005 plotline for the HBO series *Entourage* had Adrian Grenier's character Vincent Chase pursuing the lead role in a fictional Aquaman film project, it was somehow no surprise to see that same DC Comics character turn up later that year on an episode of the DC-licensed property *Smallville* (played there by Alan Ritchson). Then, to complete the circle, an "Aquaman" TV movie was made in 2006, as a pilot, but a subsequent series was not picked up in the WB-to-CW move.

Still, there were some key differences between cable and broadcast in the presentation of new series, especially in the scheduling and programming mechanics. On cable, a season of new episodes for a given program was shorter (rarely more than thirteen at a time) and its timing was more directly tailored to that program's own arc. To fans it did not matter whether a new season of *Entourage*, for example, began as part of the fall, mid-season, or summer schedule. It was its own "new season." This reflected increasing viewer orientation toward specific shows over network

loyalty and allowed for individual program stunts such as episode marathon runs or back-to-back "instant rerun" airings of each new episode. In fact, cable channels regularly timed the runs of new episodes of individual series so that there was something new in the schedule as often as possible, with only occasional overlap.

For the time in between new offerings, there were reruns. Multiple airings of available material in fact represented the bulk of the day-in, day-out cable television schedule. Repeats were so prevalent that *TV Guide* magazine had long ago switched from indicating a "rerun" in each day's slot-by-slot listings to leaving reruns unmarked and tagging the comparative handful of programs each day that were "new." Not having to fill all day with new material helped the cable bottom line. So did the dual revenue stream for cable channels (sharing not only commercial advertising

---

February 6, 2007

Forty-one-year-old Jeff Zucker (former producer of *Today* and president of NBC Entertainment) is named president and chief executive officer of NBC Universal, replacing sixty-three-year-old Robert Wright (who retains his other title as chairman of the board of NBC Universal until May 1).

June 12, 2007

ABC largely gets out of the network radio business, as Disney sells the ABC Radio Networks and twenty-two ABC radio stations (including WABC-AM, WLS-AM, and KABC-AM) to media giant Citadel Broadcasting (though Disney keeps Radio Disney and ESPN Radio). Citadel continues to use the name ABC Radio Networks under a license agreement until April 2, 2009, and continues after that to label its newscasts as being from ABC News.

June 15, 2007

After thirty-five years with CBS's daytime game show *The Price Is Right*, Bob Barker hosts his final episode. Reruns of Barker air until new host Drew Carey takes over on October 15, 2007.

July 16, 2007

Chelsea Lately. (E!). One year after the short-run *Chelsea Handler Show* comedy series for E!, the sardonic Handler returns with a Monday-through-Friday half-hour late night comedic talk show. Staking out turf in the virtually all-male late night landscape, she skewers pop culture and celebrities in interviews, monologues, and sketches, often assisted by sidekick Chuy Bravo.

July 19, 2007

Mad Men. (AMC). Debut of a highly polished original scripted series created and produced by Matthew Weiner, a former writer for *The Sopranos,* focusing on ad agencies in the early 1960s. The complex characters and situations are in the best tradition of that era's golden age of TV drama.

July 27, 2007

The Guild. Debut posting of Felicia Day's original Internet comedy series (at Watchtheguild.com) about a group of online gamers who agree to meet offline to deal with one member's real-life romantic crush. The ten-episode first season is shot on a tight budget (even incorporating online viewer micropayments) but builds an ardent following that leads to solid sponsorship for subsequent seasons.

but also cable system franchise fees, which were allotted from the monthly fee paid by individual cable subscribers).

Some cable shows also took advantage of there being fewer restrictions on cable content than on broadcast content, with the premium channels testing the boundaries the most. HBO had been key in pushing premium cable series into mainstream popular culture, enjoying an especially strong run that began with the introduction of *Sex and the City* (1999), *The Sopranos* (2000), and (in 2001) Alan Ball's funeral morgue drama *Six Feet Under* and the Steven Spielberg/Tom Hanks World War II miniseries *Band of Brothers*. However, *Sex and the City* had concluded in 2004, *Six Feet Under* had finished in 2005, and the 2006-07 season marked the end for *The Sopranos*, whose passage seemed like the closing chapter to that particularly rich era.

In addition, HBO wrapped *Deadwood* (which ended its third and final season in August 2006), the historical soap opera *Rome* (after two seasons), and the Ricky Gervais comedy *Extras* (after two seasons). That still left *Entourage*, David Simon's *The Wire* (in its penultimate season), *Big Love* (in its second season), Larry David's *Curb Your Enthusiasm* (already in production for its sixth season to start in fall 2007), and others, but *The Sopranos* powerhouse would clearly be missed. Already the series had begun its post-HBO life with reruns starting in January 2007 on A&E (with dialogue and violence scrubbed for more general audiences).

There was also a strong surge from HBO's premium channel competitor Showtime, which was on a roll with its own new generation of programs. *Weeds* (in its second season) followed single mom Nancy Botwin (Mary-Louise Parker) making ends meet in her classy California suburb by selling marijuana. That was joined later in August 2007 by *Californication*, with David Duchovny (as book writer Hank Moody) dealing with his own challenges, mixing sex and drugs and relationships in the Golden State. In the spring of 2007, Showtime introduced its own sexy historical drama, *The Tudors*, following the trysts and trials of a young, svelte King Henry VIII in sixteenth-century England. The network's most electrifying offering was *Dexter*, with Michael C. Hall (formerly David Fisher on *Six Feet Under*) in the title role of sociopath Dexter Morgan, a disturbingly likable and engaging serial killer with a sense of justice and a bag of surgical tools.

Impressive as these premium channel programs were, as an additional fee tier they had a more limited audience. Budget conscious fans sometimes waited to buy or rent the programs on DVD, months after they first aired. The most widely distributed original scripted cable series were nested in basic cable. Not surprisingly, some of those channels that seemed most comfortably close to traditional broadcasters in content were owned by those same companies, such as USA (owned by NBC Universal), FX (Fox News Corporation), and TNT (Time Warner).

Since 2002, USA's *Monk* had epitomized the network's slogan, "Characters Welcome." Brilliant but hyperphobic detective Adrian Monk (Tony Shalhoub) was on psychiatric leave from the San Francisco Police Department after the death of his wife, but his old boss, Leland Stottlemeyer (Ted Levine), regularly brought him in as a consultant. The awkward comic moments caused by Monk's dealing with his obsessions (including but not limited to germs, heights, clutter, and elevators) were far more important than the case at hand, though he solved that as well, aided in both tasks by his personal assistant Sharona Fleming (Bitty Schram), succeeded in the third season by Natalie Teeger (Traylor Howard). In the summer of 2006, a similar light touch was successfully applied to another detective series, *Psych,* in which hyperobservant Shawn Spencer (James Roday) was able to convince the Santa Barbara Police Department that he had psychic powers. (In truth, he simply

noticed details they missed.) Shawn was backed by his friend and partner, Gus (Dulé Hill), and was barely tolerated by his demanding ex-cop dad (played by Corbin Bernsen). Reruns of Fox's *House, M.D.* were also an easy fit for this cable character world, beginning in the 2006–07 season.

FX cultivated more of an edge with its signature programs and characters. In *Rescue Me* (in its third season), acerbic New York firefighter Tommy Gavin (Denis Leary) wrestled with personal demons and family issues, in between battling blazes with his Ladder 62 company. Using the provocative leading line "What don't you like about yourself?" the plastic surgeons of *Nip/Tuck* (in its fourth season) indulged and exploited the vanity and uncertainty of their clients, while treating themselves to a rich, if not always satisfying, lifestyle. Most striking, the violent, foulmouthed, double-dealing Vic Mackey (Michael Chiklis) of *The Shield* (beginning its sixth season in April 2007) took the character of the "outsider" cop to its extreme. As leader of the Strike Team in Los Angeles, he pushed the limits of legality and morality in the pursuit of his own particular take on justice. Beginning in July 2007 on *Damages*, Glenn Close (who tangled with Vic on *The Shield* in a 2005 role as Captain Monica Rawling) presented her own manipulative dark side as high-powered attorney Patty Hewes.

Even in comedy FX was "down and dirty" with the low-budget, high-energy *It's Always Sunny in Philadelphia*, set in an Irish bar and following the often crass, irreverent, and politically incorrect lives of a twenty-something foursome: brother and sister Dennis and Dee Reynolds (Glenn Howerton and Kaitlin Olson) and their friends Charlie Kelly (Charlie Day) and Mac (Rob McElhenney). For the program's second season (in the summer of 2006) they were joined by Danny DeVito as a new regular, the equally deranged Frank Reynolds, father to Dennis and Dee.

TNT had the top-rated drama series on basic commercial cable, *The Closer* (in its third season), with Kyra Sedgwick as Deputy Chief Brenda Johnson, a transplant from Georgia to Los Angeles, who specialized in high-profile cases. Though the program had a solid ensemble cast, Sedgwick's performances drove the stories, as her character artfully mixed hard-nosed, focused detective work with alluring Southern guile. By the end of the 2006–07 season, *The Closer* was joined by another female-centered crime drama, *Saving Grace*, with Holly Hunter as Grace Hanadarko, an Oklahoma City cop pulled back from personal oblivion by a guardian angel but still not ready to give up her self-destructive ways.

And so it continued across the dial, with each cable channel looking for a few signature shows and events (in between repeats), some for a broad audience, others more targeted. The Disney Channel had the two top draws for young "tweens" with *Hannah Montana* (the at home/on stage double life of a teen musical star, played by Miley Cyrus) and the made-for-TV movie "High School Musical," which was rerun endlessly on the channel as, in essence, a one-episode series that fueled an industry of tie-ins (as well as a second TV film in 2007).

On MTV, Ashton Kutcher (who graduated from Fox's *That '70s Show* to hit teen-oriented films such as "Dude, Where's My Car?") wrapped up the seventh and final season of his hidden camera prank series *Punk'd*. The partially improvised reality soap *The Hills* began its run as a follow-up spinoff to the similarly structured *Laguna Beach*, chronicling the angst of its gorgeous young California-based cast. In the process, Lauren Conrad switched from scheming bad girl to sympathetic lead.

For more polished offerings, there were straightforward British imports. AMC took the BBC's *Hustle* (a caper series starring

Robert Vaughn) while BBC America got first choice on material from the BBC network. In 2006, BBC America brought to the U.S. the previous year's British BBC revival of *Doctor Who*, with Christopher Eccleston assuming the role in the quintessential fan-favorite fantasy/science fiction series. The Sci-Fi channel snagged the U.S. rights to the next set of new episodes (with David Tennant in the lead, beginning in July 2007), adding to its own productions such as *Battlestar Galactica* and *Eureka* (Colin Ferguson as an average-guy sheriff in a town filled with genius residents).

In an era of three or four networks, most of these scripted series would have aired on one of those with the challenge to beat two or three competitors. Now programs were spread out across a television world an inch deep and a thousand miles wide. Top shows were still the top shows, significantly ahead of everything else. Beyond those, however, the proliferation of channels had essentially flattened the ratings from the middle on down, with differences between channels often measured in small increments or the makeup of a particular target audience.

There was an additional practical factor. Despite cable and satellite systems that offered channel choices numbering several dozen to several hundred, audience analysis had found that most viewers settled into watching just a core group of about seventeen channels regularly. The catch: it was a *different* core group of channels for each household. The day of everyone broadcasting to the largest possible audience might have ended, but hustling for viewers had never stopped. Every channel, broadcast and cable, worked to promote its flagship draws and to establish viewer habits. Mixing in access to specific episodes of specific shows through the emerging online services or through DVD sales and rentals only added to the pressure, blurring and by-passing any television channel identity at all.

In the 2006–07 season, though, the broadcast channels still held some advantages, most notably their ability to reach the greatest number of total viewers, including those without cable, satellite, or high-speed Internet connections. Over-the-air television was the least technically complicated way to watch TV, unchanged in six decades.

For the third season in a row, Fox won the broadcast ratings in the 18 to 49 age category. CBS won in total viewers, helped by the Super Bowl. ABC was close behind, successfully promoting the *Grey's Anatomy* spinoff *Private Practice*, along with a new multigeneration family drama, *Brothers and Sisters* (with Sally Field and Calista Flockhart leading a strong ensemble cast).

For a change, there was some good news for perennial fourth-place NBC. *Sunday Night Football* was an instant success, and the network also had several strong new scripted series, including a pair of prestige dramas and a genuine pop culture hit. *Friday Night Lights* (based on a hit film and book) presented the world of high school football as the focus of life, love, and personal human drama for adults and teens in the rural town of Dillon, Texas. Everything stopped there for the Friday night game. Kyle Chandler (as embattled team coach Eric Taylor) led a thoroughly believable cast that included Connie Britton and Aimee Teegarden (as Taylor's wife, Tami, and daughter Julie) and young performers Scott Porter (as Jason Street), Minka Kelly (as Lyla Garrity), Gaius Charles (as "Smash" Williams), and Zach Gilford (as Matt Saracen) as the young athletes and their fans.

NBC also presented views of life behind the scenes of two different fictional weekly comedy series meant to evoke its own long-running *Saturday Night Live*. The drama *Studio 60 on the Sunset Strip* (created by *The West Wing*'s Aaron Sorkin) was set at the West Coast studios of the fictional NBS network, with Matthew Perry (from *Friends*) as a big-name writer returning to

help save the show. The comedy *30 Rock* (created by former *Saturday Night Live* head writer Tina Fey) was set at the real NBC studios in New York at 30 Rockefeller Center (known as "30 Rock"), with Fey as Liz Lemon, head writer for a fictional NBC series, *The Girlie Show*. Alec Baldwin played Lemon's new boss, Jack Donaghy, GE's "Head of East Coast Television and Microwave Oven Programming."

Although both were well written, *Studio 60* ultimately did not mesh well with its comedy subject matter and came off as far too serious about issues that really did not involve the fate of the free world, and it lasted only one season. *30 Rock*, on the other hand, embraced the inherent silliness of the comedy show setting and let the humor fly. Baldwin and Fey were spot-on as professional and personal sparring partners, while the rest of the ensemble embodied their colorful characters, including Tracy Morgan and Jane Krakowski as intensely self-absorbed star actors Tracy Jordan and Jenna Maroney; Jack McBrayer as Kenneth Parcell, an eager-to-please naive NBC page; and Scott Adsit and Judah Friedlander as passionately disconnected writers Pete and Frank. Over the years, the series displayed an uncanny eye for mocking the comic absurdities of its corporate entertainment setting, from over-the-top product placement to showing the company as headed by a comatose executive or his barely articulate grown daughter. While beloved by industry insiders and critics, *30 Rock* often proved a bit too "inside" and esoteric for across-the-board ratings success.

NBC's most popular new scripted show that season was *Heroes*, created by Tim Kring (of NBC's *Crossing Jordan*, a 2001 police procedural then in its final season). The program teased viewers early on with the phrase, "Save the cheerleader, save the world" and gave the network its turn at the fantasy adventure genre with a long-form story structure that labeled each episode as a chapter in

Hayden Panettiere (who played cheerleader Claire Bennet on *Heroes*) at Denver's Invesco Field in August 2008. *(Photo by Peter Sills, Digital Focus)*

a novel. In a cross between the mysteries of *Lost* and the misunderstood mutants of the X-Men theatrical films, *Heroes* followed otherwise ordinary people who discovered they had extraordinary powers. There was a sprawling cast, but the main adventures of interest focused on Tokyo office worker Hiro Nakamura (Masi Oka), who could travel through and bend time; Texas cheerleader Claire Bennet (Hayden Panettiere), whose body repaired itself no matter the damage; Claire's stepfather, Noah Bennet (Jack Coleman), a government agent investigating people with special powers; New York paramedic Peter Petrelli (Milo Ventimiglia), who could mimic the powers of other heroes in his proximity; and clock repair expert Sylar (Zachary Quinto), who could steal the powers of other heroes, but only by cutting directly into their brains. The first season narrative set the forces of good against Sylar to prevent the future destruction of New York City.

Over subsequent seasons, the narrative thread and back stories on *Heroes* became increasingly convoluted, turning the structure into a cumbersome hindrance. That was a more immediate problem for other shows throughout the 2006–07 schedule because all of the broadcasters launched series with long-form story arcs.

On ABC there was *The Nine* (nine strangers caught for fifty-two hours in a botched bank robbery, but stretching that as a flashback over the entire season); *Six Degrees* (from *Lost*'s J. J. Abrams, intertwining lives of strangers in Manhattan); and the mid-season entries *Daybreak* (Taye Diggs as a cop framed for murder who relived one day repeatedly until he solved the crime) and *The Knights of Prosperity* (a comic caper to rob Mick Jagger's New York home).

CBS continued to favor self-contained procedurals but nonetheless slotted *Jericho*, a nuclear nightmare tale of life in a rural Kansas town after bombs were dropped on major cities throughout the U.S. With communication, transportation, and governmental infrastructure destroyed, residents were left to pick up the pieces, avoid radiation, and search for who was behind the attacks.

The CW chose the familiar *Fugitive* motif for *Runaway*, presenting a defense attorney framed for murder going on the run with his family. Fox's second season of *Prison Break* successfully used that same fugitives-on-the-run hook for its escaped characters. Also on Fox, *Vanished* followed the kidnapping of the wife of a prominent senator, while on NBC *Kidnapped* followed the kidnapping of the son of a Manhattan millionaire.

Although these series generally avoided the fantasy science fiction genre, which had largely flopped the previous season, there were still too many mysterious conspiracies and meandering plotlines. Some individual series and episodes were well done, but even the best seemed like too much to add to a schedule that already included the spinning story threads of ongoing series.

Apart from *Jericho*, none of these new long-form story shows returned for a second season, and most were pulled before all the episodes aired, annoying fans who were still interested. To solve that problem, the networks looked to their growing presence on the Internet. Instead of saddling affiliates with additional episodes of a proven flop, they could run the unaired episodes of the canceled titles online. Offering full episodes of current network fare was still a touchy subject for affiliates because it essentially cut them out of the process. Yet that online model would continue to evolve, not just with online streaming of network shows but with user-generated content through sites such as YouTube.

The 2006–07 season closed with a pair of stunning finales, one from the broadcast network world, and the other from cable.

ABC's *Lost* had split the episodes of its third season into two arcs in order to eliminate reruns interrupting the flow, airing six

episodes in the fall and the remaining sixteen beginning in February after a three-month break. That had been designed to help advance the narrative, but instead, the long gap mid-story drained its energy. In addition, a few individual fall episodes seemed to have settled into a predictable formula, especially using the element of flashing back from the island plot to the pre-crash mainland. When the May 23 two-hour season finale ("Through the Looking Glass") included a mainland storyline with a morose Jack Shephard dealing with undefined dark personal issues, it seemed superfluous, especially when contrasted with the high drama on the island. There, a ship from the outside world had been detected offshore and, for the first time, there was hope of rescue.

In the final sequence of the season, however, everything was upended. Jack went to a rendezvous point near the Los Angeles Airport to meet fellow survivor Kate Austen, whom he had not known before the crash. In this exhilarating "reveal" it instantly became clear that the scene was not a flashback to life before the crash, it was a flash forward to life *after* the rescue. Even more important, it was obvious that the escape and its aftermath had not gone well, as Jack urged Kate to join him in trying to return to the island. "We have to go back!" he cried out. That one twist reenergized the *Lost* narrative, recasting that episode's mainland scenes and teasing viewers with questions: How had they escaped? Who had escaped? What had gone wrong? Executive producers Damon Lindelof and Carlton Cuse (who wrote the episode) had taken the series to another level, creating renewed buzz and anticipation for the fourth season.

Not coincidentally the show's producers had just succeeded in getting ABC to agree to a definite end date for the series—*Lost* would run three more seasons and finish in the spring of 2010. This went against the basic grain of American broadcast television principles which were built around keeping a successful series running, open-ended, for as long as it remained profitable (even if that stretched the credibility of the premise to its breaking point, as happened in the later seasons of *The X-Files*). By knowing *Lost*'s wrap date, the producers could now methodically design the program's story-centered structure for the next three seasons.

Eighteen days after *Lost*'s 2007 game-changing season closer, it was HBO's turn with *The Sopranos* and its June 10 finale, "Made in America" (written and directed by series creator David Chase). HBO had successfully turned the finale into a major pop culture event, with blanket media coverage and a red carpet premiere party. Though on a service available in only about 30 million homes, the finale drew 11.9 million viewers, easily beating its direct competition, both broadcast and cable, and ending up the overall number-two show for the week in the Nielsen ratings, bested only by NBC's *America's Got Talent* premiere.

There had been speculation that *The Sopranos* would end in one of four ways: Tony Soprano would be killed; he would be arrested; he would "turn," testify, and go into a witness protection program; or he would get away with everything, receiving no punishment, just a quiet fade out from the series. Chase chose none of these options. The final scene was set in a New Jersey diner, with Tony, wife Carmella, and son A. J. waiting for the arrival of daughter Meadow. Ominously, they were unaccompanied and unprotected, but also unconcerned. They talked, ordered food, and selected a song from the jukebox, Journey's 1981 hit "Don't Stop Believin'," which played in the background. Throughout the scene, nondescript but potentially dangerous figures entered and left, some passing directly by their booth. Tony smiled at his family. Outside the restaurant, Meadow parallel parked her car with great difficulty and then rushed to the door of the diner. The Journey song continued and then, in mid-verse, everything went to black.

For ten seconds there was no picture and no sound. Nothing. People at viewing parties were certain that they had lost their cable signal at the worst possible time. Then, suddenly, the black turned into the closing credits. *The Sopranos* was done.

David Chase had chosen a controversial but ultimately brilliant move. He had supplied a jarring, dramatic final moment, yet still demanded that viewers use their imaginations to fill in the rest. Earlier that season (in the episode "Soprano Home Movies"), Tony's brother-in-law had pondered the possibility of a sudden ambush death that constantly hung over all their lives, observing that you probably didn't even hear it when it happened. Had that taken place in the diner? Or was this a stylistic way of showing that Tony Soprano's specific fate was less important than the life viewers had seen over six seasons? Based on that, what fate did he deserve?

The answer to that was as elusive as the future of television itself. There were countless new business considerations and technology tools now at play, making it easier for almost anyone to point, shoot, and upload a video. Over time that would no doubt introduce new styles of narrative and structure, presented by new generations of creators. However, both *Lost* and *The Sopranos* showed that straightforward, well-crafted scripted storytelling still had tremendous impact. In both programs, some of the best in the business had put their best efforts forward. In doing so, they once again transformed television into more than just a lucrative enterprise or a technical toy. This was popular art, at its finest.

68. Called Third Strike

MAD MEN WAS THE PRESTIGE program going into the fall of 2007, presenting a fictional rendering of the power and influence of the advertising business during the early 1960s. (The series took its double-meaning title from the "ad men" headquartered on Manhattan's Madison Avenue.) Beginning with its July 2007 premiere, Mad Men creator and executive producer Matthew Weiner brought to the series the self-assured sheen of HBO's just-ended Sopranos, where he had served as a writer and one of the executive producers. (Sopranos creator David Chase first gave Weiner the nod to join that series based on what was then just the spec script for Mad Men.) When Weiner put together the pilot for Mad Men in 2006, he drew from the experienced Sopranos technical team and then ramped up for the first season.

HBO had not pursued the property, though. Neither had Showtime. So Weiner landed a deal with the basic cable movie channel AMC, which had been seeking promotable original series. It was an apt pairing. Beginning as American Movie Classics in 1984, the channel had originally emphasized nostalgia in feature films from the 1930s and 1940s, and its first original scripted series in 1996 (the comedy Remember WENN) had focused on radio in the 1930s, capturing the tone and style of that era. A decade later, AMC had moved up its movie programming timeline to the post-1950s, so Mad Men allowed the channel to tap a similar classic aura surrounding the early 1960s. Those were the new "good old days."

The series was meticulous in its re-creation of the era, literally with its period props and emotionally with the personalities of its characters. Mad Men took viewers back to a time before the ubiquitous presence of computers and cell phones to a world of offices outfitted with manual typewriters, serviced by rotary dial telephones with switchboard operators, and run by male executives who expected the perks of power, including first-class travel, top-shelf liquor, and compliant women. Smoking was an assumed social activity everywhere, from boardrooms and restaurants to bedrooms and doctors' offices.

Yet there was more to Mad Men than managing the window dressing. Much like the "golden age" of original television drama in the 1950s and early 1960s, the stories on Mad Men focused on the small actions of well-developed characters facing the issues of the era. They were at a historical nexus of major change in social, political, racial, generational, and gender assumptions. The ad agency office provided the backdrop of a business in the business of communication.

Set at the fictional Sterling Cooper advertising agency on Madison Avenue, the series revolved around the company's self-assured lead ad man, Don Draper (Jon Hamm), an expert in selling clients and consumers his vision of the American Dream. During the first episode, in the course of outlining a canny new campaign hook for Lucky Strike cigarettes, Draper explained that advertising was based on "happiness," coupled with the reassurance that "whatever you do need, it's OK. You are OK."

That vision also applied to Draper himself who, over the course of the series, proved as adept at selling himself as any other product. He appeared to have the perfect life: a well-paying job, a home in the suburbs, a beautiful wife, and loving children. Yet his carefully crafted image hid deep personal secrets, including his real name, lower-class social background, and a pivotal identity switch during the Korean War. There was no mystery, though, about one telling aspect of his personality: Don Draper thrived on the sexual excitement of extramarital affairs, stirring suspicions and anguish in his wife, Betty (January Jones), who felt trapped by the era's expectation of "the good wife" and almost overwhelmed by the difficult requirements for divorce at the time.

Challenges faced by women in the workplace were an equally important theme as the series followed the paths to advancement chosen at Sterling Cooper. Peggy Olsen (Elisabeth Moss), Don Draper's new secretary in the first episode, was the embodiment of the next generation, uncertain yet excited, initially overwhelmed yet determined to make her mark. Over time she earned Draper's respect, and by the second season had won a promotion (and her own office) as a company copy writer. Joan Holloway (Christina Hendricks) was the experienced player, a striking, confident woman who made herself invaluable to the company by managing the intricacies of the office operation, earning the trust and affectionate admiration of one of the company's senior partners, Roger Sterling (John Slattery), with whom she had a long-running affair until her marriage.

During the second season, twenty-year-old Jane Siegel (Peyton List) demonstrated an alternative route to success, going from Draper's secretary to new bride to Sterling, following his divorce. Among Draper's male colleagues, ambitious young Pete Campbell (Vincent Kartheiser), from a "blue-blood" background, also married well. His wife, Trudy (Alison Brie), a New York heiress, fit easily into Campbell's social circles and also urged him to advance his career, following in the footsteps of Draper, his role model and potential rival.

Matthew Weiner carefully paced *Mad Men* to capture the era's shifting arc of history. Despite the aura of success at Sterling Cooper, stories repeatedly revealed the tension between the sometimes lumbering routine of the way things had always been done and new forces entering the commercial market (including more women in business and greater ethnic identity). Between seasons, Weiner strategically jumped the story ahead in time, picking up from that new starting point with continued real life historical and artifact details. Events such as the 1960 presidential contest between John Kennedy and Richard Nixon became part of the story, but the series treated such threads as real people in the real world might regard them: important, but viewed through the prism of their own more personal concerns. By the end of the third season, the *Mad Men* program timeline passed the assassination of President Kennedy and fully transitioned from the lingering sensibilities of the 1950s into the more controversial and confrontational phase of the 1960s.

Sterling Cooper might have been a fictional agency, but its clients usually were not. *Mad Men* consistently dropped the names of real companies and products, from Lucky Strike to London Fog to Jim Beam. Some of the cited companies such as Heineken beer even provided opportunities for product brand placement and evocative tie-in commercials during the show. Although such spots did not include ads for cigarettes (banned on television since the early 1970s), some viewers criticized the program's repeated portrayal of social smoking as the ultimate in unchecked, positive promotion of the product, circumventing the rules against such paid commercials on television. Weiner explained in an AMC "making-of" special that doing this show without smoking "would have been a joke," coming off as sanitary and phony for the time period setting.

Omnipresent smoking was not all that struck the sensibilities of twenty-first-century viewers. The heavy daily consumption of liquor (especially during business hours) and the accepted nature of extramarital sexual shenanigans in *Mad Men* also seemed almost excessive, even for the era portrayed. In a 2009 *USA Today* interview, famed real life ad executive Jerry Della Femina, who had worked on Madison Avenue during the 1950s and 1960s, observed that, if anything, in his view the show underplayed the degree of smoking, drinking, and philandering that occurred in the industry back then.

From the start, *Mad Men* won multiple awards, landing Emmys, Golden Globes, and a 2007 Peabody Award. As with *The Sopranos*, *Mad Men* showed the power of good writing to help drive a complete television package. The show ultimately served its promotional purpose for AMC, increasing awareness of the channel as including original scripted programming.

A few months after the end of *Mad Man*'s first season in October 2007, AMC introduced another new series, *Breaking Bad*, with a far different sensibility. Bryan Cranston (the harried dad from *Malcolm in the Middle*) played high school chemistry teacher Walter White, who became a drug/meth dealer after learning that he had lung cancer. Faced with the prospect of his own mortality, White embraced the news as a liberating license to do whatever he wanted. What could threaten him? He was already under a death sentence (granted, at some unspecified future date, though it was assumed to be sooner rather than later). The seven-episode first season played through March and earned its own set of awards, plus renewal.

The quick success of AMC with a pair of innovative series once again demonstrated the flexibility available to channels that originated on cable. AMC had become a hot program destination even while most of its remaining schedule consisted of old movies.

Being able to start a new season of episodes virtually anytime meant that for a particular series anytime could be the perfect time to launch. Options like that also helped cable channels in general to better deal with what became the defining force of the 2007–08 season: a writers' strike.

Since 1980, there had been two major strikes by writers (in 1981 and 1988), coinciding with the rise in the amount of programming beginning to appear on cable channels and via prerecorded video releases. Those new media outlets had been departures from the television and feature film status quo at the time, and representatives of the writers and producers argued over modifications and alternatives to existing financial agreements. The strikes had been about writers attempting to win a bigger slice

September 10, 2007
NBC further expands *Today* by adding a fourth hour to the weekday morning TV staple. At the same time, the network gives back to its affiliates one hour of afternoon programming time by axing the eight-year-old supernatural-themed soap opera *Passions*. This leaves NBC with only one hour of non-*Today* daytime programming, its final soap opera, *Days of Our Lives*.

October 1, 2007
Major League Baseball playoff games come to cable as part of a new seven-year TV contract. In order to reduce the disruptions to its fall schedule by the month-long three-round baseball playoff structure, Fox gives up the first round League Divisional Series (LDS) and one of the two second round League Championship Series (LCS). Fox keeps the remaining LCS games and the World Series. TBS takes over the LDS first round of playoffs and the other LCS series. TBS's first MLB playoff game has the home-town Colorado Rockies beat the San Diego Padres 9-8 in a one-game tiebreaker contest to choose the NL wild card team for the year. In the spring of 2008, TBS adds a Sunday afternoon national game of the week.

October 1, 2007
The debut of the NHL Network, a joint venture of professional hockey and Comcast. This new U.S. cable channel largely duplicates programming on the six-year-old Canadian cable NHL Network.

October 15, 2007
Fox launches Fox Business Network, a twenty-four-hour cable business channel to compete with NBC's CNBC.

November 20, 2007
NBC Universal closes on its acquisition of Oxygen, the seven-year-old cable channel with programming for women.

December 13, 2007
News Corp., corporate parent of Fox television, closes on its acquisition of the *Wall Street Journal* newspaper.

January 13, 2008
Terminator: The Sarah Connor Chronicles. (Fox). Just ahead of production on a new theatrical film ("Terminator Salvation"), the Terminator franchise "rewrites" its history for a television series, sending a robot back in time to a point after the second theatrical film with the mission to kill fifteen-year-old John Connor (Thomas Dekker), who will grow up to lead the human revolt against the machines. Lena Headey stars as John's mother, Sarah, who seeks to protect her son from the maniacal machine.

MON

	8:00	8:30	9:00	9:30	10:00	10:30	
	Dancing With The Stars			SAMANTHA WHO?	The Bachelor		ABC
	How I Met Your Mother	THE BIG BANG THEORY	Two And A Half Men	Rules Of Engagement	CSI: Miami		CBS
	Prison Break		K-VILLE		local		FOX
	CHUCK		Heroes		JOURNEYMAN		NBC
	Everybody Hates Chris	ALIENS IN AMERICA	Girlfriends	The Game	local		CW
	CELEBRITY EXPOSE		CONTROL ROOM PRESENTS		local		MNT

TUE

	8:00	8:30	9:00	9:30	10:00	10:30	
	CAVEMEN	CARPOOLERS	Dancing With The Stars		Boston Legal		ABC
	NCIS		The Unit		CANE		CBS
	Bones		House, M.D.		local		FOX
	The Biggest Loser			Singing Bee	Law & Order: Special Victims Unit		NBC
	Beauty And The Geek		REAPER		local		CW
	THE ACADEMY		JAIL	JAIL	local		MNT

WED

	8:00	8:30	9:00	9:30	10:00	10:30	
	PUSHING DAISES		PRIVATE PRACTICE		DIRTY SEXY MONEY		ABC
	KID NATION		Criminal Minds		CSI: NY		CBS
	BACK TO YOU	Till Death	KITCHEN NIGHTMARES		local		FOX
	Deal Or No Deal		Bionic Woman		LIFE		NBC
	America's Next Top Model		GOSSIP GIRL		local		CW
	DECISION HOUSE		MEET MY FOLKS		local		MNT

THR

	8:00	8:30	9:00	9:30	10:00	10:30	
	Ugly Betty		Grey's Anatomy		BIG SHOTS		ABC
	Survivor: China		CSI: Crime Scene Investigation		Without A Trace		CBS
	Are You Smarter Than A 5th Grader?		Don't Forget The Lyrics		local		FOX
	My Name Is Earl	30 Rock	The Office	Scrubs	ER		NBC
	Smallville		Supernatural		local		CW
	My Thursday Night Movie				local		MNT

FRI

	8:00	8:30	9:00	9:30	10:00	10:30	
	20/20		WOMEN'S MURDER CLUB		Men In Trees		ABC
	Ghost Whisperer		MOONLIGHT		Numb3rs		CBS
	Are You Smarter Than A 5th Grader?		NASHVILLE		local		FOX
	Deal Or No Deal		Friday Night Lights		Las Vegas		NBC
	WWE Friday Night Smackdown!				local		CW
	My Friday Night Movie				local		MNT

SAT

	8:00	8:30	9:00	9:30	10:00	10:30	
	Saturday Night College Football						ABC
	Crime Time Saturday		Crime Time Saturday		48 Hours Mystery		CBS
	Cops	Cops	America's Most Wanted		local		FOX
	Bionic Woman		CHUCK		Law & Order: Special Victims Unit		NBC
	local						CW
	NFL Total Access		IFL Battleground		local		MNT

SUN

	7:00	7:30	8:00	8:30	9:00	9:30	10:00	10:30	
	America's Funniest Home Videos		Extreme Makeover: Home Edition		Desperate Housewives		Brothers & Sisters		ABC
	60 Minutes		VIVA LAUGHLIN		Cold Case		Shark		CBS
	NFL Football	The O.T.	The Simpsons	King Of The Hill	Family Guy	American Dad	local		FOX
	Football Night In America		Sunday Night Football						NBC
	CW NOW	ON LINE NATION	LIFE IS WILD		America's Next Top Model		local		CW
	local								MNT

Felicia Day (as Codex, the Healer) set the scene for each episode of *The Guild* with her webcam observations detailing the latest complications with the Knights of Good online game group, starting with the unexpected appearance at her apartment of lovestruck fellow guild member, Zaboo (Sandeep Parikh). *(Courtesy of Knights of Good Productions, Inc.)*

of the emerging new media pie. Whether they had achieved that goal to the degree they had desired was still the subject of internal debate in 2007, as everyone looked toward the next new wave of emerging technologies.

Video tape had been joined by DVDs, digital video recorders, and other delivery systems. High-speed Internet connections had added the ability to bring content directly to home screens either through downloads (sometimes free, or sold through sites trafficking in digital files, such as iTunes) or through streaming video in real time (playing more like a television station, with or without commercials).

In addition, series such as *The Office, 30 Rock,* and *Lost* now produced occasional short self-contained online "webisodes" apart from the regular series, akin to bonus tracks on a DVD. There were also programs that originated online from the start, such as *The Guild*, a sitcom about online game players created by actress Felicia Day, herself a lifelong game player. Day adapted her unsold television series pilot about gaming into a live-action Internet video series, demonstrating that the essence of a good sitcom could be successfully captured in episodes that ran six to eight minutes each. *The Guild* had an ensemble cast of continuing characters, season-long story arcs, and a premiere schedule similar to that of a cable series, but online. For each season, the show rolled out about a dozen new episodes over a set period of several months and then kept them available for catch-up viewing, fueling rounds of online word-of-mouth postings. The series (at Watch-theguild.com) picked up Microsoft sponsorship in its second season including platform showcases via the company's Xbox and Zune. With minimal overhead and a program tailored to a savvy targeted audience, *The Guild* also showed how keeping creative control and ownership could result in more options on the revenue and distribution sides, such as licensing the series for DVD release.

By 2007, DVD distribution had become a reliable component in the calculus of feature film income. Television episodes, old and new, had also entered the income stream. For example, to help kick off the 2006–07 season of *24*, Fox had packaged the first four episodes for immediate DVD sale the day after the fourth one aired, creating an instant miniseries release.

Other program-related income included increased product placement, promotional partnerships, and targeted tie-ins. Teen-oriented drama and adventure series such as the CW's *Smallville* or

the new *Gossip Girl* regularly included snippets of songs that were, in turn, promoted for sale at program websites. *American Idol* was the acknowledged master in bringing these components together, packaging its brand not only for the series itself, but at each stage of the audition, performance, recording, and touring processes.

Writers saw money from these developments coming into the media entertainment system. As technology forced further changes, they wanted to be at the table as the new rules took shape.

Over the spring and summer of 2007, writers and producers positioned themselves, working through their respective negotiating representatives, the Writers Guild of America (WGA) and the Alliance of Motion Picture and Television Producers (AMPTP). They both knew the deadline facing them (the existing contract was set to expire on October 31) and that a strike after that was quite likely.

On the theatrical film side, preparations included a rush to complete scripts so that production could move forward even during a strike. Nonetheless, the feature film process followed a timeline so detached from public view that disruptions there, while costly, would be mostly out of sight to audiences. The real day-to-day exposure of any strike would come from television.

For most viewers, the prospect of a strike (if noticed at all) remained a vaguely defined background issue going into the 2007–08 season. Reinforcing that point, the traditional broadcast fall premieres rolled out, seemingly business as usual, with instant prognostications on the season.

ABC was seen as particularly strong with its returning series and new titles, including the first full season of *Private Practice*, the soapy drama *Dirty Sexy Money* (Peter Krause as an idealistic ethical lawyer representing a super-rich, morally bankrupt New York City family), the dual-personality comedy *Samantha Who?* (Christina Applegate as a woman who awakens from a coma newly nice, with no memory of how nasty she used to be), and an immediate critical favorite about death, life, and love, *Pushing Daisies*, from Bryan Fuller, a former *Heroes* executive producer. The unusual premise of *Pushing Daisies* cast Lee Pace as a shy young man who could bring the recently dead back to life with a single touch, but a second touch left them dead again for good. When he restored a woman who had been his childhood crush, it meant they could never touch again if she remained with him.

The best new show on CBS was *The Big Bang Theory* (from

Two and a Half Men producer Chuck Lorre), a breezy comedy about a pair of geeky genius apartment mates (played by Jim Parsons and Johnny Galecki) who made a quantum leap in social interaction thanks to their sweetly sexy new neighbor (played by Kaley Cuoco). On the CW, *Gossip Girl* (adapted from the best-selling young adult novels by Cecily von Ziegesar) successfully targeted its young demographic, following the soapy but stylish high school lives of privileged Manhattan teens (played by Blake Lively, Leighton Meester, Penn Badgley, Chace Crawford, and Ed Westwick), whose every scheme inevitably turned up on their cell phone screens courtesy of the unseen "gossip girl" (voiced by Kristen Bell, also the series narrator).

Riding the previous season's success of its *Heroes* fantasy, NBC's new series included: *Journeyman* (a time-travel romance); *Chuck* (Zachary Levi as the title character, a computer-tech expert at a big-box store who unwittingly becomes a secret agent after a huge cachet of top-secret government data is accidentally downloaded directly into his brain); and a high-profile remake of the 1970s *Bionic Woman* (with Michelle Ryan as Jaime Sommers in a series guided by David Eick, fresh from success with the *Battlestar Galactica* revival for the Sci-Fi channel). However, none of them matched the first season success of *Heroes*. In fact, neither did the second season of *Heroes*.

Even with positive performances by some of the new and returning shows, about a month into the 2007–08 season there was also an accumulation of bad news: disappointing ratings, behind-the-scenes production issues, and costly retooling. There were scathing reviews for a pair of outright flops: ABC's *Cavemen* (prehistoric comedy based on characters from a series of auto insurance commercials) and CBS's *Viva McLaughlin* (an over-the-top singing-and-dancing drama set in Las Vegas). There were shows that seemed to have lost their way, as with a particularly ludicrous story arc on the third season of Fox's *Prison Break* that included the "death" of Michael Scofield's girlfriend, Sara. And there were shows that simply never caught fire, such as *Cane*, CBS's multigeneration drama set in Palm Beach, which followed the fortunes of a rum-making dynasty—even with Jimmy Smits in the lead role.

Against this backdrop, the industry-anticipated jolt to the 2007–08 season began to register on Friday, October 19, when the WGA announced that it had officially received authorization from more than 90% of its voting membership to set a strike deadline anytime after the end of the month. The WGA settled on November 5. In contrast to the past, this timetable was set for highly visible impact. The strikes during the 1980s (lasting from April to July in 1981 and from March until August in 1988) had simply delayed the full arrival of those respective fall seasons, but once they began after the strikes ended, the scripted series played out without further interruption. A November strike date reflected awareness of how to effectively disrupt the heart of the television production process.

Most viewers did not realize that scripted broadcast shows usually started a new season with only a few months worth of episodes "in the can" (not the entire season) and then continued to write and produce the remaining ones as the season progressed, completing the process in time to air season finales in the spring. In addition, production of program pilots traditionally played out mid-season, with an eye toward landing a spot in the network schedules announced in the spring during the "upfront" commercial sales meetings.

A strike in early November, then, would not delay the start of the season but over time could deliver far more damage. Beginning after the broadcast networks had launched their fall programming but not before production companies had finished writing and

recording all the episodes for the season, such a strike would derail a schedule already in progress. The longer that the strike lasted, the greater the disruption to the existing season and then to the pilot process for the next season. Those implications seemed to provide maximum leverage to the writers.

On the other hand, the AMPTP side had its own priorities and leverage. Unlike during the previous strikes of the 1980s, the five main commercial broadcast networks were part of larger media conglomerates with multiple strategic entertainment interests and resources, including film studios. Standing firm against the writers sent a clear message to other potentially restive groups such as actors and directors. In the battle for the future of media, members of the AMPTP side wanted to retain their existing advantages.

These advantages included reality shows. Over the years, the WGA had tried to define work on "unscripted" reality shows as equivalent to comedy, drama, and variety writing. Those efforts had been unsuccessful, so reality programming mostly remained outside the WGA contracts. Not surprisingly, the broadcast networks planned to use such series, whose running times were particularly flexible (an hour-long "results" show could easily be stretched to ninety minutes). They also planned to tap any other non-scripted sources (including news and sports), as well as foreign productions and any other existing finished material, even series already running on cable channels.

The strike began November 5. Writers headed to the picket lines and to the Internet, using blog sites and other electronic communication for continuing updates and to launch a strong PR campaign. Members of other unions, including actors, generally honored the picket lines. Over the course of the strike only a small number of special events received waivers for writer (and performer) participation, including a benefit performance by Elizabeth Taylor for World AIDS Day in December, the Kennedy Center Honors carried by CBS on December 26, and the Screen Actors Guild SAG Awards in January 2008. Other events, such as the Grammy Awards and Golden Globes, were denied waivers.

Writers also used this "downtime opportunity" to explore online creative options that were, after all, part of why they were on strike in the first place. For example, citing Felicia Day's Internet *Guild* series as inspiration, Joss Whedon began writing what became the online original production "Dr. Horrible's Sing-Along Blog" the following year, with Neil Patrick Harris in the title role. (Appropriately, Whedon cast Felicia Day in that program as well.)

On the other side, the broadcast networks deployed every available asset to fill the time. As in past strikes, the late night talk shows were the first to shut down, immediately turning to reruns. During prime time, in the short term, the networks carefully parceled out the remaining finished episodes of their series, though it quickly became clear that the strike would not be settled soon. In mid-November, Fox canceled the new season of *24*, which had been scheduled to begin January 13 but had only a handful of hours already filmed. By early December, publications including *TV Guide* and *Entertainment Weekly* started tracking "insider reports" on how many episodes remained for each series, as the networks began looking at what could fill the mid-season gaps.

In December the late night show hosts began to face a personnel dilemma: there was network pressure to return to the air with new episodes (even without striking writers) or see large numbers of their program's non-striking support staff laid off. Citing that issue, host Carson Daly was the first to come back on December 10, with a non-scripted version of *Last Call*. (To help fill time, Daly showed pictures of the staff during the hiatus.) In January Jay Leno, Conan O'Brien, Jimmy Kimmel, Jon Stewart, and Stephen Colbert did the same, also citing staff hardships after two months off the air. David Letterman and Craig Ferguson returned as well, but unlike the others, their shows were scripted because, as owner of the production company for both series, David Letterman had come to a separate agreement with the WGA. However, Letterman did join O'Brien in sporting a "solidarity" beard.

As the strike continued, CBS slotted mid-February reruns of *Dexter* from its corporate cousin Showtime (with the serial killer's stories "cleaned up" for broadcast standards). CBS also brought back *Jericho,* which had barely escaped cancellation after one season thanks to a strong fan campaign. NBC, which had gone into the fall moving the seventh season of *Law and Order: Criminal Intent* to cable on its affiliated USA channel, brought the new episodes back to the broadcast side.

The January 13 broadcast of the annual Golden Globe awards, though, underscored the need to resolve the situation. Ordinarily a major prime time kickoff to the "awards season," the program was reduced to a glamour-free, celebrity-free half-hour televised news conference announcing the winners in each category. Audience numbers plunged from about 20 million to 6 million. Clearly there were some programs in which stand-ins would not work. Soon after the Golden Globes fiasco, the pace of talks kicked up between the WGA and AMPTP representatives, with additional high-profile events looming, especially the annual Academy Awards telecast scheduled for February 24.

After one hundred days, the strike ended at last on February 12. There was no clear-cut winner or loser, and it would take a while to judge whether the new contract provisions ultimately achieved the writers' strike goals. More immediately, the networks had to decide what to do with the remainder of the 2007–08 season, which by December had already become the season that did not matter. All the usual benchmarks, such as program ratings during the November and February sweeps, had been thrown off. It would take six to eight weeks for most shows to be up and running again, so each network had to decide, program by program, whether to close out the season or plug in as many of the remaining episodes as possible.

Entertainment publications once again ran episode guide scorecards, this time including scheduled series return dates along with projected numbers of remaining new episodes (most in the range of four to seven). Whether intended or not, this tracking of first-run episodes reinforced the message that those offerings were the only ones that mattered, especially for broadcast series. After the new episode runs were completed it was time to go on to something else. During the long negotiations of the writers' strike, the broadcast networks had pointed to the diminished value of most reruns. When viewers and the entertainment press focused on the schedule of new episodes, they only underscored that business point.

The wrap-up to the 2007–08 season was like a mini "do-over" of the fall, allowing the networks the opportunity to prune their schedules of expensive new series disappointments such as *Bionic Woman.* To win back viewer attention, network promotions stressed the return of their more familiar titles. CBS was the most aggressive, finishing off the season with new episodes, rather than keeping them as inventory for the fall, getting its shows back on the air starting March 17. The other networks paced most of their returning shows to begin later in April, leading into the May sweeps. ABC ads focused on its core shows (*Grey's Anatomy, Desperate Housewives, Lost, Ugly Betty,* and newcomer *Samantha Who?*), touting the abc.com website to "catch up on the full season."

ABC held back the new series *Dirty Sexy Money* and *Pushing Daisies,* intending to roll them out fresh in the fall. NBC similarly held back programs including the promising spy adventure *Chuck,* the police drama *Life,* and *Heroes* (which was seen as benefiting from its forced shutdown, giving the program time to retool after what had proved to be a disappointing second season). The CW's *Gossip Girl* did come back to finish out its school year just as real-life high school students were doing the same, joining the network's veteran series such as *Smallville* and *Supernatural.*

Although Fox played out the handful of remaining episodes of such series as *House* and *Bones,* the network had been least affected by the strike. *American Idol* and other reality shows were not covered by the WGA agreements, nor was its turn for the Super Bowl, so there was little surprise that Fox won its fourth straight season in the 18 to 49 demographic. For the first time Fox also won in total audience.

Final numbers on the 2007–08 network competition, though, were the least important aspect of the season. By disrupting business as usual, the writers' strike had focused extraordinary attention on the fact that broadcast television itself was no longer business as usual. Important financial issues had been brought to the table just when broadcasters were watching their longtime structure disappear. Audiences in the 18 to 49 demographic were down 10% for the season among the five English language commercial broadcast networks, while ad-supported cable numbers

February 17, 2008

Richard Belzer guests as Det. John Munch on an episode of HBO's *The Wire* ("Took"), bringing that same character (which originated in 1993 on *Homicide: Life on the Street*) to eight different series also including *The X-Files, The Beat, Arrested Development,* and three *Law and Order* titles (the original, *Special Victims Unit,* and *Trial by Jury*).

March 12, 2008

The official public launch for Hulu.com, the website set up by NBC Universal and Fox to offer commercial-supported free streaming of some of their TV shows and movies. (Hulu had begun by invitation only on October 29, 2007.) On July 6, 2009, Disney acquires an ownership interest in Hulu and begins allowing some of its TV and film material to appear on the website as well.

June 13, 2008

Tim Russert, host of *Meet the Press* since 1991 and Washington bureau chief for NBC News, dies suddenly at age fifty-eight, in the midst of a very active year for political news. Retired NBC anchorman Tom Brokaw steps in to helm *Meet the Press* through the fall presidential election, with David Gregory taking over as Russert's successor on December 14, 2008.

July 6, 2008

NBC Universal (with investment groups Bain Capital and the Blackstone Group) announces the acquisition from Landmark Communications of the twenty-six-year-old Weather Channel, one of the last of the major independent cable channels. This purchase allows NBC to shut down its rival four-year-old NBC Weather Plus service.

August 8, 2008

The summer Olympics in Beijing, China, open with an elaborate four-hour ceremony that features a cast of more than 15,000 performers. NBC televises the games to the U.S. over their sixteen-day run, while also airing portions on its affiliated cable networks USA, MSNBC, CNBC, Oxygen and Telemundo, as well as online via NBC.com.

The final session of the 2008 Democratic National Convention in Denver, Colorado *(above, left),* was held at the open-air Invesco Field football stadium, where multiple video screens allowed a capacity crowd to see Barack Obama deliver his acceptance speech. *(Photo by Peter Sills, Digital Focus)* One week after that finale, John McCain accepted the nomination at the Republican National Convention in Saint Paul, Minnesota *(right),* indoors at the Xcel Energy Center arena. *(Photo by Mark Abraham)*

were up 9%. It was doubtful that all of that change could be attributed to the strike. What's more, there were other considerations in play.

The strike had erased one of the last important distinctions between cable channels and broadcast channels. Generally, broadcasters offered a full season's worth of episodes for shows, clustered around a fall or mid-season kickoff. Because of the strike, for the 2007–08 season many of the broadcast offerings in effect ended up just like cable series, with fewer total numbers of episodes, stopping and starting in limited arcs.

Yet broadcast channels still did not receive direct payment for appearing as a channel offering on cable systems and had to rely almost exclusively on advertising revenue. Within their own corporate ownership, they were no longer the top prize. For example, as a cable-originating channel, Disney's ESPN could sell commercials and collect a portion of the cable subscriber fee, so it was potentially more lucrative than ABC.

Looking at the numbers for NBC Universal, *Variety* noted a far greater annual profit from the media company's USA cable channel (home of such series as *Monk*) than from the over-the-air NBC network (reportedly $600 million versus $100 million). Reflecting those limits, in order to fund a third season of the highly respected drama *Friday Night Lights*, NBC arranged an innovative financing partnership with satellite TV provider DirecTV. In exchange DirecTV acquired exclusive first airing of the season and, when those episodes aired on NBC months later, they would be in a cut-down form.

As revenue for cable channels grew, so did their programming budgets and audience numbers. USA was the highest rated ad-supported cable channel and only about 100,000 viewers shy of the CW broadcast network. Meanwhile, to cut its costs, the CW outsourced its Saturday morning cartoon block (as the other networks had done for years) and even looked to do the same for its Sunday evening prime time block in the fall of 2008 because it could not profitably fill the night on its own.

The distinction between broadcast and cable origination was nonexistent in the eyes of most viewers watching television via cable or satellite. Nonetheless, the media companies owning each broadcast network had to deal with the defined differences as part of the cost of doing business. There was still a percentage of U.S. television households that did not subscribe to cable or satellite (less than 20%), giving broadcast networks an advantage there. But the media conglomerates were already deep into diversification.

So were viewers. During the strike, viewers had explored other entertainment options, with choices that reflected their comfort levels with different technology. Internet offerings ranged from online streaming and downloading to social networking links to original video production. *TV Guide* reported that 48% of the population watched at least one video online during the January strike period. Others focused on more traditional venues such as DVDs, including use of the expanding Netflix mail-order video rental service, which dispatched customer-selected discs directly to subscriber households. Some viewers simply scanned the dial for alternatives to absent broadcast series, looking to all the other cable channels.

Although production on series for cable channels had also been targeted by the strike, only ongoing operations such as *The Daily Show* were visibly affected. Otherwise, any delay was not as noticeable because most scripted cable series could start and end anytime, with fewer episodes involved in any one run (generally all were completed before they began appearing on air). So *Mad Men* had ended its first season right before the strike, and previously completed episodes of *Breaking Bad* had played right through the strike period. The final dozen episodes of the highly praised HBO series *The Wire* also ran during the strike, beginning in December and ending in March. Appropriately, one of the themes of the season focused on hard-pressed news organizations dealing with upheaval in the media.

For all the challenges television had been forced to face (if not solve) as a result of the writers' strike, the need for broadcasters to fill as much time as possible with non-scripted material had also found them tapping their news departments. That need coincided with a particularly exciting presidential campaign that reached one of its key marker moments at the end of the 2007–08 season, the respective Democratic and Republican nominating conventions. From the first competitive stirrings in mid-2007 to its conclusion on election day 2008, that contest played out a narrative as engaging as any scripted series.

69. Change Is Now

THERE WAS EXTRAORDINARY INTEREST in the 2008 U.S. presidential campaign cycle, and an expanded media world was poised to meet it. Because incumbent Republican President George W. Bush was not eligible to run for a third term (and Vice President Dick Cheney broke a long tradition and chose not to seek the presidency himself), the current administration was not out discussing and defending its policies as part of an election campaign. That left the field wide open for a change in vision.

On the Democratic Party side, there were six main candidates, with Senator Hillary Clinton the early polling front-runner, along with Senator Barack Obama, Senator Joe Biden, former Senator John Edwards, Senator Chris Dodd, and Governor Bill Richardson. The Republican Party began with about a dozen contenders, but settled into a core of half that number. On name recognition alone, former New York Mayor Rudy Giuliani was most familiar, along with former Governor Mitt Romney, Senator John McCain, former Governor Mike Huckabee, and former Senator Fred Thompson.

Although the formal process of selecting a nominee would not begin until early 2008 (through voting in party primaries and caucuses), a host of sponsoring organizations and cities lured the candidates to a variety of debate settings beginning in the spring of 2007. With so many aspirants vying for attention, media exposure was seen as crucial, even for the early front-runners. From 2007 through the spring of 2008, there were more than two dozen pre-primary and primary debates among the Democratic candidates and more than twenty among the Republicans.

The debates were generally presented in conjunction with one of the all-news cable channels (CNN, MSNBC, Fox News Channel) providing the official media stage, but other organizations were also part of the mix for specific debates. Some of these included Univision, PBS, Iowa Public Television, National Public Radio, and MTV. CBS had planned a December 10 Democratic debate in Los Angeles, but that became caught up in the ongoing writers' strike at the time and was canceled. ABC landed a big draw, showcasing candidates from both parties on January 5, 2008, the weekend before the pivotal New Hampshire primary. The broadcast attracted more than 9 million viewers.

In addition to the large field of contestants, the campaign stage itself also expanded via the Internet. YouTube became the go-to site for displaying candidate video messages, commercials, and unofficial original productions. In March 2007, supporters of Barack Obama posted a seventy-four-second spot that cast Democratic favorite Hillary Clinton as the face of "Big Brother" in a parody of the famous "1984" Apple computer commercial. Less

directly political but far more deliberately seductive, in June 2007 Amber Lee Ettinger played the sexy "Obama Girl" as she lip-synched the vocal to the video "I Got a Crush … on Obama," the initial offering from BarelyPolitical.com. Those became viral hits. Recognizing the high visibility of YouTube, CNN teamed with the site the following month for the July 23 Democratic debate, taking questions submitted online as short videos. In one, a "talking snowman" asked about global warming as "the single most important issue to the snowmen of this country."

Savvy campaign operatives also used the Internet during 2007 for less showy but essential organizing and fundraising activities. They plugged into social networking sites such as Facebook and MySpace and actively courted bloggers of every stripe, creating an almost continuous cycle of mutually reinforcing online exchanges: campaign event updates and issue essays were inevitably followed by commentary threads, analysis, and links from individuals to pictures, videos, and further postings. The practice of "spin sessions" (partisan experts analyzing a just-completed event) jumped to a whole new level, with online observations running simultaneous with the event itself and continuing from there. By the time the 2008 political nominating conventions arrived, both parties had aggressively sought and credentialed more than one hundred bloggers each.

As the 2007 pre-primary debates aired through the fall, they helped to define the narrative for both parties. On the Republican side, there was the question of whether time had passed John McCain by since his heated loss to George W. Bush in the 2000 primary campaign. Eight years later, could he still be the "maverick" against the likes of Giuliani, Romney, and Huckabee? For the Democratic story, attention inevitably shifted to front-runner Hillary Clinton and challenger Barack Obama: either would represent potential history in the making as the first woman to head a major party ticket or the first black to do so.

Those compelling stories served to boost overall news interest and ratings through the fall of 2007. On the entertainment side, they also gave political humor shows strong topical hooks, with NBC's *Saturday Night Live* particularly energized. A skit on November 3 featured Amy Poehler (as Hillary Clinton) throwing a Halloween party as the presumed front-runner, with cast members playing all the other candidates except for the real Barack Obama, who came "in costume" dressed as Barack Obama and delivered the "Live from New York" line. However, the hundred-day writers' strike of 2007–08 began after that episode and pushed *Saturday Night Live* off the stage until February 2008. Later in

FALL 2008 SCHEDULE

Monday – Saturday

	8:00	8:30	9:00	9:30	10:00	10:30	
MON	Dancing With The Stars			Samantha Who?	Boston Legal		ABC
	The Big Bang Theory	How I Met You Mother	Two And A Half Men	WORST WEEK	CSI: Miami		CBS
	Terminator: The Sarah Connor Chronicles		Prison Break		local		FOX
	Chuck		Heroes		MY OWN WORST ENEMY		NBC
	Gossip Girl		One Tree Hill		local		CW
	Celebrity Expose		MAGIC'S BIGGEST SECRETS FINALLY REVEALED		local		MNT
TUE	OPPORTUNITY KNOCKS		Dancing With The Stars		Eli Stone		ABC
	NCIS		THE MENTALIST		Without A Trace		CBS
	House, M.D.		FRINGE		local		FOX
	The Biggest Loser: Families				Law & Order: Special Victims Unit		NBC
	90210		PRIVILEGED		local		CW
	Street Patrol	Street Patrol	Jail	Jail	local		MNT
WED	Pushing Daises		Private Practice		Dirty Sexy Money		ABC
	New Adventures Of Old Christine	GARY UNMARRIED	Criminal Minds		CSI: NY		CBS
	Bones		Till Death	DO NOT DISTURB	local		FOX
	Knight Rider		Deal Or No Deal		Lipstick Jungle		NBC
	America's Next Top Model		STYLISTA		local		CW
	THE TONY ROCK PROJECT	Under One Roof	THE WORLD'S FUNNIEST MOMENTS		local		MNT
THR	Ugly Betty		Grey's Anatomy		LIFE ON MARS		ABC
	Survivor: Gabon		CSI: Crime Scene Investigation		ELEVENTH HOUR		CBS
	HOLE IN THE WALL		Kitchen Nightmares		local		FOX
	My Name Is Earl	KATH & KIM	The Office	30 Rock	ER		NBC
	Smallville		Supernatural		local		CW
	My Thursday Night Movie				local		MNT
FRI	Wife Swap		Supernanny		20/20		ABC
	Ghost Whisperer		THE EX LIST		Numb3rs		CBS
	Are You Smarter Than A 5th Grader?		Don't Forget The Lyrics		local		FOX
	AMERICA'S TOUGHEST JOBS		CRUSOE		Life		NBC
	Everybody Hates Chris	The Game	America's Next Top Model		local		CW
	WWE Friday Night Smackdown!				local		MNT
SAT	Saturday Night College Football						ABC
	Crime Time Saturday		Crime Time Saturday		48 Hours Mystery		CBS
	Cops	Cops	America's Most Wanted		local		FOX
	Knight Rider		Chuck		Law & Order: Special Victims Unit		NBC
	local						CW
	My Saturday Night Movie				local		MNT

Sunday

	7:00	7:30	8:00	8:30	9:00	9:30	10:00	10:30	
SUN	America's Funniest Home Videos		Extreme Makeover: Home Edition		Desperate Housewives		Brothers & Sisters		ABC
	60 Minutes		The Amazing Race		Cold Case		The Unit		CBS
	NFL Football	The O.T.	The Simpsons	King Of The Hill	Family Guy	American Dad	local		FOX
	Football Night In America		Sunday Night Football						NBC
	IN HARM'S WAY		VALENTINE		EASY MONEY		local		CW
	local								MNT

Barack Obama *(seated)* and John McCain at their second debate, staged town-hall style on October 7, 2008, at Belmont University in Nashville, Tennessee. *(Photo by Mark Abraham)*

where both Hillary Clinton and Barack Obama remained in contention for the next four months. Obama, proclaiming himself the "candidate of change," took the lead after Super Tuesday and quickly became a media favorite, being a fresh face on the national scene with an appealing multiracial background. Still, Clinton rallied to win key states such as Ohio and Pennsylvania in March and April, keeping the battle going through spring, even though Obama's rising delegate totals meant he would probably win the nomination in the end. Previously, news organizations had frequently lamented the absence of drama in the primary and caucus process beyond the first month. Instead, in this cycle, they found themselves scrambling (and straining their budgets) to cover every Democratic contest through June, chronicling an intense back-and-forth battle.

The extended contest allowed *Saturday Night Live* the opportunity to reenter the political fray following the end of the writers' strike, giving Hillary Clinton her turn to open the show on March 1. Even more relevant to the campaign, the program raised the issue of whether the press had failed to give Obama the same degree of scrutiny directed at Clinton. Skits with Fred Armisen (as Obama) made the point, showing an awestruck press corps hanging

November, though, entertainment superstar Oprah Winfrey announced her support for Obama and, starting December 8, she campaigned for him in Iowa, New Hampshire, and North Carolina, just in front of the first caucus and primary contests.

Individual states had long looked enviously at the tremendous media attention (and associated coverage spending) focused on the first-in-the-nation Iowa caucus and New Hampshire primary. Throughout 2007 other states jockeyed to move up their own dates, in spite of national party rules against that. Most were held in check, and a handful that did violate the calendar limits were subsequently sanctioned. Through it all, the Iowa and New Hampshire state parties simply advanced their own dates as necessary to maintain their lead-off status. As a result, the formal voting began earlier than ever in a campaign cycle, with the Iowa caucus held the evening of January 3, 2008. As late as December, Clinton was comfortably ahead in national polls, though individual state surveys were much closer. The final results from Iowa had Clinton finishing third, behind Obama and just edged out by John Edwards. Five days later, Clinton won in New Hampshire after a strong showing at the ABC debate January 5.

On the Republican side, Mike Huckabee unexpectedly led the field in Iowa, but John McCain rebounded in New Hampshire and by the "Super Tuesday" contests (February 5) essentially wrapped up the race. That followed the usual pattern for recent presidential election cycles. The story was far different on the Democratic side,

September 23, 2008
The Mentalist. (CBS). Simon Baker portrays Patrick Jane, a once world-renowned psychic who later admitted he had no special powers, just keen perception and a logical mind. Jane now serves as a consultant to California police, as he helps them solve crimes. The series quickly becomes the top-rated new program of the season.

October 9, 2008
Life On Mars. (ABC). In a U.S. remake of an innovative BBC series from 2006 (which aired on BBC America in 2007), Jason O'Mara plays New York City homicide detective Sam Tyler, who is hit by a car in 2008 and inexplicably wakes up in 1973. In the pre-computer era of disco music, shaggy hair, and rampant male chauvinism on the force, Tyler continues to work as a precinct detective with everyone believing he is a transfer from another station.

January 1, 2009
Debut of the MLB Network, as Major League Baseball becomes the last of the four major U.S. team sports with its own cable channel.

January 13, 2009
On the eighth season debut of *American Idol*, songwriter-music executive Kara DioGuardi joins as a fourth judge.

January 15, 2009
After more than eight seasons as Dr. Gil Grissom, the lead forensic investigator on CBS's *CSI* series, William Petersen departs the show. His replacement, Laurence Fishburne as Dr. Ray Langston, arrived in December for the transition.

March 2, 2009
The complex game of musical chairs involving NBC's late night talk shows begins as former *Saturday Night Live* comic Jimmy Fallon replaces Conan O'Brien on the post-*Tonight* series *Late Night*.

April 2, 2009
The final episode of *ER* airs, closing out a fifteen-year run and marking the end of the last vestige of NBC's once-powerful Thursday night "must see" TV lineup.

May 20, 2009

The regular TV season concludes, with Kris Allen nosing out favorite Adam Lambert on *American Idol*. Fox wins its fifth consecutive season in the 18 to 49 demographic category, while CBS, after a one-year dip caused by the writers' strike, resumes its position as champ in overall viewers (its sixth victory in that category over the past seven years).

June 1, 2009

Changes continue at NBC, as Conan O'Brien takes over the *Tonight* show from Jay Leno, who hosted the show for seventeen years, the last fourteen as number one in its slot.

June 12, 2009

Analog television broadcasting ends in the United States (for full-power stations), seventy-three years after it supplanted the old "spinning disk" mechanical television system. With the exception of some low-power stations, American TV now broadcasts only digital signals. As part of the transition, many stations change their broadcast frequency; those in the 52 to 69 channel range are moved out, as those frequencies are to be auctioned off by the government (channels 70 to 83 having been turned over to mobile phone use back in the 1980s). As a result, while the old channel numbers (such as 2, 4, 5, 7, and up) might still be used by local stations for identification continuity, they may no longer bear any relation to a channel's frequency.

July 7, 2009

Cable's Sci-Fi network is renamed Syfy.

September 18, 2009

After seventy-two years on the air (the last fifty-seven on TV), *Guiding Light*, the longest-running entertainment program in American broadcasting, is canceled by CBS. The network is moving from soap operas to less expensive daytime fare, and it fills the time slot (beginning October 5) with a new revival of the *Let's Make a Deal* game show (hosted by comedian Wayne Brady).

September 26, 2009

MyNetworkTV ceases operating as a true TV network, becoming a mere programming service. It essentially ends original programming in favor of off-network reruns (though it does continue for one more year its one successful series, *WWE Friday Night Smackdown!*, which it inherited from the CW network in October 2008).

for one week until the Republican convention, when the acceptance speech by John McCain also attracted some 42 million viewers. However, the Republican convention had an additional draw as some 40 million viewers tuned in the previous day for the acceptance speech by McCain's just-announced vice-presidential running mate, first-term Alaska Governor Sarah Palin, the first woman on a national Republican ticket.

McCain's choice of Palin had been announced the morning after Obama's acceptance speech and caught most observers by surprise, reinforcing his image as a maverick politician. To the general public, Palin was an unknown, so there was great interest in her background and style. She rose to the occasion for the Republican convention and immediately connected as a strong stump speaker on the campaign trail, promoting herself as a tough-talking "hockey mom" who was more in tune with the average American than the politicians in Washington.

Palin was less successful facing skeptical media scrutiny of her qualifications. Because of John McCain's age (he turned seventy-two before the Republican convention) the questions really came down to her readiness to be president. Even with McCain's family history (his mother was still active at ninety-five) that was a legitimate concern. One-on-one interview sessions with ABC's Charles Gibson (September 12) and CBS's Katie Couric (September 24) cast Palin in an unfavorable light, especially on the depth of her background on foreign policy issues. For the balance of the campaign, her national news media availabilities were severely limited.

Yet the most demanding challenge to Palin's credibility came from the entertainment side, on *Saturday Night Live* and its Thursday night prime time election specials. On these, former *SNL*

John McCain's running mate, Sarah Palin, during the vice-presidential debate at Washington University in St. Louis, Missouri, on October 2, 2008. *(Photo by Mark Abraham)*

on his every word while Amy Poehler's Clinton was ignored. On the Republican side, the real John McCain appeared on the program for its May 17 season finale.

In June, after the last of the primaries clinched the nomination for Obama, Clinton conceded and acknowledged Obama as the presumptive nominee. For the August convention, Obama took a page from John Kennedy, who delivered his 1960 acceptance speech from the outdoor Los Angeles Coliseum. After three days at Denver's indoor Pepsi Center, the proceedings moved to nearby Invesco Field, allowing for greater capacity (topping 80,000) but also requiring expensive media technical relocation.

Reflecting the continuing public interest in the unfolding presidential drama, Obama's acceptance speech drew some 42 million viewers as part of the most watched political convention week in history (combining the ratings of ABC, CBS, NBC, Fox, CNN, MSNBC, Fox News Channel, and PBS). That record stood

Barack Obama was sworn in as the forty-fourth President of the United States on January 20, 2009, before a record crowd in Washington *(above)* and a global TV and Internet audience. His wife, Michelle, and their daughters, Sasha and Malia Ann, stood in witness as Chief Justice John Roberts *(far left)* administered the oath of office. *(Photos by Mark Abraham)*

writer and performer Tina Fey (who bore a striking physical resemblance to the Alaska governor) made a series of guest appearances with a dead-on impersonation of Palin, effectively exaggerating the governor's style, mannerisms, and slip-ups. For example, in citing her foreign policy qualifications, Fey-as-Palin had pointed out that she could "see Russia from my house." In a send-up of the Palin interview with Katie Couric, Fey-as-Palin dealt with a foreign policy question by asking to "use one of my lifelines. I want to phone a friend" (as contestants did on *Who Wants to Be a Millionaire?*). Eventually Palin herself appeared on *Saturday Night Live*, though there was only a brief on-camera moment when she shared the stage with Tina Fey. Ultimately, for many viewers, Fey came to define Sarah Palin, and the general consensus was that the parodies did hurt the Republican ticket's chances. More so than most journalistic criticism, the *Saturday Night Live* skits caused many voters to go beyond Palin's down-home appeal and to question her ability to serve as president.

Back on the straight political stage, Palin did well enough when tightly focused "on message" in the vice-presidential debate with Obama running mate Joe Biden, as they drew more viewers than any of the presidential debates. In the end, though, the contest was really between Barack Obama and John McCain. They made their cases in three official televised debates, in person at campaign rallies, in commercials, and online. In the closing months of the campaign, the U.S. economy suffered a series of major hits, further fermenting the desire for change (an Obama campaign theme). On election night in Chicago, just after 10:00 P.M. local time, large screen monitors tuned to CNN flashed the news to the crowds gathered for one final Democratic rally: Barack Obama had won the election. In the same spot where forty years before police and demonstrators had clashed at the 1968 Democratic convention, a new page in history had been written, with television once again flashing images for "a whole world watching."

The 2008 election cycle demonstrated the tremendous expansion already in place within the media world. To anyone interested, there were multiple opportunities to see and hear how the respective parties and their individual candidates defined themselves, simply by tuning in. Combining traditional television, radio, and print coverage with the Internet, viewers had access to video clips, detailed text analysis, charts, discussions, and even

opportunities to contribute support. News coverage had long been one of the ways television had repeatedly distinguished itself as more than just "wires in a box," and this campaign cycle continued that tradition.

For media companies, though, the question of paying for those boxes and wires (and the personnel behind them) had taken on new urgency. The fall economic downturn hit key television advertisers such as car companies. Sponsors overall were also evaluating how much of their ad budgets to direct to television, and where. Broadcast? Cable? Specific shows? One calculation put 49% of the 18 to 49 age audience watching thirty-seven ad-supported cable channels, with the four major broadcast nets grabbing only 28%. Equally striking, DVR penetration continued to rise, giving more households the ability to control their personal viewing easily.

Even new online ventures such as hulu.com (which was quickly catching on with viewers as a way to see full episodes or highlight clips from TV shows after they originally aired) offered only modest returns from advertising. Hulu was also seen in some circles as a potential threat to cable (and its monthly fees) by offering easy-to-access programming for free.

So the formula that emerged for the 2008–09 season treated overall profitability as being as important as ratings success. This led to tough negotiations by the networks for lower licensing fees and reduced production costs. Attempting to make the financial numbers work, the CW leased out Sunday nights for the fall of 2008 to an outside production company (Media Rights Capital), which supplied three hour-long series, but they were total flops. They were all gone by Thanksgiving and by the end of the season the network simply returned Sunday nights to its affiliates. Fox gave up its Saturday morning cartoon slots and replaced them with two hours of paid infomercials. Meanwhile, the affiliates faced their own local budget and ad sales challenges.

Against this backdrop, the industry at last completed the long-promised government-mandated conversion to digital broadcasting in June, at the end of the 2008–09 season. That served as both a symbolic and practical marker, changing a distribution system from the one that had been in place since the beginning of modern television. Whether or not the switch could help deal with any of the challenges facing media companies, it was one more reminder that, whatever the consequences, change was here.

70. The End of the World as We Know It

THE END OF ANALOG TELEVISION was once expected to be the defining media story of 2009 as the U.S. finished the process of putting into place a digital transmission system that rendered millions of existing TV sets obsolete for receiving over-the-air signals. Instead, despite the historic nature of that change, for the 2009–10 season that technology story quickly took a back seat to real-life high-stakes business dramas that played out in public. NBC was at the center of the most contentious tale, involving two of its biggest stars: Jay Leno and Conan O'Brien. In just seven months, the network went from touting a daring prime time experiment and a new host for one of its storied institutions to total retrenchment.

NBC had set the events in motion back in 2004 when it publicly announced a late night succession plan five years in advance and anointed Conan O'Brien the designated new *Tonight* show host, to replace Jay Leno beginning in 2009. In part, the promise of the *Tonight* show prize was a significant lure in a new contract that effectively kept O'Brien from jumping to any other network to start a competing late night program. In 2002, ABC had been in talks with David Letterman over just such a switch (bumping *Nightline*), but Letterman ultimately remained with CBS. Clearly O'Brien was an equally tempting target for such overtures.

In addition, by naming the next *Tonight* host far in advance, and by promoting O'Brien from the *Late Night* show, NBC was also attempting to avoid the messy conflicts that had followed Johnny Carson's unexpected *Tonight* show retirement announcement in 1991. Back then, the network had been faced with a choice between David Letterman (then its *Late Night* host) and Jay Leno (then Carson's permanent fill-in). Leno landed the job beginning in 1992 but an unhappy Letterman went to CBS and launched the *Late Show* opposite *Tonight*. For the next handoff, NBC did not want one of its stars again becoming a competitor.

By 2009 Leno had served as *Tonight* host for seventeen years, and NBC's plan anticipated that, like Johnny Carson, he would be ready to retire. As the reality of that once distant date approached, though, the situation grew more complicated. Jay Leno had found a comfortable groove as host, clearly enjoying the job. More important to the network, he consistently delivered strong ratings that kept *Tonight* number one in its slot, and provided a lead-in boost for O'Brien's *Late Night* and Carson Daly's *Last Call*. Leno was also a tireless promoter and popular with affiliates, some of whom wondered if it was a wise move to end such a successful arrangement.

Looking at Leno's continued success, NBC faced the real possibility that after his final *Tonight* show (as soon as his departing contract allowed) Leno would take his brand name elsewhere, same time, another channel, and go head-to-head with Conan O'Brien. Yet O'Brien's contract contained significant financial penalties if the *Tonight* show promotion did not occur; in addition, he would probably then go elsewhere himself, defeating the whole reason for the 2004 deal.

In December 2008, NBC announced a plan to keep both Leno and O'Brien at NBC: Conan O'Brien would take over the *Tonight* show, as scheduled, in June 2009 (with *Saturday Night Live* alum Jimmy Fallon stepping into O'Brien's old *Late Night* slot). Leno would return in the fall of 2009 with *The Jay Leno Show*, Monday through Friday, from 10:00 to 11:00 P.M., closing NBC's prime time schedule five nights a week. With that scenario in place, the changeover began smoothly with Conan O'Brien the sole guest on Leno's final *Tonight* show broadcast at the end of May 2009, which ended fourteen straight years of winning its time slot. O'Brien picked up the *Tonight* show reins the following Monday, with strong opening night ratings from curious first-time viewers. The real test, though, was for the long haul and whether audiences would make this version of the *Tonight* show part of their routine. In the process, a dip in the ratings was not unprecedented. When Leno and Letterman had gone head-to-head starting in the fall of 1993, it took two years for *Tonight* to pull ahead permanently.

For *The Jay Leno Show*, though, the path was new, uncertain, and somewhat controversial. On the surface, it was simply transferring a nightly *Tonight*-show-like program to an earlier period but, to that point, such a venture had never been attempted in prime time using the same host, crew, and format five nights a week. NBC CEO Jeff Zucker positioned it as a historic move. However, even if Leno brought his entire late night audience with him, it was still below the level of a successful prime time scripted series such as *Law & Order*. Nonetheless, NBC executives deemed it acceptable because this scheduling ploy was actually as much about the account books as the history books. It cost less to fill a prime time hour with a comedy-talk-variety show than with a scripted drama series. Those savings were multiplied by having the *same* show producing five new episodes each week. When drama series on the other networks went into reruns, *The Jay Leno Show* would also continue to produce new episodes and possibly even beat the competition.

Five nights of prime time with Leno's show meant five fewer

hours available for scripted drama series, and that news was not welcomed by writers and producers, who bemoaned the absence of any 10:00 P.M. slots on NBC for the next *L.A. Law*, *ER*, or *Law & Order*. In fact, for the fall of 2009, returning NBC drama series that had been running at 10:00 P.M. were kicked to an earlier time slot. NBC allowed its five-year-old series *Medium* to defect to CBS. More surprisingly, the second season of the John Wells-produced police drama *Southland* (which had done well in a short spring 2009 run) was abruptly canceled by NBC only fifteen days before it was to return (winding up instead on TNT starting in January 2010). Yet such bean-counter calculations dovetailed with general cost-cutting efforts by all the networks in the wake of the 2007–08 writers' strike season, which motivated the examination of every step of the production process. NBC had been particularly aggressive in such moves, announcing in early 2008, for example, that it planned to scrap the expensive pilot process (which could run as high as $7 million for a series that might never be produced) and take new scripted series ideas directly to the air, without pilots. If Jay Leno's prime time series worked as planned, NBC would have effectively redefined what was considered viable for broadcast network programming. Eliminating new scripted drama from the final hour of weekday prime time, NBC's schedule would more closely resemble the limited (and less expensive) presence of Fox, which ended its prime time network offerings at 10:00 P.M., not 11:00 P.M.

Jay Leno scored well in his September 14 debut, with high viewer sampling on opening night (where a tuxedo-clad Jerry Seinfeld was Leno's primary guest). As expected, those numbers dropped and settled instead into a slightly higher total as compared to his old late night slot. At first, it appeared that NBC's retention strategy for Leno and O'Brien had worked. However, that analysis was short-lived. In fact, the entire plan soon began to unravel because of, ironically, bottom line considerations, this time from affiliates.

While reduced ratings to close the last hour of prime time might have been acceptable to NBC as a network, they had a direct negative effect on one of the most lucrative times for affiliates, their local newscasts. They now had a lead-in generally weaker than the competition. NBC local news ratings dropped, sometimes dramatically. By November, affiliates were practically in open revolt, demanding a change.

That's when the real drama began.

Once again, NBC attempted to keep both stars aboard. Instead of simply canceling *The Jay Leno Show* outright, on January 10, 2010, the network announced that it wanted to move a half-hour version back to the 11:35 P.M. start time, bumping the *Tonight* show to just after midnight. That instantly transformed what had been a prime time programming issue into a late night battle.

Part of the rationale for the proposed time change was that there was ratings trouble in late night as well. Like Leno, O'Brien had settled into a higher ratings total than his old late-late slot, but not as high as this earlier setting demanded. After a strong start in June, O'Brien's *Tonight* show ratings had fallen steadily to about half of what Leno had drawn a year before, and not all of that could be attributed to the decline of the prime time/local news lead in. This allowed David Letterman's program to begin consistently to top the *Tonight* show in total viewers and occasionally in the 18 to 49 demographic. O'Brien did lower the median viewer age of the *Tonight* show by nearly ten years, though.

Conan O'Brien refused to go along with NBC's time shifting proposal, which essentially changed "Tonight" to "Tomorrow." Instead he issued an all-or-nothing press declaration on January 12 (humorously addressed to "People of Earth"), which read, in part:

October 8, 2009

Cable network Versus telecasts the first game ever of the United Football League, as the host Las Vegas Locomotives defeat the California Redwoods 30 to 17.

November 3, 2009

NBC's cult favorite from the 1980s, *V*, returns as an ABC series re-make. Morena Baccarin is Anna, leader of the seemingly friendly alien "Visitors," while Elizabeth Mitchell is FBI agent Erica Evans, who uncovers the sinister intent behind their pacific demeanor.

November 7, 2009

The Wanda Sykes Show. (Fox). After canceling both *MadTV* and Spike Feresten's *Talkshow,* Fox retains its late-Saturday night comedy presence with a one-hour talk show hosted by black stand-up comic Wanda Sykes.

November 9, 2009

Lopez Tonight. (TBS). Hispanic comic George Lopez gets his own hour-long Monday-through-Thursday late-night cable talk show.

November 19, 2009

Daytime TV superstar Oprah Winfrey announces that her twenty-five-year-old daily series will end September 9, 2011, so she can concentrate on her new cable project, OWN (the Oprah Winfrey Network) set to launch in January 2011.

November 22, 2009

More than ten years after *Seinfeld* ended its run on NBC, the iconic sitcom returns—on HBO. The seventh season finale of Larry David's tongue-in-cheek almost-autobiographical series *Curb Your Enthusiasm* presents a show-within-a-show reunion of the four main *Seinfeld* cast members (along with other series regulars). True to form, David used his real-life reunion coup as the basis for fictionalized threads throughout the season (courting the cast; writing sessions with co-creator Jerry Seinfeld). Larry David's fictional motivation for the reunion: hoping to win back his estranged TV wife, Cheryl, by casting her in the episode as George Costanza's ex-wife and love interest.

December 7, 2009

Public television's *NewsHour with Jim Lehrer* becomes the *PBS NewsHour*, adopting a two-anchor format of Lehrer accompanied by a rotation of senior correspondents Gwen Ifill, Judy Woodruff, and Jeffrey Brown. The nearly thirty-five-year-old program also combines broadcast and online newsrooms to turn out original content for both platforms.

December 8, 2009

CBS announces it will cancel its fifty-four-year-old daytime drama *As the World Turns* in September 2010, leaving the network with just two soap operas: *The Young and the Restless* and *The Bold and the Beautiful*.

December 9, 2009

Nearly a decade after the announcement of the merger of Time Warner and AOL, that unsuccessful coupling ends as America Online is spun-off from Time Warner to resume life as a stand-alone company. This follows Time Warner's less ballyhooed spin-off of its successful Time Warner Cable division on March 12, 2009.

	8:00	8:30	9:00	9:30	10:00	10:30	
M O N	Dancing With The Stars				Castle		**ABC**
	How I Met Your Mother	ACCIDENTALLY ON PURPOSE	Two And A Half Men	The Big Bang Theory	CSI: Miami		**CBS**
	House, M.D.		Lie To Me		local		**FOX**
	Heroes		TRAUMA		THE JAY LENO SHOW		**NBC**
	One Tree Hill		Gossip Girl		local		**CW**

T U E	Shark Tank		Dancing With The Stars		THE FORGOTTEN		**ABC**
	NCIS		NCIS: LOS ANGELES		THE GOOD WIFE		**CBS**
	So You Think You Can Dance?				local		**FOX**
	The Biggest Loser				THE JAY LENO SHOW		**NBC**
	90210		Melrose Place		local		**CW**

W E D	HANK	THE MIDDLE	MODERN FAMILY	COUGAR TOWN	EASTWICK		**ABC**
	New Adventures Of Old Christine	Gary Unmarried	Criminal Minds		CSI: NY		**CBS**
	So You Think You Can Dance?		GLEE		local		**FOX**
	MERCY		Law & Order: Special Victims Unit		THE JAY LENO SHOW		**NBC**
	America's Next Top Model		THE BEAUTIFUL LIFE		local		**CW**

T H R	FLASH FORWARD		Grey's Anatomy		Private Practice		**ABC**
	Survivor: Samoa		CSI: Crime Scene Investigation		The Mentalist		**CBS**
	Bones		Fringe		local		**FOX**
	COMMUNITY	Parks And Recreation	The Office	30 Rock	THE JAY LENO SHOW		**NBC**
	THE VAMPIRE DIARIES		Supernatural		local		**CW**

F R I	Supernanny		Ugly Betty		20/20		**ABC**
	Ghost Whisperer		Medium		Numb3rs		**CBS**
	BROTHERS	Till Death	Dollhouse		local		**FOX**
	Law & Order		Dateline NBC		THE JAY LENO SHOW		**NBC**
	Smallville		America's Next Top Model		local		**CW**

S A T	Saturday Night College Football						**ABC**
	Crime Time Saturday		Crime Time Saturday		48 Hours Mystery		**CBS**
	Cops	Cops	America's Most Wanted		local		**FOX**
	MERCY		TRAUMA		Law & Order: Special Victims Unit		**NBC**
	local						**CW**

	7:00	7:30	8:00	8:30	9:00	9:30	10:00	10:30	
S U N	America's Funniest Home Videos		Extreme Makeover: Home Edition		Desperate Housewives		Brothers & Sisters		**ABC**
	60 Minutes		The Amazing Race		THREE RIVERS		Cold Case		**CBS**
	BROTHERS	The Simpsons	The Simpsons	THE CLEVELAND SHOW	Family Guy	American Dad	local		**FOX**
	Football Night In America		Sunday Night Football						**NBC**
	local								**CW**

"For 60 years the 'Tonight Show' has aired immediately following the late local news ... I sincerely believe that delaying the 'Tonight Show' into the next day to accommodate another comedy program will seriously damage what I consider to be the greatest franchise in the history of broadcasting. The 'Tonight Show' at 12:05 simply isn't the 'Tonight Show.'"

The late night wars were on in earnest. For the next ten days they played out very publicly, and it seemed everyone, especially late night hosts from every network, had something to say. Jay Leno joked on his show: "NBC said they wanted drama at 10. Now they've got it." Conan O'Brien jokingly threatened to bleed NBC dry by buying the most expensive props he could find before he was booted off the network. CBS late night host Craig Ferguson described the NBC situation as "atrocious management by a once great American network," also marveling at a world in which "David Letterman and I are considered the stable ones."

By turning the cancellation of Jay Leno's prime time show into a competition between two stars for the *Tonight* show time slot, NBC essentially back-pedaled on its own six-year-old plan for an orderly transition and instead pitted the two personalities against each other. That led to some personal back-and-forth zingers, but ultimately it was NBC itself that became the punch line, chastised for executing decisions in a way that managed to make a tough situation even worse.

It was obvious that Jay Leno and Conan O'Brien could not both host a comedy program that began at 11:35 P.M., so NBC had to choose to keep one and to let the other walk. The network chose Jay Leno and announced an expensive buyout settlement with Conan O'Brien on January 21. O'Brien's last new *Tonight* show was January 22 (where he gave a classy heartfelt thank you to the network and his viewers). As part of O'Brien's departure agreement, he had to wait until September 2010 before he could return to television somewhere else.

Leno continued in prime time until February 9, after which virtually the entire regular NBC schedule (day and night) was replaced for sixteen days by wall-to-wall coverage of the Winter Olympic Games in Vancouver, Canada. On Monday, March 1, the day after the closing ceremonies, Leno returned as *Tonight* host geared to begin yet another round of the Jay versus Dave late night wars. In 2010, after nearly two decades, that conflict already seemed to belong to another era. Both men were in their sixties with established track records, having long since proven themselves in the time period. Were they really expected to engage in another protracted battle? The answer emerged in surprisingly short order: No. Soon after Leno's return, both *Tonight* and the *Late Show* were back to where they had left off in May 2009, with Leno regularly winning the time slot and Letterman comfortably ensconced with his established following. After all the drama, it was back to business as usual, at least for the immediate future.

For all its efforts to save money and to control the situation, NBC had done neither. In fact, it had hurt one of the few time periods it dominated. While recovering for this season, NBC had lost the man once considered its late night heir apparent, with no obvious replacement candidate when Jay Leno did choose to retire for good.

Conan O'Brien followed a script that ultimately departed from the traditional broadcast networks. Initial overtures from Fox ran into the practical complication of crafting an agreement acceptable on a market-by-market basis to all of Fox's individual affiliated stations, which already filled any proposed late night slot with lucrative syndicated reruns (including Fox-produced properties such as *The Simpsons*). Instead, O'Brien chose one-stop shopping with the cable channel TBS, which had a household reach just short of a broadcast network (100 million). He struck a fall 2010 deal for a Monday through Thursday 11:00 P.M. slot, with George Lopez's TBS talk show shifting to follow at midnight. This gave Conan O'Brien the opportunity to grow as part of a new generation of late night entertainment. (He turned forty-seven in 2010 while George Lopez was forty-nine.)

There were also different ratings expectations for cable, where drawing close to O'Brien's unsuccessful *Tonight* show numbers would be regarded as a huge success. More important, Conan O'Brien was expected to continue to attract a younger-skewing audience than either Jay Leno or David Letterman (who were expected to easily top his ratings). In fact, they were less his direct competition than Comedy Central's *Daily Show* and *Colbert Report*, which would play directly opposite his TBS program. All of these shows brought to the table a carefully cultivated "buzz" of hipness, which was considered a saleable cable commodity that counterbalanced lower total audience numbers. To that end, O'Brien deftly played out his time off the air until September (as imposed by his contract settlement with NBC) embarking on a cross-country stage show ("The Legally Prohibited From Being Funny on Television Tour") and communicating with fans via Twitter, where he noted: "In three months I've gone from network television to Twitter to performing live in theaters, and now I'm headed to basic cable. My plan is working perfectly."

Meanwhile, following the return of Jay Leno to late night, NBC had to scramble to fill five hours of prime time each week for the balance of the 2009–10 season. It also quickly solicited program pitches for the next fall (turning to such established names as J. J. Abrams) and once again embraced the pilot production process.

While this drama was unfolding, NBC's assets and management were under close scrutiny for another important business reason. In December 2009, just after GE agreed to buy out Vivendi's remaining 20% interest in NBC Universal, Comcast (the nation's largest cable system operator) struck a deal with GE to set up a joint venture that would merge NBC Universal (the NBC and Telemundo networks and their O&Os, along with cable channels such as USA, Bravo, CNBC, MSNBC, and Syfy, along with the Universal film studio) with Comcast's own programming assets (such as E!, Versus, the Golf Channel, and ten regional sports networks). Comcast would hold the controlling 51% ownership share in the joint venture, and GE would have the right to unload its 49% share over a ten-year period. Although the proposal faced several layers of governmental approval, the merger plan sent a clear signal that Comcast had joined the "big leagues" of the television industry with a potential concentration of powerful media assets including distribution systems for both the Internet and cable. On the content side, it was expected that, after multiple missteps in prime time programming for nearly half a decade, there would be a new focus on the NBC broadcast network side.

In the competition among the Big 4 broadcast networks, there was already considerable ground for NBC to make up, apart from the late night/prime time fiasco. CBS, ABC, and Fox had each launched successful new fall series. CBS added another procedural spin-off, *NCIS: Los Angeles* (with Chris O'Donnell and LL Cool J) and a legal drama, *The Good Wife* (with Julianna Margulies). ABC scored with three Wednesday night comedies: *The Middle* (with Patricia Heaton as a working mom), *Modern Family* (with Ed O'Neill as paterfamilias for three intersecting families), and *Cougar Town* (with Courteney Cox as a forty-something divorcee hanging with her female friends and looking for new love). Fox spun off the animated *Cleveland Show* from *Family Guy* and also successfully pulled off a scripted musical comedy-drama premise with *Glee*, which brought the youthful talent and exuberance of

December 21, 2009

Three days after Charles Gibson retired as anchor of ABC's *World News* (it dropped the "*Tonight*" from the title in July 2006), veteran Diane Sawyer steps in as his replacement. She had signed off from ABC's *Good Morning America* on December 11, with George Stephanopoulos taking over three days later as the morning show co-anchor (with Robin Roberts). In January 2010, Stephanopoulos leaves ABC's Sunday morning show *This Week,* and in March Christiane Amanpour is named as the new host, to come over from CNN in August.

January 10, 2010

Ten months after the sounds of Jimi Hendrix's "All Along the Watchtower" marked the end of the revived *Battlestar Galactica* series, the Syfy channel reconstitutes the franchise beginning with the TV movie "Battlestar Galactica: The Plan" (the story from the point of view of the Cylons) and continues January 22 with the debut of a prequel series, *Caprica.*

January 12, 2010

Changes mark the ninth-season debut of Fox's *American Idol.* Gone is mercurial judge Paula Abdul, unable to come to terms on a new contract. Replacement Ellen DeGeneres is picked after taping of the audition rounds had begun, so guest judges fill in until she makes her series debut on February 9. One day before the season begins, the most famous series judge, Simon Cowell, announces that he will leave when his contract expires at the end of the season to focus on bringing his own talent show *The X Factor* (already a hit in the U.K) to the U.S. in the fall of 2011.

February 7, 2010

"Super Bowl XLIV." (CBS). More than 106 million viewers watch the New Orleans Saints beat the Indianapolis Colts 31 to 17 in Miami, breaking the record for the most-watched U.S. TV show, held for twenty-seven years by the series finale of *M*A*S*H.* Colts fan David Letterman has the game's most talked about ad, a plug for his *Late Show*, with cameos by Oprah Winfrey and rival Jay Leno.

March 24, 2010

In the first significant 3D telecast in the U.S., regional sports network MSG presents hockey's New York Rangers defeating the New York Islanders 5 to 0 from Madison Square Garden, distributed over New York's Cablevision to the few viewers with TVs capable of displaying 3D. (It is also shown to seven hundred patrons wearing 3D glasses at a theater within Madison Square Garden.) Two weeks later, on April 8, ESPN produces what is called the first live national sports event televised in 3D: the opening round of the Masters golf tournament from Augusta, Georgia, via Comcast's cable systems. The 3D Masters serves as preparation for ESPN's 3D cable channel (ESPN 3D), set to debut on June 11 with a World Cup soccer game.

May 23, 2010

The strikingly spiritual two-and-one-half hour finale of ABC's *Lost* ("The End") wraps up the adventure but coyly avoids answers to the island's many mysteries in favor of carefully nuanced character closure. Some escape by plane, others choose to stay, and, through a "sideways" plot, all ultimately reunite in the afterlife. Coming full circle at the end, a wounded Jack Shephard winds up at the spot he first awakened, closes his eyes, and accepts his death, smiling.

American Idol to a scripted setting. (*Glee* had previewed after the May 19, 2009, episode of *American Idol.*) The series followed a fictional Midwest high school glee club, which provided a creditable reason for the characters to break repeatedly into musical numbers for rehearsals, competitive performances, and symbolic fantasies. With a repertoire that drew primarily on popular music covers (such as Journey's "Don't Stop Believin'" and Madonna's "Vogue"), *Glee* generated hit downloads, CDs, and DVDs in real life, giving Fox a cross-platform franchise that it could promote as aggressively as Disney had done with its "High School Musical."

With its new shows, returning hits, Sunday afternoon football, and an exciting World Series contest (with the New York Yankees beating the Philadelphia Phillies), Fox scored surprisingly well through the fall, winning the November sweeps. Looking toward January (and the return of *American Idol*), Fox was already assured of winning its sixth consecutive season in the 18 to 49 demographic. It was at that moment that Fox's News Corporation parent chose to aggressively revive the thorny issue of seeking compensation from cable operators for carrying its Fox broadcast channels, taking on Time Warner Cable in New York. Back in 1993, the government had ruled that over-the-air broadcasters were entitled to compensation from cable companies for retransmission of their signals, or they could pull their channels. A subsequent series of stand-offs back then were largely "solved" by cable operators paying the corporate owners of broadcasters with deals for new affiliated cable channels, but not for their broadcast channels directly.

In 2009, Rupert Murdoch's News Corporation boldly took the position that it no longer made any business sense to treat broadcast stations differently from cable channels, as the distinction between the two categories was now virtually irrelevant for the majority of viewers who received all of their television signals through cable or satellite. Therefore, just like cable channels, broadcast stations on cable should receive a second stream of revenue from cable operators (a portion of their subscriber fees) for providing a viable programming channel. At the time, the calculated fee per subscriber for an individual cable channel ranged from a few cents to the neighborhood of several dollars for the likes of an ESPN. This was in addition to the advertising income the cable channel received.

Murdoch (who was also a leading force in pushing to charge for previously free access to online content of print properties) demanded straight-out compensation for Fox's broadcast stations, and backed that assertion by threatening to pull the plug and remove his stations from Time Warner Cable on January 1. The two sides settled at the eleventh hour, with Time Warner Cable at last agreeing to pay to continue providing Fox O&Os to its viewers. Though the specific details of the agreement were not immediately made public, the message was clear to other broadcasters. Their share of the total TV audience may have been significantly reduced by hundreds of competing cable channels, but they still represented some of the main draws on the dial. In a highly competitive marketplace, they saw no reason to let cable channels thrive on dual streams of income when they were limited to just commercial revenue.

From this perspective, the broadcast networks (through their affiliates) could be thought of as another set of cable channels (and popular ones at that) that just happened to originate as free over-the-air signals. Government regulators and the overall media industry, though, did not yet subscribe to that combined view and continued to consider broadcast and cable separately in ratings calculations, sales tracking, and FCC requirements.

Friday night news analysis by columnists Mark Shields *(left)* and David Brooks *(center)* for the *PBS NewsHour* TV broadcast was often followed by additional discussion, here with correspondent Hari Sreenivasan *(right)*, recorded at the newsroom setting exclusively for the web site (newshour.pbs.org). (*Photo courtesy Mike Fritz,* PBS NewsHour*)*

That view of a split television programming world had been reflected in the extraordinary efforts to prepare the over-the-air viewing public for the final 2009 transformation of the broadcast spectrum to digital, which could not be picked up unaided by millions of existing analog television sets. Most U.S. TV stations had been broadcasting in dual formats (old analog and new digital) on two different sets of frequencies for more than a decade, as the country slowly moved toward a phase-out of the analog format. For years there had been a slowly growing information campaign detailing consumer options: subscribe to cable or satellite, by-passing the airwaves; purchase a new digital-ready set; or attach a converter box to process the digital signals between an antenna and an old set. (Congress authorized $1.5 billion to subsidize the purchase of such boxes, offering households a maximum of two $40 discount coupons each.) Millions heeded the advice, and although there was a last-minute delay postponing the change from February to June 2009, when the final shutdown of the analog transmissions took place, it proved to be less disruptive an event than had been feared for years. This was in large part because by 2009 most households were already there. In twenty-first-century America, the theoretically free access to broadcast TV was largely ignored by the overwhelming majority of viewers who had long ago ended their use of antennas.

Even the upgrade in picture quality of digital television did not seem so dramatic a change because people were already accustomed to watching digital images on high-quality monitors. By 2009 DVD players were ubiquitous and, increasingly, so were flat-screen TVs. In fact, manufacturers looking for the next "big ticket" item were already pushing 3D televisions as the new "ultimate home experience."

The broadcast television technology that had enticed viewers since Milton Berle's *Texaco Star Theater* was gone. Even the digital switchover had as an element the government's desire to reclaim some of the broadcast bandwidth to generate income by auctioning it off for other uses. In a way, the airwaves were too valuable to serve merely as a conduit for free TV signals.

On the content side, there was also the sense that television had reached one of its periodic turning points, wrapping up one era in anticipation of the next. This was the final season for a number of signature prime time series from the past decade including *24*, *Ugly Betty*, and *Lost*, while *American Idol* was losing Simon Cowell at the end of his contract. Reaching even farther back, NBC also canceled the original *Law & Order* at the end of its twentieth season, as it tied *Gunsmoke* as television's longest-running prime time drama series. In daytime television, Oprah Winfrey's announced end to her syndicated talk show in 2011 (after twenty-five years of success) had already started the jockeying to tout potential replacements. Even the late night host fracas seemed as much about a changing approach to broadcast network programming as it was about the personalities involved.

Reports on NBC's battles for its late night slots provided a striking example of how thoroughly embedded digital technology had already become in everyday viewing. Naturally, many tuned in to the respective programs each night (or watched recorded playbacks) to see the back-and-forth jokes. However, many others followed the exchanges without ever looking at their television sets, instead viewing entire episodes or highlight clips via the Internet, not just from Jay Leno and Conan O'Brien, but also from the likes of David Letterman, Jimmy Kimmel, Jimmy Fallon, *Saturday Night Live*, Comedy Central, and TV news coverage.

All of this was possible because digital images had freed video from just TV screens and video tape and allowed it to move freely from platform to platform, breaking from time-specific showcases to "anytime" access. Internet connections allowed program viewing not only on computer screens but also on small handheld devices. Television was now part of a multiplatform, integrated world of audio, video, and personal communication.

Always there, always on.

On Beyond Zebra

REVOLUTION OR EVOLUTION? At the beginning of the twenty-first century, the media business, including television, was in a quandary dealing with that puzzling question. Digital technology, combined with Internet access, had changed communication at every turn. But did that represent a revolution akin to the arrival of the printing press four centuries before (when the mass-produced printed word began to usurp individual oral traditions), or was it simply the latest evolution in more than a century of technical marvels like telephones, radios, and television itself?

Without a doubt, digital growth and the Internet signaled that life in the twenty-first century would follow a set of rules different from those of the past. Historically, though, the question of a potential revolution also harkened back a century to when the emergence of electronic communication, especially broadcasting, set off the first tremors of that era's dramatic cultural changes. Although no one knows where the new technologies will lead in the twenty-first century (as no one did back then), the twists and turns in the previous hundred years demonstrated that opportunities for strategic advantage, innovation, and competitive dominance could come from anywhere. While not an exact road map to the future, those twentieth-century changes offer a helpful, at times cautionary, journal of where we have been and point to reasonable guesses on where we are going.

The sense of a world upended began in the mid-nineteenth century when the dots and dashes of the telegraph, initially over wires, then through the airwaves, made it possible for the first time in human history for people to share in events as they happened without being anywhere near the site themselves. Ship-to-shore dots and dashes carried news of the sinking of the *Titanic* in 1912 to the mainland newspapers before the survivors arrived. When human voices followed those same paths, the personal identification with technology grew even stronger and seemed to border on magic. People did not even have to read to share in the connection.

Curious innovators, hobbyists, and tinkerers filled the airwaves with experimental transmissions in the early 1900s, while the business sides staked out revenue sources. Patents, equipment sales, message transmission, and straight-ahead commercial pitches were part of the money-making mix. Although those early listeners spent endless hours scanning the airwaves pleased with anything they could catch, the importance of content began to emerge. Without compelling, engaging, and relevant material of every sort, many of the technical gizmos would have remained little more than limited-interest workbench toys.

This was an era in which entertainment was beginning to move from the live and local to the prepackaged and national. Previously, in local areas, outside shows had been limited to occasional visits by traveling performers and vaudeville acts that played in theaters scattered throughout the country. Now, on several fronts, finished entertainment created elsewhere was appearing. Prerecorded discs and cylinders brought ready-made musical performances directly to the home. Cinema presentations (first of silent films, then of talking pictures) brought prerecorded elements to larger public venues.

Most wondrous, though, were voices through the air.

In the 1920s, local broadcast radio began to take off throughout the United States, bringing voice and music content directly into homes. Radio stations proved such a potent lure that the U.S. airwaves became a battleground of competing signals elbowing for competitive advantage with talk, music, and product pitches. There seemed an endless supply of over-the-air aspirants and the resulting crisscross cacophony of signal interference brought in the federal government to create order out of the chaos.

Establishing new rules in the late 1920s, the U.S. government set out its expectations for the technical business of broadcasting, including the right to regulate. The government instituted a process to license a limited (but significant) number of over-the-air frequencies, issuing them to private commercial operators. Parceling out stations, the government established how many were allowed in each geographical area, as well as overall ownership limits.

Unlike newspapers, broadcasters were seen as sharing a limited commodity, slices of the airwaves. While it was always possible to "add more paper" for another competing newspaper, with broadcasting there was only so much "air space." Although newspaper companies were among those that successfully pursued station licenses early on, the government soon imposed rules against "cross-media" ownership. Such actions reflected the expanded role government carved out for itself, even as the mechanics of broadcasting fell into place. From that point on, the government would sit in judgment on how well broadcasters used the limited airwaves to "serve the public interest." Stations could pursue profit, but they also had responsibilities to the public that might not be profitable at all.

Still, the U.S. did not follow the model of other countries, which from the start kept the new broadcast media limited and under more direct state control. In Great Britain, for instance, stations were part of the government-funded BBC. Set owners in

Great Britain helped to finance these broadcast services with annual fees on their equipment, beyond the purchase price.

In the U.S. structure there were hundreds of stations throughout the country, run by private interests large and small, eager to make money, primarily through advertising. By the late 1920s, another force entered the picture and accelerated the pursuit of profit: formal radio networks, pioneered by NBC and CBS (later joined by others including Mutual and ABC). In just over a decade they aggressively pursued affiliations with stations throughout the country and changed the makeup of the U.S. airwaves by the 1940s.

Although the networks themselves owned outright a limited number of stations each, their hundreds of affiliates nationwide meant that instead of several hundred stations offering several hundred different programs at one time, there were several hundred showcases all airing the *same* programs, provided by one of the networks. This changed a potentially abundant resource (the number of stations) into a far more limited and exclusive platform for a few program sources. The networks became the gatekeepers for mass media content, establishing their template for profit.

The lure for local stations was easy to see. Local network affiliates quickly came to occupy the top tier of visibility in a market, in part because they shared in a nationwide popular culture identity. While any local station could offer its own on-air talent, national radio networks created a more valuable and exclusive content commodity. They had bigger budgets and greater entertainment clout. They could attract established talent, especially movie stars, by offering an audio-only platform that could promote their latest film projects without competing directly against them. Radio networks could also create new household stars by the very nature of their national reach. Thus network affiliates could tout being the home of such marquee names as Bob Hope, Jack Benny, *Fibber McGee and Molly*, *The Lone Ranger*, *Amos 'n Andy*, and many others.

With this arrangement in place, the networks also set expectations for the home audience. Apart from the purchase price of a radio set, listeners came to regard the cost of individual programs as zero. They were free, covered by advertising. For that reason, shows and schedules were designed to provide a consistent stream of year-round advertising opportunities. So, for example, there was not just one episode of Jack Benny's program each year, there was an entire season of several dozen new weekly episodes beginning each fall, available for sponsorship.

This approach marked a departure from live stage shows and film venues, which sold admission tickets for each showing of the same material that ran repeatedly for weeks, even months. In those circles, a long run was regarded as a mark of quality. In broadcasting, there was always the need to tout something as being new. To fill the many programming slots created by this approach, the networks often settled on shows that followed predictable formula templates but could still be touted as first-run.

The U.S. network programming model, fueled by commercial dollars, helped to create, reach, and sustain a mass media audience. This benefited multiple business layers in the process: individual stations, the networks, program production companies, advertising agencies, and talent. For advertisers, the bottom line was successfully promoting their products. By the 1940s, money spent on radio advertising topped more than $100 million annually. Audiences regarded the trade-off of commercials for free entertainment as an acceptable bargain. After all, newspapers and magazines carried ads, but readers still had to purchase them.

Although radio audiences generally chose network shows, local programs remained in the mix, even on stations with network affiliations. That was in part because the government regularly reminded broadcasters of their obligation to serve the public's "interest, convenience, and necessity," especially locally. There were also some non-network stations available throughout the country.

Nonetheless, the government kept a wary eye on the consolidated power of the networks, primarily influencing them through the ongoing review of individual stations. In the early 1940s, the government effectively forced NBC to give up one of the multiple radio network chains it had formed, and NBC-Blue became ABC. Still, by the mid-1940s, the networks collectively drew about 90% of the radio audience nationwide.

Television was nurtured primarily by the same businesses involved in radio. It was not surprising that they saw the video medium as a way to replicate the money-making success of radio. Radio profits, in fact, helped to underwrite years of early television experimentation. The new medium began to step forward as a commercial force in the late 1940s and early 1950s, testing what type of content would connect with home audiences. There was dramatic growth of commercial television throughout the 1950s.

As with radio, the networks themselves owned only a limited number of television stations. However, when commercial television took off, more than 90% of the local stations chose to become network affiliates. NBC and CBS were once again the lead networks, with ABC and the short-lived DuMont network far behind. There was local programming from the individual television stations but, as with radio, the national network shows were seen as the best route to maximizing commercial success.

By 1960, television was essentially the province of just three main network programming sources, with NBC, CBS, and ABC laying affiliation claim to all but a handful of the five hundred-plus commercial stations on the air. This gave the networks a lock on video content distribution in the United States. With this leverage they could succeed in any part of the day with just about any type of program. As with radio, the hundreds of stations all aired the *same* programs provided each day by one of the networks, effectively leaving viewers with a menu choice of only three main items most of the time. This overall corporate success meant that less profitable portions of the schedule (such as news operations) could be subsidized by more lucrative offerings.

The networks did not fill every hour. Back in the 1960s, most stations, and the networks, signed off each night and signed back on each morning. However, the networks claimed many of the best slots, including all of evening prime time. Video recorders were not available for home use, so in order to see a particular program, viewers had to arrange their lives to accommodate network schedules, complete with commercials. That was television's lifeblood: the assurance to sponsors that their commercial messages had a captive audience.

Even more than radio, the television networks presented a little of everything under one "department store" programming roof. Through a combination of licensing deals, arrangements with affiliates, and their own original productions, the networks were the established gatekeepers for comedy, drama, variety, sports, soap operas, game shows, children's shows, nightly news, early morning news, news specials, daytime talk, late night talk, and, most important, high gloss ads.

In addition, CBS and NBC were especially aggressive competitors, diversifying their businesses into such areas as the phonograph record industry, book publishing, technical equipment, and consumer products. In 1964, CBS bought the New York Yankees baseball team, holding it for nearly a decade.

From the 1930s through the 1970s, then, the broadcast industry in general and the networks in particular operated as extremely successful businesses that held an influential role in everyday

American life. They also attracted considerable scrutiny from the public, the government, and other businesses. Established Hollywood film studios, for example, chafed at television's direct challenge to their theater box office take beginning in the 1950s, only to be later assuaged as they themselves began producing material directly for the medium.

The issues surrounding the networks ultimately came down to matters of money, access, and control. More people wished to have access to the broadcast airwaves with their potential for profit. Home audiences wished to exert more control over their television choices. And it seemed everybody wished to influence how the potent force of the mass media reflected and affected society. Yet even with all these challenges, the networks generally remained in control of their own destinies. Starting in the 1970s, however, their once seemingly unassailable position began to show cracks.

Through rules governing individual broadcast stations, Congress and the FCC pursued policies to chip away at what they saw as the near monopoly on content control by the networks. Two rules were introduced in 1970: the Prime Time Access rule, which required the networks to turn over outright a portion of each night's schedule for non-network shows, and the Financial Interest and Syndication ("Fin-Syn") rules, which restricted network ownership of television shows. Both of these did affect the tone and content of broadcast television in a fairly short time.

These rules also coincided with the growing success of the government's longtime effort to increase competition by increasing the number of available broadcast channels. The strategy was direct: More stations allowed more avenues of access and even set the stage for the possibility of additional competing networks. However, that approach took considerable time to bear fruit. The first major addition of channels took place back in 1952 as part of an overall technical adjustment of the spectrum allocation. At the time, the FCC added some 1,600 television channels (bringing the country's total to more than 2,000) and designated some 200 of these as earmarked for educational broadcasting.

Because most of those new channels were in a different bandwidth (UHF, not the more commonly used VHF), the new stations did not have a major impact for nearly two decades—even then, it still took a 1960s government regulation to require that all new television sets manufactured be capable of receiving both UHF and VHF. Once the number of television sets with that capability began to reach a critical mass, UHF channels became more creditable. Public/educational television stations (most of which were on UHF) were among the first to benefit and began to come into their own during the 1970s as an alternative service with programs ranging from *Masterpiece Theatre* to *Monty Python's Flying Circus*.

Additional channels also allowed growth on the commercial side. News Corporation launched the Fox network in 1987 and, seven years later, Warner Bros. offered the WB, and Paramount began UPN. These new networks actively challenged the three established networks in their over-the-air home turf. Later, at the turn of the century, one element of the government-required transition from analog to digital television was introducing the capability for still more stations, which could be squeezed in as sub-channels at each assigned broadcast frequency.

The 1970s access and ownership rules, and the realization of station growth, were a high-water mark in the government's efforts to spur competition to the established broadcast networks. At the same time, there were tremors of a different sort to the broadcast television alignment. These came from competitive business forces and from the impact of important legal rulings. They revolved around video recording and cable services.

Professional video recording equipment had been in place in the 1950s but did not reach the home market in any significant way until the 1970s. At first, home video recorders were used primarily as playback devices for theatrical feature films (purchased or rented), with the specter that the whole enterprise of off-air video recording would be judged illegal as a violation of copyright law. A U.S. Supreme Court ruling in 1984, though, allowed viewers to record television programming for their own personal use, and video became ensconced in home entertainment systems.

Over time, home video became the primary means for most people to view a theatrical feature film, and studios began to factor that into their budget calculations and release schedules. For television viewing, though, video recording hit the networks hard on multiple levels. It allowed home viewers to tear up the networks' carefully calculated program flow and arrange viewing playback to suit their own personal schedules. Video recordings also gave viewers something else to watch when nothing on the network schedule suited them. Most important, video recording and playback permitted people to fast-forward past commercial messages. This was a direct assault on the economic underpinning of the broadcast TV model, which relied on stations and networks being able to deliver to advertisers a predictable number of viewers exposed to commercials.

Parallel to the ascendance of home video, there was also the growth of cable services. Unlike the dramatic splash of home recording, cable's expansion was more quietly incremental.

For a long time cable television had been far in the media background, starting out in the 1950s and 1960s as a retransmission service of broadcast signals, primarily in rural and mountain area markets in which it was difficult to receive stations, even with an outdoor antenna. Cable brought signals via wires connected directly to homes, in the process turning free television into a fee service, though this was first viewed less as the payment for content than the cost of a technical connection. Still, while everyone else was getting television signals for free through an antenna, cable households had a new monthly "utility" bill.

Little of this mattered while cable was a blip on the radar, simply retransmitting broadcast signals. The cable industry expanded in the 1970s and 1980s, adding original content on new specialty channels while also aggressively shaping the rules of its own environment with effective actions in court, with regulatory agencies, and within political circles.

As a result, on the business side, by the mid-1980s regulations applying to cable systems and individual cable channels were surprisingly limited, many related to behind-the-scenes technical and franchise details. Departing from the broadcast model of relying solely on advertising revenue, cable channels locked in the concept of tapping dual revenue sources: they sold commercials and received licensing fees from cable systems (who, in turn, were paid by individual subscribers). Practically speaking, this established two different television systems with different sets of rules: those for broadcast and those for cable.

Broadcasting was free TV, open and available to anyone. Broadcasters had obligations for local public service, limitations on words and images that were permissible over the air, and decades of precedent for enforcement, with penalties, by the FCC.

Cable did not face the same rules. There was no assumption or requirement that cable channels would be free, nor were there expectations that each individual channel would have some kind of public affairs show or community service element. Instead, original cable content generally took the form of specialty channels. Even public service was mostly handled through special "community access" channels for local issues and services such as C-SPAN for national coverage. Twenty-four-hour cable news channels did provide coverage of important issues, but that was at their discretion, not obligation. These specialized channels were one-station networks that offered the same programming to markets throughout the country, which gave them a greater impact than if one new over-the-air channel appeared on the dial in a local market.

Cable delivery systems such as Time Warner and Comcast expanded their reach over time from the 1970s into the twenty-first century, as households signed up in part to receive some of their otherwise unavailable channels. In the process, cable distribution (later joined by satellite distribution) became the primary source of all television programming for most viewers, including access to local over-the-air affiliates of the broadcast networks. That created an oddly contradictory set-up: broadcast channels carried on cable were still bound by the over-the-air rules, while channels originating on cable were not.

The media industry routinely embraced the distinction between cable and broadcast channels when discussing such topics as ratings and market share. For cable viewers, though, it was a distinction without meaning because they clearly saw all the channels coming through the same pipeline. Viewers also noticed puzzling contradictions: some material they perceived as offensive could be penalized on one channel (a broadcast channel), but not another (a cable channel), or material that was seen as cutting-edge and explicit was allowed on one channel (a cable channel), but barred on another (a broadcast channel). It seemed that government and business had to catch up with the perceptions of the home audience.

Viewers were not the only ones who lumped all the channels together. To varying degrees, so did the corporate owners of the broadcast networks. They had been investing in cable channel ventures since the late 1970s, following an approach similar to the transition from the dominance of radio to television. By the beginning of the twenty-first century the owners of the broadcast networks had each built their own portfolio of cable channels. These holdings provided additional outlets for material (as Fox used FX) or served as upcoming talent tryouts (as NBC used MSNBC). They worked well as part of the networks' own corporate identities, which had become facets of different media conglomerates: Disney/ABC, Viacom/CBS and UPN, Universal/NBC, News Corporation/Fox, and Time Warner/WB. In addition, companies such as Comcast, which controlled cable distribution systems, also emerged as a force in their own right, carrying their own national and regional channels (especially in sports).

To viewers from the early 1950s, a snapshot of television in 2001 would have seemed revolutionary, a different landscape from their era of limited choice and limited access. Program selection was no longer just what aired on ABC, CBS, and NBC. The audience was fragmented and spread across more channels of choice. Rather than an all-in-one lineup on the broadcast networks, viewers could find single channels devoted to specific programming forms. Success still usually rested on attracting as large a number of viewers as possible, but there was also the possibility of succeeding by luring a sufficiently large number of targeted viewers to specific shows and times. Most important, video recording allowed viewers greater personal selection, so that the networks no longer had an exclusive lock on time and content.

Yet, in many ways, the heart of the television system remained intact. In the face of change, it had evolved. While television was no longer the outlet for a handful of networks, even on a typical cable service with nearly one hundred channels many of those still ultimately divided up among just a comparative handful of corporate owners. The original broadcast networks were no longer the only game in town, but the conglomerates that stood in their place seemed to have as much, or more, control and influence on the communication process. They held sway over a wide range of platforms and properties, ranging from publishing and program production to theme parks and sports teams, managing content from creation to completion, spinning off and profiting from ancillary products. Even personal video recording still drew from real time choices and was only as robust as the channel lineup it captured.

At the beginning of the twenty-first century, the media status quo was put to the test again with the rise of digital delivery systems and the Internet.

In its very design, digital technology introduced an untamed new element into the creation, display, and distribution of content. Unlike previous forms of duplication for print text, photos, audio, and video, digital formats allowed copies to be as good as the original—in fact, usually indistinguishable from the original. For that reason, through the 1980s and 1990s, the entertainment industry engaged in a tug-of-war with consumers over material, first on CDs and then on DVDs.

Consumers wanted maximum ease using content they had purchased; the industry wanted to guard against what it saw as the loss of potential sales through unauthorized duplication. This led to various types of "copy protection" codes on the discs to make it difficult for casual consumers to create digital-to-digital copies. These kept the issue at bay for a while.

Nonetheless, digital became the format of choice, in large part because it folded into the expanding information technology vision coming from such Silicon Valley powerhouses as Microsoft and Apple. In the 1990s, the computer industry had even successfully redirected the TV industry's quest for a high definition television system, replacing it with the development of a new digital transmission system that would also incorporate high definition.

As a result, broadcasters found themselves adjusting their technology to digital, from control rooms and studios to transmission towers. That process stretched into the early twenty-first century, with the result that video moved from film and video tape to digital files. On a parallel path, digital equipment on the consumer level very quickly reached a fairly high level of quality.

The Internet further pushed digital concerns.

Early Internet content was simple, in part because anything elaborate risked being too demanding for slower-speed dial-up home connections. As the number of U.S. households with access to high-speed Internet expanded, options for online content mushroomed. Digital data files became easier to upload and download. When online access migrated to cell phones and other portable communication devices, the pace picked up even more.

As with radio in the early 1900s, audio was first out of the digital box, hitting the music industry in a major way, beginning in 1999. Digital torpedoed the longtime audio distribution model. Digital downloads, file sharing, and independent sales sites broke from the standard model of reaching consumers via radio stations and stores. The alternatives transformed every Internet connection into a potential content distribution point. File-sharing sites such as Napster opened the door to exchanges of music files among fans, bypassing official sources and payments to anyone.

The next step, legal downloads, still left out the old guard. In 2003 Apple negotiated for rights to sell music in digital form through its online iTunes store as part of servicing its portable iPod playback devices. At 99¢ per song, the store was an instant success. Suddenly the lead player in musical content was an outsider apart from the established music companies. Apple's system was easy to use and customer-friendly, bringing millions of consumers to the digital download world and making iTunes the most successful source of music sales in the world.

Individual artists and specialty sites also took advantage of the online delivery system that allowed them to take their material directly to their fans—offering either downloads or direct sales of finished discs. Previously, such sales would have been limited to physical onsite promotional events or mail order. Now they could take place anytime online. However, legal downloads did not eliminate unauthorized file sharing, so that remained an open issue. What had irrevocably changed, though, was how consumers bought music.

YouTube provided a similar consumer jolt for video online, though with a different model, emphasizing user-posted video rather than downloads for sale. Anyone could upload a video to the site, tag it, and then anyone else in the world could view it. Clips became viral hits when direct links were circulated via the Internet, leading to tens of thousands (sometimes millions) of visits to specific YouTube videos.

Others saw ways for YouTube to serve their mainstream purposes. Businesses found the site a convenient way to circulate their own videos to personnel in multiple locations, or to issue video press releases. The site was also seen as a perfect medium to disseminate political campaign material, either supporting a candidate or criticizing an opponent.

Some fans also used the YouTube site to share their favorite television moments, posting excerpts from old and new shows and generally not bothering to obtain anyone's permission. Still, YouTube became an instant brand name that turned into an attractive acquisition for search giant Google (in 2006), which then looked to expand the site's mainstream reach. Some content producers concluded that the most effective way to deal with unauthorized postings was to place official highlight clips themselves (such as skits from *Saturday Night Live*). Others such as Viacom took legal action demanding that YouTube remove unauthorized postings.

Apple iTunes, which had shown the recording industry how to package and sell digital music successfully, added video sales to its site (at $1.99 per episode). Microsoft incorporated video files into its Windows software tools for multimedia entertainment recording and playback by users. Meanwhile, the established television networks and their corporate owners attempted multiple models for legal online video viewing. One of the first successful versions was hulu.com, launched by Fox and NBC Universal in 2007.

Involvement by some of the major forces in computer technology and online design signaled that the future of television now involved their concerns as much as the fortunes of longtime broadcasters and newer cable players. Television had been transformed into one more element in a torrential stream of converging digital content (video, print, audio), all under the general heading of media, all fighting for viability.

The Digital Nation was not some projection of the far future. At the end of the first decade of the twenty-first century, it was already in place. To established media companies, these advances in technology truly felt revolutionary and threatened their bottom lines by seriously limiting the leverage of three longtime tools to profit: gatekeeper access to media platforms, control of content, and the assumed reach of their advertising platforms.

Previously, advances in technology had generally served to remove barriers between average consumers and their ability to experience somebody else's packaging of news, information, and popular entertainment. That was still there with tools to download sales of music, video, and ebooks, as well as to access online stores selling just about anything. However, the new technologies also reshaped personal media options. Digital removed the entry barriers for consumers interested in creating and circulating *their own* media products including photos, video, music, and personal ob-

servational writing. With comparatively inexpensive equipment (a personal cell phone), once technically daunting tasks such as shooting a short video and distributing it had become almost as routine as driving a car (leading to countless clips posted every day at the YouTube Internet highway).

Cumulatively these consumer opportunities dimmed the aura associated with established media companies as tastemakers, historical chroniclers, and gatekeepers to access. Consumers could create, post, and sell their own material. Online social media forums stepped in as personalized publications, with individually tailored news, opinions, and video entertainment links. As a result, media companies at every level were faced with the new challenge of convincing consumers to pay for services, information, and entertainment that some had come to regard as easily accessible, instantly disposable, and something they could do on their own. Enterprising online sites took the cable concept of specialized channels to new levels, snatching specific content (as Craig's List had taken classified ads from newspapers).

These considerations extended to the professional level as well. Although producer Joss Whedon had successfully established his approach to television storytelling with *Buffy the Vampire Slayer* and *Angel* early in the 2000s, subsequent network series *Firefly* and *Dollhouse* (both on Fox) had been treated as difficult fits in the flow of broadcast network programming. In contrast, when Whedon served as his own media gatekeeper to produce "Dr. Horrible's Sing-Along Blog," he released it via the Internet in 2008 to instant success. The program was sold in download form and subsequently licensed for DVD distribution. A studio or television network did not enter into the creation, production, and presentation.

Still, going outside the established system to create original work was as old as Hollywood. The far greater challenge from digital was losing control of the distribution of produced content, no matter the source. That had torn apart financial models in every aspect of the media, from newspapers and magazines to music and movies and television. Home entertainment systems routinely included digital recording devices that let viewers easily skip commercials and also allowed the creation of huge, legally recorded personal video libraries. Armed with the proper portable technology, consumers could access video through their "smart phone" devices or even reach their own home systems from practically anywhere, wirelessly, to watch.

Consumers embraced opportunities for access everywhere. There were print publication offers to register at no cost to read publication content online, for free. Other online sites helpfully provided direct links to specific stories in multiple publications, for free. As print and video converged, online columnists regularly included links directly to sites for videos they cited or for video excerpts (often on YouTube), for free. Tech-savvy consumers who were adept at unauthorized access took distribution to the next level, finding and linking to files containing virtually any song, film, or television show, circumventing any authorized payments and circulating links, for free. In less than a decade, online consumers became accustomed to paying virtually nothing for most information and entertainment content.

Oddly, the lure of free entertainment had been one of the draws of early radio and television broadcasts in the twentieth century, with overall costs subsidized by advertising. However, in the twenty-first-century formula of free digital content, there were important differences from that previous model. Print publications were now pulled into the digital mix and tagged as free product, even though they had not given away their hard-copy publications before. Consumers often reached digital content through outside links that bypassed ads from the originating sources. Most impor-

Even in an era of compact digital equipment, fully outfitted production trucks remained components of live, multicamera high-profile events such as major awards shows, political conventions, and sports contests. *(Photo by Peter Sills, Digital Focus)*

tant, the perceived value of specific advertising placements had been undercut by, of course, digital technology.

The Internet allowed for extraordinary tracking of the reach and effectiveness of advertising by longtime ratings service Nielsen, which set up what it called its "three windows" approach to compiling viewing information: traditional television (broadcast and cable, including delayed DVR playback information), online, and mobile. There was also specialized analysis by other companies such as Google. These resources made it possible for advertisers to evaluate the nuances of particular campaigns and to reallocate their budgets accordingly. Television was still in the advertising mix, but so was the collective category of "new media" platforms.

Convergence of all these elements led, for a while in the early 2000s, to a collective lament among media organizations longing for the days of limited choice, fewer content creators, and less competition for ad dollars. And yet, ultimately, technology alone was not the sole force determining the future of media. Digital connectivity might have been revolutionary, but that did not stop companies and individuals from adapting it, using it as a tool, and countering a revolution with their own evolution.

Three national networks as content gatekeepers in the 1960s had been too few. Thousands of aspiring video producers on YouTube was far too many. One new obvious need was help in standing out from the crowd. Some strategies to this end involved shaping content with a distinctive style to match the expectations of targeted audiences. For example, news consumers who preferred less frenetic reporting could be lured by services in the style of PBS, NPR, the BBC, and C-SPAN, while others who sought more aggressively framed and packaged coverage might be drawn to the likes of an MSNBC or Fox News Channel.

Even more directly, "brand name" talent and institutions demonstrated that in a world of thousands of choices, a track record still provided an advantage. Sports leagues and franchises offered examples of luring audiences to new media venues with instantly recognized events including the Super Bowl, the World Series, and

intercollegiate March Madness basketball. Prestige award showcases (including the Oscars and Emmys) served as similar draws. Successful cable channels (such as Nickelodeon, TBS, USA, and HBO) cultivated an overall identity that extended beyond specific shows. Select high-profile individuals effectively served as their own brand-name franchises such as Will Ferrell (who launched the FunnyorDie.com streaming video website) and Oprah Winfrey (with her Oprah Winfrey Network on cable).

Apple, Google, and Microsoft demonstrated how technology companies could effectively expand into the content side through outright acquisition (YouTube), related hardware (the Xbox), and sales platforms (the iTunes store). They brought content directly to home screens, functioning like personalized television channels. Other companies such as Amazon and Netflix (which started by selling/renting video in "fixed form" DVDs) also became additional TV channel choices by integrating the option for direct delivery of video through online streaming to home entertainment systems. Very quickly these companies became part of the mix, just as NBC and CBS had emerged as new players in the early days of radio.

Longtime media concerns could still claim a degree of major gatekeeper status, not by being the only possible avenue for distribution, but by being among the most far reaching. Media conglomerates took full advantage of their consolidated portfolios of diverse holdings, which could include not only cable and broadcast channels but also cable distribution, Internet pathways, and outdoor billboards. Disney, for example, successfully promoted Miley Cyrus as Hannah Montana, backed by its broadcast, cable, radio, theme park, and touring assets. Fox's *American Idol* used similar wide-ranging talent promotion. Digital tools helped anybody with vision to create content aimed at a limited, focused audience, but when the time came to expand further, it was still the major media companies that had the mechanisms in place.

In addition, the media conglomerates and the large technology concerns were possibly in the best position to deal with several of the vexing questions that came from the material free-flowing via the Internet. For example, they had the wherewithal to pursue copyright issues. They could also shepherd news organizations (especially those associated with print publications) that feared a public accustomed to free access to news would never consent to paying for quality content again. In the heyday of broadcast network news through the 1970s, the major networks had dealt with that budget concern by simply subsidizing news operations. Such an option was still available to modern conglomerates, but they also had the potential to be patient in rolling out different types of tiered payment systems, knowing that fundamental changes took time. After all, in the early 1970s, paying for television channels would have been considered absurd, yet two decades later, most viewers had chosen that option. With aggressive executives such as News Corporation's Rupert Murdoch, there was little doubt that any possible revenue avenue would be explored, far short of waiting twenty years. Internet users paid monthly access fees and cell phone users paid monthly service fees, so there were already potential paths to build on.

Digital also provided the entertainment industry with technical opportunities to affect individuals recording and keeping content. The switch to digital transmission allowed for coding that could "flag" a program and potentially limit user options. In 2010, the FCC approved a request to allow cable companies to implement such home output control options on a test basis, blocking recording of one category of new video-on-demand movies (those that aired in the window between theatrical exhibition and release on disc). Practically speaking, this affected only a limited universe, but it did reveal a function most home viewers did not realize was now built into the system: someone else could turn off part of their personal home viewing equipment. The 1998 Digital Millennium Copyright Act also added an assortment of enforcement options and protections, but even after more than a decade of dealing with those rules, modifications and precedents were still playing out.

There were few illusions about eliminating all unauthorized downloads. However, it was important to the entertainment industry that the general public considered Internet file-sharing tools as exotic and mostly inaccessible, and to be further tempered by potentially costly consequences for using them. In line with that, the record industry aggressively pursued a "big stick" strategy, publicly prosecuting select individuals over illegal audio downloads, even though the cases often caused PR headaches and barely dented unauthorized traffic. Nonetheless, all the efforts carried the message that unauthorized file sharing, though free, was not worth the trouble, especially when official distribution channels such as Apple's iTunes were available at a comparatively reasonable fee and seen as safe and legal. Apple, in fact, was particularly effective in enticing consumers to surrender control by wrapping that strategy in the lure of its latest technology.

An industry push to "cloud computing" (storing software and data with an off-site third party rather than on a personal computer) also used a more gentle and positive approach to changing the perceptions of content management. It was sold as convenience. Rather than having legally recorded digital copies of television shows on millions of DVRs, sites such as hulu.com allowed users real-time access to material "in the cloud" but without possessing copies. When such offerings played back, the inclusion of short commercials that could not be skipped marked a retro return to watching series and movies the same way they had played on over-the-air channels in the 1950s.

Although technologies changed, there were still service expectations that remained, often just accompanied by new vocabularies. Press kits morphed into websites, social networking pages, and instant Twitter feeds. Technical experts in online search engine optimization could be as abstruse as a broadcast video engineer referencing subcarrier phase and chrominance levels. The desire to supervise the dollars-and-cents side of new business ventures meant that there would continue to be jobs for lawyers, accountants, and lobbyists. Just as in the formative days of electronic communication in the early 1900s, companies pushed to lock in favorable business rules and proprietary items (such as patents and software coding).

Looking at the emerging digital media landscape, U.S. government agencies were also determined to remain actively involved beyond the transition from over-the-air analog. Soon after assuming his position as FCC chairman in 2009, Julius Genachowski tied the purview of the commission strongly to Internet issues, getting ahead of explicit congressional authorization in some areas. (This was in contrast to cable, where the FCC found itself with limited authority when the medium emerged with full force in the 1980s.) It was possible to argue that such items as "network neutrality" and universal access to high-speed connections were akin to overseeing the broadcasting airwaves the century before. In fact, the proliferation of data-hungry wireless devices consuming bandwidth even echoed the early chaotic days of radio, when the government had sorted through competing frequency demands.

Digital connectivity was truly a revolutionary technical force driving the future of media with high-stakes social and business implications. Going forward in the twenty-first century, these concerns would be continually shaped and filtered through corporate, government, and special-issue groups with nearly a century of experience advancing their respective interests. Based on that history, there would be ongoing efforts to articulate competing visions of the future that just happened to coincide with each party's goals. One strength of the new technology world, though, was providing more avenues for the general public to enter the discussion, expressing its collective judgment on the media's performance through official forums, social network threads, and audience measurement tools. Established players might still end up writing most of the rules, but there was now the opportunity to learn more from and about users in the Digital Nation.

When it came to television, consumers had a lifetime of experience in what they expected from the medium. Surprisingly, it was not always about being a star. Thanks to ever-expanding technologies, the twenty-first-century video world provided countless opportunities for consumers to step "on screen." Yet most generally remained comfortably on the viewing side, not because they had to stay there but because they wanted to. They simply put the medium in perspective, appreciating it as another resource within their everyday lives.

Despite all the advancing technological hoopla, at the core television's greatest strength remained what was there from its beginning: the ability to free viewers from the boundaries of space and time. Either on its own or as a new integrated video element, television provided viewers with visual information and entertainment from any place in the world. At its best, this video vision of life still inspired a sense of wonder. Yet television itself was ultimately just a tool. It was up to individuals to use that tool to help stir imaginations and to pursue possibilities that might otherwise be left only in our dreams.

Index

Citations

This is a proper name, title, and selected topic index.

Names cited include on-camera performers and program participants, behind-the-scenes personnel (writers, producers, directors, executives), news subjects, public officials, and business organizations.

Character names are not indexed.

Titles cited are distinguished by the use of *italics* or "quotation marks."

Titles set in *italics* include television and radio series and miniseries, books, newspapers, and magazines.

Titles set in "quotation marks" include made-for-television movies, individual episodes of series, theatrical feature films, and plays.

Title listings that appear in the fall schedule grids are not indexed.

Selected topic citations are offered as roadmaps. Because this is a chronological history, these can help tie together elements of a story that may be spread over multiple chapters. They also make connections that might not be immediately apparent by a name or title search alone.

Page numbers

All page number references are to the main text, with two exceptions.

A page number in *italics* refers to a photo and caption appearing on that page. Example: Moon landing, *206*

A page number including a two-digit decimal refers to an item appearing on that page in a date box. Example: *Fawlty Towers*, 256.02

The decimal references in the date box citations are an index code and do not appear in the date boxes themselves. Rather, they provide a means to locate the specific date on the page which contains the citation.

For each page containing a date box, the index code references run sequentially from .01 to the last date in the box on that page. On page 256, for example, the sequence is from 256.01 to 256.07, identifying seven dates. The number 256.02 refers to the second date in that box.

Special note for page 315. On this page only there are two date boxes. The numbering begins with the first date in the first box (315.01) and continues uninterrupted through all the dates in the second date box, ending with 315.12 for a total of 12 dates on the entire page (315.01 to 315.07 in the first box; 315.08 to 315.12 in the second box).

AAFC (All-American Football Conference), 27.01

Aaker, Lee, 95

A&E (Arts and Entertainment) (cable channel), 315.09, 387, 390, 445, 448

Abbott, Bud, 24, 68–69, 85

ABC (broadcast network), 14, 15, 21.03; acquisition by Capital Cities, 326.05, 380.05; acquisition by Disney, 374–375, 380.05; as Blue network, 14, 15, 18.05, 80, 471; Disney programs in 1950s, 94–95, 103; drama anthologies, 66.05, 96; first news show, 35.06; first series hit, 50; first series, 15, 18.05; first series in top ten, 41.04; first sitcom in top ten, 118; growth limited by station clearances and affiliate lineups, 83, 84, 117; ITT merger proposal, 184–185; Jerry Lewis comedy venture, 159; late night programming, 113.03, 173.01, 179.01, 189.01, 210.04, 236.03, 237.01, 242.05, 256.07, 262, 270, 287.04; management, 48.06, 112.06, 121.01, 127, 154, 250.05, 256, 265.06, 273, 274–275, 282, 286–288; morning programming, 250.07, 257.02, 332.01, 393.01, 394.06, 399.03, 441.03, 468.01; moves from RCA building, 80; news coverage operations, 165, 188.04, *376*, 415, *415*; news documentaries, 43.07, 137–139; news magazines, 284, 345.06, 390; nightly news, 34, 48.04, 84.05, 123.01, 137, 137.04, 146.04, 173.04, 196.03, 197.03, 205.06, 220.05, 256.01, 264.06, 271.07, 279.06, 282, 311.05, 435.05, *436*, 439.06, 441.03, 468.01; nightly news in prime time, 77.03, 123.01, 137–138; nightly news late late night, 305, 357.03; nightly news late night, 173.02, 282–283, 439.04, 464; premiere week tactic, 176, 185; radio growth, 25–26; scripted series tactic in 2004, 433; second season tactic, 177; sells radio networks and stations, 447.02; stations serving as network home base, 34.06, 35.05; suspends television programming 1947–1948, 27.07, 34.06; third season tactic, 242; United Paramount merger, 61, 80, 82–83, 136; weekend programming, 49.05, 93.05, 137.03, 302.01; *Who Wants to Be a Millionaire* as schedule centerpiece, 403, 419. *See also* ABC Family Channel; Action-adventure format; ARTS; Baseball; Basketball; Boxing; Capital Cities Communications; Daytime; Disney; Football; *Good Morning America*;

Nightline; Olympic Games; Ratings; Fred Silverman; Sports

ABC Album, 83

ABC All Star News, 77.03

ABC.com, 443, 457

ABC Evening News, 197.03, 264.06

ABC Evening Report, 146.04

ABC Family Channel (cable channel), 417.03

ABC Final Report, 140.04

ABC Late Night, 256.07

ABC News This Morning, 305

ABC Nightlife, 179.01

ABC Novels for Television, 208, 242, 259, 265–266

ABC Rocks, 315.11

ABC Scope, 183, 184, 198

ABC's NFL Monday Night Football. See Monday Night Football

ABC Stage '67, 186

ABC Sunday Night Movie, 146

"ABC 2000," 406.01

Abdul, Paula, 420, 468.03

"Abe Lincoln in Illinois," 18.06

Abrams, J. J., 417, 431, 450, 467

Absolutely Fabulous, 363.02

Academy awards shows (Oscars), 78.03, 288

Acapulco, 139

Access to the media, 470–476. *See also* Prime Time Access rules

According to Jim, 417–418

Ace, Goodman, 102.01

Ackles, Jensen, 441

Ackroyd, David, 314

Acrobat Ranch, 49.05

Action-adventure format, 127, 128–129, 136, 139–140

Action in the Afternoon, 78.01

Actor's Studio, 42

Adam-12, 201

Adams, Don, 179–180

Adams, Edie, 85.01, 91

Adams, Mason, 278

Adams, Nick, 134

Adam's Rib, 242

Addams, Charles, 167

Addams Family, The, 167–168, 175

Ade, George, 9

Adelstein, Jonathan, 427

Admiral Broadway Revue, 39, 49

Adonis, Joe, 62

Adsit, Scott, 449

AdultVision (cable channel), 396

"Adventure of the Three Garridebs, The," 9

Adventures in Paradise, 129

Adventures of Champion, The, 103

Adventures of Mark and Brian, 358

Adventures of Ozzie and Harriet, The, 17, 18.02, 24, 76–77

Adventures of Rin Tin Tin, The, 95

Adventures of Robin Hood, The, 103, 163

Adventures of Sherlock Holmes, The, 387

Adventures of Superman, The, 78.04, 135, 177

Adventures of Wonder Woman, The, 272

Advertising: covering programming costs, 2, 455; sponsor control of program production, 24–25. *See also* Commercials

Advocates, The, 211

Aerosmith, 407, 426

Affiliate stations, 4, 305, 356, 345.03, 357.01, 450, 465

Affleck, Ben, 421

Afghanistan. *See* War coverage by conflict: Afghanistan

AFL (American Football League). *See* Football coverage

AfterMASH, 313–314

"Aftermath," 121

Afternoon Film Festival, 102

Agency, The, 417

Agnew, Spiro, 213, *213*, 244

Aidman, Charles, 325

Aiken, Clay, 424

Ailes, Roger, 200, 385

Alan Young Show, The, 50

Alaskans, The, 129, 140

Albert, Eddie, 167, 178.03

Albertson, Jack, 248–249

Albright, Lola, 126

Alcoa Television Playhouse, 112

Alda, Alan, 172, *234*, 234–235, 249, 312, 314

Alda, Robert, 113

Aldrich Family, The, 24, 53

Aldrin, Edwin "Buzz," Jr., 206, *206*

Alexander, Ben, 68, 195

Alexander, Jason, 345.05, 364, 371, 418

Alexander, Rod, 86

ALF, 331

Alfred Hitchcock Presents, 107, 134, 324–325, 326

Ali, Muhammad, 275

Alias, 417, 419

Alice, 261, 271, 288

All-American Football Conference (AAFC), 27.01

All-channel bill for UHF, 153–154, 295, 472

Alliance of Motion Picture and Television Producers (AMPTP), 455–457

All in the Family, 219–221, *219*, 223, 231–233, 234, 247, 255, 261, 271, 271.05, 276, 286.04. *See also Archie Bunker's Place*

All Star Revue, 68

All That Glitters, 268

"All the King's Men," 121

All Things Considered, 221.01

Allen, Debbie, 339, 438

Allen, Doug, 14

Allen, Fred, 24, 30, 34, 36, 55–56, 68, 85

Allen, Gracie, 7.03, 24, 43, 56, *57*, 125

Allen, Irwin, 189, 255

Allen, Kris, 462.01

Allen, Steve, 49.01, 59.01, 63–64, 80, 91, 92–93, 97.03, 106, 109–110, 115, 146.06, 155–156

Allen, Tim, 359

Allen, Woody, 106, 155, 221

Alley, Kirstie, 338

Alliance of Motion Picture and Television Producers (AMPTP), 455–457

Allison, Fran, 28

All My Children, 447

All of Us, 435

Ally, 403.04

Ally McBeal, 394–395, 403.04

Almost Perfect, 381

Altman, Robert, 148, 154, 233–235, 339.02

"Amahl and the Night Visitors," 66.08, 81

A.M. America, 250.07

Amanpour, Christiane, 468.01

"Amazing Falsworth, The," 324

Amazing Race, The, 423

Amazing Stories, 323–324, 326

Amazon.com streaming video, 475

Ambrose, Lauren, 412.03

AMC (American Movie Classics) (cable channel), 383, 447.05, 448–449, 452–453

Amedure, Scott, 375.02

Amen, 331

"American, The," 134

Americana Quiz, 33

American Bandstand, 80, 119–120, 155.07, 332.04

American Cable Systems, Inc., 205.03

American Chronicles, 351

American Dreams, 421

American Gothic, 381–382

"American Graffiti," 243

American Idol, 420, 423–424, 429, 434, 438–439, 442, 457, 461.04, 462.01, 468, 468.03

American Inventor, 438

American Marconi, 2, 2.03. *See also* NBC; RCA

American Minstrels of 1949, 39

American Movie Classics (cable channel). See AMC

American School of the Air, 19

American Town Meeting of the Air, 26

America Online (AOL), 407, 411.06. *See also* AOL Time Warner

America's Funniest Home Videos, 347, 387

America's Funniest People, 353

America's Got Talent, 438, 442, 450

America's Most Wanted, 339

America's Next Top Model, 430, 435, 445.05,

America's Talking (cable channel), 371, 385

America 2-Nite, 268, 271.06

Amerika, 331

Ames, Nancy, 172

Amos, John, 247, 265

Amos 'n Andy Show, The, 6.09, 7, 24, 42–43, 57–59, 77; cartoon variant *Calvin and the Colonel*, 145.05

AMPTP (Alliance of Motion Picture and Television Producers), 455–457

Amsterdam, Morey, 36, 38, 41.06, 47–48, 103, 146, *148*

Amy Fisher and Joey Buttafuoco tabloid scandal, 365

Analog television, 381.05, 462.03, 464. *See also* Digital television

And Here's the Show, 105

Anders, Bill, 206

Anderson, Daryl, 278

Anderson, Eddie "Rochester," 7.04, 84

Anderson, Gillian, 367, *367*

Anderson, Kevin, 395

Anderson, Loni, *277*, 281, 320

Anderson, Maxwell, 58.04, 66.05

Anderson, Pamela, 359, 423.07

Anderson, Paquita, 16

Anderson, Richard Dean, 327, 386

Anderson, Robert, 210

Anderson, Sam, 431

Anderson, Warner, 96

"Andersonville Trial, The," 211

Andrews, Julie, 106

Andrews, Naveen, 431

Andrews, Stanley, 77.02

Andrews, Tige, 202

Andy Griffith Show (includes *Mayberry RFD* and *The New Andy Griffith Show*), *x*, 141, *141*, 157, 167, 222, 327.03

Andy Williams Show, The, 154.05

Angel, 405, 441.06

Angel Street, 21–22

Animal Clinic, 49.05

"Animalympics," 289

Aniston, Jennifer, 362, 373, 427.01

Anna and the King, 234

"Annette," 103

Another World, 251.01, 279.03

"Answer, The," 107

Anthology form. *See* Comedy anthologies; Drama anthologies; Omnibus anthologies

"Antigone," 112

Anti-heroes, 115–117, 141

Anton, Susan, 289

Antonowsky, Marvin, 255

Anything But Love, 345.02

AOL Time Warner, 407, 411.06, 418.03, 423.01, 427.03, 443, 465.09. *See also* Time Warner

Apatow, Judd, 405, 418

"Appalachian Autumn," 235

Applegate, Christina, 334, 455

Apple iTunes, 442, 443, 473–475

Apprentice, The, 429, 434, 438

"Aquaman" as a TV property, 447

Aquanauts, The, 139

Arbus, Allan, 312

Archer, 251

Archie Bunker's Place, 286.04, 288, 292.05, 314. *See also* All in the Family

Arden, Eve, 35.03, 76

Arena football coverage, 423.02

Are You Hot? The Search for America's Sexiest People, 423

Arkin, Adam, 374

Arkin, Alan, 186

Arkin, David, 216

Arledge, Roone, 137, 220.02, 230,

256.03, 259, 265.06, 271.07, 282–283, *283*

Arli$$, 383

Armisen, Fred, 461

Armstrong, Neil, 206, *206*

Armstrong Circle Theater, 121, 159, 210

"Army Game, The," 112

Army-McCarthy hearings, 87, 89

Arnaz, Desi, ix, *x*, 37, 64–66, *67*, 75, 111, 120.04, 133.04, 135

Arnaz, Desi, Jr., ix, 201.03, 243

Arnaz, Lucie, 201.03, 243

Arness, James, 104

Arnett, Peter, 354

Arnett, Will, 427.04

Arnie, 219

Arnold, Danny, 249

Arnold, Roseanne. *See* Barr, Roseanne

Arnold, Tom, 342

"Around the World in 90 Minutes," 121

Arquette, Cliff, 84, 111

Arquette, Rosanna, 367

Arrest and Trial, 162.03

Arrested Development, 427.04, 429, 457.01

Arrow Show, The, 38–39

"Arsenic and Old Lace," 91

Arsenio Hall Show, The, 344, 361

Arthur, Beatrice, 233, *233*, 247, 326

Arthur Godfrey (various titles) 18.07, 19, 21.14, 39, 55, 118, 228.03

Arthur Murray Party, 49.04

ARTS (cable channel), 293, 293.08, 303, 315.09

Asner, Ed, 176, 217, *219*, 265, 278–279, *279*

Aspen, 272

"Assignment, The," 325

Associates, The, 286.05

Astaire, Fred, 196.04

As the World Turns, 103.05, 164, 169, 465.08

Astin, John, 167

AT&T: cable systems, 399.05, 417.04, 421.05; coaxial cable lines, 3, 10.04; radio, 1, 3.04

A-Team, The, 311–312

At Home, 16

At Home with Tex and Jinx, 29

At Issue, 184

At the Movies, 278.04

Aubrey, James, 103, 112.06, 121.03, 132.06, 133, 142, 146, 156, 158, 166–168, 175–176, 181

Auction-Aire, 45

Aurthur, Robert Alan, 97, 112, 134

Austin, Teri, 352

"Autobiography of Miss Jane Pittman," 244.01, 253

Autry, Gene, 103

Avalon, Frankie, 173.03

Avco, 196.02, 295

Avedon, Barbara, 301

Avengers, The, 137.06, 154.06, 164, 179, 196, 197; as *New*

Avengers, 264.08

Award shows. *See* Academy awards; Emmy awards; Golden Globe awards; MTV Music awards

"Awesome Servant," 139

Aykroyd, Dan, 263, 320.01

Azaria, Hank, 349

Baa Baa Black Sheep, 272

Babcock, Barbara, 301

Babes, 351

"Babes in Toyland," 91

Baby Boom, 343

Baby boom generation influence on programming, 101, 308, 335, 337, 339–340

Baccarin, Morena, 465.02

Bach, Catherine, 287

Bacharach, Burt, 15

Bachelor, The, 418, 423, 429

Bachelorette, The, 423

Bachelor Father, 117

Backe, John, 265.05, 287.05

Backus, Jim, 75, 167

B.A.D. Cats, 288

Bader, Diedrich, 381

Baer, Max, *153*, 156

Baez, Joan, 161, 203

Badgley, Penn, 456

Bailey, F. Lee, 275

Bailey, Jack, 18.08, 103.03

Bailey, Pearl, 36

Bailey, Raymond, 156

Baileys of Balboa, The, 176

Bain, Barbara, 256.04, 323

Bain, Conrad, 275, *280*

Bain Capital group, 457.04

Baio, Jimmy, 270

Baio, Scott, 274, 320

Baird, Bil, 38, 86

Baird, Cora, 38, 86

Baird, John Logie, 5, 6, 6.02, 8

Baker, Blanche, 273

Baker, Simon , 461.01

Baker, Tom, 163.02

Bakula, Scott, 344, 417.01

Balaban, Bob, 324

Balding, Rebecca, 278

Baldwin, Alec, 449

Baldwin, Daniel, 367

Ball, Alan, 412.03, 448

Ball, Lucille, ix, *x*, 35.02, 42, 50, 64–66, *67*, 75, 78.05, 109, 111, 120.04, 133.04, 135, 156, 201.03, 243, 244.06, 270.08, 331, 345.04

Balsam, Martin, 286.04

Banacek, 241

Bananarama, 321

Band Aid, 321

Band of Brothers, 448

Bank, Frank, 118

Banner, John, 181

Bannon, Jack, 278

Barbary Coast, 257

Barbeau, Adrienne, 233

Barbera, Joseph, 140–141, 154.04

Barbour, John, 285

Barclay, John, *55*

BarelyPolitical.com, 459

Baretta, 251–252, 256, 258

Barker, Bob, 447.03

Barnaby Jones, 240

Barnett, Ross, 171

Barney Blake, Police Reporter, 33

Barney Miller, 248, 249, 256, 258

Barnstable, Cyb, 276

Barnstable, Tricia, 276

Baron, Sandy, 172, 325

Barr, Roseanne, 341–342, *343*, 345.06, 388

Barrett, Rona, 293.04

Barrie, James, 91

Barris, Chuck, 179.04, 179.07, 205–206, 257.07

Barry, Gene, 125, 201, 210, 226, *226*, 367

Barry, Jack, 113, *113*, 122, 123

Barrymore, Drew, 365

Bartel, Paul, 324

Baryshnikov, Mikhail, 397

Baseball, 373.02

Baseball coverage: ABC, 78.07, 97.05, 257.05, 364.03; CBS, 97.05; CBS Yankees ownership, 163.08, 236.04; CBS $1 billion rights, 346, 354; documentary, 373.02; earthquake interruption 347.01; ESPN, 346, 350.01, 421.04; first broadcasts, 8, 10; Fox, 381.02, 394.04, 397.03, 453.02; Fox Dodgers ownership, 394.04; franchise-operated cable channel, 461.03; MSG, 296.03; NBC, 20, 97.05, 257.05, 364.03, 381.02; playoffs on cable, 453.02; TBS, 453.02

Baseball World Series by network: ABC, 270.07, 316, 347.01; CBS, 369; Fox, 386.03, 418, 468; NBC, 66.06, 136, 227.05, 258, 270.07, 275, 291, 299, 343; pooled, 30, *40*

Baseball World Series by year: (1947) 30; (1949) *40*; (1951) 66.06; (1971) 227.05; (1975) 258; (1977) 270.07; (1978) 275; (1980) 291; (1981) 299; (1983) 316; (1988) 343; (1989) 347.01; (1993) 369; (1996) 386.03; (2001) 418; (2009) 468

Basehart, Richard, 211

Bashir, Martin, 439.04

Basketball coverage by network: ABC, 418.07; CBS, 346; ESPN, 304, 421.04; first broadcast, 10; NBC 353.02, 346; NBA TV, 403.06; TNT, 344.01; USA, 304

Basketball NBA professional, 344.01, 346, 353.02, 403.06, 418.07, 419, 421.04; franchise-operated cable channel, 403.06

Basketball NCAA college, 304, 346; first college game broadcast, 10

Bateman, Jason, 427.04

Bateman, Justine, 308

Batman, 177–178

Bat Masterson, 125

Battle Report Washington, 53

"Battleship Bismarck," 48.03

Battlestar Galactica: 1978 version, 275–276; 2003 version, 427.07, 430, 435, 449, 456, 468.02
"Battlestar Galactica: The Plan," 468.02
Bavier, Frances, *x*, 141
Baxter, Anne, 293.08
Baxter, Meredith, 236.01
Bay City Blues, 316, *316*
Bays, Carter, 442
Baywatch, 347
BBC (broadcast network) British, 3.05, 8, 10.01, 163–164, 408, 470–472
BBC America (cable channel), 449, 461.02
Beacham, Stephanie, 347
Beacon Hill, 264
Bean, Orson, 108
Bearse, Amanda, 334
Beat, The, 457.01
"Beat It," 309.05
Beatles, The, 162–163, 163.01, 172.01, 189.03, 210.01, 380.03
Beatles Anthology, The, 380.03
Beat the Clock, 45, 123.05, 224
Beatts, Anne, 263, 307
Beatty, Morgan, 93.02
Beatty, Warren, 135
Beaumont, Hugh, 118, *119*
Beavers, Louise, 59
Beauty and the Beast, 336
Beavis and Butt-head, 365, 385
Bedford Diaries, The, 443
Beer, Jacqueline, 127
Beery, Noah, 251
Begala, Paul, 436, 437
Begin, Menachem, 271.01, *272*
Begley, Ed, 97
Begley, Ed, Jr., 310, *310*
Belafonte, Harry, 119, 203
Bel Geddes, Barbara, 287
Belegrin, Michelle, 445
Believe It or Not, 286
Belin, Edward, 3.06
Bell, Alexander Graham, 1
Bell, Kristen, 435, 456
Bell, Steve, 257.02, 305
Bellamy, Ralph, 143, 208
Bell and Howell Closeup, 138–139, 150
Bellisario, Donald P., 301, 344
Bell Telephone Hour, The, 24, *25*, 126.02
Belson, Jerry, 147
Belushi, Jim, 274, 417
Belushi, John, 263
Belzer, Richard, 367, 406, 457.01
Benaderet, Bea, 56, 140, 166
Benatar, Pat, 297.05
Benben, Brian, 396
Ben Casey, 144–145, 175
Bendix, William, 50, 77
Benedict, Dirk, 311
Benjamin, Richard, 194, 263, 276
Benny, Jack, 7.04, 17, 24, 43, 56, 84–85, 117, 156, 167
Benoit, Patricia, 67
Benson, 286.03
Benson, Amber, 389
Ben Stiller Show, The, 362

Benti, Joseph, 205.04
Benzali, Daniel, 379
Berfield, Justin, 405
Berg, Gertrude, 6.10, *42*, 43, 53–54, 147
Bergen, Candice, 263, 342
Bergen, Edgar, 23, 24, 27, 34, 43, 56, 103.02
Bergen, Polly, 118
Bergeron, Tom, 438
Bergman, Jules, 146.02, 206
Berle, Milton, *33*, 36, 37–38, 43.05, 66, 68, 94, 106, 121, 125, 142, 293.10, 324, 417.07
Berlin wall dismantled, 347.02
Bernard, Tom, 17
Bernardi, Herschel, 123.02, 126, 219
Bernhard, Sandra, 341
Bernie Mac Show, The, 418, 424
Bernsen, Corbin, 332, 448
Bernstein, Carl, 238, 278
Bernstein, Leonard, 52, 79
Berrenger's, 320
Berry, Chuck, 119
Berry, Ken, 180
Bessell, Ted, 188
Bessette, Lauren, 401
Best, James, 287
Best, Willie, 66
Best of Broadway, 91
Best of Saturday Night Live, 263
Best Sellers, 264–265
BET (Black Entertainment Television) (cable channel), 297.01, 413, 439.05
Betamax case, 315.07
Betty White Show, The, 271–272
Betz, Carl, 123.03
Beulah, 18.12, 58–59
Beutel, Bill, 250.07
Beverly Hillbillies, The, *153*, 156–157, 159–160, 209, 222
Beverly Hills, 90210, 351, 373
Beverly Hills Bordello, 396
Bewitched, 167, 175
Beyoncé (Knowles), 426
Bicentennial Minute, 244.04
Biden, Joe, 459, 463
Bid 'n' Buy, 122
Biel, Jessica, 389
Biff Baker, U.S.A., 163
Big Bang Theory, The, 455–456
Big Beat, 119
Big Brother, 408, 413
Big Easy, The, 386
Big Event, The, 263–265, 273, 275
Biggest Loser, The, 439, 442
Big Hawaii, 287
Big Love, 441.02, 448
Big Party, The, 134
"Big Party, The," 263–264
Big Payoff, The, 132
Big Record, The, 119
Big Shamus, Little Shamus, 288
Big Show, The, 287.01
Big Surprise, The, 101, 113
Big 3 networks (ABC, CBS, NBC), 344, 345, 382, 471–473; Big 4 (ABC, CBS, Fox, NBC), 405, 447, 467

Big Top, 51
Bilko. Also known as *Sergeant Bilko. See Phil Silvers Show*
Billboard music awards, 427
Bill Cosby Show, The, 209, 317
Bill Cosby Show, The New, 317
Bill Dana Show, The, 179
Billingsley, Barbara, 118
Bill Moyers' Journal, 227.03, 244
Billy Williams Quartet, 86
"Bing Crosby Show, The," 85.04
Bingo at Home, 122, 124
Bin Laden, Osama, 415, 424
Binns, Edward, 126
"Biography of a Bookie Joint," 150
"Biography of a Missile," 132.02, 133
Bionic Woman, The, 259, 272, 372, 456
Birney, David, 236.01
Birney, Meredith Baxter, 308
Birth episode of *I Love Lucy*, 75
Bishop, Joey, 147, 156, 189.01, 191, 210.04
Bixby, Bill, 237.04, 271.04
BJ and the Bear, 292
Black, Clint, 426
Black, Lucas, 381
Black Journal, 220
Blacklisting, 31, 52, 53–55, 108–109, 113.06, 123.02, 256.06; as censorship tool, 161–162; as drama subject 143; fear of controversy used as rationale, 53–55
Blackman, Honor, 154.06, 164, 179
Black Sheep Squadron, 272
Blackstone investment group, 457.04
Black themes and characters, (1940s) 18.12, 35.04; (1950s) 57–59, 77, 119; (1960s) 154.02, 179, 181, 183, 193, 195, 198, 201–202, 202, 205, 209, 210; (1970s) 215, 217, 220, 220.01, 227–228, 239, 241, 244.01, 247, 249, 258, 265–266, 270.02, 270.04, 273, 275, 279.02, 279.04, 280; (1980s) 297.01, 309.05, 311.04, 315.02, 317–318, 331, 334, 337, 338–339, 344, 347; (1990s) 350, 351–352, 356–357, 363.04, 381, 388, 394.07; (2000s) 418, 435
Blackwood, Nina, 297.05, 298, 327.04
Blacque, Taurean, 300
Blaiberg, Philip, 200
Blair, Henry, 17
Blair, Linda, 250.01, 253
Blake, Madge, 118
Blake, Robert, 252, 260, 326
Blanc, Mel, 84–85, 140
Blattner, Buddy, 78.07
Bledel, Alexis, 435
Bledsoe, Tempestt, 317
Blind Date, 43.06, 205
"Blithe Spirit," 21
Blocker, Dan, 134
Bloggers as content creators, 436, 459

Blondell, Gloria, 77
Bloodworth-Thomason, Linda, 331, 353, 360, 362, 365
Blue, Ben, 68
Blue Knight, The, 241–242
Blue Light, 181
"Blue Men," 126
Blue Network, 11.08, 18.05, 18.11
Blue Ribbon Bouts, 70, 136
Bob, 365
Bob and Carol and Ted and Alice, 242
Bob Crane Show, The, 246
Bob Cummings Show, The, 93.06
"Bob Hope: Laughing with the Presidents," 386.06
Bob Hope Show, The, 84.06
Bob Howard Show, The, 35.04
Bob Newhart Show, The, 271
Bob Patterson, 418
Bochco, Steven, 286.06, 300, 316, 323, 332, 337, 347, 352–353, 366, 370, 379, 407
Boesch, Rudy, 409, *409*
Bogner, Norman, 264–265
Bold and the Beautiful, The, 465.08
Bold Ones, The, 207, 209, 210, 216, 221
Bolen, Lin, 278.02
Bolger, Ray, 80, 82–83, 134
Bonanza, 134, 187, 339.07
Bond, Ward, 117
Bonerz, Peter, 271
Bonet, Lisa, 317, 339
Bonino, 84
Bonner, Frank, *277*, 280–281
Bono, 427
Bono, Cher. *See* Cher
Bono, Sonny, 260
Bonsall, Brian, 308
Booke, Sorrell, 287
Books for Our Times, 152
Boomtown, 421
Boomtown Rats, The, 321
Boone, Pat, 118
Boone, Richard, 96, 115
Booth, Connie, 256.02
Booth, Shirley, 147
Boreanaz, David, 389, *389*
Borge, Victor, 16
Borgnine, Ernest, 79, 154
Borman, Frank, 206
"Born Innocent," 250.01, 253–254
Borstein, Alex, 405
Bosley, Tom, 243, 323, 344
Bosom Buddies, 302
Bosson, Barbara, 300, 337, 353, 379
Boston Common, 380
Boston Legal, 433
Bottoms, Joseph, 273
Bottoms, Timothy, 277
Bourbon Street Beat, 129, 140
Bowes, Edward, 31
Boxing coverage: ABC, 136, 146.03, 163.09, 275; DuMont, 20, 121.08; Louis-Conn fight, 20, *23*; NBC, 10, 15, 20, 136
Boxleitner, Bruce, 315.03
Boyd, William, 44
Boyer, Charles, 94, 170

Boy George, 321
Boyle, Lara Flynn, 348
Boyle, Peter, 70
Boyle, Peter, *386*, 388
Boy Meets World, 367
Boys Are Back, The, 372
"Boys from Boise, The," 16
Bracco, Lorraine, 397
Bracken's World, 208
Braddock, Mickey, 113. *See also* Dolenz, Micky
Bradshaw, Thornton, 303
Brady Bunch, The, 210.02
Brady, Wayne, 462.05
Braga, Brannon, 441
Brambell, Wilfrid, 163, 227
Brand, Joshua, 310, 356
Brand, Neville, 129
Brand identity: broadcast networks 380, 387, 403–405; cable channels 297, 397, 400; leverage in new media platforms, 475
Brando, Marlon, 109, 279.02
Brands, X, 125
Brandy, 381
Brashun, Midge "Toughy," 44
Braugher, Andre, 366
Braun, Lloyd, 433
Brave Eagle, 103
Bravo (cable channel), 297.04, 421.06, 429, 430
Bravo, Chuy, 447.04
Breakfast Club, 17, 28, 85.05
Breaking Bad, 453, 458
Break the Bank, 26; 41.04, 45, 113
Brendon, Nicholas, 389
Brennan, Walter, 117
Brenneman, Amy, 366, 406
Brenner, 126
Breslin, Edward, 132
Breslin, Jimmy, 285
Bret Maverick, 299. See also Maverick
Brett, Jeremy, 387
"Brian's Song," 228
"Bridge on the River Kwai," 185
Bridges, Beau, 287.02
Bridges, Lloyd, 120.07, 210, 221, 265
Bridges, Steve, 443
Bridges, Todd, 275, *280*
Bridget Loves Bernie, 236.01
Brie, Alison, 452
Briggs, David, 402
Bring 'em Back Alive, 307
"Bring Me the Head of Dobie Gillis," 339.03
Brinkley, David, 103.07, 109, 112.03, 158, 172–173, 211.05, 221.04, 257.06, 285, 286.07, 302.01, 393.04
British broadcasting: begins commercial TV, 102.02, 163; royal coronation coverage of King George VI, 8; royal coronation coverage of Queen Elizabeth, 80; TV set display, *12*
British Broadcasting Corporation. *See* BBC
British broadcasting influence on U.S. commercial network

television, 221–222, 228, 264–265, 402, 408, 412.05, 420. *See also* Public Television
Britton, Barbara, 146
Britton, Connie, 449
Broadcasters: affiliate relations, 4, 305, 356, 345.03, 357.01, 450, 465; audience levels compared with cable, 429–430, 434, 449, 457–458,463; bandwidth auction, 469; content restrictions and standards, 448, 473; government oversight, 471–472
Broadcast networks. *See* ABC; CBS; CW; DuMont; Fox; i: Independent Television; Ion Television; MyNetworkTV (MNT); NBC; NET; Pax; PBS; Telemundo; United Network; Univision; UPN; WB
Broadcast networks in Britain. *See* BBC; Granada Television; ITV
Broadway Open House, 47–48, 59.06, 92. *See also Tonight*
Broadway Preview, 27.02
Broccoli, Albert, 164
Broderick, Beth, 388
Broderick, James, 126
Brodkin, Herb, 96, 126, 143
Brokaw, Tom, 264.01, 302.05, 303.04, 311.06, 347.02, 382, 390, 434.02, *436*, 457.03
Broken Arrow, 113
Brolin, James, 207, 316, 427.06
Bronco, 125, 139
Bronson, Charles, 126
"Brooch, The," 78
Brooklyn Bridge, 357–358
Brooks, Avery, 327, 363.04
Brooks, David, *469*
Brooks, James L., 281, 286.05, 333
Brooks, Mel, 49, 86, 179, 257, 347
Brosnan, Pierce, 310, 326
Brothers, Joyce, 100–101
Brothers, 315.12
Brothers and Sisters (comedy), 275
Brothers and Sisters (drama), 449
Browder, Ben, 399.06
Brown, Blair, 337
Brown, "Downtown" Julie, 327.04, 362
Brown, Georg Stanford, 394.07
Brown, James, 95
Brown, James (singer), 210.01
Brown, Jeffrey, 465.07
Brown, Jerry, 103, 284
Brown, John, 56
Brown, Tony, 220
Brownell, Herbert, 87
Bruckheimer, Jerry, 413
Bruns, Philip, 268
Bry, Ellen, 310
Brynner, Yul, 16
Brzezinski, Zbigniew, 182
Buchanan, Edgar, 166
Buchanan, Patrick, 213
Buckley, William F., 88
Buck Rogers, 276, 292
Buerk, Michael, 321
Buffalo Bill, 337
Buffy the Vampire Slayer, 388, 389,

389, 417.02, 419, 441.06
Buggles, The, 297.05
Bugs Bunny Show, The, 140
Buktenica, Ray, *249*
Buono, Victor, 178
Burden of Proof, 379
Burghoff, Gary, 234, *234*
Burke, Christopher, 347
Burke, Delta, 331
Burke, Paul, 141
Burke's Law, 367
Burnett, Carol, 145.01
Burnett, Mark, 408
"Burning Bed, The," 320.03
Burns, George, 7.03, 24, 43, 56, *57*, 117, 125, 325
Burns, Ken, 355, 373.02
Burns and Allen. See George Burns and Gracie Allen Show
Burr, Raymond, 68, 120, 196, 196.01, 326.03, 332, 344, 370.01
Burrows, Abe, 47
Burrows, James, 309
Burton, LeVar, 265, 340
Busey, Gary, 271
Busfield, Timothy, 335
Bush, George H. W., 339.01, 354–355, 356, 360
Bush, George W., 413, 414–415, 424–425, 435–437, 443, *443*, 459
Bushnell, Candace, 396
Bus Stop, 148–149
Butler, Brett, 367
Buttafuoco, Joey, 365
Butterfield, Alexander, 238
Buttons, Red, 94
Buzzi, Ruth, 192–193
By-Line, 70
Byner, John, 187
Byrd, Ralph, 61
Byrnes, Edward, 127

Caan, James, 429
Cable, 295–296, 297, 430, 445–449, 453–454, 472; as primary means for most viewers to receive stations, 468, 473; audience, 304, 344, 371, 383, 421; basic cable as broadcast competitor, 429–430, 448–449, 458, 467; community service channels, 472–473; competition to news, entertainment, 354, 421; first run from broadcast to cable, 321.03, 326, 332.04, 338, 354.03, 375.04, 386, 387; first run from cable to broadcast, 345, 388, 393, 419, 421.01; growth with limited rules, 296, 472–473; original series production schedule, 307, 361, 396, 434–435, 447; payment issues for carrying local broadcast stations, 370–371, 458, 468; primary distribution systems, 417.04, 419; reruns, 371, 383, 386–387, 400, 406–407, 413, 419, 429–430, 445, 447, 448, 453–454, 457. *See also* Dual revenue stream

Cable channels. *See* A&E; ABC Family Channel; Adult Vision; AMC; America's Talking; ARTS; BBC America; Bravo; Cable Health Network; Cartoon Network; CBN; CBS Cable; Cinemax CNBC; CNN; Comedy Central; Comedy Channel; Country Music Television; Court TV; C-SPAN; Daytime; Discovery Channel; E! Entertainment Television; Entertainment Channel; ESPN; Eye on People; Family Channel; Food Network; Fox Business Network; Fox Family Channel; Fox News Channel; Fox Sports Net; FX; HA!; HBO; Headline News/HLN; History Channel; Home and Garden Network; HSN; Learning Channel; Lifetime; Movie Channel; MSG; MSNBC; MTV; Nashville Network; National Network; Nick at Night; Nickelodeon; Oprah Winfrey Network (OWN), Outdoor Life Network; Oxygen; Playboy Channel; QVC; Sci-Fi Network; ShopNBC; Showtime; Spice; Spike TV; TBS; TNN; TNT; TV Land; USA Network; Value Vision; Versus; VH1; Weather Channel
Cable Health Network (cable channel), 315.09
Cablevision in New York City, 468.05
Cabot, Sebastian, 141, 187
Cadorette, Mary, 320.02
Caesar, Sid, 37, 39, 49, 86, 94, 105, 111, 117, 221.02
Caesar Presents, 105
Caesar's Hour, 94, 111
Cagney and Lacey, 301–302, 315, 372
"Caine Mutiny Court Martial," 106
Cain's Hundred, 148
Caldwell, L. Scott, 431
Caldwell, Taylor, 264, 274
Cale, Paula, 406
Calendar, 145.04
Calhoun, Haystack, 28
Calhoun, Rory, 125
California Fever, 288
Californians, The, 117, 123
Californication, 448
Callies, Sarah Wayne, 441
Calmer, Ned, 14
Calvin, Henry, 117
Calvin and the Colonel, 141, 145.05
Camel News Caravan, 41, 81, 158
Camel Newsreel Theater, 34, 34.05
Camp, Hamilton, 194
Campbell, Billy, 407
Campbell, Flora, 27.03
Campbell, Glen, 205
Campell, Neve, 373
Canadian hockey cable channel, 453.03

Candid Camera/Microphone, 29.06, 347
Can Do, 113
Candy, John, 264.03
Cane, 456
Cannell, Stephen J., 311, 333, 335, 370
Cannon, 226
Cannon, J. D., 225
Canova, Diana, 270
Cantor, Eddie, 14, 24, 55, 85, 94, 119
Capital Cities Communications: acquires ABC, 326.05, 328; sells ABC, 380.05
Capote, Truman, 186
Capp, Al, 60
Caprica, 468.02
Captain and Tennille, The, 260
Captain Kangaroo, 103, 320.05
Captain Nice, 188.05
Captains and the Kings, 264
Captain Video, 44, 104
Cara Williams Show, The, 176
Carbonell, Nestor, 431
Car 54, Where Are You?, 148–149
Cardellini, Linda, 405
Carell, Steve, 442
Carey, Drew, 381, 393, 447.03
Carey, Ron, 187
Caribe, 251
Carlin, George, 263
Carlson, Richard, 84.01, 163
Carlson, Tucker, 436, 437, 438
Carmichael, Hoagy, 119
Carmichael, Stokely, 183
Carne, Judy, 188, 192–193
Carnegie Corporation Report on educational television, 197
Carney, Art, *viii*, 38, 41.06, 50–51, 77.01, 97, *104*, 105, 125, 155, 178, 188.02
Caroline in the City, 380, 394
Caron, Glenn Gordon, 320
Carpenter, Charisma, 389
Carpenter, John, 402
Carpentier, Georges, 20
Carr, Martin, 197.02, 211.04, 212
Carradine, David, 242
Carradine, Keith, 429.02
Carrera, Barbara, 327
Carrey, Jim, 314, 350
Carrier, Corey, 358
Carroll, Diahann, 202
Carroll, James J., 62
Carroll, Leo G., 84.04, 169
Cars, The, 320.01
Carsey, Marcy, 317, 341, 347, 367, 387
Carson, Jack, 55–56
Carson, Johnny, 80, 85.06, 93–94, 103.06, 120.02, 155–156, 228.04, 274, 282, 286, 288, 292.02, 360, 361
Carson, Rachel, 150
Carson's Cellar, 80
Carter, Chris, 367, *367*
Carter, Dixie, 331
Carter, Jack, 39, 49
Carter, Jimmy, 264.04, *272*, 289, 292.04

Carter, Lynda, 320
Carter, Ralph, 247
Carteris, Gabrielle, 351
Cartoon Network (cable channel), 365, 371
Cartoons: daytime, 58.02, 103.01, 132.04, 242.02, 354.04, 359.05, 399.08, 421.01, 458, 463; prime time, 140–142, 145.05, 348–349, *349*, 365, 383–385, *385*, 388, 405, 435.01, 442, 467
Cartwright, Angela, *83*, 117
Cartwright, Nancy, *349*
Caruso, David, 366, 421
Carvey, Dana, 360
Carville, James, 360
Casablanca, 102, 311.01
Case, Steve, 407
Casey, Bernie, *316*
Casey, Bob, 53
Cash, Johnny, 211
Cash and Carry, 21
"Casino Royale," 93.04
Cass, Peggy, 148
Cassavetes, John, 96
Cassidy, Jack, 194, 211
Cassidy, Shaun, 381, 441
Cassidy, Ted, 168
Castellaneta, Dan, 333, 349, *349*
Castro, Fidel, 126.03, 139, 391
Cates, Phoebe, 316
Cattrall, Kim, 396
Caulfield, Emma, 389
Cavalcade of Sports. See Gillette Cavalcade of Sports
Cavalcade of Stars, 39, 44, 48–49, 50–51, 104, 105, 180
Cavemen, 456
Cavett, Dick, 155.02, 186, 197.01, 205.05, 210.04, 237.01, 250.06, 263, 264
CBN (Christian Broadcast Network) cable channel, 296–297, 339.07
CBS (broadcast network), 3, 6.05, 10.05, 27.05, 471; acquisition by Viacom, 406.05, 407, 439.05, 442; acquisition by Westinghouse, 375, 380.04, 394.02; all-remote strategy, 28, 29.01, 32–33, 34.07; baseball $1 billion rights, 346, 354, 369; California (Hollywood) television production site established, 78; daytime programming, 58.05, 66.01, 67.02, 67.05, 86, 103, 103.05, 359.03; demographics challenges, 308, 372–373, 381–382, 387–388, 407; documentaries, 58.06, 97.08, 98, 121.06, 122, 132.02, 133, 139, 150, 197.02, 211.04, 212, 214, 228, 230, 331.01; drama anthologies, 25, 33, 41, 48.03, 78–79, 93.04, 96–97, 107, *111*, 112, 121, 129, 325–326; experimental television station W2XAB, 7.02, 7.08, 11.01, 10–11; eye logo, 66.02; feed goes dark, 338.03; heated competition

with NBC, 42, 75, 81; late late news, 305, 357.03, 375.01; late night programming 70, 205.08, 228.02, 264.08, 278.01, 344.04, 350.02, 353.04, *363*, 361, 369, 415, 456–457, 464–467; loses affiliates to Fox, 369, 372, 381; loses NFL football, 369, 394; management, (pre-1940s) 6.08; (1940s) 21.07, 24; (1950s) 103, 112.06, 121.02, 121.03, 122, 132.06, 133; (1960s) 155.03, 163.05, 176, 183, 205.02, 209; (1970s) 210.06, 211.02, 227.02, 228.07, 237.03, 256, 261–262, 265.05, 272, 279.05; (1980s) 287.05, 311.03, 329, 347.03; (1990s) 353.01, 354, 375.06, 380.04, 387.08, 394.05; morning country variety beats *Today*, 113.02, 120.05; morning programming, 103.04, 145.04, 205.04, 237.05, 244.02, 320.05, 403.05, 418.04; news coverage operations, 10.04, 18, 72, 158–159, 164, 415; news magazines, 145.04, 200, 283–285, 330, 390; nightly news, 14, 34, 34.07, 41, 158, 271.01, 271.02, 292.08, *293*, 338.03, 339.01, 364.04, 375.05, 434.04, *436*, 445.01; Operation 100 tactic, 209; "Paley's Comet" talent raids, 42–43; radio stations ownership numbers, 386.07; sitcom strategy, 35.02, 35.03, 42–43, 56–58, 66, 75, 146, 157, 166–167; *60 Minutes* begins, 200; Smothers Brothers fired, 203; weekend daytime programming, 79, 279.01, 421.01; Yankees ownership, 163.08, 236.04. *See also* Baseball; Basketball; Color television; Football; Olympic Games; Ratings; Silverman, Fred; Sports; Viacom
CBS Cable (cable channel), 303–304, 309.02
CBS Corporation, 439.05, 442
CBS Early Morning News, The, 305
CBS Evening News, The, 163.01, *293*, 338.03, 339.01, 364.04, 375.05, 434.04, 445.01
CBS Film Theater of the Air, 44, 145
CBS Innertube, 443
CBS Late Movie, 228.02
CBS Morning News, The, 163.01, 205.04, 244.02
CBS News Hour, 184, 198, 200
CBS Playhouse, 202, 235
CBS Reports, 132.02, 133, 150, 176, 197.02, 228, 286.08
CBS Television News, 14, 18,
CBS Thursday Night Movies, 178.05
CBS World News Roundup, 10.05
Celanese Theater, 66.05
Celebrity Exposé, 445
Celebrity news TV magazine shows, 284–285, 303

Censorship in variety show performances: Bob Dylan, 155.04; Eddie Cantor, 14; Smothers Brothers, 203
Centennial, 275, 291
Central Park West/CPW, 381
Cera, Michael, 427.04
Cerf, Bennett, 21
Cesana, Renzo, 70
Chad Mitchell Trio, 162
Chains of Love, 411
Chamberlain, Richard, 144, 291
Chambers, Justin, 433
Champion, Gower, 39
Champion, Marge, 39
Chancellor, John, 140.07, 154.01, 211.05, 221.04, 257.06, 271.01, 303.04, 373.02
Chance of a Lifetime, 104
Chandler, Kyle, 357, 433, 449
Changing Rooms, 386.01
Channel numbers: channel one removed from broadcasting allocation, 35.01; renumbered for digital allocations, 381.05, 462.03
Channels. *See* Broadcast networks; Cable channels
Channing, Carol, 134, 221.02
Channing, Stockard, 406
Chao, Rosalind, 313
Chao, Stephen, 359.02
Chapin, Lauren, 118
Chapman, Graham, 250
Chappell, John, 314
Charade Quiz, 33
Charades, 11.07, 12
Charles, Gaius, 449
Charles, Glen, 309
Charles, Les, 309
Charles, Prince of Wales, 390
Charles, Ray, 318, 321; Ray Charles singers, 102.01
Charles in Charge, 320
Charles M. Storm theater company, 16
"Charlie Brown Christmas, A," 179.03
Charlie's Angels, 261, 270.03, 293.01
Charmed, 405, 435
Charteris, Leslie, 164
Chartoff, Melanie, 351
Chase, Chevy, 262, 263, 361, 366, 369
Chase, David, 397, 450–451, 452
Chase, Ilka, 47
Chayefsky, Paddy, 42, 79, 97, 265.01
Checkers speech, 73
Checkmate, 141
Cheers, 308–309, 311, 326, 332, 338, 363, 364.02, 368
Chelsea Handler Show, The, 447.04
Chelsea Lately, 447.04
Chen, Joan, 348
Chen, Julie, 408, 413, 418.04
Cheney, Dick, 354, 359.02, 436, 459
Cheney, Lynne, 359.02

Cher, 255, 332, 427
Chernin, Peter, 386.04
Cherry, Marc, 433
"Chess Game, The," 79
Chesterfield Sound Off Time, 68
Chesterfield Supper Club. See Supper Club
Chet Huntley Reporting, 150–151
Chevalier, Maurice, 106
Chevrolet on Broadway, 42
Chevy Chase Show, The, 369
Chevy Mystery Show, The, 133.08
Chevy Show, 106
Cheyenne, 102, 104, 106, 125, 127, 128, 139
Chianese, Dominic, 399
Chicago Hope, 374, 393.03
Chicago television, 28, 43.01, 43.04, 44, 48.05, *55*; cut back, 49, 59
Chicken Soup, 347
Chico and the Man, 248–249, 260
Chiklis, Michael, 448
Child, Julia, 152
Children's Television Workshop, 209, 211
Childress, Alvin, 57
China Beach, 336–337
China visit coverage of Richard Nixon (1972), *229*
CHiPs, 272, 291
"Choice," 173–174
Chris-Craft, 406.04
Christiansen, Robert, 244.01, 253
"Christmas Carol, A," 16, 30
"Christmas Carol II: The Sequel," 325
"Christmas Memory, A," 186
Christopher, William, 235, 313
Chrysler Theater, 210
Chuck, 456, 457
Chumley, Norris, 303
Chung, Connie, 364.04, 375.05, 413
Churchill, Sarah, 67.01, 79
Cigarette advertising, 47; banned, 220.06, 221–222, 453
Cimarron City, 125
Cinema verite style documentaries, 138–139, 150, 274
Cinemax (cable channel), 297.03
Circus Boy, 113
Cisco Kid, 59.03
Citadel Broadcasting acquires ABC radio stations, 447.02
Civil rights coverage, 171
Civil War, The, 355
Civilisation, 221
C.J., 316
Claire, Helen, 34
Clancy Brothers, 162
Clapp, Gordon, 366
Clarissa Explains It All, 388
Clark, Bobby, 55–56
Clark, Dick, 80, 119–120, 132.03, 133, 314, 322, 332.04, 406.01, 421
Clark, Fred, 56
Clark, Harry, 97
Clark, Jack, 162.02
Clark, Kenneth, 221

Clark, Marcia, 375–376
Clark, Ramsay, 200
Clark, Roy, 205
Clark, Susan, 315.02
Clarke, Sarah, 417
Clarkson, Kelly, 420
Clary, Robert, 181
Class of '96, 362, 363.05
Clavell, James, 291
Clayson, Jane, 403.05
Clayton, Jan, 95
Cleese, John, 250, 256.02
Cleghorne!, 381
Cleghorne, Ellen, 381
Clennon, David, 338
Cleveland Show, The, 467
Cliffhangers, 275
Climax, 91, 93.04, 107, 112, 121, 163
Clinton, Bill, 359–360, *360*, 385, *391*, 391–393, *400*, 400–401, 403.07; plays sax on *Arsenio Hall*, 360. *See also* Whitewater coverage
Clinton, Hillary Rodham, 359, 459–462
Clooney, George, 374
Clooney, Rosemary, 38, 118
Close, Glenn, 316, 448
Closer, The, 448
Closeup, Bell and Howell, 138–139, 150
Cloud computing as video source, 476
Clovers, The, 119
CMT (Country Music Television) (cable channel), 375, 435.03, 439.05
CNBC (cable channel), 345.03, 377, 385, 393, 403.01, 429, 453.04, 457.05
CNN (cable channel), 287.06, 297–298, 305, 354–355, 390, 415, 424, *430*, 436–437, 442, 459, 463, 468.01
CNN Headline News/CNN-2. *See* Headline News/HLN (cable channel); HLN (cable channel)
Coach, 345.01
Coast to Coast, 274
Coaxial cable links, 9–10, 10.04, 15, 20, 21.08, 21.10, 28, 34.02, 59; coast-to-coast connection completed, 63; east/west traffic, 48–49; Midwest network links, 34.02, 40–41; Public television links, 212
Cobb, Buff, 64, 81
Cobb, Lee J., 52, 154.03, 217
Coburn, James, 139
Coca, Imogene, 39, 49, 86, 117
Cochran, Johnnie, 375–376
Cochran, Ron, 146.04, 173.04
Code of ethics (NAB): broadcasting seal, 70–71, 79; family hour added, 254–256
Coe, Fred, 18.06, 21–22, 27, 29, 30, 41, 66, 79, 84, 90–91, 107, 112, 121
Coffield, Kelly, 350
Cohen, Sacha Baron, 423.03

Cohn, Roy, 89
Colantoni, Enrico, 435
Colasanto, Nicholas, 309
Colbert, Claudette, 9
Colbert, Stephen, 443, *443*, 456
Colbert Report, The, *443*, 467
Colbys, The, 320, 327
Cold Case, 429, 434
Cole, Gary, 344, 381
Cole, Michael, 201
Cole, Nat King, 118–119
Coleman, Dabney, 268, 337
Coleman, Gary, 275, *280*
Coleman, Jack, 450
Coleman, John, 305
Coles, Kim, 350
Colgate Comedy/Variety Hour, 55–56, 68–69, 85, 94, 101
Colgate Theater, 42
College Bowl, 60
Collingwood, Charles, 86, 108, 198
Collins, Dorothy, 49.03, 112.02
Collins, Joan, 303
Collins, Michael, 206
Collins, Phil, 319, 321
Collins, Stephen, 343, 388
Collyer, Bud, 112.07
Colonel Humphrey Flack, 87
Color television, 6; conflict between RCA/NBC and CBS color systems, 11, 11.10, 27–28; development of RCA/NBC "compatible" system, 11.06, 27–28, 48.02, 61, 81, 85.03; FCC-approved CBS "non-compatible" system, 61–62, 81, 221.03; FCC reverses itself to RCA-NTSC compatible color system, 81; growth of color, 59.03, 81–82, 90, 102.04, 102.07, 134, 145.02, 146, 154.03, 154.04, 172.02, 176–177, 179.02, 188.04
Colson, Charles, 230, 238, 244
Coltrane, Robbie, 387
Columbia, 296.01
Columbo, 225, 226–227, *226*, 323, 343, 387; introduced, 133.08
Combat!, 154
Combs, Holly Marie, 405
Comcast, 205.03, 347.07, 417.04, 421.05, 447, 473; bid for NBC Universal, 467; hockey joint venture, 453.03; properties, 447; regional sports, 447; Video on demand, 442. *See also* E! Entertainment; Golf Channel; QVC; Versus
Comeback, The, 434–435
Comeback Story, The, 83
Comedy anthologies, 209, 210, 271, 325
Comedy Central (cable channel), 353.03, 360, 371, 385, 388, 393, 423.06; nightly news, 385, 399.02, 439.05, 443, 456–458, 467
Comedy Channel (cable channel), 353.03
Comedy Hour, 84.06
Comedy Playhouse, 227

Comedy Spot, 146
Comedy variety as topical forum, 187, 202–203, 250–251, 263, 350
"Comic Relief," 371
Commander in Chief, 442
Commander Jamaica, 164
Commercial campaigns: Apple "1984," 315.08, 459; Bulova watch first commercial, 12–13; Kraft cheese campaign, 29; Lyndon Johnson daisy campaign ad, 173; Obama "1984" campaign ad, 459; "Swift boat" anti-Kerry campaign ad, 436–437; Texaco middle ad, 36
Commercials, 2, 12–13, 14, 22–23; Arthur Godfrey delivery style, 19; ban on cigarette commercials, 220.06, 221–222; commercial free news coverage, 164, 415; co-op sponsorship, 48; direct sponsorship, 48–49; *Mad Men* advertising tie-ins, 452–453; Microsoft online series sponsorship, 455; participating sponsorship, 49; skipping commercials with recording systems, 442, 472; Super Bowl as a commercial showcase, 426–427, 468.04; sponsor program control in Golden Age of radio, 24–25; sustaining sponsorship, 19, 48
Communications Act of 1934, 7.09. *See also* Telecommunications Act of 1992, 1996
Como, Perry, 18.03, 24, 39, 41.07, 95, 102.01, 105, 118, 125
Compton, Walter, 29.04, 34
Conaway, Jeff, 281
Concentration, 122, 285
Condit, Gary, 413
Condon, Eddie, 101
Confession, 126
Conflict, 102
Conger, Darva, 406.03
Congress: coverage of 1947 opening ceremonies, 27.06; 1979 live coverage begins via C-SPAN, *275*
Congressional hearings: quiz show scandal, 131–132; sex and violence and network influence, 128; 148–149, 201, 207
Conn, Billy, 20, 21.13, *23*
Connolly, Kevin, 429.07
Connors, Chuck, 125, 162.03, 265
Connors, Mike, 195
Conrad, Lauren, 448
Conrad, Michael, 300, *301*
Conrad, Robert, 129, 179, *180*, 191, 225
Conrad, William, 67.03, 104, 226
Conried, Hans, *177*, 276
Conroy, Frances, 412.03
Considine, Bob, 110
Constantine, Michael, 209
Consumer generated content and sales, 474–476
Contender, The, 438

Content distributed free, 471, 474, 476

Content ratings. *See* Rating program content.

Continental, The, 70

Controversial programming: avoiding controversy , 78–79, 98, 107, 112, 121, 126, 133, 134 295; *Beavis and Butt-head* cartoon violence, 365; "Born Innocent" rape sequence, 253; casual sex and single motherhood (Dan Quayle criticizes *Murphy Brown*), 358–359; "fleeting expletives," 427; news coverage "telling both sides," 182; Jack Paar, 133.03; protest music by Bob Dylan, 155.04; protest music by Pete Seeger, 161–162, 187; Ronald Reagan TV biography film, 427; religious issues on *Nothing Sacred*, 395; "risqué" behavior in early television, 14, 21.12, 47; *South Park*, 385; "Sticks and Bones" antiwar drama, 237; Super Bowl Janet Jackson "wardrobe malfunction," 426–427; violence on *Bus Stop*, 148–149; White House Correspondents' Dinner routine by Stephen Colbert, 443

Conversation, 114

Converse, Frank, 195

Convoy, 177

Conway, Tim, 154, 204

Coogan, Jackie, 168

Cook, Fielder, 112, 235

Cooke, Alistair, 79, 211

Cooper, Alice, 236.03

Cooper, Anderson, 436, 437

Cooper, Gary, 78.03, 139

Cooper, Gladys, 170

Cooper, Gordon, 155.06

Coote, Robert, 170

Copage, Marc, 202

Coppola, Francis Ford, 273

Copps, Michael, 427

Cop Rock, 352–353

Cops, 345

Copyright issues with digital, 443, 476

Corbett, Harry, 163, 227

Corbett, John, 397

Corby, Ellen, 236

Corcoran, Noreen, 117

Corday, Barbara, 301

Corey, Wendell, 155

"Corky and White Shadow," 103

Corley, Pat, 342–343

Corner Bar, The, 246

Coronation Street, 163, 197

Corporation for Public Broadcasting (CPB), 198, 212, 221.01, 229, 238

Correll, Charles, 6.09, 42, 57–58, 145.05

Cos, 260, 317

Cosby, 332, 387

Cosby, Bill, 179, 260, 285, 317–318, *319*, 351, 387

Cosby Show, The, 317–318, *319*, 326, 338–339, 351, 387

Cosell, Howard, 113.04, 220.02, 230, 242, 256.03, 257, 259, 293.02

Cossack, Roger, 379

Costas, Bob, 383

Costello, Frank, 62

Costello, Lou, 24, 68–69, 85

Costner, Kevin, 326

Cotten, Joseph, 101

Cougar Town, 467

Coulson, Catherine, 348

Countdown, 436

Counterattack, 31, 52

Coupling, 429

Country Music Television (CMT) (cable channel), 375, 435.03, 439.05

Couric, Katie, 353.05, 387.02, 445.01, 462

Court Martial, 126

Court of Current Issues, 33, 37

Court TV (cable channel), 354.02, 365, 375, 377, 379

Cover Up, 320

Cowan, Louis G., 34, 59, 99, 101, 111, 121.02, 122–123, 132, 132.06, 133

Coward, Noel, 21, 106

Cowell, Simon, 420, 438, 468.03, 469

Cowlings, Al, 370.02

Cox, Archibald, 244

Cox, Courteney, 373, 467

Cox, James, 2, 3.03

Cox, Ronny, 352

Cox, Wally, 66–67, 91

Coy, Wayne, 46

CPW/Central Park West, 381

Cracker, 387, 395

Crane, Bob, *177*, 181

Crane, David, 373

Crane, Les, 156, 173.01, 179.01

Cranston, Bryan, 405, 453

Crawford, Broderick, 102.06, 215

Crawford, Chace, 456

Crawford, Joan, 323

Crawford, Johnny, 125

Crenna, Richard, 76, 117, 176

Crichton, Michael, 373

Crime hearings: hands on screen, 62; political career leverage, *60*

Crime in the Streets, 96

Crime series, (1950s) 120–121, 126, 129–130; (1970s) 225–226, 251; (1980s) 299, 309–310, 318–319, 331–332, 336; (1990s) 353, 397–400

Crime Story, 331–332

Crime Syndicated, 62

Crimetime After Primetime, 353.04, 375.01, 386

Criminal Minds, 442

Cronkite, Walter, 53, 67.06, 73, 77.07, 85.07, 86, 121, 137, 146.02, 151, 158, 163.01, 164, 172–173, 179.02, 181, 199, 203, 206, 228, *229*, 238, 271.01, *272*, 274, 282–283, 293.06, *293*, 343

Crosby, Bing, 24, 56, 85.04, 106,

159, 226

Crosby, Cathy Lee, 286

Crosby, Denise, 340

Crosby, Mary, 287

Cross, David, 380.02, 383, 427.04

Cross, Marcia, 433

Crossfire, 385, 436, 437

Crossing Jordan, 449

Crossley, Archibald, 4

Crossley ratings service, 4

Crotty, Burke, 10

Crusade in Europe/Pacific, 43.07, 137

Cryer, Jon, 346, 429

Crystal, Billy, 270, 396

CSI: Crime Scene Investigation, 413, 417, 421, 434, 442, 445, 461.05

CSI: Miami, 421, 434, 445

CSI: New York, 434

C-SPAN (cable channel), 275, 297, *357*, 390, *424*, 443, *443*; begins C-SPAN 2, 327.05

Cugat, Xavier, 132

Cullen, Bill, 112.05

Cullum, John, 363

Culp, Robert, 179

Cummings, Robert, 75, 97

Cuoco, Kaley, 421, 456

Curb Your Enthusiasm, 411.03, 448, 465.06

Curry, Mark, 367

Curtain Call, 79

Curtin, Jane, 263, 314–315, 380

Curtis, Jamie Lee, 345.02

Curtis, Thomas, 237, 238

Cusack, Joan, 326

Cuse, Carlton, 450

Cusick, Henry Ian, 431

Custer, 194

Cuthbert, Elisha, 417

CW (broadcast network), 441.06, 442, 445, 445.05, 458, 463, 462.06

Cybill, 381

Cyrus, Miley, 448

D.A., The, 225

Da Ali G Show, 423.03

d'Abo, Olivia, 338

Daddy's Girls, 372

Dagmar, 48

Dagmar's Canteen, 48

Daily, Bill, 271

Daily Show, The, 385, 399.02, 399.07, 437, 443, 467; affected by writers' strike, 456, 458

Dale, Alan, 444

Daley, John Francis, 405

Daley, Richard J., 199

Dallas, 287, 288, 291–292, 302, 303, 327, 330–331

Daly, Carson, 397.04, 417.05, 456, 464

Daly, James, 207

Daly, John, 48.04, 84.05, *93*, 123.01, 137–138, 137.04, 189.06

Daly, Timothy, 350.03

Daly, Tyne, 302, 315, 406

Damages, 448

Damon, Cathryn, 270

Dana, Bill, 109, 179, 189.02, 294

Dan August, 239

Dancing with the Stars, 438–439

D'Andrea, Tom, 77

Danes, Claire, 373.01

Danger, 80

Danger Man, 137.01, 164, 170

Daniels, Stan, 281, 286.05

Daniels, William, 310, 367

Dann, Mike, 209, 210.06, 211.02

Danner, Blythe, 343–344

Danny, 418

Danny Kaye Show, The, 186

"Danny Match," 58.02

Danny Thomas Show, The. See Make Room for Daddy/Danny Thomas Show

Danson, Ted, 309, 316, 387

Dante, Joe, 323

Danza, Tony, 281, 320

Darcel, Denise, 47

Daria, 383–385, *385*

Darin, Bobby, 119

"Darker Than Dark," 323

Dark Justice, 353.04

Dark Skies, 388

Darnell, Mike, 406.03

Dateline NBC, 357.06, 363.03

Dating Game, The, 179.04, 205–206

Dave Clark Five, The, 162

David, Larry, 287.04, 345.05, 363, 411.03, 448, 465.06

David Brinkley's Journal, 150–151

David Cassidy: Man Undercover, 241

David Frost Show/Revue, 205.07, 210.03, 224

David Letterman Show, 287.07

Davidson, Amy, 421

Davidson, David, 96, 107

Davidson, John, 286, 287.08

Davidson, Tommy, 350

David Susskind Show, 267

Davies, Michael, 402

Davis, Ann B., 93.06, 210.02

Davis, David, 271

Davis, Geena, 442

Davis, Jim, 287

Davis, Joan, 75

Davis, Judy, 427.06

Davis, Kristin, 396

Davis, Ossie, 273

Davis, Peter, 228

Davis (Reagan), Nancy, 126.01

Davis, Sammy, Jr., 80, 109, 134, 193

Davis, Tom, 263

"Davy Crockett," 95

Dawber, Pam, 277, 331

Dawson, Richard, 181, 193

Dawson's Creek, 405, 441.06

Day, Charlie, 448

Day, Dennis, 7.04, 24, 84

Day, Doris, 201.02

Day, Felicia, 447.06, 455, *455*, 456

Daybreak, 450

Day in Court, 123.05, 126

"Day of Absence, A," 198

Days and Nights of Molly Dodd, The, 337, 338

Days of Our Lives, 453.01
"Days of Wine and Roses, The," 123.04
Daytime (cable channel), 303.03, 315.09
Daytime game shows, 18.08, 58.01, 67.04, 85.06, 103.02, 103.03, 112.05, 112.07, 120.02, 120.06, 123.05, 163.03, 188.03, 257.07
Daytime sitcom reruns, 189.04, 270.08, 359.03
Daytime talk and variety shows, 58.03, 59.01, 62, 85.01, 86, 146.01, 155.02, 196.02, 205.05, 228.02, 228.05, 287.07, 287.08, 303.01, 331.02, 381.03, 411
DBS (Direct Broadcast Satellite), 315.05
Deacon, Richard, 118, 147
Deadly Games, 380
Deadwood, 429.02, 448
Dealer's Choice, 285
Deal or No Deal, 439, 442
Dean, Dizzy, 78.07
Dean, Howard, 436; "rebel yell" speech, 436
Dean, James, 80
Dean, Jimmy, 113.02, 120.05
Dean, John, 238
Deane, Meredith, 407
Dean Martin Show, The, 178.04
Dear John, 343
Death in fictional series: *Archie Bunker's Place*, 292.05; *Chico and the Man*, 249; *Dallas*, 327; *Lost*, 468.06; *M*A*S*H*, 235; *The Sopranos*, 399
Death in real life news reports: Scott Amedure, 375.02; Don Harris, 278.05; John F. Kennedy, 164–165; John F. Kennedy, Jr., 401; John Lennon, 293.02; Mother Teresa, 390; 1972 Olympic Games, 230; off-air shooting, 70; on-air shooting, 46; Lee Harvey Oswald, 165; Benny "Kid" Paret in boxing match, 146.03; Frank Reynolds, 311.05; Franklin D. Roosevelt, 19; Diana Spencer, 390; Vietnam execution, 199
"Death Is My Neighbor," 80
"Death of a Salesman," 326.01
Death of real life series performers: Redd Foxx, 357.02; Freddie Prinze, 249; George Reeves, 135
Death Valley Days, 77.02
Debates. *See* Political coverage of debates
Debost, Michel, 293.08
DeCamp, Rosemary, 93.06
DeCarlo, Yvonne, 168
Deeley, Cat, 438
Defenders, The, 143–144
De Forest, Lee, 1, 2.08
DeGeneres, Ellen, 387.07, 395, 427.01, 468.03
Deintermixture proposal, 153–154
Dekker, Thomas, 453.07
DeKova, Frank, 180
Delancey, John, 340

Delaney, Kim, 366, 421
Delany, Dana, 336
DeLay, Tom, 438
Delugg, Milton, 48
Del-Vikings, The, 119
De Matteo, Drea, 434
Demographics: changing demographics of the 1950s TV audience, 98, 101, 114, 123; "relevancy" season, 215–217; series canceled for missing preferred audience, 209, 222; series retained for attracting preferred audience, 234, 236, 311; Spanish-language households, 444–445; targeting women, 44, 315.02, 406–407, 453.05; targeting younger generation viewers, (1960s) 187, 188, 194–195, 201–203, 207, 209; (1970s) 215–217, 217–221, 256–259, 262–263; (1980s) 333–334, 335; (1990s) 350, 351–352, 359.05, 362, 364, 365, 369.02, 372, 373, 380, 388–389, 403–405; (2000s) 412.06, 418–419, 420, 421–423
Dempsey, Jack, 20
Dempsey, Patrick, 433
Denison, Anthony, 331
Dennis Day Show, The, 84
Dennis James Sports Parade, 10
Dennis the Menace, 134, 321.06
Denny, Reginald, 356
Denoff, Sam, 147, 246, 255
Denver, Bob, 135, 167
Depp, Johnny, 333
Depth of field, 20
Deputy, The, 134
De Ravin, Emilie, 431
Derek, Bo, 445
Dern, Laura, 387.07
De Rossi, Portia, 427.04
Derounian, Steven, 131
Designing Women, 331, 359.03
Desilu Playhouse, 129
Desilu production company, 65, 128
Desire, 445, 445.02
Desperate Housewives, 433, 435
Destination television, 394. *See also* Must See TV on NBC
Devane, William, 256.06
"Devil Wears Prada, The," 444
DeVito, Danny, 281, 309, 448
Devlin Connection, The, 317
Devo, 308
DeVol, Frank, 271.06
Dewey, Thomas, 35
DeWilde, Brandon, 83
DeWitt, Joyce, 270
Dexter, 448, 457
Dey, Susan, 332, 363
Dhiegh, Khigh, 251
Diagnosis Murder, 367, 372, 382, 397.01
Diamond Jubilee, 101
Diana, 242.03
Dick, Andy, 362, 375.03
Dick Cavett Show, The, 197.01, 270.06

Dick Clark Beech-Nut Show, The, 119–120
Dickens, Charles, 16
Dickinson, Angie, 251
Dick Powell's Zane Grey Theater, 113
Dick Tracy, 25, 60–61, 68
Dick Van Dyke Show, The, 146–147, *147*, *148*; *The New*, 227.01, 234
Diddy, P. (Sean Combs), 426
Different World, A, 338–339
Diff'rent Strokes, 275, *280*, 292
Diggs, Taye, 435, 450
Digital Millennium Copyright Act, 476
Digital television: 393.02, 397.07, 423.04; conversion from analog, 381.04, 381.05, 462.03, 463, 464, 469; delivery system, 473–476; DVDs, 387.05, 455; flag content, 476; music files, 442, 473. *See also* High Definition Television
Digital Video Recorders. *See* DVR recording
Diller, Barry, 210, 328, 357.04, 394.03, 418.02
Diller, Phyllis, 159
Dillon, Kevin, 429.07
Dillon, Melinda, 325
DiMaggio, John, 405
Dinah Shore Show, The, 66.07
DioGuardi, Kara, 461.04
DirecTV satellite TV, 423.05; *Friday Night Lights* split cost, 458
Dirty Sexy Money, 455, 457
Discovery Channel (cable channel), 321.05, 399.01, 421.01
Discovery People (cable channel), 399.01
Disney, 315.07, 374–375, 380.05, 403, 413, 417.03, 429, 434.05, 447, 458; Betamax case, 315.07; cross platform promotion, 441.01, 447, 475; first TV special, 59.02; Hulu.com venture, 457.02; Radio Disney, 447.02; sells ABC radio stations, 447.02; targeting "tweens," 441.01, 448
Disney, Walt, 59.02, 94–95
Disney Channel (cable channel), 311.02
Disneyland, 94–95. *See also* Walt Disney
Divorce Court, 126
Dixon, Helen, 93
Dixon, Ivan, 181
Dobie Gillis. See Many Loves of Dobie Gillis
Dobyns, Lloyd, 250.04, 284, 305
Doc Corkle, 75
Doctors, The, 207, 210
Doctor Who, 163.02, 449
Documentaries, 139, 150–151, 212. *See also* ABC; CBS; Fox; Networks; News; Public Television
Dodd, Chris, 459

Dodd, Jimmie, 103
Doherty, Shannen, 351, 373, 405
Dolan, A., 5
Dole, Bob, 382, *382*, 385
Dolenz, Micky, 188. *See also* Braddock, Mickey
"Doll, The," 324
Domestic Life, 314
Dominican Republic. *See* War coverage by conflict: Dominican Republic
Domino, Fats, 119
Donahue, Elinor, 118, 351
Donahue, Phil, 196.02, 305
Donahue, Troy, 140
Donaldson, Sam, 345.06
Donna Reed Show, The, 123.03, 181
Don't Call Me Charlie, 154
"Don't Stop Believin'" (Journey recording), 450, 468
Doogie Howser, M.D., 347
Doohan, James, 190
"Doomsday Flight," 185
Doors, The, 187
Doris Day Show, The, 201.02
Dorn, Michael, 340
Dorsey Brothers, The, 105–106
Dot Comedy, 411.05
Dotto, 120.06, 121.05, 122–124, *125*
"Double Door," 29
Double or Nothing, 15
Double run strategy, 393
Doug, 354.04
Dough Re Mi, 122
Douglas, Donna, *153*, 156
Douglas, Mike, 51, 146.01, 156, 287.08
Douglas, Paul, 137.03
Douglas Edwards and the News, 34
Doumanian, Jean, 292.07
Dow, Tony, 118
Down You Go, 59, 99, 104
Downey, Robert, Jr., 326
Downey, Roma, 373.03
Downs, Hugh, 86, 111, 154.01, 155–156, 221.04, 284
Doyle, David, 261
Do You Trust Your Wife?, 103.02, 120.02
Dozier, William, 78.06, 177–178
Dragnet, 43.08, 67–68, 81, 96, 195, 421
Dragon, Daryl (The Captain), 260
Drama, 9, 16; longest running prime time drama series, 469; long form story arcs, 433, 441–442, 450; MTM ensemble productions, 278–280; sponsors avoid controversy in series, 98, 107, 112, 121, 126, 133, 134; topical subject matter, 143–144, 195–196, 278–280; wholesome image series, 319–320, 382, 388–389
Drama anthologies: (1940s) 14, 18.06, 21–22, 25, 27.02, 27.08, 29, 33, 41, 42, 43.02, 44, 48.03; (1950s) 48.07, 58.04, 66.05, 67.01, 78, 79, 82–83, 90–91,

Drama anthologies: (1950s) *(cont.)* 93.04, 96, 97, 101, 102, 102.07, 111, 112, 113.07, 120.01, 121, 121.09, 123.04, 126.01, 129, 132.01, 133.02; (1960s) 133.05, 134, 140.05, 143, 148–149, 159, 185–186, 209–210, 211; (1970s) 221, 241, 271; (1980s) 316, 323–326; limitations of the form, 98, 112, 143, 159, 325

Dramedy style, 287.02, 337

Draper, Paul, 52

Draper, Polly, 335

Dream On, 371, 373, 396, 397

Dream resolutions: *Dallas* shower scene, 327; *Newhart* finale, 350.04; *St. Elsewhere* finale, 339.06

Dreier, Alex, 204

Drescher, Fran, 369.03

Drew, Robert, 138–139

Drew Carey Show, The, 381, 434.03

Drewry, John, *96*, *195*

Dreyfuss, Richard, 418

"Dr. Horrible's Sing-Along Blog," 456, 474

Dr. I.Q., 24

Dr. Kildare, 144–145, 169

Dr. Quinn, Medicine Woman, 365

Drudge, Matt, 391, 401

Drury, James, 154.03

Dual revenue stream (commercials and cable fees), 370–371, 403.07, 430, 442, 447–448, 458, 468, 472–473

Duchovny, David, 349, 367, 371, 407, 448

Duck Factory, The, 314

Duckman, 371

Duel (Deuel), Peter, 188, 217

"Duel," 323

Duet, 333

Duff, Gordon, 97

Duff, Howard, 201

Duffy, Julia, 307

Duffy, Patrick, 287, 325, 327, 330

Duffy's Tavern, 24

Duggan, Andrew, 129, 147, 236

Duke, Patty, 112, 132, 210

Dukes of Hazzard, The, 287, 288

DuMont, Allen B., 11, 105, 121.04

DuMont (broadcast network), 11–12, 15–16, 21.09, 21.10; biggest series successes, 50–51, 66; drama, 14, 44; experimental station W2XWV, New York, 11.04; management, 121.04; news, 29.04, 34, 59.04, 93.02; Paramount ownership issue, 10.07, 11–12, 39–40, 61, 80, 105; schedule growth, 31, 39, 43; Pittsburgh station WDTV used for leverage, 39, 104; shuts down as TV network, 104–105, 121.04; telecenter venture, 87, 105. *See also* Boxing; Football; Wrestling

Dundee and the Culhane, 194

Dunkleman, Brian, 420, 423

Dunn, Michael, 179

Dunninger, Joseph, 39

Dunphy, Don, 163.09

Duopoly policy, 407

DuPont's Cavalcade of America, 24

DuPont Show of the Month/Week, 120.01, 145.01, 159

Dupuis, Roy, 386

Duran Duran, 321

Durante, Jimmy, 24, 49.02, 55–56, 85, 94, 134

Durocher, Leo, 106

Dushku, Eliza, 389

Dussault, Nancy, 257.02

Duvall, Robert, 235, 344.05

DVD format, 387.05; sales impact on series, 435.01, 455

DVR recording, 429–430, 439, 442, 473–476

Dylan, Bob, 155.04, 321

Dynasty, 303, 320, 327

Dysart, Richard, 332

E! Entertainment Television (cable channel), 377, 383, 387, 390, 447, 447.04, 467; late night talk show, 447.04

Eagles, The, 369

Early Show, The, 403.05, 418.04

Early Today, 403.01

Earnhardt, Dale, 412.01

Earn Your Vacation, 85.06

Earthquake in San Francisco, 347.01

East of Eden, 292

Easton, Elliot, 347.06

East Side, West Side, 159–160

Eastwood, Clint, 125, 324

Eaton, Evelyn, 23

Ebersol, Dick, 292.07

Ebert, Roger, 278.04

Ebsen, Buddy, 95, *153*, 156, 240

Eccleston, Christopher, 449

Edelstein, Lisa, 434

Eden, Barbara, 178.06

Edge, Bob, 30

Edge, The, 362

Edge of Night, The, 103.05

Edison, Thomas, 4

Edmonds, Kenneth "Babyface," 406.06

Ed Sullivan Show, The, 102.03, 155.04, 162, 222; as *Toast of the Town*, 36, 37–38, 52, 55, 68–69, 90, 102.03

Ed Thorgensen and the News, 59.04

Ed Wynn Show, The, 49–50, 125

Educational television. *See* Public Television

Education of Max Bickford, The, 418

Edwards, Anthony, 363, 374

Edwards, Douglas, 18, 28, 34–35, 34.07, *35*, 41, 158, 339.05

Edwards, John, 459, 461

Edwards, Ralph, 11.03, 13, 58.01

Edwards, Stephanie, 250.07

Edwards, Vincent, 145

Effron, Zac, 441.01

Efron, Marshall, 221

Egypt and Israel summit meeting, 271.01, *272*

Ehrlichman, John, 273, 285

Eick, David, 456

Eigen, Jack, 30

Eight Is Enough, 286

8 Simple Rules for Dating My Teenage Daughter, 421

87th Precinct, 148

Eikenberry, Jill, 332

Einstein, Bob, 187, 262

Eisele, Donn F., *204*

Eisenhower, Dwight, *viii*, ix, 21.08, 71–72, 73–75, 76, 87, 97.01, 131, 132, 173

Eisley, Anthony, 129

Eisner, Michael, 374, 429, 434.05

Ekberg, Anita, 102

Elam, Jack, 271

Eleanor and Franklin, 242

Electric Company, The, 317

Electronic television transmission system, 6–7, 6.04, 9–10, 10.01

Eleventh Hour, The, 155

Elgin Hour, The, 96

Elizabeth (queen of England), 80

Elizabeth R, 211

Elizondo, Hector, 374

Ellen, 387.07, 395

Ellen DeGeneres Show, The, 421.01

Ellerbee, Linda, 305, 330, 343

Elliot, Bob, 351

Elliot, Chris, 351

Elliott, Ramblin' Jack, 161

Ellis, Steve, 15

Ellison, Harlan, 325

"Elvis," 281

Elvis, 348

"Elvis and the Beauty Queen," 292

Emanuel, Ari, 429.07

Emanuel, Rahm, 429.07

Emergency, 225

Emerson, Faye, 38, 47

Emerson, Hope, 126

Emerson, Michael, 431

Emery, Bob, 28–29

Emmy awards shows, 43.03, 97.03, 299; includes cable, 344–345

Empty Nest, 343

Engel, Georgia, 271–272

English, Diane, 342, 363, 365

Ennis, John, 380.02

"Enough Rope," 133.08

Enright, Dan, 122–123, 131

Ensign O'Toole, 154

Enterprise, 417.01, 419

Entertainment Channel, The (cable channel), 315.09

Entertainment shows as forums for public discourse, 187, 217, 231–235, 353, 356–358

Entertainment Tonight, 303

Entourage, 429.07, 435, 447, 448

Epps, Omar, 434

Epstein, Brian, 162

Equalizer, The, 327

Equal Time law, 138, 385

E/R (sitcom), 320

ER, 373–374, 393.03, 394

Erickson, Frank, 62

Ernie Kovacs Show, The, 77.05

Ervin, Sam, 238

Escalating costs for series renewals, 394

ESP, 122, 123, 124

ESPN (cable channel), 279.07, 297, 315.10, 338.01, 346, 350.01, 421.04, 439.02, 441.05, 447; ESPN-2, 371; ESPN HD, 423.04; ESPN 3D, 468.05

ESPN Radio, 447.02

Estrada, Erik, 272

Ethnic characters in crime series, 130, 239–241

Ethnic characters in sitcoms, 43, 77–78, 247–250

Ettinger, Amber Lee (Obama Girl), 459

Eureka, 449

Evans, Bergen, 59, 99

Evans, Linda, 303, 327

Evans, Maurice, 79, 178

Evans, Mike, 247

Evening Magazine, 285

Evening Shade, 353

Everett, Chad, 207, 317

Everwood, 421.02

Everybody Hates Chris, 439.01

Everybody Loves Raymond, 386, 388, 417, 434

Everything Money Can't Buy, 246

Evigan, Greg, 339

Executive Suite, 287

Exile, The, 353.04

Explorers, The, 268

Extras, 448

Extreme Football League (XFL) coverage, 412

Extreme Makeover: Home Edition, 433, 439

Extreme sports on MyNetworkTV, 445

Eye on People (cable channel), 387.06, 399.01

Eyewitness, 150–151

EZ Streets, 388

Fabares, Shelly, 123.03, 345.01

Fabian, 119, 148

Facebook, 459

Face of Sweden, 152

Face the Nation, 93.05, 445.01

Facts of Life, 292

Fadiman, Clifton, 47

Fafara, Stanley, 118

Fager, Jeff, 429.05

"Fahrenheit 9/11," 437

Fairbanks, Jerry, 30–31, 50, 75

Fairchild, Morgan, 445

Fair Exchange, 156

Fairness Doctrine, 87–88. *See also* Equal Time law

Falco, Edie, 397

Falcon Crest, 302–303

Falk, Peter, 226, *226*

Falkenburg, E. A. "Jinx," 29, 47

Fallon, Jimmy, 263, 461.06, 464

Fall premieres: effects of September 11, 415–418; last minute strategies, 260; premieres spread over a month, 175–176,

239; premieres spread over a week, 162.01, 172.02, 175–177, 185

Falsey, John, 310, 356

"Fame Is the Name of the Game," 185

Family, 259

Family Affair, 187

Family Channel, The (cable channel), 339.07, 413; as ABC, 417.03; as Fox, 394.08, 417.03

Family Dog, 326

Family Guy, 405, 435.01, 442, 467

Family Holvak, The, 255

Family hour programming rules, 254–256, 261

Family Matters, 347

Family Ties, 308, 318, 326, 338

Famous Film Festival, 102, 145

Famous Teddy Z, The, 346

Fantasy Island, 271, 286, 288, 292.03

Faraway Hill, 27.03, 28

Farina, Dennis, 331

Farley, Chris, 263

Farnsworth, Philo T., 6–7, 6.04

Farr, Jamie, 312, 313

Farrell, Charles, 66

Farrell, Mike, *234*, 235, 406

Farrow, Mia, 169

Farscape, 399.06

Fashion House, 445, 445.02

Fat Albert and the Cosby Kids, 317

Fatal Vision, 332

Father Dowling Mysteries, The, 344

Father Knows Best, 93.03, 118

Father Murphy, 299

Faulk, John Henry, 27.04, 85.07, 86, 108–109, 113.06, 256.06

Faulkner, William, 78

Faustino, David, 334

Fawcett, Farrah, 261, 270.03, 320.03

Fawlty Towers, 256.02

Fay, 255

Faye, Herbie, 106

Faye, Joey, 15

Fayed, Dodi, 390

Faylen, Frank, 135

FBI, The, 178.07, 195, 234

FCC, 7.09, 10–11, 294, 470–476; bandwidth auction, 469; chairmen, 140.02, 155.05, 184, 427, 476; fines against stations, 427; fourth commercial network efforts, 294–295; network ownership, 407, 427; public interest, convenience, and necessity, 3, 294, 470; radio ownership, 382, 386.07; signal interference, 37

See also: ABC: ITT merger proposal; ABC: United Paramount merger; All Channel bill for UHF; Cable; Channel numbers; Color television; Deintermixture proposal; Digital television; DuMont Paramount ownership issue; Duopoly policy; Equal Time law; Fairness Doctrine; Family hour programming rules; Financial Interest and Syndication Rules; Freeze on station applications; Frequency allocation issues; Game shows; High Definition Television; Must Carry requirement for cable; Prime Time Access rules; Program ownership rules; Public Television; Retransmission consent settlement between cable and broadcasters; Secondary stations; Signal interference issue; Stations; UHF; VHF

Fear Factor, 412, 418, 423

"Fear on Trial," 256.06

Federal Communications Commission. *See* FCC

Federal Radio Commission. *See* FCC

Feig, Paul, 405

Feldon, Barbara, 180

Felicity, 405, 441.06

Felix the Cat statue, 6

Fell, Norman, 270

Felony Squad, 195, 201

Female themes and characters, (1960s) 164, 188, 179, 201.02; (1970s) 217–219, 232, 233, *233*, 242.03, *249*, 249–250, 258, 261; (1980s) 301–302, 314–315, 331, 332, 333, 336, 341–342, 342–343; (1990s) 365, 367, 373, 386, 396–397

Femina, Jerry Della, 453

Fenn, Sherilyn, 348, 397

Fenneman, George, 60

Feresten, Spike, 445.04, 465.03

Ferguson, Colin, 449

Ferguson, Craig, 434.03, 457, 467

Ferguson, Warren J., 255

Fernwood 2-Nite, 268

Ferrara, Jerry, 429.07

Ferrell, Will, 263, 475

Ferrera, America, 444

Ferrigno, Lou, 271.04

Ferris Bueller, 351

Fessenden, Reginald, 1, 2.07

Fey, Tina, 263, 449, 463

Fibber McGee and Molly, 18.12, 24, 59

Field, Sally, 449

Fields, Joel, 444

Fifty Grand, 78

Fight of the Week, 146.03, 163.09

Fillion, Nathan, 251.03

Finales: *As the World Turns*, 465.08; *Cheers*, 364.02; *Ellen*, 395; *ER*, 461.07; *Frasier*, 429, 429.04; *Friends*, 429, 429.03, 430; *The Fugitive*, 189.05, 190–191; *The Guiding Light*, 462.05; *Howdy Doody*, 133.09, 135; Johnny Carson on *Tonight*, 360; *The Larry Sanders Show*, 395; *Lost*, 468.06, 469; *Lucy-Desi Comedy Hour*, 133.04; *M*A*S*H*, 312; *Mary Tyler Moore*, 265.03; *The Price Is Right* (Bob Barker finale), 447.03; *Roseanne*, 388; *Seinfeld*, 395; *Sex and the City*, 420.01, 430; *Sopranos*, 450–451; *Ted Mack*, 211.05; *What's My Line?*, 189.06

Financial Interest and Syndication Rules (Fin-Syn), 211.01, 222, 350, 369–370, 380.01, 394

Finch, Peter, 265.01

"Fine Tuning," 324

Fink, H. Julian, 121.09

Fireball Fun-for-All, 39

Fired Up, 388, 394

Firefly, 421, 421.03

Fireside Theater, 42, 50, 78

First Camera, 330

First Churchills, The, 211

Firsts in TV, radio, and media history:
first ad (print) for a ready-made TV set, 6.06
first airing of "The Wizard of Oz" on TV, 111
first appearance of the word "television," 2.04
first baseball game on TV (Japan), 8
first baseball game on TV (U.S.), 10
first black host of a network television series (Bob Howard), 35.04
first black network correspondent (Mal Goode), 154.02
first Bob Hope major TV appearance, 48.08
first broadcast network series rerun on cable days later (*Hi Honey, I'm Home*), 354.03
first broadcast network series to continue with new episodes on cable (*Paper Chase*), 306–307
first cable channel exclusively for one sport (basketball), 403.06
first cable series to beat prime time broadcast competition (*The Sopranos*), 419
first cartoon show on Saturday morning network TV (*Mighty Mouse*), 103.01
first children's show TV hit (*Small Fry Club*), 29
first color television image, 6
first color television sets (compatible) on sale, 85.03
first commercial on U.S. radio, 3.04
first commercial on U.S. TV, 12
first commercial television broadcast in the U.S., 11.07
first commercial U.S. high definition digital television station (WRLD), 381.04
first coverage of the U.S. Congress, 27.06
first coverage of the U.S. Congress live via C-SPAN, *275*
first daytime network television program (*Swift Home Service Club*), 29
first daytime soap opera on network television (*These Are My Children*), 43.04, 44
first demonstration in public of a working television system, 5, 6.02
first demonstration of an all-electronic television system, 6.04
first demonstration of an experimental television system in the U.S., 6.01
first Elvis Presley appearance on network television, 106
first Emmy awards presentation, 43.03
first female network news anchor (Pauline Frederick), 34, 137
first female to solo anchor a nightly broadcast network news show (Katie Couric), 445.01
first image orthicon camera broadcast, 21.06
first intercity TV transmission in U.S., 5, 7
first James Bond media appearance, 93.04
first late late night show (*Midnight Special*), 237.02
first late night network program (*Perry Como*), 39
first late night weeknight news, 140.04
first made-for-TV movie ("See How They Run"), 172.04
first million-dollar newswoman (Barbara Walters), 264.06, 282
first Miss America live television coverage, *93*
first mobile TV vans in Germany, 8
first mobile TV vans in the U.S., 9
first murder broadcast as it occurred (Lee Harvey Oswald), 165
first network produced news show, 18
first nightly network news show, 29.04
first one-minute series (*Bicentennial Minute*), 244.04
first opera written for television ("Amahl and the Night Visitors"), 66.08
first outdoor scene on TV, 6
first play for television, 6
first political convention official acceptance speech live on radio (Franklin Roosevelt in Chicago at 1932 Democratic convention), 7.05
first political convention televised (Republicans in Philadelphia in 1940), 11.05, 12

Firsts in TV, radio, and media history (cont.)
first presidential election coverage on radio (1920 on KDKA), 2, 3.03
first presidential inauguration carried live coast to coast (Dwight Eisenhower), 75
first presidential news conference filmed for TV, 97.01
first president to appear on TV (Franklin Roosevelt), 10
first professional football game in prime time, 27.01
first professional sport with weekly network coverage (football), 41.03
first radio entertainment program, 2.07
first radio programming via national network, 6.03
first ratings report with basic cable beating the broadcast networks, 393
first series to play on four broadcast networks (Arthur Murray Party), 49.04
first sitcom made for cable (Brothers), 315.12
first sitcom on weekly TV (Mary Kay and Johnny), 34.03
first soap opera in daytime TV to run ninety minutes (Another World), 279.03
first soap opera in daytime TV to run sixty minutes (Another World), 251.01
first soap operas in daytime TV to run thirty minutes (As the World Turns), 103.05
first soap opera series for TV (Faraway Hill), 27.03, 28–29
first space pictures sent live, 155.06
first sports extravaganza for TV (Louis-Conn), 20, 21.13, 23
first television station (W2XCW) regularly operating in U.S., 5–6
first Telstar beaming of live TV to Europe, 145
first 3D live national sports event telecast (Masters golf), 468.05
first 3D significant sports telecast (hockey), 468.05
first variety show on network TV (Hourglass), 21.11, 22–23
first video recorder for home use, 173.07
first video tape used on a network TV show, 112.02
First Tuesday, 198, 200
Fischer, Jenna, 442
Fish, 249
Fishburne, Laurence, 461.05
Fisher, Amy, 365
Fisher, Eddie, 55, 95, 118
Fisher, Peter, 320
Fisher, Terry Louise, 332

Fishman, Hal, 171
Fishman, Michael, 341
Fitzgerald, Ella, 119
Flaherty, Joe, 264.03, 405
Flamingo Road, 292, 302
Flanders, Ed, 310
Flanders, Ralph, 88
Flannery, Sean Patrick, 358
Flash, The, 353, 387
Fleiss, Mike, 406.03, 418
Fleming, Eric, 125
Fleming, Ian, 93.04, 163–164, 169
Fleming, Jim, 70
Flintstones, The, 140–141
Flip Wilson Show, The, 220.01
Flo, 288
Flockhart, Calista, 395, 449
Flops: Bob Patterson, 418; Cavemen, 456; Chicken Soup, 347; Dot.comedy, 411.05; Life with Lucy, 331; Turn-On, 204–205; Viva McLaughlin, 456; XFL telecasts, 412; You're in the Picture, 142
Floren, Myron, 101
Flowers, Gennifer, 359
Fly by Night, 353.04
Flying Blind, 362
Flying Nun, The, 195
Flynn, Joe, 154
Foley, Dave, 375.03
Foley, Scott, 405
Fonda, Henry, 33, 134, 164, 264
Fontaine, Frank, 38, 155
Food Network (cable channel), 415, 438
Football coverage:
college, 21.01, 21.06, 66.03, 136, 137, 304
college by network/channel: ABC, 137; NBC 21.01, 21.06, 136; WTBS, 304
first broadcasts, 10
professional by league: AAFC, 27.01; AFL, 137, 178.01; Arena Football League, 423.02; NFL, 41.03, 66.04, 84.03, 112.01, 136, 201.04, 220.02, 293.02, 293.03, 315.01, 338.01, 372, 394, 397.02, 419, 421.04, 427.05, 441.05, 447, 449; UFL, 465.01; USFL, 309.03; XFL, 412
professional by network: ABC, 41.03, 66.04, 178.01, 220.02, 293.02, 315.01, 309.03, 429, 441.05; CBS, 112.01, 136, 394, 397.02; DuMont, 27.01, 66.04, 84.03, 112.01; ESPN, 338.01, 394, 419, 421.04, 441.05, 447; franchise-operated cable channel, 427.05, 445.07; Fox, 372, 394; NFL Network, 427.05, 445.07; NBC, 178.01, 201.04, 293.03, 372, 412, 423.02, 441.05, 447, 449; Versus, 465.01
Super Bowl as a broadcast exclusive event, 426, 447; as commercial sponsorship

showcase, 426–427; as half time entertainment showcase, 426–427; as program lead in, 311, 337, 364.01, 366, 433
Super Bowl by network: ABC, 321.01, 447; CBS 188.06, 359, 407, 426–427, 468.04; Fox 387.03, 418; NBC 188.06, 311, 364.01, 426;
Super Bowl by year: (1967) 188.06; (1983) 311; (1984) 315.08; (1985) 321.01; (1992) 359, 426; (1993) 426; (1997) 387.03; (2001) 407; (2002) 418; (2004) 426–427; (2005) 427; (2010) 468.04
television rights costs: (1990) 354; (1994) $1.58 billion by Fox, 369, 372; (1998) 394
See also "Heidi" incident in football coverage
Foote, Horton, 79, 97
Forbes, Kathryn, 43
Ford, Benson, 52
Ford, Betty, 245
Ford, Faith, 342
Ford, Gerald, 151, 245, 263, 264.04, 303, 382
Ford, John, 101
Ford, Paul, 106
"Ford 50th Anniversary," 90
Ford Star Jubilee, 106, 111, 112.04
Ford Star Time, 134
Forever Fernwood, 268
Forrest, Frederic, 333
Forrest, Steve, 252
Forsyte Saga, The, 197, 211
Forsythe, John, 117, 172.04, 261, 303, 357.05
Forte, Will, 437
For the People, 189
Fortune Hunter, 372
48 Hours, 331.01
"48 Hours on Crack Street," 331.01
For Your Pleasure, 33
Foster, Meg, 302
Fountain, Pete, 101
Four-in-One, 216, 221, 323. See also NBC Mystery Movie
Four Seasons, The, 314
Four Star Playhouse, 94, 170
Four Star Productions, 94, 128, 170
Four Star Revue (All Star Revue), 55–56, 68, 85
Fox, Matthew, 373, 431
Fox, Michael J., 308, 326, 388
Fox (broadcast network), 327.01, 328, 332–333, 365.05, 436, 472; acquires NFL football rights, 369, 372; affiliate lineup grows, 332, 350, 369, 372; Dodgers ownership, 394.04; first sweeps win, 423–424; Hulu.com venture, 457.02; management, 328, 357.04, 359.02, 364.04, 386.04; late night comedy, 380, 445.04, 465.03, 467; late night talk, 332–333, 361, 467; MyNetworkTV venture, 442,445; news, 380.06, 413; news magazines, 364.05;

weekend cartoon slots, 463. See also American Idol; Baseball; Football; NASCAR coverage; News Corporation; Ratings
Fox Business Network (cable channel), 453.04
Fox Family Channel (cable channel), 394.08, 417.03
Fox News Channel (cable channel), 385, 390, 415, 424, 425, 459
Fox Sports Net (cable channel), 386.05
Foxworth, Robert, 216
Foxx, Jamie, 350, 388
Foxx, Redd, 205, 227, 270.04, 287.03, 357.02
Frakes, Jonathan, 340
Franciosa, Tony, 185, 201, 210
Francis, Anne, 179
Francis, Arlene, 43.06, 83, 86, 205
Francis, Connie, 119
Francis, Genie, 302.02
Franciscus, James, 126, 162.07, 225
Franco, James, 405
Franken, Al, 263, 385
Franken, Stephen, 135
Frank McGee Report, The, 178.08
Frank Sinatra Show, The, 68
Frank's Place, 337, 338
Frann, Mary, 307
Franz, Dennis, 300, 316, 316, 326, 366
Frasier, 368, 429, 429.04, 430
Frawley, Jim, 188
Frawley, William, 65–66, 67
Freaks and Geeks, 405
Freberg, Stan, 106
Freddy Martin Show, The, 64
Freddy's Nightmares, 344
Frederick, Pauline, 34, 137
Freed, Alan, 119–120, 132.05, 133
Freed, Bert, 133.08
Freedman, Albert, 124, 131–132
Freeman, Al, 210
Freeman, Orville, 197.02
Freeze on station applications, 37, 46, 51–52, 61, 63, 71
French, Dawn, 333
French, Victor, 319
French Chef, The, 152, 197
Frequency allocation issues, 27, 462.03, 472. See also UHF; VHF
Fresh Prince of Bel-Air, The, 351–352
Freston, Tom, 429.06
Frewer, Matt, 331
Frey, Glenn, 319, 369
Friday Night Lights, 449
Friday Night Videos, 306
Fridays, 287.04
Friedlander, Judah, 449
Friedman, Bruce Jay, 237.04
Friendly, Fred, 41.05, 58.06, 88, 132.02, 133, 163.05, 181–183
Friends, 373, 394, 417–418, 429, 429.03, 430, 434; finale ratings, 429.03
Friends and Lovers, 271
Froman, Jane, 95

Frontier, 103, 104
Front loading strategy, 260
Front Page, 364.05
Front Row Center, 38
Frost, David, 164, 172, 205.07, 224, 228.05, 250, 265.04
Frost, Mark, 348
F Troop, 180
Fugitive, The, 160–161, 162.05, 189.05, 190–191
Fuhrman, Mark, 376
Fujisaki, Hiroshi, 379
Fulbright, William, 183, 184
Fulbright hearings on the Vietnam War, 183, 184
Fuller, Bryan, 455
Fuller, Buckminster, 197.01
Fuller, Robert, 225
Fuller, Simon, 420, 438
Full House, 339, 347
Fullmer, Don, 163.09
Funicello, Annette, 103, 119, 173.03
FunnyorDie.com, 475
Funt, Allen, 29.06, 347
Furness, Betty, 70, 73
Futterman, Dan, 406
Futurama, 405
FX (cable channel), 371, 430, 448

Gabor, Eva, 134, 167, 178.03
Gabor, Zsa Zsa, 155, 192
Gail, Max, 249
Galactica: 1980, 276. *See also Battlestar Galactica*
Galecki, Johnny, 341, 456
Gallagher, Megan, 337
Gallant Men, 154
Gallery, 79
Galsworthy, John, 112, 211
Gambon, Michael, 331.04
Game shows, 11.03, 41.04, 43.06, 59–60, 85.07, 109, 121.05, 162.02, 163.03, 179.04, 179.07, 189.06, 205–206, 224, 402–403, 408; big money giveaway shows on radio, 26, 29.05; big money giveaway shows on television, 99–101, 113–114, 162.02, 402–403, 406.02, 439; government ban on giveaway shows, 45, 93.01, 99. *See also* Quiz show scandal
Games People Play, 286
Gandolf, Ray, 330
Gandolfini, James, 397
Gangbusters, 26
Garber, Victor, 417
Garbo, Greta, 102
Garcia, Jorge, 431
Gardner, Erle Stanley, 11.09, 120
Gardner, Hy, 110
Garland, Judy, 106, 159
Garlin, Jeff, 411.03
Garner, James, 115, 127, 139–140, 225, 250.02, 251, 299
Garner, Jennifer, 417
Garofalo, Janeane, 362
Garrett, Brad, *386*, 388
Garrison, David, 334
Garrison, Greg, 264

Garroway, Dave, 28, 44, 49, 69–70, 91, 102.05, 140.07
Garroway at Large, 44, 59
Garry Moore Show, The, 49.02
Garth, Jennie, 351
"Gathering, The," 113
"Gathering Night, The," 78
Gavilan, 317
Gay themes and characters, 229, 231, 236, 259, 270, 302, 303, 315.12, 320, 341, 350, 375.02, 387.07, 395, 399.04, 405; "That Certain Summer," 236
Gazzara, Ben, 162.03
GE. *See* General Electric
Geary, Cynthia, 363
Geary, Tony, 302.02
Gedrick, Jason, 379
Geer, Will, 236
Gelbart, Larry, 287.02, 313, 337
Geldof, Bob, 321
Gellar, Sarah Michelle, 389, *389*
Geller, Bruce, 188.01
Genachowski, Julius, 476
General Electric: acquires RCA and NBC, 327.06, 328; acquires Vivendi/Universal, 429; early radio, 1, 3.02, 7.06; early television, 5–6, 11.02; sells NBC Universal, 467. *See also* RCA
General Electric Theater, 107, 126.01, 126.04
General Hospital, 302.02, 447
Gentle Ben, 192
Geographically Speaking, 29
George, Anthony, 141
George, Gorgeous, 28
George, Phyllis, 285
George Burns and Gracie Allen Show, The, 7.03, 56, 75
George Burns Comedy Week, 325–326
George Jessel's Show Business, 83
George VI (king of England), 8
Gerard, Danny, 358
German TV, 8, *8*
Gershwin, George, 7
Gervais, Ricky, 412.05, 448
Get a Life, 351
Get Christie Love, 251
Gets, Malcolm, 380
Get Smart, 179–180, 205, 209
Getty, Estelle, 326
Getty oil company begins ESPN, 279.07
Ghost Whisperer, 441
Gibbs, Marla, 247, 326
Gibbsville, 260
Gibson, Charles, 332.01, 394.06, 399.03, 439.06, 441.03, 462, 468.01
Gibson, Henry, 192–193
Gifford, Frank, 242, 259
Gilbert, Melissa, 255
Gilbert, Sara, 341
Gilford, Zach, 449
Gillen, Aidan, 399.04
Gillette Cavalcade of Sports, 15, 18.01, 20, 133.07, 136
Gilliam, Terry, 250
Gilligan's Island, 167, 175, 278.03

Gilmore Girls, 435
Gilpin, Peri, 368
Gilroy, Frank, 97
Gimbel's department store demo, 20
Girl About Town, 33
Girlfriends, 435
"Girl on the Run," 127
Girls on Top, 333
Giuliani, Rudy, 415, 459
"Give My Regards to Broadway," 134
Glamour-Go-Round, 47
Glaser, Paul Michael, 258
Glass, Ron, 249
Gleason, Jackie, *viii*, 37–38, 39, 50–51, 77, 77.01, 101, *104*, 105–106, 111, 125, 142, 155, 188.02, 257.04
Glee, 467–468
Glen Campbell Goodtime Hour, 205
Glenn, John, 122, 146.02, 397.07
Gless, Sharon, 302, 315, 353
Gloria, 309.01
Gobel, George, 105
Godfather Saga, The, 273, 291
Godfrey, Arthur, *17*, 18–19, 18.07, 21.14, 24, 39, 47, 61, 66, 67.02, 228.03; fires Julius La Rosa, 85–86
Goldberg, Gary David, 308, 357, 388
Goldberg, Leonard, 252, 258, 259, 261, 271
Goldberg, Whoopi, 321.04, 340, 371
Goldberg, William, 301
Goldbergs, The, 7, 6.10, *42*, 43, 53–54, 77
Golden, William, 66.02
Golden Age of Radio, 7, 24–26
Golden Age of TV Drama (1950s), 79, 96–98, 143
"Goldengirl," 289
Golden Girls, The, 326
Golden Globe awards shows, 427; truncated by 2008 writers' strike, 457
"Golden Moment, The," 289
Golden Palace, The, 365
Goldenson, Leonard, 142
Goldman, Ronald, 370.02, 375
Goldwater, Barry, 172–174
Golf Channel (cable channel), 467
Golf in 3D, 468.05
Gomer Pyle, USMC, 97, 167, 175, 222
"Gone With the Wind," 10, 58, 264, 266, 281, 327.02, 344.01
Gong Show, The, 257.07
Good, Jack, 126.07, 172.01
"Goodbye, Farewell and Amen," 312
Goode, Mal, 154.02
Goode Behavior, 388
Good Grief!, 351
Goodman, Dody, 111, 268
Goodman, John, 341, *343*
Goodman, Len, 438
Goodman, Mark, 297.05

Good Morning, 103.04
Good Morning America, 257.02, 274, 283, 332.01, 393.01, 394.06, 399.03, 403.02, 439.06, 441.03, 468.01
Good News, 388
Goodson, Mark, 34, 67.04, 109, 112.07, 128, 256.06, 286
Goodson-Todman, 128
Good Times, 247, 255
Good Wife, The, 467
Goodwin, Bernard, 105
Goodwin, Ginnifer, 441.02
Goodyear Television Playhouse, 79
Google, 445.06, 474–475; YouTube acquisition, 445.06, 474
Goranson, Lecy, 341
Gorbachev, Mikhail, 356
Gordon, Bruce, 129
Gordon, Gale, 35.02, 35.03, 76, 156, 201.03, 331
Gordon-Levitt, Joseph, 380
Gore, Al, 413
Gorham, Christopher, 444
Gorme, Eydie, 93
Gorshin, Frank, 178
Gosden, Freeman, 6.09, 42, 57–58, 145.05
Gosfield, Maurice, 106
Gossip Girl, 456, 457
Gothings, Ezekiel, 71
Gottlieb, Dick, 46
Gould, Chester, 60
Gould, Elliott, 233, 263, 320, 325, 396
Gould, Harold, 194
Gould, Jack, 36, 44, 121, 132–132
Grable, Betty, 91
Grace, Maggie, 431
Grace, Topher, 405
Grace Under Fire, 367
Grade, Lew, 196
Graham, Fred, 329
Graham, Lauren, 435
Grammer, Kelsey, 309, 368
Granada Television (broadcast network) British, 163
Grand Ole Opry, The, 24
Grandstaff, Tracy, *385*
Grant, Lee, 255
Grateful Dead, The, 325
Grauer, Ben, 10, 20, 27, 35, 52
Graves, Peter, 188.01, 344.02
Graves, Teresa, 251
Gray, Billy, 118
Gray, Donald, 120
Gray, Erin, 308
Gray, Linda, 287
Gray, Macy, 427.01
Gray, Tamyra, 420
Great American Dream Machine, 221
Great Britain. *See* British broadcasting
Great Debate between Nixon and Kennedy, 138
Great Depression slows U.S. TV growth, 7–8
Greatest American Hero, The, 311
Great Gildersleeve, The, 24

Great Performances, 286.01
Greed, 408
Green, Brian Austin, 351
Green, Seth, 389, 405
Green Acres, 167, 178.03, 222
Greenbriar Boys, The, 161
Greene, Felix, 198, 230
Greene, Lorne, 80, 134, 265, 276
Greene, Michele, 316, 332
Green Hornet, The, 25
Greenwood, Bruce, 310
Gregory, David, 457.03
Gregory, James, 249
Grenier, Adrian, 429.07, 447
Grey, Joel, 55, 80
Grey's Anatomy, 433, 442, 449
Grieco, Richard, 333
Grier, David Alan, 350, 426
Grier, Pam, 394.07
Griff, 241
Griffin, Merv, 64, 155.02, 156,
   173.06, 205.07, 205.08, 228.02,
   228.05, 327.07
Griffith, Andy, *x*, 97, 141, *141*,
   156, 167, 215, 217, 327.03, 332
Griffith, Emile, 146.03
Groening, Matt, 333, *349*, 405
Groh, David, 250
Gross, Michael, 308
Growing Pains, 327
Guarini, Justin, 420
Guedel, John, 34.01, 60
Guestward Ho, 141
Guiding Light, The, 10.02, 67.05,
   169, 197.05, 462.05
Guilbert, Ann Morgan, 147
Guild, The, 447.06, 455, *455*, 456
Guillaume, Robert, 270, 286.03
Guinness, Alec, 286.01
Gulager, Clu, 221
Gumbel, Bryant, 302.05, 387.02,
   403.05, 418.04
Gunsmoke, 67.03, 104, 107, 113,
   114, 125, 145.03, 194, 225,
   251.05, 469
Gunty, Morty, 146
Guthrie, Woody, 161
Guy, Jasmine, 339
"Guyana Tragedy: The Story of Jim
   Jones," 288
Gwynne, Fred, 147–148, 168

HA! (cable channel), 353.03
Hack, Shelley, 286.02, 293.01
Hackett, Buddy, 125
Haden, Nate, 445
Hagen, Jean, 83, 117
Haggis Baggis, 122, 124
Hagman, Larry, 178.06, 287, 327
Haid, Charles, 300
Hailey, Arthur, 316
Hale, Alan, Jr., 163, 167
Hale, Barbara, 120, 326.03
Haley, Alex, 265–266, 279.02
Half and Half, 435
Hall, Andria, 364.05
Hall, Arsenio, 334, 344, 360, 361,
   366, 369, 438
Hall, Brad, 380
Hall, George, 358
Hall, Michael C., 412.03, 448

Hall, Monty, 59, 122, 163.03, 206
Halley, Rudolph, 62
Halliday, Richard, 91
Hallmark Hall of Fame, 67.01, 79
Hamel, Veronica, 300
Hamer, Rusty, 83, *83*
Hamill, Mark, 271
Hamilton, George, 208
Hamilton, Linda, 336
Hamilton, Neil, 33, 51, 178
Hamlin, Harry, 332
Hamm, Jon, 452
Hammer, Jan, 319
Hammerstein, Oscar, 69
Hamner, Earl, 235
Hampton, Walter, 80
Handler, Chelsea, 447.04
"Hands of Murder," 44
Hangin' with Mr. Cooper, 367
Hank, 181
Hank McCune Show, The, 50
Hanks, Tom, 302, 448
Hanna, William, 140–141, 154.04
Hannah Montana, 448
Hannigan, Alyson, 389, 442
Hannity, Sean, 424, 436
Happy Days, 243, 257, 258,
   270.05, 277, 286, 301, 314
Hardball, 385
Hardin, Ty, 125
Harding, Tonya, 371
Harding, Warren, 2, 3.03
"Hardy Boys, The," 103
Hargitay, Mariska, 406
Harkness, Richard, 35
Harmon, Angie, 353
Harmon, Kelly, *316*
Harmon, Mark, 310, 429
Harper, Valerie, 218, *218*, 249, *249*
Harper Valley PTA, 292
Harrelson, Woody, 309, 326
Harriman, Averell, 213
Harrington, Pat, Jr., 47, 109
Harris, Don, 278.05
Harris, Estelle, 364
Harris, Mel, 335
Harris, Neil Patrick, 347, 442, 456
Harris, Oren D., 131
Harris, Percy, 59
Harris, Rosemary, 273
Harris, Samantha, 438
Harris, Susan, 255, 268–270
Harris, Tony, 364.05
Harris Against the World, 172.03
Harrison, Benjamin, 41
Harrison, George, 162
Harrison, Linda, 208
Harrison, Rex, 101
Harry, Jackee, 367
Harry, Prince, 390
Harry-O, 251
Hart, John, 283, 298
Hart, Melissa Joan, 388
Hartford, John, 187
Hartman, David, 207, 257.02,
   332.01
Hartman, Paul, 80, 82–83
Hartman, Phil, 263, 375.03
Hartnell, William, 163.02
Hartnett, Vincent, 54, 108–109
Hartz, Jim, 244.05, 264.01

"Harvest of Shame," 139
Harvey, Paul, 71, 137
Harvey, Steve, 388, 438
Hasel, Joe, 41.03, 44
Haskell, Jack, 44
Hasselhoff, David, 347
Hatch, Richard, 409, *409*
Hatcher, Teri, 433
Hathaway, Anne, 444
Hathaways, The, 148
Hauck, Charlie, 286.05
Have Gun Will Travel, 115–116,
   125
Hawaii, 434
Hawaiian Eye, 129, 140
Hawaii Five-O, 201, *203*
Hawk, Susan, 409
Hawkins, 241
Hawkins, Screamin' Jay, 119
Hawn, Goldie, 193
Hayek, Selma, 444
Hayes, Harold, 284
Hayes, Helen, 69, 90
Hayes, Sean, 405
Haynes, Lloyd, 209
Haynes, Pamela, 220
Haynes, Peter Lind, 38
Hays, Will, 70
Haysbert, Dennis, 417, 442
Hayward, Leland, 90, 164
Haywire, 351
Hayworth, Rita, 200
Hazel, 147
HBO (cable channel) Home Box
   Office, 236.02, 256.05, 296,
   302.03, 353.03, 371, 383,
   412.03, 429.01, 429.02, 429.07,
   434–435, 437, 441.02, 448;
   competitive advantages and
   disadvantages, 400; *Seinfeld*
   reunion, 465.06; *Sopranos*
   finale, 450–451
HDTV. *See* High Definition
   Television
Head, Anthony Stewart, 389
Headline News/HLN (cable
   channel), 302.04, 305, 412.06
Headmaster, 215–217
"Head of the Family," 146
Headey, Lena, 453.07
"Healer, The," 112
He and She, 194–195
Hear It Now, 58.06, 63. *See also I
   Can Hear It Now; See It Now*
Hearn, Chick, 142
Hearst, 303.03, 315.09
Hearts Afire, 362–363
Heaton, Patricia, *386*, 388, 467
Hee-Haw, 205, 219, 222, 224,
   256.06
Hegyes, Robert, 258
"Heidi" incident in football
   coverage, 201.04
Heights, The, 362
Heigl, Katherine, 433
Helgenberger, Marg, 337, 413
Hell Town, 326
Hello, Larry, 275
Helmond, Katherine, 270, 320
"Hemingway," 145.01
Hemingway, Ernest, 78

Hemingway, Mariel, 331
Hemsley, Sherman, 247, 331
Henderson, Florence, 210.02
Henderson, Skitch, 38, 93
Hendricks, Christina, 452
Hendry, Ian, 137.06, 164
Henner, Marilu, 281, 353
Hennessy, Jill, 353
Henning, Paul, 93.06, 118, 156,
   162.06, 166–167, 178.03
Henry, Bill, 103.07
Henry, Buck, 172, 179, 263, 276
Henson, Jim, 211, 264.02, 399.06
Henson, John, 383
Henteloff, Alex, 272
Hercules: The Legendary Journeys,
   387
Here's Lucy, 201.03, 244.06,
   270.08
Here's Morgan, 21.12
Herlihy, Ed, 29, 81
Herman, Pee-Wee, 332
Heroes, 449–450, *449*, 455, 456,
   457
Herskovitz, Marshall, 335, 373.01,
   407
Hervey, Jason, 338
Hesseman, Howard, *277*, 280, 325
Heston, Charlton, 41, 48.03, 320
Hewitt, Don, 34.07, 63, 200, 415,
   429.05
Hewitt, Jennifer Love, 373, 441
Hexum, Jon-Erik, 320
Hickman, Dwayne, 93.06, 135
Hickok, Wild Bill, 103
Hickox, Harry, 167
Hicks, Catherine, 388
Hicks, George, 137
Higgins, Joel, 308
High Definition Television
   (HDTV), 381.04, 381.05,
   393.02, 397.07, 423.04
"High School Musical," 441.01,
   448, 468
"High Tor," 106
Highway Patrol, 102.06
Highway to Heaven, 318, 319–320
Hi Honey, I'm Home, 354.03
Hiken, Nat, 106, 147–148
Hilgemeier, Ed, 123
Hill, Anita, 356, *357*
Hill, Arthur, 225
Hill, Dulé, 448
Hill, George Roy, 112
Hill, Steven, 188.01, 353
Hillenburg, Stephen, 399.08
Hiller, Bill, 285
Hillerman, John, 272, 301
Hilliard, David, 212
Hilliard, Harriet. *See* Nelson,
   Harriet (Hilliard)
Hills, The, 448
Hill Street Blues, 293.05, 299–301,
   301, 326
Hindenburg disaster, 10.03
Hines, Cheryl, 411.03
Hines, Gregory, 324
Hirsch, Judd, 281, 343
Hispanic themes and characters,
   248–249
Hiss, Alger, 73, 151

History Channel, The (cable channel), 373.04

Hitchcock, Alfred, 107, 134, 143, 324–325

Hitler, Adolf, 8

HLN (cable channel). *See* Headline News/HLN

Hockey, 10, 421.04, 439.02; franchise-operated cable channel, 453.03; 3D telecast, 468.05

Hoffman, Dustin, 326.01

Hoffman, Gertrude, 66

Hogan, Frank, 123

Hogan, Paul, 423

Hogan's Heroes, *177*, 180–181, 222

Holbrook, Hal, 210, 216, 236

Holden, William, 241

Holliday, Judy, 91

Holliman, John, 354

Holloway, Josh, 431

Hollywood competes with New York for television production, 49–50, 57–59, 67–68, 75–78, 87, 94, 101, 102, 104–105, 107, 121, 128–129; uses other media to promote films, 471

Hollywood Film Theater, 113.01, 145

Hollywood Palace, 159, 162

Hollywood Screen Test, 33

Hollywood Special, 146. *See also ABC Sunday Night Movie*

Hollywood Squares, 188.03, 224

Hollywood Television Theater, 211, 237.04

Holmes, Rupert, 383

Holmes and Yo Yo, 261

Holocaust, 273

Holyfield, Evander, 438

Holzman, Winnie, 373.01

Home, 86

Home and Garden Network (cable channel), 415

Home Box Office. *See* HBO

Homeboys in Outer Space, 388

"Homecoming," 235–236

"Home for Dinner," 325

Homefront, 357

Home Improvement, 359

Home shopping, 321.07, 357.04, 412.04

Home videotaping allowed, 315.07, 472

Homicide: Life on the Street, 364.01, 366–367, 387, 388, 406, 418.06, 457.01

Homicide: Second Shift, 387.04

Homing pigeons replaced by wireless, 2.05

Honeymooners, The, *viii*, 101, *104*, 105–106, 111, 188.02, 257.04. *See also Flintstones*

Honey West, 179

Hong Kong, 139

Hooks, Robert, 195

Hooperman, 337

Hooper ratings service, 24, 31

Hoopes, Wendy, *385*

Hootenanny, 161–162

Hoover, Herbert, 5, 7

Hoover, J. Edgar, 212

Hopalong Cassidy, 44, 50

Hope, Bob, 24, 27, 48.08, 55–56, 68, 78.03, 82, 84.06, 106, 109, 117, 192, *195*, 262, 350, 386.06

Hope, Leslie, 417

Hopkins, Telma, 387

Hopper, Dennis, 115, 348

Hopper, William, 120

Horn, Bob, 80

Hornsby, Don, 47

Horta, Silvio, 444

Horton, Edward Everett, 132.04, 180

Horton, Peter, 335

Horton, Robert, 117

Hotel, 316

Hot l Baltimore, 247, 251.02

Hot Pursuit, 320

Hour Glass, 21.11, 22–23

House Calls, 288

Houseman, John, 129, 277–278, 306–307, *307*, 308

House, M.D., 434, 448

House Party, 18.04, 60

House Un-American Activities Committee. *See* HUAC televised public hearings

Hovis, Larry, 181

Howar, Barbara, 285

Howard, Bob, 35.04

Howard, Ken, 280

Howard, Ron, *x*, 141, 243, 257, 427.04

Howard K. Smith: News and Comment, 150–151

Howard, Traylor, 448

Howdy Doody, 31–32, 103, 133.09, 135

Howe, Quincy, 35

Howell, Arlene, 129

Howerton, Glenn, 448

How I Met Your Mother, 442

How the West Was Won, 273

HSN (Home Shopping Network) (cable channel), 321.07

HUAC televised public hearings, 31

Hubbel, Dick, 13

Huckabee, Mike, 459, 461

Hudgens, Vanessa, 441.01

Hudson, Rock, 134, 225, 317, 320

Huffington, Arianna, 385

Huffman, Felicity, 433

Huggins, Roy, 115, 160, 250.02

Hughes, Robert, 284

Hugo, Victor, 160

Hull, Warren, 29.05, 59

Hullabaloo, 173.03

Hulu.com, 457.02, 463, 474, 476

Hume, Brit, 385

Humphrey, Hubert, 35, 121, 199, 200

"Hunger in America," 197.02

Hunnam, Charlie, 399.04

Hunt, Bonnie, 421

Hunt, Gareth, 264.08

Hunt, Helen, 363

Hunter, Alan, 297.05

Hunter, Holly, 448

Hunter, Jeffrey, 189

Hunter, Tab, 141, 268

Hunter, The, 163

Huntley, Chet, 97.07, 103.07, 109, 112.03, 145.01, 158, 172–173, 211.05, 228

Huntley-Brinkley Report, The, 112.03, 158–159, 163.01, 172, 178.08, 179.02

Hurok, Sol, 106

Hurricane Katrina coverage, 437

Hurt, Marlin, 18.12, 58–59

Hussein, Saddam, 354

Hustle, 448–449

Hutchins, Will, 115, 127

Hutton, Betty, 90

Hutton, Ina Ray, 101

Hyams, Peter, 324

Hyatt, Bobby, 83

Hyde-White, Wilfrid, 286.05

Hyman, Mac, 97

Ian, Janis, 263

Ian and Sylvia, 162

I Can Hear It Now, 41.05. *See also Hear It Now; See It Now*

Iconoscope developed, 6

Idle, Eric, 250

I Dream of Jeannie, 177, 178.06

Ifill, Gwen, 456.07

Iger, Robert, 434.05

"I Have a Dream" civil rights speech, 171

i: Independent Television (broadcast network), 435.04

I Led Three Lives, 84.01, 163

Iler, Robert, 397

I'll Fly Away, 356–357

I Love Lucy, 64–66, 68, 75–78, 101, 105, 111–112, 113–114, 117, 123, 189.04, 244.06; birth, ix, 75; as *Lucy-Desi Comedy Hour*, 120.04

I Love to Eat, 16

I'm a Celebrity, Get Me Out of Here, 423

Image orthicon camera, 20, *21*, 21.04

I Married Joan, 75, 79

"I Met Him in Paris," 9

Immortal, The, 210

Impeachment proceedings: Clinton, 400–401; Nixon, 244–245

Imperioli, Michael, 399

Inaba, Carrie Ann, 438

Ina Ray Hutton Show, 101

"Incident in an Alley," 107

In Concert, 236.03, 262

Incredible Hulk, The, 271.04, 272

"Incredible Jewel Robbery, The" 126.04

"Incredible World of Horace Ford, The," 97

Indelicato, Mark, 444

Infinity broadcasting company, 386.07

INK, 387

In Living Color, 350, 361–362, 426

"Inner Light, The," 340

In Search Of, 286

"Inside Beverly Hills," 107

"Inside North Vietnam," 198

International Magazine, 152

Internet, 473–476; America Online, 407, 411.06; Drudge 391, 401; runs unaired episodes of canceled shows, 450; "viral" events, 425, 436, 437, 443, 459, 474; website TV tie-ins, 270.05, 387.04, 388, 400, 442–443

Internet TV. *See* ABC.com; Amazon.com streaming video; BarelyPolitical.com; CBS Innertube; Hulu.com; FunnyorDie.com; JibJab.com; NBC.com; Newshour.pbs.org; Thirteen.org; Watchtheguild.com; Webisodes; YouTube.com

Interns, The, 215–217

In the Heat of the Night, 339

In the House, 388

"In the Presence of Mine Enemies," 134

In Town Today, 27

Invasion, 441

Invention of television, 5–7

Invitation to Art, 152

Ion Television (broadcast network), 435.04

Iowa Public Television, 459

Iran-Contra investigation, 332.02, 339.01

Iran Crisis, 283. *See also Nightline*

Iran hostage crisis, 282–283

Iraq War. *See* War coverage by conflict: Persian Gulf War

I Remember, 303

Iron Chef, 438

Ironside, 196, 196.01

Islanders, The, 139

I Spy, 179, 186, 317

Issues and Answers, 137.03

Ito, Lance, 375–376, 377–379

It Pays to Be Ignorant, 25

It's a Good Life, 323

It's Always Sunny in Philadelphia, 448

It's a Miracle, 397.01

It's About Time, 188

It's Garry Shandling's Show, 331.03, 345

It's Like, You Know, 403

It's News to Me, 85.07

It's Not Easy, 314

It's Polka Time, 101

It Takes a Thief, 196.04

ITT and ABC merger proposal, 184–185

ITV (broadcast network) British, 102.02. 402, 408

Ivanhoe, 163

I've Got a Secret, 67.04

Ives, Burl, 112, 210

Jack and Bobby, 435

Jack and Jill, 405

Jackass, 411

Jack Benny Program, The, 7.04, 84–85

Jack Carter Show, The, 49

Jackie Gleason Show, The, 77.01, 209
Jackie Thomas Show, The, 342
Jack Paar Show, The, 29.02, 85.01, 161, 163, 227, 237.01
Jackpot Bowling, 142
Jackson, Charles E., 124
Jackson, Felix, 97
Jackson, Gregory, 303, 305
Jackson, Janet, 426–427
Jackson, J. J., 297.05, 327.04
Jackson, Kate, 261, 286.02, 315.03
Jackson, Keith, 220.02, 309.03
Jackson, Michael, 309.05, 311.04, 321, 426
Jackson, Randy, 420
Jackson, Sammy, 167
Jackson, Sherry, 83, *83*
Jacobs, Lawrence-Hilton, 258
Jacobs, Mike, 15
Jaffe, Sam, 145
JAG (Judge Advocate General), 434
Jagger, Dean, 162.07
Jagger, Mick, 450
Jail, 445
James at 15, 272
James Bond, 163–164; first media appearance, 93.04; *James Bond, Secret Agent*, 164; *Remington Steele* casting complication, 326
James, Dennis, 10, 21, 27.01, 28
James, Harry, 91
James, Sheila, 135
Jamie, 82–83
Jamie Foxx, 388
Janis, Conrad, 276, 277
Jankowski, Gene, 262
Janney, Allison, 406
Janssen, David, 120, 160–161, 190–191, 225, 251
Jarvis, Graham, 268
Jay Leno Show, The, 464–467
Al-Jazeera news, 425
"Jazz Singer, The," 134
Jeff, D. J. Jazzy, 351
Jeffersons, The, 247, 255, 261, 288
Jeni, Richard, 373
Jenkins, Charles Francis, 6.01, 11
Jenkins, Ken, 357
Jennifer Slept Here, 314
Jennings, Peter, 173.04, 196.03, 230, 250.07, 271.07, 282, 283, 311.05, 390, 430, 435.05, *436*, 439.06
Jennings, Waylon, 287
Jenny, 383
Jenny Jones Show, The, 375.02
Jensen, Ann "Red," 44
Jensen, Ashley, 444
Jensen, Karen, 208
Jericho, 450, 457
Jerry Lewis Show, The, 159
Jessel, George, 80, 82–83
Jesus of Nazareth, 264
Jetsons, The, 141, 154.04
Jewel in the Crown, The, 315.06
Jewison, Norman, 159
JibJab.com, 437
Jiggling strategy, 272
Jillian, Ann, 314

Jimmy Dean Show, The, 113.02, 120.05
Jimmy Kimmel Live, 421.07
Joanie Loves Chachi, 301
Joan of Arcadia, 429
Job, The, 418
Joe and Sons, 255
Joe Forrester, 241
Joe Millionaire, 423
Joey, 434–435
Joey Bishop Show, The, 188, 189.01
John, Elton, 332–333
John Davidson Show, The, 287.08
"Johnny and Mr. Do-Right," 58.02
Johnny Carson Show, The, 94; 103.06
John Paul II (pope), 391
Johnson, Arte, 192–193
Johnson, Chic, 39
Johnson, Don, 319, 382
Johnson, Eric, 21.02
Johnson, Laurence, 108–109
Johnson, Lyndon, 164, 172–174, 184, 197–198, 199
Johnson, Nicholas, 184
Johnson, Robert L., 297.01
Johnson, Russell, 167
Johnson, Van, 185
Johnston, Kristen, 380
Jonathan Winters Show, The, 112.03
Jones, Carolyn, 167
Jones, Davy, 188
Jones, Dean, 204
Jones, Edgar Allan, Jr., 126
Jones, James Earl, 160, 279.02, 286.06
Jones, January, 452
Jones, Jenny, 375.02, 411
Jones, Jim, 278.05
Jones, Paula, 391, 401
Jones, Quincy, 321
Jones, Shirley, 210
Jones, Spike, 68–69
Jones, Terry, 250
Jones, Tommy Lee, 344.05
Jordan, Michael, 375, 394.05
Journey, 450, 468
Journeyman, 456
"Journey of Robert Kennedy, The," 210
Joyce, Yootha, 242.01
Judge, Mike, 365, 388
Judging Amy, 406
Julia, 202
"Julius Caesar," 41
Jump, Gordon, *277*, 280
Jump the Shark website, 270.05
June Taylor dancers, 50–51, 77.01, 125
Junior Jamboree, 28
Justice, 96
Justice Department: investigates NBC station trade, 97.06, 108, 109; network strategy of ceding some program controls, 128; Paramount case, 10.06
Justice for All, 219
Just Our Luck, 314
Just the Ten of Us, 347

Juvenile Court, 126
Juvenile Jury, 25

K–station call letters:
  KABC New York radio, 447.02
  KDKA Pittsburgh radio, 3.03
  KDKA Pittsburgh television, 39. *See also* WDTV
  KYW Philadelphia, 9. *See also* W3XE
Kaczmarek, Jane, 405
Kaelin, Kato, 376, 380
Kahn, Madeline, 314
Kaiser, Henry, 112
Kaiser Aluminum Hour, 112
Kalember, Patricia, 354.01
Kaltenborn, H. V., 17, 24, 35
Kanakaredes, Melina, 406, 434
Kaplan, Gabe, 257, 260
Karen, 172.03
Karloff, Boris, 91
Karmazin, Mel, 386.07, 394.05, 407, 429.06
Karn, Richard, 359
Karras, Alex, 315.02
Kartheiser, Vincent, 452
Kate and Allie, 314–315
Kate Smith Show, The, 58.03
Katt, William, 326.03
Katz, Mickey, 55
Kauffman, Marta, 373
Kaufman, Andy, 281
Kaufman, George S., 47
Kavner, Julie, *249*, 250, 333, *349*
Kaye, Caren, 272
Kaye, Danny, 172
Kaye, Sammy, 101
Kay Kyser's Kollege of Musical Knowledge, 25, 51
Keating, Larry, 56
Keaton, Buster, 50
Keaton, Diane, 337
Keeshan, Bob, 32, 103
Kefauver, Estes, *60*, 62, 95
Keitel, Harvey, 324
Keith, Brian, 96, 187, 251
Keith, Richard, *x*
Kellerman, Sally, 235
Kelley, David E., 365, 374, 394–395, 433
Kelley, DeForest, 190
Kelley, Malcolm David, 431
Kellner, Jamie, 370, 373
Kelly, Jack, 115
Kelly, Minka, 449
Kelly, Roz, 260
Kelsey, Linda, 278
Kelton, Pert, 51, 52, 77.01, 105
Kelton, Richard, 276
Kendrick, Alexander, 163.01
Kennan, George, 183
Kennedy, Bob, 122
Kennedy, Caroline, *165*
Kennedy, Carolyn (Bessette), 401
Kennedy, Edward "Ted," 286.08
Kennedy, George, 225
Kennedy (Onassis), Jacqueline, 84.02, *165*
Kennedy, John F., 84.02, 120.03, 137.02, 138, 139, *145*, 158–159, *161*, 164–165, 172.05;

assassination and funeral coverage, 164–165, *165*
Kennedy, John, Jr., *165*, 401
Kennedy, Mimi, 357
Kennedy, Robert, 199, 201
Kenny, Tom, 380.02, 399.08
Kent State, 292
Keppel, Judith, 402
Kercheval, Ken, 287
Kerr, Elizabeth, 277
Kerrigan, Nancy, 371
Kerry, John, 436–437
Kesten, Paul, 27
Kevin Hill, 435
Keymah, T'Keyah Crystal, 350
Key West, 363.05
Khan, 251
Khan, Chaka, 319
Khomeini, Ayatollah Ruhollah, 283
"Kick the Can," 323
Kick up the Eighties, A, 333
"Kid Champion," 58.02
Kidnapped, 450
Kid Rock, 426
Kidvid adventures on film (1950s), 95, 103, 117
Kiernan, Walter, 137
Kilborn, Craig, 399.02, 399.07, 434.03
Kilborn, Greg, 385
Kiley, Richard, 96, 97, 227
Kilian, Victor, 267
Killian, James, 238
Kim, Daniel Dae, 431
Kim, Yunjin, 431
Kimbrough, Charles, 342
Kimmel, Jimmy, 421.07, 456
Kinescope (kine), 6, 31, 49–50
King, 273
King, Alan, 246
King, B. B., 286.05
King, Billie Jean, 242
King, John Reed, 15
King, Larry, 321.03, 343, 360, 385
King, Martin Luther, Jr., 171, 198, 201
King, Rodney, 354.02, 356
King, Wayne, 101
King Family, 205
King of the Hill, 388
King's Row, 102
King World TV syndication, 439.05
Kinison, Sam, 334
Kinnear, Greg, 383
Kinney, Kathy, 381
Kinter, Robert, 48.06, 53, 109, 121.07, 142, 145.02, 179.05, 183
Kipling, Rudyard, 78
Kirby, Durward, 47, 49.02, 187
Kirshner, Don, 236.03
Kirshner, Ricky, 427
Kissinger, Henry, 182, 303
Kitt, Eartha, 178
Klein, Paul, 272, 273, 274–275
Klein, Robert, 221.02, 325
Klemperer, Werner, 181
Klimt, Gustav, 293.08
Klondike, 139
Kluge, John, 121.04

Klugman, Jack, 143, 220.03, 264.05
Knight, Gladys, 221.02, 319
Knight, Ted, 217, *218*
Knight, T. R., 433
Knight, Wayne, 362, 364, 380
Knights of Prosperity, The, 450
Knots Landing, 288, 302
Knotts, Don, 97, 109, 141, *141*, 325
Knowles, Beyoncé, 426
Knox, Terence, 310, 336
Koenig, Dennis, 313
Koenig, Walter, 190
Kojak, 239–240, 261
Kolb, Clarence, 66
Komack, James, 248, 258, 260
Koop, Ted, 93.05
Koppel, Ted, 283, 361, 366, 382, 401, 425, 439.04
Korea. *See* War coverage by conflict: Korea
Korman, Harvey, 325
Kotto, Yaphet, 366
Kovacs, Ernie, 51, 59.05, 69–70, 77.05, 91, 110, 133.04, 149, *149*; style embraced, 192, 250
Kraft Music Hall, 24, 29, 125
Kraft Television Theater, 27.08, 29, 79, 97, 112, 121, 121.09
Krakowski, Jane, 449
Krasinski, John, 442
Krause, Peter, 412.03, 455
Kreitzer, Catherine, 100
Kring, Tim, 449
Kristofferson, Kris, 331
Kroft, Steve, 359
Kudrow, Lisa, 373, 434
Kukla, Fran and Ollie, 28, 43.01, 59.05, 113.05
Kulp, Nancy, 156
Kung-Fu, 242–243
Kunis, Mila, 405
Kupcinet, Irv, 110
Kuralt, Charles, 151, 279.01, 285, 304
Kurtz, Swoosie, 302, 354.01
Kutcher, Ashton, 405, 448
Kyle MacDonnell Sings, 33
Kyser, Kay, 24, 25, 51

Lace, 316
Lace II, 320
Lack, Andrew, 412.02, 417
Ladd, Cheryl, 270.03
Ladies Be Seated, 15, 18.05
Lady Diana. *See* Spencer, Diana
"Lady in the Dark," 90
Lafavore, Michael, 427
La Femme Nikita, 386
Laguna Beach, 448
Lahti, Christine, 331
Laine, Frankie, 38
Laire, Judson, 43
L.A. Law, 332
Lamb, Brian, 297
Lamb, Claudia, 267
Lamb, Edward, 88
Lambert, Adam, 462.01
Lamp Unto My Feet, 41.01
Landau, Martin, 256.04, 323

Lander, David, 258
Landis, John, 309.05, 323
Landmark Communications, 457.04
Landon, Michael, 134, 255, 299, 319
Landsburg, Alan, 286
Lane, Allan "Rocky," 137.05
Lane, Charles, 166
Laneuville, Eric, 310
Lang, Fritz, 5
Lansbury, Angela, 320, 372
Lansing, Robert, 148
Lanson, Snooky, 49.03
Lanza, Mario, 91
Laramie, 134
Larkin, Sheila, 216
La Rosa, Julius, 85–86
Larry King Live, 321.03
Larry Sanders Show, The, 361, 371, 383, 395, 396, 397
Larson, Glen A., 301
LaSalle, Eriq, 374
Lasser, Louise, 267–268, *269*
Lassie, 29.03, 95, 222, 224
Lassie, *96*
Last Call, 417.05, 456, 464
"Last Notch," 97, 103
"Last One, The," 339.07
Last Resort, The, 286, 308
Last Word, The, 305
Las Vegas, 429
Las Vegas Show, The, 189.02, 294
Late Late Show, The, 375.01, 399.07, 434.03
Late Night: Jimmy Fallon, 461.06, 464; David Letterman, 303.01, 329, 361; Conan O'Brien, 369.02, 434.01, 461.06, 464
Later, 383
Later Today, 403.01, 411.01
Late Show (David Letterman), *363*, 369, 381, 456–457, 464–467, 468.04
Late Show, The (Joan Rivers), 332–333, 334
Lauer, Matt, 387.02
Laugh-In, 192–193, 201.01, 203–205, 250, 270.01
Laughlin, Tom, 126
Laugh track added to filmed series, 50
Lauren, Tammy, 357
Laurence, John, 214
Lauria, Dan, 338
Laurie, Hugh, 434
Laurie, Piper, 123.04, 348
Laverne and Shirley, 258, 260, 277, 286, 288, 314
Law & Order, 353, 375, 387, 388, 406, 417, 434, 442, 457.01, 469
Law & Order: Criminal Intent, 457
Law & Order: Special Victims Unit, 406
Law & Order: Trial by Jury, 457.01
Lawford, Peter, 120
Lawless, Lucy, 387
Lawless Years, The, 129
Lawman, 125
Law of the Plainsman, 134
Lawrence, Gertrude, 9

Lawrence, Sharon, 366, 388
Lawrence, Steve, 93
Lawrence Welk (various titles), 101, 111, 224
Lawyers, The, 210
LAX, 434
Lazenby, George, *203*
Leachman, Cloris, 95, 218, *218*
Lear, Norman, 56, 154.05, 195, 219–220, 227, 231, 233, 247–248, 251.02, 255, 258, 267–268, 271.06, 272, 279.04, 357.05
Learned, Michael, 236
Learning Channel, The (cable channel), 386.01
Leary, Denis, 418, 448
Leave It To Beaver, 117–118, *119*, 309.04
Le Beauf, Sabrina, 317
LeBlanc, Matt, 373, 434
Lee, Gypsy Rose, 52, 53
Lee, Jason, 442
Lee, Peggy, 119
Lee, Stan, 423.07
Leeves, Jane, 368
Legal dramas, 96, 120–121, 126, 143, 210, 215–217, 225, 226, 332, 353, 379, 394–395, 433
Legs, 274
Lehrer, Jim, 238, 257.01, *261*, 311.07, 391, *391*, 465.07
Lembeck, Harvey, 106
Lemmon, Jack, 51
Lennon, John, 162, 293.02
Lennon Sisters, 101
Leno, Jay, 361, 364.02, 366, 369, 377, *379*, 381, 397.06, 434.01, 456, 462.02, 464–467, 468.04
Leo and Liz in Beverly Hills, 326
Leonard, Jack E., 59.06, 91
Leonard, Robert Sean, 434
Leonard, Sheldon, 147
Leonard, William, 279.05
Leoni, Téa, 362, 388
Lerman, Logan, 435
Lescoulie, Jack, 70, 110
Les Crane Show, The, 173.01
Lester, Jerry, 39, 47–48, 50, 64, 68, 92, 156
Let's Make a Deal, 163.03, 206, 224, 462.05
Letter to Your Serviceman, 15
Levenson, Sam, 38
Levi, Zachary, 456
Levin, Gerald, 386.02, 407, 418.03
Levine, Samm, 405
Levine, Ted, 448
Levinson, Barry, 364.01, 366–367, 383
Levinson, Richard, 133.08, 195, 210, 226, 241, 320, 323
Levitt, Saul, 211
Levy, Chandra, 413
Levy, Eugene, 264.03, 325
Lewinsky, Monica, 391–393
Lewis, Al, 168

Lewis, Anthony, 230
Lewis, Emmanuel, 315.02
Lewis, Huey, 320.01
Lewis, Jennie, 48. *See also* Dagmar
Lewis, Jenny, 358
Lewis, Jerry, 36, 38, 47, 55–56, 69, 85, 94, 101, 109, 134, 159, 336
Lewis, Jerry Lee, 119
Lewis, John L., 21
Lewis, Richard, 345.02, 411.03
Lewis, Robert Q., 58.05, 03.06
Leydenfrost, Regan (Mrs.), 124
Liberace, 123.05
Liebman, Max, 39, 48.08, 49, 86, 90–91, 106, 121
Lieutenant, The, 189
Life, 457
Life and Legend of Wyatt Earp, The, 103–104, *108*
Life Begins at 80, 104
Life Goes On, 347
"*Life* Goes to the Movies," 264
"Life in Hell," 333
Life Is Worth Living, 68, 104
Lifeline, 274
Life of Leonardo da Vinci, 228
Life of Riley, 24, 50, 77–78
Life on Mars, 461.02
Lifetime (cable channel), 315.09, 332.03, 338, 406–407, 447
Life with Bonnie, 421
Life with Lucy, 331
Life with Luigi, 43, 77
Light, Judith, 320
Lightfoot, Leonard, 308
Lights Out, 21, 25
"Light That Failed, The," 78
Lillie, Bea, 69
Lilly, Evangeline, 431
Limbaugh, Rush, 393
Linc's, 394.07
Lindelof, Damon, 431, 450
Linden, Hal, 249, 372
Lindsay, Robert Howard, 79
Lines of resolution in television images, 5
Lineup, The, 96
Link, William, 133.08, 195, 210, 226, 241, 320, 323
Linkletter, Art, 18.04, 24, 60, 107, 162
Linville, Larry, 235
"Lion Walks Among Us, A," 148
Lippmann, Walter, 133
"Lippmann on Leadership," 133
Lip synch technique in performing, 17
Lipton, Peggy, 201
Liquid Television, 365
List, Peyton, 452
Lithgow, John, 324, 380
Little, Rich, 188
Littlefield, Warren, 354
Little House on the Prairie, 255, 291
Little Men, 397.01
"Little Peace and Quiet, A," 325
Live Aid fundraiser, 321–322
Live episode of *ER*, 393.03
"Live from New York, it's *Saturday Night*," 263, 459

Live local entertainment supplanted by national media, 470
Live local programming supplanted by movies released to television, 103
Lively, Blake, 456
Live origination from Los Angeles, 63
Live productions and their inherent problems, 91
"Living End, The," 134
Living Single, 388
LL Cool J, 467
Lloyd, Norman, 310
Lobo, 292
Local stations via satellite, 403.07
Lockhart, June, 95
Locklear, Heather, 301, 303, 359.04
Loeb, Philip, *42*, 43, 52, 53–55
Loggia, Robert, 347
Lombardo, Guy, 101
Lomond, Britt, 117
Lon, Alice, 101
London, Julie, 225
Lone Ranger, The, 7.07, 25, 26; *47*, 50
Lonesome Dove, 344.05
Long, Huey, 57
Long, Loretta, 220
Long, Matt, 435
Long, Richard, 129
Long, Shelley, 309, 332, 364.02
Longest running prime time network drama series (*Gunsmoke, Law and Order*), 469
Longest running soap opera in broadcasting (*The Guiding Light*), 462.05
Longet, Claudine, 263
Longoria, Eva (Parker), 433
Longstreet, 225
Loomis, Henry, 237
Loose Change, 272
Lopez, George, 465.04, 467
Lopez, Vincent, 101
Lopez Tonight, 465.04
Lord, Jack, 201, *203*
Lord, Marjorie, *83*, 117
Lorne, Marion, 67
Lorre, Chuck, 456
Lorre, Peter, 93.04, 163
Lost, 431–433, 450, 468.06, 469
Lost in Space, 189
Lotsa Luck, 246
Lou Grant, 278–280, *279*, 288, 291
Louis, Joe, 20, 21.13, *23*
Louis-Conn fight, 20, *23*
Louis-Dreyfus, Julia, 350.05, 364, 380, 417.06
Louise, Tina, 167
Love, American Style, 209, 243
Love and War, 363
Love Boat, The, 271, 292.03
Lovejoy, Frank, 120
Love Nest, The, 246
Love of Life, 66.01, 169
Love on a Rooftop, 188
Love, Sidney, 302
"Love Song of Barney

Kempinsky," 186
Love Story, 87
Love That Bob, 93.06
Lovell, Jim, 206
Lovitz, Jon, 326
Lowe, Rob, 406, 429
Lowrey, Malcolm, 25
Lucas, George, 275, 358
Lucille Ball and Desi Arnaz Show, 120.04
"Lucy Meets the Moustache," 133.04
Lucy Show, The, 156, 244.06
Ludlum, Robert, 265
Lum and Abner, 26, 43
Lumley, Joanna, 264.08, 363.02
Lunden, Joan, 393.01
Lupino, Ida, 94
Lutes, Eric, 380
Lux Radio Theater, 24, 25, 78
Lux Video Theater, 78–79, 112
Lynch, David, 348–349, 351
Lynn, Bambi, 86
Lyon's Den, The, 429
Lythgoe, Nigel, 438

Mabius, Eric, 444
Mac, Bernie, 418
MacCorkindale, Simon, 316
MacDonnell, Kyle, 33
MacFarlane, Seth, 405, 435.01
MacGyver, 327
Mack, Ted, 31, 211.06
MacKenzie, Gisele, 118
MacLachlan, Kyle, 397
MacLaine, Shirley, 264
MacLeod, Gavin, 217, *218*, 271
MacMurray, Fred, 141
Macnee, Patrick, 137.06, 154.06, 164, 179, 242.03, 264.08
MacNeil, Robert, 178.08, 229, 238, 257.01, *261*, 311.07
MacNeil-Lehrer NewsHour/Report, The, *261*, 311.07
MacNicol, Peter, 357.05
MacRae, Gordon, 36, 94
MacRae, Sheila, 188.02
Macy, Bill, 233
Macy, William, 374
Mad About You, 363
Madden, John, 369, 372, 441.05
Made-for-TV movies, 185–186, 228, 242; as series pilots, 226, *226*; topical and controversial, 210, 242, 253
"Made in America" (*Sopranos*), 450–451
Madison Square Garden Network. *See* MSG
Mad Men, 447.05, 452–453
Madonna, 320.01
MADtv, 380, 445.04, 465.03
Magazines (1950s) with TV listing information, 70, 78.05
Maggart, Brandon, 315.12
Magic Carpet, 16
Magnum, P.I., 301
Maharis, George, 141
Maher, Bill, 371, 388, 437
Mahoney, Jock, 125
Mahoney, John, 368

Mail Story, The, 96
Major Dad, 346
Major League Baseball (MLB). *See* Baseball
Majors, Lee, 225, 243, 260
"Make Me Laugh," 323
Make Room for Daddy/Danny Thomas Show, *83*, 83–84, 117
Making of the Band, 411
Malcolm and Eddie, 388
Malcolm in the Middle, 405
Malden, Karl, 344
Malkovich, John, 326.01
Malone, Dorothy, 169
Malone, Joe, 333
Malone, John, 370
Malone, Ray, 48
Mama, 43, 44
Mamet, David, 442
Man About the House, 242.01
Man and the City, 225
Mancini, Henry, 126, 133
Mancuso, FBI, 347
Mandan, Robert, 270, 320.02
Mandel, Howie, 310, 351, 439
Mandel, Loring, 112
Mandrell, Barbara, 292
Manetti, Larry, 301
"Man from Hope, The," 360
Man from U.N.C.L.E., The, 169–170
Manimal, 316
"Man Is Ten Feet Tall, A," 97
Mann, Michael, 318, 331
Manna, Charly, 164
Manning, Martha, 16
Mannix, 195–196, 219, 234, 256.07
Mansfield, Jayne, 110, 155
Man Show, The, 421.07
Mantooth, Randolph, 225
Manulis, Martin, 112, 235
Man with a Camera, 126
Many Loves of Dobie Gillis, The, 134–135, 339.03
March, Hal, 56, 99, 131
Marchand, Nancy, 79, 278, *279*, 398
March of Time, 137
Marconi, Guglielmo, 1, 2.01, *3*
Marconi Wireless Telegraph Company, 1, 2.01, 2.02
"Marcus-Nelson Murders, The," 239
Marcus Welby, M.D., 207, 259
Margulies, Julianna, 374, 467
Marinaro, Ed, 300
Market area for broadcast stations, 3
Markham, 126
Markle, Fletcher, 25
Mark Saber, 120
Married ... with Children, 333–334
Marriott, Evan Wallace, 423
Mars, Kenneth, 194
Marsh, Daniel, 46
Marshal Dillon, 145.03
Marshall, E. G., 143, 207, 210, 374
Marshall, Garry, 147, 220.03, 233, 243, 258, 274, 276–277, 343
Marshall, Penny, 258, 260
Marshall, Peter, 188.03

Marsters, James, 389
Martha Raye Show, The, 85
Martian invasion radio hoax (1938), 10.08
Martin, 388
Martin, Andrea, 264.03
Martin, Dean, 36, 38, 47, 55–56, 69, 85, 94, 101, 118, 159, 178.04, 262
Martin, Dick, 192–193, 270.01
Martin, Freddy, 64, 101
Martin, Kiel, 300
Martin, Mary, 90, 91
Martin, Millicent, 164
Martin, Nora, 14
Martin, Quinn, 129–130, 160, 178.07, 190, 226, 240
Martin, Ross, 133, 179, *180*
Martin, Steve, 262, 325
Martin, Tony, 68, 95, 119
Martinez, Tony, 117
Martin Kane, Private Eye, 68
"Marty," 79
Marvin, Lee, 120, 134
Marx, Chico, 60, 126.04
Marx, Groucho, 34.01, 43, 60, 126.04
Marx, Harpo, 126.04, 145.01
Marx Brothers career finale ("Incredible Jewel Robbery"), 126.04
Mary Hartman, Mary Hartman, 267–268, *269*
Mary Kay and Johnny, 33, 34.03
Mary Tyler Moore Show, The, 217, *218*, 249–250, 265.03, 271, 278
*M*A*S*H*, 233–235, *234*, 255, 261, 271, 312, 313, 468.04
Mason, Jackie, 344, 347
Massey, Raymond, 144
Masterpiece Theater, 211, 221, 227.04, 264, 315.06
Masterson, Danny, 405
Matalin, Mary, 385
Mathers, Jerry, 118, *119*
Matheson, Richard, 324
Matheson, Tim, 325
Matinee Theater, 121
Matlock, 332
Matson, Boyd, 338.04
Matthews, Chris, 385, 436
Matthews, Larry, 146, *147*
Matt Houston, 307
Maude, 233, *233*, 247
Maverick, 115, 125, 127, 128, 140–141; as *Bret Maverick*, 299
Max Headroom, 331, 387
Maxwell, Elsa, 111
May, Donald, 140
May, Elaine, 164
Mayberry RFD. See Andy Griffith Show
Mayehoff, Eddie, 75
Mayo, Whitman, 228
"Mayor and the Manicure, The," 9
Mayron, Melanie, 335
Mays, Tom, 47
McAuliffe, Christa, *325*
MCA/Universal, 304, 394.03. *See also* Universal
McBrayer, Jack, 449

McCain, John, *458*, 459–463, *461*
McCallum, David, 169
McCann, Chuck, 187
McCarthy, Eugene, 199
McCarthy, Jenny, 383
McCarthy, Joseph, 52, 87–89, 93.05; docudrama "Tail Gunner Joe," 264
McCarthy, Kevin, 208
McCarthy, Mary, 39
McCarthy, Richard, 200
McCartney, Paul, 162, 163, 285, 322, 418, 427
McClanahan, Rue, 326
McCloud, 221, 225
McClure, Doug, 141, 154.03
McCord, Kent, 201
McCormack, Eric, 405
McCormack, Patty, 112
McCormick, Pat, 155.02
McCrary, J. R. "Tex," 29, 47
McCune, Hank, 50
McCutchen, Richard S., 100
McDaniel, Hattie, 59
McDaniel, James, 352, 366
McDermott, Dylan, 395
McDowell, Ronnie, 348
McEachin, James, 241
McElhenney, Rob, 448
McFadden, Cynthia, 439.04
McFadden, Gates, 340
McGavin, Darren, 134
McGee, Frank, 134, 178.08, 206, 211.05, 221.04, 244.03
McGinley, Ted, 334
McGinnis, Joe, 200
McGiveney, Maura, 204
McGoohan, Patrick, 137.01, 164, 170, *193*, 196–197, 227
McGovern, George, 229, 236, 237
McGraw, Charles, 102
McGwire, Mark, 397.03
McHale's Navy, 154
McKay, Gardner, 129
McKay, Jim, 51, 121, 136, 137, 230
McKean, Michael, 258, 396
McKellar, Danica, 338
McKinny, Laura Hart, 376
McLaughlin, Kyle, 348–349
McMahon, Ed, 51, 120.02, 156, 275, 314, 438
McMahon, Vince, 412
McMillan and Wife, 225–226
McMullen, Jay, 150
McMurray, Sam, 333
McMurtry, Larry, 344.05
McNamara, Robert, 181
McNeill, Don, 17, 85.05
McQuade, Arlene, 43
McQueen, Butterfly, 59
McQueen, Steve, 125, 143
McRaney, Gerald, 346
McRee, Lisa, 393.01, 399.03
McShane, Ian, 429.02
Meadows, Audrey, *viii*, 77.01, *104*, 105, 257.04
Meaney, Colin, 340
Meany, Kevin, 353
Meara, Anne, 286.04
Mechanical television system, 5–6, *6*

Media conglomerate synergy and cross-ownership, 406–407, 447–448, 458, 473–476
Media One cable system acquired by AT&T, 417.04
Media Rights Capital (CW Sunday programming arrangement), 463
Medic, 96
Medical Center, 207
Medical dramas, 96, 144–145, 154–155, 207–208, 310–311, 373–374
Medical Investigation, 434
Medium, 465
Meester, Leighton, 456
Meet McGraw, 120
Meet Mr. McNutley, 94
Meet My Folks, 445
Meet the Press, 21.02, 25, 30, 289, 363.01, 457.03
Melgar, Gabriel, 249
Melis, Jose, 85.01
Melody Street, 87
Meloni, Christopher, 406
Melrose Place, 359.04, 387
Melton, James, 36
Melvin, Allan, 106
"Memphis by Morning," 112
Men at Law, 217
Menendez brothers coverage, 365
Menotti, Gian-Carlo, 66.08
Mentalist, The, 461.01
Mercury Theater, 10.08
Meredith, Burgess, 49, 52, 323
Meredith, Don, 220.02
Meredith, James, 171
Meriwether, Lee Ann, *93*, 178
Merkerson, S. Epatha, 353
Merman, Ethel, 90
Merrill, Gary, 97
Merv Griffin Show, The, 155.02, 173.06, 205.07
Messing, Debra, 405
Metcalf, Laurie, 341
Metcalfe, Burt, 313
Metromedia, 105, 121.04. 295; DuMont roots, 121.04; stations acquired by News Corporation for Fox, 327.01, 328;
Meyers, Seth, 437
MGM film library acquired by Turner broadcasting, 327.02
MGM Parade, 102
Miami Vice, 318–319, 344
Michael, George, 321
Michael Nesmith in Television Parts, 321.04
Michael Richards Show, The, 411.04
Michaels, Al, 347.01, 441.05
Michaels, Loren, 316, 262–263, 326, 415
Michaels, Mia, 438
Michaels, Nick, 306
Michener, James, 58.04
Mickey Mouse Club, The, 103, 126.08
Microsoft: partnership with NBC, 382; sponsorship of online *Guild* series, 455
Microwave links, 9

Middle, The, 467
Midler, Bette, 320.01, 360
Midnight Caller, 344
Midnight Special, The, 237.02, 262
Mid-season schedule changes tactic, 175–176, 430
Midwestern coaxial cable network, 41.02, 43.01
Mifune, Toshiro, 291
Mighty Mouse Playhouse, 103.01
"Migrants," 211.04, 212
"Mikado, The," 79
Mike Douglas Show, The, 146.01
Mike Wallace Interviews, 113.03
Milano, Alyssa, 365, 405
Milch, David, 366, 429.02
Miles, Sylvia, 146
Milland, Ray, 94, 126
Millennium coverage, 406.01
"Millennium 2000," 406.01
Miller, Alan, 303
Miller, Arthur, 52, 326.01
Miller, Christa, 381
Miller, Dennis, 263, 326
Miller, George, 323
Miller, J. P., 123.04
Miller, Marvin, 97.02
Miller, Mitch, 134, 140.01
Miller, Wentworth, 441
Millionaire, The, 97.02
"Million Dollar Ripoff, The," 260
Mills, Alley, 338
Mills, Heather, 438
Milner, Martin, 141, 201
Miner, Worthington, 14, 15, 33, 36, 41, 43, 44, 79, 96, 103, 112, 133.05, 140.05
Miniseries format, 241, 242, 264, 265, 268, 273, 275, 288, 291, 311, 316, 320, 331, 355; strengths and flaws, 273
Minnelli, Liza, 159, 264, 427.04
Minow, Newton, 140.02, 142, 143, 149, 152, 153–154, 155.05, 165
Mintz, Eli, *42*, 43
"Miracle on Ice," 292
"Miracle on 34th St.," 101
"Miracle Worker, The," 112, 132
Mirror of reality style of program, 17
Mischer, Don, 427
Misfits of Science, 326
Miss America Pageant, *93*, 435.03
Mission: Impossible, 188.01, 219, 344.02
Missus Goes A' Shopping, 15
Mitchell, Chad, 162
Mitchell, Elizabeth, 431, 465.02
Mitchell, George, 434.05, 429
Mitchell, Guy, 118, 119
Mitchell, Warren, 179.06, 195
Mixed Bag New Wave, 303, 309.02
MLB Network/MLB.com, 461.03
MNT. *See* MyNetworkTV
Mobil Oil Corporation funds *Masterpiece Theater*, 211
Mobil Showcase Network, 268
Modern Family, 467
Mod Squad, The, 201–202, 236
Moesha, 381
Mole, The, 417, 418

Molly Dodd. See Days and Nights of Molly Dodd
Monaco, Kelly, 438
Monaghan, Dominic, 431
Monash, Paul, 148
Monday Night Fights, 121.08
Monday Night Football, 220.02, 242, 291, 293.02, 307, 315.01, 321.01, 347, 394, 421, 429, 441.05, 447
Monday Night Special, 228
Moneychangers, The, 265
Monk, 419, 430, 448
Monkees, The, 188
Monroe, Vaughn, 38
Monsoon, Gorilla, 28
Montalban, Ricardo, 271
Montgomery, Elizabeth, 167
Montgomery, George, 125
Montgomery, Robert, 48.07, 94
Monty Python's Flying Circus, 210.03, 250–251, 250.03, 295
Moon landing coverage, 206, *206*
Moonlighting, 320–321, 327
Moonves, Leslie, 375.06, 387.08, 429.06
Moore, Clayton, *47*, 50
Moore, Dudley, 372
Moore, Garry, 49.02, 58.05, 64, 67.04, 186–187
Moore, Mandy, 438
Moore, Mary Tyler, 146–147, *147*, 217–219, *218*, 234, 276
Moore, Michael, 437
Moore, Monte, 296.03
Moore, Roger, 129, 139, 155.01, 164
Moore, Tim, 57
Moore, Tom, 154
Moran, Erin, 243
Moran, Terry, 439.04
Moranis, Rick, 264.03
Morey Amsterdam Show, The, 41.06
Morgan, Edward P., 165, 198, 212
Morgan, Gary, 146
Morgan, Harry, 195, *234*, 235, 313
Morgan, Henry, 21.12, 164, 172
Morgan, Jane, 76
Morgan, Russ, 38
Morgan, Tracy, 449
Morgan, Wesley, 77
Morganthau, Henry III, 163–164
Moriarty, Michael, 273, 353
Mork and Mindy, 277, 286, 288
Morning Show, The, 86, 103
Morris, Garrett, 263
Morris, Howard, 49, 86, 94, 179
Morris, Kathryn, 429
Morrison, Brian, 233
Morrison, Herbert, 10.03
Morrison, Jennifer, 434
Morrow, Jeff, 97
Morrow, Rob, 344, 350.06, 363
Morse, Barry, 160, 256.04
Morse, David, 310, *310*
Morse, Samuel, 1
Mosley, Roger E., 301
Moss, Elisabeth, 452
Moss, Frank, 120–121
Most Deadly Game, 222

Mostel, Zero, 52
Mother's Day, 123.05
Mother Teresa, 390
"Motown 25: Yesterday, Today, and Forever," 311.04
Mouseketeers, The, 103
Movie Channel, The (cable channel), 332.03, 326.02
Movie of the Week, 209, 210, 228, 236, 256.07
Movies: feature films in prime time, 102, 102.05, 112.04, 113.01, 145, 146, 178.05, 185, 194, 441.04; first made-for-TV movie, 172.04; from British sources, 44, 102, 102.05; made-for-TV movies as series pilots, 210; movie characters migrate to radio, 18.10, 29.03; pre-1948 movies released to television, 103; topical themes in theatrical films playing on television, 194
Mowbray, Alan, 87
Mowry, Tamera, 367
Mowry, Tia, 367
Moyers, Bill, 227.03, 229, 304
Mr. and Mrs. North, 22, 24,225
Mr. District Attorney, 24, 68
Mr. Dugan, 279.04
Mr. Ed, 137.05
Mr. I Magination, 44
Mr. Lucky, 133
Mr. Novak, 162.07
Mr. Peepers, 66–67, 75
Mr. President, 333
"Mr. Roberts," 33
Mr. Rogers' Neighborhood, 197
Mrs. Columbo, 275
Mrs. G Goes to College, 147
Mr. Show, 380.02, 383
Mr. Smith, 316
Mr. Solo, 169
Mr. T, 311
Mr. T and Tina, 260–261
Mr. Terrific, 188.05
MSG (cable channel), 296.01, 297, 297.02, 304
MSNBC (cable channel), 382, 415, 429, 436, 442, 457.05, 459
M Squad, 120
MTV (cable channel), 297.05, 298, *298*, 306, 326.02, 327.04, 332.03, 365, 383–385, *385*, 439.05, 448, 459; 1992 election coverage, 360; 2008 election coverage, 459; first game show, 338.05; Live Aid broadcast, 321–322; Music awards shows, 320.01, 419; *The Real World*, 359.01; Super Bowl halftime show, 426–427; *Unplugged*, 347.06; veejays, 297.05, 327.04
"Much Ado About Nothing," 237
Mudd, Roger, 165, 173, 245, 286.08, 292.08, 303.04, 311.06
Muggs, J. Fred, 80, 86
Muir, Jean, 53–55
Mulgrew, Kate, 373
Mull, Martin, 268, 271.06, 314, 325, 341
Mullally, Megan, 405

Mullavey, Greg, 267–268, *269*
Mulligan, Richard, 270, 343
Multi-cam process for filmed series, 50
Municipal Court, 126
Muniz, Frankie, 405
Munsel, Patrice, 118
Munsters, The, 168
Munsters Today, The, 344
Muppet Show, The, 264.02
Murder. *See* Death
"Murder by the Book," 323
Murder One, 379
Murder, She Wrote, 320, 344, 372, 381, 382
Murdoch, Rupert, 328, 332, 359.02, 386.04, 423.05, 468, 476
Murphy, Brian, 242.01
Murphy, Eddie, 263, 292.07, 357.02
Murphy, Mary, 438
Murphy, Michael, 339.02
Murphy Brown, 342–343, 359; criticism by Dan Quayle, 358–359
Murray, Arthur, 49.04
Murray, Bill, 263
Murray, Don, 97
Murray, Jan, 38
Murray, Ken, 36
Murrow, Edward R., 10.05, 18, 24, 35, 41.05, 58.06, 63, 74, 79, 84.02, *87*, 88, 126.03, 132.02, 133, 139, 152, 158, 163.04, 173.05, 212; "Harvest of Shame," 139; reports on Joseph McCarthy, 88
Musante, Tony, 241
Music, Lorenzo, 271
Musical drama in *Cop Rock*, 352–353
Music Bingo, 122
Music Scene, 210.01
Music variety format: fifteen minute length, 33, 35.04, 41.07, 66.07, 102.01, 118; grows in prime time, 118–119
Music videos, 309.05, 315.11, 321.04
Must carry requirement for cable, 296; 370–371
Must See TV on NBC, 318, 368, 405
Mutual Broadcasting System radio network (MBS), 7.07, 18.08, 25; breakthrough news interview show *Meet the Press*, 21.02, 25; purchased by Westwood One, 326.04
My Big Fat Obnoxious Fiancé, 429
Myers, Dee Dee, 385
Myers, Mike, 263
Myerson, Bess, *93*
My Favorite Husband, 35.02, 42, 64, 76
My Favorite Martian, 167
My Friend Irma, 42, 66
My Hero, 75
My Little Margie, 66, 84
My Living Doll, 176
My Mother the Car, 178.02

My Name Is Earl, 442, 447
MyNetworkTV (MNT) (broadcast network), 442, 445, 445.02, 462.06
Myrer, Anton, 264
My Sister Sam, 331
MySpace, 459
My So-Called Life, 373.01
Mystery Science Theater, 371, 385–386
"My Sweet Charlie," 210
My Three Sons, 141
My Two Dads, 339
My Wife and Kids, 417

NAB (National Association of Broadcasters), 70–71, 254–256
Nabors, Jim, x, *141*, 167, 209, 222
Nader, Ralph, 263
Nadler, Teddy, 123
Nakamoto, Mark, 421
Naked City, 126, 141
Naked Truth, The, 388, 394
Nakia, 251
Namath, Joe, 220.02
Name of the Game, 201
Name That Tune, 122, 132, 285
Nancy Walker Show, The, 261
Nanny, The, 369.03
Narz, Jack, 123–124, *125*
NASCAR coverage, 412.01; Earnhardt death, 412.01
Nash Bridges, 382
Nashville Network, The (cable channel), as TNN, 411.02
National Amusements Inc. acquires Viacom, 332.03
National Basketball Association (NBA). *See* Basketball
National Football League (NFL). *See* Football
National Hockey League (NHL). *See* Hockey
National Network, The (cable channel), as TNN, 411.02
National Public Radio (NPR), 221.01, 391, 459; as brand name, 475
National Velvet, 141
Naudet, Jules, 414
Navy Log, 106, 120.03
Nazi TV in Germany, 7.10, 8
NBA Inside Stuff, 353.02, 418.07
NBA TV/NBA.com, 403.06
NBC (broadcast network), 3, 6.03, 9, 471; acquisition by GE, 327.06, 328; arena football venture, 423.02; as Blue and Red networks, 3, 11.08, 13–14, 471; Burbank (California) television production site established, 78; comedy variety program strategy, (1950s) 55–56, 68–69, 85–86, 94, 106, 111; (1960s) 192–193; (1970s) 262–263; daytime programming, 43.04, 58.03, 87, 155.02, 287.07, 397.06; drama anthologies, 18.06, 21–22, 27.02, 27.08, 29, 41, 44, 78–79, 97, 107, 112, 121, 323–325; experimental

television station W2XBS, 6.07; Hulu.com venture, 457.02; late night programming, 39, 41.07, 47–48, 59.06, 91–93, 110–111, 133.03, 155–156, 263, 292.02, 303.01, 306, 329, 357.01, 360, 361, 369, 379, 434.01, 456–457, 464–467; late late night programming, 242.04, 293.04, 293.09, 303.01, 305, 357.03, 361, 369.02, 397.06; management, 7.01, 48, 48.01, 69, 85.02, 86–87, 103.08, 107, 109, 121.07, 179.05, 210.05, 228.01, 257.03, 272, 273, 274–275, 279.05, 293, 299, 328, 329, 353–354, 412.02, 447.01; morning programming, 69–70, 80, 140.07, 154.01, 221.04, 244.03, 244.05, 264.01, 264.07, 302.05, 338.04, 353.05, 359.05, 363.01, 370.03, 387.02, 403.01, 411.01, 421.01, 453.01, 457.03; NBC.com, 387.04; NBC Week tactic, 172.02; news coverage operations, 10.03, 18, 18.09, 34.05, 158–159, 178.08, 179.02, 251.04, 382, 413, 415; news documentaries, 77.04, 133–134, 139, 171, 212; news magazines, 200, 250.04, 263, 284–285, 330, 357.06, 363.03, 390, 393–394; nightly news, 34, 41, 109, 112.03, 158, 178.08, 211.05, 221.04, 257.06, 286.07, 292.08, 303.04, 311.06, 347.02, 434.02, *436*; Olympic Games boycott, 289–290; Olympic Games rights deal through 2012, 394; radio network sold, 338.02; station trade with Westinghouse (Cleveland/Philadelphia), 97.06; *Today* as top money maker, 86; Universal merger, 429; USA cable profit tops NBC network, 458; weekend daytime programming, 79, 359.05, 421.01; weekend late night programming, 250.04, 262–263; XFL venture, 412. *See also* Baseball; Basketball; Boxing; Bravo; CNBC; Color television; Football; GE; MSNBC; Must See TV; NBC.com; Olympic Games; Oxygen; Pax; Ratings; RCA; Silverman, Fred; Sports; Telemundo; *Today*; *Tonight*; Vivendi/Universal Entertainment; Weather Channel; Wrestling coverage
NBC.com, 387.04, 443, 457.05
NBC Comedy Hour, 106
NBC Comics, 58.02
"NBC: First 50 Years," 264
NBC Magazine, 285
NBC Mystery Movie, 221, 225–227, 264.05. *See also Four-in-One*
NBC News, 112.03
NBC News at Sunrise, 403.01
NBC News Overnight, 305, 357.03
NBC News Update, 251.04

NBC Nightly News, 211.05, 257.06, 303.04, 311.06, 434.02
NBC Nightside, 397.06
NBC Novels for Television, 75, 264–265, 275, 311
NBC Saturday Night at the Movies, 146, 185
NBC Television Newsreel, 18
NBC Television Theater, 18.06, 21–22
NBC Universal, 429, 473
NBC Weather Plus service, 457.04
NBC White Paper, 139
NCIS (Naval Criminal Investigative Service), 429, 434
NCIS: Los Angeles, 467
Neal, Patricia, 236
Neal, Roy, 146.02
Nearing, Vivienne, 114, 131, 132
Neill, Sam, 331
Nelly, 426
Nelson, Barry, 93.04, 163
Nelson, Craig T., 345.01
Nelson, David, 17, 76–77
Nelson, Ed, 169
Nelson, Harriet (Hilliard), 17–18, 18.02, 76–77
Nelson, Judd, 388
Nelson, June (Blair), 77
Nelson, Kris (Harmon), 77
Nelson, Ozzie, 17–18, 18.02, 76–77
Nelson, Rick, 17, 76–77
Nelson, Tracy, 308, 344
Nemec, Corin, 351
Nesmith, Michael, 188, 321.04
Nessen, Ron, 263
NET (broadcast network). *See* Public Television
Netflix mail order video, 458; as streaming video, 475
NET Playhouse, 211
"Network," 265.01, 278.02
Networks, 3. *See also* Broadcast networks; Cable channels
Neuwirth, Bebe, 368
New Andy Griffith Show, The, 217
New Avengers, The, 264.08
New Christy Minstrels, 162
New Dick Van Dyke Show. See Dick Van Dyke Show
Newell, Patrick, 196
Newhart, 307, 350.04
Newhart, Bob, 147, 271, 307, 350.04, 365
Newlywed Game, The, 179.07, 205–206
Newman, Edwin, 163.01, 321.02, 394.06
Newman, Kevin, 399.03
Newman, Laraine, 263, 325
Newman, Paul, 80, 106, 112
Newman, Phyllis, 172
Newman, Randy, 352
Newmar, Julie, 176, 178
New Revue, 81
News: affiliate and network tensions, 213–214, 305; available in color, 179.02; available twenty-four hours a day, 287.06, 297–298; cinema verite style documentaries, 138–

139, 150, 274; conflicts with Johnson administration, 181–183; conflicts with Nixon administration, 212, 213–214, 228–230, 236–238, 244–245; demands entry at political news conference, 72; early radio and television news, 10.03, 17–18; effects of news coverage on story itself, 165, 354–35, 377, 401; instant analysis controversy, 213–214, 237, 244; longest continuous period for TV coverage of one news event, 415; Murrow takes a stand on Joseph McCarthy, 88; one minute news, 251.04, 339.05; policy of network news independence, 137–138; prime time nightly news, 77.03, 123.01; program lengths expand to sixty minutes, 205.04, 311.07; program lengths expand to thirty minutes, 158–159, 178.08, 188.04, 282; programming to fill strike gaps, 458; tabloid feel and celebrity coverage, 413; what constitutes news?, 401. *See also* ABC, CBS, CNN, Fox, NBC, Public Television
News and Views, 35.06, 137
News Corporation, 472, 473; acquires DirecTV, 423.05; acquires stations from Metromedia, 328; acquires Twentieth Century Fox, 328; acquires *Wall Street Journal*, 453.06; fee payment conflict with Time Warner Cable, 468. *See also* Fox
News from Washington, 29.04, 34
Newshour.pbs.org, 442, *469*
NewsHour with Jim Lehrer, The, 391, *391*, 401, *430*, 459, 442; as *PBS NewsHour*, 465.07, *469*
New Show, The, 316
NewsRadio, 375.03
Newton, Becki, 444
New York drama versus Hollywood drama. *See* Hollywood competes with New York
New York Undercover, 388
Next Great Champ, The, 438
NFL Network/NFL.com, 427.05, 445.07
NHL Network/NHL.com, 453.03
Nicholas, Nichelle, 190
Nichols, 225
Nichols, Mike, 164
Nick at Nite (cable channel), 321.06, 354.03, 387, 415
Nickelodeon (cable channel), 296.02, 297, 321.06, 326.02, 332.03, 354.03, 354.04, 385, 388, 415, 439.05; fills broadcast Saturday morning cartoon slots, 421.01; reruns of newly made broadcast first-run series, 354.03
Nielsen, Leslie, 208, 210, 303.02
Nielsen ratings service, 56; DVR

tracking, 439; manipulating the process, 176; overnight, 242; turnaround time, 90; "three windows" tracking, 475; twice-monthly books procedure, 177; Univision tracking, 444–445
Night Court, 126, 314, 326
Night Gallery, 221, 323
Nightline, 283, 361, 366, 382, 401, 425, 439.04, 464
"Nightmare at 20,000 Feet," 323
Nightside, 357.03, 397.06
Night Stalker, The, 228
Nightwatch, 305, 357.03
Nilsson, Harry, 187
Nimoy, Leonard, 189–190, 339
Nine, The, 450
1968 Democratic Convention in Chicago. *See* Political coverage of conventions
90 Bristol Court, 172.03, 210
Nip/Tuck, 448
Niven, David, 94, 170
Nixon, Cynthia, 339.02, 396
Nixon, Pat, 73, *245*
Nixon, Richard, ix, 31, 73, 87, 137.02, 138, 151, 155, 192–193, 199, 200, 201.01, *212*, 212–214, 228–229, *229*, 230, 236–238, *243*, 243–245, *245*, 265.04; resignation speeches, 245. *See also* Watergate coverage
Nixon, Trisha, 73
Nizer, Louis, 108–109
Noah's Ark, 111
Noble, Edward, 11.08, 14
No Holds Barred, 286
Nolan, Kathy, 91, 117
Nolte, Nick, 259
Noncommercial television. *See* Public Television
"Noon on Doomsday," 107
Norris, Chuck, 365
North, Jay, 134
Northern Exposure, 350.06, 353, 363
Norton, Cliff, 44
Norville, Deborah, 347.04, 353.05
Norwood, Brandy. *See* Brandy
Noth, Chris, 353, 397
Nothing Sacred, 395
"No Time for Sergeants," 97, 97.04
No Time for Sergeants, 167
Nouri, Michael, *316*
Novello, Don, 262
Now, 212
Nowhere Man, 380
NPACT coverage for PBS: of Nixon impeachment, 244–245; of Watergate, 238
NPR (National Public Radio), 221.01, 391, 459; as brand name, 475
'N Sync, 407, 426
NTSC color process, 81
Numbers. *See* Television numbers
Nurses, The, 155
Nutt House, The, 347
Nydell, Ken, 44
Nye, Louis, 109
NYPD, 195

NYPD Blue, 366, 419, 430

O&Os (owned and operated) stations, 4, 382, 386.07, 407
Obama, Barack, *430*, *458*, 459–463, *461*, *463*
Obama, Malia Ann, *463*
Obama, Michelle, *463*
Obama, Sasha, *463*
Obama Girl (Amber Lee Ettinger), 459
Ober, Ken, 338.05
O'Brian, Hugh, 104
O'Brien, Conan, 361, 366, 369.02, 434.01, 456–457, 461.06, 462.02, 464–467
O'Brien, Edmund, 185
O.C., The, 429
O'Connor, Carroll, 219–220, *219*, 339
O'Connor, Donald, 68, 85, 94
Odd Couple, The, 220.03
Odenkirk, Bob, 380.02, 383
O'Donnell, Chris, 467
O'Donnell, Gene, 33
O'Donnell, Rosie, 381.03, 411
O'Donoghue, Michael, 263
"Offer, The," 227
Office, The (U.K. version), 412.05
Office, The (U.S. version), 434, 442, 455
O'Flaherty, Terry, 140.06
Ogilvy, Ian, 278.01
Oh, Sandra, 433
O'Hanlon, Redmond, 100
O'Hara, Catherine, 264.03, 325
O'Hara, John, 260
O'Hara, U.S. Treasury, 225
Oh Boy, 126.07
Oh Grow Up, 403
Ohlmeyer, Don, 289
Oh Madeline, 314
O'Hurley, John, 438
Oka, Masi, 450
O'Keefe, Walter, 43.03
Olbermann, Keith, 436
Olin, Ken, 316, 335, 388
Olivier, Laurence, 102.05
O'Loughlin, Gerald, 217
Olsen, Ashley, 339
Olsen, Mary-Kate, 339
Olsen, Merlin, 299
Olsen, Ole, 39
Olson, Johnny, 15
Olson, Kaitlin, 448
Olympic Games coverage by network and cable channel: ABC, 136, 230, 259, 288, 289, 316; CBS, 136, 359, 371, 394; CNBC, 457.05; MSNBC, 457.05; NBC, 275, 289–290, 343, 359, 394, 442, 457.05, 467; NBC.com, 457.05; Oxygen, 457.05; Reichs Rundfunk (Germany), 8; Telemundo, 457.05; USA, 457.05
Olympic Games coverage of Summer Games by year/location: 1936 Berlin, 8; 1960 Rome, 136; 1972 Munich, 230; 1976 Montreal, 259; 1980

Olympic Games coverage of Summer Games by year/location: 1980 (cont.) Moscow, 275, 289–290; 1988 Seoul, 343; 1992 Barcelona, 359; 2008 Beijing, 457.05

Olympic Games coverage of Winter Games by year/location: 1960 Squaw Valley, 136; 1976 Innsbruck, 259; 1980 Lake Placid, 288, 289; 1984 Sarajevo, 316; 1992 Albertville, 359; 1994 Lillehammer, 371; 1998 Nagano, 394; 2006 Turin, 442; 2010 Vancouver, 467

Olympic Games TripleCast cable package, 359

Olyphant, Timothy, 429.02

O'Mara, Jason, 461.02

Omnibus, 79, 140.03

Omnibus anthologies, 79, 102.05, 134, 140.03, 145.01, 186, 263

Once and Again, 406–407

Once an Eagle, 264

O'Neal, Ryan, 169

One Day at a Time, 258, 260, 261, 271, 314

One Foot in the Grave, 387

"One Hour in Disneyland," 59.02

100 Grand, 162.02

O'Neill, Ed, 334, 421, 467

O'Neill, Eugene, 66.05

O'Neill, Thomas "Tip," 275

"One Left Over," 79

One Man's Family, 7

One-minute series, 244.04, 251.04, 339.05

One Tree Hill, 429, 435

Online. See Internet

Onorati, Peter, 352–353

Ontkean, Michael, 348

Operation 100 strategy by CBS, 209

Operation Prime Time (OPT), 268, 295

Operation: Success, 37

Oppenheimer, Alan, 343

Oppenheimer, Jess, 35.02, 65–66

Oppenheimer, J. Robert, 88

Oprah Winfrey Network (OWN) (cable channel), 465.05, 475

Oprah Winfrey Show, The, 331.02

O'Quinn, Terry, 431

Orbach, Jerry, 353

O'Reilly, Bill, 385, 424, 436

O'Reilly, Harry, 357

Original Amateur Hour, The, 31, 211.06

Orlando, Tony, 260

Ormandy, Eugene, 33

Ortiz, Ana, 444

Osbourne, Ozzy, 418

Osbournes, The, 418–419

Oscars. See Academy awards shows

Osmond, Donny, 438

Osmond, Ken, 118

Osmond Brothers, The, 154.05

O'Sullivan, Richard, 242.01

Oswald, Lee Harvey, 165

Our Miss Brooks, 35.03, 49.01, 76

Our Private World, 169

Our Secret Weapon—The Truth, 53

"Our Town," 106

"Our World," 189.03

Our World, 330

Outdoor Life Network (cable channel), 439.02

Outer Limits, The, 162.04, 189, 375.04, 386

Overnight. See NBC News Overnight

Owen Marshall, 225

Owens, Buck, 205

Owens, Gary, 193

Owens, Jesse, 8

OWN (Oprah Winfred Network) (cable channel), 465.05

Owned and operated stations. See O&Os

"Ox-Bow Incident, The," 101

Oxygen (cable network), 453.05, 457.05

Oz, 383

Paar, Jack, 29.02, 34, 64, 68, 85.01, 86, 111, 133.03, 155, 156, 172, 237.01, 242.05

Pabst Blue Ribbon Bouts, 136

Pace, Lee, 455

Pacific Blue, 386

Padalecki, Jared, 441

Page, LaWanda, 228

Page, Patti, 79, 118–119

Pahlavi, Mohammed Reza (shah), 283

Palance, Jack, 111, 112, 211

Paley, William, 3–4, 6.08, 13, 21.07, 24, 42–43, 61, 72, 194, 238, 244, 265.05, 287.05, 288, 305, 311.03, 329, 353.01, 354

"Paley's Comet" talent raids, 42–43

Palillo, Ron, 258

Palin, Michael, 250

Palin, Sarah, 462–463, 462

Pallisers, The, 264

Paltrow, Bruce, 280, 310

Panettiere, Hayden, 449, 450

"Panic Button," 121

Pantomime Quiz, 43.03, 45

Papenfuss, Tony, 307

Paper Chase, The, 277–278, 306–307, 307

Papp, Joseph, 237

Pappas, Ike, 329

Paramount: acquires MSG, 304; acquired by Viacom, 370.04, 439.02, 442; interest in DuMont, 10.07, 11–12, 39–40, 61, 80, 105; starts UPN, 370, 472

Paramount Case legal action, 10.06, 34.08, 40, 429

Parent 'hood, The, 373

Paret, Benny "Kid," 146.03

Parikh, Sandeep, 455

Paris, 286.06, 288

Paris, Jerry, 147

Paris 7000, 208

Parker, Corey, 362

Parker, Eva Longoria, 433

Parker, Fess, 95

Parker, Mary-Louise, 448

Parker, Nicole Ari, 406.06

Parker, Noelle, 365

Parker, Robert B., 327

Parker, Sarah Jessica, 308, 362, 396

Parker, Trey, 385

Parker Bowles, Camilla, 390

Parker Lewis Can't Lose, 351

Parks, Bert, 26, 34, 41.04, 44, 113, 122

Parks, Van Dyke, 84

Parrish, Helen, 23

Parsons, Jim, 456

Parsons, Luther, 41

Parsons, Richard, 418.03

Partners in Crime, 320

Parton, Dolly, 339

Party of Five, 373

Passions, 453.01

Pastore, John, 148–149, 201, 207

Pastore, Vincent, 399

Pastorelli, Robert, 342, 395

Pate, Jonas, 441

Pate, Josh, 441

Patinkin, Mandy, 374, 442

"Patrolling the Ether," 14

Pat Sajak Show, The, 344.04, 350.02

"Patterns," 97–98

Patterson, Melody, 180

Paul, Henri, 390

Paul, Ralph, 122, 125

Pauley, Jane, 264.07, 302.05, 347.04, 357.06, 363.03, 382

Paul Sand in Friends and Lovers, 271

Paulsen, Pat, 187, 262

Paulson, Sarah, 381

Paul Whiteman's TV Teen Club, 39

Pax (broadcast network), 397.01, 403.03, 413, 435.04

Paxson, Lowell "Bud," 397.01, 403.03

Paxson Communications, 403.03

Paxton, Bill, 441.02

Paxton, Tom, 161

Pay TV, 295–296

PBL, 198

PBS (broadcast network). See Public Television

PBS NewsHour, 465.07, 469

Peabody award winners, 96, 195, 283

Peaceable Kingdom, 346

"Peanut Is a Serious Guy, The," 14

Peanuts franchise, 179.03

Pearl, 291, 387

Pearson, Drew, 26, 35

Peckinpah, Sam, 141

Peet, Amanda, 405

Pennies from Heaven, 352

Pennington, Ty, 433

People, 285

People Are Funny, 15, 18.04, 60

Pep, Willie, 15

Peppard, George, 241, 311

Percy, Charles, 138

Perfect Strangers, 347

Perlman, Rhea, 309, 387

Perlman, Ron, 336

Perot, Ross: 1992 presidential campaign, 360; 1996 presidential campaign, 385

Perrine, Valerie, 237.04, 285

Perrineau, Harold, 431

Perry, Luke, 351, 389

Perry, Matthew, 373, 449

Perry Como, 102.01, 111

Perry Mason, 11.09, 120–121, 125, 143, 326.03, 332, 370.01

"Perry Mason Returns," 326.03

Persian Gulf War. See War coverage by conflict: Persian Gulf War

Persky, Bill, 147, 255

Personal video recording systems. See DVR recording; TiVo recording system

Person to Person, 84.02, 126.03

Pete and Gladys, 141

Peter Gunn, 123.02, 126

Peter Loves Mary, 141

"Peter Pan," 91, 106

Petersen, Paul, 123.03

Petersen, William, 413, 461.05

Peterson, Seth, 406

Petrillo, James C., 17, 32

Petrocelli, 251

Petticoat Junction, 162.06, 166–167, 172, 174, 209

Pettit, Tom, 198

Petty, Tom, 427

Peyton Place, 168–169, 172, 174, 175, 177, 208

Philbin, Regis, 189.01, 402, 408

Philco Television Playhouse, 41, 79, 97, 98

Phil Donahue, 196.02

Philipps, Busy, 405

Phillips, Julianne, 354.01

Phillips, Stone, 357.06

Phil Silvers Show, The, 106. Also known as Sergeant Bilko; You'll Never Get Rich. See also Top Cat

Phyllis, 261, 271

Piaf, Edith, 56

Pick and Pat, 39

Pickens, James, Jr., 433

Picket Fences, 365

Pickles, Cristina, 310

Pierce, David Hyde, 357.05, 368

Pierce, Fred, 250.05, 256. 275, 286, 288

Pierson, Wayne, 8

Pietz, Amy, 380

Pig Sty, 373

Pilot production, 29, 456–457, 465, 467

Pinchot, Bronson, 325

Pinky and the Brain, 381

Pinza, Ezio, 68, 84

Piscopo, Joe, 292.07

Pistols 'n' Petticoats, 187

Piven, Jeremy, 429.07

Place, Mary Kay, 267

Plainclothesman, The, 104

Plana, Tony, 444

Plato, Dana, 280

Platt, Edward, 180

Platypus Man, 373

Playboy Channel, The (cable channel), 396

Playhouse 90, *111*, 112, 121, 123.04, 126, 129, 133.02, 134
"Playing for Time," 291
Play of the Week, 132.01, 133.05, 140.05
Play the Game, 21
Playwrights '56, 107, 112
Pleasence, Donald, 227
Pleshette, Suzanne, 271, 314, 350.04, 372
PM East/PM West, 140.06, 146.06
PM Magazine, 285
Poehler, Amy, 263, 459, 462
Poitier, Sidney, 79, 97
Police Squad!, 303.02
Police Story, 241, 251
Police Woman, 241, 251
Political coverage of conventions: 1932 Chicago, 7.05; 1940 Philadelphia, 11.05, 12; 1944 Chicago, 14; 1948 Philadelphia, 34–35; 1952 Chicago, 67.06, 67.07, *69*, 72; 1956 Chicago, 103.07, 1964 San Francisco, 173; 1968 Chicago, 199, 202; 1968 Miami Beach, 197.04; 1972 Miami Beach, 229–230; 1980 New York, 298; 1984 Dallas, San Francisco, 322; 1996 San Diego, 382, *382*; 2004 Boston, *430*, 436, *436*; 2004 New York, 436; 2008 Denver, Saint Paul, 458, *458*, 462
Political coverage of debates: 1960, 137.02, 138; 1976, 264.04; 1980, 292.04; 1992, 360; 2008, 459, 461, *461*, *462*, 463; strike cancellation, 459
Political coverage of election campaigns: 1920, 2, 3.03; 1928, 6; 1932, 8; 1940, 12; 1948, 34–35; 1952, ix, *60*, 62, 71, 73; 1956, 95; 1964, 172–173, 174; 1968, 192–193, 199, 200, 201.01; 1972, 236–237; 1980, 382, 385; 2000, 413; 2004, 435–437, *436*; 2008, 459–463, *461*, *462*; computer projections and exit polls, 73, 172–173, 292.06; fund-raising telethon, 228.06, 229; Supreme Court Florida recount ruling, 413
Political coverage of inaugurations: 1949 Truman, 41; 1953 Eisenhower, *viii*, ix, *76*; 1981 Reagan, 293.07; 1997 Clinton, *360*; 2009 Obama, *463*;
Political coverage of news conferences, 97.01, *145*, *161*
"Political Obituary of Richard Nixon, The," 151
Political satire, 164, 172, 174, 187, 221, 263, 339.02, 357.05, 437, 443, 459, 461–463
Political television commercials: 1952 Eisenhower, 73; 1964 Johnson, 173; 2004 Kerry, 436–437; 2008 Obama, 459
Pollan, Tracy, 308
Pollard, Michael J., 135
Pompeo, Ellen, 433

Ponce, Poncie, 129
Pons, Lily, *25*
Pool coverage, 35. *See also* Baseball World Series
Pop Idol, 420
Pop Stars, 411
Popular, 405
Porter, Cole, 69
Porter, Scott, 449
Post, Markie, 326, 362
Poston, Tom, 109, 307
Potter, Dennis, 331.04
Potts, Annie, 331
Povich, Maury, 406.02
"P.O.W.," 96
Powell, Colin, 354, 424
Powell, Dick, 94
Powell, Jonathan, 286.01
Powell, Michael, 427
Powers, Ron, 253
Powers of Matthew Star, The, 307
Powers That Be, The, 357.05
Practice, The, 395, 403, 433
Prato, Gino, 100
Prentiss, Paula, 194
Prepon, Laura, 405
"Prescription: Murder," 226, *226*
Presidential Timber, 34
Presley, Elvis, 106, 109–110, 133.06; "comeback special," 201.05; "from the waist up," 110
Presley, Priscilla, 348
Preston, Billy, 172.01, 263
"Presumption of Innocence," 121.09
Pretender, The, 388
Price, George, 36
Price, Vincent, 122, 123, 178
Price Is Right, The, 109, 112.05, 122, 285, 447.03
Pride of the Family, 83
Priestley, Jason, 347, 351
Prime Time Access rules, 222, 223–224, 231, 246, 253–254, 264.02, 295, 472; first run syndication in prime time access periods, 224, 285; requirements end, 381.06; waiver for Fox, 350
Prime time hours, 47
Prime Time Live, 345.06
Prime Time Sunday, 284–285
Prince, 427
Principal, Victoria, 287
Prinze, Freddie, 248–249, 260
Prison Break, 441, 450, 456
Prisoner, The, *193*, 196–197
Private Practice, 433, 449, 455
Probst, Jeff, 409, *409*
Producers' Showcase, 90–91, 97, 106, 114
Professional Father, 118
Profiler, 388
Profiles in Courage, 172.05
Program content warnings on-screen, 254, 269–270, 366, 393.05. *See also* Rating program content
Program ownership rules, 222, 334, 350
Program Playhouse, 44
Project 20, 139

Protectors, The, 210
Providence, 406
Provine, Dorothy, 129, 140
Provost, Jon, 95
Pryor, Richard, 263, 270.02
Psych, 448
Psychiatrist, The, 216–217, 221, 323
"PT-109," 120.03
Public Broadcasting Act of 1967, 198, 295
Public Prosecutor, 30–31
Public Television (NET and PBS), 71, 126.05, 151, 152, 205.01, 211, 295; affiliate servicing, 151, 205.01, 212; cable competition, 387; conflict with Nixon administration, 237–238; documentaries, 184, 198, 227.03, 244, 315.04, 321.02, 355, 373.02; from NET to PBS, 220.04, 221; funding, 152–153, 221; New York City presence, 151; news magazines, 184, 198, 212, 221; nightly news, 257.01, *261*, 311.07, 465.07, *469*; NPACT coverage of Watergate and Nixon impeachment, 238, 244–245; number of stations, 71, 151; online, 465.07, *469*; political convention coverage, *430*; reliance on British offerings, 152, 211, 221, 251; 2008 political campaign debates, 459; Spanish language V-me partnership, 444; Vietnam coverage, 213–214. *See also* *NewsHour*
Pulitzer Prize Playhouse, 58.04
Pulliam, Keshia Knight, 317
Punk'd, 448
Puppet Television Theater, 31
Purcell, Dominic, 441
Purcell, Sarah, 285
Pushing Daisies, 455, 457
Push, Nevada, 421
Putnam, George, 34
Puzo, Mario, 273

Al-Qaeda, 415, 424
QB VII, 242
Quantum Leap, 344
Quark, 276, 277
Quayle, Dan, 358–359
Queen for a Day, 25, 18.08, 103.03, 109
Queer as Folk, 399.04
Queer Eye for the Straight Guy, 430
Quincy, M.E., 264.05, 292, 387
Quinn, Anthony, 225
Quinn, Colin, 338.05
Quinn, Louis, 127
Quinn, Martha, 297.05, 298
Quinn, Sally, 237.05, 244.02
Quinn Martin productions, 129–130, 160–161
Quinto, Zachary, 450
Quiz Kids, 15
Quiz show scandal, 122–124; Congressional hearings, 131–

132; consequences, 132.06, 132–133; grand jury involvement, 124, 130–131; laws violated, 131, 132; subsequent increase in news and public affairs, 132.02, 133–134, 138
QVC (cable channel), 321.07, 357.04, 447

Rabe, David, 237
Rachins, Alan, 332
Racial tension news coverage, 171, 356, 375–376
Racket Squad, 68
Radio: adapting to rise of television, 45–46; comedy variety, 41.06, 55–56; early growth, 2, *2*, 2.07; games and quizzes, 33–34, 34.01, 41.04, 58.01; as Hollywood promotional platform, 471; ownership, 382, 386.07; payola scandal, 132.03, 132.05, 133; simulcast, 67.02; situation comedy, 56–58; as TV program source, 15, 18.05, 21, 33, 39, 43.06, 48.08, 49.03, 67.02, 77.02, 85.05
Radio Act of 1927, 2–3, 7.09
Radio Disney, 447.02
Radner, Gilda, 263
Radnor, Josh, 442
Radulovich, Milo, 88
Rafferty, Bill, 285
"Raid on Entebbe," 264
Raimi, Sam, 381, 387
Rains, Claude, 112
Ramis, Harold, 264.03
Randall, Sue, 118
Randall, Tony, 67, 220.03, 302
Randolph, Amanda, 57–58
Randolph, John, 308
Randolph, Joyce, *viii*
"Ransom for a Deadman," 227
Rap music, 351–352
Rashad, Phylicia, 317, *319*, 387
Rather, Dan, 158, 165, 199, 245, 283, 285, *285*, *293*, 338.03, 339.01, 364.04, 375.05, 390, 407, 413, 424, 434.04, *436*, 437
Rating program content, 382, 385, 387.01, 393.05
Ratings for broadcasters by network:
ABC as number one, 258–259, 260–261, 281, 374, 403; other, 128, 136, 145, 175, 185, 286–288
CBS as number one, 75, 156, 157, 159, 166–167, 209, 222, 288, 303, 316, 343, 371, 413, 421, 424, 429, 433–434, 439, 442, 449, 462.01 ; other, 370; "wrong" demographic ratings, 308, 372–373, 381–382, 387–388, 407
Fox demographic ratings success, 394, 424, 429; number one in 18 to 49, 434, 439, 442, 449, 457, 462.01, 468; number one total audience, 457

Ratings for broadcasters by
network (*cont.*)
  NBC as number one, 4, 37, 75,
    222, 318, 327, 329, 343, 379–
    380, 387, 394, 421, 424, 429;
    other, 145, 365, 434, 442, 449–
    450
Ratings for cable beat broadcasters,
  393, 413, 419
Ratings of highest rated:
  entertainment series, 266;
  individual episode, 292, 312,
  468.04; live news event, 377;
  most watched U.S. TV show,
  468.04; political nominating
  conventions, 462
Ratings points and shares, 37
Ratings services. *See* Crossley;
  Hooper; Nielsen; and Trendex
  ratings services
Ratings shift from total audience to
  target demographics, 293, 370,
  372, 382, 394, 409–411, 413
Ratings sweeps process, 281
Ratings tracking of broadcast
  networks adds Spanish-language
  data, 444–445
Ratzenberger, John, 309
Rawhide, 125
Raw Is War, 405
Rawls, Lou, 205
Ray, Johnny, 80
Rayburn, Gene, 93
Ray Charles singers, 102.01
Raye, Martha, 68, 85, 86, 106
RCA, 2, 3.02, 7.01, 7.06, 315.09;
  acquired by GE, 327.06; RCA-
  NTSC color process adopted, 81.
  See also NBC
RCA Victor Show, 84
Reagan, Nancy (Davis), 126.01,
  303
Reagan, Ron, Jr., 364.05
Reagan, Ronald, 107, 126.01,
  292.04, 292.06, 293.06, 302, 303
"Reagans, The," 427.06
Reality programming: (1970s) 285–
  286; (1980s) 339, 344, 345, 346,
  347; (1990s) 358, 359.01;
  (2000s) 406.03, 408–412, 418–
  419, 438–439; naked exposure
  gimmick, 409, 412;
  "nice" (positive) settings, 438–
  439; not covered by WGA
  contracts, 456; scheduling
  season flow, 438–439
Real McCoys, The, 117–118, 127,
  156
Real McKay, The, 51
Real People, 285–286, 291, 292
Real Sex, 396
Real Time, 437
"Real West, The," 139
Real World, The, 359.01
Reason, Rex, 140, 200
Reasoner, Harry, 145.04, 165, 181,
  220.05, 256.01, 264.06, 271.07,
  282, *285*
Rebel, The, 134
Rebel Billionaire: Branson's Quest
  for the Best, The, 438

Red Channels, 52, 53–54
Redford, Robert, 134
Redgrave, Lynn, 288, 347, 397
Redgrave, Vanessa, 291
Red Shoe Diaries, The, 371, 396
Red Skelton Show, The, 75–76, 107,
  209
Redstone, Sumner, 332.03, 370.04,
  407, 429.06, 442
Reed, Donna, 123.03
Reed, Robert, 143, 210.02
Reed, Shanna, 346
Reese, Della, 373.03
Reeves, George, 78.04, 126.06, 135
Regalbuto, Joe, 286.05, 342
Regina, Paul, 315.12
Regis and Kathy Lee, 402
Reichs Rundfunk, 8
Reid, Daphne Maxwell, 337, 346
Reid, Elliott, 172
Reid, Tim, *277*, 280, 337, 346, 367,
  394.07
Reiner, Carl, 49, 86, 94, 146–147,
  227.01, 246, 220, 246, 263
Reiser, Paul, 339, 363
Relay II satellite, 163.06
Relevancy programming season
  (1970–71), 215–217
Religious themes and programs,
  41.01, 236.01, 395; prime time
  sermons by Bishop Sheen, 68,
  104; religious identity in drama
  and comedy, 357–358
Remember the Days, 28
Remember WENN, 383, 452
Remington Steele, 308, 309–310,
  321, 326
Remini, Leah, 388
Remote Control, 338.05
Renaldo, Duncan, 59.03
Ren and Stimpy Show, The, 354.04
Renegade, 386
Reporter, The, 176
Repurposing, 406–407
"Requiem for a Heavyweight," *111*,
  112
Reruns: cable's use of reruns, 297,
  386–387, 400, 429–430, 447–
  448, 453–454; cost-saving
  measure by networks, 393; in
  daytime, 189.04, 270.08, 359.03;
  Disney rerun schedule for 1954
  series, 95; double runs, 393;
  edited for content (*Sopranos*),
  448; effects of family hour, 255;
  element in first Fox schedule,
  333; eliminated for *24* and *Lost*,
  441; in network prime time,
  112, 145.03; repurposing, 406–
  407; strike filler, 239, 456–457;
  in syndication, 106, 447; *TV
  Guide* change in identification
  of, 447; value of series, 75–76,
  361–362, 369–370, 429–430,
  439–441, 457
"Rescue from Gilligan's Island,"
  278.03
Rescue Me, 448
Rescue 911, 346
Restless Gun, 117
Retransmission consent settlement

between cable and broadcasters,
  370–371; rules and agreements,
  387.06
Rettig, Tommy, 95
Return of the Saint, 278.01
"Return to Mayberry," 327.03, 332
Reuben, Gloria, 374
Reynolds, Burt, 134, 239, 353
Reynolds, Frank, 197.03, 205.06,
  220.05, 271.07, 282, 283, 311.05
Reynolds, Marjorie, 77
Rhea, Caroline, 388
Rhenquist, William, 401
Rhimes, Shonda, 433
Rhinemann Exchange, The, 265
Rhoda, 249–250, *249*, 261, 271
Rice, Elmer, 66.05
Rich, John, 147
Richard, Cliff, 162
Richard Diamond, 120, 146
Richard Pryor Show, The, 270.02
Richards, Keith, 322
Richards, Michael, 287.04, 345.05,
  350.05, 364, 411.04
Richardson, Bill, 459
Richardson, Patricia, 359
Richie, Lionel, 321
Richman, Mark, 148
Rich Man, Poor Man, 242, 259,
  260
Rickles, Don, 325
Rifkin, Ron, 417
Rifleman, The, 125–126, 127
Rigg, Diana, 179, 196, 242.03
Riggs, Bobby, 242
Riley, Jack, 271
Ringside with Tex and Jinx, 29
*Rin Tin Tin. See Adventures of Rin
  Tin Tin*
Ripley, Robert, 286
Rise and Shine, 69
Ritchard, Cyril, 91, 97
Ritchson, Alan, 447
Ritter, John, 270, 320.02, 337, 363,
  421
Ritz Brothers, The, 68
Rivera, Geraldo, 284, 377, 393, 395
Rivera Live, 377
Riverboat, 134
Rivers, Joan, 332–333, 334
Rivers, Johnny, 170
Roaring Twenties, The, 140
Roar of the Rails, 43
Robbins, Harold, 208
Roberts, Brian, 347.07, 421.05
Roberts, Ralph, 205.03, 347.07,
  421.05
Robert MacNeil Report, 257.01,
  261
Robert Montgomery Presents,
  48.07, 112
Roberts, Doris, 310, *386*, 388
Roberts, John, *463*
Roberts, Pernell, 134
Roberts, Robin, 441.03, 468.01
Roberts, Tanya, 293.01
Robertson, Cliff, 78.06, 123.04
Robertson, Deirdre, 377
Robertson, Rev. Pat, 296, 339.07
Robinson, Anne, 408
Robinson, Bartlett, 11.09

Robinson, Holly, 333
Robinson, Hubbell, 186
Robinson, Larry, 43
Robinson, Max, 271.07, 282
Roble, Chet, *55*
RoboCop, 387
Rocco, Alex, 346
Rock, Blossom, 168
Rock, Chris, 263, 350, 439.01
Rockford Files, The, 250.02, 251,
  372
Rock music shows and
  performances, 119–120, 126.07,
  133.06, 155.07, 172.01, 173.03,
  201.05, 210.01, 236.03, 262,
  306, 321–322, 348
Rock 'n' Roll Revue/The Big Beat,
  119
Rockwell, Rick, 406.03
Rockwell, Robert, 76
Rocky and His Friends, 132.04
Rocky King, 104
Roday, James, 448
Rod Brown of the Rocket Rangers,
  78.06
Roddenberry, Gene, 188–190, 339
Rodeo coverage, 27.04
Rodgers, Richard, 69, 77.04
Rogen, Seth, 405
Rogers, Kenny, 321
Rogers, Roy, 25, 103
Rogers, Wayne, 234–235, 288
Rogers, Will, Jr., 86, 103.04
Rogers, William, 131
Rogues, The, 170
Rolle, Esther, 233, 247
Rolling Stones, The, 162, 427
Romano, Ray, *386*, 388
Rome, 448
"Romeo and Juliet," 14, 114
Romero, Cesar, 80, 178
Romney, Mitt, 459
Rooftop Singers, The, 162
Rookies, The, 252, 256
Room for One More, 147
Room 222, 209
Rooney, Andrew, 145.04, 221
Roosevelt, Franklin D., 7.05, 8, 10,
  12, 13, 19, *19*, 73
Root, Stephen, 375.03
Roots, 242, 265–266; *The Next
  Generations*, 279.02, 281
Ropers, The, 286
Rose, Reginald, 97, 112, 143
Roseanne, 341–342, *343*, 388
Roseanne. *See* Barr, Roseanne
Rose Marie, 146, *148*
Rosenberg, Leo H., 2, 12
Rosenberg, Richard, 244.01, 253
Rosenzweig, Barney, 301
Rosie O'Donnell Show, The, 381.03
Ross, Joe E., 106, 147–148
Ross, Marion, 243, 358
Roswell, 405
Roth, David Lee, 332
Rough Riders, 125
Roundtree, Richard, 241
Rountree, Martha, 21.02, 25
Rousters, The, 317
Route 66, 141, 321.06

Rove, Karl, 436
Rowan, Dan, 192–193, 203, 270.01
Rowan and Martin's Laugh-In. See Laugh-In
Royal Family, The, 357.02
Royal Showcase, 68
Roy Rogers, 25
Rudd, Hughes, 237.05
Rude Awakening, 396–397
Ruggles, The, 50
Rugrats, 354.04, 385
Rumsfeld, Donald, 436
Runaway, 450
Rundgren, Todd, 297.05
Rupp, Debra Jo, 405
Rusk, Dean, 183
Russell, Connie, 44
Russell, John, 125
Russell, Keri, 405
Russell, Kurt, 386
Russell, Mark, 285
Russell, Nipsey, 205
Russert, Tim, 457.03
"Russian for Beginners," 152
Russ Morgan Show, The, 101
Ryan, Irene, *153*, 156
Ryan, Leo, 278.05
Ryan, Michelle, 456

Sabrina, the Teenage Witch, 388
Sachs, Andrew, 256.02
Sadat, Anwar, 271.01, *272*
Safer, Morley, 182, 283, *285*
Sagal, Katey, 334, 405, 421
Sagansky, Jeff, 347.03
Saget, Bob, 339, 347, 442
Saint, Eva Marie, 106
Saint, The, 155.01, 164, 278.01
Saint James, Susan, 185, 201, 226, 314
Sajak, Pat, 344, 344.04, 350.02, 353.04
Salant, Richard, 163.05, 183, 213, 279.05
Salt, Jennifer, 270
Saltzman, Harry, 164
Samantha Who?, 455
Sand, Paul, 271
Sanders, George, 178
Sanders, Jay O., 313
Sanders, Lugene, 77
Sanders, Richard, *277*, 281
Sanderson, William, 307
Sandler, Adam, 263
Sandy, Gary, *277*, 280
Sandy Duncan Show, The, 234
Sanford, Isabel, 247
Sanford, 287.03
Sanford and Son, 227–228
Sanford Arms, 270.04
San Francisco International Airport, 221
Sarge, 225
Sarnoff, David, 1, 2.06, 3.01, 3.02, 5, 7.01, 8, 9–10, 13, 179.05, 210.05, 228.01
Sarnoff, Robert, 107, 109, 121.07, 142, 210.05, 257.03
Saroyan, William, 79
Satellite: retransmission of local stations, 403.07; sexual adult

entertainment, 396; technical growth, 146.07, 163.06
Satellite companies: Direct Broadcast Satellite (DBS), 315.05; DirecTV, 423.05, 458
"Satins and Spurs," 90
Saturday Night Live, 251, 262–263, 292.07, 326, 360, 415, 427, 437, 449, 459–463 461.06
Saturday Night Live with Howard Cosell, 256.03
Saturday Night Revue, 48–49
Saudek, Robert, 172.05
Saunders, Jennifer, 333, 363.02
"Savage," 323
Savage, Ben, 367
Savage, Fred, 337
Savalas, Telly, 170, 239–240, 325
Saved by the Bell, 359.05
Saviano, Josh, 338
Saving Grace, 448
Sawyer, Diane, 345.06, 399.03, 441.03, 468.01
Sawyer, Joe, 95
Saxon, John, 207
Scales, Prunella, 256.02
Scarecrow and Mrs. King, 315.03, 321
Scene of the Crime, 353.04
Schafer, Natalie, 167
Schaffner, Franklin, 112
Scheider, Roy, 369.01
Schenkel, Chris, 259
Scherer, Ray, 178.08
Scherer-MacNeil Report, The, 178.08
Schieffer, Bob, 434.04, 445.01
Schiff, Richard, 406
Schine, G. David, 89
Schlamme, Thomas, 406
Schlatter, George, 192, 205, 270.01, 285–286
Schlitz Playhouse, 78
Schmitz, Jonathan, 375.02
Schneider, Jack, 176, 183
Schneider, John, 287
Schorr, Daniel, 173, 230
Schram, Bitty, 448
Schroder, Ricky, 308
Schuck, John, 226
Schultz, Dwight, 311
Schulz, Charles, 179.03
Schwarzkopf, H. Norman, 354
Schweitzer, Mitchell D., 131
Schwimmer, David, 338, 373
Science fiction and fantasy format, 78.04, 78.06, 162.04, 163.02, 331, 336, 344, 367, *367*, 381–382, 388
Sci-Fi Network (cable channel), 365, 385–386, 387, 394.01, 421.03, 427.07, 429, 430, 435, 449, 456, 462.04. *See also* Syfy
Scolari, Peter, 302, 307
Scott, Bill, 132.04
Scott, Debralee, 267
Scott, George C., 159–160, 211, 256.06
Scott, Ridley, 315.08
Scott Music Hall, The, 79

Screen Director's Playhouse, 101
Screen Gems/Columbia Pictures, 128
SCTV Network 90, 293.09. *See also Second City TV*
Seacrest, Ryan, 420
Sea Hunt, 120.07
Seales, Franklyn, 308
SeaQuest DSV, 369.01
Search for the Nile, 228
Search for Tomorrow, 66.01, 169, 197.05
Season length: measured from September, 381.01, 383; start season anytime, 439–441, 447–448
Secondary stations, 292.01
Second City TV, 264.03. *See also SCTV Network 90*
Second season tactic from ABC, 177
Secret Agent, 170
"Secret Cinema," 324
Sedgwick, Kyra, 448
Seeger, Pete, 52, 161, 187, 203
"See How They Run," 172.04
See It Now, 63, 74, 79, *87*, 88, 97.08, 98, 121.06, 122, 133. See also *Hear It Now*
See What You Know, 21
Segal, Alex, 58.04, 66.05, 79, 96
Segel, Jason, 405, 442
Segelstein, Irwin, 231
Seinfeld, 350.05, 363–364, 394, 395, 465.06; reunion on HBO's *Curb Your Enthusiasm*, 465.06; as *Seinfeld Chronicles*, 345.05
Seinfeld, Jerry, 345.05, 350.05, 363–364, 394, 395, 465, 465.06
"Selena ¡VIVE!" (Univision), 444
Sellecca, Connie, 316
Selleck, Tom, 301
"Selling of the Pentagon, The," 228
Senator, The, 210, 216–217
Sentinel, The, 380
September 11, 2001, impact of televised attacks, 414–415, *415*
"Serenity," 421.03
Sergeant Bilko. See Phil Silvers Show
Sergeant Preston of the Yukon, 25, 103
Sergei, Ivan, 405
Serling, Rod, 77.06, 97–98, 107, *111*, 112, 121, 134, 143, 185, 221, 323
Sesame Street, 211, 220
Sessions, 396
Sevareid, Eric, 129, 158, *229*, 271.02
"Seven Against the Wall," 129
700 Club, The, 296–297
"Seven in Darkness," 210
Seventh Avenue, 264–265
7th Heaven, 388–389, 445.05
79 Park Avenue, 272
77 Sunset Strip, 127, 128, 139
Severance, Joan, 336
Sevigny, Chloe, 441.02
Sex and the City, 396–397, 400, 429.01, 430, 448

Sexual images and values, 47, 208–209, 233, 237.04, 242.01, 250.01, 253, 256, 261, 268–272, 273, 300–301, 302–303, 309, 316, 334, 339, 362–364, 363.02, 366–367, 368, 386, 396–397, 399–400, 406–407
Seyfried, Amanda, 435
Seymour, Jane, 365
Shackelford, Ted, 288
Shadel, Bill, 137.04
Shaft, 241
Shakespeare, William, 41, 321
Shalhoub, Tony, 448
Shandling, Garry, 321.04, 331.03, 345, 361, 395
Shane, Irwin, 14
Shankman, Adam, 438
Shannon, Del, 331
Shares in ratings calculations, 37
Sharkey, Ray, 336
Shatner, William, 121, 143, 189, 211, 257, 301, 346, 433
"Shatterday," 325
Shaud, Grant, 342
Shaughnessy, Charles, 369.03
Shaver, Helen, 287.02
Shaw, Bernard, 354
Shaw, Irwin, 259
Shawn, Dick, 91
Shearer, Harry, 349
Sheen, Charlie, 429
Sheen, Fulton J., 68
Sheen, Martin, 236, 406
Shepherd, Cybill, 316, 320, 381
Sheridan, Nicollette, 433
Sherlock Holmes TV adaptations, 9, 387
Sherman, Allan, 156
Sherman, Bobby, 172.01
Shield, The, 430, 448
Shields, Arthur, 43.02
Shields, Brooke, 388
Shields, Mark, *469*
Shimada, Yoko, 291
Shimerman, Armin, 389
Shindig, 172.01, 175
Shogun, 291
ShopNBC (cable channel), 412.04
Shopping with Martha Manning, 16
Shore, David, 434
Shore, Dinah, 24, 66.07, 95, 106, 113.07, 118
Short, Martin, 264.03, 286.05
Shower of Stars, 91
Showtime (cable channel), 257.08, 315.12, 326.02, 332.03, 345, 371, 386, 399.04, 427.06, 439.05, 448, 457
Shriver, Maria, 338.04
Shroyer, Sonny, 287
Shukovsky, Joel, 342
Shuster, Rosie, 263
Sierra, Gregory, 249
Sigler, Jamie-Lynn, 397
Signal interference issue, 37
Signature, 303
Sikking, James B., 300
Sikron, Jerry, 70
Sikron, John, 70

Silent Force, 222
"Silent Night, Lonely Night," 210
Silents Please, 149
"Silent Spring of Rachel Carson," 150
Silk Stalkings, 386
Silliphant, Stirling, 141
Silva, Zack, 445
Silver, Ron, *249*, 336
Silverheels, Jay, *47*
Silver King broadcasting company, 394.03
Silverman, Ben, 444
Silverman, Fred: at ABC, 256–259, 260–261, 265, 269, 272; at CBS, 155.03, 209, 210.06, 211.02, 219, 220, 223, 231; at NBC, 273, 274–275, 288, 289–293, 299; at production company, 326.03, 332, 339
Silverman, Jonathan, 380
Silvers, Phil, 38–39, 106, 109
Silver Spoons, 308
Silver Theater, 50
Simon, Carly, 162
Simon, David, 418.06
Simon, Lucy, 162
Simon, Neil, 49, 86, 220.03
Simon, Paul, 263
Simpson, Nicole Brown, 370.02, 375
Simpson, O. J., 263, 265, 315.01; Bronco chase, 370.02; trial coverage, 375–376, *376*, 377–379
Simpsons, The, 333, *349*, 349–350, 351, 388
Simulcasts of radio and television, 6, 9
SIN (Spanish International Network) (broadcast network), 444
Sinatra, Frank, 24, 30, 56, 68, 106, 118–119, 133.06, 159, 178.05
Sinclair, Upton, 264
Sing Along with Mitch, 140.01
Singer, Marc, 320.04
"Singer Presents Elvis," 201.05
Singing Detective, The, 331.04
Singled Out, 383
Single Guy, The, 380
Sirico, Tony, 399
Sirtis, Marina, 340
Siskel, Gene, 278.04
Sister Kate, 347
Sister, Sister, 367, 373, 388
Sisters, 354.01
Sitcoms: affected by family hour, 255–256; comedy drama combination, 231–235, 287.02, 337–338; comfort viewing after September 11, 2001, 417–418; family, 43, 44, 118, 247, 387–388; format fades in ratings in 1980s, 314, 317–318; format revived by *Cosby Show*'s success, 317–318; "mirror of reality" structure, 17; MTM ensemble style, 217–219, 271, 280–281, 307; obstacle course comedy, 57, 246, 271; radio's

biggest Golden Age hit comedy, 6.09; rural humor, 117–118, 141, 157; science fiction parody, 276, 388; TGIF lineup on ABC, 347, 388, 403; topical, 209, 219–220, 231–233, 246–250, 271, 337; working class, 105, 146.05, 163, 179.06, 195, 219–221, 334, 341–342, 381, 412.05; workplace family, 146, 217–219, 271, 280–281, 307, 308–309
"Sit In," 139
Six Degrees, 450
Six Feet Under, 412.03, 448
Six Million Dollar Man, The, 243, 259
$64 Question, The, 64, 99
$64,000 Challenge, The, 101, 122–124, 132
$64,000 Question, The, 98, 99–101, 107, 109, 122–124, 131–132
60 Minutes, 198, 200, 219, 283–285, *285*, 291, 330, 359–360, 372, 429.05, 437
Six Wives of Henry VIII, 221, 228
Skelton, Red, 17, 24, 43, 68, 75–76, 93, 117, 221.05
Skerritt, Tom, 365
Sklar, Jason, 411.05
Sklar, Randy, 411.05
Sky King, 25
SlamBall, 423.07
Slap Maxwell Story, The, 337, 338
Slater, Bill, 30
Slattery's People, 176
Sloan, Everett, 97–98
Small Fry Club, 29
Smallville, 419, 421.02, 435, 447
Smart, Jean, 331, 442
Smart Guy, The, 388
Smith, Alfred E., 6
Smith, "Buffalo" Bob, 31–32, 39
Smith, Harry, 418.04
Smith, Howard K., 52, 137.02, 150–151, 165, 183, 205.06, 220.05, 237, 256.01, 279.06
Smith, Jaclyn, 261
Smith, Kate, 7, 24, 58.03, 64
Smith, Kurtwood, 405
Smith, Roger, 127
Smith, Will, 351–352
Smith, William Kennedy, 354.02
Smith, Yeardley, *349*
Smithers, Jan, *277*, 281
Smits, Jimmy, 332, 456
Smoking on television, 48, 220.06, 221–222, 453
Smothers, Dick, 187
Smothers, Tom, 187, 202–203
Smothers Brothers, 187, 202–204, 224
Smothers Brothers Show, The, 162, 187, 202–204, 211.03, 224, 262
Smothers Brothers Summer Show, The, 211.03
Smulders, Cobie, 442
Sneak Previews, 278.04
Snip, 260
Snodgrass, James, 124, 131
Snoops, 346
Snow, Tony, 380.06

Snyder, Tom, 242.04, 284, 292.02, 293.04, 303.01, 375.01, 399.07
Soap, 268–270, 286.03
SOAPnet, 445–447
Soap operas: daytime, 43.04, 67.05, 197.05, 251.01, 279.03, 302.02, 397.06, 453.01, 462.05, 465.08; expand to thirty minutes, 103.05; expand to sixty minutes, 251.01; expand to ninety minutes, 279.03; parodies, 267–270; prime time, 144–145, 154–155, 168–169, 207–208, 211, 259, 287–288, 302–303, 320, 327, 351, 433; as telenovelas, 444–445, 445.02
Sobol, Edward, 18.06
Social networks. *See* Facebook; MySpace; Twitter
Solomon, Bruce, 268
Somerhalder, Ian, 431
Somers, Suzanne, 270
"Something About Amelia," 316
Something Is Out There, 343
Sonny and Cher Show, The, 261
Sonny Spoon, 343
Soo, Jack, 249
Sophocles, 112
"Soprano Home Movies," 451
Sopranos, The, 397–400, 419, 430, 448, 450–451, 452
Sorbo, Kevin, 387
Sorkin, Aaron, 403, 406, 417, 449
Sorvino, Paul, 353
Sothern, Ann, 90, 178.02
"Soul," 205
Soul, David, 225, 258, 311.01, 316
Soul Food, 406.06
Southland, 465
South of Sunset, 369
South Park, 385
Soviet Union dissolution, 356
So You Think You Can Dance, 438–439
"Space Barton," 58.02
Space coverage: *Apollo 7*, *204*; *Apollo 8*, 206; *Apollo 11*, 206, *206*; *Apollo 15*, 221.03; *Challenger* explosion, *325*; first color transmission, 221.03; first live TV transmission, 155.06; first orbital, 146.02; Moon landing, 206, *206*; space shuttle mission on HDTV, 397.07
Space Ghost, 371
Space: 1999, 256.04, 267
Spacey, Kevin, 336
Spader, James, 433
Spanish language networks. *See* SIN; Telemundo; Univision; V-me
Spanjers, Martin, 421
Spano, Joe, 300
Sparks, 388
Speak Up, America, 286
Spear, Sammy, 50
Spectaculars and big budget specials on NBC, 48.08, 90–91, 106, 111, 263–265
Speedman, Scott, 405
Spelling, Aaron, 201, 252, 258,

259, 261, 271, 301, 303, 351, 359.04, 388
Spelling, Tori, 351
Spencer, Bob, 269
Spencer, Jesse, 434
Spencer, Lady Diana, 390
Spencer, John, 406
Spenser: For Hire, 327
Spice (cable channel), 396
Spielberg, Steven, 323–324, 369.01, 448
Spike TV (cable channel), 423.07, 439.05, 445
"Spin and Marty," 103
Spin City, 388
Spiner, Brent, 340
Spinks, Leon, 275
Spinning disk mechanical television system, 5–6, *6*
Spinoffs as programming strategy, 166–167
Spiridellis, Evan, 437
Spiridellis, Gregg, 437
Spivak, Lawrence, 21.02, 25
Split Enz, 297.05
SpongeBob SquarePants, 399.08
Sponsorship. *See* commercials
Sports: all-sports cable, 296.01, 279.07; as promotional tool for the entire schedule, 346; escalating licensing rights, 346; NBC Olympics deal, 394. *See also* specific sports: Arena football; Basketball; Baseball; Boxing; Football; Hockey; NASCAR; Rodeo; Roller derby; *SlamBall*; Tennis; Wrestling. *See also* specific networks and cable channels: ABC, CBS, ESPN, Fox, NBC, MSG, TNT
Sports anthology programs: ABC, 137; CBS, 133.01; NBC, 271.03, 289
Sports Focus, 113.04
Sports franchise-operated cable channels. See Baseball; Basketball; Hockey; Football
Sports Night, 403
Sportsworld, 271.03, 289
Springer, Jerry, 411, 438
Springsteen, Bruce, 321, 427
Spy format in the 1960s, 163–164, 169–170, 196
Square Pegs, 307–308
Squeeze, 347.06
Sreenivasan, Hari, *469*
Stack, Robert, 129, 201, 210, 344
Stacke, Win, *55*
Stafford, Jo, 95
Stage Show, 105–106
Staggers, Harley O., 228
Stained Glass Windows, 41.01
Stand by for Crime, 42
Stanis, BernNadette, 247
Stans, Maurice, 230
Stanton, Bob, 30
Stanton, Frank, 21.07, 24, 81, 132–133, 142, 227.02, 228, 228.07, 237.03
Stapleton, Jean, *219*, 219–220, 292.05

Star, Darren, 381, 396
Stargate SG-1, 386
Starger, Martin, 256
Starr, Kenneth, 391–393, 400–401
Starr, Ringo, 162, 262
Star Search, 438
Starsky and Hutch, 257–258
"Star Spangled Revue," 48.08
Star Trek, 188–190, 286.09;
    animated series, 242.02. *See also*
    Enterprise
Star Trek: Deep Space Nine,
    363.04
Star Trek: Enterprise, 417.01, 419,
    430, 435, 435.02
Star Trek franchise, 242.02, 286.09,
    339–340, 363.04; ends new
    episode run since 1986, 435.02
Star Trek: The Next Generation,
    339–340;
Star Trek: Voyager, 370, 373
Stassen, Harold, 34–35
State of the Union broadcast 1947,
    27.06
Stations: ownership limits, 427;
    secondary, 292.01; super
    stations, 265.02, 296; via
    satellite, 403.07
Stations by call letters. *See* K–
    station call letters; W-station
    call letters
Statistics. *See* Television numbers
"Steambath," 237.04
Stearns, Johnny, 33
Stearns, Mary Kay, 33
Steiger, Rod, 79, 121
Steinberg, David, 203, 210.01
Steinbrenner, George, 236.04
St. Elsewhere, 308, *310*, 310–311,
    339.06
Stempel, Herbert, 113, 123, 131
Stephanopoulos, George, 360,
    468.01
Stephens, James, 277, 306, *307*
Stephens, Laraine, 208
Stephenson, Skip, 285
Steptoe and Son, 146.05, 163, 197,
    227
Stern, Bill, 10
Stern, Carl, 244
Stern, Daniel, 337, 418
Stern, Howard, 383
Stern, Isaac, 303
Steve Allen Show, The, 49.01,
    59.01, 146.06
Steve Harvey's Big Time, 435, 438
Steve Harvey Show, The, 388
Stevens, Connie, 129
Stevens, Craig, 126
Stevens, Robert T., 89
Stevens, Rusty, 118
Stevenson, Adlai, 73, 87, 142
Stevenson, McLean, 234, 275
Stewart, Byron, 311
Stewart, French, 380
Stewart, Horace, 58
Stewart, Jimmy, 184, 241
Stewart, Jon, 371, 399.02, 437,
    456
Stewart, Lee, 80
Stewart, Patrick, 340

Stewart, Rod, 297.05, 320.01
St. Gerard, Michael, 348
"Sticks and Bones," 237
Stiers, David Ogden, 312
Stiles, Ryan, 381
Stiller, Ben, 362
Stiller, Jerry, 344, 364
Still the Beaver, 309.04. *See also*
    Leave It To Beaver
Sting, 426
Stivers, Robert, 122
Stockwell, Dean, 344
Stone, Harold J., 54
Stone, Matthew, 385
Stone, Sid, 36
"Stone Pillow," 331
Stop the Music, 33–34, 44, 45,
    93.01, 99
Storch, Larry, 38, 39, 180
Storefront Lawyers, 215–217; as
    Men at Law, 217
Storm, Gale, 66
Storm, Hannah, 418.04
Stranger, The, 87
Strauss, Peter, 259, 260
Straw, Syd, 347.06
Streep, Meryl, 273, 444
Streets of San Francisco, 256, 261
Streisand, Barbra, 159
Strictly Come Dancing (U.K.), 438
Strike It Rich, 29.05, 59–60, 85,
    120.06
Strikes: actors 1980, 290–291,
    292.03, 293; actors 2001, 411;
    musicians with Petrillo ban, 17,
    22–23, 32–33; writers 1973,
    239, 242; writers 1981, 293.07,
    299; writers 1988, 339.04, 343,
    344.02; writers 2001, 411;
    writers 2007–08, 453–458, 459–
    461
Strike waivers in 2007, 456
Stringer, Howard, 329
Stringfield, Sherry, 366, 374
Striperella, 423.07
Strong, Brenda, 433
Struck by Lightning, 286
Struthers, Sally, 211.03, 220
Studdard, Ruben, 424
Studio One, 25, 41, 48.03, 78, 79,
    96–97, 101, 112, 121, 143
Studio 60 on the Sunset Strip, 449
Studs' Place, 48.05, *55*
Stunting strategy, 260
Suddenly Susan, 388, 394
Sues, Alan, 193
Sugarfoot, 115, 125, 127, 139
Sullivan, Barry, 323
Sullivan, Ed, 36, 37–38, 52, 68–69,
    109–110, 115, 155.04, 159, *195*,
    209, 221.02
Sullivan, Erik Per, 405
Sullivan, Kathleen, 305
Summerall, Pat, 369, 372
Summerfield, Arthur, 96
"Sunday in Town," 91
Sunday Morning, 279.01
Sunday Night Football, 447, 449
Sunday Showcase, 134
Sunday Sports Spectacular, 133.01
Sunset Beach, 397.06

Sunshine, 246
Super, The, 246
Super Bowl. *See* Football
Superboy, 344
*Superman. See Adventures of
    Superman*
Supernatural, 441
Super stations via cable, 265.02,
    296
Supertrain, 275
Supper Club, 18.03, 39, 41.07
Supreme Court: ban on giveaway
    game shows, 93.01, 99; Florida
    recount ruling in 2000 election,
    413; home video recording
    allowed, 315.07; Paramount
    Case, 34.08
Surface, 441
Surfside Six, 140
Survivor, 408–411, *409*, 418, 423,
    439, 442
Survivors, 208
"Susan and God," 9
Susann, Jacqueline, 41.06
Suspense, 24, 70
Susskind, David, 96, 109, 120.01,
    121, 132.01, 133.05, 159, 195,
    256.06, 285
Sussman, Kevin, 444
Sutherland, Donald, 233, 389
Sutherland, Kiefer, 417
Sutherland, Kristine, 389
Sutton, Frank, 167
*Suzanne Pleshette Is Maggie
    Briggs*, 314
Swann, Lynn, 309.03
Swanson, Kristy, 389
S.W.A.T., 251, 252, 256
Swayze, John Cameron, 41, 81,
    109, 158
Sweating Bullets, 353.04
Swedish TV *Big Brother*, 408
Sweepstake$, 275
"Swift boat veterans" 2004
    campaign ad against Kerry, 436–
    437
Swift Home Service Club, 29
Swift Justice, 381
Swiss Family Robinson, 255
Swit, Loretta, 235, 302
Switch, 259, 260
Syfy (cable channel), 462.04,
    468.02. *See also* Sci-Fi network
    (cable channel)
Sykes, Wanda, 465.03
Syler, Rene, 418.04
Syndication: first run material, 30–
    31, 59.03, 77.02, 78.04, 102.06,
    120.07, 132.01, 137.05, 140.05,
    264.02, 264.03, 267–268, 294–
    295, 322, 326, 344, 347; formula
    for timeless productions, 129

Tab Hunter Show, The, 141
Tabloid feel to television, 365, 371,
    391–393, 411
Taeger, Ralph, 139
Taft, Robert, 72
"Tail Gunner Joe," 264
Take a Good Look, 149
Takei, George, 190

Take It or Leave It, 99
Talent Associates, 121, 128, 159,
    195
Tales from the Darkside, 326
"Tales of Anne Boleyn," 79
Tales of the Red Caboose, 44
Tales of the 77th Bengal Lancers,
    113
Tales of Wells Fargo, 113
Talk shows: daytime first run
    syndication, 146.01, 196.02,
    205.07, 228.02, 228.05, 287.08,
    327.07, 331.02, 375.02, 381.03,
    427.01, 465.05, 469; late night
    first run syndication, 140.06,
    146.06, 155–156, 173.06, 344
Talk Show with Spike Feresten,
    445.04
Talk Soup, 383
Talley, Jill, 380.02
Talman, William, 120
Tamblyn, Amber, 429
Tambor, Jeffrey, 361, 427.04
Tamez, Jose, 444
Tammy Grimes Show, The, 187,
    205
Tanner '88, 339.02
Tapert, Rob, 387
Target the Corruptors, 148
Tarkenton, Fran, 286, 315.01
Tarrant, Chris, 402
Tarses, Jay, 337
Tartikoff, Brandon, 299, 308, 309,
    316, 317, 318, 320, 326–327,
    329, 335, 353–354
Tate, 134
TAT/Tandem productions, 275
Tattingers, 343–344
Taxi, 278, 281, 286, 309, 314
Taylor, Arthur, 228.07, 254, 256,
    261
Taylor, Elizabeth, 121, 456
Taylor, Kent, 125
Taylor, Meshach, 331
Taylor, Regina, 356
Taylor, Rod, 139
TBS (cable channel), 447, 467
TCI cable system, 370–371,
    399.05, 417.04
"Teddy," 286.08
Teegarden, Aimee, 449
Tele-Communications, Inc. *See*
    TCI cable system
Telecommunications Act of: 1992,
    370; 1996, 382, 386.07. *See also*
    Communications Act of 1934
Telemundo (broadcast network),
    418.01, 429, 444–445, 457.05
Telenovelas, 444–445, 445.02
Telethon: for cancer research
    (1949), 43.05; for Democratic
    Party (1972), 228.06, 229
Televised hearings: *See* Army-
    McCarthy hearings; Crime
    hearings; Fulbright hearings on
    the Vietnam War; HUAC
    televised public hearings;
    Impeachment proceedings; War
    coverage by conflict: Vietnam;
    Watergate coverage
Televised trials, 354.02

Television (documentary), 321.02

Television absence: six weeks of no TV in New York City (1946), 21.09

Television numbers: cable subscribers, 293, 304, 413; channels viewers choose to watch, 449; sets, 20, 26–28, *28*, 31, 98, 101; stations, 20, 21.03, 26–28, 31, 63, 71, 472; stations needed for multiple viable broadcast networks, 294–295, 442, 445, 471, 472; video recorders, 293, 304; share of audience to broadcast networks, 293, 358, 387, 388, 393, 445, 463, 468

Television Parts. See Michael Nesmith in Television Parts

Television Playhouse, 107, 113.07. *See also Alcoa Television Playhouse; Goodyear Television Playhouse; Philco Television Playhouse*

Television profits, 63, 122, 393, 394; exceed radio profits, 63; subsidized by radio profits, 7, 44, 45–46, 51–52

Television Roof, 10

Television seen as competition to Hollywood film studios, 31, 41, 48.07, 94–95, 128

Television Workshop, 14

Telstar I satellite, 146.07, *146*

Temptation Island, 411–412

Tenafly, 241

Tennant, David, 449

Tennille, Toni, 260

Tennis coverage, U.S. Open, 338.03

"Tennis—The Battle of the Sexes," 242

Tenspeed and Brownshoe, 288

Ten Who Dared, 268

Terkel, Studs, 48.05, 49, *55*

Terminator: The Sarah Connor Chronicles, 453.07

Testimony of Two Men, 268

Texaco Star Theater, 24, 36, 37, 66, 68

Texan, The, 125

Tex and Jinx, 29

Texas Wheelers, The, 271

"That Certain Summer," 236

That Girl, 188

That '70s Show, 405, 448

That's Incredible, 286, 288, 291

That's My Line, 286

That Was the Week That Was/TW3, 164, 171–172, 174

That Wonderful Guy, 51

Theater Guild of the Air, 26, 80

Theater of the Mind, 44

Theron, Charlize, 427.04

These Are My Children, 43.04, 44

They Stand Accused, 104, 120

Thiessen, Tiffani-Amber, 373

Thin Man, The, 24, 120

Thinnes, Roy, 216

3rd Rock from the Sun, 380

"Third season" tactic by ABC, 242

Thirteen.org (WNET, New York), 444

.38 Special, 297.05

30 Rock, 449

thirtysomething, 335, 338

"This Land" (music political parody), 437

This Is Show Business, 47

This Is Your Life, 224

This Week (ABC): Christiane Amanpour, 468.01; David Brinkley, 302.01, 393.04; George Stephanopoulos, 468.01

This Week (PBS), 227.03

Thomas, Betty, 300

Thomas, Clarence, 356, *357*

Thomas, Craig, 442

Thomas, Danny, 17, 34, 55–56, 68–69, 80, 82–84, *83*, 117, 125, 156

Thomas, Dave, 264.03

Thomas, Jay, 363

Thomas, Larry, 364

Thomas, Lowell, 11.07, 13, 17

Thomas, Marlo, 188

Thomas, Philip Michael, 319

Thomas, Richard, 235

Thomas, Rob, 435

Thomason, Harry, 331

Thomerson, Tim, 286.05

Thomopoulos, Tony, 275, 286, 288

Thompson, Andrea, 413

Thompson, Fred, 353, 459

Thompson, J. Walter, 14, 15

Thompson, Lea, 380

Thomsett, Sally, 242.01

Thorgensen, Ed, 34, 59.04

Thorn Birds, The, 311

Thorne-Smith, Courtney, 417–418

Thorson, Linda, 196

Those Amazing Animals, 286, 291

"Those Were the Days," 219

Those Whiting Girls, 105

3D television transmissions, 468.05, 469

Three Dog Night, 210.01

Three for the Road, 255

Three of a Kind, 333

Three's a Crowd, 320.02

Three's Company, 270–271, 286, 314

Three to Get Ready, 69–70

Threshold, 441

Thriller, 309.05

Thrills and Chills, 14

"Through the Looking Glass" (*Lost* episode), 450

"Thunder on Sycamore Street," 97

Thurmond, Strom, 35, 245

Tick, The, 418

Tic Tac Dough, 109, *113*, 122, 131

Tiger, Dick, 163.09

Tighe, Kevin, 225

Till Death Us Do Part, 179.06, 195, 197, 219

Tillstrom, Burr, 28, 172

Tilton, Charlene, 287

Timberlake, Justin, 407, 426–427

Time and Again, 382

Time for Ernie, 59.05

Time-Life: begins HBO, 236.02, 296; as producer and distributor, 43.07, 137–138, 251, 285; USA, 304; Warner merger, 347.05. *See also* Time Warner

"Time Out," 323

Time shifting control by viewers, 429–430, 439–441, 472–476

Time Warner, 347.05, 473; acquires Turner Broadcasting, 386.02; AOL merger, 407, 411.06; AOL split, 427.03, 465.09. *See also* AOL Time Warner

Time Warner Cable, 447, 468, 473

Tinker, Grant, 271, 272, 280, 293, 299, 327, 328, 329, 347, 353

Tinker, Mark, 280, 310

Tinker, Tailor, Soldier, Spy, 286.01

Tiny Tim, 192

Tisch, Laurence, 329, 353.01, 354, 375, 380.04

Titanic, 3.01, 470

TiVo recording system, 439

T. J. Hooker, 301

TNN (cable channel): as The Nashville Network, 375, 411.02; as The National Network, 411.02, 412, 423.07

TNT (cable channel), 344.01, 448, 465

Toast of the Town. See Ed Sullivan Show

Today, 69–70, 80, 86–87, 120.05, 123, 131, 156, 244.03, 244.05, 264.07, 274, 283, 305, 338.04, 347.04, 353.05, 359.05, 360, 363.01, 370.03, 387.02, 403.01, 411.01, 453.01; anchors, 140.07, 154.01, 221.04, 302.05, 338.04, 347.04, 445.01, 445.03

Todd, Mike, 56, 121

Todman, Bill, 67.04, 112.07, 128, 286

Toma, 241, 252

Toma, Dave, 241

Tom, Dick, and Mary, 172.03

Tomlin, Lily, 187, 193, 262, 263

Tomorrow, 242.04, 292.02; *Coast-to-Coast*, 293.04

Tonight: as *America After Dark* 110–111; Steve Allen era, 91–93, 106, 109; Johnny Carson era, 155–156, 228.04, 255, 262, 274, 282, 286–287, 291, 292.02, 357.01, 360, 361; Jay Leno era, 361, 364.02, 369, 377, *379*, 381, 397.06, 434.01, 462.02, 464–467; Conan O'Brien era, 434.01, 462.02, 464–467; Jack Paar era, 110–111,155. *See also Broadway Open House*

Tonight! America After Dark, 110–111

Tonight on Broadway, 33

Tonioli, Bruno, 438

Tony Orlando and Dawn Rainbow Hour, 260

Top Cat, 141

Top Dollar, 122, 132

Topper, 18.10, 84.04

Tork, Peter, 188

Torn, Rip, 361

Tors, Ivan, 120.07, 139

Tortorici, Peter, 375.06

Toscanini, Arturo, 33

Totally Hidden Video, 347

Total Request Live, 397.04, 417.05

To Tell the Truth, 112.07, 224

Touched by an Angel, 373.03, 382, 388, 397.01

Touch of Grace, A, 246

Tour of Duty, 336

"Town Has Turned to Dust, A," 121

Townsend, Robert, 373

Tracey Ullman Show, The, 333, *333*, 334

Trachtenberg, Michelle, 389

Trading Spaces, 386.01, 433

Traffic Court, 126

"Trail of Tears, The," 211

Travanti, Daniel J., 300

Travelers, The," 79

Travis, Nancy, 381

Travolta, John, 257–258, 260

Treacher, Arthur, 173.06

Treasure Hunt, The New, 285

Trendex ratings service, 90

Treyz, Ollie, 121.01, 127, 136, 140, 142, 154

Trials deal with cameras in the courtroom, 375–376, 379

Trials of O'Brien, The, 181, 226

Trials of Rosie O'Neill, The, 353

Tripp, Paul, 44

Tripplehorn, Jeanne, 441.02

Troup, Bobby, 225

Trout, Robert, 173

Trudeau, Garry, 339.02

Truex, Ernest, 83

Trujillo, Molina Rafael, 133

"Trujillo, Portrait of a Dictator," 133

Truman, Harry S., ix, 19, 21.05, 27.06, 34–35, 41, 63, *65*, 87

Trump, Donald, 429

Truth or Consequences, 11.03, 11.07, 13, 15, 24, 58.01, 223–224

Tucci, Stanley, 336, 379

Tucker, Forrest, 180

Tucker, Michael, 332

Tudors, The, 448

Tufts, Sonny, 192

"Tunnel, The," 150

"Turkey for the President, A," 126.01

Turner, Frederick J., 116

Turner, Janine, 363

Turner, Lana, 208

Turner, Ted, 265.02, 287.06, 296–298, 302.04, 305, 327.02, 344.01, 386.02, 423.01

Turner, Tina, 319, 320.01

Turner Broadcasting acquires MGM film library, 327.02, 344.01. *See also* Time Warner

Turning Point, 375

"Turn of the Screw," 134

Turn-On, 204–205

Turturro, Nicholas, 366

TV Guide magazine, 78.05, 296.04, 427, 427.02, 439.03, 445;

change in rerun identification, 447

TV Land (cable channel), 380.07, 387, 439.05, 447

TV's Bloopers and Practical Jokes, 314

Twain, Shania, 426

"Twelve Angry Men," 97

Twelve O'Clock High, 175

Twelvetrees, Helen, 15

Twente, Sanford B., 46

Twentieth Century, 137

Twentieth Century Fox, 128, 328

20th Century Fox Hour, The, 101

24, 417, 419, 424, 441, 442

Twenty-One, 113–114, 117, 122–124, 131–132, 406.02, 408

21 Jump Street, 333

Twenty Questions, 25, 45

20/20, 284, 330

Twerp, Joe, 80

Twilight Zone, The, 134, 325–326; movie, 323

Twin Peaks, 348–349

Twitter, 467, 476

Two and a Half Men, 429, 434, 456

240-Robert, 288

227, 326

Tyler, Richard, 53

Tyson, Cicely, 159–160, 244.01, 253, 263, 265, 273

Tyson, Ian and Sylvia, 162

Uggams, Leslie, 265

Ugly Betty, 444–445, 469

UHF: frequency allocation issue, 11.10, 27–28; number of stations, 71; public television, 71, 151; required on new TV sets, 153–154, 163.07, 472

Ullman, Tracey, 333, *333*, 334

Unauthorized downloads of video and audio, 443, 473–476

Uncle Buck, 353

"Uncle Ed and Circumstance," 101

Uncle Jim's Question Bee, 13

Undeclared, 418

"Under the Volcano," 25

Unhappily Ever After, 373

Union Square, 394

Unit, The, 442

United Artists, 296.01

United Football League (UFL), 465.01

United Network (broadcast network), 189.02, 294

United States, 287.02, 337

Unit 4 production team, 112

Universal Studios, 172.04, 208, 429; Betamax court case, 315.07; made-for-TV movies, 185–186; Operation Prime Time, 268

Universal Television, 304, 394.01, 394.03, 418.02. *See also* MCA/Universal; NBC Universal; USA Network; Vivendi/Universal Entertainment

Univision (broadcast network), 444-445, 459

Unsolved Mysteries, 344

Untouchables, The, 129–130, 139

UPN (broadcast network), 370, 373, 380–381, 397.05, 405, 406.04, 419, 442, 435, 439.05, 441.06, 442, 445.05, 472; demographic targeting of black ethnics, 388, 435; management, 370; wrestling, 405 435; XFL, 412

Upstairs, Downstairs, 211, 227.04, 264

Up to the Minute, 357.03

Ure, Midge, 321

Urich, Robert, 270, 317, 327, 331, 344.05

Urie, Michael, 444

Uris, Leon, 242

USA for Africa, 321

USA Network (cable channel), 297.02, 304, 371, 386, 387, 394.01, 394.01, 394.03, 406, 419, 429, 430, 445, 448, 457, 457.05, 458, 472; "Characters Welcome" slogan, 448; profits for cable vs. NBC broadcast network, 458

USFL (United States Football League) coverage, 309.03

U.S. Steel Hour, The, 82, 97, 97.04, 103, 107, 159, 210; as *Theater Guild of the Air*, 26, 80

Utley, Garrick, 182

U2, 321, 418, 426

V: 1983 version, 311, 320.04; 2009 version, 465.02

Valderrama, Wilmer, 405

Valentine, Karen, 209

Valentine's Day, 185

Vallee, Rudy, 7

Valli, June, 119

Value Vision (cable channel), 412.04

Vance, Vivian, *x*, 65–66, *67*, 156

Van Doren, Charles, 113–114, 122, 123–124, 131–132

Van Dyke, Barry, 367

Van Dyke, Dick, 86, 123.05, 146–147, *147*, *148*, 227.01, 367, 372

Van Dyke, Jerry, 159, 178.02, 215, 345.01

"Vanessa in the Garden," 324

Vanished, 450

Vanocur, Sander, 200, 229, 284

Vanoff, Nick, 287.01

Van Susteren, Greta, 379

Van Zandt, Steven, 399

Vargas, Elizabeth, 439.06, 441.03

Vartan, Michael, 417

Vast Wasteland speech, 142; aftermath, 143, 147–148, 149, 150, 151,

Vaudeo format, 36, 287.01

Vaughn, Robert, 169, 449

V-chip technology requirement, 382

Vegas, 434

Ventimiglia, Milo, 450

Ventura, Jesse, 412

Vereen, Ben, 265

Verne, Jules, 95

Vernon, Jackie, 187

Veronica Mars, 435, 443

Veronica's Closet, 394

Versus (cable channel), 439.02, 465.01, 467

Vertical integration, 369, 407. *See also* Paramount Case legal action

VHF: frequency allocation, 27–28; number of stations increased in bandwidth, 71

VH1 (cable channel), 320.06, 439.05

Viacom, 222, 332.03; acquires CBS, 406.05, 407, 439.05, 442; cable properties, 257.08, 296, 326.02, 332.03, 353.03, 370.04, 394.01, 406.04, 411.02, 413, 423.06, 423.07, 426, 439.05; as CBS spinoff, 222; management, 429.06; splits off CBS, 439.05, 442; sues Google/YouTube, 474

Victor, David, 225

Victory at Sea, 77.04

Vidal, Gore, 97

Video on Demand (VOD), 442

Video online: copyright issues, 443, 475–476; sales by Apple iTunes, 443, 474; user control, 443, 474–476

Video tape recording, 80, 121, 132.01, 146.03; Betamax case, 315.07; first network series use, 112.02; helps supplant live television, 112.02; home use, 173.07, 315.07, 429–430; instant replay, 137, 146.03; Oswald shooting, 165; Rodney King, 356; sales impact 291

Vieira, Meredith, 445.03

Vietnam. *See* War coverage by conflict: Vietnam

Vietnam: A Television History, 315.04

Vietnam Perspective, 182

Vietnam service by George W. Bush and John Kerry (2004 political campaign), 436–437

Vietnam Weekly Review, 182

Vigoda, Abe, 249

Violence in series, 60–61, 129–130, 148–149, 201, 240–241, 250.01, 251–252, 397–400

"Violent World of Sam Huff, The" 137

Virginian, The, 154.03, 185

"Visit to a Small Planet, A," 97

Viva McLaughlin, 456

Vivendi/Universal Entertainment, 418.02, 429, 467

Vivyan, John, 133

V-me (broadcast network), 444

Voice of Firestone, The, 24

Voland, Herbert, 188

Volstad, John, 307

Von Zell, Harry, 56

Von Ziegesar, Cecily, 456

Voohees, Donald, *25*

Voyage to the Bottom of the Sea, 175

W – station call letters

W2XAB New York, 7.02, 7.08, 7–8, 11.01. *See also* WCBW; WCBS

W2XBS New York, 6, 6.07, 9–10, 12. *See also* WNBC, WNBT

W2XCW Schenectady, 5–6. *See also* WRGB

W2XWV New York, 11.04, 11.11, 12. *See also* WABD, WNEW

W3XE Philadelphia, 9. *See also* KYW

WABC New York, 78.02. *See also* WJZ

WABC New York radio, 447.02

WABD New York, 11.11, 12, 21.09. *See also* W2XWV; WNEW

WBKB Chicago, 13. *See also* WLS

WCBS New York, 12, 27.05. *See also* W2XAB; WCBW

WCBW New York, 12, 27.05. *See also* W2XAB; WCBS

WDTV Pittsburgh, 39, 104. *See also* KDKA (television)

WEAF New York, 3.04

WFIL Philadelphia, 34.06

WGBH Boston, 152

WGN Chicago, 296

WJZ New York, 35.05. *See also* WABC

WLS Chicago, 10.03, 13. *See also* WBKB

WLS Chicago radio, 447.02

WMAL Washington, D.C., 34.06

WNBC New York, 12. *See also* W2XBS; WNBT

WNBT New York, 12–13. *See also* W2XBS, WNBC

WNDT New York, 152. *See also* WNET

WNET New York, 220.04, 444. *See also* WNDT

WNEW New York, 12. *See also* W2XWV; WABD

WRGB Schenectady, 5. *See also* W2XCW

WRLD-HD Raleigh, 381.05

WTBS Atlanta, 296, 387. *See also* WTCG

WTCG Atlanta, 265.02. *See also* WTBS

Wade, Ernestine, 57–58

Wagner, Lindsay, 259, 260, 277, 346

Wagner, Robert, 196.04

Wagon Train, 117, 125

Wahl, Ken, 335

Waite, Ralph, 236

"Waiting to Explode" on *Dateline*, 363.03

Waitresses, The, 308

Wakefield, Jack, 146

Walden, Robert, 278, 315.12

Walker, Clint, 102, 125, 127

Walker, David, 298

Walker, Herschel, 309.03

Walker, Jimmie, 247
Walker, Jimmy (mayor), 7
Walker, Nancy, 226, 250
Walker, Texas Ranger, 365
"Walk in My Shoes," 139
Walk Through the 20th Century, A, 303
Wallace, George C., 171
Wallace, Marcia, 271
Wallace, Mike, 64, 81, 101, 113.03, 140.06, 146.06, 200, 230, 283, *285*
Walsh, Frank, 85
Walsh, John, 339
Walsh, Kate, 433
Walston, Ray, 168, 365
Walt Disney (also as *Disney, Disneyland, Walt Disney's Wonderful World of Color*), 59.02, 94–95, 127, 145.02, 223, 234, 254
Walter, Jessica, 427.04
Walters, Barbara, 264.06, 264.07, 271.01, 271.07, 282, 375
Waltons, The, 235–236, 339.07
Wambaugh, Joseph, 241, 251
Wanda Sykes Show, The, 465.03
Wanted: Dead or Alive, 125
War: defining a "television war," 181–183, 424–425; twenty-four-hour coverage, 354–355, 425
War and Peace, 228
War and Remembrance, 344.03
War coverage by conflict:
 Afghanistan (1979), 289–290
 Afghanistan (2002), 424, 435
 Dominican Republic, 182
 Korea, *51*, 53, 70, 74
 Persian Gulf War (1991), 354–355; ground campaign, *355*
 Persian Gulf War (2003), *424*, 424–425, 435–436, 439.06, 441.03; embedded correspondents, 425; "Mission Accomplished," 435
 Vietnam, *170*, 181–183, *182*, 184, 228–230; Cambodia invasion, *212*, 212–214; Cam Ne village burning, 181–182; congressional hearings, 183, 184, 221.01; documentary history, 315.04; domestic anti-war demonstrations, 198, 212–214; Fred Friendly quits over coverage policy, 183; Kent State killings, 214; ratings for war coverage in 1966, 183; Tet offensive, 198–199; U.S. forces depart, 251.03, 252
 World War I, 1–2
 World War II, 13–14; V-E day, 18
Warburton, Patrick, 364, 418
Ward, Billy, 119
Ward, Burt, 178
Ward, Jay, 132.04
Ward, Robin, 326
Ward, Sela, 354.01, 407
"Ward Eight," 77.06
Waring, Fred, 39
Warner, Malcolm-Jamal, 317

Warner/Amex, 296.02, 297.05, 320.06, 326.02
Warner Bros. Presents, 102, 106
Warner Bros. studio, 127, 128–129, 139–140, 472. *See also* CW; Time-Life; Time Warner; Warner/Amex; Warner Communications; WB
Warner Communications, 347.05
"War of the Worlds," 10.08
War of the Worlds, 344
Warren, Earl, 14
Warren, Michael, 300
Warren, Robert Penn, 121
Warwick, Dionne, 321
Washington, Denzel, 310, *310*
Washington: Behind Closed Doors, 273
Washington Week in Review, 197, 238
Wass, Ted, 270
Watching Ellie, 417.06
Watch Over Me, 445
Watchtheguild.com, 455
Watergate coverage, 229–230, 237–238, *243*, 244–245
Waters, Ethel, 59
Waters, John, 367
Waterston, Sam, 353, 356
Watson, Barry, 389
Watson, Patrick, 303
Wax, Ruby, 333
Wayans Bros., The, 373, 388
Wayans, Damon, 326, 350, 417, 426
Wayans, Keenan Ivory, 350, 361
Wayans, Kim, 350
Wayans, Marlon, 350, 373
Wayans, Shawn, 350, 373
Wayne, David, 178, 287
Wayne, John, 104, 192
WB (broadcast network), 370, 373, 380–381, 397.05, 405, 419, 421.02, 435, 472; demographic target of black ethnics, 373, 381, 388, 405; demographic target of teens, 388–389, 405; Internet promotion with AOL, 443; management 373; signs off, 441.06. *See also* CW
Weakest Link, The, 408, 413
Weather Channel, The (cable channel), 304, 457.04
Weaver, Dennis, 221, 225, 323
Weaver, Fritz, 273
Weaver, Pat, 48–49, 48.01, 69, 85.02, 86–87, 90–92, 98, 102.05, 102.07, 103.08, 106–107, 109, 121, 128, 186
W.E.B., 278.02
Webb, Jack, 43.08, 67–68, 111, 195, 201, 225
Weber, Steven, 350.03
Webisodes, 455
Webster, 315.02
Webster, Don, 230
Weddings on TV: fictional, 250, 302.02; real life, 390
Weeds, 448
Weekend, 250.04, 262, 284–285
We Got It Made, 314

Weigert, Robin, 429.02
Weinberger, Ed., 281, 286.05
Weiner, Matthew, 447.05, 452–453
Weisberger, Lauren, 444
Weitz, Bruce, 300
Welch, Jack, 328
Welch, Raquel, 288
Welcome Aboard, 38
Welcome Back, Kotter, 257–258
Weld, Tuesday, 135
Welk, Lawrence, 101, 221.06
Welles, Orson, 10.08, 41, 52, 264, 321
We'll Get By, 246, 249
Wells, Carveth, 29
Wells, Dawn, 167
Wells, H. G., 10.08, 344
Wells, John, 406, 465
Welsh, Ken, 349
Wendt, George, 309
Werner, Tom, 317, 341, 347, 367, 387
West, Adam, 177
West, Billy, 405
West, Shane, 407
Westerner, The, 141
Westerns: "adult" Westerns, 67.03, 103–104, 115–117; historical setting and themes, 116; live afternoon adventures, 78.01; matinee-style heroics, 44, 50; program dominance, 77.02, 113, 115–117, 125, 134, 145.03, 154.03; revivals of the form, 251.05, 257, 344.05, 365, 429.02; violence 141-142, 207, 429.02
West 57th, 330
Westin, Av, 198, 205.06
Westinghouse: acquires CBS, 375, 380.04; acquires Infinity broadcasting, 386.07; divests of NBC, 7.06; early radio, 1, 2, 3.03; spins off CBS, 394.02; talk shows, 295
Weston, Jack, 78.06, 148
West Point Story, The, 113
Westwick, Ed, 456
West Wing, The, 406, 417, 430
Westwood One: acquires Mutual Broadcasting radio, 326.04; acquires NBC Radio, 338.02; CBS Radio, 386.07
Wettig, Patricia, 335
We've Got Each Other, 271
WGA (Writers Guild of America), 455–457. *See also* Strikes: writers
What I Like About You, 435
"What Makes Sammy Run," 134
What Makes You Tick, 53
"What To Do During an A-Bomb Attack," 53
"What's It All About, World?," 204
What's My Line?, 45, 189.06, 224, 286
Whedon, Joss, 389, 417.02, 421, 421.03, 456, 474
Wheels, 272
Whelan, Julia, 407
When the Whistle Blows, 288

When Things Were Rotten, 257
"Where It's At," 186
Where's Raymond?, 83
Where's the Fire?, 246
Whispering Smith, 141
White, Betty, 218, 271–272, 326
White, Jaleel, 347
White, John, 126.05
White, Paul, *35*
White, Slappy, 205
Whitehead, Clay, 229, 236–237
White House Correspondents' Association dinner 2006, 443, *443*
White House Office of Telecommunications Policy, 228–229
Whiteman, Paul, 39
White Shadow, The, 280, 288, 291
Whitewater coverage, 393, *400*, 400–401
Whitford, Bradley, 406
Whitmore, James, 325
Who, The, 187, 297.05, 427
Who Do You Trust?, 120.02. *See also Do You Trust Your Wife?*
Whodunnit?, 275
Who invented television, 5–7
"Who Invited Us?," 212
Whose Line Is It Anyway?, 371, 393
Who Shot J. R.? (*Dallas*), 292
"Who Speaks for the South?," 133
Who's the Boss?, 320, 327
Who's Watching the Kids?, 274
Who's Who, 285
Who Wants to Be a Millionaire, 402–403, 411, 419
"Who Wants to Marry a Multi-Millionaire," 406.03
Wicked, Wicked Games, 445
Wide Wide World, 102.05
Wide World of Entertainment, 237.01
Wide World of Sports, 137, 230, 259, *283*
Wiglesworth, Kelly, 409, *409*
Wilcox, Larry, 272
Wilcox, Paula, 242.01
Wilder, Laura Ingalls, 255
Wilder, Thornton, 58.04, 106, 311
Wild Kingdom, 224
Wild Wild West, The, 179, *180*
Wilkinson, Bud, 200
Will & Grace, 405
Willard, Fred, 271.06, 285, 325
William, Prince, 390
Williams, Andy, 60, 93, 154.05
Williams, Anson, 243
Williams, Brian, 382, 434.02
Williams, Cara, 176
Williams, Cindy, 258, 260
Williams, Clarence, III, 201
Williams, Dick Anthony, 357
Williams, Frances E., 337
Williams, Grant, 129
Williams, Guy, 117
Williams, Malinda, 406.06
Williams, Mason, 187
Williams, Matt, 341
Williams, Robin, 270.01, 277, 367, 371

Williams, Spencer, 57
Williams, Steven, 333, 394.07
Williams, Tyler James, 439.01
Williams, Van, 129, 140
Williams, Vanessa, 406.06, 444
Williamson, Kevin, 405
Willis, Bruce, 320, 325
Willkie, Wendell, 12
Wilson, Chandra, 433
Wilson, Charles, 61
Wilson, Demond, 227, 270.04
Wilson, Don, 7.04, 84
Wilson, Earl, 110
Wilson, Flip, 193, 220.01, 236
Wilson, Hugh, 337
Wilson, Lanford, 251.02
Wilson, Lois, 53
Wilson, Marie, 42, 66
Wilson, Peta, 386
Wilson, Rainn, 442
Wilson, Terry, 117
Wilson, Theodore, 270.04
Wilson, Woodrow, 1
Winchell, Paul, 39
Winchell, Walter, 18, 24, 35, 129–130, 137
Window on Main Street, 147
"Winds of Change, The" 134
Winds of War, The, 311, 344.03
Winfield, Paul, 273
Winfrey, Oprah, 331.02, 360, 411, 461, 465.05, 468.04, 469, 475
Wingo, 122
Wings, 350.03
Winkler, Henry, 243, 257, 260, 427.04
Winner Take All, 45
Winning Lines, 408
Winston, Hattie, 357
Winters, Jonathan, 112.02
Win with a Winner, 122
WIOU, 353
Wire, The, 418.06, 419, 448, 457.01, 458
Wireless telegraphy, 1–2, 2.05, 470. *See also* Marconi, Guglielmo; *Titanic*
Wire Service, 113
Wise, Ray, 348
Wiseguy, 335–336
Wiseman, Frederick, 198

Without a Trace, 421, 434
"Wizard of Oz," 111, 112.04
Wizbar, Frank, 79
WKRP in Cincinnati, 277, 278, 280–281, 288
Wolf, Dick, 353, 421
Wolf, Scott, 373
Wolfman Jack, 237.02, 262
Wolper, David, 210, 265
Wolverton, Charles A., 81
Wonder, Stevie, 321, 426
Wonderfalls, 429
"Wonderful World of Christmas, The," 145.01
Wonder Woman, 272
Wonder Years, The, 337–338
Wood, Evan Rachel, 407
Wood, Natalie, 83
Wood, Peggy, 43
Wood, Robert, 205.02, 209, 219, 222
Wood, Ron, 322
Woodruff, Bob, 439.06, 441.03
Woodruff, Judy, 465.07
Woods, James, 273
Woods, Jim, 296.03
Woods, Mark, 48.06, 51
Woodward, Bob, 238, 278
Woodward, Edward, 327
Wopat, Tom, 287, 346
"Wordplay," 325
Working Stiffs, 286
World in Your Home, The, 16
World News, 468.01
World News Now, 357.03
World News Tonight, 271.07, 274, 282–283, 311.05, 435.05, 439.06, 441.03; as *World News*, 468.01
World Premiere Movie, 250.01
World's Fair (1939) New York broadcast, 10, *13*
World transmissions: Atlantic, 146.07; "Our World," 189.03; Pacific, 163.06
World War I. *See* War coverage by conflict: World War I
World War II. *See* War coverage by conflict: World War II
World Wide 60, 134
World Wrestling Entertainment

(WWE), 435, 462.06
Worley, Jo Anne, 192
Wouk, Herman, 344.03
Wrangler, 189
Wray, Fay, 83
Wrestling coverage: CW, 441.06, 462.06; DuMont, 28; MyNetworkTV, 462.06; NBC, 10, 15; UPN, 405, 435, 441.06
Wright, Chalky, 15
Wright, Max, 331
Wright, Robert, 328, 329, 412.02, 447.01
Wright, Teresa, 112
Writers Guild of America (WGA). *See* Strikes: writers; WGA
Wuhl, Robert, 383
Wussler, Robert, 272
WWE Smackdown! (Friday Night Smackdown!), 435, 462.06; as *WWF Smackdown!*, 411.02
WWF (World Wrestling Federation), 411.02
Wyatt, Dana, 29
Wyatt, Jack, 126
Wyatt, Jane, 172.04
Wyatt Earp. See Life and Legend of Wyatt Earp
Wyle, Noah, 374
Wyman, Jane, 302
Wyman, Thomas, 287.05, 311.03, 329
Wynn, Ed, 9, 50, 55–56, 111, 112, 125
Wynn, Keenan, *111*, 112, 287

Xena: Warrior Princess, 387
X Factor, The, 438, 468.03
X-Files, The, 367, *367*, 418.05, 457.01
XFL football coverage, 412

Yancy Derringer, 125
"Yanki No!," 138
Yarborough, Barton, 67–68
Yarbrough, Glenn, 162
Yellow Rose, 316
Yerkovich, Anthony, 318
York, Jeff, 129
Yorkin, Bud, 154.05, 195, 219, 227, 247

Yo soy Betty, le Fea, 444
Yothers, Tina, 308
You Are There, 77.07, 80
You Asked For It, 83
You Bet Your Life, 34.01, 60
You'll Never Get Rich. See Phil Silvers Show
Young, Alan, 24, 36, 137.05
Young, Bob, 196.03, 197.03
Young, Gig, 102, 170
Young, Loretta, 94, 123
Young, Robert, 93.03, 118, 147, 207
Young, Roland, 18.10
Young and the Restless, The, 465.08
Younger, Beverly, *55*, 166
Young Indiana Jones Chronicles, The, 358
Young Lawyers, 210, 217
Youngman, Henny, 36
Young Rebels, 217, 222
You're in the Picture, 142
Your Hit Parade, 24, 49.03, 81, 118
Your Show of Shows, 39, 49, 56, 86
Your Show Time, 42, 43.02
Your Tropical Trip, 64–65
Youth Court, 126
YouTube.com, 443, 445.06, 450, 459, 474–475; acquired by Google, 445.06

Zappa, Frank, 263
Zeffirelli, Franco, 264
Zenith, 295–296
Zielinski, Bruno, 101
Ziering, Ian, 351
Zimbalist, Efrem, Jr., 21, 127, 178.07, 310
Zimbalist, Stephanie, 309
Zinnemann, Fred, 101
Ziv, Frederick, 34.04, 75
Ziv productions, 34.04, 59.03; 84.01, 113, 128, 129
Zmed, Adrian, 301
Zorro, 117
Zucker, Jeff, 447.01, 464
Zweibel, Alan, 263, 345
Zwick, Edward, 335, 373.01, 407
Zworykin, Vladimir, 6–7

508

Photograph by Martin Rich

Harry Castleman never really watched as much television as you might think, he just has a good memory. When not writing books, Harry is a lawyer with the firm of Michienzie & Sawin in Boston, specializing in business, real estate, probate and intellectual property law. He has co-authored seven other popular culture books with Wally Podrazik, and also co-authored another book about applying and going to law school. He previously worked as a media producer for the Democratic National Committee, press secretary for the Florida Democratic Party, and as a media consultant to political campaigns both nationally and in Florida. Harry has also been a guest lecturer on TV history at Boston University's College of Communication and has been interviewed on radio and television stations concerning television and music history. He graduated from Northwestern University (where Harry met Wally) and Boston University School of Law. Harry is thrilled that he twice got to share with his daughter the excitement of watching the Red Sox win the World Series. He now can't imagine life without a wide-screen high-definition television but still relies on his daughter to program his cell phone. Harry is enjoying the second decade of the twenty-first century more than he ever expected.

Photograph by Peter Sills, Digital Focus

Walter J. Podrazik loves making media work. As a project planner and consultant, Wally has experienced firsthand history-in-the-making handling media logistics at such high profile events as the Democratic party's quadrennial presidential nominating conventions. As a communication analyst and writer, Wally has provided insights online, in print, on radio and television, at conferences, and in a variety of education forums. A graduate of the School of Communication at Northwestern University, Wally has taught writing, communication, and media history, and is a visiting lecturer at the University of Illinois at Chicago (UIC). Wally has collaborated on seven other books with Harry Castleman. Separately, he has also provided historical narrative and analysis on pioneer interactive projects such as *The Great Debate*, a joint production of UIC and Chicago's Museum of Broadcast Communications, where Wally has been a consulting curator. He also serves as creative resources director for Heartland Historical Research Service, specializing in researching and packaging local and personal history. Wally is happily married and enjoys watching television at his family homestead (built in 1872), occasionally imagining a pre-TV world there without *Lost*, *Columbo*, *Fawlty Towers*, and *Buffy the Vampire Slayer*.